The Montana Constitution in the State Constitutional Tradition

The Montana Constitution in the State Constitutional Tradition

Anthony Johnstone

Carolina Academic Press
Durham, North Carolina

Library of Congress Cataloging-in-Publication Data

Names: Johnstone, Anthony, author.
Title: The Montana Constitution in the state constitutional tradition / by Anthony Johnstone.
Description: Durham, North Carolina : Carolina Academic Press, LLC, [2021]
Identifiers: LCCN 2021043791 (print) | LCCN 2021043792 (ebook) | ISBN 9781531022143 (paperback) | ISBN 9781531022150 (ebook)
Subjects: LCSH: Constitutional law—Montana. | Montana. Constitution (1972) | Constitutional law—United States—States. | LCGFT: Casebooks (Law)
Classification: LCC KFM9400 .J64 2021 (print) | LCC KFM9400 (ebook) | DDC 342.786/02—dc23/eng/20211005
LC record available at https://lccn.loc.gov/2021043791
LC ebook record available at https://lccn.loc.gov/2021043792

Carolina Academic Press
700 Kent Street
Durham, North Carolina 27701
(919) 489-7486
www.cap-press.com

Printed in the United States of America

Contents

Foreword xiii
What State Constitutions can Teach xiii
The New State Constitutional Scholarship xv
This Casebook's Method xvii
Acknowledgments xviii
A Note on Editing xx
Disclosures xx

Part I · Introduction

Chapter 1 · Origins of the Montana Constitution 3
A. The State Constitutional Tradition 4
1. Ideological Origins of State Constitutions 4
Gordon S. Wood, *Foreword: State Constitution Making in the American Revolution* 5
Daniel J. Elazar, *The Principles and Traditions Underlying State Constitutions* 6
Notes on the Origins of State Constitutions 9
2. Contemporary State Constitutionalism 11
William J. Brennan, Jr., *State Constitutions and the Protection of Individual Rights* 12
James A. Gardner, *The Failed Discourse of State Constitutionalism* 14
Daniel B. Rodriguez, *State Constitutional Failure* 15
Jeffrey S. Sutton, *Why Teach—and Why Study—State Constitutional Law* 18
Notes on State Constitutionalism 21
B. Framing the Montana Constitution 21
The Enabling Act of 1889 22
1. The 1889 Statehood Constitution 23
Larry M. Elison & Fritz Snyder, *The Montana State Constitution* 23
Notes on the 1889 Constitution and Statehood 26
2. Drafting the 1972 Constitution 27
Tyler Stockton, *Originalism and the Montana Constitution* 28
Note on Drafting the 1972 Constitution 33
3. Ratifying the 1972 Constitution 35
Burger v. Judge 35

Notes on Ratifying the 1972 Constitution 38
C. Constitutional Revision 38
Anthony Johnstone, *The Constitutional Initiative in Montana* 40
Harper v. Greely 41
Marshall v. Cooney 48
Montana Ass'n of Counties v. State 54
Notes on Constitutional Revision 63

Chapter 2 · Interpretation & Enforcement 67
A. State Constitutional Independence (Herein of Criminal Procedure) 68
1. Independent and Adequate State Grounds 68
State v. Robinette 69
Ohio v. Robinette 71
State v. Robinette 74
Notes on Independent and Adequate State Grounds 75
2. Lockstepping With and Distinguishing Federal Constitutional Law 77
State v. Covington 77
Notes on Lockstepping With and Distinguishing Federal Constitutional Law 80
3. Identifying and Distinguishing Sibling State Constitutions 81
State v. Bullock 82
State v. A Blue in Color, 1993 Chevrolet Pickup 86
Notes on Identifying and Distinguishing Sibling State Constitutions 92
B. Constitutional Remedies 94
1. Sovereign Immunity 94
Anthony Johnstone, *Immunity Confusion: What Is Article II, Section 18 About?* 95
2. Constitutional Torts 101
Dorwart v. Caraway 102
Sunburst School District No. 2 v. Texaco, Inc. 117
Notes on Constitutional Torts 121
3. Attorneys' Fees 121
Western Tradition Partnership, Inc. v. Attorney General 122
Notes on Attorneys' Fees 128

Part II · Structure

Chapter 3 · Legislative Powers, Duties, and Limits 131
A. Legislative Process and Public Purposes 133
White v. State 133
Kottel v. State 140
Notes on Legislative Limits 145

B. Special Legislation 149
Rohlfs v. Klemenhagen 149
Notes on Special Legislation 159

Chapter 4 · Executive Powers 163
A. The Divided Executive Branch 165
William Marshall, *Break up the Presidency? Governors, State Attorneys General, and Lessons from the Divided Executive* 165
Bullock, Governor v. Fox, Attorney General 167
Board of Regents of Higher Education v. Judge 170
Notes on the Horizontal Division of Powers 178
B. Delegation of Powers 184
State ex rel. Judge v. Legislative Finance Committee 184
MEA-MFT v. McCulloch 186
In the Petition to Transfer Territory from High School District No. 6, Lame Deer, Rosebud County, Montana 190
Notes on the Delegation of Powers 193

Chapter 5 · Judicial Powers 199
A. Judicial Independence 201
Anthony Johnstone, *A Past and Future of Judicial Elections: The Case of Montana* 201
Coate v. Omholt 208
Reichert v. State 215
McLaughlin v. Montana State Legislature 221
Notes on Judicial Independence 229
B. Justiciability 234
Reichert v. State 235
McLaughlin v. Montana State Legislature 239
Notes on Justiciability 240
C. Open Courts 245
David Schuman, *The Right to a Remedy* 246
Meech v. Hillhaven West 248
Notes on Open Courts 277

Chapter 6 · Local Government 281
A. The Scope and Preemption of Local Power 282
D & F Sanitation Service v. City of Billings 282
American Cancer Society v. State 287
Notes on the Scope and Preemption of Local Power 294
B. The Structure of Local Government 301
Phillips v. City of Whitefish 301
Notes on the Structure of Local Government 311

Chapter 7 · Education 315
A. The School System & Equal Opportunity 316
Bartmess v. Board of Trustees of School District No. 1 316
Kaptein v. Conrad School District 322
Notes on the School System and Equal Opportunity 328
B. Public School Funding 329
Helena Elementary School District No. 1 v. State 330
Columbia Falls Elementary School District No. 6 v. State 337
Notes on Public School Funding 348

Chapter 8 · Elections & Voting 351
A. The Right to Vote 353
Hannah Tokerud, *The Right of Suffrage in Montana: Voting Protections Under the State Constitution* 353
Driscoll v. Stapleton 354
Weinschenk v. State 358
Notes on the Right to Vote 362
B. Districting and Representation 365
Caitlin Boland Aarab & Hon. Jim Regnier, *Mapping the Treasure State: What States Can Learn from Redistricting in Montana* 365
League of Women Voters v. Commonwealth 369
Notes on Districting and Representation 382

Part III · Rights

Chapter 9 · Introduction to the Declaration of Rights 387
A. The Structure of Constitutional Rights 388
Thomas J. Bourguignon, *The Poacher, the Sovereign Citizen, the Moonlighter, and the Denturists: A Practical Guide to Inalienable Rights in Montana* 388
Butte Community Union v. Lewis 391
Notes on the Structure of Constitutional Rights 395
B. Inalienable Rights Applied and Revisited 396
Wadsworth v. State 397
Wiser v. State 405
Montana Cannabis Industry Association v. State 409
Notes on Inalienable Rights 414
C. A Clean and Healthful Environment 419
Montana Environmental Information Center v. Department of Environmental Quality 420
Cape-France Enterprises v. Estate of Peed 431
Park County Environmental Council v. Department of Environmental Quality 436
Notes on a Clean and Healthful Environment 447

Chapter 10 · Dignity & Equality 457
A. Frameworks for Dignity and Equality 458
Matthew O. Clifford & Thomas P. Huff, *Some Thoughts on the Meaning and Scope of the Montana Constitution's "Dignity Clause" with Possible Applications* 458
Notes on Frameworks for Dignity and Equality 462
B. Equal Protection of the Laws 464
State v. Egdorf 464
Arneson v. State 466
Oberson v. United States Department of Agriculture, Forest Service 472
Notes on Equal Protection 482
C. The Human Rights Act, Race, and Culture 483
1. Montana's Tentative Approach to Race (and Culture) 484
Dupuis v. Board of Trustees 485
State v. Shook 486
Notes on Race, Culture, and Human Rights 489
2. Other State Approaches to Race 492
Malabed v. North Slope Borough 492
Sheff v. O'Neill 497
Notes on Other State Approaches to Race Discrimination 505
D. Gender, Sex, and Emerging Issues 505
1. Sex Discrimination (and State Action) 506
In the Matter of Will of Cram 506
Notes on Sex & Gender Classifications and State Action 509
2. "Sex," Sexual Orientation, and Suspect Classifications 514
Snetsinger v. Montana University System 514
Donaldson v. State 520
Notes on "Sex," Sexual Orientation, and Suspect Classifications 530

Chapter 11 · Privacy 533
A. The Origins and Scope of Individual Privacy 534
State v. Long 534
State v. Nelson 549
Notes on Origins and Scope of Individual Privacy 557
B. Privacy as Autonomy 563
Gryczan v. State 563
Armstrong v. State 574
Notes on Privacy as Autonomy 592
C. Privacy's Frontiers and Dignity, Revisited 595
Walker v. State 595
Baxter v. State 609
Notes on Privacy's Frontiers and Dignity, Revisited 626

Chapter 12 · Freedoms of Religion and Expression 629
A. Freedom of Religion 630
1. Free Exercise and Establishment of Religion 631
Big Sky Colony, Inc. v. Montana Department of Labor and Industry 631
Notes on Free Exercise and Establishment of Religion 640
2. Other Religion Clauses and "the Play in the Joints" 644
Espinoza v. Montana Department of Revenue 644
Notes on Separationism and the Play in the Joints 657
B. Freedom of Speech, Press, and Expression 665
1. A Distinct Freedom of Expression? 666
City of Billings v. Laedeke 668
City of Helena v. Krautter 671
Notes on a Distinct Freedom of Expression 673
2. The Current Scope of the Freedom of Expression 675
State v. Dugan 675
Notes on the Current Scope of Freedom of Expression 684
3. Religion, Speech, and Civil Rights, Revisited 686
Griffith v. Butte School District No. 1 687
Notes on Religion, Speech, and Civil Rights, Revisited 695

Chapter 13 · Rights to Participate & Know 697
A. The Rights to Participate and Know 698
Peter Michael Meloy, *Double and Nothing: Open Government in Montana Under Article II, Section 9 and Section 10* 698
Bryan v. Yellowstone County Elementary School District No. 2 706
Notes on the Rights to Participate and Know 717
B. Limits on the Right to Know 721
1. Implicit Limits on the Right to Know 721
Nelson v. City of Billings 721
Notes on Implicit Limits on the Right to Know 732
2. Privacy and the Merits of Public Disclosure 736
Billings Gazette v. City of Billings 736
Notes on Privacy and the Merits of Public Disclosure 753

Chapter 14 · Due Process of Law and Other Guarantees 757
A. Due Process of Law 757
1. "Procedural" Due Process 759
State v. Stanko 759
In the Matter of the Mental Health of K.G.F. 764
Notes on Procedural Due Process 770

2. "Substantive" Due Process 773
State v. Egdorf 773
Notes on Substantive Due Process 775
B. Other Rights in the Montana Constitution 777
1. The Declaration of Rights 778
Buhmann v. State 779
Notes on the Declaration of Rights 784
2. Rights Elsewhere in the Montana Constitution 787
Emily Zackin, *Looking for Rights in All the Wrong Places: Why State Constitutions Contain America's Positive Rights* 788
Notes on Rights Elsewhere in the Montana Constitution 790

Index 793

Foreword

Why publish a casebook with an audience of one course at one law school—as I like to call it, "The Only Montana Constitutional Law Course in the Universe"? (To their credit, the Montana Board of Bar Examiners maintains a basic one-hour segment on state constitutional law, and the State Bar of Montana includes a similar segment in its occasional Law School for Legislators.) States, and their constitutional law, matter as much now as they ever have. This casebook offers a record of one state's distinctive constitutional culture, as well as a model for the law school classroom study of state constitutions generally. Its goal is to place the Montana Constitution in the state constitutional tradition to the benefit of both.

What State Constitutions can Teach

American democracy lives in the states. Throughout our history, states have served as forums for progress and resistance, deliberation and mass movements, consensus and dissent. These laboratories of democracy work within a structure of surprisingly diverse state constitutions. In these provincial expressions of popular sovereignty, we find a federal republic's DNA: stolid Yankee artifacts of the Founding Era, populist reflections of the Jacksonian Era, traces of Reconstruction and its failure, Progressive Era innovations in government power and direct democracy, and an optimistic Post-War mix of modern management and bold activism.

Each of the 50 state constitutional texts, debated, written, and ratified by ordinary Americans across two centuries, speaks eloquently to our common concerns, old and new. State constitutions deal in issues ranging from open government to privacy, from fair trials to victims' rights, from bearing arms to a healthy environment. They respond to citizens' alienation from the political class with extraordinary deliberations on shared commitments. And they speak in home-grown dialects as varied as the American landscape, from baroque Alabama (376,000 words) and rangy Texas (87,000 words) to reticent Iowa (11,100 words) and spartan Vermont (8,600 words). Each of these state's traditions is sustained by the constitutional law and culture of the states, a vast and underexplored repository of democratic practice.

The state constitutional tradition can renew our national political deliberations at a time when a hyper-partisan Congress, divided state governments, and deep polarization reaching sorted suburbs call for civic renewal. When so many national discussions take place in self-selected media, among self-selected circles, with self-selected facts, state constitutions offer Americans a common civic vocabulary they can call their own. Increased engagement with home-grown constitutionalism offers opportunities to reinvigorate political reforms at the state level and reimagine our national politics.

The challenge is to rediscover a common civic vocabulary of American principles, and a common civic forum for democratic practices. State constitutions speak such a vocabulary; they structure such forums. Each state serves as an irreducible component of our federal political order, providing a platform for political mobilization to lead or restrain the progress of the nation. It is easy to conceive the states as laggards on the most important questions of slavery or gay rights, for example. Yet many states also challenged the federal government from the other side of these policies. Consider Pennsylvania's resistance to the Fugitive Slave Act, or Hawaii's early exploration of marriage equality. Little progress is accomplished at the national level that has not first been subject to deliberation and action at the state level.

State constitutions grew with the nation, providing an archeological record of democratic practice. The record of American democracy is written in our state constitutions. In these provincial expressions of popular sovereignty, for example, we find access to justice descended directly from Magna Carta, declaring "open courts" and guaranteeing remedy "without denial or delay." (*See, e.g.*, Ohio Const. Art. I, § 16.) Most states catalog inalienable rights such as "life, liberty, and the pursuit of happiness," among others, recalling the natural rights principles of the Declaration of Independence. (*See, e.g.*, Mo. Const. Art. I, § 2.) The earliest state constitutions have survived since the Founding Era in New England, including the world's oldest written constitution in Massachusetts. (*See, e.g.*, Mass. Const. (1780); N.H. Const. (1793); Vt. Const. (1793).) These are not dusty artifacts; they are living law, contested in capitols and courtrooms, still governing.

States serve as laboratories of democracy across all policy domains, but none as important as democracy itself. Through the Jacksonian and Antebellum Eras, as suffrage expanded, states introduced new protections for legislative deliberation such as the single-subject rule (*see, e.g.*, Or. Const. Art. IV, § 20), public purpose requirements (*see, e.g.*, Wis. Const. Art. VIII, § 7), and prohibitions on special legislation (*see, e.g.*, Nev. Const. Art. IV, § 20). Of those that survived, Reconstruction Era constitutions strengthened the executive branch at the expense of legislatures, followed by Progressive Era reforms such as special regulatory agencies for oversight of industry and positive rights to education and welfare. After the turn of the twentieth century, state constitutions also established the American practice of direct democracy, including in the amendment of the constitutions themselves.

The dynamism of state politics, including the new avenue of popularly initiated state constitutional reforms, led to a flourishing of state constitutional revisions after World War II. Some of these new constitutions modernized government by cleaning up the accretion of legislative constraints and special-purpose agencies that had ceased to serve their original purposes. In the wake of the Reapportionment Revolution launched by the one-person, one-vote rule of *Reynolds v. Sims* (1964), refreshed democratic energy spurred innovative guarantees such as open government and express rights to privacy, the right to a healthful environment, and even a cosmopolitan right to individual dignity descended from international law.

While this history of state constitutionalism merits scholarly attention from a political development perspective, its greatest value is that it is with us today. These documents, and their ambitious provisions, are the foundation for the law of the land in America. State constitutions structure our democratic practice from the bottom up, and sustain today's most pressing debates affecting education, welfare, public finance, liberty, equality, criminal justice, judicial independence and accountability, and politics itself. Yet these foundational texts' common heritage is unheralded, and links are missing between the origins and migration of provisions across the states.

The New State Constitutional Scholarship

Recent years have witnessed a renaissance of state constitutional scholarship that begins to draw some of these connections. More than four decades ago Justice Brennan wrote *State Constitutions and the Protection of Individual Rights*, 90 HARV. L. REV. 489 (1977), a post-Warren Court call for civil libertarians to seek refuge in the development of state constitutions, albeit according to Justice Brennan's increasingly frequent dissenting views on the federal Constitution. A cottage industry of state constitutional scholarship followed, framed by Professor Daniel J. Elazar's *The Principles and Traditions Underlying State Constitutions*, 12 PUBLIUS 11 (1982). Professor Alan Tarr in UNDERSTANDING STATE CONSTITUTIONS (Princeton University Press 2000), Professor John J. Dinan in THE AMERICAN STATE CONSTITUTIONAL TRADITION (University Press of Kansas 2006), and Professor Robert F. Williams in THE LAW OF AMERICAN STATE CONSTITUTIONS (Oxford University Press 2009) began more comprehensive studies of state constitutions' legal content. Meanwhile, Oxford University Press's 50-State series of state constitution guides spotlights individual states in detail, usually at the expense of placing that detail in a broader context.

In the last few years, many more commentators have engaged state constitutions as a way to escape a kind of theoretical stalemate in federal constitutional law. In particular, Professor Sanford Levinson's FRAMED: AMERICA'S 51 CONSTITUTIONS AND THE CRISIS OF GOVERNANCE (Oxford University Press 2012), and Sixth Circuit Judge Jeffrey Sutton's duology 51 IMPERFECT SOLUTIONS: STATES AND THE MAKING OF AMERICAN CONSTITUTIONAL LAW (Oxford University Press 2018) and WHO DECIDES?: STATES AS LABORATORIES OF CONSTITUTIONAL EXPERIMENTATION (Oxford University Press 2021), offer a constructive critique of federal constitutional law rooted in the ingenuity of state constitutional structures and rights, respectively. In a series of articles beginning with *State Constitutional Theory and its Prospects*, 28 N.M. L. Rev. 271 (1998), Professor Daniel Rodriguez establishes a separate discourse of state constitutional design and power, connected with but independent of federal constitutional discourse. Professor Emily Zackin's Looking for Rights in All the Wrong Places: Why State Constitutions Contain America's Positive Rights (Princeton University Press 2013) pulls away from the federal frame to emphasize the distinctive features of state constitutional rights.

In 2010, the Conference of Chief Justices resolved to encourage all law schools to offer a course on state constitutional law. The resolution noted that "the overwhelming majority" of constitutional law courses "are taught from the perspective of the federal Constitution." Yet "state constitutions contain different structures of government, unique provisions, and substantive provisions or declarations of rights that are often greater than" federal rights, and "being a competent and effective lawyer requires an understanding of both the federal Constitution and state constitutional law." Two national state constitutional law casebooks have emerged from this and similar charges. Professor Williams's State Constitutional Law: Cases and Materials (LexisNexis, 5th ed. 2015, with Lawrence Friedman), originally supported by the U.S. Advisory Commission on Intergovernmental Associations, sweeps in a broad range of diverse commentaries and cases, paying particular attention to interpretive methodologies. Judge Sutton joins Former Delaware Justice Randy J. Holland, former Kansas Solicitor General (and former U.S. Attorney for the District of Kansas) Stephen R. McAllister, and Professor Jeffrey M. Shaman in State Constitutional Law: The Modern Experience (West Academic, 3d ed. 2020), a casebook focused more on the development over time and diversity of state constitutional doctrine in a smaller selection of subjects.

Notably, both of these books draw on some Montana law for principal cases. Holland et al. incorporate *Arneson v. State* (Mont. 1993) on equal protection, *Columbia Falls Elem. School Dist. No. 6 v. State* (Mont. 2005) on school funding, and *State v. Bullock* (Mont. 1995) on privacy and criminal procedure. Williams and Friedman include *Butte Community Union v. Lewis* (Mont. 1986) on welfare rights. Yet these selections, while demonstrative of the impact Montana has on state constitutional discourse nationwide, do not begin to capture the distinctiveness of Montana constitutional law. Depending on the count, Montana's 1972 Constitution (a successor to the 1889 Statehood Constitution) is the third or fourth newest constitution in the union, and the last thoroughly innovative text to come from the post-war modernization of state constitutions. Nearly half of states provide some form of constitutional environmental protection, but only a handful treat it as a judicially enforceable self-executing right. An enumerated right of individual privacy, while not unique to Montana, is shared by some ten states and meaningfully enforced by only a few. The right of individual dignity appeared first in Puerto Rico's 1952 Constitution, inspired by the Universal Declaration of Human Rights, and only Illinois, Louisiana, and Montana adopted it, all in the early 1970s.

This Casebook's Method

The proper study of Montana constitutional law, or any state's constitutional law, requires more than either a state-specific treatise or a general casebook. To be useful to students and practitioners, a state constitutional casebook demands a practical balance of depth and breadth. For depth, it should explore the origins, development, and (where it exists) "black letter" doctrine of key provisions in the Montana Constitution through the canonical constitutional modalities of text, structure, history, practice, policies, and principles. Here in Montana, we are fortunate that our law students are also prolific scholars of Montana Constitutional law. This casebook will incorporate this scholarship with a hope to inspire more. Even an exhaustive analysis of Montana's law in isolation, however, does not sufficiently serve the reader. This is especially true in Montana, where a new constitution, relatively low caseload of constitutional matters, and a single appellate court combine in sparse coverage of many important areas of constitutional doctrine.

Breadth comes from the study of similar provisions in other state constitutions, and how different courts facing different issues at different times develop different doctrines. Drawing on the methods of comparative constitutionalism at the international level, this approach looks for parent and sibling relationships among state constitutions. For example, much of Montana's 1889 Statehood Constitution derived from the 1876 Colorado Constitution, and the 1870 Illinois Constitution before that. Many provisions that are taken to be unique to Montana, such as the dignity right of Article II, section 4, have fascinating lineages and siblings in other states, and even other countries. Not only is Montana's dignity provision descended from Puerto Rico, and post-war Germany before that, but guarantees similar to Montana's clean and healthful environment have found their way into the constitutions of South Africa and other nations. Particularly where the Montana courts have not encountered an issue, those other states can provide useful precedent and context for Montana constitutional analysis. This casebook will not endeavor to draw all such connections, but it will provide a basic methodology and some leads to future students and practitioners.

The book begins with an introduction to state constitutional history and methodologies. Part I situates the Montana Constitution in the American system of dual sovereignty and the political and social factors that shaped the legal framework at both ratifications and in subsequent amendments. Within this context, the introduction concludes by exploring the bases of state constitutional distinctions (and potential distinctions from the federal Constitution), including variations in text, local history, and policy and principal determinants of open-ended provisions, as well as the courts' deliberate or incidental moves to "march in lock-step" with federal constitutional law. It also introduces some practical considerations in enforcing state constitutional law that frame its future development. Part II examines the structure of Montana law and government, with particular attention to distinctions between state and federal institutions such as legislative duties (beyond powers), the divided (not unitary) executive, the elected (not appointed) judiciary, subsidiary (not sovereign) local governments, and express rights of popular governance and free suffrage not found at the federal level. Part III turns to the rights guarantees that open the Montana Constitution in Article II, their original and interpreted scopes, and the Montana Supreme Court's varied approaches to judicial scrutiny.

Each section begins with the provision(s) covered alongside the popular explanation of the provision in the official voter information guide at ratification (or, where applicable, amendment), *in italics*. The voter information guide is the most accessible, and arguably the most reliable, source of original meaning at the time of adoption. Where a provision's background is not otherwise addressed in the principal cases, each section introduces the provision's origins in the 1972 Constitutional Convention, the 1889 Constitution, and where available, other sibling or parent constitutions. Next, principal cases demonstrate the provision's application and, often, alternative approaches expressed in concurrences or dissents. Consistent with the casebook's broader methodology, where Montana law is underdeveloped, some principal cases come from other jurisdictions. Finally, each section concludes with notes considering commentary on the provision or its siblings elsewhere, contrasting views expressed in Montana or other jurisdictions, and some emerging issues. Many notes highlight past student scholarship and ask questions to encourage future student scholarship.

Acknowledgments

The University of Montana Blewett School of Law is one of the smallest law schools in the nation, and its Montana Constitutional Law course is just one elective of many valuable courses that (in the words of our mission) "[e]mphasize those areas of law significant to the Rocky Mountain West." More than many scholarly projects, this one is sustained by the mission and continuous support of the School of Law over the past decade. This includes the whole community of alumni, students, faculty, and staff. Deans Irma Russell, Greg Munro, and Paul Kirgis have encouraged and supported this and related work since Dean Russell allowed me to co-teach my first seminar on the Montana Constitution in 2012. That experience with the great (and then recently retired) Justice Jim Nelson, week after week of sitting with students wrestling with his sophisticated and principled approach to the law, catalyzed my dedication to this project. More than 200 students in the Montana Constitutional Law course sustained my interest and introduced me to new applications of the law through moot courts and research papers, many of which are cited in this book. Over this same time, it has been my privilege to serve as faculty advisor to the MONTANA LAW REVIEW, which plays an essential role in the criticism and development of Montana constitutional law, and provides a platform for student scholarship that has helped maintain a fresh outlook on our state Constitution. Several students went beyond their coursework and publications to serve as formal or informal research assistants on this book and related research, and I am grateful for the tireless effort and attention to detail of Amber Henning, Joshua Van Swearingen, Haley Nelson, Zachary Rogala, Anne Sherwood, Samir Aarab, Constance

Van Kley, Jesse Flickinger, Rebecca Stursberg, Qasim Abdul-Baki, Victoria Nickol, Elizabeth Webster, Kim Wein, and last but not least McKenna Ford, who has borne the burden of getting the book to press. Special thanks to Carolina Academic Press, including David Herzig for seeing the value in this book—and seeing past its first sentence—and Susan Trimble and her team for their patient shaping and reshaping of a novice author's first attempt at a book.

Many of my introductions to the issues in this book came from the practice of law. Jim Goetz gave me my first taste of practice in Montana as a law student. Judge Sidney Thomas offered me two formative opportunities of a lifetime—to clerk in Montana and work in the Ninth Circuit under a mentorship marked by his humane wit. Julie North, Vincent Warren, and Beth Brenneman gave me the opportunity to encounter Montana Constitutional Law for the first time as a lawyer in the unlikely setting of a New York City litigation practice. Chief Justice Mike McGrath, then Attorney General, and Chief Judge Brian Morris, then State Solicitor, brought me out to Montana for good and fed me a rich diet of constitutional litigation in what is and should remain the best law firm in Montana. Attorney General and later Governor Steve Bullock allowed me to continue to support and defend the Montana Constitution with mixed success. Throughout my training as a state lawyer, innumerable colleagues patiently and generously let me interrupt their brief writing to work through state constitutional questions, and sometimes even let me join them in court. They include Chris Tweeten, Pam Bucy, Ali Bovingdon, Jim Wheelis, Jennifer Anders, Mark Mattioli, Tammy Hinderman, Stuart Segrest, Jon Ellingson, Jim Molloy, Jennifer Hurley, and especially Peter Bovingdon, who taught me how to teach even as we learned the law together. After I left state government and they joined it, Dale Schowengerdt and Raph Graybill each led me to and followed me down countless constitutional rabbit holes, apparently in our spare time. Caitlin Borgmann regularly prompted me toward deeper understandings of how constitutional rights function in Montana. When I started teaching the Montana Constitution, Betsy Griffing and Jack Tuholske gave me a head start with their materials and insight about what issues mattered most in the classroom. Martha Sheehy reminded me and my students that the Right of Participation and the Right to Know come before the Right of Privacy in the Declaration of Rights, as well as how funny—and sometimes ridiculous—it can be to practice under the Montana Constitution.

Then there are the delegates. Few constitutional law professors get to know the authors of the constitution they study. I knew the good civic sense of Mae Nan Ellingson, an old family friend, before I could write. Only later could I appreciate the greatness of her contributions to the Montana Constitution as its youngest framer, a skilled practitioner of its most technical aspects, and its champion for five decades and counting. Once in a while, Mae Nan would ask me a question about the constitution she helped write, in the way she would question her fellow delegates at the convention: politely, with a deceptive simplicity, and often leading to a revelation for the respondent even though she knew the answer the whole time. Bob Campbell and I met in a classroom convened in a truck trailer near Boulder, Montana. It was my first Law Day, with the Equal Protection Clause as our subject, and I did not know he would be my co-teacher until he showed up and started passing out signed copies of the Montana Constitution. There was little for me to do but to sit back and hear Bob's stories bring the convention to life for the students, the teacher, and me. Many times since, Bob has done the same in my classroom, and just like those Jefferson County High School students, the law students became quick fans of this unlikely constitutional superstar, lining up for autographs after class. Over the years, I have been privileged to meet, learn from, practice before, and even get served a complaint by several more delegates, including Jean Bowman, Wade Dahood, Gene Harbaugh, Bob Kelleher, Jerome Loendorf, Michael McKeon, C.B. McNeil, and Arlyne Reichert. I hope this work is worthy of their legacy.

Finally, I am indebted to my family's enduring support. To my grandparents and their grandparents for a heritage of quiet beauty, grand mountains, and vast plains; my parents for providing me innumerable opportunities through their moral, intellectual, and general sustenance; my wife for a quality of life filled with her constant love, encouragement, patience, as well as occasional line-edits; and our children for every hour I spent with this book and not with them. May this book do its part to improve the quality of life, equality of opportunity, and secure the blessings of liberty for them and future generations.

A Note on Editing

For ease in reading, the text abridges most cases and commentary. Ellipses (. . .) denote omissions within a paragraph, and asterisks (***) denote omissions of entire paragraphs or across paragraphs. The text also omits most citations and footnotes, including citations to the records of the Constitutional Convention. Citations, when they occur, typically include only the court and date except when the Montana Supreme Court uses its public domain citation format (introduced in 1998). Except for United States Supreme Court case citations, the cited court is inserted into the parenthetical following the case name even where the citing case or commentary has excluded it.

Disclosures

The author served as counsel for the state at some stage in the proceedings in the following cases featured in this casebook: *Baxter v. State* (Mont. 2009); *Big Sky Colony, Inc. v. Montana Department of Labor and Industry* (Mont. 2012); *Columbia Falls Elementary School District No. 6 v. State* (Mont. 2005); *Donaldson v. State* (Mont. 2012); *Espinoza v. Montana Department of Revenue* (Mont. 2018); and *Western Tradition Partnership, Inc. v. Attorney General* (Mont. 2012). *Immunity Confusion: What Is Article II, Section 18 About?* (Chapter 2) is a condensed version of a paper prepared for Farmers and Ranchers for Montana (FARM), an organization supporting the water rights compact between Montana and the Confederated Salish and Kootenai Tribes, and the views expressed in it are the author's.

Part I

Introduction

Chapter 1

Origins of the Montana Constitution

> We the people of Montana grateful to God for the quiet beauty of our state, the grandeur of our mountains, the vastness of our rolling plains, and desiring to improve the quality of life, equality of opportunity and to secure the blessings of liberty for this and future generations do ordain and establish this constitution.
>
> *Preamble is new. The old Preamble is deleted.*
>
> MONT. CONST., PREAMBLE

We begin the book with a history of state constitutions and an introduction to the state constitutional tradition. The oldest written constitution still in effect is not the United States Constitution, but the Massachusetts Constitution drafted by John Adams and ratified in 1780. The ratifications of our earliest state constitutions predated the United States of America itself, as the colonies organized for independence. After independence, the new states tested their innovative models of written constitutions for more than a decade before the eventual framers of the United States Constitution convened at Philadelphia in 1787. These early state constitutions served as a model for the federal Constitution and subsequent state constitutions, including the Montana Constitution. John Adams was not exaggerating the states' contributions when he boasted "I made a Constitution for Massachusetts, which finally made the Constitution of the United States."

Our latter-day founding fathers and mothers, the delegates to the 1972 Constitutional Convention, were heirs of this tradition and students of this history. In framing the Montana Constitution, they carried on some parts of this tradition by readopting provisions from the 1889 "Statehood" Montana Constitution, they revived other parts of this tradition by bringing in provisions from other states, and they broke with some parts of this tradition by synthesizing new constitutional principles for their time and place in late twentieth century Montana. Unlike John Adams, they could benefit from hundreds of state and national constitutions that had been ratified and replaced in the intervening two centuries, including the Constitution of the United States. Unlike the United States Constitution, which is notoriously difficult to amend, the framers of the Montana Constitution also understood and expected that their work would be revisited and revised by future generations. Understanding this historical discourse among state constitutions, and between them and the federal Constitution, is essential to understanding the Montana Constitution and how Montanans continue to revise it today.

A. The State Constitutional Tradition

Over nearly two-and-a-half centuries a state constitutional tradition arose from the recurring American practices of establishing governments. Early state constitutions recorded variations on the unwritten constitutionalisms of the day while incorporating innovations rooted in each new state's distinctive political culture. In turn, these served as models for future constitutions both in new states and in revisions of preexisting state constitutions. Courts and other legal actors looked across states to draw on legal developments in other jurisdictions with a shared constitutional heritage. Meanwhile, federal constitutional law recurred often to legal principles born in the states and, eventually, states began to borrow from federal sources. This complicated and dynamic relational network forms the basis for state constitutional law today.

1. Ideological Origins of State Constitutions

The state constitutional tradition precedes the federal Constitution, which arose from but did not displace its state progenitors. The first state constitutions reflected distinct political cultures and maintained diverse structures of government after ratification of the federal Constitution. As the new nation grew, new states introduced constitutional innovations to meet the needs of different places and times. States revised their constitutions as the nation matured, drawing on emerging political theories, constitutional provisions from other states, and even some ideas from the federal Constitution. Over more than two centuries, this discourse within states, across states, and between states and the national government developed a uniquely American state constitutional tradition.

Gordon S. Wood, a leading historian of the founding era, draws the connection between the original state constitutions and the idea of American independence. He writes, "[t]he Declaration of Independence, though drawn up by the Continental Congress, was actually a declaration by 'thirteen united States of America' proclaiming that as 'Free and Independent States they have full Power to levy War, conclude Peace, contract Alliances, establish Commerce, and to do all other Acts and Things which Independent States may of right do,'" including draft constitutions. Daniel Elazar, a political scientist, developed the conventional classification of state constitutions based on each state's political culture. He describes a mix of three founding-era constitutional traditions translated and remixed through the political history of each state at the time of its constitutional framing. As you read Professors Wood and Elazar, consider Montana's place in the state constitutional tradition, and why a reader might look back to the first state constitutions to understand the Montana Constitution today.

Gordon S. Wood, *Foreword: State Constitution Making in the American Revolution*

24 Rutgers L.J. 911, 913, 914, 917 (1993)

The era of the American Revolution was the most creative and significant period of constitutionalism in modern Western history, but this time was creative and significant not because of the Constitution that looms so large in our lives today. Rather, the American Revolution was creative and significant because of the revolutionary state constitutions that preceded the Constitution by more than a decade. Not only did the formation of the new state constitutions in 1776 establish the basic structures of our political institution, their creation also brought forth the primary conceptions of America's political and constitutional culture that have persisted to the present.

The office of our governors, the bicameral legislatures, tripartite separation of powers, bills of rights, and the unique use of constitutional conventions were all born during the state constitution-making period between 1775 and the early 1780s, well before the federal constitution of 1787 was created. In fact, the structure and form of the new federal government of 1787 was the direct product of what had taken place in the making of the state governments during the previous decade. In the first crucial years of independence, the states, not the federal government, were the focus of interest for most Americans. ***

The Continental Congress had prepared the way for constitution-making as early as May 1776. On May 10, the Congress advised the colonies to adopt new governments "where no government sufficient to the exigencies of their affairs have been hitherto established." ... Although the revolutionaries in 1776 knew they would establish republics in place of the British royal governments, they did not know precisely what form their new governments would take. There was therefore some confusion and dispute over the arrangement of governmental institutions. There was no doubt, however, about what institution was the most dangerous and most to be feared: the rulers or governors.

The revolutionaries' central aim was to prevent power, which they identified with the governors, from encroaching on liberty, which was the possession of the people or their representatives in the legislatures. Most sought to create a balance between power and liberty, the rulers and the ruled. Thus, in all the state constitutions, the much-feared governors were radically weakened and the popular assemblies or houses of representatives greatly strengthened. ***

The separation of the legislature from the executive was one of the two important ways in which the American and English constitutional systems came to differ during the American Revolution. The other was over the meaning and purpose of a constitution.

The American revolutionaries virtually established the modern idea of a written constitution. There had, of course, been written constitutions before in Western history, but the Americans did something new and different. They made written constitutions a practical and everyday part of governmental life. They showed the world how written constitutions could be made truly fundamental and distinguishable from ordinary legislation, and how such constitutions could be interpreted on a regular basis and altered when necessary. Further, they offered the world concrete and usable governmental institutions' for carrying out these constitutional tasks. ***

These were extraordinary contributions that Americans of the revolutionary era made to the world — the modern idea of a constitution as a written document, the device of a convention for creating and amending constitutions, the process of popular ratification, and the practice of judicial review. The sources of these constitutional achievements lay deep in Western history. For centuries, people had talked about fundamental law and the placing of limits on the operations of government. But not until the American Revolution had anyone ever developed such regular and everyday institutions not only for controlling government and protecting the rights of individuals, but also for changing the very framework by which government operated. And all these remarkable achievements were realized or, at least in the case of judicial review, begun prior to the formation of the federal constitution in the ten short years or so following the Declaration of Independence. Indeed, the creation of the federal constitution in 1787 would not have been possible without the previous constitution-making of the states. It was the revolutionaries' experience with their state constitutions, not with their central government, that had the greatest effect on the constitutionalism of the world.

Daniel J. Elazar, *The Principles and Traditions Underlying State Constitutions*

12 Publius 11, 18–23 (1982)

There appear to be six constitutional patterns among the American states. These patterns are rooted in the original constitutional conceptions of the founding era [an early *Whiggish* conception furthering republican virtue, a Madisonian *federalist* conception refining interest group politics, and a Hamiltonian *managerial* conception facilitating efficient administration] plus differences among the types and goals of pioneers who first settled the Northern, Middle, and Southern colonies of the New World. Subsequent migrations carried the constitutional ideas of these sections westward and, in some cases, resulted in significant changes as settlers mixed, confronted new environments and sets of governmental problems, and framed their constitutions at different times, thereby incorporating conceptions of government prevalent at the times of their writing.

The Commonwealth Pattern

The commonwealth pattern derives largely from the constitutions of the states of greater New England. They are basically philosophic documents designed first and foremost to set a direction for civil society and to express and institutionalize a theory of republican government. Based on seventeenth and eighteenth-century Puritan and Whiggish ideas about constitution making, this pattern is the oldest in America. It emphasizes the constitution as a covenant establishing a civil society and setting forth its frame of government. These constitutions, as brief or briefer than the federal document, concentrate on setting forth the philosophic basis for popular government, guaranteeing the fundamental rights of the individual and delineating the elements of the state's government in a few broad strokes. Frames of government in the classic American sense, they have shown greater longevity and, at least in the case of Massachusetts, greater longevity than the U.S. Constitution. ***

Eight states outside of New England whose political character was formed by New Englanders have followed the commonwealth pattern. All are still operating under their original constitutions. Although the youngest among them—those admitted as states in the latter half of the nineteenth century—have somewhat longer constitutions than their sisters formed earlier, as a rule they are also relatively short. Their greater length is accounted for in the somewhat more detailed restrictions placed on the institutions of state government and in the granting of constitutional status to state educational and welfare institutions. Minnesota's constitution is a good example of this variation of the commonwealth pattern.

The Commercial Republic Pattern

A second pattern has prevailed in the Middle states (the northern states just south of New England and the states to the west of them which they have influenced, including most of the very large ones). These states have built their constitutions upon a series of compromises required by the conflict of ethnic and commercial interests and ideals created by the flow of various streams of migrants into their territories, and the early development of commercial cities.

The pattern in each is much the same. As each stream of migrants has been able to demand a government modeled after the one its people knew "back home" or a fundamental law that would protect its socioeconomic interests, the state's constitution has been replaced or revised accordingly.... Illinois is an example of this tradition.

The Southern Contractual Pattern

The Southern states developed a third pattern of constitution making, one which began with a general penchant for changing constitutions and was enhanced by the need to do so because of the disruption of constitutional continuity caused by the Civil War. Except for North Carolina and Tennessee, none of the eleven states of the former Confederacy has had less than five constitutions, most of which embodied the constitutional changes of secession, reconstruction, and the restoration of white supremacy. Alabama, for example, adopted a constitution upon its admission to the Union in 1819, a revised document when it seceded from the Union in 1861, and still another when it sought to be restored to full rights in 1865. Then it adopted two constitutions during Reconstruction (1868 and 1875) and finally a constitution ratifying white supremacy in 1901. ***

Constitutions of the Southern contractual pattern are unique in other and related ways. They are the only group to formally acknowledge the supremacy of the U.S. Constitution (a product of Reconstruction). At the same time, most of them contain (and retain) many provisions particularly regarding elections, civil rights, and legislative apportionment—which have been invalidated by U.S. Supreme Court decisions. In general, the Southern contractual pattern has looked upon state constitutions as instruments designed to perpetuate a particular social system based on slavery or racial segregation. As political instruments, Southern state constitutions are designed to diffuse the formal allocation of authority among many offices in order to accommodate the swings between oligarchy and factionalism characteristic of Southern state politics. Perhaps because of the fluctuating balance of factions in many of the Southern states, their citizens have also been more tempted to write into their constitutions materials normally included in ordinary legislation. Texas is a prime example of this pattern.

The Civil Code Pattern

Louisiana is the one state that operates within a constitutional pattern of its own. Because of its original French background, its constitutions have been more like the basic civil codes of European countries—long, detailed, and not particularly revered. The Pelican State has had eleven different constitutions since 1812. Its tenth constitution, adopted in 1921, contained some 256,500 words, over six times as many as the average state document. As of 1965, it has been amended 439 times. The Louisiana constitutional tradition provides, in effect, a continuing referendum on all basic governmental decisions in the state and its localities. In 1974, however, 36 percent of the registered voters turned out to adopt (by 58 percent) a more modernized constitution containing only 29,704 words.

The Frame of Government Pattern

The fifth pattern is to be found exclusively among the less populated states of the Far West. In these states, the constitutions are frames of government first and foremost. They explicitly reflect the republican and democratic principles dominant in the nation in the late nineteenth century when their first constitutions were written, and then go on to specify the structure of state government and the distribution of powers within it in the style of the times. Their constitutions tend to be businesslike documents of moderate length that reflect the relative homogeneity of the states themselves. ***

Montana is a good example of this frame of government pattern. Admitted as a state in 1889, its original constitution reflected the frame of government approach when it was at its height. In 1972, the state adopted a constitution after what experts in the field consider to be a model process of constitution writing and ratification. While the new constitution incorporates many of the recommendations of constitutional reformers, it also appears to remain faithful to the frame of government pattern, adapting it to late twentieth century ideas.

The constitutional tradition of the Treasure State has tended to emphasize limited government except on certain matters of economic development. After World War II. Montana emerged from almost a century of well-nigh colonial status under the control of the Anaconda Company and, later, Montana Power. In part, the new constitution of 1972, which replaced the state's original document of 1889, symbolized the new independence of the state and the assertion of power by the general citizenry.

The Managerial Pattern

Alaska and Hawaii, the two newest states, reflect a sixth constitutional pattern, one developed in the last half of the twentieth century. Their constitutions come closest to fitting the model designed by today's constitutional reformers. This reform model emphasizes conciseness, broad grants of powers to the state executive branch, and relatively few structural restrictions on the legislature. Their constitutions also feature articles dealing with local government, natural resource conservation, and social legislation. In all of this, they reflect the Hamiltonian managerial model, albeit without being aware of it. While, as a model, it is as old as the republic itself, only in the twentieth century has it entered the mainstream of American constitutional development and only in the newest states could it serve as the basis for their constitutional foundations. ***

Directions

In order to understand constitutional design in the states ... much needs to be done to properly examine and articulate the explicit and implicit political theories and philosophic assumptions of the American state constitutions as manifested by the three constitutional traditions, as they have found expression in these six different patterns.

The object of such efforts should be to reconstruct the inner logic of the state constitutions so as to understand their basic theoretical conceptions of government, its proper role in society, and the very purposes of the constitutions. In this respect, each constitution must be treated as a package made up of diverse elements, including compromises, which together shape a fundamental role for government in the state. ...

To understand the theoretical assumptions of each constitution it will be necessary to look at each provision and concept in five ways: (1) by itself as stated in the constitution, (2) in relation to the other provisions of the constitution, (3) in relation to earlier constitutions or founding documents, (4) in comparison with similar provisions in other state constitutions, and (5) in relation to its actual interpretative use.

Notes on the Origins of State Constitutions

1. The structures of the first state constitutions, which were written during the nascent states' engagement in the Revolutionary War, represented a political reaction to the Crown's rule. Many of these ideas flowed across state constitutions of the

time, into the drafting of the federal Constitution, and down to modern state constitutions, including Montana's. What use is this early history to lawyers practicing the Montana Constitution?

2. How might Professor Elazar's categories and comparative methodology inform the legal meaning of the Montana Constitution (and other state constitutions), particularly where that meaning might draw on broad historical, structural, and principled arguments?

3. Professor Elazar directs state constitutional analysts to consider the text and context of state constitutional provisions. Like the interpretive conventions for the federal Constitution, that context includes structure "in relation to the other provisions of the constitution," history "in relation to earlier constitutions or founding documents," and precedent "in relation to its actual interpretative use." Unlike the interpretative conventions for the federal Constitution, however, state constitutional analysis also looks to "comparison with similar provisions in other state constitutions," because those provisions may arise from the same state constitutional tradition. What can a practitioner tell about the meaning of one state constitutional provision by a comparison with other state constitutions? Consider Patrick L. Baude, *Interstate Dialogue in State Constitutional Law*, 28 RUTGERS L.J. 835, 836–39 (1997):

> My argument here is that there are meaningful local epics, profound in their contribution to identity and meaningful in the world of constitutional interpretation. These epics are not specific to a state but apply to a group of states, sometimes a region; they are distinctly less than national in scope. An epic is, after all, a kind of narrative, a species of literature. In American literature generally, we are all familiar with the greatness of regional traditions. Faulkner, Dreiser and Hawthorne paint different pictures of the human condition, pictures which both derive their meaning from, and help to create, regional contexts of meaning quite different from each other. It would not be incongruous to find similar meaningful variations in the constitutions of Mississippi, Indiana and Massachusetts. ***
>
> [For this article] I collected a comprehensive list of the occasions on which a state's highest court referred to the constitution of another state. If state constitutions were randomly varied across the country, one would not expect to see significant differences in regional patterns. And there certainly are signs in these data that regionalism or geographical proximity is not the consuming explanation of the occasions on which one state consults the constitutional learning of another state. For example, twenty-nine states refer to the constitution of California more often than to any other state and these states that refer most to California are as removed as Massachusetts and Louisiana. If state constitutions were rated by U.S. News and World Report, California would be the reputation leader, followed very distantly by Virginia and Wisconsin, with three firsts apiece.

> Of course, states are likely to cite decisions of the states on which their own constitutions may have been modeled. The Oregon constitution, for example, bears a close resemblance to the Indiana constitution, and accordingly, Oregon's most frequent reference to an out-of-state constitution is Indiana. But even this pattern is far from universal. In California, for example, "of the 137 sections of the original Constitution 66 were adopted from the Constitution of Iowa and 19 from the Constitution of New York." Even so, the California Supreme Court cites Illinois ahead of New York and nine states ahead of Iowa. Similarly, Kentucky, whose constitution is especially indebted to Pennsylvania's, is more likely to refer to its neighbors Missouri and Tennessee. Turnabout being fair play, Louisiana's constitution was modeled on Kentucky's, but the Louisiana Supreme Court is more likely to consult California and Alabama....
>
> Still, the data reported in the table do show several strong regional patterns. Consider a few examples from the West. Fifty-nine percent of Montana's references are to Alaska, California, Oregon, Washington, Arizona and Colorado. The Utah Supreme Court is most likely to refer to California, Arizona, Colorado, Oregon and Montana. Alaska is most likely to refer to California, Washington and Hawaii; while Hawaii, in turn, is most likely to refer to California, Alaska and Oregon. The Washington Supreme Court is most likely to refer to California, Oregon and Colorado, as is the Idaho Supreme Court.

Professor Baude's complete tally of the Montana Supreme Court's references to other state constitutions as of 1997 was in descending order: Alaska (9); California (8); Oregon (6); Washington (5); Arizona and Colorado (4); Michigan and Ohio (3); Minnesota, New York, North Dakota, Pennsylvania, Texas, and Wyoming (2); and Arkansas, Florida, Hawaii, Illinois, Massachusetts, Nevada, Tennessee, and West Virginia (1). What does this tell us about Montana constitutional law?

2. Contemporary State Constitutionalism

In 2010, the Professionalism and Competence of the Bar Committee of the Conference of (State) Chief Justices "encourage[d] all law schools to offer a course on state constitutional law." They explained "state constitutions contain different structures of government, unique provisions, and substantive provisions or declarations of rights that are often greater than federally guaranteed individual rights and liberties," and declared that "being a competent and effective lawyer requires an understanding of both the federal Constitution and state constitutional law." The Chief Justices' argument for studying state constitutional law is authoritative but surprisingly recent.

The most famous elaboration of this argument comes from Justice William Brennan, who served as the leading voice for civil liberties on the United States Supreme

Court as an associate justice from 1956 to 1990. Justice Brennan, who served on the Supreme Court of New Jersey from 1951 to 1956, became the first state judge appointed to the United States Supreme Court since Benjamin Cardozo left the Chief Judgeship of the New York Court of Appeals (its highest court) in 1932. The Warren Court, marked by the elaboration of broad federal constitutional rights, ended with the replacement of Chief Justice Earl Warren by Chief Justice Warren Burger by President Nixon in 1969. Several years into the increasingly moderate Burger Court, Justice Brennan published a call for lawyers to turn to state constitutions and courts for further development of individual rights. It remains one of the most cited law review articles of all time. A quarter-century after Justice Brennan's article, law professor James Gardner revisited its "New Judicial Federalism" promise of an independent state constitutionalism that could stand up to, or even shape, American constitutional law as determined by the United States Supreme Court. Professor Daniel Rodriguez turns from these rights-centered debates to the less comparable and arguably more fundamental questions of how state constitutions structure government powers, to what ends, and whether those structures are successful in accomplishing those ends.

Another notable judicial observer of state constitutions from the opposite end of the ideological spectrum from Justice Brennan is Jeffrey Sutton. Judge Sutton is a former Solicitor General of Ohio and current judge on the United States Court of Appeals for the Sixth Circuit who also teaches state constitutional law. (Like other such professors, this author included, he has recognized that much of the content for his course comes from state constitutional cases he lost while representing the state.) He offers a practical rationale—verging on ethical duty—for studying state constitutional law. As you read Justice Brennan, Professor Gardner, Professor Rodriguez, and Judge Sutton, consider the proper place of state constitutions in American law schools and legal practice, why we require an understanding of federal but not state constitutional law, and what effects this may have on both subjects.

William J. Brennan, Jr., *State Constitutions and the Protection of Individual Rights*

90 Harv. L. Rev. 489, 491, 500-02 (1977)

... [S]tate courts cannot rest when they have afforded their citizens the full protections of the federal Constitution. State constitutions, too, are a font of individual liberties, their protections often extending beyond those required by the Supreme Court's interpretation of federal law. The legal revolution which has brought federal law to the fore must not be allowed to inhibit the independent protective force of state law—for without it, the full realization of our liberties cannot be guaranteed. ***

[E]xamples abound where state courts have independently considered the merits of constitutional arguments and declined to follow opinions of the United States Supreme Court they find unconvincing, even where the state and federal constitutions are similarly or identically phrased. As the Supreme Court of Hawaii has observed, "while this results in a divergence of meaning between words which are the same in both federal and state constitutions, the system of federalism envisaged by the United States Constitution tolerates such divergence where the result is greater protection of individual rights under state law than under federal law . . ." Some state courts seem apparently even to be anticipating contrary rulings by the United States Supreme Court and are therefore resting decisions solely on state law grounds. For example, the California Supreme Court held, as a matter of state constitutional law, that bank depositors have a sufficient expectation of privacy in their bank records to invalidate the voluntary disclosure of such records by a bank to the police without the knowledge or consent of the depositor; thereafter the United States Supreme Court ruled that federal law was to the contrary.

And of course state courts that rest their decisions wholly or even partly on state law need not apply federal principles of standing and justiciability that deny litigants access to the courts. Moreover, the state decisions not only cannot be overturned by, they indeed are not even reviewable by, the Supreme Court of the United States. We are utterly without jurisdiction to review such state decisions. ***

This pattern of state court decisions puts to rest the notion that state constitutional provisions were adopted to mirror the federal Bill of Rights. The lesson of history is otherwise; indeed, the drafters of the federal Bill of Rights drew upon corresponding provisions in the various state constitutions. Prior to the adoption of the federal Constitution, each of the rights eventually recognized in the federal Bill of Rights had previously been protected in one or more state constitutions. And prior to the adoption of the fourteenth amendment, these state bills of rights, independently interpreted, were the primary restraints on state action since the federal Bill of Rights had been held inapplicable.

The essential point I am making, of course, is not that the United States Supreme Court is necessarily wrong in its interpretation of the federal Constitution, or that ultimate constitutional truths invariably come prepackaged in the dissents, including my own, from decisions of the Court. It is simply that the decisions of the Court are not, and should not be, dispositive of questions regarding rights guaranteed by counterpart provisions of state law. Accordingly, such decisions are not mechanically applicable to state law issues, and state court judges and the members of the bar seriously err if they so treat them. Rather, state court judges, and also practitioners, do well to scrutinize constitutional decisions by federal courts, for only if they are found to be logically persuasive and well-reasoned, paying due regard to precedent and the policies underlying specific constitutional guarantees, may they properly claim persuasive weight as guideposts when interpreting counterpart state guarantees. I suggest to the bar that, although in the past it might have been safe for counsel to raise only federal constitutional issues in state courts, plainly it would be most unwise these days not also to raise the state constitutional questions. ***

James A. Gardner, *The Failed Discourse of State Constitutionalism*

90 Mich. L. Rev. 761, 804–05, 812, 837 (1992)

The overwhelming impression left by an examination of state constitutional decisions is that state courts by and large have little interest in creating the kind of state constitutional discourse necessary to build an independent body of state constitutional law. With a handful of exceptions, the decisions fail to address state constitutional issues squarely and independently from federal constitutional jurisprudence, and show no sign of any discourse of distinctness that would allow participants in the legal system to craft intelligible arguments about the nature of any differences between the state and federal constitutions.

By engaging in extensive lockstep analysis, many courts have also created an atmosphere in which it is unnecessary to distinguish between the state and federal constitutions because they are generally held to have the same meaning. This reduces state constitutional law to a redundancy and greatly discourages its use and development. In the few cases in which courts hold the state and federal constitutions to be distinct, they often seem to have done so in a way that is so idiosyncratically result-oriented as to provide little basis for further intelligible debate about the nature of the differences between the two documents that account for the court's departures from federal norms. Certainly, litigants can hardly be confident about replicating the results of such cases in factually distinct circumstances. ***

When he was still on the Oregon Supreme Court, Hans Linde complained that "[a] generation of lawyers . . . seems literally speechless" when faced with questions of state constitutional law. In view of the actual condition of state constitutional law, however, such silence seems understandable enough when lawyers lack a language in which to speak, or at best have a language that is too impoverished to allow them to say anything worthwhile. ***

[T]he cause of the problem is a failure that goes much deeper than the actions of the Supreme Court, the state bar, or the law schools. All these groups, as well as state courts themselves, are responding to the same underlying phenomenon: the failure of state constitutionalism itself to provide a workable model for the contemporary practice of constitutional law and discourse on the state level. In particular, state courts do not talk about state constitutions in the way New Federalism advocates because to do so would be to talk in a way that, under present conditions, simply makes no sense. ***

Americans have a communal identity, but it is a national and not a state identity. We debate our fundamental values and our identity through constitutional discourse, but we do so on a national level, as a national community. Residency in one state rather than another is not viewed as an aspect of individual or group identity, or if it is, it has come to represent aspects of identity that are not bound up with the types of decisions that make us who we are in any kind of essential way. As long as this continues to be the case, state constitutional law is likely to remain marginal to legal life, and future battles over the nature of the American character and communal identity will have to be fought, like their predecessors, on a national level in the forum of federal constitutional law.

Daniel B. Rodriguez, *State Constitutional Failure*

2011 U. Ill. L. Rev. 1243, 1254–61

A. State Constitutions and U.S. Constitutionalism

. . . State constitutions are important elements in the collective structure of U.S. constitutionalism. While this structure is built upon the union of states created in the late eighteenth century, it remains unequivocally so that many aspects of public governance in the United States are dealt with primarily, and in some cases even exclusively, by state governments under the rubric of state constitutions. This is not merely the result of inattention on the part of the national government; of course, public power under state constitutional direction does more than fill a lacuna in the general scope of public power nationally. As political scientist Donald Lutz insightfully explains, state constitutions are best understood as part of a larger constitutional framework constructed by the framers of a much earlier generation, a framework which was discernibly and intentionally left incomplete. Just as the constitutional amendment process would be expected to help accomplish the objective that this "experiment that needed careful control and some means for future adjustment," so, too, would "[p]utting significant power in the hands of state government" through a rich, evolving process of state constitutionalism. State constitutional power, in this account, is not the power which is simply left over when federal power under the U.S. Constitution runs out; rather, state constitutions function to complete the constitutional text.

This is an idealized rendering, to be sure, of what state constitutionalism is or can become. The question remains of how successful state constitutions are in performing these ambitious tasks. Scholars have expressed skepticism about the general condition of modern state constitutionalism, noting that the state constitutional law is "a vast wasteland of confusing, conflicting, and essentially unintelligible pronouncements," and that states constitutions are "mostly anchor and little sail." In a somewhat related vein, influential critics of U.S. federalism devalue the U.S. Constitution's historic demarcation of federal and state powers, believing that such a scheme is deeply anachronistic. Both views are orthogonal to my main point, however, which is that state constitutions remain relevant as documents which forge state and local government, empower institutions to act on behalf of the respective people of the fifty states, regulate the conduct of important state institutions, and prescribe individual rights. And while it is fashionable to attribute the renaissance in state constitutional studies to Justice William Brennan's lodestar 1977 Harvard Law Review article, state constitutions have been critical parts of U.S. legal architecture since the beginning of the republic. They remain so today.

B. Ends and Means

State constitutions in the U.S. system have several overlapping functions. At the very least, state constitutions configure the arrangements of intrastate governance and limit the exercise of state and local governmental power. State-to-state differences mean that the specific objectives of a particular constitution will track the hopes, dreams, and plans of the state citizenry. Yet, we can generalize in useful ways about the governance objectives of state constitutions across the nation. A core function of all state constitutions is to arrange government institutions and processes in order to further the objectives of the polity. These arrangements will involve both the creation of powers—as in the creation of the police power in order to establish plenary authority to govern—and the delineation of limits to the exercise of those powers.

To what end are these broad powers directed? Certainly toward the safeguarding of public welfare, at least insofar as such "safeguarding" is within the purview of state, rather than national governance. There is a more ambitious rendering of state governmental power, however, which finds support in the modern historiography of state constitutional development. Various scholars note that the eighteenth century project of constitution making was an essentially progressive one, with the goal being to facilitate social and economic progress through an active government. Progressive state government—which Daniel Elazar goes so far as to see that state constitutions are concerned with moral perfectionism—was embodied in state constitutions precisely because the national Constitution had more limited aims. This is not the only way to see the origins of state constitutional development to be sure; and this is not the place to resolve the complex debate over the global purposes of state constitutional development in the eighteenth and nineteenth centuries. But I note the debate only to highlight the point that an ambitious view of state constitutional functions does sharpen our perspective about state constitutional performance. If we have high aims for constitutional achievement, we will have a particular picture in mind for how we want our constitutions to perform. Moreover, we will have special concerns about the capacity of state constitutions, as distinct from the federal constitution and other national sources of law, to realize these objectives within the structure of U.S. politics.

C. Control and Governance

State constitutions are not only about authorizing public authorities to wield power, they are concerned as well with structuring appropriate limits on that power. In our attention to constitutionally created public authority, we should not lose sight of the fact that "[p]ower is also limited through specific prohibitions on decision outcomes reached by those in power." The constitutional law of the states is fundamental law. It sets out (sometimes in general and other times in specific terms) the parameters of state and local governance. State constitutions create the basic instruments of intrastate governance. They do so not only by the delineation of the scope and limits of official authority but also through the express establishment of appropriate institutions to facilitate the state's variegated policy objectives. To whatever ends these institutions direct their energies, a core function of state constitutions is the establishment of these complex local governing institutions....

D. "A Polity Within a Polity": Identity and Interest

The principal function of state constitutions is to create instruments of governance by creating institutions which yield public power on behalf of the state and, moreover, to create the rules of the game in which these institutions operate. But to what purpose is this structure directed? Presumably, it is toward the welfare and well-being of the state's polity. At some level of generality, this is undoubtedly true. "State constitutions," writes Robert Post, "face a fundamental challenge: They must constitute a polity within a polity. They must establish a distinctive political culture within the confines of the encompassing and transcendent political culture of the nation."

States, however, are not islands on their own; they are nested not only in a federal system with constraints set by the national Constitution but also in a system with forty-nine other states respectively. State constitutions help to facilitate intrastate communities of interest. This concept trades on the idea commonly discussed in the ample literature on constitutionalism generally, that is, that constitutions function to ratify and promote the cultural identity of a common people with shared interests. While the prevailing view of the national Constitution is that the U.S. constitutional order, by design and effect, promotes this national identity, it is far less obvious that state constitutions can and do have a similar objective. The notion that each state constitution reflects the distinct identity of its people is almost certainly misleading. Few believe that the differences among state citizens are sufficiently salient and intractable to warrant distinct constitutional mechanisms to foment real difference. We can reject here—as others have rejected plausibly before—that there are meaningful intrastate communities of identity that the (constitutional) law ought to value.

The community-building idea, however, can be reformulated in a way that makes better sense of state constitutional purpose. We need to sort out identity from interest. We should understand that community in the intrastate context is not principally a community of identity, but one of interest.

Communities of interest are collections of individuals assembled within geographically or legally defined borders who share common, collective interests. Employees of a company are an example of this; students in a university setting are another. Individuals in these settings may be enormously diverse and share little in common other than matters attending particularly to the work or educational setting. Still, these settings are enormously important and enduring. The communities of interest that are configured within the employment or educational settings are, while not limitless, important. More to the point, they are protected to a greater or lesser degree through state constitutional and statutory law.

State citizenship both defines and fosters communities of interest. Individuals yoked together as citizens of a state—even if this citizenship is transient—have common agendas and objectives. For example, the decision of land-grant colleges and universities to restrict access to state residents (or, at the very least, accord favorable financial treatment to in-state residents) will generate a common interest in maintaining this system against efforts to widen access. State citizenship is an artificial construct; it hardly matters in the grand ways that national citizenship does, for example, in eligibility for military service or certain governmental employment. But that it matters at all—as it clearly does in key contexts—is enough to generate communities of interest.

This point is relatively straightforward: state citizens have interests that derive distinctly from this citizenship and will, on occasion, drive political judgment and strategy. What is less apparent is precisely how state constitutions facilitate these communities of interest. State constitutions function in part to protect, preserve, and further these communities of interest. Of course, these communities are ever evolving; they are contingent on shifting judgments and allegiances both within the community and by outside decision makers whose views bear on the prerogatives of these communities. A state constitution functions successfully where it furthers intrastate interest communities, taking full account of the dynamic nature of these communities.

The main way state constitutions do so is twofold. First, state constitutions delineate the franchise and thereby make clear whose interests matter for the purpose of state policy making. Second, and relatedly, state constitutions and the institutions they create establish mechanisms of access to political power and influence. Only state citizens can vote in state elections; accordingly, state political officials will, to the extent possible, respond to the interest of these citizens; they will presumably do so at the expense of folks just passing through. The exportability of state and local taxes is just a complex economic version of this rather obvious insight. In the state political context, you are, like the contestants on *Project Runway*, either in or you're out. Whenever you have folks on both sides of the divide, you have communities of interest.

State constitutions are frameworks in which key matters of state governance are carried out. They structure the (incomplete) mechanisms for authorizing and limiting public power and they facilitate communities of interest within the state. ***

Jeffrey S. Sutton, *Why Teach—and Why Study—State Constitutional Law*

34 Okla. City U. L. Rev. 165, 165–66, 172–78 (2009)

Imagine an NCAA tournament basketball game. Your favorite team is down by one point. With no time left on the clock, the opposing team commits a two-shot foul on your star player. How would you react if the player took just one of the two free throws offered him? Strange, yes? A two-shot foul normally would give the player two chances to make one free throw, which would tie the game, and one chance to make both free throws, which would win the game. Not a bad situation to be in. But if a coach told his player to take just one of the free throws, he would reduce the team to the hope of at best forcing overtime. Any coach who made such a decision would be ridiculed out of the profession, particularly if his team lost the game.

If you think this scenario is utterly implausible, so do I. But that leaves us with some explaining to do. Why is it that when we switch from basketball to American law, we find so many lawyers willing to give up the second free throw? Under our legal system, whenever a state or local government enacts a dubious law, lawyers and clients have two chances, not one, to invalidate it. They may invoke the United States Constitution to strike the law, and they may invoke that State's constitution to strike the law. Yet, in my experience as a federal judge, a private practitioner and a lawyer for the State of Ohio, that is not what most lawyers do. ***

Let me shift from speculating why state constitutional law is not offered at most law schools to explaining why it ought to be. Start with lawyers' duties to their clients—to solve a client's problem by prevailing in a case. When, in the words of Justice Kennedy, "[t]he Framers split the atom of sovereignty," they created a system of government that features two sets of sovereigns, that produced fifty-one constitutions and that in the end places two sets of constitutional limitations on the validity of (nearly) every state and local law. Lawyers are problem solvers, and when a state or local law stands in the way of a client's objective, it generally will matter little to the client whether the lawyer manages to strike the law on federal or state grounds.

A constitutional claimant needs to win just once. No State permits a law invalidated under its constitution to be enforced; and the Supremacy Clause of the United States Constitution prohibits any State from enforcing laws invalidated under the Federal Constitution. A necessary consequence of a system of dual sovereignty is that it permits serial, or at least dual, claims of unconstitutionality. While federal judges are not known for giving legal advice, it seems to me that the first reason for teaching, and the first reason for studying, state constitutional law is simple: Lawyers are paid to solve problems for their clients, and one way to do that is to win cases. A lawyer paid to help a client win a case usually will have some explaining to do if he opts to take just one shot, rather than two, at knocking out a state or local law.

State constitutional law not only gives the client two chances to win, but, in many cases, it also will give the client a *better* chance to win.... The United States Supreme Court, in the first place, is at a considerable disadvantage relative to the state courts when it comes to defining constitutional rights and crafting constitutional remedies in many areas of the law. Because the Supreme Court must announce rights and remedies for fifty States, one National Government and over 300 million people, it is far more constrained than a state supreme court addressing a difficult problem for one State and, say, fifteen-million people.... In some settings, the challenge of imposing a constitutional solution on the whole country at once will increase the likelihood that federal constitutional law will be underenforced or that a "federalism discount" will be applied to the right. State courts face no such problem in construing their own constitutions.

State courts also have a freer hand in doing something the Supreme Court cannot: allowing local conditions and traditions to affect their interpretation of a constitutional guarantee and the remedies imposed to implement that guarantee. Does anyone doubt that . . . the Montana Supreme Court might look at property rights differently from other States or the United States Supreme Court? . . . State constitutional law respects and honors these differences between and among States by allowing fifty constitutions to be interpreted differently to account for these differences in culture, geography and history.

A mistaken or an ill-conceived constitutional decision is also easier to correct at the state level than it is at the federal level. Not only do the state courts have a narrower jurisdiction and smaller populations that their decisions will affect, but the people at the state level have other remedies at their disposal: an easier constitutional amendment process and, for better or worse, judicial elections. It thus is an area where a court can feel more free to experiment—to be the familiar "laboratories of experimentation" that Justice Brandeis described.

Perhaps the most significant comparative advantage that state courts have over federal courts—and the key reason it sometimes will be easier to win in state rather than federal court—is that the legal and equitable complexities of many issues do not lend themselves to one-size-fits-all solutions. . . . Many lawyers, law professors and law students, when coming across difficult areas of constitutional law, insist that there are no right answers to these questions or, worse, that policy preferences underlie judges' answers to these questions.

As to these vexing areas of the law, what better time to permit the state courts to adopt their own interpretation of parallel (or somewhat parallel) constitutional guarantees found in their own constitutions? When difficult areas of constitutional litigation arise—equal protection, free exercise or property rights—why should we assume that the United States Supreme Court is a Delphic Oracle, that it is the only supreme court in the country able to offer an insightful solution to a difficult problem? . . . In these settings, it may be more appropriate to have fifty-one imperfect solutions rather than one imperfect solution—particularly when imperfection may be something we invariably will have to live with in a given area.

In some cases, moreover, the only way a lawyer can win is through the state constitution because it is the only constitution with a provision on point. State constitutions have a variety of clauses found nowhere in the United States Constitution: single-subject clauses; uniform-law clauses; and right-to-remedies clauses. And some state constitutions have exotic clauses found in few, if any, [other] state constitutions.

So far, I have given two reasons why students ought to study state constitutional law: (1) every lawyer should prefer to have two arrows in her quiver rather than just one; and (2) it often will be easier to vindicate a state constitutional right in state court than a federal constitutional right in the United States Supreme Court.

There is a third reason: It may facilitate the development of federal constitutional law. The development of state constitutional law as a subject, and its revitalization as a litigation tool, may be the best thing that could happen for federal constitutional law. For too long, we have lived in a top-down constitutional world, in which the United States Supreme Court announces a ruling, and the state supreme courts move in lockstep in construing the counterpart guarantees of their own constitutions.

Why not do the reverse? ***

Notes on State Constitutionalism

1. Why would state constitutions, which are the law of the land (subject only to federal supremacy) for every American in all fifty states, require these relatively recent defenses of their relevance?

2. Is Justice Brennan's argument merely tactical, or is there reason to believe that state high courts may reliably protect individual rights better than the United States Supreme Court?

3. Professor Gardner finds that state courts have not delivered on Justice Brennan's promise of a "New Judicial Federalism" and is doubtful that they can deliver on that promise in the contemporary United States. Throughout the later materials are claims by justices and others that Montana's constitutional law is distinctive in important ways. Is it? Can it be? How and why might Montana constitutional law distinguish itself from national constitutional law at both the federal and state levels?

4. Professor Rodriguez suggests state constitutions cannot foster distinct state identities, but can sustain a state's communities of interest. What are some examples of such interests located within states, and how responsive can (or should) state constitutionalism be to those interests?

5. After reading Judge Sutton's arguments for state constitutional law, why would a professionally responsible lawyer not consider a state constitutional claim, at least in a case when they are considering a federal constitutional claim?

B. Framing the Montana Constitution

Montana's first constitution was written in a premature rush to statehood over a week in 1866 and was lost before publication somewhere between Helena and Washington, D.C. As a territory established in 1864, Montana was subject to direct or indirect federal control over all government functions. Residents of the territory voted for a territorial legislature, but both the governor and the three-member supreme court were appointed by the President. These officials typically came from "the East" and gained their positions through political patronage. Within two decades, Montanans again clamored for a new constitution, hopeful that a growing population would merit statehood, and convened in Helena to compose the 1884 Constitution. Again, the effort was premature, though within five years, Montanans' dreams of statehood were finally realized under an 1889 Constitution that closely resembled the draft of 1884. The legal precursor to the "Statehood" Montana Constitution is the 1889 Enabling Act, which set the terms under which Montana and its sibling states (North Dakota, South Dakota, and Washington) would enter the Union. Note the specific issues addressed in the Enabling Act, and how many of them have carried forward through the 1889 Constitution into the current Montana Constitution.

The Enabling Act of 1889 ("AN ACT to provide for the division of Dakota into two States and to enable the people of North Dakota, South Dakota, Montana, and Washington to form constitutions and State governments and to be admitted into the Union on an equal footing with the original States, and to make donations of public lands to such States")

25 Stat. 676 (1889)

Be it enacted by the Senate and House of Representatives of the United States of America in Congress assembled, That the inhabitants of all that part of the area of the United States now constituting the Territories of Dakota, Montana, and Washington, as at present described, may become the States of North Dakota, South Dakota, Montana, and Washington, respectively, as hereinafter provided. ***

SEC. 3. That all persons who are qualified by the laws of said Territories to vote for representatives to the legislative assemblies thereof, are hereby authorized to vote for and choose delegates to form conventions in said proposed States . . .

SEC. 4. That the delegates to the conventions elected as provided for in this act shall meet at the seat of government of each of said Territories . . . on the fourth day of July, eighteen hundred and eighty-nine, and, after organization, shall declare, on behalf of the people of said proposed States, that they adopt the Constitution of the United States; whereupon the said conventions shall be, and are hereby, authorized to form constitutions and States governments for said proposed states, respectively. The constitutions shall be republican in form, and make no distinction in civil or political rights on account of race or color, except as to Indians not taxed, and not be repugnant to the Constitution of the United States and the principles of the Declaration of Independence. And said conventions shall provide, by ordinances irrevocable without the consent of the United States and the people of said States:

First. That perfect toleration of religious sentiment shall be secured and that no inhabitant of said States shall ever be molested in person or property on account of his or her mode of religious worship.

Second. That the people inhabiting said proposed States do agree and declare that they forever disclaim all right and title to the unappropriated public lands lying within the boundaries thereof, and to all lands lying within said limits owned or held by any Indian or Indian tribes; and that until the title thereto shall have been extinguished by the United States, the same shall be and remain subject to the disposition of the United States, and said Indian lands shall remain under the absolute jurisdiction and control of the Congress of the United States . . .

Third. That the debts and liabilities of said Territories shall be assumed and paid by said States, respectively.

Fourth. That provision shall be made for the establishment and maintenance of systems of public schools, which shall be open to all the children of said States, and free from sectarian control.

[Sections 5–7 address the division of Dakota Territory into North and South Dakota.]

SEC. 8. . . . [T]he constitutional conventions which may assemble in North Dakota, Montana, and Washington shall provide in like manner for submitting the constitutions formed by them to the people of said proposed States, respectively, for ratification or rejection at elections to be held in said proposed States on the said first Tuesday in October. . . . And if the constitutions and governments of said proposed States are republican in form, and if all the provisions of this act have been complied with in the formation thereof, it shall be the duty of the President of the United States to issue his proclamation announcing the result of the election in each, and thereupon the proposed States which have adopted constitutions and formed State governments as herein provided shall be deemed admitted by Congress into the Union under and by virtue of this act on an equal footing with the original States from and after the date of said proclamation. ***

1. The 1889 Statehood Constitution

The 1889 Statehood Constitution was a means to an end: statehood, with full representation in Congress and, more importantly to Montanans, representation in the state executive and judicial branches. Yet that document structured eight decades of political development that built the State of Montana and set the stage for work on a new state constitution. In their definitive guide to the Montana Constitution, University of Montana Law Professors Larry Elison and Fritz Snyder explain the development of the Montana Constitution from statehood to the 1972 Constitutional Convention.

Larry M. Elison & Fritz Snyder, *The Montana State Constitution*

Part I, Montana Constitutional History (2001)

Montana's constitutional development traces primarily to two periods: the 1880s, which culminated in the Constitution of 1889, under which Montana was admitted to statehood; and the 1960s and early 1970s, which culminated in Montana's Constitution of 1972. Each constitution reflects the period in which it was framed; even though largely patterned after existing state constitutions, each had roots in Montana's own political, economic, and social experience.

In the territorial period (1864–1889), the primary constitutional goal was to achieve statehood and gain freedom from the restraints of federal territorial administration. Fundamental law for the Territory of Montana was the 1864 Organic Act, amended in 1867 and modified by subsequent federal law. The principal features included: congressional authority over the composition, length, and frequency of sessions of the territorial legislative assembly and the power of annulment over territorial enactments; presidential appointment of the territorial governor and secretary, which was overwhelmingly partisan and usually a reward for service outside of Montana; presidential appointment of the territorial chief justice and two associate justices; and an elected, non-voting delegate to the House of Representatives. ***

For a territory to be admitted into the union as a state, the territory had to first adopt and ratify a constitution. The drive for statehood commenced with an irregular and ill-fated constitutional convention convened in April 1866 by Acting Governor Thomas F. Meagher. The legislative assembly was in its second session; the territory's settlers numbered fewer than 20,000, still largely clustered in the mining centers of southwestern Montana. Fifty-five delegates met in Helena for six days and produced a constitutional document. The delegates borrowed from the proposed Colorado Constitution of 1865, which relied upon the Kansas Constitution of 1859. The document was never printed or submitted to the electorate. The only copy of the document was lost, and what details are known are derived from press reports. This early convention did little more than give notice of a serious commitment to seek statehood.

From 1883 on, pressures for statehood mounted in Montana as its population increased, its economy became more diverse, its communities grew and dispersed, and railroad lines provided new east-west and north-south links to the rest of the nation.

In 1883 the Montana territorial legislative assembly passed a House Joint Resolution providing for a constitutional convention.... The convention assembled in Helena on January 14, 1884, with instructions to adopt rules and draft a constitution which would be submitted to Montana voters at the 1884 general election.

The delegates brought experience in territorial government in Montana and elsewhere to the convention. Lawyers predominated, joined by delegates with mining, stock raising, farming, and other experience. Democrats outnumbered Republicans. The majority had been in Montana since the early 1860s and many had moved from mining to other occupations. William A. Clark, prominent as a mine owner and banker, was elected chairman. ***

A first reading of Montana's 1884 Constitution suggests special attention directed toward what would appear to be uniquely Montana (e.g., the tax exemption for mining claims, the right to cross private property for reservoirs and ditches, and the treatment of public land grants). Further study reveals that the Colorado Constitution had similar provisions derived from other constitutions. Colorado's models had been the recent constitutions of Illinois and Pennsylvania, documents written in

1870 and 1873. The Illinois and Pennsylvania constitutions were responsive to abuses characterized by legislative favors to developing industries and by hundreds of private bills and special local laws. The Montana Constitution of 1884 and the succeeding statehood Constitution of 1889 descended from and took on the character of most late-nineteenth century state constitutions, hallmarks of which were procedural and substantive restrictions on the legislature, a fragmented executive, and emphasis on proscriptive detail rather than fundamental law.

Territorial Delegate Joseph K. Toole presented the ratified 1884 Constitution to both sessions of the forty-ninth Congress (1885–1887), but Montana statehood remained mired in the broader politics of the admission of western states and the unresolved question of whether the Dakota Territory would be admitted as one or two states. By 1884 the Montana Territory had a population of about 135,000, which was adequate to support statehood, but the more significant issue was political. Other territories, including Dakota, Wyoming, Idaho, Washington, New Mexico, Arizona, and Utah, were also contesting for statehood. All faced delays based partly on specific local circumstances, but chiefly on partisan congressional considerations stemming from Democratic and Republican concern about preserving existing balances of political power. At that time Democrats controlled the Montana Territory. From 1884 through 1888 on the national level, the Republican Senate regularly blocked admittance of Democratic-controlled territories, while the Democratic House prevented the admission of Republican controlled territories. The impasse ended with the party conventions of 1888, when the Democrats adopted a plank for statehood for Montana, Dakota, Washington, and New Mexico, and the Republicans added Wyoming, Idaho, and Arizona. The long-awaited congressional action came early the following year. On February 22, 1889, President Cleveland signed an Omnibus Bill, authorizing Montana, Washington, North Dakota, and South Dakota to call constitutional conventions and submit ratified constitutions to Congress.

Montana responded quickly to congressional authorization. On July 4, 1889, 75 delegates convened in Helena to draft a constitution.... The lines of continuity to the 1884 convention and constitution were numerous.... Although each provision was debated, nearly 90 percent of the text of the 1884 Constitution was re-adopted.

The 1889 Constitution was enacted more as a tool to achieve statehood than to provide a well-thought-out structure of governance for the new state. The delegates, not surprisingly, were driven by self-interest and concerns about government abuse of power. Typical of state constitutions of its time, it minimized the powers of the executive branch and maximized the powers of the legislature. It forced the governor to work with myriad boards and commissions, particularly a powerful Board of Examiners consisting of the governor, the secretary of state, and the attorney general. The Board of Examiners had the powers now entrusted to the Department of Administration, which included the power to examine, and approve or reject claims against the state. ***

Montanans ratified the 1889 Constitution by an overwhelming 91.6 percent vote, 24,676 to 2,274. The document contained approximately 28,000 words. President

Benjamin Harrison proclaimed Montana the Union's forty-first state on November 8, 1889. The election for state legislators was far more contentious, and Montana commenced statehood with both houses evenly divided between Democrats and Republicans. The Montana Senate ultimately sent four senators to Washington, D.C., where the Republican majority promptly seated the two Republicans, Senators Wilbur Fisk Sanders and T.C. Power. The two Democrats returned to Montana.

... The Montana Constitutional Convention Memorandum notes that between 1889 and 1972 more than 500 amendments were introduced in the legislature, and of that number 61 were approved by the legislature for submission to the voters. (One amendment in 1904 was divided into two amendments when the secretary of state placed it on the ballot, increasing the number of amendments to 62.) Of the 62 approved, one was vetoed by the governor and four more were invalidated by the supreme court prior to the election in which they would have been considered. Of the 58 amendments submitted for voter approval, 18 were rejected and 40 were approved, of which three were annulled by the supreme court for procedural irregularities, leaving 37 amendments approved and in effect.... The 157 sections of the 1889 Constitution were increased to 181 through amendments.

In Montana, as elsewhere in the nation, the early years of the twentieth century produced increased demands for government services and programs. [By mid-century,] [v]eteran politicians, as well as newcomers to the political process, realized that structural changes were necessary....

Notes on the 1889 Constitution and Statehood

1. The 1972 Constitution adopted many of the provisions from Montana's 1889 "Statehood" Constitution. How might this account of the 1889 Constitution's origins and sources inform the legal meaning of the current Montana Constitution? Where the 1972 text carries over from the 1889 version, or from intervening amendments, there may be nearly a century of historical judicial interpretations. When and how should these pre-1972 cases inform the modern reader of the Montana Constitution's current meaning?

2. The first section of the Montana Constitution contains an important incident of statehood carried over from the 1889 Constitution:

> **Compact With The United States.** All provisions of the enabling act of Congress (approved February 22, 1889, 25 Stat. 676), as amended and of Ordinance No. 1, appended to the Constitution of the state of Montana and approved February 22, 1889, including the agreement and declaration that all lands owned or held by any Indian or Indian tribes shall remain under the absolute jurisdiction and control of the congress of the United States, continue in full force and effect until revoked by the consent of the United States and the people of Montana.
>
> *Makes it clear that the new constitution does not affect any agreements made with the United States Government when Montana first became a state.*

This reflects the state's continued adherence to the terms of statehood, including the express reservation of federal power over "all lands owned or held by any Indian or Indian tribes." Embedded in this Compact "with the United States" is a history of settler colonization of Indigenous lands through war against and removal of Indigenous peoples. They have since time immemorial lived on the lands now occupied by Montana and continue to have a crucial presence in the area today. The project of Montana as a territory and then a state is inextricably intertwined with this history. A later chapter addresses the status of Indigenous people under the Montana Constitution, though as the Compact suggests, the broader issue of tribal-state relations is a subject of Federal Indian Law. For now, note that the Montana Constitution begins by disclaiming any jurisdiction over Indian country (as defined in various ways by federal law). This does not, however, mean that Indigenous people in Montana are strangers to its state constitutional powers and rights outside of Indian country, such as the duty to preserve Indigenous peoples' cultural integrity and the prohibition of discrimination based on Indigenous culture. Whenever and wherever the State of Montana acts, it is bound by both the federal and state constitutions.

2. Drafting the 1972 Constitution

When one hundred elected delegates convened in Helena, Montana in the late winter of 1972, they and those around them understood that they were making history. For a lawyer, this history serves as an important source of constitutional meaning. Throughout this book, the Montana Supreme Court and others will come back to the drafting history as relevant and sometimes dispositive of questions arising under the Montana Constitution. Although the generally available eight-volume transcripts of the Constitutional Convention are the most commonly cited historical source in the courts, they are not as definitive as they may seem. The Montana Legislature assembled and published those volumes seven years after the Convention, in 1979, so the delegates as drafters and the voters as lawmakers had to rely on other sources in their deliberations and debates. These include the contemporary reports of the Convention in newspapers and published commentaries, as well as an exhaustive set of background materials that provided a rich intellectual foundation for the drafting process. These also include the records of the ratification campaign itself in official and unofficial pamphlets actually relied upon by Montanans in casting their votes. Tyler Stockton, a law student at the time, reexamines the documentary history of the 1972 Constitution in the following article (originally a paper in the Montana Constitution course). Although Stockton offers some suggestions about how to use constitutional sources consistent with a theory of original meaning, he also explains the basic process and players producing both the Montana Constitution and a broad written record of the debates that surrounded it.

The recorded deliberations and debates on the 1972 Constitution are all the more important because of the narrow margin by which Montanans ratified the document. Indeed, while a slight majority of Montanans who voted on ratification supported the new constitution — a margin of nearly three thousand voters — that majority was only a plurality of all voters in the election. More than seven thousand voters who cast ballots on options for a bicameral legislature, gambling, and capital punishment failed to cast a vote for or against the constitution. State and federal courts rejected challenges to ratification arising from this confusion. In subsequent calls for a constitutional convention, held every twenty years in 1990 and 2010 pursuant to Article XIV, section 3, wide majorities of Montanans repeatedly voted in favor of retaining the 1972 Constitution. Still, the narrow margin of ratification serves as a reminder that every argument made for the Montana Constitution and each of its provisions, whether on the floor of the Convention or in the pages of a pamphlet, may have been essential to its adoption.

Tyler Stockton, *Originalism and the Montana Constitution*

77 Mont. L. Rev. 117, 119–25, 143–48 (2016)

In 1967, the Montana Legislature ordered the Legislative Council to evaluate the Montana Constitution. The Legislative Council's report recommended substantial changes to the constitution with a focus on creating an "active, dynamic government." In response, the Montana Legislature created a Constitutional Revision Commission in 1969 to study the Montana Constitution and provide recommendations for improvement. The Commission determined a constitutional convention was necessary, a decision that was supported by numerous other groups. A referendum for a new constitutional convention passed 133,482–71,643 in November of 1970.

During the period between the referendum and the convention, the Montana Legislature tasked a team of researchers to compile notes and compare other state constitutions to aid the upcoming convention in drafting the proposed constitution. Chaired by Alexander Blewett, this team of researchers was known as the Montana Constitutional Convention Commission. The Commission produced a series of research papers organized into two groups: Constitutional Convention Studies and Research Memorandums. The studies covered various topics, providing background information for modern constitution drafting and the provisions found in other new constitutions across the United States. The memorandums covered topics not worthy of an official report, such as the rules for operating a convention. The researchers compiled over 2,300 pages of materials evaluating constitutions across the United States, the principles of constitutional law, and other various topics.

On January 17, 1972, a hundred delegates elected from across the state met in Helena to begin drafting the proposed constitution. The convention lasted for over two months and the delegates extensively debated each provision in the document. Each delegate's own knowledge and experience — including individual delegate proposals for provisions — the reports prepared by the Montana Constitutional Convention Commission, and the earlier reports by the Constitutional Revision Commission and the Legislative Council Convention informed the Convention debates. The constitution's emphasis on direct participation in governmental decisions was a reflection of the delegates' populist worldview. As Constitutional Convention President Leo Graybill noted, the Constitutional Convention "overlooked no opportunity to publicize its activities and to encourage public participation." Every vote and meeting (including all committees) "were open to the public and the press." This openness created an extensive amount of news coverage and public notice regarding the Convention and the decisions made therein. The delegates signed the proposed constitution on March 24, 1972.

After the Convention approved the proposed constitution, the delegates created a voter education committee to use the remaining funds provided by the Montana Legislature for educational efforts regarding the new constitution. To fund the voter education, the committee planned to spend a remaining $15,000 from the Legislature's grant to the Constitutional Convention and another $30,000 from a HUD grant. However, Oscar S. Kvaalen brought a class action suit to bar the committee's educational efforts, arguing the Constitutional Convention's power ended upon its conclusion and therefore it could not conduct the educational initiative. The Montana Supreme Court granted Kvaalen's request:

> [W]e hold that the Constitutional Convention itself possesses no power or authority to receive or expend public funds for voter education beyond the specific requirements and authority found in the Enabling Act; that these requirements in the Enabling Act have already been satisfied; and that the Convention lacks power or authority to receive or expend further public funds for voter education in the manner proposed by the committee.

The enabling act for the Constitutional Convention had only authorized the Secretary of State to send out a Voter Information Pamphlet—also called the "explanatory notes" to the proposed constitution—and that was the extent of the power granted by the Montana Legislature. The Court, however, made it clear that the ruling did not prohibit delegates from pursuing education efforts on their own.

The Voter Information Pamphlet was 24 pages long and provided explanations for each provision in the proposed constitution. The first page of the pamphlet prominently noted it was the "Official Publication of the 1972 Constitution Proposed by the 1971–1972 Montana Constitutional Convention," its publication was expressly required by "Chapter 206, 1971 Laws of Montana," and it was financed by an appropriation of the Montana Legislature. The Secretary of State distributed the Voter Information Pamphlet to all registered voters. Due to the Court's ruling in *Kvaalen* [*v. Graybill* (Mont. 1972)], the Voter Information Pamphlet was the only official explanation of the proposed constitution.

Following *Kvaalen*, the delegates, along with other advocacy groups both for and against the proposed constitution, immediately began funding their own educational efforts across Montana. A group of delegates formed the Concerned Citizens for Constitutional Improvement and funded a pamphlet titled *The Proposed 1972 Constitution for the State of Montana*, which was commonly known as the Roeder Pamphlet because it was drafted by Dr. Richard B. Roeder and Dr. Pierce C. Mullen.

The pamphlet was distributed across all of Montana as a newspaper insert. The Roeder Pamphlet contained detailed descriptions of the provisions and explanations of what they meant. It also contained a note at the end that it had been reviewed for "accuracy, style, and objectivity" by Mrs. Margaret S. Warden, Mrs. Thomas Payne, and Mr. Fred Martin.

On the other side of the state, Gerald J. Neely, a Billings lawyer, published a pamphlet titled *A Critical Look: Montana's New Constitution* and sent it to a distribution list developed during the Constitutional Convention. Mr. Neely had been a United Press International string reporter throughout the Constitutional Convention and had published a newsletter during the Constitutional Convention known as the Con Con Newsletter. The pamphlet contained commentary on what the proposed constitution meant. Neely's commentary has been referred to as a fairly neutral document reflecting on the proposed constitution.

Throughout the Constitutional Convention and the ratification process, Montana newspapers published extensive articles on the proposed document. News coverage came primarily from the Associated Press, the Lee State Bureau, and the Tribune State Bureau. The Tribune printed 430 stories covering over 5,300 column-inches between January 17, 1972 and March 24, 1972. The Missoulian ran 347 stories for a total of 4,300 column-inches. The Gazette ran 271 stories covering 3,200 column inches. Each of these papers also ran numerous editorials: the Tribune ran 26, the Missoulian 22, and the Gazette 13. Newspapers and news agencies dedicated five full-time reporters to the Constitutional Convention: the Associated Press had one, the Tribune Capitol Bureau had two, and Lee Newspapers State Bureau (serving the Gazette, the Standard, the Missoulian, and the Independent Record) had two. And, although there was no television press assigned to the Convention, Cable TV provided 25 hours of coverage. During the ratification period between the Constitutional Convention and the June 6, 1972, vote, the Associated Press released a ten-article series and the Lee State Bureau carried a 21-article series explaining the new constitution.

Opposition material came primarily from the Farm Bureau Federation, the Taxpayers Association, and some unions. Opponents used newspaper coverage, radio, and television to air their objections. The Associated Press noted "most of the opposition focused on the taxation article." Supporting the tax opposition was the highway lobby, which included unions, oil companies, and Montana's AAA. Particularly, they disagreed with the proposal to allow the diversion of earmarked highway funds by a three-fifths vote of the Montana Legislature.

Finally, proponents and opponents engaged in a varying array of private correspondence and local advocacy. The AFL-CIO, one of the unions supporting the constitution, produced a flyer debunking rumors about the proposed constitution. The Montana Common Cause endorsed the proposal with a letter hoping for a unicameral legislature, annual legislative sessions, and a strong right to know provision. The Montana League of Cities and Towns penned a letter to one of the delegates noting the proposed constitution was an "excellent document" that would be a "foundation on which Montana can progress in the future." The Montana Farm Bureau opposed the taxing provisions, noting the proposed document would "eliminate the requirement that taxes be collected uniformly." The Associated General Contractors of America published a letter to their members in Montana noting the proposed document had a "watered-down proposal" for the anti-diversion amendment.

Following a brief and intense period after the Constitutional Convention's proposal on March 24, 1972, the voters ratified the new constitution on June 6, 1972, by a thin margin: 116,415–113,883. In 1979, the Montana Legislature, the Montana Legislative Council, and the Constitutional Convention's Editing and Publishing Committee published the entirety of the Constitutional Convention in a series of eight volumes. The series, titled 1971–1972 Montana Constitutional Convention, contained a brief history of the Convention, the proposals made by individual delegates, the Committee Proposals for each section of the proposed constitution, and a verbatim transcript of the entire Constitutional Convention.

In 2008, Professor Robert Natelson, with the aid of the libraries at Montana State University and the University of Montana, the Montana Historical Society, and various delegates, pulled many of the above noted ratification materials together and digitized the collection. The materials are now available online at the William J. Jameson Law Library at the University of Montana School of Law.

* * *

[Based on originalist theory, Stockton critiques practitioners' and courts' common reliance on the "original intent" of the delegates as expressed in Constitutional Convention Transcripts published after ratification. He argues the Constitution's public meaning for the voters at the time of ratification, not the expressed intentions of the drafters in the later transcription, should determine the intent of the constitutional text. Yet, as of 2016, "the Court has cited or referred to the Constitutional Convention transcripts at least 164 times. The Court has referred to only 13 other ratification-era sources and only four of those references come after the transcripts were published."

Stockton suggests an improved approach to Montana constitutional sources based on several factors rooted in interpretive theory: "(1) timeframe of the document; (2) reliance versus contract understanding; (3) timing and distribution of the publication; (4) public versus private understanding; and (5) character of the author." According to Stockton the most reliable sources of meaning are, in descending order of priority:]

> 1. *Voter Information Pamphlet.* The Voter Information Pamphlet meets each and every factor and carries considerable weight. The Voter Information Pamphlet was the only official, government-sponsored document published regarding the constitution. It was distributed to all registered voters.

2. *Roeder Pamphlet.* The Roeder Pamphlet meets many of the same factors as found in the Voter Information Pamphlet, with the exception of one: government publication. The Roeder Pamphlet was not an official publication, but it did come from a very reliable source. Dr. Richard Roeder, one of the princip[al] authors of the pamphlet and a convention delegate, was a well-known Montana State University history professor who later co-authored *Montana: A History of Two Centuries*. Further, the pamphlet had extensive distribution across Montana. The pamphlet was inserted into almost every newspaper across the state in time for voters to read and understand.

3. *Neely Pamphlet.* Gerald Neely, a Billings attorney, authored *A Critical Look: Montana's New Constitution*, a document now known as the Neely Pamphlet. During the Constitutional Convention, Neely published a newsletter and worked as a United Press International reporter on the Convention. Although the extent of the pamphlet's distribution is unknown, the subscription nature of it, built through the prior newsletters Neely published during the Constitutional Convention, at least points to a somewhat wide distribution. Neely's status as a recognized attorney and his work as a reporter during the Convention also lends extensive weight to the character of the author.

4. *Constitutional Convention Transcripts.* The actual Constitutional Convention transcripts are missing some important factors necessary to give them considerable interpretive weight. While clearly a founding-era document, the transcripts were not available in published form until 1979, well after the ratification. This gives rise to problems with public understanding and reliance theory. The transcripts' lack of availability during ratification means there was very limited public knowledge of the minute-by-minute transcripts and therefore they could not have informed public meaning or been used as a reliance-based document.

5. *Montana Constitutional Convention Commission Reports.* Similar to the Constitutional Convention transcripts, the Commission Reports, though founding-era documents, had limited availability. The focused nature of the reports—"for the Convention"—implies a very limited distribution. The Commission Reports were published to aid the delegates, not the public, in preparing for the Constitutional Convention. Therefore, the dual lack of reliance and informing public meaning limits their function to informing the delegates themselves.

6. *1889 Constitution.* The 1889 Constitution has limited, but important, interpretive weight. As Montana's constitution leading up to the 1972 Constitutional Convention, the 1889 Constitution was a very well-known and thoroughly interpreted document. The 1889 Constitution was a founding-era document, appropriately timed because it was in place until the new

constitution was ratified and widely distributed. The Voter Information Pamphlet also created extensive reliance on the 1889 Constitution itself. When provisions in the proposed constitution were left unchanged from the 1889 Constitution or had minor modifications, the Voter Information Pamphlet noted such and provided no further explanation.

7. Ratification Era Newspaper Articles & Opinion Pieces. Throughout the Constitutional Convention and the ensuing ratification process, newspapers across Montana published various articles regarding the Convention, the proposed constitution, and its meaning. These articles carry the character weight found in journalism and ought to be regarded as reliable sources. Newspaper articles functioned as reliance-based documents that individuals would have used to understand the proposed constitution and therefore would have provided a public meaning on the topics and provisions covered.... Therefore, depending on the geographic distribution, newspaper articles should be weighed equal with the statewide pamphlets or below them.

8. Varying Private Documents, Correspondence, or Association Materials. The Documentary History of the Ratification of the Montana Constitution Collection housed at the Jameson Law Library contains a broad array of newsletters, letters, memorandums, and other correspondence from delegates, private citizens, and various associations both supporting and opposing the 1972 Constitution. Although clearly timely and founding-era documents, most of these materials were quite limited in distribution. Many were letters within specific advocacy organizations or private correspondence responding to an inquiry. As such, these factors lower the weight of these materials to contract-based understanding or smaller, public meanings.

9. Opposition Materials. During the ratification debate, there was significant opposition to the proposed constitution. Opposition largely rallied around taxation issues and was prevalent in newspaper, radio, and television coverage. However, even though the vote was close, the opponents lost. Opponents could have had two major disagreements with the proposed constitution: differences over meaning and impact; or differences over policy choice as a whole. Either way, the opponent's interpretation was not the dominant meaning and the proposed policy choices were rejected.

Note on Drafting the 1972 Constitution

1. The best analyses of constitutional text will draw on several sources of legal meaning where available, and avoid "streetlight effects," when someone who loses his keys in the park at night goes to a streetlight to look for them because the light is better there. What role should relatively recent debates by the framers and ratifiers — including some Montanans who still engage in public life (and occasionally

appear as plaintiffs in constitutional cases) — play in interpreting disputed constitutional text? Is it possible the delegates who framed the Constitution might have originally intended some of its text to bear an esoteric (and potentially controversial) legal meaning while hoping the public originally (mis)understood the text to be less controversial for ratification's sake?

Sample ballot and explanation from the Roeder Pamphlet.

3. Ratifying the 1972 Constitution

After a hard-fought campaign, the ratification election led to an unusual result. In an attempt to prevent ratification from being derailed by politically controversial proposals concerning a unicameral legislature, legalized gambling, and the death penalty, the Constitutional Convention proposed these issues as separate votes on the ratification ballot. Of the votes to ratify, the new constitution narrowly passed. In Butte, however, only 47 percent of voters approved the constitution even as 73 percent of voters favored the side issue of legalized gambling. The deviation contributed to a final tally in which the new constitution won only a plurality of total votes cast. Opponents of the new constitution mobilized for one last campaign in the courts. After a close rejection of their claims 3-2 at the Montana Supreme Court in the summer of 1972, the parties headed to federal court. On July 11, 1973, ten days after the new constitution's effective date, a three-judge panel of the United States Court for the District of Montana unanimously rejected the federal constitutional challenge.

Burger v. Judge

364 F. Supp. 504 (D. Mont. 1973)

Before BROWNING, Circuit Judge, and MURRAY and JAMESON, District Judges.

PER CURIAM:

Plaintiffs seek a declaratory judgment "that the proposed Constitution for the State of Montana was declared adopted in violation of the Fourteenth Amendment to the Constitution of the United States, Article IV, Section 4 of the Constitution of the United States, and the Voting Rights Act of 1965 (42 U.S.C. Section 1973) and is, therefore, void." . . .

At a special election on June 6, 1972 the electors of Montana voted on four propositions submitted by a Constitutional Convention held pursuant to (1) the authority of Section 8 of Article XIX of the Montana Constitution; (2) the vote of the electors of Montana at the general election on November 3, 1970; and (3) the Enabling Act of the Legislative Assembly of the State of Montana, Chapter 296, Session Laws of 1971, as amended by Chapter 1, Laws of First Extraordinary Session, 1971.

[The Court explained the ballot design and questions.]

237,600 electors voted at the special election on June 6, 1972. Of this number 116,415 voted for the proposed constitution (Proposition 1) and 113,883 voted against it. A total of 7,302 persons voted neither for nor against the proposed constitution, but voted on one or more of the other propositions. Thereupon the Governor of Montana proclaimed that the proposed constitution had been approved and adopted.

Original proceedings were instituted in the Supreme Court of Montana by William F. Cashmore and Stanley C. Burger (one of the plaintiffs in this action), relators, against the Governor of Montana "seeking a declaratory judgment that the proposed 1972 Montana Constitution was not ratified and adopted because it was not 'approved by a majority of the electors voting at the election' as required by

Article XIX, Section 8 of the present Montana Constitution." *State ex rel. Cashmore v. Anderson* [(Mont. 1972)]. The Supreme Court of Montana in its opinion on August 18, 1972, held, inter alia:

> "Accordingly, we hold that 'approval by a majority of the electors voting at the election' as used in Article XIX, Section 8, of the Montana Constitution means approval by a majority of the total number of electors casting valid ballots on the question of approval or rejection of the proposed 1972 Montana Constitution. We hold that it does not refer to or include those electors who failed to express an opinion by a vote on that issue. The Secretary of State's certificate shows 116,415 votes in favor of the proposed constitution and 113,883 votes against the proposed constitution and no one contends these figures are incorrect. As these figures carry a presumption of correctness by statute, and as there is nothing to indicate otherwise, we hold that the proposed 1972 Montana Constitution was approved by the required majority and the Governor's proclamation thereof was correct. [Fn. Two of the five justices dissented, and "would hold that the *** language 'a majority of the electors voting at the election', means just what it says", and that "the natural significance" of this language "is that to determine whether the proposed constitution was adopted, you count the total number of electors voting at the election, and one half plus one must have voted for the measure or it fails."]

A Petition for a Writ of Certiorari to the Supreme Court of the United States filed by Burger was denied without comment by an order entered February 20, 1973. This action followed. ***

We turn now to the merits of the controversy.... Plaintiffs rely upon the Montana court's interpretation "to prove that the representations made by Montana officials prior to the election, and on the Ballot, as to what effect an elector's voting decision would have, were actually wrong." They argue that 7,302 electors were "misled by the change of rules, after the election was over," were "disenfranchised by the misleading and erroneous information," and "that the Federal Constitution and law will protect them from such action."

In support of their contention that the 7,302 electors were misled, plaintiffs rely upon (1) the official ballot; (2) an official publication mailed to all voters; (3) a newspaper supplement, 197,500 copies of which were distributed by the 13 leading newspapers in the state; (4) an analysis prepared by the Montana Constitutional Convention Commission in 1971; (5) debate in the Constitutional Convention; and (6) Section 17(9) of Ch. 296, 1971 Session Laws.

The plaintiff Burger voted against the proposed constitution. The plaintiff Garrettson was one of the 7,302 electors who did not vote on the constitution. (Proposition One). He testified in his deposition that he voted for a bicameral legislature, gambling, and the death penalty, and that he understood that if the proposed constitution failed "the alternate issues also fail." He failed to vote on the proposed constitution for two reasons: first, because he did not know enough "about the issues involved", and second, because he felt that if he did not vote, "it was a vote against it." He had read the ballot and the newspaper supplement. Garrettson's wife voted as he did. There was no further testimony with respect to any other electors.

With respect to the official ballot, plaintiffs rely upon the recitals that, "If the proposed constitution fails to receive a majority of the votes cast, alternate issues also fail," and "The proposed constitution will include a bicameral (2 houses) legislature unless a majority of those voting in this election vote for a unicameral (one house) legislature in Issue 2." The reference to the "majority of those voting in this election" simply follows the language of the then existing constitution providing that no revision, alteration or amendment shall take effect unless approved by "a majority of the electors voting at the election". It is obvious that if the proposed constitution failed to pass, the alternate issues would also fail. The ballot contains and underscores the statement "PLEASE VOTE ON ALL FOUR ISSUES." ***

There is no suggestion that any publication or statement, either official or unofficial, was intended to misrepresent any facts or deceive or mislead the voters. The official ballot and publication followed the language of the existing constitution. The other statements at most contained an erroneous interpretation of an ambiguous provision in the Montana Constitution—an interpretation deemed correct by two of the five justices of the Montana Supreme Court.

In no document was there any advice or suggestion that the electors should not vote on the proposed constitution. On the contrary, the unofficial as well as the official publications urged a vote on all four issues. Additionally the newspaper supplement and other unofficial statements cautioned the electors that if they did not vote on the constitution (or any of the other issues) they would aid in its defeat. While this interpretation of the language in the existing constitution was subsequently held erroneous, it was made in good faith and was not an unreasonable interpretation when it was made. In any event, it is clear that all electors who were in fact opposed to the proposed constitution could have expressed their disapproval by voting against it.

This is not a case where any electors were deprived of a right to vote or where there was any debasement or dilution in their votes. Nor is it a case where the voters were misled with respect to the content or meaning of any of the issues submitted to them. The 7,302 electors clearly had a right and opportunity to vote on the proposed constitution and in fact were urged to do so.

If, under these circumstances, any electors were in fact misled, they were simply mistaken as to the effect of their abstention from voting and not deprived of any right or opportunity to vote in violation of Article IV, Section 4 of the Constitution of the United States, the Fourteenth Amendment to the Constitution, or the Voting Rights Act of 1965 (42 U.S.C. § 1973).

The motion to dismiss accordingly has been granted.

Notes on Ratifying the 1972 Constitution

1. After the Montana Supreme Court rejected a request to spend remaining convention funds on voter information in *Kvaalen*, convention president Leo Graybill complained to the newspapers that "it is ironic that efficiency is rewarded with a blast by the court." Graybill, a Great Falls lawyer often credited with mediating many of the deepest disagreements arising in the convention, was called before the Montana Supreme Court for an unusual public apology during the ratification campaign. *See In re Graybill* (Mont. 1972). University of Montana Political Science Professor Ellis Waldron, a member of the 1971 Constitutional Convention Commission, later concluded that in the years before the Convention, the Supreme Court had been "notably 'activist' in its willingness to become involved in the processes of constitutional revision, and notably 'conservative' in its view of the power of the people and their constituted representatives to change basic constitutional rules." *See* Ellis Waldron, *The Role of the Montana Supreme Court in Constitutional Revision*, 35 MONT. L. REV. 227, 229 (1974). What is a state supreme court's proper concern with rewriting the state constitution?

2. The Supreme Court of the United States affirmed *Burger v. Judge* on December 3, 1973, and the 1972 Montana Constitution was settled as the law of the land. This formative episode recalls the narrow margins in several states for the ratification of the United States Constitution: ten or fewer delegate votes in New Hampshire, Virginia, New York, and Rhode Island. Does the close and controversial ratification result bear any meaning for the constitution's effect?

C. Constitutional Revision

Self-government. The people have the exclusive right of governing themselves as a free, sovereign, and independent state. They may alter or abolish the constitution and form of government whenever they deem it necessary.

No change except in grammar. Gives Montanans the right to govern themselves and to determine their form of government.

MONT. CONST. Article II, § 2

Amendment by legislative referendum. Amendments to this constitution may be proposed by any member of the legislature. If adopted by an affirmative roll call vote of two-thirds of all the members thereof, whether one or more bodies, the proposed amendment shall be submitted to the qualified electors at the next general election. If approved by a majority of the electors voting thereon, the amendment shall become a part of this constitution on the first day of July after certification of the election returns unless the amendment provides otherwise.

Revises 1889 constitution. Legislature may propose constitutional amendment by a vote of two-thirds of total membership rather than two-thirds of each house. Provides for July effective date for amendments.

MONT. CONST. Article XIV, § 8

Amendment by initiative. (1) The people may also propose constitutional amendments by initiative. Petitions including the full text of the proposed amendment shall be signed by at least ten percent of the qualified electors of the state. That number shall include at least ten percent of the qualified electors in each of at least one-half of the counties. ***

New provision. Ten percent of voters may propose constitutional amendments by petition.

MONT. CONST. Article XIV, § 9

Submission. If more than one amendment is submitted at the same election, each shall be so prepared and distinguished that it can be voted upon separately.

New provision. Self-explanatory.

MONT. CONST. Article XIV, § 11

We might be in danger of flooding the Montana Constitution with amendment after amendment that would be better put in the statutes, and we'll have a Constitution that looks like California and Louisiana.

Del. Robert Vermillion, 1972 Montana Constitutional Convention

One important distinction between the federal Constitution and most state constitutions, including the Montana Constitution, is the ease of amendment. Article V of the United States Constitution requires two-thirds of Congress to propose and three-fourths of the States to ratify any amendments (resulting in only 17 amendments over more than two centuries), or a convention for proposing amendments called by two-thirds of states and ratified by three-fourths of states (something that never has happened). Nearly every state provides for ratification of constitutional amendments by a simple majority vote of the electorate, and Montana is one of sixteen states providing for proposal of constitutional amendments by popular initiative through a petition process.

The Montana Constitution has been amended the second fewest number of times of any current state constitution, at a far lower rate than the rate for the most actively amended constitutions. Since 1972, Montanans amended the Constitution at an average rate of once each year, but nearly all of those amendments were referenda; Montanans approved initiated amendments less than once every seven years. These rates fall below the median state rate of nearly one-and-one-half constitutional amendments per year, including one initiated amendment every five years in the sixteen states that provide for the direct constitutional initiative.

Before we consider the Montana Constitution in detail, it is worth examining the dynamics of constitutional amendment. Unlike in federal constitutional law, popular amendment of the state constitutional text is a realistic option for Montanans. This power can constrain both the legislature and the courts, so its potential exercise adds a new dimension to constitutional politics in the state.

Montana law regulates constitutional revision in several ways to promote deliberation over proposed amendments. Constitutional signature and title requirements, elaborated by statutory submission and election laws, regulate the process of balloting constitutional amendments referred to the voters by the Legislature (constitutional referenda) and constitutional amendments initiated by petition from voters (constitutional initiatives). The constitutional "separate amendment" rule requires each amendment to "be so prepared and distinguished that it can be voted upon separately." Although the voter explanation of the separate amendment rule calls it "self-explanatory," the rule has become a difficult and controversial constraint on constitutional revision. As you read the cases below, consider the Supreme Court's role in refereeing the rules of constitutional amendment, and how tensions between popular sovereignty and judicial review that emerged in the development of the 1972 Montana Constitution may reemerge in the amendment process.

Anthony Johnstone, *The Constitutional Initiative in Montana*

71 Mont. L. Rev. 325, 380–82 (2010)

The Montana Constitution provides innovative structural checks and individual rights that constrain the popular will in service to its aspirations of "quality of life, equality of opportunity and . . . the blessings of liberty." It is also fundamentally a democratic document that owes its current form and continuation to the consent of a simple majority of voters. Popular sovereignty therefore motivates the Montana Constitution, not only as an original matter in the theory of its conception, but also as a contemporary matter in the practice of its amendment. The constitutional initiative originated and operates as a direct expression of popular sovereignty.

The power to amend the Constitution by petition and majority vote is a solution to the basic problem of inflexible and unresponsive state government that motivated the 1972 Constitutional Convention. Delegates understood, however, that the use of that power also can cause the same problems it is intended to solve. The flexibility and responsiveness that the Constitution enables in state government, when translated into the process of amending the Constitution itself, can lead back to the eventual inadequacy of the 1889 Constitution or lead on to the political sclerosis of "a Constitution that looks like California." Delegates in convention and proponents in ratification recognized that the best way to accommodate needed textual flexibility without compromising future responsiveness was "reliance on the legislature": in a word, politics.

Although the Montana Constitution is amended more often than its predecessor, it is amended less often than many other state constitutions with similar amendment processes. The Legislature, not petitioners, dominates the amendment process, and only three constitutional initiatives are now part of the constitutional text. Strict enforcement of procedural rules and signature gathering reforms maintain the integrity of the petition and the vote against fraud or mistake, although too strict enforcement of the Separate Amendment Rule threatens a judicial veto of otherwise proper amendments. Montanans strongly endorsed the text of their Constitution when it last came to a vote, and they rarely seek to overrule its interpretation by the Supreme Court. Today, the Montana Constitution keeps remarkably close to its original form as one of the shortest state constitutions.

This may change. An increasingly easy supply of qualified initiatives balloted by professional signature gatherers will be more sensitive to popular demand for amendments. Demand, in terms of approval of amendments by the people, will depend on the state government's responsiveness. If the Legislature is unable or, in the case of constitutional referenda, unwilling, to resolve policy issues, or if the Supreme Court is too willing to reject the Legislature's resolution of policy issues, then demand for constitutional amendments may increase. Based on the number of proposed and nearly approved amendments in the past, a significant increase in either supply or demand could tip the Montana Constitution toward the length of the inflexible document it replaced, but with less of a possibility for revision.

The paradox of the constitutional initiative is that it guarantees popular sovereignty over the Constitution to an extent that government under the Constitution can become unresponsive to the people. The Montana Constitution avoided this fate in its first four decades, but it continues to pose the question of its future in the amendment provisions of Article XIV. The delegates who authored and the voters who ordained the Constitution understood that the answer to that question depends on the people to whom they entrusted it. The Montana Constitution can enable politics as an enduring set of basic principles, or it can preempt politics as a contested list of detailed policies. It cannot do both, as long as the constitutional initiative gives the people the last word.

Harper v. Greely

234 Mont. 259 (1988)

HARRISON, Justice.

*** Over the fifteen years since adoption of Montana's 1972 Constitution, no provision in that Constitution has received more attention than Article XII, which relates to the economic assistance and social rehabilitative services to those in need. *** This philosophy of caring for the needy is not new to Montana, Art. X, sec. 5 of our original Constitution of 1889, State Institutions and Public Buildings, was directed to this very problem. Art. X, sec. 5 Mont. Const. (1889) read:

> The several counties of the state shall provide as may be prescribed by law for those inhabitants, who, by reason of age, infirmity or misfortune, may have claims upon the sympathy and aid of society.

That section and the numerous cases interpreting it served this state for over eighty years through depressed times, including the Great Depression of the 1930s. It was not until Montana's 1972 Constitutional Convention met that a new philosophy of caring for those in need evolved in this state. The new article, Art. XII, sec. 3, again is directed at institutions and assistance. Section 3(3) states the philosophy of the 1972 Constitution:

> (3) The legislature shall provide such economic assistance and social and rehabilitative services as may be necessary for those inhabitants who, by reasons of age, infirmities, or misfortune may have need for the aid of society.

From this subsection comes the understandings and misunderstandings of the people of this state as to whether this section guarantees a constitutional right to public assistance for the citizens of this state. *In Butte Community Union v. Lewis* (Mont. 1986), Mr. Justice Morrison writing for the majority noted:

> There is no constitutional right to welfare within the Montana Constitution's Declaration of Rights. Further, the right to welfare is not a right upon which constitutionally guaranteed rights depend. In fact, welfare is more properly characterized as a benefit. Since welfare is not a fundamental right, strict scrutiny does not apply and the State need show something less than a compelling state interest in order to limit that right.

It should be noted that in this opinion Mr. Justice Sheehy, while specially concurring, stated:

> I do not wish to be bound by the statement in the majority opinion that fundamental rights under the Montana Constitution must be found within the Declaration of Rights, Art. II. The Article holds itself open to unenumerated rights which may not be denied to the people.

Butte Community Union.

In a later case, *Butte Community Union v. Lewis* (Mont. 1987), authored by Mr. Justice Sheehy, we affirmed the district court's finding unconstitutional a law passed by the Legislature, noting:

> The legislature, in determining where sacrifices, are necessary, should regard "welfare benefits grounded in the constitution itself are deserving of great protection." *Butte Community Union v. Lewis.* The State may legitimately limit its expenditures for public assistance, public education or any other program even-handedly applied. It may not limit its expenditures by the expedient of eliminating classes of eligible individuals from public assistance without regard to their constitutionally grounded right to society's aid when needed, through misfortune, for the basic necessities of life. We do not

> hereby declare that inhabitants have a constitutional right to public assistance. We do declare that the legislature, in performing its duty under Art. XII, § 3(3), must not act arbitrarily between classes of entitled persons.

Butte Community Union II.

It is clear from this background it was the inability of the Legislature to write an act which would pass constitutional muster which led to its attempts to control the expenditures and the operations of the welfare programs.

In 1987, the 50th Legislature of the State of Montana adopted a proposed amendment to the Constitution, House Bill 637 (Ch. 343, 1987 Mont. Laws). This legislation refers to the voters of Montana a proposed amendment to Art. XII, sec. 3, Mont. Const.... House Bill 637 was designated Constitutional Referendum No. 18 [C-18] by the Secretary of State's Office, and is scheduled to be placed on the general election ballot for presentation to the Montana voters on November 8, 1988. [W]e are asked to remove this referendum.

The appellants present the issue regarding the ballot title and statements of implication (the "for" and "against" statements) which will appear on the ballot, alleging they are untrue, misleading and unconstitutional. Section 13-27-501(3), MCA, provides that the ballot title for the legislative referendum proposing to amend the Constitution is to be the title of the legislative proposal itself. The title which will appear on the ballot reads as follows:

> AN ACT TO SUBMIT TO THE QUALIFIED ELECTORS OF MONTANA AN AMENDMENT TO ARTICLE XII, SECTION 3, OF THE MONTANA CONSTITUTION TO ALLOW THE LEGISLATURE GREATER DISCRETION IN PROVIDING ECONOMIC ASSISTANCE AND SOCIAL AND REHABILITATIVE SERVICES TO THOSE IN NEED; AND PROVIDING AN EFFECTIVE DATE.

The statements of implication from HB 637, reads as follows:

> [] FOR allowing the legislature greater discretion to determine the eligibility, duration, and level of economic assistance and social services to those in need.
>
> [] AGAINST allowing the legislature greater discretion to determine the eligibility, duration, and level of economic assistance and social services to those in need.

*** The principal issue in this litigation concerns the ballot title and the statements of implication ("for" and "against") which appear on the ballot. Section 13-27-501(3), MCA, provides that the ballot title for the initiative referendum proposing to amend the Constitution is the title of the legislation itself. The title herein to be voted upon is the same title as the legislative act, exactly as used in HB 637 when introduced into the legislative process. We note throughout the legislative history of this Bill there were committee hearings, debates, and discussions concerning the merits of the proposed constitutional change, and there were no amendments, or even proposed amendments to the title. It emerged from the legislative process in exactly the same fashion it was entered. The words of the statement of implication were provided for in that legislation and have previously been noted. Throughout the committee hearings, debates and discussions in the legislative process concerning the merits of the constitutional change, neither the plaintiffs' testimony at the hearings nor any member of the Legislature offered any amendments concerning the title or ballot language throughout the legislative history of HB 637.

The appellants strenuously argue that the statutory standard which applies to both the initiative and referendum begun by petition, should equally apply to constitutional referenda originating from the Legislature. They argue that § 13-27-312(4), MCA, controls. That section states:

> The statement of purpose and the statements of implication must express the true and impartial explanation of the proposed ballot issue in plain, easily understood language and may not be arguments or written so as to create prejudice for or against the measure.

We are called upon to answer the question of what standard is to be applied to this legislative referendum. Because we find that the legislative referendum is a product of the Legislature and is passed in the form of a bill, its title should be examined according to the same standard applied to other legislation. If it results in greater deference being given to the ballot language which derives from the legislation rather than the petition, then that is appropriate due to the differences between the two sources. This distinction has been noted by this Court in *State ex rel. Montana Citizens for the Preservation of Citizens' Rights v. Waltermire* (Mont. 1987), where Mr. Justice Sheehy, writing for the majority, noted:

> There is evident wisdom in what the constitutional framers provided with respect to publication where initiatives are concerned. In the other two cases, that of convention and of legislative referenda, the proposed amendments are carefully worked over by contending parties whose governmental business at the time is to construct either a constitution or propose amendments to it. In the case of an initiative by the people, not enough adverse input occurs to justify the conclusion that a careful study has been made of the proposed amendment prior to its submission.

Article V, sec. 11(3) of the Montana Constitution states in pertinent part: "Each bill . . . shall contain only one subject, clearly expressed in its title."

. . . *State v. McKinney* (Mont. 1904) . . . set forth five principles for the construction of the titles by Montana courts:

> First. The purposes of this constitutional provision are to prevent the legislature from the enactment of laws surreptitiously; to prevent "logrolling" legislation; to give to the people general notice of the character of proposed legislation, so they may not be misled; to give all interested an opportunity to appear before committees of the legislature and be heard upon the

> advisability of the proposed legislation; to advise members of the legislature of the character of the proposed legislation, and give each an opportunity to intelligently watch the course of the proposed Bill; to guard against fraud in legislation, and against false and deceptive titles. These purposes have been so plainly announced by this court in numerous opinions that a statement of the rule and a citation of cases would seem sufficient. (Citations omitted.)
>
> Second. While all the provisions of the constitution are "mandatory and prohibitory" (Art. III, Sec. 29), yet the courts, bearing in mind that the legislature is a co-ordinate [sic] branch of the government and that its action, if fair, should be sustained, have given this section of the constitution a liberal construction, so as to not interfere with or impede proper legislative functions. (Citations omitted.)
>
> Third. The legislature is the judge, to a great extent, at least, of the title which it will prefix to a Bill; and the court has no right to hold a title void because, in its opinion, a better one might have been used. (Citations omitted.)
>
> Fourth. The title is generally sufficient if the body of the Act treats only, directly or indirectly, of the subjects mentioned in the title, and of other subjects germane thereto, or of matters in furtherance of or necessary to accomplish the general objects of the Bill, as mentioned in the title. Details need not be mentioned. The title need not contain a complete list of all matters covered by the Act. (Citations omitted.)
>
> Fifth. If the court, after an application of all these principles, is still in doubt as to the constitutionality of the Bill, it should sustain the Act. (Citations omitted.) . . .

In applying the constitutional requirement of "clearly expressing the subject" in the title, and employing the rules of construction developed under case law, the ballot title in question here is legally sufficient. With the background of the legislative hearings and a vote by two-thirds of the members of the Legislature, we conclude that they understood the issue and voted accordingly. Specific reference is made in the title to Art. XII, sec. 3, Mont. Const., and that the subject matter involves the provision of economic assistance and social and rehabilitative services to those in need. The explanation of the effect of the proposal is left to the Attorney General's explanatory statement which is given each voter the time of the election.

Two years ago, on three separate occasions, we refused to intervene in the initiative process prior to submission of the initiatives to the voters of Montana. Recognizing that these cases involved the initiative rather than the referendum process, they are yet applicable to the present case and should be considered.

Art. II, sec. 1 and 2, Mont. Const. (1972), read:

> Section 1. Popular sovereignty. All political power is vested in and derived from the people. All government of right originates with the people, is founded upon their will only, and is instituted solely for the good of the whole.

> Section 2. Self-government. The people have the exclusive right of governing themselves as a free, sovereign, and independent state. They may alter or abolish the constitution and form of government whenever they deem it necessary.

The initiative and referendum process enable the people to peacefully accomplish the goals of these two sections of our constitution by allowing important issues to be placed before the people for a popular vote. To deny the right to vote would thwart these provisions.

As we have noted, there are important distinctions between the constitutional amendments proposed through the initiative process (by the people) and constitutional amendments proposed through the referendum process (by the legislature). Our reasoning in refusing to intervene in the initiative process prior to the vote of the people is applicable in this case. In fact, such reasoning has greater weight in relation to the referendum because of the safeguards already built into the referendum process. While the appellants cite precedent in which this Court granted pre-election review and enjoined an election, we distinguish these cases. In *State ex rel. Steen v. Murray* (Mont. 1964), the challenged initiative was unconstitutional on its face. In *State ex rel. Harper v. Waltermire* (Mont. 1984), the challenge to the initiative went to the text of the initiative rather than to its title. ***

We held in *State ex rel. Montana Citizens for the Preservation of Citizens' Rights v. Waltermire* (Mont. 1986), that:

> The right retained by the people of Montana to change our Constitution by initiative is unique. The people do not have such a right under the federal Constitution nor under many state constitutions. In Montana this right of constitutional change by initiative was first inserted in the 1972 Constitution. As we stated in our opinion in *State ex rel. Mont. School Board Ass'n. v. Waltermire* [(Mont. 1986)], we should decline to interfere with this right of constitutional change by initiative unless it appears to be absolutely essential.

*** In conclusion, we find that the ballot language and the abbreviated form complained of by the appellants is not legally deficient. While the language may not be the best conceivable statement, it does not appear purposely misleading, and does identify the measure on the ballot so that a Montana voter, drawing on both official and unofficial sources of information and education, will exercise his or her political judgment.

The District Court's order that appellants' complaint be dismissed is affirmed.

SHEEHY, Justice, dissenting:

I dissent and would take jurisdiction to remove this shabby referendum from the ballot.

I begin by agreeing with the District Court judge that this referendum is flagrantly deceitful. Its true intent, to deprive this Court of our constitutional basis for rebuffing the legislature's discriminatory acts, is trickily masked in self-effacing language: ". . . to allow the legislature *greater discretion* in *providing* economic assistance and social and rehabilitative services to those is [sic] need." (Emphasis added.) The legislature does not intend to "provide;" it intends to "eliminate."

Greater discretion? The legislature now has absolute discretion to determine the eligibility, duration and levels of aid to the needy. The only limitation upon its discretion is its constitutional duty to avoid invidious discrimination *between* members of the same needy classes. *Butte Community Union v. Lewis* (Mont. 1987). The legislature, unwilling to assume the burden of acting constitutionally, wants the voters to remove the constitution.

Under the present constitution, the aged, the infirm, the unlucky, who without fault need the aid of society, must be given economic assistance by the legislature. Art. XII, § 3(3), 1972 Mont. Const. The legislature wants to get rid of that "must" but it does not want to tell the voters directly. Instead, the legislature proposes a referendum with its true intent couched in vague and illusory wording.

. . . The Attorney General's Explanatory Statement will not appear on at least 67 percent of the state ballots. The county clerks of enough counties have requested permission to omit the Attorney General's Explanatory Statement because of lack of space on the ballot or machines. ***

Where in the ballot are the aged informed that their present group *right* to state aid, if needy, is stripped away by the ballot issue, and their lot cast to the whim of the legislators? They are not informed.

Where in the ballot are the sick, the crippled, the infirm told that their present group *right* to state aid, if needy, will be gone with the wind? They are not told.

Where in the ballot does it state that a Montanan's present group *right* to state aid in case of faultless poverty will be lost? It is not stated.

In the face of such deceit, this Court should condemn the referendum, and take it off the ballot for at least these reasons:

(1) By hiding its true purpose, the referendum prevents the free exercise by Montana voters of their right of suffrage. (Art. II, § 13, 1972 Mont. Const.)

(2) By hiding its true purpose, the referendum prevents the public right of opportunity to participate in the operation of state agencies. (Art. II, § 8, 1972 Mont. Const.)

(3) By hiding its true purpose, the referendum deprives the public of its right to examine public documents. (Art. II, § 9, 1972 Mont. Const.)

(4) By hiding its true purpose, the referendum deprives the public of its right to pursue life's basic necessities. (Art. II, § 3, 1972 Mont. Const.)

(5) By hiding its true purpose, the referendum deprives the needy aged, infirm and misfortunate persons of due process of law. (Art. II, § 17, 1972 Mont. Const.)

Because of the foregoing failings, the voters will not be given an opportunity to exercise their franchise in a knowing, conscientious manner. In *Burgan and Walker v. State Highway Commission* (Mont. 1943), this Court enjoined a referendum before the election because of its evident constitutional deficiencies. That situation exists here. Our judicial duty is to enjoin or prevent the submission of this mendacity to the people.

HUNT, J., joins in the foregoing dissent of SHEEHY, J.

Marshall v. Cooney

293 Mont. 274 (1999)

Justice W. WILLIAM LEAPHART delivered the Opinion of the Court.

¶ 1 Plaintiffs challenge the constitutional validity of Constitutional Initiative 75 (CI-75) in an original application for declaratory judgment and injunctive relief.

¶ 2 We hold that CI-75 violates Article XIV, Section 11, of Montana's Constitution. ***

Factual and Procedural Background

¶ 5 On November 3, 1998 Montana voters approved CI-75. As enacted, CI-75 amended Article VIII of the Montana Constitution by adding a new Section 17 that began:

> Section 17. People's right to vote on taxes-fairness in tax elections-enforcement.
>
> (1) No new tax or tax increase may be enacted unless first approved by a majority of the electors voting on the measure in the geographic area subject to the tax.

In response to CI-75, Plaintiffs made an original application for declaratory judgment and injunctive relief. This Court accepted jurisdiction in December, 1998.

¶ 6 In their original application for declaratory judgment and injunctive relief, Plaintiffs set forth seven Counts. Count one alleges that CI-75 violates Article XIV, Section 11, of the Montana Constitution because the provisions of CI-75 make more than one amendment to the Montana Constitution. Count two alleges that CI-75 violates Article V, Section 11(3), of the Montana Constitution because CI-75 has multiple subjects. Count three alleges that CI-75 violates Article XIV, Sections 1–7, of the Montana Constitution because CI-75 constitutes a revision of the Montana Constitution without a Constitutional Convention having been called. Count four alleges that the ballot presented to the electorate violated the right to due process guaranteed by Article II, Section 17, of the Montana Constitution because the ballot did not describe the entirety of the measures proposed by CI-75. Count five appears to allege that in violation of Article II, Section 4, of the Montana Constitution, Plaintiffs have been discriminated against in the exercise of their political rights on account of their social origin or political ideas. Count six alleges that in violation of Article II, Section 17, of the Montana Constitution certain plaintiffs were prohibited from exercising their right to political speech and association in connection with their opposition to CI-75, and thus denied their right to substantive due process. Count seven alleges that in violation of Article II, Sections 6–7, of the Montana Constitution certain plaintiffs were denied their right to political speech and association in connection with their opposition to CI-75. ***

Discussion

¶ 8 Whether CI-75 violates the separate-vote provision in Article XIV, Section 11, of the Montana Constitution.

¶ 9 Because the issue is dispositive, we address Plaintiffs' argument that CI-75 has two or more constitutional amendments in violation of Article XIV, Section 11, of the Montana Constitution. Article XIV, Section 11, provides:

> Submission. If more than one amendment is submitted at the same election, each shall be so prepared and distinguished that it can be voted upon separately.

Art. XIV, Sec. 11, Mont. Const.

¶ 10 Plaintiffs argue that CI-75 violates Article XIV, Section 11, of the Montana Constitution because it either explicitly or implicitly amends at least twelve sections of Montana's Constitution. Further, CI-75 is defective because of its provision that if there is an "irreconcilable" conflict between any part of it and the Montana Constitution, CI-75 prevails. Plaintiffs contend that the effect of CI-75's "irreconcilable conflict" clause is that existing constitutional rights, such as the right to a trial by jury and to a speedy trial, have become conditional rights with effect only so long as the people approve taxes necessary to provide service. ***

¶ 17 . . . Article XIV, Section 11 provides that "[i]f more than one amendment is submitted at the same election, each shall be so prepared and distinguished *that it can be voted upon separately.*" Art. XIV, Sec. 11, Mont. Const. (emphasis added). Thus, the plain language of Article XIV, Section 11, is that each constitutional amendment shall be voted upon separately. Article V, Section 11(3), provides in pertinent part that "[e]ach bill, except general appropriation bills and bills for the codification and general revision of the laws, shall contain only one subject, clearly expressed in its title." Art. V, Sec. 11(3), Mont. Const.

¶ 18 However, Defendants urge that this Court be guided by the unity of subject rule, which the Court developed in [*State v. Board of Comm'rs* (Mont. 1906) (hereafter "*Teague*"), *State v. Alderson* (Mont. 1914) (hereafter "*Hay*"), and *State v. Cooney* (Mont. 1924)], and conclude that Article XIV, Section 11, means not what it plainly says but rather that a constitutional initiative containing more than one amendment is valid provided that it has unity of subject and that its parts are germane to that subject. We disagree. We conclude that the requirement, in Article XIV, Section 11, of a separate vote has a substantively different meaning from the single-subject requirement set forth in Article V, Section 11(3). For several reasons, we further conclude that *Teague*, *Hay*, and *Cooney* should be distinguished from the present case.

¶ 19 First, under the Montana Constitution in effect when *Teague, Hay* and *Cooney* were decided, amendments could be proposed in either house of the legislature but no provision was made for constitutional initiatives. See Art. XIX, Sec. 9, Mont. Const. (1889) (providing that "[a]mendments to this Constitution may be proposed in either house"). The Montana Constitution thereby guaranteed that legislators would debate and deliberate upon any proposed constitutional amendment. For present-day constitutional initiatives, however, there is no guarantee that Montana voters will have similar deliberative opportunities. As the Court in *Sawyer Stores v. Mitchell* (Mont. 1936), commented:

> it is instructive to note the difference in the conditions under which a measure is submitted to the electorate of this state. The members of the Legislature meet for the purpose of considering legislation, and for a period of sixty days that, with a few exceptions, is their sole business. The members of that body have the advantage of conference, that is, of conferring together and each gaining from the other such information as each may possess concerning a given measure.... The voter to whom a measure is submitted has a business or occupation other than that of the consideration of legislation. The measure is submitted to the banker, the merchant, the farmer, the lawyer, the laborer, the housewife.

We conclude that the separate-vote requirement of Article XIV, Section 11, is a cogent constitutional recognition of the circumstances under which Montana voters receive constitutional initiatives. Nor is the Montana Constitution alone in its recognition of the importance of the separate-vote requirement. CI-75 itself also affirms the import of the separate-vote requirement; it provides that "each ballot issue shall encompass only a single tax."

¶ 20 Second, the constitutional amendment that the Court considered in *Hay* affected only one provision of the Constitution. *See Hay* (commenting "[o]nly one provision of the Constitution was changed"). In the present case, CI-75 affects multiple parts of Montana's Constitution.

¶ 21 Third, for purposes of Article XIV, Section 11, the unity of subject rule that the Court applied in *Hay* and *Cooney* is unworkable. Under the Court's rationale in *Hay*, for example, a constitutional initiative to "improve Montana's government" could amend virtually every part of Montana's Constitution but have one single subject. The unity of subject rule set forth in *Hay* and *Cooney* is so elastic that it could swallow Montana's entire Constitution. We decline to affirm such a rule.

¶ 22 In *Armatta* [*v. Kitzhaber* (Or. 1998)], we find support for our conclusion that the plain meaning of the Montana Constitution's separate-vote requirement is substantively different from its single-subject requirement. As previously discussed, the court in *Armatta* compared two constitutional provisions that are similar to Article XIV, Section 11, and Article V, Section 11(3), of Montana's Constitution. The *Armatta* court concluded

> the separate-vote requirement of Article XVII, section 1, imposes a *narrower* requirement than does the single-subject requirement of Article IV, section 1(2)(d). Such a reading of the separate-vote requirement makes sense, because the act of amending the *constitution* is significantly different from enacting or enabling *legislation.*

We agree that a separate-vote requirement for constitutional amendments is a different and narrower requirement than is a single-subject requirement. As the *Armatta* court remarked, a constitutional amendment may be valid under the single-subject rule but fail under the separate-vote requirement.

¶ 23 We hold that Article XIV, Section 11, has a substantively different meaning from that of Article V, Section 11(3) of the Montana Constitution. We hold further that the plain meaning of Article XIV, Section 11, requires a separate vote for each constitutional amendment. To the extent that this holding is in conflict with *Hay, Teague,* and *Cooney,* those decisions are overruled.

¶ 24 Having determined that Article XIV, Section 11, requires a separate vote on each proposed constitutional amendment, we consider whether CI-75 violates that constitutional requirement. We conclude that CI-75 specifically amends three parts of Montana's Constitution. First, CI-75 expressly provides that "Article VIII of the Constitution [Revenue and Finance] . . . is amended." Second, CI-75 amends Article II, Section 18, providing that "[n]otwithstanding any legislative limitation created pursuant to Article II, Section 18, sovereign immunity does not shield public officials or employees from appropriate civil liability for violation of this section." Third, CI-75 provides that "[n]otwithstanding the referendum exception of Article VI, Section 10, before a bill imposing new or increased taxes is referred to the people the governor shall have the veto power." Because CI-75 expressly amends three parts of Montana's Constitution but does not allow a separate vote for each amendment, we hold that CI-75 violates Article XIV, Section 11, of Montana's Constitution. *Compare Sawyer Stores* (commenting that "a [ballot] submission is void where two propositions have been submitted so as to have one expression of the voter answer both propositions, and this for the reason that voters might thereby be induced to vote for both propositions who would not have done so if the question had been submitted singly").

¶ 25 Although CI-75 has a severability clause, we reject the notion that objectionable parts of CI-75 may be severed, leaving a valid constitutional amendment in place. During oral argument, Defendants contended that some parts of CI-75 could be severed. The suggestion that offending parts of CI-75 can be severed misconstrues the separate-vote requirement in Article XIV, Section 11. Article XIV, Section 11, expressly contemplates the submission of constitutional amendments; it embodies the constitutional determination that each submitted amendment shall be voted upon separately. Thus, as a matter of logic, any severance of CI-75 could not cure its constitutional defect because the defect lies in the *submission* of CI-75 to the voters of Montana with more than one constitutional amendment.

¶ 26 In *Cit. for Pres. of Cit. R. v. Waltermire* (Mont. 1987), this Court concluded:

> There are three ways in which our state constitution may be amended, (1) through legislative referendum (Article XIV, Section 8), (2) through a further constitutional convention (Article XIV, Section 1) or, as in this case, (3) by initiative (Article XIV, Section 9). Although the people of this state have retained the exclusive right of governing themselves, and the right to alter or abolish the constitution or form a government whenever they deem it necessary (Article II, Section 12), it is nonetheless true that as long as the State Constitution is in effect, the people may amend the constitution by initiative only in the manner provided by the constitution. "The sovereignty of the people is itself subject to those constitutional limitations which have been duly adopted and remain unrepealed."

With our holding today we do no more and no less than affirm the clear intent of the people of Montana, as set forth in Montana's Constitution, that constitutional amendments be voted upon separately. ***

Justice JAMES C. NELSON specially concurs.

¶ 28 I concur in the Court's decision as far as it goes. I would also hold, however, that, in addition to Article VIII, Article II, Section 18 and Article VI, Section 10, CI-75 also clearly amends Article IX, Section 2(2), Article XII, Section 1(2) and Article XIII, Section 2, and thus requires a separate vote on these amendments. I disagree with footnote 2 to the Court's opinion to the extent that it may be read as implying otherwise.

¶ 29 Article IX, Section 2(2) provides:

> The legislature shall provide for a fund, to be known as the resource indemnity trust of the state of Montana, to be funded by such taxes on the extraction of natural resources as the legislature may from time to time impose for that purpose.

This constitutional provision unambiguously requires the legislature to impose taxes on the extraction of natural resources from time to time for the purpose of funding the resource indemnity trust. This constitutional provision also necessarily reposes in the legislature the sole power to determine the nature, frequency and amount of such tax in order to fulfill its constitutional obligation to fund the trust. While CI-75 would apparently not prohibit the legislature from continuing the type and level of taxation for the trust extant at the time CI-75 was adopted, CI-75 clearly would prohibit the legislature from either increasing such tax or changing the nature of the tax (i.e. creating a "new tax") without submitting the increase or new tax to the voters. Such a voting requirement—backed up by CI-75's supremacy clause—changes the present constitutional scheme by giving the voters veto power over a legislative decision to fund the trust to a greater extent or in a manner different from that presently in existence. The requirements of CI-75 are totally inconsistent with the constitutional obligation of the legislature under Article IX, Section 2(2), to not only impose, but to determine as well the nature, frequency and amount of the tax in order to fund the resource indemnity trust. Article IX, Section 2(2) in its present form, cannot co-exist with the competing obligations imposed upon the legislature by CI-75. Accordingly, CI-75 amends Article IX, Section 2(2) and this amendment should have been voted upon separately when CI-75 was submitted to the voters.

¶ 30 Similarly, Article XII, Section 1(2) provides:

> Special levies may be made on livestock and on agricultural commodities for disease control and indemnification, predator control, and livestock and commodity inspection, protection, research and promotion. Revenue derived shall be used solely for the purposes of the levies.

This constitutional provision empowers the legislature to make certain levies on livestock and agricultural commodities for the various purposes set out. CI-75 amends this constitutional provision on the same rationale discussed above with respect to Article IX, Section 2(2). Pursuant to Article XII, Section 1(2), as Governor Racicot's brief *amicus curiae* demonstrates, the legislature has established a number of fees and has given the Department of Livestock authority to set many of them. Again, while the existing fee structure may be continued, no new, different or increased fee may be imposed by the legislature without voter approval. As with Article IX, Section 2(2), CI-75 effectively strips the legislature of its constitutional power under Article XII, Section 1(2) to determine the nature, frequency and amount of levies which it may choose to impose for the purposes set out in this constitutional provision. This amendment of Article XII, Section 1(2) was required to be separately voted upon by the provisions of Article XIV, Section 11.

¶ 31 Finally, Article XIII, Section 2 is also amended by CI-75. This part of the constitution provides:

> Consumer counsel. The legislature shall provide for an office of consumer counsel which shall have the duty of representing consumer interests in hearings before the public service commission or any other successor agency. The legislature shall provide for the funding of the office of consumer counsel by a special tax on the net income or gross revenues of regulated companies.

As with its obligation to fund the resource indemnity trust by tax levies, the legislative obligation to provide for and fund, by way of a special tax, the office of consumer counsel is equally clear. The rationale demonstrating why CI-75 amends Article XIII, Section 2 has already been discussed and will not be reiterated here. Suffice it to say that the amendment to Article XIII, Section 2 imposed by CI-75 was required to be separately voted upon.

¶ 32 In summary, I agree with the Court's opinion as far as it goes. I would hold, however, that CI-75 also amended Article IX, Section 2(2), Article XII, Section 1(2) and Article XIII, Section 2, of Montana's Constitution and that Article XIV, Section 11 required a separate vote on these amendments as well.

Justices TERRY N. TRIEWEILER and WILLIAM E. HUNT, SR., join in the foregoing special concurrence.

Montana Ass'n of Counties v. State

2017 MT 267

Justice LAURIE MCKINNON delivered the Opinion and Order of the Court.

¶ 1 Petitioners challenge the constitutionality of Constitutional Initiative 116 (CI-116), commonly known as Marsy's Law, in an original petition for declaratory judgment and injunctive relief. The merits of CI-116 and the policy choices behind it are not at issue in this case. The only question before this Court is whether the procedure by which CI-116 was submitted to voters conformed to Montana's constitutional requirements. ***

Factual and Procedural Background

¶ 5 On November 8, 2016, a majority of Montana voters approved CI-116, a constitutional amendment proposed by popular initiative. As enacted, CI-116 amended Article II of Montana's Constitution by adding a new Section 36, titled Rights of Crime Victims. By way of description, CI-116 contains four sections. CI-116(1) enumerates eighteen rights to which crime victims are entitled. These rights are meant "[t]o preserve and protect a crime victim's right to justice, to ensure a crime victim has a meaningful role in criminal and juvenile justice systems, and to ensure that a crime victim's rights and interests are respected and protected by law in a manner no less vigorous than the protections afforded to a criminal defendant and a delinquent youth." ...

¶ 6 CI-116(2) provides the manner in which victim's rights are to be recognized and effectuated.... CI-116(3) ensures that the enumerated rights "may not be construed to deny or disparage" other victims' rights and provides that CI-116 "applies to criminal and youth court proceedings, is self-executing, and requires no further action by the Legislature." ... CI-116(4) provides definitions for "crime" and "victim." ...

Discussion

*** ¶ 13 Montana's 1972 Constitution provided citizens with a new way to amend their Constitution: by popular initiative. The addition was consistent with the overall theme of the 1972 Constitutional Convention of constructing a flexible Constitution subject to popular control.... The Constitutional Revision Committee (Committee) proposed the initiative power because it believed the power was "an inherent right in a body politic whose Constitution is to be the embodiment of the will of the people." The Committee wanted to ensure the 1972 Constitution provided a constitutional revision process that "hit a happy and workable medium."

¶ 14 Consequently, while providing for initiative power, the 1972 Constitution also imposed limitations on the initiative process. Such limitations included signature gathering and geographic distribution requirements. Mont. Const. art. XIV, § 9(1). The Committee determined limitations were necessary because it was "not unreasonable to demand strict standards when dealing with something as fundamental and important as Constitutional change." The Committee noted another check on the constitutional amendment process: the separate-vote requirement. Indeed, the official voter pamphlet for the new Constitution explained to voters that the only limit on how constitutional amendments may be submitted at an election was the requirement that each amendment "be clearly designated on the ballot so that they can be voted on separately."

¶ 15 The separate-vote requirement is one of eleven sections in Article XIV directing the manner in which Montana's Constitution may be revised.... The separate-vote requirement was "designed to aid voters in casting their votes on Constitutional issues, and as a check on the possible action of grouping several issues under one innocuous title." The separate-vote requirement has a long history in Montana. Montana's 1884 and 1889 Constitutions both contained a separate-vote requirement, and the requirement was adopted unanimously during the Constitutional Convention of 1972. The separate-vote requirement has two well-recognized objectives. The first is to avoid voter confusion and deceit of the public by ensuring proposals are not misleading or the effects of which are concealed or not readily understandable. The second is to avoid "logrolling" or combining unrelated amendments into a single measure which might not otherwise command majority support. By combining unrelated amendments, approval of the measure may be secured by different groups, each of which will support the entire proposal in order to secure some part, even though not approving all parts of a multifarious amendment.

¶ 16 This Court's interpretation of the separate-vote requirement has narrowed over time as the processes by which the Constitution can be amended have changed. In the early twentieth century, before Montana's Constitution could be amended by initiative, we held the separate-vote requirement satisfied as long as all provisions of the proposed constitutional amendment related to one subject matter or a single plan. *See, e.g., State ex rel. Corry v. Cooney* (Mont. 1924) (concluding the separate-vote requirement satisfied if "the operation of the amendment relates to a single plan or purpose"); *State ex rel. Hay v. Alderson* (Mont. 1914) (holding the separate-vote requirement satisfied as long as all parts of the proposed constitutional amendment "may be logically viewed as parts or aspects of a single plan"); *State ex rel. Teague v. Bd. of Comm'rs* (Mont. 1906) (holding a proposed amendment constitutional under the separate-vote requirement because it was not "three separate propositions" but instead was "only one matter and one subject").

¶ 17 We revisited our *Cooney, Hay,* and *Teague* separate-vote reasoning and jurisprudence following ratification of the 1972 Constitution and introduction of the petition by popular initiative. Notably, our 1999 decision in *Marshall v. State* overruled *Cooney, Hay, and Teague* to the extent those decisions failed to recognize a distinction between the single-subject and separate-vote requirements. ***

¶ 23 While *Marshall* is significant for its explanation of the separate-vote requirement in the context of an amendment by initiative, particularly in distinguishing the separate-vote requirement from the less arduous single-subject requirement, the Court invalidated CI-75 based on the express language of the initiative itself, which specifically amended other provisions of the Constitution. We determined these express amendments each needed a separate vote pursuant to Article XIV, Section 11. While explaining that CI-75 also affected other parts of the Constitution by limiting legislative spending, we did not incorporate these implied amendments into our reasoning because our discussion of the three express changes was sufficient to demonstrate CI-75's violation of the separate-vote requirement. In deciding *Marshall* in this manner, we left unanswered what is a "separate amendment" for purposes of the separate-vote requirement. *** We endeavor now to answer the question left open in *Marshall*; that is, how to determine whether an amendment by initiative contains two or more separate amendments in violation of Montana Constitution, Article XIV, Section 11.

¶ 25 . . . The separate-vote requirement states, "If more than one amendment is submitted at the same election, each shall be so prepared and distinguished that it can be voted upon separately." Mont. Const. art. XIV, § 11. The clear import of this provision is that voters must be allowed to express their separate opinion as to each proposed constitutional amendment. Accordingly, this Court is obligated to ensure that voters have the opportunity to cast separate votes for separate amendments. At the same time, we must apply the separate-vote requirement in a manner that does not encumber the right of the people to amend the Constitution.

¶ 26 There is considerable variance in the way other state courts interpret their separate-vote requirements. *See Cambria v. Soaries* (N.J. 2000). At one end of the spectrum are states that make only a slight distinction between the broader single-subject requirement and the separate-vote requirement, requiring the parts be rationally or logically related to each other. *See Fugina* [*v. Donovan* (Minn. 1960)]. Other states have adopted a more narrow interpretation, but are still deferential to the single-subject analysis and do not make a measurable distinction between single-subject and separate-vote requirements. *See, e.g., Missourians to Protect the Initiative Process v. Blunt* (Mo. 1990); *Milwaukee Alliance Against Racist and Political Repression v. Elections Bd. of Wis.* (Wis. 1982); *Carter v. Burson* (Ga. 1973); *Ohio ex rel. Roahrig v. Brown* (Ohio 1972). The narrowest interpretation of the separate-vote requirement clearly distinguishes it from the single-subject requirement by requiring there be a single subject to the proposed amendment and parts so interdependent that they constitute a whole and cannot be separated. *See Kerby* [*v. Luhrs* (Ariz. 1934)] ("[T]he different changes contained in the proposed amendment [did not] cover matters necessary to be dealt with in some manner, in order that the Constitution, as amended, shall constitute a consistent and workable whole on the general topic embraced in that part which is amended, and if, logically speaking, they should stand or fall as a whole, then there is but one amendment submitted."). *See also Lee v. Utah* (Utah 1962); *Farris v. Munro* (Wash. 1983); *Armatta v. Kitzhaber* (Or. 1998). ***

¶ 28 We conclude that the proper inquiry is whether, if adopted, the proposal would make two or more changes to the Constitution that are substantive and not closely related. This conclusion is based upon the language of Article XIV, Section 11; our decision in *Marshall* distinguishing between the single-subject and separate-vote requirements in the context of constitutional amendment by initiative; our conclusion that the single-subject requirement contained in Article V, Section 11(3), is inapplicable to constitutional amendments; and the transcripts of the 1972 Constitutional Convention. Furthermore, if a proposed constitutional amendment adds new matter to the Constitution, that proposition is at least one change in and of itself. *See, e.g., Oregon v. Rogers* (Or. 2012). Then, "if a measure has the effect of modifying an existing constitutional provision, it proposes at least one additional change to the constitution, whether that effect is express or implicit." *Rogers*.

¶ 29 Our separate-vote inquiry begins by focusing on the changes CI-116 makes to the Montana Constitution.... Consideration of whether the proposed constitutional changes are closely related gives appropriate effect to the separate-vote requirement by ensuring each constitutional amendment receives its own vote without unduly restricting constitutional change. Other states have applied similar closely-related analyses to proposed constitutional amendments and upheld the amendments as constitutional, demonstrating that a properly constructed constitutional amendment could certainly be found constitutional pursuant to our reasoning today.

¶ 31 We turn now to the text of CI-116 to determine whether its submission to Montana voters violated the separate-vote requirement. CI-116 expressly amends Article II of the Montana Constitution by adding a new Section 36, providing for specific crime victim rights. Adding a new constitutional provision constitutes one change. CI-116 does not expressly mention, repeal, or otherwise modify any other areas of the Constitution. However, CI-116 implicitly substantively changes multiple provisions of Montana's Constitution, some of which we now discuss.

A. CI-116(1)(a) Provides a New Due Process Right for Crime Victims.

*** ¶ 33 The first right CI-116 provides to a crime victim is the right "to due process and to be treated with fairness and respect for the victim's dignity." CI-116(1)(a). Accordingly, subsection (1)(a) of CI-116, standing on its own, creates a new due process guarantee for, specifically, crime victims. This new due process right for crime victims is a change in itself because, unlike our existing due process clause, it identifies a particular group of persons entitled to due process protections. Identifying and defining a group of persons who are entitled to expressly enumerated due process protections may also implicitly change other areas of the Constitution by effectuating a substantive change which is not closely related to a victim's due process right, thus violating the separate-vote requirement. Although it is difficult to imagine that a proposed provision granting a due process guarantee to crime victims would not be closely related to Montana's existing grant to persons of a due process guarantee as contained in Montana Constitution, Article II, we decline to speculate on whether submission of only CI-116(1)(a) would violate the separate-vote requirement. By way of illustration, the definition in CI-116 of "crime" and "victim," appears broader through its inclusion of various individuals and types of proceedings than that ascribed to "person" as embodied in our existing constitutional provision. Nonetheless, for purposes of our decision today, it is clear that CI-116 as a whole enumerates many other crime victim rights that are not closely related to our existing due process guarantee contained in Article II, Section 17. Consequently, it is unnecessary to determine whether CI-116(1)(a) is closely related to Article II, Section 17, as CI-116(1)(a) undisputedly adds matter to an existing constitutional provision and constitutes one change in itself.

B. CI-116(1)(j) and (2) Affect Montana Constitution Article VII, Section 2(3)'s Grant of Power to the Supreme Court to Regulate Attorney Conduct.

*** ¶ 36 CI-116 changes a prosecutor's duties in a criminal adjudication. CI-116 requires prosecutors to confer with a victim for the purposes of preserving and protecting the victim's right to justice, ensuring the victim has a meaningful role in the justice system, and ensuring the victim's rights and interests are respected and protected in a manner as vigorous as the protections afforded to a criminal defendant. CI-116 also gives prosecutors the option to, at the victim's request, seek enforcement of the victim's rights. CI-116 changes the way a prosecutor must handle a criminal case in which there is a victim, thus affecting the Supreme Court's power under Article VII, Section 2(3), to make rules governing attorney conduct. We conclude Montana Constitution Article VII, Section 2(3), is substantively changed by CI-116(1)(j) and (2), and that the provisions relating to crime victims' rights are not closely related to this Court's constitutional authority to regulate attorney conduct. Accordingly, asking the people in one vote to substantively change multiple provisions of the Constitution which are not closely related violated the separate-vote requirement.

C. CI-116(1)(g) and (i) Affect Montana Constitution Article II, Section 21's Right to Bail.

*** ¶ 38 ... CI-116 affords victims the right to "notice of and to be present at all proceedings involving the ... release ... of the defendant or youth," CI-116(1)(g), and the right "to be heard in any proceeding involving the release ... of the defendant or youth," CI-116(1)(i). Thus, CI-116 changes an accused's right to bail provided in Montana Constitution Article II, Section 21, by constitutionally prohibiting a court from releasing a defendant or youth on bail until all victims, including kinship and those having a "substantially similar relationship" to the victim, are present and heard by the court. CI-116 constitutionally requires a court not release a defendant until the victim appears and is heard, substantively affecting Article II, Section 21's requirement of bail upon sufficient surety. We conclude Montana Constitution Article II, Section 21 is substantively changed by CI-116(1)(g) and (i), because CI-116(1)(g) and (i) add new constitutional requirements to the preexisting bail provision. The constitutional provision regarding an accused's right to bail is not closely related to victims' rights and the separate-vote requirement was violated when voters were asked to consider these multiple amendments in one measure.

D. CI-116(1)(g) and (i) Affect Montana Constitution Article II, Section 20's Criminal Procedure Rules.

*** ¶ 41 CI-116 . . . requires courts give the victim notice of, allow the victim to be present at, and give the victim the opportunity to be heard at various hearings. These rights given to the victim add steps to the procedures a court is constitutionally required to take under Article II, Section 20, in initiating proceedings against a defendant and drawing a grand jury. We conclude Article II, Section 20, of Montana's Constitution is substantively changed by CI-116(1)(g) and (i) and that the preexisting constitutional provision related to initiation of criminal proceedings is not closely related to crime victims' rights.

E. CI-116(1)(e) and (f) Affect Montana Constitution Article II, Section 24's Rights of the Accused.

¶ 42 Article II, Section 24, of Montana's Constitution provides rights of the accused. . . . As a "corollary to [Article II, Section 24's] fundamental right to defend," a defendant has "the right to conduct investigations and otherwise prepare a defense to the charges." *State v. Couture*, 2010 MT 201. ***

¶ 44 CI-116 changes the accused's constitutional rights enumerated in Article II, Section 24. CI-116(1)(e) changes a defendant's right to discover any information he or she may be entitled to under Article II, Section 24, that "could be used to locate or harass the victim or that contains confidential or privileged information about the victim." CI-116(1)(f) also changes a defendant's right to discover information he or she may be entitled to under Article II, Section 24, by giving victims and those close to the victim as defined in CI-116(4)(b)(i) the right to "refuse an interview, deposition, or other discovery request." We conclude Montana Constitution, Article II, Section 24, is substantively changed by CI-116(1)(e) and (f). Further, sections (1)(e) and (f) are not closely related to our preexisting constitutional provision establishing basic constitutional rights of the accused, including the right to discover information, meet accusers, and prepare a defense.

F. CI-116(1)(f) and (4)(b) Affect Montana Constitution Article II, Section 9's Right to Know and Section 10's Right of Privacy.

*** ¶ 46 . . . The public's right to know, Article II, Section 9, is balanced against the individual's right of privacy, Article II, Section 10 . . . .

¶ 47 CI-116(1)(f) provides a crime victim with the right "to privacy, including the right to refuse an interview, deposition, or other discovery request and to set reasonable conditions on the conduct of any interaction to which the victim consents." Thus, CI-116 creates an entirely new privacy interest for victims, extended family members, and others with "similar relationships."

¶ 48 CI-116 affects Article II, Section 10's right of privacy and the balancing test between the right of privacy and the right to know. Aside from providing a new constitutional right to a particular class of persons—crime victims—which is a change in itself to the Constitution, CI-116 affects the balancing test employed between two preexisting constitutional provisions, the right of privacy and the right to know. Further, CI-116 gives the right of privacy to extended family members and others with similar relationships to the victim. Finally, CI-116(4)(b) specifically defines a victim as a "person" who suffers direct or threatened harm. In contrast, the term "person," as recognized by the Delegates, includes corporations and other non-human entities. Accordingly, "persons" entitled to a right to privacy under CI-116 would be different than under the constitutional provisions of Article II, Section 9, the public's right to know, and Section 10, an individual's right of privacy. We conclude Montana Constitution Article II, Sections 9 and 10, are substantively changed by CI-116(1)(f) and (4)(b) and that the people should have been afforded the right to vote on each amendment separately.

¶ 49 To summarize, CI-116 adds a new Section 36 to Article II of Montana's Constitution, substantively changing the Constitution by enumerating rights for victims. The preexisting constitutional provisions that are substantively changed by CI-116 include Article VII, Section 2(3)'s grant of power to the Supreme Court to govern attorney conduct; Article II, Section 21's right to bail; Article II, Section 20's criminal procedure rules; Article II, Section 24's rights of the accused; Article II, Section 9's right to know; and Article II, Section 10's right of privacy.

¶ 50 Some of these provisions are related in the broad sense that they are implicated during a criminal prosecution. For example, Article II, Section 21's right to bail, Article II, Section 20's criminal procedure rules, and Article II, Section 24's rights of the accused all seek to protect an accused's fundamental rights during a criminal proceeding. However, a broad relationship between various provisions or a broad single subject does not satisfy the narrower interpretation of the separate-vote requirement we adopted in *Marshall* because voters did not have the opportunity to convey their opinions as to each constitutional provision changed by CI-116 .... Further, not all of the affected provisions share even the broad connection of relating to a criminal prosecution or victim's rights. For example, attorney conduct, Article VII, Section 2(3), is not closely related to the right of privacy, Article II, Section 10, and neither of those provisions is closely related to the accused's right to bail, Article II, Section 21. Each of these amendments should have been presented to the electorate individually. Separate votes on each change would have protected the integrity of the vote and ensured that voters had complete control over each amendment made to the Montana Constitution. ***

Conclusion

¶ 54 We hold Montana Constitution, Article V, Section 11(3)'s single-subject requirement does not apply to constitutional amendments. Therefore, we do not address MACo's argument that CI-116 violates Article V, Section 11(3). We expand upon our analysis of Montana Constitution, Article XIV, Section 11 's separate-vote requirement and hold a proposed constitutional amendment violates the separate-vote requirement if it substantively changes two or more parts of the Constitution that are not closely related. Applying that analysis to CI-116, we hold CI-116 violates the separate-vote requirement and is therefore void in its entirety.

Justice JIM RICE, dissenting.

¶ 55 I believe the Court has adopted a deeply flawed test for application of the submission requirement of Article XIV, Section 11, of the Montana Constitution, which is not rooted in the text of the Constitution. The effect of this decision may be to significantly undermine, if not eliminate, the right of Montanans to amend the Constitution by initiative. This is not merely my opinion, but the experience of other courts. Respectfully, I believe the Court has failed to "apply the separate-vote requirement in a manner that does not encumber the right of the people to amend the Constitution." ***

¶ 56 Before discussing these concerns, I begin with the threshold concern that the Court has, in my view, violated justiciability principles by exercising original jurisdiction of this constitutional challenge. ***

¶ 63 ... [W]e cannot now know if our interpretational duty to harmonize these constitutional provisions is possible to fulfill. Without a specific claim and a factual record, it is impossible to properly determine whether a constitutional conflict exists that cannot be reconciled.... Without a factual record, the Court cannot determine whether it is possible to balance competing constitutional interests, a duty we are often compelled to perform. How particular constitutional rights will be weighed and balanced with other such rights is a matter that can only be decided in the factual context of an actual, concrete legal dispute. ***

¶ 66 While I could stop at this point, my deep concerns about the Court's new test for application of the separate-vote requirement of Article XIV, Section 11, lead me to discuss the merits of the Court's constitutional analysis. ***

¶ 69 [U]nder the Court's new test, if a constitutional initiative adds new language to the constitution, "that proposition is at least one change in and of itself." Then, if the initiative "has the effect of modifying" an existing constitutional provision in a way that is deemed "unrelated" to the new text, whether such modification is express or implied, then such an "effect" must also be counted as "one additional change to the constitution," requiring a separate vote. Applying the new test here, the Court concludes that CI-116 is invalid in seven different ways, reasoning that the initiative "affects" seven different existing provisions of the Montana Constitution, each of which required a separate vote, in addition to the vote taken on the text of CI-116 itself, for a total of eight votes.

¶ 70 This new formula, whereby a textual "proposition" is counted as "one change in and of itself," while the measure's "effect" upon an existing constitutional provision is counted as a second change, is inconsistent with the language of Article XIV, Section 11, which is premised upon the concept of "amendments," not "propositions" and "effects." The distinction is illustrated by the Court's analysis of the right to privacy.

¶ 71 CI-116 provides that crime victims have the right "to privacy, including the right to refuse an interview, deposition or other discovery request and to set reasonable conditions on the conduct of any interaction to which the victim consents." CI-116(1)(f). Applying its new test to this clause, the Court first reasons that CI-116 "provid[es] a new constitutional right to ... crime victims" which is a "change in itself[.]"Then the Court reasons that this new clause also "substantively change[s]" Article II, Section 9, the public's right to know, and Section 10, an individual's right to privacy, which requires a separate vote because of how it "affect[s]" the two constitutional provisions, thus concluding that the clause must receive a separate vote for its adoption. However, what has been lost in the application of the test's components is that the two concepts identified by the Court are two sides of the same amendment coin: one side is the new text, while the other side is the effect of the new text. Article XIV, Section 11, does not require separate votes for text and effect, but for wholly separate amendments, and we should analyze the issue in that way—as we did in *Marshall.*

¶ 72 To be clear, I agree with the Court that a constitutional initiative could have the effect of amending one or more articles of the Constitution even though the initiative's text does not expressly identify or add new language to the amended articles. Thus, I concur with the Court's assessment that in *Marshall,* we left open the possibility that such an initiative could run afoul of Article XIV, Section 11. My disagreement lies in the test adopted by the Court for identifying these separate amendments. As recognized by other courts, the Court's test is problematic because it will lead to the invalidation of challenged constitutional initiatives that do not actually effectuate multiple amendments, severely undermining citizen rights.

¶ 74 This precipitous invalidation of initiatives likely will occur under the Court's analysis here. I note again the Court's analysis of CI-116's right to privacy provision. If CI-116, in its entirety, would have provided only that victims have a right "to privacy, including the right to refuse an interview, deposition, or other discovery request and to set reasonable conditions on the conduct of any interaction to which the victim consents," *see* CI-116(1)(f), and said nothing else, it would nonetheless still violate the separate-vote requirement under the Court's test, and be invalid. This is because it adds a new section to the Constitution—requiring one vote—and also constitutes an "unrelated" implied change to the existing privacy provision—requiring a second vote. Few initiatives will survive the microsco[p]ic judicial review created herein.

¶ 75 Instead, we should use the test that is consistent with the language of Article XIV, Section 11, our constitutional history, and our case law. [Fn. The Court states that the 1972 Constitution changed the separate-vote requirement because the new constitution allowed amendment by initiative. However, nothing in the text or history of the separate-vote requirement would support this contention. Rather, the 1972 drafters unanimously adopted the same separate amendment rule from the prior constitution, Mont. Const. Conv. Proc. Vol. I, 354 (1972) (hereafter Committee

Report), and made only stylistic changes to the rule. See Mont. Const. Conv. Proc. Vol. IV, 1195 (1972) . . . The purpose of allowing popular initiatives was to avoid "cumbersome procedural detail," which had been a "burden to often-popular Constitutional change," and to preclude the Supreme Court from voiding proposed amendments because of a "slight procedural irregularity." Mont. Const. Conv. Proc. Vol. I, 362 (1972).]

In *Marshall* . . . we employed an analysis founded upon our own Constitution, which is premised on whole "amendments." We made a straight-forward determination that the text of CI-75 amended the Constitution in three ways—without regard to the numerous concepts employed here by the Court. The same approach can be used for initiatives that amend the Constitution without the use of explicit language. . . . The question is, does the initiative substantively constitute more than one amendment? Such an approach would not invalidate an initiative merely because it contained text that changed or revised more than one article of the Constitution, as long as those revisions were part of one complete, substantive amendment. Further, this straight-forward, constitutionally-based approach would avoid the flawed formulaic approach of assessing the text and the effect separately.

¶ 76 Most importantly, so holding would affirm the promise of Article II, Section 2, of the Montana Constitution, whether the courts think it good policy or not:

> The people have the exclusive right of governing themselves as a free, sovereign, and independent state. They may alter or abolish the constitution and form of government whenever they deem it necessary.

¶ 77 I dissent.

Justice BETH BAKER joins in the dissenting Opinion of JUSTICE RICE.

Notes on Constitutional Revision

1. In *Armatta v. Kitzhaber*, a source of the Court's reasoning in *Marshall* and *MACo*, Oregon's supreme court adopted an unusually strict new rule to invalidate a wide-ranging crime victim's rights initiative that probably would have failed under most of the less restrictive interpretations of the Separate Amendment Rule. Under *Armatta*, the Oregon courts invalidated nearly every proposed constitutional initiative for a decade. *See generally* Cody Hoesly, Student Author, *Reforming Direct Democracy: Lessons from Oregon*, 93 Cal. L. Rev. 1191 (2005) ("The Court's recent application of [the Separate Amendment Rule] has greatly affected direct democracy in Oregon. . . . Should the court adhere to *Armatta* and its reasoning, most initiative amendments are likely to fail.").

2. One scholar of direct democracy, Professor Daniel Lowenstein, leveled a similar criticism against *Marshall*:

> To limit a constitutional amendment to modifying not more than one provision of the existing constitution hardly recommends itself as sound public

> policy. Such a mechanical test makes proposed changes contingent on the way the existing constitution happens to be organized. It would encourage drafters of amendments to ignore loose ends that might be serious but that could only be tied up by referring to various existing constitutional articles or sections, and it would seriously impede many perfectly legitimate proposed constitutional amendments.

He doubted that "the Montana courts will impose such an absurd limitation on the Legislature when it proposes constitutional amendments." Daniel H. Lowenstein, *Initiatives and the New Single Subject Rule*, 1 Election L.J. 35 (2002). Meanwhile, scholarship by Professors Richard Hasen and John Matsusaka on the single subject rule (a similar restriction applicable to statutes) finds that in states where courts aggressively enforce the rule against initiatives, decisions track individual judges' partisan views of the initiative's merit. John G. Matsusaka & Richard L. Hasen, *Aggressive Enforcement of the Single Subject Rule*, 9 Election L.J. 399 (2010).

3. What is the rule of *Marshall* and *MACo*? If it prohibits any amendment containing revisions of more than one part of the constitution no matter how closely related, is it constitutionally impossible, for example, to change the title of State Auditor to Commissioner of Securities and Insurance? *See* C-42 ("AN ACT SUBMITTING TO THE QUALIFIED ELECTORS OF MONTANA AN AMENDMENT TO ARTICLE IV, SECTION 8, ARTICLE VI, SECTIONS 1, 2, 3, 4, 6, AND 7, AND ARTICLE X, SECTION 4, OF THE MONTANA CONSTITUTION TO PROVIDE THAT THE NAME OF THE STATE AUDITOR BE CHANGED TO THE INSURANCE COMMISSIONER."). What is the implied amendment rule of Justice Nelson's concurrence in *Marshall*? Would it, for example, prohibit a personhood amendment defining "person" to include the unborn in the due process provision of Article II, section 17 if doing so limited the abortion rights the Montana Supreme Court has located in the privacy provision of Article II, section 10? If such rights arise from "a compact of overlapping and redundant rights and guarantees," are some constitutional provisions (and the law the Supreme Court has located in them) effectively non-amendable? *See Armstrong v. State*, 1999 MT 261, ¶ 71.

4. Do the rules of *Marshall* and *MACo*, and the reasoning behind them, also apply to amendments referred to the people by the Legislature? (The "separate amendment" limit of Article XIV, section 11 makes no distinction between the two.)

5. In 2006, CI-97 proposed a state spending limit similar to the tax limit proposed by CI-75. In an attempt to narrow the amendment to a single section of the Constitution, and avoid any implied amendments, the proposed text ran for more than 1200 words and contained exceptions for every spending program in the Constitution. Before it could reach any separate amendment issues, the Supreme Court decertified CI-97 and associated ballot issues due to fraud in the petition process. *See Montanans for Justice v. State ex. rel. McGrath*, 2006 MT 277.

6. What should we take from the low rate of amendment of the 1972 Montana Constitution relative to other states? Given the money-driven politics of ballot issues, and imperfect process of translating popular opinion into constitutional text, what, if anything, do constitutional amendments tell us about how Montanans perceive their Constitution? How can the law protect the integrity of the amendment process, respecting the will of the people without fulfilling Delegate Vermillion's fears of "a Constitution that looks like California and Louisiana"? (Is there anything wrong with that?)

Chapter 2

Interpretation & Enforcement

Popular sovereignty. All political power is vested in and derived from the people. All government of right originates with the people, is founded upon their will only, and is instituted solely for the good of the whole.

Identical to 1889 constitution. Expresses the philosophy that government is founded on the will of the people and is for their good.

Mont. Const. Art. II, § 1

This Constitution, and the Laws of the United States which shall be made in Pursuance thereof; and all Treaties made, or which shall be made, under the Authority of the United States, shall be the supreme Law of the Land; and the Judges in every State shall be bound thereby, any Thing in the Constitution or Laws of any State to the Contrary notwithstanding.

The "Supremacy Clause."

U.S. Const. Art. VI, cl. 2

Oath of office. Members of the legislature and all executive, ministerial and judicial officers, shall take and subscribe the following oath or affirmation, before they enter upon the duties of their offices: "I do solemnly swear (or affirm) that I will support, protect and defend the constitution of the United States, and the constitution of the state of Montana, and that I will discharge the duties of my office with fidelity (so help me God)." No other oath, declaration, or test shall be required as a qualification for any office or public trust.

Shortened version of oath contained in 1889 constitution.

Mont. Const. Art. III, § 3

Like all state constitutions, the Montana Constitution establishes the sovereignty and expresses the foundational legal principles of a particular "people." Those principles are often, but not always, shared with other American constitutions — state and federal — through common texts, structures, histories, precedents and practices, policies, and principles. In answering specific questions under any constitution, it can be difficult to discover where the voice of one "We the people" stops and another starts. Public officials, while they swear an oath to support both the federal and state constitution, need to know where their allegiance to one constitution ends and the other constitution begins, to understand when federal law preempts state constitutional powers or rights, "the Constitution ... of any State to the Contrary notwithstanding," and to define the independent scope of their powers and people's rights under state constitutional law. Practitioners also need to draw these lines to know when public officials cross them, and to help distinguish unfavorable authority that may also be unfaithful to the governing state constitution. The first section considers where and how state and federal courts delineate the scope of state constitutional law.

Even when state constitutional rights (and powers and duties) are clearly defined, however, they may mean little if there is no remedy against the state for constitutional violations. Nearly every successful constitutional claim in this book results in only non-enforcement of the law against the claimant. When are state officials immune from suit for damages, or suit at all, for violations of the state constitution? That question is the subject of the second section, and it is an important consideration for constitutional lawyers and their clients in their willingness and ability to bring constitutional cases.

A. State Constitutional Independence (Herein of Criminal Procedure)

The Montana Constitution is situated "vertically" with respect to federal constitutional law and "horizontally" with respect to other state constitutional law. On the vertical axis, the United States Constitution and federal law may displace state constitutional law under the Supremacy Clause. In many cases beyond its preemptive scope, however, federal constitutional law determines state constitutional law through the practice of state court "lockstepping" with, or following without significant exception, the federal Constitution. This occurs even when state constitutional law is free to develop independently between the "floor" of federal rights (mostly incorporated through the "no state shall" prohibition of the Fourteenth Amendment) and the "ceiling" of preemptive power under the Supremacy Clause. Often state courts, including the Montana Supreme Court, will "march in lock-step" in constitutional domains where federal constitutional law generally does not reach, such as state separation of powers. This subsection explores the scope of state constitutional independence through several criminal procedure cases. As you read the cases, consider why constitutional criminal procedure has become such a busy intersection of federal and state constitutional law.

1. Independent and Adequate State Grounds

The vertical relationship between federal and state constitutions is demonstrated by the *Ohio v. Robinette* trilogy. These cases apply the "independent and adequate state ground" rule for when the Supreme Court, in its review of state supreme court decisions, may reverse a judgment of a state court because of an incorrect holding on federal grounds. State constitutional decisions often refer to federal law, but if a lower court decides a case on an "independent and adequate state ground" the Supreme Court — a court of federal question jurisdiction — will not review that decision. Many state constitutional cases are won by establishing an "independent and adequate state ground," avoiding review by the Supreme Court, and ensuring the state courts get the last word. As you will see, there is a trick to making clear the state court wants to have the last word.

State v. Robinette

73 Ohio St. 3d 650 (1995)

PFEIFER, J. The issue in this case is whether the evidence used against Robinette was obtained through a valid search. We find that the search was invalid since it was the product of an unlawful seizure. We also use this case to establish a bright-line test, requiring police officers to inform motorists that their legal detention has concluded before the police officer may engage in any consensual interrogation.

In order to justify any investigative stop, a police officer "must be able to point to specific and articulable facts which, taken together with the rational inferences from those facts, reasonably warrant that intrusion." *Terry v. Ohio* (1968). Absent any additional articulable facts arising after the stop is made, the police officer must tailor his detention of the driver to the original purpose of the stop. *State v. Chatton* (Ohio 1984). ***

When the motivation behind a police officer's continued detention of a person stopped for a traffic violation is not related to the purpose of the original, constitutional stop, and when that continued detention is not based on any articulable facts giving rise to a suspicion of some separate illegal activity justifying an extension of the detention, the continued detention constitutes an illegal seizure. *Chatton, supra.* ***

However, this case contains a feature not discussed in *Chatton*: Robinette consented to the search of his vehicle during the illegal seizure. Because Robinette's consent was obtained during an illegal detention, his consent is invalid unless the state proves that the consent was not the product of the illegal detention but the result of an independent act of free will. *Florida v. Royer* (1983). The burden is on the state to prove that the consent to search was voluntarily given. ***

In this case there was no time lapse between the illegal detention and the request to search, nor were there any circumstances that might have served to break or weaken the connection between one and the other. The sole purpose of the continued detention was to illegally broaden the scope of the original detention. Robinette's consent clearly was the result of his illegal detention, and was not the result of an act of will on his part. Given the circumstances, Robinette felt that he had no choice but to comply.

This case demonstrates the need for this court to draw a bright line between the conclusion of a valid seizure and the beginning of a consensual exchange. A person has been seized for the purposes of the Fourth Amendment when a law enforcement officer, by means of physical force or show of authority, has in some way restrained his liberty such that a reasonable person would not feel free to walk away. *United States v. Mendenhall* (1980). ***

Therefore, we are convinced that the right, guaranteed by the federal and Ohio Constitutions, to be secure in one's person and property requires that citizens stopped for traffic offenses be clearly informed by the detaining officer when they are free to go after a valid detention, before an officer attempts to engage in a consensual interrogation. Any attempt at consensual interrogation must be preceded by the phrase "At this time you legally are free to go" or by words of similar import.

While the legality of consensual encounters between police and citizens should be preserved, we do not believe that this legality should be used by police officers to turn a routine traffic stop into a fishing expedition for unrelated criminal activity. The Fourth Amendment to the federal Constitution and Section 14, Article I of the Ohio Constitution exist to protect citizens against such an unreasonable interference with their liberty.

MOYER, C.J., and WRIGHT and RESNICK, JJ., concur.

FRANCIS E. SWEENEY, SR., J., dissenting. I am disturbed by the majority's requirement that police officers must now recite certain words before a consensual interrogation may begin. This "bright-line" test appears unique to Ohio and vastly undercuts our law enforcement's ability to ferret out crime. Furthermore, the majority's test is contrary to well-established state and federal constitutional law.

The United States Supreme Court has made it clear that not every encounter between a police officer and citizen is a seizure. *Florida v. Bostick* (1991). Instead, the encounter becomes a seizure and is subject to Fourth Amendment scrutiny only when the encounter loses its consensual nature. Traditionally, the crucial test has always been "whether, taking into account all of the circumstances surrounding the encounter, the police conduct 'would have communicated to a reasonable person that he was not at liberty to ignore the police presence and go about his business.'" *Id.* . . .

The United States Supreme Court has consistently applied this legal standard in cases dealing with consensual encounters. In fact, in *Bostick, supra,* the Supreme Court struck down a per se rule adopted by the Florida Supreme Court that all routine bus searches were unconstitutional. The Supreme Court remanded the case to the state court to apply the totality-of-the-circumstances test. ***

Despite this well-established test, the majority now holds that before a police officer may engage in consensual interrogation, the officer must inform the individual that "at this time you legally are free to go." . . .

I would instead apply the totality-of-the-circumstances test to this case. ***

This technique of requesting consent following an initial valid detention is employed on a daily basis throughout this nation to interdict the flow of drugs. While I certainly do not advocate giving police officers carte blanche in their treatment of traffic violators, when the original stop is permissible, the police should be permitted to make inquiries that are not coercive. The majority's bright-line test undercuts police authority and severely curtails an important law enforcement tool that is sanctioned by state and federal constitutional law. ***

DOUGLAS and COOK, JJ., concur in the foregoing dissenting opinion.

Ohio v. Robinette

117 S. Ct. 417 (1996)

Chief Justice REHNQUIST delivered the opinion of the Court.

We are here presented with the question whether the Fourth Amendment requires that a lawfully seized defendant must be advised that he is "free to go" before his consent to search will be recognized as voluntary. We hold that it does not. ***

We must first consider whether we have jurisdiction to review the Ohio Supreme Court's decision. Respondent contends that we lack such jurisdiction because the Ohio decision rested upon the Ohio Constitution, in addition to the Federal Constitution. Under *Michigan v. Long* (1983), when "a state court decision fairly appears to rest primarily on federal law, or to be interwoven with the federal law, and when the adequacy and independence of any possible state law ground is not clear from the face of the opinion, we will accept as the most reasonable explanation that the state court decided the case the way it did because it believed that federal law required it to do so." *Id.* Although the opinion below mentions Art. I, § 14, of the Ohio Constitution in passing (a section which reads identically to the Fourth Amendment), the opinion clearly relies on federal law nevertheless. Indeed, the only cases it discusses or even cites are federal cases, except for one state case which itself applies the Federal Constitution. ***

We now turn to the merits of the question presented. We have long held that the "touchstone of the Fourth Amendment is reasonableness." *Florida v. Jimeno* (1991). Reasonableness, in turn, is measured in objective terms by examining the totality of the circumstances. *** In applying this test we have consistently eschewed bright-line rules, instead emphasizing the fact-specific nature of the reasonableness inquiry. ***

The Supreme Court of Ohio having held otherwise, its judgment is reversed, and the case is remanded for further proceedings not inconsistent with this opinion.

Justice GINSBURG, concurring in the judgment.

*** From their unique vantage point, Ohio's courts observed that traffic stops in the State were regularly giving way to contraband searches, characterized as consensual, even when officers had no reason to suspect illegal activity. One Ohio appellate court noted: "[H]undreds, and perhaps thousands of Ohio citizens are being routinely delayed in their travels and asked to relinquish to uniformed police officers their right to privacy in their automobiles and luggage, sometimes for no better reason than to provide an officer the opportunity to 'practice' his drug interdiction technique."

Against this background, the Ohio Supreme Court determined, and announced in Robinette's case, that the federal and state constitutional rights of Ohio citizens to be secure in their persons and property called for the protection of a clear-cut instruction to the State's police officers: An officer wishing to engage in consensual interrogation of a motorist at the conclusion of a traffic stop must first tell the motorist that he or she is free to go. ***

Today's opinion reversing the decision of the Ohio Supreme Court does not pass judgment on the wisdom of the first-tell-then-ask rule. This Court's opinion simply clarifies that the Ohio Supreme Court's instruction to police officers in Ohio is not, under this Court's controlling jurisprudence, the command of the Federal Constitution. The Ohio Supreme Court invoked both the Federal Constitution and the Ohio Constitution without clearly indicating whether state law, standing alone, independently justified the court's rule. The ambiguity in the Ohio Supreme Court's decision renders this Court's exercise of jurisdiction proper under *Michigan v. Long* (1983), and this Court's decision on the merits is consistent with the Court's "totality of the circumstances" Fourth Amendment precedents. I therefore concur in the Court's judgment.

I write separately, however, because it seems to me improbable that the Ohio Supreme Court understood its first-tell-then-ask rule to be the Federal Constitution's mandate for the Nation as a whole. "[A] State is free as a matter of its own law to impose greater restrictions on police activity than those this Court holds to be necessary upon federal constitutional standards." *Oregon v. Hass* (1975). But ordinarily, when a state high court grounds a rule of criminal procedure in the Federal Constitution, the court thereby signals its view that the Nation's Constitution would require the rule in all 50 States. Given this Court's decisions in consent-to-search cases such as *Schneckloth v. Bustamonte* (1973), however, I suspect that the Ohio Supreme Court may not have homed in on the implication ordinarily to be drawn from a state court's reliance on the Federal Constitution. In other words, I question whether the Ohio court thought of the strict rule it announced as a rule for the governance of police conduct not only in Miami County, Ohio, but also in Miami, Florida.

The first-tell-then-ask rule seems to be a prophylactic measure not so much extracted from the text of any constitutional provision as crafted by the Ohio Supreme Court to reduce the number of violations of textually guaranteed rights. In *Miranda v. Arizona* (1966), this Court announced a similarly motivated rule as a minimal national requirement without suggesting that the text of the Federal Constitution required the precise measures the Court's opinion set forth.... Although all parts of the United States fall within this Court's domain, the Ohio Supreme Court is not similarly situated. That court can declare prophylactic rules governing the conduct of officials in Ohio, but it cannot command the police forces of sister States. The very ease with which the Court today disposes of the federal leg of the

Ohio Supreme Court's decision strengthens my impression that the Ohio Supreme Court saw its rule as a measure made for Ohio, designed to reinforce in that State the right of the people to be secure against unreasonable searches and seizures.

The Ohio Supreme Court's syllabus and opinion, however, were ambiguous. Under *Long*, the existence of ambiguity regarding the federal-or state-law basis of a state-court decision will trigger this Court's jurisdiction. *Long* governs even when, all things considered, the more plausible reading of the state court's decision may be that the state court did not regard the Federal Constitution alone as a sufficient basis for its ruling.

It is incumbent on a state court, therefore, when it determines that its State's laws call for protection more complete than the Federal Constitution demands, to be clear about its ultimate reliance on state law. Similarly, a state court announcing a new legal rule arguably derived from both federal and state law can definitively render state law an adequate and independent ground for its decision by a simple declaration to that effect. A recent Montana Supreme Court opinion on the scope of an individual's privilege against self-incrimination includes such a declaration:

> "While we have devoted considerable time to a lengthy discussion of the application of the Fifth Amendment to the United States Constitution, it is to be noted that this holding is also based separately and independently on [the defendant's] right to remain silent pursuant to Article II, Section 25 of the Montana Constitution." *State v. Fuller* (Mont. 1996).

An explanation of this order meets the Court's instruction in *Long* that "[i]f the state court decision indicates clearly and expressly that it is alternatively based on bona fide separate, adequate, and independent grounds, [this Court] will not undertake to review the decision."

On remand, the Ohio Supreme Court may choose to clarify that its instructions to law enforcement officers in Ohio find adequate and independent support in state law, and that in issuing these instructions, the court endeavored to state dispositively only the law applicable in Ohio. To avoid misunderstanding, the Ohio Supreme Court must itself speak with the clarity it sought to require of its State's police officers. The efficacy of its endeavor to safeguard the liberties of Ohioans without disarming the State's police can then be tested in the precise way Our Federalism was designed to work.

Justice STEVENS, dissenting.

The Court's holding today is narrow: The Federal Constitution does not require that a lawfully seized person be advised that he is "free to go" before his consent to search will be recognized as voluntary. I agree with that holding. Given the Court's reading of the opinion of the Supreme Court of Ohio, I also agree that it is appropriate for the Court to limit its review to answering the sole question presented in the State's certiorari petition. As I read the state-court opinion, however, the prophylactic rule announced in the second syllabus was intended as a guide to the decision of future cases rather than an explanation of the decision in this case. I would therefore affirm the judgment of the Supreme Court of Ohio because it correctly held that respondent's consent to the search of his vehicle was the product of an unlawful detention. Moreover, it is important to emphasize that nothing in the Federal Constitution—or in this Court's opinion—prevents a State from requiring its law enforcement officers to give detained motorists the advice mandated by the Ohio court. ***

State v. Robinette

80 Ohio St. 3d 234 (1997)

LUNDBERG STRATTON, J. The first issue that we must determine is whether this court's prior holding should be reaffirmed under the adequate and independent ground of the Constitution of the state of Ohio.

When the United States Supreme Court incorporated the federal Bill of Rights into the Fourteenth Amendment, the United States Constitution became the primary mechanism to safeguard an individual's rights. As a result, state court litigation of constitutional issues was based primarily upon the authority of the United States Constitution.

However, more recently, there has been a trend for state courts to rely on their own constitutions to provide broader protection for individual rights, independent of protections afforded by the United States Constitution. A state may impose greater restrictions on police activity pursuant to its own state constitution than is required by federal constitutional standards. This movement toward enforcing state constitutions independently has been called the "New Federalism."

Despite this wave of New Federalism, where the provisions are similar and no persuasive reason for a differing interpretation is presented, this court has determined that protections afforded by Ohio's Constitution are coextensive with those provided by the United States Constitution.

The language of Section 14, Article I of the Ohio Constitution and the Fourth Amendment is virtually identical. Accordingly, this court has interpreted Section 14, Article I of the Ohio Constitution as affording the same protection as the Fourth Amendment. ***

Thus, case law indicates that, consistent with *Robinette II*, we should harmonize our interpretation of Section 14, Article I of the Ohio Constitution with the Fourth Amendment, unless there are persuasive reasons to find otherwise. ***

Accordingly, we find that Section 14, Article I of the Ohio Constitution affords protections that are coextensive with those provided by the Fourth Amendment and, therefore, the Ohio Constitution does not require a police officer to inform an individual, stopped for a traffic violation, that he or she is free to go before the officer may attempt to engage in a consensual interrogation. Further, under Section 14, Article I of the Ohio Constitution, we find that the totality-of-the circumstances test is controlling in an unlawful detention to determine whether permission to search a vehicle is voluntary. Once an individual has been unlawfully detained by law enforcement, for his or her consent to be considered an independent act of free will, the totality of the circumstances must clearly demonstrate that a reasonable person would believe that he or she had the freedom to refuse to answer further questions and could in fact leave.

Therefore, pursuant to the totality of the circumstances, we find that Robinette did not voluntarily consent to allow [Officer] Newsome to search his automobile. As a result, the evidence collected in that search is inadmissible.

MOYER, C.J., and RESNICK and PFEIFER, JJ., concur.

FRANCIS E. SWEENEY, SR., J., dissenting. . . . Upon remand, the majority now applies the correct test (totality of the circumstances), but, in my opinion, still reaches the wrong result. ***

DOUGLAS, J., concurs in the foregoing dissenting opinion.

Notes on Independent and Adequate State Grounds

1. Each state supreme court may, subject to its duty to its state constitution, decide for itself whether or not to "march lock-step" with federal constitutional law. When a state court does so, it abandons any independent state grounds for its decision and subjects its interpretation to review by federal courts. This includes the United States Supreme Court on direct review as well as other federal courts on collateral review or under diversity jurisdiction. In effect, a lock-stepping state is saying: "whatever you do with your interpretation of federal constitutional provision X is good enough for our state constitutional provision Y." Why would a state supreme court do this? At least where the court borrows a federal "totality-of-the-circumstances" test in part due to policy arguments, should the totality of the circumstances include the distinct law enforcement policies and practices of the state?

2. For a sharper response to the Supreme Court's strict requirement of clearly articulated independent and adequate state grounds, see *State v. Jackson* (Mont. 1983) (Sheehy, J., dissenting):

> In our original opinion in this case, we had examined the rights guaranteed our citizens under state constitutional principles, in the light of federal constitutional decisions. Now the United States Supreme Court has interjected itself, commanding us in effect to withdraw the constitutional rights which we felt we should extend to our state citizens back to the limits proscribed by the federal decisions. Effectively, the United States Supreme Court has intruded upon the rights of the judiciary of this sovereign state.
>
> Instead of knuckling under to this unjustified expansion of federal judicial power into the perimeters of our state power, we should show our judicial displeasure by insisting that in Montana, this sovereign state can interpret its constitution to guarantee rights to its citizens greater than those guaranteed by the federal constitution. ***

> [T]he United States Supreme Court has no business contravening the final decisions of a state judiciary where no federal right guaranteed to all citizens has been offended. Constitutional rights are guaranteed to persons, not states. Here the State has complained to the United States Supreme Court because its own state judiciary has protected the constitutional rights of one of its citizens, and extended those rights beyond what the State perceives as the federal limits. It has always been the rule that the states could extend federal constitutional rights past the boundaries of the federal limitations as defined by the federal judiciary, but could not delimit such constitutional rights to a lesser degree than would be permitted under federal rules. In other words, the United States Supreme Court historically has intervened to make sure that persons who seek to vindicate federal rights have been fairly heard.... No federal rights of a citizen were denied in our original opinion in this case.
>
> The general public may have a perception that courts operate in a degree of permanency, interpreting constitutions and laws unchangingly. That perception is most misleading. The shades of opinion and the quality of a court's interpretations are transient, depending in large measure upon the changing personnel making up the court, and the ability of its members to withstand the tides of public opinion. The most illustrative example of this transiency is the United States Supreme Court itself. Its vagaries of opinions in the fields of civil rights, human rights, education, and the rights of states in the past 20 years must be astounding to any student of judicial history. The result of the decision in *Michigan v. Long* will be, as Justice Stevens said, a swelling increase in the number of cases the United States Supreme Court will be called on to interpret, where states complain that their own judiciaries have granted greater rights than the federal decisions have allowed. The great likelihood is that the United States Supreme Court must in the future reverse its position and adopt a stance that adequate state grounds for its decision are independent of federal grounds unless it clearly appears from the state's opinion otherwise. We should at least attempt to force the United States Supreme Court to come to that proper stance.
>
> If a majority of this Court had the will to press the issue, we could put the question to the United States Supreme Court four-square, that this State judiciary has the right to interpret its constitution in the light of federal decisions, and to go beyond the federal decisions in granting and preserving rights to its citizens under its state constitution. That is the route I would take in this case.

Justice Sheehy quoted from Justice Stevens' dissent in *Michigan v. Long* at length, replacing the state's name for effect:

> In this case the State of [Montana] has arrested one of its citizens and the [Montana] Supreme Court has decided to turn him loose. The respondent

> is a United States citizen as well as a [Montana] citizen, but since there is no claim that he has been mistreated by the State of [Montana], the final outcome of the state processes offended no federal interest whatever. [Montana] simply provided greater protection to one of its citizens than some other State might provide or, indeed, than this Court might require throughout the country.

Michigan v. Long (1983) (Stevens, J., dissenting); *see also Delaware v. Van Arsdall* (1986) (Stevens, J., dissenting) ("The Court's decision to monitor state-court decisions that may or may not rest on nonfederal grounds is not only historically disfavored but risks the very confrontations and tensions a more humble jurisdictional stance would avoid . . .").

2. Lockstepping With and Distinguishing Federal Constitutional Law

Even when a state court gets the last word on the meaning of a state constitution, however, it may fall back on federal law anyway. The Montana Supreme Court, and lawyers who appear before it, generally start with the federal Constitution as a baseline for interpreting similar provisions of the Montana Constitution. Instead of asking what the Montana Constitution means in the first instance, the Court often starts with what the United States Supreme Court has held the federal Constitution means, even when that meaning is itself contested among the federal justices.

The Montana Supreme Court often recites: "we refuse to 'march lock-step' with the United States Supreme Court where constitutional issues are concerned, even if the applicable State Constitution provisions are identical or nearly identical to those of the United States Constitution." *State v. Johnson* (Mont. 1986). Yet gravitational forces of uniformity, persuasiveness, and even convenience pull the courts and other practitioners toward the deeper reservoir of federal constitutional law when no other easy state constitutional answer is at hand. *State v. Covington* works through the Montana Supreme Court's decision to interpret Montana's constitution in lock-step with federal law.

State v. Covington

2012 MT 31

Justice BRIAN MORRIS delivered the Opinion of the Court.

*** ¶ 14 Issue 1: Whether the existence of facts, including a prior conviction, that trigger the application of the sentence enhancement process of § 46-18-219(1)(b)(iv), MCA, must be submitted to the jury?

¶ 15 Covington argues that the right to a jury trial requires that any fact used to enhance a sentence beyond a statutory maximum, including prior convictions, must be submitted to the jury. Covington concedes the United States Supreme Court has rejected his interpretation of the right to a jury trial under the Sixth Amendment to the United States Constitution. *Almendarez-Torres v. U.S.* (1998). The Court decided in *Almendarez-Torres*, with a 5-4 vote, that a court may determine that a prior conviction exists to enhance a sentence beyond the statutory maximum without infringing on a defendant's right to a jury trial. Covington contends, however, that the Court has called into doubt *Almendarez-Torres* in subsequent decisions.

¶ 16 Covington primarily bases his argument on Justice Thomas's concurrence in *Apprendi v. New Jersey* (2000) (Thomas, J., concurring). The Court determined in *Apprendi* that the right to a jury trial under the Sixth Amendment to the United States Constitution dictated that any fact used to enhance a sentence beyond the statutory maximum must be found by the jury rather than the court. Justice Thomas, who joined the majority in *Almendarez-Torres*, also joined the majority in *Apprendi*. He wrote a concurrence in *Apprendi*, however, in which he stated that *Almendarez-Torres*—a case in which he had cast the decisive fifth vote—had been decided incorrectly.

¶ 17 Covington further argues that *Apprendi* itself called into doubt *Almendarez-Torres*'s viability. The Court in *Apprendi* stated that "it is arguable that *Almendarez-Torres* was incorrectly decided" and also noted "that a logical application of our reasoning today should apply if the recidivist issue were contested." *Apprendi*. The Court declined, however, to overturn *Almendarez-Torres*. . . . ***

¶ 19 Covington concedes that *Almendarez-Torres* remains good law. Covington argues, however, that Article II, § 24 and § 26 of the Montana Constitution provide a stronger right to a jury trial than does the Sixth Amendment to the United States Constitution. *Woirhaye v. Montana Fourth Judicial Dist. Court*, 1998 MT 320 . . . . We disagree.

¶ 20 The Montana Constitution may provide greater protection, in certain circumstances, than the United States Constitution. *State v. Hardaway*, 2001 MT 252. For example, this Court specifically has determined that the Montana Constitution provides a person with an enhanced right to a jury trial. *Woirhaye*, ¶ 14. The Court also has determined, however, that a defendant must establish sound and articulable reasons that the Montana Constitution affords greater protection for a particular right. *See State v. Rosling*, 2008 MT 62.

¶ 21 A party may establish sound and articulable reasons when it demonstrates that the Montana Constitution contains unique language, not found in its federal counterpart, that dictates this Court should recognize the enhanced protection. *See State v. Ellis*, 2009 MT 192 (noting that the Montana Constitution provided an enhanced right to privacy in light of the Constitution's expressed, rather than implicit, right to privacy); *see also Buhmann v. State*, 2008 MT 465 (determining that the Montana Constitution did not provide enhanced rights for regulatory takings due to the absence of any language in Article II, § 29 that specifically addressed regulatory takings). A party also may establish, through convention transcripts and committee reports, that the delegates to the Montana Constitutional Convention intended to provide the alleged, broader protection. *See State v. Goetz*, 2008 MT 296 (determining that the Montana Constitution provides enhanced protection against electronic monitoring due to the delegates' expressed fear, as stated in the convention records, of technology's infringement on individual privacy). A party further may illustrate his claim for broader protection by establishing that the right must not be read in isolation, but rather, in conjunction with rights that are uniquely Montanan. *See State v. Bullock* (Mont. 1995) (determining that the Montana Constitution provided additional protection against illegal searches and seizures because Article II, § 11 must be read in conjunction with the expressed right of privacy in Article II, § 10). We accordingly will undertake a unique, state constitutional analysis only when the defendant has satisfied his burden of proof that a unique aspect of the Montana Constitution, or the background material related to the provision, provides support for the greater protection that he seeks to invoke.

¶ 22 For example, the Court addressed the constitutionality of a statute that provided that a person, charged with a misdemeanor and tried in justice court, could receive only one jury trial. *Woirhaye*, ¶ 11. This interpretation left a defendant who had appealed to the district court for trial de novo with one bench trial and one jury trial. This Court agreed that this interpretation of the statute violated the defendant's right to a jury trial under the Montana Constitution. *Woirhaye*, ¶ 26.

¶ 23 The United States Supreme Court previously had determined that a two tiered, criminal justice system did not infringe on an individual's right to a jury trial under the Sixth Amendment to the United States Constitution when it provided only one jury trial. *Woirhaye*, ¶ 12, citing *Ludwig v. Massachusetts* (1976). The Court in *Woirhaye* examined the history and text of Montana's right to a jury trial to determine that the Montana Constitution provided greater protection for an accused's right to a jury trial than the United States Constitution provided. *Woirhaye*, ¶ 17.

¶ 24 The Court cited two reasons to support its determination that the statute implicated greater protection under the Montana Constitution. First, the delegates to the Montana Constitutional Convention sought to provide more expansive rights to a jury trial for misdemeanor defendants. *Woirhaye*, ¶ 17. Delegates to the 1972 Constitutional Convention expressed a desire that even misdemeanor defendants must be found guilty by a unanimous verdict rather than the two thirds system adopted in the 1889 Constitution. Second, defendants who appealed from a guilty verdict in justice court were entitled only to trial de novo in district court. The statute failed to provide defendants with a right to appeal any specific legal or evidentiary issues. For example, the question of whether a jury had been selected fairly in justice court could not be reviewed in district court. *Woirhaye*, ¶ 22. As a result, this system could deprive a person from receiving a fair jury trial at justice court at the same time that it deprived a defendant of any jury trial in the district court. *Woirhaye*, ¶ 22.

¶ 25 Covington has failed to provide any reason for us to determine that the Montana Constitution offers some greater protection on the issues that must be found by the jury than the United States Supreme Court determined in *Almendarez-Torres* that the United States Constitution requires to be found by a jury. Covington has failed to articulate how his claim implicates any enhanced right afforded under the Montana Constitution when the District Court determined the existence of his prior robbery conviction. He cites nothing in the background materials to indicate that the delegates to Montana's Constitutional Convention contemplated some enhanced protection for the narrow issue presented here. Covington provides no argument as to what injustice would be prevented by requiring a jury to determine the existence of a prior conviction in order for the court to use the prior conviction for sentence enhancement purposes to § 46-18-219, MCA. Covington further fails to articulate what safeguard a jury provides to the criminal justice system when the fact of a prior conviction is at issue. Simply put, Covington failed to meet his burden of establishing that the District Court infringed on an enhanced right to a jury trial under the Montana Constitution. ***

Notes on Lockstepping With and Distinguishing Federal Constitutional Law

1. The relevant text of Article II, sections 24 (Rights of the Accused) and 26 (Trial by Jury) is nearly identical to the 1889 Constitution, and does not vary significantly from the Sixth Amendment. What does it mean for the Montana Constitution to "provide greater protection, in certain circumstances, than the United States Constitution"? When did it do so and why?

a. Assuming that the text of the federal Constitution is authoritative in interpretation of the Montana Constitution's jury trial right (why?), is the baseline for that interpretation the original meaning of the Sixth Amendment in 1791 or as it was incorporated by the Fourteenth Amendment in 1868? The United States Supreme Court did not recognize the incorporation of the Sixth Amendment jury trial right until a century later in *Duncan v. Louisiana* (1968). Is the right date 1968?

b. Alternatively, should the interpretive baseline be Sixth Amendment case law as it was developed by the United States Supreme Court as of 1889 when Montanans first ratified the right of "trial by jury" in the state constitution? Or in 1972 when Montanans decided to retain the right in the current constitution? If any of these sources lead to a different answer, why should a relatively recent 5-4 federal decision called into question by the justices themselves be the "right answer" under the Montana Constitution?

2. According to the Court, "sound and articulable reasons" for recognizing greater protections include distinct text, distinct history, or distinct context. *See also State v. Nixon*, 2013 MT 81 (applying *Covington* analysis to the self-incrimination and double jeopardy protections of Article II, section 25). Is this an exclusive list? Should historical evidence of distinctions include public meaning sources beyond

the delegates' intent? These are three of the six conventional methods of constitutional interpretation. *See* PHILIP BOBBITT, CONSTITUTIONAL FATE (1982) (identifying historical, textual, doctrinal, structural, prudential (policy-oriented) and ethical (principled) modalities of American constitutional practice). What about the Court's interpretation of, or other officials' practices under, similar constitutional text under the 1889 Constitution? Is there room for policy-based or principled distinctions that arise from Montana's local values?

3. Compare the approach of Washington (and several other states), summarized in *State v. Gunwall* (Wash. 1986):

> The following nonexclusive neutral criteria are relevant in determining whether, in a given situation, the Washington State Constitution should be considered as extending broader rights to its citizens than the United States Constitution: (1) the textual language; (2) differences in the texts; (3) constitutional history; (4) preexisting state law; (5) structural differences; and (6) matters of particular state or local concern.

Washington is Montana's twin (or quadruplet) state, created in the same 1889 Enabling Act. Does that make its approach to constitutional interpretation any more persuasive?

4. Levels of generality sometimes decide questions of constitutional law. *See, e.g., Washington v. Glucksberg* (1997) (rejecting a liberty interest in physician-assisted suicide under a "careful description" and refusing to consider more general dignity-based descriptions of the interest). Here, the Montana Supreme Court requires evidence "the delegates to Montana's Constitutional Convention contemplated some enhanced protection for the narrow issue presented here," as opposed to more general descriptions of the role of the jury in Montana criminal practice that might distinguish the basic protections of the incorporated Sixth Amendment. Most hard cases in constitutional law arise from situations falling outside of the narrow issues the framers and ratifiers might have considered. Many such narrow issues have not been addressed by the United States Supreme Court either. Should the meaning of state constitutional provisions with federal analogues turn on whether any particular narrow issue arises first before the United States Supreme Court (in which case, the state supreme court will "march in lock-step" with the decision, without more) or the state supreme court (in which case, the state supreme court will decide the issue independently and presumably will stand by its decision even if the United States Supreme Court decides the federal analogue provides less protection)?

3. Identifying and Distinguishing Sibling State Constitutions

There is a second important "horizontal" relationship among state constitutions. Arguably, the other states, from which much of Montana's (and most federal) constitutional text is derived, offer a more faithful approach to state constitutional meaning than "lock-stepping" with whatever current federal constitutional doctrine may say. The forces that pull practitioners toward federal constitutional law seem to be stronger than the attraction exerted by the dispersed state constitutional tradition, so interstate constitutional exchange is less prominent than lock-stepping. Still the independent development of constitutional law under similar (and often related) state constitutional provisions offers practitioners an alternative, and potentially more faithful, set of answers to a state's open constitutional questions. *Bullock* and *Blue Pickup* feature similar approaches to cross-state analysis that lead to different results.

State v. Bullock

272 Mont. 361 (1995)

TRIEWEILER, Justice.

At about 6:30 a.m. on October 31, 1991, while returning home from work, Chuck Wing observed what he estimated was a large six or seven point antlered bull elk on Boulder Hill near Boulder, Montana. He recognized that the elk was in Hunting District 380 where hunters were allowed to shoot only "spikes" unless they had a special permit. As Wing observed the elk, he heard a gunshot, saw the elk fall, and observed two men and a boy standing near a pickup truck in the vicinity of the fallen elk. He believed the pickup belonged to defendant Eddie J. Peterson. He then observed the three people drag the elk to the truck and load it without field-dressing it. Wing reported the incident to Jefferson County Sheriff Tom Dawson, who, in turn, relayed the information to Game Warden Chris Anderson, an employee of the Montana Department of Fish, Wildlife, and Parks. Anderson traveled from Helena to Boulder that morning to investigate the incident.

Anderson first interviewed Wing who related the above information. He then drove to Peterson's home in Boulder, but Peterson was not at home. Anderson returned to the sheriff's office where he learned that Peterson had a cabin in Basin Creek. Rather than try to give directions, Dawson agreed to accompany him to the cabin. To reach Peterson's cabin, it is necessary to travel approximately seven miles on a one-lane forest service road which is bounded by forest on both sides. At least one sign along that road indicates that the road is bordered by private property and advises the public to remain on the road.

Peterson's property is separated from the road by a fence. There is a gate which provides access to his property from the forest service road. "No Trespassing" signs are posted on trees on each side of the gate. His cabin is located at the end of a private road 334 feet from the forest service road. Between the forest service road and Peterson's cabin, the terrain is slightly elevated in a way that conceals Peterson's cabin and the other structures on his property. He moved his cabin beyond the hill at an earlier time so that it would not be evident to passersby.

When Anderson and Dawson reached Peterson's property, the gate was open. They entered the property through the gate and drove approximately 180 feet down Peterson's private road. As they descended the crest of the hill between his cabin and the forest service road, they first observed a large bull elk hanging from a tree in an area about 126 feet from Peterson's cabin. The elk could not be seen from the public road, nor was there evidence that it could be seen from any other public location. Peterson testified that the elk was hanging between his cabin, several vehicles, and a guest sleeping cabin.

The parties agreed that, in the past, anyone who wished to enter Peterson's property or drive on his private road had called to ask permission. In fact, the Jefferson County Sheriff's Office had done so a few days earlier prior to conducting a search for lost hunters. On the date in question, neither Dawson nor Anderson asked or received permission to be on Peterson's property. Neither had they secured a search warrant, in spite of the fact that Anderson testified in Justice Court that he believed there was probable cause that a crime had been committed, that Peterson was involved, and that Peterson still possessed evidence of that crime. ***

ISSUE 3

Does Article II, Section 11, of the Montana Constitution, prohibit warrantless searches and seizures, under the circumstances in this case, on private land that falls outside the curtilage of a dwelling? ***

The Fourth Amendment to the United States Constitution provides that:

> The right of the people to be secure in their persons, houses, papers, and effects, against unreasonable searches and seizures, shall not be violated, and no Warrants shall issue, but upon probable cause, supported by Oath or affirmation, and particularly describing the place to be searched, and the persons or things to be seized.

Article II, Section 11, of the Montana Constitution, provides similarly that:

> The people shall be secure in their persons, papers, homes and effects from unreasonable searches and seizures. No warrant to search any place, or seize any person or thing shall issue without describing the place to be searched or the person or thing to be seized, or without probable cause, supported by oath or affirmation reduced to writing.

Pursuant to these provisions, searches conducted without warrants are presumed to be unreasonable subject to a few delineated exceptions. The State contends that a search of open fields was either never intended for protection pursuant to these amendments, or is an exception to the warrant requirement, depending on which precedent is considered.

Because of what appear to be seeming inconsistencies in the decisions of the United States Supreme Court, our prior willingness to apply those decisions under circumstances which were different than those presented in this case, and contrary decisions in other jurisdictions based on the same high regard for privacy that prevails in this State, we deem it appropriate to trace the origins of the "open fields" doctrine, and reconsider its applicability to Article II, Section 11, of the Montana Constitution.

The open fields doctrine was first established in *Hester v. United States* (1924). In *Hester*, the Court held that the Fourth Amendment protects "persons, houses, papers, and effects," and is not extended to the open fields. Shortly thereafter, the Supreme Court clarified that the Fourth Amendment provides protection from invasion of one's house or curtilage. *Olmstead v. United States* (1928).

Subsequently, however, that Court recognized that the Fourth Amendment protects people—not places—from unreasonable searches. *Katz v. United States* (1967). In *Katz*, the Court stated that the Fourth Amendment protects individual privacy against certain kinds of government intrusion, but its protections go further and often do not relate to privacy. A person's right to privacy, or right to be let alone, is largely left to the law of the states. What a person knowingly exposes to the public is not protected, but what an individual seeks to preserve as private, even in an area accessible to the public, may be constitutionally protected. Finally, the Court discredited the previous notion that property interests control the government's right to search and seize. However, the two-part test that this Court has followed . . . to determine whether a search is unlawful was set forth in Justice Harlan's concurring opinion in *Katz* (Harlan, J., concurring). That test requires that (1) a person have an actual expectation of privacy; and (2) the expectation must be one society is willing to recognize as reasonable.

In a seeming return to concepts discredited in *Katz*, the Court reaffirmed notions grounded in *Hester* in *Oliver v. United States* (1984). *Oliver* was based on two similar fact patterns where law enforcement officials ignored "No Trespassing" signs and fences, entered private property, and observed illegal drug activity. The Court held that the specific language of the Fourth Amendment does not include open fields. The amendment's protection extends only to the curtilage area immediately surrounding one's home. Following *Oliver*, it appears that if an area is not curtilage, it is an open field unprotected by the Fourth Amendment. Despite the Court's intent to eliminate case-by-case determinations, the *Oliver* Court did not discuss how courts were to determine the distinction between curtilage and open fields.

Based on this omission, the Supreme Court suggested a four-part test for determining the extent of the curtilage area in [*United States v. Dunn* (1987)]. *** However, based on this State's Constitution, and its expressed regard for individual privacy, we decline to follow the U.S. Supreme Court's distinction between curtilage and open fields, and therefore, will not consider the applicability of the *Dunn* criteria to this case. Although we have not previously followed *Dunn*, we have, in the past, applied the "open fields" doctrine in cases which are factually distinguishable from this case.

Before Montana's Constitution was amended in 1972, the doctrine was discussed in several cases. We initially followed *Hester* and held that the constitutional protections of Montana's analogous provision to the Fourth Amendment do not extend to an open field. [W]e held that open pastures and farm lands are not protected by the Fourth Amendment, or Montana's analogous constitutional provision.

Following the amendment of Montana's Constitution in 1972, and after *Katz,* this Court began to analyze the open fields doctrine differently. In *State v. Charvat* (Mont. 1978), relying on *Hester,* this Court held that neither the Fourth Amendment, nor Article II, Section 11, of the Montana Constitution, extended protection to open fields. However, because *Katz* was decided after *Hester,* we stated that the determination of whether an intrusion was unreasonable depended upon whether one had an actual (subjective) expectation of privacy that society would recognize as reasonable. This Court, like the Court in *Katz,* cited authority for the proposition that the focus of search and seizure analysis is no longer on common law property concepts. ***

As [earlier cases] illustrate, we have followed the principles established in *Katz,* but have applied the "open fields" doctrine to our consideration of whether a person's expectation of privacy is one that society would consider reasonable. However, we have not had occasion to consider reasonableness under precisely the circumstances presented in this case.

Nor have we discussed the distinction between curtilage and open fields, or the impact of *Dunn* on Montana's constitutional guarantee of freedom from unreasonable searches. Therefore, we look to other jurisdictions which have addressed the open fields doctrine as applied to state constitutional provisions similar to ours under circumstances similar to those presented in this case.

In 1988, the Oregon Supreme Court held that that state's nearly identical right to be free from unreasonable searches and seizures provided broader privacy protection in open fields than the United States Supreme Court had provided pursuant to the Fourth Amendment. *State v. Dixson/Digby* (Or. 1988).... [T]he Oregon court established the following test to enable police to determine whether an uninvited intrusion on private property constitutes a search under that state's constitution which requires a warrant: ... "A person who wishes to preserve a constitutionally protected privacy interest in land outside the curtilage must manifest an intention to exclude the public by erecting barriers to entry, such as fences, or by posting signs."

The Court of Appeals of New York has also refused to follow the United States Supreme Court's distinction between curtilage and an open field. *People v. Scott* (N.Y. 1992).... After thoughtful consideration ... the New York Court held that: "[W]here landowners fence or post 'No Trespassing' signs on their private property or, by some other means, indicate unmistakably that entry is not permitted, the expectation that their privacy rights will be respected and that they will be free from unwanted intrusions is reasonable." ***

Finally, and most recently, a Washington Court of Appeals found additional protection based on its state constitution. *State v. Johnson* (Wash. 1994).... The court first stated that the Washington Constitution provides more protection than the Fourth Amendment, partly because Washington has a strong tradition of protecting private property from unwanted intrusions and recognized criminal trespass for similar conduct.... It held that fields that are fenced and posted with no trespassing signs are protected, and therefore, that the agents' entry was an unreasonable intrusion into Johnson's private affairs.

Like our sister states, Montana has a strong tradition of respect for the right to individual privacy.... Because Montana's Constitutional protections [in the nearly identically worded protection against unreasonable searches and seizures of Art. II, section 11, as well as the express protection of individual privacy in Art. II, section 10] have an existence which is separate from the Federal Constitutional protections it is necessary to offer an independent analysis of the privacy and search and seizure provisions of the Montana Constitution. ***

We conclude that in Montana a person may have an expectation of privacy in an area of land that is beyond the curtilage which the society of this State is willing to recognize as reasonable, and that where that expectation is evidenced by fencing, "No Trespassing," or similar signs, or "by some other means [which] indicate[s] unmistakably that entry is not permitted" (*Scott*), entry by law enforcement officers requires permission or a warrant. As in our prior decisions, however, this requirement does not apply to observations of private land from public property. To the extent that our prior decisions in *Charvat* [and other cases] are inconsistent with this holding, they are overruled. ***

State v. A Blue in Color, 1993 Chevrolet Pickup

2005 MT 180

Justice PATRICIA O. COTTER delivered the Opinion of the Court. ***

¶ 3 On August 6, 2002, after a several-month investigation of Pelvit, and based on information he was operating a methamphetamine lab, agents of the Eastern Montana Drug Task Force (EMDTF), conducted a warrantless "trash dive" on garbage cans located along a public alley on an open wooden rack behind Pelvit's residence. EMDTF agents removed an opaque trash bag from one of the unlocked garbage cans and discovered inside it pseudoephedrine boxes with corresponding empty blister packs and empty Naptha cans. Naptha is a solvent known to be used in the manufacture of methamphetamine.

¶ 4 These items formed the basis for the issuance of a search warrant. The search of Pelvit's residence, pickup, and boat occurred on August 9, 2002. The State thereafter petitioned to institute forfeiture proceedings against Pelvit's pickup, boat, and boat trailer, because the search turned up drug-related evidence in these places. Pelvit was also charged with federal drug offenses. ***

¶ 6 Did the District Court err in concluding the warrantless search of Pelvit's trash bags did not violate his right to privacy under Article II, Sections 10 and 11 of the Montana Constitution, and on that basis denying Pelvit's motion to suppress?

¶ 7 Pelvit maintains he exhibited both an objective and subjective expectation of privacy in the contents of his trash, which society is willing to recognize as reasonable. Pelvit claims he took steps to conceal the contents of his trash by putting it in opaque bags in cans located on the rear of his property. He argues a search warrant was required to authorize the search of his trash, and that since one was not obtained, the search was illegal and the items seized should have been suppressed. Pelvit proceeds to argue that the evidence found in his truck and boat should have been suppressed pursuant to the "fruit of the poisonous tree" doctrine, because it would not have been discovered but for the unlawful warrantless search of his trash. Pelvit maintains that *State v. Siegal* [(Mont. 1997)], in which we held the warrantless use of thermal imaging violated the defendant's right to privacy, is controlling. Pelvit also points to several cases from other state supreme courts in support of his argument.

¶ 8 The State counters that Pelvit abandoned his trash, and as a result, he had no actual or subjective expectation of privacy in it. In support of this argument, the State points out Pelvit took no steps to secure the trash; rather, he placed it in an unlocked garbage can set out in a public alley for collection. Further, the State asserts society is not willing to recognize Pelvit's claimed expectation of privacy in his trash as reasonable. The State distinguishes Siegal and cites language from that decision to support its position.

¶ 9 The Fourth Amendment to the United States Constitution protects citizens against unreasonable searches and seizures. Montanans have a heightened expectation of privacy, pursuant to the protections found at Article II, Sections 10 and 11 of the Montana Constitution. An impermissible search and seizure occurs within the meaning of Article II, Section 10 of the Montana Constitution when a reasonable expectation of privacy has been breached. However, where no reasonable expectation of privacy exists, there is neither a "search" nor a "seizure" within the contemplation of Article II, Sections 10 and 11 of the Montana Constitution.

¶ 10 To determine whether Pelvit had a reasonable expectation of privacy in his trash, we consider: (1) whether he had an actual expectation of privacy in his trash; (2) whether society is willing to recognize that expectation as objectively reasonable; and (3) the nature of the State's intrusion. Analyzing the first two factors, the United States Supreme Court in *California v. Greenwood* (1988), held the Fourth Amendment does not prohibit a warrantless search and seizure of trash left for collection in an area accessible by the public, reasoning that a person has no reasonable expectation of privacy, which society is willing to recognize, in items knowingly exposed to the public. However, given Montanans' heightened expectation of privacy pursuant to our Constitution, we will look to our case law in analyzing this inquiry. ***

¶ 14 Voluntary relinquishment of one's interest in an item or one's control over that item is akin to the legal concept of abandonment. . . . We have stated that when a person intentionally abandons his property, that person's expectation of privacy with regard to that property is abandoned as well. Moreover, as did the United States Supreme Court in *Greenwood*, this Court has frequently stated that what a person knowingly exposes to the public is not protected by the Montana Constitution. ***

¶ 16 Even if we assume for the sake of argument that Pelvit had an actual expectation of privacy in the garbage he placed for collection, we must still determine whether society would be willing to recognize that expectation as objectively reasonable. In analyzing this inquiry, we logically look to society's experience with respect to garbage placed in an alley for the trash collector. While garbage bags oftentimes remain intact until their contents are collected by a designated hauler, it is also common to see homeless people, stray pets and wildlife, curious children, and scavengers rummaging through trash set out for collection, in hopes of finding food, salvageable scrap, or deserted treasure. *See Greenwood*. The wind and the elements are also factors, particularly in Montana. Routinely, cans are knocked over, bags are exposed to the predations of dogs and raccoons, and garbage is found strewn across streets and alleyways. In short, society's experience with trash left at the alley or curb for collection is anything but consistent with an objective expectation of privacy.

¶ 17 We conclude that when Pelvit placed his garbage at the alley's edge for collection, he abandoned his garbage; as a result, he had no expectation of privacy in it that society would be willing to accept as reasonable. Absent such a reasonable expectation of privacy, there is neither a "search" or "seizure" within the contemplation of Article II, Sections 10 and 11 of the Montana Constitution. We further conclude that the burden of proving that garbage has been abandoned by the defendant shall be on the State. However, this conclusion does not end our analysis, as this decision will guide the conduct of police in the future, and will also have an impact upon the expectations of a public that is compelled, for lack of easy and lawful alternatives, to use public refuse collection services.

¶ 18 While we do not believe the public would accept as reasonable an expectation of privacy in abandoned garbage, neither do we believe the public would be entirely comfortable with the image of police officers overtly foraging through curbside garbage. Nor do we believe the public would embrace the idea of police officers conducting random and arbitrary fishing expeditions through garbage cans, in the hopes of finding contraband. Garbage is unique in the sense that, while we may have abandoned it, if we want it hauled away, we are generally obligated to comply with local refuse ordinances by placing it for collection in a particular place. In exchange for such compliance, it seems only fair that certain constraints — inoffensive to legitimate law enforcement interests — should limit the nature and extent of permissible government intrusions into it. Therefore, so as to strike a balance between such public concerns and the needs of law enforcement, we deem it appropriate to qualify our holding. In doing so, we borrow from the analysis of the Indiana Supreme Court set forth in its March 24, 2005, opinion in the case of *Litchfield v. State* (Ind. 2005).

¶ 19 In *Litchfield* . . . the Court imposed two constraints: first, for such a seizure to be reasonable, the garbage must be quickly retrieved by officers "in substantially the same manner as the trash collector would take it." In other words, officers cannot openly rummage through a person's garbage at the curb or in the alley, to the embarrassment or indignity of the owner. Second, so as to prevent wholesale or random searches, officers must have an articulable individualized suspicion that a crime is being committed, essentially the same as is required for a "Terry stop" of an automobile, in order to justify the garbage seizure. We conclude that these constraints are reasonable and justified; they balance the State's interest in conducting a legitimate investigatory search against the public's expectation that, if they place their garbage for collection as the law requires, curbside chaos will not ensue. We therefore incorporate these limitations into our decision today. ***

¶ 21 In conclusion, given the undisputed facts before us, we determine that the State met its burden of proving Pelvit abandoned his trash. We further conclude that the seizure of the garbage was conducted in a reasonable and unobtrusive manner, and that the police had sufficient particularized suspicion to justify the warrantless search of Pelvit's garbage. Therefore, the District Court did not err in denying Pelvit's motion to suppress this evidence. ***

Justice JAMES C. NELSON concurs.

¶ 24 I have signed our Opinion because we have correctly applied existing legal theory and constitutional jurisprudence to resolve this case on its facts.

¶ 25 I feel the pain of conflict, however. I fear that, eventually, we are all going to become collateral damage in the war on drugs, or terrorism, or whatever war is in vogue at the moment. I retain an abiding concern that our Declaration of Rights not be killed by friendly fire. And, in this day and age, the courts are the last, if not only, bulwark to prevent that from happening.

¶ 26 In truth, though, we are a throw-away society. My garbage can contains the remains of what I eat and drink. It may contain discarded credit card receipts along with yesterday's newspaper and junk mail. It might hold some personal letters, bills, receipts, vouchers, medical records, photographs and stuff that is imprinted with the multitude of assigned numbers that allow me access to the global economy and vice versa.

¶ 27 My garbage can contains my DNA.

¶ 28 As our Opinion states, what we voluntarily throw away, what we discard—i.e., what we abandon—is fair game for roving animals, scavengers, busybodies, crooks and for those seeking evidence of criminal enterprise.

¶ 29 Yet, as I expect with most people, when I take the day's trash (neatly packaged in opaque plastic bags) to the garbage can each night, I give little consideration to what I am throwing away and less thought, still, to what might become of my refuse. I don't necessarily envision that someone or something is going to paw through it looking for a morsel of food, a discarded treasure, a stealable part of my identity or a piece of evidence. But, I've seen that happen enough times to understand—though not graciously accept—that there is nothing sacred in whatever privacy interest I think I have retained in my trash once it leaves my control—the Fourth Amendment and Article II, Sections 10 and 11, notwithstanding. ***

Justice W. WILLIAM LEAPHART dissenting.

¶ 39 Since I find the Court's analysis both internally incoherent and inconsistent with our privacy jurisprudence, I dissent. ***

¶ 41 . . . [M]uch of society's growing awareness of, and determination to combat, identity theft stems precisely from our expectation that our garbage will remain private, and from the outrage that a stranger's violation thereof naturally inspires. ***

¶ 43 [Abandonment through voluntary relinquishment of control], of course, is not what we do when we leave our household refuse for collection. The act itself links the garbage ineluctably to us, as does the latter's appearance on our property in our garbage can, and this connection continues at least until our trash is commingled with that of others. This distinction, unappreciated by the Court, is a crucial one, because by disclaiming any connection to the marijuana-filled duffel bags, [another defendant] naturally disclaimed all privacy interest in them, as well. Leaving garbage for collection, by contrast, constitutes at most proprietary renunciation, not absolute disavowal.

¶ 45 . . . We have defined "abandonment" as "the giving up of a thing absolutely, without reference to any particular person or purpose." *Moore v. Sherman* (Mont. 1916). When we haul our household refuse out for collection, however, we have both a person and a purpose in mind. We intend nothing more nor less than that the garbage collector will dispose of it for us at the designated location. "By definition, there cannot be an abandonment to a particular person[.]" 1 C.J.S. Abandonment § 3b (citing *Moore*; *Norman v. Corbley* (Mont. 1905)).

¶ 46 The Court then compounds its error with this vague, sweeping, and entirely unsupported assertion: "Voluntary relinquishment of one's interest in an item or one's control over that item is *akin* to the legal concept of abandonment." Maj. Op., ¶ 14 (emphasis added). The passage serves as the means by which to nudge the practice of leaving one's garbage for collection into the category of "abandonment," a characterization which I have already demonstrated to be legally erroneous. It is useful, however, to examine the statement further.

¶ 47 The Court has already conceded that Pelvit relinquished only "immediate control" of his garbage. Maj. Op., ¶ 13. Remembering and retrieving items which we have unintentionally or rashly discarded is a fairly common action, and one which we could hardly perform if we enjoyed no control over our garbage whatsoever.

Therefore, it must be the cession of "immediate control" that is akin (whatever that may mean) to the legal concept of abandonment.

¶ 48 Now consider the common practice of parking one's car in the driveway and leaving it there to enter one's home. This surely constitutes a relinquishment of "immediate control" over the vehicle. On the Court's view, then, this amounts to abandonment, and should result in a loss of all privacy protection in the car. Maj Op., ¶ 14 ("[w]e have stated that when a person intentionally abandons his property, that person's expectation of privacy with regard to that property is abandoned as well"). Does it in fact do so? No. *State v. Tackitt*, 2003 MT 81 (privacy protection extends to automobile parked at residence). Or consider mailing a letter. Does placing the letter in the mailbox for collection by the postman disqualify it for privacy protection? No, not even under the United States Constitution, a document which affords but meager privacy protection in comparison with our State Constitution. *California v. Greenwood* (1988) (Brennan, J., dissenting).

¶ 49 Even if Pelvit abandoned his garbage, moreover, this would not necessarily mean that he abandoned all privacy interest therein, the Court's assertion to the contrary notwithstanding. Maj. Op., ¶ 14. Not even the United States Constitution equates proprietary abandonment with abandonment of privacy interests. ***

¶ 50 The Court's position is a throwback to the old abandonment-and-curtilage analysis that *Katz* superseded almost four decades ago. *Katz v. United States* (1967). The fact that we now base our three-pronged test for impermissible governmental intrusions upon *Katz* only highlights the absurdity of the Court's stance. *See State v. Bullock* (1995). ***

¶ 51 While it is true that we have held Article II, Section 10, of our Constitution not to protect whatever privacy interest the citizen might claim in objects which he has knowingly exposed to the public, Maj. Op., ¶ 14, it is also beside the point, for Pelvit did not knowingly expose his garbage to public view. He put it into opaque garbage bags, put the bags into garbage cans, and closed the cans. See Maj. Op., ¶ 3. To imply, as the Court does, that Pelvit knowingly exposed his garbage to the public at large is thus to credit Montana's citizenry with X-ray vision.

¶ 52 Though perhaps not to the extent of imputing super-human powers to our citizens, the Court similarly overstates its case when it claims that garbage cans "[r]outinely . . . are knocked over" and their contents "strewn across streets and alleyways." Our cities' thoroughfares are not, I am happy to report, awash in garbage. In any event, as the Vermont Supreme Court wrote in *State v. Morris*:

> [T]he mere possibility that unwelcome animals or persons might rummage through one's garbage bags does not negate the expectation of privacy in the contents of those bags any more than the possibility of a burglary or break-in negates an expectation of privacy in one's home or car, or the possibility that an operator or party-line caller will listen in on a telephone conversation negates an expectation of privacy in the contents of the conversation,

> or the possibility that a cleaning person or house guest will exceed the scope of a visit negates an expectation of privacy in a hotel room or home.

State v. Morris (Vt. 1996). As we stated in *State v. Hamilton*, 2003 MT 71, "[t]he reality that certain people lack respect for the property of another is no reason to diminish the expectation of privacy we protect so jealously in Montana."

¶ 53 It is therefore odd to find the Court requiring that, before officers can seize and search garbage, they must have an "articulable individualized suspicion that a crime is being committed" in the interests of balancing the State's interest in conducting a legitimate investigatory search against the public's expectation that, "if they place their garbage for collection as the law requires, curbside chaos will not ensue." Maj. Op. ¶ 19. When the Court has spent the better part of its opinion attempting to show that Pelvit did not have a reasonable expectation of privacy in his garbage, it is internally inconsistent for the Court to continue characterizing this intrusion as a seizure and search and, on that basis, to impose a requirement of "articulable individualized suspicion." If, as the Court posits, Pelvit had no reasonable expectation of privacy in the garbage, then there was neither a seizure nor search of the garbage and no legal constraints are constitutionally required. Either Pelvit had an expectation of privacy or he did not. I would conclude that he did. ***

Chief Justice KARLA M. GRAY joins in the foregoing dissent of Justice LEAPHART.

Notes on Identifying and Distinguishing Sibling State Constitutions

1. Article II, section 10 of the Montana Constitution provides "The right of individual privacy is essential to the well-being of a free society and shall not be infringed without the showing of a compelling state interest." Notwithstanding the Court's emphasis on this distinct textual protection, the Montana Supreme Court applies a slightly modified version of the United States Supreme Court's "reasonable expectation of privacy" test from *Katz v. United States* (1967). Does the Montana Supreme Court in *Bullock* simply disagree with the United States Supreme Court on its policy-laden application of an essentially federal rule of reasonableness? If so, should that justify overruling prior cases where the state court, presumably equipped with the same "strong tradition of respect for the right to individual privacy," embraced a different rule?

2. In departing from its own precedent, the Montana Supreme Court in *Bullock* looked to the decisions of several other states. While New York, Oregon, and Washington all might resemble Montana in some ways relevant to the right to privacy (which ways?), what if neighboring states Idaho and Wyoming took the other side of the debate? *Cf. State v. Beck* (Idaho 2014); *Pellatz v. State* (Wyo. 1986).

3. The *Katz* test embraces judicial policymaking (as does, arguably, the "unreasonable searches and seizures" text of the federal Fourth Amendment and Montana's Article II, section 11). Along with the Montana analogue, it requires that (1) a person have an actual expectation of privacy; and (2) the expectation must be one society is willing to recognize as reasonable. What does "society" mean in the crucial second, "objective," part of the test? When Montana's courts hold an expectation of privacy is reasonable, are they referring to American society, Montana society, or some other society hypothesized by the framers (or the court)?

4. The Montana Supreme Court refers repeatedly to the "discredited" property-based concept of privacy underlying the open fields doctrine. Does a federal critique (in *Katz*) of a federal doctrine (in *Hester*) necessarily discredit Montana's independent state constitutional doctrine? What if Montana's right of privacy was based in property more than "reasonable expectations"? *See Welsh v. Pritchard* (Mont. 1952) (quoted in the 1972 Constitutional Convention discussion of Article II, section 10, and discussed in Chapter 11). Wouldn't the defendants in *Bullock* benefit at least as much from a property-based concept of privacy?

5. Compare the Montana Supreme Court's analysis in *Blue Pickup* to *Bullock*. What accounts for the Court's recognition of a broader "reasonable expectation of privacy" in the latter than the former?

6. Consider California Supreme Court Justice Goodwin Liu's summary of garbage privacy under state constitutions:

> In 1988, the Supreme Court in *California v. Greenwood* held that police may search trash left at the curbside of a home without a warrant because "society would not accept as reasonable [the] claim to an expectation of privacy in trash left for collection in an area accessible to the public." Although many state courts have adopted this rule as a matter of state constitutional law, several have not—and the weight of their analysis has focused on how the Court in *Greenwood* failed to properly understand what individuals and society consider private. The New Hampshire Supreme Court found Justice Brennan's dissent in *Greenwood* more persuasive and concluded that "society is prepared to recognize th[e] expectation [of privacy in one's trash] as reasonable." The Washington Supreme Court opined that "[w]hile a person must reasonably expect a licensed trash collector will remove the contents of his trash can, this expectation does not also infer an expectation of governmental intrusion." The Vermont Supreme Court, describing *Greenwood* as "misguided," held that "unconstrained government inspection of people's trash is not consistent with a free and open society." Notably, the court said there is no reason that "any state court should refrain from following a different path from that taken by the United States Supreme Court unless the court can rely on unique state sources—historical, legislative or otherwise." And the New Jersey Supreme Court, finding *Greenwood*'s reasoning "dubious" and "disturbing," concluded that *Greenwood* was "flatly

> and simply wrong as [to] . . . the way people think about garbage." The court did not rely on state-specific sources, making clear that "there is no 'unique New Jersey state attitude about garbage.'"

Goodwin Liu, *State Constitutions and the Protection of Individual Rights: A Reappraisal*, 92 N.Y.U. L. Rev. 1307, 1317 (2017). Why should New York, Oregon, and Washington persuade the Montana Supreme Court in *Bullock* while it rejects the reasoning of New Hampshire, New Jersey, Vermont—and Washington—in *Blue Pickup*?

7. Pelvit lost his property to state forfeiture proceedings, but he lost his liberty to a federal prosecution. The investigation leading to both was conducted by a joint drug task force consisting of local, state, and federal law enforcement officials. Although federal officials in Montana are not sworn to or bound by the Montana Constitution, state and local officials are. Assume this case went the other way. If state officials on the task force violated Pelvit's state constitutional rights, why should that violation save his property in state court and not his liberty in federal court? Conversely, can a state court enforce the state constitution against federal officials on behalf of a Montanan? *See* Riley M. Wavra, *State Constitutional Rights Be Damned: Reconsidering the Indifference to State Constitutional Violations in Federal Criminal Proceedings*, 82 Mont. L. Rev. 237 (2021) (arguing for the exclusion of evidence in federal prosecutions when state or local law enforcement officers obtained it through a violation of the defendant's state constitutional rights).

8. Why might Justice Nelson have penned his concurrence?

B. Constitutional Remedies

> **State subject to suit.** The state, counties, cities, towns, and all other local governmental entities shall have no immunity from suit for injury to a person or property, except as may be specifically provided by law by a 2/3 vote of each house of the legislature.
>
> *New provision abolishing the doctrine of sovereign immunity ("the King can do no wrong") and allowing any person to sue the state and local governments for injuries caused by officials and employees thereof.*
>
> **Mont. Const. Art. II, § 18, *as amended by* Const. Ref. 2 (1974)**

1. Sovereign Immunity

This section begins with an overview of federal and state sovereign immunity, and in particular, the arguments made for "waiving" the state's sovereign immunity in Article II, section 18. Even when waived, however, the liability of state and local officials is further circumscribed by common law traditions resting on tort policy rationales borrowed from federal law. Although there are important distinctions between federal and state immunities, including the potential scope of qualified immunity, consider whether the courts' reimposition of these immunities after the 1972 Constitution might have been a surprise to the framers.

Anthony Johnstone, *Immunity Confusion: What Is Article II, Section 18 About?*

MONTANA LAWYER (March 2017)

Article II, section 18 of the Montana Constitution ("State subject to suit") says "[t]he state, counties, cities, towns, and all other local governmental entities shall have no immunity from suit for injury to a person or property, except as may be specifically provided by law by a 2/3 vote of each house of the legislature." Lawyers commonly understand this provision to waive the state's "sovereign immunity," except when a supermajority of the legislature confers such immunity by statute. ***

Sovereign immunity and related doctrines grew from roots in the common law long before Montana statehood. There are two main strands of immunities at play in claims brought against a state and its officers. First, sovereign immunity protects a state from jurisdiction in a court without its consent, and from entity liability for damages in civil suits. It arises from principles of sovereignty in constitutional law, including popular sovereignty, under which the source of the law may not be subjected to the law. Second, personal immunity protects state officers from personal liability for damages in civil suits for actions taken as state officers. It arises from public policy concerns in tort law, under which a fear of civil suits may interfere with an officer's faithful execution of his duties. Personal immunity can be absolute depending on an officer's function, and can be qualified depending on whether the officer acted in good faith. The forms of sovereign immunity that come to Montana law through the Montana Constitution, the legislature, and judicial decisions draw on these various immunities.

I. Constitutional sovereign immunities can protect states from either jurisdiction, or liability, or both.

The concept of sovereign immunity arrived in the United States from English law, under which "no suit or action can be brought against the king . . . because no court can have jurisdiction over him." Such jurisdiction would imply a superior power of courts over the king, which is inconsistent with the supreme power of the king as sovereign. In the Federalist Papers, Alexander Hamilton assured the states that the ratification of the United States Constitution would not alter the sovereign immunity "now enjoyed by the government of every State in the Union," because "[i]t is inherent in the nature of sovereignty not to be amenable to the suit of an individual without its consent." Sovereign immunity stands "on the logical and practical ground that there can be no legal right as against the authority that makes the law on which the right depends." The implications of sovereign immunity include both jurisdictional and liability immunities.

A. Federal sovereign immunity protects states from both jurisdiction and liability.

The question of whether the states consented to suit in federal court under the new Constitution soon arose in a case brought by a citizen of North Carolina against the State of Georgia. A majority of justices in that case held that Georgia was subject to suit, relying on the text of Article III, section 2 ("The judicial Power [of the United States] shall extend . . . to Controversies . . . between a State and Citizens of another State"), as well as new American principles of popular sovereignty (the people not their governments are sovereign). The states, apparently surprised at the Court's conclusion, within two years ratified the Eleventh Amendment: "The Judicial power of the United States shall not be construed to extend to any suit in law or equity, commenced or prosecuted against one of the United States by Citizens of another State, or by Citizens or Subjects of any Foreign State." Although the Constitution speaks only to suits against states by citizens of other states, the Supreme Court now recognizes general state sovereign immunity against federal jurisdiction and most federal law regardless of the plaintiffs' state citizenship, except when expressly abrogated by Congress and the Constitution. The federal courts' extension of sovereign immunity beyond the text of the Eleventh Amendment has drawn critics, but is well-established.

Sovereign immunity of states under federal law exists independent of state law and is motivated by both jurisdictional and liability concerns. With respect to jurisdiction, sovereign immunity "prevent[s] the indignity of subjecting a State to the coercive process of judicial tribunal at the instance of private parties." With respect to liability, sovereign immunity prevents a state from "the prospect of being thrust, by federal fiat and against its will, into the disfavored status of a debtor, subject to the power of private citizens to levy on its treasury or perhaps even government buildings or property which the State administers on the public's behalf." Consistent with these concerns, federal constitutional sovereign immunity has limits. States can consent to suit through powers originally delegated in the United States Constitution such as the federal judicial power of Article III and the congressional civil rights enforcement power of the Fourteenth Amendment, or through legislation or other official waiver of sovereign immunity from suit in state, federal, or tribal courts. Furthermore, state officers acting on behalf of a state remain subject to suit in their official capacity for injunctive or declaratory relief, even when a judgment would have the effect of enjoining or declaring invalid the execution of state law. As described below, sovereign immunity under federal law also does not prevent some damages claims against state officers in their personal capacity, as long as the claim does not result in a judgment against the state treasury.

B. Montana's sovereign immunity also protects the state from both jurisdiction and liability.

Like the Eleventh Amendment, Montana's original 1889 Constitution addressed state sovereign immunity only indirectly. Prior to statehood, the territorial supreme court recognized sovereign immunity against a contract claim in 1868, holding, "unless permitted by some law of this Territory, or of the general government, no citizen of this Territory can sue it." The statehood constitution assumed rather than expressed sovereign immunity in state courts, providing for a Board of Examiners to consider "all claims against the state" before the legislature acted upon them. As the Montana Supreme Court later put it, "the legislature found itself in the unpalatable position of acting as judge, jury, and responsible party in determining and settling such tort claims." In 1963, the legislature limited sovereign immunity by deeming the purchase of liability insurance for either state or local governments to waive immunity to the extent of the insurance coverage. The Montana Supreme Court unanimously reaffirmed the doctrine on the eve of the 1972 Constitutional Convention, citing the legislature's attempts to limit sovereign immunity as evidence of its continued existence.

1. Article II, § 18 concerns only state liability immunity from tort damages.

For a brief period, Montana abolished a form of sovereign immunity through its new 1972 Constitution. Several delegates introduced a proposed provision in the Declaration of Rights: "The State of Montana and its subdivisions shall be subject to the same liabilities as a natural person." The Judiciary Committee referred the proposal to the Bill of Rights Committee. That committee proposed "Non-Immunity from Suit" as new Section 18 to the Declaration of Rights: "The state and its subdivisions shall have no special immunity from suit. This Provision shall apply only to causes of action arising after June 1, 1973." The committee report noted trends in citizen concern, legal scholarship, and sixteen state judiciaries that "the doctrine no longer has a rational justification in law." The committee's conclusions found support in the influential Bill of Rights study prepared for the delegates by Rick Applegate, who reviewed modern criticism of the ancient doctrine yet also noted the difficulties presented by abolition. Indeed, the committee found sovereign immunity "repugnant to the fundamental premise of the American justice: all parties should receive fair and just redress whether the injuring party is a private citizen or a governmental agency."

In the floor debate, the delegates focused on tort liability, despite expressing broader concerns about sovereign immunity. Delegate Marshall Murray introduced the proposal by explaining "the doctrine of sovereign immunity, which we are attempting to do away with by this particular provision, really means that the king can do whatever he wants but he doesn't have to pay for it; and we'd like to do away with that doctrine." Delegate Wade Dahood explained how the Supreme Court and legislature both seemed to defer to the other in hesitating to abolish sovereign immunity, even if "it's an inalienable right to have remedy when someone injures you through negligence and through a wrongdoing, regardless of whether he has the status of a governmental servant or not." As debate proceeded, Delegate Otto Habedank proposed, and the convention unanimously approved, a limit on the abolition's scope to "suit for injury to a person or property," which he understood to include tort actions, leaving the legislature "free to make [the immunity waiver] more open if they desire to in the future." Later, the Style and Drafting Committee retitled the provision "State subject to suit," and clarified the scope of "The State of Montana and its subdivisions" to include "The state, counties, cities, towns, and all other local governmental entities." In retrospect, this clarification of the provision's application to tort liability was fateful. It sacrificed the broader principle originally suggested by the text "no special immunity to suit," in favor of a narrower right to recover tort damages from the state treasury.

The People of Montana ratified the new Constitution, including the sovereign immunity provision, described as a "[n]ew provision abolishing the doctrine of sovereign immunity ('the King can do no wrong') and allowing any person to sue the state and local governments for injury caused by officers and employees thereof." The legislature responded to the abolition of sovereign immunity with the Montana Comprehensive State Insurance Plan and Tort Claims Act. At the same time, critics speculated about the fiscal and administrative impacts of governmental liability. In 1974, the Montana Legislature proposed, and the voters ratified, the power to invoke sovereign immunity by legislative supermajorities. Professors Larry M. Elison and Fritz Snyder comment, "[t]he people accepted the proposed change" to sovereign immunity in the ratification of the 1972 Constitution, but "[e]ffective lobbying by tradition-bound politicians and frightened government employees quickly reversed the change." Still, they did so through ratification by 55% of voters at the 1974 general election. The ballot language for the amendment explained, "[p]resently the Constitution of Montana provides that the state, counties, cities, towns, and all other local governmental entities shall have no immunity from suit for injury to person or property. This amendment would allow specific exceptions to the waiver of sovereign immunity by a 2/3 vote of each house of the legislature." The provision now reads, as amended:

> Section 18. State subject to suit. The state, counties, cities, towns, and all other local governmental entities shall have no immunity from suit for injury to a person or property, except as may be specifically provided by law by a 2/3 vote of each house of the legislature. [This provision shall apply only to causes of action arising after July 1, 1973.]

Thus, sovereign immunity, which once arose only in common-law judicial decisions, gained express constitutional status in a backlash against an attempt to abolish it.

2. Article II, § 18 does not affect other forms of liability immunity, or jurisdictional immunity.

Montana courts generally read Article II, Section 18 consistent with its text and history to focus on tort liability against the state itself. The legislature recognizes an arguably broader waiver in statute, including both state tort liability and liability for torts "of its employees acting within the scope of their employment or duties whether arising out of a governmental or proprietary function except as specifically provided by the legislature under Article II, section 18, of The Constitution of the State of Montana." The legislature also acted to provide immunity from exemplary and punitive damages, and capped governmental liability for tort damages.

Alongside its assumption of liability for officers acting within the scope of their duties, the legislature enacted several forms of what might more accurately be termed personal immunities for legislative, judicial, and certain quasi-legislative executive decisions. These provisions immunize not just the state when sued as an entity, but also immunize state employees when sued in their personal capacities. Relatedly, the legislature "provide[s] for the immunization, defense, and indemnification of public officers and employees civilly sued for their actions taken within the course and scope of their employment." This immunization and indemnification of state officers in their personal capacities exceeds the traditional scope of sovereign immunity under federal law, at least to the extent the personal capacity claims do not clearly seek damages from the public treasury.

The remaining jurisdictional and liability immunity outside of tort claims is not diminished by the Montana Constitution, or subject to Article II, Section 18. Beyond the scope of that provision's tort immunity waiver, the general rule of sovereign immunity applies: "a state cannot be sued in its own courts without its plain and specific consent to suit either by constitutional provision or by statute." The state waives sovereign immunity and consents to suit on certain claims, including contract claims. Where there is no consent to suit, or where the state affirmatively confirms immunity, however, the law recognizes the state's sovereign immunity untouched by the state constitution's limited abolition of tort immunity.

II. Common-law personal immunities, not sovereign immunity, provide liability immunity to state officials.

American courts adapted the doctrine of personal immunities from English common law. For example, the United States Supreme Court recognized judicial immunity as early as 1872 in a case arising from a trial of one of the alleged participants in President Abraham Lincoln's assassination. In holding the trial judge immune from civil suit, the Court cited English law for the absolute immunity of a judge's actions in his official capacity: "This provision of the law is not for the protection or benefit of a malicious or corrupt judge, but for the benefit of the public, whose interest it is that the judges should be at liberty to exercise their functions with independence, and without fear of consequences." A related "qualified" immunity developed in the common law where "absolute" immunity is unavailable, yet officers act in good faith pursuit of the law. In these cases the Court recognizes that "the general costs of subjecting officers to the risks of trial—distraction of officials from their governmental duties, inhibition of discretionary action, and deterrence of able people from public service," outweigh the benefit of holding even careless public officials liable for abuse of power.

Personal immunities are distinct from sovereign immunity, because they arise from public policy embedded in tort law rather than sovereignty principles recognized in constitutional law. As the United States Court of Appeals for the Ninth Circuit recently summarized:

> As a general matter, individual or "[p]ersonal-capacity suits seek to impose personal liability upon a government official for [wrongful] actions he takes under color of . . . law," and that were taken in the course of his official duties. *Kentucky v. Graham* (1985). By contrast, official capacity suits ultimately seek to hold the entity of which the officer is an agent liable, rather than the official himself . . . for this reason, an officer sued in his official capacity is entitled to "forms of sovereign immunity that the entity, qua entity, may possess." An officer sued in his individual capacity, in contrast, although entitled to certain "personal immunity defenses, such as objectively reasonable reliance on existing law," cannot claim sovereign immunity from suit, "so long as the relief is sought not from the [government] treasury but from the officer personally." *Alden v. Maine* (1999).

Thus, damages claims against the state as an entity are subject to sovereign immunity, conditional on compliance with Article II, section 18 for tort liability. Damages claims against officers may be subject to personal immunities, either absolute or qualified.

Montana has adopted both forms of personal immunity, absolute and qualified, with its inheritance of the common law. State agencies and their officers enjoy quasi-judicial immunity from damages suits in their discretionary decisions to initiate and adjudicate administrative proceedings. Reiterating the English common law principle, the Montana Supreme Court has explained, "[l]ike judicial immunity, quasi-judicial immunity benefits the public—not the person being sued—by ensuring that quasi-judicial officers exercise their functions unfettered by fear of legal consequences; also like judicial immunity, quasi-judicial immunity extends only to acts within the scope of the actor's jurisdiction and with the authorization of law." Where this quasi-judicial immunity does not apply, an additional layer of common law immunity is provided by qualified immunity, which "operates to shield government officers performing discretionary functions from liability for civil damages when their conduct does not violate clearly established statutory or constitutional rights of which a reasonable person would have known."

Montana courts consistently distinguish these common-law personal immunities of individuals from constitutional state sovereign immunity, including the state's immunity from tort liability addressed by Article II, section 18. These "are different concepts and are supported by different considerations of public policy," the latter arising from ancient principles of sovereignty, the former arising from modern tort doctrine's common-law adaptation to the ebb of those ancient principles as applied to public officers. Thus, the "1972 Montana Constitution did not abolish prosecutorial immunity," or the related quasi-judicial immunity, as these immunities are "separate and distinct from sovereign immunity," and therefore are "unaffected by the language of Art. II, Sec. 18." Because of this distinction, and because "quasi-judicial immunity is not a subject of Montana statutory law," there is no requirement for the legislature to act under the supermajority requirement of Article II, section 18 for quasi-judicial immunity to protect state officers otherwise subject to these common-law personal immunities.

Conclusion

Sovereign and personal immunities are a complex inheritance of both constitutional and common law. Article II, section 18 of the Montana Constitution concerns only one strand of sovereign immunity doctrine, the tort liability of the state. Although there may be good arguments in law and justice for abolition, federal and state courts have long established the sovereign and personal immunities that were untouched by the state constitutional waiver of tort liability immunity. These include the state's jurisdictional immunity from suit without its consent, the state's liability immunity from suit for damages outside tort, and state officers' liability immunity from suit for damages arising from their performance of official duties. Under established law, the state may confirm or waive these other judicially recognized immunities without consideration of Article II, section 18 or its supermajority rule.... Recognition of these various sovereign and personal immunities, and their distinct sources and purposes, may help to clarify the resolution of legal problems that arise when a state and its officers land in court.

2. Constitutional Torts

Substantively, Montana courts have recognized constitutional tort claims for damages, subject to any grant of sovereign immunity under Article II, section 18 and the courts' own development of common law personal immunities. Constitutional claims may sound in tort, with damages available, where the constitutional right is "self-executing" (that is, not requiring implementation by the legislature) and there is no other adequate remedy at law. Both of these elements are hotly debated, and the scope of constitutional tort doctrine is largely yet to be established.

Dorwart v. Caraway

312 Mont. 1 (2002)

Justice TERRY N. TRIEWEILER delivered the Opinion of the Court.

¶ 1 This matter was previously before the Court in *Dorwart v. Caraway*, 1998 MT 191 (*Dorwart I*). There, we held that the Plaintiffs' state constitutional rights to due process, privacy and the right to be free from unreasonable searches and seizures were violated. We remanded to the District Court for the Twenty Second Judicial District in Stillwater County for further consideration of the Plaintiffs' claims for damages and attorney's fees caused by the violation of those rights. ***

¶ 8 The Plaintiff, Russell Dorwart, was named as a defendant in two separate Stillwater County Justice Court actions. Default judgments were entered against him in both actions and writs of execution were issued to enforce those judgments on March 12 and April 9, 1991, respectively.

¶ 9 On the evening of April 11, 1991, while operating his motor vehicle, Russell Dorwart was stopped by the Defendant, Deputy Sheriff Danny Ames, and served with the two writs of execution. Ames also arrested Dorwart for driving under the influence of alcohol, seized the pickup truck and transported Dorwart to the Stillwater County Jail. After Dorwart was incarcerated in the jail, either Ames or the Defendant, Deputy Sheriff Paul Caraway, advised Dorwart that the two of them were going to his home to seize property pursuant to the writs of execution. They were advised by Dorwart that the only unlocked door was the back door but that they should be careful not to let his cat out when they entered his home. Dorwart also advised the deputies that his wallet and driver's license were on the dashboard of his mother's car, which was parked in his driveway. Although the deputies claim to have interpreted Dorwart's remarks as permission to enter his home, they did not directly ask his permission nor did he grant it. Caraway and Ames worked for the Defendant, Stillwater County Sheriff Cliff Brophy.

¶ 10 Ames and Caraway proceeded to Dorwart's residence, entered the house and the garage, and seized various items of personal property pursuant to the writs of execution. They also took Dorwart's wallet from the dashboard of the car. ***

¶ 13 Dorwart's pickup truck, its contents and his wallet were returned to him several days later. On April 18, 1991, Dorwart filed in Justice Court a Motion for Release of Property and to Quash the Writs of Execution, supported by an Affidavit of Exemption and other affidavits, asserting that the personal property which Ames and Caraway had seized from his house and garage was either exempt from execution or did not belong to him. On September 30, 1991, the Justice Court ordered that all of the property seized from Dorwart's house and garage be returned to its rightful owners. Dorwart subsequently retrieved the property from the jail. ***

¶ 18 In *Dorwart I*, we held that because Caraway and Ames did not have a search warrant, Dorwart did not consent to their entry of his home, and there were no exigent circumstances nor any other established exception to the search warrant requirement, the deputies' entry into Dorwart's home and seizure of his property violated his right to be free from unreasonable searches and seizures pursuant to Article II, Section 11 of the Montana Constitution. We also specifically held that neither the writs of execution themselves nor Montana's postjudgment execution statutes pursuant to which the writs were issued expressly directed or authorized the deputies to enter Dorwart's home to effectuate seizure of his property. ***

¶ 20 We also held that because Montana law in Title 25, Chapter 13, Part 6, of the Montana Code Annotated provides that certain property is exempt from execution to enforce a judgment, Montana debtors have a property interest in those statutory exemptions protected by the due process guarantees of the Montana Constitution found at Article II, Section 17; and that Montana's post-execution statutes violated Dorwart's right to due process because they did not provide him notice of the seizure of his property, of the availability of statutory exemptions from execution, of where to locate additional information about exemptions, of the procedures by which to claim his exemptions, and because he was not provided with a prompt hearing at which to claim his property exempt from execution. However, after concluding that Dorwart's state constitutional right to due process had been violated, we mistakenly omitted remanding to the District Court for further consideration of that claim.

¶ 21 Finally, a majority of this Court concluded that at the time of Ames' and Caraway's entry into Dorwart's home to execute on his property, the law regarding his constitutional rights to privacy, to be free from searches and seizures and to due process as it interrelated with the law regarding postjudgment execution, had not been clearly established. Therefore, we affirmed the District Court's summary dismissal of Dorwart's claims for common law trespass and conversion, for damages pursuant to 42 U.S.C. § 1983, and for attorney's fees.

¶ 22 In conclusion, we stated:

> Thus, we conclude that Dorwart's arguments regarding entitlement to attorney's fees on his claims under Article II, Sections 10 and 11 of the Montana Constitution must be remanded in conjunction with our remand of those constitutional claims for further proceedings.

Dorwart I, ¶ 134.

¶ 23 However, because Dorwart has at all times claimed violations of not just Article II, Sections 10 and 11, but also Article II, Section 17, and because our prior opinion established violations of all three sections to the Montana Constitution, our remand should properly have included consideration of Dorwart's claim for violation of his right to due process guaranteed by Article II, Section 17. ***

Issue 1

¶ 30 Does violation of rights guaranteed by the Montana Constitution give rise to a cause of action for damages?

¶ 31 By 1998, twenty-one states had recognized an implied cause of action for state constitutional violations. Three additional states had indicated that they would do so under certain narrow circumstances. A private cause of action has been recognized in a twenty-fifth state by federal courts and four states have enacted statutes which authorize causes of action for violation of state constitutional rights. Seven states have specifically rejected state constitutional causes of action. See Gail Donoghue & Jonathan I. Edelstein, *Life After Brown: The Future of State Constitutional Tort Actions in New York*, 42 N.Y.L. Sch. L.Rev. 447, 447 n. 2 (1998). Furthermore, the majority of legal scholarship on the topic of state constitutional tort actions has favored an expansive right of action. The analytical framework for consideration of claims for violation of state constitutions varies from state to state. However, any discussion of a claim for violation of constitutional rights begins with *Bivens* [*v. Six Unknown Named Agents of Fed. Bureau of Narcotics* (1971)].

¶ 32 In *Bivens*, the plaintiff complained that federal narcotics agents entered his apartment, arrested him, manacled him in front of his family, and threatened to arrest his entire family. He was then taken to a federal courthouse where he was interrogated, booked, and subjected to a visual strip search. He filed a complaint for damages for his warrantless search and arrest and for the agents' unreasonable use of force. That complaint was dismissed by the district court. The dismissal was affirmed by the Second Circuit Court of Appeals. However, the U.S. Supreme Court granted certiorari and reversed the dismissal. On appeal, the defendant federal agents contended, as do the Defendants in this case, that Bivens' exclusive remedy should be pursuant to state tort law. They contended that because he had a state tort remedy, there was no need for a cause of action to vindicate his constitutional rights. The Supreme Court disagreed and distinguished common law torts from the violation of constitutional rights. In language repeatedly cited by state courts considering the same issues, the Court stated:

> Respondents seek to treat the relationship between a citizen and a federal agent unconstitutionally exercising his authority as no different from the relationship between two private citizens. In so doing, they ignore the fact that power, once granted, does not disappear like a magic gift when it is wrongfully used. An agent acting albeit unconstitutionally in the name of the United States possesses a far greater capacity for harm than an individual trespasser exercising no authority other than his own. Accordingly, as our cases make clear, the Fourth Amendment operates as a limitation upon the exercise of federal power regardless of whether the State in whose jurisdiction that power is exercised would prohibit or penalize the identical act if engaged in by a private citizen. It guarantees to citizens of the United States the absolute right to be free from unreasonable searches and seizures carried out by virtue of federal authority. And 'where federally protected rights have been invaded, it has been the rule from the beginning

> that courts will be alert to adjust their remedies so as to grant the necessary relief.' [Citations omitted.]

Bivens, 403 U.S. at 391–92.

¶ 33 The Court proceeded to make the following distinction between those interests protected by state laws regulating trespass and those protected by the constitutional right to be free from unreasonable searches and seizures:

> The interests protected by state laws regulating trespass and the invasion of privacy, and those protected by the Fourth Amendment's guarantee against unreasonable searches and seizures, may be inconsistent or even hostile. Thus, we may bar the door against an unwelcome private intruder, or call the police if he persists in seeking entrance. The availability of such alternative means for the protection of privacy may lead the State to restrict imposition of liability for any consequent trespass. A private citizen, asserting no authority other than his own, will not normally be liable in trespass if he demands, and is granted, admission to another's house. But one who demands admission under a claim of federal authority stands in a far different position. The mere invocation of federal power by a federal law enforcement official will normally render futile any attempt to resist an unlawful entry or arrest by resort to the local police; and a claim of authority to enter is likely to unlock the door as well. 'In such cases there is no safety for the citizen, except in the protection of the judicial tribunals, for rights which have been invaded by the officers of the government, professing to act in its name. There remains to him but the alternative of resistance, which may amount to crime.' [Citations omitted.]

Bivens, 403 U.S. at 394–95.

¶ 34 The Supreme Court held that while the Fourth Amendment did not expressly provide for its enforcement by an award of money damages for its violation, "[h]istorically, damages have been regarded as the ordinary remedy for an invasion of personal interests in liberty. . . . [F]ederal courts may use any available remedy to make good the wrong done." *Bivens*, 403 U.S. at 395–96 (citations omitted).

¶ 35 The Supreme Court held that:

> Having concluded that petitioner's complaint states a cause of action under the Fourth Amendment, we hold that petitioner is entitled to recover money damages for any injuries he has suffered as a result of the agents' violation of the Amendment.

Bivens, 403 U.S. at 397.

¶ 36 Subsequently the Supreme Court has held that money damages can be recovered for violations of the Fifth Amendment's guarantee of due process and the Eighth Amendment's prohibition against cruel and unusual punishment.

¶ 37 The general principle of *Bivens* and its progeny is set out clearly in Restatement (Second) of Torts § 874A (1979), which provides:

> When a legislative provision protects a class of persons by proscribing or requiring certain conduct but does not provide a civil remedy for the violation, the court may, if it determines that the remedy is appropriate in furtherance of the purpose of the legislation and needed to assure the effectiveness of the provision, accord to an injured member of the class a right of action, using a suitable existing tort action or a new cause of action analogous to an existing tort action.

¶ 38 Section 874A, comment a, makes clear that the term "legislative provision" includes a constitutional provision. ***

¶ 44 We conclude that the *Bivens* line of authority buttressed by § 874A of the Restatement (Second) of Torts are sound reasons for applying a cause of action for money damages for violations of those self-executing provisions of the Montana Constitution. We also conclude that those rights protected by Article II, Sections 10, 11 and 17 of the Montana Constitution are self-executing.... We conclude that this result is further compelled by our own statutory law and, in particular, §§ 1-1-109 and 27-1-202, MCA. Section 1-1-109, MCA, provides that:

> The common law of England, so far as it is not repugnant to or inconsistent with the constitution of the United States or the constitution or laws of this state, is the rule of decision in all the courts of this state.

Section 27-1-202, MCA, provides that:

> Every person who suffers detriment from the unlawful act or omission of another may recover from the person in fault a compensation therefor in money, which is called damages.

¶ 45 Either statute standing alone reinforces our decision based on the legislative policy of this state. However, when considered together, and with the right found at Article II, Section 16 of the Montana Constitution to a remedy for every injury, this body of statutory and constitutional law permits no other result. ***

¶ 48 For these reasons, we conclude that the District Court correctly held that a cause of action for money damages is available for violation of those rights guaranteed by Article II, Sections 10 and 11 of the Montana Constitution. In addition, we conclude that a direct cause of action for money damages is available for violation of the Plaintiffs' rights guaranteed by Article II, Section 17 of the Montana Constitution, and remand for further consideration of the Plaintiffs' claims for damages pursuant to all three sections of Article II.

Issue 2

¶ 49 Did the Defendants have statutory immunity based on the facts in this case pursuant to § 2-9-103(1), MCA?

¶ 50 Section 2-9-103(1), MCA, provides as follows:

> If an officer, agent, or employee of a governmental entity acts in good faith, without malice or corruption, *and* under the authority of law *and* that law is subsequently declared invalid as in conflict with the constitution of Montana or the constitution of the United States, neither he nor any other officer or employee of the governmental entity he represents nor the governmental entity he represents is civilly liable in any action in which he, such other officer, or such governmental entity would not have been liable had the law been valid. [Emphasis added.]

¶ 51 The District Court held that because Ames and Caraway acted in reliance on the law and because neither acted with "malice or corruption," all Defendants were entitled to immunity as a matter of law pursuant to § 2-9-103(1), MCA. The problem with the District Court's analysis is twofold. First, Caraway and Ames, based on their own testimony, did not rely on anything they assumed to be true [under the case law]. They relied on the writ of execution and on Dorwart's admonishment to use the back door and not let the cat out. Second, we did not conclude that postjudgment execution statutes were unconstitutional for authorizing entry into Dorwart's home. We held that there was nothing in the writ of execution or the statutes pursuant to which they were issued which did authorize entry into Dorwart's home. Neither was there any language in the writ of execution nor in the execution statutes which authorized seizure of nonexempt property owned by Dorwart or others....

¶ 52 Therefore, Caraway and Ames did not enter Dorwart's home and seize nonexempt property pursuant to a statute which has since been held unconstitutional. The execution statute pursuant to which they entered the home did not authorize their entry in the first place and did not authorize their seizure of nonexempt property. For these reasons, we conclude that § 2-9-103(1), MCA, is inapplicable to their conduct and they were not provided with statutory immunity. However, we also conclude that to the extent any claim for damages for violation of Dorwart's right to due process is based on a failure to provide him with the notice of exempt property and a timely hearing required by our prior decision, those claims are a result of the execution statutes' constitutional inadequacy and recovery for those procedural inadequacies is barred by the statutory immunity provided by § 2-9-103(1), MCA. The District Court's dismissal of the Plaintiffs' claims based on statutory immunity is otherwise reversed.

Issue 3

¶ 53 Should this Court create qualified immunity analogous to federal qualified immunity as applied in claims pursuant to 42 U.S.C. § 1983, and, if so, were Defendants in this case entitled to summary judgment on that basis?

¶ 54 Damages may be recovered for violation of federal constitutional rights pursuant to 42 U.S.C. § 1983. That section provides that:

> Every person who, under color of any statute, ordinance, regulation, custom, or usage, of any State ... subjects, or causes to be subjected, any citizen of the United States or other person within the jurisdiction thereof to the

> deprivation of any rights, privileges, or immunities secured by the Constitution and laws, shall be liable to the party injured in an action at law, suit in equity, or other proper proceeding for redress....

¶ 55 However, in *Harlow* [*v. Fitzgerald* (1982)], the Supreme Court held that qualified or good faith immunity is sometimes necessary to balance the competing values of damages for violation of a constitutional right and the vigorous exercise of official authority. The Court held that:

> [G]overnment officials performing discretionary functions generally are shielded from liability for civil damages insofar as their conduct does not violate clearly established statutory or constitutional rights of which a reasonable person would have known. [Citations omitted.]

Harlow, 457 U.S. at 818.

¶ 56 We applied qualified immunity to bar the Plaintiffs' claims based on § 1983 in *Dorwart I*. There we held that the law on which Dorwart relied in asserting his federal claim was not clearly established at the time that it was violated. Caraway and Ames were entitled to qualified immunity for Dorwart's § 1983 search and seizure claim. ***

¶ 59 In amicus briefs filed by Wade Dahood, Chairman of the Bill of Rights Committee of the 1972 Montana Constitutional Convention, and the Montana Trial Lawyers Association, Amici contend that the adoption of qualified immunity in Montana would ignore fundamental differences between federal law and our state constitution. They contend that the federal government has reserved sovereign immunity except to the extent that it is waived, but that the Montana Constitution abolishes sovereign immunity except to the extent that it is readopted by two-thirds of the Legislature, citing Article II, Section 18 of the Montana Constitution. They contend that federal qualified immunity is a common law construct arising from the long tradition of sovereign immunity as recognized by the Supreme Court. ***

¶ 65 [T]here is no comparable immunity found in Montana for the acts of state employees in violation of state constitutional rights. In fact, contrary to the federal presumption of immunity, the Montana State Constitution at Article II, Section 18, prohibits immunity in the following language:

> The state, counties, cities, towns, and all other local governmental entities shall have no immunity from suit for injury to a person or property, except as may be specifically provided by law by a two-third vote of each house of the legislature.

¶ 66 We need not decide in this case whether by a two-thirds vote of the Legislature qualified immunity can in fact be created which would render unenforceable other provisions of the same constitution. The Legislature clearly has not done so and that argument is not before us.

¶ 67 Furthermore, Article II, Section 16 of the Montana Constitution provides that "[c]ourts of justice shall be open to every person, and speedy remedy afforded for every injury of person, property, or character."

¶ 68 [Q]ualified immunity is not a defense to the merits of a claim but frees a wrongdoer from liability whether or not he or she acted wrongly. Therefore, the adoption of qualified immunity in Montana would also be inconsistent with the constitutional requirement that courts of justice afford a speedy remedy for those claims recognized by law for injury of person, property or character.

¶ 69 For these reasons, we conclude that qualified immunity, as established by federal law and applied by this Court in *Dorwart I*, to bar those claims filed by plaintiffs pursuant to 42 U.S.C. § 1983 is not applicable to those claims filed by the Plaintiffs for violation of those rights guaranteed by the Montana State Constitution.

Issue 4

¶ 70 Did the District Court err when it denied Plaintiffs' claim for an award of attorney's fees?

¶ 71 Dorwarts contend that the violation of their state constitutional rights entitled them to an award of attorney's fees in addition to whatever damages might be proven and recoverable. In support of that argument, Plaintiffs contend that attorney's fees are recoverable in successful claims pursuant to 42 U.S.C. § 1983 and that fees are necessarily recoverable for vindication of state constitutional rights by analogy and because the cost of bringing a claim might otherwise outweigh the expected benefits. ***

¶ 74 . . . Based on the issue as it has been framed by the parties' arguments and the authorities presented to us, we conclude that no authority has been established for an award of attorney's fees to the Plaintiffs in this case. Therefore, we affirm the District Court's denial of Plaintiffs' claim for attorney's fees.

Summary

¶ 75 We conclude that the rights at issue in this case, Article II, Sections 10, 11, and 17 of the Montana Constitution, are self-executing and that pursuant to the English Common Law as adopted by the State of Montana, § 874A of the Restatement (Second) of Torts, and analogous federal law, including *Bivens*, in combination with the clear intent of those delegates to the Montana Constitution that courts be open for redress of injuries to person, property, or character, that a claim for damages from violation of the specified state constitutional rights can be presented as a cause of action in Montana. We furthermore conclude that § 2-9-103(1), MCA, is not a defense to the Plaintiffs' claims based on the facts in this case and make no determination about its constitutionality. We conclude that qualified immunity as described by the U.S. Supreme Court in *Harlow* is not a defense to claims for damages for violation of Montana constitutional rights. And, finally, we conclude that based on the arguments and authorities presented in this case, the Plaintiffs are not entitled to the recovery of attorney's fees.

¶ 76 The right to privacy to be left alone is precious. It is essential to our quality of life. No one was more aware of that than the authors of our Constitution who went to great and conspicuous lengths to preserve it in the face of what they correctly anticipated would be increasing political pressure and the developing technological ability to erode it.

¶ 77 Invasion of individual privacy by a fellow citizen is a bad thing. Invasion by the state or its agents is worse. A culture of governmental disregard for the right to privacy would be worst of all. To avoid that possibility in the face of sometimes short-sighted popular and political sentiment will take a vigilant judiciary with a full arsenal of remedies. Today, in recognition of this year's thirtieth anniversary of our state constitution and those far-sighted delegates who crafted it, we add the cause of action for damages to that arsenal.

¶ 78 For these reasons, we affirm in part and reverse in part the District Court's order of summary judgment.

Justice JAMES C. NELSON specially concurs.

*** ¶ 85 ... Montana's Constitution guarantees rights that are not provided for in the federal constitution—the right to a clean and healthful environment, the right to pursue life's basic necessities, the right to enjoy and defend one's life and liberties (all protected under Article II, Section 3); the right of dignity (Article II, Section 4); the right of public participation in the operation of governmental agency decision making (Article II, Section 8); the right to examine government documents and to observe the deliberations of government entities (Article II, Section 9); the right of individual privacy (Article II, Section 10); the rights of persons not adults (Article II, Section 15); the right of access to the courts and to full legal redress (Article II, Section 16); the waiver of sovereign immunity (Article II, Section 18); rights regarding the initiation of criminal proceedings, criminal detention, imprisonment for debt and rights of the convicted (Article II, Sections 20, 23, 27 and 28 respectively); the right to an award of attorney fees in eminent domain cases (Article II, Section 29); and others.

¶ 86 ... [I]t is important that the right of direct action to protect these distinctive Montana constitutional rights not be restricted by jurisprudence that is limited to a few constitutional rights that are common to both the constitutions of the United States and Montana or that were historically actionable at common law.

¶ 87 As stated in *Dorwart I*, the constitutional rights violated in the case at bar were those guaranteeing the right to be free from unreasonable searches and seizures under the Fourth Amendment and Article II, Sections 10 and 11 of Montana's Constitution and the right to due process of law protected by the Fourteenth Amendment and Article II, Section 17. At least as the federal law now stands, *Bivens* and the line of cases following it support our decision here to create a remedy for the violations of these rights. ***

¶ 92 Given this direction of the U.S. Supreme Court, *Bivens* eventually may well be interpreted out of any meaningful existence. Moreover, as noted, *Bivens* is already limited to constitutional torts committed by governmental officers under color of law; involving searches and seizures, cruel and unusual punishment or some due process violations; and where the injured person lacks an alternative remedy. These limitations make it analytically difficult to provide citizens with the broader and, in some cases, unique, protections afforded by Montana's Constitution should a case arise in some other context; involve some other class of defendant or injured plaintiff; involve a constitutional right not historically actionable under common law; involve a right where the common law remedy has been superseded or suspended by statute; or involve a right for which the statutory remedy created is inadequate. ***

¶ 94 In his amicus curiae brief, Wade Dahood, Esq., formerly the Chairman of the Bill of Rights Committee (Committee) at the Constitutional Convention, argues persuasively that when the Constitution's "Declaration of Rights was framed, [the Committee] intended it to stand on its own footing and to provide individuals with fundamental rights and protections far broader than those available through the federal system." This statement is supported by reference to the Committee's February 22, 1972 transmittal letter to the Convention delegates which states that "new safeguards" had been added to the Declaration [Bill] of Rights "to meet the changing circumstances of contemporary life" and that:

> In presenting this proposed Declaration of Rights, the committee notes that the guidelines and protections for the exercise of liberty in a free society come *not from government but from the people who create that government.*
>
> It is that spirit which has motivated this committee to insure for Montana's future, through this bill of rights, a more responsible government that is Constitutionally commanded never to forget that *government is created solely for the welfare of the people* so that the people can more fully enjoy the heritage of American liberty within the structure of that government.

(emphasis added).

¶ 95 Taking these admonitions to heart, this Court has, for example, applied the broader protections of Montana's Constitution in a number of contexts involving individual privacy (*Gryczan v. State* (Mont. 1997)) and personal autonomy (*Armstrong v. State*, 1999 MT 261); involving search and seizure (*State v. Bullock* (Mont. 1995); *State v. Siegal* (Mont. 1997); *State v. Elison*, 2000 MT 288); involving the environment (*Montana Envtl. Info. Ctr. v. Department of Envtl. Quality*, 1999 MT 248); and involving the right of participation and the right to know (*Common Cause v. Statutory Comm. to Nominate Candidates for Comm'r of Political Practices* (Mont. 1994); *Great Falls Tribune Co. v. Great Falls Pub. Schs.* (Mont. 1992); *Associated Press v. Board of Pub. Educ.* (Mont. 1991); *Jarussi v. Board of Trustees* (Mont. 1983).

¶ 96 Furthermore, and acknowledging the Committee's statement that no part of the Constitution is more important, we have repeatedly recognized the rights found in Montana's Declaration of Rights as being "fundamental," *Butte Community Union v. Lewis* (Mont. 1986), meaning that these rights are significant components of liberty, any infringement of which will trigger the highest level of scrutiny, and, thus, the highest level of protection by the courts.

¶ 97 We have also observed the obvious logical corollary to these rules: "[c]onstitutional rights that cannot be enforced are illusory. It is as if those rights cease to exist as legal rights." The importance of being able to enforce one's constitutional rights through the courts and to receive meaningful redress for public or private injury cannot be overstated. If an individual's constitutional rights can be violated by the government, by the government's officers, or, where so protected, by a private person, secure in the knowledge nothing will come of the wrongdoing, then it follows that the constitution provides no protection at all. It is but a collection of elegant words without substance; it is a shield made of little more than aspirations and hopes.

¶ 98 As Attorney Dahood argues in his amicus brief, in order to avoid this result and in order to give Montana's constitutional guarantees teeth, the framers intended that the people retain the ability to protect their rights—both enumerated and unenumerated—through direct actions in the courts. This conclusion follows from the Committee's proposal of Article II, Section 34 to the Convention delegates and the subsequent adoption of this provision. Article II, Section 34 states:

> Unenumerated rights. The enumeration in this constitution of certain rights shall not be construed to deny, impair, or disparage others retained by the people.

¶ 99 In proposing the adoption of this Section, the Committee did two things. First, it recognized that the rights enumerated in Montana's Constitution were not exclusive—i.e. that there are unenumerated rights or "rights beyond those specifically listed" which are retained by the people. Second, and important for our purposes here, the Committee considered this Section to be ". . . a crucial part of any effort to revitalize the state government's approach to civil liberties questions . . . [and that this Section] . . . may be the source of innovative judicial activity in the civil liberties field."

¶ 100 The proceedings of the Constitutional Convention reveal no debate on Article II, Section 34. It was adopted unanimously on the straightforward, yet eloquent recommendation of Delegate Eck, who stated: "I think that [this Section] is completely self-explanatory. There are rights which are not enumerated which the people of Montana should not be denied." ***

¶ 103 Frankly, I can think of no better application of Article II, Section 34 than in the case at bar.

¶ 104 As the Committee recognized, the "protections for the exercise of liberty in a free society come *not from government but from the people who create that government* [and that] *government is created solely for the welfare of the people.*" Montana Constitutional Convention, Vol, II, 619 (emphasis added). Indeed, Article II, Section 1 of the Constitution of Montana could not be more clear:

> *All* political power is vested in and derived from the people. *All* government of right originates with the people, is found upon *their* will *only*, and is instituted *solely* for the good of the whole.

(Emphasis added).

¶ 105 The intent of the framers and the language of the Constitution is incontrovertible: all government is derived from and originates with the people; government is created and instituted solely for the good and welfare of the people. Thus, and with those core principles in mind, it makes perfect sense that, as they did in Article II, Section 34, the people would retain unto themselves rights beyond those which are enumerated in their Constitution. Recognizing that they are the wellspring of all government which they choose to impose upon themselves, the people also positively declared their intent not to restrict their liberties to those textually set out in their Constitution.

¶ 106 Correspondingly, it takes no leap of logic to conclude that one of the unenumerated rights which the people would necessarily retain is the power — the right, if you will — to protect from government infringement their ability to fully exercise those liberties which they specifically guaranteed unto themselves in their Declaration of Rights.

¶ 107 As already noted, constitutional rights that cannot be enforced are illusory; they simply cease to exist; they offer no protection whatsoever. Therefore, it follows that to ensure that the government which they created did not, like Frankenstein's monster, turn on its creator, the people would, as they did, implicitly retain the right to directly access the courts to protect and enforce their other constitutional liberties. ***

¶ 109 . . . [W]ithout retaining the right of direct action for constitutional violations, the core premise under which the people adopted their Constitution — that government derives from and originates with them — would, itself, be meaningless, because it could not be enforced.

¶ 110 For these reasons, I would hold that the people have reserved unto themselves under Article II, Section 34 of the Constitution of Montana, the unenumerated right to sue their government, its agents, and, in some cases, their fellow citizens, directly in the courts of this state for violations of their fundamental rights protected under Montana's Constitution.

¶ 111 Moreover, I would hold that this unenumerated right of direct action for damages for constitutional violations is a stand-alone right guaranteed by Article II, Section 34, independent of the enumerated rights of access to the courts and to full legal redress guaranteed by Article II, Section 16 and independent of the right to defend one's life and liberties guaranteed by Article II, Section 3. Indeed, Article II, Section 34 unambiguously makes this distinction in providing that the enumeration of certain rights in the constitution "shall not be construed to deny, impair or disparage others retained by the people."

¶ 112 In my view, the real efficacy of this Article II, Section 34 cause of action is to ensure that the enumerated fundamental rights are protected from diminution, limitation and restriction. This stand-alone right of direct action for constitutional violations would protect the most basic and most important rights that Montanans enjoy. These are the rights that:

> shield . . . each individual from the excesses of government, from the tyranny of the majority, and from the sorts of abuses perpetrated by persons, firms, corporations, associations, organizations, and institutions that, in pursuit of their own interests and agenda, effectively would deprive the people of those things essential to their humanity and to their lawful individual pursuits.

Associated Press, ¶ 55 (Nelson, J., concurring).

¶ 113 Returning to Attorney Dahood's amicus brief, he states:

> In placing Article II, Sec. 34 in the 1972 Constitution, the framers wanted to make clear that it was "crucial" that the judiciary had the power to recognize unenumerated rights when necessary to protect and secure those which are enumerated. A direct cause of action to protect the specified rights is one of those "unenumerated rights."

I could not agree more. ***

Justice TERRY N. TRIEWEILER concurs in the foregoing special concurrence.

Justice W. WILLIAM LEAPHART, specially concurring.

¶ 115 A number of the briefs filed in this appeal, noting that the deputies testified that they were "commanded by the judge" to go seize the property, expressed a concern that officers should be protected in the performance of their duties when they are acting in reliance on a court order. I write separately to address that concern and point out that the parties did not specifically raise, and thus the Court does not address, the question of quasi-judicial immunity, which is separate and distinct from qualified immunity. In doing so, however, I do not express an opinion as to whether the doctrine of quasi-judicial immunity would change the result in this case. ***

¶ 116 Under our 1972 Constitution, the government is not immune from suit unless the legislature enacts a statute by a two-thirds vote of each house. Art. II, Sec. 18, Mont. Const. Pursuant to that provision, the legislature enacted § 2-9-112, MCA, which provides as follows:

> Immunity from suit for judicial acts or omissions. (1) The state and other governmental units are immune from suit for acts or omissions of the judiciary.
>
> (2) A member, officer, or agent of the judiciary is immune from suit for damages arising from his lawful discharge of an official duty associated with judicial actions of the court.
>
> (3) The judiciary includes those courts established in accordance with Article VII of The Constitution of the State of Montana. ***

¶ 120 As to officers who rely and act upon a judge's order, there is nothing in this opinion which abrogates the doctrine of quasi-judicial immunity. As we concluded . . . , "[c]ourts have consistently held that officials acting pursuant to a facially valid court order have a quasi-judicial absolute immunity from damages for actions taken to execute that order."

Justice TERRY N. TRIEWEILER concurring.

¶ 121 Frankly, I do not understand the point of Justice Leaphart's concurring opinion and write separately to caution the parties and the District Court from attaching too much significance to it. To do so would only lead to further error, expense and delay before finally resolving this decade-long dispute on the merits.

¶ 122 First, Justice Leaphart points out that the parties have not raised quasi-judicial immunity. Then he claims he has no opinion about its application. One would assume that would be the end of the discussion. However, as if the facts in this case cry out for some defense, he then proceeds to brief that issue for the parties and tout the policy considerations behind it.

¶ 123 Having read the entire record, including the testimony of the Defendants, I can assure the parties that, Justice Leaphart's unsolicited coaching aside, there is no factual nor legal basis for the application of quasi-judicial immunity to this case. To test those waters would only lead to further error, further appeal and further delay. Considering the Defendants' representations at oral argument about the hardship that protraction of this case has caused them, that would not seem to be in anyone's best interests.

¶ 124 It is also necessary to respond to the dissent of Justice Rice. Justice Rice concludes that statutory immunity is applicable because Deputy Sheriffs Ames and Caraway acted under "authority of law" when they entered Dorwart's house. We, of course, have previously concluded that there was no statute, court order or prior decision of this Court which granted that authority. ***

¶ 138 It is clear from the entire context of the deputies' testimony that they have justified their entry into and search of Dorwart's home and seizure of his exempt property for two reasons. First, they contend the writs authorized them to do so. However, we have now held twice that they did not. Second, they contend that Dorwart gave them permission to enter and search his home. However, it is clear that he did not. He was never even asked for his permission.

¶ 139 To suggest that somewhere in this series of uninformed mistakes, there lies a defense such as quasi-judicial or statutory immunity is a disservice to the Defendants, those who are advocating on their behalf, and law enforcement in general who will surely repeat the Defendants' mistakes if encouraged to do so based on misinformation. ***

Chief Justice KARLA M. GRAY, dissenting.

¶ 141 . . . I dissent from the Court's discussion of — and holding on — due process. ***

¶ 161 [O]ur cases standing for the proposition that due process is a flexible concept which should be tailored to the circumstances of each case are legion. In light of... our cases, it is inconceivable to me that a private constitutional due process cause of action can exist which, among other things, would improperly permit a jury to determine the constitutional and ever-flexible question of what process is due.

¶ 162 I understand the Court's desire to breathe life into the provisions of the Montana Constitution. Where that desire properly can be pursued under the law, I support it. For all the reasons stated herein, I cannot support any portion of the Court's analysis of the due process issue....

Justice JIM RICE, concurring in part and dissenting in part.

¶ 163 I concur with this Court's decision on Issue 1, that Article II, Sections 10 and 11 of the Montana Constitution are self-executing, and provide the basis for a right of action for damages for violation thereof. Regarding the Article II, Section 17 claim, I join Chief Justice Gray's dissent. I respectfully dissent from this Court's determination on Issue 2 that the Defendants are not entitled to statutory immunity pursuant to § 2-9-103(1), MCA. Based on the plain language and plain meaning of the statute, I would affirm the District Court's conclusion that the Defendants are entitled to immunity thereunder and, therefore, would not address Issue 3 or Issue 4.

¶ 164 Section 2-9-103(1), MCA, declares:

> If an officer, agent, or employee of a governmental entity acts in good faith, without malice or corruption, and under the authority of law and that law is subsequently declared invalid as in conflict with the constitution of Montana or the constitution of the United States, neither he nor any other officer or employee of the governmental entity he represents nor the governmental entity he represents is civilly liable in any action in which he, such other officer, or such governmental entity would not have been liable had the law been valid. ***

¶ 177 Under the plain language of § 2-9-103(1), MCA, the deputies must act under authority of law which subsequently must be "declared invalid as in conflict with the constitution of Montana or the constitution of the United States." In adopting the execution warrant requirement as a procedural safeguard, this Court in *Dorwart I* implicitly declared that *Ramsey* [*v. Burns* (Mont. 1902)] was no longer a valid source of authority for Ames' and Caraway's actions.

¶ 178 Based on the foregoing, I would conclude that the statutory requirements have been clearly met and that Ames and Caraway are entitled to statutory immunity pursuant to § 2-9-103(1), MCA....

¶ 179... I conclude that, after its substantial and able review of the issues raised herein, the District Court correctly ruled that a right of action exists for the constitutional violations at issue here, but that the officers under these circumstances were shielded from the claim by statutory immunity.

Sunburst School District No. 2 v. Texaco, Inc.

2007 MT 183

Justice BRIAN MORRIS delivered the Opinion of the Court.

*** ¶ 10 Texaco operated a gasoline refinery just outside the town of Sunburst, Montana, from 1924 until 1961. Gasoline leaked from pipes at the refinery for many years and contaminated the surrounding soil. The gasoline spread to the subsurface groundwater and eventually migrated underneath the town of Sunburst. The contamination came to Texaco's attention as early as 1955 when escaping fumes from the underground plume caused a house in the town of Sunburst to explode. The accident prompted Texaco to conduct a partial cleanup of the contamination in the soil and groundwater. Texaco extracted some gasoline over the next few years, but left a significant amount of pollution. ***

¶ 15 Texaco . . . entered into an investigative work plan with DEQ [Montana's Department of Environmental Quality] to examine the groundwater conditions. Texaco hired an environmental contractor, Tri-Hydro, Inc. (Tri-Hydro), to investigate the groundwater and to evaluate remediation alternatives. Following the completion of Tri-Hydro's investigation, Texaco proposed to DEQ in May 2003 that it remediate the groundwater contamination through monitored natural attenuation (MNA).

¶ 16 MNA involves simply monitoring the level of benzene in the groundwater with the expectation that the environment naturally will degrade the benzene over a period of years. Opinions on the degradation period for benzene through MNA ranged from 20 to 100 years to reach contamination levels below the maximum level allowed by the DEQ regulations. Texaco selected MNA as its proposed remediation method based, in part, upon its cost effectiveness. Tri-Hydro estimated that MNA would cost approximately $1 million compared with active remediation plans identified by Tri-Hydro that potentially could cost over $30 million. In 2003, DEQ proposed, for public comment, that Texaco use MNA to conduct the remediation. ***

¶ 19 Sunburst filed this action against Texaco on February 22, 2001. Sunburst alleged numerous causes of action, including trespass, strict liability for abnormally dangerous activity, public nuisance, violation of the constitutional right to a clean and healthful environment, wrongful occupation of property, and constructive fraud. . . . The court found that Texaco's liability for trespass extended to all the Sunburst plaintiffs who owned property above the contamination plume. As a result, the court instructed the jury to determine the amount of damages to award to all of the Sunburst plaintiffs who owned property above the plume, including the reasonable costs of environmental investigation, the cost of any future environmental investigation, and damages for the loss of use and enjoyment of Sunburst's properties. The court also instructed the jury to award all costs that reasonably would be necessary to restore the plaintiffs' property to the condition it would have been absent Texaco's contamination. Finally, the court instructed the jury to award damages if Texaco had violated Sunburst's constitutional right to a clean and healthful environment.

¶ 24 The jury awarded Sunburst compensatory damages of approximately $16 million. The jury's special verdict included awards of $170,000 for wrongful occupation of property, $371,000 for constructive fraud, $350,000 for the costs of environmental investigation, and a single award of $226,500 for private nuisance, public nuisance and constitutional tort. The jury specified the amount awarded to each individual plaintiff for wrongful occupation and constructive fraud, but combined the award for private nuisance, public nuisance, and constitutional tort.

¶ 25 Sunburst requested a lump sum award for restoration because they argued cleanup represented a single expense that could not be apportioned among the plaintiffs. Sunburst maintained that they actually intended to use any award of restoration costs to remediate the property, rather than to divide any award among the plaintiffs. The jury awarded a lump sum of $15 million for restoration damages.

¶ 26 The jury also found Texaco had acted with actual fraud or actual malice and therefore was liable for punitive damages. Following the jury's verdict, the District Court held a separate hearing to calculate the amount of punitive damages to be awarded. Texaco submitted a proposed jury instruction for the punitive damages phase that directed the jury to consider whether its actions comported with state regulations or had been approved by a state regulator. The court denied the instruction, reasoning that it was "the same issue" that the court earlier had decided regarding the admissibility of evidence concerning DEQ. The jury awarded Sunburst $25 million in punitive damages.

¶ 27 Sunburst filed a post-trial motion for attorney's fees and costs based upon the fact that the plaintiffs had acted as private attorneys' general in vindicating an important constitutional right. The District Court determined that Sunburst could recover attorney's fees, but did not settle on an amount. This appeal followed.

Discussion

(1) Restoration Damages

*** ¶ 38 We agree with Sunburst that an award of restoration damages must be available to compensate a plaintiff fully for damages to real property when diminution in value fails to provide an adequate remedy. Sunburst has demonstrated in this case that the diminution in market value approach fails to provide adequate compensation. Sunburst brought an action for contamination of the plaintiffs' personal residences with benzene, a well-known carcinogen. A personal residence represents the type of property in which the owner possesses a personal reason for repair.... [T]he personal reasons for repair are usually the owner's desire to enjoy and live in their homes. These reasons prove compelling and we adopt them as part of our analysis under Montana law.

¶ 39 One plaintiff, Sunburst School District, owns property that does not constitute a personal residence. The Sunburst School District operates a public school on the property. We still deem an award of restoration damages to be appropriate, however, in light of the fact that the responsible party could not remediate the groundwater beneath the personal residences owned by the other plaintiffs without also treating the groundwater beneath the school. The presence of the district as a collateral beneficiary does not defeat an award of restoration damages. ***

¶ 49 The jury awarded Sunburst $15 million in restoration damages. Testimony at trial established that the properties located above the contamination plume have an aggregate market value of approximately $2 million. A strict cap on restoration damages applied to the Sunburst property barely would cover the cost of MNA, Texaco's preferred remediation method, estimated at approximately $1 million. The costs of the active remediation plans identified by Texaco's consultants could approach $30 million. The jury's award of $15 million in restoration damages falls comfortably within these two extremes, and we deem it to be reasonable compensation. For these reasons and under these circumstances, we conclude that the District Court properly allowed the jury to make an award of restoration damages to Sunburst that exceeded the value of the damaged property. ***

(3) Constitutional Tort

¶ 60 Texaco challenges the District Court's decision to instruct the jury to award monetary damages, pursuant to Article II, Section 3, of the Montana Constitution, for any alleged constitutional tort. The availability of a cause of action presents a question of law that we review to determine if it is correct. *Dorwart v. Caraway.*

¶ 61 The Montana Constitution provides that all persons have a "right to a clean and healthful environment." Art. II, Sect. 3, Mont. Const. The right to a clean and healthful environment constitutes a fundamental right. *MEIC v. Dept. of Environmental Quality* [(Mont. 1999)]. Texaco argues, however, that Article II, Section 3, cannot support a private cause of action for monetary damages as it is not "self-executing." As a result, Texaco contends that "the Montana Constitution places responsibility for environmental remedies squarely in the hands of the Legislature." Texaco asserts that CECRA [the Comprehensive Environmental Cleanup and Responsibility Act] serves as the Legislature's adopted remedy for environmental violations.

¶ 62 Sunburst points to our decision in *Dorwart* to support its claim that a private party must be able to bring an action seeking monetary damages against another private party for a violation in order to vindicate a fundamental constitutional right. The parties fully briefed this question and presented oral argument to the Court. In fact, we expressly framed the issues to be presented at oral argument to include whether "the right to a clean and healthful environment is self-executing?" This Court repeatedly has recognized, however, that courts should avoid constitutional issues whenever possible. We deem it possible in light of our decision in *Dorwart* to resolve this case without resort to determining whether Article II, Section 3, is self-executing and consequently could support a private cause of action for monetary damages.

¶ 63 The plaintiff in *Dorwart* brought an action against Stillwater County and several police officers stemming from an alleged illegal search and seizure. The plaintiff sought monetary damages based on alleged common law violations and alleged violations of Article II, Sections 10, 11, and 17 of the Montana Constitution. We recognized that common law causes of action intended to regulate relationships among and between individuals may not always be adequate to redress the type of damage caused by the invasion of constitutional rights by government actors. We noted that a police officer's actions are likely to be more harmful than those resulting from the conduct of a private citizen. We further reasoned that Article II, Section 16 of the Montana Constitution afforded speedy remedy for every injury of person, property, or character. As a result, we held that recognition of a constitutional tort was necessary to provide citizens with an adequate remedy due to the fact that an injury inflicted by a government agent differs from the injury inflicted by a private individual.

¶ 64 Thus we concluded in *Dorwart* that the absence of any other remedy supported the establishment of a constitutional tort. We now have adopted Restatement (Second) of Torts § 929, to allow for the recovery of restoration damages. By their very nature, restoration damages would restore a private party back to the position that it occupied before the tort. An award of restoration damages serves to ensure a clean and healthful environment. Sunburst has not demonstrated that the common law restoration damages would not address adequately any potential damages caused by Texaco's contamination. Accordingly, we conclude that the District Court erred in instructing the jury on the constitutional tort theory where, as here, adequate remedies exist under statutory or common law. ***

Justice JAMES C. NELSON, concurring in part and dissenting in part.

*** ¶ 95 I read the Opinion to hold that we are not rejecting, *per se*, a constitutional tort for violation of the fundamental right to a clean and healthful environment since here, having adopted Restatement (Second) of Torts § 929 and cmt. b (allowing restoration damages for injury to real property), an award of damages for violation of Article II, Section 3, would be redundant. I concur in the Court's Opinion on this limited basis, recognizing that a future case may present a factual and legal scenario that might well require us to address the constitutional tort theory on the merits. ***

Chief JUSTICE KARLA M. GRAY, concurring in part and dissenting in part.

¶ 128 I concur in the results the Court reaches on all issues, but do not join in several aspects of the Court's reasoning, particularly where the Court fails to address either the record before us or the arguments presented and where it unnecessarily relies on authorities from other jurisdictions. I respectfully, but vigorously, disagree with the Court's characterization of Texaco's Article II, § 3-related argument in Issue 3 as a challenge to any damages other than the restoration costs award, or to the viability of Sunburst's constitutional tort claim. ***

Notes on Constitutional Torts

1. In *Dorwart* the Court applies statutory "good faith immunity" but rejects common law "qualified immunity" with a suggestion it may be unconstitutional under Article II, section 16. What is the difference between the two immunities?

2. While concurring in *Dorwart* and separately analyzing Article II, section 34's "unenumerated rights," Justice Nelson relies on Larry M. Elison and Fritz Snyder's THE MONTANA STATE CONSTITUTION: A REFERENCE GUIDE (2001). Consider the following excerpt:

> [t]he section could be used as the basis for the introduction of a theory of natural law or an expansion of the use of substantive due process or judicial finding of unstated individual rights hidden in the self-reliant, free-thinking, idiosyncratic Montanan mythology. Presumptively, this could limit state police power and enlarge existing rights or create new rights.... While plenary state legislative power and unenumerated rights might appear to be in conflict or contradictory, they are not. In a state constitution a provision on unenumerated rights as a balance against state police power is a potentially useful idea, but something of an anomaly. Historically, within the context of state governments in a federal system, the limitations on plenary legislative power are the specific prohibitions and restrictions found in a constitutional declaration of rights. *Adding unenumerated rights to specific prohibitions and restrictions could transfer to the people indirectly, and to the courts directly, additional means of checking plenary legislative power.*

The language from section 34 is identical to that in Article III, § 30 of the 1889 Constitution, and nearly identical to language in the Ninth Amendment of the United States Constitution ("the Constitution" there versus "this constitution" in Montana). What role does the 1972 Constitutional Convention discourse surrounding section 34 play in establishing an "unenumerated right of direct action for damages for constitutional violations"? Is there such a right?

3. In *Sunburst*, the Montana Supreme Court adopts a new remedy of restoration damages then holds this new remedy is sufficiently adequate to preclude recognition of a constitutional tort. In the future, why might a plaintiff with an innovative tort claim bring a parallel constitutional tort claim, even if they do not expect to recover under the Constitution?

3. Attorneys' Fees

As a practical matter, questions of immunity and liability are irrelevant to a constitutional plaintiff if she cannot pay a lawyer to bring her claims in the first place. While federal civil rights law imposes broad restrictions on recovery through sovereign and personal immunities, it also incentivizes those civil rights claims that can be brought by awarding attorneys' fees to the prevailing party in most cases. Montana has no such provision, although the courts have developed some quasi-constitutional doctrine requiring attorneys' fees awards in limited cases. Thus, the Montana lawyer faces a choice between the broader state constitutional civil rights actions with uncertain payouts of tort liability and attorneys' fees, or the more established federal civil rights actions that can provide both damages and attorneys' fees against a state, but only where sovereign and personal immunities do not bar the claim.

Western Tradition Partnership, Inc. v. Attorney General

367 Mont. 112 (2012)

Justice BETH BAKER delivered the Opinion of the Court.

¶ 2 *** Briefly stated, Plaintiffs Western Tradition Partnership—now known as American Tradition Partnership—Champion Painting, and Montana Shooting Sports Foundation (collectively referred to as ATP) sought a declaratory ruling that § 13-35-227(1), MCA, violated their rights to free speech guaranteed by the United States and Montana Constitutions by prohibiting political expenditures by corporations on behalf of or opposing candidates for public office. ATP argued that the U.S. Supreme Court's decision in *Citizens United v. FEC* (2010), barred Montana from prohibiting independent and indirect corporate expenditures on political speech, and that Montana's century-old ban on independent corporate expenditures therefore was invalid.

¶ 3 The Attorney General defended the law's constitutionality on the grounds that the law invalidated in *Citizens United* was distinguishable from the Montana statute, that corporate rights could not be asserted against states in the same manner as against Congress, and that Montana has a compelling interest in requiring business corporations to use segregated funds for campaign expenditures. The Attorney General argued that § 13-35-227(1), MCA, is narrowly tailored because it still allows for lobbying, testimony, and other direct contacts and that the Commissioner of Political Practices has interpreted the law to exclude voluntary associations. ***

¶ 5 On appeal, this Court reversed. A majority of the Court agreed with the Attorney General's position that *Citizens United* did not foreclose Montana from prohibiting independent corporate expenditures on behalf of candidates. Based on the record developed in the District Court, this Court concluded that the State had a compelling interest that justified the imposition of statutory restrictions that the Court determined were narrowly tailored to meet its objectives. We did not reach ATP's claim for fees, as it was mooted by our reversal of the District Court's summary judgment ruling. Two members of the Court dissented on the ground that Montana's statute did not pass constitutional muster under *Citizens United*. *Western Tradition Partn.* (Mont. 2011) [Baker & Nelson, JJ., dissenting]. The U.S. Supreme Court summarily reversed, ruling that "[t]here can be no serious doubt" that the holding of *Citizens United* applies to the Montana statute.

¶ 6 We return now to ATP's cross-appeal and consider whether it is entitled to recover its attorneys' fees from the State of Montana under either the UDJA [Uniform Declaratory Judgments Act] or the private attorney general doctrine. [Fn. Although ATP's renewed motion for fees also seeks a fee award under 42 U.S.C. § 1988, as prevailing parties in a proceeding to enforce 42 U.S.C. § 1983, this argument was not raised in or decided by the District Court and we decline to consider it.] ATP seeks a total award of $138,403.01. ***

Discussion

¶ 8 Did the District Court abuse its discretion in declining to award attorneys' fees?

¶ 9 Montana follows the American Rule that, absent a specific statutory or contractual provision, a prevailing party generally is not entitled to recovery of its attorneys' fees in prosecuting or defending the action. We have recognized equitable exceptions to the American Rule, but construe these exceptions narrowly "lest they swallow the rule." We have rejected the expansion of such equitable exceptions when the effect would "drive a stake into the heart of the American Rule."

1. Statutory Basis for Fees

¶ 10 Montana law provides that a prevailing party may recover attorneys' fees against the State of Montana only if "the court finds that the claim or defense of the state ... was frivolous or pursued in bad faith." Section 25-10-711(1)(b), MCA. A claim or defense is frivolous or in bad faith "when it is 'outside the bounds of legitimate argument on a substantial issue on which there is a bona fide difference of opinion.'" In this case, the District Court did not find the Attorney General's position to be frivolous or in bad faith. To the contrary, the court determined that the State's arguments "were made in good faith and were supported by briefs that were meticulously researched, well written, and well argued."

¶ 11 ATP argues that, despite its finding of good faith, the District Court erred by failing to award fees under § 27-8-313, MCA, which serves as statutory authority for an award of fees in this case. That section does not specifically provide for an award of attorneys' fees to a prevailing party, but does give a court the ability to grant "supplemental relief" in a case brought under the Uniform Declaratory Judgments Act when the court determines such relief to be "necessary or proper." While § 27-8-313, MCA, may provide a statutory basis for awarding fees, its reach is narrow. In order to avoid "eviscerat[ing]" the American Rule, we have determined that an award of fees to the prevailing party is not warranted "in every garden variety declaratory judgment action[.]"

¶ 12 Accordingly, we have required courts analyzing a claim for fees in a declaratory judgment proceeding to make a threshold determination that equitable considerations support an award of attorneys' fees. If that threshold determination is met, we apply a three-part "tangible parameters test" to determine whether an award of fees is necessary or proper as required by § 27-8-313, MCA. The District Court concluded that, although the Uniform Declaratory Judgments Act provided authority for an award of fees, the court did not find it "necessary and proper to do so in this case." Because equitable considerations also inform the analysis of ATP's claim for fees under the private attorney general doctrine, we will consider these arguments together.

2. Private Attorney General Doctrine

¶ 13 The private attorney general doctrine is one of a handful of equitable exceptions this Court has recognized to the American Rule. This doctrine "is normally utilized when the government, for some reason, fails to properly enforce interests which are significant to its citizens." *Montanans for the Responsible Use of the Sch. Trust v. State ex rel. Bd. of Land Comm'rs* [(Mont. 1999)] *(Montrust).* It, too, has been invoked sparingly. Since first recognizing the doctrine in 1989, we have only twice used it to award or uphold the award of fees, and just once to a party prevailing against the State.

¶ 14 We held in *Montrust* that three factors should be considered in determining whether to award fees under the private attorney general doctrine: "(1) the strength or societal importance of the public policy vindicated by the litigation, (2) the necessity for private enforcement and the magnitude of the resultant burden on the plaintiff, (3) the number of people standing to benefit from the decision." *Montrust,* ¶ 66 (*quoting Serrano v. Priest* (Cal. 1977)). We have limited the award of fees under the doctrine to cases "vindicating constitutional interests." We have declined to apply the doctrine when the litigation primarily served a party's own pecuniary interests. We also consider whether an award of fees would be unjust under the circumstances.

¶ 15 ATP argues that it has vindicated important free speech rights that benefit all Montana citizens and corporations and will result in adding more thoughts and views to the state's political discourse. The Attorney General, conversely, argues that there is substantial overlap between ATP's view of the public interest and its own pecuniary interests, and that the District Court was justified in declining to award fees in this case.

¶ 16 The constitutional principles underlying this litigation cannot be doubted. The U.S. Supreme Court's order reaffirmed that "political speech does not lose First Amendment protection simply because its source is a corporation." Our cases applying the private attorney general doctrine reflect the caution, however, "that the first factor not become for courts 'assessments of the relative strength or weakness of public policies furthered by their decisions . . . a role closely approaching that of the legislative function.'" The separation of powers between the branches requires us to use the same caution to avoid interference with the executive function as well.

¶ 17 "The Attorney General is the legal officer of the state and shall have the duties and powers provided by law." Mont. Const. art. VI, § 4(4). It is the duty of the Attorney General "to prosecute or defend all causes in the supreme court in which the state or any officer of the state in the officer's official capacity is a party or in which the state has an interest." Section 2-15-501(1), MCA. As an executive officer of the State of Montana, the Attorney General determines when to prosecute or to defend cases in which the State has an interest. Thus, if a challenge is brought to a state statute, the Attorney General has discretion to decide whether or not to defend its constitutionality. The courts necessarily must use caution in awarding fees against the State in a "garden variety" declaratory judgment action that challenges the constitutionality of a statute that the Attorney General, in the exercise of his executive power, has chosen to defend.

¶ 18 The legislature has cabined this executive discretion by authorizing the courts to impose fees when the State's defense is frivolous or in bad faith. Section 25-10-711(1)(b), MCA. While not dispositive, this standard also serves as a guidepost in analyzing a claim for fees under the private attorney general doctrine....

¶ 19 *Montrust,* however, was not a "garden variety" constitutional challenge to a legislative enactment. It involved unique issues raising the State's breach of fiduciary duties imposed by the Montana Constitution and federal enabling laws under which the federal government's grant of lands to Montana for support of common schools constitutes a trust for which the State is the trustee. As trustee, the State is obligated to obtain full market value for the school trust lands; the statutes in question were held to violate the State's constitutional obligation and its duty of undivided loyalty to the trust beneficiary. In contrast, we observed in *Finke* [*v. State ex rel. McGrath* (Mont. 2003)] that fees against the State would not be appropriate under the private attorney general doctrine where "the only potential liability of the State for fees would lie for the actions of the Legislature in enacting an unconstitutional bill."

¶ 20 In this case, the District Court did not abuse its discretion in determining that the State mounted a good faith defense to § 13-35-227(1), MCA. While the Attorney General did not prevail, it is difficult to conclude that his arguments were frivolous when five members of this Court were convinced of their merit. In the final analysis, even though ATP vindicated principles of constitutional magnitude, the State's defense also was grounded in constitutional principles and in an effort to enforce interests the executive deemed equally significant to its citizens. The Attorney General defended a statute with deep roots in the State's history, enacted by initiative of the people to combat corruption that had resulted in the bribery of state judges and the embarrassment of seeing one of the State's U.S. Senators unseated for also accepting bribes. The challenge was brought in a time of shifting legal landscapes, the contours of which still have not finally been defined. Under these circumstances, the predicate for an award of fees under the private attorney general doctrine—"when the government, for some reason, fails to properly enforce interests which are significant to its citizens"—has not been established.

Conclusion

¶ 21 We reverse a district court for abusing its discretion only "when it acts arbitrarily without employment of conscientious judgment or exceeds the bounds of reason[,] resulting in substantial injustice." For the reasons discussed above, and given the District Court's express determination that the State's defense was meticulously researched, well presented, and made in good faith, we cannot conclude that equitable considerations required it to award fees against the State under either the Uniform Declaratory Judgments Act or the private attorney general doctrine.

¶ 22 The District Court's order declining to award attorneys' fees to the Cross-Appellants is affirmed.

Justice JAMES C. NELSON, dissenting.

¶ 23 I dissent from the Court's denial of attorneys' fees under the private attorney general doctrine. I believe the Court errs in three respects.

¶ 24 First, the District Court provided two distinct analyses of ATP's two distinct theories for seeking attorneys' fees: one under the private attorney general doctrine and the other under the Uniform Declaratory Judgments Act (§ 27-8-313, MCA). This Court provides zero analysis of the District Court's actual decision under the private attorney general doctrine. Moreover, the Court fails to conduct its own distinct analysis under this doctrine pursuant to the three *Montrust* factors. Instead, the Court merges the private attorney general analysis into the Uniform Declaratory Judgments Act analysis and thereby creates a sort of one-size-fits-all procedural "smoothie" for analyzing attorneys' fees requests under these two distinct doctrines.

¶ 25 Second, the Court further confuses matters by injecting § 25-10-711, MCA, into this case. That statute provides an independent basis for an award of attorneys' fees. It states:

> (1) In any civil action brought by or against the state, a political subdivision, or an agency of the state or a political subdivision, the opposing party, whether plaintiff or defendant, is entitled to the costs enumerated in 25-10-201 and reasonable attorney fees as determined by the court if:
>
> (a) the opposing party prevails against the state, political subdivision, or agency; and
>
> (b) the court finds that the claim or defense of the state, political subdivision, or agency that brought or defended the action was frivolous or pursued in bad faith.
>
> (2) Costs may be granted pursuant to subsection (1) notwithstanding any other provision of the law to the contrary.

Section 25-10-711, MCA. If ATP had sought an award of attorneys' fees pursuant to this provision, then ATP would have been required to show (a) that it prevailed against the State and (b) that the State's defense was "frivolous or pursued in bad faith." What the Court apparently fails to appreciate, however, is the fact that ATP did not seek an award of attorneys' fees based on this statute. ATP relied, rather, on the private attorney general doctrine and the Uniform Declaratory Judgments Act. Hence, ATP was not required to show that the State's defense was "frivolous or pursued in bad faith." It was required, rather, to establish the elements of the two doctrines upon which it relied.

¶ 26 Notably, the district court in *Montrust* denied an award of attorneys' fees under § 25-10-711, MCA, because the action involved "neither frivolous conduct, extreme conduct, nor bad faith by the State." On appeal, the State asserted the very proposition stated [in] today's Opinion — namely, that a prevailing party may recover attorneys' fees against the State only if the court finds that the claim or defense of the State was frivolous or pursued in bad faith. In other words, the State suggested that § 25-10-711, MCA, is a blanket limitation on an award of attorneys' fees against the State under any theory — what the Court effectively holds in today's decision. The statute contains no such language, however, and we therefore rejected the State's proposition and instead adopted the private attorney general doctrine as a theory of recovery distinct from the entitlement to, and limitations on, an award of attorneys' fees under § 25-10-711, MCA. We concluded that *Montrust* was entitled to attorneys' fees under the private attorney general theory, regardless of the district court's determination that the action involved "neither frivolous conduct, extreme conduct, nor bad faith by the State." The Court's contrary approach in its decision today throws this entire area of law into a state of utter disarray.

¶ 27 Third, the Court denies relief under ATP's private attorney general theory based entirely on a sentence in the District Court's order that was not part of the District Court's reasoning under that theory. Specifically, the District Court observed that "[t]he State's arguments were made in good faith and were supported by briefs that were meticulously researched, well written, and well argued." This statement might be relevant if ATP were pursuing a claim for attorneys' fees under § 25-10-711, MCA. ATP is not relying on this statute, however, as noted above. Furthermore, the District Court provided the foregoing quoted statement as its rationale for concluding that an award of attorneys' fees was not proper under ATP's Uniform Declaratory Judgments Act theory. The District Court provided an entirely separate analysis of the private attorney general theory; this Court simply chooses not to address the District Court's specific reasoning under that theory.

¶ 28 In short, and with due respect, I believe it is wrong — not to mention patently unfair — for this Court to reject ATP's argument for attorneys' fees based on the criteria of a statute (§ 25-10-711, MCA) that ATP never even invoked. The Court completely muddles this area of law by blending the private attorney general doctrine and the Uniform Declaratory Judgments Act doctrine into a single analysis and then superimposing on that analysis the "frivolous or pursued in bad faith" criterion of § 25-10-711, MCA — contrary to our approach in *Montrust*. With this Opinion, we have effectively done away with the private attorney general doctrine. Like the majority of the United States Supreme Court in *Citizens United v. FEC* (2010), this Court has now remade this case so as to remake the law pertaining to the private attorney general doctrine. ***

Notes on Attorneys' Fees

1. In addition to *Western Tradition Partnership*, the Court also rejected attorneys' fees in *Baxter v. State* (Mont. 2009), explaining "[t]he private attorney general doctrine applies when the government fails to properly enforce interests which are significant to its citizens. The private attorney general doctrine, however, applies only when constitutional interests are vindicated. Our holding today is statute-based. Therefore, without the vindication of constitutional interests, an award of fees under the private attorney general doctrine is not warranted." Does this rule make sense? Consider Jesse Kodadek, *Expensive Free Speech*: Western Tradition Partnership *and the Silencing of the Private Attorney General Doctrine*, 75 Mont. L. Rev. 275 (2014) (arguing the Court has weakened the private attorney general doctrine in recent cases by mistakenly conflating the common law purposes of the doctrine with the limits on statutory attorneys' fees).

2. In addition to the restriction on sovereign immunity, the Declaration of Rights provides in Art. II, § 16:

> **The administration of justice.** Courts of justice shall be open to every person, and speedy remedy afforded for every injury of person, property, or character.... Right and justice shall be administered without sale, denial, or delay.

This provision is covered in the chapter on the Judicial Power and cited by the Court in *Dorwart* as a reason not to recognize qualified immunity. Does this impose any additional limits on judicially recognized official immunities or legislatively imposed limits on attorneys' fees?

Part II

Structure

Chapter 3

Legislative Powers, Duties, and Limits

Article V, Section 1. Power and structure. The legislative power is vested in a legislature consisting of a senate and a house of representatives. The people reserve to themselves the powers of initiative and referendum.

No change except in grammar.

Article V, Section 11. Bills. (1) A law shall be passed by bill which shall not be so altered or amended on its passage through the legislature as to change its original purpose. No bill shall become law except by a vote of the majority of all members present and voting.

(2) Every vote of each member of the legislature on each substantive question in the legislature, in any committee, or in committee of the whole shall be recorded and made public. On final passage, the vote shall be taken by ayes and noes and the names entered on the journal.

(3) Each bill, except general appropriation bills and bills for the codification and general revision of the laws, shall contain only one subject, clearly expressed in its title. If any subject is embraced in any act and is not expressed in the title, only so much of the act not so expressed is void.

(4) A general appropriation bill shall contain only appropriations for the ordinary expenses of the legislative, executive, and judicial branches, for interest on the public debt, and for public schools. Every other appropriation shall be made by a separate bill, containing but one subject.

(5) No appropriation shall be made for religious, charitable, industrial, educational, or benevolent purposes to any private individual, private association, or private corporation not under control of the state.

(6) A law may be challenged on the ground of noncompliance with this section only within two years after its effective date.

(1) No change except in grammar. (2) Changes 1889 constitution by requiring recorded votes on all actions which affect passage of a bill. (3) (4) (5) No change except in grammar. (6) New provision. After it is two years old a law cannot be challenged in court because of technical errors in the way it was passed.

Article V, Section 12. Local and special legislation. The legislature shall not pass a special or local act when a general act is, or can be made, applicable.

No change except in grammar.

Article VIII, Section 1. Tax purposes. Taxes shall be levied by general laws for public purposes.

Revises 1889 constitution by eliminating references to particular kinds of revenue sources (such as property taxes. license fees. and income taxes) and continues the legislative power to determine tax structures.

Unlike the federal Constitution's enumeration of "All legislative Powers herein granted," state constitutions provide for the legislature's general or "plenary" power. This does not mean that state legislatures are unlimited. Montana's Constitution, like many state constitutions, begins with a Declaration of Rights before any grants of power as a reminder that government exists to protect individual liberties. Beyond the Declaration of Rights, the Montana Constitution reshapes the general legislative power with both limits and duties. We will address some of the duties, such as the duty to provide "a clean and healthful environment" (Article IX, section 1) and "a basic system of free quality public elementary and secondary schools" (Article X, section 1) in later chapters.

Most state constitutions also go beyond the federal Constitution by imposing procedural limits on legislatures, requiring a more transparent deliberative process, and prohibiting omnibus legislation. In theory, these provisions enable the public to track the path of policy through the legislature and hold their representatives accountable for votes on specific issues. Under Article 5, section 11, each bill "shall contain only one subject, clearly expressed in its title," its purpose may not change in its passage through the legislature, and all votes in committee or on the floor must be recorded and made public. This final publicity requirement is an innovation in the 1972 Constitution, coming after concerns that backroom deals brokered by powerful interests such as the Anaconda Company made public deliberations an afterthought once the fix was in.

The primary substantive limit on state legislative power is that it must be exercised for public purposes. In Federalist 44, James Madison gave early expression to Americans' suspicion of their state legislatures:

> The sober people of America are weary of the fluctuating policy which has directed the public councils. They have seen with regret and with indignation, that sudden changes and legislative interferences in cases affecting personal rights, become jobs in the hands of enterprizing and influential speculators; and snares to the more industrious and less informed part of the community. They have seen, too, that legislative interference, is but the first link of a long chain of repetitions; every subsequent interference being naturally produced by the effects of the preceding. They very rightly infer, therefore, that some thorough reform is wanting which will banish

> speculations on public measures, inspire a general prudence and industry, and give a regular course to the business of society.

State constitutional law long has been concerned with this potential for capture of public policy and resources by special interests. The Montana Constitution establishes the public purpose principle in several provisions, including appropriations (Article V, section 11(5)), taxes (Article VIII, section 1), and general legislation (Article V, section 12). What is or is not a public purpose is routinely debated in the Legislature. The question is debated less often in the courts. These debates balance the constitutional concern of public purpose with the more practical demands of political dealmaking and, for the court, deference to a legislative branch that is kept closer to the people through shorter terms and smaller districts.

A. Legislative Process and Public Purposes

White v. State

233 Mont. 81 (1988)

McDONOUGH, Justice.

*** We find and declare that House Bill 700, also referred to as the "Science and Technology Development Board Seed Capital Bond Act", is unconstitutional for the reasons set forth below.

I.

... Section 2 of HB 700 expresses the Act's purpose:

> The legislature finds and declares that:
>
> (1) it is the policy of the state of Montana to promote the health, safety, and general welfare of all the people of the state;
>
> (2) such policy will be furthered through strengthening and diversifying the state's economy by facilitating a public-private sector partnership to encourage scientific and technological development within the state in order to keep pace with a changing economic structure and to create new jobs and expand business opportunities; and
>
> (3) such strengthening and diversification will be fostered by assisting in the acceleration of development of technology in the state through the making of technology investments.

Section 90-3-402, MCA. House Bill 700 was enacted to expand the powers of the Montana Science and Technology Development Board (the Board), which was created by the legislature in 1985 "to strengthen and diversify Montana's economy by establishing a public-private sector partnership to encourage scientific and technological development within the state in order to keep pace with a transforming economic structure and to create new jobs and expand small business opportunities."

Section 90-3-101, MCA. House Bill 700 provides the Board with bonding authority to raise money for certain types of "technology investments"; seed capital projects, start-up capital projects and expansion capital projects. Section 15 of the Act provides that the Board shall make at least 20 percent of the "Technology Development Account", funded from bond sales, available for investment in certified Montana capital companies that make technology investments. Section 90-3-415, MCA.

The proceeds received by the Board as the return on its technology investments are to be placed in the "Technology Investment Program Debt Service Fund" to repay the bonds. Section 90-3-404, MCA. Security for bond obligations is provided by the Coal Severance Tax Permanent Trust Fund. Section 90-3-416, MCA.

On November 19, 1987 the Board adopted a resolution that bonds should be issued in accordance with the provisions of HB 700. The Board has been advised that without a Supreme Court ruling that the Act is constitutional, bond counsel cannot render an unqualified opinion that the bonds would be a valid and binding obligation upon the state, and without such an opinion the bonds cannot be successfully marketed.

II.

The defendants concede . . . that plaintiffs, as taxpayers, have standing under the rule articulated in *Grossman v. State* (Mont. 1984). They also concede that this is an appropriate case for the exercise of this Court's original jurisdiction. The three major factors necessary for a valid exercise of our original jurisdiction are: (1) where constitutional issues of major statewide importance are involved, (2) where the questions involved are purely legal questions of statutory or constitutional construction, and (3) where urgency and emergency factors exist making the normal appeal process inadequate. *State ex rel. Greely v. Water Court* (Mont. 1984). We hold that all of these factors have been established.

III.

The plaintiffs contend that HB 700 violates Article V, Section 11, paragraph (5) of the Montana Constitution, which provides:

> No appropriation shall be made for religious, charitable, industrial, educational or benevolent reasons to any private individual, private association or private corporation not under control of the state.

*** In order to gain perspective on this issue, we will examine the authorities cited by both parties in chronological order. While plaintiffs cite *Hill* [*v. Rae* (Mont. 1916)] as being dispositive, it was decided in 1916 and was therefore based on the 1889 constitution. Our consideration of this issue is guided sufficiently by the cases decided post-1972.

Huber [*v. Groff* (Mont. 1976)] was decided in 1976, and concerned legislation enabling the state Board of Housing to sell bonds to help provide housing for low-income individuals and families. The proceeds from bond sales were to be used in two programs: (1) to loan money to private lenders on the condition that they in turn lend it to low-income individuals or families, or (2) to purchase mortgages on the condition that the money had been loaned to low-income individuals or families. We held that the Housing Board was a public corporation, deriving its powers directly from the legislature and following duties prescribed by the legislature. Article V, Section 11(5) was therefore held inapplicable.

Our 1984 decision in *Grossman* upheld legislation providing that proceeds from the sale of coal severance tax revenue bonds would be loaned to local government entities to finance water development projects. We cited our decision in *Huber*, and held that appropriations to public entities were constitutional even though the money might ultimately benefit private individuals or businesses through its use by the state agency. The state funds involved in *Grossman* ultimately benefitted private companies and cooperatives that leased new or improved hydroelectric facilities.

However, we established a limit to this principle two years later in *Hollow* [*v. State* (Mont. 1986)]. *Hollow* involved the use of bond proceeds by the Montana Economic Development Board to fund economic development projects. The Development Board was authorized to establish a project guaranty program, under which it could make commitments to guaranty payments on loans, leases or other credit arrangements required for funded projects in return for a fee. The Board further was authorized to make loans from the Montana in-state investment fund, made up in part of funds from coal severance taxes, to its capital reserve account (securing the bonds issued) and its guaranty fund (securing the loans and other credit arrangements). We held that the use of state tax revenues to secure the private obligations of project participants and the bonds providing funds for the benefit of their businesses violated Art. V, § 11(5), as well as Art. VIII, § 1 and Art. VIII, § 13(1) of the Montana Constitution. We distinguished *Huber* in that the legislation in *Huber* specifically did not pledge the credit of the state to secure the bonds being issued. The *Hollow* legislation in effect directly pledged the credit of the state to secure the bonds and guaranties being used to benefit private business ventures.

House Bill 700 establishes a program similar to that in *Hollow*. The Science and Technology Development Board is empowered to funnel bond proceeds into private business ventures through technology investments. Defendants rightly argue that the Board is a public corporation, as were the boards in the above cases. Therefore, funds initially appropriated for the Board's use would not be appropriated to "any private individual, private association, or private corporation not under control of the state" in violation of Art. V, § 11(5). However, the significance of this argument would diminish greatly once bonds were issued.

*** Section 16(3) [of the Act] ... ultimately requires the legislature to make up the difference between the return received by the Board on the investment of bond proceeds and the obligations arising from the bonds. By providing that the legislature shall deposit coal severance tax funds into the Board's debt service fund and assess taxes in order to continue such deposits as needed, § 16(3) in effect pledges the credit of the state to secure the bonds issued by the Board, the proceeds of which are to be used for the benefit of private businesses. As we said in *Hollow*, "What we do not and cannot condone is the direct use of tax monies by legislative provision which in effect directly pledges the credit of the state to secure the bonds involved in this case." We hold, therefore, that § 16(3) of HB 700 violates Art. V, § 11(5) of the Montana Constitution, and is therefore void.

IV.

Plaintiffs assert that HB 700 unconstitutionally delegates legislative power to the Board, violating Article V, Section 1 of the Montana Constitution which provides:

> The legislative power is vested in a legislature consisting of a senate and a house of representatives....

The plaintiffs' position is that HB 700 grants the Board too much discretion. They argue that the powers granted to the Board are not circumscribed sufficiently; i.e., there are no standards or rules from the legislature to guide the Board in making technology investments. *** The defendants assert that HB 700 delegates administrative authority to the Board, not legislative power. Defendants cite *Huber* for the standard that determines whether legislation results in an unconstitutional delegation of legislative power:

> ... Concerning adequate standards and guides in delegation of legislative power, this court has stated the rule as follows: If the legislature fails to prescribe with reasonable clarity the limits of power delegated to an administrative agency, or if those limits are too broad, its attempt to delegate is a nullity.
>
> On the other hand a statute is complete and validly delegates administrative authority when nothing with respect to a determination of what is the law is left to the administrative agency, and its provisions are sufficiently clear, definite, and certain to enable the agency to know its rights and obligations.

Defendants ... distinguish *Douglas* [*v. Judge* (Mont. 1977)], where the Board of Natural Resources and Conservation was authorized to make loans to farmers and ranchers "for any worthwhile project...." Defendants say HB 700 stands in sharp contrast to the legislation in *Douglas* and does not grant the same unguided discretion.

The constitutional tests applied in *Douglas* and *Huber* were similar in their purpose of preventing the delegation of unbridled authority to an administrative board. Defendants are correct, however, in their assertion that the very lax legislation in *Douglas* was quite different from that in *Huber*. In *Huber*, ... [t]he size of the family, total income available for housing, availability and cost of housing and ability to enter the housing market at the "going rate" were all objective criteria requiring only observation and arithmetical calculation.

The considerations to be used by the Science and Technology Development Board in making technology investments are set forth in Section 13 of HB 700:

> (1) Technology investments may be made from money in the technology development account only upon a favorable determination by the board of:

(a) the relevance of the proposed technology development project to the purposes of this part;

(b) the prospects for collaboration on the project between public and private sectors of the state's economy in mineral technology, agricultural technology, forestry technology, biotechnology, microelectronics and computer sciences, energy technology, information sciences, and materials science;

(c) the prospects for achieving commercial success in general and for creating significant numbers of new jobs in the state in particular;

(d) the quality of the specific product and business development methodology proposed;

(e) the suitability of any proposed milestone for evaluating progress of technology development project results; and

(f) the availability of matching funds required under 90-3-301(2).

(2) In this evaluation process, the board shall consider the investment's:

(a) job creation potential;

(b) potential benefit for existing industry;

(c) potential for creating new industry; and

(d) involvement of existing institutional research strength or whether it involves a newly targeted technology area with development potential.

These considerations do not rise to the level of the objective criteria offered in *Huber*. They are more akin to general policy considerations underlying the entire technology investment program.

For example, "the prospects for achieving commercial success in general and for creating significant numbers of new jobs in the state in particular" are considerations at the heart of the legislature's decision to empower the Board to sell bonds. They are not objective criteria guiding the investment of bond proceeds. In *Huber*, the legislation at issue went beyond simply directing that individuals and families of lower income should receive housing assistance. The objective guidelines listed above were supplied to guide the administration of that project. Likewise in *Grossman*, the legislation directed that the feasibility of hydroelectric projects should be considered, and then went on to list objective standards (e.g., estimated costs of necessary improvements, debt servicing requirements and ability of customers to lease improved facilities) by which to judge feasibility. In the case at bar, HB 700 does not set forth the law under which the Board would function. No legislatively defined "policy, standard or rule" is effectively given.

House Bill 700 also fails to "prescribe with reasonable clarity the limits of power delegated" to the Board. The statement of purpose in Section 2 asserts that "strengthening and diversification" of Montana's economy "will be fostered... through the making of technology investments." The linchpin of the legislation is thus the grant of authority to the Board to make technology investments. Yet the term "technology investment" is not well defined in HB 700 . . . . Technology investment is defined only as "an award of funds for a technology development project." On the basis of this definition, the form that such an award might take is left almost entirely to the imagination of the Board. As the plaintiffs point out, the guidelines laid out by HB 700 do not prohibit the Board from holding private corporate capital stock, an arrangement which could violate Art. VIII, Section 13(1) of the Montana Constitution.

Another area where definition is lacking is the terms on which technology investments are to be made. When making an "award of funds," the Board is required to negotiate a "return-on-investment agreement." However, return on investment appears to be as murky a concept as technology investment. Section 23 of HB 700 states that the Board shall enter into return-on-investment agreements requiring payment of "a return that [the Board] considers commensurate with the risk of its original investment." As with the criteria for investment discussed above, the Board is left to define a policy that should have been contained in HB 700 . . . . In *Huber*, we noted a rule promulgated by the Housing Board showing its ability to place a figure on the income limit for "persons and families of lower income" pursuant to the objective criteria present in that case. However, constitutional law does not allow for an administrative board to legislate the limits of its own power, which the Board in the present case has been required to do in order to give some meaning to the vague terms of HB 700.

Sections 12, 13, 14, 15, and 22 of HB 700 delineate the operations of the Board and the powers it may exercise. Through vagueness or incorporation of inadequately defined operative terms, all of these sections delegate legislative authority to the Board. They violate Art. V, § 1 of the Montana Constitution, and are therefore void.

V.

Plaintiffs assert that the title of the Act violates Article V, Section 11(3) of the Montana Constitution, which requires that

> [e]ach bill, except general appropriation bills and bills for the codification and general revision of the laws, shall contain only one subject, clearly expressed in its title. If any subject is embraced in any act and is not expressed in the title, only so much of the act not so expressed is void.

The plaintiffs argue the title to HB 700 is vague. They assert it is not specific about the details concerning the money committed from the coal severance tax permanent trust fund and it does not mention the Montana capital companies.

The defendants state that the test for compliance with this provision of the Montana Constitution is simply whether the title is of such character as to mislead the public [or members of the legislature] as to the subject embraced. *Montana Automobile Association v. Greely* (Mont. 1981). They argue the title gives fair and accurate notice of the subject of the Act to interested parties, and the title need not provide details regarding every aspect of the legislation in order to pass constitutional muster.

The full title of HB 700 is as follows:

> An Act providing authority to the Montana Science and Technology Development Board to issue science and technology development seed capital fund bonds to finance technology investments; creating necessary funds and accounts; making statutory appropriations of certain money; authorizing transfer of a portion of the coal severance tax permanent trust fund; providing for audits of the board; amending Sections 17-7-502, 90-3-203, 90-3-302, and 90-3-304, MCA; and providing an immediate effective date.

At no point does this title mention the fact that Section 16(3) of the Act pledges the credit of the State of Montana to secure the bonds to be issued. This would be a subject of importance to legislators preparing to vote on HB 700. As § 16(3) contains a subject of importance not embraced in the title of HB 700, it violates Art. V, § 11(3) of the Montana Constitution, and is therefore void.

VI.

Both parties note the presence of Section 27 in HB 700, which provides for severability:

> If a part of this act is invalid, all valid parts that are severable from the invalid part remain in effect. If a part of this act is invalid in one or more of its applications, the part remains in effect in all valid applications that are severable from the invalid applications.

In *Greely*, we reviewed Montana case law dealing with severability. The essential principle of severability is that a statute is not entirely voided by inclusion of one or more unconstitutional sections, unless those sections are "necessary to the integrity of the statute or [were] the inducement to its enactment." Our invalidation of Sections 12, 13, 14, 15, 16(3) and 22 of HB 700 removes the legislative grant of authority to the Board for making technology investments. Those portions of HB 700 remaining are thus rendered meaningless. Accordingly, we declare House Bill 700 to be void in its entirety, as it suffers from constitutional defect in its core provisions. For this reason, it will be unnecessary for us to proceed to the remaining issues posed by the plaintiffs.

SHEEHY, Justice, concurring:

I concur wholly with the foregoing opinion. It may help to demonstrate the unconstitutional use of state funds for private purposes if we examine some of the investments that are permitted by the law or committed by the Board. ***

Among other commitments, the Board had committed for the period between November 1, 1986 and December 1, 1987 the following "investments" under technology transfer: [e.g., $50,600 to Montana Wool Growers for "Transfer of Sheep Management Technology"].

Clearly, each of the foregoing commitments is the use of state monies for private purposes, because there is no provision for reimbursement nor a dollar for dollar match. However well intended the objectives may have been, these uses of state monies through private agencies clearly offend the Montana Constitution.

Kottel v. State

312 Mont. 387 (2002)

Justice JAMES C. NELSON delivered the Opinion of the Court.

*** ¶ 5 Under § 20-25-301, MCA, Montana has one state-wide university system which is supervised by the Board of Regents. This university system includes vocational technical schools (vo-techs), officially called colleges of technology, located in Cascade, Lewis and Clark, Missoula, Silver Bow, and Yellowstone counties. Under § 20-25-439(1), MCA, (the vo-tech levy), both real and personal property in these five counties is subject to a mandatory tax of 1.5 mills that provides partial funding for the vo-techs. The amounts generated by the vo-tech levy are deposited into the general fund to be distributed to the vo-techs for educational purposes on the basis of budgets approved by the Board of Regents. The Board of Regents is not required to allocate to a particular vo-tech an amount of funding equal to that generated by the vo-tech levy in the corresponding county. The funds generated by the vo-tech levy provide less than five percent of the total annual funding for vo-techs. In addition to the vo-tech levy and university appropriations approved by the Legislature under § 17-7-138, MCA, and § 20-25-422, MCA, there is also a state-wide 6-mill levy authorized under § 20-25-423, MCA, that provides partial funding for the entire university system.

¶ 6 The Taxpayers in this case reside in Cascade County, own property subject to the vo-tech levy, and paid the tax under protest pursuant to § 15-1-402, MCA. The Taxpayers then instituted this declaratory judgment action, asserting that the vo-tech levy is unconstitutional because it is only required and levied in the five counties where the vo-techs are located even though the vo-techs are part of the state-wide university system. The State answered and asserted that the vo-tech levy is not unconstitutional because it is rationally related to a legitimate government purpose. ***

¶ 11 Montana's vo-tech system originated in 1917 when the Legislature authorized the then State Board of Education to cooperate with local school districts and county school boards in the establishment and maintenance of vo-techs in the public schools of the state.... Initially, funding for vo-techs came from federal sources.... In 1969, the Legislature designated the present day vo-techs and gave local counties with vo-techs discretionary authority to levy a 1 mill property tax to support the vo-tech in their community.... After gradually increasing the taxing authority to 1.5 mills over the years, the Legislature made the vo-tech levy mandatory in 1986. ***

¶ 13 In 1987, the Legislature transferred control of the vo-techs to the Board of Regents. Local administrative control was removed from the counties and placed with the Board of Regents.... Further, the amounts generated by the vo-tech levy were placed under control of the Board of Regents rather than the local districts.... In 1995, the Legislature merged the vo-techs into the state university system, removed all statutory references to "vocational technical centers" as separate entities, and instead designated vo-techs as units of either Montana State University or the University of Montana. This allowed the Board of Regents to rename the vo-techs as "colleges of technology." . . .

¶ 14 The Taxpayers assert this history demonstrates a long tradition of local control, funded in part by the local, discretionary tax embodied in § 20-7-324(1)(b), MCA (1985), the earlier version of § 20-25-439, MCA. The Taxpayers further note the system of local control was converted to a state-run system at almost the same time as the vo-tech levy was converted to a mandatory state tax. The Taxpayers assert that the removal of local control should have been accompanied by a removal of the five-county vo-tech levy or possibly expansion of the vo-tech levy to all counties with university system operations or to all 56 counties. At any rate, the Taxpayers assert that retention of the mandatory vo-tech levy in only five counties results in a statute that violates the tax provisions of Article VIII, Sections 1 and 3 and the equal protection provisions of the Montana and federal Constitutions because the property owners in these five counties carry a disproportionate share of the burden to support the state-wide university system. ***

¶ 16 B. Did the District Court err in holding that, for purposes of this case, equal protection analysis and the requirements of Article VIII, Sections 1 and 3 are the same?

¶ 17 Because the Taxpayers challenge the meaning of the current 1972 Constitution based on provisions from the 1889 Constitution, we first set out the provisions in issue. Article XII of the 1889 Constitution is entitled "Revenue and Taxation." Section 1 reads:

> The necessary revenue for the support and maintenance of the state shall be provided by the legislative assembly, which shall levy a uniform rate of assessment and taxation, and shall prescribe such regulations as shall secure a just valuation for taxation of all property, except that specially provided for in this article.

Article XII, Section 11 of the 1889 Constitution reads:

> Taxes shall be levied and collected by general laws and for public purposes only. They shall be uniform upon the same class of subjects within the territorial limits of the authority levying the tax.

Article VIII of the 1972 Constitution is entitled "Revenue and Finance." Section 1, entitled "Tax purposes" reads:

> Taxes shall be levied by general laws for public purposes.

Article VIII, Section 3 of the 1972 Constitution entitled "Property tax administration" reads:

> The state shall appraise, assess, and equalize the valuation of all property which is to be taxed in the manner provided by law.

Further, the 1972 Constitution equal protection clause is in Article 2, the Declaration of Rights. It reads:

> Section 4. Individual dignity.... *No person shall be denied the equal protection of the laws.* Neither the state nor any person, firm, corporation, or institution shall discriminate against any person in the exercise of his civil or political rights on account of race, color, sex, culture, social origin or condition, or political or religious ideas. (emphasis added)

In contrast, unlike the 1972 Constitution, the 1889 Constitution did not contain an equal protection clause.

¶ 18 Given these provisions, the parties agree that the word "uniform" no longer appears in the plain language of the 1972 Constitution. However, the parties disagree over the meaning of relevant case law and the history of the Constitutional Convention, both of which we discuss below. ***

¶ 20 The Taxpayers... assert that these [pre-1972] cases incorporate the uniformity doctrine into the phrase "general laws" in Article VIII, Section 1 and the phrase "equalize" in Article VIII, Section 3. *** Assuming then that the uniformity doctrine is part of the 1972 Constitution, the Taxpayers argue that § 20-25-439(1), MCA, violates the uniformity doctrine because it is not uniform within the same class of subjects within the territorial limits of the authority levying the tax. Specifically, they assert that despite the fact that § 20-25-439(1), MCA, is a tax mandated by the state and the fact that the university system is one state-wide system supervised by the Board of Regents under § 20-25-301, MCA, the tax is not levied on a state-wide basis, but only in five of Montana's 56 counties. Therefore, the five vo-tech counties are not treated uniformly with other counties, but are required to carry a heavier tax burden to support the state-wide vo-tech system than the burden carried by the rest of the state. ***

[W]e conclude that the uniformity doctrine as interpreted under the 1889 Constitution provided for equal protection in the area of taxation and accordingly is still embodied in our 1972 Constitution. *** [N]either uniformity requirements nor equal protection prevent the state from making classifications that result in different state taxes among the various counties of the state, as long as those classifications are rationally related to legitimate government purposes.

c. Constitutional Convention History

¶ 35 In addition to precedent, the Constitutional Convention history also supports our conclusion here. *** [T]he particular history of Article VIII, Section 1 indicates that the omission of the second sentence of previous Article XII, Section 11, was still intended to preserve equal protection requirements. The Committee expressed its specific intent regarding the current Article VIII, Section 1, as follows:

> The first sentence [of Art. XII, Sec. 11] is now proposed section 1. The uniformity philosophy in the second sentence was eliminated, *primarily because uniformity of taxation is already required of the states through the 14th Amendment to the United States Constitution.* The proviso also unnecessarily thwarts taxation programs, and *has caused considerable*

> *consternation in other states.* The Pennsylvania Supreme Court invalidated an inheritance tax program as violative of the uniformity provision. The Illinois uniformity clause was interpreted to prohibit a graduated income tax in that state. (emphasis added).

Rather than resurrect the "ironclad" rule of uniformity expressly rejected 53 years earlier, this history indicates that the delegates intended to eliminate any future confusion that could be caused by retaining the uniformity language as it existed in Article XII, Section 11 of the 1889 Constitution. See also V Mont. Const. Conv., Verbatim Transcript, 1378 ("[W]e have also eliminated the uniformity clause.... under the present Constitution it's been unattainable.") Further, this history does not express an intent to nullify the state's extensive tax jurisprudence, but instead demonstrates that the framers acted with a knowledge of existing Montana and federal law. ***

¶ 39 Accordingly, based on our review of case law and Constitutional Convention history, we conclude that the framers intended to preserve the uniformity rule only as it is equivalent to equal protection requirements and also intended to remove any confusion that could lead to other conclusions, such as the position asserted by the Taxpayers in this case....

3. The Analysis is the Same Under Article VIII, Sections 1 and 3, and Under Equal Protection for this Case ***

¶ 41 Normally, we follow the rule that we do not construe a provision to create surplus language. Said another way, interpretations that give effect to all the language are preferred over interpretations that treat language as void. Under this rule, Article VIII, Sections 1 and 3, must have meaning independent from the equal protection clause. However, our review of the case law above indicates that the analysis is often the same. Said another way, the question of whether a law is a "general law" is simply another approach to the question of whether a law violates equal protection by unfairly discriminating against a specific person. Further, the question of whether property appraisals are "equalized" is another approach to the question of whether an appraisal system violates equal protection.

¶ 42 The same parallel also applies to the analysis of whether a law is "special" in violation of Article V, Section 12. *Linder v. Smith* (Mont. 1981) (reasonable classifications will be upheld against a "special legislation" challenge or against an equal protection challenge); *D & F Sanitation Serv. v. Billings* (Mont. 1986) (a law is special if it does not "operate equally upon all of a group of objects which, having regard to the purpose of the legislature, are distinguished by characteristics sufficiently marked and important to make them a class by themselves.") Therefore, for purposes of this case, there is no difference between Article VIII, Sections 1 and 3 and equal protection analysis.

¶ 43 This conclusion is supported by the rule that language is presumed to have the same meaning throughout a document. In the Montana Constitution, the word "general" is used throughout. In each instance, other than referring to the Attorney General or general elections, the word "general" is used to require a law that does not single out particular individuals for special treatment. For example, Article V, Section 12, reads: "The legislature shall not pass a special or local act when a general act is, or can be made, applicable." This provision assures equal protection by requiring general laws. See also Art. XIII, Sec. 1(1) ("Corporate charters shall be granted, modified, or dissolved only pursuant to general law."); Art. X, Sec. 11(2) ("No such land or any estate or interest therein shall ever be disposed of except in pursuance of general laws providing for such disposition."); Art. V, Sec. 11("(3) Each bill, except general appropriation bills and bills for the codification and general revision of the laws, shall contain only one subject, clearly expressed in its title.... (4) A general appropriation bill shall contain only appropriations for the ordinary expenses of the legislative, executive, and judicial branches, for interest on the public debt, and for public schools.").

¶ 44 Further, identical analysis under the general laws provision of Article VIII, Section 1 and under equal protection is also supported by history from the Constitutional Convention. The Committee Comments on the Majority Proposal state: "The requirement of general laws for public purposes extends to all tax programs, both state and local. Although those two requirements are already imposed on the state by the federal Constitution, repetition in the state document emphasizes their importance." II Mont. Const. Conv. 588. See also II Mont. Const. Conv. 579 ("From a pure, theoretical viewpoint, the Constitution does not have to say a thing about taxation.... Anything in a state Constitution on the subject of taxation is either redundant (reiterating a power already possessed by the state) or restrictive.")

¶ 45 Therefore, even though we hold that the District Court erred when it determined the uniformity doctrine is no longer included in our current Constitution, we also conclude that the District Court was correct in holding that the analysis under Article VIII, Sections 1 and 3, and under equal protection is the same for purposes of this case. We now turn to the issue of whether § 20-25-439(1), MCA, violates equal protection.

*** [W]e note that the Taxpayers do not assert that the state equal protection clause provides greater protection than the federal Constitution. *** The State asserts that ... the rational basis test applies because no constitutionally significant interests are implicated.

¶ 51 We agree that rational basis analysis applies. We have already addressed the issue of what level of scrutiny generally applies to tax classifications. In *Montana Stockgrowers Ass'n v. Department of Revenue* (Mont. 1989), the Stockgrowers asserted that constitutionally significant interests were implicated because agricultural interests are specifically mentioned in Article XII, Section 1. We disagreed and held that an equal protection challenge to the property tax treatment afforded livestock was subject to the rational basis test.... Therefore, no constitutionally significant interests are implicated that require greater than rational basis analysis.

3. The Vo-Tech Levy Has a Rational Basis

¶ 53 Having determined that the vo-tech levy is to be reviewed for a rational basis, we now turn to the merits.... In considering the property taxes at issue in *Montana Stockgrowers* we stated:

> Equal protection of the law is seldom, if ever, obtained; and because of the very frailty of human agencies, the authorities all recognize the right of the legislative branch of government to make reasonable classifications of subjects, for property or occupation taxes and if the classification is reasonable, and if all of the subjects within a given class are accorded the same treatment, the legislation cannot be said to deny to anyone within such class the equal protection of the law, even though the burden imposed upon him may be more onerous than that imposed upon a member of another class. But to justify such discriminatory legislation, and avoid the condemnation of the Fourteenth Amendment to the federal Constitution, the classification must be reasonable-that is, must be based upon substantial distinctions which really make one class different from another.

¶ 55 In sum, we will uphold a tax classification under the rational basis test if (1) the tax classification is reasonable, not arbitrary; and (2) the statute applies equally to all who fall within the same classification. Further, a classification is reasonable if any reasonably conceivable state of facts provides a rational basis for it. ***

¶ 58 . . . [T]he vo-tech levy is rational because the vo-techs have historically relied on it to raise revenue and because the vo-techs are distinguishable from other parts of the university system. Further, the fact that local residents tend to attend the vo-techs in order to receive a broad cross-section of workforce related courses serves as a "reasonably conceivable state of facts" that provides a rational basis for the vo-tech levy. Therefore, the counties with vo-techs are not arbitrarily selected from the rest of the state because vo-tech counties do not stand in the same relation to the greater privileges conferred on those counties by vo-techs than the rest of the state. Accordingly, the disability of the vo-tech levy is rationally imposed.

Notes on Legislative Limits

1. *White*, like *Grossman* and other cases, was "a test case designed to obtain a final judgment on the validity of coal severance tax revenue bonds so that if valid, the bonds will be marketable." This explains the "kitchen sink" approach to the claims. The Court expanded the justiciability of such cases so the bonds could be issued without a cloud over their constitutionality. In *Grossman*, the Court noted "Legal niceties must bend on occasion to the reality of the market. The living law moves with the times." Is issuing a declaratory judgment on the marketability of bonds to private investors a proper exercise of the judicial power?

2. *White* presents both procedural and substantive challenges to legislative power. The procedural "single-subject" challenge to legislation raises similar questions to the "separate amendment" rule for constitutional amendments examined in Chapter 1. Many state courts take a highly deferential approach to challenges based on legislative procedure. Under the "enrolled bill rule," for example, courts do not question even blatant violations of legislative procedure once a bill has been formally "enrolled" by the signatures of the appropriate legislative officials. As with the single-subject rule, Montana courts have rejected the deferential approach to

enrolled bills. In *O'Bannon v. Gustafson* (Mont. 1956), parents of a killed worker claimed equitable tolling of a claim deadline for workers compensation benefits because a statute eliminating that tolling apparently had not been "printed for the use of the members" as required by Article V, section 22 of the 1889 Constitution. Although the Court had "early recognized the danger of reviewing legislative procedure and . . . tended to follow the strict English rule of not allowing judicial review of a legislative enactment," it declined to defer under the enrolled bill rule: "[t]he constitutional mandate not having been followed by the legislative body in its action on the purported statute, and this fact appearing affirmatively in the journals, the statute fails as unconstitutional." (It pays to attend to legislative procedure!)

3. As will be discussed in the next chapter, the Montana Supreme Court applies a more rigorous non-delegation standard than the "intelligible principle" currently required of legislative delegations under the federal Constitution. Should an overly broad delegation from the legislature to the executive aggravate or mitigate public purpose concerns for legislation? At some point, to accomplish most legislative policies, the government through the executive branch must do business by spending tax money on privately provided goods and services. Why might executive branch spending raise fewer "public purpose" concerns than the legislative appropriations policed by the requirements in *White*, *Grossman*, and other cases?

4. In *Grossman v. State*, the Court also addressed a challenge under Art. VIII, section 1 of the 1972 Montana Constitution, which provides: "Taxes shall be levied by general laws for public purposes." The plaintiff contended "that the funds used to service a debt of coal severance tax bonds are generated by the general taxing powers of the state and that the funds will not be used for public purposes but rather for financing special local purposes." The Court responded:

> These contentions are weightless. The question of whether a particular purpose for which taxes may be levied and collected is a public purpose is for the legislature in the first instance, and the courts will indulge every reasonable presumption of favor of the legislative decision in this respect. The words "public purposes" are synonymous with "governmental purposes."
>
> . . . It is enough to say that for the most part the loans are authorized to provide financial aid for city water systems, water distribution systems, water supply treatment facilities, sewage treatment, construction to provide reliable supplies of water, and plans to alleviate water shortages. In one case a rural water system is authorized where presently water must be hauled for both domestic and stock water purposes. In each case the legislature has found specifically the public purpose involved, in some instances to resolve health hazards to the residents being served, to prevent health problems, to improve the quality of ground water, to improve the water supply performance, and to stabilize water supplies.
>
> It is clear that the purposes of the loans for which the $17,044,735 is authorized affects the inhabitants of the particular areas as communities,

> and not merely as individuals. The use of the loan proceeds will clearly be for public purposes.

Is it true, against the background of concerns motivating public purpose and special legislation provisions, that "public purposes" are synonymous with "governmental purposes"? Is the Court drawing the line at the private beneficiary or private function of the government funds? Prisons serve a public purpose, but could the Legislature direct tax money to a private prison company as long as it was "under control of the state" through the Department of Corrections? What about the purchase of a privately owned power plant for environmental or energy generation reasons?

5. Is economic development a public purpose? Consider *Town of Beloit v. County of Rock* (Wis. 2003):

> CROOKS, J.
>
> *** The court of appeals held that the Town of Beloit (town) has the statutory authority to spend public tax monies to develop and sell property in the Heron Bay subdivision, and that the town's goals in developing the subdivision constitute legitimate and valid public purposes.
>
> We affirm the court of appeals decision. In *Libertarian Party of Wisconsin v. State* (Wis. 1996), this court held that creating jobs and enhancing the tax base were legitimate and valid reasons, along with others, for finding a legislative public purpose in the expenditure of public funds to build the Milwaukee Brewers' Miller Park. Accordingly, we hold that the combination of the town's enunciated goals of creating jobs, promoting orderly growth, increasing the tax base, and preserving and conserving an environmentally sensitive area for the benefit of the citizens of the town is a legitimate and valid public purpose under Wisconsin statutes, case law, and the United States and Wisconsin Constitutions. ***
>
> ABRAHAMSON, C.J., dissenting.
>
> *** An expenditure is for a public purpose if it provides a direct advantage or benefit to the public at large. It is not for a public purpose if the advantage to the public is indirect, remote, or uncertain. ***
>
> The combination of goals enunciated by the majority opinion as constituting a legitimate and valid public purpose for the Town of Beloit's expenditures properly includes a list of benefits that might conceivably, in some circumstances, provide a direct benefit to taxpayers and thereby satisfy the public purpose doctrine. An expenditure of funds that is legitimately designed to create jobs, promote orderly growth, increase the tax base, and preserve an environmentally sensitive area is made for a public purpose.
>
> I dissent in this case, however, to express my conviction that some of the goals on which the majority opinion rests its conclusion are merely assertions unsupported by the facts of this case while others are admittedly hoped for but distant outcomes, not justifications. The public purpose

doctrine becomes a charade if a town may justify expenditures by merely offering enough of the proper buzzwords, "job creation," "orderly growth," "increasing the tax base," and "environment concerns," without any facts to back up the assertions. Moreover, judicial review cannot begin and end simply with the recitation of those buzzwords, without any analysis.

*** The majority opinion lists job creation as an express goal of the town's expenditure in this case, despite the fact that the town did not articulate that benefit as a goal in its stipulation, brief, or oral argument. *** The majority opinion includes this noble public goal based solely upon a single affidavit from the town's attorney, asserting in broad terms, not necessarily related to this subdivision development, that "the Town of Beloit has a history of leading development for the benefit of its citizens. The purpose of development has been to develop jobs, a greater tax base for the community and places for citizens to live." No evidence appears in the record of the types of jobs that would be created in this case, who would receive those jobs, or how long those jobs would last.

The court's emphasis on the public purpose of preservation of an environmentally sensitive strip of land along the Rock River also amounts to reliance on buzzwords. *** [I]t is unclear why any expenditure of funds for subdivision improvement is necessary for environmental protection of land the town owns along the river. The monies expended go to the development of the sites, not the creation or enforcement of any environmental easement or covenant. According to the parties' stipulation, the public can access these lands for recreation and enjoyment at the present time. To conclude that the town is justified in expending funds for sewer, water, roads, gas, electricity, storm sewer management and any other appurtenances necessary for development of the subdivision for sale for homes because the public would benefit from no development on a particular strip of town-owned land is doublespeak.

The two other goals in the combination of objectives the majority opinion says supports the expenditures for a public purpose are the promotion of orderly growth and increasing the tax base. The town, however, makes no showing of the relationship of the subdivision to orderly growth. Orderly growth is accomplished by a master plan, zoning codes, and regulation of private land developers. The Town of Beloit has such a master plan in place. How the town is promoting orderly growth by development of the subdivision is therefore unclear. The majority opinion appears to have accepted the town's mere suggestion of promoting orderly growth. It certainly cannot base its conclusion on facts because the record is devoid of any such facts.

The final objective of the expenditures is to increase the tax base. The tax base will increase if the lots are sold and houses are constructed. Yet the stipulation states that the "Town has not sold any portion of the Heron Bay

> Lands as of this date. The Town has no guarantee that anyone will purchase any of the future residential lots. . . ." An enhanced tax base from the sale of land and the construction of homes is an indirect, remote, and uncertain benefit of the expenditure in the present case and is not a sufficient public purpose to justify the town's running a for-profit real estate development business and engaging in the non-traditional enterprise of building residential home sites.

6. Assuming the delegates' intent (as opposed to the meaning of the words the People adopted) controls the interpretation of the general taxation requirement in *Kottel*, is the relevant inquiry federal equal protection doctrine as of 1972, federal equal protection doctrine at the time a case is decided, or the distinct equal protection doctrine of the Montana Supreme Court as of ratification? If the latter, is it for the Court to decide that general taxation is not a "constitutionally significant interest" deserving heightened scrutiny when, after all, the delegates decided to keep the restriction in the Constitution? As we will see, the Court does not apply the "any reasonably conceivable state of facts" standard for rational basis review in other cases. Why should it do so with respect to fiscal policy?

7. In apparent dicta, the Court in *Kottel* also suggests on textual grounds that restrictions on "special" as opposed to "general" legislation and related provisions should follow federal equal protection doctrine. Although the 1889 Constitution did not guarantee "equal protection of the laws," it was adopted more than two decades after ratification of the Fourteenth Amendment's Equal Protection Clause, and the 1972 Constitution continues to govern legislation, taxes, and appropriations by distinct provisions focused around the difference between "public purposes" or "general laws" on one hand and "special legislation" on the other. These provisions now stand alongside a separate guarantee of equal protection, and are framed as limits on legislative powers, not individual rights. Is there any role left for these uniquely state constitutional provisions in Montana?

B. Special Legislation

Rohlfs v. Klemenhagen

354 Mont. 133 (2009)

Justice JOHN WARNER delivered the Opinion of the Court.

¶ 1 Plaintiffs Cary and Terra Rohlfs brought suit against Klemenhagen, L.L.C., doing business as the Stumble Inn, to recover damages incurred as the result of an automobile accident involving a patron of the Stumble Inn. The Twenty-First Judicial District Court, Lake County, granted Stumble Inn's motion to dismiss based on a provision of Montana's Dram Shop Act, § 27-1-710(6), MCA, that requires a claimant give notice to the potential defendant of intent to sue to within 180 days of the alleged furnishing alcohol to an intoxicated person. The Rohlfs appeal. ***

¶ 5 A little over a year after the accident, in July 2007, the Rohlfs filed their complaint, alleging Stumble Inn is liable to them for the injuries caused by Warren because its employees served alcohol to him shortly before the accident while he was visibly intoxicated, in violation of § 27-1-710(3)(b), MCA. Stumble Inn moved to dismiss the complaint based on § 27-1-710(6), MCA, that provides:

> A civil action may not be commenced under this section against a person who furnished alcohol unless the person bringing the civil action provides notice of an intent to file the action to the person who furnished the alcohol by certified mail within 180 days from the date of sale or service. The civil action must be commenced pursuant to this section within 2 years after the sale or service.

¶ 6 In response to the motion to dismiss, the Rohlfs concede they did not give the notice required by § 27-1-710(6), MCA, to Stumble Inn within 180 days. The Rohlfs argued to the District Court that the notice provision may not be enforced because it is unconstitutional special legislation and violates their right to equal protection of the law. ***

¶ 9 Issue 1: Is § 27-1-710(6), MCA, special legislation prohibited by Article V, Section 12, of the Montana Constitution?

¶ 10 The Montana Constitution provides:

> The legislature shall not pass a special or local act when a general act is, or can be made, applicable.

Mont. Const. art. V, § 12.

¶ 11 . . . The central point of the Rohlfs' argument is that § 27-1-710(6), MCA, is prohibited special legislation as there is nothing unique about cases against bar owners under the Dram Shop Act, as compared to negligence cases generally, which makes evidence and witnesses more likely to disappear quickly. Thus, the Rohlfs assert the 180-day notice provision in § 27-1-710(6), MCA, has singled out "dram shop plaintiffs" for a unique procedural disability that is arbitrary and does not arise from any distinction that can withstand constitutional muster.

¶ 12 In the constitutional context, a law is not local or special if it operates in the same manner upon all persons in like circumstances. If a law operates uniformly and equally upon all brought within the circumstances for which it provides, it is not a local or special law. On the other hand, a law is special legislation if it confers particular privileges or disabilities upon a class of persons arbitrarily selected from a larger group of persons, all of whom stand in the same relation to the privileges or disabilities. ***

¶ 13 Class legislation may be constitutional if the class established is germane to the purpose of the law and is characterized by some special qualities or attributes which reasonably render the legislation necessary. In other words, if the classification is reasonable and the law operates equally upon every person or thing within the given class, it is not unconstitutional. Reasonable classifications of persons will be upheld against a special legislation challenge. A presumption exists in favor of a law being constitutional and the classification being reasonable.

¶ 14 Section 27-1-710(6), MCA, does set up a class: those who seek to recover from a person or entity who furnished alcohol to a visibly intoxicated person who later caused an injury. This does not mean the statute is unconstitutional. It is constitutional if the established class is reasonable and treats all those equally that are within the class.

¶ 15 At common law, a purveyor of alcohol could not be held liable for injuries caused to a third party by his intoxicated patron or guest. The reason behind this rule was the idea that the consumption, rather than the furnishing of the alcoholic beverage, proximately caused the injury. However, in *Nehring v. LaCounte* (Mont. 1986), this Court held that to exempt a purveyor of alcohol from liability without regard to his own negligence or fault was a Neanderthal approach to dram shop liability and rejected the common law rule.

¶ 16 After *Nehring*, the Legislature enacted § 27-1-710, MCA, commonly referred to as the Dram Shop Act, with the stated purpose to set statutory criteria governing the liability of a person or entity that furnishes an alcoholic beverage for injury or damage arising from an event involving the person who consumed the beverage. Section 27-1-710(1), MCA. In 2003, the Fifty-eighth Legislature enacted subsection (6) of the statute, adding the 180-day notice requirement the Rohlfs now attack.

¶ 17 In this instance, the legislative history reveals what motivated the Legislature to add the notice provision in question. In summary, the proponents of the notice requirement testified it is oftentimes difficult, if not impossible, to gather and preserve evidence concerning an event where a potential defendant was not present and may not be aware created potential liability. The legislators were also told that insurance coverage for liability created by the Dram Shop Act was not readily available because the gathering of evidence and location of witnesses was difficult. The Legislature accepted these arguments, and in its wisdom decided the 180-day notice requirement was appropriate to help alleviate the problem. Thus, it adopted subsection (6) to fix a time within which notice of a claim must be given, so that recollections are reasonably intact and witnesses are still available.

¶ 18 The dissent passionately disagrees with the Legislature's policy decision to create a class of tort defendants that serve alcohol and then establish a shorter period within which members of that class may commence a lawsuit. However, the fact finding process and motivation of legislative bodies is entitled to a presumption of regularity and deferential review by the judiciary. It is not the function of the courts to second-guess the legislature and substitute their judgment on the policy of limiting the ability to bring suit against one who furnishes alcoholic beverages. Adherence to this principle is not fawning or groveling before the legislature, it is respect for the role of the policymaking body in our system of government. The courts are limited to a determination of whether it is reasonable to differentiate between the classes created by the legislation in question. Here, those classes are tort claims against a defendant directly involved in the incident causing damage and those where the defendant is not present and may not be aware that an incident occurred until being served with a complaint.

¶ 19 The class created under § 27-1-710(6), MCA—plaintiffs who utilize a statutory scheme to bring an action against a defendant that is not immediately aware it may be held liable—is germane to the purpose of requiring members of this class notify a potential defendant of their claim. This class of plaintiffs is characterized by the special nature of the Dram Shop Act, which creates a statutory claim that arises even though defendants may not be aware they are alleged to have caused an injury. The notice provision operates equally upon every person who seeks redress under the Dram Shop Act, be it against a bartender, a tavern owner, a club or organization holding some sort of an event, or a social host who has friends to dinner. The wisdom of the notice requirement of § 27-1-710(6), MCA, is subject to debate. However, it operates uniformly and equally upon all brought within the circumstances for which it provides. ***

¶ 21 Issue 2: Is § 27-1-710(6), MCA, unconstitutional as a violation of equal protection of the law required by Article II, Section 4, of the Montana Constitution?

¶ 22 Article II, Section 4, of the Montana Constitution guarantees that "[n]o person shall be denied the equal protection of the laws." The Rohlfs contend that § 27-1-710(6), MCA, denies them equal protection of the law because it unconstitutionally imposes a burden on plaintiffs who bring suit under the Dram Shop Act that is not imposed on other general negligence plaintiffs. ***

¶ 30 The Rohlfs ignore the fact that the entirety of § 27-1-710, MCA, applies not only to tavern owners, but to all who might give or sell an alcoholic beverage to another. They argue the Legislature has no rational basis for requiring them to give notice to Stumble Inn within 180 days of serving alcohol to Warren because the proposition that tavern owners somehow have more difficulty preserving potential witness testimony than other negligence defendants is fundamentally flawed. The Rohlfs claim the fundamental flaw is that the Legislature was presented with insufficient evidence that tavern owners have more difficulty locating witnesses and preserving evidence than other defendants in civil actions. According to the Rohlfs, § 27-1-710(6), MCA, is really a gratuitous windfall for the tavern industry. ***

¶ 33 It cannot be gainsaid that the government has a legitimate interest in establishing rules for the conduct of litigation and in setting periods of limitation for particular types of claims. See Title 27, Chapter 2, MCA, Statutes of Limitations. While it is not necessary that the rationale behind a particular statute be apparent on its face in order for it to pass constitutional muster, in this case the rationale is known. In an action under the Dram Shop Act, the plaintiff has the burden of proof. Nevertheless, the plaintiff has immediate knowledge of the incident and the ability to begin an investigation and preserve evidence. On the other hand, the defendant most likely was not present at the incident and may not know an incident occurred. The people's representatives determined it is appropriate that a potential defendant should have notice of a possible claim within six months, so that he, she, or it could, like a plaintiff, locate witnesses and preserve potential evidence. There is a rational basis for the 180-day notice requirement.

¶ 34 Other special periods of limitation have survived an equal protection challenge. In a discrimination context, this Court held that 180-day statute of limitations was a rational way preventing stale claims and ensuring that claims are filed before essential evidence disappears. Concerning medical malpractice claims by a minor, this Court held that a statute of limitations that applied only to minors had a rational basis and did not violate Article II, Section 4 — the equal protection clause of the Montana Constitution.

¶ 35 We conclude that § 27-1-710(6), MCA, is rationally related to a legitimate government purpose and therefore does not violate Article II, Section 4, of the Montana Constitution.

Justice BRIAN MORRIS concurs.

*** ¶ 40 I would have been willing to consider an as applied challenge to the notice provision in light of the fact that the principals of Klemenhagen, L.L.C. d/b/a Stumble Inn likely had actual knowledge of the accident and its role in serving alcohol to Warren in the 11 hours preceding the accident almost immediately after the accident. Rohlfs's formal notice under § 27-1-710(6), MCA, simply would have informed these principals what they already knew. The principals likely could not have demonstrated prejudice from the Rohlfs's failure to comply strictly with the notice provision under those circumstances. Compliance with the notice provision under those circumstances would have been a useless act. It is axiomatic that "neither law nor equity require useless acts."

Justice W. WILLIAM LEAPHART, dissenting.

¶ 41 I dissent. As the Court's opinion notes, the purpose of § 27-1-710(6), MCA, is to provide a purveyor of alcohol notice of a potential claim arising out of an incident at which the purveyor "most likely was not present." Opinion, ¶ 33. Under the facts of the present case, it is clear that the Stumble Inn was, in fact, on notice of the incident. . . . ***

Justice PATRICIA O. COTTER dissents.

*** ¶ 45 I write to address the notice provision from the perspective of the victim. . . . It bears repeating that Article V, Section 12 of the Montana Constitution provides that the Legislature shall not pass a special act "when a general act is, or can be made, applicable." For the many decades before this notice provision came into being, the statutes of limitations operated generally, uniformly, and successfully upon all tort victims, regardless of whether their injuries stemmed from negligence or recklessness. There is absolutely nothing in the legislative history demonstrating that the general act could no longer "be made applicable" to the particular class of persons victimized by overserved intoxicated persons. If Article V, Section 12 is to mean anything, it must mean that if the general law works, then no special act should be passed. The general law has always worked; therefore, the Legislature violated this constitutional precept when it passed a special act disadvantaging victims of overserved drunk drivers.

¶ 46 The notice provision is plainly unconstitutional special legislation. I would therefore reverse the order of the District Court and remand this case for trial on its merits. I dissent from our refusal to do so.

Justice JAMES C. NELSON, dissenting.

¶ 47 . . . The 180-day notice provision of § 27-1-710(6), MCA, is unconstitutional special legislation, plain and simple. The 2003 Legislature admittedly bestowed this privilege on a small subset of negligence defendants — those who allegedly served alcoholic beverages to underage or visibly intoxicated consumers — so that these defendants would have a special defense to civil claims which other, similarly situated negligence defendants do not have. Conversely, those who are injured by these defendants' negligent conduct have an extra burden in obtaining a remedy — a burden which other, similarly situated plaintiffs do not have. This is quintessential special legislation; and in holding otherwise, the Court "gives mere lip service" to the constitutional provisions and then "twists the provisions . . . to reach the desired conclusion" that legislation specially enacted to give special protection to an apparently special group is not "special" itself. ***

¶ 50 [T]o the point of the Rohlfs' constitutional challenge, there is no evidence anywhere in the record supporting the proposition that alcohol purveyors have a special need (in comparison to similarly situated tort defendants) to know that they are going to be sued so that they might gather evidence and interview witnesses. In point of fact, Stumble Inn was in a better position to know that it might be sued and to prepare its defense than a distant tire manufacturer would have been had the accident been caused by defective tires. Yet, while the Rohlfs could hold the tire manufacturer responsible for placing a defective product in the stream of commerce, they are denied their right to hold Stumble Inn responsible for loading up its patron with alcohol for eleven hours and then unleashing him on unsuspecting motorists. Stumble Inn will certainly be delighted to learn that this Court has endorsed the special legislation mandating this result. ***

¶ 101 Here, the Rohlfs cite Article V, Section 12 of Montana's 1972 Constitution in arguing that the 180-day notice provision is unconstitutional. This provision states that "[t]he legislature shall not pass a special or local act when a general act is, or can be made, applicable." Article V, Section 26 of Montana's 1889 Constitution contained a substantially similar prohibition.

¶ 102 A special statute is

> one which relates to particular persons or things of a class, or one made for individual cases and for less than a class, or one which relates and applies to particular members of a class, either particularized by the express terms of the Act or separated by any method of selection from the whole class to which the law might, but for such limitation, be applicable.

State ex rel. Redman v. Meyers (Mont. 1922); *accord Lowery v. Garfield County* (Mont. 1949). Unconstitutional class legislation "includes all laws that rest upon some false or deficient classification, and the vice in such laws is that they do not embrace all of the class to which they are naturally related." "It is not, therefore, what a law includes, but what it excludes, that determines whether it is special." A law makes an improper discrimination if it confers particular privileges or imposes peculiar disabilities upon a class of persons arbitrarily selected from a larger number of persons all of whom stand in the same relation to the privileges conferred or the disabilities imposed. Special laws are objectionable "for not extending to the whole subject to which their provisions would be equally applicable, and thus permitting a diversity of laws relating to the same subject."

¶ 103 In *Redman*, this Court struck down § 1038, RCM (1921), as special legislation. Section 1038 stated that all school districts which have been or may be divided by the creation of a new county under the New County Acts are joint school districts subject to the laws relating to the management and control of joint school districts. Section 1038 operated only upon existing districts divided by the creation of new counties, and only such new counties as had been or might be created under the New County Acts. It excluded from its operation all existing districts which had been or might be divided by the creation of new counties by direct legislative enactment. But the fact that § 1038 applied only to some school districts did not necessarily render it invalid. Rather, the question was whether the law "operate[d] equally upon all of a group of objects which, having regard to the purpose of the legislature, are distinguished by characteristics sufficiently marked and important to make them a class by themselves." Applying this test, the Court observed that

> [t]here is not any difference in the situation or circumstances of a school district divided by the creation of a new county under the New County Acts and one divided by the creation of a new county by direct legislative enactment. The first is included in the operation of section 1038, and the last is excluded, apparently without any reason, and in the absence of anything which distinguishes the excluded districts from those included.... Section 1038 is a special statute under all of the authorities, and the attempted classification found in it is purely arbitrary and artificial.

The Court further concluded that a general law could be made applicable: the general statute for the creation of joint school districts. Thus, the Court held that § 1038 was void.

¶ 104 In *Lowery*, this Court likewise struck down Chapter 100, Laws of 1943, as special legislation. Under § 9024, RCM (1935), a party claiming adverse possession must show that the land has been occupied and claimed continuously for a period of ten years and that the party or her predecessors, during such period, have paid all taxes levied upon said land. For those claiming right under a tax deed, however, Chapter 100 reduced the period of possession by eight years and eliminated the requirement that taxes be paid during the period of adverse possession. After reciting the rules for determining whether a statute is special legislation, the Court concluded that

> Chapter 100, Laws of 1943, is clearly a special law. It applies to certain persons and individuals and leaves all others in the same circumstances subject to the provisions of the general statute on adverse possession. The right of the legislature to shorten the Statute of Limitations for the period of adverse possession is not questioned but it must apply to all classes claiming adversely and the same requirements during the period of adverse possession must be required of all persons and classes.

¶ 105 The 180-day notice provision is unconstitutional for the same reasons the *Redman* and *Lowery* statutes were. First, as to the classification at issue here, Stumble Inn argues that we should define the class narrowly as just "those persons that might be impacted by alcohol service claims." Essentially, Stumble Inn would define the class as dram-shop plaintiffs and defendants. Stumble Inn then argues that because all such plaintiffs are equally disadvantaged by the notice provision, and because all such defendants are equally benefited by it, the provision is not special legislation. This approach, however, is pure sophistry. If the relevant class for special legislation analysis were simply the class encompassed by the legislation, then a special legislation challenge would never succeed. Notably, we rejected this same approach in *Oberson v. U.S. Dept. of Agriculture* (Mont. 2007), where the Forest Service argued that the "legislature here treated all snowmobilers identically, and thus created no distinction or classification that warrants equal protection review." We noted that the general class is defined as those who are similarly situated with respect to the governmental purpose. The statute at issue in *Oberson* sought to prevent frivolous lawsuits by immunizing snowmobile area operators from the inherent risks of the sport over which the operator had no control. Yet, all operators who provide a venue for an inherently dangerous sport are similarly situated with respect to the mischief the statute proposed to remedy. Thus, we held that the snowmobile liability statute classified snowmobile area operators and snowmobilers and treated them differently from other similarly situated groups.

¶ 106 Here, the purpose of the law is to alert an otherwise unaware dram-shop defendant that an accident for which he may bear some liability has occurred within the previous six months and that the victim intends to sue. That way, the defendant knows to interview witnesses before they disappear or their memories degrade, to gather and preserve evidence, and to prepare a defense. Given this purpose, I agree with the Court's observation that the 180-day notice provision distinguishes defendants directly involved in the incident causing damage from defendants who are not present and may not be aware that an incident occurred until being served with a complaint.

¶ 107 The question, then, is whether the 180-day notice provision "embrace[s] all of the class to which [it is] naturally related" or whether it "confers particular privileges or imposes peculiar disabilities upon a class of persons arbitrarily selected from a larger number of persons all of whom stand in the same relation to the privileges conferred or the disabilities imposed." As noted, a variety of tort defendants are similarly situated with respect to the mischief the 180-day notice provision proposes to remedy. Product manufacturers and slip-and-fall defendants, as well as snowmobile area operators, are but three examples of defendants who are "not present and may not be aware that an incident occurred until being served with a complaint." Yet, the 180-day notice provision does not embrace these defendants. These defendants, rather, are subject to the generally applicable statute of limitations and do not enjoy the benefit of a 180-day notice provision. Conversely, the plaintiffs in those cases are not subject to the added notice requirement. It must also be reiterated here that no evidence was presented to the Legislature substantiating the tavern industry's claim that alcohol purveyors are in a class of their own vis-à-vis the difficulties in defending against a claim arising out of an incident at which the defendant was not present.

¶ 108 In sum, the 180-day notice provision applies to certain persons and entities and leaves all others in the same circumstances subject to the provisions of the general statute of limitations.... The notice provision classifies dram-shop defendants and confers on them a special privilege not enjoyed by similarly situated defendants. Conversely, it imposes a peculiar disability on a class of persons (dram-shop plaintiffs) arbitrarily selected from a larger group of similarly situated persons (plaintiffs injured by absent defendants who are unaware of the incident). Yet, there is no evidence that the three-year statute of limitations generally applicable to all such absent defendants cannot be made applicable to dram-shop defendants. I consequently would hold that the notice provision is unconstitutional special legislation in violation of Article V, Section 12.

¶ 109 In reaching the opposite conclusion, the Court's analysis founders due largely to the Court's confusion about the class at issue here. Initially, the Court correctly identifies the class as tort plaintiffs bringing claims against defendants who were not present at the injury-causing incident and, thus, may not be aware that the incident occurred until being served with a complaint. But then the Court defines the class narrowly as tort plaintiffs seeking redress under the Dram Shop Act. Based on this latter classification, the Court reasons that because all dram-shop plaintiffs are "uniformly and equally" disadvantaged by the notice provision, the provision is not special legislation. This approach is incorrect for two reasons.

¶ 110 First, the Court errs by defining the class in such a fashion as to yield a self-sustaining classification — i.e., by defining the class as those who are burdened by the challenged law and then upholding the law because it discriminates against all of these people "uniformly and equally." Our caselaw makes clear that the relevant class consists of all persons who are similarly situated with respect to the law's purpose.... The relevant class here, therefore, is not dram-shop plaintiffs; it is all tort plaintiffs injured by an absent defendant who is unaware of the injury-causing incident. The notice provision arbitrarily singles out dram-shop plaintiffs and treats them differently from these similarly situated tort plaintiffs.

¶ 111 Second, the Court's approach is based on the fundamentally mistaken proposition that a cause of action against a purveyor of alcoholic beverages is "a statutory claim" or "utilize[s] a statutory scheme." As explained above, dram-shop liability developed under the common law. Thus, a plaintiff does not "seek[] redress under the Dram Shop Act." Rather, a dram-shop claim is simply a common law negligence action against a purveyor of alcoholic beverages. *** Thus, the Court's premise in ¶ 19 that dram-shop plaintiffs are somehow a class of their own because they are utilizing a statutory scheme is incorrect, and the entire foundation of the Court's special legislation analysis crumbles—as it should. The 180-day notice provision is special legislation. ***

¶ 113 Stumble Inn served alcoholic beverages to a visibly intoxicated patron who then got into his car and, a quick 157 feet of burnt rubber later, smashed into Cary Rohlfs, causing Cary serious injuries. Stumble Inn knew about the accident; Stumble Inn knew that its patron was involved; Stumble Inn knew (or should have known) that Cary might sue the tavern for its negligent conduct; and Stumble Inn knew (or should have known) that it needed to start interviewing witnesses and preserving evidence. Stumble Inn does not contend that it is unable to mount a defense to the Rohlfs' claims. Rather, Stumble Inn seeks to deny the Rohlfs their day in court, and seeks to avoid having to answer for its actions, simply because the Rohlfs did not mail a notice of intent to sue within 180 days of the accident. The Rohlfs' observation that § 27-1-710(6), MCA, is "a gratuitous windfall for the tavern industry" is well-taken on the facts presented here.

¶ 114 The Court characterizes the lawmakers who enacted the 180-day notice provision as the "people's representatives." It is doubtful that the Rohlfs and other victims of drunk drivers will share this view; more likely, they will view them as the "alcohol purveyor's representatives." As the historical account of dram-shop liability reveals, the Legislature has readily obliged the tavern industry's demands (and those of certain event sponsors, such as the Montana Chamber of Commerce, the Helena Chamber of Commerce, the Montana University System, and Downtown Helena, Inc.) for exemptions from the common law rules of negligence applicable to everyone else. Indeed, the tavern industry and its supporters have been immensely successful in stemming the tide of modern tort doctrine with legislatively conferred privileges and immunities over the past 24 years. And with each new special protection, the accountability of those who sell or furnish intoxicating beverages lessens and the law governing dram-shop liability concomitantly regresses. Indeed, the present policy of protecting purveyors of alcohol at the expense of the victims of drunk drivers can only be characterized as "Neanderthal." ***

¶ 117 The 180-day notice provision is "a protection bill" for those in the business of dispensing alcoholic beverages. It is a "back-eddy" running counter to the mainstream of modern tort doctrine. But most of all, it is special legislation benefiting and burdening a discrete group of persons while leaving all other similarly situated persons subject only to the provisions of the generally applicable statute of limitations. The Rohlfs have met their burden of making a "plain showing of unconstitutionality." . . .

Notes on Special Legislation

1. Although the 1972 Voter Information Pamphlet indicated the 20-word draft of Article V, section 12 presented "[n]o change except in grammar," it condensed an 1889 provision that ran thirty times longer:

> The legislative assembly shall not pass local or special laws in any of the following enumerated cases, that is to say: For granting divorces; laying out, opening altering or working roads or highways; vacating roads, town plats, streets, alleys or public grounds; locating or changing county seats; regulating county or township affairs; regulating the practice in courts of justice; regulating the jurisdiction and duties of justices of the peace, police magistrates or constables; changing the rules of evidence in any trial or inquiry; providing for changes of venue in civil or criminal cases; declaring any person of age; for limitation of civil actions, or giving effect to informal or invalid deeds; summoning or impaneling grand or petit juries; providing for the management of common schools; regulating the rate of interest on money; the opening or conducting of any election or designating the place of voting; the sale or mortgage of real estate belonging to minors or others under disability; chartering or licensing ferries or bridges or toll roads; chartering banks, insurance companies and loan and trust companies; remitting fines, penalties or forfeitures; creating, increasing or decreasing fees, percentages or allowances of public officers; changing the law of descent; granting to any corporation, association or individual the right to lay down railroad tracks, or any special or exclusive privilege, immunity or franchise whatever; for the punishment of crimes; changing the names of persons or places; for the assessment or collection of taxes; affecting estates of deceased persons, minors or others under legal disabilities; extending the time for the collection of taxes; re-funding money paid into the State treasury; relinquishing or extinguishing in whole or in part the indebtedness, liability or obligation of any corporation or person to this State, or to any municipal corporation therein; exempting property from taxation; restoring to citizenship persons convicted of infamous crimes; authorizing the creation, extension or impairing of liens; creating offices, or prescribing the powers of duties of officers in counties, cities, township or school districts; or authorizing the adoption or legitimation of children. In all other cases where a general law can be made applicable, no special law shall be enacted.

In *Article V, Section 12 of the Montana Constitution: Restoring Meaning to a Forgotten Provision*, 79 MONT. L. REV. 115 (2018), Constance Van Kley puts the provision in context:

> The text of the 1889 provision reveals two patterns. First, some prohibitions provide for the separation of powers, both vertically—giving local governments greater control over local affairs—and horizontally—preventing the Legislature from doing the work of the court. These provisions are largely

> unnecessary in modern Montana.... Second, the provision restricts legislation passed in favor of the politically powerful. Some of these enumerated restrictions are highly specific.... Unlike the first category of enumerated restrictions, the concerns reflected in this second group remain relevant today.

What would a reinvigorated special legislation doctrine look like?

2. In *Grossman*, the Court rejected a special legislation challenge to the water development bonding bill:

> We would be skirting the issue if we did not readily admit that the effect of §§ 5 and 6, Ch. 705, Laws of Montana (1983), is special or local. The 22 projects authorized for loans under the bond program by the legislation relate to particular municipalities or particular governmental subdivisions on the basis of individual cases for less than a class and apply to particular members of a class particularized by the express terms of the act. Thus the sections seem to come within the definition of "special law...." Yet we do not find §§ 5 and 6, Ch. 705, Laws of Montana (1983), to be special or local acts which are prohibited by Art. V, § 12.
>
> It is important to realize that the language of 1972 Mont. Const., Art. V, § 12, is not absolutely prohibitory. The legislature is enjoined from passing a special or local act only when a general act is or can be made applicable. We cannot imagine how the legislature could draft a general act of state-wide application providing for the issuance and sale of revenue bonds and at the same time keep a handle on the way the bond proceeds are to be spent or loaned except through its direct authorization of projects. ***

3. How is a court to distinguish whether a legislature's enactment of a special law is deserving of deference? For a famous example of such deference, *Grossman* cited *Hotel Dorset Company v. Trust for Cultural Resources of City of New York* (N.Y. 1978), which upheld "a legislative act which provided support for financially troubled museums in the state of New York" despite the fact "it benefited only the Museum of Modern Art in the City of New York." In a passage quoted in *Grossman*, the New York Court of Appeals held:

> If the subject matter of the legislation is of sufficient importance to the State generally, the legislation cannot be deemed a local law even though it deals directly with the affairs of the municipality. This has been an accepted principle for many years, and there is ample showing from the legislative findings alone that the maintenance of cultural institutions is a State concern. *** We should not strain ourselves to find illegality in such programs. The problems of a modern city can never be solved unless arrangements like these ... are upheld, unless they are patently illegal ...

Compare Anderson v. Bd. of Comm'rs of Cloud County (Kan. 1908):

> The inherent vice of special laws is that they create preferences and establish irregularities. As an inevitable consequence, their enactment leads to

improvident and ill-considered legislation. The members whose particular constituents are not affected by a proposed special law become indifferent to its passage. It is customary, on the plea of legislative courtesy, not to interfere with the local bill of another member; and members are elected, and re-elected, on account of their proficiency in procuring for their respective districts special privileges in the way of local or special laws. The time which the Legislature would otherwise devote to the consideration of measures of public importance is frittered away in the granting of special favors to private or corporate interests or to local communities. Meanwhile, in place of a symmetrical body of statutory law on subjects of general and common interest to the whole people, we have a wilderness of special provisions, whose operation extends no further than the boundaries of the particular school district or township or county to which they were made to apply. For performing the same services the sheriff or register of deeds or probate judge of one county receives an entirely different compensation from that received by the same officer of another county. The people of one community of the state are governed, as to many subjects, by laws wholly different from those which apply to other localities. Worse still, rights and privileges, which should only result from the decree of a court of competent jurisdiction after a full hearing and notice to all parties in interest, are conferred upon individuals and private corporations by special acts of the Legislature, without any pretense of investigation as to merits, or of notice to adverse parties.

Commenting upon the evils of special legislation, Mr. Samuel P. Orth, in the Atlantic Monthly for January, 1906 (volume 97, p. 69), uses this language: "The Romans recognized the distinction between private bills and laws. To them special laws were *privilegia* or *constitutionis privelegia*. In England they used to say, when a public bill was passed: '*Le roi le veut*'—it is the king's wish; and of a private measure: '*Soit fait comme il est désire*'—let it be granted as prayed for. Here is the gist of the matter: A public law is a measure that affects the welfare of the state as a unit; a private law is one that provides an exception to the public rule. The one is an answer to a public need, the other an answer to a private prayer. When it acts upon a public bill, a Legislature legislates; when it acts upon a private bill, it adjudicates. It passes from the function of a lawmaker to that of a judge. It is transformed from a tribune of the people into a justice shop for the seeker after special privilege.

See also Benderson Development Co. v. Sciortino (Va. 1988):

It is true that for a long period of our history, the Equal Protection clause was interpreted by both federal and state courts in language that bore marked similarities to the analysis we made of statutes under the special-laws prohibition contained in the Virginia Constitution. But the two are not the same. The Fourteenth Amendment to the Federal Constitution, of

> which the Equal Protection clause is a part, was declared ratified in 1868, during the period of Reconstruction. Its purpose was the prevention of racial discrimination by state legislatures. Although it was, in later years, extended to apply to other kinds of state legislation, the Supreme Court of the United States has, based upon considerations of federalism, been markedly deferential to state laws which make economic classifications, when those laws have been challenged on Equal Protection grounds.... By contrast, the special-laws prohibitions contained in the Virginia Constitution are aimed squarely at economic favoritism, and have been so since their inception. *** Their purpose was to correct the perception that the General Assembly, in the nineteenth century, devoted an excessive amount of its time to the furtherance of private interests, and to counter the "sway that moneyed interests were seen to hold over state legislatures at the turn of the century."

Several cases considered in this chapter frame allegedly special-interest legislation as equal protection issues rather than special legislation or public purpose issues. In Chapter 10, we'll see how rational basis review under equal protection in Montana can have surprising "bite" in a few areas, but generally the courts defer to legislative assessments of the public interest. If special-interest legislation—the kind that worried Madison and, perhaps, Montana's constitutional framers—is pervasive, is this a reason for courts (or conscientious legislators) to restore meaning to the "special legislation" prohibition, or to leave politics to the "political" branches?

4. One justification offered for judicial deference to legislatures, even under constitutional provisions that expressly call for inquiries into whether laws serve public purposes or special interests, is the apparently superior "democratic pedigree" of legislatures relative to courts. *See, e.g., State ex rel. Dean v. Brandjord* (Mont. 1939) ("In the Constitution the people of Montana, wisely or not, entrusted the appropriation power to the legislature, since it is the branch closest to the people."). As we'll see in Chapter 5, however, the "countermajoritarian difficulty" associated with judicial review does not translate directly from federal to state constitutional discourse, because in Montana, as in many states, state judges are elected at the statewide and district levels. More generally, due to partisan entrenchment and various foreseeable distortions in legislative elections, state legislatures may not be particularly representative of "the people" relative to the executive and judicial branches, or to local governments. If these other officials enjoy at least as much popular legitimacy as a legislature, should state courts decrease their deference to state legislatures and reassess the doctrines of legislative limits explored in this and later chapters, such as non-delegation, local government powers, and election rules? *See* Miriam Seifter, *Countermajoritarian Legislatures*, 121 COLUM. L. REV. 1733 (2021).

Chapter 4

Executive Powers

Article III, Section 1. Separation of powers. The power of the government of this state is divided into three distinct branches — legislative, executive, and judicial. No person or persons charged with the exercise of power properly belonging to one branch shall exercise any power properly belonging to either of the others, except as in this constitution expressly directed or permitted.

Identical to 1889 constitution except for substitution of the word "branches" for "departments". This distinguishes the three branches of government from the 20 departments in the executive branch.

Article VI, Section 4. Duties. (1) The executive power is vested in the governor who shall see that the laws are faithfully executed. He shall have such other duties as are provided in this constitution and by law.

(2) The lieutenant governor shall perform the duties provided by law and those delegated to him by the governor. No power specifically vested in the governor by this constitution may be delegated to the lieutenant governor.

(3) The secretary of state shall maintain official records of the executive branch and of the acts of the legislature, as provided by law. He shall keep the great seal of the state of Montana and perform any other duties provided by law.

(4) The attorney general is the legal officer of the state and shall have the duties and powers provided by law.

(5) The superintendent of public instruction and the auditor shall have such duties as are provided by law.

Only change is subsection (2), which is a new provision allowing legislature to make lieutenant governor full time. Deletes provision that lieutenant governor be president of senate.

Perhaps the single greatest difference between federal and state constitutional structures is the divided executive at the state level. In the federal government, Article II, section 1 specifies "[t]he executive Power shall be vested in a President of the United States of America." State constitutions, originally shaped by revolts against the colonial governor, not only shifted power from the executive to the legislature but also diffused executive power across multiple officials.

Given the divided executive and an express separation of powers requirement, power conflicts can arise along several dimensions. The first is familiar to students of the federal Constitution, and involves improper "horizontal" exercise of one branch's powers by another (for example, the executive by the legislative or vice versa). The second occurs "vertically" or "diagonally" within a branch or across branches under non-delegation rules, such as when the legislature delegates its policymaking or appropriations authority to an executive branch official (*see White v. State*, in Chapter 3). The third is unique to the divided executive, when one executive branch officer comes into conflict with another officer or board (such as the Board of Regents).

Montana's executive branch is divided among five independent statewide officers. As the Montana Constitution contemplates, the Legislature has by law provided various duties to executive officers. For example, the Governor's powers and duties include:

> **2-15-201. Powers and duties of governor.** (1) In addition to the duties prescribed by the constitution, the governor shall:
>
> (a) supervise the official conduct of all executive and ministerial officers;
>
> (b) ensure that all offices are filled and that the duties of the offices are performed or, in default of the performance, apply a remedy that the law allows. If the remedy is imperfect, the governor shall acquaint the legislature with the issue at its next session. ***
>
> (3) The governor is the sole official organ of communication between the government of this state and the government of any other state or of the United States.
>
> (4) Whenever any suit or legal proceeding is pending against this state that may affect the title of this state to any property or that may result in any claim against the state, the governor may direct the attorney general to appear on behalf of the state and may employ additional counsel that the governor may judge expedient.
>
> (5) The governor may require the attorney general or the county attorney of any county to inquire into the affairs or management of any corporation existing under the laws of this state.
>
> (6) The governor may require the attorney general to aid the county attorney in the discharge of the county attorney's duties. ***
>
> (10) The governor may require any officer or board to make special reports, upon demand, in writing. ***

The Attorney General's general duties include:

> **2-15-501. General duties.** It is the duty of the attorney general:
>
> (1) to prosecute or defend all causes in the supreme court in which the state or any officer of the state in the officer's official capacity is a party or in which the state has an interest; ***
>
> (5) to exercise supervisory powers over county attorneys in all matters pertaining to the duties of their offices and from time to time require of

them reports as to the condition of public business entrusted to their charge. The supervisory powers granted to the attorney general by this subsection include the power to order and direct county attorneys in all matters pertaining to the duties of their office....

(6) when required by the public service or directed by the governor, to assist the county attorney of any county in the discharge of the county attorney's duties or to prosecute or defend appropriate cases in which the state or any officer of the state in the officer's official capacity is a party or in which the state has an interest;

(7) to give an opinion in writing, without fee, to the legislature or either house of the legislature, to any state officer, board, or commission, to any county attorney, to the city attorney of any city or town, or to the board of county commissioners of any county of the state when required upon any question of law relating to their respective offices.... [T]he attorney general's opinion is controlling unless overruled by a state district court or the supreme court. ***

Although the executive officers commonly come from different parties, major legal disputes between them are rare. Open conflicts, when they occur, typically arise from their work together as the Board of Land Commissioners, a constitutional body charged with administering state trust lands for the benefit of schools. Sharper divisions have arisen in other states with similarly divided executives. As you read the following materials, consider whether and how a divided executive enhances or diminishes the efficacy and accountability of executive functions in state government.

A. The Divided Executive Branch

William Marshall is a law professor who in practice has served as legal counsel to both a state attorney general and a President. Here, he explores the characteristic dynamics of the divided executive in state governments, which he develops into a critique of "unitary executive" arguments and a proposal for an independent federal attorney general.

William Marshall, *Break up the Presidency? Governors, State Attorneys General, and Lessons from the Divided Executive*

115 Yale L.J. 2446, 2451–52, 2467–68 (2006)

As the nation matured, many states created independent attorneys general and afforded the Office even greater autonomy by making it a popularly elected position. Again, the states' purpose was to weaken the power of a central chief executive and further an intrabranch system of checks and balances. Thus, the Minnesota Supreme Court observed, in reference to the state's 1851 constitution, that:

> Rather than conferring all executive authority upon a governor, the drafters of our constitution divided the executive powers of state government among six elected officers. This was a conscious effort on the part of the drafters, who were well aware of the colonial aversion to royal governors who possessed unified executive powers.

Accordingly, as the nineteenth century unfurled, most new states provided in their constitutions for the popular election of an attorney general (and other executive branch officials) while many of the established states amended their constitutions to the same end. As a result of this trend, at present, forty-three state attorneys general are elected and forty-eight are free from gubernatorial control. Notably, no state has reversed direction and made its Attorney General subservient to the Governor. ***

The . . . state experience with the divided executive and the independent Attorney General hold a number of lessons. First, as its architects intended, the divided executive model disperses power and checks executive branch excess. Second, under the divided executive, the Office of the Attorney General is, or can be, appropriately independent of gubernatorial control. Neither ethical constraints nor structural concerns, properly understood, demand that the Attorney General exclusively represent the Governor's interests. Third, by insulating the Attorney General's legal authority from gubernatorial control, the divided executive protects against executive branch overreaching by dedicating an executive officer to uphold the rule of law. Additionally, as the example of intrabranch litigation suggests, attorney general independence promotes fuller decision-making before governmental action by assuring consideration of a wider range of concerns than if the Governor acted alone. Fourth, the divided executive can be constructed to accommodate a variety of interests. A state, for example, may protect the right of an attorney general to exercise independent legal judgment against the Governor's position in a particular matter while still requiring the Attorney General to advance the interests of the Governor when her disagreement is based on pure policy or upon any other factor deemed to fit best within the final authority of the Governor. In this way, the Governor's prerogatives can be accommodated as well.

This then leads to a final lesson. The proponents of the federal unitary executive have argued that other structures are destined to fail because they would lead to weakened executives fraught with internal conflict and lack of accountability. The state experience has shown, however, that this has not occurred. After all, the divided executive has been the rule, rather than the exception, in virtually every state for most of the nation's history, yet there is little to suggest that it has created endemic dysfunction. The final lesson from the state experience with the divided executive, in short, is that, despite the doubts of the unitarians, the structure has been proven to work.

Bullock, Governor v. Fox, Attorney General

2019 MT 50

Chief Justice MIKE MCGRATH delivered the Opinion of the Court.

¶3 The parties do not dispute the facts. The sole dispute between the parties is a matter of law. The Attorney General believes that Montana law requires the Department of Fish, Wildlife and Parks (FWP) to seek final approval from the Board of Land Commissioners (Land Board) for conservation easement transactions pursuant to its Habitat Montana Program (Habitat Montana), while the Governor and FWP Director do not. ***

¶7 On September 18, 2017, the Land Board voted down an amendment to the Keogh Ranch Conservation Easement, and on February 20, 2018, the Land Board indefinitely postponed consideration of the approximately $6.1 million, 25,000-acre Horse Creek Conservation Easement near Wibaux, Montana. FWP did not resubmit the projects. Instead, Governor Bullock directed FWP to finalize the Horse Creek Conservation Easement without the Land Board's final approval. While § 87-1-209(1), MCA, requires final approval from the Land Board for "land acquisition involving more than 100 acres or $100,000 in value," Governor Bullock reasoned that "land acquisition" did not include conservation easement acquisition; Montana law did not obligate FWP to bring its conservation easement transactions before the Land Board.

¶8 On August 1, 2018, Senate President Scott Sales requested an Attorney General opinion as to whether § 87-1-209(1), MCA, required the Land Board's final approval on FWP's conservation easement transactions. On October 15, 2018, Timothy C. Fox, in his official capacity as Attorney General of Montana, issued an Opinion (A.G. Opinion) precluding FWP from finalizing conservation easement transactions of more than 100 acres or $100,000 in value without the Land Board's final approval.

¶9 While an A.G. opinion binds state agencies, an A.G. opinion does not bind the courts, which have the authority to overrule opinions incorrectly interpreting the law. This Court is not bound by an A.G. Opinion. Section 2-15-501 (7), MCA ("the attorney general's opinion is controlling unless overruled by a state district court or the supreme court"). ***

Historical Background: The Constitutional Convention of 1972

¶16 While the issues presented concern justiciability and statutory interpretation, full appreciation of this decision requires an understanding of the historical context preceding and enshrined in Montana's 1972 Constitution.

¶17 Montana became a state on November 8, 1889, operating under a constitution (1889 Constitution) hastily drafted with statehood in mind. "One interest above all dominated [the delegates to the 1889 Constitutional Convention's] thinking-the mining industry." At the time, Montana's politics revolved around copper, the railroad, timber, and the likes of Marcus Daly and William A. Clark. Private economic interests determined the language adopted in the 1889 Constitution, and set "the tenor of later contests, including a major battle in the Clark-Daly [f]eud and the cause of the scattering of state institutions."

¶18 In 1970, Montanans voted for a constitutional convention, and in 1972, one hundred delegates from across the State met in Helena, Montana, and embarked on creating a new constitution. Central to the 1972 Constitutional Convention (1972 Con Con) was a desire to re-organize the executive power, which according to the delegates, "had been whittled to insignificance by creation of more than 160 state agencies with little executive or legislative supervision," and to re-establish "the fundamental concept of checks and balances by separate branches of government." The delegates took on the "1889 Constitution's inherent contradiction — the delegation of executive power to the governor, yet restricting that power due to diffusion in Constitutional boards" — and clarified it.

The Constitution adopted by the 1972 Con Con and ratified by the people on June 6, 1972, provides, "[t]he executive power is vested in the governor who shall see that the laws are faithfully executed." Mont. Const. art. VI, § 4 (1). The drafters of this language commented:

> [Due to] the people having decisively voted to implement a well-ordered executive department of government in place of the 103 or more boards, bureaus, commissions, etc., it is clear that a strong and responsive chief executive is desired. W[e] have clarified his powers and duties accordingly.

The drafters further commented:

> Previously, the divided powers of boards of elective officials, such as the board of examiners, made a mockery of [the provision]: 'The supreme executive power of the state shall be vested in the governor, and shall see that the laws are faithfully executed.' The governor, under reorganization and in this article, has the responsibility and the accountability to the electorate and the legislature. This fundamental principle of delegation of power is an important breakthrough in the continuing effort for effective, responsible, viable and efficient government. The state's chief executive will be chief in fact, not in rhetoric.

¶20 The delegates determined that the attorney general would be an independent, elected officer of the executive. The Montana Constitution provides: "The attorney general is the legal officer of the state and shall have the duties and powers provided by law." Mont. Const. art. VI, § 4 (4). The drafters of this language noted, "[A]gain it is hoped this office will not be made a policy maker."

¶21 The Montana Constitution established the board of land commissioners (Land Board), consisting of the governor, superintendent of public instruction, auditor, secretary of state, and attorney general, with "the authority to direct, control, lease, exchange, and sell school lands and lands which have been or may be granted for the support and benefit of the various state educational institutions, under such regulations and restrictions as may be provided by law." Mont. Const. art. X, § 4.

¶22 It is with the historical context of the 1972 Con Con in mind that this Court determines whether the issue presented is justiciable and whether "land acquisition" per § 87-1-209(1), MCA, includes conservation easement acquisition. ***

¶29 Initially, the Attorney General argues that Governor Bullock and FWP Director Williams lack standing to sue in their official capacities because the Governor and FWP Director did not suffer concrete or personalized injuries. . . .

¶30 Case-or-controversy standing derives from Article VII, Section 4 (1), of the Montana Constitution, and Article III, Section 2, of the United States Constitution. Article VII, Section 4 (1), of the Montana Constitution, limits Montana courts to deciding "cases at law and in equity," while Article III, Section 2, of the United States Constitution, limit courts to deciding only "cases or controversies." This Court has said that federal precedent interpreting Article III, Section 2, of the United States Constitution, is persuasive authority for interpreting the justiciability requirements of Article VII, Section 4 (1), of the Montana Constitution. ***

¶33 Significantly, the Montana Constitution provides: "The executive power is vested in the governor who shall see that the laws are faithfully executed." Mont. Const. art. VI, § 4(1). A princip[al] objective of the 1972 Con Con was to produce a constitution vesting the executive power in the governor "in fact, not in rhetoric." To this end, the drafters of the 1972 Constitution were unequivocal. And this Court has held that the "Executive branch is ultimately the responsibility of the Governor," whose constitutional duty is "to see that the laws passed by the Legislature are properly executed" with history in mind. *MEA-MFT v. McCulloch*, 2012 MT 211.

¶34 Moreover, following the approval of the Montana Constitution in 1972, the Legislature passed the Executive Reorganization Act, § 2-15-101, et seq., MCA. In 1995, this Court held:

> the [c]onstitutional status of the governor as the State's chief executive officer and, subject only to the Constitution and other State laws, require the governor to formulate and administer the policies of the executive branch with 'full powers of supervision, approval, direction, and appointment over all departments and their units.'

State Pub. Employee's Ass'n v. Office of the Governor (Mont. 1995) (quoting § 2-15-103, MCA).

¶35 The Governor and FWP Director allege personal concrete injury sufficient to support standing because the A.G. Opinion precluded them from effectuating the constitutional and statutory duties of their respective offices. They contend only the Governor and FWP Director have the authority and ability to sign the papers closing the real estate transaction that creates a conservation easement pursuant to Habitat Montana. We agree. Their injuries are personal, concrete, and redressable. ***

¶47 Finally, the Attorney General cites *State ex rel. Olsen v. Pub. Serv. Comm'n* (Mont. 1955), arguing that it is the attorney general's exclusive prerogative "to control and manage all litigation on behalf of the state." However, the 1972 Constitution controls, stating "the attorney general is the legal officer of the state and shall have the duties and powers provided by law." Mont. Const. art. VI, § 4(4). The delegates to the 1972 Con Con noted the potential for conflict within the executive branch, and stated: "it is hoped [the Attorney General's] office will not be made a policy maker." *Convention Committee Proposal.*

¶48 Rather than usurp the Attorney General's constitutional authority, dismissal of this action for lack of standing would usurp the Governor's constitutional and statutory authority, and thus, Director Williams's statutory authority, effectively immunizing the A.G. Opinion from review. ***

¶63 This Court assumes original jurisdiction over the issue presented and finds the issue presented justiciable. The Governor and FWP Director have standing within prudential limits to petition this Court. The Court is well within the sphere of its constitutional authority to interpret the statutory meaning of § 87-1-209 (1), MCA. The plain and ordinary meaning of "land acquisition" does not encompass conservation easement acquisition, and § 87-1-209 (1), MCA, does not require FWP to finalize its conservation easement transactions with the Land Board.

Board of Regents of Higher Education v. Judge

168 Mont. 433 (1975)

CASTLES, Justice.

This is an original proceeding for a declaratory judgment brought by the Board of Regents of Higher Education of the State of Montana against the Governor of the State. The Board of Regents seeks definitive rulings on the constitutionality of two bills passed during the 1975 legislative session and signed into law by the Governor. House Bill 271 appropriates monies to the university system for the biennium. Senate Bill 401 provides for a legislative finance committee to approve budget amendments....

The Legislative Finance Committee and the Legislative Audit Committee of the Montana Legislative Assembly moved to intervene. Hereinafter these committees will be referred to in the singular as the Finance Committee. Such intervention was granted, and no challenge is made to the status of legislative committees as party litigants. The Associated Students of Montana State University and University of Montana were allowed to submit a brief and appear as amicus curiae. ***

The issues to be resolved in this action are as follows:

1) whether Section 1(3) of House Bill 271, in light of the provisions of Senate Bill 401 is an unconstitutional infringement on the powers and duties of the Board of Regents;

2) whether (a) the certification requirement contained in the origination clause of Section 12 of House Bill 271 is unconstitutional as an improper legislative infringement on the management authority of the Board of Regents, and (b) whether Section 12(6) of House Bill 271 is unconstitutional as a direct invasion of the

management prerogatives granted to the Board of Regents by Article X, Section 9 of the Montana Constitution. ***

Prior to discussing Issue No. 1, it will be helpful to give some background. House Bill 271 appropriates money to the university system for the biennium by various line items from various state operating funds. The Commissioner of Higher Education, the University of Montana, Montana State University, and the various other college units are each appropriated certain funds.

For example, the University of Montana is appropriated $17,782,106.00 for the year ending June 30, 1976, in ten line items [for "instruction," "research," "public service," "academic support," "student services," etc.], drawn from specified funds including the state general fund. . . .

[1. Legislative Finance Committee Approval of Regents Budget Amendments.]

H.B. 271 provides for budget amendment by the Regents whenever funds become available from sources outside the general fund for new or expanded programs, or in transfers of not more than 15% of any appropriation of a single unit of the university system to another unit, and expending balances remaining at the end of the first fiscal year during the second fiscal year.

Additional monies are appropriated by section 3 of H.B. 1, (Special Session) Laws of 1975, which adds an additional section to H.B. 271, Section 13 as previously quoted. The contingency of additional appropriations by budget amendments is taken from the Regents by definition in H.B. 271, Section 1(3), "Approved budget amendment' means approval by the board of regents *unless otherwise provided by law* ***.' (Emphasis supplied.)

S.B. 401 provides that no state agency shall expend in excess of an appropriation except under authority of a budget amendment approved by the legislative finance committee. Thus both by the section 13 amendment in the Special Session to H.B. 271 and by S.B. 401, the authority for budget amendments is in the legislative finance committee.

Thus, the question and conflict arises between the Regents and the legislative finance committee.

The Regents urge that line item appropriations of general fund monies by the legislature to the Board of Regents infringe on the authority of the Board granted by the Constitution of Montana 1972. Their position is hinged on this language contained in Article X, Section 9, 1972 Montana Constitution:

> (2)(a) The *government and control* of the Montana university system is vested in a board of regents of higher education which shall have *full power, responsibility, and authority to supervise, coordinate, manage and control* the Montana university system ***. (Emphasis supplied.)

The Regents . . . went so far as to state that indeed the university system and its Board of Regents was a fourth branch of government. In support of that construction, the

Regents note particular changes in the 1972 constitutional provision which, they insist, are indicative of the intent of the framers to vest complete control in the Regents to the exclusion of legislative and executive bodies.

First, the 1889 Constitution vested control and supervision in the state board of education, but limited its powers to those which "shall be prescribed and regulated by law." Art. XI, Sec. 11. Thus, the Regents urge that a board regulated by law is clearly under the control of the law-making body to some extent. The qualifying phrase is absent in the 1972 Montana Constitution, indicating that the powers of the Regents are not to be prescribed by the legislature. Second, the language of the new provision is much stronger and more comprehensive than that of the old provision. Under the 1889 Constitution, the board of education was given "general control and supervision' of the university system; under the 1972 Montana Constitution, the Board of Regents was given 'full power, responsibility, and authority to supervise, coordinate, manage and control the Montana university system ***."

At this point we observe that if Article X, Section 9, 1972 Montana Constitution, was read literally without reference to the rest of the Constitution, the Regents' argument and position would be correct; but, as will be hereinafter developed, the Constitution is not so read.

Article III, Section 1, 1972 Montana Constitution, reads:

> 'The power of the government of this state is divided into *three distinct branches*-legislative, executive, and judicial. No person or persons charged with the exercise of power properly belonging to one branch shall exercise any power properly belonging to either of the others, *except as in this constitution expressly directed or permitted.* (Emphasis supplied.)

Article V, Section 1, 1972 Montana Constitution, reads:

> *The legislative power is vested in a legislature* consisting of a senate and house of representatives. The people reserve to themselves the powers of initiative and referendum. (Emphasis supplied.)

Article VIII, Section 12, 1972 Montana Constitution, reads:

> *The legislature shall by law insure strict accountability of all revenue received and money spent by the state* and counties, cities, towns, and all other local government entities. (Emphasis supplied.)

It is the opinion of this Court that these provisions of the 1972 Montana Constitution and Article X, Section 9, should stand together. To be sure, that constitutional provision, like most, is couched in broad language, but it must not be read or construed in isolation. *** Our task then is to harmonize in a practical manner the constitutional power of the legislature to appropriate with the constitutional power of the Regents to supervise, coordinate, manage and control the university system. At the outset we note that there is not always a clear distinction between these powers and therefore limit our ruling here to these specific legislative enactments.

It is also necessary when speaking to issues arising out of the appropriation process to clarify our conception of the funds subject to that power. Previous rulings of this Court have limited the scope of appropriation to the general fund. Statutory changes, as well as the 1972 Montana Constitution, cause us to reexamine that definition at this time. ***

The 1972 Constitution also broadens the scope of the appropriation power. Article VI, Section 9, commands the governor to submit a budget to the legislature "setting forth in detail *for all operating funds* the proposed expenditures and estimated revenue of the state." (Emphasis supplied.)

Article VIII, Section 9, 1972 Montana Constitution states:

> Appropriations by the legislature shall not exceed anticipated revenue.

Section 12 of the same Article provides:

> *The legislature shall by law insure strict accountability of all revenue received and money spent by the state* and counties, cities, towns, and all other local governmental entities. (Emphasis added.)

Thus the legislative appropriation power now extends beyond the general fund and encompasses all those public operating funds of state government. *** However we emphasize that the power to appropriate does not extend to private funds received by state government which are restricted by law, trust agreement or contract.

These [public operating] funds — subject to the appropriation process — concern us in the Regents' challenge to the approved budget amendment requirement of Section 1(3) of H.B. 271. If the approval of budget amendments by the Finance Committee is a proper exercise of the legislative appropriation power, then the Regents as part of state government are subject to those requirements. But, as developed in this Court's opinion in the companion case, *State ex rel. Judge v. Legislative Finance Committee* (Mont. 1975), also decided today, the power to approve budget amendments in S.B. 401 constitutes an unconstitutional delegation of legislative power to the Finance Committee. Thus for the reasons enumerated in that opinion, the Regents' challenge to the approved budget amendment requirement of H.B. 271 succeeds.

[2. Legislative Conditions on Appropriations to the Regents.]

To reach the Regents' constitutional challenge of the certification requirement in the origination clause of Section 12 of H.B. 271, we must consider the power of the legislature to make line item appropriations.

We repeat the provision of H.B. 271:

> Section 12. The provisions set forth in this section are limitations on the appropriations made in this act. *It is the purpose of the legislature in enacting this bill only to appropriate funds and to restrict and limit by its provisions the amount and conditions under which the appropriations can be expended.*

> Except as otherwise provided in this act, the expenditures of appropriations are hereby contingent upon the board of regents certifying to the budget director that the university units shall comply completely with the following general and specific provisions ***. (Emphasis supplied.)

If the legislature cannot make line item appropriations for the university system, it does not have the authority to require certification by the Regents. The position of Amicus, which was adopted by the Regents in oral argument, is that the "autonomy" and "uniqueness" of the Regents precludes line item appropriations by the legislature. However, we find no constitutional limitations or judicial interpretation of this Court to bottom such a conclusion. The Regents' assertion of autonomy based on an isolated analysis of one article of Montana's Constitution does not show a basic violation of fundamental law of this long standing legislative practice. Even the Regents' cases from other jurisdictions cited in support of this principle, two of which we discuss later, do not challenge the authority of the legislature to itemize appropriations.

An early Michigan case, *Sterling v. Regents of University of Michigan* (Mich. 1896) sets the precedent for regent autonomy according to the Regents, but this Court notes this discussion in the decision which illuminates the background of the constitutional provision giving the regents control over "expenditures from the university interest fund" (similar to the Montana Trust and Legacy Fund, Article XXI, 1889 Constitution):

> *It is significant that*, at the time of the adoption of the constitution, this fund constituted the sole support of the university, aside from fees which might be received from students. *The state had made no appropriations for its support, and there is nothing to indicate that any such appropriations were contemplated.* (Emphasis supplied.)

The present Michigan Constitution grants the regents control of "expenditures from the institution's funds." Based on this provision regent autonomy recently prevailed over these legislative appropriation bills described in *Regents of University of Michigan v. State of Michigan* (Mich. Ct. App. 1973):

> Furthermore a careful reading of 1972 P.A. 260 discloses that the Legislature has in no way abandoned its intention to substitute its judgment for that of the constitutionally created boards of control. ***
>
> Whether it be under the guise of the police power or a reporting requirement, the simple fact remains that the *legislature still is attempting* through 1972 P.A. 260 to do the same thing it sought to do through 1971 P.A. 122 and prior acts: i.e., *determine who shall teach and who shall not, who shall learn and who shall not.* (Emphasis supplied.)

Regent autonomy has not been asserted over the bare legislative power to appropriate in the above instances. That power, by implication in these cases and expressly in others cited by the Regents, is secure even in Michigan with its strong constitutional provision and long judicial recognition of autonomy of the regents. We recognize here that while Montana's Constitution is not as explicit or broad as that of Michigan, the principle of regent independence was definitely intended by the drafters of the 1972 Montana Constitution. At the same time, just as in Michigan, legislative control of higher education through the appropriation process remains. The Regents are a constitutional body in Montana government subject to the power to appropriate and the public policy of this state. For a discussion of the impact of the 1972 constitutional provision see: Schaefer, *The Legal Status of the Montana University System under the New Montana Constitution*, 35 Mont. Law Review 189 [(1974)].

Going hand in hand with the power to appropriate has been legislative exercise of control over expenditures through itemization. Historically the English Parliament during the reign of William in the seventeenth century appropriated sums for particular purposes with penalties for disobedience. After two years of lump sum appropriations the United States Congress in 1793 began to itemize expenditures in its appropriation acts. In Montana too, itemization of appropriations is well established. Laws of Montana, Second Session 1891, pp. 129, 130. In addition to these historical bases, itemization of appropriations is vital to the legislative decisionmaking process involved in providing a balanced budget (Article VIII, Section 9), in providing a system of strict accountability (Article VIII, Section 12), and in fulfilling the audit responsibility of Article V, Section 10. Also, Article X, Section 9(1) provides that:

> It (state board of education) shall submit unified budget requests.

These constitutional bases justify the legislature's use of line items in its appropriations.

However, the legislature cannot do indirectly through the means of line item appropriations and conditions what is impermissible for it to do directly. Line item appropriations become constitutionally impermissible when the authority of the Regents to supervise, coordinate, manage and control the university system is infringed by legislative control over expenditures. On their face, the budget items and corresponding line items of H.B. 271 are reasonably related to the purpose of providing funds for necessary services and the other responsibilities of the legislature enumerated above.

[2(a). Certification of private funding.]

Within these parameters we now consider the certification requirements of Section 12, House Bill 271.

That section, as previously quoted, requires the Regents to certify full compliance to certain conditions to the budget director. Without such certification of compliance the appropriations in the bill are null and void. At the same time the Regents concede that the conditioning of appropriations has been a traditional and recognized legislative prerogative. Despite this, the Regents contend that compliance with numerous conditions erodes their authority granted them by the Constitution. But, the Regents' argument sheds little light on specific intrusions; hence our ruling here is necessarily limited due to the facts presented us.

We think this description adopted by Minnesota in *State ex rel. U. of Minnesota v. Chase* (Minn. 1928) to be a realistic approach to the issue of the propriety of legislative conditions to university system appropriations:

> *** At the one extreme, the Legislature has no power to make effective, in the form of a law, a mere direction of academic policy or administration. *At the other extreme it has the undoubted right within reason to condition appropriations as it sees fit. "In such case the regents may accept or reject such appropriation. *** If they accept, the conditions are binding upon them."* (Emphasis supplied.)

As noted above, the Regents are not mentioned in either Article III, Section 1, which creates the three branches of government, nor in Article V, which limits the powers of the legislature. Similarly, the legislature is not mentioned in Article X, Section 9(2), which entrusts the government and control of the university system to the Regents. By no rule of construction then can the powers of one be exercised or encroached upon by the other. In other words, the conditioning of university system appropriations by the 1975 Montana legislature and the summary procedure for compliance were proper exercises of its appropriation powers to the extent the conditions do not infringe on the constitutional powers granted the Regents. This means the conditions must be individually scrutinized to determine their propriety. The fact that there are numerous conditions and a requirement of blanket compliance does not in itself infringe upon the Regents' constitutional powers.

Nevertheless we cannot neglect the fact that certain of the certification requirements do exceed the limits to the exercise of the appropriation power which we have outlined above. We note particularly these provisions of Section 12, H.B. 271:

> (4) *All moneys* collected or received by university system units subject to this act *from any source* whatsoever, including federal grants for research and operations, *and any moneys received from a foundation* shall be deposited in the state treasury pursuant to the provisions of Title 79 R.C.M.1947, *except that the department of administration may, pursuant to section 79-603, R.C.M.1947, permit any university system unit subject to this act to retain in its possession moneys that would otherwise be deposited in the state treasury, provided that the anonymity of private foundation donors shall be maintained and that private donations shall not be used as an offset to general fund appropriations.* (Emphasis supplied.)

Based on our earlier discussion of the legislative appropriation power, certification cannot be used as a bootstrapping device to gain legislative control over private moneys. As noted heretofore, private moneys restricted by law, trust agreement, or contract are beyond the appropriation power. To the extent then that the certification requirement of Section 12(4) attempts to exert any control over such private moneys or to grant any discretion over such funds to the department of administration, it is unconstitutional.

[2(b). The Legislature's regulation of presidents' salaries.]

The Regents' challenge to Section 12(6) of House Bill 271 on its face, in the final issue presented to this Court, provides us an opportunity to more fully define the limits within which the legislature may condition appropriations to the university system. That section provides:

> (6) *Salary increases for presidents of units of the university system and for the commissioner of higher education* shall not exceed five percent (5%) each year of the biennium using the respective fiscal year 74–75 salaries previously approved by the regents as the basis for determining such increases. (Emphasis supplied.)

The question presented is whether this condition is a direction of academic policy or administration by the legislature. The Regents argue this condition represents an effort to abrogate the powers and prerogatives granted expressly and absolutely to them by the 1972 Montana Constitution. The Governor and Finance Committee assert the condition is a proper exercise of the legislative appropriation power.

The problem of delineating the area forbidden to the legislature in conditioning appropriations of the university system is not easily resolved, as was noted by the Michigan Court of Appeals in *Regents of University of Michigan v. State* (Mich. Ct. App. 1973):

> While it must be recognized that the legislature's power to make appropriations to a constitutional university does not include and is separate from the power to control the affairs of such a university, the legislature can within reason attach conditions to its university appropriations. If a constitutional university accepts such conditioned funds, it is then bound by the conditions. *There are not many decisions in this area, however, so the line between conditions the legislature can validly attach and those it cannot has not been drawn in a distinct fashion.* Conditions which require the university to follow prescribed business and accounting procedures have generally been found to be valid. The courts have also sustained conditions which require, on penalty of losing part of the appropriation, annual reports to the governor, and fair and equitable distribution of an appropriation among the departments of the university or maintenance of university departments. It has also been held that the legislature can properly make non-teaching employees subject to the state's workmen's compensation law, and can require loyalty oaths by the teachers. On the other side of the line, a condition that the university move a certain department of the school has been held to be invalidly attached, an attempt to limit the amount of funds that can be spent for a given department is likewise an invalid condition. It is clear that limits should be placed on the use of the conditioned appropriation, for without such limits the legislature could use the conditioned appropriation to strip the university of its constitutional authority." (Emphasis supplied.)

Clearly any decision with respect to appropriations affects the management of the university system to some degree. We assume the 1972 Constitutional Convention was aware of this fact when it drafted Article V. That Article, as was noted, does not limit the legislature's power to appropriate funds for the university system. Therefore, we look to the impact of the appropriation condition on the management and control exercised by the Regents.

Returning now to the restrictions contained in Section 12, we note no legislative explanation of the breadth of the restrictions. Neither is there any provision for the Regents to object. The Regents either comply or forego the funds. Seemingly minor conditions could ultimately affect academic, administrative and financial matters of substantial importance to the system.

But, control over college president salaries is not a "minor" matter. It does dictate university personnel policy. That such effect was meant need only be found in the final sentence of the bill following Section 6 which states "The regents shall grant classified university employees salaries in accord with House Joint Resolution 37, forty-fourth legislature." Such a limitation on significant expenditures indicates a complete disregard for the Regents' constitutional power.

Inherent in the constitutional provision granting the Regents their power is the realization that the Board of Regents is the competent body for determining priorities in higher education. An important priority is the hiring and keeping of competent personnel. The limitation set forth in Section 12(6), H.B. 271, specifically denies the Regents the power to function effectively by setting its own personnel policies and determining its own priorities. The condition is, therefore, unconstitutional.

Notes on the Horizontal Division of Powers

1. Note the checks and balances at issue in *Bullock v. Fox*. The Legislature created the Habitat Montana program, the Governor (through the Department of Fish, Wildlife, and Parks) proposed a policy under it (a transaction based on a particular reading of the statute), then the Land Board rejected the proposal. The Governor then moved forward with the transaction, a legislative leader sought the Attorney General's opinion, and that opinion rejected the Governor's claim of power. The Supreme Court rejected the Attorney General's opinion, allowing the Governor to move forward. Legislative leadership, which doubted the legality of the Governor's policy, could not clarify the statute without enactment of an amendment and the Governor's signature, a veto override, or a successful referral of a ballot issue to the voters. The Land Board, which opposed the transaction on policy grounds, also could not block the Governor. The legislative leadership or Land Board needed either a court or the Attorney General to issue an opinion to block it, and the Land Board is chaired by the Governor, so the legislative leadership sought an Attorney General opinion. (Why didn't the legislative leadership or Land Board just go to court directly?) Once the Attorney General issued an opinion, the Governor's only remedy was the third branch—the courts.

2. In *Bullock v. Fox*, the Governor could not expect the Attorney General to go to court as the constitutional "legal officer of the state," because the two officials had different views of the state's interest. In some states, nearly all lawyers representing the state (with the possible exception of the Governor's legal counsel) report to the Attorney General, including lawyers for agencies like the Department of Fish, Wildlife, and Parks. In a few states, the Attorney General actually reports to (and is appointed by) the Governor. How would *Bullock v. Fox* have played out under these arrangements? Montana's division of powers occupies an intermediate position, with agency lawyers routinely designated "assistant attorneys general" who litigate positions dictated by agency directors, almost all of whom report to the Governor or other elected officials besides the Attorney General.

3. Increasingly, Montana's Governor, like those of other states, is bringing or joining cases that resemble cases the Attorney General might bring, sometimes alongside another state's attorney general. *See, e.g., Bullock v. Internal Revenue Service* (D. Mont. 2019) (on behalf of the Department of Revenue, and with the State of New Jersey, challenging federal revenue procedure relating to donor disclosure of 501(c)(4) organizations). Does the Attorney General's constitutional duty as the "legal officer of the state" limit others' claims to represent state agencies or officials in prosecuting and defending state interests? How should a court determine who speaks for Montana? Should it matter? *See* Anthony Johnstone, *A State Is a "They," Not an "It": Intrastate Conflicts in Multistate Challenges to the Affordable Care Act*, 2019 B.Y.U. L. Rev. 1471, 1498–1507.

4. After *Board of Regents v. Judge*, can the Board of Regents really have "full power, responsibility, and authority to supervise, coordinate, manage and control the Montana university system" when the Legislature holds the purse strings? How might the Legislature react if it lacks control over university budgets, and how might the Board of Regents respond? How do you think governors have maintained their recent control over "tuition freezes" under *Board of Regents*?

5. What is the proper scope of the Board of Regents control under Article X, section 9 beyond fiscal policy? The core and primary purpose of the Board of Regents powers is, as the other states' cases suggest, academic freedom. How far does this go? For example, could the legislature allow or prohibit the carrying of firearms on Montana University System campuses? *See Board of Regents v. State*, No. 1-DV-21-0598 (Mont. 1st Dist. filed May 27, 2021).

6. Consider *Sheehy v. Commissioner of Political Practices*, 2020 MT 37. Regent Sheehy appealed the Commissioner's finding that she violated the Montana Code of Ethics at a Board of Regents meeting by asking "is there anything else we can do as Regents to support" the decennial referendum on the six-mill statewide property tax levy, which provides about 10% of funding for the Montana University System. The Court held Regent Sheehy did not violate the Code of Ethics:

> ¶11 Under the 1972 Montana Constitution, the Board is vested with the "government and control of the Montana university system" and is

"responsible for long-range planning, and for coordinating and evaluating policies and programs for the state's educational systems." Mont. Const. art. X, § 9. The Board has the "full power, responsibility, and authority to supervise, coordinate, manage and control the Montana university system. . . ." Mont. Const. art. X, § 9.

¶12 The 1972 Montana Constitution also established that the "legislature shall provide a code of ethics prohibiting conflict between public duty and private interest for members of the legislature and *all* state and local officers and employees." Mont. Const. art. XIII, § 4 (emphasis added). As provided in the Montana Constitutional Convention Notes, the Ethics Code provision applies to not only legislators but also "*other public officials*." Mont. Const. art. XIII, § 4 (emphasis added). Indeed, the framers' concern centered on conflicts of interest arising between public duty and private interest. As such, the Ethics Code enacted by the Legislature in 1977 is an aspect of Montana's Sunshine Laws and is liberally interpreted in favor of openness. ***

[The Court held Regent Sheehy was a "public employee" because she was a "member . . . of a board, commission, or committee with rulemaking authority" covered by the Code of Ethics. However,]

¶29 Regent Sheehy's statements were authorized by law as they were inherently part of her constitutional and statutory duties as a Board of Regents member. Implied in the Board of Regents' broad powers to "supervise, coordinate, manage, and control the [MUS]," is the power to do all things necessary and proper to the exercise of its general powers which would necessarily include support of a major financing source for the MUS. As prescribed by Article X, Section 9(2)(a), of the Montana Constitution, and § 20-25-301, MCA, a Board of Regents member has not only the power, but also the constitutional and statutory duty to ensure the health and stability of the MUS. Obviously included in such duties is ensuring the financial stability of the MUS. Supporting the passage of the 6-Mill Levy is hardly different than submitting a budget request to the Legislature, which the Board is required to do under Article X, Section 9(1), of the Montana Constitution; rather, instead of submitting the budget request indirectly to the Legislature, the request is sent directly to the people of Montana through the 6-Mill Levy ballot initiative. Accordingly, supporting and discussing the 6-Mill Levy, a major financing source for the MUS, is inherently an action authorized by law and properly incidental to Regent Sheehy's duties.

Justice McKinnon, specially concurring and rejecting the majority holding that regents were "public employees" by law, elaborated on the Board of Regents' constitutional independence:

¶35 . . . Under the 1889 Montana Constitution, the legislature had the absolute authority to define the powers and duties of the Board: "The general control and supervision of the state university . . . shall be vested in a state board of education, whose powers and duties shall be prescribed and regulated by law." Mont. Const. of 1889, art. XI, § 11. However, under the 1972 Montana Constitution, the Board's status was transformed from one of legislative devise to a constitutional department with the authority to "supervise, coordinate, manage and control the Montana university system." *See* Mont. Const. art. X, § 9(2)(a) . . . .

¶36 . . . A review of the 1972 constitutional convention debate over Mont. Const. art. X, § 9, is helpful in determining the intent of the framers regarding the bounds of the Board's authority. The 1972 constitutional convention debate on Article X, Section 9, reveals the delegates' intention to place the Montana University System (MUS) beyond the political influence of the legislature, entrusting it instead to a Board which should be directly responsible and answerable to the people. The Education and Public Lands Committee (Education Committee) of the 1972 constitutional convention was responsible for proposing changes to the Montana Constitution which are now contained in Article X. In its report to the convention, the Education Committee provided a number of fundamental reasons for the establishment of a separate Board of Regents of higher education, chiefly because:

> Higher education is not simply another state service; the administrative structure of higher education cannot be considered an ordinary state agency. The unique character of the college and university stands apart from the business-as-usual of the state. Higher learning and research is a sensitive area which requires a particular kind of protection not matched in other administrative functions of the state.

The Education Committee's original proposal named the Board as "a body corporate," to "be considered a legal entity which has powers as a board rather than as individuals and which is perpetuated as a separate administrative entity." However, the framers ultimately declined to retain the Board's description as "a body corporate," fearing such language risked establishing a fourth branch of government, and reasoning that the words "supervise, coordinate, manage and control" were sufficient to establish the Board's independence. ***

¶39 [Prior cases], although informative, do not resolve whether a neutral law of state-wide concern prescribing requirements for ethical behavior, and not pertaining to an exclusively higher education affair, can be expanded to include Regents or, conversely, infringes upon the Board's autonomy. Among other states with similarly vested higher education governing boards, legislative enactments have been held unconstitutional, or inapplicable to the higher education system, where those statutes encroached upon the powers of the governing board as laid out in its constitutional mandate. For example, statutes requiring a board to move a college to a different location, *Sterling v. Regents of Univ. of Michigan* (Mich. 1896); changing the governance form of a college, *People ex rel. Hastings v. Kewen* (Cal. 1886); and restricting the manner of a board's employment of professors, officers, agents, or employees via a state-wide anti-nepotism statute, *Dreps v. Bd. of Regents of Univ. of Idaho* (Idaho 1943), were each held unconstitutional or inapplicable to the higher education governing board.

¶40 In contrast, there are examples of legislative enactments which were upheld as proper exercises of legislative authority. For instance, in *Branum v. Bd. of Regents of Univ. of Michigan* (Mich. 1966), the Michigan board of regents asserted that, although the legislature had waived the governmental immunity of the state by statute in certain actions, the legislature did not have the authority to waive the immunity of the board. Although Michigan is generally regarded as having the most independently operated higher education system in the country, the Michigan court ultimately denied the board's assertions....

¶41 These cases upholding legislative enactments as a proper exercise of the legislature's authority each embrace the same notion, informative to the discussion here. The Board may exercise all powers connected with the proper and efficient internal governance of the MUS; however, the constitutional grant of authority does not inhere the absolute power of self-government, and there are limitations and checks on the Board's power. The Board cannot abridge rights protected by the federal or state constitutions, and is subject to state legislation enforcing state-wide standards for public welfare, health, and safety. ***

¶44 If we were to read Mont. Const. art. X, § 9(2)(a), literally, and without reference to the rest of the Constitution, that provision alone could arguably grant full autonomy to the Board, and severely limit the legislature's ability to expand the Ethics Code to include Regents. However, other provisions of the Montana Constitution place reasonable restraints upon the specific grant of autonomy in Article X, § 9. [T]he Board retains its reasonable constitutional autonomy but is still subject to the legislative functions of appropriation, audit, setting by statute Regents' terms of office, assigning additional educational institutions to the control of the Board, and permissible delegations of legislative authority. Additionally, the executive branch has indirect controls over the Board through the power of appointment of Regents, the governor's ex officio membership on the Board, and the constitutional power of the governor to request and obtain information in writing under oath from all officers and managers of state institutions. *See* Mont. Const. art. VI, § 15; Hugh V. Schaefer, *The Legal Status of the Montana University System under the New Montana Constitution*, 35 Mont. L. Rev. 189, 198 (1974). ***

¶47 Because the Board executes the laws of the state, and is one of two bodies which make up the State Board of Education, it is part of the executive branch of government. As members of the executive branch, individual Regents are susceptible to the same conflicts of interest as other executive branch officers and employees charged with carrying out the law. The power vested in the Board under Mont. Const. art. X, § 9, is not so broad as to destroy or limit the general power of the legislature to enact laws mandated by other constitutional provisions. Just as the legislature cannot pass laws which directly infringe upon the Board's authority to supervise, coordinate, manage and control the MUS, the Board cannot renounce permissible exercises of legislative authority by ignoring constitutional mandates of separation of powers or eschewing ethics standards applicable to other executive branch members of like distinction. The Ethics Code is a law enacted for the general welfare of the public, and is of a broad scope, meant to prohibit transgressions which abuse the public's trust and violate public duty. Where, as here, the statute is not aimed at the Board alone, or at any activities under the authority of the Board, there is no reason to permit individual Regents to use their independence to frustrate the clearly established public policy of the people of Montana. The application of the Ethics Code to Regents does nothing to take away powers or duties conferred to the Board under the Constitution. While the Board is meant to function as a cooperative body, each Regent is answerable for any individual indiscretions that are unbecoming of the offices they hold as part of the collective Board. As such, the legislature possesses the authority to include Regents in the requirements of the Ethics Code. ***

¶71 To conclude, I would hold that the legislature has the authority to extend the Ethics Code to apply to Regents. I would further hold that Regents are "public officers" under the Ethics Code, not subject to COPP's enforcement jurisdiction. Instead, I would reiterate that, as public officers, Regents are answerable to the public for violations of the Ethics Code, and other violations of their duties to the public, through the provisions of the Recall Act. Regent Sheehy's statements were part of her duties as a member of the Board, and she is answerable to Montana citizens through the public's right to know and observe the public meetings of its governing bodies.

7. In *Board of Regents v. Judge*, the Board of Regents sued the Governor to enjoin him from withholding payments to the Montana University System, although the Board's real adversary was the Legislature that enacted the restrictions on university spending. The same day the court decided *Board of Regents*, it decided *State ex rel. Judge v. Legislative Finance Committee*, below, where the Governor challenged the Legislature's attempt to restrict his own spending authority over funds already appropriated. (The Court rejected the Committee's argument that the Governor was estopped from challenging the restrictions in a bill he had just signed into law.)

B. Delegation of Powers

State ex rel. Judge v. Legislative Finance Committee

168 Mont. 470 (1975)

CASTLES, Justice.

This is an original proceeding brought by plaintiff Governor of Montana for declaratory relief pursuant to section 93-8901 et seq., R.C.M. 1947, involving the constitutionality of several legislative enactments establishing and empowering defendant Legislative Finance Committee and its office of Legislative Fiscal Analyst. *** Specifically this challenge involves three enactments of the Forty-fourth Legislature.

(1) Senate Bill No. 333, Chapter 448, Laws of Montana, 1975—The Legislative Finance Act—provides for the creation of the interim legislative finance committee whose membership is made up of four members of the senate finance committee, two members from the senate at large, four members of the house appropriation committee, and two members from the house at large. The act also creates the office of legislative fiscal analyst and specifies the duties of both the analyst and the committee.

(2) Senate Bill No. 401, Chapter 510, Laws of Montana, 1975, as set forth in the companion case, grants the legislative finance committee review and approval authority over budget amendments which are therein defined as expenditures by state agencies in excess of their appropriations.

(3) House Bill No. 1 (Special Session), Laws of Montana, 1975, specifically appropriates funds from sources other than the general fund which were not available for consideration by the legislature and modifies each of the appropriation bills of the Forty-fourth Legislature to insure that such funds are approved by the legislative finance committee in the form of a budget amendment before they are made available to the state agency for expenditure. ***

[(2)-(3). Budget amendments by Legislative Finance Committee.]

. . . [W]e first consider the budget amendment authority given the Finance Committee under S.B. 401 and H.B. 1 (Special Session). Initially we find that the legislature in H.B. 1 (Special Session), Laws of Montana, 1975, did intend and did accomplish the appropriation of monies received from sources other than the general fund which were not available for consideration by the legislature. What remains is a categorization and constitutional evaluation of the function of that committee.

There can be no doubt that the legislature, sitting in session, could determine whether or not to release money already appropriated from a source other than the general fund and not available for consideration by an earlier session of that same legislature. Such a determination is an integral part of the final appropriation decision. The power to appropriate is a long established, well-recognized power of the legislature. Further, these nongeneral fund monies are public operating funds of state government subject to the appropriation process. See companion opinion *Board of Regents v. Judge, supra*.

Alternatively the legislature might, as it has often done in other areas, make a policy determination and delegate to an executive agency or officer the duty to later implement the legislature's policy determination.

The legislature has the power to establish interim committees to gather information upon which the legislature can evaluate past actions or use as a basis for future decisions. Article V, Section 10, 1972 Montana Constitution.

But, the 1975 Montana Legislature in its enactment of S.B. 401 and H.B. 1 (Special session) empowering the Finance Committee to approve budget amendments delegated a power properly exercisable only by either the entire legislature or an executive officer or agency, to one of its interim committees. Such a hybrid delegation does not pass constitutional muster. The power in question here resides in either the entire legislative body while in session or, if properly delegated, in an executive agency. Clearly the action of the Finance Committee does not constitute the action of the entire legislature. Article V, Section 11, 1972 Montana Constitution. Just as clear is the fact that Article V, Section 9, 1972 Montana Constitution ["No member of the legislature shall, during the term for which he shall have been elected, be appointed to any civil office under the state"], would disqualify these legislators from membership on the Finance Committee if it were an executive agency. Therefore those sections of S.B. 401 and H.B. 1 (Special Session) empowering the Finance Committee to approve budget amendments are declared invalid as unconstitutional delegations of legislative power.

This determination that S.B. 401, Chapter 510, Laws of Montana, 1975, is unconstitutional necessarily denies the Finance Committee any power over those requests enumerated in section 1(3), H.B. 271, before us in the companion case *Board of Regents v. Judge, supra*. Since we have found the appropriation to have been made by the legislature, which both parties concede, the discretion regarding the disposition of these nongeneral fund unanticipated revenues resides within the executive branch.

[(1) Creation of the Legislative Finance Committee & Legislative Fiscal Analyst.]

Next we consider S.B. 333, which the Governor alleges to be an infringement on the executive branch and therefore violative of the separation of powers clause of Article III, Section 1, 1972 Montana Constitution. ***

To what extent then does S.B. 333 violate the separation of powers in view of the command of Article VI, Section 9, 1972 Montana Constitution, for the governor to "submit to the legislature at a time fixed by law, a budget for the ensuing fiscal period setting forth in detail for all operating funds the proposed expenditures and estimated revenue of the state." Again, our determination here is limited to a consideration of S.B. 333 on its face, due to the concession of factual issues by the Governor.

Basic to the resolution of this issue is the fact that the budget in Montana is a legislative budget not an executive budget notwithstanding Article VI, Section 9. Article V and Article VIII, 1972 Montana Constitution, vest the power to approve appropriation bills and a budget in the legislative branch. Article V, Sections 1, 11; Article VIII, Sections 9, 12, 14, 1972 Montana Constitution. In other words the legislature has the power to adjust and finalize the budget. Given that power and responsibility the legislature through an interim committee may require such information from the other branches of government as is reasonably necessary to form a rational basis for its budget determinations.

The Governor's assertion that Section 7 of S.B. 333 infringes on the executive branch because it requires a disclosure of information held by state agencies, including a copy of the preliminary budget, is of little substance. Indeed, should the executive branch withhold from the legislature or one of its interim committees any information reasonably necessary for budget decisions, it in fact would be interfering with the legislature to the extent of violating the separation of powers doctrine. Once prepared the preliminary budget is arguably a public document and should be available not only to the Finance Committee but to the general public as well under Article II, Section 9, 1972 Montana Constitution.

While an apparent unnecessary duplication of effort in the preparation of two budgets and an apparent lack of cooperation may exist between the executive and the legislature in this matter, which results in a waste of taxpayers' money, these are insufficient grounds upon which to find a legislative enactment constitutionally invalid. ***

MEA-MFT v. McCulloch

366 Mont. 266 (2012)

Chief Justice MIKE McGRATH delivered the Opinion of the Court.

*** ¶ 6 LR-123 was enacted by the Montana Legislature in 2011 as Senate Bill 426. It proposed a vote in the November 2012 general election on whether to provide a tax credit and potential tax refund, or outright State payment, to individuals in years in which there is a certain level of projected surplus revenue. LR-123 provides that if the unaudited ending State general fund balance exceeds 125% of the projected fund balance and this excess balance over 125% is at least $5 million, then a taxpayer could claim the tax credit as to taxes owed for the current year, and could receive a payment from the State if the credit exceeds tax liability and even if the individual had no tax liability.

¶ 7 The dispute in this case arises from the calculations required to determine whether the credit-refund threshold is reached. While LR-123 assigns various duties to the Department of Administration, the primary dispute is over the role assigned to the Legislative Fiscal Analyst. The Legislative Fiscal Analyst (LFA) is an individual employed by the Legislative Finance Committee and serves at its pleasure, § 5-12-205, MCA. The Finance Committee is a permanent joint committee of the

Montana Legislature, § 5-12-201, MCA. Section 1(7)(a) of LR-123 requires the LFA to calculate a projected general fund balance by August 1 for the end of the current fiscal year. This calculation involves a projection to be determined by a consideration of anticipated revenues and transfers, the impacts of enacted legislation, anticipated supplemental appropriations and anticipated reversions. The LFA is directed to calculate the projected general fund balance by adding the unassigned fund balance from the most recent completed fiscal year to the anticipated revenues and transfers, less the level of appropriations and transfers, supplemental appropriations and anticipated reversions for the most recent completed fiscal year. The constitutional issue in this case turns upon whether LR-123 impermissibly delegates legislative power to an employee (the LFA) of one of the Legislature's committees (the LFC). ***

¶ 9 A critical component of LR-123 is the requirement that the LFA determine the amount of the budgeted general fund balance. An affidavit by the LFA presented in the District Court proceedings sets out in detail the numerous separate steps, some involving other sub-steps, required to make this calculation. The calculation requires the LFA to project and anticipate fund balances, revenues, transfers, appropriations and reversions to arrive at a conclusion. That conclusion determines whether funds are paid into the State coffers or are paid out. ***

¶ 21 Article III, section 1 of the Montana Constitution divides the government into legislative, executive and judicial branches, and provides that "[n]o person or persons charged with the exercise of power properly belonging to one branch shall exercise any power properly belonging to either of the others, except as in this constitution expressly directed or permitted." Article V, section 1 of the Montana Constitution provides that the "legislative power is vested in a legislature consisting of a senate and a house of representatives." Article VI, section 4 provides that the "executive power is vested in the governor who shall see that the laws are faithfully executed."

¶ 22 LR-123 delegates to the Legislative Fiscal Analyst, a staff person employed by a legislative committee, the power and duty to determine the projected general fund balance, which would involve two dozen separate steps or calculations, and requires discretionary projections of balances, revenues, transfers, appropriations and reversions. Based upon these calculations and projections, LR-123 empowers the LFA to determine whether money comes into the State treasury in taxes or is paid out in cash payments or refunds. The District Court held that these were functions of either the Legislature itself, or of an Executive branch official acting under responsibilities properly delegated by the Legislature. The District Court ruled that "LR-123 is unconstitutional as a violation of the separation of powers envisioned by the Montana Constitution and as an unlawful delegation of the power of the Legislature."

¶ 23 This Court considered a similar issue in *Judge v. Legislative Finance Committee* (Mont. 1975). In that case the Legislature enacted a provision requiring the Legislative Finance Committee to approve budget amendments to allow executive branch agencies to spend money from the State treasury that was not otherwise appropriated by the Legislature itself. This Court recognized that "[t]he power to appropriate is a long established, well-recognized power of the legislature" and that the "public operating funds of state government [are] subject to the appropriation process."

¶ 24 Because of the public nature of the funds and the Legislature's role in the appropriation process, expenditure of funds to meet budget amendments could only be authorized by the entire Legislature while in session or through a duty properly delegated to an executive branch agency or officer. Since the Legislature had not appropriated the money itself and had not properly delegated that duty to an executive branch agency or officer, the budget amendment provision improperly delegated power to the Legislative Finance Committee. The "hybrid delegation" of authority to the Committee did not "pass constitutional muster." Action by the Legislative Finance Committee was not action by the Legislature, and neither was it action by the Executive branch. Therefore the provision was stricken as an unconstitutional delegation of legislative power.

¶ 25 The same considerations govern our analysis of LR-123. Here the authority to determine when State funds should be paid out is not delegated to the Legislative Finance Committee, but to its individual agent, the Legislative Fiscal Analyst, who serves at the pleasure of the Committee, § 5-12-205(2), MCA. This delegation is therefore yet another step removed from the Legislature itself. If action by the Legislative Finance Committee did not constitute the exercise of the legislative power in the *Judge* case then clearly neither does action by the Committee's staff, the Legislative Fiscal Analyst.

¶ 26 The separation of governmental powers into equal branches is a fundamental precept of the American constitutional form of government. The drafters of the Montana Constitution, commenting on Article III, stated that "dividing the powers of government among three branches of state government is essential to any constitution." The separation of powers in the Montana Constitution is "designed to act as a check on an overly ambitious branch of government."

¶ 27 The District Court's discussion regarding separation of powers considered an act similar to LR-123 that was rejected by the United States Supreme Court. In *Bowsher v. Synar* (1986), the Court invalidated a law that required the Comptroller General to estimate federal revenues and expenditures and then specify the deductions in spending required to reach a balanced budget. The Comptroller General is an agent of Congress and the Court found that as such he could not exercise what the Court determined to be executive powers without running afoul of the constitutional requirement for a separation of the three branches of government.

> [W]e view these functions as plainly entailing execution of the law in constitutional terms. Interpreting a law enacted by Congress to implement the legislative mandate is the very essence of "execution" of the law. Under § 251, the Comptroller General must exercise judgment concerning facts

> that affect the application of the Act. He must also interpret the provisions of the Act to determine precisely what budgetary calculations are required. Decisions of that kind are typically made by officers charged with executing a statute.

¶ 28 Likewise, in Montana each branch of government is equal, coordinate and independent, in that powers belonging to one branch may not be exercised by another. The District Court found that under LR-123, as in *Bowsher,* the LFA would be required to exercise "independent judgment and evaluation" with respect to the numerous estimates and projections. We agree with the District Court that such judgment and interpretation of the Act are functions plainly entailing execution of the law and are thus consistent with executive branch functions that are routinely required to implement legislative enactments. The Executive branch is ultimately the responsibility of the Governor.

¶ 29 In this case the Legislative Fiscal Analyst is clearly an employee or agent of the Legislature, serving "at the pleasure" of the Legislative Finance Committee. Section 5-12-205(2), MCA. Under the separation of powers established in Article III, section 1 of the Montana Constitution, the Legislative Fiscal Analyst may not "exercise any power properly belonging" to the Executive or Judicial branches of government. It is the exclusive power of the Legislature to enact the laws of this State, and the exclusive power of the Executive branch to implement and enforce those laws. Under Article VI, section 4 of the Montana Constitution it is the responsibility of the governor to see that the laws passed by the Legislature are properly executed.

¶ 30 For the reasons stated above, we have affirmed the decision of the District Court. LR-123 on its face violates both Article V, section 1 of the Montana Constitution as an unlawful delegation of legislative power, and Article III, section 1 of the Montana Constitution as a violation of the separation of powers of the independent branches of government. ***

¶ 32 LR-123 is unconstitutional on its face and therefore may not appear on the ballot in November 2012.

Justice BETH BAKER, dissenting.

¶ 33 I would conclude that the issues raised in the Plaintiffs' complaint are not ripe for resolution, and therefore would have reversed the District Court's June 5, 2012 Opinion and Order. I now dissent from this Court's ruling on Issue One of the appeal and would not reach Issue Two absent approval of LR-123 by a majority of voters casting ballots in the general election. ***

¶ 38 It is ironic that the constitutional defect on which the Court's decision rests is the Legislature's violation of the principle of separation of powers. Opinion, ¶ 30. While the Court faults the Legislature for attempting to short-cut the constitutional process, it too is being unfaithful to that process by deciding the validity of a proposed law. ***

Justice JIM RICE and Justice PATRICIA O. COTTER join in the dissenting Opinion of Justice BAKER.

In the Petition to Transfer Territory from High School District No. 6, Lame Deer, Rosebud County, Montana, to High School District No. 1, Hardin, Big Horn County, Montana

303 Mont. 204 (2000)

Justice WILLIAM E. HUNT, Sr. delivered the Opinion of the Court.

*** ¶ 3 Lame Deer High School District (LDHSD) was created in 1993 after extensive hearings and testimony. *** The assessed taxable valuation of the territory belonging in LDHSD is approximately $2,111,689.

¶ 6 In 1994, individuals residing in both Rosebud and Big Horn Counties, but outside of the Northern Cheyenne Indian Reservation (collectively "Respondents"), petitioned their respective County Superintendents of Schools requesting a territory transfer from [the Lame Deer High School District (LDHSD)] back to the Colstrip and Hardin High School Districts. Both County Superintendents of Schools held hearings, and both granted the Respondents' requests to transfer territory from LDHSD pursuant to § 20-6-320, MCA. [The transfer sought to be made here will remove approximately $1.6 million through the Rosebud County territory transfer, and approximately $325,000 will be removed by the Big Horn County territory transfer. Transferring both the Rosebud and Big Horn territories from LDHSD would leave the district with only $161,000 in taxable valuation, all within the Northern Cheyenne Indian Reservation.] ***

¶ 13 Section 20-6-320, MCA, grants local county superintendents the power to transfer territory from one school district to another. Section 20-6-320, MCA, gives the county superintendents the authority to alter the boundaries of school districts, constituting a delegation of legislative power. The legislature may constitutionally delegate its legislative functions to an administrative agency, but it must provide, with reasonable clarity, limitations upon the agency's discretion and provide the agency with policy guidance.

¶ 14 Article III, Section 1, of the 1972 Montana Constitution (formerly Article IV, Section 1, 1889 Montana Constitution) provides:

> Separation of powers. The power of the government of this state is divided into three distinct branches — legislative, executive, and judicial. No person or persons charged with the exercise of power properly belonging to one branch shall exercise any power properly belonging to either of the others, except as in this constitution expressly directed or permitted.

¶ 15 In *Bacus v. Lake County* (Mont. 1960) we set the standard for a delegation of legislative power. We stated the rule as follows:

> The law-making power may not be granted to an administrative body to be exercised under the guise of administrative discretion. Accordingly, in delegating powers to an administrative body with respect to the administration of statutes, the legislature must ordinarily prescribe a policy, standard, or rule for their guidance and must not vest them with an arbitrary and uncontrolled discretion with regard thereto, and a statute or ordinance which is deficient in this respect is invalid.

A statute granting legislative power to an administrative agency will be held to be invalid if the legislature has failed to prescribe a policy, standard, or rule to guide the exercise of the delegated authority. If the legislature fails to prescribe with reasonable clarity the limits of power delegated to an administrative agency, or if those limits are too broad, the statute is invalid. ***

¶ 17 The legislature has established a number of conditions which must be satisfied before a petition may be considered by a county superintendent of schools. Satisfaction of these conditions, however, does not require granting of a petition. Section 20-6-320, MCA (1993), is as follows:

(1) A majority of registered electors of a high school district who reside in territory that is a part of a high school district may petition the county superintendent to transfer the territory in which they reside to another high school district if:

> (a) the territory to be transferred is contiguous to the high school district to which it is to be attached;
>
> (b) the territory to be transferred is not located within 3 miles, over the shortest practical route, of an operating school of the high school district from which it is to be detached;
>
> (c) the transfer of the territory will not reduce the taxable value of the district to less than $300,000 unless the remaining territory of the high school district contains not less than 50,000 acres of nontaxable Indian land;
>
> (d) the board of trustees of the school district that would receive the territory has approved the proposed transfer in writing; and
>
> (e) the territory proposed to be transferred to another high school district has not been included in a petition filed under this section in the previous 3 years. ***

This statute's only directive on whether to grant or deny a petition is that "the decision must be based on the effects that the transfer would have on those residing in the territory proposed for transfer as well as those residing in the remaining territory of the high school district." Section 20-6-320(6), MCA (1993). The territory transfer statute does not constrain a county superintendent's discretion in whether to grant or deny a transfer. The decision is left up to the county superintendent's unguided judgment.

¶ 18 While this statute sets forth some criteria, the satisfaction of these conditions does not limit a county superintendent's discretion in granting or denying a petition once the procedural requirements have been met. This statute fails to provide any checks on the discretion of the county superintendent of schools in deciding whether to grant a territory transfer. The statute's only directive is that the county superintendent should make the decision based on the effects felt by those transferred and those remaining. Section 20-6-320(6), MCA (1993). The legislature has provided no criteria for balancing the effects felt by the parties involved in a school district territory transfer. Instead, the decision is left solely to the whim of the local county superintendents.

¶ 19 It is this broad grant of discretion to a county superintendent of schools, unchecked by any standard, policy or rule of decision, that renders the territory transfer statute unconstitutional. In *Bacus* we stated that "the standard must not be so broad that the officer or board will have unascertainable limits within which to act." If the legislature had limited a county superintendent to the role of fact finder or if the legislature had set forth the specific criteria to be weighed when deciding to grant or deny a petition, the statute would have conformed to constitutional requirements.

¶ 20 We hold that § 20-6-320, MCA, is an unconstitutional delegation of legislative power. . . .

Justice JAMES C. NELSON specially concurs.

*** ¶ 30 Subsection (6) completely fails to provide any objective legislative standard, policy, instruction, criteria, or requirements as to what sort of "effects" are to guide the county superintendent in exercising his or her power to grant the petition to transfer or to deny the petition. There is no legislative direction as to what "effects" the county superintendent, at a minimum, is to consider. *** Moreover, the statute fails to provide any legislative direction as to how, substantively, the county superintendent is to evaluate the types of "effects" that transfer might implicate. *** The statute does not set out who — the petitioners or the opponents of transfer — bears the burden of proof of the "effects." . . .

¶ 33 In short, one cannot read subsection (6) without being reminded of the old fast-food commercial:

Customer: "What's in the chicken sandwich?"

Counter person: "Parts."

Customer: "What kind of parts?"

Counter person: "Parts is parts."

In context, the same question can be asked: What's in this statute? Unfortunately, the answer is the same: "Effects is effects."

¶ 34 Under this statute, the Legislature has effectively given the county superintendent carte blanche to make virtually any decision he or she wishes. *** As a result, this scheme allows, if not encourages, arbitrary and capricious decisions based on political expediency instead of on considerations emphasizing thoughtful and fiscally responsible school district administration and, most importantly, insuring the best educational opportunity for the students affected.

*** ¶ 48 Under this statute, the county superintendent can make his or her decision for a good reason, for a bad reason, or for no reason at all. Provided his or her decision is based on the "effects" of the transfer on the residents of the territories involved and assuming he or she says his or her decision is based on the "effects," legally it matters not what or how he or she decides. *** Moreover, any judicial review of his or her decision—our appellate review included—is necessarily little more than an exercise in the judiciary substituting its judgment for that of the county superintendent's. Since the statute fails to include any objective, legislative policy, standard, or rule of decision as to what "effects" are to be considered, reviewing courts have no basis for determining whether the county superintendent met or missed the mark. There is no yardstick by which to determine whether his or her decision was arbitrary or capricious; wrong or right.

¶ 50 In short, the county superintendent's decision may have no real meat in it at all. It might well be made up of little more than beaks and claws and gizzards and eyeballs. But, under this statute, that's all right because "Parts is parts," and "Effects is effects." ***

Justice W. WILLIAM LEAPHART joins in the forgoing special concurrence.

Justice KARLA M. GRAY, dissenting [omitted].

Notes on the Delegation of Powers

1. Why enforce a non-delegation rule? Are there justiciable standards for how much delegation of legislative power is too much? Delegation issues often arise in emergencies. For example, the *Bacus* case discussed above involved a public health statute. Consider the various executive power issues that arose in states' responses to the COVID-19 pandemic. In *Trump for President v. Bullock* (D. Mont. 2020), the federal district court considered whether the Governor's emergency authorization of mail-ballot elections unconstitutionally exercised legislative powers vested by Mont. Const. art. IV, § 3 (the "legislature shall provide by law the requirements for . . . administration of elections") and U.S. Const. art. II, § 1 ("Each State shall appoint, in such Manner as the Legislature thereof may direct, a Number of [Presidential] Electors . . ."):

> Notably, the provisions of Montana law permitting an election to be conducted by mail ballot provide that "a regularly scheduled federal, state, or county election" cannot "be conducted by mail ballot." Mont. Code Ann. § 13-19-104(3)(a). Montana's statutory framework regarding the administration of elections cannot be read in isolation, however, and particular attention to the emergency powers afforded to the Governor must be paid. Specifically, the Montana Legislature has provided Governor Bullock with

> the power to "suspend the provisions of any regulatory statute prescribing the procedures for conduct of state business or orders or rules of any state agency if the strict compliance with the provisions of any statute, order, or rule would in any way prevent, hinder, or delay necessary action in coping with the emergency or disaster." Mont. Code Ann. § 10-3-104(2)(a). ***
>
> The Court is convinced that the statute at issue here, Montana Code Annotated § 13-19-104(3)(a), which forbids local officials from conducting a "regularly scheduled federal, state or county election" by mail ballot, is precisely the sort of regulatory statute that falls within Governor Bullock's statutory suspension power. After all, the administration of federal, state, and local elections is quintessentially state business. [T]he Court has no trouble concluding that suspension of Montana Code Annotated § 13-19-104(3)(a) is necessary to facilitate Montana's effective response to the COVID-19 pandemic. The provisions on which Governor Bullock relies in issuing the Directive not only provide him with such authority, but likewise constitute a fundamental part of the legislative enactments governing the time, place, and manner of elections in Montana and how electors are appointed.

Compare *Midwest Institute of Health v. Governor* (Mich. 2020), which held that the governor's invocation of the Michigan Emergency Powers of the Governor Act (EPGA) to "promulgate reasonable orders, rules, and regulations as he or she considers necessary to protect life and property" was an unconstitutional delegation of legislative power to the executive branch under the Michigan Constitution's separation of powers provision:

> The consequence of such illusory "non-standard" standards in this case is that the Governor possesses free rein to exercise a substantial part of our state and local legislative authority—including police powers—for an indefinite period of time. There is, in other words, nothing within either the "necessary" or "reasonable" standards that serves in any realistic way to transform an otherwise impermissible delegation of *legislative* power into a permissible delegation of *executive* power. This is particularly true in the specific context of the EPGA, a statute that delegates power of immense breadth and is devoid of all temporal limitations. These facets of the EPGA—its expansiveness, its indefinite duration, and its inadequate standards—are simply insufficient to sustain *this* delegation. While, in the context of a less-encompassing delegation, the standard might be sufficient to sustain the delegation, that is not the case the Court entertains today.

Would the Michigan law be permissible under the Montana Constitution? Would the Montana law be permissible under the Michigan Constitution? The plaintiffs in *Trump* did not raise any state constitutional claims. Would the Montana law be permissible under the Montana Constitution? (In 2021 the Montana Legislature substantially limited the governor's and local health officials' emergency powers, including under Mont. Code Ann. § 10-3-104.)

2. The implementation of statutory policy through agency regulations, consistent with the requirements of public participation and due process, is the domain of administrative law under the Montana Administrative Procedure Act. *See generally* William L. Corbett, *Montana Administrative Law Practice: 41 Years After the Enactment of the Montana Administrative Procedure Act*, 73 MONT. L. REV. 339 (2013).

3. Certain legislative committees provide oversight of administrative rules and can review rulemaking proceedings under the Montana Administrative Procedure Act. *See* Mont. Code Ann. § 2-4-402. Beyond these conventional oversight responsibilities, the Legislature also has provided for a "legislative poll" process to "veto" administrative rules.

> **2-4-403. Legislative intent—poll.** (1) If the legislature is not in session, the committee may poll all members of the legislature by mail to determine whether a proposed rule is consistent with the intent of the legislature. ***
>
> **2-4-404. Evidentiary value of legislative poll.** If the appropriate administrative rule review committee has conducted a poll of the legislature in accordance with 2-4-403, the results of the poll must be admissible in any court proceeding involving the validity of the proposed rule or the validity of the adopted rule if the rule was adopted by the agency. If the poll determines that a majority of the members of both houses find that the proposed rule or adopted rule is contrary to the intent of the legislature, the proposed rule or adopted rule must be conclusively presumed to be contrary to the legislative intent in any court proceeding involving its validity.

Does this violate the separation of legislative and executive powers? Consider *State ex rel. Barker v. Manchin* (W. Va. 1981):

> What the Legislature has attempted to do here is to invest itself with the power to promulgate rules having the force and effect of law outside the constitutional limitations imposed upon the legislative branch in the exercise of that power. In effect, the Legislature abdicates in favor of the executive its power to make rules and then asserts that because the rule-making power so delegated is legislative in nature, it may step into the role of the executive and disapprove or amend administrative regulations free from the constitutional restraints on its power to legislate. The statutory scheme brings to mind the Old Testament quotation from Job I:21, "The Lord gave, and the Lord hath taken away." The Legislature at one time created and delegated powers and responsibilities to the Department of Mines and at a later time attempted to take away some of those important powers and responsibilities and to lodge them in the hands of the Legislature and its personnel. Such a mechanism for legislative review of executive action may properly be called an "extra-legislative control device" for it permits the Legislature to act as something other than a legislative body to control the actions of the other branches. This is in direct conflict with our constitutional requirement of separation of powers. The power of the Legislature in

> checking the other branches of government is to legislate. While the Legislature has the power to void or to amend administrative rules and regulations, when it exercises that power it must act as a legislature through its collective wisdom and will, within the confines of the enactment procedures mandated by our constitution. It cannot invest itself with the power to act as an administrative agency in order to avoid those requirements.

West Virginia's review process involved a committee "veto" not involving the full legislature. Would polling all legislators out of session cure the constitutional defect? *Compare Mead v. Arnell* (Idaho 1990) (affirming "the Idaho Legislature may rescind the rules promulgated by an executive department board or agency by concurrent resolution").

4. Legislative vetoes typically invalidate an administrative rule after disapproval, or failure to approve, by the legislature or a committee. Montana's legislative poll does something different: it gives rise to a conclusive presumption that the rule is "contrary to the legislative intent in any court proceeding involving its validity." Does this violate the separation of legislative and judicial powers? A separate law allows an interim legislative committee to suspend an administrative rule until the adjournment of the next legislative session. *See also* Mont. Code Ann. § 2-4-306. This may render some rules unenforceable for nearly two years given the Legislature's biennial sessions. Does this raise problems similar to the legislative veto?

5. How much should federal separation-of-powers law inform state separation-of-powers law? In *Contingency and Universalism in State Separation of Powers Discourse*, 4 Roger Williams U. L. Rev. 79 (1998), Robert A. Schapiro observes "in the separation of powers area state courts have nowhere to hide" in lock-step interpretation because "[f]ederal law provides no constitutional floor." He continues:

> Whatever the relative strength of the executive, legislative, and judicial departments, a striking feature of the national government is the overall strength of each branch. *** By contrast, significant, additional checks thwart the exercise of power by each part of state government. Executive branches of state governments often have a more diffused assignment of authority. States commonly elect several members of the executive branch, affording independence to other executive officers in addition to the governor. This dispersal acts as an internal check on the state executive power. State constitutions also place significant substantive and procedural limits on state legislatures. To say that the United States Congress enjoys only enumerated powers, while state legislatures exercise plenary power, would be to emphasize theory over practice. The chief limitations on Congress's legislative authority are the external limits established by the Bill of Rights. In addition to these strictures, state legislatures often face additional requirements, such as prohibitions on local or special legislation or germaneness requirements. Further, substantive due process limits on state legislatures' economic and social policies have outlived *Lochner*'s demise in the federal system. Finally, state courts have tended to be less assertive in defining and

> enforcing constitutional rights. This reluctance may be traceable to the courts' greater electoral accountability. Indeed, the reluctance to engage in independent interpretation of the state constitution exemplifies the relative passivity of state courts. . . .

In federal and state constitutional law, the classic separation of powers case involves conflicts between the legislative and executive branches, but separation of powers principles govern the relationships between all three branches: legislative and executive, legislative and judicial, and executive and judicial. A system of checks and balances arms each branch with certain powers over other branches, such as the legislature's power to appropriate funding (or not), the executive's power to enforce the laws (or not), and the judiciary's power to review the acts of the other branches (or not). We will consider more of these relationships in the next chapter.

Chapter 5

Judicial Powers

Article VII, Section 1. Judicial power. The judicial power of the state is vested in one supreme court, district courts, justice courts, and such other courts as may be provided by law.

Revises 1889 constitution by allowing the legislature to establish "inferior" courts, such as a small claims court, as well as intermediate courts of appeal. Reference in 1889 constitution to senate as court of impeachment is deleted.

Article VII, Section 2. Supreme court jurisdiction. (1) The supreme court has appellate jurisdiction and may issue, hear, and determine writs appropriate thereto. It has original jurisdiction to issue, hear, and determine writs of habeas corpus and such other writs as may be provided by law.

(2) It has general supervisory control over all other courts.

(3) It may make rules governing appellate procedure, practice and procedure for all other courts, admission to the bar and the conduct of its members. Rules of procedure shall be subject to disapproval by the legislature in either of the two sessions following promulgation.

(4) Supreme court process shall extend to all parts of the state.

(1) No change except in grammar. (2) No change except in grammar (3) allows Supreme Court to make rules governing itself, other courts, and lawyers. Legislature may veto the rules. (4) No change except in grammar.

Article VII, Section 8. Selection. (1) Supreme court justices and district court judges shall be elected by the qualified electors as provided by law....

Revises 1889 constitution. Contested election of judges is not changed, however if a judge in office does not have an opponent in an election, his name will be put on the ballot anyway and the people asked to approve or reject him. If rejected, the governor appoints another judge. When there is a vacancy (such as death or resignation) the governor appoints a replacement but does not have unlimited choice of lawyers as under 1889 constitution. He must choose his appointee from a list of nominees and the appointment must be confirmed by the senate—a new requirement.

Article II, Section 16. The administration of justice. Courts of justice shall be open to every person, and speedy remedy afforded for every injury of

> person, property, or character. No person shall be deprived of this full legal redress for injury incurred in employment for which another person may be liable except as to fellow employees and his immediate employer who hired him if such immediate employer provides coverage under the Workmen's Compensation Laws of this state. Right and justice shall be administered without sale, denial, or delay.
>
> *Adds to 1889 constitution by specifically granting to a person injured in employment the right to sue a third party causing the injury. except his employer or fellow employee when his employer provides coverage under workmens compensation laws.*

Federal courts, with their life tenure, limited jurisdiction, and interpretative focus on federal statutory and constitutional law, are the outlier in the American judiciary. Nearly all of the courts in the country are state courts, many of them elected, with general jurisdiction and common-law powers. Montana judges' electoral pedigree raises questions of judicial independence and accountability that do not occur in the federal judiciary. Their independence is not only formal in the separation of powers, but also political. In the ordinary course, state judges attain their appointment and retention from the electorate, like the so-called "political" branches of the legislature and executive. The corollary of this independence from the other branches is accountability to the electorate, which raises questions about the judicial role not present in the federal judiciary, including conflicts of interest.

State courts' jurisdiction also makes them relatively powerful policymakers even outside the domain of constitutional law. Their broad procedural, substantive, and inherent powers, combined with their political independence, can make for sharper separation of powers conflicts with the other branches. State courts also develop different conceptions of "the judicial power" among themselves and relative to the federal standard in matters of justiciability and related doctrines. The open-textured vesting of "judicial power" and broad terms of state jurisdictional statutes leaves state courts ample space to depart from lock-step federal notions of standing, ripeness, mootness, advisory opinions, and political questions. State courts vary in their assertions of authority to hear cases and controversies, and some state laws expressly authorize advisory opinions and other exercises of jurisdiction that depart from the Article III model. Montana's Constitution does not offer clear textual deviations from the federal standards of judicial power, aside from a distinct guarantee that "Courts of justice shall be open to every person." Given these distinctions, how much should or do state courts deviate from federal judicial practices?

A. Judicial Independence

Anthony Johnstone, *A Past and Future of Judicial Elections: The Case of Montana*

16 J. App. Pro. & Practice 47, 50–59, 63–72, 124, 130–31 (2015)

*** II. A History of Montana's Judicial Elections and Judicial-Election Reforms

Judicial selection in Montana is both distinct from and representative of its practice across the states. Montana's 150-year-old judiciary began in territorial days, when outside judges appointed in Washington, D.C., produced resentment among Montanans even as these territorial judges helped the new territory develop toward statehood. The state's first constitution responded to this popular resentment by providing for judicial elections. In the Progressive Era, the state adopted typical campaign-finance and nonpartisan election reforms, but only after exceptional agonies of corporate corruption. By the second half of the twentieth century, Montana had joined many other states in reconsidering judicial elections, though it did so through the extraordinary means of popular deliberation through a constitutional convention. Montana, in short, is a microcosm of judicial election reform in the American states.

A. The Territorial Origins of Montana's Elected Judiciary

Twenty-five years of territorial status forged Montana's attitude toward its courts. In the gold rush that opened Montana's territorial history, customary miners' courts and the storied vigilantes dispensed civil and criminal justice. Territorial justices, appointed by the President, "owed allegiance to the federal government and to political parties, yet at the same time were not insensitive to pressures within the territory itself." These tensions played out when Territorial Secretary Thomas Meagher, a Union Democrat serving as acting governor, pushed for statehood in 1866 with a constitutional convention and two extraordinary legislative sessions. When a two-member majority of the territorial court, both Republicans, declared the acts of the extraordinary sessions null and void, the state legislature redistricted those justices to the wilderness. Congress responded with a rare nullification of all laws enacted in the extraordinary sessions. To make clear its "irritation toward the Democratic populace of this ill-mannered western province," the Republican Congress also revoked the legislature's judicial districting power and raised the territorial judges' salaries by $1000.

Once the territorial government settled in, "Montana gained recognition as having one of the most efficient court systems among western territories." Yet territorial justices were "[h]ampered ... by an unfamiliarity with mining law, and by resentment stemming from local political cleavages and the dislike of 'foreign' officials." Despite the quality of some territorial justices, residents chafed at their lack of democratic legitimacy. Montanans complained about "'breaking in' pilgrim Judges from Eastern States who have known nothing of our people, laws and customs." On the eve of the second Montana constitutional convention in 1884, one newspaper editorial captured the popular complaint that

> [t]he President has nominated another carpetbagger for Associate Justice of the Supreme Court of Montana. Seventy-five thousand people in the Territory to make laws for themselves, and a Hoosier sent out from Indiana to tell us what we have done. How long, oh Lord; how long!

The proposed 1884 Constitution, the unsuccessful predecessor of the 1889 Constitution that secured statehood, reflected this suspicion of outside influence. In its memorial to Congress, the convention sought statehood to redress "the policy which has so long prevailed of sending strangers to rule over us and fill our offices." The convention's address to voters detailed the grievances. Notably, the address devoted more lines to the Judicial Department than it devoted to the legislative and executive branches combined. The proposed judicial system responded to popular distrust of outsider territorial justices:

> The present system is manifestly wrong again; by it the people have no voice in selecting the judges. They are sent to us from the far off East, probably in deference to the traditional idea that it was from thence all of the "wise men" came.... The character of our litigation is such that, however learned in the law our eastern judge may be, he will find himself much embarrassed in his new field.

Under the proposed state constitution, justices would be "elected by the people" for six-year terms, and would be "required to have resided in the State or Territory at least two years prior to their election." When Montana finally attained statehood in 1889, the convention's address to voters was shorter, as the Constitution proposed was similar in all its fundamental provisions to the Constitution of 1884, which had been ratified by a large majority. Still, the judicial provisions retained primary importance as the only article specifically recommended in the address: "yet we think in this the judiciary system is better suited to the wants and interests of our people." The 1889 Constitution contained several stylistic and procedural changes, but retained the elected terms and residency requirements for justices.

B. The Copper Kings and Their Influence on Montana's Judicial Elections Today

With statehood, Montana's judiciary transitioned from federal appointees unfamiliar with mining law to elected officials all too familiar with the corporate overreach and corruption that came to be known as the War of the Copper Kings. The mining industry matured with outside investment of capital from the so-called Copper Kings: the 1884 and 1889 Constitutional Convention President (and disgraced United States Senator) William A. Clark; the head of the giant Anaconda Copper Mining Company Marcus Daly; and the aggressive young industrialist F. Augustus Heinze. ***

Heinze waged a more focused battle, largely in the courts, to extend his mining holdings in Butte and defend them against industry consolidation by the

Amalgamated Copper Company, which had purchased Daly's Anaconda interests in 1889. Heinze met mixed results as a defendant in federal court, and through a series of corporate maneuverings turned to state court, where he could more easily influence the judges. In 1900, with his support for the re-election of William Clancy and the election of Edward Harney for the Second Judicial District Court, the state trial court with jurisdiction over Butte, Heinze did just that. For their four-year terms, "[w]ith his allies sitting on the local courts, Heinze could easily drive the titans of Standard Oil to absurd lengths" of vexatious litigation that kept Amalgamated—a holding company formed by Standard Oil officers—at bay while Heinze, sometimes literally, mined ore out from under the company's feet. Indeed, "in a burlesque of judicial dignity, William Clancy found in Heinze's favor with monotonous regularity."

After years of delaying cases to the strategic advantage of Heinze, Judge Clancy dealt two devastating blows to Amalgamated on October 22, 1903: first, awarding ownership of the strategically crucial Minnie Healy mine from Amalgamated to Heinze; and second, enjoining the Amalgamated from holding its Montana subsidiaries. Amalgamated responded in kind, shutting down its Montana operations and throwing more than 15,000 employees out of work. Governor Joseph Toole, elected in 1900 with the support of Clark and Heinze, eventually capitulated to Amalgamated's demand. He called a special session to enact an unprecedented "Fair Trials" law allowing the peremptory substitution of a district judge. [A one-substitution variation of the law, still called the "Clancy Law," remains in effect, providing that "[e]ach adverse party is entitled to one substitution of a district judge." Mont. Code Ann. § 3-1-804(1).] ***

The War of the Copper Kings left lasting scars on the integrity of state government in Montana, including its courts. Shortly after it ended, President Roosevelt's Solicitor General worried about bringing the so-called smoke-wars litigation to end the deadly pollution of forest and farmlands by Amalgamated's smelter, noting that "[t]he suit will be filed in a territory which has heretofore been the battleground between the Amalgamated and Heinze interests . . . where open confessions of sales of political and even judicial influence were lightly looked upon." A mining trade publication observed at the time that "[t]he judiciary of a State has been debauched, its politics mired, its people obsessed, while two parties of mine owners have twisted our awkward mining laws to the acquirement of territory and the destruction of property." Going forward, Amalgamated's successor the Anaconda Company "dominated Montana after 1906 like no other single company dominated any other state, with the possible exception of the tiny Dupont satrapy of Delaware." This corporate domination lasted decades, until a mix of political and social changes in the 1960s brought calls for reform, and eventually a new state constitution. ***

1. A Call for a New Constitution

The judiciary, including judicial selection, emerged as a central concern of constitutional reformers. In a 1967 "Blueprint for Modernization," Professors David Mason and William Crowley proposed a comprehensive revision of the state's judicial system, criticizing the 1889 judicial article as "designed for a horse and buggy society . . .

cumbersome, inefficient and expensive." The Blueprint's primary focus was judicial administration and organization, particularly of the inferior courts. Yet it included an option to enact alternatives to judicial elections, "[i]f the legislature should see fit at some time in the future to adopt the Missouri Plan [of merit selection] or some variant thereof." The Legislative Council stopped short of criticizing judicial elections, but noted that the method of judicial selection presented "a basic question," and that the Missouri Plan had been recommended by the American Judicature Society, the American Bar Association, and the National Municipal League. ***

2. The Constitutional Convention of 1972

The convention's proceedings were notable for a general atmosphere of bipartisanship. Yet the Judiciary Committee's votes substantially divided along party lines, even to the extent that party "trumped the divide between lawyers and non-lawyers on the Committee." Democrats controlled the Committee six members to three, though in their work they broke into a working majority of five Democrats supporting the majority proposal, and three Republicans and a Democrat supporting a minority proposal.

The majority report retained much of the 1889 Constitution's provisions, including judicial elections. The minority report proposed a modified merit plan, in which "the governor of the state shall nominate a supreme court or district court judge from nominees selected in the manner provided by law," with one opportunity for a contested election after appointment, followed by retention elections for each succeeding term of office. In extensive commentary, the minority observed "that today, few, if any, of the voters are at all acquainted with the judicial candidates," and "the present system of elected judiciary utterly and completely fails to attain" the informed electorate necessary for "the survival of democratic institutions." At the same time, the minority was "especially apprehensive of the future political character of [Montana's] judges," citing "statistics revealing that an overwhelming majority" of the judges (but not supreme court justices) had "been appointed by the governor." This modified Missouri Plan of commission nomination, executive appointment, and voter retention reflected elements of the so-called Montana Plan, but added the intervening opportunity for a contested election after appointment.

Despite the legal establishment's support for a merit plan more like the minority's hybrid proposal, the Judiciary Committee's poll of nearly 500 lawyers in the state found that a slight majority favored judicial elections; over a hundred members of the Montana Trial Lawyers Association favored elections by more than a two-to-one margin. Delegate John M. Schiltz, a former legislator and an unsuccessful candidate for chief justice in 1970, made a case for judicial elections based on personal and political history. In Montana, he explained, "we have strong corporate influence; where, if I can elect a Governor, and through that office nominate and appoint the district and the Supreme Court judges, I can run this state.... I can own it." Noting how the Anaconda Company and its former affiliate the Montana Power Company could dominate appointment processes, including the Constitutional Convention Commission itself, he concluded that

> you cannot pick a committee in the State of Montana that will be totally free of that kind of influence. And I am afraid of it, and if I have to choose between one or the other, I'm going to the electorate every time, because I had a chance . . . to be elected. With another few bucks, I might have made it.

Delegate James C. Garlington, also a lawyer, argued for judicial appointment. "There is clear agreement on the part of all that we do need good judges," he noted, "[t]he question is how to recruit them." He expressed "utmost sympathy" for judicial candidates who "must undergo the type of ordeal that Mr. Schiltz very feelingly described." He suggested that such an ordeal makes judicial office unattractive for most lawyers "who have any kind of a stable, private practice" because the judicial candidate "must sever himself completely from the private practice of law," and should he return to practice after losing a campaign, "he then begins at absolute rock bottom . . . no clients, no office, no library, no nothing." ***

In a series of sharply divided votes the delegates eventually rejected both the majority and minority proposals and adopted Article VII, section 8, whose original text suggests its complicated origins. In a concession to merit selection, its first section provides "replacement . . . for any vacancy" by the governor's appointment "from nominees selected in the manner provided by law," subject to senate confirmation. Its second section provides for retention elections as the default, but permits contested elections. Its third section provides for an election "[i]f an incumbent does not run." The result, in other words, was the maintenance of contested judicial elections, but with a merit plan of appointment by nominees from a selection committee in case of vacancies. Based on a campaign that noted, revealingly "[c]ontested election of judges is not changed," the people narrowly ratified the 1972 Constitution, including the new judicial article.

3. Public Financing for Judicial Elections

A collateral consequence of the debate at the Constitutional Convention was a failed proposal for public financing of judicial campaigns. The Judiciary Committee proposed a section requiring the legislature to "appropriate funds for the contested general election campaign expenses of candidates for the offices of justices of the supreme court and district court judges." Unlike the primary selection proposal, the public-financing proposal enjoyed broad support on the committee. Public financing of judicial elections was not raised in any of the pre-convention studies, and appeared to originate with the Judiciary Committee itself. Because the majority and minority proposals both contemplated contested non-partisan judicial elections, the entire committee recognized "the same problems we have always had" with judges running for office. These included

> (1) the necessity that the judge demean himself and his position by seeking campaign funds;
>
> (2) the fact that the wrong people can make contributions;
>
> (3) the fact that lawyers are the biggest contributors and solicitors of campaign funds to the detriment of themselves than the candidate;

(4) the fact that the candidate with the most money to spend is the more likely to win regardless of merit; and

(5) the fact that the appearance of justice suffers in the process.

The committee's solution to these problems prompted a prescient discussion of campaign finance in judicial elections. ***

The delegates gave the public-financing proposal preliminary approval by a narrow margin, but voted later that day to reconsider the proposal, and opened a deeper debate on the issue. *** Opponents, however, doubted that the legislature would provide sufficient funding, and asked why only the judiciary should have public campaign financing entrenched in the constitution. *** By the end of the day's debate, several delegates moved to adjourn and take "a chance to think about this overnight," but those motions were defeated. Then the delegates voted to delete the provision.

Two weeks later, with the judiciary article reported out of the Style and Drafting Committee, Delegate Rick Champoux recalled an earlier point made by Delegate Schiltz: "[I]f we don't provide the expenses for these judges, somebody else will, and that other group will be, in the main, large companies that come before this court, whether they do it directly or indirectly." In response, the delegates suspended the rules to reconsider the proposal, but only as applied to supreme court justices. Judges "are supposed to decide fairly and evenly between all of us after they get elected," Delegate Graybill reminded the delegates during the debate that followed, pointing out that "[i]t's one thing to support a senator or a congressman and have him help you out with a bureaucracy; it's another thing to support a judge and have him help you out with a decision."

Delegate Garlington, however, had already advised against an unprecedented constitutional provision for public financing: "[I]t seems to me the proper judgment here is to leave this to such time as it may genuinely prove in our own state to be an evil that needs correction, and then our people's representatives, the Legislature, can do so." And Delegate Dave Drum observed that public financing might upset the long-standing tradition of the lawyers-money primary, whereby "you may wind up with the gentleman as a Supreme Court justice who the legal fraternity generally thinks will be the best judge." Others raised fiscal concerns that voters might reject a new constitution with spending mandates that seemed to have been included "in order to finance all the political aspirations of our lawyers wanting to run for Supreme Court justice or other higher offices." Delegate Dahood responded by arguing that "[t]he taxpayer, above all, should have paramount interest in this proposal" because "[h]e is the one that is affected by the quality of justice, more than anyone else." This time, the delegates adopted the proposal by fifty-five votes to thirty-two.

All that remained was final consideration of the judicial article. The Convention adopted the first thirteen sections—including the compromise judicial-selection section—by wide margins. But when the Convention reached the final section of the judicial article, on campaign expenses, the ayes fell three votes short of a majority. The Convention sent the Sergeant to find absent delegates, and voted upon their return to reconsider. But in a final vote, with all but three of the delegates present, the public-financing proposal fell short again. After an agonizing series of debates, what would have been a major innovation in state judicial elections failed by just two votes. ***

Financing of Contested Montana Judicial Campaigns: 1990–2014

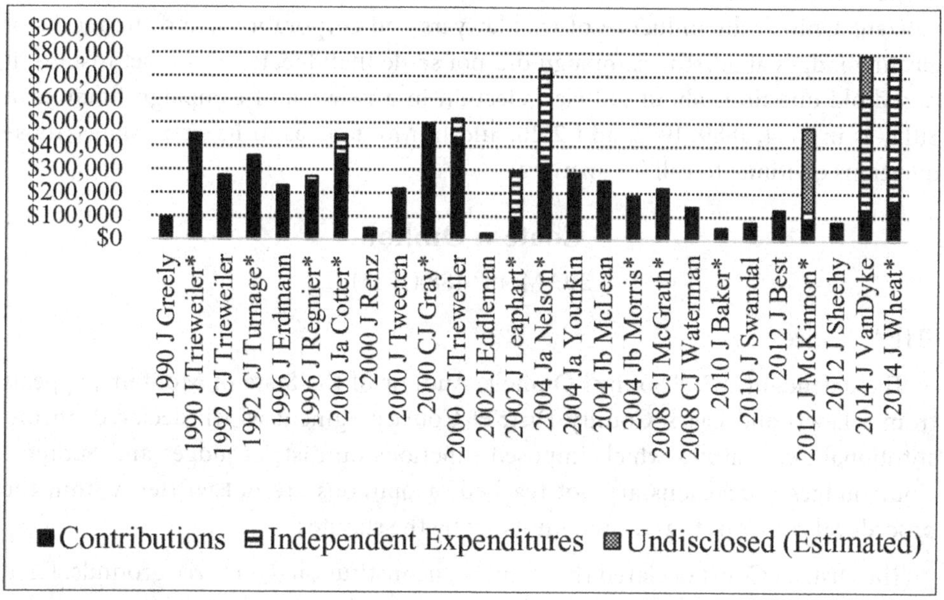

[* denotes candidate who won the race]

*** VI. Conclusion

State courts, no less than federal courts, pose critical questions of independence and accountability under the rule of law. There is no one right answer to those questions for all jurisdictions. Montana's answer reflects a territorial suspicion of outside influence, a progressive-era concern about corporate corruption, and an extraordinarily deep deliberation among ordinary citizens about competing models for judicial selection in the formation of its 1972 constitution. The result is a hybrid model sharing elements of contested election, retention election, merit, and (with strong gubernatorial representation on the nominating commission) straight appointment models. After the invalidation of its partisan-endorsement prohibition, Montana now also shares some elements of a partisan-election model, for better or worse.

As in other states with similar models of judicial elections, Montana's model is being tested by a new normal in politics. More than any other recent development,

Citizens United disrupted the traditional practice of judicial elections in Montana. The Montana Supreme Court itself invited the justices to consider the implications of that case for judicial elections in [*Western Tradition Partnership v. Attorney General* (Mont. 2011)], but the United States Supreme Court declined. In the aftermath, corporate expenditures, super PACs, dark money, and even national political parties flooded Montana's relatively small supreme court campaigns with exactly the sort of out-of-state corporate influence Montanans had fought against for the last 150 years. This prompted a vigorous public debate, in the context of the [2014] campaign between Mike Wheat and Lawrence VanDyke, about the Montana Constitution and Citizens United, the influence of trial lawyers and corporations, and the merits of electing judges at all. The campaign did not settle that debate, of course. Instead, it raised old questions about judicial selection in a new era of campaign finance. In 2014, as in 1864, 1889, 1972, and 2010, and in Montana as in its sister states, those questions continue to call for answers.

Coate v. Omholt

203 Mont. 488 (1983)

SHEA, Justice.

The defendant, E.V. "Sonny" Omholt, Auditor of the State of Montana, appeals from a Lewis and Clark County District Court judgment which declared unconstitutional two statutes which imposed sanctions on district judges and Supreme Court judges if decisions are not reached or opinions are not written within the procedural constraints and time limits set by the statutes.

The District Court declared the statutes unconstitutional on three grounds. First, in attempting to regulate the internal operations of the judiciary by imposing procedures and time limits for reaching decisions, the statutes violated the separation of powers doctrine as set forth in Article III, § 1 of the Montana Constitution. Second, by requiring the forfeiture of one month's pay for a violation, the statutes violated Article VII, § 7(1) of the Montana Constitution which provides that judicial salaries must not be diminished during a term of office. Third, the forfeiture of pay provisions violated the impairment of contract clauses of Art. I, § 10 of the United States Constitution and Art. II, § 31, of the Montana Constitution. We affirm.

The statutes involved, sections 3-2-104 (applicable to Supreme Court justices) and 3-5-212, MCA (applicable to district judges), operate in essentially the same way. . . .

Both statutes provide that decisions must be reached or opinions written within 90 days of submission. If not, another procedure is invoked to allow 30 more days to reach the decision or write the opinion. On or before the 90th day of submission, a district judge or Supreme Court justice, must file an affidavit to the chief justice giving the case name and number and the reason for delay. The parties involved in the case must be given a copy of the affidavit. Upon timely filing of the affidavit, the judge or justice has an automatic 30 more days to reach a decision or to write the opinion. To justify further delay a judge or justice must file another affidavit to the Supreme Court before the expiration of the 120th day, which affidavit must establish good cause for the delay. A majority of the Supreme Court must determine whether additional time should be given to reach the decision or to write the opinion.

The statutes are imprecise as to when or how a violation occurs if the affidavits are timely filed. However, if no affidavit is filed on or before the 90th day of submission, or on or before the 120th day of submission, a violation is automatic. It appears also that if an affidavit is timely filed but good cause is not shown for an extension of time beyond the 120 days, either the Supreme Court by a majority vote, or a party to the case, may refer the case to the judicial standards commission.

Upon the commission receiving the matter it appears that further proceedings and a hearing are contemplated before the commission, although the statute does not so state. Nonetheless, once the judicial standards commission has acted and made a recommendation to the Supreme Court, it appears that the Supreme Court must then sit as a court of review to determine whether the commission's recommendation was proper. If there has been a failure to file an affidavit, it appears the commission must find a violation, and it further appears the Supreme Court would likewise have to find a violation. On the other hand, if the question is one of good cause for the delay, it appears that the commission and this Court are granted some discretion in determining whether a violation has occurred.

If a violation is found this Court is compelled by statute to direct the state auditor to withhold a month's pay from the district judge or justice—this pay is forfeited.

Part I. Separation of Powers

The essential question is whether the legislature, in enacting time limits and setting forth the enforcement procedures for judicial decision-making, has exercised a power that properly belongs to the judicial branch of government. We conclude that, based on the separation of powers clause of our state constitution, that the question of when cases shall be decided and the manner in which they shall be decided, is a matter solely for the judicial branch of government.

The separation of powers provision, contained in the general government section of Art. III, § 1, 1972 Montana Constitution, provides:

> The power of the government of this state is divided into three distinct branches—legislative, executive, and judicial. No person or persons charged with the exercise of power properly belonging to one branch shall exercise any power properly belonging to either of the others, except as in this constitution expressly directed or permitted.

By this provision, each branch of government is made equal, coordinate, and independent. By this we do not mean absolute independence because "absolute independence" cannot exist in our form of government. It does mean, however, "... that the powers properly belonging to one department shall not be exercised by either of the others." With only one exception, the Supreme Courts of those states called on to answer the question have declared that the essential nature of a constitutional court encompasses the right to determine when a judicial decision will be made.

These holdings are best summarized in a law review article entitled, *Legislative Control Over Judicial Rule-Making: A Problem in Constitutional Revision* (1958), 107 U. Pa. L. Rev. 1, 31–32:

> What the holdings do suggest is that there is a third realm of judicial activity, neither substantive nor adjective [procedural] law, a realm of "proceedings which are so vital to the efficient functioning of a court as to be beyond legislative power." This is the area of minimum functional integrity of the courts, "what is essential to the existence, dignity and functions of the court as a constitutional tribunal and from the very fact that it is a court." Any statute which moves so far into this realm of judicial affairs as to dictate to a judge how he shall judge or how he shall comport himself in judging or which seeks to surround the act of judging with hampering conditions clearly offends the constitutional scheme of the separation of powers and will be held invalid.

The courts have recognized as the authors state, that certain judicial functions require that the courts alone determine how those functions are to be exercised. Even assuming the right under many state constitutions, and indeed, the need for the legislature to be involved in rule-making where the courts and the legislature have concurrent rule-making power, the authors state:

> Grant the necessity for concurrent jurisdiction in the field of procedure, immediately another problem presents itself. Should there not be some realm of judicial administration entirely free from legislative supervision? Or shall the legislature be permitted to dictate to the courts every detail of their internal regimen: command appellate courts to issue written opinions in every case, declare within what time cases shall be heard, deny to the court the power to issue its mandate until a prescribed period of time after judgment shall have elapsed? *There are spheres of activity so fundamental and so necessary to a court, so inherent in its very nature as a court, that to divest it of its absolute command within these spheres is to make meaningless the very phrase judicial power.*" (Emphasis added.)

To the questions posed above the courts have answered with virtual unanimity that the separation of powers doctrine does not permit the legislature to intrude. For example, in *Houston v. Williams* ([Cal.] 1859), the court struck down a statute which required that in all cases the California Supreme Court must render a written opinion with reasons. The court said:

> If the Legislature can require the reasons for our decisions to be stated in writing, it can forbid their statement in writing, and enforce their oral announcement, or prescribe the paper upon which they shall be written, and the ink which shall be used. And yet no sane man will justify any absurd pretension, but where is the limit to this power if its exercise in any particular be admitted?

*** And, of course, other decisions have struck down legislation imposing time limits for judicial action. . . .

The federal courts have struck down provisions of the Federal Speedy Trial Act on grounds that the requirements for trial within the statutory deadlines constitute an unconstitutional encroachment of the judiciary. The provisions were held to infringe on the constitutionally autonomous power of the judiciary—that is, to violate the separation of powers doctrine.

We make no attempt to catalog and discuss all the cases bearing on this issue. ***

The last clause of the separation of powers provision, Art. III, §1, declares that one branch shall not exercise a power belonging to another branch "... except as in this constitution expressly directed or permitted." Even by the most liberal construction standards we cannot read either Art. VIII, §12 ["The legislature shall by law insure strict accountability of all revenue received and money spent by the state and counties, cities, towns, and all other local governmental entities."], or Art. VII, §11 ["The legislature shall create a judicial standards commission consisting of five persons and provide for the appointment thereto of two district judges, one attorney, and two citizens who are neither judges nor attorneys...."], to mean that the drafters of these provisions intended that time limits on judicial decision-making would be imposed....

Perhaps the trial court best described the effect of sections 3-2-104 and 3-5-212, MCA, in comparing them with an attempt by the judiciary to interfere with the internal operations of the legislature:

> The totality of the effect of Chapter 375 is to interfere with the internal operations of the judiciary in the same manner as if the judiciary would impose limitations on the legislature as to its internal operations, such as the number of committees, the time within which a committee must act, the time each legislator must attend the sessions, limiting the time of discussion, limiting the time one bill must pass from one house to the other and the like. All of these legislative functions are internal with the legislature and the constitution authorizing the legislature to govern its affairs without interference from the other constitutional branches of government.

Part II. Diminution of Salary and Impairment of Contract

Although our decision on the separation of powers issue is dispositive, we nonetheless proceed to the two additional grounds on which the trial court held the statutes to be unconstitutional—diminution of salary and impairment of salary. The salary forfeiture provisions clearly violate these constitutional provisions.

The penalty provisions of both statutes require a one month's forfeiture of pay in the event of a violation. Section 3-2-104, MCA, which applies to Supreme Court justices, provides in part that the Supreme Court "... shall order that the state auditor not issue a warrant for payment of services for 1 month, which pay is forfeited by the justice." Section 3-5-212, which applies to district judges, provides in part that the Supreme Court "... shall order that the state auditor not issue a warrant for payment of services for 1 month, which pay is forfeited by the judge." The trial court held that these statutes constitute both an unconstitutional diminution of salary and an unconstitutional impairment of contract.

The state constitutional prohibition against diminution of judicial salaries during terms of office provides that "[a]ll justices and judges shall be paid as provided by law, but salaries shall not be diminished during terms of office." Art. VII, § 7(1). The federal constitutional prohibition against impairment of contracts, Art. I, § 10, provides in part: "no state shall . . . pass any . . . law impairing the obligation of contracts . . ." The state constitutional prohibition against impairment of contracts, Art. II, § 31, provides: "[n]o . . . law impairing the obligation of contracts . . . shall be passed by the legislature."

In arguing that the prohibition against reduction of judicial salaries is not violated, defendant in effect argues that the legislature can do indirectly what it is prohibited from doing directly. Defendant concedes that the statute mandates a reduction in salary but argues that if the judiciary imposes the sanctions rather than the legislature, the constitution is not violated. This argument, of course, ignores the fact that the judicially-imposed reductions are mandated by the statutes.

And assuming that the legislature can indirectly violate the constitution by imposing the duties on the Supreme Court to forfeit the salaries of judges who do not comply with the challenged statutes, the defendant next argues that the contract impairment clauses of the United States and Montana Constitutions are not violated because the legislature has reserved to itself the authority to condition payment of salaries on performance of all services required. As applied here, defendant claims that the legislature can withhold judicial salaries if a judge does not reach a decision within the time limits set by the challenged statutes.

A constitutional provision prohibiting diminution of salaries during the term of office is designed to remove from lawmakers the temptation to exert control over the other branches by promise of reward in the form of increased compensation or threats of punishment by way of reduced salaries. *State ex rel. Jackson v. Porter* (Mont. 1920). In *Jackson*, we so interpreted the 1889 provision which applied to all elected public officers. The 1889 Constitution also contained a provision applying only to judges. Art. VIII, § 29, expressly prohibited the salaries of judges from being increased or decreased. The provision with respect to all public officials was not carried over to our 1972 Constitution; however, a similar provision applying to judges was, of course, placed in the 1972 Constitution. Art. VII, § 7 of our present Constitution, although now applying only to judicial compensation, still embodies the fundamental policy considerations set forth in *Jackson*. . . .

We will not, as the defendant urges, sanction an indirect violation of the Constitution by upholding a scheme for reduction of salaries mandated by the legislature but administered by the courts. We must, therefore, conclude that the challenged statutes violate Art. VII, § 7 of our Constitution forbidding a reduction of judicial salaries during a term of office.

Assuming, however, that it is permissible to indirectly violate an express mandate of the Constitution, the statutes challenged here nonetheless cannot survive a challenge that they violate the impairment of contract clauses of our State and Federal Constitutions.

In *Olson v. Cory* (Cal. 1980), the California Supreme Court interpreted the impairment clauses as it affects the judiciary's right to salary set by statute. The court held that a judge entering office does so partly in consideration of the salary benefits then offered by the state for that office. The court held that if those salary benefits are reduced by the legislature during a judge's term of office or during the unexpired term of a predecessor judge, the judge is nonetheless entitled to the contract for benefits during the remainder of the term. In applying the impairment clause the court stated:

> Public employment gives rise to certain obligations which are protected by the contract clause of the Constitution. [Citations omitted.] Promised compensation is one such protected right. [Citations omitted.] Once vested, the right to compensation cannot be eliminated without unconstitutionally impairing the contract obligation. [Citations omitted.] When agreement of employment between the state and public employees have been adopted by governing bodies, such agreements are binding and constitutionally protected.

*** In effect, defendant argues that the legislature can withhold or forfeit the salaries of all state officials covered by the statute. Suffice to say that this interpretation will undoubtedly come as a great shock to those state officials who claim a right to their salaries without a requirement that they file affidavits or perform their duties within a specified time.

We have held that the challenged statutes violate Art. VII, § 7(1), which empowers the legislature to set judicial salaries subject to the restriction that such salaries cannot be reduced during a term of office. The legislature cannot directly establish an annual salary by one statute and then indirectly take away any part of that salary by a statute that imposes a forfeiture because an affidavit has not been filed or a decision has not been filed within the time limits set by the challenged statutes. These forfeiture provisions just as clearly violate the impairment of contract clauses of the State and Federal Constitutions.

Part III. The Application of Article VII, § 2(3)

In light of our holdings in Parts I and II declaring the challenged statutes to be unconstitutional, we think it important to discuss the role of the courts and the legislature as they relate to rule-making for the courts. The roles are specified in Art. VII, § 2(3), which provides:

> It [the Supreme Court] may make rules governing appellate procedure, practice and procedure for all other courts, admission to the bar and conduct of its members. Rules of procedure shall be subject to disapproval by the legislature in either of the two sessions following promulgation.

The 1889 Constitution did not contain such a provision. The judicial article was silent on the role of the Supreme Court in making appellate rules of practice or civil rules of practice. It was simply assumed that the legislature had unrestricted authority to legislate in this area. In fact, before the 1972 Constitution, any authority of the Supreme Court in adopting either appellate rules of procedure or civil rules of procedure, came expressly from the legislature, with the legislature reserving the right to repeal any rules promulgated pursuant to this legislative authorization. See sections 3-2-701 through 3-2-708, MCA, enacted in 1963. Clearly, with the adoption of the 1972 Constitution, sections 3-2-701 through 3-2-708, were impliedly repealed, for Art. VII, § 2(3) vests the rule-making authority in the Supreme Court subject only to legislative veto. This provision changed the roles of the Supreme Court and the legislature.

We have had only one occasion to interpret this clause in an opinion. In *Matter of McCabe* (Mont. 1975), the issue was whether the legislature or this Court could set the standards for admission to the bar. In interpreting Art. VII, § 2(3), we held that this Court has the exclusive control over admission to the bar and conduct of members of the bar. Concerning the remaining portion of (3) we stated:

> The second sentence of subdivision (3) obviously means, without the necessity for any strained construction, that as to rules of appellate procedure and rules of procedure for other courts, such as the Montana Rules of Civil Procedure, the promulgation of such rules is subject to disapproval by the legislature.

Without question, Art. VII, § 2(3) vests in the Supreme Court the authority to adopt rules for appellate procedure and trial and appellate procedures "for all other courts." Just as clearly, the legislature is empowered to veto any such rules promulgated by this Court. However, once a legislative veto is exercised, the legislature is not empowered to fill the vacuum by enacting its own legislation governing appellate procedure or lower court procedure.

We have held in Part I of this opinion that the challenged statutes constitute a direct infringement on the functional and constitutional integrity of the judiciary as a separate branch of government, and therefore that the statutes violate the separation of powers clause (Art. III, § 1) of our State Constitution. The constitutional provision giving rule-making power to the Supreme Court and veto power to the legislature, does not encompass the kind of legislation embodied in the challenged statutes. We held that time limits within which judicial decisions must be reached, fall within what we recognized as the ". . . third realm of judicial activity, neither substantive nor adjective [procedural] law, a realm of 'proceedings which are so vital to the effective functioning of the courts as to go beyond legislative power.'" 107 U. Pa. L. Rev. at 31–32. The internal operations of the courts, this third realm of judicial proceedings, are not subject to legislative veto:

> A constitutional [provision such as Art. VII, § 2(3)] which expressly reserves ultimate authority over procedure to the legislature need not be feared as sanctioning legislative invasion of this last judicial stronghold. . . . So long

> as a constitution maintains the fundamental separation of powers [Art. III, § 16, 1972 Mont. Const.] this area of functional independence of the judiciary will be preserved in the very grant of judicial power.

107 U.Pa.L.Rev. at 33. If we held, however, that the separation of powers doctrine was not violated, we would then be required to examine the statutes in light of Art. VII, § 2(3), which gives only the veto power to the legislature. The question would be whether the legislature, in the face of Art. VII, § 2(3), could validly enact statutes setting time limits (with sanctions other than a forfeiture or loss of judicial salary) for the judiciary to reach its decisions. Again, we would be required to strike down the legislation as having gone beyond the authority conferred on the legislature as provided for in this constitutional provision.

The trial court aptly described the situation that would exist if the statutes were considered to be procedural rules and therefore necessarily subject to the requirements and restrictions of Art. VII, § 2(3):

> Chapter 375 [sections 3-2-104 and 3-5-212] is a statute which attempts to govern the internal conduct of judicial business. Like the rules governing conduct of members of the bar, it is not a procedural rule within the meaning of the Montana Constitution, Article VII, Section 2(3). Even if the Supreme Court adopted the language of Chapter 375 as a procedural rule, the legislature has only the power, under Article VII, of the Montana Constitution to disapprove.

It is therefore clear that if in Parts I and II of this opinion we did not find the constitutional violations complained of, we would nonetheless be required to hold that the legislature exceeded its constitutional power under Art. VII, § 2(3) in enacting the legislation.

For all of these reasons we hold the challenged statutes to be unconstitutional. The judgment of the District Court is affirmed.

Reichert v. State

365 Mont. 92 (2012)

Justice JAMES C. NELSON delivered the Opinion of the Court.

¶ 1 The State of Montana appeals from the decision of the First Judicial District Court, Lewis and Clark County, ordering Secretary of State Linda McCulloch to decertify Legislative Referendum No. 119 (LR-119) and enjoining the Secretary of State from presenting LR-119 on the June 5, 2012 primary election ballot.

¶ 2 We address the following issues on appeal:

1. Whether the non-retiring justices on this Court should recuse themselves from participating in the decision of this appeal.

[The justiciability and severability issues are addressed in the next section.]

3. Whether LR-119 is constitutionally defective.

Background

*** ¶ 6 Under current law, the justices are elected on a statewide basis. See § 3-2-101, MCA. LR-119 would change the law so that each justice is elected from one of seven districts of approximately equal population. The districts created under LR-119 follow county lines — for example, the Fifth Supreme Court district would consist of Lincoln, Sanders, Flathead, Glacier, and Toole Counties. The district numbers correspond to the justices' current seat numbers, with Chief Justice McGrath's seat being assigned to the seventh district (Missoula, Lake, and Mineral Counties). The justices would be required to reside and be registered to vote in their respective districts at the time they are elected, and electors in a given district could vote only for that district's justice. Consequently, rather than voting for each of the seven Supreme Court justices as they come up for election in two-year intervals, electors could vote for only one of the justices, who would come up for election every eight years. The chief justice would then be chosen from among the seven justices by majority vote of the justices.

¶ 7 LR-119, therefore, would effect three changes concerning the qualifications and selection of justices. First, LR-119 adds a residency and voter-registration requirement: a candidate for a seat on the Supreme Court must be a "qualified elector" of the district from which the candidate is elected. (Once elected, a justice is not required to reside within that district during the justice's service in office.) Second, LR-119 creates seven Supreme Court districts and requires that each justice be elected from a separate district. Only voters in a given district are eligible to vote for that district's justice. Third, LR-119 changes the method of selecting the chief justice from a statewide election to a selection by the seven justices from among their number.

Procedural History

¶ 8 Plaintiffs are Montana citizens, taxpayers, and electors [Fn. Reichert, Dahood, and Bowman were delegates to the 1972 Montana Constitutional Convention] who historically have participated in elections for justices of the Montana Supreme Court and who reside in each of the seven districts proposed by LR-119 . . . .

¶ 9 Meanwhile, on January 9, seven individual Montana legislators (Legislators) filed a motion to intervene in the action as party defendants pursuant to M.R. Civ. P. 24. [Fn. One of the legislators is identified as the primary sponsor of SB 268 (Senator Joe Balyeat). The other six legislators (Representatives Mark Blasdel, Ryan Osmundson, Mathew Rosendale, and Kelly Flynn, and Senators Edward Walker and Greg Hinkle) supported SB 268 and voted for its passage. The legislators reside in each of the seven districts proposed by LR-119.] ***

Discussion

¶ 22 Before we may address the substantive merits of whether LR-119 is invalid, there are two threshold issues which must be considered and resolved. First, Legislators have raised the question whether certain justices of this Court should recuse themselves from this case. This question is obviously antecedent to all other issues on appeal, and we thus address it first (commencing at ¶ 23). Second, the State has raised the question whether Plaintiffs' challenge to LR-119 is justiciable. The judicial power of Montana's courts is limited to justiciable controversies—meaning that our courts do not resolve abstract differences of opinion or advise what the law would be upon a hypothetical state of facts. Hence, issues of justiciability—such as whether the plaintiff has standing and whether the dispute is ripe or moot—are antecedent, as well, to any discussion of the substantive merits of the parties' claims. We therefore address the justiciability question after the recusal question (commencing at ¶ 52). Then, having resolved the recusal question, and having concluded that this case is justiciable, we reach the merits of Plaintiffs' challenge to LR-119 under Issue 3 (commencing at ¶ 61).

¶ 23 Issue 1. Whether the non-retiring justices should recuse themselves.

¶ 24 Legislators argue in their amicus brief that all non-retiring justices of this Court should recuse themselves.... That issue is raised solely by Legislators. This Court has long held, however, that amici curiae cannot raise separate issues not raised by the parties. One reason for this rule is that "[t]he theories and arguments in the case should not be changed by amici at the expense of the litigants by injecting new and extraneous issues in the case." *Crabtree v. Mont. State Lib.* (Mont. 1983) (Haswell, C.J., specially concurring). Moreover, there is "[t]he everpresent danger that issues and arguments ... not considered significant or controlling by the litigants themselves will not be adequately briefed or argued on appeal." ...

¶ 26 The general rule, therefore, is that "[s]ince amici curiae are not parties and cannot assume the functions of parties, nor create, extend or enlarge issues, we ... consider[] the briefs of amici only insofar as they coincide with the issues raised by the parties to the action." We have deviated from this rule only in rare instances. *See e.g. Crabtree* ("While it is not our custom to address separately issues not raised by the parties, we depart from that practice here because of the widespread impact that the Library and amicus argue our opinion will have on the hiring practices within state and local levels of government.") ...

¶ 27 In the present case, while we reaffirm the general rule stated above, we conclude that the importance of the recusal issues raised by Legislators makes this one of the rare instances in which we should consider a question raised by amici but not by the parties themselves. Because the analysis under the Due Process Clause provides useful context for the analysis under the Montana Code of Judicial Conduct, we shall first address Legislators' arguments premised on constitutional standards, and then their arguments premised on the ethical standards set forth in the Code.

Constitutional Standards

¶ 28 Legislators analogize the present case to *Caperton v. A.T. Massey Coal Co.* (2009). In *Caperton,* the Supreme Court held that due process "require [s] recusal when 'the probability of actual bias on the part of the judge or decisionmaker is too high to be constitutionally tolerable.'" "The inquiry is an objective one. The Court asks not whether the judge is actually, subjectively biased, but whether the average judge in his position is 'likely' to be neutral, or whether there is an unconstitutional 'potential for bias.'" . . .

¶ 29 This Court has not heretofore considered the application of these principles to a claim that a justice (or justices) or a judge (or judges) must be recused from a case in the interest of due process. As Legislators concede, the foregoing standards "protect *the parties'* basic right to a fair trial in a fair tribunal." Again, Legislators are not "parties" to this action, and neither Plaintiffs nor the Attorney General has expressed fairness concerns here. Nevertheless, as noted, given the peculiar significance of the recusal issue in this case, we shall address the due process question.

¶ 30 . . . According to Legislators, the alleged interest of the four not-presently-retiring justices is their "potential" to seek reelection in the future. *** The Due Process Clause does not mandate recusal simply because LR-119 "could possibly" prevent a justice, who "potentially" may decide in the future to seek reelection, from getting reelected. . . . In this regard, the traditional common-law rule, which the Due Process Clause incorporated, required recusal when the judge had a direct, personal, substantial, pecuniary interest in a case, but did not permit disqualification for bias or prejudice. . . . Instead, matters of kinship, personal bias, state policy, remoteness of interest, and prejudice were left to statutes and judicial codes. In Montana, such matters are addressed and governed by the 2008 Montana Code of Judicial Conduct. And "[b]ecause the codes of judicial conduct provide more protection than due process requires, most disputes over disqualification will be resolved without resort to the Constitution. Application of the constitutional standard . . . will thus be confined to rare instances." *Caperton*. ***

¶ 37 Returning now to the present case, we first note that the interest identified by Legislators as necessitating recusal is not exclusive to the four not-presently-retiring justices. In the event of a justice's disqualification, "[a] district judge shall be substituted." Mont. Const. art. VII, § 3(2). A district judge, however, also has "the potential" to run for a seat on this Court in the future, "could possibly" be prevented by LR-119 from getting elected, and thus (under Legislators' theory) has an "interest" in the outcome of this case. Under a logical extension of Legislators' argument, no judge in this state — indeed, no otherwise qualified person with "the potential" to run for Supreme Court justice — could sit on this case. Hence, applying the rule of necessity, none of the justices would be disqualified.

¶ 38 But more importantly, "the potential" to run for reelection in the future, coupled with the fact that LR-119 "could possibly" prevent a justice from getting reelected if he or she were unable to garner the required number of votes to win in a particular district, does not constitute a "direct, personal, substantial, and pecuniary" interest. Indeed, any interest the justices might conceivably have in this case is "highly speculative and contingent." It is sheer conjecture at this point whether the adoption of district-based elections under LR-119, in lieu of statewide elections under the current system, would help or hinder a justice's chance for reelection. It is also sheer conjecture whether LR-119 will become law, whether the four justices will seek reelection, and whether anyone will run against them. . . . The fact that the justices have "the potential" to seek reelection and "could possibly" be hindered in their reelection bids by LR-119 (assuming it passes) does not create the sort of "extreme," "extraordinary," "exceptional," and "rare" circumstances that the Supreme Court has indicated must exist before a due process violation will be found. *** Having explained, in some detail, why this case is not one of those "rare instances," we now turn to Montana's Code of Judicial Conduct.

Code of Judicial Conduct ***

¶ 50 In sum, the ultimate question here is whether the four justices' impartiality "might reasonably be questioned." Mont. Code of Jud. Conduct, Rule 2.12(A). The fact that the justices have "the potential" to run for reelection, coupled with the fact that LR-119 "could possibly" hinder their reelection bids, does not establish that the justices' impartiality might reasonably be questioned. Legislators have presented no other legal theories for recusal. And neither Legislators nor the parties have pointed to any actual evidence of bias, prejudice, or unethical conduct on the part of any justice or judge sitting on this case. Absent evidence to the contrary, the "presumption of honesty and integrity in those serving as adjudicators" stands. ***

¶ 61 Issue 3. Whether LR-119 is constitutionally defective.

The Constitutional Provisions

¶ 62 Article VII, Section 9 of the Montana Constitution specifies the "[q]ualifications" of Supreme Court justice and district court judge. It states:

> A citizen of the United States who has resided in the state two years immediately before taking office is eligible to the office of supreme court justice or district court judge if admitted to the practice of law in Montana for at least five years prior to the date of appointment or election. Qualifications and methods of selection of judges of other courts shall be provided by law.

Mont Const. art. VII, § 9(1). Thus, to be eligible to the office of Supreme Court justice or district court judge, the person must (1) be a citizen of the United States, (2) have resided in Montana for two years immediately before taking office, and (3) have been admitted to the practice of law in Montana for at least five years prior to the date of appointment or election. Article VII, Section 9(1) contemplates that the qualifications for these offices are dictated solely by the Constitution. This much is apparent from the last sentence of Article VII, Section 9(1), which states that "[q]ualifications and methods of selection of judges of *other* courts shall be provided *by law*" (emphases added), a clear indicator that the Legislature may establish the qualifications and methods of selection of judges of other courts, but the qualifications and methods of selection of Supreme Court justices and district court judges are set by the Constitution alone and consist of the foregoing three criteria—no more, no less. Even without the last sentence, however, this Court has held that the Legislature may not add to or subtract from the constitutional qualifications to hold a particular office. ***

¶ 64 The language and structure of these sections demonstrate that the Constitution intends Supreme Court justices to be elected and serve on a statewide basis, district court judges to be elected and serve on a district-wide basis, and justices of the peace to be elected and serve on a countywide basis. *** Given this statewide jurisdiction, it would be incongruous to interpret the Constitution as contemplating a Supreme Court made up of justices who are elected from districts and implicitly "represent" regional interests. Such an interpretation would be inimical to the judicial function.

> Courts are not representative bodies. They are not designed to be a good reflex of a democratic society. Their judgment is best informed, and therefore most dependable, within narrow limits. Their essential quality is detachment, founded on independence. History teaches that the independence of the judiciary is jeopardized when courts become embroiled in the passions of the day and assume primary responsibility in choosing between competing political, economic and social pressures.

Dennis v. United States (1951) (Frankfurter, J., concurring in affirmance of the judgment). Legislative and executive officials serve in representative capacities, as agents of the people, whose primary function is to advance the interests of their constituencies. Judges, in contrast, "are not political actors. They do not sit as representatives of particular persons, communities, or parties; they serve no faction or constituency. . . . Even when they develop common law or give concrete meaning to constitutional text, judges act only in the context of individual cases, the outcome of which cannot depend on the will of the public." *Republican Party of Minn. v. White* (2002) (Ginsburg, Stevens, Souter, & Breyer, JJ., dissenting). The obligation of Supreme Court justices is to interpret and apply the law on a uniform basis statewide. The requirements and protections of the Constitution and the law do not vary from one county or district to another. They are the same whether one is from Yaak, Broadus, Wisdom, or Plentywood. Ethical rules do not permit judges to "represent" particular constituencies or interest groups. *See* Mont. Code of Jud. Conduct, Rule 2.2 (Impartiality and Fairness), Rule 2.3 (Bias, Prejudice, and Harassment). These principles are implicit in the constitutional design, which establishes the office of Supreme Court justice as one subject to selection by electors statewide.

LR-119's Amendments ***

¶ 82 In sum, LR-119 would create new qualifications for the office of Supreme Court justice by requiring each justice to be a "qualified elector"—i.e., a registered voter and resident—of the Supreme Court district from which the justice is elected or appointed. In addition, LR-119 would alter the structure of the Supreme Court by converting it from a statewide elected institution into a district-based representative body. Correspondingly, LR-119 would eliminate the right presently held by all Montana voters to select all seven justices of the Supreme Court. Legislators argue extensively in their amicus brief that the process of electing justices from smaller, local districts from around the state has "inherent value." However, this case is not about the wisdom or "value" of the changes proposed by LR-119. The point, rather, is that these changes constitute amendments to the Constitution, which cannot be achieved by means of a statutory referendum. Accordingly, we hold that LR-119 is facially unconstitutional.

McLaughlin v. Montana State Legislature

2021 MT 178

Justice BETH BAKER delivered the Opinion of the Court.

¶3 . . . [T]he Montana Legislature asked [Court Administrator for the Montana Judicial Branch] Beth McLaughlin to provide information on a poll she facilitated of the Montana Judges Association pertaining to Senate Bill 140, a bill then under consideration by the Legislature. She responded to the request but had not retained and did not provide narrative responses that some of the judges had included. Under an unsigned April 8, 2021 subpoena from the Chair of the Senate Judiciary Committee, the Legislature directed Montana Department of Administration Director Misty Ann Giles to appear the following afternoon and produce without subject matter limitation "[a]ll emails and attachments sent and received by Court Administrator Beth McLaughlin between January 4, 2021 and April 8, 2021." The Subpoena also requested "[a]ny and all recoverable deleted emails" McLaughlin sent or received during the same time period. The subpoena excluded only "any emails and attachments related to decisions made by the justices in disposition of final opinion." The subpoena did not identify the purpose or subject of the inquiry. Though not served, McLaughlin learned of the subpoena when she received a "courtesy copy" late afternoon on April 9, 2021. By that time, Director Giles already had provided several thousand pages of e-mail messages to the Legislature. ***

Discussion

Legislative Power to Investigate

¶6 The Montana Constitution divides the power of government "into three distinct branches—legislative, executive, and judicial." Mont. Const. art. III, § 1. "The legislative power is vested in a legislature consisting of a senate and a house of representatives." Mont. Const. art. V, § 1. Like the United States Constitution, Montana's Constitution contains "no enumerated constitutional power [in the Legislature] to conduct investigations or issue subpoenas," but it is well-established that a legislative body "has power 'to secure needed information' in order to legislate." *Trump v. Mazars USA, LLP* (2020). "This 'power of inquiry—with process to enforce it—is an essential and appropriate auxiliary to the legislative function.'" *Mazars*; *see also* 43 Mont. Op. Att'y Gen. 60 at 222 (1990) ("The legislative power described by Article V, section 1 of the Montana Constitution contains the inherent power of investigation."). "This has been recognized from the earliest times in the history of U.S. legislation, both federal and state, and from even earlier epochs in the development of British jurisprudence." Mason's Manual of Legislative Procedure (2010 ed.).

¶7 The Montana Legislature has by statute set forth its authority to issue subpoenas "requiring the attendance of any witness before either house of the legislature or a committee of either house" and the requisite form of the subpoenas so issued.

Section 5-5-101, MCA. A witness subpoenaed by the Legislature "cannot refuse to testify to any fact or to produce any paper concerning which the witness is examined for the reason that the witness's testimony or the production of the paper tends to disgrace the witness or render the witness infamous." Section 5-5-105(2), MCA. *See also* § 5-11-107, MCA (providing that a statutory or interim committee of the legislature "may hold hearings, administer oaths, issue subpoenas, compel the attendance of witnesses and the production of papers, books, accounts, documents, and testimony, and cause depositions of witnesses to be taken in the manner prescribed by law for taking depositions in civil actions in district court" and allowing enforcement of the same by "the district court of any county[.]").

¶8 A legislature's "power to obtain information is 'broad' and 'indispensable.'" Courts generally must indulge a presumption that the legislative activity has as its object a legitimate goal toward possible legislation. But the Legislature's investigative power, broad as it is, "is not unlimited." *Mazars*. The Supreme Court has stated,

> Congress may only investigate into those areas in which it may potentially legislate or appropriate, it cannot inquire into matters which are within the exclusive province of one of the other branches of the Government. Lacking the judicial power given to the Judiciary, it cannot inquire into matters that are exclusively the concern of the Judiciary. Neither can it supplant the Executive in what exclusively belongs to the Executive.

Barenblatt v. United States (1959).

¶9 The legislative branch is not a law enforcement agency; its inquiry "must be related to, and in furtherance of, a legitimate task of the [Legislature]." To serve a "valid legislative purpose," the subpoena "must 'concern[] a subject on which legislation "could be had."'' "The investigatory power of a legislative body is limited to obtaining information on matters that fall within its proper field of legislative action." Mason's Manual of Leg. Procedure, § 797.7 at 567. "Investigations conducted solely for the personal aggrandizement of the investigators or to 'punish' those investigated are indefensible." And "'there is no congressional power to expose for the sake of exposure.'" ***

Legislative Purpose and Scope of Subpoenas

¶20 We accordingly turn to the merits of the controversy presented, whether the stated legislative purposes of the subpoenas for the Court Administrator's records are "related to, and in furtherance of, a legitimate task of the [Legislature]," and whether, consistent with the separate powers the Constitution confers on each branch, the subpoenas seek only information within the scope of such a task.

¶21 We look to the purposes the Legislature identifies. The April 8 subpoena to Director Giles did not identify any purpose for which the subpoena was issued. The April 14 subpoena to McLaughlin stated:

> This request pertains to the Legislature's investigation into whether members of the Judiciary or employees of the Judicial Branch deleted public

> records and information in violation of state law and policy; and whether the current policies and processes of the Judicial Standards Commission are sufficient to address the serious nature of polling members of the Judiciary to prejudge legislation and issues which have come and will come before the courts for decision.

*** We distill these variously stated purposes to three principal categories: (1) the Judicial Branch's records retention policy and practices; (2) the Court Administrator's use of state e-mail to communicate with judges and the Montana Judges Association about matters pending before the Legislature; and (3) the statements and conduct of members of the judiciary.

¶22 <u>Records Retention</u>

¶23 We address the asserted legislative purpose relating to judicial records retention first. ***

¶28 The Legislature unquestionably may seek data from the court administrator "relating to the business transacted by the courts." Section 3-1-702(2), MCA. In light of the statutes and Judicial Branch policies [that do not require retention of e-mails], however, the Legislature has not "adequately identif[ied] its aims and explain[ed]" the connection between the subject of its investigation — alleged violations of state law and policy — and the evidence offered — unretained e-mails. Investigating potential violation of unspecified state law or policy is not a valid legislative purpose to justify the subpoenas.

¶29 Importantly, "other sources could reasonably provide" information that would be relevant for understanding Judicial Branch records retention, such as the branch's publicly available e-mail policy, public statements by members of the Judicial Branch, or inquiries to the relevant Judicial Branch and information technology staff. The Legislature has not suggested that the Judicial Branch's policies are not available to the public, that its efforts to seek information on Judicial Branch policy and practice have been rebuffed, or that it is otherwise incapable of understanding Judicial Branch retention practices and policies without resorting to a subpoena of Judicial Branch electronic correspondence. ***

¶31 We therefore conclude that the Legislature's first proffered legislative purpose — an investigation into Judicial Branch members' e-mail retention practices as an alleged violation of state law or policy — is not a legitimate purpose of the Legislative Branch of government. It is based on an unsubstantiated premise that Judicial Branch members are required to retain all e-mails and fails to show that compelling production of thousands of unredacted Judicial Branch messages, rather than undertaking other forms of inquiry, will advance its consideration of legislation on the matter of a judicial records retention policy. The Legislature's subpoenas cannot be supported by this alleged legislative purpose.

¶32 <u>Use of State Resources to "Lobby"</u>

¶33 The Legislature identifies a second legislative purpose in its response to the Petition as seeking to determine "whether the Court Administrator has performed tasks for the Montana Judges Association during taxpayer funded worktime in violation of law and policy" and "members of the judicial branch improperly using government time and resources to lobby on behalf of a private entity." This purpose was not expressed in either subpoena. ***

¶35 ... [Montana's lobbying law] excludes actions of public officials acting in their governmental capacities from the definition of "lobbying." As public officials acting in their governmental capacities, district court judges therefore are not "lobbying" when they inform members of the Legislature of how proposed legislation will affect the function of the Judicial Branch. *** In that same vein, Rule 3.1 of the Montana Code of Judicial Conduct allows judges to use court "premises, staff, stationery, equipment, or other resources" for "incidental use for activities that concern the law, the legal system, or the administration of justice," because "[j]udges are uniquely qualified to engage in the extrajudicial activities that concern" such matters. Mont. Code of Jud. Conduct 3.1 & Comment 1.

¶37 Because the Legislature has not articulated a legitimate legislative purpose related to lobbying and predicates it on an erroneous legal premise, this suggested purpose is insufficient to support the legislative subpoenas at issue.

¶38 Statements by Judges

¶39 The Legislature's third proffered legislative purpose supporting the subpoenas relates to the statements and conduct of members of the judiciary—in particular, the practice by district court judges of responding to polls used by the Montana Judges Association to determine whether to take a policy position on proposed legislation affecting the Judicial Branch. The Legislature suggests that such responses indicate improper judicial "bias" or what it terms "pre-judging" with regard to pending legislation that, if enacted and subsequently challenged in court, judges could potentially be asked to determine as a matter of constitutional law or statutory interpretation. ***

¶40 Article VII, section 11, of the Montana Constitution addresses the removal and discipline of judges. *** "The judicial power of the state is vested in one supreme court, district courts, justice courts, and such other courts as may be provided by law." Mont. Const. art. VII, § 1. The Constitution bestows the Supreme Court with general supervisory control over all other courts and vests authority in the Supreme Court for the discipline or removal from office of "any justice or judge." Mont. Const. art. VII, §§ 2(2), 11(3). Although the Legislature is required to establish the Judicial Standards Commission, Article VII, section 11, delegates implementation of its provisions to the Commission by rulemaking and confers upon the Legislature only the development of provisions regarding confidentiality of the Commission's proceedings. To maintain the independence of the judiciary, the Constitution commits the oversight of judges to the judicial branch of government. The Legislature's stated purpose of "[i]nvestigation into whether members of the Judiciary ... [have acted] in violation of state law and policy" thus does not pertain to an "area[] in which it may potentially legislate or appropriate." The Judicial Standards Commission, not the Legislature, investigates allegations of judicial misconduct. Mont. Const. art. VII, §11(2). Any concern about a judge or justice "pre-judging" a case or making statements about matters pending or that could come before the courts would be within the exclusive authority of the Judicial Standards Commission and the Supreme Court. *See* Mont. Code Jud. Cond. Rule 2.11(A) ("A judge shall not make any public statement that might reasonably be expected to affect the outcome or impair the fairness of a matter pending or impending in any court, or make any nonpublic statement that might substantially interfere with a fair trial or hearing.").

¶42 Again, the Legislature fails to "adequately identif[y] its aims and explai[n]" how the "the evidence offered" connects to the legislative purpose it puts forth. The Legislature asserts that district court judges engage in "pre-judging" amounting to "bias" when they respond to polls used by the Montana Judges Association to determine whether to take a position, as a matter of policy, on proposed legislation affecting the function of the judiciary. *** In using the term "bias," the Legislature does not indicate that it wishes to investigate whether any judges had developed views on legal matters, the absence of which the United States Supreme Court found to be not only impossible but an undesirable indication of incompetence. [*See Republican Party v. White* (2002).] Neither has the Legislature explained how the practice of responding to Montana Judges Association polls could suggest partiality for or against any given party or a lack of open-mindedness by district court judges. Failing to show any nexus between the target of the subpoenas — polling of district court judges on their policy positions on proposed legislation that could affect the judiciary — with the supporting allegations of "pre-judging" or "bias," the Legislature has not "adequately identif[ied] its aims and explain[ed]" how the information sought relates to a valid legislative purpose or to any matter not constitutionally committed to the oversight of the Judicial Standards Commission. Perhaps more importantly, the Legislature's asserted legislative purpose of addressing the "serious nature" of conducting such polls is undercut by the First Amendment principles at play. And in fact, the practice the Legislature seeks to investigate is encouraged by established canons of judicial conduct that recognize judges' "special expertise" in matters concerning the law, the legal system, and the administration of justice and allow judges expressly to "share that expertise with governmental bodies and executive or legislative branch officials." Mont. Code of Jud. Conduct 3.2(A) & Comment 1.

¶46 Examining the two subpoenas insofar as they concern conduct of the Court Administrator or of other Judicial Branch employees, the Legislature has failed to provide a single legitimate legislative purpose tied to matters "concern[ing] a subject on which 'legislation could be had.'" The asserted legislative purpose — both expressed in the April 14 subpoena and in the Legislature's filings with the Court — is to determine whether individuals violated the law. Enforcement of the law is not a "legitimate task" of the legislative function. More pointedly, the conduct the Legislature alleges does not, as a matter of law, constitute the purported legal violations it uses to support its asserted legislative purposes. And there is, of course, no legislative "power to expose for the sake of exposure.'"

¶47 Finally, beyond the failure of a legitimate legislative purpose, the subpoenas sweep far too broadly. The subpoenas compel production of ***all*** of McLaughlin's e-mails within the designated time frame, not just those limited to the purposes the Legislature now articulates. The subpoenas' breadth is vast; they demand information without limitation to "public records" or "public information" and encompass all personnel-related matters, which may include confidential medical information and potential employee disciplinary matters; information regarding Youth Court matters, which are confidential by law—§§ 41-5-215 through -221, MCA; information regarding confidential matters before the Judicial Standards Commission; information in which third parties have protected privacy interests, such as disability accommodations requested by members of the public; information about potential on-going security risks to individual judges, including communications with law enforcement; and confidential information related to ongoing cases and judicial work product. In sum, the subpoenas are sweepingly overbroad and exceed the legislative power to "obtain[] information on matters that fall within its proper field of legislative action." Mason's Manual of Leg. Procedure, § 797.7 at 567.

¶48 In addition, the subpoenas fail to safeguard the process that ordinarily attends the issuance of such compelled process. As observed, the first subpoena was served on Director Giles only and demanded production within a twenty-four-hour period. Contrast this with Rule 45(c) and (d) of the Montana Rules of Civil Procedure, which requires service of a subpoena "no less than 10 days before the commanded production of [information]" (M. R. Civ. P. 45(c)(1)); requires the party responsible for issuing the subpoena to "take reasonable steps to avoid imposing undue burden or expense on a person subject to the subpoena" (M. R. Civ. P. 45(d)(1)); affords opportunity for the subject of the subpoena to object (M. R. Civ. P. 45(d)(2)(B)); and requires the subpoena to be quashed or modified if it "requires disclosure of privileged or other protected matter, if no exception or waiver applies" (M. R. Civ. P. 45(d)(3)(A)(iii)). Director Giles, in turn, failed to consider the significant confidentiality and privacy interests implicated when she began her blanket release of the entirety of McLaughlin's e-mails without giving McLaughlin notice or an opportunity to review the materials and raise any such concerns or seek protection of such interests in a court of law. These basic safeguards guarantee minimum standards of due process and should have been understood and respected by both the legislative and executive branch officials involved. [The Court later holds, "Legislative subpoenas to a governmental officer reaching information that may be protected by law require that the matter first be submitted to a court for *in camera* review of the affected information and an order for any necessary redactions. Further, before releasing any requested records or seeking court review, the governmental officer should have the opportunity to review the requested records to determine if any constitutionally protected privacy rights could be implicated."]

¶49 In short, the two subpoenas fail to offer evidence that would "establish that a subpoena advances a valid legislative purpose," seek information that "other sources could reasonably provide," are far "broader than reasonably necessary" to serve the stated goals, and jeopardize the protected constitutional rights of others. *Mazars* instructs us to "carefully scrutiniz[e]" subpoenas that do "not represent a run-of-the-mill legislative effort" but originate from a "political branch" with "incentives to use subpoenas for institutional advantage" over another independent branch. These concerns undoubtedly are implicated here.

¶50 This is not to say that the Court Administrator is insulated from revealing information to the legislative branch of state government. Far from it. As noted, the Legislature has enacted statutes that require her to submit regular reports to the Legislature regarding budgetary matters, as well as requested information about "business transacted by the courts." Section 3-1-702(2), MCA. In addition, the Legislature has vested its Legislative Auditor with broad authority to conduct financial and compliance audits of all agencies and to examine their "books, accounts, activities, and records, confidential or otherwise[.]" Sections 5-13-303, -309, MCA. The Legislative Auditor's authority encompasses review of the Judicial Standards Commission. Section 3-1-1125, MCA. The Legislature thus has provided for alternative means by which to obtain information and to determine accountability of administrative matters in the Judicial Branch.

¶51 Is there nonetheless, as the Legislature suggests, a place for discussion among the branches if it desires more dialogue with the Court or information from the Judicial Branch? Likely so. But that is not what this Petition is about and not what the Legislature suggested when it resorted to direct subpoena without opening any such discussion with the Judicial Branch and without even giving McLaughlin notice of the first subpoena. Inquiries for information through these means might have averted interbranch confrontation — and could in the future — had the Legislature pursued a path of "negotiation and compromise" before it subpoenaed the broad swath of McLaughlin's records at issue without any notice to the Judicial Branch. ***

Conclusion

¶55 For the foregoing reasons, we conclude that the April 8, 2021, subpoena issued by the Chair of the Senate Judiciary Committee to Director Misty Ann Giles and the April 14, 2021, subpoena issued by the Senate President and Speaker of the House to Court Administrator Beth McLaughlin do not serve a valid legislative purpose, are impermissibly overbroad, and therefore are invalid.

Justice LAURIE McKINNON, specially concurring. ***

¶65 We are asked to determine whether the Legislature's subpoena is within the legislative power, a question that raises serious separation of powers concerns about how a legislative committee may investigate the judicial branch. . . . Montana's Separation of Powers provision is contained in Article III, Section 1, of Montana's 1972 Constitution. It provides:

> The power of the government of this state is divided into three distinct branches — legislative, executive, and judicial. No person or persons charged with the exercise of power properly belonging to one branch shall exercise

any power properly belonging to either of the others, except as in this constitution expressly directed or permitted. ***

¶69 The scope of legislative authority over the judicial branch is illustrated by several scenarios. First, the legislature has the power to define the substantive law that courts must apply; however, the judiciary must ensure that those laws do not violate individual rights. If the legislature disagrees with a court's decision it may enact a statute to reverse the effect of the decision, provided it does not change the result of the specific case. Thus, the legislature has substantial investigatory power to investigate the appropriateness of proposed new substantive laws. The legislature also has substantial, although not unlimited nor undisputed, power to regulate the procedures utilized by courts—the distinction being drawn between substantive and procedural rulemaking. Additionally, the legislature, through its control of the appropriations process, has substantial authority over both the judicial branch budget and the administrative structure by which the judicial branch is managed. Given the legislature's authority to create, modify, and fund the bureaucracy by which the judicial branch manages itself, the legislature has substantial authority over changes in the structure of the judicial branch and what changes should be made to advance its policy objectives.

¶70 Weighed against the legislature's authority to investigate is the equally weighty authority of the judicial branch to maintain its independence from the political influences of the legislature. The Framers clearly intended the courts would operate independently from the political and partisan interests and influences of both the executive and legislative branches. There must be a constitutional separation of powers by recognizing that the legislature's investigatory authority does not extend to investigating the duties or the performance of judicial branch employees while performing judicial branch work-related functions....

¶71 When addressing a separation of powers issue, it is important to understand the branches are to work together to secure a workable government for its citizens while respecting each branch's autonomy. "Though faithful to the precept that freedom is imperiled if the whole of legislative, executive, and judicial power is in the same hands, The Federalist No. 47 (J. Madison), the Framers understood that a 'hermetic sealing off of the three branches of Government from one another would preclude the establishment of a Nation capable of governing itself effectively.'" A key contention in Justice Robert H. Jackson's concurring opinion in *Youngstown Sheet & Tube Co. v. Sawyer* (1952) was that "[w]hile the Constitution diffuses power the better to secure liberty, it also contemplates that practice will integrate the dispersed powers into a workable government. It enjoins upon its branches separateness but interdependence, autonomy but reciprocity."

¶72 In the spirit of integrating diverse powers of government and providing citizens with a "workable government," judges have frequently testified before the legislature on matters concerning judicial administration, representation of indigent defendants, habeas corpus appeals, exclusionary rule modifications, judge's use of legislative history, juvenile delinquency reform, criminal justice reform, and civil justice reform. Judicial input on matters that relate so integrally to the operation of the judicial branch clearly benefits both the courts and the legislature. Restricting these opportunities would have a serious adverse effect on the ability of the judicial and legislative branches to offer its citizens a workable government that integrates each branch's diverse powers. ***

Justice DIRK SANDEFUR, concurring. ***

¶82 Regardless of competing interests pertinent in the two political branches of government and society in general, or the dominant will of any majority political faction at any particular time, the continued survival and vitality of our constitutional democracy, and all of the personal and societal freedoms, protections, and other benefits it provides, depend on the preservation of and respect for the distinct functions of all three co-equal branches of government, without any usurpation or interference with one by another. This simple, self-evident principle is more important than ever when, as now, a single political faction overwhelmingly controls the two partisan branches of state government, rendering it quite expedient to irresponsibly attack and attempt to undermine the only non-partisan branch in an effort to attain unitary, unfettered—in effect, authoritarian—power, unconstrained by constitutional limits. ***

Notes on Judicial Independence

1. The Montana Supreme Court elaborated upon the early statehood history of the judiciary and the origins of the unusual "Clancy Rule" in *Patrick v. State* (Mont. 2011):

> ¶ 18 The story begins in 1889, in Butte, Montana, with the arrival of a young surveyor named F. Augustus Heinze. Though an ambitious man, Heinze had neither the wealth of W.A. Clark or Marcus Daly, nor their political connections. However, what Heinze lacked in resources he made up for in a keen understanding of the law governing the ownership of ores within the earth. Prior to Heinze's arrival, the Silver Bow County Courts had avoided litigation regarding ownership of the ores beneath the richest hill on earth; Heinze singularly changed that.
>
> ¶ 19 Armed with his favorite legal weapon, the injunction, Heinze commenced filing lawsuits, asserting that various ore bodies reached an apex on his claims. Generally, under the apex theory, or rule of extra-lateral rights, if an ore vein apexed on a claim, that claim's owner could chase the vein below ground, without regard to the claim's above-ground confines. Heinze was not ashamed to purchase a tiny un-owned swath of land and immediately assert that ore being mined on a neighboring claim actually apexed on his. Although such conduct might not ultimately prove legally successful, Heinze's cases had a habit of remaining tied up in the courts for years. Heinze filed over 100 lawsuits, and between 1901 and 1902 he was involved in 14 separate actions before the Montana Supreme Court. Furthermore,

these lawsuits were not cheap. Heinze was known to have 37 lawyers on staff, and forced his opponents to spend millions on legal fees and associated costs. Moreover, while legal action was pending, Heinze was not above sending his workers into the earth to mine the contested ore, using the proceeds to maintain his expensive legal bills.

¶ 20 However, injunctions alone could not make Heinze rich. Rather, his true power has historically been perceived to have resided in the form of two men: District Court Judges William Clancy and E.W. Harney. Clancy was something of a judge-of-the people, popular with the bartenders, miners and "the lower level of Butte society." A "burlesque of judicial dignity, William Clancy found in Heinze's favor with monotonous regularity." In one notable case, Clancy determined that three valuable ore veins, the Anaconda, St. Lawrence and Neversweat, apexed in a 75-foot-long triangular sliver of land owned by Heinze. Harney, for his part, handed down one of Heinze's greatest victories, ownership of the disputed Minnie Healy Mine, amidst allegations of bribery, and revelation of a clandestine relationship with a public stenographer with ties to Heinze.

¶ 21 Historians disagree over whether Judges Harney and Clancy were corrupt, inept, or merely fiercely loyal to Heinze. However, regardless of their motives, continual rulings in Heinze's favor invited the antipathy of the Amalgamated Copper Company. By that time a bloated leviathan of a world-wide mining entity, Amalgamated grew increasingly frustrated with its inability to crack Heinze's hold upon the Silver-Bow judiciary. When legal action failed, Amalgamated resorted to bribery, offering Harney $250,000 to sign an affidavit that Heinze had purchased his loyalty. Even when Amalgamated succeeded in removing Judge Harney from the lawsuit concerning ownership of the Minnie Healy Mine and obtained a new trial, the case was remanded to Judge Clancy, who subsequently ruled in Heinze's favor.

¶ 22 Amalgamated realized that "recourse" to the law was both costly and unsuccessful and opted for a new approach: "extortion." On October 3, 1903, Amalgamated announced a shutdown of all Montana operations, except for the company's newspapers, casting an estimated four-fifths of Montana wage earners into unemployment. Amalgamated's demand was simple: the Governor was to call an extraordinary session of the Montana Legislature in order to enact legislation that would put an end to the troublesome Heinze litigation. On November 10, Governor Toole, "yielding to the exigency of the hour," called a special session. In response, the Legislature passed the "Fair Trial Bill," and Amalgamated resumed work throughout Montana. The new law permitted a party to automatically obtain judicial substitution by filing an affidavit upon the belief that a fair and impartial hearing or trial was not possible before the presiding judge. By the next year, Judges Clancy and Harney were voted from the bench.

> ¶ 23 Ultimately, Heinze resists being cabined as angel or villain. Describing the moral conundrum he posed, a contemporaneous magazine explained, "[h]is course has been without moral justification, but not wholly without excuse. Indeed, the most depressing feature of the conflict to an unprejudiced onlooker is the fact that had he been a more scrupulous man, he would long since have been wiped off the slate." In 1906, Amalgamated did finally erase Heinze. The company purchased his mining interests and secured the dismissal of eighty pending lawsuits. Four years later, he died penniless in New York City. Despite this ultimate defeat, Augustus Heinze's short but successful vexation of the all-powerful Amalgamated provided the impetus for a judicial substitution statute that remains in effect over one century later.

2. Although judicial elections provide a form of accountability by the courts to the people, other branches also may attempt to check and balance the judicial branch. Consider the "three realms" of judicial power referenced in *Coate v. Omholt*: substantive, procedural, and inherent, and the conflicts with other branches that might arise in each realm.

a. The first two "realms" of judicial power that interact with the legislative power are substantive and procedural law. The question of the judiciary's control over substantive law through common law adjudication is addressed in the "Open Courts" section below. Procedural law is governed by Art. VII, section 2(3):

> It [the Supreme Court] may make rules governing appellate procedure, practice and procedure for all other courts, admission to the bar and conduct of its members. Rules of procedure shall be subject to disapproval by the legislature in either of the two sessions following promulgation.

The Court in *Coate* reads the Legislature's powers narrowly as a "veto," which may be exercised only over rules of procedure, not practice or bar matters, and implicitly prevents the Legislature from enacting such rules on its own. Yet two entire Titles of the Montana Code Annotated address "Civil Procedure" (Title 25) and "Criminal Procedure" (Title 46). Some of these rules are codified from court orders, such as the Rules of Civil Procedure at Title 25, chapter 20. Must all other rules codified in these titles also originate in the Supreme Court? Once codified, may the Supreme Court decide to "amend" or "repeal" any of them subject to the legislative "veto" of Article VII, section 2(3)?

b. What is a "rule of procedure"? *Compare People v. McKenna* (Colo. 1978) (upholding "rape shield" statute as outside of the court's exclusive rulemaking power "in view of [its] mixed policy and procedural nature"), *with Opinion of the Justices (Prior Sexual Assault Evidence)* (N.H. 1997) (invalidating law creating a rebuttable presumption that evidence of a defendant's prior sexual assaults shall be admissible "[b]ecause the proposed bill directly conflicts with Rule [of Evidence] 404(b), a rule concerning a uniquely judicial function").

c. What is the scope of the "third realm" of judicial power, "activity so fundamental and so necessary to a court, so inherent in its very nature as a court, that to divest it of its absolute command within these spheres is to make meaningless the very phrase judicial power"? As in the federal government, the legislature wields the power of the purse over the courts, including the power to create additional lower courts and judgeships. Does the legislature enjoy any additional powers to regulate the judiciary? Unlike state university presidents in *Board of Regents v. Judge* (Mont. 1975), the justices' salaries are set by the legislature, as is the overall funding of the judicial system. Could a failure to fund the judicial system adequately (according to the courts) violate the judiciary's inherent constitutional powers? Consider *Commonwealth ex rel. Carroll v. Tate* (Pa. 1971):

> A Legislature has the power of life and death over all the Courts and over the entire Judicial system. Unless the Legislature can be compelled by the Courts to provide the money which is reasonably necessary for the proper functioning and administration of the Courts, our entire Judicial system could be extirpated, and the Legislature could make a mockery of our form of Government with its three co-equal branches—the Executive, the Legislative and the Judicial.

In *Tate*, the court compelled the City of Philadelphia to fund the Court of Common Pleas of Philadelphia.

3. What is the holding (or holdings) of *Coate v. Omholt*? Like federal courts, state courts often seek to avoid constitutional questions:

> No question brought before this Court is of greater delicacy than one that involves the power of the legislature to act. If it becomes indispensably necessary to the case to answer such a question, this Court must meet and decide it; but it is not the habit of the courts to decide questions of a constitutional nature unless absolutely necessary to a decision of the case.

Baxter v. State (Mont. 2009) (Warner, J., concurring). In *Coate*, the Court appears to answer several constitutional questions unnecessarily, since finding the law unconstitutional on any one ground would be sufficient to invalidate it. The Court also starts with the broadest challenge (separation of powers), before reaching the same conclusion on narrower grounds (diminution of salary and rulemaking powers), with a detour to the state and federal contracts clauses. If the salary forfeiture law "clearly violate[s]" the diminution of salary prohibition, why should the Court reach any of the other questions? Are the broader holdings an appropriate exercise of the judicial power?

4. The Court in *Reichert* goes out of its way to emphasize that Montana's elected courts are not "representative bodies," citing the unelected federal Supreme Court and state judicial ethics rules on impartiality. Is representation inconsistent with impartiality? In view of the history of judicial selection in Montana, why does the Montana Constitution establish elected courts if not to ensure that they are

representative of Montanans? Does representation help explain (justify?) when and how Montana's courts break from lock-step interpretation of similar federal constitutional provisions?

5. Like most separation of powers cases, *McLaughlin* identifies the limits of one branch's powers and discusses the extent of another branch's power. Here, the Legislature's power is limited by legislative (not executive or judicial) purposes, while the Court's power extends to protect judicial privilege as well as third-party rights of due process and privacy. If you were a legislator who shared the concerns of the committee that issued the subpoenas, what would your next move be? Is interbranch negotiation more likely before a subpoena to the other branch, after a subpoena, or after a judgment quashing the subpoena?

6. One theme in *Reichert* and *McLaughlin* is a concern expressed by legislators that the justices are acting as judges in their own case. According to *McLaughlin*, the Judicial Standards Commission provided by Article VII, section 11, and staffed by two judges, one attorney, and two lay citizens, is the primary means of investigating and disciplining judges for misconduct in office. Is it the exclusive means? If a judge violates lobbying laws, public information laws, or even criminal laws within the scope of their official duties, when and how can the executive branch investigate? The Legislature retains the power of impeachment, including for judicial officers, and "shall provide for the manner, procedure, and causes for impeachment." Art. V, § 13. What is the appropriate investigative scope of this essentially legislative power? *See Mazars* (2020) (Thomas, J., dissenting) ("Congress' legislative powers do not authorize it to engage in a nationwide inquisition with whatever resources it chooses to appropriate for itself.... If Congress wishes to obtain these documents, it should proceed through the impeachment power.").

7. If the shoe were on the other foot in *McLaughlin*, could a legislator (or legislative staffer) assert a parallel privilege against an investigation undertaken by the executive or judicial branches? Article V, section 8 privileges legislators "from arrest during attendance at sessions of the legislature and in going to and returning therefrom, unless apprehended in the commission of a felony or a breach of the peace" and immunizes them from being "questioned in any other place for any speech or debate in the legislature," though many legislative activities might fall outside this provision. Note also that, like the judicial branch, the legislative branch bears primary responsibility for disciplining its own members under its own rules: "Each house may expel or punish a member for good cause shown with the concurrence of two-thirds of all its members." Art. V, § 10.

8. In *Brown v. Gianforte* (Mont. 2021), the Court upheld the Legislature's grant of direct judicial appointment powers to the Governor, subject to Senate confirmation, and abolition of the Judicial Nomination Commission established in 1973 under Article VII, section 8(2), which provides in the case of a judicial vacancy, "the governor shall appoint a replacement from nominees selected in the manner provided by law." Writing for the Court, Justice Shea bypassed detailed textual analysis

to emphasize the apparent purpose of this provision: "The manifest constitutional objective of Article VII, Section 8(2) was the appointment of good judges." Comparing the vetting processes under the former commission and new gubernatorial process, the Court concluded direct appointment as contemplated by the law fulfilled that objective. Justice McKinnon, dissenting, cited the text of the provision and the Voter Information Pamphlet, which explained to the ratifiers "the governor appoints a replacement but does not have unlimited choice of lawyers as under the 1889 constitution" and "must choose his appointee from a list of nominees."

B. Justiciability

Like other structural analogues in the federal Constitution, Article III justiciability does not bind state courts under their own constitutional grants of judicial power. The open-textured vesting of "[t]he judicial power" in state courts presents similar issues of justiciability as arise under the federal Constitution, though under different text than Article III "cases" and "controversies." In Montana, "[t]he supreme court has appellate jurisdiction" as well as "original jurisdiction [over] writs of habeas corpus and such other writs as may be provided by law." Art. VII, § 2. District courts possess general jurisdiction "in all criminal cases amounting to felony and all civil matters and cases in law and equity." Art. VII, § 4. On the eve of the 1972 Constitutional Convention, the Montana Supreme Court, like many other state supreme courts, recognized its jurisdiction as extending as far as limited advisory opinions in some matters of judicial supervision and beyond. *See In re Advisory Opinion to Commission on Practice* (Mont. 1971) (clarifying "ex voluntate" the duties of the Commission on Practice with respect to criminal convictions of attorneys); *In re Montana Trust and Legacy Fund* (Mont. 1964) (issuing advisory opinion to the Montana Legislative Council under the requirements of the 1889 Constitution, Article XXI, section 17).

Since 1972, the Montana Supreme Court has patterned its justiciability doctrine after the federal courts. In practice, however, the courthouse doors open a little wider to litigants in Montana. For example, in *Montana Ass'n of Counties* (Chapter 1) and *White v. State* (Chapter 3), the justices recognized a pre-enforcement challenge and taxpayer standing, respectively, in cases the federal courts may have dismissed. The two opinions below concern justiciability in two of the judicial independence cases from the previous section. Under federal justiciability doctrine, *Reichert* is arguably unripe (if the plaintiffs have standing at all), and *McLaughlin* is arguably moot. Consider how the cases conceive of a distinct "judicial power" under the Montana Constitution, and whether this broader conception of justiciability makes sense in these politically sensitive and high stakes interbranch disputes, directly and indirectly, with the legislative branch.

Reichert v. State

365 Mont. 92 (2012)

Justice JAMES C. NELSON delivered the Opinion of the Court.

*** ¶ 2 We address the following issues on appeal:

2. Whether Plaintiffs' constitutional challenge to LR-119 is justiciable. ***

Principles of Justiciability and Ripeness

¶ 53 As stated above, the judicial power of Montana's courts is limited to "justiciable controversies." In general terms, a justiciable controversy is one that is "definite and concrete, touching legal relations of parties having adverse legal interests" and "admitting of specific relief through decree of conclusive character, as distinguished from an opinion advising what the law would be upon a hypothetical state of facts, or upon an abstract proposition." *Chovanak v. Matthews* (Mont. 1948) (emphasis omitted). To be justiciable, the parties must have existing and genuine (rather than theoretical) rights or interests, the questions must be presented in an adversary context, and the controversy must be one upon which a court's judgment will effectively and conclusively operate, as distinguished from a dispute invoking a purely political, administrative, philosophical, or academic conclusion. This limitation on judicial power derives primarily from the Montana Constitution, which limits the courts to deciding only cases and controversies, but also from the courts themselves, which have adopted discretionary limitations on the exercise of judicial power for prudential reasons. While the constitutional case-or-controversy requirement must always be met, prudential rules may be subject to exceptions.

¶ 54 The central concepts of justiciability have been elaborated into more specific doctrines—advisory opinions, feigned and collusive cases, standing, ripeness, mootness, political questions, and administrative questions—each of which is governed by its own set of substantive rules. At issue here is ripeness, which is concerned with whether the case presents an "actual, present" controversy. The basic purpose of the ripeness requirement is to prevent the courts, through avoidance of premature adjudication, from entangling themselves in abstract disagreements. Ripeness is predicated on the central perception that courts should not render decisions absent a genuine need to resolve a real dispute; hence, cases are unripe when the parties point only to hypothetical, speculative, or illusory disputes as opposed to actual, concrete conflicts.

¶ 55 In analyzing ripeness, it is helpful to understand its relationship to standing and mootness. To meet the constitutional case-or-controversy requirement for standing, the plaintiff must clearly allege a past, present, or threatened injury to a property or civil right, and the injury must be one that would be alleviated by successfully maintaining the action. Note that standing may rest not only on past or present injury, but also on threatened injury. Ripeness and mootness, in turn, can be seen as "the time dimensions of standing." Ripeness asks whether an injury that has not yet happened is sufficiently likely to happen or, instead, is too contingent or remote to support present adjudication, whereas mootness asks whether an injury that has happened is too far beyond a useful remedy. ***

Application to Present Case ***

¶ 58 Starting with the constitutional component of ripeness, the Legislature has placed a referendum on the June 5 ballot concerning the election of Supreme Court justices. If passed, the statutory changes outlined in the referendum are effective immediately. They will change the manner in which justices are elected to Seats 5 and 6 (presently held by Justice Nelson and Justice Morris, respectively), which are up for election this year. The deadline to file as a candidate for those seats was March 12. While all registered voters in the state may vote in the June primary election for the candidates running for Seats 5 and 6, only registered voters in the Fifth and Sixth Supreme Court districts, respectively, will be permitted to vote for those seats in the November general election (if LR-119 is adopted). Plaintiffs challenge LR-119 as impermissibly amending the constitutionally established qualifications for, and selection of, Supreme Court justices by creating a residency requirement and thereby disenfranchising Plaintiffs. They allege a threatened injury because LR-119, should it pass, will deprive them of their right to vote for each seat on the Supreme Court. For those Plaintiffs who do not reside in the Fifth and Sixth Supreme Court districts, the disenfranchisement will occur this election cycle. The issues presented are definite and concrete, not hypothetical or abstract, and this case thus presents a controversy in the constitutional sense.

¶ 59 Turning to prudential considerations, we must weigh the fitness of the issues for judicial decision and the hardship to the parties of withholding court consideration. In this regard, this Court has noted that "[j]udicial intervention in referenda or initiatives prior to an election is not encouraged." We have reasoned that to effectively protect and preserve the rights which Montanans have reserved to themselves to change the laws or the Constitution through the initiative process, Mont. Const. art. III, § 4, art. XIV, § 9, and to approve or reject by referendum legislative acts (except appropriations of money) and proposed constitutional amendments, Mont. Const. art. III, § 5, art. XIV, § 8, pre-election judicial review should not be routinely conducted. Such deference and restraint do not apply, however, where a challenged measure is facially defective. *** [Fn. Besides facial invalidity, courts will entertain pre-election challenges where the measure "was not properly submitted under the election laws."] Where a measure is facially defective, placing it on the ballot does nothing to protect voters' rights. It instead creates a sham out of the voting process by conveying the false appearance that a vote on the measure counts for something, when in fact the measure is invalid regardless of how the electors vote. Placing it on the ballot would also be a waste of time and money for all involved—putting the Secretary of State, local election officials, and ultimately taxpayers to the expense of the election; putting proponents and opponents to the expense of needless campaigning; and putting voters to the task of deciding a ballot issue which this Court already knows cannot stand even if passed. Deferring decision to a later date so the measure can go forward is senseless. It consumes resources with no corresponding benefit. Nothing in ripeness doctrine mandates such an approach. Indeed, "the prudential concerns of the ripeness doctrine [are] not implicated" where "the possible constitutional infirmity [is] clear on the face" of the measure.

¶ 60 In the present case, the record is factually adequate to enable the court to make the necessary legal determinations. The question presented is purely one of law, and no additional facts will aid the court in its inquiry. As explained below under Issue 3, the constitutional infirmity is clear on the face of the measure in that LR-119 attempts to amend the Constitution by means of a statutory referendum. Furthermore, as explained under Issue 4, the constitutionally infirm portions of LR-119 cannot be severed from the remainder of the referendum. The issues are fit for judicial decision, and the hardship of withholding consideration of those issues would be great for the reasons just discussed. Accordingly, we conclude that Plaintiffs' challenge to LR-119 is ripe. ***

Justice BETH BAKER, concurring in part and dissenting in part.

*** ¶ 93 We have long recognized "the principle that 'initiative and referendum provisions of the Constitution should be broadly construed to maintain the maximum power in the people.'" . . . Instead, the Court rules on constitutionality of legislation only if, and after, a duly-enacted law has been challenged. Here, displaying "lack of confidence in the knowledge of the voters," and contrary to well-established tenets of judicial review, the Court has preempted the legislative referendum process to reach the merits of the constitutional issues.

¶ 94 Although this Court has entertained pre-election challenges to ballot issues, historically we have done so sparingly. *** [W]hen the legislature has prescribed a specific process for a court challenge to a ballot measure, we have refused to intervene prior to the election if that process was not followed. [T]he Legislature has expressly preserved "the right to challenge a constitutional defect in the substance of an issue *approved by a vote of the people*." Section 13-27-316(6), MCA (emphasis added).

¶ 96 Withholding consideration of the alleged constitutional defect in LR-119 until after the election—and then, obviously, only if the measure passed—would comport with the process set forth in the statute and remain true to the restraint that characterizes our consideration of constitutional challenges. "[T]he constitutional requirement of a 'case or controversy' contemplates real controversies and not abstract differences of opinion." Among the categories subsumed in the "case or controversy" requirement are the doctrine of ripeness and the refusal to issue advisory opinions. "The doctrine of ripeness 'requires an actual, present controversy, and therefore a court will not act when the legal issue raised is only hypothetical or the existence of a controversy merely speculative.'" We have followed the guiding principle that "courts should avoid constitutional issues whenever possible." The Court cites to no case in which a court has determined a statute to be ripe for constitutional challenge before it was enacted. Prior to approval by the voters, the constitutional dispute at issue regarding residency qualifications and district elections for Supreme Court justices does not rise above an abstract difference of opinion.

Depending on the election results, there may never have been a constitutional issue to consider.

¶ 97 The Court determines that LR-119 presents unique grounds for pre-election review because of its effect in the current election cycle, observing that the measure threatened to disenfranchise voters outside the Fifth and Sixth Supreme Court Districts. (Opinion ¶ 58.) The Court's concerns, however, conflate the merits of the constitutional issues with the timing of their consideration. The legislature clearly was within its authority to order a special election in conjunction with the June 5 primary election. Mont. Const. art. III, § 6. At that election, all Montana voters would have been given the opportunity to vote on LR-119, and all Montana voters would have been able to vote for all Supreme Court positions on the ballot. If, and only if, LR-119 passed would anyone's right to vote have been affected in the general election. As illustrated by the efficiency with which this appeal was briefed, considered and decided, we easily could have held the appeal in abeyance, awaited certification of the June 5 election results, and decided the case—if necessary—within a few weeks. The only impact may have been a few weeks of lost statewide campaigning time by successful primary candidates, but they are not even parties to the challenge. Ironically, the only "disenfranchisement" of voters results from the Court's decision to remove LR-119 from the ballot.

¶ 98 The Court's ruling that the measure's facial invalidity requires its immediate consideration also is unconvincing. First, the District Court acknowledged, and the Plaintiffs do not appear to dispute, that not all provisions of LR-119 are facially unconstitutional. The District Court agreed that the Montana Constitution does not prohibit the legislature from creating Supreme Court districts or from having the Chief Justice selected by the other members of the Court. Whether or not these provisions, if constitutional, could be severed from the measure would have been appropriate and better suited for consideration only if the referendum passed and became law.

¶ 99 Finally, the Court holds that it would have been a "waste of time and money" to place the measure on the ballot. (Opinion ¶ 59.) Although I agree that delays in this case, including the State's inexplicable failure to secure a stay of the District Court's decision, were regrettable and have made the process tortuous and more costly than necessary, these types of emergencies are not uncommon in election matters and the court system is equipped to deal with them. I cannot ascribe "no corresponding benefit" (Opinion ¶ 59) to the fulfillment of our Constitution's guarantee of the right of initiative and referendum. The "consum[ption of] resources" in this case (Opinion ¶ 59) is not sufficient to outweigh the people's right to vote. The Court's decision to protect the voters from a measure referred by the legislature is patronizing and elevates judicial economy above respect for the constitutional process and the people's role in it.

¶ 100 We should decline to interfere with the initiative and referendum process "unless it appears to be absolutely essential." *Mont. Citizens for the Preservation of Citizens' Rights* [(Mont. 1986)]. Because a decision on the constitutional issues could have been rendered quickly following the primary election had the referendum passed, the Court's interference now is not, in my view, "absolutely essential." I dissent.

McLaughlin v. Montana State Legislature

2021 MT 178 (2021)

Justice BETH BAKER delivered the Opinion of the Court.

Justiciability of the Controversy

¶14 ... [W]e turn first to the Legislature's first Motion to Dismiss. The Motion makes three points, which in the aggregate argue that the case does not present a justiciable controversy as the matter is vested exclusively with the Legislature and, because the subpoenas pertain to the Judicial Branch, the Court has an insurmountable conflict of interest that requires it to refrain from adjudicating the dispute. The Legislature concludes that this Court "must refuse to further interfere with a duly authorized legislative investigation" and "has no authority but to dismiss this Petition." McLaughlin responds that in the constitutional system of checks and balances, implemented through Montana statutes and rules, the Legislature enacts statutes, the legislative subpoena power must be "adjunct to the legislative process," and the judiciary determines the permissible scope and enforcement of subpoenas.

¶15 We addressed the conflict-of-interest argument in our Opinion and Order denying the Legislature's motion to disqualify the members of this Court from presiding in this proceeding. ["The Legislature has unilaterally attempted to create a disqualifying conflict for every duly constituted and elected member of this Court, during the pendency of a proceeding before the Court, by issuing a subpoena to every presiding justice in the case which is nearly identical to the subject of the litigation — McLaughlin's subpoena. It is well recognized that a party's unilateral acts personally attacking or suing the judge for acts taken in his or her judicial capacity do not create a proper basis for recusal. Recusal under such circumstances would permit a party to avoid a particular judge simply by attacking or suing him. Here, the Legislature itself has created the conflict by issuing a subpoena to each justice during a pending proceeding involving the same issues raised in a legislative subpoena. The Legislature's unilateral act of issuing subpoenas to the justices during the pendency of this case is not ground for recusal of every member of this Court. A judge is required to act in a manner that promotes "public confidence in the independence, integrity, and impartiality of the judiciary, and shall avoid impropriety and the appearance of impropriety." M.C. Jud. Cond. 1.2. Were the Court to succumb to the Legislature's request and evade our responsibilities and obligations as a Court, we are convinced that public confidence in our integrity, honesty, leadership, and ability to function as the highest court of this State would be compromised."] We do not address it further. ***

¶17 The judiciary has an unflagging responsibility to decide cases and controversies, even those that involve the authority of a coordinate branch of government or the courts' own functions. *See Coate v. Omholt* (Mont. 1983) (declaring unconstitutional two statutes that directed the State Auditor to withhold a month's pay from district court judges and supreme court justices if decisions were not reached or opinions written within certain procedural and time constraints set by statute); *see also Gabler v. Crime Victims Rights Bd.* (Wis. 2017) (Wisconsin Supreme Court declaring unconstitutional a law authorizing a special executive branch board to investigate and adjudicate complaints against the judiciary, including the ability to seek equitable relief and forfeiture against judges); *State ex rel. Kostas v. Johnson* (Ind. 1946) ("A court of general jurisdiction, whether named in the Constitution or established in pursuance of the provisions of the Constitution, cannot be directed, controlled, or impeded in its functions by any of the other departments of the government. The security of human rights and safety of free institutions require the absolute integrity and freedom of action of courts."). Though not a frequent subject of litigation, disputes over the scope of legislative subpoena power are squarely within the authority of the courts.

¶18 What is more, this Court on several occasions has been called upon to resolve disputes about its own authority. *See, e.g., Matter of McCabe* (Mont. 1975) (holding that the Supreme Court, not the Legislature, had authority to set standards for admission to the bar and conduct of members of the bar); *Goetz v. Harrison* (Mont. 1969) (entertaining an original proceeding filed against all members of the Supreme Court to determine the constitutionality of the Montana statutory "diploma privilege" for admission to the bar and to consider the Court's corresponding rule under its "exclusive" and "inherent jurisdiction, in all matters involving admission of persons to practice law in this state"). Even when a constitutional provision is non-self-executing because it commits authority to the Legislature, "the courts, as final interpreters of the Constitution, have the final 'obligation to guard, enforce, and protect every right granted or secured by the Constitution. . . .'" *Columbia Falls Elem. Sch. Dist. No. 6 v. State* (Mont. 2005); *Marbury v. Madison* (1803) ("It is emphatically the province and the duty of the judicial department to say what the law is."). ***

[Earlier in the opinion, the Court noted: "On June 22, 2021, Legislative leadership notified both McLaughlin and Department of Administration Director Misty Ann Giles by letter that the Legislature had withdrawn the subject subpoenas. The Legislature then moved to dismiss this action as moot. McLaughlin opposed the motion. On June 29, this Court denied the motion because it did not address documents already in the Legislature's possession and the issues the withdrawn subpoenas raised fall within the public interest and voluntary cessation exceptions to mootness."]

Notes on Justiciability

1. In *Reichert*, what does it mean for a ballot measure (or any proposed law) to be "facially defective"? According to the Court, "[w]here a measure is facially defective, placing it on the ballot does nothing to protect voters' rights. It instead creates a sham out of the voting process by conveying the false appearance that a vote on the measure counts for something, when in fact the measure is invalid regardless of

how the electors vote." Would the Court ever review the substantive constitutionality of a bill before enactment to avoid a "waste of time and money"? Consider Carina Wilmot, Reichert v. State ex rel. McCulloch *and the Open Door for Increased Pre-Election Substantive Judicial Review*, 74 MONT. L. REV. 441 (2013):

> One potential approach to address a referendum's potential defect(s) is for the Court to differentiate challenges to procedural sufficiency, legal sufficiency, and substantive constitutionality. The procedural challenges, following Montana law, could continue to be made pre-election to avoid mootness issues. Even if struck down by the Court, defects in procedural sufficiency might be remedied and brought again to ballot by following proper procedure.... The Court could redefine the current facial constitutionality review to be a pre- or post-election legal sufficiency review. "Legal sufficiency" review would include review as currently defined by the Constitution and statutes [e.g., single subject or separate amendment challenges]. Legal sufficiency review could be done either pre- or post-election.... Similar to a procedurally insufficient measure, a legally insufficient measure could be remedied and proposed again.... Although the Court currently reviews all substantive considerations of statutory referenda to determine if they are "facially unconstitutional," the third type of review would be a post-election substantive review. There are various reasons why it is preferable to wait until after a proposal is enacted before conducting a substantive review. Post-election substantive reviews are viable for statutes that are challenged for constitutional defects, regardless of whether the statutes were enacted by a bill, initiative, or referendum. [E.g., general violations of constitutional structure or rights not specific to the initiative process.] Here ... the measures would not be able to be brought again, even with revisions, because they are unconstitutional on their merits. No ripeness analysis would be necessary as a post-election-only analysis would keep the judiciary within its role of hearing challenges only to enacted law and not allow the judiciary to offer advisory opinions.

2. Do prudential or constitutional considerations control the ripeness inquiry in *Reichert*? In other words, if Justice Baker is correct that the Court could resolve the issue (and prevent any potentially imminent injury to the parties) in a post-election case (after the primary election on the initiative, but before the general election on the justices), that would meet constitutional justiciability standards (and defeat them in this case) why would prudential considerations matter at all? Does the justiciability analysis change if, as Justice Baker notes in *Reichert*, the Legislature provided a process to do exactly that? (Is such a provision a substantive or procedural rule for purposes of the Court's rulemaking powers?)

3. Note the plaintiffs in *Reichert* include several delegates to the 1972 constitutional convention. This is unusual but not unprecedented, particularly in matters concerning the judiciary provisions. *See, e.g., Cross v. VanDyke* (Mont. 2014); *Committee for an Effective Judiciary v. State* (Mont. 1984). Should a delegate-plaintiff matter to the

Court's deliberations? Why would plaintiffs seek to join with one or more delegates? Legislators also often seek to intervene in defense of state laws or other legislative action, as they did in *Reichert* and *McLaughlin*. Are they proper parties?

4. Perhaps, given the greater popular accountability (representation?) of Montana's state courts, they should be more willing to exercise their judicial powers than their federal counterparts. Consider Helen Hershkoff, *State Courts and the "Passive Virtues": Rethinking the Judicial Function*, 114 HARV. L. REV. 1833 (2001):

> Forty years ago, Alexander M. Bickel coined the term the "passive virtues" to describe various "jurisdictional techniques" that allow the Supreme Court to avoid or delay deciding controversial public issues. These techniques, which comprise the doctrine of justiciability, mediate concerns that Article III judges, unelected and of limited competence, will make decisions irrevocably binding future democratic majorities.... Although justiciability doctrine derives from the "case or controversy" requirement of Article III, commentators nevertheless tend to discuss this conception of the judicial function in universal or essential terms, as if Article III courts represent the institutional possibilities of courts more generally.
>
> State courts, however, are not bound by Article III, and judicial practice in some states differs—and differs radically—from the federal model. Some state courts issue advisory opinions, grant standing to taxpayers challenging misuse of public funds, and decide important public questions even when federal courts would consider the disputes moot. Moreover, functions that seem intuitively nonjudicial in the federal system are assigned to the judicial branch in some states, and judicial officers discharge them comfortably. State judges in Tennessee appoint the attorney general, and some state constitutions establish sheriffs as part of the judicial, and not the executive, branch. Elsewhere (although only occasionally) state judges initiate investigations into public conditions without any request from a party or the public. In addition, as common law courts, all state courts play an accepted policymaking role in a broad range of complex areas, including disputes related to state indebtedness, territorial annexation, and redistricting. ***
>
> State and local governments are highly vulnerable to the rent-seeking behavior of factional coalitions. *** Many state constitutions explicitly treat the problems that populism and privatism create for democratic lawmaking through provisions that regulate the nongovernmental exercise of power and its use for private ends. The state action doctrine is broader in most state judicial systems, and the doctrine of private delegation is more robust. Moreover, state constitutions include a diverse array of antifaction controls that do not appear in the federal Constitution: public-purpose requirements that limit taxation and bond indebtedness to nonprivate uses, bans on special legislation, and limits on public credit.... These open-ended constitutional terms typically depend on the courts for enforcement of the public interest broadly understood....

Federal standing rules and the zone of interest test that the Court has developed tend to favor special interest alliances at the expense of diffuse groups seeking to promote the public interest. A reconfigured state justiciability doctrine, by allowing taxpayers and others opportunities to enforce the structural restraints of state constitutions, could serve as an important filtering device against special-interest, rent-seeking behavior at the state and local levels.

This doctrine could play a different but equally important role when groups seek to enforce state constitutional provisions that are themselves no more than partisan victories over the public interest. Although state constitutions generally ban special and local legislation, commentators note that some statute-like provisions serve to entrench political advantage. In these situations, state justiciability doctrine could filter out litigation that is essentially "private action with an official stamp"—the efforts of dominant groups to ratify their political privilege through the courts. In both situations, justiciability doctrine could afford the state court a role in helping reduce partisan control over public resources.

5. One clear departure from federal justiciability doctrine is Montana's storied writ of supervisory control. Professor Larry Howell chronicles its origins and influence in *"Purely the Creature of the Inventive Genius of the Court"*: State ex rel. Whiteside *and the Creation and Evolution of the Montana Supreme Court's Unique and Controversial Writ of Supervisory Control*, 69 Mont. L. Rev. 1, 2–6 (2008):

State Senator Fred Whiteside knew he was in the eye of a political hurricane when he rose to address a joint session of the Montana Legislature in Helena on January 10, 1899. He was, after all, in the midst of exposing what Montana's preeminent historian, the late Michael P. Malone, labeled "one of the most remarkable, most sordid political spectacles in the history of the United States." Just hours before, on the night of January 9, Whiteside had appeared before a special joint legislative committee, where he testified about a brazen scheme to bribe state legislators into electing infamous "copper king" William Andrews Clark to the United States Senate. Clark, through his hirelings, had openly offered legislators as much as $10,000 each for their votes and was committed to spending $1,000,000 if necessary, a staggering sum at the time. Clark's son Charles, his campaign treasurer, summed up their election strategy this way: "We'll send the old man to the Senate or to the poorhouse."

What Whiteside had no way of knowing, however, was that reverberations from his whistle-blowing would still be felt more than a century later. On July 3, 2007, the Montana Supreme Court issued an order repealing the existing Montana Rules of Appellate Procedure. In its initial order proposing to amend the Rules, the Court explained that the previous rules "have been amended piece-meal over the years and, in many instances, are confusing, internally inconsistent, and comport neither with this Court's jurisprudence nor with current appellate practice and procedure in this State." In short, the Court concluded its rules were outdated. The new rules, which became effective October 1, 2007, alter the old rules in many fundamental ways, including changing the terminology applied to parties, the method of counting time, and even the office where the notice of appeal is filed.

The most interesting substantive change, however, is not new at all. Instead, Rule 14(3), concerning the Court's power of supervisory control over lower courts, actually takes the Court full circle, back to the beginning of the previous century when the state was just a decade old and Fred Whiteside was a household name. Considered "the most turbulent period in the entire political history of the commonwealth," it was a time when Montana was known primarily not for its rugged mountains and vast open spaces, but rather for the "massive corruption of the machinery of government" brought on by the infamous War of the Copper Kings. In late 1900, at the end of one of the more tumultuous years of this turbulent time, the Montana Supreme Court issued a decision bearing Whiteside's name that still ranks among its more significant and controversial. In *State ex rel. Whiteside v. District Court of First Judicial District*, the Court announced the creation of a "distinctive" new writ of supervisory control, a previously unknown judicial tool that would allow the Court great latitude "to control the course of litigation in the inferior courts." This past summer, after applying various tests and standards for issuing the writ for much of the last century, the Court finally codified in Rule 14(3) the original supervisory control test it announced in *Whiteside* 108 years ago.

Unlike the traditional common law writs, such as prohibition, certiorari, or mandamus, which generally could only issue to a lower court that either exceeded or refused to exercise its jurisdiction, this new supervisory writ allowed the Supreme Court to intervene in litigation in trial courts even when those courts "were proceeding within their jurisdiction." By inventing this new writ, the Court in 1900 addressed what is still considered today one of the thorniest issues in appellate law: how to allow immediate review of crucial but discretionary interlocutory rulings that otherwise could not be appealed until after trial under the final judgment rule. Through its new writ, the Court effectively resolved that dilemma three-quarters of a century before a commission appointed by the American Bar Association would recommend that appellate courts across the country adopt some similar method of discretionary interlocutory review.

The judicial foresight that led to the writ's creation is all the more remarkable considering the political and social turmoil afflicting the state—and the Supreme Court—at the time. The writ was a direct result of, and a creative method of dealing with, the state's pervasive corruption, a fact that has been overlooked by both legal scholars and historians. A close examination of Montana cases from this period reveals that the Court invented the writ primarily to control a corrupt Butte judge who was presiding over some of the most significant litigation in America—the legal battles between the copper kings over the vast ore deposits under "the richest hill on earth" at a time when the spread of electricity and telephones made copper one of the world's most important natural resources.

After the War of the Copper Kings ended in the early 1900s, and with it much of the corruption that had led to the writ in the first place, the Montana Supreme Court struggled with the writ's creation for most of the twentieth century. The struggle reached its peak a half-century after Chief Justice Theodore Brantly's opinion in *Whiteside*, when another Montana chief justice derided the writ of supervisory control as "purely the creature of the inventive genius of the court without being prescribed or authorized by either the Codes, the statutes or any other written law of this state." That criticism resurfaced at the 1972 Montana Constitutional Convention when the Judiciary Committee proposed abolishing the writ, calling it an "unseemly avoidance of the express provisions of the 1889 Constitution." Fortunately, convention delegates rejected that recommendation, choosing instead to ratify and even strengthen the Supreme Court's supervisory control powers. Approval of the 1972 Constitution by voters therefore should have put to rest any lingering questions about the writ's legitimate place in Montana jurisprudence. With the new Montana Rules of Appellate Procedure, the Court has gone further yet, in effect paying judicial homage to Brantly's opinion in *Whiteside*, albeit without acknowledging the test's origins.

Article VII, section 2 provides "[t]he supreme court . . . has original jurisdiction to issue, hear, and determine writs of habeas corpus and such other writs as may be provided by law." By statute, those writs include "mandamus, certiorari, prohibition, injunction, and habeas corpus," plus "all other writs necessary and proper to the complete exercise of its appellate jurisdiction." Mont. Code Ann. § 3-2-202. Is the writ of supervisory control constitutional? Beyond these legislatively recognized writs, is its original jurisdiction constitutional?

C. Open Courts

Magna Carta, the thirteenth century charter of liberties agreed to by English kings, guarantees a basic form of equal justice under law: "We will not sell, or deny, or delay right or justice to anyone." Like many state constitutions, and unlike the United States Constitution, the Montana Constitution incorporates this guarantee into a right to open courts. In an age of statutes, however, the substance of any "speedy remedy afforded for every injury of person, property, or character," is more likely to be codified by state legislatures than developed by common law courts. State courts, however, may resist statutory limits on their common law authority to provide a remedy for wrongs. The open courts guarantee may be read to provide some grounds for this resistance. Professor David Schuman discusses the unlikely role of Magna Carta's descendants in today's tort reform battles. *Meech v. Hillhaven West* remains the definitive account of Montana's Article II, section 16. The questions the Montana Supreme Court leaves open in *Meech* are subject to perennial debates in both the legislature and the courts.

David Schuman, *The Right to a Remedy*

65 Temple L. Rev. 1197, 1199–1203 (1992)

Part I: Background

A. History and Sources

Modern remedy clause litigation centers around such relatively recent innovations as workers' compensation schemes, no-fault insurance plans, medical malpractice damage caps, and product liability statutes of repose—issues distant indeed from the clause's origins. Yet because these origins sometimes provide the materials from which judges fashion decisions, they merit a brief review.

The remedy clause derives ultimately from Magna Carta, where it took the form of a promise extracted from King John to reform his courts. These institutions had fallen into disrepute for their practice of selling writs—the most powerful and efficient writs fetching the highest prices. Hence, King John's promise: "To no one will we sell, to no one will we refuse or delay, right or justice." In the hands of Lord Coke, whose influential commentary on Magna Carta was among the most frequently read legal texts in colonial America, the King's promise underwent a radical change and emerged in pertinent part as follows: "[E]very Subject of this Realm, for injury done to him in [goods, land or person], . . . may take his remedy by the course of the Law, and have justice and right for the injury done him, freely without sale, fully without any denial, and speedily without delay." In this form, the remedy clause was urged upon the Framers of the Federal Bill of Rights, but to no avail. The right did, however, appear in several of the original state constitutions, and from there was copied into the constitutions of many states later admitted.

B. Texts

Today, the citizens of thirty-nine states can claim a constitutional "right to a remedy." The language granting this right differs from constitution to constitution but it typically guarantees that for injuries of a certain type, a person shall have access to a remedy through the state's legal apparatus. Connecticut's clause is typical: "All courts shall be open, and every person, for an injury done to him in his person, property or reputation, shall have remedy by due course of law. . . ."

Some constitutions vary the injuries for which a remedy is guaranteed: Florida and South Carolina include general entitlement to a remedy for "any injury" or "wrongs sustained" without limitation, and Illinois guarantees a remedy for injuries to privacy. Further, whereas in most states the provision is phrased as a command (a person "shall" have remedy), in Maryland, Rhode Island, and Vermont, it is a suggestion (every person "ought" to have a remedy for injury). Frequently additional rights accompany or modify the remedy guarantee: the right to a speedy and complete remedy, freely and without sale, in open court; or the right to sue the state. Judicial opinions, however, rarely account for textual or contextual particularities, despite the fact that, for example, a guarantee like Louisiana's specifying an "adequate" remedy may, as a matter of plain meaning, require a different interpretation than a guarantee like Illinois's specifying a "certain" remedy. A statute replacing traditional workplace personal injury torts with a no-fault workers' compensation scheme provides injured employees a degree of "certainty" at the occasional expense of "adequacy," and is therefore less problematic under the latter constitution than the former.

C. Scope of Usage

"Right to remedy" arguments appear in a variety of contexts. Most commonly, litigants use the guarantee to attack an adversary's immunity from legal action. Some of these immunities such as spousal, intra-familial and sovereign, derive from the common law, but more often they are statutory. While most immunities attacked as violations of the remedy guarantee confer complete immunity, some are partial, as in limits or caps on damages obtainable in medical malpractice actions, or in sovereign immunity statutes that set an upper limit on recoveries against the state.

All of the immunities listed thus far eliminate or limit some subset of a larger cause of action; for example, they affect negligence claims brought by employees against employers, but not all negligence claims. The remedy clause is also used, however, against immunities that result from legislative elimination of an entire traditional cause of action. Thus, plaintiffs have used remedy guarantees to attack statutes eliminating "alienation of affection" or so-called "heart balm" suits.

In all these cases, injured parties invoked the remedy guarantee to attack substantive legislative policy choices. An example of a substantive remedy clause attack would be a suit challenging a legislatively revised workers' compensation scheme in which certain events (on-the-job injuries) will no longer be remediable in tort. Likewise, an automobile guest passenger statute could offend the remedy guarantee if it barred recovery for certain legislatively identified victims; a damage cap could also be called a violation of the remedy clause if it set limits on the extent of the remediable injury. All of these challenges deploy the remedy clause against legislation that defines certain types of events as non-injuries.

In procedural remedy clause cases, on the other hand, plaintiffs attack legislation that is aimed at some characteristic of the litigation process itself, regardless of its substantive content. Examples include attacks on statutes of limitations or statutes of repose. The two types of attack—substantive and procedural—frequently overlap, for example when the attack focuses on a medical malpractice statute of repose. Insofar as the challenge alleges that the legislature cannot immunize medical malpractice, the challenge is substantive; insofar as the challenge alleges that the legislature cannot set time limits on litigation, the challenge is procedural. Again, the cases rarely focus on whether the statute under attack is substantive, procedural or both. This oversight seems particularly unfortunate in jurisdictions which infer from the remedy clause's history as a guarantee of fair judicial process that it does not constrain legislatures. The more logical inference would be that the remedy clause applies against all impediments to fair judicial process, be they legislative or judicial in origin. In other words, history more logically supports a "substantive/procedural" distinction than a "legislative/judicial" one. ***

Meech v. Hillhaven West

238 Mont. 21 (1989)

McDONOUGH, Justice.

This opinion concerns questions certified to this Court by the United States District Court for the District of Montana, Great Falls Division, Honorable Paul G. Hatfield presiding. The questions are as follows:

(1) Is the Montana Wrongful Discharge From Employment Act, §§ 39-2-901 to 39-2-914, MCA, unconstitutional in that it serves to wrongfully deprive an individual falling within the purview of the Act from his or her right to "full legal redress" within the meaning of Article II, § 16 of the Montana Constitution?

(2) Are those provisions of the Montana Wrongful Discharge From Employment Act which expressly prohibit recovery of noneconomic damages, and limit the recovery of punitive damages, violative of an individual's right to "full legal redress" within the meaning of Article II, § 16 of the Montana Constitution?

We answer "No" to both questions.

Petitioner Meech's action in the United States District Court claims damages for wrongful termination from employment, breach of the implied covenant of good faith and fair dealing, and intentional or negligent infliction of emotional distress. Meech also seeks punitive damages for allegedly oppressive, malicious, and unjustifiable conduct on the part of Meech's former employer, respondent Hillhaven. The claims grew from the alleged wrongful discharge of Meech by Hillhaven. Hillhaven moved to dismiss asserting that the Montana Wrongful Discharge From Employment Act (Act) precluded Meech's common-law claims. Meech responded to the motion by contending that the Act violated Article II, § 16 of the Montana Constitution. Certification of the questions presented here followed. Before fully answering the questions, a brief summary of the Act aids in understanding the issues.

The Act provides the exclusive remedy and procedure for actions formerly governed to a great extent by common-law requirements:

> Preemption of common-law remedies: Except as provided in this part, no claim for discharge may arise from tort or express or implied contract.

Section 39-2-913, MCA. . . . In place of the prior governing statutes and the common-law causes of action it abrogates, the Act provides a statutorily defined cause of action for wrongful discharge.

The Act broadly defines "discharge" to include constructive discharge. Section 39-2-903, MCA. Covered employees may sue for discharges defined as wrongful under the Act. Section 39-2-904, MCA. Three causes of action for "wrongful" discharge exist under the Act: discharge in retaliation for an employee's refusal to violate public policy or for reporting a violation of public policy, discharge in violation of the express provisions of the employer's written personnel policies, and discharge for reasons other than good cause as defined in the Act. The Act limits the time for bringing a cause under its provisions to one year from the date of discharge. Section 39-2-904, MCA.

The Act establishes the extent of employers' liability for wrongful discharge. Under the Act, plaintiffs have no claim to damages for "pain and suffering, emotional distress, compensatory damages, or punitive damages, or any form of damages, except as provided for in subsections (1) and (2) [of § 39-2-905, MCA]." Subsections (1) and (2) of § 39-2-905, MCA, provide damages for lost wages and fringe benefits, together with interest thereon for a period not to exceed four years from the date of discharge. The Act defines the value of employee paid pension plans, insurance coverage, vacation time, and sick time as fringe benefits. Subsection (2) provides for an award of punitive damages where claimants can show by clear and convincing evidence actual malice or actual fraud. Interim earnings, including those the claimant could have earned with reasonable diligence, are to be subtracted from the award for lost wages. Section 39-2-905(1), MCA. The Act also provides an incentive for arbitration as an alternative mechanism for settling employment disputes. Section 39-2-913, MCA.

Meech in essence argues that the Act denies his fundamental right to full legal redress under Article II, § 16 of the Montana Constitution. Meech also contends that the Act violates equal protection by denying the fundamental right to full legal redress to a class of claimants without demonstrating that the classification furthers a compelling state interest. Hillhaven answers that the Act does not violate equal protection of the laws or infringe on a fundamental right to full legal redress because Article II, § 16 of the Montana Constitution guarantees only a right of access to courts to seek a remedy for wrongs recognized by common-law or statutory authority, and the legislature may alter common-law causes of action to promote a legitimate state interest. We agree with Hillhaven and overrule *Corrigan* [*v. Janney* (Mont. 1981)], *White* [*v. State* (Mont. 1983)], and *Pfost* [*v. State* (Mont. 1986),] insofar as they hold that Article II, § 16 of the Montana Constitution guarantees a fundamental right to full legal redress.

I.

The Act does not Violate the Fundamental Right of Full Legal Redress, Because no such "Fundamental Right" is Created by Article II, Section 16.

*** A. Historically, Courts Have Construed Constitutional Guarantees in Light of the Particular Abuses Those Guarantees Seek to Prevent. ***

Construing our speedy remedy guarantee in light of the particular abuses the framers sought to correct supports the argument that the clause does not guarantee a fundamental right to "full legal redress." The predecessor to Article II, § 16, was Article III, § 6 of the 1889 Montana Constitution, which reads as follows:

> Courts of justice shall be open to every person, and a speedy remedy afforded for every injury of person, property, or character; and that right and justice shall be administered without sale, denial, or delay.

*** Article III, § 6, was not placed in the Constitution as a directive to the legislature. Rather, the guarantee was directed at the courts, and it was framed to provide for equality in the administration of justice. . . . The Magna Carta's chapter 40, which contains language similar to the last segment of Article III, § 6, reads as follows:

> To no one will We sell, to none will We deny or delay, right or justice.

The language of the first part of Article III, § 6, providing for a speedy remedy for injury to person, property, and character, resembles commentary on Chapter 40 by the influential 17th century expositor on the common law, Sir Edward Coke:

> And therefore every Subject of this Realm, for injury done to him in *bonis, terris, vel persona* [i.e., goods, lands, or person], by any other Subject, be he Ecclesiastical, or Temporal, Free or Bond, Man or Woman, Old or Young, or be he outlawed, excommunicated, or any other without exception, may take his remedy by the course of the Law, and have justice and right for the injury done him, freely without sale, fully without any denial, and speedily without delay.

Schuman, *Oregon's Remedy Guarantee*, 65 Or.L.Rev. 35, 39 (1986) (quoting E. Coke, Second Institute 55–56 (4th ed. 1671)). Coke's version of Chapter 40 influenced the content of remedy clauses in many state constitutions:

> The constitutions of thirty-seven states contain passages which, in substance, provide that the courts "shall be open to every person, and speedy and certain remedy afforded for every wrong and for every injury to person, property, or reputation." . . . [I]t appears most likely that the highly influential Sir Edward Coke, commenting on the Magna Carta more than four centuries after its adoption, was primarily responsible for the contemporary forms of the various certain-remedy provisions.

Note, *Constitutional Guarantees of a Certain Remedy*, 49 Iowa L.Rev. 1202, 1202–03 (1964).

Coke's interpretation of the Magna Carta is, in a broad sense, faithful to its origins. The English feudal nobility sought through Chapter 40 to eliminate abuses in the writ system which governed King's courts. The abuses in the system made the price of the writ obtained by a would-be litigant a determinant of the quality of justice received. See generally W. McKechnie, The Magna Carta: A Commentary on the Great Charter of King John (2d ed. 1914). The goal of ending the abuses present in the English writ system eventually lead to the embodiment of a greater constitutional principle:

> It is evident that the Magna Carta did not put down the practice of charging heavy fees for writs. Yet this chapter [Chapter 40], although so frequently misunderstood and exaggerated, is still of considerable importance.... [I]t has been interpreted as a universal guarantee of impartial justice to high and low; and because, when so interpreted, it has become in the hands of patriots in many ages a powerful weapon in the cause of constitutional freedom.

W. McKechnie, The Magna Carta: A Commentary on the Great Charter of King John 397–98 (2d ed. 1914).

The recognition of the historical meaning of guarantees derived from Chapter 40 as mandating that the courts provide equal access to justice, led to limited interpretations of remedy clauses when plaintiffs claimed the provisions constricted the legislature. The concurring opinion in *Davidson* [*v. Rogers*] (Or. 1978) by Justice Linde set out the rationale for a limited interpretation of the guarantees in remedy clauses as follows:

> The guarantee in article I, section 10, of a "remedy by due course of law for injury done [one] in his person, property, or reputation" is part of a section dealing with the administration of justice. It is a plaintiffs' clause, addressed to securing the right to set the machinery of the law in motion to recover for harm already done to one of the stated kinds of interest, a guarantee that dates by way of the original state constitutions of 1776 back to King John's promise in Magna Carta chapter 40:... It is concerned with securing a remedy from those who administer the law, through courts or otherwise.

Put another way:

> The guarantee tells those who *apply* the law when and how they must do so. It says nothing to *lawmakers*, except insofar as they attempt to interfere with the administration of justice.

Schuman, *Oregon's Remedy Guarantee*, 65 Or.L.Rev. 35, 67 (1986) (emphasis in original).

In *Shea* [*v. North Butte Mining Co.* (Mont. 1919)], this Court succinctly explained this point holding that Article III, § 6, did not constrict the legislature's power to replace common-law personal injury actions with actions provided by workers' compensation legislation:

> A reading of the section discloses that it is addressed exclusively to the courts. The courts are its sole subject-matter, and it relates directly to the duties of the judicial department of the government. It means no more nor less than that, under the provisions of the Constitution and laws constituting them, the courts must be accessible to all persons alike, without discrimination, at the time or times and the place or places for their sitting,

> and afford a speedy remedy for every wrong recognized by law as being remedial.

Both *Stewart* [*v. Standard Publishing* (Mont. 1936)] and *Reeves* [*v. Ille Electric Co.* (Mont. 1976)] quoted *Shea* for the proposition that the remedy guarantee, as a mandate aimed exclusively at the courts, does not constrict legislative powers.

We agree with *Shea*, *Stewart*, and *Reeves* on this point. The history of the guarantee indicates that framers of state constitutions inserted remedy clauses to insure equal administration of justice. Clauses insuring equal administration of justice are aimed at the judiciary, not the legislature. Therefore, the history of our provision supports Hillhaven's argument that our remedy guarantee does not create a fundamental right to full legal redress. Such a reading of the remedy guarantee also accords with another rule recognized in *Shea*: No one has a vested right to any rule of common law.

B. No One Has a Vested Right to a Rule of Common Law.

The controversy posed by the first question from the United States District Court hinges also on whether Article II, §16, prohibits the legislature from exercising its plenary power to abrogate the common-law tort causes of action alleged by Meech. The general rule on the constitutional authority of state legislatures is that:

> [T]he people, through the legislature, have plenary power, except in so far as inhibited by the Constitution, and the person who denies the authority in any given instance must be able to point out distinctly the particular provision of the Constitution which limits or prohibits the power exercised.

Missouri River Power Co. v. Steele (Mont. 1905). The general rule is also that no one has a vested interest in any rule of common law. Therefore, as a general proposition, the legislature, under its plenary power to act for the general welfare, may alter common-law causes of action. The legislative action may not, however, infringe on constitutional rights. We have already pointed out that historically, Article II, §16, does not constrict the power of the legislature to alter common-law causes of action. The more specific issue here is whether the legislature may alter or abrogate causes of action sounding in tort. ***

As Prosser [and Keeton on Torts §1, at 2–4 (5th ed. 1984)] demonstrates, wrongs recognized at law are corrected as provided by law. Legislatures in the Anglo-American system have long been held to possess the authority to expand or reduce claims and remedies available at common law. O.W. Holmes, The Common Law 112 (1881). The law of Montana has long recognized that the courts and the legislature establish the substantive law governing tort claims. Early Montana statutes contemplated passage of legislation altering the common law. For example, §1-1-109, MCA, first enacted as part of the Bannack Statutes, states:

> The common law of England, so far as it is not repugnant to or inconsistent with the constitution of the United States or the constitution or *laws* of this state, is the rule of decision in all the courts of this state. (Emphasis added.)

Similarly, Montana law provides that there "is no common law in any case where the law is declared by statute." Section 1-1-108, MCA. And statutes in derogation of the common law are "to be liberally construed with a view to effect their objects and to promote justice." Section 1-2-103, MCA.

The legislature's exercise of its power to alter the common law supports in a large part our legal system. And as pointed out by Hillhaven, much of the legislation altering the common law concerns the legislature's decisions on the remedies, redress, or damages obtainable in various causes of action. For example, the legislature has arguably expanded liability in adopting comparative negligence in § 27-1-702, MCA. Similarly, in § 27-1-715, MCA, the legislature has provided a remedy where none previously existed by ordering courts to hold owners of vicious dogs strictly liable in particular circumstances. Recognition of human rights violations under Title 49 of the Montana Code Annotated, prohibition of certain trade practices in the insurance industry under Title 33 of the Montana Code Annotated, and expansion of parents' liability for children's torts (§ 40-6-237, MCA) are also instances where the legislature has acted to expand available causes of action, remedies, redress, and damages. Other examples undoubtedly exist, and where these legislative expansions govern causes of action, courts and administrative bodies are bound to follow their mandate.

Legislative decisions to expand liability to further various policy objectives are debated and passed almost routinely. In a like manner, for policy reasons, the Legislature debates and passes statutes that take away causes of action and/or constrict liability. The following are examples: abolition of a cause of action for alienation of affection (§ 27-1-601, MCA), abolition of a cause for breach of promise to marry (§ 27-1-602, MCA), protection for certain persons against a cause of action for libel (§ 27-1-804, MCA), liability limitations for those rendering emergency care at an accident scene (§ 27-1-714, MCA), liability limitations for those furnishing alcoholic beverages (§ 27-1-710, MCA), liability limitations for persons donating food for charity (§ 27-1-716, MCA), liability limitations for agents and volunteers of nonprofit corporations, (§ 27-1-732, MCA), and liability limitations for nonprofit organizations sponsoring rodeos and other events, (§ 27-1-733, MCA). Laws on livestock in open range constitute another legislative limit on liability of parties who are arguably tort-feasors. Section 60-7-202, MCA. Landowners also benefit from legislative limits on liability. For example, under § 23-2-321, MCA, a landowner owes only a duty for acts or omissions that constitute willful or wanton misconduct to individuals making recreational use of surface waters flowing over or through the landowner's property. Similarly, from a remedy and redress standpoint, property owners benefit from statutory provisions exempting certain property from execution. The Index to the Montana Code Annotated lists over sixty types of property statutorily exempt from execution. These and other statutes constrain liability and limit remedies and redress available at law.

In actions governed by the common law, this Court has also established limitations and expansions of liability. For example, in *Miller v. Fallon County* (Mont.

1986), this Court abrogated interspousal tort immunity. Similarly, this Court, acting in its role as lawmaker, recently imposed on employers the duty of good faith and fair dealing. *Gates v. Life of Montana Insurance Company* (Mont. 1982). In another decision, breach of the duty of good faith and fair dealing arising from obligations in a lease justified an award of punitive damages. *Nicholson v. United Pacific Insurance Co.* (Mont. 1985).

This Court has also refused to expand common law. For example, this Court has affirmed a trial court's decision disallowing evidence of emotional harm to a shareholder where the tort was committed against the shareholder's corporation. *Moats Trucking Co. v. Gallatin Dairies* (Mont. 1988). Another case held that the guarantee under Article II, § 16, does not abrogate a statute of limitations defense. *State v. Perry* (Mont. 1988).

The above cited examples of legislative and judicial limitations illustrate that the law, for a variety of policy reasons, refuses to provide a cause of action, remedy and redress for every injury. This proposition is expressed in Latin as *damnum absque injuria*, meaning a "loss which does not give rise to an action for damages against the person causing it." Black's Law Dictionary 345 (4th ed. 1979). The legislation at issue here similarly alters common-law rights and duties and arguably denies a cause of action, remedy, and redress for injuries recognized at common law. If Article II, § 16, guarantees a fundamental right to full legal redress as embodied in common-law causes of action, then a myriad of legislation altering common law in a restrictive manner, as well as the Act, denies this fundamental right. *Shea* addressed this issue:

> If the contention of counsel should be upheld, the consequence would be that the legislature would be stripped of all power to alter or repeal any portion of the common law relating to accidental injuries or the death of one person by the negligence of another.
>
> It is true the legislature cannot destroy vested rights. Where an injury has already occurred for which the injured person has a right of action, the legislature cannot deny him a remedy. But at this late day it cannot be controverted that the remedies recognized by the common law in this class of cases, together with all rights of action to arise in [sic] future may be altered or abolished to the extent of destroying actions for injuries or death arising from negligent accident, so long as there is no impairment of rights already accrued.

As *Shea* demonstrates, if Article III, § 6, is read as only a directive to the courts to provide for equal administration of justice, then the rule that the legislature may alter the common law does not conflict with the speedy remedy guarantee. Therefore, the general rule that no one has a vested interest in a rule of common law refutes Meech's argument that the Act unconstitutionally deprives him of his fundamental right to full legal redress.

C. The 1972 Amendment to Article III, § 6, did not Recognize or Create a Fundamental Right to Full Legal Redress.

In 1972, Article III, § 6 of the 1889 Constitution was amended and inserted in the current Constitution as Article II, § 16. The amendment added to the Article as underscored below:

> Courts of justice shall be open to every person, and speedy remedy afforded for every injury of person, property, or character. No person shall be deprived of this full legal redress for injury incurred in employment for which another person may be liable except as to fellow employees and his immediate employer who hired him if such immediate employer provides coverage under the Workmen's Compensation Laws of this state. Right and justice shall be administered without sale, denial, or delay.

In *Reeves*, the amended version of Article III, § 6 of the 1889 Constitution was held not to constrict the legislature's decision to alter common law:

> As indicated in *Shea* and *Stewart*, the legislature is not constitutionally prohibited from eliminating common law rights which have not accrued or vested. The Constitution does not freeze common law rights in perpetuity.

There was no comment in *Reeves* on the amendment to Article III, § 6.

1. The Wording Itself. *White* [*v. State* (Mont. 1983)] and *Pfost* [*v. State* (Mont. 1986)], without discussing governing precedent, reached the opposite conclusion construing Article II, Section 16 of the 1972 Montana Constitution on issues involving governmental immunity and equal protection. *White* held that Article II, § 16, "guarantees that all persons have a speedy remedy for every injury," and thus the classification resulting from a cap on tort damages awarded against state governmental entities violated equal protection. *White* then concluded that the legislation violated the guarantee because no compelling state interest justified denying the fundamental right to full legal redress for all injuries.

In *Pfost*, this Court faced an equal protection challenge to an amended version of the damages cap at issue in *White*. *Pfost* cited *White* and again held that Article II, Section 16, provides a "constitutional right to full legal redress for injury." The phrase "full legal redress" from Article II, § 16, played an important role in this determination:

> The use of the clause "this full legal redress" has major significance. It obviously and grammatically refers to the "speedy remedy afforded for every injury of person, property, or character." The adjective "this" means the person, thing or idea that is present or near in place, time or thought or that has just been mentioned. Webster's New Collegiate Dictionary (1981). The constitutional framers thus construed a "speedy remedy" as comprehending "full legal redress." A state constitutional right to full legal redress was thereby created. Any state statute that restricts, limits, or modifies full legal

> redress for injury to person, property or character therefore affects a fundamental right and the state must show a compelling state interest.

There are flaws in this reasoning. As pointed out by Justice Weber's dissent in *White*, rules on the construction of constitutional guarantees favor interpretations of the guarantees in line with former judicial decisions where a constitutional convention has approved a similar or identical provision in a new constitution. If "this full legal redress" refers to the speedy remedy in the first clause, then the two references are identical and the Convention approved *Shea's* and *Stewart's* definition of the guarantee. *Shea* and *Stewart* leave little doubt that our remedy provision does not guarantee a fundamental right to a particular cause of action, remedy, or redress. As discussed below, the delegates narrowly drafted the amendment to accomplish the single purpose of limiting the lawmakers' power in restricting third party actions in workers' compensation law. ***

The maxim, "For every wrong there is a remedy" thus bestows upon the person who may be wronged the right to seek redress to be made whole again in an action, whereas the facts which entitle a claimant to legal redress is denominated the "cause of action." Remedy is neither "redress" nor "relief." Remedy is "[t]he means by which a right is enforced or the violation of a right is prevented, redressed, or compensated." Black's Law Dictionary 1163 (5th ed. 1979). Therefore, the Act does not deny full legal redress or a speedy remedy. It simply defines what constitutes the facts which must be established to obtain remedy and redress in the context of wrongful discharge.

Similarly, the guarantee of a "speedy remedy" in the first clause of Article II, § 16, means such remedy as is provided by law. This "full legal redress," following the guarantee of a speedy remedy, refers to the equal right to be made whole again by what the law defines as a cause of action and its elements. Legal requirements and restrictions, as discussed more fully below, may be part of the entire package the law calls a cause of action, remedy, and redress. These restrictions and requirements are not established by our Constitution. Rather, it is the duty of the courts and the legislature to establish what constitutes available causes of action, remedies, and redress. Thus, we disagree with the notion that the proper grammatical and definitional construction of the words in Article II, § 16 of the Montana Constitution supports the existence of a fundamental right to redress so that the legislature may not alter causes of actions except by a showing that the legislation serves a compelling state interest. There must be the basis or underpinning of a cause of action and remedy as defined by the lawmakers before one arrives at the point of redress.

2. The "Intent of the Framers." Basic rules of construction favor deriving the meaning of Article II, § 16, from its face. From our discussion above, and apart from what is referred to later in this opinion as the *Ashcraft* amendment, it is apparent that the words of Article II, § 16, only mandate that the courts provide equal access to causes of action and remedies established by the courts or the legislature. However, even if an ambiguity exists, the debates at the 1972 Constitutional Convention reinforce our initial conclusion.

White's and *Pfost's* interpretation of the effect of the 1972 amendment to the remedy provision ignores the specific meaning ascribed to the provision during debates at the 1972 Constitutional Convention. Moreover, the majority's analysis in these decisions overlooks the explanation of the amendment in the Official Text with Explanation of the Proposed 1972 Constitution, a document circulated to inform voters of the content of the Constitution prior to the vote on its adoption in 1972. Our beginning discussion focuses on the proceedings at the Constitutional Convention.

The record from the Constitutional Convention of 1972 demonstrates that the addition to Article III, § 6, was meant to address a specific problem created by this Court's interpretation of a workers' compensation statute:

> DELEGATE MURRAY: The committee voted unanimously to retain this section with one important addition. The provision as it stands in the present Constitution guarantees justice and a speedy remedy for all without sale, denial or delay. The Committee felt, in light of a recent interpretation of the Workmen's Compensation law, that this remedy needed to be explicitly guaranteed to persons who may be employed by one covered by Workmen's Compensation to work on the facilities of another. Under Montana law, as announced in the recent decision of *Ashcraft versus Montana Power Company* (1971) the employee has no redress against third parties for injuries caused by them if his immediate employer is covered under the Workmen's Compensation law. The committee feels that this violates the spirit of the guarantee of a speedy remedy for all injuries of person, property or character. It is this *specific denial, and this one only*, that the committee intends to alter with the following additional wording: [Delegate Murray reads the amendment].

(emphasis added). Following Delegate Murray's explanation of the *Ashcraft* amendment, Delegate Habedank moved for its deletion:

> DELEGATE HABEDANK: Mr. President [Chairman], ladies and gentlemen. I have no objection to this being in here if you put it in here with full knowledge of what you are doing. The decision in the *Ashcraft* case, which I heard and which was brilliantly argued by Mr. Dahood, made quite a change in what a lot of us thought the law was. However, they were interpreting a specific statute of the State of Montana. All that is necessary to change their interpretation is to amend the statute of the State of Montana. And you, if you adopt this particular provision, are writing into the Constitution by vote of a majority of this group what I consider to be strictly statutory matter.

Delegate Habedank also expressed concern that the addition would extend liability for workers' injuries beyond correcting the decision in Ashcraft:

> As I view this amendment, it will not allow anyone to recover from anyone else without negligence on the part of the person being charged. However, it will eliminate the ability of you as an owner to hire an independent contractor, require him to carry Workmen's Compensation as a part of the coverage, and be assured that you will not be sued on a third party claim.

Delegate Dahood, Chairman of the Convention's Bill of Rights Committee, responded to both arguments made by Habedank:

> I have heard this argument in the Supreme Court, an argument that had no basis in logic. I have heard it by several defense counsel who represent the best of corporate interests, that this is going to affect the individual property owner, and if he hires a contractor, he is going to be exposed to a liability that is unprecedented and they did not experience before. This is totally untrue. This section is *doing nothing more*, and the wording has been *very precisely selected to make sure that it does nothing more*, than place the injured working man back in the status that he enjoyed prior to 1971, a very basic constitutional right which he enjoyed for 80 years in the State of Montana.... Regardless of all this conflict, this technicality, having to use the word "Workmen's Compensation" in this particular section, which we didn't want to do, because the minute we did it we knew that somebody would jump up and say it's legislative, but if you're going to draft something with precision and you want to make sure that all *that you're doing is returning the law to what it was prior to this decision a year ago*, you are compelled, sometimes, in fashioning this precise language to use language that may be seized upon by someone else as legislative. It is not. It is giving back a basic constitutional right that the citizen of Montana had prior to that particular decision.

(emphasis added).

It is perhaps ironic that the convention delegates amended the Constitution to correct this Court's restrictive interpretation of a legislative enactment, and subsequently this Court in *White* and *Pfost* interpreted the addition to constrict the power of the legislature to alter the common law. At any rate, the testimony before the Convention demonstrates that the amendment to Article II, Section 16, was to operate in only one particular area of law. Specifically, the addition prevents lawmakers, that is both the courts and the legislature, from denying workers' compensation claimants a cause of action against negligent third parties for job related injuries. The amendment did not seek to define "full legal redress" as a fundamental right which could not be altered by the legislature. The delegates sought to overturn *Ashcraft*, not *Shea*. The entire discussion presupposes the existence of legislative powers to alter causes of action, remedies, and redress.

The narrow purpose the delegates ascribed to the change in the remedy guarantee is further reflected in the Proposed 1972 Constitution for the State of Montana, Official Text with Explanation, circulated to the voters prior to the vote on adopting the 1972 Constitution. According to the explanation in the voters' information pamphlet, the amendment:

> Adds to 1889 constitution by specifically granting to a person injured in employment the right to sue a third party causing the injury, except his employer or fellow employee when his employer provides coverage under workmens [sic] compensation laws.

Proposed 1972 Constitution for the State of Montana, Official Text with Explanation, at 6.

In summary, the history of our remedy guarantee, the rule that the legislature may alter the common law, and the wording of Article II, § 16, support Hillhaven's assertions that no fundamental right exists to the common-law claims asserted by Meech. The role the judiciary must maintain in interpreting constitutional limitations affecting the plenary power possessed by the people through their legislature, and through their initiative and referendum powers, also supports Hillhaven's assertions.

D. Deriving A New Fundamental Right From Article II, § 16, Violates Separation of Powers.

Both courts and legislatures make the substantive law. The Montana Legislature derives its power to make law from the Constitution's grant of plenary power in Article V, § 1:

> The legislative power is vested in a legislature consisting of a senate and a house of representatives. The people reserve to themselves the powers of initiative and referendum.

One conclusion which could be drawn from an application of *White* and *Pfost* to the legislation at issue in this case is that while the legislature may play a role in expanding common-law causes of action, its attempts to restrict causes of action newly created by this Court fails under the guarantee in Article II, § 16. Yet, the general rule states otherwise:

> [A] constitutional provision that courts of justice shall be open to every person, and speedy and certain remedy afforded for every wrong and for every injury to person, property, or reputation, *is not intended as a limitation upon the legislative branch of the government* where the legislation involved deals with rightful subjects of legislation.

16A Am.Jur.2d Constitutional Law § 616, at 564 (2d ed. 1979) (emphasis added).

The interpretation of Article II, Section 16, called for by Meech would prevent the legislature and the people through the initiative process from restricting or modifying the common law relative to injuries of person, property, or character.... This Court would act as the ultimate authority in a vast, expanding, and ever changing field of law governing important social and economic rights and duties. It could exclude the legislature from deciding: What are injuries to an individual's person, property, or reputation; what wrongs are actionable; what remedies are available;

and what redress will be given. The present appeal presents this separation of powers issue.

. . . We agree with Chief Justice Turnage's dissent in *Pfost* on this aspect of the issue:

> There further can be no question that our courts are open to every person and speedy remedy afforded for every injury of person, property, or character; however, this does not mean that the people have been denied the right to act through their legislature in providing a system of law that may set forth the scope and extent of the remedies provided by law. For this Court to decide otherwise requires a denial of the doctrine of separation of powers in Article III, Section 1, of the Montana Constitution.

E. Meech's Arguments Are Inapposite.

Meech has several contentions addressing the arguments supporting Hillhaven's position. First, Meech points out that in *State ex rel. Montana Citizens for the Preservation of Citizens' Rights v. Waltermire* (Mont. 1987), this Court declared null and void the effect of a voter initiative passed in 1986 amending Article II, § 16, to overrule *White* and *Pfost*. The amendment was held invalid because of an error in the voter information pamphlet. Meech asserts that the fundamental right to full legal redress remains in Montana law because the legislature passed the Act under the authority of the invalid amendment.

This proposition depends on the continued vitality of *White* and *Pfost*. We are overruling *White* and *Pfost* and any decisions relying on *White* and *Pfost* to the extent that they hold Article II, § 16, guarantees a fundamental right to a particular cause of action, remedy, or redress.

Meech further contends that the legislation at issue in *Shea* must be distinguished from the Act. Meech asserts that in *Shea*, the modification of common law benefited workers, but here, according to Meech, the legislation only "creates employers' defenses and eliminates many employees' claims for recovery." We disagree that the Act must be distinguished from the legislation at issue in *Shea* for the purpose of testing its constitutionality under Article II, § 16. *Shea* analyzed the trade-off in employees' and employers' interests as a result of the passage of workers' compensation legislation, but the holding rested on an interpretation of Article III, § 6, as only a mandate to the courts to provide for the equal administration of justice. Thus, *Shea* does not require this Court to analyze whether the Act provides an adequate trade for the loss of common-law wrongful termination claims.

However, this Court's decision in *Corrigan* could be construed as placing this jurisdiction in with those that require an adequate substitute for legislative acts abrogating common-law remedies. See B.R. Burke, *Constitutional Initiative 30: What Constitutional Rights did Montanans Surrender in Hopes of Securing Liability Insurance*, 48 Mont.L.Rev. 53, 66 (1987). Even if Montana law required an adequate substitute for legal remedies abrogated by the legislature, as explained below, we disagree that no adequate remedy for common-law wrongful discharge exists under the Act. Therefore, we do not reach the issue.

In conclusion, we answer, "No" to the first question submitted by the United States District Court. Article II, § 16, does not render the Act unconstitutional as depriving an individual, in this case Meech, of a fundamental right to the common-law actions he alleges.

II.

The Act Survives Equal Protection Scrutiny because it is Rationally Related to a Legitimate State Interest.

The second question certified from the United States District Court concerns the validity of the Act's specific limitations on damages. The issue as framed is whether the Act's prohibition on the recovery of noneconomic damages and punitive damages violates Article II, § 16. Our discussion in answer to this question necessarily extends to an analysis of the equal protection guarantee found in Article II, § 4 of the Montana Constitution.

White and *Pfost* interpreted Article II, § 16, as guaranteeing a fundamental right of full legal redress for "all recognized compensable components of injury, including the right to be compensated for physical pain and mental anguish and the loss of enjoyment of living." *White*, 661 P.2d at 1275. These decisions then went on to hold that the legislation at issue violated the equal protection guarantee because no compelling state interest justified denying the fundamental right found in Article II, § 16, to the class of claimants affected by the damages limitation at issue. Here, the question involving the Act's damages limitation is similar, and more properly framed as:

> Do the limitations on the recovery of certain damages in the Act violate equal protection because the Act unconstitutionally burdens a class of claimants seeking damages for wrongful discharge?

Selection of the proper equal protection test is our first task in determining this issue.

As discussed in the previous section, no fundamental right to "full legal redress" exists under Article II, § 16. Meech alleges no other infringement of fundamental rights by operation of the Act, and no suspect classifications are involved. The strict scrutiny test applies only where legislative classifications infringe on a fundamental right, or where the legislature employs suspect classifications such as race or national origin to define the benefited or burdened class. *See* J.E. Nowak, R.D. Rotunda, & J.N. Young, Constitutional Law Ch. 16, § I, at 596–98 (2d ed. 1983). Therefore, the strict scrutiny test does not apply.

We also refuse to employ middle tier scrutiny to analyze classifications created under the Act. The United States Supreme Court has employed the middle tier criterion in only a few situations which are not applicable here. *See generally Butte Community Union v. Lewis* (Mont. 1986). This Court's decisions have applied the test only where specific directives in the Montana Constitution protected interests in education and welfare. Our interpretation of Article II, § 16, as only a directive to the courts distinguishes the interest at issue here from the interests at stake in those cases.

We determine that the proper level of scrutiny for the classifications created by the Act's limitation on employers' liability is provided by the rational basis test. We further find that the Act's provisions on damages pass equal protection muster because the Act's disparate treatment of similar claims is rationally related to a legitimate state interest.

Until recently, the fundamental body of law governing available damages in the employment area has been contract law. Courts, by virtue of their power to alter the common law, have expanded employers' liability by recognizing tort claims in the employment context. The legislature has now acted to reverse this trend by restricting damages for wrongful discharge. This decision to limit liability "emerges as a classic example of an economic regulation—a legislative effort to structure and accommodate 'the burdens and benefits of economic life.'" *Duke Power Co. v. Carolina Environmental Study Group* (1978). A statutory "limitation on recovery is a classic economic regulation, ... [which] must be upheld if it is reasonably related to a valid legislative purpose." *Boyd v. Bulala* (W.D. Va.1986) (finding heightened scrutiny inappropriate for reviewing liability-limitation under requirements of Virginia's remedy guarantee). ***

This Court, too, in *Reeves*, recognized that the rational basis test applied to analyzing whether liability-limitations imposed through a special statute of limitations for architects and builders violated equal protection:

> The test of the constitutionality of class legislation is whether the classification has some reasonable, just and practical basis and whether the law operates equally upon every person within the class. [citations omitted] A statute will not be stricken down upon constitutional grounds unless its violation of the fundamental law is clear and palpable, and the classification it makes is illusory and unreal. [citation omitted] Applying these tests, section 93-2619, R.C.M.1947, does not violate equal protection of the laws.

We hold that these decisions provide the proper rule on which equal protection test applies to analyzing the Act. ***

The remedy provision in the Act, set out below, arguably classifies wrongful discharge claimants based on the magnitude of harm:

> Remedies. (1) If an employer has committed a wrongful discharge, the employee may be awarded lost wages and fringe benefits for a period not to exceed 4 years from the date of discharge, together with interest thereon. Interim earnings, including amounts the employee could have earned with reasonable diligence, must be deducted from the amount awarded for lost wages.

> (2) The employee may recover punitive damages otherwise allowed by law if it is established by clear and convincing evidence that the employer engaged in actual fraud or actual malice in the discharge of the employee in violation of 39-2-904(1).
>
> (3) There is no right under any legal theory to damages for wrongful discharge under this part for pain and suffering, emotional distress, compensatory damages, punitive damages, or any other form of damages, except as provided for in subsections (1) and (2).

Section 39-2-905, MCA. Claimants alleging only wage loss within a four year period, and only noneconomic damages, are not adversely affected by the Act's remedy provision. Claimants seeking damages extending beyond four years, or claimants suffering from noneconomic harm such as emotional distress, are foreclosed from pursuing their claims by the Act's remedy provision. Meech asserts that this difference in available remedies violates equal protection guarantees. In addition, Meech argues that the Act unconstitutionally limits the availability of punitive damages.

The general rule on the plenary power of the legislature in determining the availability of punitive damages refutes Meech's argument that the Act unconstitutionally limits such damages:

> There is no vested right to exemplary damages and the legislature may, at its will, restrict or deny the allowance of such damages.

22 Am.Jur.2d Damages § 239, at 326 (2d ed. 1965). See also *White* (tort claimants have no constitutional right to punitive damages). We hold that the Act's provision on punitive damages is constitutional.

We also hold that the Act's classification of claims by available remedies passes equal protection muster. Again, these types of limitations are not new to law. Limitations on recovery for wrongful death, for recovery against common carriers, and limits for damages on baggage claims are classic examples of liability-limitations. As explained below, we conclude that that the Act rationally relates to promoting a legitimate state interest.

The legislative history of the Act demonstrates that lawmakers perceived an unreasonable financial threat to Montana employers from large judgments in common-law wrongful discharge claims. Testimony in legislative hearings also indicated to legislators that large judgments in common-law wrongful discharge cases could discourage employers from locating their businesses in Montana. The Act's limitation on damages is intended to alleviate these threats. Therefore, the Act passes muster on this leg of the test because promoting the financial interests of businesses in the State or potentially in the State to improve economic conditions in Montana constitutes a legitimate state goal.

We also conclude that the Act relates rationally to promoting Montana's economic interests. Some awards for common-law wrongful discharge have included wages which extend far into the claimant's employment future. The effect of the

Act's limitations on damages to four years lost wages rationally relates to reducing this potential liability. Moreover, the limit itself is not irrational or so arbitrary that the classification it creates violates equal protection. As a matter of policy, the legislature determined that four years should be the maximum period for consideration of wage loss reasoning that claimants could generally be expected to find similar employment by the end of this period. The time period in any given claim is necessarily speculative. However, statistics before the legislature supported the conclusion that most wrongful discharge claimants with reasonable diligence will obtain other employment within the four year period. Therefore, judicial deference for the time period at issue is appropriate. The same sort of analysis applies to the Act's limitations on damages for pain and suffering and emotional distress; the restriction on recovery rationally relates to the legislature's legitimate purpose of limiting employers' liability for wrongful discharge.

It could be surmised too that this particular limitation relates rationally to another legitimate legislative aim, that is, it provides for greater certainty in defining an employer's duties by recalling a contract law limitation on damages for pain and suffering. See e.g., § 27-1-310, MCA. As a corollary to this purpose, a greater certainty of the rights of employees also exists under the Act as a result of the "good cause" requirement.

For example, in computing contract damages according to the contemplation of the parties, recovery for

> mental anguish is not, as a general rule, allowed.... the courts evidently believe that the mental suffering which accompanies a breach of contract is too remote for compensation.

22 Am.Jur.2d Damages § 195 (2d ed. 1965). Montana follows the general rule by prohibiting damages for emotional or mental distress in most contract actions. Section 27-1-310, MCA. In contrast, the law generally permits a broader measure of damages in personal injury actions:

> There is no fixed rule or exact standard by which damages can be measured in personal injury cases. The law does not assume that a particular injury calls for a definite amount of compensation, for just compensation may vary widely in different cases, even where the physical injury is the same, especially where the injury is permanent, or where pain and suffering are involved. When a plaintiff suffers pain, fright, or humiliation because of a tort, dollars are awarded as "compensation" but not as the *equivalent* of what was suffered. Because of this lack of equivalence in a major portion of many personal injury awards, precise rules of damages are impossible to state.

22 Am.Jur.2d Damages § 86 (2d ed. 1965) (emphasis in original). Montana also follows the general rule on damages for personal injury:

> For the breach of an obligation not arising from contract, the measure of damages, except where otherwise expressly provided by this code, is the

> amount which will compensate for all the detriment proximately caused thereby, *whether it could have been anticipated or not.*

Section 27-1-317, MCA (emphasis added).

The differences in calculating personal injury damages and contract damages points out a problem with the emergence of tort claims in the employment relationship. Tort claims for at-will employees compensate for these workers' inability to control the term of their employment. Employers, however, are unable to plan for the extensive liability which may arise from damages available in these claims. Testimony in legislative hearings indicated that this is a source of great discontent in the Montana business community. The Act's limitation on noneconomic damages applies long-standing contract law in an attempt to solve this problem by dictating a more objective measure of damages. Under the Act, employers benefit because their potential liability is made more certain. Meanwhile, employees' control over the manner in which they are discharged remains, in part, as a result of the Act's "good employees' cause" requirement. The Act, in making this trade, is in no sense irrational. Therefore, classifications in the Act satisfy the requirements of the rational basis test.

Finally, we address the argument mentioned above that *Shea* requires the legislature to provide adequate substitutes for causes of action abrogated by statute. The Court in *Duke Power* faced a similar contention based on the Due Process Clause of the United States Constitution.... [It] resolved the argument for requiring a quid pro quo as follows:

> Initially, it is not at all clear that the Due Process Clause in fact requires that a legislatively enacted compensation scheme either duplicate the recovery at common law or provide a reasonable substitute remedy. However, we need not resolve the question here since the Price-Anderson Act does, in our view, provide a reasonably just substitute for the common law or state law remedies it replaces.

Here, too, the benefits of the Act for employees are not illusory. Therefore, we need not reach the issue as posed by Meech because the Act provides a reasonably just substitute for the common-law causes it abrogates. ***

In some situations the Act may benefit employees by eliminating common-law defenses formerly available. For example, in *Prout v. Sears* (Mont. 1989), a majority of this Court explained that under prior Montana law, an employer could defend a discharge suit by claiming that the employee was let go for no cause:

> At the same time we give effect to the employment application and record time card. These give the employer the right to fire without cause.

Under the Act, the no-cause defense for discharging an employee who has worked beyond the probationary period is unavailable to most employers. Instead, employers may be subject to discharge only for good cause defined as:

> "Good Cause" means reasonable job-related grounds for dismissal based on failure to satisfactorily perform job duties, disruption of the employer's operation, or other legitimate business reason.

Section 39-2-903(5), MCA. Similarly, the good-cause provision may provide greater protection for an employee whose employer has carefully avoided giving objective manifestations of continued employment, a requirement for maintaining a cause of action for violation of the covenant of good faith and fair dealing under the former law. Imposition of a good-cause requirement in discharge may also provide greater employee protection in situations, as in *Prout*, where employers sought to disclaim in the employment contract any objective manifestations of continued employment. The Act's provision allowing claims for prejudgment interest also betters the prior common-law provisions for recovery.

In addition to the amount awarded for lost wages, pensions, insurance benefits, and vacation time may be considered as fringe benefits under the statute. Section 39-2-903(4), MCA. All fringe benefits which would have accrued during the four year period following the discharge are available as damages under the Act. Therefore, the Act contemplates allowing some recovery for wrongful discharges which would otherwise deny retirement benefits, and more.

To summarize, greater certainty in the law may alleviate problems experienced by both employers and employees. As explained by one commentator:

> [T]he employees who benefit [under common-law cause of action] are few and far between, first, because of the difficulties involved in staying the course of a lengthy and expensive judicial process, and second, because of limitations inherent in the legal doctrines adopted by the courts.

Gould, *Stemming the Wrongful Discharge Tide: A Case for Arbitration*, 13 Emp. Rel.L.J. 404, 413 (1988). Therefore, Meech's argument that the Act provides an inadequate trade for prior common-law actions fails to provide authority for finding the Act unconstitutional.

In conclusion, Montana's remedy clause seeks to guarantee equal access to courts to obtain remedies for injuries as provided by governing law. It does not, however, impart a definition of what the law considers a remedy or full legal redress. Nor does it empower this Court to exclude the legislature from defining what are legal injuries.

Finally, we make clear here that the proper test to apply to the Act's classifications burdening one class and not another, is the rational basis test. The classifications created under the Act at issue here survive scrutiny under this test, and even if Montana law required a quid pro quo for the old causes of actions, the Act provides a reasonable substitute. Thus, we answer "No" to both questions posed by the United States District Court.

TURNAGE, C.J., and GULBRANDSON and WEBER, JJ., concur.

SHEEHY, Justice, dissenting:

This is the blackest judicial day in the eleven years that I have sat on this Court. Indeed it may be the blackest judicial day in the history of the state. Certainly this decision is more regressive than the ill-boded *Ashcraft v. Montana Power Company*

(Mont. 1971), which deprived injured workers of their full legal redress against third party tortfeasors. The decision today cleans the scalpel for the legislature to cut away unrestrainedly at the whole field of tort redress. Perhaps worse by this decision today, the Court throws in the sponge as a co-equal in our tripartite state government.

I.

For the reader to understand the drastic ramifications of the "Wrongful Discharge From Employment Act" the whole of the Act must be set out. The legislation passed as Ch. 641, Laws of Montana (1987) .... The bracketed numbers thereon indicate the present number of the code sections of the Act as they now appear in Montana Code Annotated.

The contraction of what was once in this state the tort of wrongful discharge is found principally in three sections of the Act, Section 4 [§ 39-2-904, MCA], Section 5 [§ 39-2-905, MCA] and Section 8 [§ 39-2-913, MCA].

Under Section 4 of the Act [§ 39-2-904, MCA] grounds for wrongful discharge are limited to three possibilities:

> (1) It was in retaliation for the employees refusal to violate public policy or for reporting a violation of public policy;
>
> (2) The discharge was not for good cause and the employee had completed the employers probationary period of employment; [under the Act, a probationer has absolutely no right of recourse for a wrongful discharge] or
>
> (3) The employer violated the express provisions of its own written personnel policy.

The attorneys in this case supporting the Wrongful Discharge From Employment Act filed briefs claiming that it provided great new rights for discharged workers. Not true. Each of the elements listed above was established by this Court in decisions heretofore made and each was fully available to wrongfully discharged employees, including probationers. *** The elements of wrongful discharge, as found in the Act, therefore, are but restatements of cases based on some judicial policy heretofore promulgated by this Court. While perforce, the legislature had to recognize at least those three elements of wrongful discharge, it took care to provide that no significant amount of damages could be recovered by a wrongfully discharged employee even under those elements. A wronged employee's remedies are nearly emasculated under the Act.

Section 5 of the Act [§ 39-2-905, MCA] describes the recoverable remedies for a wrongfully discharged employee. He or she may recover no more than four years of lost wages and fringe benefits from both of which are deducted amounts the employees earned or could have earned with reasonable diligence during that period. Since Section 6 of the Act [§ 39-2-911, MCA] limits suits to one year from the date of discharge, the employee's loss is wholly speculative.

Section 5 of the Act completely wipes out any right of any discharged employee to damages for pain and suffering, emotional distress, compensatory damages or any other form of damages except the four years of mitigated lost wages and fringe benefits. These stricken elements of damages are traditionally allowed against tort-feasors, elements which we have supported in any number of cases, as proper items of recovery.

Finally, to make certain that a wronged employee would have to take his or her lumps without a legal basis for proper recovery, the legislature adopted Section 8 [§ 39-2-913, MCA] which states that no claim for discharge may arise from a tort or express or implied contract except as provided in the Act itself. The real purpose of Section 8 is to negate by elimination any possible employee claim of tort based upon an implied covenant of good faith and fair dealing in the employment contract. This provision takes Montana out of the mainstream of American legal thought.

Restatement (Second) of Contracts, § 205, provides:

> Duty of good faith and fair dealing. Every contract imposes upon each party a duty of good faith and fair dealing in its performance and its enforcement.

... We have also found a remedy for the breach of the implied covenant in the employment cases noted above....

The implied element of "good faith" connotes a moral quality "honesty of person, freedom from fraudulent intent, and faithfulness to duty or obligation."

The nature and extent of an implied covenant of good faith and fair dealing is measured in any particular contract by the justifiable expectations of the parties to the contract.

The approval by this Court in this case of the elimination by the legislature of the element of good faith and fair dealing in employment contracts has the effect of reversing all of the employment cases this Court has handed down in the last decade. The elimination has a profound effect on the recovery of punitive damages. Although the Act here in question provides [Section 5(2)] for punitive damages in case of actual fraud or actual malice on the part of the employer, unless an employee can show an implied covenant of good faith and fair dealing in his employment contract, he will find no basis upon which punitive damages can be awarded to him.

The legislature, in effect, has converted the tort of wrongful discharge into a sort of contract action by the adoption of the Wrongful Discharge From Employment Act. The legislature refused, nonetheless, to provide all the elements of the damages allowable for breach of contract which ordinarily would compensate the party aggrieved for all of the detriment proximately caused by the breach and in the ordinary course of things likely to result therefrom. Section 27-1-311, MCA. ***

It is evident that the Wrongful Discharge From Employment Act adopted by the Montana legislature purporting to give a wronged employee some rights, instead, took away any possible right of meaningful recovery. The ominous implications of this Act for all employees not working under a union contract cannot be overstated. The longer the employee works for an employer, the greater reliance the employee places upon the employer's proffer of fringe benefits and retirement allowances, then the more the employee is at risk to be discharged, because the economic result of a wrongful discharge to the employer, even if the employee's suit under the Act should be successful, is nothing but paltry damages to the employee and possible profit to the employer. The lack of legislative clout of the unorganized workers, although they may comprise a majority of the workers in this state, is demonstrated in that this patently unfair legislation in 1987 passed the State Senate without a no vote on third reading, and with but 16 no votes out of 100 in the State House of Representatives.

II.

When law can do no right [Then] it be lawful that law can bar no wrong.

—William Shakespeare, King John (Magna Carta's John) Act III, Scene i.

Four centuries ago William Shakespeare stated in capsule the view of the majority of this Court in upholding the Act. The majority view is that the legislature can abolish any right of recovery and when it does courts are barred from awarding "full legal redress" under Art. II, Sec. 16, Montana State Constitution. So holding, the majority airily overrule *Pfost v. State* (Mont. 1986); *White v. State* (Mont. 1983), *Corrigan v. Janney* (Mont. 1981). We submit that not only are these reversals overbroad, but they are clearly in error.

First let us examine the overruled cases. *Corrigan v. Janney*, supra, involved an appeal from a summary judgment granted in the District Court against a plaintiff in a wrongful death case. Janneys had leased living quarters to the Corrigans, and the leased premises were defectively wired so that Max Corrigan came in contact with the faucet on a bathtub and received an electrical shock which ultimately caused his death. The District Court, reading earlier cases of this Court, decided that there was no cause of action by a tenant against the landlord for such a defect and granted summary judgment. This Court held (Harrison, J.) that there is in modern day usage a need for rental houses to be suitable for human occupation and that a cause of action for wrongful death in this case did exist. The Court cited Art. II, Sec. 16 of the Constitution and went on to state:

> It would be patently unconstitutional to deny a tenant *all* the causes of action for personal injuries or wrongful death arising out of the alleged negligent management of rental premises by a landlord. If this action were to be taken away, a substitute remedy would have to be provided. Arguably, the repair and deduct statute provides an alternative remedy for damage to the leasehold interest. However, in no way can it be considered an alternative remedy for damages caused by personal injury or a wrongful death. (Emphasis supplied.)

Justice Harrison then noted a controlling statute and went on to state:

> In summary, we overrule *Dier v. Mueller* and hold that our Constitution requires that plaintiff have a form of redress for wrongful death and survivor damages. We hold that § 58-607 R.C.M. (1947), is controlling and that

> one is responsible for injury occasioned to another by want of ordinary care subject to the defenses and contributory negligence or assumption of risk.

Thus *Corrigan* held that § 58-607 provided a statutory basis for recovery in this wrongful death case, and that Art. II, Sec. 16 constitutionally guaranteed the right of redress in that case. Why the majority overrules that case is beyond my conjecture.

In *White v. State*, Karla White sued the State of Montana alleging that the State was grossly negligent in permitting an allegedly violent and dangerous person to escape from the mental hospital at Warm Springs and to remain free for a period of 5 years without serious attempts to locate and reincarcerate the escaper. Karla was brutally attacked by this individual about 5 years after he had escaped from Warm Springs.

The legislature meanwhile had passed § 2-9-104, MCA, which provided that any governmental unit, including the State, was not liable for noneconomic damages, nor for any economic damages in excess of $300,000 for any one claimant. If this statute were upheld, Karla's right of recovery, premised upon severe emotional injuries which she received from the attack but insignificant economic damages, would be effectively wiped out. The District Court held that the statutory limitation on governmental liability for damages was unconstitutional and granted summary judgment in favor of Karla. The State appealed to this Court, which said:

> Article II, Section 16 of the Montana Constitution guarantees that all persons shall have a "speedy remedy . . . for every injury of person, property, or character." In *Corrigan v. Janney* (Mont. 1981), this Court held that it is "patently unconstitutional" for the legislature to pass a statute which denies a certain class of Montana Citizens their causes of action for personal injury and wrongful death. We affirm and redefine our holding in *Corrigan v. Janney, supra*; we hold that the Montana Constitution guarantees that all persons have a speedy remedy for every injury. The language "every injury" embraces *all recognized compensable components of injury including the right to be compensated for physical pain and mental anguish and the loss of enjoyment of living.* Therefore, strict scrutiny attaches. (Emphasis supplied.)

In *White*, this Court found no compelling state interest to classify tortfeasor victims on whether they had been injured by a nongovernment tortfeasor or by a government tortfeasor. The Court struck down a statute which allowed recovery to plaintiffs damaged economically up to $300,000, but totally denied recovery for noneconomic damages; and further, the statute classified victims of government tortfeasors by the severity of the victim's injuries.

It should be clear to all that § 2-9-104, MCA, denied the equal protection of the law to White because the statute discriminated between tortfeasors injured by government agents or by private defendants; and as between persons injured by government tortfeasors, it discriminated on the basis of economic and noneconomic damages. Certainly this Court in *White* enforced the state constitutional mandate to courts that "Right and justice shall be administered without . . . denial . . ." Art. II, Sec. 16.

Before adverting to *Pfost v. State*, we set out for the convenience of the reader the full text of Art. II, Sec. 16, of the State Constitution:

> Courts of justice shall be open to every person, and speedy remedy afforded for every injury of person, property, or character. No person shall be deprived of this *full legal redress* for injury incurred in employment for which another person may be liable except as to fellow employees and his immediate employer who hired him if such immediate employer provides coverage under Workmens' Compensation Laws of this state. Right and justice shall be administered without sale, denial, or delay. (Emphasis added.)

Pfost v. State involved a plaintiff who had been injured when his truck-tractor collided with a bridge on an extremely icy and hazardous highway. He alleged no precautions had been taken by the State to remedy the hazardous condition although three separate wrecks had occurred prior to Pfost's arrival. Pfost suffered injuries which eventually made him a quadriplegic. He sought compensatory damages of 6 million dollars. In the meantime, the legislature had adopted a new statute regarding the liability of the State in tort cases, limiting any or all recovery to $300,000 for a single person. Section 2-9-107, MCA. Pfost's medical expenses alone exceeded that sum. The District Court held the statute to be unconstitutional as a denial of equal protection and the State appealed. In *Pfost*, we followed *White v. State*, holding that Art. II, Sec. 16, 1972 of Montana Constitution, granted a fundamental right to access to courts for a full legal redress and on the basis of equal protection found that § 2-9-107, MCA, discriminated improperly between those with minor injuries and those with catastrophic injuries resulting from the tort of a government agent. In passing on the language of Art. II, Sec. 16, *supra*, we stated:

> The use of the clause "this full legal redress" has major significance. It obviously and grammatically refers to the "speedy remedy afforded for every injury of person, property, or character." The adjective "this" means the person, thing, or idea that is present or near in place, time, or thought or that has just been mentioned. Websters New Collegiate Dictionary (1981). The constitutional framers thus construed a "speedy remedy" as comprehending "full legal redress." A state constitutional right to full legal redress was thereby created. Any state statute that restricts, limits, or modifies full legal redress for injury to person, property, or character therefore affects a fundamental right and the State must show a compelling state interest if it is to sustain the constitutional validity of the statute.

Pfost, 713 P.2d at 503.

The majority object to our grammatical interpretation in *Pfost* of Art. II, Sec. 16, as "flawed." Perhaps the majority have rules of grammar of which this writer is unaware, but we will leave it to the teachers of English that the clause "this full legal redress" refers in Art. II, Sec. 16 to the "speedy remedy afforded for every injury of a person, property, or character." Grammatically, we insist that "speedy remedy" comprehended "full legal redress."

Speaking in the vein of grammatical construction, the majority ask us to construe the term "full legal redress" in the second sentence of Art. II, Sec. 16 as applying only to injured workmen who have claims against third parties for their injuries. The majority contend that the purpose of the inclusion of the second sentence was only to protect injured workmen and had no effect on the remainder of Art. II, Sec. 16. In this sense, the majority grammatically misconstrue the article. Under its plain language the right of "full legal redress" is not given only to Workers' Compensation claimants. Rather, the right of "full legal redress" is emphatically granted to Workers' Compensation claimants too. The framers intended to make certain that included in Art. II, Sec. 16 was a specific provision which also extended the speedy remedy comprehending full legal redress to Workers' Compensation claimants who might have separate causes of action against third parties, not their employers or fellow employees.

Ashcraft v. The Montana Power Company (Mont. 1971) was the reason for the insertion by the framers of the second sentence in Art. II, Sec. 16, to make certain that Workers' Compensation claimants had the right of full legal redress, too. Ashcraft was a laborer working for a construction company which as an independent contractor was performing work on the job for the general employer, Montana Power Company. Ashcraft was injured through the alleged negligence of the Montana Power Company. He recovered Workers' Compensation benefits through his employer, and sought to sue Montana Power Company as a third party tortfeasor. This Court held that Ashcraft had no cause of action for his injuries against the third party tortfeasor, Montana Power Company. *Ashcraft* and several cases of its progeny following, were at the forefront when Art. II, Sec. 16 was considered by the constitutional framers in 1972. The second sentence of Art. II, Sec. 16 was inserted specifically to overrule *Ashcraft*.

When the provisions of Art. II, Sec. 16 came before the Constitutional Convention for eventual adoption, Delegate Habedank, as indicated in the majority opinion, made a motion to strike the second sentence of the section upon the grounds that the sentence was merely legislative, and its subject was better left to the legislature.

Even more interesting in connection with the Constitutional Convention is that the author of the majority opinion here, a respected member of the Constitutional Convention, stood and opposed Delegate Habedank's motion to delete the second sentence of Art. II, Sec. 16. He stated:

> DELEGATE McDONOUGH: Mr. Chairman, I also support the committee's proposal. In Eastern Montana there's a lot of accidents in the oil field, and practically all the work is subcontracted out or contracted out, and we never dreamed — and Mr. Habedank, I am sure, admits himself he never dreamed, because he's defended these law suits — that the Supreme Court would rule in this manner. And I support the committee proposal because it just — it was a very bad law and it should be restored.

There is an inconsistency between the statements of Delegate McDonough in support of Art. II, Sec. 16, and his statements as the author of the majority opinion as expressed today. If, as he now espouses, Art. II, Sec. 16 gives only a right of access to the courts, but not to a full legal redress, the legislature could make the second sentence of Art. II, Sec. 16, meaningless by simply abolishing the remedies available to third party plaintiffs as they have abolished the tort remedies of the employees in this case. Such a view was unexpressed by any delegate to the Convention. In the light of his opinion today, the commendable efforts of Delegate McDonough to support Art. II, Sec. 16 were not worth the candle. The injured workman now has no more guaranty of a legislature allowing full legal redress than the merest employee relying on implied covenants. ***

A major premise of the majority opinion is that Art. II, Sec. 16 is addressed to the courts, and because the section is not addressed to the legislature, the legislature is free to act without restraint except for a minimal rational test. That concept ignores the last sentence of Art. II, Sec. 16, which tells the courts that "right and justice shall be administered without denial." The courts must consider first the right and then justice, and neither must be denied.

A full legal remedy, state the majority, is not a fundamental right; and so bring themselves to deny the essence of a fundamental right. The right of a citizen to claim justice from his state, is, we should agree, a fundamental right; else the right of petition for redress from grievances is meaningless. State protection of citizens from injustice, a fortiori, is also a fundamental right; else the right of petition is toothless.

A legal remedy that delivers only 25% justice automatically also delivers 75% injustice. Assuming a wrong-doing employer, a legal remedy that delivers to the long-term employee only four working years of justice delivers also the balance of a working lifetime of injustice. For justice is not divisible. Either the result is just or it is unjust, just as a single fact is true or else it is untrue. There is no middle to justice, for injustice takes up where partial justice ends. In defining justice, we do not mess with Mr. In-Between. As surely as there are fundamental rights, there are surely no fundamental half-rights. The right of access to courts is only part of the fundamental right; the right to a full legal remedy completes the part to make a whole. The two, access to the courts and full redress, indivisibly make one fundamental right, and together they are the essence of justice. They must coexist to complete the fundamental right to justice.

The least plausible argument of the majority in this case is that the legislature has the power to limit remedies, and that this Court may not interfere if the legislature so acts. If this were true in all cases, the public in this state would have no protection from free-wheeling legislatures. Fortunately, if the Court does its job, our state constitutional system is designed to contain legislative action within constitutional limits. That design requires the state courts to rein in a rampant legislature. Especially must an appellate court (in Montana the only appellate court is this Court) be watchful to safeguard the rights of the public in state constitutional disputes.

Our appellate jurisdiction has a two-fold purpose: First, we assure state litigants that the decision makers at the first level, the district courts, will make correct decisions, not in isolation, but with the connected support of the state legal system. The review for correctness reinforces the dignity and acceptability of the trial court's decisions, and controls any adverse effects of shortcomings at the first level. The second purpose of this appellate court is equally important. Our institutional review of the workings of trial courts serves to announce, clarify and harmonize the rules of decision and the application of laws in the state legal system. Necessarily, institutional review is both creative and political; to say that legislatures, and not courts, make law ignores the facts of appellate life.

The final arbiter of what the state law in Montana shall be is this Court, under Art. II, Sec. 16, not the legislature. We are given that power, to be used judicially. The Justices in the majority do not seem to realize it, but in approving without objection or by inaction the Wrongful Discharge From Employment Act of 1987, they are making law. They have blessed what should be repugnant to a court—a savage curtailment of redress for wrongs, and they excuse their inaction by ceding overall power to the legislature. Though the State Constitution requires courts of justice (not the legislature) to afford a speedy remedy for every injury of person, of property, or of character, the majority have taken a detour from the road to remedy. They have declined to insist on not only a speedy remedy, but on full legal redress for wrongfully discharged employees. They have made law by being passive, and deserve no praise. A toothless court, when abstaining from its duty, is making law and is as great a threat to a just government as an unrestrained legislature.

This is not to say that this Court sits as a super legislature, governing by its discretion the policy, wisdom, and direction of legislative acts. When, however, the legislature acts invidiously to discriminate between persons similarly situated, as will be demonstrated below, Art. II, Sec. 16 imposes a duty upon this Court to make certain that right and justice are not denied.

III.

Having determined that Meech has no fundamental right to a full legal redress here, the majority sustain the equal protection implications of the Wrongful Discharge From Employment Act by applying the rational test. This leads the majority to the irrational result that it is rational to make the state safe for unscrupulous employers. ***

At its core, the Wrongful Discharge From Employment Act is nothing more than a cap on recoverable damages available to wronged employees. In that sense, the type of law we are looking at here is no different than the types presented to us in *White* and *Pfost*, supra. ***

The Wrongful Discharge From Employment Act cannot be sustained as an equal protection under the rational basis test because it discriminates adversely between persons similarly situated and it discriminates vertically as well as horizontally.

Equal protection permits reasonable classifications only if those similarly situated in relevant respects are treated similarly. An Act is excessively underinclusive if it excludes persons who are similarly situated.

The majority opinion does not begin to state the number of ways in which employees similarly situated are discriminated against under the Wrongful Discharge From Employment Act. Horizontally, the discriminations include at least these:

> 1. A union worker is not affected by the Act; only non-union workers are covered. Thus a union worker who is discharged for "whistle blowing" has larger rights of recovery than a non-union worker discharged for the same reason.
>
> 2. Workers whose discharge is the result of a violation of the Human Rights Act, the Equal Employment Opportunity Act, the Pension Reform Act of 1974 (ERISA), the Pregnancy Disability Act and any number of other state or federal acts are not covered under the Wrongful Discharge From Employment Act. Such employees' full rights of recovery are not taken away under this Act.
>
> 3. The Act discriminates against long term employees by severely limiting their damages which might be large in magnitude.
>
> 4. A worker on probation is entirely precluded from any action for wrongful discharge.

In addition, the Act is vertically discriminatory in that it imposes upon wrongfully discharged employees the burden of subsidizing a better business climate for wrongdoing employers.

It is not a legitimate state purpose to protect employers from their unscrupulous acts as against the traditional rights of individuals to earn their livelihood. Our state constitution includes among inalienable rights "pursuing life's basic necessities, enjoying and defending their lives and liberties, acquiring, possessing and protecting property, and seeking their safety, health and happiness in all lawful ways. In enjoying these rights, all persons recognize corresponding responsibilities." Art. II, § 3, 1972 Mont. Const.

Thus, no case can be made on a rational basis to sustain a law the principal purpose of which is to subsidize, protect or enhance the acts of wrongdoers.

Because of its manifest discrimination, because it serves no legitimate state purpose, and because it cannot survive a proper balancing test as between the rights of employers and of individuals to pursue life's basic necessities, the Wrongful Discharge From Employment Act of 1987 violates the Equal Protection Clause of the 1972 Montana Constitution, Art. II, § 4. ***

IV.

Generally, when a legislative act is invalid because of a discrimination, the act also violates other provisions of the state constitution. That is true in this case. The majority dismisses without proper discussion the due process implications of the Wrongful Discharge From Employment Act.

It is usually a due process argument that an Act which limits the rights of recovery of injured parties must provide a reasonably adequate substitute, or quid pro quo, as the majority calls it. The majority, having adopted the irrational conclusion that the Wrongful Discharge From Employment Act was valid, is driven to a further irrationality in determining that the substitution of mitigated recovery provided to wronged employees in the Act was adequate. Not unlike Polonious in Hamlet, the majority can find in a cloud a camel's shape, a weasel's, or very like a whale.

In determining the adequacy of the substituted recovery in the Act, the majority confined itself to examination of the mitigated four years of damages as against what might be recovered for loss of wages or fringe benefits. The majority paid no attention in determining adequacy to the elimination of compensatory damages, damages for emotional or mental distress, and damages arising from the breach of the implied covenant of good faith and fair dealing. By so examining, the majority managed to escape the best indication of the inadequacy of the recoverable damages in the Act demonstrated by the cases that have come to this Court. The results in [recent] cases . . . show the injury done by the Act to plaintiffs through the elimination of common law tort remedies. The Act simply does not survive an adequacy test when properly admeasured against the former law in Montana.

Other constitutional provisions probably affected by the majority decision but not referred to by the majority opinion and thus not pertinent to this dissent are the right to trial by jury, and the privilege and immunity clauses of the state constitution. Art. II, § 26; Art. II, § 31, 1972 Mont. Const. Oregon looks to Art. I, § 20 of its constitutional Privileges and Immunities Clause rather than to equal protection tests to determine the validity of a statute. There the court inquires into whether the challenged statute affects a "privilege or immunity"—that is, "some advantage" to which a person "would be entitled but for a choice made by government authority." *Salem v. Bruner* (Or. 1985). In a recent case in Washington, *Sofie v. Fireboard Corporation* (Wash. 1989), the Supreme Court of that state found, because of the language in Washington's Tort Reform Act, a violation of the state constitutional provision of the right to trial by jury. Arguments with respect to similar clauses in our state constitution could be made in this case, but were not raised in briefs nor decided by the majority. They are therefore open to future discussions.

V.

If Art. II, § 16 of the Montana Constitution does anything, it imposes upon the judiciary the duty to guard the state constitution. In its decision today, this Court sidesteps that duty and reverses not only the cases mentioned in the majority opinion but a long line of cases in the past 15 years that have established solid boundaries for employers and employees, while adhering to the at-will principle declared in our statutes. In yielding our duty to the vagaries of the legislature, we have disadvantaged a large portion of the Montana labor market in the guise of a better business climate. The Wrongful Discharge From Employment Act of 1987 is economically and socially regressive. The majority opinion is legally regressive. Because of the unwillingness of the majority to act properly in a constitutional case, regressiveness is the order of the day.

I would hold the Wrongful Discharge From Employment Act of 1987 to be invalid on the basis that under an equal protection test it cannot meet even a rational scrutiny. The only basis for the Act that I can find is that as between business and the workers, the legislature discriminatingly prefers business. That is not a constitutional basis on which to found a statute.

HUNT, J., concurs.

HARRISON, Justice, dissenting.

While I agree with much that is said by the majority in this opinion, the totality of this opinion in reversing so many cases this Court has previously decided, necessitates my filing this dissent.

I cannot concur with all that has been said in the dissent of Mr. Justice John C. Sheehy, yet I find I must agree with Justice Sheehy regarding *Corrigan v. Janney* (Mont. 1981). I feel that it is totally unnecessary to reverse *Corrigan* which established that when a cause of action is grounded on statute the plaintiff has a fundamental right to full legal redress under that statute.

Notes on Open Courts

1. *Meech* raises several issues about the rule of law in state common-law courts. Trace carefully the various disputes. What was the relationship between the legislature and judiciary in providing remedies under the 1889 Constitution? How does the insertion of the second sentence of Article II, section 16 in the 1972 Constitution change that relationship? If section 16 guarantees a baseline right to a remedy, what is that baseline? The majority overrules the cases the dissent relies upon, but those same cases overrule earlier cases the majority relies upon. Is there a fixed baseline of constitutionally guaranteed remedies or is it common law judicial policymaking all the way down?

2. Consider Professor Schuman's critique of *Meech* and perspective on how other states read similar "right to a remedy" provisions.

> Courts have on occasion looked to the remedy clause's origins for help in interpreting its current meaning. In *Meech v. Hillhaven West, Inc.*, for example, the Supreme Court of Montana used an historical analysis to sustain a statute precluding general and punitive damages in most actions for wrongful discharge. Reviewing scholarship on the remedy clause, the

court concluded that the purpose of the guarantee was to prevent judicial abuse, not legislative abuse: the remedy clause "is addressed exclusively to the courts. It means no more nor less than that, under the provisions of the Constitution and laws constituting them, the courts must be accessible to all persons alike, without discrimination, . . . and afford a speedy remedy for every wrong recognized by law as being remedial." In other words, "[t]he guarantee tells those who apply the law when and how they must do so. It says nothing to lawmakers, except insofar as they attempt to interfere with the administration of justice." Legislatures are absolutely free, then, to declare what is or is not a legally cognizable injury; once they do, then the remedy clause guarantees that persons suffering the injury have equal access to the state's judicial system.

This holding demonstrates one of the dangers of historical analysis. The *Meech* majority relied on the history of the remedy guarantee as a response to corrupt English courts at the time of Magna Carta—approximately 550 years before the first American state constitutions. By the last quarter of the eighteenth century, during which the American remedy guarantees first appeared, the focus of popular distrust had shifted from the King's courts to the people's representatives. After an unsuccessful early period during which state constitutions contained expansive grants of authority to the legislative branch, the people, disillusioned by what they perceived as legislative corruption (capture by private interest), enacted a "second wave" of state constitutions stripping legislatures of many of their prerogatives and vesting increased power in the judiciary. Looking to the history of the remedy guarantee to determine what "evils" it was intended to "cure" thus leads to diametrically opposite interpretations, depending on which "history" is relevant. At the time of Magna Carta, the evil was corrupt courts, supporting the *Meech* majority's theory that legislatures remain free to define what "injuries" are "legal" and thereby must be afforded a remedy; the object of the constitutional provision is merely to see to it that the judicial system operates fairly. But at the time that many modern American remedy guarantees themselves, or their direct predecessors, were brought into existence, the evil was renegade legislatures that had, for example, deprived injured creditors of their judicial remedies against debtors by passing legislation impairing existing contractual obligations. This history supports the *Meech* dissenter's contention that the clause empowers appellate courts to correct the occasional excesses of overzealous legislatures, a position in fact adopted by the Supreme Court of Kentucky in construing that state's remedy guarantee as giving expression to the Kentucky framers' desire to restrict "the almost unlimited power of the General Assembly." The issue is complicated even further in the case of a state like Montana. In that state, the original 1889 constitution dates from a populist era during which distrust of elitist courts ran high, and the remedy guarantee was amended in 1972 to counteract supposedly high-handed judicial interference with legislative innovation. And what about a state like Oregon, where the constitutional bill of individual rights was taken in toto and verbatim from Indiana, without any significant discussion or debate? Thus, the origins and history of the remedy guarantee may play some role in a contemporary interpretation, but the precise nature of that role is not clear and may, in fact, vary from state to state. ***

PART III: TEXT, CONTEXT, AND INTERPRETATION

None of the existing solutions to the remedy clause problem is completely satisfactory. The various rule approaches are all, to some extent, blunt instruments. Allowing a legislature to eliminate remedies at will seems to fly in the face of the guarantee's plain language, and runs the risk of majoritarian abuse. To distinguish between common law and legislative causes of action is to elevate form over substance. Moreover, to protect pre-constitutional remedies and not modern ones is to prevent modern courts and legislatures from purging anachronisms such as heart-balm statutes. To allow elimination contingent upon some adequate quid pro quo is not a solution to the remedy clause problem, but a restatement of it, because the determination of the quid pro quo's adequacy is little more than a determination of whether or not a remedy has in fact been lost. And the problems with various balancing tests are well-known. They permit courts to act like legislatures, accommodating competing policy claims; they provide no guidance to legislators or litigants; and they call for the comparison of incommensurables. ***

[T]he best interpretation of the remedy guarantee in one state may differ radically from the best interpretation in another state, even when the wording of the two provisions is identical. That is because, as legal scholars have belatedly discovered, a text's meaning cannot be separated from its speaker, its audience, its genre—from its context. Thus, the command to provide a remedy for injuries means one thing if the words occur in the charter of a people noted for distrust of renegade legislatures and something quite different in the charter of a populist community with an historical anti-judicial bias. Thus, the appropriate inquiry is not, "What does the remedy guarantee mean?," but "What does the remedy guarantee mean in the constitution of State X?."

Both the majority and the lead dissent in *Meech* make various attempts to ground their constitutional and remedial reasoning in Montana law, but at critical points, both also resort to outside authorities. Does either side have the better claim to legitimacy?

Chapter 6

Local Government

Article XI, Section 4. General powers. (1) A local government unit without self-government powers has the following general powers:

(a) An incorporated city or town has the powers of a municipal corporation and legislative, administrative, and other powers provided or implied by law.

(b) A county has legislative, administrative, and other powers provided or implied by law.

(c) Other local government units have powers provided by law.

(2) The powers of incorporated cities and towns and counties shall be liberally construed.

New provision allowing legislature to grant legislative, administrative and other powers to local government units.

Article XI, Section 6. Self-government powers. A local government unit adopting a self-government charter may exercise any power not prohibited by this constitution, law, or charter. . . .

New provision allowing local government units to share powers with the state and to have all powers not specifically denied. At present local governments have only those powers specifically granted.

Article XI, Section 8. Initiative and referendum. The legislature shall extend the initiative and referendum powers reserved to the people by the constitution to the qualified electors of each local government unit.

New provision directing legislature to give residents the power to initiate local ordinances by petition or to petition to vote on ordinances passed by local governments.

Unlike states, which enjoy a separate sovereignty in relation to the federal government under the United States Constitution, local governments are subdivisions of state governments created under and ruled by state law. Many states including Montana, however, provide localities an opportunity for "home rule," a grant of significant policymaking autonomy and departure from the traditional rule that municipal corporations only possessed the powers expressly granted them by the state. Once recognized, however, such autonomy may be limited in certain policy spheres or withdrawn altogether. Although the terms of these political debates differ from the "states' rights" debates of our American federalism, many issues of local control remain as controversial within states as they do among states.

A. The Scope and Preemption of Local Power

By default, Montana local governments have those powers "provided or implied by law" under Article XI, section 4. By local option, a local government can adopt a "self-government charter" authorizing it to exercise any power not prohibited by law. To borrow a rangeland metaphor, local governments start "fenced in" by state law and cannot exceed those express or implied powers. Self-governing localities, however, enjoy the benefits of roaming through all policy domains unless "fenced out" by express prohibitions in state law. As discussed below, self-government is still the minority rule in Montana. Very few counties adopt self-government, in part because their roles are primarily law-enforcing rather than law-making within their jurisdiction. Many more municipalities adopt self-government, consistent with their general purposes of securing the health, safety, and welfare of local communities. Whether or not a locality is self-governing, its powers depend in part on how broadly or narrowly permissions or prohibitions of state law are construed. Consider how the Montana Supreme Court approaches its interpretation of state law in the following cases, and how that approach shapes local control.

D & F Sanitation Service v. City of Billings

219 Mont. 437 (1986)

SHEEHY, Justice.

*** The parties stipulated to the facts in this case. Plaintiffs are Montana corporations authorized by the Public Service Commission to collect garbage in and outside the Billings city limits. They brought this action for damages and an injunction against the City of Billings for violating section 7-2-4736, MCA. . . :

> PRESERVATION OF EXISTING GARBAGE OR SOLID WASTE SERVICE IN THE EVENT OF ANNEXATION. A municipality that annexes or incorporates additional area receiving garbage and solid waste disposal service by a motor carrier authorized by the public service commission to conduct such service may not provide competitive or similar garbage and solid waste disposal service to the area for 5 years following annexation except upon a proper showing to the public service commission that the existing carrier is unable or refuses to provide adequate service to the annexed or incorporated area, and after the expiration of 5 years, the municipality may provide such service only if a majority of the residents of the annexed or incorporated area request in writing to the municipality that such service be provided by the municipality. If a proper showing is made that the existing carrier is unable or refuses to provide adequate service to the annexed or incorporated area

or if a majority of the residents request service from the municipality, the municipality may assume sole jurisdiction for the garbage and solid waste disposal service to the entire annexed or incorporated area.

The City of Billings has provided garbage service to annexed areas on the following basis:

a) when totally undeveloped, vacant lands are annexed, the City provides all subsequent garbage services;

b) when developed lands are annexed that are receiving no garbage services, the City provides all subsequent garbage services;

c) when developed lands are annexed on which some persons are receiving private garbage services, those persons cannot receive City garbage service for 5 years, but the City provides garbage collection services to all subsequent residents in the area.

The garbage collected by the plaintiffs, is taken to the city landfill. City customers of the plaintiffs are assessed a disposal fee by the City. County customers are assessed a fee by the county, which is remitted to the City. ***

We begin with respondent's first contention that section 7-2-4736, MCA violates 1972 Mont. Const., Art. II, § 31. That section states: "No ex post facto law nor any law impairing the obligation of contracts, or making any irrevocable grant of special privileges, franchises, or immunities, shall be passed by the legislature." . . .

We defined a franchise as a "special privilege conferred by the government on an individual which does not belong to the citizens generally." *Glodt v. City of Missoula* (Mont. 1948). Section 7-2-4736, MCA confers a special privilege or franchise upon the private garbage haulers. However, we agree with the District Court that the franchise granted is not irrevocable. The privilege can be terminated by either a showing that the private carrier is unable or refused to provide adequate service; or by written request of a majority of residents after a set period of time. Thus even if section 7-2-4736, MCA does grant a franchise, it is not an irrevocable one within the meaning of 1972 Mont. Const., Art. II, § 31. We hold section 7-2-4736 is constitutional under 1972 Mont. Const., Art. II, § 31.

Respondent next contends section 7-2-4736, MCA violates the equal protection clause of the Montana Constitution which states: "No person shall be denied the equal protection of the laws." 1972 Mont.Const., Art. II, § 4. Respondent makes an allegation that the law places a greater tax on annexed taxpayers as opposed to unannexed taxpayers. "A privilege conferred upon one class is a discrimination in favor of that class and against all others." *Hill v. Rae* (Mont. 1916). But the mere fact it is discriminatory is not necessarily unlawful. The greater part of all legislation is discriminatory in some manner. An analysis of whether a privilege violates equal protection requires a determination as to whether the classification is legally permissible and if the classification is reasonable.

This statute is not subject to strict scrutiny because it does not burden a fundamental right or constitute invidious discrimination against a suspect classification. The test here is whether the classification is rationally related to a legitimate governmental interest.

The legislature sought to protect the investments of motor carriers in enacting section 7-2-4736, MCA. Generally, prior to annexation, land areas are sparsely populated. They do not represent the most attractive business to private carriers. Yet the need for garbage disposal services is not met by the City. Therefore the legislature sought to make unannexed areas a more attractive business proposal by allowing the private carriers time to recoup their investments after annexation. This is a legitimate governmental objective. The classification of people in annexed areas using private garbage services prior to annexation bears a rational relation to the governmental purpose of encouraging private garbage service in unannexed areas. We hold this statute does not violate equal protection.

Finally, respondent contends section 7-2-4736, MCA violates 1972 Mont. Const., Art. V, § 12 which states: "The legislature shall not pass a special or local act when a general act is, or can be made, applicable." A general law need not be a law which operates on all persons. "The word 'general' comes from the Latin 'genus' and relates to the whole kind, class or order; hence a law which affects a class of persons less than all may be a general law." *Leuthold v. Brandjord* (Mont. 1935). Special laws are laws made for individual cases, or for less than a class; local laws are special as to place. Such laws are prohibited in order to prevent a diversity of laws on the same subject. The test for a special law is: "Does it operate equally upon all of a group of objects which, having regard to the purpose of the legislature, are distinguished by characteristics sufficiently marked and important to make them a class by themselves?" *State ex rel. Redman v. Meyers* (Mont. 1922). We have already determined the legislative purpose to encourage private garbage service to unannexed areas is a sufficiently important governmental interest to justify the classification. Section 7-2-4736, MCA is not a special or local law. This statute is a general law which does not violate 1972 Mont. Const., Art. V, § 12. We find section 7-2-4736, MCA to be constitutional.

The next issue raised on cross-appeal and on appeal is the interpretation of section 7-2-4736, MCA. Appellants contend the plain meaning of section 7-2-4736, MCA is to prohibit all competitive garbage service by a city in an annexed area for a period of five years after annexation. They argue the statute refers to "annexed area" but does not differentiate between old and new customers as the City does. Therefore they argue all new residents of an annexed area must use private garbage services for a period of five years after annexation.

Respondent contends the language of the statute and the intent of the legislature is to preserve existing garbage services, but not to force subsequent residents in annexed areas to use private garbage services. Therefore, the City has been providing garbage services to subsequent residents in annexed areas. Respondent also contends that where a statute grants a franchise to a corporation the words of grant must be construed against the grantee.

We hold the District Court was correct in interpreting the statute to mean that the private garbage carriers may continue to provide services to those customers it had prior to annexation only. We hold the City is correct in its interpretation for three reasons. First, the purpose of the statute is to allow the private garbage haulers to recoup their investment for providing an essential service. The investment in providing services prior to annexation is only as great as the need for services at that time and therefore section 7-2-4736, MCA should be limited to existing customers at the time of annexation. Second, section 7-2-4736, MCA grants a franchise to the private garbage haulers. In the grant of a franchise by the government the grantee takes only what is clearly given by the grant, and nothing by implication. Thus the statute must be interpreted to refer only to customers existing at the time of annexation. Third, if a governmental grant of a franchise is susceptible to two meanings, the meaning which works the least harm to the public must be adopted. The interpretation restricting the scope of the statute to existing services works the least harm to the public and must be adopted. ***

The [next] issue on appeal is whether the legislature by enacting section 7-2-4736, MCA has pre-empted the field of garbage regulation. The appellants contend the legislature has evidenced its intent to pre-empt municipalities from collecting garbage by authorizing the PSC to grant certificates of operating authority to garbage carriers. Appellant argues municipalities have only such power as is granted by the legislature, and if the legislature chooses to pre-empt a field, the city is powerless to act. Appellants contend that local regulation was not intended by the legislature since no statutory authority exists for the regulation of garbage as Billings does.

Prior to the 1972 Montana Constitution, it was fundamental that cities were subordinate political subdivisions of the State. Cities had only those powers expressly given to them by the legislature. Thus if the state legislature deemed a subject to be a matter of statewide concern, it could enact laws on the subject and pre-empt local governments from the field.

However, the 1972 Montana Constitution changed the role and power of local governments in Montana. The new Constitution provides local governments with the option of adopting a self-government charter or retaining general government powers. If a local government adopts a charter, the local government may exercise any power not prohibited by the Constitution, law or the charter. 1972 Mont. Const., Art. XI, § 6. This section grants local governments, which formerly had only such powers granted to them, the authority to share powers with the state government. "[T]he 'shared powers' concept does not leave the local unit free from state control; it does, however, change the basic assumption concerning the power of local government. At present, that [sic] assumption is that local government *lacks* power unless it has been specifically granted. Under the shared powers concept, the assumption is that local government *possesses* the power, unless it has been specifically denied." 1972 Mont. Const., Con. Committee Notes (1972), Vol. II, pp. 796–97. (Emphasis in original.) Hence, if a local government did adopt self-government powers under the 1972 Constitution, then [pre-1972 cases] would no longer apply. If a local government choose to retain general government powers, the local government would have only the powers given to it by the legislature and those cases would still be applicable.

We take judicial notice under Rule 202(b)(2), M. R. Evid., that Billings voters adopted a self-government charter on November 14, 1976. With the adoption of the charter, the City of Billings assumed self-government powers. The City may exercise any power or provide any service except those specifically prohibited by the constitution, law, or the charter. Section 7-1-102, MCA. Because of this we expressly overrule statements in *City of Billings v. Weatherwax* (Mont. 1981), that municipalities have only such power as is granted them by the legislature. This was the law under the 1889 Constitution. It is not the law under the 1972 Constitution. Under the new Constitution, the City of Billings has all powers save those expressly prohibited.

The only way the doctrine of pre-emption by the state can co-exist with self-government powers of a municipality is if there is an express prohibition by statute which forbids local governments with self-government powers from acting in a certain area. The doctrine of implied pre-emption, by definition, cannot apply to local governments with self-government powers. We look then to the statutes to determine if there has been an express prohibition against local governments regulating garbage.

The powers specifically denied to local governments are enumerated in section 7-1-111, MCA. "A local government unit with self-government powers is prohibited the exercise of the following: . . . (4) any power that prohibits the grant or denial of a certificate of public convenience and necessity." Garbage disposal service operators are required to get a certificate of public convenience and necessity issued by the PSC prior to doing business. Section 69-12-314, MCA. The certificate grants the carriers the right to operate their business upon the public streets.

The decision of the voter of the City of Billings, that the City should provide garbage pick-up services for its residents in no way prohibits the grant or denial of a certificate of public necessity. The City has not refused to allow garbage service companies to operate despite their certificate, nor has the City allowed garbage service companies to operate without a certificate. The City is simply exercising its self-government powers to provide a service for its residents and taxing them for that service. This is clearly within the self-government powers of Billings and does not conflict with state law.

American Cancer Society v. State

325 Mont. 70 (2004)

Justice W. WILLIAM LEAPHART delivered the Opinion of the Court.

*** ¶ 7 The parties agree that, in the recent past, four charter government cities with self-governing powers (Helena, Missoula, Bozeman, and Great Falls) have adopted local ordinances limiting—or prohibiting altogether—the smoking of tobacco products in buildings open to the public. Only one, Helena, has adopted an ordinance that applies, without limitation, to premises with state licenses for the operation of video gambling machines (VGMs). In response to these ordinances, the Legislature enacted HB 758 that imposes a surcharge fee on VGMs and exempts establishments that have VGMs on the premises from local government smoking ordinances that are more stringent than the Montana Clean Indoor Air Act of 1979 (MCIAA), §§ 50-40-101 to 109, MCA. Petitioners brought this action to request that we declare HB 758 unconstitutional under various provisions of the Montana Constitution.

¶ 8 We address the constitutional issues before us pursuant to well-established principles. We presume a legislative enactment to be constitutional. *Powder River County v. State*, 2002 MT 259. "The question of constitutionality is not whether it is possible to condemn, but whether it is possible to uphold the legislative action...." *Powder River County*, ¶ 73. Thus, a legislative enactment will not be declared invalid unless it conflicts with the constitution beyond a reasonable doubt. *Powder River County*, ¶ 73. "The party challenging a statute bears the burden of proving that it is unconstitutional beyond a reasonable doubt and, if any doubt exists, it must be resolved in favor of the statute." *Powder River County*, ¶ 74.

Discussion

¶ 9 Under the 1972 Montana Constitution, then-existing local governing units retained the same powers they had under the 1889 Montana Constitution (i.e. those powers specifically provided by law), although the 1972 Montana Constitution, Article XI, Section 4(2), mandated that such powers be liberally construed. The 1972 Montana Constitution then created a new category of local government by allowing local governing units to adopt self-governing charters. In contrast to local governing units without self-governing powers, which are creatures of the state that have only those powers conferred by law, a local governing unit with a self-governing charter can exercise any power not prohibited by the constitution, law, or charter. Montana Constitution, Article XI, Section 6, provides:

> Section 6. Self-government powers. A local government unit adopting a self-government charter may exercise any power not *prohibited* by this constitution, law, or charter. This grant of self-government powers may be extended to other local government units through optional forms of government provided for in section 3.

(Emphasis added.) ***

¶ 10 To maintain the presumption that the locality retains all powers the Legislature does not prohibit, the Legislature must expressly—and not impliedly—delineate those prohibitions. As we previously decided, "[t]he only way the doctrine of pre-emption by the state can co-exist with self-government powers of a municipality is if there is an express prohibition by statute which forbids local governments with self-government powers from acting in a certain area. The doctrine of implied pre-emption, by definition, cannot apply to local governments with self-government powers." *D & F Sanitation Serv. v. City of Billings* (Mont. 1986). All prohibitions must be explicit. *D & F Sanitation Serv.*

¶ 11 In the case sub judice, the Legislature has exempted VGM establishments from local ordinances that are more restrictive than the MCIAA.

> Section 1. Premises with video gambling machines—local smoking ordinance no more restrictive than state law. An establishment that has been granted a permit under Title 23, chapter 5, part 6, for the placement of video gambling machines on the premises is *exempt* from any local government ordinance that is more restrictive than the provisions of Title 50, chapter 40, part 1.

Section 7-1-120, MCA (emphasis added).

¶ 12 The question we must address is whether this exemption constitutes an express prohibition that forbids local governments with self-government powers from acting in a certain area. *See Gregory v. Ashcroft* (1991) (discussing the need for unmistakable clarity when Congress intends to preempt powers of the states):

> [I]f Congress intends to alter the "usual constitutional balance between the States and the Federal Government," it must make its intention to do so "unmistakably clear in the language of the statute." . . . Congress should make its intention "clear and manifest" if it intends to pre-empt the historic powers of the States. . . . "In traditionally sensitive areas, such as legislation affecting the federal balance, the requirement of clear statement assures that the legislature has in fact faced, and intended to bring into issue, the critical matters involved in the judicial decision."

¶ 13 We analyze this question by determining, first, whether an exemption is the same as a prohibition and, second, whether the city ordinances regulating smoking in buildings open to the public constitute the regulation of gambling.

¶ 14 The Legislature can effect a prohibition under Article XI, Section 6, through express prohibitory language. See § 7-1-111, MCA ("A local government unit with self-government powers is prohibited from exercising the following: . . ."). Alternatively, a legislative prohibition can arise through a direct inconsistency between a state legislative act and the legislation of a self-governing unit. For example, the City of Billings could not supersede the state statutory requirement that charges against a suspended firefighter must be presented to the city council for a hearing. *Billings Firefighters Local 521 v. City of Billings*, 1999 MT 6.

¶ 15 On the question whether § 7-1-120, MCA, contains express prohibitory language, the State argues that, although the legislature did not use the word "prohibited," the exemption created by the statute is tantamount to a prohibition. We disagree. To exempt is not to prohibit. A prohibition cuts off the power to act in the first instance. *See Ortiz v. Pennsylvania* (Pa. 1996), wherein the home-rule municipalities of Philadelphia and Pittsburgh adopted ordinances banning assault weapons. The Pennsylvania Supreme Court declared the ordinances banning assault weapons were invalidated by a subsequent state law specifically denying municipalities any power to "in any manner regulate" the lawful ownership of firearms. In contrast to such an express "prohibition," an "exemption" assumes that there is authority or power to act and grants freedom or immunity from that power. The American Heritage Dictionary 1046 (William Morris, ed., 1969) (defining prohibit as "1. To forbid by authority. 2. To prevent or debar."); The American Heritage Dictionary 622 (4th ed., 2000) (defining the adjective exempt as "1. Freed from an obligation, a duty, or a liability to which others are subject; excused: persons exempt from jury duty; income exempt from taxation; a beauty somehow exempt from the aging process."). In other words, an exemption is an exception to, not a denial of the power to act.

¶ 16 The Legislature has very clearly delineated fourteen powers that self-governing municipalities are "prohibited" from exercising. Section 7-1-111, MCA. It has also set forth five specific powers that local governments with self-government powers are "prohibited" from exercising "unless the power is specifically delegated by law. . . ." Section 7-1-112, MCA. Together, these two statutes constitute prohibition through express statutory language. The power to regulate indoor smoke, however, is not listed in either of these prohibitory statutes. See §§ 7-1-111 to 112, MCA. We hold that, in passing § 7-1-120, MCA, the Legislature did not effect an express prohibition of self-governing powers.

¶ 17 The State contends that it has pre-empted the area of state licensed VGMs and that the city ordinances are inconsistent with that pre-emption. The Legislature has provided through express statutory language that local governments with self-government powers are "prohibited" "the power to regulate any form of gambling, lotteries, or gift enterprises." Section 7-1-112(5), MCA. The question is, have the cities, in passing clean air ordinances, attempted to regulate a "form of gambling" in contravention of the express prohibition? The answer is no. The cities did not regulate gambling or video gaming in any sense of the word. They regulated clean indoor air. If the regulation of clean indoor air incidentally impacts VGM establishments, that does not mean that they have been regulated qua VGM establishments. Rather, they have been regulated as buildings open to the public. The city ordinances have incidental impacts on all buildings open to the public. This includes buildings housing state regulated and licensed enterprises, for example drug stores, chiropractic offices, and law offices. In prohibiting indoor smoking, the cities have not infringed upon the state regulation of pharmacists and chiropractors or upon this Court's regulation of attorneys. Were a city ordinance to require that owners of buildings (including VGM establishments) keep their sidewalks clear of snow, we would not conclude that the cities have regulated gambling.

¶ 18 In conclusion, we hold that the challenged statute, § 7-1-120, MCA, does not set forth a prohibition of self-governing powers under Article XI, Section 6, of the Montana Constitution. Accordingly, it does not preempt any no-smoking ordinances adopted by any self-governing entity. Since § 7-1-120, MCA, has no force and effect, we need not address the other constitutional challenges under Montana Constitution Article V, Section 11(3) and Article II, Sections 1 and 2.

¶ 19 In concluding that the Helena ordinance is more restrictive than the MCIAA, Justice Warner's dissent depicts the MCIAA as protecting the "right" or privilege of proprietors to designate areas as smoking. This analysis ignores the fact that the MCIAA was enacted to advance the Legislature's "constitutional obligations under Article II, section 3 . . ." (right to a clean and healthy environment) and "Article XI of the Montana Constitution. . . ." Section 50-40-102, MCA. Contrary to the dissent's characterization, the MCIAA does not confer any rights or privileges on proprietors. Rather, it requires that proprietors place appropriate signs in designated areas. That this requirement is merely a means to an end (separating nonsmokers from smokers), rather than a right or a privilege, is illustrated by the fact that a proprietor who fails to comply is subject to criminal sanctions. Section 50-40-109, MCA. It would be ironic indeed if the MCIAA, designed to promote a clean and healthy environment, was interpreted as a declaration of rights for proprietors of VGM establishments. ***

Justice W. WILLIAM LEAPHART specially concurring.

¶ 22 In the Court's opinion we conclude that § 7-1-120, MCA, does not expressly "prohibit" the cities from exercising self-governing powers. I write this special concurrence to point out that, in addition, § 7-1-120, MCA, does not, by its terms, have any effect on the anti-smoking ordinances in question. In briefing this matter, the parties and various amici have all assumed that the ordinances in question are "more restrictive" than the provisions of the Montana Clean Indoor Air Act, §§ 50-40-101 to 109, MCA (MCIAA), in that the ordinances deny access to smokers who would otherwise be guaranteed access to "some public places," including VGM establishments. Denial of this supposedly guaranteed smoker access to VGM establishments resulted in a loss of revenue from VGMs. To protect that source of revenue, the Legislature passed § 7-1-120, MCA. Upon close examination, it is apparent that the Legislature's assumption that the MCIAA guarantees access to smokers is entirely unfounded. ***

¶ 30 Section 7-1-120, MCA, seeks to protect smoker access and state revenue by exempting VGM establishments from any local ordinances that are "more restrictive" than the provisions of the MCIAA. It assumes, as the MCIAA so states in its purpose clause, that the MCIAA requires that "smoking areas" be reserved in some public places for those who choose to smoke. However, the substantive provisions of the MCIAA are permissive rather than mandatory and do not actually require that managers or proprietors reserve any areas for smokers. Since the MCIAA does not restrict managers or proprietors to guaranteeing smoking areas, the Helena ordinance is not "more restrictive." An ordinance cannot be deemed more restrictive than legislation which is not restrictive.

¶ 31 "Every reasonable doubt as to the existence of a local government power or authority shall be resolved in favor of the existence of that power or authority." Section 7-1-106, MCA. Accordingly, although § 7-1-120, MCA, exempts VGM establishments from ordinances that are "more restrictive" than the MCIAA, that exemption has no application to the ordinances in question. Since § 7-1-120, MCA, does not interfere with the enforcement of the ordinances adopted by the self-governing units, it does not implicate Article XI, Section 6, or Article II, Sections 1 or 2, of the Montana Constitution.

Justice PATRICIA O. COTTER concurs.

¶ 33 As the Court points out at ¶ 10 of its Opinion, *D & F Sanitation* stands for the proposition that the State may preempt action of local governments with self-government powers only "if there is an express prohibition by statute which forbids local governments with self-government powers from acting in a certain area." Clearly, HB 758 by its terms does not expressly prohibit cities with self-governing powers from regulating smoking in public establishments. To the contrary, we can conclude from the specificity of HB 758 that the Legislature had no intention of prohibiting these cities from regulating smoking in most public buildings. The sole concern of the Legislature was with buildings containing video gaming machines. Thus, if anything, HB 758 reflects the Legislature's tacit agreement that self-governing cities may exercise the power to regulate smoking in most local facilities.

¶ 34 Nothing in the Constitution or the laws of this state gives the Legislature the authority to at once allow the exercise of a power by a self-governing city, while declaring that certain entities or establishments shall be exempt from the operation of that otherwise valid—that is, unprohibited—exercise of self-government power. If anything, in granting a special privilege to the video gaming industry by exempting it from the operation of a local smoking ordinance which by its terms is applicable to all local public buildings, the Legislature has arguably violated Article II, Section 31 of the Montana Constitution which prohibits any law which makes an irrevocable grant of special privileges, franchises, or immunities. For this reason, in addition to those set forth in the Court's Opinion, I concur in the result reached by the Court.

Justice JAMES C. NELSON joins in the concurrence of Justice PATRICIA O. COTTER.

Chief Justice GRAY concurring in part and dissenting in part.

¶ 37 I dissent... from the Court's decision to address whether the ordinances enacted by these self-governing local governments are valid vis-a-vis the express prohibition on the exercise of the power to regulate a form of gambling contained in

§ 7-1-112(5), MCA, and its conclusion that they are. The Court's determination that Section 1 of HB 758 does not constitute an express prohibition on the powers of self-governing local governments is dispositive of the issues regarding the constitutional validity of the legislative enactment—HB 758—over which we accepted jurisdiction. As a result, the Court's discussion of whether the local ordinances regulate a form of gambling in violation of § 7-1-112(5), MCA, is obiter dictum in its entirety.

¶ 38 Furthermore, I observe that the issues over which this Court accepted original jurisdiction are limited—with the exception of the attorneys' fees issue—to issues relating to whether the Legislature's passage of HB 758 is constitutional. None of the issues accepted by the Court involves the validity of the local ordinances themselves. We are all aware that several legal actions pending in at least one district court directly challenge the validity of the local indoor smoking ordinances on various grounds. It is entirely possible that the issue of whether the local ordinances violate § 7-1-112(5), MCA, has been raised in at least one of these district court actions. In my opinion, the Court's discussion, in dicta, of whether the local ordinances constitute the regulation of a form of gambling could potentially foreclose the ability of the parties in those actions to raise and thoroughly present the merits of this issue which is beyond the scope of this proceeding. ***

Justice JOHN WARNER dissents.

¶ 40 I think I can understand what the result of the Court's decision is, including the special concurrences. That is: Helena casino operators cannot allow smoking in their gaming rooms, in spite of § 7-1-120, MCA. Thus, the Petitioners are successful in this part of the litigation. However, I must confess I am not sure why.

¶ 41 First, the Court's Opinion. This case does not present a smoking versus non-smoking question. It is a case of a city versus the Legislature. It is the law that in a power struggle between the Legislature and a self-governing municipality, the Legislature wins. Mont. Const., Art. XI, § 6. It seems the Court agrees the Legislature has the power to prohibit Helena from banning smoking in casinos-it just did it wrong. It had to "prohibit," not "exempt."

¶ 42 I agree with the Court's Opinion to the point where *Billings Firefighters Local 521* is cited for the correct proposition that a legislative prohibition can arise through a direct inconsistency between a state legislative act and the legislative act of a self-governing unit. Beyond that point, while I stand in awe of the Court's ability to weave words toward a result, I must disagree.

¶ 43 Helena's ordinance prohibits smoking in casinos in the city—no exceptions. House Bill 758, codified as § 7-1-120, MCA, states that casinos are exempt from all city ordinances that are more strict than the Clean Indoor Air Act, Title 50, chapter 40, part 1. The Clean Indoor Air Act allows a proprietor to designate his casino as a place where smoking is allowed. Section 50-40-104(1)(c), MCA. Ergo: even though Helena's ordinance states there will be no smoking within the city's casinos, the Legislature says a proprietor may allow smoking in his Helena casino. To me, this is a direct inconsistency between a state legislative act and the legislative act of a self-governing unit. The Legislature trumps Helena—that's the law.

¶ 44 I think what Justice Leaphart's special concurrence says is: since the MCIAA does not prohibit smoking in casinos, but only requires designation of smoking and non-smoking areas, § 7-1-120, MCA, is not more restrictive than the MCIAA. This is so because § 7-1-120, MCA, does not state that smoking is allowed but only states that an ordinance cannot be more restrictive than the MCIAA. Thus, the reasoning goes, even though § 7-1-120, MCA, may be valid; it is meaningless.

¶ 45 Again, I am forced to disagree. The proprietor of a casino is clearly allowed to designate a portion, or all, of his establishment as "Smoking Allowed," at his option. Section 50-40-104(1)(c), MCA. Helena's ordinance states that the proprietor does not have such option; his premises is "No Smoking" by law. I offer the following to illustrate the obvious:

Figure 1

Figure 2

¶ 46 The casino depicted in Figure 1 is more restricted than the one in Figure 2. Ergo: Helena's ordinance, which states "No Smoking" is more restrictive than the MCIAA, which states "Smoking Optional." Section 7-1-120, MCA, is not meaningless. It has the very real effect of exempting the proprietor of a casino from the restriction of Helena's ordinance. Under the statute, a proprietor can exercise his right to post a sign that says smoking is allowed, and smoking is then allowed.

¶ 47 Justice Cotter's special concurrence would conclude that § 7-1-120, MCA, is special legislation in violation of Article XI, Section 31, of the Montana Constitution, because it grants a special privilege, franchise, or immunity to tavern owners with gaming machines, and denies such to other businesses without gambling. To reach this conclusion, the concurrence states, without citation of authority, that nothing in the Constitution or the statutes gives the Legislature the power to allow self-governing cities to ban smoking in establishments without gaming licenses, and to deny this authority to such cities in regard to establishments with gaming licenses. I must disagree yet again.

¶ 48 Article III, Section 9, of the Montana Constitution gives the Legislature the authority to allow gambling by law; it has done so. The regulation of gambling is a matter of state-wide concern. There is no disagreement in this case that the State of Montana has the authority to regulate gambling and that it has done so. Title 23, Chapter 5, MCA. The statute in question here applies only to gaming premises, and is a part of the regulation of those premises. I would conclude that the power to regulate gambling includes the power to regulate the premises wherein it is conducted. The decision whether to allow smoking where gambling is allowed is within the power of the State.

¶ 49 The evidence that smoking, and second-hand smoke, is detrimental to health appears to be overwhelming. However, we do not have before us the question of whether smoking is or is not bad for health; the answer to which question seems obvious. Still, the citizens of Montana have the right to be foolish, and some choose to exercise that privilege. What we do have before us is whether the Legislature's power to regulate gambling can be usurped by Helena. It cannot. Whether the Legislature has unwisely exercised its power in this area is a matter of policy for it alone to decide; and the citizens of Helena, this Court, and the rest of Montana's citizens, must live with its decision or get it to change the law. Of course, none of us are required to patronize establishments that allow smoking.

¶ 50 I dissent.

Justice JIM RICE joins in the foregoing dissent.

Notes on the Scope and Preemption of Local Power

1. A local government may adopt a charter providing self-government powers by initiative or referendum of local voters "with the approval of a majority of those voting on the question." Mont. Const. Art. XI, § 5. In an echo of the Montana Constitution's "periodic submission" provision requiring a vote on the state Constitution every 20 years, Article XI, section 9 requires "an election in each local government to determine whether a local government will undertake a review procedure once every ten years after the first election."

2. According to the MSU Local Government Center:

> [A]ll but eight of the 35 local government charters now in effect in Montana have been the result of Local Government Review. Laurel, Libby, Lima, Red Lodge, Troy, West Yellowstone and Whitefish successfully sought self-governing powers by means of charter adoption outside of the Voter Review process, generally to accomplish a local goal otherwise not possible to achieve as a "general powers" government.

Eight of the now existing charters were adopted during the first and mandatory Voter Review cycle; only two gained approval in the 1986 cycle; eight were approved in the 1994–1996 cycle and in the 2004–2006 cycle nine new charters were adopted. Here too we should note that 28 (80 percent) of the 35 charter governments are located in the western half of the state where one might expect to encounter the greatest community and local government stress associated with the rapid population growth experienced in western Montana during the several past decades.

In passing, it is perhaps noteworthy that only three (5 percent) of Montana's 56 county governments (including the two consolidated governments) now operate with a self-government charter, whereas some 32 (25 percent) of the state's municipalities now operate with a charter. Ironically, it would seem that, of the several forms of local government possible in Montana (and nationally for that matter) none would benefit more from clarification of governmental roles, responsibilities and relationships than the familiar and even venerated commission form of Montana county government. Given the fact that Montana voters have approved only four of the 63 county charter proposals that have been placed on the ballot during the four cycles of Local Government Review, one of which was repealed (Madison County), we can only infer that the familiar courthouse structures of county government are generally trusted by their voters who apparently view them as generally adequate to deal with the modern problems that counties must confront.

With respect to electoral requirements, it is perhaps a bit surprising that half of the charters call for continuation of electoral districts wherein the candidate must reside, as a qualification for election to the governing body. Interestingly, two of these eleven communities also elect one council/commission member at large, in addition to the election of the remaining members by ward. Perhaps less surprising is the uniform abandonment of partisan elections in all of the municipal charters. On the other hand, few would have guessed that a Montana county government, and perhaps especially the Butte-Silver Bow government, would abandon the election of local officials by party label. Yet, all three county charters now call for nonpartisan elections for both the commissioners, the chief executive officers and the elected department heads.

Finally, we note that the majority of charters impose a taxing limitation of some kind on their local government. Most typically, the charter limits the property tax mill levy to a specific amount or to the statutory mill levy limit of a local government possessing only "general powers."

Ken Weaver & Judith Mathre, *Local Government Charters, in* MONTANA'S LOCAL GOVERNMENT REVIEW (Rev. ed. 2008). A list of current charters is available from Montana State University's Local Government Center.

3. Both *D & F Sanitation* and *American Cancer Society* address the statutory catalog of powers denied and powers requiring delegation to self-governing localities. The powers denied by Mont. Code Ann. § 7-1-111 include:

> (1) any power that applies to or affects any private or civil relationship, except as an incident to the exercise of an independent self-government power; ***
>
> (4) any power that prohibits the grant or denial of a certificate of compliance or a certificate of public convenience and necessity pursuant to Title 69, chapter 12;
>
> (5) any power that establishes a rate or price otherwise determined by a state agency;
>
> (6) any power that applies to or affects any determination of the department of environmental quality with regard to any mining plan, permit, or contract;
>
> (7) any power that applies to or affects any determination by the department of environmental quality with regard to a certificate of compliance;
>
> (8) any power that defines as an offense conduct made criminal by state statute, that defines an offense as a felony, or that fixes the penalty or sentence for a misdemeanor in excess of a fine of $500, 6 months' imprisonment, or both, except as specifically authorized by statute;
>
> (9) any power that applies to or affects the right to keep or bear arms, except that a local government has the power to regulate the carrying of concealed weapons; ***
>
> (11) any power that applies to or affects the standards of professional or occupational competence established pursuant to Title 37 as prerequisites to the carrying on of a profession or occupation; ***
>
> (13) any power that applies to or affects landlords, as defined in 70-24-103, when that power is intended to license landlords or to regulate their activities with regard to tenants beyond what is provided in Title 70, chapters 24 and 25. This subsection is not intended to restrict a local government's ability to require landlords to comply with ordinances or provisions that are applicable to all other businesses or residences within the local government's jurisdiction.
>
> (14) subject to 7-32-4304, any power to enact ordinances prohibiting or penalizing vagrancy;
>
> (15) subject to 80-10-110, any power to regulate the registration, packaging, labeling, sale, storage, distribution, use, or application of commercial fertilizers or soil amendments, except that a local government may enter into a cooperative agreement with the department of agriculture concerning the use and application of commercial fertilizers or soil amendments.

This subsection is not intended to prevent or restrict a local government from adopting or implementing zoning regulations or fire codes governing the physical location or siting of fertilizer manufacturing, storage, and sales facilities.

(16) subject to 80-5-136(10), any power to regulate the cultivation, harvesting, production, processing, sale, storage, transportation, distribution, possession, use, and planting of agricultural seeds or vegetable seeds as defined in 80-5-120. This subsection is not intended to prevent or restrict a local government from adopting or implementing zoning regulations or building codes governing the physical location or siting of agricultural or vegetable seed production, processing, storage, sales, marketing, transportation, or distribution facilities. ***

(19) any power to require a fee and a permit for the movement of a vehicle, combination of vehicles, load, object, or other thing of a size exceeding the maximum specified in 61-10-101 through 61-10-104 on a highway that is under the jurisdiction of an entity other than the local government unit;

(20) any power to enact an ordinance governing the private use of an unmanned aerial vehicle in relation to a wildfire.

The powers denied (but subject to delegation by the Legislature) are provided by Mont. Code Ann. § 7-1-112:

(1) the power to authorize a tax on income or the sale of goods or services, except that, subject to 15-10-420, this section may not be construed to limit the authority of a local government to levy any other tax or establish the rate of any other tax;

(2) the power to regulate private activity beyond its geographic limits;

(3) the power to impose a duty on another unit of local government, except that nothing in this limitation affects the right of a self-government unit to enter into and enforce an agreement on interlocal cooperation;

(4) the power to exercise any judicial function, except as an incident to the exercise of an independent self-government administrative power;

(5) the power to regulate any form of gambling, lotteries, or gift enterprises.

See also Mont. Code Ann. § 7-1-106 ("The powers and authority of a local government unit with self-government powers shall be liberally construed. Every reasonable doubt as to the existence of a local government power or authority shall be resolved in favor of the existence of that power or authority."). What might these denials of local government power suggest about the political relationship between the state Legislature and localities?

4. The Legislature also purports to limit the exercise of local powers elsewhere throughout the code. *See, e.g.,* Mont. Code Ann. §§ 45-8-351 (Restriction on local

government regulation of firearms); 80-8-120 (Local pesticide regulation); 2-17-603 (Government competition with private internet services providers prohibited—exceptions); 69-12-342 ("A local government... may not impose a tax or fee on, require a license for, or impose any other operational requirements on transportation network carrier services."); 16-11-311 ("A local government may by ordinance adopt regulations on [youth access to tobacco products] that are no more stringent than [the Youth Access to Tobacco Products Control Act]."). One such restriction was at issue in *City of Missoula v. Fox*, 2019 MT 250, involving a city's attempt "to close a loophole in federal law" by requiring background checks for firearm transfers in the city:

> ¶10 The Attorney General issued an Opinion that concluded that cities with self-government powers were "prohibited by Montana state law from enforcing a local regulation or ordinance requiring background checks on firearm sales or transfers," and reasoning that cities could not exercise "any power that applies to or affects the right to keep or bear arms" pursuant to § 7-1-111(9), MCA. 57 Op. Att'y Gen. No. 1, 9 (2017). The Attorney General also cited § 45-8-351(1), MCA, which generally provides a city "may not prohibit, register, tax, license, or regulate the purchase, sale or other transfer (including delay in purchase, sale, or other transfer), ownership, possession, transportation, use, or unconcealed carrying of any weapon, including a rifle, shotgun, handgun, or concealed handgun," and concluded that the Ordinance was not permissible under the statutory exception to this prohibition. ***
>
> ¶17 The Attorney General argues § 45-8-351, MCA, must be read and harmonized with § 7-1-111(9), MCA, which provides that a local government with self-governing powers "is prohibited from exercising... any power that applies to or affects the right to keep or bear arms...." Missoula answers that the District Court correctly determined the Ordinance was validly enacted pursuant to the language within § 45-8-351(2)(a), MCA, which authorizes cities to "prevent and suppress... the possession of firearms by convicted felons, adjudicated mental incompetents, illegal aliens, and minors."... Thus, as the Ordinance itself explains, the entirety of its regulatory scheme is premised upon, in isolation, the wording in subsection (2) of the statute that grants cities the power "to prevent and suppress... the possession of firearms by convicted felons, adjudicated mental incompetents, illegal aliens, and minors." ***
>
> ¶21 However, the Ordinance, as well as the City's arguments and the District Court's order, fails to account for the remaining language within § 45-8-351, MCA, and thus fails to properly apply the standards of statutory interpretation. "Possession" of firearms is only one of multiple functions the statute explicitly prohibits cities from regulating under subsection (1); the others are "purchase," "sale," "other transfer," "ownership," "transportation," and "use." Nothing within the language of subsection (2) permits

cities to regulate these other functions in any manner, yet the Ordinance does so. Although purporting to merely suppress the "possession" of firearms by convicted felons, adjudicated mental incompetents, illegal aliens, and minors, the scheme of the Ordinance goes much further. It requires that "every firearm transfer... in the City of Missoula, shall be subject to background check." City of Missoula, Mont., Municipal Code § 9.60.030 (2016). Thus, at a minimum, it regulates, in violation of subsection (1), the "purchase," "sale," and "other transfer" of firearms; and not merely by those who are convicted felons, adjudicated mental incompetents, illegal aliens, and minors, but by everyone who engages in a transaction with a private, unlicensed dealer and who does not qualify for an exception under the Ordinance.

¶22 As the Attorney General notes, the District Court's interpretation of the exception in subsection (2) is overbroad. As the Ordinance offers, its background check requirements for firearm transactions is intended to be a "prevention mechanism to serve as a deterrent" to the possession of firearms. City of Missoula, Mont., Municipal Code § 9.60.010 (2016). Under such a rationale, virtually any kind of regulation could be justified as being a "deterrent" to possessing firearms and would permit the exception within subsection (2) to swallow the rule in subsection (1), an absurd result. Harmonizing and reading the statute holistically does not permit such a rendering....

¶23 As the District Court noted, the powers of self-governing local governments must be liberally construed, but this presumption cannot override specific legislative preemption, as here. The express statutory prohibition upon cities in § 45-8-351(1), MCA, is a limitation on Missoula's self-governing powers.

5. Consider Richard Briffault, *The Challenge of the New Preemption*, 70 Stan. L. Rev. 1995, 1997–99 (2018):

This decade has witnessed the emergence and rapid spread of a new and aggressive form of state preemption of local government action. Traditionally, preemption consisted of a judicial determination of whether a new local law conflicted with preexisting state law. Classic preemption analysis harmonized the efforts of different levels of government in areas in which both enjoy regulatory authority and determined the degree to which state policies could coexist with local additions or variations. Classic preemption disputes continue to arise, but the real action today is the *new preemption*: sweeping state laws that clearly, intentionally, extensively, and at times punitively bar local efforts to address a host of local problems.

The new preemption runs the gamut from firearms regulation to sanctuary cities, from workplace equity to environmental protection and public health. New preemption measures frequently displace local action without replacing it with substantive state requirements. Often propelled by trade association and business lobbying, many preemptive laws are aimed not at coordinating state and local regulation but at preventing any regulation at all.

Several states have adopted *punitive preemption* laws that do not merely nullify inconsistent local rules—the traditional effect of preemption—but rather impose harsh penalties on local officials or governments simply for having such measures on their books. Others have considered proposals that are tantamount to *nuclear preemption*, effectively blowing up the ability of local governments to regulate without affirmative state authorization.

The rise of the new preemption is closely connected to the interacting polarizations of Republican and Democrat, conservative and liberal, and nonurban and urban. To be sure, Democratic states preempt Democratic cities; preemptive laws constrain small towns; and some measures impose progressive values on conservative communities. But the preponderance of new preemption actions and proposals have been advanced by Republican-dominated state governments, embrace conservative economic and social causes, and respond to—and are designed to block—relatively progressive local regulations. Since 2011, Republicans have dominated state government. As of 2016 Republicans controlled both houses of thirty-two state legislatures and had trifectas—control of the legislature and the governorship—in twenty-five states. Even as a majority of states are controlled by Republicans, most cities, particularly big cities, are led by Democrats. Thirty-three of the fifty largest cities have Democratic mayors; fourteen of those are in Republican trifecta states. The not-so-irresistible force of cities pushing progressive agendas increasingly runs into the immovable object of conservative state resistance, manifested by aggressive preemption. ***

Much of the criticism of the new preemption has focused on how conservative state lawmakers are blocking progressive local initiatives. But the concerns raised by the current state challenges to local self-government transcend the politics of the particular issues at stake. In this highly polarized era, local autonomy can reduce conflict by permitting diverse communities to take different approaches to different problems while also generating usable information about how debated public policies work in practice. State power is necessary to address the external effects of local action and the costs of varying local laws as well as to ensure that the scale of government action is consistent with the scope of economic and social problems. But our system ought to maintain some legal space for local self-determination concerning problems that arise at the local level.

Does the procedural rule that the Legislature must specifically deny powers to self-governing localities, as interpreted by the Montana Supreme Court, sufficiently guarantee the substantive principle of local "self-government"?

B. The Structure of Local Government

The Montana Constitution provides alternative forms of local government, and offers one of several possible templates combining the executive and legislative powers into a single county commission. *See* Mont. Const. Art. XI, § 3; Mont. Const. Art. XI, § 9. These powers, combined with the initiative and referendum powers granted in Article XI, section 8, set the stage for responsive local governments, at least as an original matter. The interaction of these powers with legislative preemption encourages innovative and diverse policies at the local level but also invites legislative reactions that impose statewide uniformity. Consider how these forces play out in the following case.

Phillips v. City of Whitefish

375 Mont. 456 (2014)

Justice JIM RICE delivered the Opinion of the Court.

¶ 1 . . . Plaintiffs filed this action after voters in Whitefish passed a referendum repealing Resolution 10-46, which authorized the City to enter into an interlocal agreement with the County concerning planning and zoning authority over a two-mile area surrounding the City, commonly referred to as the extraterritorial area (ETA), or the "donut." On cross-motions for summary judgment, the District Court held that the Resolution was not subject to the right of voter initiative and referendum. ***

Factual and Procedural Background

¶ 6 A city may adopt a growth policy and implement zoning and subdivision regulation in an area beyond the city limits only if the county has not "adopted zoning or subdivision regulations" in that area. Section 76-2-310(1), MCA. Likewise, a city may enforce its zoning and subdivision regulations in the extended area only "until the county board adopts a growth policy. . . and accompanying zoning or subdivision resolutions that include the area." Section 76-2-311(1), MCA. Thus, by statute, a city's authority to zone and regulate outside its boundaries is limited to instances where the county has not exercised its authority, and only until the county does so.

¶ 7 State law also provides geographical limits for a city's exercise of zoning and subdivision authority outside its boundaries. As a city designated by statute of the second class, according to its population, § 7-1-4111(2), MCA, Whitefish could extend its regulations for up to two miles beyond the city limits, § 76-2-310(1)(b), MCA. State law also allows local governments to create joint planning boards, § 76-1-112(1), MCA, and to enter into interlocal agreements concerning joint provision and maintenance of various services, § 7-11-104, MCA.

¶ 8 The history of this matter begins in 1967, when the City and County jointly created the Whitefish City-County Planning Board (Planning Board). The Planning

Board was given planning jurisdiction over the area extending four and one-half miles from city limits, and the City exercised exclusive zoning authority in the area up to one mile beyond city limits, in accordance with then-applicable law and the consent of the County. These jurisdictional areas for planning and zoning were set without a formal interlocal agreement.

¶ 9 In 2005, after two years of negotiation, the City and County entered a formal agreement. This 2005 interlocal agreement (2005 IA) reduced the Planning Board's jurisdictional area from four and one-half miles to two miles outside the city limits, while providing for the City's exclusive authority to establish and enforce zoning, subdivision, floodplain, and lakeshore protection regulations, as well as authority to adopt and amend a growth policy, for an area two miles beyond the city limits. By its terms, the 2005 IA could not be altered or terminated without the mutual consent of the parties.

¶ 10 In 2008, the City adopted the Critical Areas Ordinance (CAO), which imposed zoning restrictions in the donut to protect lakes, streams, wetlands, and drainage areas from development. The County opposed the CAO and advised the City that if it was adopted, the County would withdraw from the 2005 IA. Following the adoption of the CAO, the County passed a resolution to withdraw from the 2005 IA. The City filed a lawsuit (2008 lawsuit) that sought to uphold the 2005 IA, and for a declaration that the County could not unilaterally withdraw from the agreement.... The District Court denied a preliminary injunction that would have prevented the County from taking any planning or zoning action in the donut during the pendency of the lawsuit, and summarily declared the 2005 IA to be unenforceable. On appeal, this Court reversed that ruling as a premature decision on the merits, entered an injunction, and remanded for trial. *City of Whitefish v. Bd. of Co. Commrs. of Flathead Co.*, 2008 MT 436.

¶ 11 After remand, the City and County sought an extension of time from the District Court to allow opportunity for settlement discussions.... The City formally undertook consideration of the new agreement (2010 IA) by way of Resolution 10-46. On November 15, 2010, the City Council passed Resolution 10-46, which authorized the City Manager to sign the 2010 IA on behalf of the City. At the same meeting, the City Council passed Resolution 10-47, which authorized the City to seek dismissal of the 2008 lawsuit. On November 30, 2010, the County Commissioners adopted a resolution identical to Resolution 10-46 authorizing the County to enter the 2010 IA. As required by the 2010 IA, the City and County filed a joint motion to dismiss the 2008 lawsuit, offering to the District Court that the litigation was moot because the 2010 IA was fully in effect and specifically replaced the 2005 IA. Intervenors in that case opposed dismissal. The District Court dismissed the action on July 11, 2011, reasoning that the 2010 IA had rendered the 2005 IA void and resolved the issues between the parties.

¶ 12 After passage of Resolutions 10-46 and 10-47 by the City Council, citizens who would become Intervenors in this case, and other City residents unhappy with the decision, began collecting signatures to put a referendum on the ballot to repeal Resolution 10-46, which had authorized the City to enter the 2010 IA. The referendum petition was approved as to form and compliance with state law on January 11, 2011. Sufficient signatures were gathered, and on April 24, 2011, the County Election Department certified the ballot measure for the November election. The Referendum explained that the 2010 IA permitted termination by either party without cause, but did not reference Resolution 10-47 or the dismissal of the 2008 lawsuit. In light of the development of this challenge to the 2010 IA and the likelihood of further legal disputes, the County passed a resolution on June 22, 2011, giving notice to the City that it was withdrawing from the 2010 IA.

¶ 13 The Referendum seeking repeal of Resolution 10-46 was placed on the ballot and voted on by City residents. Citizens residing in the donut were not permitted to vote on the Referendum. The Referendum passed by a two-to-one margin in the November 2011 election. Following the election, the City deemed the 2010 IA as rescinded and no longer in effect. The City further took the position that after the 2010 IA was revoked, the 2005 IA was reinstated in its entirety, and the City was authorized once again to exercise exclusive jurisdiction in the donut.

¶ 14 The present lawsuit challenging the validity of the Referendum was filed by Plaintiffs, residents of both the City and the County, on December 20, 2011, four days after the Flathead County Clerk and Recorder certified the results of the Referendum. Plaintiffs claimed the citizens' power of referendum and initiative did not extend to Resolution 10-46 because the decision to enter into the agreement was contractual and administrative in nature. The City filed a third-party complaint against the County, alleging that the County breached the 2010 IA by taking steps to adopt zoning regulations prior to the expiration of the one-year notice period and, on the assumption that the 2005 IA had been reinstated, that the County had breached the 2005 IA by unilaterally withdrawing from it. The County counterclaimed against the City, alleging it breached the 2010 IA by failing to carry out the required mediation process, and that such breach excused the County from any further performance under the 2010 IA. The District Court granted an unopposed motion to intervene by the Intervenors, who sought to defend the citizens' passage of the Referendum. ***

Standard of Review

*** ¶ 17 The City argues that we must give the Referendum a "presumption of constitutionality and validity" because after passage it was a legislative enactment and must be afforded the same presumption granted to a law enacted by the Legislature. Based on this presumption, the City argues we must apply an "unconstitutional beyond a reasonable doubt" standard. While we have previously determined that this standard does not apply to proposed ordinances and referendums, we have not directly addressed its application to referendums or initiatives after they have been passed. Here, the Referendum rescinded a prior action; it did not create a new law or dictate a future action. Additionally, to deem the Referendum a "validly passed legislative enactment" would put the analytical cart before the horse where the central issue before us is the validity of the Referendum in rescinding Resolution 10-46. We therefore conclude that this standard is not appropriate here, and instead review the District Court's conclusions of law regarding the character of Resolution 10-46, which, in turn, determines the legality of the Referendum, for correctness.

Discussion

*** ¶ 28 2. Did the District Court err by determining that Resolution 10-46 was an administrative act by the City that was not subject to repeal by referendum?

¶ 29 The powers of government are separated into three branches: legislative, executive, and judicial. Mont. Const. art. III, § 1. At the state level, the separation of powers clause prohibits any person belonging to one branch from exercising any power belonging to either of the others, unless the Constitution expressly provides otherwise. Mont. Const. art. III, § 1. The power to make and repeal laws resides in the legislative branch. Mont. Const. art. V, § 1. The Montana Constitution also "reserves to the people of this State the powers to challenge and enact laws through the referendum and initiative processes." *Whitehall v. Preece*, 1998 MT 53 (citing Mont. Const. art. V, § 1 ("The people reserve to themselves the powers of initiative and referendum.")). This power of referendum and initiative is limited to "any act of the legislature except an appropriation of money." Mont. Const. art. III, § 5(1). No similar power is granted over acts of the judiciary or the executive branch.

¶ 30 In contrast to the powers of state entities, "[l]ocal governing bodies are empowered to exercise legislative, administrative, and other powers pursuant to Article XI, Section 4, Mont. Const." *Whitehall*, § 19. Article XI, Section 8 requires the Legislature to extend the power of referendum and initiative "to the qualified electors of each local government unit." The Legislature has codified the power of referendum over the actions of local governments in § 7-5-131, MCA, which provides that "[r]esolutions and ordinances within *the legislative jurisdiction and power* of the governing body of the local government" may be repealed by referendum. (Emphasis added.)

¶ 31 In *Whitehall*, § 17, we explained that "[t]his Court has long recognized a distinction between legislative and administrative or quasi-judicial acts in relation to the powers of initiative and referendum; legislative acts have been held subject to referendum, while administrative or quasi-judicial acts have not." This distinction "applies in virtually all other jurisdictions" and is based upon the "sound rationale" that "referenda on executive and administrative actions would hamper the efficient administration of local governments." *Whitehall*, § 21 (quotation omitted). The efficiency rationale is balanced against the obligation to broadly construe initiative and referendum powers to maintain maximum power in the people. *Whitehall*, § 18. Thus, fundamentally, whether the citizens of Whitefish had the ability by referendum to repeal Resolution 10-46 hinges on whether the action by the City was administrative or legislative in nature. ***

¶ 33 Though it is easy to state a rule recognizing the power of referendum or initiative over legislative matters and rejecting such power over administrative matters, determining whether a particular local government action is legislative or administrative can be difficult. We noted in *Whitehall*, § 26, that the "denomination of an act of local government as a resolution or as an ordinance is not dispositive as to whether the act is legislative or administrative; that determination is fact-driven." We then adopted guidelines stated by the Supreme Court of Kansas to aid in distinguishing legislative and administrative acts of government. These guidelines are:

> 1. An ordinance that makes new law is legislative, while an ordinance that executes an existing law is administrative. Permanency and generality are key features of a legislative ordinance.
>
> 2. Acts that declare public purpose and provide ways and means to accomplish that purpose generally may be classified as legislative. Acts that deal with a small segment of an overall policy question generally are administrative.
>
> 3. Decisions which require specialized training and experience in municipal government and intimate knowledge of the fiscal and other affairs of a city in order to make a rational choice may properly be characterized as administrative, even though they may also be said to involve the establishment of a policy.
>
> 4. No one act of a governing body is likely to be solely administrative or legislative, and the operation of the initiative and referendum statute is restricted to measures which are quite clearly and fully legislative and not principally executive or administrative.

Whitehall, ¶ 28 (*quoting Wichita v. Kan. Taxpayers Network* (Kan. 1994)).

¶ 34 Encapsulating the issue, the fourth guideline posits that an act of a governing body is not likely to be either solely legislative or solely administrative, underscoring that these cases are not black and white, and contain a mixture of considerations. Referendum is to be restricted to acts that have a "fully" legislative purpose, and are not "principally" administrative. This overarching principle prompts the parties' arguments over what Resolution 10-46 and the 2010 IA actually were and actually did—their substance and effect.

*** It is clear that the settlement of the lawsuit and the approval of the 2010 IA by the Council, as implemented by Resolution 10-46, were inextricably tied together. Although Resolution 10-47 technically authorized the City to seek dismissal of the 2008 lawsuit, approval of the 2010 IA by Resolution 10-46 was expressly conditioned upon such dismissal and would not have been honored by the City if dismissal had not been granted by the court. Plaintiffs are correct that, beyond authorization to enter the 2010 IA, Resolution 10-46 was substantially related to the agreement to settle the 2008 lawsuit over the 2005 IA.

¶ 39 The first *Whitehall* guideline recognizes that legislative actions are typically permanent or general in character while those actions that are temporary or limited in effect are administrative. If the action declares a new policy or plan it is generally legislative. If the action pursues a plan previously adopted by the local government, or by a superior legislative body, it is administrative. *Whitehall*, § 28.

¶ 40 City and Intervenors contend that the 2010 IA constituted a new policy that made significant, generally applicable changes to land-use and zoning policies. They argue that by eliminating the mutual consent provision, and allowing the County to withdraw for any reason with only one year's notice, the City "relinquished its sole jurisdictional authority over the ETA" and "in essence transferred control of planning and zoning in the ETA from the City to the County." Because of the potential impact on zoning and planning, the City argues that our holding in *Greens* [*at Fort Missoula, LLC v. City of Missoula* (Mont. 1995)] is dispositive.

¶ 41 In *Greens*, after Fort Missoula was purchased by a private developer and annexed to the city of Missoula, the city enacted an ordinance that rezoned the Fort to allow residential housing. We affirmed that the ordinance was legislative, and subject to the power of referendum, because rezoning and zoning are equally legislative in character.

¶ 42 However, *Greens* and other cases holding zoning decisions to be legislative are not determinative here. Resolution 10-46 and the 2010 IA are not zoning ordinances; they do not actually zone or rezone any property, or make any such land-use decisions. It is important to recognize, as explained above, that any planning authority the City could hope to exercise in the donut was subject to the County's primary statutory authority to act. Sections 76-2-310(1), -311(1), MCA. Although we are not deciding in this case whether zoning authority was the proper subject of an interlocal agreement, nonetheless the action here was simply an amendment to an interlocal agreement that had provided, at most, consensual authority from the County for the City to act. Not only did the IA amendments not actually zone, but they also did not alter the contractual designation of which local government had current authority to zone in the donut. Land-use authority in the donut under the 2010 IA remained with the City, while an unspecified power of oversight in the County was added. What the amendments did was to provide a new mechanism that could potentially lead to a change in the City's permissive authority in the future, including ultimate termination of the interlocal agreement between the City and County. Generally, a municipality has the same general power of contract, including the power to settle a dispute over the contract, as do private individuals.

¶ 43 The parties' arguments overlap into the second guideline—whether an action is one declaring a public purpose or only a small segment of a policy question. The City and Intervenors contend that the 2010 IA effectively brought about a broad alteration in land-use authority in the donut broadly because the termination provision rendered the City's authority illusory—subject only to the County's whims. However, this argument requires speculation beyond the record. . . . Setting aside the fact that the purpose of the 2010 IA was to settle litigation, on this record it is difficult to conclude that the 2010 IA itself effectuated a new zoning policy. Rather, an agreed-upon process between two local governments was established that could lead to a future change in policy after the IA had run its course.

¶ 44 *Whitehall* is instructive. There, the town was required by the Public Service Commission to explore options for reducing its water consumption. The town had a flat-rate billing system for water and did not monitor individual usage. The town passed resolutions approving submission of an application to a grant program; authorizing the town to borrow funds from a U.S. Department of Agriculture program; and authorizing the mayor to enter into a contract for additional grant funding to fund a water system improvement project. Subsequently, the town passed an ordinance requiring a water meter to be installed for each water user, and providing that water use would be billed based on actual use rather than by flat rate. Citizens attempted to place a referendum on the ballot to repeal the ordinance requiring water meters and use billing, and the town council filed suit challenging the proposed referendum. We found the first guideline to be inconclusive because, while previous enactments set out the overall purpose of pursuing a water improvement project, the requirement for installing a water meter was added for the first time in the challenged ordinance. Nonetheless, we determined the challenged ordinance was administrative because it only dealt with a portion of the overall policy question as to how to improve the town's water system to provide water to consumers. Likewise, here, the few 2010 amendments dealt with only a portion of the 2005 IA, and with a portion of the overall question of zoning in the donut, an issue with many other complexities.

¶ 45 The third guideline considers specialized knowledge necessary for the municipal action. "[L]ocal enactments have been held nonreferable where they involve questions upon which the governing body of the local government has far better background, information, and access to the facts than the general electorate." Sandra M. Stevenson, Antieau on Local Government Law vol. 6, § 89.06, at 89-18 (2d ed., Matthew Bender & Co. 2009). Other jurisdictions have recognized that the decision to settle a lawsuit requires investigation and analysis, and appropriately lies within the discretion and business judgment of the local government.

¶ 46 The potential costs to the City of continuing the 2008 lawsuit, the assessment of the outcome of that litigation, including the potential that the County's primary statutory authority to zone in the donut would ultimately prevail, the cost/benefit analysis of seeking a cooperative relationship with the County, and the posture the City would maintain under the 2010 IA in order to pursue its future goals were factors that made the decision to enter the agreement a technical one requiring intimate knowledge of the City's affairs, financing, and long-term goals. The decision required specialized knowledge in many areas and required the technical expertise and discretionary judgment of City officials and their advisors.

¶ 47 The last guideline primarily provides direction about how the guidelines should be weighed.... While we carefully consider the legislative aspects of all local government decisions in a dispute such as this in order to preserve the maximum power of the people, the power of referendum does not extend to all acts of local governments that bear legislative implications. As noted above, if the action of the local government is principally administrative, it will be considered administrative for this purpose, despite having legislative characteristics.

¶ 48 The Dissent would abandon application of the *Whitehall* factors as "vague, confusing, and awkward to apply," Dissent,¶ 52, thereby overruling our precedent and charting a new course—a proposition that none of the parties have advocated. As support for the theory that we no longer need to engage in troublesome balancing, the Dissent offers the characteristics of numerous enactments of the Legislature, Dissent, ¶¶ 53–44, but fails to recognize that all actions of a state legislature are inherently legislative by their very nature. Except for certain appropriation measures, all actions of the Legislature are subject to challenge by citizen initiative. Mont. Const. art. III, § 5(1) ("The people may approve or reject by referendum *any act* of the legislature except an appropriation of money." (emphasis added)). In contrast, local governing bodies act with multiple powers, not merely legislative, and the multi-faceted nature of their actions thus requires an analysis to determine if the purpose of a challenged action is fully or primarily legislative in nature. Otherwise—and this would inevitably be the net result of the Dissent's theory—without an analytical balancing, virtually all actions with policy implications would be subject to challenge. For example, in *Whitehall*, the ordinance requiring water meters, being inherently an act of legislation, albeit a small part of a larger issue, would necessarily be subject to challenge, and we therefore should have upheld the citizen's initiative there that sought to overturn the City's ordinance. However, we disagree that "[t]here can be no argument that adoption of an interlocal agreement is a legislative act," Dissent ¶ 59 (see § 7-11-104, MCA (authorizing interlocal agreements for "any administrative service, activity, or undertaking or to participate in the provision or maintenance of any public infrastructure facility, project, or service")), or that all "significant policy changes" are legislative actions subject to challenge by initiative, Dissent, ¶ 60.

¶ 49 Applying the *Whitehall* factors here, the 2010 IA was an amendment to the previous interlocal agreement between the City and the County. By its terms, it provided a limited duration. The agreement was driven by a desire of neighboring and concurrent local governments to settle contentious issues and pursue a course of cooperation. Fundamentally concerning the settlement of litigation, the decision to enter the 2010 IA and resolve the 2008 lawsuit, with limited assurances about the ultimate duration and outcome of the agreement, was a decision that required specialized knowledge and experience of the City's fiscal and other affairs. These factors weigh in favor of being considered an administrative action. We acknowledge that the 2010 IA and Resolution 10-46 also held legislative implications, including the addition of unspecified County oversight over the City's authority and the possibility that the City's authority, though contingent in nature, could be impacted in the future. However, no zoning was enacted or affected by the action, and the City's zoning authority was initially retained. Balanced together, we conclude that the

City's action had significant administrative characteristics that made it principally administrative in nature, and that the legislative function did not predominate.

Conclusion

¶ 50 We affirm the District Court's determination that Resolution 10-46 was not subject to the power of referendum. As we have determined that the Referendum did not validly rescind the City's authority to enter into the 2010 IA, we do not address whether the 2005 IA has been reinstated.

Chief Justice MIKE McGRATH dissenting.

¶ 51 While I concur with the majority's resolution as to Issue 1, I dissent as to the resolution of Issue 2. The Whitefish City Council's Resolution 10-46 was a legislative enactment and was thus subject to referendum by the voters.

¶ 52 The distinction between legislative and administrative acts is essentially whether the act creates new law (legislative) or executes an already existing law (administrative). *Whitehall v. Preece*, 1998 MT 53. The majority's decision that Resolution 10-46 was an administrative measure derives from application of the four factors in the *Whitehall* case, which in turn were adopted from the Kansas decision in *Wichita v. Kan. Taxpayers Network* (Kan. 1994). The problem with the four factors is that they are vague, confusing, and awkward to apply. Even the Kansas Supreme Court has since found that identifying the line between administrative and legislative actions is difficult. In a subsequent decision that Court decided that few actions are ever solely administrative or solely legislative; that the four factors set out in *Kansas Taxpayers* should be modified (by recognizing that the fourth factor is a statement of policy that is not helpful as a guideline for evaluating a specific set of facts); and by adopting a new fourth factor involving delegated decision-making power. *McAlister v. City of Fairway* (Kan. 2009).

¶ 53 The four (or now three) *Kansas Taxpayers/Whitehall* factors are also confusing, and can unreasonably restrict the voters' right to participate in the referendum process. Factor 1 states, in part, that "permanency and generality are key features of a legislative ordinance." While that may be true, temporary measures may be wholly legislative as well. The Montana Legislature, for example, periodically enacts statutes that will expire on a certain date or will become effective only upon the happening of a certain event. *See e.g.* § 27-1-703, MCA, which is designated as "temporary" and the second § 27-1-703, MCA, set to become "effective on occurrence of contingency." When the people, through referendum, exercise the legislative power, that power should not be more limited than the power exercised by the Legislature.

¶ 54 Factor 2 states that provisions "that deal with a small segment of an overall policy question generally are administrative." This does not even seem to be generally true, since statutes enacted by the Legislature frequently deal with small segments of larger groups or larger policy questions. *See e.g.* § 39-71-117(1)(d), MCA, which revised the Workers Compensation Act definitions of "employer" so as to bring within the umbrella of the Act "a religious corporation, religious organization, or religious trust receiving remuneration from nonmembers for agricultural production, manufacturing, or a construction project conducted by its members on or off the property of the religious corporation, religious organization or religious trust." The representative who introduced this legislation, as well as other legislators, freely conceded that the amendment was directed specifically toward Hutterite religious colonies, and unquestionably and extremely small segment of state "employers." *Big Sky Colony, Inc. v. Mont. Dep't of Labor & Indust.*, 2012 MT 320.

¶ 55 More importantly, however, Factor 2 does not allow for consideration of amendatory measures, such as Resolution 10-46. Looking again to the Montana Legislature, it routinely enacts statutes which are clearly legislative acts, but which are amended in future years in ways large or small. These amendatory actions are no less legislative than the ones that enacted the original entire statute. Factor 2 is therefore misleading and incorrect. An action that amends a prior legislative action will almost always also be a legislative action. These same considerations and criticisms apply to the first sentence of Factor 1 as well, wherein it states that an action which "makes new law is legislative." While generally true, that statement overlooks amendatory measures and confuses the situation when amendatory measures are being considered.

¶ 56 Factor 3 seems to be describing a situation in which governmental officials are called upon to apply training, experience and specialized knowledge to make decisions in specific situations as between several alternatives. This could describe discretionary decisions such as settlement of a lawsuit.

¶ 57 However, the fact that Resolution 10-46 was adopted as part of the settlement of a lawsuit with the County has little or nothing to do with whether the resolution itself is administrative or legislative. While the decision to settle the lawsuit per se may be administrative, it was undertaken in the separate Resolution 10-47. There is no reason why the City could not agree, as it did, to undertake a legislative act as part of the consideration for the settlement. [Fn. It is not unusual for the Montana Legislature to enact legislation as part of the settlement of a lawsuit. For example, that occurred when the Legislature enacted a statewide system for defense of indigent defendants charged with crimes. *See* § 47-1-101 et seq., MCA; and James Park Taylor, Bespeaking Justice: A History of Indigent Defense in Montana, 68 Mont. L.Rev. 363, 381–84 (2007).] That is exactly what it did here. The City, as part of the settlement, agreed to approve and adopt the Restatement of Cooperative Interlocal Agreement with the County, making two important changes as to the term of the agreement and withdrawal from the agreement. Whether the Resolution is viewed as an action re-adopting the Interlocal Agreement or as an action amending the Interlocal Agreement, it is still a legislative measure.

¶ 58 The courts that have considered this administrative act/legislative act divide agree, as does the majority in this case, that the determination is ultimately "fact driven." Opinion, ¶ 33. Because of the fact driven nature of such determinations, some courts have simply adopted a case-by-case approach, guided by underlying principles of separation of powers and historical examples of recognized legislative power, when considering the legislative/administrative question.

¶ 59 The facts of this case show the unmistakable legislative nature of the act at issue. The City Council of Whitefish adopted Resolution 10-46, which by its title, approved the "restatement" of the City-County Interlocal Agreement concerning zoning. There can be no argument that adoption of an interlocal agreement is a legislative act, because the agreement gave the City authority to zone in the donut, or, phrased alternatively, created new law. Since adoption of a zoning ordinance would be a legislative act, it follows that an act granting such authority must also be a legislative act. Further, even if Resolution 10-46 simply adopted the agreement again, it would not lose its legislative nature.

¶ 60 Resolution 10-46 adopted two significant policy changes in the agreement, to provide for a five-year term and to allow withdrawal of a party. As noted above, amendment of a prior legislative enactment is itself a legislative act.

¶ 61 The facts here admit to but one conclusion, that Resolution 10-46 was a legislative measure. I dissent.

Justices PATRICIA COTTER and MICHAEL E. WHEAT join the Dissent of Chief Justice MIKE McGRATH.

Notes on the Structure of Local Government

1. Consider Michelle Tafoya, *Reframing the Framework: Direct Democracy, State Constitutional Interpretation, and the Legislative-Administrative Question in Montana*, 77 Mont. L. Rev. 151, 170, 173–74, 177, 179–80 (2016):

> A. We Should Not be in Kansas Anymore: *Whitehall*, Meet the Montana Constitution ***
>
> The *Phillips* majority's continued reliance on the Kansas-adopted *Whitehall* factors is ultimately misplaced because, unlike Montanan voters, the Kansas electorate has no constitutional guarantee to initiative and referendum at the state or local government level. Instead, the Kansas Legislature must delegate and define this authority for Kansas voters. Unlike Montana, the legislative initiative and referendum movement in Kansas was short-lived and largely unsuccessful. While populist, democratic, and progressive leaders attempted to amend the Kansas Constitution to include the right to initiative and referendum, a guarantee to direct citizen lawmaking never materialized. The 1909 Kansas Legislature eventually passed a bill establishing initiative and referendum in all the state's cities. However, the Kansas Supreme Court has a long history of strictly confining the operation of this statute, which sets out the requirements for local initiative and referendum

ordinance proposals "on a narrow range of subjects." As a result, "[i]n Kansas, the initiative and referendum process... has long been judged on a more demanding basis than in some other locales."

Unlike Kansas, the right to initiative and referendum in Montana is reflected, but not created, in statute. Under the Montana Constitution, "[t]he people reserve to themselves the powers of initiative and referendum." The root of this power dates back to the turn of the last century when a bipartisan legislature and the Montana electorate joined together to amend the 1889 Constitution and engender direct citizen participation in state governmental decision-making. The drafters of the 1972 Montana Constitution not only intended to retain this guarantee, but expressly extended the people's lawmaking power, previously authorized only in statute, "to the qualified electors of each local government unit." A review of Montana's constitutional convention and ratification process also reveals the uncontroversial nature and clear meaning of the initiative and referendum provisions contained in Articles III, V, and XI. In the end, the initiative and referendum power in the constitution reflects the delegates' desire to entrust the people with this power and provide the electorate with a "check that the people of Montana want."

The long history and acceptance of the express initiative and referendum provisions in Montana's fundamental and organic law demand that this power reserved to the people be liberally interpreted. If Montana is to adhere to the "principle that initiative and referendum provisions of the Constitution should be broadly construed to maintain the maximum power in the people," the Montana Supreme Court should no longer adhere to Kansas's stricter doctrine that has admittedly "never adopted a 'liberal' view of the matters which should be subject to initiative and referendum, but quite the contrary." The fundamental flaw in the *Whitehall* and *Phillips* decisions is not in the Court's use of extrinsic jurisprudence to help it interpret Montana's initiative and referendum provisions. Rather, when the Court considered whether to adopt the persuasive precedent of other courts, it erred by not turning to decisions with "well-reasoned and meaningful" analysis "made by courts of last resort in sister states with similar constitutional provisions." In failing to do so, the *Whitehall* and *Phillips* decisions also failed to follow the Court's own precedent that holds extra-jurisdictional cases "practically without value" when "[t]hey construe constitutional provisions altogether unlike our own." ***

Montana case law after the adoption of Article XI, Section 8 in the 1972 Constitution and before the adoption of the *Whitehall* factors provides the first and most important guidepost in formulating a more appropriate framework for the legislative-administrative question. Also persuasive is Oregon case law interpreting what is now Article IV, Section 1 of the 1857 Oregon Constitution. Oregon's precedent is somewhat limited on this subject. However, the Colorado Supreme Court's interpretation of the legislative-administrative question is additionally useful here because Montana, Oregon, and Colorado have similar historical backgrounds on this subject. Like Montana, Colorado modeled its provision after Oregon's constitutional amendment, and today both states share almost identical local government initiative and referendum provisions. Finally, like the Montana Supreme Court, the highest courts in Oregon and Colorado have long held the view that the constitutional guarantee to initiative and referendum at the local level should be liberally construed. ***

By combining Montana, Oregon, and Colorado jurisprudence, a more streamlined approach emerges which allows for a broader interpretation of Article XI, Section 8 of the Montana Constitution. To determine if the subject matter of an ordinance is legislative or administrative in nature-and thus eligible for initiative and referendum-the Montana Supreme Court should adopt the following framework:

1. An ordinance that enacts a new law of general applicability is legislative, while an ordinance that executes or implements an existing, general law is administrative. Where an original act is legislative, an amendment to that act is likewise legislative.

2. A court's decision may be informed by historical examples of recognized legislative power. If a local government act is sufficiently analogous and finds longstanding parallels in statutes enacted by the Montana Legislature, it should be deemed a legislative act. If, on the other hand, the act is analogous to an act the legislature typically delegates to an executive body, it should be deemed an administrative act.

2. The local government article of the 1972 Constitution contained some of the most-debated provisions of the convention and ratification campaign. Is the reality of local government law, as espoused by both the Montana Legislature and Supreme Court in this chapter, faithful to the Montana Constitution's dynamic view of localism?

Chapter 7

Education

Article X, Section 1. Educational goals and duties. (1) It is the goal of the people to establish a system of education which will develop the full educational potential of each person. Equality of educational opportunity is guaranteed to each person of the state.

(2) The state recognizes the distinct and unique cultural heritage of the American Indians and is committed in its educational goals to the preservation of their cultural integrity.

(3) The legislature shall provide a basic system of free quality public elementary and secondary schools. The legislature may provide such other educational institutions, public libraries, and educational programs as it deems desirable. It shall fund and distribute in an equitable manner to the school districts the state's share of the cost of the basic elementary and secondary school system.

Revises 1889 Constitution. Expresses the goal of the State to educate all of its citizens regardless of their ages. Creates a right to equal educational opportunity and specifically recognizes unique heritage of Indians.

Article X, Section 7. Nondiscrimination in education. No religious or partisan test or qualification shall be required of any teacher or student as a condition of admission into any public educational institution. Attendance shall not be required at any religious service. No sectarian tenets shall be advocated in any public educational institution of the state. No person shall be refused admission to any public educational institution on account of sex, race, creed, religion, political beliefs, or national origin.

Last sentence revises 1889 Constitution which merely forbade denying any person entrance to a university because of his or her sex by broadening the language to include all public educational institutions and to include other kinds of discrimination. Other changes in grammar only.

Article X, Section 8. School district trustees. The supervision and control of schools in each school district shall be vested in a board of trustees to be elected as provided by law.

New provision which guarantees control of schools to local boards. Deletes requirement in 1889 Constitution that elections for school district officers must be separate from state and county elections.

Since the early nineteenth century, public education has been a primary responsibility of states. The provision of "common schools" is required by many state enabling acts, including Montana's. A guarantee of local control of schools by school boards creates tensions with state (and federal) government efforts to ensure adequate educational standards. Even with the support of school trust lands granted to or vested in the state from the United States at statehood, school funding raises persistent issues of adequacy and equity, exacerbated by the guarantee of local control and the uneven capacity of districts to raise local property tax revenue for education.

Over all of this stands the state constitutional commitment to "a basic system of free quality public elementary and secondary schools," and "equality of educational opportunity," as well as "the preservation of [American Indians'] cultural integrity." Although the text puts the Legislature at the center of the state's educational duties, the courts could not help but be drawn into complicated questions of educational policy. The Montana Supreme Court has struggled to define the legal scope of these commitments, and to what extent they give rise to individually enforceable rights.

A. The School System & Equal Opportunity

The Montana Constitution declares a goal of "a system of education which will develop the full educational potential of each person," and also contains a guarantee of "[e]quality of educational opportunity." This open language, which unlike other provisions, is not charged to any one branch or level of government, leaves much to the legislative process, school boards, and, perhaps, to the courts. The following cases intersect this broad constitutional language with the minute details of extracurriculars. Consider how much a state constitution, and state courts under it, can or should say about a local school board's decisions concerning the supervision and control of its schools.

Bartmess v. Board of Trustees of School District No. 1

223 Mont. 269 (1986)

WEBER, Justice.

Relators are citizens and taxpayers of Lewis and Clark County and parents of students enrolled in the two Helena high schools. They object to the rule adopted by respondents requiring a student to maintain a 2.0, or "C", grade average for the preceding nine weeks in order to participate in extracurricular activities in the following nine week grading period. Extracurricular activities are those which do not earn credit toward graduation, including athletics, band, choir, speech, drama, cheer-leading, drill team, student council, and holding class office. The 2.0 rule does not apply to special education students or students with learning disabilities. ***

The relators contend that the right to participate in extracurricular activities is fundamental and that the strict scrutiny standard therefore applies. The United

States Supreme Court has held that education is not a fundamental right guaranteed by the federal Constitution. *San Antonio School District v. Rodriguez* (1973). Based on that holding, we conclude that participation in extracurricular activities is not a fundamental right under the U.S. Constitution. However, that does not preclude a finding that the right is fundamental under Montana's Constitution.

The relators cite *Moran v. School District # 7, Yellowstone County* (D. Mont. 1972). In that case, Federal District Judge Murray said this Court had recognized extracurricular activities as an "integral part of the total educational process." The court there overturned a school rule which denied a married high school student the right to participate in extracurricular activities. Since that case involved the right to marriage, there was a separate ground for heightened constitutional scrutiny. While we agree that extracurricular activities are part of the educational process, the case is not authority because of the marriage aspect.

The *Moran* decision was based on language in a case which relators also cited, *McNair v. School Dist. No. 1* (Mont. 1930).

> Under the heading "Education," our Constitution declares that "it shall be the duty of the legislative assembly of Montana to establish and maintain a general, uniform and thorough system of public, free, common schools." . . . [I]t is clear that the solemn mandate of the Constitution is not discharged by the mere training of the mind; mentality without physical well-being does not make for good citizenship—the good citizen, the man or woman who is of the greatest value to the state, is the one whose every faculty is developed and alert.

That case arose out of a taxpayer's objection to the construction of a gymnasium and athletic field. This Court held the school board had been granted the authority to provide such facilities. The 'solemn mandate of the Constitution' discussed in *McNair* has been reworded in our 1972 Constitution, Art. X, § 1(3): "The legislature shall provide a basic system of free quality public elementary and secondary schools." The emphasis in *McNair* was that education should attempt to improve mental, physical, and moral powers.

The *McNair* case demonstrates that physical and moral development are important aspects of education. The state has an important interest in seeing that its young citizens receive a basic quality education under Art. X, § 1, Mont. Const. (1972): "It is the goal of the people to establish a system of education which will develop the full educational potential of each person." The provisions of Art. X demonstrate that there are constitutional rights and obligations which extend to all sides of the question of education. There is the right to equality of educational opportunity guaranteed to each person. There is the goal to establish a system of education which will develop the full educational potential of each person. There is a requirement that the State's educational goals recognize and preserve the cultural heritage of American Indians. The legislature is obligated to provide a basic system of free quality education. The state board of education is responsible for long-range planning, coordination and evaluation of the systems with regard to such rights and obligations. The school trustees are vested with the authority to discharge these obligations and protect the rights.

Our review of the educational provisions of the Montana Constitution demonstrates the extreme importance attached to the various elements of education by the people of Montana in adopting the Constitution. This review suggests that the various aspects of education under our Montana Constitution could be classed as "fundamental" because of the critical importance of developing the full educational potential of each citizen. ***

[However,] our analysis of the educational provisions of our Montana Constitution demonstrates there are competing and in some cases contradictory viewpoints which must be considered in determining whether the educational aspects of extracurricular activities are a right under our Constitution. We conclude that the only standard of constitutional review which allows a careful balancing of these competing interests is middle-tier analysis. We therefore hold that the middle-tier constitutional analysis is to be applied in determining whether the 2.0 rule violates students' right to participate in existing extracurricular activities. We further hold that this right is not a fundamental right under the Montana Constitution; but that such right is clearly subject to constitutional protection and that a middle-tier analysis is to be applied for constitutional equal protection purposes.

The standard of review used under Montana's middle-tier constitutional analysis is a "balancing of the rights infringed and the governmental interest to be served by such infringement." *Butte Community Union v. Lewis* (Mont. 1986). As in *Butte Community Union*, our first inquiry is whether the classification is reasonable. Specifically, is the classification of students eligible to participate in extracurricular activities on the basis of a 2.0 rule reasonable? Then we must examine whether the government interest in making this classification based upon academic grades is more important than the students' interest in participating in existing extracurricular activities. In other words, the school district must demonstrate that its classification is substantially related to an important governmental objective.

The action of the trustees places attaining minimum grades in academic subjects above participating in non-academic or extracurricular activities for which no graduation credits are given. The 2.0 rule does not apply to special education students or students with learning disabilities. While it is not based on studies showing improved grades for students operating under such a rule, it cannot be denied that the rule is an incentive for those students who wish to participate in extracurricular activities. It also promotes adequate time to study for those students who have not maintained a 2.0 grade average. We conclude that the classification is a reasonable one.

The priority given to academic over non-academic work to the extent found here does not contradict this Court's statement in *McNair* that physical and moral education are also important. We are not able to conclude, as the relators urge, that an opportunity to participate in extracurricular activities is more important than the achievement of average academic performance. We conclude that the government interests in developing the full educational potential of each person and providing a basic system of quality public education by the enactment of the 2.0 rule outweigh the students' interest in participating in existing extracurricular activities.

We hold that the District Court did not err in holding that participation in existing extracurricular activities is not a fundamental right. We further hold that the 2.0 rule does not violate the Constitution of the State of Montana.

Affirmed.

MORRISON, Justice, specially concurring:

I concur in the result but the majority Opinion is not entirely clear on a central issue.

First we must decide whether education is a fundamental right. The United States Supreme Court has held that education is not a fundamental right guaranteed by the federal Constitution. *San Antonio School District v. Rodriguez* (1972). In *Rodriguez,* it was argued that education is fundamental because it is essential to the effective exercise of First Amendment freedoms and the right to vote. The Court disagreed, stating "[W]e have never presumed to possess either the ability or the authority to guarantee to the citizenry the most effective speech or the most informed electoral choice."

In the recent case of *Plyler v. Doe* (1981), the Supreme Court reaffirmed its holding in *Rodriquez* that education is not a fundamental right guaranteed by the federal Constitution. Despite its holding, the Court placed great emphasis on the importance of education:

> But neither is it merely some governmental "benefit" indistinguishable from other forms of social welfare legislation. Both the importance of education in maintaining our basic institutions, and the lasting impact of its deprivation on the life of the child, mark the distinction. The "American people have always regarded education and [the] acquisition of knowledge as matters of supreme importance." *Meyer v. Nebraska* (1923).

This Court is not bound by the decisions of the United States Supreme Court where independent state grounds exist for developing expanded rights under our state Constitution. ***

The right to education is not enumerated in Montana's Declaration of Rights but is found in Art. X, § 1, Mont. Const. (1972). This section provides in part: "It is the goal of the people to establish a system of education which will develop the full educational potential of each person," and further directs the legislature to "provide a basic system of free quality public elementary and secondary schools."

The official committee comment to Art. X, § 1, opens with a statement stressing the importance of education in Montana:

> Education occupies a place of cardinal importance in the public realm. The educational system is charged with the task of shaping and cultivating

> the mind of each succeeding generation and with developing the capacities for cultural and technical advancement of society.
>
> For many, denial of a basic education would result in either illiteracy or severely retarded growth. Such individuals would be restricted from exercising, in a meaningful way, fundamental rights guaranteed in the Declaration of Rights such as the right to vote, right of participation, and right to know. Education is essential to even the most elemental exercise of many rights guaranteed by the Montana Constitution.

Education cannot be characterized as merely a benefit as was welfare in *Butte Community Union, supra.* The right to an education is not restricted in any manner. One need not qualify. Education is for all. Pursuant to Art. X, § 1, the legislature must provide a basic system of public schools, and each person is guaranteed equality of educational opportunity. In view of this constitutional mandate and the fact that education is essential to the exercise of other constitutionally guaranteed rights, we should clearly hold that basic education is a fundamental right under the Montana Constitution. ***

Regardless of whether the extracurricular activity is academic or non-academic, the state has a compelling interest in seeing that its young citizens receive a basic quality education. While the 2.0 rule is not based on studies showing improved grades by students operating under such a rule, there can be no denying it is sound incentive for those students who desire to engage in extracurricular activities. Further, it assures adequate time to study for those students affected by the rule.

Montana's strong commitment to providing a quality system of education is clear under our Constitution. The state's compelling interest in educating its citizens is reflected in Art. X, § 1, Mont. Const. (1972): "It is the goal of the people to establish a system of education which will develop the full educational potential of each person." Respondents' 2.0 rule is a policy designed to achieve this constitutional directive.

The supervision and control of the public schools in each district is vested in a board of trustees pursuant to Art. X, § 8. The trustees' action does not deny educational opportunity, whether academic or nonacademic, to any students. Rather it seeks to create priorities within the curriculum to the end that students will receive the best education possible. ***

I would hold that respondents' 2.0 rule is a constitutionally sound method of furthering the state's compelling interest in educating its citizens.

SHEEHY, Justice, dissenting:

*** The single issue in this case is the constitutional validity of the academic requirement rule for participation in extracurricular activities adopted by the Helena High School District.

Until today, this Court had followed the rule that a student's right to participate in extracurricular activities was constitutionally protected. To be sure, that was not the majority rule among the several states, but in Montana, we held unswervingly to that rule, based on our special constitutional provisions and the interpretation of this Court in *McNair v. School Dist. No. 1* (Mont. 1930). ***

In brief and in oral argument, the School Board concedes that extracurricular activities are "a fundamental ingredient of the educational process," but, without further explanation contends that the "fundamental ingredient" is not constitutionally protected. Some may distinguish a fundamental ingredient from a fundamental right, but it takes a quantum jump.

Thus, it was the law in this state until today that participation in extracurricular activities was a fundamental ingredient of the educational process; that school boards which issue bonds or otherwise finance through taxpayers the erection of athletic fields and gymnasiums or other provisions for extracurricular activities do so as part of the educational process; and that fees cannot be charged by the School Board if a given course or activity is reasonably related to recognized academic or educational goal. That was the state of the law when the constitutional framers in 1972 in the new constitution adopted Art. X, § 1, which provides:

> (1) It is the goal of the people to establish a system of education which will develop the full educational potential of each person. Equality of educational opportunity is guaranteed to each person of the state.

We have been shown no record from the 1972 Constitutional Convention that would indicate that the constitutional framers wanted to divert extracurricular activities in schools from the other educational goals. Indeed, the language used by the constitutional framers in 1972 seems to encompass physical development in the term "educational potential." For this must be true, if nothing else is, that the end of our educational system must be to develop students physically, mentally and morally to meet the challenges of life.

Of the approximately 2,500 students attending both Helena high schools, more than 500 of them, with the approval of this Court, are ousted by the eligibility rule from any extracurricular activities. If these students found little to relish in classrooms heretofore, their tedium will never be relieved by the sweet mix of association with their peers in other school endeavors, now branded as "nonessential"—drama, debate, cheerleading, drill team, student government, class and/or organizational officers, and yes, interscholastic track, football, basketball and golf. It is now possible for a student to graduate from either of Helena's high school without ever being eligible for any extracurricular activity!

We have never had before us a scheme of government so patently discriminatory. This Court has followed convoluted equal protection analyses *ad absurdum* to a silly result. Now a Helena High School girl with a 1.98 grade average and a good soprano voice is excluded from singing with the Helena Starlighters. A Gary Cooper or a Myrna Loy, both Helena products, may now be excluded from the Helena drama classes. A student can sign up for Spanish, but that student cannot belong to the Spanish Club, even with a passing grade in Spanish, if his or her overall average is less than "C." In any test of fair dealing, those results should instantly be held irrational, but this Court does not want to apply rationality standards. It wants to talk about strict scrutiny and middle term reviews to deny these students perhaps the only time in their lives to use their God-given skills to run in track, to twirl batons, to play in bands.

We should not resort to high-flown concepts of equal protection law, which are with us today and tomorrow are gone with the wind, to deny constitutional protection to these affected students. Even if we reverse this Court in its prior decisions by holding that no fundamental right is involved, or by holding that we do not have an inherently suspect class, equal protection still requires that the rule be rationally related to a legitimate state interest.

The only stated purpose for the rule set out in the agreed statement of facts is that the rule is "to encourage higher academic achievement to students who wish to participate in extracurricular activities." A rule which places physical, educational and moral development below mental education slaps at the three legs upon which the educational stool is built.

This rule is not rationally related to its object for two reasons: it is guilty of bad breadth, and it is not rationally related to its intended purpose.

When I say bad breadth, I mean that this rule is so overbroad that it must eventually be modified by the School District trustees, and indeed it has already been modified once. Its intended purpose, to encourage greater academic achievement, is not supported by any evidence in the agreed statement of facts or otherwise. It is built more on wish than fact. No rational relationship has been shown.

It is noteworthy that the exclusion of high school students from extracurricular activities is so drastic that it is one of the punishments allowed to trustees for students who show open defiance of authority, deface school buildings or threaten other persons. Section 20-5-201, MCA. Thus has the School Board placed students who earn a grade point average of less than 2.0 in the category of the rebellious and defiant. It is patently irrational.

HUNT, concurs.

Kaptein v. Conrad School District

281 Mont. 152 (1997)

LEAPHART, Justice.

Kathy and Marvin Kaptein (Kapteins) are residents and taxpayers in Conrad, Montana. In October of 1995, the Kapteins filed suit in the Ninth Judicial District Court, Pondera County, asking the court to enter a judgment requiring that the Conrad School District Board of Trustees allow their 7th grade daughter, Tami, to participate in the public school sports programs. Tami was, and is, a student at the Conrad Christian School. The private school in which Tami is enrolled offers ski days and arranges for basketball practices and an intramural game. The Conrad area offers some additional athletic programs which Tami participates in, for example, soccer and softball. In addition, Tami seeks to play on the public school athletic teams for social purposes related to friendship and team camaraderie. Tami participated in the public school girls' sports program during the 1994–95 school year. This participation was without the approval of the Superintendent or the Board of Trustees. Her participation in the public school program was terminated upon discovery by the Board of Trustees. The Board of Trustees refused to allow Tami to further participate in the public school sports programs since the Board's policy limited participation to students enrolled full time in public school. The Kapteins contend that the school's policy is unconstitutional under the provisions of Article X, Section 1 of the Montana Constitution. . . .

Discussion

The Kapteins based their constitutional argument on Article X, Section 1, of the Montana Constitution, which states:

> It is the goal of the people to establish a system of education which will develop the full educational potential of each person. Equality of educational opportunity is guaranteed to each person of the state.

Citing our decision in *State, ex rel., Bartmess v. Board of Trustees* (Mont. 1986), Kapteins contend that Tami has a constitutionally protected right to participate in public school extracurricular activities and that this Court should apply a middle-tier analysis in balancing Tami's right to participate against the governmental interests to be served by infringing that right. The School District takes the position that middle-tier analysis is not appropriate in this case and, even if middle-tier analysis were applied, the school's educational interests in permitting only students enrolled in the school district to participate in school-sponsored extracurricular activities outweighs any right that Tami may have to participate. ***

Kapteins suggest that we should decide this case solely upon the basis of Tami's right to participate in extracurricular activities; that we should not consider any "worse case scenarios," and that we can. . . narrowly craft a decision recognizing a right to participate only in certain nonacademic activities such as sports, shop, band and art. Given that Kapteins are asserting a constitutional right to the "full educational potential of each person" under Article X, Section 1, of the Montana Constitution, Tami's appeal cannot be decided in such a vacuum. If Tami's right to participate in extracurricular activities outweighs the School District's interest in limiting participation to enrolled students, then Tami will not be the only nonenrolled person entitled to partake of the public school programs. Home-schoolers, dropouts and adults would have a right equal to that of private school students such as Tami Kaptein to participate in school programs on a part-time or piecemeal basis. Furthermore. . . there would be nothing preventing a private school from unilaterally deciding to transport its entire student body to the public school for purposes of taking an academic course such as computer science. ***

We determine that Kapteins' claim of a right to participate, like the relators in *Bartmess*, must be analyzed under a middle-tier analysis. We recognized in *Bartmess* that a student's right to participate in extracurricular activities, although not a fundamental right, is "clearly subject to constitutional protection." Under a middle-tier analysis there must be a "balancing of the rights infringed and the governmental interest to be served by such infringement." Thus, in the present context, the right to participate must be balanced against the School District's interests in restricting participation to students enrolled in the public school system. Consistent with the middle-tier analysis conducted in *Bartmess*, we must first determine whether the classification based upon enrolled students is reasonable. We then examine whether the governmental interest in making this classification based upon enrollment is more important than Tami Kaptein's interest in participating in existing extracurricular activities.

As to the "reasonableness" of classifying students based upon whether they are enrolled in the public school system, we note that Article X of the Montana Constitution places a heavy emphasis on the concept of an educational "system." Article X, Section 1(1), states that it is the goal of the people to "establish a system of education which will develop the full educational potential of each person." Article X, Section 1(3), provides: "The legislature shall provide a basic system of free quality public elementary and secondary schools." Article X, Section 9(1), creates a state board of education responsible for planning and evaluating programs for the state's "educational systems."

Article X, Section 9(3), creates a board of public education "to exercise general supervision over the public school system. . . ." Given this heavy emphasis on the creation, supervision and quality of the state's educational "system," we hold that the School District's classification of students based upon whether they are enrolled in the public school "system" is entirely reasonable.

We must then examine the School District's interest in making this classification and weigh that interest against Tami Kaptein's interest in participating.

The School District has set forth an extensive list of "educational reasons" for its policy of restricting participation to enrolled students. We will not delve into the particulars of that list other than to note that the primary "educational reason" propounded by the School District is that of providing a unified program in which required academic courses, elective courses and extracurricular activities are "integrated" so as to complement each other. The Board takes the position that the integrating of the academic and extracurricular activities does not lend itself to participation by nonenrolled students. This rationale finds ample support in our decision in *Bartmess*. ***

In the present case, we are likewise unable to conclude that a private school student's interest in participating in extracurricular activities is more important than the School District's policy decision that, in order to effectively integrate academics and extracurricular activities, it needs to restrict participation to those students who are enrolled in the public school system. ***

NELSON, Justice, specially concurring.

*** Beyond the narrow issues addressed in *Bartmess* and in the instant case... I do not want my agreement with our opinion to be read as any sort of concession that a Montanan's rights under Article X, Section 1, of the Montana Constitution, to equal educational opportunity and to "a basic system of free quality public elementary and secondary" education are anything but fundamental rights.

As our opinion points out, Montanans, uniquely, are constitutionally guaranteed important equal public education rights. Moreover, the legislature is obligated by our constitution to provide the mechanism that will enable each person in this State to exercise those rights to effectuate the goal of the people of this state "to establish a system of education which will develop the full educational potential of each person." Art. X, Sec. 1, Mont. Const.

In that context, and as to those rights, I believe that such rights are, indeed, fundamental. In truth, when one considers the obvious fact that, without a quality education, a person's ability to exercise his or her other constitutional rights is severely circumscribed, then it becomes readily apparent just how fundamental the educational rights set forth in Article X, Section 1, really are. In our modern, technological, information-oriented society one's constitutional right to seek gainful employment, to vote, to express one's views, to pursue life's basic necessities, to acquire and possess property and to seek safety, health and happiness, all, in a very real sense, depend upon a person's education. And these are but just a few of the constitutional rights which Montanans enjoy. Simply put, educational rights are fundamental because they are rights without which other constitutional rights would have little meaning. *See Butte Community Union v. Lewis* (1986).

Second, as to the precise question at issue in the instant case, I would also conclude that Article X, Section 6, of the Montana Constitution prevents a public school district from allowing sectarian school students to participate in district activities. This provision of Montana's Constitution provides:

> Aid prohibited to sectarian schools. (1) The legislature, counties, cities, towns, *school districts*, and public corporations *shall not* make any direct or indirect appropriation or payment from any public fund or monies, or any grant of lands or other property for any sectarian purpose or to *aid any* church, *school*, academy, seminary, college, university, or other literary or scientific institution, *controlled in whole or in part by any church, sect, or denomination*. (Emphasis added).

Article X, Section 6, which was carried over from our 1889 Constitution, represents the Constitutional Convention's strong and continuing belief in the necessity to maintain Montana's public school systems apart from any entanglements with private sectarian schools and to guard against the diversion of public resources to sectarian school purposes. As Delegate Burkhardt stated:

> The primary and significant advantage secured by the present provision is the unequivocal support it provides for a strong public school system. The traditional separation between church and state, an important part of

> the American social framework, has also become a fundamental principle of American education. The growth of a strong, universal, and free educational system in the United States has been due in part to its exclusively public character.... Any diversion of funds or effort from the public school system would tend to weaken that system in favor of schools established for private or religious purposes.

If Tami is allowed to participate in the public school sports programs, it is clear to me that the School District will be providing aid, either directly or indirectly, to the Conrad Christian School in violation of this express prohibition of Montana's Constitution. This is so because sectarian schools derive their operating funds, for the most part, from tuition or church resources. To the extent that a sectarian school determines that it cannot afford, for example, a volleyball program, or a chemistry lab, or a band from these private sources, such schools can shift the financial burden of such programs to the public treasury by sending sectarian school students to the public school volleyball program, chemistry lab or band. In short, the public school district ends up effectively subsidizing the sectarian school's educational program. This is precisely what Article X, Section 6, prohibits—indirect aid to sectarian schools.

Moreover, Montana's constitutional prohibition against aid to sectarian schools is even stronger than the federal government's. The former expressly prohibits either direct or indirect aid, while the latter prohibits aid which is found to be "direct." ... [C]*ompare State ex rel. Chambers v. School District No. 10* (Mont. 1970) (Article XI, Section 8, of Montana's 1889 Constitution, the predecessor of Article X, Section 6, prevents the busing of parochial students even though busing was permissible under the federal constitution).

Accordingly, while I concur fully in our analysis and in our opinion, I am also convinced that Montana's Constitution expressly prohibits what Tami and the Conrad Christian School hoped to accomplish in this litigation. The School District may not allow her to participate in its programs unless she enrolls in the public school system.

LEAPHART, J., concurs in the foregoing special concurrence.

GRAY, Justice, concurring in part and dissenting in part.

Notwithstanding my disagreement with the Court's analysis of the issue before us, I concur in the result the Court reaches. The basis of my disagreement is set forth briefly below, followed by a brief statement of my view regarding the appropriate constitutional basis on which this case should be resolved. In this latter regard, I join in Justice Nelson's reasoning that Article X, Section 6, of the Montana Constitution clearly prohibits the Conrad School District from allowing Tami to participate in public school sports.

The critical facts of this case are that Tami is enrolled in the Conrad Christian School, a sectarian educational facility; she is not enrolled in the Conrad public school system. Tami seeks to play on public school athletic teams for social purposes and camaraderie. The School District refused to allow her to do so pursuant to its policy limiting participation to students enrolled full time in the public school.

Under these facts, Tami asserts a constitutional right to participate under Article X, Section 1, of the Montana Constitution. The Court relies on *Bartmess* in concluding that Tami has such a constitutional right. It then applies the *Bartmess* middle-tier scrutiny and concludes that the School District's policy decision to restrict participation in extracurricular activities in order to effectively integrate academics and extracurricular activities is more important than Tami's interest in participating. It holds that the School District's policy does not violate the Montana Constitution.

While I agree that the policy does not violate the Montana Constitution, it is my view that *Bartmess* is inapplicable under the facts now before us with regard to both the constitutional right to participate and the resulting application of middle-tier scrutiny. In *Bartmess*, the challenge to the 2.0 GPA rule for participation in extracurricular activities was asserted by students enrolled full time in the public schools. We held that a public school student's right to participate in extracurricular activities offered by the public school system in which the student is enrolled is entitled to some degree of constitutional protection.

Unlike in *Bartmess*, however, the right being asserted by Tami is totally separate and apart from any asserted right to participate in the overall educational system of the School District. She has a right, of course, to attend public schools but has chosen not to do so. Thus, she does not have the same right to participate as the students in *Bartmess*. I simply do not perceive any tie to Article X, Section 1, of the Montana Constitution such as existed in *Bartmess* and, as a result, middle-tier scrutiny is not appropriate.

In any event, the Montana Constitution contains a provision which affirmatively precludes the School District from permitting Tami to participate and which, therefore, provides the appropriate basis on which to resolve the present case. That provision—Article X, Section 6, of the Montana Constitution—is discussed in Justice Nelson's special concurring opinion and needs no further discussion here. I join in that portion of Justice Nelson's opinion.

Tami advances several cases, including a recent United States Supreme Court case, which she contends establish that no constitutional problems involving separation of church and state arise by allowing her to participate in public school athletics. In particular, she relies on *Zobrest v. Catalina Foothills School Dist.* (1993), in which the Supreme Court held that the "no establishment of religion" clause in the First Amendment to the United States Constitution does not bar a public school district from providing a sign language interpreter to accompany a deaf student to classes at a sectarian school where the service was part of a general governmental program. As Justice Nelson points out, however, the First Amendment generally prohibits only direct aid. Article X, Section 6, of the Montana Constitution, on the other hand, prohibits school districts from extending both direct and indirect aid to sectarian schools. Thus, the federal and sister state cases on which Tami relies have no application to the unique and broad proscription contained in the Montana Constitution regarding aid to sectarian schools.

I join the Court in affirming the District Court, although I would accomplish that result under a different analysis.

Notes on the School System and Equal Opportunity

1. The title of Article X, section 1, the provision at issue in these cases, is "Educational Goals and Duties." Is the Court correct to treat these state duties as individual rights? What turns on the distinction, if anything? What would change in *Bartmess* and *Kaptein* if education were considered a "fundamental right"?

2. As the Court often does, it resorts to equal protection analysis of the state's educational goals and duties, and settles on a middle-tier scrutiny "balancing test." Is such a test more or less protective of educational interests than requiring the state to fulfill its duties regardless of the strength of competing interests?

3. In *Bartmess*, Justice Sheehy discusses several cases that elaborated the scope of the right to education under the 1889 Montana Constitution. *See, e.g., Perkins v. Trask* (Mont. 1933) (a swimming pool in a school was a performance of an educational duty by the school trustees); *Flathead Lake Methodist Camp v. Webb* (Mont. 1965) ("The end of education may be to develop either the mental, physical, or moral qualities."). Justice Sheehy also described *Granger v. Cascade County School Dist.* (Mont. 1972), decided shortly after ratification of the 1972 Constitution (but before its effective date):

> In that case Cascade County School District had imposed fees in the grade school and high school for such items as workbooks, chemistry notebooks, manual arts materials, musical instrument rentals, summer school, and others. The fees were attacked by the plaintiffs on the grounds that the constitutional requirement of a "thorough system" of public, free schools encompass all categories of activities in the school and no such fees can be imposed. There this Court reaffirmed its statement that education may be directed to mental, moral and physical powers, and provided this test:
>
> Is a given course or activity reasonably related to a recognized academic and educational goal of the particular school system? If it is, it constitutes part of the free, public school system commanded by Art. XI, Sec. 1 of the Montana Constitution and additional fees or charges cannot be levied, directly or indirectly, against the student or his parents. If it is not, reasonable fees or charges may be imposed.
>
> In addition, the federal district court in Montana construed our holding in *McNair* and its following cases as granting a constitutionally protected right to participate in extracurricular activities. In *Moran v. School Dist. No. 7, Yellowstone County* (D. Mont. 1972), the federal court, recognizing the holding in *McNair*, stated: "it is apparent that the right to attend school includes the right to participate in extracurricular activities." . . .

Who gets to define what is included in the school "system" required by the Constitution?

B. Public School Funding

Educational funding was one of many controversies giving rise to innovative constitutional claims around the framing of the 1972 Constitution. In *Granger v. Cascade County School Dist.* (Mont. 1972), the Court observed:

> The recent California case, *Serrano v. Priest* (Cal. 1971), is persuasive concerning the meaning of a general and uniform system of public, free, common schools as used in Art. XI, Sec. 1, of our Constitution. This case has national significance in the entire area of school financing. It challenged the method of financing schools by local property taxes where legislative classifications discriminate on the basis of wealth. In that case, the court rejected the argument that the constitutional requirement for a "system of (free) common schools" compels uniform education expenditures. The court said: "we have never interpreted the constitutional provision to require equal school spending; we have ruled only that the educational system must be uniform in terms of the prescribed course of study and educational progression from grade to grade." *See also Rodriguez v. San Antonio Independent School District* (W.D. Texas 1971) [finding Texas's school funding system unconstitutional, reversed by the Supreme Court in 1973].
>
> This language in *Serrano* goes to the crux of the problem in the instant case. Any definition of a "thorough system of public, free, common schools" must take into consideration the wide diversity of spending throughout Montana's school districts. Certain course and activity opportunities in Cascade County School District No. 1 are not available in other Montana districts. As long as the individual student is not deprived of equal access to educational courses and activities reasonably related to recognized academic and educational goals of the particular school system, the constitutional mandate is not violated.

Notwithstanding the passage quoted above, *Serrano* recognized a fundamental right to an education and held that California's school funding system violated the federal Equal Protection Clause. After *Rodriguez*, the California Supreme Court rooted these rights in the state constitution, and *Serrano* became a model for future school funding challenges, including in Montana.

In a pair of cases, local school districts, joined by teachers' unions and parents of students, claimed Montana's school funding system was unconstitutional for two distinct reasons. Like the *Rodriguez* and *Serrano* cases, though under the state constitution, *Helena Elementary* (1989) challenged the "equity" of a state's school funding system. The equity claim raised in that case is based on the disparate funding of local schools by the state relative to their need. In contrast, *Columbia Falls* (2005) is a challenge to the "adequacy" of a state's school funding system, or the overall amount of funding necessary to provide a constitutionally adequate education statewide. As you read the cases, consider the differences between the two claims, the proof needed to establish them, and the appropriate remedy.

Helena Elementary School District No. 1 v. State

236 Mont. 44 (1989)

WEBER, Justice.

*** In the 1985–86 school year, there were 545 school districts in Montana with a total student enrollment of 153,869. These included 382 elementary and 163 secondary districts. Nearly 45% of Montana schools have enrollments of less than 100 students.

The six-week-long trial included extensive evidence and testimony about the complex combination of federal, state, and local sources through which Montana's public elementary and secondary schools are funded. In addition to the General Fund, each school district uses up to nine other types of budgeted funds. These include transportation funds, teacher retirement funds, debt service funds, and building reserve funds. Some of these depend upon voted levies and all are primarily funded on a district or county level. School districts also have nonbudgeted funds including food service, traffic education, rental funds, sick leave reserves, block grants, building funds, endowment funds, and interlocal agreement funds. Expenditures from these nonbudgeted funds may only be made from cash on hand.

The General Fund, which provides 70% of school funding in Montana, includes several components. In 1949, the Montana Legislature enacted the Montana School Foundation Program. Under that program, every two years the legislature sets "Maximum General Fund Budget Without a Vote" (MGFBWV) schedules for elementary and secondary school districts in the state. Eighty per cent of the MGFBWV is funded by county and state equalization revenues. These equalization revenues are derived from levies of 45 mills on all taxable property in each county and state aid from such sources as earmarked revenues, surplus county Foundation Program revenue, and direct legislative appropriations.

The remaining 20% of the funding of MGFBWV is through permissive mill levies of up to 6 mills for elementary districts and 4 mills for high school districts. These levies are made without a vote. If the school district is unable to obtain the MGFBWV level through permissive levies and other specified nonlevy revenue, state permissive equalization revenues are used to make up the difference.

The evidence shows that, in 1985–86, most school districts adopted budgets in excess of the MGFBWV. They utilized a third stage of funding under which monies were obtained primarily from property tax levies voted by each school district. Other revenues which were used in this third level of funding included vehicle taxes, interest income, tuition income, and federal "874" funds. By 1985–86, 35% of all General Fund budgets were obtained from this level of funding. In contrast, in 1950, the Foundation Program furnished 81.2% of all general fund revenues in Montana, leaving less than 20% of revenues to be obtained by local levies and other sources.

Plaintiffs presented voluminous evidence to support their theory that the system of funding public education in Montana is unconstitutional. The evidence established great differences in the wealth of the various school districts and, more significantly, established disparities of spending per pupil as high as 8 to 1 in comparisons between similarly-sized school districts. We affirm the following unchallenged findings of the District Court:

> Several Plaintiff witnesses had experience either as teachers or administrators in other Montana districts, including some relatively wealthier districts. Mr. Walt Piipo, for example, currently Superintendent at Drummond, was previously Superintendent for Geraldine schools. The two school districts are very close in size, at both the elementary and high school levels. Geraldine's taxable valuation, however, is more than twice that of Drummond's. The tax efforts for the elementary schools are comparable, while Geraldine levies more General Fund mills than does Drummond at the high school level. Consequently, Geraldine spends approximately $1,000 more per [student] than Drummond at the elementary level, and over $2,000 more per [student] at the high school level. Approximately 40% of Geraldine's General Fund revenues derive from the voted levy, while at Drummond, the voted levy supplies approximately 15% of General Fund revenue. This illustrates the fact that wealthier districts are able to rely to a greater extent on the voted levy to generate revenues for the General Fund. ***
>
> [An expert] Study Team identified clear differences between the schools in each of the pairs. They found that the better funded schools tended to offer more enriched and expanded curricula than those offered in the schools with less money. The richer schools were also better equipped in the areas of textbooks, instructional equipment, audio-visual instructional materials, and consumable supplies. With respect to buildings and facilities, the districts with more money were better able to maintain their facilities than were the poorer districts. ***
>
> In sum, the comparative evidence establishes that spending differences among similarly sized school districts in the State result in unequal educational opportunities for students. Furthermore, the comparative evidence verifies the fact that the deficiencies and problems identified by Plaintiff witnesses are part of a consistent pattern in lower-spending districts, and that such deficiencies and problems are not consistently found in relatively higher spending districts. ***

The District Court concluded that education is a fundamental right under Montana's Constitution. It concluded that, under the 1985–86 system of funding public elementary and secondary schools, disparities in per pupil spending among schools as a result of disparities in local property wealth do not even pass the rational basis test of equal protection analysis. It concluded that the concept of local control is not related to the spending disparities now present. It further concluded that the State's budgetary difficulties do not constitute a legal defense to these inequalities.

The court also concluded that the Montana School Accreditation standards do not define the constitutional right to education. It concluded that the treatment of federal "874" funding for schools with Indian enrollment exacerbates the inequalities present in the school finance system. The court ordered that the present system of school funding may remain in effect until October 1, 1989, and retained jurisdiction, but left to the Legislature the task of fashioning a constitutional funding system. ***

I

Does Montana's system of funding the public schools violate the education article, Art. X, of the Montana Constitution?

Art. X, Sec. 1, Mont. Const., provides:

> (1) It is the goal of the people to establish a system of education which will develop the full educational potential of each person. Equality of educational opportunity is guaranteed to each person of the state.
>
> (2) The state recognizes the distinct and unique cultural heritage of the American Indians and is committed in its educational goals to the preservation of their cultural integrity.
>
> (3) The legislature shall provide a basic system of free quality public elementary and secondary schools. The legislature may provide such other educational institutions, public libraries, and educational programs as it deems desirable. It shall fund and distribute in an equitable manner to the school districts the state's share of the cost of the basic elementary and secondary school system.

By referring to the discussions in the transcript of the 1972 Montana Constitutional Convention, the State contends the provision in subsection (1) that "[e]quality of educational opportunity is guaranteed to each person," is an aspirational goal only. We disagree with that contention. In interpreting the Constitution, as in statutory construction, this Court must first look to the plain meaning of the words used. In the first sentence of Art. X, Sec. 1(1), the framers of the Constitution clearly stated the "goal" of the people to establish a system of education which will develop the full educational potential of each person. In the next sentence, the framers did not use the term "goal." Instead they stated that equality of educational opportunity "is guaranteed" to each person of the state. As we review our Constitution, we do not find any other instance in which the Constitution "guarantees" a particular right. We conclude that the plain meaning of the second sentence of subsection (1) is that each person is guaranteed equality of educational opportunity. The plain meaning of that sentence is clear and unambiguous.

The State argues that the last sentence of subsection (3) limits the Legislature's duty in connection with the guarantee of equal educational opportunity. It points out that Foundation Program funds are conceded by all parties to have been distributed in an equitable manner, and then suggests that because the State has distributed such funds in an equitable manner as required under the last sentence of subsection (3), the Legislature has met its constitutional obligations as required under Art. X, Sec. 1.

Art. X, Sec. 1(3), Mont. Const., requires that the Legislature shall provide a basic system of free quality education, that it may provide various types of educational institutions and programs, and that the state's share of the cost of the basic system shall be distributed in an equitable manner. There is nothing in the plain wording of subsection (3) to suggest that the clear statement of the obligations on the part of the Legislature in some manner was intended to be a limitation on the guarantee of equal educational opportunity contained in subsection (1). The guarantee provision of subsection (1) is not limited to any one branch of government. Clearly the guarantee of equal educational opportunity is binding upon all three branches of government, the legislative as well as the executive and judicial branches. We specifically conclude that the guarantee of equality of educational opportunity applies to each person of the State of Montana, and is binding upon all branches of government whether at the state, local, or school district level. We hold that the last sentence of subsection (3) is not a limiting provision on the guarantee of equal educational opportunity contained in subsection (1).

The evidence presented at the trial of this case clearly and unequivocally established large differences, unrelated to "educationally relevant factors," in per pupil spending among the various school districts of Montana. The evidence also demonstrated that the wealthier school districts are not funding frills or unnecessary educational expenses. Plaintiffs' expert witnesses testified that discrepancies in spending as large as the ones present in Montana translate, in their opinions, into unequal educational opportunities. There was also unrebutted testimony that Foundation Program funding falls short of even meeting the costs of complying with Montana's minimum accreditation standards.

The State attempted to present an argument at trial that equality of educational opportunity is more appropriately measured by output, that is, by analysis of the success of students from the different school districts, rather than by input of dollars. The District Court concluded that the State had failed to submit convincing evidence on the output theory of measurement. We agree with that conclusion on the basis of this record. The District Court found similarly unpersuasive the argument that statewide fiscal difficulties in the last few years somehow excuse the disparities in the spending per pupil in the various school districts. We agree with the District Court that such fiscal difficulties in no way justify perpetuating inequities.

The State also argued that the Constitutional directive of local control of school districts, Art. X, Sec. 8, Mont. Const., requires that spending disparities among the districts be allowed to exist. That section provides:

> School district trustees. The supervision and control of schools in each school district shall be vested in a board of trustees to be elected as provided by law.

While Section 8 does establish that the supervision and control of schools shall be vested in the board of trustees, there is no specific reference to the concept of spending disparities. Further, as made especially apparent after the passage of Initiative 105, the spending disparities among Montana's school districts cannot be described as the result of local control. In fact, as the District Court correctly found, the present system of funding may be said to deny to poorer school districts a significant level of local control, because they have fewer options due to fewer resources. We conclude that Art. X, Sec. 8, Mont. Const., does not allow the type of spending disparities outlined in the above quoted findings of fact.

In 1972, when our Constitutional Convention met, approximately 65% of General Fund revenues were funded through the Foundation Program. Con.Con.Tr. 2157. The transcript of the debate on Art. X, Sec. 1(3), Mont. Const., clearly expresses the delegates' concern with that level of funding. See, for example, Con.Con.Tr. 1981–86, 2152–59.

We conclude that as a result of the failure to adequately fund the Foundation Program, forcing an excessive reliance on permissive and voted levies, the State has failed to provide a system of quality public education granting to each student the equality of educational opportunity guaranteed under Art. X, Sec. 1, Mont. Const. We specifically affirm that portion of the District Court's Conclusion of Law 17 which holds that the spending disparities among the State's school districts translate into a denial of equality of educational opportunity. We hold that the 1985–86 system of funding public elementary and secondary schools in Montana is in violation of Article X, Section 1 of the Montana Constitution.

In analyzing school funding under an equal protection analysis pursuant to the provisions of Art. II, Sec. 4, Mont. Const., the District Court concluded that education is a fundamental right and also made numerous and extensive findings of fact and adopted a number of conclusions of law. Because we have concluded that the school funding system is unconstitutional under Art. X, Sec. 1, Mont. Const., we do not find it necessary to consider the equal protection issue. We therefore make no decision with regard to the findings of fact and conclusions of law relating to the equal protection of the laws analysis of the District Court, and in particular do not rule upon the determination by the District Court that education is a fundamental right.

Several of the parties suggested that in the event we concluded the school funding was unconstitutional, we should spell out the percentages which are required on the part of the State under the Foundation Program and for the districts under the voted levy system. We are not able to reach that type of a conclusion. As previously indicated, the 1985–86 school funding involved more than 20 different funds. The control of such funds is primarily in the Legislature. Our opinion is not directed at only one element of the system of funding public schools in Montana, as we recognize that the Legislature has the power to increase or reduce various parts of these elements, and in addition to add other elements for such funding.

While this opinion discusses spending disparities so far as pupils are concerned, we do not suggest that financial considerations of that type are the sole elements of a quality education or of equal educational opportunity. There are a number of additional factors which are a significant part of the education of each person in Montana, including but not limited to such elements as individual teachers, classroom size, support of the parents of students, and the desire and motivation on the part of the student which moves him or her to seek earnestly after an education. By not discussing these elements, we do not in any way suggest they are irrelevant, for the financing of education is only one aspect of equal educational opportunity. Our opinion is intentionally limited to the elements discussed in the opinion.

II

Should this Court clarify the District Court's findings regarding the accreditation standards promulgated by the Montana Board of Public Education?

Under Art. X, Sec. 9(3), Mont. Const., the Montana Board of Public Education (Board) has general supervisory power over the public school system. The Board has adopted statewide accreditation standards for elementary and secondary schools. Those standards require teachers to be certified by the State, limit teachers' class loads, outline a minimum instructional program (for example, courses required for high school graduation), and establish minimum size, maintenance, and safety standards for school facilities. The Board argues that these standards establish the instructional component of a basic system of free quality public elementary and secondary schools. *** We therefore hold that findings of fact 262 and 270 and conclusion of law 18 shall be amended to read as follows:

> [Finding of Fact 262.] The testimony of superintendents, teachers, and trustees clearly establishes that from the professional educators' perspective, the minimum accreditation standards do not fully define a quality education.
>
> [Finding of Fact 270.] In sum, the Montana School Accreditation Standards are minimum standards upon which quality education must be built.
>
> [Conclusion of Law 18.] Thus, the Montana School Accreditation Standards do not fully define either the constitutional rights of students or the constitutional responsibilities of the State of Montana for funding its public elementary and secondary schools.

III

Did the District Court err in its findings and conclusions relating to consideration in the equalization process of federal "874" funding?

Public Law 81-874 ("874") was enacted by the United States Congress in 1950. It provides federal payments to school districts which serve children who reside on or whose parents are employed on federal property, including Indian lands, or who have a parent on active duty in the military.

Hays-Lodge Pole asserts that, contrary to the District Court's finding, Public Law 81-874 has as one of its purposes assisting with the special problems in Indian education and is not only a federal effort to replace lost tax revenue resulting from the federal presence. It argues also that the court's finding that, in some districts, "874" funding has been used as tax relief is irrelevant and shows only the State's neglect of the special needs of Indian children. It contends that "874" funding is closely tied to the need on and near Indian reservations for additional school funding because of the extraordinary educational difficulties present—language barriers, poverty, unemployment, and cultural differences. It maintains that any inequity present in "874" districts will vanish when the Montana funding system is equalized without consideration of "874" funding and that the history of neglect of Indian education justifies judicial protection of the benefits provided by "874" funding. Hays-Lodge Pole argues that the District Court erred in ruling that the Legislature may consider "874" funding in equalization.

This issue is resolved by the federal statutory requirement that the United States Secretary of Education must approve of Montana's equalization plan before "874" funding may be taken into account. 20 U.S.C.A. § 240(d) (Supp. 1988). The District Court recognized this requirement in its finding no. 235, and found that Montana's system had not secured that federal approval. We specifically affirm the District Court's Conclusions No. 20:

> 20. A state may factor P.L. 81-874 revenue into its school finance equalization system only if the system meets the federal definition of an equalized program, subject to the determination of the Secretary of Education. [*See Gwinn Area Community Schools v. State of Michigan* (6th Cir.1984).] Montana presently does not and may not factor P.L. 81-874 revenue into the Foundation Program equalization formula, because Montana's system does not meet the federal definition of an equalized program.

Art. X, Sec. 1(2), Mont. Const., states as follows with regard to our American Indians:

> The state recognizes the distinct and unique cultural heritage of the American Indians and is committed in its educational goals to the preservation of their cultural integrity.

That provision establishes a special burden in Montana for the education of American Indian children which must be addressed as a part of the school funding issues. We do invite the attention of the Legislature and the executive branch to Montana's failure to meet the federal equalization requirements. As a part of the changes to be made in Montana's school funding system, it may be appropriate to meet the federal equalization requirements in order that "874" funding may be factored into the State's equalization formula. ***

IV

Did the District Court err in denying plaintiffs' attorney fees?

Plaintiffs argue that they are entitled to recover their reasonable attorney fees under the "common fund" doctrine. This Court has described that doctrine as one which:

> . . . provides that when a party through active litigation creates, reserves or increases a fund, others sharing in the fund must bear a portion of the litigation costs including reasonable attorney fees. The doctrine is employed to spread the cost of litigation among all beneficiaries so that the active beneficiary is not forced to bear the burden alone and the "stranger" (i.e., passive) beneficiaries do not receive their benefits at no cost to themselves.

Means v. Montana Power Co. (Mont. 1981). *See also Serrano v. Priest* (Cal. 1977).

The District Court concluded that the common fund doctrine did not apply in this case because no common fund was created from which attorney fees and expert witness fees could be paid. In a similar manner, under the "substantial benefit" concept which has grown out of the common fund doctrine, the District Court concluded that no substantial benefit had resulted from its opinion and that no such benefit would accrue unless the Legislature acts. We conclude that the District Court properly denied attorney fees. We affirm the District Court's denial of plaintiffs' request for attorney fees.

V

We approve the District Court's rationale that "in order to provide the Legislature with the opportunity to search for and present an equitable system of school financing," the holdings in this case should not become immediately effective. We modify the reservation of jurisdiction by the District Court to provide that this Court specifically retains jurisdiction until July 1, 1989, and on that date the holdings of this opinion shall become fully in effect for all school terms commencing after that date.

Columbia Falls Elementary School District No. 6 v. State

326 Mont. 304 (2005)

Justice W. WILLIAM LEAPHART delivered the Opinion of the Court.

*** ¶ 10 A coalition of schools, education groups, and parents (the Coalition) brought this action contending that the State has acted unconstitutionally in administering and funding Montana's constitutionally-mandated public school system. After a three-week trial, the District Court found serious problems with the current school system, relating both to the manner in which the State funds its public schools and the educational product the schools are delivering. The District Court concluded that the current system violates the Public Schools Clause of Article X, Section 1(3), and the Indian Education Clause of Article X, Section 1(2). The District Court also concluded that the current school system does not violate the Equal Protection Clause of the Montana Constitution and that the Coalition should not be awarded attorney fees. ***

Issue One

¶ 13 Whether a challenge to the adequacy of the State's funding of a basic system of free quality public elementary and secondary schools presents a non-justiciable political question.

¶ 14 The State, relying on *Baker v. Carr* (1962), asserts that questions arising under Montana Constitution Article X, Section 1(3), are non-justiciable under the political question doctrine. That section provides: "The legislature shall provide a basic system of free quality public elementary and secondary schools." Of course, in interpreting our own Constitution, this Court need not defer to the United States Supreme Court. Nonetheless, given the dearth of Montana precedent on the political question doctrine and the State's reliance on federal doctrine, we look to the federal precedent for guidance in developing our own doctrine.

¶ 15 Both the United States Supreme Court and this Court recognize that non-self-executing clauses of constitutions are non-justiciable political questions. *Baker*, 369 U.S. at 217 (listing one factor of the federal political question doctrine as "the impossibility of deciding without an initial policy determination of a kind clearly for nonjudicial discretion"); *State ex rel. Stafford v. Fox-Great Falls Theatre Corp.* (Mont. 1942).

¶ 16 To determine whether the provision is self-executing, we ask whether the Constitution addresses the language to the courts or to the Legislature. If addressed to the Legislature, the provision is non-self-executing; if addressed to the courts, it is self-executing. Louisiana's Constitution once provided that "Gambling is a vice and the Legislature shall pass laws to suppress it." In *Stafford*, we agreed with the Louisiana Supreme Court's conclusion that provisions beginning "the Legislature shall" are non-self-executing provisions; as such, in Louisiana, gambling was legal unless the Legislature enacted a provision making it illegal.

¶ 17 Like the Louisiana clause, Montana's Public Schools Clause constitutes a directive to the Legislature: "The legislature shall provide a basic system of free quality public elementary and secondary schools." Since the Public Schools Clause is non-self-executing, it presents a political question which, in the first instance, is directed to the Legislature and is non-justiciable. That determination, however, does not end the inquiry. As here, (1) once the Legislature has acted, or "executed," a provision (2) that implicates individual constitutional rights, courts can determine whether that enactment fulfills the Legislature's constitutional responsibility. *City of Boerne v. Flores* (1997) (determining, under the First Amendment, that the Religious Freedom Restoration Act of 1993 violates the Constitution despite Congress specifically implementing the Act through Section 5 of the Fourteenth Amendment, that provides that "[t]he Congress shall have power to enforce, by appropriate legislation, the provisions of this article.").

¶ 18 Like Section 5 of the Fourteenth Amendment of the United States Constitution, provisions that directly implicate rights guaranteed to individuals under our Constitution are in a category of their own. That is, although the provision may be non-self-executing, thus requiring initial legislative action, the courts, as final interpreters of the Constitution, have the final "obligation to guard, enforce, and protect every right granted or secured by the Constitution. . . ." Thus the question whether Article X, Section 1(3), presents a "justiciable" controversy cannot be addressed in a vacuum. The clause must be read in the context of any correlative individual rights guaranteed under the Montana Constitution.

¶ 19 In this case, the requirement that the Legislature shall provide a basic system of free quality public schools, must be read in conjunction with Section 1 of Article X, which guarantees a right to education. *Kaptein ex rel. Kaptein v. Conrad Sch. Dist.* (Mont. 1997). In the case *sub judice*, the Legislature has addressed the threshold political question: it has executed Article X, Section 1(3), by creating a basic system of free public schools. As the final guardian and protector of the right to education, it is incumbent upon the court to assure that the system enacted by the Legislature enforces, protects and fulfills the right. We conclude this issue is justiciable.

Issue Two

¶ 20 Whether the District Court erroneously concluded that the current school funding system violates Article X, Section 1(3), by failing to provide adequate funding for Montana's schools.

¶ 21 Article X, Section 1(3), of the Montana Constitution mandates that "[t]he legislature shall provide a basic system of free quality public elementary and secondary schools. . . . It shall fund and distribute in an equitable manner to the school districts the state's share of the cost of the basic elementary and secondary school system." As we have just stated, the Legislature has made an initial policy determination regarding this language. It has created a public school system and a method of funding the system. Although Article X, Section 1(3), is textually committed to the Legislature in the first instance, once the Legislature acts we are not barred from reaching the question of whether the Legislature has fulfilled its constitutional obligation to "provide a basic system of free quality public elementary and secondary schools."

¶ 22 Although the Legislature has made an initial policy determination by establishing a public school system (the relevant consideration under the Political Question Doctrine), it has not made a determination as to the meaning of "quality." Because the Constitution mandates that the Legislature provide a quality education, we determine that the Legislature can best construct a "quality" system of education if it first defines what is a "quality" system of education. In addition, even though we here defer to the Legislature as to what constitutes "quality," given the unchallenged findings of the District Court we do conclude that the educational product of the current school system is constitutionally deficient and that the Legislature currently fails to adequately fund Montana's public school system.

¶ 23 The Montana Legislature created the current education funding system in 1993 with House Bill (HB) 667. The Legislature did so in response to a court challenge to the former system. Unlike in the current proceedings, that challenge was brought under the Equality of Educational Opportunity Clause. Mont. Const. Art. X, Sec. 1(1). We addressed the challenge in *Helena Elementary Sch. Dist. No. 1 v. State* (Mont. 1989), where we concluded that the spending disparities among the State's school districts constituted a denial of equality of educational opportunity as guaranteed by Article X, Section 1(1) of the Montana Constitution.

¶ 24 HB 667 sought to address those inequities. It did this by relying on a regression analysis designed to address spending and taxing disparities among school districts. Central to the funding system it instituted is the "general fund." The general fund is the largest and most important part of a school district's overall budget. Each school district's general fund budget includes a basic entitlement lump sum from the State, the Average Number Belonging (ANB) entitlement, locally raised funds, and special education funds. A school district's general fund budget has a built-in maximum and minimum, computed using a formula. Tellingly, most school districts currently either exceed their maximum budgets or are budgeting over 98 percent of the 100 percent they are allowed to spend. At trial some educators stated that their districts could not provide what they considered a "quality" education unless they were allowed to spend more than their general fund maximum.

¶ 25 This funding system is not correlated with any understanding of what constitutes a "quality" education. The evidence for this is two-fold. First, as the State admitted at oral argument, in passing HB 667, the Legislature did not undertake a study of what the Public Schools Clause demands of it. That is, it did not seek to define "quality." As stated above, since the Legislature has not defined "quality" as that term is used in Article X, Section 1(3), we cannot conclude that the current funding system was designed to provide a quality education. Second, as found by the District Court, the Legislature, in creating the spending formula of HB 667, did not link the formula to any factors that might constitute a "quality" education.

¶ 26 The District Court found that the "major problems" with HB 667 were: it provided no mechanism to deal with inflation; it did not base its numbers on costs such as teacher pay, meeting accreditation standards, fixed costs, or costs of special education; increases in allowable spending were not tied to costs of increased accreditation standards or content and performance standards; relevant data was already two years old when the bill was passed; and no study was undertaken to justify the disparity in ANB dollars dispensed to high schools as compared to elementary schools. From these credible findings we must conclude that the Legislature did not endeavor to create a school funding system with quality in mind. Unless funding relates to needs such as academic standards, teacher pay, fixed costs, costs of special education, and performance standards, then the funding is not related to the cornerstones of a quality education. We also note that in *Helena Elementary* we stated that "the accreditation standards establish a minimum upon which quality education can be built" but "do not fully define either the constitutional rights of students or the constitutional responsibilities of the State of Montana for funding its public elementary and secondary schools."

¶ 27 Without an assessment of what constitutes a "quality" education, the Legislature has no reference point from which to relate funding to relevant educational needs. In the absence of a threshold definition of quality, we cannot conclude that the system is adequately funded as required by Article X, Section 1(3).

¶ 28 The above analysis is essentially prospective in nature—that is, it states what the Constitution demands of the Legislature and what the Legislature must do to fashion a constitutional education system. Nonetheless, in order to address the Coalition's claims we have to address the educational product that the present school system provides, not just the manner in which the Legislature funds that school system. Even given the absence of a definition of "quality" education, the District Court's findings demonstrate that whatever legitimate definition of quality that the Legislature may devise, the educational product of the present school system is constitutionally deficient and that the Legislature currently fails to adequately fund Montana's public school system.

¶ 29 The evidence that the current system is constitutionally deficient includes the following unchallenged findings made by the District Court: school districts increasingly budgeting at or near their maximum budget authority; growing accreditation problems; many qualified educators leaving the state to take advantage of higher salaries and benefits offered elsewhere; the cutting of programs; the deterioration of school buildings and inadequate funds for building repair and for new construction; and increased competition for general fund dollars between special and general education.

¶ 30 The State counters by arguing that the District Court should have considered output measures, such as test scores, in determining whether the current system is constitutional, and that under such measures Montana compares very favorably with other states. Indeed, Montana's students often do perform quite well on standardized achievement tests. However, current test scores do not tell the whole story. First of all, a "system" of education includes more than high achievement on standardized tests. We have noted elsewhere, for example, that school districts have an interest in integrating their academic programs with extracurricular activities. *Kaptein*. Secondly, it may be that test scores are not attributable to the current educational system. The voluminous evidence presented at trial and summarized in the preceding paragraph established that although Montana's students are testing well when compared with students in similar states, there are serious concerns as to whether this level of achievement will continue. With the District Court's findings of fact in mind, it may be that the achievement registered by Montana's students is not because of the current educational system.

¶ 31 Therefore, because the Legislature has not defined what "quality" means we cannot conclude that the current system is designed to provide a "quality" education. Article X, Section 1(3), explicitly requires the Legislature to fund a "quality" educational system. Therefore we defer to the Legislature to provide a threshold definition of what the Public Schools Clause requires. We also conclude, however, that given the unchallenged findings made by the District Court, whatever definition the Legislature devises, the current funding system is not grounded in principles of quality, and cannot be deemed constitutionally sufficient.

Issue Three

¶ 32 Whether the District Court erred in concluding that the State has violated Article X, Section 1(3), by not paying its share of the cost of the public school system.

¶ 33 In light of our holding on issue number two above, we decline to address this issue.

Issue Four

¶ 34 Whether the District Court erred in concluding that the State has violated Article X, Section 1(2), by not recognizing the cultural heritage of American Indians in its educational goals.

¶ 35 The District Court concluded that the State has failed to recognize the distinct and unique cultural heritage of American Indians and that it has shown no commitment in its educational goals to the preservation of Indian cultural identity, as demanded by Article X, Section 1(2). It relied on our opinion in *Helena Elementary*, when we held that the "provision establishes a special burden in Montana for the education of American Indian children which must be addressed as part of the school funding issues." *Helena Elementary.* The State does not contest these conclusions. "This Court will not endeavor to review a matter when appellant has directed no argument toward it." Therefore, we merely recognize that the findings and conclusions of the District Court regarding Article X, Section 1(2), of the Montana Constitution stand unchallenged. ***

Issue Seven

¶ 40 Whether an award of attorney fees is appropriate.

¶ 41 The District Court denied an award of attorney fees to the Coalition, citing our denial of attorney fees in *Helena Elementary.* It is true that we denied attorney fees in that case. However, as the Coalition correctly points out, our decision there was based on the "common fund" doctrine. Since *Helena Elementary*, we decided *Montanans for the Responsible Use of the School Trust v. State ex rel. Board of Land Commissioners*, 1999 MT 263 (*Montrust*). In *Montrust* we awarded attorney fees pursuant to the private attorney general doctrine. The District Court erred in not addressing this change in our attorney fees jurisprudence. Therefore, we vacate the District Court's denial of attorney fees and remand for reconsideration in light of *Montrust.*

Justice JIM NELSON concurs.

¶ 42 I concur in our Opinion, although I perceive a need for further remarks regarding our power to enforce non-self-executing constitutional rights.

¶ 43 First, in *General Agric. Corp. v. Moore* (Mont. 1975), our view of what sort of provision is and is not self-executing was softened somewhat from the definition we adopted in *State ex rel. Stafford v. Fox-Great Falls Theatre Corp.* (Mont. 1942). In *General Agric.*, we stated:

> A provision is self-executing when it can be given effect without the aid of legislation and there is nothing to indicate that legislation is contemplated in order to render it operative.... The fact that a right granted by a constitutional provision may be better or further protected by supplementary legislation does not of itself prevent the provision in question from being self-executing; nor does the self-executing character of a constitutional provision necessarily preclude legislation for the better protection of the right secured, or legislation in furtherance of the purposes, or of the enforcement, of the provision.

Accordingly, I am not necessarily of the view that constitutional provisions beginning with the words "the legislature shall" must all be denominated as non-self-executing.

¶ 44 Second, with the exception of rights protected under Article II of the Montana Constitution, there are those who might read our Opinion as suggesting that the legislature must always act upon a non-self-executing constitutional directive before a justiciable claim arises regarding the implementation of that provision. This raises a question: if the legislature fails or refuses to implement a non-self-executing constitutional directive, may a justiciable claim regarding the proper implementation of that clause eventually ripen?

¶ 45 As early as 1900, this Court considered the problem posed by legislative inaction with respect to non-self-executing clauses. The case of *State ex rel. Whiteside v. First Judicial Dist. Ct.* (Mont. 1900), dealt with the Court's constitutionally granted power of supervisory control as established in Article VIII, Section 2 of the 1889 Constitution. This section provided that such power was to be exercised "under such regulations and limitations as may be prescribed by law." The Court questioned whether the power of supervisory control would be dormant in the absence of legislation indicating specific procedures for the exercise of that power. While acknowledging that such legislative inaction would represent an ostensible limitation on the exercise this power, the Court flatly rejected the notion that such a constitutionally granted power could be rendered ineffective by the legislature's failure to enact guidelines for its use. *Whiteside*. In doing so, the Court noted that "the legislature cannot decrease the powers granted by the Constitution." *Whiteside*. This view pays due respect to the paramount nature and inherently positive force of constitutionally established powers, as well as constitutionally granted rights.

¶ 46 When, in adopting their constitution, the people provided that a provision shall be implemented by the legislature, it cannot be gainsaid that the people had the right to expect, and do expect that branch of government to, in good faith, carry out its constitutionally imposed obligation to legislate. In truth, non-self-executing constitutional directives may be, for all intents and purposes, nullified by a legislature which chooses to ignore such directives. Simply put, non-self-executing clauses, whether delineating a power or establishing a right, are not rendered ineffective by a legislative failure to enact laws in furtherance of such clauses. ***

¶ 48 Starting with the assumption, as does our Opinion, that non-self-executing constitutional mandates are, by their very nature, enacted with the expectation that the legislature will act to implement the directive, a justiciable claim must, at some point, arise if the legislature fails or refuses to fulfill its obligation. Indeed, choosing not to act, is an act in and of itself.

¶ 49 The only real question is, at what point in time is there an unacceptable failure or refusal? I submit that that issue is best resolved on a case-by-case basis, taking into consideration the nature of the right, the length of time during which the legislature has failed or has refused to act, and the reason for its failure or refusal to legislate. ***

¶ 52 As we stated in *General Agric.*:

> The supremacy of constitutional mandates is too well established to require citation.... A written constitution is not only the direct and basic expression of the sovereign will, it is also the absolute rule of action and decision for all departments and offices of government with respect to all matters covered by it, and must control as it is written until it is changed by the authority which established it. No function of government can be discharged in disregard of or in opposition to the fundamental law. The state constitution is the mandate of a sovereign people to its servants and representatives. No one of them has a right to ignore or disregard its mandates, and the legislature, the executive officers, and the judiciary cannot lawfully act beyond its limitations.

¶ 53 Indeed, no branch of government has, in default of its constitutional obligation to act, the power to, *de facto*, write out of the constitution important rights and guarantees which the people sought to secure unto themselves, believing when they did so, that their elected officials would, in good faith, honor their command.

¶ 54 With those caveats, I concur.

Justice PATRICIA O. COTTER joins in the concurrence of Justice JAMES C. NELSON.

Justice JIM RICE specially concurring.

¶ 55 I concur with the holding of the Court on all issues and write to offer alternative reasoning for affirming the District Court on Issues 1 and 2.

¶ 56 The State's argument that this is a political question reserved for the Legislature is well supported by case authority from other states. However, I agree with the Court's resolution and would add that this question was essentially resolved sixteen years ago by *Helena Elementary Sch. Dist. No. 1 v. State* (Mont. 1989), wherein the Court first undertook judicial review of the constitutional issues related to school funding under the 1972 Montana Constitution. School funding has been analyzed pursuant to that decision ever since. It may have been more appropriate for the State to raise the political question defense at that time, but, in any event, I believe the Court's decision is clearly consistent with the expectations of the Constitutional Convention delegates, who rejected an amendment which would have placed school funding within the exclusive province of the Legislature, offered by Delegate McDonough:

> [W]hat is distribution in an "equitable manner"; and what is "full funding" of the educational program? Now, that should be left with the Legislature and the Legislature only, and nobody else. They're the representatives of the people up here to decide fiscal matters, not the Supreme Court of Montana and not anybody else. It's the Legislature that has this power, and the Legislature should have it....
>
> ... There's going to be problems from time to time, but if you leave [the words] in as they are now worded, you're going to have more problems of constitutional-legal construction on any lawsuits relative to the application of these last two sentences [of Article X, Section 1(3)].

Mont. Const. Conv. Tr., Vol. VI at 1963. The delegates' rejection of the proposed amendment set the Constitution on a course that would make Delegate McDonough's observations prescient: school funding was made an issue of constitutional dimension which requires the involvement, within their respective spheres, of both the legislative and judicial branches in order to resolve "problems of constitutional-legal construction."

¶ 57 Turning to the substance of school funding under Issue 2, the Court concludes that "the Legislature can best construct a 'quality' system of education if it first defines what is a 'quality' system of education" based upon educationally relevant factors. See § 22. This is undoubtedly logical, but I would nonetheless refrain from suggesting how to "best construct" the educational system, and upon what factors it must do so, believing it to be an inappropriate judicial comment on the Legislature's prerogative, if I was not convinced that the "suggestion" was, in fact, constitutionally compelled. Truly, the debates of the delegates demonstrate that, in assigning to the Legislature the task of designing the system, they intended the Legislature to assess the educational needs of the state before deciding funding issues. "After the state has assessed the needs and established what a minimum program ought to be, we feel that the state ought then to provide, by whatever means it sees fit, for the funding of the program." [Del. Harbaugh.] "Once the needs for a basic quality system of elementary and secondary schools have been realistically assessed, the state has the obligation to guarantee...." [Del. Habedank.]

¶ 58 Clearly, the power to determine what constitutes a quality system was granted to the Legislature. "We are saying to the Legislature, 'We have untied your hands. We want you to set up a basic elementary and secondary education. You have full power to decide what that is going to be; but when you get it done, the state's share of it, as you determine it'—we give the Legislature full power there to determine its share, too—we haven't tied their hands—'shall be funded. . . .'" [Del. Habedank.] Based on these indications from the delegates, I concur that the Court's directives—to define a quality system based upon relevant factors—are appropriately given.

¶ 59 I agree with the Court's focus on the word "quality," but the Constitution also uses two other important terms in regard to educational funding requirements—"basic" and "state share." These terms are employed to shape the Legislature's duty with regard to educational funding. "Basic" occurs twice in describing the system the Legislature must create. Extensive explanation of the meaning of "basic" was given by Delegate Habedank, who offered the motion to add the term to the Constitution in these two places. In summary, the intention was:

> [T]o require the Legislature to do full funding of a basic educational program and that the frills and the things beyond the basic program, as the Legislature determines it, can still remain with the people. . . . .
>
> . . . [T]he public is concerned. They are very concerned. And the delegation here. . . evidenced its concern about educational theorists coming in with every type of—shall we call it "screwball education proposal" and insisting that this be in here, and it was felt that "basic" would help.

Delegate Habedank, Mont. Const. Conv. Tr., Vol. VI at 1962, 2154.

¶ 60 Next, the delegates inserted "state share" into the Constitution to further define the Legislature's obligation. The first sentence of Article X, Section 1(3), states that the Legislature "shall provide a basic system of free quality public" schools. The third sentence of this section states that the Legislature "shall fund. . . the state's share" of the cost of this basic system. From these provisions we understand that the Legislature must "provide"—to establish or make available—a basic system of quality education, but that the Legislature must "fund" only the "state's share" of this system. Indeed, the District Court concluded that "the State is not paying *its share* of the cost of the basic elementary and secondary school system." (Emphasis added.)

¶ 61 These provisions of the Constitution arose out of the delegates' concern that the Legislature had historically failed to fully fund the Foundation Program, the then-existing vehicle for state support of public education, or state share. ("It is only when our state Legislature fails to meet the obligation under the foundation program that we begin to get these real inequities built into it. For instance, the state right now is funding only about 65 percent, and the other 35 percent has to go back on local property tax levies." [Del. Blaylock.]) Although acknowledging that other revenue sources, including local levies, were also necessary in order to fund a basic system of quality education, the intent was to require the Legislature to fund only the state's share of that cost:

> I think there's fear here that we're asking the state to do all of the financing for education. This is not what we're trying to do. I think what we're trying

> to do here is to do what the foundation program has not done. I don't think we're trying to eliminate levies at the local level. I don't foresee this, and I would hate to see it come. I think at the local level, still there should be ability—or the people should be able to have a higher quality of education [than] in some other community. And I really think the underlying fear here is that the state is going to provide the total financing, and this is not true. We're asking for the full funding [of the foundation program]; and when we're asking that, we're talking, really, in the sense that we have in the past in this area.

Delegate Woodmansey, Mont. Const. Conv. Tr., Vol. VI at 1968.

> I think it's also essential that the Legislature should have the power to require school districts to tax for a portion of their educational program in order to keep control of education at a local level, in order to allow people to know what is being spent for education, and this is what my proposal also does.

Delegate Habedank, Mont. Const. Conv. Tr., Vol. VI at 2153.

¶ 62 In my view, the District Court's conclusion that school funding is constitutionally inadequate is supported primarily by the evidence demonstrating that the system has once again fallen into the condition criticized by the delegates, and against which they reacted—namely, that the state's share of the cost of education has steadily eroded to the point of insufficiency. This condition was also critically noted by the Court in *Helena Elementary*. In inflation-adjusted dollars, state aid declined between 1991 and 2003 by 17 percent, and local taxes have increased by 120 percent to pay for the cost of education. The state share of the general fund declined to 60.95 percent in 2003. Thus, while the funding system created under HB 667 addressed the constitutional problem caused by disparities in funding between school districts—the primary issue in *Helena Elementary*—it nonetheless failed, over time, to maintain state support and satisfy the state's duty to fund its share of education, thus running afoul of a separate constitutional mandate. The evidentiary focus on such factors as deterioration of school buildings and the departure of educators is appropriate in assessing the health of the system, but such factors are merely symptoms of the underlying disease: the state's failure to fully fund its share of educational costs. This is a long term, systemic and fundamental flaw which I believe violates the last sentence of Article X, Section 1(3).

¶ 63 In conclusion, the Court has noted that this decision stands on its own and does not necessarily affirm the entirety of the District Court's order. The District Court's yeoman efforts are to be saluted, and we simply do not have time to address each matter ruled upon in its lengthy decision. I would make one exception and offer comment thereon. In Finding of Fact No. 186, the District Court found that the constitutional mandate to the Legislature does not depend on the state's fiscal capacity, citing *Helena Elementary*. However, in *Helena Elementary*, we found "unpersuasive the argument that statewide fiscal difficulties in the last few years somehow excuse the disparities in the spending per pupil in the various school districts." *Helena*

Elementary. In other words, limited resources did not excuse the unequal distribution of those resources. That is not the problem here. While legislators cannot avoid school funding problems because of financial concerns, it should also be stated that the school funding obligation, as with any financial obligation, even one of constitutional dimension, is necessarily circumscribed by the State's "fiscal capacity." Indeed, this was acknowledged by the delegates: "the committee realizes that economic resources of the state limit this [educational] goal." [Del. Harbaugh.]

¶ 64 The extensive quotations from the transcripts of the constitutional convention herein are made with the understanding that the statement or intention of one delegate does not necessarily equate with the intention of the delegates as a body or of the Great Work they created. However, a comparison of the words of the Constitution with a study of the entirety of the debates allows one to glean the delegates' intentions with regard to the issue of educational funding with, in my view, a high degree of confidence. I believe the quotations herein accurately reflect those intentions.

¶ 65 I concur.

Chief Justice KARLA M. GRAY joins in the special concurring opinion of Justice Rice.

Notes on Public School Funding

1. Like the *Rodriguez* case brought under the federal Constitution, *Helena Elementary* is a challenge to the "equity" of a state's school funding system. Such systems are complex fiscal efforts shared among state, local, and often federal governments (and taxpayers). On one hand, school boards have their own constitutionally guaranteed local control over budgeting. On the other hand, the federal government makes independent decisions about compensating for wealth disparities (sometimes resulting from reduced local property tax bases on federal or tribal lands). How can the state best ensure the constitutional "equality of educational opportunity" across these diverse funding decisions—only some of which are in the state's control—and to what extent should the court take these external funding factors into account?

2. In contrast, *Columbia Falls* is a challenge to the "adequacy" of a state's school funding system. This raises similar questions around "the state's share of the cost of the basic elementary and secondary school system." How should the Legislature fund "a basic system of free quality public elementary and secondary schools" when it need not and cannot fund the full amount required for such a system?

3. The Montana Constitution charges the Board of Public Education with "general supervision over the public school system." Mont. Const. Art. X, § 9(3)(a). Why *shouldn't* the Board's accreditation standards suffice as the minimum constitutional requirements for equal educational opportunity in Montana? If neither the Board nor the Court can define an equitable school funding system that binds the Montana Legislature under the Constitution, who can?

4. What is the nature of the "special burden in Montana for the education of American Indian children" the state bears under Article X, section 1(2) and how does it relate to the broader equality of educational opportunity issues in *Helena Elementary*? How do you read the state's duties to remedy the violation of section 1(2) in *Columbia Falls*? In 1999, the Montana Legislature enacted the following:

> **20-1-501. Recognition of American Indian cultural heritage—legislative intent.** (1) It is the constitutionally declared policy of this state to recognize the distinct and unique cultural heritage of American Indians and to be committed in its educational goals to the preservation of their cultural heritage.
>
> (2) It is the intent of the legislature that in accordance with Article X, section 1(2), of the Montana constitution:
>
> (a) every Montanan, whether Indian or non-Indian, be encouraged to learn about the distinct and unique heritage of American Indians in a culturally responsive manner; and
>
> (b) every educational agency and all educational personnel will work cooperatively with Montana tribes or those tribes that are in close proximity, when providing instruction or when implementing an educational goal or adopting a rule related to the education of each Montana citizen, to include information specific to the cultural heritage and contemporary contributions of American Indians, with particular emphasis on Montana Indian tribal groups and governments.
>
> (3) It is also the intent of this part, predicated on the belief that all school personnel should have an understanding and awareness of Indian tribes to help them relate effectively with Indian students and parents, that educational personnel provide means by which school personnel will gain an understanding of and appreciation for the American Indian people.

See Carol Juneau & Denise Juneau, *Indian Education for All: Montana's Constitution at Work in Our Schools*, 72 MONT. L. REV. 111 (2011). Assuming this policy is fulfilled by the state and schools (is it enforceable?), does this provision of "Indian Education for All" satisfy the commitment "to the preservation of [American Indians'] cultural integrity"? What other policies should such a commitment require (or prohibit) in public education?

5. The governance of the Montana University System under the Board of Regents is addressed by *Board of Regents of Higher Education v. Judge* (1975) in Chapter 4. Compare the provisions governing schools and the university system, and the relative autonomy granted by each. How are they alike and what accounts for the differences? To what extent should principles drawn from one level of education in the Montana Constitution inform the other? Note that many provisions of Article X, including the "full educational potential" goal and "equality of educational

opportunity" guarantee of section 1(1), and the "cultural heritage of the American Indians" commitment of section 1(2), are applicable to the entire system of education, including both local public schools and the state university system.

Chapter 8

Elections & Voting

Article II, Section 13. Right of suffrage. All elections shall be free and open, and no power, civil or military, shall at any time interfere to prevent the free exercise of the right of suffrage.

Identical to 1889 constitution.

Article IV, Section 1. Ballot. All elections by the people shall be by secret ballot.

Revises 1889 constitution by adding the word "secret."

Article IV, Section 2. Qualified elector. Any citizen of the United States 18 years of age or older who meets the registration and residence requirements provided by law is a qualified elector unless he is serving a sentence for a felony in a penal institution or is of unsound mind, as determined by a court.

Revises 1889 constitution. Provides legislative rather than constitutional requirements for residence and registration. Convicted felon loses voting rights only while incarcerated. (18 is voting age established for ALL elections by 26th amendment to U.S. Constitution ratified June 30, 1971 [sic]).

Article IV, Section 3. Elections. The legislature shall provide by law the requirements for residence, registration, absentee voting, and administration of elections. It may provide for a system of poll booth registration, and shall insure the purity of elections and guard against abuses of the electoral process.

Revises 1889 constitution. Provides legislative rather than constitutional establishment of requirements which are often affected by (and sometimes in conflict with) federal law and court decisions. When necessary to comply with federal requirements it is much easter to change the law than to amend the Constitution. Second sentence specifically authorizes legislature to provide for voter registration at time and place of voting—rather than in advance of election.

Article V, Section 14. Districting and apportionment. (1) The state shall be divided into as many districts as there are members of the house, and each district shall elect one representative. Each senate district shall be composed of two adjoining house districts, and shall elect one senator. Each

> district shall consist of compact and contiguous territory. All districts shall be as nearly equal in population as is practicable.
>
> (2) In the legislative session following ratification of this constitution and thereafter in each session preceding each federal population census, a commission of five citizens, none of whom may be public officials, shall be selected to prepare a plan for redistricting and reapportioning the state into legislative districts and a plan for redistricting the state into congressional districts. ***
>
> *(1) New provision for single-member house districts. Two house districts constitute a senatorial district. (2) . . . new provision which establishes a five member commission to recommend a reapportionment plan after each U.S. census.*

Election laws mark the transition between constitutional structure and constitutional rights. Elections are the means by which voters constitute state government under the Montana Constitution. In doing so, Montana's voters enjoy an express right to suffrage in "free and open" elections. The federal Constitution does not guarantee a right to vote in those terms. Instead, it protects against certain forms of discrimination in voting, but leaves the question of who may vote to states. Even in federal elections, voting rights are derivative of state qualifications. Article I, section 2 provides "the Electors in each State shall have the Qualifications requisite for Electors of the most numerous Branch of the State Legislature." Americans' right to vote is therefore guaranteed primarily by state constitutions, which provide general qualifications for "electors" or voters. Like many state constitutions, Montana's Constitution further provides an affirmative "right of suffrage" in its Declaration of Rights, complemented by a requirement that the legislature "shall insure the purity of elections and guard against abuses of the electoral process." Today's debates between expanding the franchise and subjecting restrictions on voting to constitutional scrutiny on the one hand, and restricting the franchise in the name of electoral integrity on the other, are thus embedded in the text of the Montana Constitution and other state constitutions. Not surprisingly, state courts strike different balances.

Beyond the right to vote, state constitutions attend to equally weighty structural questions of representation and redistricting for both federal and state offices. In American practice, elected legislatures redraw their own district lines, as well those of congressional districts, every decade. This is a temptation toward Gerrymandering, the problem of drawing constituencies to maximize the benefit to one candidate or party (or detriment to the other), and few legislatures are able to resist. Some states address this problem through constitutional adjudication. One of the Montana Constitution's innovations is the delegation of redistricting to an appointed commission that acts independently of political officeholders.

A. The Right to Vote

Hannah Tokerud, *The Right of Suffrage in Montana: Voting Protections Under the State Constitution*

74 Mont. L. Rev. 417, 417–18, 420–21, 439 (2013)

In Montana, the right of suffrage is expressly granted by the state constitution. Article II, section 13 of the Montana Constitution states: "All elections shall be free and open, and no power, civil or military, shall at any time interfere to prevent the free exercise of the right of suffrage." This clause would appear to bar any act, law, or practice that would prevent free and open elections. But what does it mean for an election to be "free and open"? ***

The history of the 1889 Convention clarifies what the delegates understood the phrase "free and open" to mean. The delegates understood "open" to be consistent with secret ballots. "Open" seems to refer not to the ballot form but to the actual accessibility of the voting process. The elections were to be in public, free to everybody, and open to everybody. By open to everybody, the delegates meant open to eligible voters, as "everybody" in 1889 did not include women, "idiots and insane" persons, and felons. It is harder to say what "free" meant to the delegates. "Free" seems to have meant without restraint as opposed to without cost because Montanans added an economic qualification for voting in certain types of elections to the constitution in 1932. The U.S. Supreme Court declared such provisions unconstitutional and invalid, and the Montana Legislature recognized this by eliminating the requirement and by voting to submit a proposed constitutional amendment, which would have deleted the provision. Therefore, to the 1972 Convention delegates, "free" probably meant both without cost and without restraint.

In the 1972 Bill of Rights Committee Comments to the proposed section 13, committee members stated the section should be unchanged to guarantee that elections remain free and open. The Committee noted the proposed provision was the same as that in the 1889 constitution. The Committee further commented that the provision supplemented the General Government Committee on Suffrage and Elections's proposals but did not replace them. No delegate proposals were received. In March 1972, the Montana Constitutional Convention adopted the provision unanimously. ***

The delegates' discussion of Article IV, section 3, allowing the legislature to establish a system of poll booth registration, highlights that they understood the idea behind the vote to be that "when you put a restriction on it, that is, a restriction passed by a Legislature—they must register 40 days before or they do not have that right—then you are depriving, artificially, people of their vote, and when you deprive people of their vote, you deprive them of their rights." Delegate Dahood was not concerned about the possibility of voter fraud and argued:

> Our law, and the wisdom that formed the basis for our law, provides not only judicial thinking but, by statute in this state, that all citizens are presumed

> to be honest, and we must deal with all of our citizens on the basis that we presume that when they participate in the functions of citizenship, they shall participate in an honest manner and in an honest endeavor.

[Ms. Tokerud concludes by applying the "free and open elections" clause to a hypothetical voter ID requirement and, under strict scrutiny, suggests "the potential for voter fraud would probably be insufficient to justify" the requirement.]

Driscoll v. Stapleton

2020 MT 247

Justice BETH BAKER delivered the Opinion of the Court. ***

¶3 BIPA [the Ballot Interference Prevention Act] was introduced in the 2017 Montana Legislature with an asserted purpose of protecting election integrity and instilling voter confidence in the election process. The bill's sponsor said during legislative committee hearings that he had brought the bill because of voters' suspicions and concerns he had received over ballot-collection activity. The bill received no public testimony in support but significant testimony in opposition. No one testified to specific instances of voter fraud or ballot tampering. BIPA passed both houses of the Legislature, and Montana voters approved it as a legislative referendum on November 6, 2018. It has not yet been in effect for a statewide general election.

¶4 Under BIPA's provisions, absentee ballots, voted or unvoted, may be collected from individual voters only by certain persons, including election officials, postal workers, or the voter's family members, household members, caregivers, or acquaintances. Section 13-35-703, MCA. With the exception of election officials and postal workers, these enumerated individuals are limited to collecting and conveying up to six ballots during an election cycle; they must sign a registry upon delivery of the ballots, providing their name, address, phone number, relationship to each voter, the voter's name, and the voter's address. Sections 13-35-703(3), 13-35-704, MCA. Violation of BIPA's restrictions carries a fine of $500 for each ballot collected unlawfully. Section 13-35-705, MCA. ***

¶19 Here, the Secretary argues the District Court erred by applying strict scrutiny when evaluating BIPA. The right to vote in any manner, the Secretary maintains, is not absolute and must be balanced against the regulatory power the constitution confers on the Legislature. The Montana Constitution directs the Legislature to "provide by law the requirements for residence, registration, absentee voting, and administration of elections" and to "insure the purity of elections and guard against abuses of the electoral process." Mont. Const. art. IV, § 3. In light of this directive, the Secretary urges this Court to adopt the more flexible balancing approach set forth in *Anderson v. Celebrezze* (1983), and *Burdick v. Takushi* (1992).

¶20 At this stage of the proceedings, we find it unnecessary to set forth a new level of scrutiny. The case is not before us on a full evidentiary record for evaluation of the ultimate merits. We conclude that, for purposes of resolving the instant preliminary injunction dispute, the level of scrutiny is not dispositive to the issues presented on appeal.

¶21 Noting that voters have come to rely on ballot-collection services, Democrats argue that BIPA will disproportionately affect the right of suffrage for certain subgroups, including Native Americans, rural and elderly voters, students with full-time jobs, low-wage workers, working parents, disabled voters, and first-time voters. Democrats presented evidence of increased Native American voter turnout between the 2014 and 2018 elections due to the efforts of organizations like Western Native Voice that do ballot-collection work on reservations. The District Court found that the evidence of various factors contributing to unequal access to the polls for Native American voters would be exacerbated by BIPA, burdening this subgroup's constitutional right to vote.

¶22 The Secretary asserts on appeal, as he did before the District Court, that the State has important interests to ensure voter confidence in the electoral process and to guard against abuses of that process. But he did not present evidence in the preliminary injunction proceedings of voter fraud or ballot coercion, generally or as related to ballot-collection efforts, occurring in Montana. More importantly, the Secretary has pointed to no evidence in the preliminary injunction record that would rebut the District Court's finding of a disproportionate impact on Native American voters, and he leaves the contention largely undisturbed in his briefing on appeal. The Secretary's only suggestion is a general one—that the alternative means of returning ballots or of voting in person remain equally available to all voters. But this does not address Democrats' evidence that the burden on Native American communities is disproportionate, and the Secretary fails to refute the District Court's finding.

¶23 The Secretary has not demonstrated clear error in the District Court's finding of sufficient evidence for a preliminary injunction of a disproportionate burden to Native American voters' right against "interfere[nce with] . . . the free exercise of the right of suffrage." Mont. Const. art. II, § 13. Democrats' evidence was sufficient to make a prima facie showing of the harm BIPA may impose on Native American voters in particular. On review of the preliminary injunction record, we conclude that the District Court did not err in finding prima facie evidence that BIPA may unconstitutionally burden the right of suffrage, particularly with respect to Native American communities, or in concluding that the Secretary did not demonstrate an interest that weighed more heavily than the burdens Democrats assert. The court thus did not manifestly abuse its discretion in concluding that a preliminary injunction should issue, even under the *Anderson-Burdick* balancing standard.

¶24 Finally, the District Court did not err by finding a possibility of irreparable injury absent an injunction against BIPA. We are mindful that BIPA was passed in the 2018 general election and has not yet been in effect for a statewide general election. Democrats presented evidence of election officials' concerns about the strain BIPA puts on them leading up to Election Day, especially in rural counties, and the record before us shows uncertainty regarding BIPA's effects on such things as a ballot-collector mailing another voter's ballot, the use of after-hours ballot drop-boxes, or the need for election officials to question every person returning a ballot. In light of Democrats' evidence, and absent evidence of fraudulent ballot collection in Montana elections, preliminarily enjoining BIPA pending full consideration will minimize the harm to all parties and maintain the status quo pending final resolution on the merits.

¶25 In sum, we conclude that the District Court did not manifestly abuse its discretion by granting the preliminary injunction against enforcement of BIPA. ***

Justice DIRK SANDEFUR concurring in part and dissenting in part. ***

¶35 ... Here, the District Court ultimately concluded that Plaintiffs made an unrebutted prima facie showing that they will likely prevail on the merits of their predicate claim that BIPA unconstitutionally burdens or interferes with the fundamental right to vote of a specified class of Montana voters under Article II, Section 13 of the Montana Constitution. Not so. ***

¶44 Plaintiffs' generalized voting-cost-increase theory, and accompanying anecdotal observations and concerns of election officials and political organizations, proves no more than a highly speculative *possibility* that some unquantifiable segment of absentee voters, who used previously available mass ballot collection services, *might choose* not to vote rather than timely mail their absentee ballot or use a BIPA-qualified family/friend collector like all other Montanans who choose to vote absentee. Regardless of any disproportionate nature of the independently-caused circumstances that may hamper voter turnout in Montana, the evidentiary record in this case is devoid of any substantial non-speculative evidence that BIPA will likely be a cause of any significant decrease in absentee voter turnout among the broad spectrum of Montana voters as alleged by Plaintiffs. The key findings of fact of the District Court regarding the alleged substantial interference or burden on the *right* of the specified class of Montanans to vote are thus clearly erroneous.

¶49 Here... despite the lack of any formal evidentiary showing by the State, BIPA is a voter-approved enactment.... [S]tatewide voter approval of BIPA is indicative of a compelling state interest insofar that it is indicative of the common understanding and mandate of the electorate for such legislation. Moreover, . . . the State supported its assertion of BIPA's manifest purposes (*i.e.*, "to prevent voter fraud, protect voters from harassment, ensure voters feel secure in the voting process, and protect public integrity in the elections") by citing the District Court to various federal and state authorities recognizing important state interests in maintaining the integrity of and public confidence in the electoral process and protecting against *the risk* of voter fraud, including absentee voter fraud. The State further cited the District Court to similar enactments in other states, as well as two published papers, and the recommendations of a bipartisan commission providing additional factual support consistent with BIPA and the cited federal and state authorities. Of significant note, this Court has similarly recognized, without requirement for evidentiary support, that "Montana has a compelling interest in imposing reasonable procedural requirements tailored to ensure the integrity, reliability, and fairness of its election processes." *Larson v. State* (Mont. 2019). As similarly noted by the Supreme Court, "[c]ommon sense, as well as constitutional law, compels the conclusion that government must play an active role in structuring elections; as a practical matter, there must be a substantial regulation of elections if they are to be fair and honest and if some sort of order, rather than chaos, is to accompany the democratic processes." *Burdick v. Takushi* (1992).

¶50 . . . [T]he District Court further inexplicably failed to even note that the State made an irrefutable showing that the Montana Senator (Al Olszewksi) who sponsored the BIPA referendum testified to the legislature, *inter alia*, that he was motivated by the stated concerns of a small sample of constituents that they had been solicited at their homes by third-party ballot collectors, fearfully relented to the collectors' offers to turn-in their absentee ballots, and were later concerned about the propriety of doing so. Thus, . . . based on the totality of the legal and factual information cited by the State below, the State made an ample showing to the District Court of a legitimate and compelling state interest related to BIPA. ***

¶56 The Majority's application of intermediate scrutiny is further erroneous because it is essentially based on the same erroneous procedural and substantive bases that the District Court applied strict scrutiny. As a threshold matter, it is irrefutable that election laws invariably burden the fundamental voting and associational rights of individual voters to some degree, whether governing "registration and qualifications of voters, the selection and eligibility of candidates, or the voting process itself." *Burdick*. As we and other courts have previously recognized, it is further irrefutable without need for evidentiary proof, that Montana has compelling state interests in preserving the integrity of our election laws, maintaining public confidence therein, and protecting against *the risk* of voting fraud, including absentee voting fraud. To suggest otherwise is sophistry of the highest order. Thus, upon application of intermediate scrutiny, the Majority's analysis is ultimately erroneous for the same reasons as the District Court's analysis, *i.e.*, Plaintiffs failed to satisfy their threshold burdens under § 27-19-201(1), MCA, of making a prima facie showing that BIPA will likely substantially burden or interfere with the voting rights of the specified class *and* that BIPA is likely *not* substantially related to an important government interest. ***

¶58 . . . While Montana certainly has a strong public policy interest in providing voters the most convenient and most preferable manner in which to vote, it remains the constitutional prerogative of the Legislature and/or electorate to address that interest. On their preliminary showing in this case, Plaintiffs have manifestly failed to make a prima facie showing that the failure to do so is of constitutional magnitude or dimension. ***

Justice JIM RICE joins in the concurring and dissenting Opinion of Justice Sandefur.

Weinschenk v. State

203 S.W.3d 201 (Mo. 2006)

PER CURIAM.

After a 2006 statute was enacted requiring registered voters to present certain types of state- or federally-issued photographic identification in order to cast regular ballots, Ms. Kathleen Weinschenk and others sued the state to block enforcement of the law on the grounds that it interfered with the fundamental right to vote as protected by the Missouri and United States constitutions. Ms. Weinschenk and the others claimed that the new law required them and other voters—particularly those who are low-income, disabled or elderly and who do not have driver's licenses—to spend money to obtain the necessary documents such as birth certificates in order to obtain the requisite photo ID. The trial court declared the law unconstitutional. ***

This Court agrees that SB 1014's Photo-ID Requirement violates Missouri's equal protection clause, Mo. Const. art. I, sec. 2, and Missouri's constitutional guarantee of the right of its qualified, registered citizens to vote. Mo. Const. art. I, sec. 25; art. VIII, sec. 2. While this Court fully agrees with Appellants that there is a compelling state interest in preventing voter fraud, the evidence supports the trial court's conclusion that the Photo-ID Requirement is not narrowly tailored to accomplish that purpose. ***

SB 1014's Photo-ID Requirement prohibits otherwise qualified and lawfully registered Missourians from voting if they present only out-of-state picture identification, social security cards, utility bills, school or work IDs, or other documents that served as proper identification under the version of section 115.427 in effect prior to the enactment of SB 1014. As amended by SB 1014, section 115.427 now requires that Missourians present as identification a document issued by the state or federal governments that contains the person's name as listed in the voter registration records, the person's photograph, and an expiration date showing that the ID is not expired. In practical effect, the only documents that most Missourians would have that could meet these requirements are a Missouri driver's or non-driver's license or a United States passport. ***

The Missouri Constitution expressly guarantees that "all elections shall be free and open; and no power, civil or military, shall at any time interfere to prevent the free exercise of the right of suffrage." Mo. Const. art. I, sec. 25. Additionally, rather than leaving the issue of voter qualification to the legislature, the Missouri Constitution has established an exclusive list of qualifications necessary to vote in Missouri. Mo. Const. art. VIII, sec. 2 ("All citizens of the United States. . . over the age of eighteen who are residents of this state and of the political subdivision in which they offer to vote are entitled to vote at all elections by the people, if. . . they are registered within the time prescribed by law"). These constitutional provisions establish with unmistakable clarity that the right to vote is fundamental to Missouri citizens.

The express constitutional protection of the right to vote differentiates the Missouri constitution from its federal counterpart. Federal courts also have consistently held that the right to vote is equally fundamental under the United States Constitution. *See, e.g., Reynolds v. Sims* (1964) ("The right to vote freely for the candidate of one's choice is of the essence of a democratic society"). But, the right to vote in state elections is conferred under federal law only by implication, not by express guarantee. *See Harper v. Virginia State Bd. Elections* (1966) ("the right to vote in state elections is nowhere expressly mentioned" in the United States Constitution).

Moreover, the qualifications for voting under the federal system are left to legislative determination, not constitutionally enshrined, as they are in Missouri. *Compare* U.S. Const. art. I, sec. 2 (providing that "Electors" shall be equivalent to those for state positions) *with* Mo. Const. art. VIII, sec. 2 (establishing exclusive qualifications for voting in Missouri). *Compare also* U.S. Const. amend. XV (protecting right to vote from abridgment "on account of race, color or previous condition of servitude") *with* Mo. Const. art. I, sec. 25 (protecting right to vote from all "power, civil or military" that "interferes to prevent the free exercise of the right of suffrage").

Due to the more expansive and concrete protections of the right to vote under the Missouri Constitution, voting rights are an area where our state constitution provides greater protection than its federal counterpart. . . . Of course, some regulation of the voting process is necessary to protect the right to vote itself. Such regulations are in place in all state and federal elections, and the Missouri Constitution further specifically delegates to the legislature the right to regulate registration. Mo. Const. art. VIII, sec. 5. In addition, many matters may tangentially affect voting, such as rules regarding who may run for office and how candidates are listed on ballots. For this reason, the extent of the burden this statute imposes on the right to vote must be evaluated before determining the level of scrutiny it will receive.

The record supports the trial court's determination that SB 1014's Photo-ID Requirement places a burden on the right of Missourians to vote. As set out at length above, it requires each of the individual plaintiffs in this case to present a Missouri driver's license, a Missouri non-driver's license, or a United States passport on election day in order to vote. The record reveals that between 3 and 4 percent of Missouri citizens (estimates vary from 169,215 to 240,000 individuals) lack the requisite photo ID. Appellants concede that many of these citizens, including all of the individual plaintiffs in this case, are eligible to vote and, in many cases, are already registered to vote. Nevertheless, under the new law these eligible registered voters will not be able to cast a regular ballot (or after 2008 any ballot at all) unless they undertake to obtain one of the requisite photo IDs. This will constitute a dramatic increase in provisional ballots over the previous law, as only 8,000 provisional ballots were cast statewide in the 2004 general election. As conceded by Appellants, denial of the right to vote to these Missourians is more than a *de minimis* burden on their suffrage. ***

In light of the substantial burden that the Photo-ID Requirement places upon the right to vote, the statute is subject to strict scrutiny. This is consistent with the past decisions of Missouri courts, which have uniformly applied strict scrutiny to statutes impinging upon the right to vote. ***

Recognizing that the State does have compelling interests in preserving electoral integrity and combating voter fraud, the issue becomes whether the record shows that the type of Photo-ID Requirement enacted in SB 1014 "is necessary to accomplish a compelling state interest." Because, for the reasons set out above, this Court has found that the Photo-ID Requirement imposes a severe burden on the right to vote, it can survive strict scrutiny only by showing it is necessary to accomplish a compelling state interest or that it is "narrowly drawn to express the compelling state interest at stake."

Yet, Appellants do not demonstrate that SB 1014's requirement of state or federally issued, non-expired photo IDs is strictly necessary or narrowly tailored to accomplish the State's asserted interests. To the contrary, Appellants concede that the only type of voter fraud that the Photo-ID Requirement prevents is in-person voter impersonation fraud at the polling place. It does not address absentee voting fraud or fraud in registration. While the Photo-ID Requirement may provide some additional protection against voter impersonation fraud, the evidence below demonstrates that the Photo-ID Requirement is not "necessary" to accomplish this goal. As the trial court found: "No evidence was presented that voter impersonation fraud exists to any substantial degree in Missouri. In fact, the evidence that was presented indicates that voter impersonation fraud is not a problem in Missouri."

The only evidence that Appellants marshal of voter impersonation fraud occurred prior to the enactment of identification requirements in 2002. The 2002 identification law, enacted in response to the federal HAVA law, required voters to present some proof of identity or residence when they arrived at the polling place. The list of acceptable identification under the 2002 requirements is much broader than the three types of photo ID that SB 1014 allows and included a utility bill, bank statement, expired passport, out-of-state driver's license, and other commonly available documents of identification.

Although Appellants protest that some of the approved identification documents under the 2002 law do not provide proof of eligibility to vote, neither does the Photo-ID Requirement. The Photo-ID Requirement assists in prevention of voter impersonation, but the evidence reveals that the 2002 requirements, which are much less restrictive on the right to vote, have been sufficient to prevent this type of fraud. These facts compel the conclusion that the Photo-ID Requirement is not "necessary to accomplish a compelling state interest."

The conclusion that the Photo-ID Requirement is not necessary to serve the State's asserted end should not be taken as an indication that the State's interest in combating voter fraud is insubstantial. Indeed, legislative efforts to combat the types of voter fraud and opportunities for voter fraud that persist in Missouri, such as absentee ballot fraud, voter intimidation, and inflated voter registration rolls, should be encouraged. Where the legislature places a heavy burden on the right to vote, however, the

Missouri Constitution requires that the burden be justified by a compelling interest and the statute be narrowly tailored or necessary to accomplish the statutory goals. The Photo-ID Requirement could only prevent a particular type of voter fraud that the record does not show is occurring in Missouri, yet it would place a heavy burden on the free exercise of the franchise for many citizens of this State.

Appellants also urge that the State has a compelling interest in combating perceptions of voter fraud. While the State does have an interest in combating those perceptions, where the fundamental rights of Missouri citizens are at stake, more than mere perception is required for their abridgement. Perceptions are malleable. While it is agreed here that the State's concern about the perception of fraud is real, if this Court were to approve the placement of severe restrictions on Missourians' fundamental rights owing to the mere perception of a problem in this instance, then the tactic of shaping public misperception could be used in the future as a mechanism for further burdening the right to vote or other fundamental rights. Moreover, the public could believe that the new law has prevented fraud in Missouri elections, whereas the type of fraud that has been shown to exist—fraud in registration and in absentee ballots—is not addressed by the Photo-ID Requirement and may still need resolution. The protection of our most precious state constitutional rights must not founder in the tumultuous tides of public misperception. ***

V. Conclusion

The Missouri Constitution provides a specific provision that enshrines the right to vote among certain enumerated constitutional rights of its citizens. SB 1014's Photo-ID Requirement creates a heavy burden on the right to vote and is not narrowly tailored to meet a compelling state interest, so it falls afoul of the Missouri Constitution's equal protection clause, Mo. Const. art I., sec. 2, and of Missourians' specific constitutional protection of the right to vote. Mo. Const. art. I, sec. 25. For these reasons, the trial court judgment is affirmed.

STEPHEN N. LIMBAUGH, JR., Judge, dissenting.

*** Although I would not reach the merits of the claim against the permanent provisions of the MVPA due to lack of ripeness, I cannot leave unchallenged the majority's incomplete recitation of the facts pertaining to the existence of voter fraud and the need for a photo ID system to combat that fraud. According to the majority, there has been no fraud in the polling places; thus no need to prevent it. But the evidence, in part, is this: In an investigative report issued after the 2000 presidential election by outgoing Secretary of State Rebecca McDowell Cook, and introduced in evidence in this case, "135 people who were not registered to vote were permitted to vote at a polling place without a court order and without apparent authorization from [an election] Board Official." A subsequent report from then Secretary of State Matt Blunt noted, as even the plaintiffs have acknowledged here, that 79 voters registered from vacant lots, 45 people voted twice, and 14 votes were cast by the "dead." Further, as set out in a pending complaint filed in federal court by the United States Department of Justice against the State of Missouri and cited to the trial court and this Court without objection, there is a stunningly large number of duplicate and ineligible voter registrations throughout the state.... Although the majority agrees that there is some evidence of voter fraud at the voter registration stage, they discount that evidence as if it had no connection with fraud at the polling place. But why else does voter registration fraud occur if not to vote persons fraudulently registered? And if, as in the DOJ report, there are more voters registered to vote than persons eligible to vote, the requirement to present a photo ID will at least eliminate those who attempt to vote in the place of others and those who attempt to vote more than once. It must be said, too, that even if there were no substantial evidence of existing voter impersonation fraud, legislatures are permitted to respond to the potential for such fraud, and they may do so "with foresight" rather than "reactively." In any event, as the Carter-Baker Commission recently concluded, "there is no doubt that [in-person voter fraud] occurs" and that such fraud "could offset the outcome of close elections."

For the foregoing reasons, I would reverse the judgment of the trial court.

Notes on the Right to Vote

1. As *Driscoll* indicates, the Supreme Court has not settled on an analytical framework for free and open election claims. Ms. Tokerud finds, "Oftentimes, the right to vote has simply been included in a laundry list of provisions cited to prove a particular point, such as the progressive nature of the Montana Constitution." For example, in *Finke v. State ex rel. McGrath* (Mont. 2003), the Supreme Court invalidated a law that only allowed "record owners of real property" in a proposed special building code jurisdiction to vote in an election establishing that jurisdiction. The court explained:

> ¶ 14 The election provisions of SB 242 are challenged on several constitutional grounds—as violations of Article II, §§ 4, 13 and 17 and Article V, § 11(3) of the Montana Constitution, and as violations of the Fifth and Fourteenth Amendments of the U.S. Constitution. Article II, § 4 of the Montana Constitution guarantees equal protection of the laws; Article II, § 13 guarantees the unencumbered right of suffrage; and Article II, § 17 guarantees due process of law. Article V, § 11(3) requires that each bill contain only one subject that is clearly expressed in its title. The Fifth and Fourteenth Amendments of the U.S. Constitution guarantee that no person shall be deprived of life, liberty or property without due process of law. Additionally, the Fourteenth Amendment guarantees all persons equal protection of the laws.
>
> ¶ 15 This Court has noted that "[b]ecause voting rights cases involve a fundamental political right, the [U.S.] Supreme Court generally evaluates state legislation apportioning representation and regulating voter qualifications under the strict scrutiny standard." ***

2. The United States Supreme Court has, sometimes reluctantly, applied broad equal protection principles on a sliding scale to regulate who can vote (vote denials, *see Harper v. Virginia Board of Elections* (1966)), how votes count (vote dilution, *see*

Reynolds v. Sims (1964)), and how votes are counted (vote administration, *see Bush v. Gore* (2000)). Assuming the distinct text of Article II, section 13 requires something more than lockstepping with federal (and state) equal protection analysis, what is required (or prohibited) in "free and open elections" under Article II, section 13? Factually, what must a plaintiff establish to demonstrate a burden on voting rights, and when there is a burden, what must the government establish to demonstrate a sufficient state interest? Legally, what is the appropriate level of scrutiny, and how does the Article IV, section 3 legislative duty to "insure the purity of elections and guard against abuses of the electoral process" factor into the analysis? In *Driscoll*, the Montana Supreme Court expressed a concern about additional burdens on Native American voters and voters in other groups. How should such a disparate impact weigh in the analysis? Would it be more or less problematic under a "free and open elections" analysis if a law had a disparate impact on a particular political party? If a law intentionally targeted a particular political party?

3. In 2005, Indiana enacted a voter identification law similar to the one at issue in *Weinschenk*. In a challenge brought under the Equal Protection Clause, the United States Supreme Court upheld the law in *Crawford v. Marion County Election Board* (2008):

> In sum, on the basis of the record that has been made in this litigation, we cannot conclude that the statute imposes "excessively burdensome requirements" on any class of voters. ***
>
> It is fair to infer that partisan considerations may have played a significant role in the decision to enact [the voter ID law]. If such considerations had provided the only justification for a photo identification requirement, we may also assume that [the law] would suffer the same fate as the poll tax at issue in *Harper*. But if a nondiscriminatory law is supported by valid neutral justifications, those justifications should not be disregarded simply because partisan interests may have provided one motivation for the votes of individual legislators. The state interests identified as justifications for [the law] are both neutral and sufficiently strong to require us to reject petitioners' facial attack on the statute. The application of the statute to the vast majority of Indiana voters is amply justified by the valid interest in protecting "the integrity and reliability of the electoral process."

Plaintiffs then turned to state court under the Indiana Constitution's guarantee that "All elections shall be free and equal." In *League of Women Voters of Indiana v. Rokita* (Ind. 2010), the state court held:

> The burdens occasioned by the Voter ID Law serve numerous substantial interests relating to the use of technology to modernize and to protect the integrity and reliability of the electoral process. We find that the requirements of the Indiana Voter ID Law, while enhancing the procedural burdens associated with the voting process, are not sufficiently unreasonable.

Because it is not alleged in the present case, we need not determine whether an as-applied challenge may be maintained if a claim were presented and proven that reasonable government assistance was not actually available to adequately relieve either the cost or hardship of obtaining photo ID. ***

We conclude that it is clear on the face of the complaint that the plaintiffs, as a matter of law, are not entitled to the relief sought. It is within the power of the legislature to require voters to identify themselves at the polls using a photo ID.

This result may contrast with a somewhat analogous case in our sister state of Missouri, *Weinschenk v. State* (Mo. 2006). In that case, particular voters sued to block enforcement of a 2006 Missouri statute requiring registered voters to present certain types of photo ID to vote. Ms. Kathleen Weinschenk and the others claimed that the new law required them and other voters—particularly those who are low-income, disabled, or elderly, and who do not have driver's licenses—to spend money to obtain the necessary documents such as birth certificates in order to obtain the requisite photo ID in violation of the Missouri Constitution's provisions relating to equal protection and the right to vote. The Missouri Supreme Court held that while "there is a compelling state interest in preventing voter fraud, the evidence supports the trial court's conclusion that the Photo-ID Requirement is not narrowly tailored to accomplish that purpose." Accordingly, it found the statute unconstitutional.

Not only do the constitutions of Indiana and Missouri vary, but also our statute differs from Missouri's—notably, a requisite photo ID can be obtained from the Indiana Bureau of Motor Vehicles at no cost, Ind.Code § 9-24-16-10—and we do not mean to suggest that the facts present in the Missouri case would necessarily warrant declaring the Indiana Voter ID Law unconstitutional. But we do not foreclose such as-applied claims. Here the plaintiffs seek a declaration that it is unconstitutional to require voters to identify themselves at the polls using a photo ID. This is relief to which the plaintiffs are not entitled. But in affirming the trial court, we do so without prejudice to future particularized as-applied claims.

We affirm the judgment of the trial court granting the appellee's motion to dismiss and rejecting the plaintiffs' claims that the Indiana Voter ID Law contravenes Article 2, Section 2 or Article 1, Section 23 of the Indiana Constitution.

B. Districting and Representation

Montana is the first state to regain its second seat in Congress, after losing it in the 1990 reapportionment cycle. This casts Montana's districting process under a national spotlight, and tests the state's distinct bipartisan commission process for drawing district lines without significant legislative involvement. In guaranteeing fair representation at both the state and federal level, state constitutions can provide both procedural protections (like a redistricting commission) and substantive protections (like a right of suffrage). Consider how effectively these procedural and substantive protections may withstand the strong partisan forces that seek to shape Montana's legislative districts, and whether it is possible or desirable to achieve a non-partisan or bi-partisan system of representation under a state constitution.

Caitlin Boland Aarab & Hon. Jim Regnier, *Mapping the Treasure State: What States Can Learn from Redistricting in Montana*

76 Mont. L. Rev. 257, 260–63, 268–70, 276–80 (2015)

III. MONTANA'S CHOICE: A COMMISSION

A. Montana Chooses a Commission

Before adopting the 1972 constitution, Montana left redistricting to the state legislature—a system that repeatedly failed. As a result, delegates to Montana's 1972 Constitutional Convention considered a new system. During a debate about the merits of forming a nonlegislative redistricting commission, Delegate Carman Skari of Chester summarized the legislature's track record:

> The Montana experience was that in 1965 the Legislature was unable to reapportion. About a dozen bills were introduced, and not a single one was accepted. Consequently, it fell to the federal District Court to reapportion the state. In 1971 the Legislature drew up one plan which was invalid because of a 37 percent [population] variance. After working through the regular session [and] one special session, the Legislature finally came up with the present plan in the second special session.

It was clear to the delegates that Montana needed a new system. ***

The Montana Constitution is the source of Montana's redistricting powers and objectives:

> The state shall be divided into as many districts as there are members of the house, and each district shall elect one representative. Each senate district shall be composed of two adjoining house districts, and shall elect one senator. Each district shall consist of compact and contiguous territory. All districts shall be as nearly equal in population as is practicable.

Redistricting is conducted by a Districting and Apportionment Commission that is comprised of five citizens and formed immediately preceding the release of decennial census data. The majority and minority leaders of the Montana House and Senate each choose one commissioner and those four commissioners then pick a fifth commissioner to serve as chairman of the Commission. If the four legislatively appointed commissioners fail to agree on a fifth commissioner, a majority of the Justices on the Montana Supreme Court appoint the chairman. None of the commissioners may be public officials. The Commission develops a plan for congressional and legislative districts based on the federal census data and constitutional redistricting criteria. The Commission submits its redistricting plan to the legislature for nonbinding recommendations and then files the plan with the Montana Secretary of State. The plan becomes law upon filing. ***

B. Developing Redistricting Criteria

The 2010 Commission, like all previous Commissions, needed to redistrict and reapportion Montana's legislative districts according to mandatory constitutional and discretionary criteria. There are four mandatory criteria for legislative districts: (1) population equality and maximum population deviation; (2) compact and contiguous districts; (3) protection of minority voting rights and compliance with the Voting Rights Act; and (4) race cannot be the predominant factor to which the traditional discretionary criteria are subordinated.

1. Constitutionally Mandated Criteria

The Montana Constitution is the source of the first two mandatory criteria: the districts must be "as nearly equal in population as is practicable" and must "consist of compact and contiguous territory." *** The second criterion, compact and contiguous territory, allows the Commission to use a "general appearance test"—that is, does the district in question look compact and contiguous or does it instead resemble the salamander-shaped district that led to the coining of the term "gerrymander"? *** The Voting Rights Act says a "political process leading to nomination or election in [a] State" may not be imposed or applied so that racial or language minorities "have less opportunity than other members of the electorate to participate in the political process and to elect representatives of their choice." *** The fourth criterion, that race cannot be the predominant factor to which the traditional discretionary criteria are subordinated, is a distillation of the United States Supreme Court's holding in *Shaw v. Reno* [(1993)].

2. Developing Discretionary Criteria through Public Process

As long as the four mandatory criteria are satisfied, Commissions have some flexibility in deciding which discretionary criteria to adopt. [The 2010] Commission officially adopted the following discretionary criteria: (1) follow the lines of political units; (2) follow geographic boundaries; and (3) keep communities of interest intact. ***

V. Montana's Successes

Redistricting in Montana following the 2010 census was quantitatively successful: it resulted in districts that are as equal as practicable and, with a population deviation of less than one percent in both House and Senate districts, it nearly achieved the "one person, one vote" ideal. But Montana had other, more normative successes that make it a model for other states seeking similar outcomes. In short, Montana set and achieved worthy goals: the 2010 redistricting process (1) was perceived as legitimate; (2) was bipartisan; and (3) resulted in competitive elections.

The delegates to Montana's Constitutional Convention preferred a commission approach to redistricting over a legislative approach largely for a single reason: the delegates wanted to limit the potential for boundaries drawn on the basis of political self-interest. The delegates intuitively understood that self-interest decreases legitimacy and that public perception of government institutions matters. Two separate mechanisms operate to ensure that public and not private interests motivate the redistricting commissioners. First, Montana's constitution requires that "none of [the members of the Districting and Apportionment Committee] may be public officials." And second, Montana is one of only two states that has a redistricting commission truly independent of the state legislature. Montana's redistricting plan becomes law upon filing with the Secretary of State and without legislative action. The success of these mechanisms in eliminating self-interested line-drawing is borne out anecdotally. The print media that followed the work of the 2010 Commission noted that the Commission responded to public input, successfully reached an initial 5-0 consensus on the House districts, and generally created a plan that did not advantage one party over another. "Longtime political hounds in Montana saw the process as much less rancorous than in decades past," the Helena Independent Record opined. And Bob Brown, former Montana Secretary of State and State Senate president wrote, "[t]he Republicans got as fair a deal as the Democrats." Montana's recent experience makes clear that a commission approach can achieve public legitimacy. States should consider prioritizing the public perception of their redistricting processes because the perceived legitimacy of governmental institutions has wide-ranging effects on many aspects of the democratic process.

The second goal of Montana's redistricting system—bipartisanship—recognizes that American politics is, and for the foreseeable future will be, a two-party system. A common criticism of the commission approach is that "[d]istricting by bipartisan commission. . . does not take the politics out of redistricting. Rather, it replaces the potential for partisan gerrymandering with the potential for bipartisan, or 'consensual' gerrymandering, in which mapmakers design safe seats for both parties' incumbents." The transcript of Montana's Constitutional Convention supports the view that commissions do not take the politics out of redistricting. The delegates themselves said they "recognized that redistricting and reapportionment has political repercussions" and as a result the Montana constitution "provides for bipartisanism in the method of selection of the first four members [of the commission]." But the delegates envisioned both bipartisanship and impartiality. It is the fifth member of the commission who "becomes the key vote." "[H]is selection by the other four members is to insure impartiality."

The combination of bipartisanship and impartiality is a better model for redistricting commissions than a nonpolitical or nonpartisan commission because the former accepts politics as inevitable and values fairness over equality. Fair is "just or appropriate in the circumstances," whereas equal is "being the same in quantity, size, degree, value." The Supreme Court's emphasis on the "one person, one vote" ideal implies that equality should be the goal of redistricting. But valuing fairness allows decision makers to consider relevant circumstances and to support one party over another if doing so is appropriate. Valuing equality, on the other hand, leads to mathematical formulas and an objectification of the subjective. Protecting "communities of interest" cannot be reduced to a formula and political consensus cannot be achieved by a computer. Valuing nonpartisanship over bipartisanship is an attempt to depoliticize an inherently political process, an attempt to turn a human process into an automated process. The 2010 Commission is proof that a bipartisan commission with a tie-breaking presiding officer can produce political consensus as well as fair results statewide—fair to citizens, fair to communities, and fair to political parties. States should strive for fairness and political consensus as well as constitutional equality and Montana is a model for all three.

The nearly universal distaste for gerrymandering is rooted in the public's conception of what a democratic election should be. Voters choose legislators; legislators do not choose voters. The political science literature is enlightening on this point:

> [W]hile political scientists have noted a significant decline in party identification, anti-incumbent sentiment is prevalent. Therefore, it may be less important, from the voter's perspective, whether he is represented by a Republican or Democrat than whether he is represented by a long-term incumbent in a safe seat or an official who knows he resides in a competitive district.

Redistricting commissions should strive to enable competitive elections within legislative districts because competitive districts are the opposite of the gerrymandered "safe seats."

The 2014 elections demonstrated that the new Montana legislative districts were competitive. Despite a sweeping tide of national Republican victories, Montana Democrats increased their numbers in the House by two seats and retained their Senate numbers. Ballotpedia, an interactive almanac of U.S. politics, has developed a "competitiveness index" by which it ranks the states according to the competitiveness of their legislative races. Their analysis ranked the 2014 Montana legislative elections as the fifth most competitive in the country. In 2012, Montana was ranked tenth and in 2010 it was ranked twelfth. Thus, in the first election conducted with the 2010 Commission's new districts, Montana increased its electoral competitiveness.

The 2014 elections put Montana's new legislative districts to the test and proved that a bipartisan redistricting process can produce competitive elections.

VI. Conclusion

In order for a redistricting plan to pass constitutional muster, it need only adhere to the Supreme Court's "one person, one vote" conception of political equality. But if states want a fuller conception of political equality to underlie their redistricting processes, a bipartisan redistricting commission like Montana's has much to recommend it. Montana nearly achieved the "one person, one vote" ideal, developed a bipartisan plan, and held competitive elections. But the goal of this article was not to persuade other states that Montana's approach to redistricting is objectively the best. After all, as Daniel Lowenstein and Jonathan Steinberg wrote in their oft-cited article on legislative districting, "there are no coherent public interest criteria for legislative districting independent of substantive conceptions of the public interest, disputes about which constitute the very stuff of politics." Rather, this article sought to illustrate Montana's redistricting goals, why the goals are worthy of pursuit, and Montana's recent success in achieving them. If other states share Montana's conception of the public interest, our redistricting model is worth exploring.

League of Women Voters v. Commonwealth

178 A.3d 737 (Pa. 2018)

JUSTICE TODD

It is a core principle of our republican form of government "that the voters should choose their representatives, not the other way around." In this case, Petitioners allege that the Pennsylvania Congressional Redistricting Act of 2011 (the "2011 Plan") does the latter, infringing upon that most central of democratic rights—the right to vote. Specifically, they contend that the 2011 Plan is an unconstitutional partisan gerrymander. While federal courts have, to date, been unable to settle on a workable standard by which to assess such claims under the federal Constitution, we find no such barriers under our great Pennsylvania charter. The people of this Commonwealth should never lose sight of the fact that, in its protection of essential rights, our founding document is the ancestor, not the offspring, of the federal Constitution. We conclude that, in this matter, it provides a constitutional standard, and remedy, even if the federal charter does not. Specifically, we hold that the 2011 Plan violates Article I, Section 5—the Free and Equal Elections Clause—of the Pennsylvania Constitution. ***

Pennsylvania's congressional districts are drawn by the state legislature as a regular statute, subject to veto by the Governor. While this process is dictated by federal law, it is delegated to the states. The federal Constitution's Elections Clause provides that "[t]he Times, Places and Manner of holding Elections for Senators and Representatives, shall be prescribed in each State by the Legislature thereof," unless Congress should "make or alter such Regulations." U.S. Const. art. I, § 4, cl. 1. Pursuant to the Elections Clause, Congress passed 2 U.S.C. § 2a, which provides that, following the decennial census and reapportionment, the Clerk of the House of Representatives shall "send to the executive of each State a certificate of the number of Representatives to which such State is entitled" and the state shall be redistricted "in the manner provided by the law thereof." 2 U.S.C. § 2a.

The 2011 Plan, Senate Bill 1249, was enacted on December 22, 2011, setting forth Pennsylvania's 18 congressional districts. In the November 2010 general election, voters elected Republicans to majorities in both houses of the General Assembly and elected a Republican, Tom Corbett, as Governor. Thus, in 2011, the Republican-led General Assembly was tasked with reconstituting Pennsylvania's congressional districts, reducing their number by one, and adjusting their borders in light of population changes reflected by the 2010 Census. ***

Of the 67 counties in Pennsylvania, the 2011 Plan divides a total of 28 counties between at least two different congressional districts: Montgomery County is divided among five congressional districts; Berks and Westmoreland Counties are each divided among four congressional districts; Allegheny, Chester, and Philadelphia Counties are each divided among three congressional districts; and Cambria, Carbon, Clarion, Crawford, Cumberland, Delaware, Erie, Greene, Huntingdon, Lackawanna, Lancaster, Lawrence, Lebanon, Luzerne, Monroe, Northampton, Northumberland, Perry, Somerset, Tioga, and Washington Counties are each split between two congressional districts. Additionally, whereas, prior to 1992, no municipalities in Pennsylvania were divided among multiple congressional districts, the 2011 Plan divides 68, or 2.66%, of Pennsylvania's municipalities between at least two Congressional districts. ***

D. Electoral History

*** In the three elections since the 2011 Plan was enacted, Democrats have won the same five districts, and Republicans have won the same 13 districts. In the 2012 election, Democrats won five congressional districts with an average of 76.4% of the vote in each, whereas Republicans won the remaining 13 congressional districts with an average 59.5% of the vote in each, and, notably, Democrats earned a statewide share of 50.8% of the vote, an average of 50.4% per district, with a median of 42.8% of the vote, whereas Republicans earned only a statewide share of 49.2% of the vote.

In the 2014 election, Democratic candidates again won five congressional races, with an average of 73.6% of the vote in each, whereas Republicans again won 13 congressional districts, with an average of 63.4% of the vote in each. In 2014, Democrats earned a 44.5% statewide vote share in contested races, whereas Republicans earned a 55.5% statewide vote share in contested races, with a 54.1% statewide share vote in the aggregate.

In the 2016 election, Democrats again won those same five congressional districts, with an average of 75.2% of the vote in each and a statewide vote share of 45.9%, whereas Republicans won those same 13 districts with an average of 61.8% in each and a statewide vote share of 54.1%. ***

V. Analysis

We begin our analysis of the challenge to the 2011 Plan with the presumption that the General Assembly did not intend to violate the Pennsylvania Constitution, "in part because there exists a judicial presumption that our sister branches take seriously their constitutional oaths." Accordingly, a statute is presumed to be valid, and will be declared unconstitutional only if the challenging parties carry the heavy burden of proof that the enactment "clearly, palpably, and plainly violates the Constitution." Upon review, and for the following reasons, we are persuaded by Petitioners and the other presentations before us that the 2011 Plan clearly, plainly, and palpably violates the Free and Equal Elections Clause of our Constitution.

A. Free and Equal Elections Clause

Pennsylvania's Constitution, when adopted in 1776, was widely viewed as "the most radically democratic of all the early state constitutions." Indeed, our Constitution, which was adopted over a full decade before the United States Constitution, served as the foundation—the template—for the federal charter. Our autonomous state Constitution, rather than a "reaction" to federal constitutional jurisprudence, stands as a self-contained and self-governing body of constitutional law, and acts as a wholly independent protector of the rights of the citizens of our Commonwealth. *** Moreover, the Free and Equal Elections Clause has no federal counterpart ***

1. Language

Article I, Section 5 of the Pennsylvania Constitution, entitled "Elections," is contained within the Pennsylvania Constitution's "Declaration of Rights," which, as noted above, is an enumeration of the fundamental individual human rights possessed by the people of this Commonwealth that are specifically exempted from the powers of Commonwealth government to diminish. As noted above, this section provides:

> Elections shall be free and equal; and no power, civil or military, shall at any time interfere to prevent the free exercise of the right of suffrage.

Pa. Const. art. I, § 5. This clause first appeared, albeit in different form, in our Commonwealth's first organic charter of governance adopted in 1776, 11 years before the United States Constitution was adopted. By contrast, the United States Constitution—which furnishes no explicit protections for an individual's electoral rights, nor sets any minimum standards for a state's conduct of the electoral process—does not contain, nor has it ever contained, an analogous provision.

The broad text of the first clause of this provision mandates clearly and unambiguously, and in the broadest possible terms, that all elections conducted in this Commonwealth must be "free and equal." In accordance with the plain and expansive sweep of the words "free and equal," we view them as indicative of the framers' intent that all aspects of the electoral process, to the greatest degree possible, be kept open and unrestricted to the voters of our Commonwealth, and, also, conducted in a manner which guarantees, to the greatest degree possible, a voter's right to equal participation in the electoral process for the selection of his or her representatives in government. Thus, Article I, Section 5 guarantees our citizens an equal right, on par with every other citizen, to elect their representatives. Stated another way, the actual and plain language of Section 5 mandates that all voters have an equal opportunity to translate their votes into representation. This interpretation is consistent with both the historical reasons for the inclusion of this provision in our Commonwealth's Constitution and the meaning we have ascribed to it through our case law.

2. History

Our Commonwealth's centuries-old and unique history has influenced the evolution of the text of the Free and Equal Elections Clause, as well as our Court's interpretation of that provision. Although the general character of our Commonwealth during the colonial era was reflective of the fundamental desire of Pennsylvania's founder, William Penn, that it be a haven of tolerance and non-discrimination for adherents of various religious beliefs, the manner in which the colony was governed from its inception nevertheless excluded certain groups from participation in its official government. Roman Catholics, for example, could not hold office in the colony from 1693 to 1776, due to the requirement in the Charter of Privileges, a precursor to our Constitution in which Penn set forth the manner of governance for the colony, that every candidate for office was required to swear "that he did not believe in the doctrine of transubstantiation, that he regarded the invocation of the Virgin Mary and the saints as superstitious and the Popish Mass as idolatrous." Thus, although successive waves of European immigrants were attracted to the Pennsylvania colony after its founding by the promise of religious tolerance, not every group which settled in Pennsylvania was afforded the equal legal right to participate in its governance. Related thereto, the colony became divided over time by the geographical areas in which these immigrants settled, as well as their religious beliefs. ***

These various groups began to align themselves into nascent political factions which, by the 1760s, exerted varying degrees of control over the colonial government.... Although these political alliances remained intact until the early 1770s, they began to unravel with the tensions occasioned by the general colonial revulsion at the heavy-handed tactics of the British Crown—e.g., the imposition of the Stamp Act and the use of writs of assistance to enforce the Revenue Act—which ultimately culminated in the Revolutionary War. [B]y the early 1700s, colonial government remained dominated by the counties of Philadelphia, Chester, and Bucks, even though they had been eclipsed in population by the western regions of the colony and the City of Philadelphia. Although, in an effort to placate these groups, the assembly granted a concession by giving the west 28 seats in the assembly, while retaining 30 for the east, this did little to mollify the fervor of these groups for further reform.

The opportunity for such reform arose with the formal adoption of the Declaration of Independence by the Continental Congress in 1776. This same Congress also adopted a resolution suggesting that the colonies adopt constitutions in the event that they had "no government sufficient to the exigencies of their affairs." For the Pennsylvania colony, this was the catalyst which enabled the reformers from the western regions and the City of Philadelphia, who were now known as "the radicals," to achieve the calling of a constitutional convention. This convention, which was presided over by Benjamin Franklin, who also was serving at the same time in the Continental Congress, adopted our Commonwealth's Constitution of 1776, which, for its time, was considered very forward thinking. Many of its provisions reflected the prevailing sentiment of the radical delegates from the frontier and the City of Philadelphia for a devolution of centralized political power from the hands of a very few, in order to form a government more directly responsive to the needs of the people. Thus, it adopted a unicameral legislature on the belief that bicameral legislatures with one house dominated by elites who were elected on the basis of monetary or property qualifications would thwart the will of the people, as expressed through their representatives in the lower chamber, whose members were elected by those whose right of suffrage was not similarly constrained. Even though concerned with foundational matters such as the structure of government, the delegates, in response to their experience of being excluded from participation in the colonial government, included two explicit provisions to establish protections of the right of the people to fair and equal representation in the governance of their affairs.

The first requirement was that representation be proportional to population and that reapportionment of legislative seats be done every seven years. As noted by one commentator, this was the direct product of the personal history of the majority of the delegates, and the requirement of equal representation was, thus, intended to protect future individuals against the exclusion from the legislative process "by persons who gained power and intended to keep it."

Concomitant with this requirement, the delegates also deliberately incorporated into that Constitution the Declaration of Rights—which they considered to be an integral part of its framework—and therein the first version of Article I, Section 5, which declared that "all elections ought to be free; and that all free men having a sufficient evident common interest with, and attachment to the community, have a right to elect officers, or to be elected into office." Pa. Const. of 1776, art. I, § VII.

This section reflected the delegates' desire to secure access to the election process by all people with an interest in the communities in which they lived—universal suffrage—by prohibiting exclusion from the election process of those without property or financial means. It, thus, established a critical "leveling" protection in an effort to establish the uniform right of the people of this Commonwealth to select their representatives in government. It sought to ensure that this right of the people would forever remain equal no matter their financial situation or social class.

Opposition to the new Constitution arose almost immediately, driven chiefly by the Quakers, Episcopalians, and Germans who had not fought in the Revolution, and the commercial interests in the City of Philadelphia. [P]opular dissatisfaction with the chaotic state of the Commonwealth's governance grew to such a degree that the Republicans gained control of the General Assembly in 1788, and, in November 1789, they passed legislation to call a constitutional convention.... Their work yielded a Constitution which, while making the structural reforms to the Commonwealth's government favored by the Republicans, such as the adoption of a bicameral legislature and the creation of the office of chief executive with veto power over legislation, also preserved the principle cherished most by the Constitutionalists—namely, popular elections in which the people's right to elect their representatives in government would be equally available to all, and would, hereinafter, not be intentionally diminished by laws that discriminated against a voter based on his social or economic status, geography of his residence, or his religious and political beliefs.

Consequently, popular election of representatives was maintained by the new Constitution, and applicable in all elections for both houses of the bicameral legislature. Importantly, consistent with the evident desire of the delegates to neutralize the factors which had formerly given rise to such rancorous division amongst the people in the selection of their representatives, the language of Article I, Section 5 was revised to remove all prior ambiguous qualifying language. In its place, the delegates adopted the present language of the first clause of Article I, Section 5, which has remained unchanged to this day by the people of this Commonwealth. It states, simply and plainly, that "elections shall be free and equal."

When viewed against the backdrop of the intense and seemingly unending regional, ideological, and sectarian strife detailed above, which bitterly divided the people of various regions of our state, this provision must be understood then as a salutary effort by the learned delegates to the 1790 convention to end, once and for all, the primary cause of popular dissatisfaction which undermined the governance of Pennsylvania: namely, the dilution of the right of the people of this Commonwealth to select representatives to govern their affairs based on considerations of the region of the state in which they lived, and the religious and political beliefs to which they adhered. These historical motivations of the framers have undergirded our Court's interpretation of the Free and Equal Elections Clause throughout the years since its inclusion in our Constitution.

3. Pennsylvania Case Law

As one noted commentator on the Pennsylvania Constitution, Charles Buckalew, himself a delegate to the 1873 Constitutional Convention, opined, given the aforementioned history, the words "free and equal" as used in Article I, Section 5 have a broad and wide sweep:

> They strike not only at privacy and partiality in popular elections, but also at corruption, compulsion, and other undue influences by which elections may be assailed; at all regulations of law which shall impair the right of suffrage rather than facilitate or reasonably direct the manner of its exercise, and at all its limitations, unproclaimed by the Constitution, upon the eligibility of the electors for office. And they exclude not only all invidious discriminations between individual electors, or classes of electors, but also between different sections or places in the State.

Our Court has ascribed the same expansive meaning to the terms "free and equal" in Article I, Section 5. Although our Court has infrequently relied on this provision to strike down acts of the legislature pertaining to the conduct of elections, the qualifications of voters to participate therein, or the creation of electoral districts, our view as to what constraints Article I, Section 5 places on the legislature in these areas has been consistent over the years. Indeed, nearly 150 years ago, in considering a challenge to an act of the legislature establishing eligibility qualifications for electors to vote in all elections held in Philadelphia, and specifying the manner in which those elections are to be conducted, we recognized that, while our Constitution gives to the General Assembly the power to promulgate laws governing elections, those enactments are nonetheless subject to the requirements of the Free and Equal Elections Clause of our Constitution, and, hence, may be invalidated by our Court "in a case of plain, palpable and clear abuse of the power which actually infringes the rights of the electors."

In answering the question of how elections must be made equal, we stated: "Clearly by laws which shall arrange all the qualified electors into suitable districts, and make their votes equally potent in the election; so that some shall not have more votes than others, and that all shall have an equal share in filling the offices of the Commonwealth." Thus, with this decision, our Court established that any legislative scheme which has the effect of impermissibly diluting the potency of an individual's vote for candidates for elective office relative to that of other voters will violate the guarantee of "free and equal" elections afforded by Article I, Section 5. This interpretation is wholly consonant with the intent of the framers of the 1790 Constitution to ensure that each voter will have an equally effective power to select the representative of his or her choice, free from any discrimination on the basis of his or her particular beliefs or views. ***

4. Other Considerations

In addition to the occasion for the adoption of the Free and Equal Elections Clause, the circumstances in which the provision was adopted, the mischief to be remedied, and the object to be obtained, as described above, the consequences of a particular interpretation are also relevant in our analysis. Specifically, partisan gerrymandering dilutes the votes of those who in prior elections voted for the party not in power to give the party in power a lasting electoral advantage. By placing voters preferring one party's candidates in districts where their votes are wasted on candidates likely to lose (cracking), or by placing such voters in districts where their votes are cast for candidates destined to win (packing), the non-favored party's votes are diluted. It is axiomatic that a diluted vote is not an equal vote, as all voters do not have an equal opportunity to translate their votes into representation. This is the antithesis of a healthy representative democracy. Indeed, for our form of government to operate as intended, each and every Pennsylvania voter must have the same free and equal opportunity to select his or her representatives. As our foregoing discussion has illustrated, our Commonwealth's commitment to neutralizing factors which unfairly impede or dilute individuals' rights to select their representatives was borne of our forebears' bitter personal experience suffering the pernicious effects resulting from previous electoral schemes that sanctioned such discrimination. Furthermore, adoption of a broad interpretation guards against the risk of unfairly rendering votes nugatory, artificially entrenching representative power, and discouraging voters from participating in the electoral process because they have come to believe that the power of their individual vote has been diminished to the point that it "does not count." A broad and robust interpretation of Article I, Section 5 serves as a bulwark against the adverse consequences of partisan gerrymandering.

5. Conclusion

The above analysis of the Free and Equal Elections Clause—its plain language, its history, the occasion for the provision and the circumstances in which it was adopted, the case law interpreting this clause, and consideration of the consequences of our interpretation—leads us to conclude the Clause should be given the broadest interpretation, one which governs all aspects of the electoral process, and which provides the people of this Commonwealth an equally effective power to select the representative of his or her choice, and bars the dilution of the people's power to do so.

B. Measurement of Compliance with Article I, Section 5

We turn now to the question of what measures should be utilized to assess a dilution claim under the Free and Equal Elections Clause of the Pennsylvania Constitution. Neither Article 1, Section 5, nor any other provision of our Constitution, articulates explicit standards which are to be used in the creation of congressional districts. However, since the inclusion of the Free and Equal Elections Clause in our Constitution in 1790, certain neutral criteria have, as a general matter, been traditionally utilized to guide the formation of our Commonwealth's legislative districts in order to prevent the dilution of an individual's vote for a representative in the General Assembly. These standards place the greatest emphasis on creating representational districts that both maintain the geographical and social cohesion of the communities in which people live and conduct the majority of their day-to-day affairs, and accord equal weight to the votes of residents in each of the various districts in determining the ultimate composition of the state legislature.

Significantly, the framers of the 1790 constitution who authored the Free and Equal Elections Clause also included a mandatory requirement therein for the legislature's formation of state senatorial districts covering multiple counties, namely that the counties must adjoin one another. Also, the architects of that charter expressly prohibited the division of any county of the Commonwealth, or the City of Philadelphia, in the formation of such districts. Pa. Const. of 1776, § 7. Thus, as preventing the dilution of an individual's vote was of paramount concern to that august group, it is evident that they considered maintaining the geographical contiguity of political subdivisions, and barring the splitting thereof in the process of creating legislative districts, to afford important safeguards against that pernicious prospect.

In the eight-plus decades after the 1790 Constitution became our Commonwealth's fundamental plan of governance, many problems arose from the corruption of the political process by well-heeled special interest groups who rendered our representative democracy deeply dysfunctional by weakening the power of an individual's vote through, inter alia, their selection, and financial backing in the electoral process, of representatives who exclusively served their narrow interests and not those of the people as a whole. One of the methods by which the electoral process was manipulated by these interest groups to attain those objectives was the practice of gerrymandering, popular revulsion of which became one of the driving factors behind the populace's demand for the calling of the 1873 Constitutional Convention.

As noted by an eminent authority on Pennsylvania constitutional law, by the time of that convention, gerrymandering was regarded as "one of the most flagrant evils and scandals of the time, involving notorious wrong to the people and open disgrace to republican institutions." Although the delegates to that convention did not completely eliminate this practice through the charter of governance which they adopted, and which the voters subsequently approved, they nevertheless included significant protections against its occurrence through the explicit adoption of certain requirements which all state legislative districts were, thereafter, required to meet: (1) the population of such districts must be equal, to the extent possible; (2) the district that is created must be comprised of compact and contiguous geographical territory; and (3) the district respects the boundaries of existing political subdivisions contained therein, such that the district divides as few of those subdivisions as possible. Pa. Const. of 1874, art. 2, § 16. Given the great concern of the delegates over the practice of gerrymandering occasioned by their recognition of the corrosive effects on our entire democratic process through the deliberate dilution of our citizenry's individual votes, the focus on these neutral factors must be viewed, then, as part of a broader effort by the delegates to that convention to establish "the best methods of representation to secure a just expression of the popular will." Consequently, these factors have broader applicability beyond setting standards for the drawing of electoral districts for state legislative office.

The utility of these requirements to prevent vote dilution through gerrymandering retains continuing vitality, as evidenced by our present Constitution, adopted in 1968. In that charter, these basic requirements for the creation of senatorial districts were not only retained, but, indeed, were expanded by the voters to govern the establishment of election districts for the selection of their representatives in the state House of Representatives. Pa. Const., art. 2, § 16.

Because these factors are deeply rooted in the organic law of our Commonwealth, and continue to be the foundational requirements which state legislative districts must meet under the Pennsylvania Constitution, we find these neutral benchmarks to be particularly suitable as a measure in assessing whether a congressional districting plan dilutes the potency of an individual's ability to select the congressional representative of his or her choice, and thereby violates the Free and Equal Elections

Clause. In our judgment, they are wholly consistent with the overarching intent of the framers of the 1790 Constitution that an individual's electoral power not be diminished through any law which discriminatorily dilutes the power of his or her vote, and, thus, they are a measure by which to assess whether the guarantee to our citizenry of "free and equal" elections promised by Article, I Section 5 in the selection of their congressional representative has been violated. Because the character of these factors is fundamentally impartial in nature, their utilization reduces the likelihood of the creation of congressional districts which confer on any voter an unequal advantage by giving his or her vote greater weight in the selection of a congressional representative as prohibited by Article I, Section 5. Thus, use of these objective factors substantially reduces the risk that a voter in a particular congressional district will unfairly suffer the dilution of the power of his or her vote.

Moreover, rather than impermissibly lessening the power of an individual's vote based on the geographical area in which the individual resides—which, as explained above, Article I, Section 5 also prohibits—the use of compactness, contiguity, and the maintenance of the integrity of the boundaries of political subdivisions maintains the strength of an individual's vote in electing a congressional representative. When an individual is grouped with other members of his or her community in a congressional district for purposes of voting, the commonality of the interests shared with the other voters in the community increases the ability of the individual to elect a congressional representative for the district who reflects his or her personal preferences. This approach inures to no political party's benefit or detriment. It simply achieves the constitutional goal of fair and equal elections for all of our Commonwealth's voters. Finally, these standards also comport with the minimum requirements for congressional districts guaranteed by the United States Constitution, as interpreted by the United States Supreme Court.

In sum, we conclude that the evidence detailed above and the remaining evidence of the record as a whole demonstrates that Petitioners have established that the 2011 Plan subordinates the traditional redistricting criteria in service of achieving unfair partisan advantage, and, thus, violates the Free and Equal Elections Clause of the Pennsylvania Constitution. Such a plan, aimed at achieving unfair partisan gain, undermines voters' ability to exercise their right to vote in free and "equal" elections if the term is to be interpreted in any credible way.

An election corrupted by extensive, sophisticated gerrymandering and partisan dilution of votes is not "free and equal." In such circumstances, a "power, civil or military," to wit, the General Assembly, has in fact "interfere[d] to prevent the free exercise of the right of suffrage." Pa. Const. art. 1, § 5.

VI. Remedy

Having set forth why the 2011 Plan is constitutionally infirm, we turn to our January 22, 2018 Order which directed a remedy for the illegal plan. Therein, our Court initially invited our sister branches—the legislative and executive branches—to take action, through the enactment of a remedial congressional districting plan; however, recognizing the possibility that the legislature and executive would be unwilling or unable to act, we indicated in our Order that, in that eventuality, we would fashion a judicial remedial plan. ***

[I]t is beyond peradventure that it is the legislature, in the first instance, that is primarily charged with the task of reapportionment. However, the Pennsylvania Constitution, statutory law, our Court's decisions, federal precedent, and case law from our sister states, all serve as a bedrock foundation on which stands the authority of the state judiciary to formulate a valid redistricting plan when necessary. ***

Concurring and Dissenting Opinion [of] Justice BAER

. . . I continue to join the Majority's conclusion that the Pennsylvania Congressional Redistricting Act of 2011 (2011 Plan) violates the Pennsylvania Constitution, as originally set forth in the first sentence of Paragraph First of the Court's January 22nd Order. Moreover, I concur with the Majority's erudite explication of Article I, Section 5 of the Pennsylvania Constitution (the Free and Equal Election Clause), Pa. Const. art. I, § 5, and the Court's ultimate conclusion that the 2011 Plan violates the rights protected by that provision. ***

> Elections shall be free and equal; and no power, civil or military, shall at any time interfere to prevent the free exercise of the right of suffrage.

Pa. Const. art. I, § 5. This language obviously does not address the size or shape of districts. Moreover, there is nothing inherent in a compact or contiguous district that insures a free and equal election, as is evidenced by claims of unconstitutional gerrymandering raised in challenges to redistricting plans of other states which employ maps created in compliance with the traditional districting criteria of compact and contiguous territory, equality of population, and minimization of municipal line division.

Accordingly, I am unwilling to engraft into the Pennsylvania Constitution criteria for the drawing of congressional districts when the framers chose not to include such provisions despite unquestionably being aware of both the General Assembly's responsibility for congressional redistricting and the dangers of gerrymandering. It is not this Court's role to instruct the Legislature as to the "manner of holding elections," including the relative weight of districting criteria.

I nonetheless agree with the Majority's holding that the Free and Equal Election Clause protects against the dilution of votes because "a diluted vote is not an equal vote." . . . I conclude that the Free and Equal Clause is violated by the use of extreme partisan gerrymandering by the Legislature and Governor because it constitutes unconstitutional interference by a civil power "to prevent the free exercise of the right to suffrage" through vote dilution. Pa. Const. art. I, § 5. ***

Dissenting Opinion [of] Chief Justice SAYLOR

In summary, I believe that: the present exercise of extraordinary jurisdiction was improvident; this Court's review would benefit from anticipated guidance from the

Supreme Court of the United States; awaiting such guidance is particularly appropriate given the delay, until 2017, of Petitioners' challenge to a 2011 redistricting plan; and the appropriate litmus for judicial review of redistricting should take into account the inherently political character of the work of the General Assembly, to which the task of redistricting has been assigned by the United States Constitution.

Further, I respectfully disagree with the majority opinion in many other material respects. Initially, I certainly have no cause to differ with the broader strokes comprising the bulk of the opinion, including the historical accounts and the confirmation of "a voter's right to equal protection in the electoral process for the selection of his or her representatives in government," Majority Opinion, which is a right that is also recognized under federal constitutional law. *See Vieth v. Jubelirer* (2004) (plurality) (expressing agreement with a dissenting Justice that severe partisan gerrymanders are inconsistent with democratic principles and may violate the Equal Protection Clause, albeit maintaining that the judiciary is incapable of devising manageable standards for the assessments of degree).

The Supreme Court of the United States has also emphasized, however, that redistricting is committed to the political branch and is inherently political. In this regard, the application of constitutional principles governing individual rights in the context of legislative redistricting is sui generis, given the inevitable tension between the power allocated to the Legislature to make political choices and the individual rights of voters relative to the exercise of the franchise. Moreover, in terms of the individual-rights component—and contrary to the majority's perspective—there is no right to an "equally effective power" of voters in elections.

Given the political character of redistricting, the pervading question relating to partisan considerations, with which courts have had great difficulty, is "how much is too much?" Rather than engaging this question in these conventional terms, the majority proceeds to overlay factors delineated by the Pennsylvania Constitution in relation to state-level reapportionment upon congressional redistricting. Since these considerations are not constitutional commands applicable to congressional redistricting, the majority's approach amounts to a non-textual, judicial imposition of a prophylactic rule. ***

From my point of view, the majority opinion fails to sufficiently account for the fundamental character of redistricting, its allocation under the United States Constitution to the political branch, and the many drawbacks of constitutionalizing a non-textual judicial rule. For my own part, I would abide by the Court's previous determination, in the redistricting setting, that the Free and Equal Elections Clause provides no greater protection than the state charter's Equal Protection Clauses, which have been deemed coterminous with the protection provided by the United States Constitution. I find that the majority's focus on a limited range of traditional districting factors allocates too much discretion to the judiciary to discern violations in the absence of proof of intentional discrimination. Instead, I believe that, under the state and federal charters, the discretion belongs to the Legislature, which should be accorded appropriate deference and comity, as reflected in the majority's initial articulation of the presumption of constitutionality and the heavy burden borne by challengers.

Justice MUNDY joins this dissenting opinion.

Dissenting Opinion [of] Justice MUNDY

I respectfully dissent. Today the Majority announces that the Pennsylvania Congressional Redistricting Act of 2011 clearly, plainly and palpably violates the Pennsylvania Constitution on the basis of the Free and Equal Elections Clause. See generally Pa. Const. art. I, § 5. The claim here is not that voters were unable to cast their vote, but rather that the power of the individual voters was diluted, thus preventing them from electing candidates of their choice. The Majority concedes, "[n]either Article 1, Section 5, nor any other provision of our Constitution, articulates explicit standards which are to be used in the creation of congressional districts." Nevertheless, the Majority holds that "certain neutral criteria" are to be utilized in drawing congressional districts in this Commonwealth. ***

Recognizing that the Pennsylvania Constitution does not articulate explicit standards to be used in the creation of congressional districts, the Majority fashions a three part test: "(1) the population of such districts must be equal, to the extent possible; (2) the district that is created must be comprised of compact and contiguous geographical territory, and (3) the district respects the boundaries of existing political subdivisions contained therein, such that the district divides as few of those subdivisions as possible." These vague judicially-created "neutral criteria" are now the guideposts against which all future congressional redistricting maps will be evaluated, with this Court as the final arbiter of what constitutes too partisan an influence. ***

... I also have grave concerns about the Majority's remedy. I agree with the Majority that we have the authority to direct the legislative and executive branches of our government to draw new maps to remedy any violation of law. However, I am troubled by the Majority's decision to strike down the 2011 congressional map on the eve of the 2018 midterm election. Particularly its disregard for precedent which supports deferring redistricting until after the 2018 election. I further share the concerns expressed by the dissenting opinion of Chief Justice Saylor and the dissenting portion of the concurring and dissenting opinion of Justice Baer that this is a political process the General Assembly should be afforded the full opportunity and adequate time to address. I write further only to address the remedy suggested by the Majority of bestowing the task of drawing a new Congressional map onto itself in the face of a clear legislative alternative. ***

The Elections Clause of the Federal Constitution states that "[t]he Times, Places and Manner of holding Elections for Senators and Representatives, shall be prescribed in each State by the Legislature thereof; but the Congress may at any time by Law make or alter such Regulations, except as to the Places of chusing Senators." U.S. Const. art I, § 4, cl. 1. The Elections Clause at its core, grants the authority to draw a state's congressional districts to the state legislatures, Congress, or an independent redistricting commission. As the Supreme Court of the United States recognized, "redistricting is a legislative function, to be performed in accordance with the State's prescriptions for lawmaking, which may include the referendum and the Governor's veto." It is a truism that this Court possesses neither legislative function, nor authority. While this Court is certainly the final arbiter of the meaning of the Pennsylvania Constitution, it may not remedy any violations of our state charter, in a manner, that the Federal Constitution prohibits. After all, federal law is supreme. U.S. Const. art. VI, cl. 2. ***

For the foregoing reasons, I respectfully dissent.

Notes on Districting and Representation

1. The Pennsylvania Supreme Court broke with its own precedent to set standards for the drawing of congressional districts under the "free and equal" elections clause. How does the court use history to justify its result? Is the fascinating history of the early Pennsylvania Constitutions (themselves grandparents of many state constitutions, including Montana's) pertinent to the interpretation of the state's current Constitution, ratified in 1968?

2. Among the dissenters' concerns about the court's proposed remedy, Justice Mundy expresses a concern that the court's order violates the Elections Clause, which gives "the Legislature" of states power to determine "[t]he Times, Places and Manner of holding Elections for Senators and Representatives." Some defendants petitioned the U.S. Supreme Court for a writ of certiorari on the following questions:

> 1. Whether the Pennsylvania Constitution's substantive provisions and whatever interpretation Pennsylvania courts afford them, however atextual, can restrict time, place, and manner rules Pennsylvania's lawmakers have passed to govern congressional elections pursuant to Article I, § 4, cl. 1, of the United States Constitution, known as the "Elections Clause."
>
> 2. Whether the Pennsylvania Supreme Court, which has no lawmaking authority, may, consistent with the Elections Clause, adopt a redistricting plan as a remedy solely for state-law violations and, if so, whether it may, consistent with the Elections Clause, craft redistricting policy wholesale in creating that remedy.

The Supreme Court denied the petition without comment.

Similar claims arose before and after the 2020 presidential election under the Electors Clause, Art. II, § 1, which provides in part, "Each State shall appoint, in such Manner as the Legislature thereof may direct, a Number of Electors...." *See, e.g., Trump for President v. Hertz* (D. Mont. 2020) (rejecting Electors Clause challenge to

Governor's authorization of a statewide mail ballot election under emergency powers statute); *Pennsylvania Democratic Party v. Boockvar* (Pa. 2020) (extending statutory deadline for mail ballots and rejecting Electors Clause challenge), *cert. denied* (2021). In the latter case, Justices Thomas, Alito, and Gorsuch dissented from the denial of certiorari, asking the Supreme Court to decide "whether the Elections or Electors Clauses of the United States Constitution, Art. I, § 4, cl. 1; Art. II, § 1, cl. 2, are violated when a state court holds that a state constitutional provision overrides a state statute governing the manner in which a federal election is to be conducted," and suggesting they would answer the question in the affirmative. *See Republican Party of Pennsylvania v. Degraffenreid* (2021); *but see* Vikram David Amar & Akhil Reed Amar, *Eradicating* Bush-*League Arguments Root and Branch: The Article II Independent-State-Legislature Notion and Related Rubbish*, 2021 SUP. CT. REV. (Forthcoming 2022) (rejecting the claim on originalist, state practice, and federal precedential grounds).

Part III

Rights

Chapter 9

Introduction to the Declaration of Rights

Article II, Section 1. Popular sovereignty. All political power is vested in and derived from the people. All government of right originates with the people, is founded upon their will only, and is instituted solely for the good of the whole.

Identical to 1889 constitution. Expresses the philosophy that government is founded on the will of the people and is for their good.

Article II, Section 2. Self-government. The people have the exclusive right of governing themselves as a free, sovereign, and independent state. They may alter or abolish the constitution and form of government whenever they deem it necessary.

No change except in grammar. Gives Montanans the right to govern themselves and to determine their form of government.

Article II, Section 3. Inalienable rights. All persons are born free and have certain inalienable rights. They include the right to a clean and healthful environment and the rights of pursuing life's basic necessities, enjoying and defending their lives and liberties, acquiring, possessing and protecting property, and seeking their safety, health and happiness in all lawful ways. In enjoying these rights, all persons recognize corresponding responsibilities.

Revises 1889 constitution by adding three rights relating to environment, basic necessities, and health. The last sentence is also new and provides that in accepting rights people have obligations.

State constitutions are a font of rights for American constitutional law. The first American bills of rights originated in state constitutions and served as a source for the federal Constitution and subsequent state constitutions. State constitutional guarantees enumerate many more rights than the federal Constitution. Montana's protections for human dignity, privacy, open government, and a clean and healthful environment stand out as distinctive but not unique expressions of modern rights. Although several other state constitutions contain similar guarantees that the federal Constitution lacks, Montana's courts demonstrate local pride in these expressions of arguably universal principles. As a doctrinal matter, however, lockstepping with federal constitutional law is common, and conversation with other states providing similar guarantees is rare, for now.

It is difficult for judges, lawyers, and law students alike to escape the pervasive rights discourse in American constitutional law. This is a discourse about federal constitutional rights, drafted by famous men with fraught backgrounds at auspicious historical moments in terms of "due process," "equal protection," and "the freedom of speech." More than this, it is framed by a sturdy yet relatively recent doctrine of fundamental rights guarded by tiered judicial scrutiny—enforced by life-tenured judges—ranging from the presumptively fatal strict scrutiny to the presumptively toothless rational basis test. Despite the ancient roots and contemporary applications of Montana's Declaration of Rights, its courts have fit state constitutional rights into this conventional federal model of scrutiny tiered around fundamental rights, sometimes uneasily, and even when the Montana right has no peer in the federal Constitution.

A. The Structure of Constitutional Rights

The Declaration of Rights begins with three apparent abstractions about popular sovereignty, self-government, and inalienable rights. Here, the Montana Constitution most resembles its early American ancestors, and most distinguishes itself from the federal constitutional form. In historical context, these first three sections describe the fundamental terms of the social contract and the obligations of government to protect natural rights. It reflects conventional constitutional law in its purest form, while adhering to the Enabling Act's requirements that the state constitution "not be repugnant to the constitution of the United States *and* the principles of the Declaration of Independence." Yet a closer examination reveals striking references to "a clean and healthful environment" and "pursuing life's basic necessities," both additions from the 1970s to a text rooted in the 1770s. The beginning of the Montana Constitution is where courts have struggled most to realize the text's meaning.

Thomas J. Bourguignon, *The Poacher, the Sovereign Citizen, the Moonlighter, and the Denturists: A Practical Guide to Inalienable Rights in Montana*

77 MONT. L. REV. 5, 9–14 (2016)

*** A contradiction lies at the heart of any inalienable rights provision in a written constitution. Inalienable rights are natural rights that are inherent and exist prior to, and separate from, any written laws. According to Alexander Hamilton's theory, inalienable rights do not need to be found "among old parchments, or musty records" because they are written "by the hand of divinity itself." However, the more modern, positivist theory is that there are no universal, natural laws—or as Justice Holmes said, "you can not argue a man into liking a glass of beer. . . ."

Most state constitutions include a section on inalienable rights; however, the inclusion of a list of inalienable rights appears to be self-defeating. For instance, why codify rights that exist outside of any attempt at codifying law? Isn't there a risk of leaving some of them out? Why not just state in the constitution, "All humans have inalienable rights," and allow the courts to define what those rights are?

And what happens when a state chooses to draft its inalienable rights provision as Montana has: with a fairly long and specific list of enumerated inalienable rights? Is Article II, section 3 of the Montana Constitution a recognition of universal and unchangeable tenets of natural law, as stated by Hamilton; or is it positive law, as Justice Holmes would argue, enacted by a particular group of delegates at a particular time? ***

Eight hundred years ago, King John of England deprived his people of rights with such frequency and intensity that the nobility rose up against him and forced him to sign a charter subsequently known as Magna Carta, granting rights from the king to the people. One famous passage of Magna Carta has served as the precursor to many inalienable rights provisions:

> Chapter 39. No free man shall be taken, imprisoned, disseised, outlawed, banished, or in any way destroyed, nor will We proceed against or prosecute him, except by the lawful judgment of his peers and by the law of the land.

Magna Carta's due process or inalienable rights provision has been characterized in two manners: first, as the Seventeenth Century legal scholar Edward Coke argued, Magna Carta was a restatement of even more ancient positive laws already in place in England; and second, as early Americans and the framers of the Constitution argued, Magna Carta was an attempt at codifying or incorporating natural law concepts.

American colonists used passages of Magna Carta in some early colonial governments. For instance, the Concessions and Agreements of West New Jersey, dated March 13, 1677, stated,

> That no Proprietor, freeholder or inhabitant of the said Province of West New Jersey, shall be deprived or condemned of life, limb, liberty, estate, property or any ways hurt in his or their privileges, freedoms or franchises....

The Declaration and Resolves [of the First Continental Congress], dated October 14, 1774 stated,

> That the inhabitants of the English colonies in North-America, by the immutable laws of nature... have the following RIGHTS:... That they are entitled to life, liberty and property....

Such statements of inalienable rights became regular provisions to include in charters and constitutions during the Revolutionary Era. The Virginia Declaration of Rights, dated June 7, 1776, and drafted principally by George Mason, used language that would be highly influential to states in drafting their constitutions:

> That all men are by nature equally free and independent, and have certain inherent rights, of which, when they enter into a state of society, they cannot,

> by any compact, deprive or divest their posterity; namely, the enjoyment of life and liberty, with the means of acquiring and possessing property, and pursuing and obtaining happiness and safety.

Perhaps the most famous formulation of inalienable rights is from the second paragraph of the Declaration of Independence, drafted principally by Thomas Jefferson:

> We hold these Truths to be self-evident, that all Men are created equal, that they are endowed by their Creator with certain unalienable Rights, that among these are Life, Liberty, and the Pursuit of Happiness. . . .

The Bill of Rights to the United States Constitution departed from Jefferson's phrasing and used a phrase more similar to the one used by the First Continental Congress. The Fifth Amendment states, "No person shall. . . be deprived of life, liberty, or property, without due process of law. . . ."

Inspired by these foundational documents, the states drafted inalienable rights provisions in their respective constitutions. . . . Most states used natural law principles in inserting inalienable rights provisions into their constitutions. But do the court systems tend to enforce those principles as natural rights, or do courts enforce only the literal text? Legal scholar R.A. Helmholz recounts Randy Barnett's quip that two things are true of natural law: everyone believes in it, and it makes no difference. Helmholz then studies a number of court cases in America before concluding that Barnett was, more or less, correct.

III. Background Concepts Regarding the Montana Constitution

By some accounts, the inalienable rights provision in Article II, section 3 of the Montana Constitution is not a substantive provision but rather is a "primarily hortatory" statement or a statement of political philosophy. If so, it is best read along with the two provisions preceding it, both of which are broad statements that [in the words of Professors Larry Elison and Fritz Snyder] have little "practical value."

Compared to some of the inalienable rights provisions in older documents, Montana's 1972 Constitution includes a fairly long inalienable rights provision. . . . Article II, section 3 (hereinafter the Inalienable Rights Clause) consists of three sentences. The first sentence is a general statement recognizing (as opposed to granting) that people possess inalienable rights. This statement and the verb "include" in the second sentence allow for the recognition of unenumerated rights.

The second sentence consists of a list of five clauses, each of which provides one or more inalienable rights. Because the primary verb in the sentence is "include," the implication is that the list that follows is not comprehensive but merely several specific examples of inalienable rights. In theory, this is true. In practice, however, the Court has been slow to recognize unenumerated inalienable rights. Of the five clauses in the second sentence of the Inalienable Rights Clause, the first two are simple clauses: the right to a clean and healthful environment, and the right of pursuing life's basic necessities. The next three clauses are each compound clauses: (i) enjoying and defending their lives and liberties; (ii) acquiring, possessing and protecting property; and (iii) seeking their safety, health and happiness. The second sentence concludes with the limiting phrase "in all lawful ways," which appears to mean that all of the rights listed in the sentence are only recognized to the extent that the person asserting the right is acting within the scope of the law. Note how this second sentence includes a number of "temporizing" terms that limit the scope of the right: for instance, there is not a broad right to life's basic necessities but rather a narrow right to pursue life's basic necessities.

The third sentence, the "Corresponding Responsibilities Clause," asserts that by "enjoying" the inalienable rights listed in the second sentence (and the unenumerated ones implied in the first), all persons "recognize corresponding responsibilities," whatever those may be. ***

Butte Community Union v. Lewis

219 Mont. 426 (1986)

MORRISON, Justice.

*** In response to a complaint filed by Butte Community Union in February of 1984, the Honorable Arnold Olsen issued a preliminary injunction June 29, 1984, prohibiting the Department of Social and Rehabilitation Services (SRS) from implementing proposed regulations establishing AFDC guidelines as the guidelines for determining general assistance (GA) benefits. Thereafter, the 1985 Montana Legislature enacted House Bill 843 establishing cash payment levels for GA recipients in accordance with Judge Olsen's order. House Bill 843 also eliminates GA payments to able-bodied individuals under thirty-five who have no minor dependent children and substantially restricts GA payments to able-bodied individuals between thirty-five and fifty who have no minor dependent children. ***

We hold that Dave Lewis, as a public official, should be permanently enjoined from implementing the pertinent provisions of HB 843. However, our reasons for this injunction differ markedly from those of the trial judge. We find that the Montana Constitution does not establish a fundamental right to welfare for the aged, infirm or misfortunate. However, because the constitutional convention delegates deemed welfare to be sufficiently important to warrant reference in the Constitution, we hold that a classification which abridges welfare benefits is subject to a heightened scrutiny under an equal protection analysis and that HB 843 must fall under such scrutiny.

Respondent contends that the result of this legislation is forbidden by the Constitution. Respondent argues the Legislature must fund welfare for the misfortunate. However, because the legislation at issue today is discriminatory in nature, determining its constitutionality calls for equal protection analysis. It is not necessary that we address the broader question of whether there is a constitutional directive to the Legislature for the funding of welfare which can not be avoided under any set of circumstances.

The fourteenth amendment to the Federal Constitution and article II, section 4 of the Montana Constitution provide that "[n]o person shall be denied the equal protection of the laws." The equal protection clause guarantees that similar individuals will be dealt with in a similar manner by the government. J. Nowak, R. Rotunda and J.N. Young, Constitutional Law, Chpt. 16, § 1 (2d ed. 1983).

Equal protection analysis traditionally centers on a two-tier system of review. If a fundamental right is infringed or a suspect classification established, the government has to show a "compelling state interest" for its action. If the right is other than fundamental, or the classification not suspect, the government has only to show that the infringement or classification is rationally related to a governmental objective which is not prohibited by the Constitution. J. Nowak, *supra*.

In the instant case, the trial judge held the right to welfare to be fundamental. We can not agree. In order to be fundamental, a right must be found within Montana's Declaration of Rights or be a right "without which other constitutionally guaranteed rights would have little meaning." *In the Matter of C.H.* (Mont. 1984). Welfare is neither.

Art. XII, § 3(3) of the 1972 Montana Constitution, the section on which the trial judge relies, is not part of the Declaration of Rights. Art. II, § 3 is the only section in the Declaration of Rights which arguably could create a right to welfare. It states:

> Inalienable rights. All persons are born free and have certain inalienable rights. They include the right. . . of pursuing life's basic necessities. . . .

Mont. Const., art. II, § 3 (1972). The official committee comment to that provision states:

> The intent of the committee on this point is not to create a substantive right for all for the necessities of life to be provided by the public treasury.

There is no constitutional right to welfare within the Montana Constitution's Declaration of Rights. Further, the right to welfare is not a right upon which constitutionally guaranteed rights depend. In fact, welfare is more properly characterized as a benefit. Since welfare is not a fundamental right, strict scrutiny does not apply and the State need show something less than a compelling state interest in order to limit that right.

Traditionally courts have applied a "rational basis" test for equal protection analysis where a fundamental right is not implicated. Rational basis is easily satisfied. The more stringent test, strict scrutiny requiring the state to show a compelling state interest, is seldom satisfied.

The United States Supreme Court only recently has begun to recognize the problem the two-tier system creates. Initially, the Court was particularly concerned with gender-based discrimination. Unable, or unwilling, to recognize gender as a suspect class, the Court still recognized that Congress should not be able to discriminate between the sexes on any "conceivable basis." The Court therefore adopted, in *Craig v. Boren* (1976), the middle-tier of review for analyzing gender-based discrimination. The Court said such discrimination will be upheld only when the government can show that the classification it has used is "substantially related" to an "important governmental objective."

Variations of this middle-tier test, or at least a failure to apply either of the other tests, have been recognized in discrimination cases involving illegitimate children; limitations on the right to vote; and mandatory retirement for police officers, to name a few.

Yet, the United States Supreme Court has consistently refused to apply this middle area of review to welfare and other social economic cases. *** We will not be bound by decisions of the United States Supreme Court where independent state grounds exist for developing heightened and expanded rights under our state constitution. This position was last articulated by our Court in *Pfost v. State* (Mont.1985). Justice Sheehy writing for the majority said:

> Art. II, § 4, of our State Constitution provides in part that "[n]o person shall be denied the equal protection of the laws." Art. II, § 4, 1972 Mont. Const. That provision of our State Constitution, though similar in wording to the last clause of the Fourteenth Amendment of the Federal Constitution provides a separate ground on which rights of persons within this state may be founded, and under accepted principles of constitutional law such rights must be at least the same as and may be greater than rights founded on the federal clause. Thus, states may interpret their own constitutions to afford greater protections than the Supreme Court of the United States has recognized in its interpretations of the federal counterparts to state constitutions. Federal rights are considered minimal and a state constitution may be more demanding than the equivalent federal constitutional provision. This is true even though our state constitutional language is substantially similar to the language of the Federal Constitution.

We proceed to develop our own middle-tier test for determining whether HB 843 violates the Montana Constitution. We do so because although a right to welfare is not contained in our Declaration of Rights, it is sufficiently important that art. XII, sec. 3(3) directs the Legislature to provide necessary assistance to the misfortunate. A benefit lodged in our State Constitution is an interest whose abridgement requires something more than a rational relationship to a governmental objective.

A need exists to develop a meaningful middle-tier analysis. Equal protection of law is an essential underpinning of this free society. The old rational basis test allows government to discriminate among classes of people for the most whimsical reasons. Welfare benefits grounded in the Constitution itself are deserving of great protection.

In reviewing the textual discussions by constitutional authorities and the insightful dissents of Justices Marshall, Brennan, Powell, and Stevens [in earlier welfare rights cases] we have distilled a test we think is sound. Where constitutionally significant interests are implicated by governmental classification, arbitrary lines should be condemned. Further, there should be balancing of the rights infringed and the governmental interest to be served by such infringement.

We hold that a finding that HB 843 is constitutional requires the State to demonstrate two factors: 1) that its classification of welfare recipients on the basis of age is reasonable; and 2) that its interest in classifying welfare recipients on the basis of age is more important than the people's interest in obtaining welfare benefits.

A reasonable classification is one which is not arbitrary. The State has failed to show that misfortunate people under the age of 50 are more capable of surviving without assistance than people over the age of 50. Broad generalizations, concluding that those who are 49 years of age can retrain or relocate while those who are days older cannot, are arbitrary.

Next, the State's objective in enacting HB 843—saving money—must be balanced against the interest of misfortunate people under the age of 50 in receiving financial assistance from the State. The trial record does not show the State to be in such a financially unsound position that the welfare benefit, granted constitutionally, can be abrogated.

This Court does not pass on the merits of welfare. The respective members of the Court may well have different views about the public policy justifying public assistance. These matters are not properly treated by an appellate court. Our task is simply to determine constitutionality of the statute. On that subject we are of one mind.

We find the provisions of HB 843, which restrict or deny general assistance benefits to "able-bodied persons under the age of fifty who do not have minor dependent children", to be unconstitutional. A permanent injunction is hereby issued prohibiting Dave Lewis, Director of SRS, from implementing those provisions.

SHEEHY, Justice, specially concurring:

In addition to my concurrence with the majority opinion, I wish to state some observations.

For the purposes of this case, I am willing to concede that a fundamental right to welfare for the individuals affected does not exist. There is however a constitutionally-mandated duty upon the legislature to provide economic assistance "as may be necessary" for the misfortunate who need the aid of society. Art. XII, § 3(3). When that duty is shirked by the legislature, upon whatever pretense, the class discriminated against has at least a constitutional right for redress in the courts. I am unable to distinguish the fine line between "fundamental right" for the discriminated class and the constitutional right for redress.

I do not wish to be bound by the statement in the majority opinion that fundamental rights under the Montana Constitution must be found within the Declaration of

Rights, Art. II. The Article holds itself open to unenumerated rights which may not be denied to the people. Art. II, § 34.

[HUNT, Justice, joins the concurrence of Justice SHEEHY.]

GULBRANDSON, Justice, specially concurring.

I concur in the result and in the decision that the right to welfare is not a fundamental right but I do not concur in the adoption of a middle-tier standard of review in this case.

In my view, the legislation under attack does not meet the existing rational basis test and should therefore be declared unconstitutional. Thus, I do not perceive a need to adopt an additional test requiring a higher standard of review for legislation that may be enacted in the future. It appears that the newly adopted test, described as a middle-tier standard of review, actually replaces the rational basis test, even though no party to the action argued for its adoption.

In my opinion, the majority, by requiring the legislature to establish a factual record in its classification procedure, may have limited possible future legislative alternatives, because of time constraints existing in this matter, to the point where adequate welfare benefits may not be available to the needy.

TURNAGE, Chief Justice, [joins in the concurrence of Justice GULBRANDSON.]

Notes on the Structure of Constitutional Rights

1. Is *Butte Community Union* about equal protection under Article II, section 4, inalienable rights under Article II, section 3, or express positive rights to assistance under (the original) Article XII, section 3? Or does the case simply march lock-step with Justices Marshall's and Brennan's dissents arguing for heightened scrutiny of wealth and welfare classifications regardless of a textual basis for such heightened scrutiny in the federal Constitution? If the latter, what work does Article XII, section 3 do in the opinion? Note the Bill of Rights Committee Report locates some of the Court's concerns elsewhere in Article II, section 4: "Social origin or condition," it explains, "was included to cover discriminations based on status of income and standard of living." Why does this provision not appear in the Court's discussion?

2. The "intermediate scrutiny" adapted by the Court for legislative duties differs from the federal test for intermediate scrutiny of legislative classifications. It attempts to distinguish the strict scrutiny sometimes applied to "fundamental rights" (a strand of federal equal protection doctrine), as well as the rational basis test supported by Justice Gulbrandson. When if ever is this formulation likely to lead to a different result than rational basis scrutiny? Is a right subject to intermediate scrutiny more or less protective than a duty to "provide such economic assistance and social and rehabilitative services as may be necessary for those inhabitants who by reason of age, infirmities, or misfortune may have need for the aid of society"? *See* Article XII, § 3(3). How would this case come out under the Court's approach to the educational duties (and guarantee) in *Columbia Falls*, excerpted in Chapter 7?

3. The Court cites the committee comment for the Article II, section 3 "pursuing life's basic necessities" right, but not the similar background for Article XII, section 3(3). That committee comment frames the provision as addressing the sources rather than the levels of welfare funding:

> The original section placed the burden of taxation upon the several counties of the state to provide by tax levy for their indigents. The proposed section changes this to provide that the legislative assembly shall decide where this tax burden should rest, counties as at present or a state wide levy, or some combination thereof. The testimony taken on this matter showed conclusively that welfare recipients tend to congregate in the larger cities of our state, partly because of better job opportunities, and partly because of better welfare facilities. It was shown that the welfare recipients from the smaller counties tend to gather in Great Falls, Anaconda, Butte, Missoula, Billings, etc., imposing a disproportionate burden on the taxpayers of these counties. The proposed section would allow the legislature to place this burden on a state wide basis if it so chose and thus correct this inequity. Your committee considered the possibility of providing that it would be "the duty of the State to provide economic assistance. . .", but we believed that this should be equally as restrictive as the existing section and believe the matter should be one for legislative discretion.

Similarly, the 1972 voter information pamphlet explains that section 3, "Revises 1889 constitution which states that the 'several counties' must provide welfare. Revision leaves it up to the legislature to determine whether the state, county or a combination of the two must provide welfare." Should that change the Court's interpretation?

4. *Butte Community Union* sparked the constitutional amendment effort discussed in *Harper v. Greely*, Chapter 1.

B. Inalienable Rights Applied and Revisited

The Montana Supreme Court's engagement with inalienable rights peaked around the turn of the 20th century with a series of cases that advanced then retreated from an ambitious substantiation of the right "of pursuing life's basic necessities." Compare this effort to the *Lochner* Era of early substantive due process cases in federal constitutional law at the turn of the 19th century, and consider whether one or both are supported by the relevant texts and contexts. Another line of cases emerging from this period involves vindication of the right to a "clean and healthful environment," a provision amplifying associated legislative duties, and is addressed in the following section.

Wadsworth v. State

275 Mont. 287 (1996)

NELSON, Justice.

Wadsworth began working as a real estate appraiser for DOR [the Montana Department of Revenue] in 1974. On September 14, 1981, DOR enacted conflict-of-interest rule 81-2 precluding DOR appraisers from engaging in independent fee appraisals, real estate sales, or brokerage activities during their off-duty hours. Conflict-of-interest rule 81-2 provides:

> The very nature of this Division's work requires that our employees attain a high level of credibility and objectivity as viewed by the taxpaying public. When situations arise, such as conflicts of interest, that jeopardize either requirement, the integrity of the Department as well as the respective appraisal and assessor offices is detrimentally affected. Examples of conflicts of interest include, but are not limited to, fee appraising, selling real estate (excluding the sale of one's personal residence or property), and operating or working for a real estate firm.
>
> In such undertakings, the actual risk of and/or appearance of impropriety that occurs cannot be tolerated. Engaging in such activities will bring about immediate disciplinary action and may result in termination.

In December of 1981, Wadsworth received a letter informing him of the conflict-of-interest rule. He filed a grievance claiming that the rule is discriminatory, unfair, and unconstitutional. ***

In March of 1989 [after several rounds of judicial review], DOR directed Wadsworth to comply with the conflict-of-interest rule within 30 days. Wadsworth commenced a new grievance with DOR complaining of disciplinary action directed at him for violating the conflict-of-interest rule. The hearing examiner found that Wadsworth had to divest himself of his private fee appraisal business or face discharge. In a letter dated November 27, 1989, the Director of DOR adopted a final decision wherein he accepted the decision of the hearing officer, confirmed the policy statement in rule 81-2, sustained Wadsworth's 9-day suspension without pay, and indicated that Wadsworth had 30 days to divest himself of his interests in fee appraising and selling real estate. On February 16, 1990, DOR terminated Wadsworth from his employment for refusing to give up his outside employment activities.

In November of 1990, Wadsworth filed a wrongful discharge suit in the District Court of the Eighth Judicial District, Cascade County. *** In submitting the case to the jury, the District Judge included instructions on fundamental rights and that fundamental rights may not be infringed by the State without a showing of a compelling state interest. The jury rendered a verdict in Wadsworth's favor awarding him $85,000 in damages. DOR appeals the final judgment rendered following the jury trial.

Discussion ***

2. Whether Wadsworth has a fundamental constitutional right to the opportunity to pursue employment and, if so, whether the State provided a compelling interest for infringing upon that right? ***

In the instant case, Wadsworth claimed that the conflict-of-interest rule unconstitutionally infringed upon his fundamental right to the opportunity to pursue employment. Wadsworth presented a question of law—i.e. whether he had a fundamental constitutional right and whether the State showed a compelling interest for infringing upon that right. Thus, the question before the District Court was a legal issue containing no implicit questions of fact. ***

Wadsworth asserts that Article II, section 3 of the 1972 Montana Constitution establishes the inalienable right to pursue life's basic necessities which right necessarily includes the opportunity to earn a living, and that DOR wrongfully terminated him because he asserted this constitutionally protected right. Article II of Montana's constitution, entitled Declaration of Rights, enumerates various rights, among which are certain "inalienable rights" set forth at section 3. That section provides:

> All persons are born free and have certain inalienable rights. They include the right to a clean and healthful environment and the rights of pursuing life's basic necessities, enjoying and defending their lives and liberties, acquiring, possessing and protecting property, and seeking their safety, health and happiness in all lawful ways. In enjoying these rights, all persons recognize corresponding responsibilities.

While section 3 does not refer to "fundamental rights" per se, nevertheless, we have held a right may be "fundamental" under Montana's constitution if the right is either found in the Declaration of Rights or is a right "without which other constitutionally guaranteed rights would have little meaning." *Butte Community Union v. Lewis* (1986) (holding that Montana's constitution does not create a right to welfare). The inalienable right to pursue life's basic necessities is stated in the Declaration of Rights and is therefore a fundamental right.

While not specifically enumerated in the terms of Article II, section 3 of Montana's constitution, the opportunity to pursue employment is, nonetheless, necessary to enjoy the right to pursue life's basic necessities. As a practical matter, employment serves not only to provide income for the most basic of life's necessities, such as food, clothing, and shelter for the worker and the worker's family, but for many, if not most, employment also provides their only means to secure other essentials of modern life, including health and medical insurance, retirement, and day care. We conclude that without the right to the opportunity to pursue employment, the right to pursue life's basic necessities would have little meaning, because it is primarily through work and employment that one exercises and enjoys this latter fundamental constitutional right. Accordingly, we hold that the opportunity to pursue employment, while not specifically enumerated as a fundamental constitutional right under Article II, section 3 of Montana's constitution is, notwithstanding, necessarily encompassed within it and is itself a fundamental right because it is a right "without which other constitutionally guaranteed rights would have little meaning." . . .

This interpretation of Montana's constitution is supported by the decisions of other jurisdictions which have held their state constitutions to encompass a fundamental right to the opportunity to pursue employment. For example, the right to pursue any proper vocation under the personal liberty clause of Indiana's state constitution is a fundamental right. *Kirtley v. State* (Ind. 1949) (holding that a statute regarding the sale of tickets interfered with the liberties and the personal and property rights of a ticket owner). In *Kirtley*, the Indiana Supreme Court construed Indiana's personal liberty clause to confer not only freedom from servitude and restraint, but also "the right of everyone to be free in the use of their powers in the pursuit of happiness in such calling as they may choose subject only to the restraints necessary to secure the common welfare."

Similarly, in Florida, "[t]he right to work, earn a living and acquire and possess property from the fruits of one's labor is an inalienable right." *Lee v. Delmar* (Fla. 1953). In *Lee*, the Florida Supreme Court held that a resolution prohibiting a real estate salesperson from operating part-time was invalid as depriving the salesperson of his inalienable right to work and earn a living and as an excess of power granted to the Real Estate Commission. In *Town of Milton v. Civil Service Commission* (Mass. 1974), citing *Truax v. Raich* (1915), the Supreme Court of Massachusetts stated that "[i]t is certainly true that the opportunity to earn a living is a fundamental right in our society." But the court also clarified that "[i]t is an equally basic axiom that there is no right to public employment." *Milton* (discussing durational residency requirements).

Likewise, we distinguish the right to a particular job or employment from the right to pursue life's basic necessities through employment. "While the legislature may elect not to confer a property interest in [public] employment, it may not constitutionally authorize the deprivation of such an interest, once conferred, without appropriate procedural safeguards." *Boreen v. Christensen* (Mont. 1994). In essence, absent a contract, policy, regulation, or statute providing a specified term of employment, an employee does not have a property interest in a particular job. The Oregon Supreme Court made this germane distinction in *Minielly v. State* (Or. 1966), by stating:

> The conclusion to be drawn. . . would appear that while a person does not have a constitutional right to be employed by the public, the government is not free to place unconstitutional prerequisites upon the securing of public employment nor does it have the right to ignore the constitution if it desires to terminate such employment.

Accordingly, while Article II, section 3 of Montana's constitution encompasses the right to the opportunity to pursue employment generally as a necessary incident of the fundamental right to pursue life's basic necessities, that provision of our constitution does not, without more, grant a right or property interest in any particular job or employment.

Wadsworth makes no claim to the contrary. Wadsworth does not claim a constitutional right to his state job, but instead claims that by pursuing employment in addition to his job with the State, he has the constitutional right to pursue life's basic necessities, to acquire property, and to be free from the State's interference with his lawful activities. Wadsworth claims that the State has infringed these fundamental rights, not that it deprived him of a right to a specific job.

The State argues that because cities or counties may restrict employees' ability to work in outside jobs by placing restrictions on the residency of their employees, DOR may similarly restrict Wadsworth's ability to pursue employment by placing restrictions on the type of outside employment he may pursue. It is true that cities may place police officers in a separate category and impose residence requirements on the officers because the duties and interests protected by police are of a sufficiently distinct character from those of other governmental employees. However, cases discussing residency requirements have no application to the instant case because they hinge on the right to travel and do not discuss the right to life's basic necessities or the right to the opportunity to pursue employment. ***

Having concluded that the opportunity to pursue employment is a fundamental right as a necessary incident to the fundamental right to pursue life's basic necessities, we must next determine the level of scrutiny to apply to the infringement of that right. In determining what level of scrutiny to apply to legislation or to a rule in question, we first determine what rights are involved. "The extent to which the Court's scrutiny is heightened depends both on the nature of the interest and the degree to which it is infringed." Thus the nature of the individual interest affected dictates which standard of review to apply. The most stringent standard, strict scrutiny, is imposed when the action complained of interferes with the exercise of a fundamental right or discriminates against a suspect class. Strict scrutiny of a statute is required only when the classification impermissibly interferes with the exercise of a fundamental right.

Strict scrutiny of a legislative act requires the government to show a compelling state interest for its action. When the government intrudes upon a fundamental right, any compelling state interest for doing so must be closely tailored to effectuate only that compelling state interest. In addition to the necessity that the State show a compelling state interest for invasion of a fundamental right, the State, to sustain the validity of such invasion, must also show that the choice of legislative action is the least onerous path that can be taken to achieve the state objective. ***

In the instant case, while DOR's conflict-of-interest policy or rule is at issue rather than a statute, we, nevertheless, apply strict scrutiny analysis since the operation of that rule implicates Wadsworth's fundamental right to the opportunity to pursue employment. The constitutionality of the conflict-of-interest rule itself is not the issue, but rather whether the State has infringed Wadsworth's fundamental right without providing a compelling interest for doing so.

As we have held, employment is a necessary means to pursue life's basic necessities, without which the latter fundamental constitutional right could not be enjoyed. As such, the right to the opportunity to pursue employment is itself a fundamental right and is encompassed within the right to pursue life's basic necessities as declared under Article II, section 3 of Montana's constitution. Because the opportunity to work and to make a living is a fundamental right, it is incumbent upon the state to demonstrate a compelling interest before it may constitutionally infringe upon that right. Necessarily, demonstrating a compelling interest entails something more than simply saying it is so.

Based on the record established in the trial court, we conclude that, as a matter of law, the State failed to demonstrate a compelling interest for the conflict-of-interest rule restricting Wadsworth's ability to pursue employment opportunities and thus pursue life's basic necessities. Simply because the State alleges a compelling interest, does not obviate the necessity that the State prove the compelling interest by competent evidence.

Here, the State adopted the conflict-of-interest rule for the singular purpose of avoiding the appearance of impropriety of real estate appraisers. The evidence at trial established that there were no complaints about any appearance of impropriety when State appraisers appraised property outside of their DOR employment. Mr. Groepper, the Administrator of the Property Assessment Division, stated that none of the grievants nor anyone else had been or was being accused of any actual wrongdoing. The only semblance of a complaint consisted of a letter that Paul Pistoria wrote DOR stating that Wadsworth handed out his private business card while working for the Department. DOR presented no case in which an appearance of impropriety arose; DOR could not demonstrate that Wadsworth jeopardized the integrity of or detrimentally affected DOR or the appraisal or assessor offices in any way. In fact, no one ever expressed a lack of confidence in the integrity of the Property Tax Division or expressed a belief that outside employment activities undermined public confidence....

Dennis Burr, the DOR Administrator of the Property Tax Division, issued the conflict-of-interest rule but never enforced it. Nick Lazanas, the Director of the Cascade County Appraiser Office also chose not to enforce the rule; he did not believe in it nor did he see a reason for it. Additionally, the State's expert witness, Gaylord Aldinger, a member of the International Order of Assessing Officers, admitted that his organization's code of ethics did not preclude outside employment activities, and that in his state, he was not aware of any abuse of official duties by the activities in question. Moreover, the record is ambivalent as to whether the State considered the relevant constitutional provision before it applied the conflict-of-interest policy.

That is not to say that the State could never demonstrate a compelling interest for the conflict-of-interest rule or for some other rule restricting the outside employment of its employees. In this case, on the record here and as a matter of law, it simply did not.

In this regard we note that Article XIII, section 4 of Montana's constitution requires the legislature to provide a code of ethics prohibiting conflict between public duty and private interest for, among others, state and local employees. We also note that the legislature has, pursuant to that constitutional mandate, enacted standards of conduct for public officers and employees, including a code of ethics, at Title 2, Chapter 2, MCA. Neither DOR nor Wadsworth raise any issue as to the application of either Article XIII, section 4 or those standards of conduct and code of ethics in this appeal. Notwithstanding, in the interest of completeness, we acknowledge both this constitutional provision and its implementing statutes and point out that there was no allegation made or evidence in this case that Wadsworth's conduct was at anytime ever in violation of these statutes.

We hold that, because the State did not demonstrate a compelling interest for applying the conflict-of-interest rule at issue here, the State wrongfully terminated Wadsworth's employment. ***

TRIEWEILER, Justice, specially concurring.

. . . I specially concur with the majority's resolution of Issue 2 because although I agree with the result arrived at in that section of the Court's opinion, I disagree that the District Court erred by submitting underlying factual issues to the jury.

The majority correctly concludes that the opportunity to pursue employment is one of life's basic necessities, and therefore, a fundamental right guaranteed by Article II, Section 3, of the Montana Constitution. I also agree that before the State can interfere with that fundamental right, it must establish a compelling state interest for doing so and that whether a particular interest, if proven, is "compelling" is a question of law. However, where the very facts which form the basis for the State's alleged interest are disputed, the resolution of that dispute involves a question of fact.

For example, in this case, the State alleged that its conflict of interest rule served the interest of avoiding the appearance of impropriety by real estate appraisers. Had that fact been established by competent evidence, the determination of whether that fact established a compelling state interest would have been an issue of law. However Wadsworth, and numerous others who were qualified by training and experience, testified that the conflict of interest rule was unnecessary and bore no relationship to public confidence in real estate appraisers. Therefore, whether there was any relationship between the conflict of interest rule and public confidence raised an issue of fact which must necessarily be decided by the finder of fact—in this case, the jury. As pointed out by the majority, § 26-1-202, MCA, provides as follows:

> If a trial is by jury, all questions of fact other than those mentioned in 26-1-201 must be decided by the jury, and all evidence thereon must be addressed to them, except as otherwise provided by law. If the trial of a question of fact is not by jury, all evidence thereon must be addressed to the trial court, which shall decide such question.

That underlying questions of fact were at issue is evident from the majority's opinion. In analyzing whether proof was offered of a compelling state interest, the majority opinion repeatedly refers to the evidence at trial. Evidence is considered for the sole purpose of resolving factual issues which are the unique responsibility of juries or the district court, as the case may be.

What the majority has, in effect, held is that in every case involving a constitutional issue with an underlying factual component, this Court is in the best position to resolve the factual issue de novo on appeal. ***

In *Collier v. Civil Service Commission* (Tex.Ct.App. 1989), the Texas Court of Appeals was asked to decide whether "nepotism" rules adopted by the Civil Service Commission for the city of Wichita Falls violated the equal protection clause of the Texas Constitution. The nepotism rule provided that no person could be employed by the fire department if a member of that person's immediate family was already employed by the department. The city contended that the rule was necessary in order to avoid impairment of one firefighter's judgment when placed in a situation where a member of that person's family was in peril.

The Texas court held that to decide the constitutional issue raised by the petitioners, several fact issues must first be resolved, including whether the rule advances legitimate government objectives. (A similar rational basis test would be applied by our Court if a fundamental interest was not at issue.) In holding that underlying factual issues must be resolved by the finder of fact before the constitutional issue could be resolved, the Texas court stated as follows:

> Deciding the constitutionality of a statute necessarily involves several related fact questions. *See* Pine, [*Speculation and Reality: The Role of Facts in Judicial Protection of Fundamental Rights*, 136 U. Pa. L. Rev. 655 (1988)], 666-67. For example, Wichita Falls argues the nepotism rule will prevent a firefighter's unavoidable impairment of judgment in a situation where a member of his immediate family is involved in a perilous situation. Appellants argue strong emotional bonds exist between firefighters even if they are not related by blood or marriage. These issues are relevant to whether the nepotism rule will advance the governmental objective of improving the safety of the fire department, but this court does not have any special knowledge of emotional ties between firefighters or the dangers found within burning buildings. This question involves social and emotional issues, but it is still a question of fact. Social facts may be developed through expert testimony, "Brandeis briefs" or requests for judicial notice. We are unwilling to base our decision on the unsupported generalizations contained in the briefs. ***

Likewise, in this case, a factual issue was raised by the State's contention that its conflict of interest rule was necessary in order to retain public confidence in its real estate appraisers. Before the District Court or this Court could decide whether that need constituted a compelling state interest, someone first had to decide whether the allegation was true. Under our statutory system for resolving factual issues, that responsibility belonged to the jury. Therefore, I would conclude that the District Court did not err when it submitted that issue to the jury based on the proper instructions.

I otherwise agree with the majority opinion, including its conclusion that if the District Court did err by submitting issues regarding a compelling state interest to the jury, the error was harmless.

HUNT, J., joins in the foregoing concurring opinion.

ERDMANN, Justice, specially concurring.

*** I do not agree with the majority's conclusion that Wadsworth has a fundamental right to pursue a particular job. The majority finds a fundamental right in the right to pursue employment in order to pursue life's basic necessities. The majority, however, fails to construe the meaning of "life's basic necessities." In fact, there was no discussion in the majority opinion as to whether Wadsworth's second job was needed in order for him to obtain these basic necessities. Life's basic necessities cannot and should not be an infinite term. One person's necessity can be another person's luxury. The right to pursue employment is fundamental to the extent that employment provides those necessities.

In the majority's opinion, Wadsworth has successfully evaded his responsibility of limiting his right to the basic necessities. In fact, Wadsworth failed to produce any evidence as to the basic necessities of which he was deprived. A more plausible right encompassing Wadsworth's right to pursue employment would therefore be his right to acquire property. The right to acquire, possess, and protect property is also an inalienable right. Mont. Const. art. II, § 3. However, the right to pursue a particular job in order to acquire property is not fundamental.

The majority distinguishes the right to pursue employment generally as a necessary incident of the fundamental right to pursue life's basic necessities from a right or property interest in any particular job or employment. Absent a specified term of employment, this Court has held that an employee does not have a property interest in a particular job. *Boreen v. Christensen* (1994). Nor should a right to acquire property impart a fundamental right to pursue employment in a particular job. In this respect, I see no significant difference in the right to hold a particular job and the right to pursue a particular job.

In *Cecil v. Allied Stores* (Mont. 1973), nonretail sellers claimed a legislative act that denied them the right to charge the same finance charges as retail sellers was a violation of their constitutionally protected right to acquire property. Similar to the present case, the plaintiffs in *Cecil* argued that the act inhibited their ability to make money so that they may acquire property. This Court held that so long as the legislative classifications of the act are constitutional, it does not violate the right to acquire property.

As for the right to pursue a particular job, this Court has held that the practice of certain professions is not a fundamental right. *Petition of Morris* (Mont. 1978). In *Morris*, the petitioner claimed that unification of the bar deprived him of his inalienable right to earn a living. The Court held "[a]n individual has no inalienable right to earn a living practicing law. It is neither a vested right nor a property right. The practice of law is a privilege burdened with conditions." The practice of real estate appraising is similar to the practice of law in that both provide a needed service that is regulated by a professional board and is subject to certain educational and ethical standards.

Finally, the inalienable rights set forth in our constitution's declaration of rights impart corresponding responsibilities. Mont. Const. art. II, § 3. Delegates to the 1971–72 Constitutional Convention expressed concern that people were accepting rights without recognizing that they create obligations. The convention committee concluded that the inclusion of such a statement would not infringe or impair the rights granted in the Declaration of Rights but would only accord a tone of responsibility to their exercise. Mont. Const. Conv. (1971–72) vol V, 1637. In this case, the majority has failed to acknowledge any corresponding responsibility on the part of Wadsworth in exercising his rights.

I would have found that Wadsworth did not have a fundamental right in pursuing a second job as a real estate appraiser. Therefore, the analysis of Wadsworth's pursuit of that particular employment should not be subject to strict scrutiny but scrutiny of a lesser degree.

Wiser v. State

2006 MT 20

Justice JIM RICE delivered the Opinion of the Court. ***

¶ 7 The long struggle between denturists and dentists is well documented in the annals of the legislative, executive, and judicial branches of Montana government. This Court has adjudicated disputes between these two professions no less than three times. Raging since the mid-1980s, the battle at its core is the regulation of the denturity profession by the State Board of Dentistry, which, in the eyes of denturists, is dominated by dentists who actively oppose denturity.

¶ 8 Authorized for licensure by the Montana Legislature in 1984, denturists were originally regulated by a Board of Denturity created by the Freedom of Choice in Denture Services Act of 1984. However, in 1987, the Legislature dissolved the Board of Denturity, placing denturists under the licensing and regulatory authority of the Board of Dentistry (BOD). Regulatory conflicts between denturists and dentists ensued thereafter.

¶ 9 Between 1987 and 1991, the BOD restricted denturists by (a) requiring dentist referrals, (b) restricting when denturists can insert dentures, (c) requiring three-part certificate of work forms from dentists before certain denturity procedures could be performed, and (d) by bringing suit against denturists engaging in bite-examination work with patients. Denturists, fearing the systematic erosion of their profession and livelihoods, challenged all of these actions, and at times prevailed. At times the BOD prevailed.

¶ 10 The roots of the present controversy run to 1985, when the Legislature passed § 37-29-403, MCA, requiring denturists to refer partial denture patients to dentists "as needed." Not surprising, the "as needed" language was disputed almost immediately. Dentists claimed that all partial denture patients had to be referred to a dentist before denturists could proceed with treatment, while denturists claimed referrals were in the discretion of the denturist. Unfortunately for the denturists, the BOD agreed with the dentists, and promulgated Rule 8.17.800, ARM, interpreting § 37-29-403, MCA, as requiring that denturists refer all partial denture patients to dentists before providing partial denture services (the Partial Denture Rule). Litigation ensued. ***

¶ 12 Appellant denturists and denture patients challenge the constitutionality of both the Partial Denture Rule and the statutory framework which places the profession of denturity under the regulatory thumb of the BOD. The District Court rejected both challenges, upholding both the constitutionality of the Partial Denture Rule, and the placement of denturity under the control of the Board of Dentistry. ***

Discussion

Issue 1: Does the Board of Dentistry's Partial Denture Rule impermissibly infringe upon the state constitutional privacy right of denture patients?

¶ 14 Appellants assert that BOD restrictions on denturity, specifically the Partial Denture Rule set forth in Rule 24.138.416, ARM, requiring dentist referrals before denturists may perform partial denture work, infringe upon the right of patients to seek the medical professional of their choice. Citing *Armstrong v. State* (Mont. 1999), Appellants argue that the restrictions violate their right to privacy guaranteed in Article II, Section 10 of the Montana Constitution.

¶ 15 The right to privacy is a fundamental right guaranteed by the Montana Constitution. However, it does not necessarily follow from the existence of the right to privacy that every restriction on medical care impermissibly infringes that right. *Armstrong* described the right to health care as a

> fundamental privacy right to obtain a particular lawful medical procedure from a health care provider that has been determined by the medical community to be competent to provide that service and who has been licensed to do so.

¶ 16 Thus, while recognizing that the right to privacy was implicated in health care choices, *Armstrong* nonetheless specifically defined the right as guaranteeing access to a chosen health care provider who has been determined "competent" by the medical community and "licensed" to perform the procedure desired. *Armstrong* did not hold that there is a right to see a health care provider who is not licensed to provide the services desired.

¶ 17 Appellants rely heavily on *Andrews v. Ballard* (S.D.Tex. 1980), a case which held that patients have a broad right to health care which includes the fundamental right to seek treatment from acupuncturists who have not been licensed or approved by the relevant licensing or medical board. The court in *Andrews* struck down the statute at issue there, which limited the practice of acupuncture to licensed doctors, because it did not serve a "compelling" state interest. Appellants correctly note that we cited *Andrews* favorably in *Armstrong*. However, we cited *Andrews* for the general proposition that individuals have the right to obtain and reject medical treatment, a holding we do not disturb today, and not for the proposition that patients have a fundamental right to obtain medical care from professionals who have not been determined by the regulating authority to be qualified to provide the desired service.

¶ 18 A conclusion that Montanans have a fundamental right to seek medical care from un-licensed professionals would force the State and its licensing boards to demonstrate a compelling state interest in order to license and regulate health care professionals. The State would, in effect, "shoulder the burden of demonstrating that no less restrictive set of qualifications for a license could serve the state's interest in protecting the health of its citizens." Under such a rule, regulation of health care professions necessary for the public's protection would become very difficult, if not impossible, for the State to undertake.

¶ 19 It is clear that the State of Montana has a police power by which it can regulate for the health and safety of its citizens. *State v. Skurdal* (Mont. 1988). Furthermore, this Court has recognized that the State's exercise of its police powers often implicates individual rights. *State v. Rathbone* (Mont. 1940). However, when the rights affected are not fundamental, we do not utilize strict scrutiny review, requiring a compelling state interest. Instead, the State need only demonstrate a rational basis for the regulation.

¶ 20 Here, Appellants argue that the right to obtain medical care free of regulation is a fundamental right, and that the State's regulation of that right must be supported by a compelling state interest. As noted above, we disagree with Appellants' contention that the fundamental right extends that broadly, and therefore, Appellants' argument must fail. Furthermore, because Appellants did not argue, and the District Court did not decide, if the Partial Denture Rule was rationally related to a legitimate state interest, we decline to reach that issue today.

Issue 2: Does the Board of Dentistry's Partial Denture Rule impermissibly infringe upon denturists' state constitutional right to pursue employment?

¶ 21 Article II, Section 3 of the Montana Constitution guarantees to Montanans the right to pursue, "life's basic necessities. . . in all lawful ways." Art. II, Sec. 3, Mont. Const. This Court has held that this section provides a fundamental right to the citizen to pursue employment. *Wadsworth v. State* (1996). Relying on *Wadsworth*, Appellant denturists argue that they have a fundamental right to practice denturity free of regulation.

¶ 22 Although *Wadsworth* demonstrates that Appellants have a fundamental right to "pursue" denturity as a profession, it does not follow thereafter that denturists have a fundamental right to practice denturity free of all regulation. The regulatory purpose in promulgating the Partial Denture Rule was stated by the BOD as follows:

> The Board has considered all the comments, both written and oral. Giving great weight to its obligation to protect the public, the Board concludes that it is in the best interests of the Montana public to require by rule that prior to the preparation or fitting or [sic] partial dentures, denturists shall refer all partial denture patients to a dentist for examination, evaluation and/or treatment that the dentist may deem necessary prior to the insertion of the partials. The consequences of insertion of partials into an inadequately prepared, or compromised, mouth may be serious dental problems for the patient.

Although we do not address in this case the validity or rationality of the Board's expressed reason for the rule, we cite to the BOD's reason to illustrate that the rule does not bar denturity, and that Appellants remain free to pursue the profession. With regard to partial denture work, § 37-29-403, MCA, authorizes denturists to see patients as long as they obtain a dentist's referral first. These conditions render this case distinguishable from *Wadsworth.*

¶ 23 In *Wadsworth*, this Court evaluated a Department of Revenue (DOR) rule forbidding state real estate appraisers from doing appraisal work in their free time. State appraisers challenged the rule as violating their constitutional right to pursue employment. This Court agreed, holding that the state appraisers had a fundamental right to pursue employment, and further holding that the state rule forbidding independent employment violated that right. However, the DOR employees in *Wadsworth* were completely proscribed from independently appraising, barred from pursuing employment in their free time by the DOR rule. Here, denturists remain free to pursue denture work generally, and further, are not completely proscribed from performing partial denture work. The Partial Denture Rule merely requires a dentist's referral.

¶ 24 As mentioned in the above discussion concerning privacy rights, the State of Montana holds police power to regulate for the health and welfare of its citizens. Furthermore, the idea that the right to pursue employment and life's other "basic necessities" is limited by the State's police power is imbedded in the plain language of the Constitution. Article II, Section 3 states that citizens have the right to pursue "life's basic necessities... *in all lawful ways.*" Art. II, Sec. 3, Mont. Const. (emphasis added). The Constitution is clear. While it granted the fundamental right to pursue employment, it also circumscribed that right by subjecting it to the State's police power to protect the public's health and welfare. "[L]iberty is necessarily subordinate to reasonable restraint and regulation by the state in the exercise of its sovereign prerogative—police power." Accordingly, while one does have the fundamental right to pursue employment, one does not have the fundamental right to practice his or her profession free of state regulation promulgated to protect the public's welfare.

¶ 25 Appellants argued to both the District Court and to this Court that their right to pursue denturity free of regulation was a fundamental right, and that infringement upon that right had to be reviewed with strict scrutiny. For the reasons above, we disagree. Furthermore, because Appellants did not argue, and the District Court did not decide, that the Partial Denture Rule failed minimal or rational basis review, we decline to take up that issue today. ***

Montana Cannabis Industry Association v. State

2012 MT 201

Justice MICHAEL E. WHEAT delivered the Opinion of the Court. ***

¶ 2 In 2004, Montana voters approved the use of medical marijuana through the passage of I-148, the Medical Marijuana Act. The 2004 Medical Marijuana Act left in place those provisions in the Montana criminal code that make it illegal to cultivate, possess, distribute or use marijuana, while simultaneously protecting authorized users of medical marijuana from being prosecuted. Section 50-46-201(1), MCA (2009) (repealed 2011). In 2011, the Montana Legislature, in response to a drastic increase of caregivers and medical marijuana users, passed House Bill 161, which repealed I-148. The Governor vetoed House Bill 161, and in response, the Legislature enacted Senate Bill 423, which repealed the 2004 Medical Marijuana Act and replaced it with the Montana Marijuana Act ("MMA"), § 50-46-301 et seq., MCA, which dramatically changed the landscape for the cultivation, distribution, and use of marijuana for medical purposes.

¶ 3 On May 13, 2011, the Plaintiffs filed a lawsuit seeking to both temporarily and permanently enjoin the implementation of the MMA in its entirety. Based on a motion filed with the complaint, the District Court immediately entered a temporary restraining order blocking implementation of § 50-46-341, MCA, which prohibited the advertising of "marijuana or marijuana-related products" and which was scheduled to take effect that day. By stipulation, the temporary restraining order remained in effect pending the preliminary injunction hearing. A hearing on the preliminary injunction was held June 20 through 22, 2011.

¶ 4 On June 30, 2011, the District Court issued its Order on Motion for Preliminary Injunction. In its Order, the District Court enjoined the following relevant subsections of § 50-46-308, MCA:

> (3)(a)(i) A provider or marijuana-infused products provider may assist a maximum of three registered cardholders.
>
> (ii) A person who is registered as both a provider and a marijuana-infused products provider may assist no more than three registered cardholders.

(b) If the provider or marijuana-infused products provider is a registered cardholder, the provider or marijuana-infused products provider may assist a maximum of two registered cardholders other than the provider or marijuana-infused products provider.

(4) A provider or marijuana-infused products provider may accept reimbursement from a cardholder only for the provider's application or renewal fee for a registry identification card issued under this section.

. . .

(6) A provider or marijuana-infused products provider may not:

(a) accept anything of value, including monetary remuneration, for any services or products provided to a registered cardholder;

(b) buy or sell mature marijuana plants, seedlings, cuttings, clones, usable marijuana, or marijuana-infused products[.]

¶ 5 The District Court preliminarily enjoined a number of sections of the MMA; however, only §§ 50-46-308(3), (4), (6)(a) and (6)(b), MCA, are pertinent to this opinion. The District Court found that these sections substantially implicated the Plaintiffs' fundamental rights to pursue employment, to seek one's own health in all lawful ways, and to privacy. Because the sections substantially implicated the Plaintiffs' fundamental rights, the District Court applied a strict scrutiny analysis, and determined that the Plaintiffs would suffer irreparable harm if the court did not enjoin these provisions. ***

¶ 16 In order to determine if a constitutional right has been lost, a court must first determine which of the established levels of scrutiny is appropriately applied: strict scrutiny, middle-tier scrutiny or the rational basis test. Legislation that implicates a fundamental constitutional right is evaluated under a strict scrutiny standard, whereby the government must show that the law is narrowly tailored to serve a compelling government interest. If a law or policy affects a right conferred by the Montana Constitution, but is not found in the Constitution's declaration of rights, we apply middle-tier scrutiny. If neither strict scrutiny nor middle-tier scrutiny apply, the rational basis test is appropriate. Pursuant to the rational basis test, the statute must be rationally related to a legitimate government interest. ***

1. Right to Employment

¶ 18 The District Court determined that because the State has declared medical marijuana a legal product in Montana, with an established licensing and distribution system through providers, then the MMA's prohibition of remuneration substantially implicates the fundamental right to employment. The right of the opportunity to pursue employment is a fundamental right that is embodied within Article II, Section 3 of the Montana Constitution. . .

While the right to the opportunity to pursue employment is not specifically enumerated, it is a fundamental right because it is a right without which other constitutionally guaranteed rights would have little meaning. This right, though, is limited. It does not "grant a right or property interest in any particular job or employment." *Wadsworth.*

¶ 19 We clarified the boundaries of the right to pursue employment in *Wiser v. State.* In *Wiser,* denturists challenged the constitutionality of a Board of Dentistry rule requiring that denturists refer all partial denture patients to dentists before providing partial denture services. The denturists, in part, relied upon the right to pursue employment to challenge the rule. In concluding that the rule did not warrant strict scrutiny analysis, this Court noted,

> [T]he idea that the right to pursue employment and life's other 'basic necessities' is limited by the State's police power is imbedded in the plain language of the Constitution. Article II, Section 3 states that citizens have the right to pursue "life's basic necessities... *in all lawful ways.*" Art. II, Sec. 3, Mont. Const.

Continuing, this Court observed that "[t]he Constitution is clear. While it granted the fundamental right to pursue employment, it also circumscribed that right by subjecting it to the State's police power to protect the public health and welfare."

¶ 20 Here, the District Court concluded that the MMA's prohibition of the right to sell medical marijuana substantially implicated the fundamental right to pursue employment. However, under *Wadsworth* and *Wiser,* although individuals have a fundamental right to pursue employment, they do not have a fundamental right to pursue a particular employment or employment free of state regulation.

¶ 21 In this case, the legislature, in its exercise of the State's police powers, decided that it would legalize the limited use of medicinal marijuana while maintaining a prohibition on the sale of medical marijuana. This action prohibits employment as a medical marijuana provider, but as noted in *Wadsworth,* an individual has no property interest in a "particular job or employment." Providers, who are ultimately horticulturists, remain free to pursue horticulture work generally, and further, are not proscribed from practicing the art of horticulture—including hydroponic horticulture—for profit. Thus, the MMA does not implicate the fundamental right to employment, and we reverse the District Court's holding on this issue.

2. Right to Seek Health

¶ 22 The District Court next concluded that denying providers compensation and limiting the number of cardholders that each provider can serve will substantially implicate Montanans' fundamental right to seek their health in a lawful manner because such restrictions deny access to medical marijuana, which is otherwise a legal product. The fundamental right to seek health is found in Article II, Section 3 of the Montana Constitution and provides that Montanans have a fundamental right to "seek[] their safety, health and happiness *in all lawful ways.*" (Emphasis added.) As with the right to pursue employment, the Constitution is clear that the right to seek health is circumscribed by the State's police power to protect the public's health and welfare.

¶ 23 In pursuing one's own health, an individual has a fundamental right to obtain and reject medical treatment. But, this right does not extend to give a patient a fundamental right to use any drug, regardless of its legality. No court has acceded to this type of affirmative access claim, and Plaintiffs cite to none. *See Abigail Alliance for Better Access to Developmental Drugs v. Von Eschenbach* (D.C.Cir. 2007).

¶ 24 Thus, we conclude, in pursuing health, an individual does not have a fundamental affirmative right of access to a particular drug. A patient's "selection of a particular treatment, or at least a medication, is within the area of governmental interest in protecting public health," and regulation of that medication does not implicate a fundamental constitutional right. *Rutherford v. U.S.* (10th Cir. 1980). Because the fundamental right to seek one's own health is not implicated, the District Court erred when it applied a strict scrutiny analysis.

3. Right to Privacy

¶ 25 The District Court also concluded that the restrictions substantially implicated the fundamental right to privacy found in Article II, Section 10, of the Montana Constitution. In reaching its decision, the District Court relied exclusively on *Armstrong v. State* (Mont. 1999). The State argues that the District Court's reliance on Armstrong was misplaced because of our subsequent holding in *Wiser*, § 20, and because it is factually distinguishable. We agree with the State.

¶ 26 In *Armstrong*, the plaintiffs challenged a state law prohibiting certified physicians assistants from performing abortions. This Court struck down the law because it infringed on an individual's personal autonomy protected by the right to privacy. In so holding, this Court noted that the purpose of the law was clearly "to make it as difficult, as inconvenient and as costly as possible for women to exercise their right to obtain, from the health care provider of their choice, a specific medical procedure" protected by both the U.S. and Montana constitutions.

¶ 27 This Court concluded in *Armstrong* that the right to health care is a fundamental privacy right, but only to the extent that it protects an individual's right to obtain a particular lawful medical procedure. In *Wiser*, this Court circumscribed its holding in *Armstrong* when we stated that "it does not necessarily follow from the existence of the right to privacy that every restriction on medical care impermissibly infringes that right." The *Wiser* Court additionally determined that an individual does not have a fundamental right to obtain medical care free of regulation. Thus, while the right to privacy is certainly implicated when a statute infringes upon a person's ability to obtain or reject a lawful medical treatment, it does not follow that the right to privacy is necessarily implicated when a statute regulates a particular medication. ***

¶ 32 We agree with [federal and other states'] cases, and conclude the right to privacy does not encompass the affirmative right of access to medical marijuana.

The Plaintiffs may decry that the Legislature gutted I-148, but it was within the Legislature's right to do so, and the new medical marijuana framework does not suddenly raise the affirmative right to access a particular drug to a fundamental right protected by our Constitution. Moreover, the Plaintiffs cannot seriously contend that they have a fundamental right to medical marijuana when it is still unequivocally illegal under the [federal] Controlled Substances Act. We accordingly reverse the District Court's holding that the MMA substantially implicates the Plaintiffs' fundamental right to privacy.

Justice JAMES C. NELSON, dissenting. ***

¶ 49 *** I believe the decisions of the District Court and this Court amount to advisory opinions. But because the Court has nevertheless chosen to discuss the merits of the issues on appeal, I briefly note my concern with certain aspects of the Court's analysis.

¶ 50 For starters, the Court overlooks two fundamental principles relevant to Plaintiffs' claims. First, this Court has held repeatedly that the rights enumerated in Article II of Montana's Constitution (the Declaration of Rights) are fundamental constitutional rights. Second, this Court has also held that strict scrutiny applies to an alleged infringement of a fundamental right. Here, Plaintiffs' claims are premised on Article II, Sections 3 and 10. Because Article II, Sections 3 and 10 are contained in the Declaration of Rights, it necessarily follows that they are fundamental rights to which strict scrutiny applies. The Court is thus wrong in directing the District Court to analyze Plaintiffs' claims using a "rational basis" standard. We do not apply rational-basis review to legislation which regulates the exercise of a fundamental right. ***

¶ 52 The real question in this appeal... is whether the constitutional provisions upon which Plaintiffs rely include the rights they claim. In this regard, I have grave concerns with the Court's suggestions that the rights enumerated in Article II, Section 3 are circumscribed by the State's police power. If this proposition were true, then the constitutional rights at issue would be rendered meaningless. After all, the Montana Constitution generally, and the Declaration of Rights especially, serve as a restraint on governmental power. Such restraint does not exist if, as the Court appears to hold, the parameters of constitutional rights are dictated by the State's police power as defined by changing compositions of the legislative and executive branches. Again, the Montana Constitution is the supreme law of this State and its mandate must be followed by each of the three branches of government—not the other way around.

¶ 53 In this regard, I believe the Court overreads our decision in *Wiser v. State*. There, the appellant denturists claimed they had a fundamental right to practice denturity "free of regulation." We rejected that claim, noting that the State has police power to regulate for the health and welfare of its citizens and that the fundamental right to pursue employment and life's other "basic necessities" is subject to the State's power to protect the public's health and welfare. We also noted that the regulatory provision at issue did not bar denturity; to the contrary, it left the appellants free to pursue the profession. Our holding was simply that "while one does have the fundamental right to pursue employment, one does not have the fundamental right to practice his or her profession free of state regulation promulgated to protect the public's welfare." I signed the *Wiser* opinion and still agree with this holding. I disagree, however, with the Court's expansion of *Wiser*'s holding in the present case to stand for the proposition that the parameters of the Article II, Section 3 rights are dictated, circumscribed, or trumped by the State's police power.

¶ 54 In my view, Plaintiffs' constitutional claims may be resolved on a much narrower ground. The Supremacy Clause, again, dictates that federal law "shall be the supreme Law of the Land; and the Judges in every State shall be bound thereby, any Thing in the Constitution or Laws of any State to the Contrary notwithstanding." U.S. Const. art. VI, cl. 2. In my view, it is wholly implausible to suggest that Article II, Sections 3 and 10 guarantee the right to engage in conduct which federal law proscribes—here, selling and using marijuana. Indeed, Article II, Section 3 recognizes "the rights of pursuing life's basic necessities, enjoying and defending their lives and liberties, acquiring, possessing and protecting property, and seeking their safety, health and happiness *in all lawful ways*" (emphasis added). And the Court itself recognizes, near the end of the Opinion, that "Plaintiffs cannot seriously contend that they have a fundamental right to medical marijuana when it is still unequivocally illegal under the Controlled Substances Act." This is more than enough to revolve Plaintiffs' claims, and I thus question the judiciousness of the Court's discussion of the State's police power, not to mention the Court's wholesale adoption of federal and out-of-state caselaw to interpret and limit the constitutional rights at issue. It is unnecessary to assess whether Montana's medical marijuana laws pass muster under the Montana Constitution. Because federal law and the Supremacy Clause render Plaintiffs' activities unlawful regardless, they have no state constitutional rights to vindicate in this case.

Notes on Inalienable Rights

1. Would *Wadsworth* have come out differently if the Legislature, in pursuit of its Article XIII, section 4 duty to establish a code of ethics for public employees, had enacted the same conflict-of-interest rule? What if the Court had applied merely rational-basis scrutiny?

2. Justice Trieweiler argues that the application of constitutional scrutiny is a matter of fact for the jury. In what ways might a jury be better than judges at determining the fit and justification of a challenged law? What problems might arise?

3. What is the precise source and scope of a right "of pursuing life's basic necessities" that includes "the right to the opportunity to pursue employment"? Is this a negative right of non-interference with private employment or a positive right to public employment? If the latter, why is the pursuit of life's basic necessities guaranteed for public employees in the professional class, but not for minimum-wage

workers whose own pursuit of basic necessities might be advanced by a constitutionalized "living wage" for public (or private) employment? What makes the latter result less plausible than *Wadsworth*?

4. Consider the possible distinctions between *Wiser* and *Wadsworth*. Is the regulation at issue in *Wiser* more or less burdensome than the regulation at issue in *Wadsworth*? Does *Wiser* read *Wadsworth* as applying an enumerated or unenumerated right? If unenumerated, why would it be limited to the Article II, section 3 proviso of "all lawful ways"? (Why wouldn't the same limit apply to the right recognized in *Wadsworth*?) Can you think of a case in which the *Wadsworth* right would apply, other than in *Wadsworth*? Is *Wadsworth* still good law?

5. Do you agree with Justice Nelson in *MCIA* that a decision holding that the State of Montana cannot enforce its state law restrictions on medical marijuana would be "meaningless"? When might it not be meaningless to a medical marijuana business, even if the business is violating federal law?

6. The Court struggles through *Butte Community Union*, *Wadsworth*, *Wiser*, and *MCIA* to reconcile the "inalienable rights" beginning of section 3 with the police power "all lawful ways" end of section 3. The language of modern "fundamental rights" and tiered scrutiny are anachronisms that may not fit the subtler functions of natural rights reflected in state constitutional law. For some context, consider Steven G. Calabresi, Sarah E. Agudo & Katherine L. Dore, *The U.S. and the State Constitutions: An Unnoticed Dialogue*, 9 N.Y.U. J.L & LIBERTY 685, 689, 698, 702–03 (2015):

> It turns out that in 1791, seven of the fourteen State[s] all contained Lockean Natural Rights Guarantees in their State Bills of Rights which provided in effect that:
>
> > Article I. All men are born free and equal, and have certain natural, essential, and unalienable rights; among which may be reckoned the right of enjoying and defending their lives and liberties; that of acquiring, possessing, and protecting property; in fine, that of seeking and obtaining their safety and happiness.
>
> Thus, at least half the States, in 1791, recognized Lockean Natural Rights Guarantees as being deeply rooted in their history and tradition. This raised the disturbing possibility that the rights that are rooted deeply in American history and tradition might be the very same natural law rights that Judge Bork, Attorney General Meese, and Justice Scalia had been criticizing.... It turned out that the deeply rooted in history and tradition test is just circular and takes you back to Lockean natural law, since that is the belief that is deeply rooted in American history and tradition. ***
>
> When we turn to the modern era, we find that in 2010 that thirty-one states out of fifty, more than a three-fifths majority, contain Lockean Natural Rights Guarantees in their state constitutions. *** One other indicia of

> state protection of unenumerated individual rights is the presence in state constitutions of analogues to the federal Ninth Amendment. Not a single state had a Ninth Amendment analogue in its state constitution or bill of rights in 1791, but by 1868 eighteen of the thirty-seven state constitutions had such analogues. These "baby" Ninth amendment analogues declared that the enumeration of rights in state constitutions should not be construed to impair or deny other rights in state constitutions. By 2010, Ninth Amendment analogues in state constitutions increased to thirty-two states out of fifty, and 64% of the American people lived in states with "baby" Ninth Amendments.
>
> The growing popularity of Ninth Amendments like the growing popularity of Lockean Natural Rights Guarantees shows widespread public support for both liberty and unenumerated constitutional rights. This ought, at least, to support what Professor Randy Barnett has called a presumption of liberty.
>
> The presence of Ninth Amendment analogues in more than a three-fifths majority of the state constitutions in states with 64% of the American people counters the widely expressed theory that the federal Ninth Amendment was meant only to not preempt other state constitutional rights. It suggests instead that the federal and state Ninth Amendments mean what they say in protecting a presumption of liberty. Thus, one thing state constitutional law can teach federal constitutional lawyers is that the "deeply rooted in history and tradition" test is circular and does not work.

Professor Randy Barnett's "presumption of liberty," informed by the natural rights tradition reflected in Article II, section 3, rejects the conventional strict scrutiny analysis of favored fundamental rights adopted by most American jurists, including the Montana Supreme Court:

> Implicit in [constitutions] is the principle that the people retain their natural rights when they surrender to government the executive power to enforce their rights. A conception of the police power that is consistent with this principle would have the following components: (1) a *prohibition* of an act is proper when the act violates the rights of others (e.g., murder, rape, robbery, theft, trespass)—because such an act wrongfully violates the rights of another person, it is not properly called a "liberty"; (2) a *regulation* of liberty is proper when it is necessary to protect the rights of others from the risk of violation—for example, health and safety laws; and (3) to establish that a regulation of liberty is "necessary" would require the government to show some degree of fit between means and ends and that the measure is not simply a pretext for restricting the exercise of liberties of which the legislature disapproves.
>
> This approach to protecting liberty generally resembles how courts now protect the enumerated natural rights of speech, press, and assembly. The

prohibition of wrongful acts, such as fraud, defamation or trespass are constitutional notwithstanding that the acts being prohibited are speech or assembly. Regulations of rightful exercises of speech or assembly in the form of rules governing "time, place, and manner" are proper insofar as there is an appropriate fit between means and ends, they do not place an undue burden on the exercise of these rights, and they are not pretexts for prohibiting speech of which the government disapproves.

While there is much more to be said about this approach, this brief sketch reveals the following features:

(1) Instead of distinguishing those liberties that merit enhanced protection from those that do not, this approach seeks to identify the proper powers of federal and state governments.

(2) Rather than place an insurmountable burden of justification on the government that is fatal in fact as "strict scrutiny" is sometimes said to be, a presumption of liberty would be genuinely rebuttable.

(3) Only laws restricting the rightful exercise of a liberty—a small subset of all legislation—are scrutinized under this approach (although laws that do not restrict liberty might be scrutinized on other grounds, such as those suggested by the other two paragraphs of footnote four [of *United States v. Carolene Products Co.* (1938)]).

One potential price of extending judicial protection to liberty generally is the reduction of the protection now afforded to those preferred liberties that are deemed to be fundamental. But it is not at all clear that the proposed degree of scrutiny is any more permissive than the way the Supreme Court now protects the freedoms of speech and press in practice while purporting to apply "strict scrutiny." Of course, a court could always preserve a two-tiered approach by which the government must justify its restrictions on liberties as described above, but meet an increased burden when laws trench upon rights deemed to be fundamental. Because such an approach would only disparage rather than completely deny the other rights retained by the people, it would be a significant improvement over the modem doctrine of fundamental rights, especially as expounded by the *Glucksberg* Two-Step [of enforcing only carefully defined rights, deeply rooted in tradition, from *Washington v. Glucksberg* (1997)].

Randy E. Barnett, *Scrutiny Land*, 106 MICH. L. REV. 1479, 1499–1500 (2008). Would this approach make more sense of Article II, section 3 and the *Wadsworth* line of cases?

7. Compare Article II, section 3 with *Allgeyer v. Louisiana* (1897), which set the stage for judicial scrutiny of state regulations under the federal Due Process Clause in *Lochner v. New York* (1905):

> The liberty mentioned in that amendment means not only the right of the citizen to be free from the mere physical restraint of his person, as by incarceration, but the term is deemed to embrace the right of the citizen to be free in the enjoyment of all his faculties; to be free to use them in all lawful ways; to live and work where he will; to earn his livelihood by any lawful calling; to pursue any livelihood or avocation, and for that purpose to enter into all contracts which may be proper, necessary and essential to his carrying out to a successful conclusion the purposes above mentioned.

Would *Lochner*-type review of regulations (economic and otherwise) focused on the fit between an exercise of the police power and its justification be a better fit under state inalienable rights provisions?

8. Like the Supreme Court in *Lochner* itself, some states locate substantive *Wadsworth*-like "rights to make a living" in due process clauses. Consider *Patel v. Texas Dep't of Licensing* (Tex. 2015), which involved a challenge to a state licensing requirement for commercial eyebrow threading under Article I, section 19 of the Texas Constitution ("No citizen of this State shall be deprived of life, liberty, property, privileges or immunities, or in any manner disfranchised, except by the due course of the law of the land."):

> Following the lead of our prior jurisprudence, we conclude that the Texas due course of law protections in Article I, § 19, for the most part, align with the protections found in the Fourteenth Amendment to the United States Constitution. But, that having been said, the drafting, proposing, and adopting of the 1875 Constitution was accomplished shortly after the United States Supreme Court decision in the *Slaughter-House Cases* [(1872)] by which the Court put the responsibility for protecting a large segment of individual rights directly on the states. Given the temporal legal context, Section 19's substantive due course provisions undoubtedly were intended to bear at least some burden for protecting individual rights that the United States Supreme Court determined were not protected by the federal Constitution. That burden has been recognized in various decisions of Texas courts for over one hundred and twenty-five years. We continue to do so today: the standard of review for as-applied substantive due course challenges to economic regulation statutes includes an accompanying consideration as reflected by cases referenced above: whether the statute's effect as a whole is so unreasonably burdensome that it becomes oppressive in relation to the underlying governmental interest. ***
>
> ... To become a licensed esthetician, threaders must take at least 750 hours of instruction in a Commission-approved training program, and take State-prescribed practical and written examinations [at a cost of $3,500 to $9,000 for tuition alone]. Those training programs must devote at least 225 hours of instruction to facial treatments, cleansing, masking, and therapy; 90 hours to anatomy and physiology; 75 hours to electricity, machines, and

> related equipment; 75 hours to makeup; 50 hours to orientation, rules, and laws; 50 hours to chemistry; 50 hours to care of clients; 40 hours to sanitation, safety, and first aid; 35 hours to management; 25 hours to superfluous hair removal; 15 hours to aroma therapy; 10 hours to nutrition; and 10 hours to color psychology.... The record reflects that fewer than ten of the 389 Commission-approved Texas beauty schools teach threading techniques, and only one of those devotes more than a few hours to them. *** [T]he Threaders contend that as many as 710 of the required 750 training hours for an esthetician license are not related to properly training threaders in hygiene and sanitation, considering the activities they actually perform. The State argues that the Threaders greatly exaggerate the number of unrelated hours, but concedes that as many as 320 of the curriculum hours are not related to activities threaders actually perform. [For comparison, Texas requires Emergency Medical Technicians get only 140 hours of training.] ***
>
> [T]he admittedly unrelated 320 required training hours, combined with the fact that threader trainees have to pay for the training and at the same time lose the opportunity to make money actively practicing their trade, leads us to conclude that the Threaders have met their high burden of proving that, as applied to them, the requirement of 750 hours of training to become licensed is not just unreasonable or harsh, but it is so oppressive that it violates Article I, § 19 of the Texas Constitution.

How would the Texas Supreme Court's "unreasonably burdensome" measure of a law's fit apply in *Wadsworth*, *Wiser*, or *MCIA*?

C. A Clean and Healthful Environment

The 1972 Montana Constitution includes "the right to a clean and healthful environment" foremost among the inalienable rights. Controversy surrounded its inclusion and followed it decades later. The argument for calling a new constitutional convention in 2010 highlighted, but did not substantiate, a leading criticism of the provision:

> The "clean and healthful environment" provision... has been expanded by Montana's overzealous courts to prohibit any public or private activity which "implicates" the environment, unless you can prove a compelling state interest permitting it. Thus, Montana's constitution empowers judges and bureaucratic rulemakers to micro-meddle in your property rights, business affairs, and personal conduct.... When Montana's expansive constitution is placed in the hands of our overzealous courts, the net result is assault with a deadly weapon on Montana's economy and jobs.... Many believe it's no coincidence that the frightening downhill slide of Montana wages coincided with the activist judicial application of Montana's 1972 Constitution.

Yet after nearly fifty years, it is fair to say "the right to a clean and healthful environment" has fulfilled neither the hopes of its champions nor the fears of its detractors. Advocates and courts have struggled to articulate the scope of the right and the scrutiny it requires under the Declaration of Rights, while paying relatively little attention to its intersection with Article XI legislative duties. With conflicts between natural resource conservation and development at the forefront of Montana politics and policy, and the catastrophic effects of climate change no longer merely on the horizon, consider what work the right to a clean and healthful environment can or should do in Montana, and how.

Montana Environmental Information Center v. Department of Environmental Quality

296 Mont. 207 (1999)

Justice TERRY N. TRIEWEILER delivered the Opinion of the Court.

¶ 1 The Plaintiffs, Montana Environmental Information Center (MEIC), Clark Fork-Pend Oreille Coalition, and Women's Voices for the Earth, filed an amended complaint in the District Court for the First Judicial District in Lewis and Clark County in which the Department of Environmental Quality (DEQ) for the State of Montana was named as the Defendant and in which Seven-Up Pete Joint Venture (SPJV) subsequently intervened. Plaintiffs alleged, among other claims, that to the extent § 75-5-317(2)(j), MCA (1995) allows discharges of water from watering well or monitoring well tests, which degrade high quality waters without review pursuant to Montana's nondegradation policy found at § 75-5-303(3), MCA (1995), that statute is void for a violation of Article IX, Section 1(1) and (3) of the Montana Constitution. Plaintiffs sought an injunction suspending the exploration license that had been issued by DEQ to SPJV for pump tests to be performed at the site of its proposed gold mine. Both parties moved for summary judgment and following the submission of affidavits and oral testimony, the District Court held that absent a finding of actual injury, § 75-5-317(2)(j), MCA (1995) was not unconstitutional as applied and entered judgment for the DEQ. The Plaintiffs appeal from the judgment of the District Court. We reverse and remand for further review consistent with this opinion. ***

¶ 6 Seven-Up Pete Joint Venture has submitted an application for a massive open-pit gold mine in the upper Blackfoot River valley, near the confluence of the Landers Fork and Blackfoot Rivers. Plaintiffs' complaint alleged that in the summer of 1995, DEQ illegally amended SPJV's mineral exploration license to allow for the discharge of groundwater containing high levels of arsenic and zinc into the shallow aquifers of the Blackfoot and Landers Fork Rivers, without requiring nondegradation review pursuant to § 75-5-303(3), MCA (1995), and to the extent that it was authorized to do so, pursuant to § 75-5-317(2)(j), MCA (1995), the latter statute violates the right to a clean and healthy environment guaranteed by Article II, Section 3 of Montana's

Constitution, and the clear nondegradation policy established by Article IX, Section 1 of Montana's Constitution. ***

¶ 28 The District Court held that Article II, Section 3 of the Montana Constitution does provide a fundamental right to a clean and healthy environment, and that parties such as the Plaintiffs are entitled to bring a direct action in court to enforce that right. The District Court interpreted the Plaintiffs' challenge to § 75-5-317, MCA (1995) as an "applied" challenge based on the fact that Plaintiffs do not contend the statute is unconstitutional in all conceivable applications. However, the District Court held that before strict scrutiny applies, Plaintiffs must demonstrate that a right guaranteed by the constitution has been abridged and that in this case they did not do so because:

¶ 29 1. There is no proof that discharges from the mixing zones (as opposed to discharges from the ground) exceeded water quality standards;

¶ 30 2. Plaintiffs have demonstrated no significant changes to the quality of water on either the surfaces of the Landers Fork or Blackfoot Rivers;

¶ 31 3. Before a constitutional violation can be shown, Plaintiffs must demonstrate that the waters of the Blackfoot and Landers Fork are so affected that public health is threatened or applicable water quality standards are violated to the extent that there is a significant impact on either river. Absent a finding of actual injury, as defined, § 75-5-317, MCA, is not unconstitutional as applied.

¶ 32 In an order denying the Plaintiffs' request for an order temporarily restraining further pumping tests, the District Court noted the following factual findings which formed the basis for its conclusions:

¶ 33 1. The existing level of arsenic in the Landers Fork River is .0015 mg/l. The State expected the arsenic in the well water which was to be discharged into the infiltration gallery to be at a level of .014 mg/l and be reduced to .006 mg/l by the end of the mixing zone.

¶ 34 2. SPJV, however, concluded that the level of arsenic discharged into the infiltration galleries is .009 mg/l, far below the standard for aquatic life and the human health standard and that there will be no detectable change in the ambient level of arsenic in water 50 feet downstream from the point of discharge.

¶ 35 3. Based on these figures, there is no evidence of threat to public health, no violation of water quality standards, and no significant impact on the Landers Fork River or the Blackfoot River. ***

Constitutional and Statutory Framework

¶ 46 Appellants contend that § 75-5-317(2)(j), MCA (1995), violates their rights guaranteed by Article II, Section 3 and Article IX, Section 1 of the Montana Constitution.

¶ 47 Article II, Section 3 provides in relevant part that:

> All persons are born free and have certain inalienable rights. They include the right to a clean and healthful environment....

Mont. Const. art. II, § 3.

¶ 48 Article IX, Section 1 provides in relevant part as follows:

> (1) The State and each person shall *maintain and improve* a clean and healthful environment in Montana for present and future generations. ***
>
> (3) The legislature shall provide adequate remedies for the protection of the environmental life support system *from degradation* and provide adequate remedies to *prevent unreasonable depletion and degradation* of natural resources.

Mont. Const. art. IX, § 1 (emphasis added).

¶ 49 Although enacted prior to the constitutional provisions relied on, the Plaintiffs contend that the nondegradation policy for high quality waters established by § 75-5-303, MCA, of Montana's Water Quality Act is reasonably well designed to meet the constitution's objectives and that it is the minimum requirement which must be satisfied for a discharge which degrades the existing quality of Montana water. The relevant portions of that statute provide:

> (1) Existing uses of state waters and the level of water quality necessary to protect those uses must be maintained and protected.
>
> (2) Unless authorized by the department under subsection (3) or exempted from review under 75-5-317, the quality of high quality waters must be maintained.
>
> (3) The department may not authorize degradation of high quality waters unless it has been affirmatively demonstrated by a preponderance of evidence to the department that:
>
> (a) degradation is necessary because there are no economically, environmentally, and technologically feasible modifications to the proposed project that would result in no degradation;
>
> (b) the proposed project will result in important economic or social development and that the benefit of the development exceeds the costs to society of allowing degradation of high quality waters;
>
> (c) existing and anticipated use of state waters will be fully protected; and
>
> (d) the least degrading water quality protection practices determined by the department to be economically, environmentally, and technologically feasible will be fully implemented by the applicant prior to and during the proposed activity.

§ 75-5-317, MCA (1995).

¶ 50 Plaintiffs contend that the Constitution's environmental protections were violated by the legislature in 1995, when it amended § 75-5-317(2)(j), MCA to provide a blanket exception to the requirements of nondegradation review for discharges from water well or monitoring well tests without regard to the harm caused by those tests or the degrading effect that the discharges have on the surrounding or recipient environment.... ***

¶ 52 Because discharges containing carcinogenic parameters, (i.e., discharged water containing concentrations of arsenic equal to .009 mg/l) greater than those in the receiving water (i.e., .003 mg/l) were allowed in this case, Plaintiffs contend that the discharges should not have been exempt from nondegradation review by DEQ's own standards and that they have, therefore, demonstrated the necessary harm for strict scrutiny of the blanket exemption provided for in § 75-5-317(2)(j), MCA.

¶ 53 DEQ and SPJV on the other hand, contend that even before the 1995 amendment to § 75-5-317, MCA, which exempted well tests from nondegradation review, well tests were exempted from nondegradation review by ARM 16.20.713(i), the predecessor to what is currently ARM 17.30.716, which incorporates the exemptions found at § 75-5-317(2)(j), MCA by reference.

Constitutional Analysis

¶ 54 In order to address the issue raised on appeal, it is necessary that we determine the threshold showing which implicates the rights provided for by Article II, Section 3 and Article IX, Section 1 of the Montana Constitution and the level of scrutiny to be applied to each provision. DEQ and SPJV contend, and the District Court agreed that actual danger to human health or the health of the environment must first be demonstrated. The Plaintiffs contend that Montana's constitutional provisions are intended to prevent harm to the environment; that degradation to the environment is all that need be shown; and that degradation was established in this case based on the DEQ's own adopted standard.

¶ 55 We have not had prior occasion to discuss the level of scrutiny which applies when the right to a clean and healthful environment guaranteed by Article II, Section 3 or those rights referred to in Article IX, Section 1 are implicated. Nor have we previously discussed the showing which must necessarily be made to establish that rights guaranteed by those two constitutional provisions are implicated. However, our prior cases which discuss other provisions of the Montana Constitution and the debate of those delegates who attended the 1972 Constitutional Convention, guide us in both respects.

¶ 56 In *Butte Community Union v. Lewis* (Mont. 1986), we held that:

> If a fundamental right is infringed or a suspect classification established, the government has to show a "compelling state interest" for its action.....
>
> ... in order to be fundamental, a right must be found within Montana's Declaration of Rights or be a right "without which other constitutionally

guaranteed rights would have little meaning." *In the Matter of C.H.* (Mont. 1984).

Butte Community Union, 219 Mont. at 430, 712 P.2d at 1311.

¶ 57 We held, however, that a middle-tier level of scrutiny will be applied when a right is implicated which, though not contained in our declaration of rights, is referred to in our constitution even though the constitutional provision in question is merely directive to the legislature. We held that:

> A benefit lodged in our State Constitution is an interest whose abridgement requires something more than a rational relationship to a governmental objective.....
>
> ... Where constitutionally significant interests are implicated by governmental classification, arbitrary lines should be condemned. Further, there should be balancing of the rights infringed and the governmental interest to be served by such infringement.

Butte Community Union, 219 Mont. at 434, 712 P.2d at 1313–14.

¶ 58 We held that when a government classification is challenged as a violation of equal protection and a constitutionally significant interest is implicated, middle-tier scrutiny requires that the State demonstrate two factors: "(1) that its classification... is reasonable; and (2) that its interest in classifying... is more important than the people's interest in obtaining [constitutionally significant benefits]." *Butte Community Union*, 219 Mont. at 434.

¶ 59 We elaborated on the level of scrutiny for statutes or rules which implicate rights guaranteed in our declaration of rights in *Wadsworth v. State* (Mont. 1996). There we held that, "the inalienable right to pursue life's basic necessities is stated in the Declaration of Rights and is therefore a fundamental right." *Wadsworth*, 275 Mont. at 299.

¶ 60 We also held in *Wadsworth* that the nature of interest affected by state action dictates the standard of review that we apply and that: "[t]he most stringent standard, strict scrutiny, is imposed when the action complained of interferes with the exercise of a fundamental right or discriminates against a suspect class." *Wadsworth*, 275 Mont. at 302.

¶ 61 In *Wadsworth*, we gave the following explanation of what is required by strict scrutiny:

> Strict scrutiny of a legislative act requires the government to show a compelling state interest for its action. When the government intrudes upon a fundamental right, any compelling state interest for doing so must be closely tailored to effectuate only that compelling state interest. In addition to the necessity that the State show a compelling state interest for invasion of a fundamental right, the State, to sustain the validity of such invasion,

> must also show that the choice of legislative action is the least onerous path that can be taken to achieve the state objective.

Wadsworth, 275 Mont. at 302.

¶ 62 Finally, in language relevant to this case, we held in *Wadsworth* that, "while DOR's conflict of interest policy or *rule* is at issue rather than a statute, we, nevertheless, apply strict scrutiny analysis since the operation of that *rule* implicates Wadsworth's fundamental right to the opportunity to pursue employment." *Wadsworth*, 275 Mont. at 303 (emphasis added).

¶ 63 Applying the preceding rules to the facts in this case, we conclude that the right to a clean and healthful environment is a fundamental right because it is guaranteed by the Declaration of Rights found at Article II, Section 3 of Montana's Constitution, and that any statute or rule which implicates that right must be strictly scrutinized and can only survive scrutiny if the State establishes a compelling state interest and that its action is closely tailored to effectuate that interest and is the least onerous path that can be taken to achieve the State's objective.

¶ 64 State action which implicates those rights provided for in Article IX, Section 1 would normally not be subject to strict scrutiny because those rights are not found in Montana's Declaration of Rights. Those rights would normally be subject to a middle-tier of scrutiny because lodged elsewhere in our state constitution. However, we conclude that the right to a clean and healthful environment guaranteed by Article II, Section 3, and those rights provided for in Article IX, Section 1 were intended by the constitution's framers to be interrelated and interdependent and that state or private action which implicates either, must be scrutinized consistently. Therefore, we will apply strict scrutiny to state or private action which implicates either constitutional provision.

¶ 65 A thorough review of the discussion and debate among the delegates to our 1972 Constitutional Convention leads us to the further conclusion that the nature of the environmental rights provided by Articles II and IX cannot be interpreted separately, but that it was the delegates' intention that the two provisions compliment each other and be applied in tandem. Therefore, we look to the records of the convention discussion and debate to determine the showing that must be made before the rights are implicated and strict scrutiny applied.

¶ 66 Article IX, Section 1 was reported to the floor of the constitutional convention by the Natural Resources and Agricultural Committee on March 1, 1972. As originally proposed, however, Article IX, Section 1(1) required that "the state and each person. . . maintain and enhance the Montana environment for present and future generations." It did not provide, as does the current provision, the obligation to "maintain and improve a clean and healthful environment." Mont. Const. art. IX, § 1(1). The provision, as introduced, was thought by members of the committee to be the strongest environmental protection provision found in any state constitution. Delegate McNeil explained that descriptive adjectives were not included preceding the word environment such as healthful or unsoiled, because the majority felt that the current Montana environment encompassed all of those descriptive adjectives. He further explained that descriptive adjectives were not originally included because:

> The majority felt that the use of the word "healthful" would permit those who would pollute our environment to parade in some doctors who could say that if a person can walk around with four pounds of arsenic in his lungs or SO2 gas in his lungs and wasn't dead, that that would be a healthful environment. We strongly believe the majority does that our provision or proposal is stronger than using the word "healthful."

¶ 67 In discussing the interrelationship of subsections (1) and (3), Delegate McNeil stated:

> Subsection (3) mandates the Legislature to provide adequate remedies to protect the environmental life-support system from degradation. The committee intentionally avoided definitions, to preclude being restrictive. And the term "environmental life support system" is all-encompassing, including but not limited to air, water, and land; and whatever interpretation is afforded this phrase by the Legislature and courts, there is no question that it *cannot be degraded.*

(emphasis added).

¶ 68 There were delegates including Delegate Campbell who felt that without descriptive adjectives, such as "clean and healthful" prior to the term "environment," Article IX, Section 1 lacked the force that the majority had intended. However, the proponents of Section 1 as introduced, insisted that the subsection require that the environment not only be maintained but improved.

¶ 69 Delegate McNeil explained the committee's concern about including "clean and healthful" as follows:

> [T]he majority felt this would permit degradation of the present Montana environment to a level as defined in Illinois, which may be clean and healthful. *And our intention was to permit no degradation* from the present environment and affirmatively require enhancement of what we have now.

(emphasis added),

¶ 70 In further discussing the interrelationship between subsections (1) and (3) of Article IX, Delegate McNeil stated:

> The majority proposal before you now does recommend, as did Mr. Lindbergh, government monitoring. It goes further than that and directs the Legislature to provide remedies to prevent degradation. *This is anticipatory.*

(emphasis added).

> *The proposal mandates the legislature to prevent degradation* and to prevent unreasonable depletion. Now, that includes private property.

(emphasis added).

¶ 71 Delegates such as Mae Nan Robinson who agreed in substance with the preceding statements by Delegate McNeil suggested amendments but only for the purpose of assuring greater protection of the current environment. Delegate Robinson stated:

> I contend that if you're really trying to protect the environment, you'd better have something whereby you can sue or seek injunctive relief before the environmental damage has been done; it does very little good to pay someone monetary damages because the air has been polluted or because the stream has been polluted if you can't change the condition of the environment once it has been destroyed.

¶ 72 In defending the section as proposed, proponents explained that:

> The reason that the majority did not support a separate section saying "the right to sue", the paragraph 3 of our report states, "The Legislature is directed to provide adequate remedies for the protection of the environmental life support system from degradation and to provide adequate remedies to prevent unreasonable depletion of natural resources." Now, to those of us that studied what we were doing for a long time before we did it, we felt that this, in itself, is a lot stronger than, certainly, the proposal we're looking at right now [a proposed right to sue provision].

¶ 73 In concluding remarks in opposition to amending the committee majority's proposed Article IX, Section 1, Delegate McNeil gave the following explanation for the language being recommended:

> We did not want the Supreme Court of this state or the Legislature to be able to say that the environment in Montana, as we know right now, can be degraded to a healthful environment. So our purpose in leaving that word out was to strengthen it. I would like also to remind the delegates that the Illinois provision does not contain subparagraph 3 of the majority proposal, [Article IX, Section 1(3)] which speaks precisely to the point that concerned Jerry Cate so much, and that is there is no provision by which the Legislature can prevent and this is anticipatory can prevent unreasonable depletion of the natural resources. I submit if you will read that majority proposal again and again, you will find that it is the strongest of any constitution....

¶ 74 Delegate Foster also gave the following defense of the language as originally proposed:

> I feel that if we, as a Constitutional Convention of Montana, use our line of defense on the environment on the basis of healthful, then we, in fact,

> might as well forget it, because what I'm concerned about in Montana is not a healthful environment. This country is going to have to address itself to the question of a healthful environment. What I'm concerned about is an environment that is better than healthful. If all we have is a survivable environment, then we've lost the battle. We have nothing left of importance. The federal government will see to it one way or another, if it's in its power, that we have an environment in which we can manage to crawl around or to survive or to in some way stay "alive". But the environment that I'm concerned about is that stage of quality of the environment which is above healthful; and if we put in the Constitution that the only line of defense is a healthful environment and that I have to show, in fact, that my health is being damaged in order to find some relief, then we've lost the battle; so I oppose this amendment.

¶ 75 In the end advocates for adding the descriptive language "clean and healthful" prevailed. However, it was not on the basis that they wanted less protection than articulated by Delegates McNeil and Foster, it was because they felt the additional language was necessary in order to assure the objectives articulated by Delegates McNeil and Foster. It was agreed by both sides of the debate that it was the convention's intention to adopt whatever the convention could agree was the stronger language.

¶ 76 Although Article IX, Section 1(1), (2), and (3) were all approved by the convention on March 1, 1972, the right to a clean and healthful environment was not included in the Bill of Rights until six days later on March 7, 1972. On that date, Delegate Burkhart moved to add "the right to a clean and healthful environment" to the other inalienable rights listed in Article II, Section 3 of the proposed constitution. He explained his intention that it interrelate with those rights provided for and previously adopted in Article IX, Section 1. He also stated that it was his intention through the addition of this right to the Bill of Rights to give force to the language of the preamble to the constitution. Burkhart stated: "I think it's a beautiful statement, and it seems to me that what I am proposing here is in concert with what's proposed in that Preamble. . . ." Delegate Eck concurred that including the additional language in Article II, Section 3, was consistent with the intention of the Natural Resources Committee when it reported Article IX, Section 1. The right to a clean and healthy environment was, therefore, included as a fundamental right by a vote of 79 to 7. We have previously cited with approval the following language from 16 C.J.S. Constitutional Laws § 16 (1984):

> The prime effort or fundamental purpose, in construing a constitutional provision, is to ascertain and to give effect to the intent of the framers and of the people who adopted it. The court, therefore, should constantly keep in mind the object sought to be accomplished. . . and proper regard should be given to the evils, if any, sought to be prevented or remedied. . . .

General Agric. Corp. v. Moore (Mont. 1975).

¶ 77 We conclude, based on the eloquent record of the Montana Constitutional Convention that to give effect to the rights guaranteed by Article II, Section 3 and Article IX, Section 1 of the Montana Constitution they must be read together and consideration given to all of the provisions of Article IX, Section 1 as well as the preamble to the Montana Constitution. In doing so, we conclude that the delegates' intention was to provide language and protections which are both anticipatory and preventative. The delegates did not intend to merely prohibit that degree of environmental degradation which can be conclusively linked to ill health or physical endangerment. Our constitution does not require that dead fish float on the surface of our state's rivers and streams before its farsighted environmental protections can be invoked. The delegates repeatedly emphasized that the rights provided for in subparagraph (1) of Article IX, Section 1 was linked to the legislature's obligation in subparagraph (3) to provide adequate remedies for degradation of the environmental life support system and to prevent unreasonable degradation of natural resources.

¶ 78 We conclude, therefore, that the District Court erred when it held that Montana's constitutional right to a clean and healthy environment was not implicated, absent a demonstration that public health is threatened or that current water quality standards are affected to such an extent that a significant impact has been had on either the Landers Fork or Blackfoot River.

¶ 79 We conclude that the constitutional right to a clean and healthy environment and to be free from unreasonable degradation of that environment is implicated based on the Plaintiffs' demonstration that the pumping tests proposed by SPJV would have added a known carcinogen such as arsenic to the environment in concentrations greater than the concentrations present in the receiving water and that the DEQ or its predecessor after studying the issue and conducting hearings has concluded that discharges containing carcinogenic parameters greater than the concentrations of those parameters in the receiving water has a significant impact which requires review pursuant to Montana's policy of nondegradation set forth at § 75-5-303, MCA. The fact that DEQ has a rule consistent with § 75-5-317(2)(j), MCA (1995), is of no consequence. As we have previously held in *Wadsworth*, the constitution applies to agency rules as well as to statutes.

¶ 80 We conclude that for purposes of the facts presented in this case, § 75-5-303, MCA is a reasonable legislative implementation of the mandate provided for in Article IX, Section 1 and that to the extent § 75-5-317(2)(j), MCA (1995) arbitrarily excludes certain "activities" from nondegradation review without regard to the nature or volume of the substances being discharged, it violates those environmental rights guaranteed by Article II, Section 3 and Article IX, Section 1 of the Montana Constitution. [Fn. In fact, the delegates to the 1972 Constitutional Convention were very much aware of legislation passed during the previous year, such as requirements for nondegradation review and indicated that they felt that legislation was consistent with their own efforts to engraft environmental protection to Montana's Constitution.] Our holding is limited to § 75-5-317(2)(j), MCA (1995), as applied to the facts in this case. We have not been asked to and do not hold that this section facially implicates constitutional rights.

¶ 81 Based on these holdings, we reverse the judgment of the District Court and remand to the District Court for strict scrutiny of the statutory provision in question, and in particular for a determination of whether there is a compelling state interest for the enactment of that statute based on the criteria we articulated in *Wadsworth v. State.*

¶ 82 The judgment of the District Court is reversed and this case is remanded for further proceedings consistent with this opinion.

Justice W. WILLIAM LEAPHART, specially concurring.

¶ 83 I concur in the result reached by the Court and specifically with the conclusion that the right to a clean and healthful environment is a fundamental right guaranteed by the Declaration of Rights found at Article II, Section 3 of the Montana Constitution. Having so concluded, the Court goes on to declare that "state or private action which implicates either [Article II, Section 3 or Article IX, Section 1 of the Montana Constitution], must be scrutinized consistently. Therefore, we will apply strict scrutiny to state or private action which implicates either constitutional provision." I agree that state action implicating the rights guaranteed by Article II, Section 3 or Article IX, Section 1, must be subject to strict scrutiny. Although Article IX, Section 1, clearly imposes an obligation on private entities, as well as the state, to maintain and improve a clean and healthy environment, I would not, in the context of this appeal, address the question of private action. In resolving this appeal, we are not addressing private action. Rather, we are addressing state action; that is, the constitutionality of a state statute. The conclusion that we will apply strict scrutiny analysis to private action is dicta which, I submit, may well prove unworkable in the future. As we state in this opinion, strict scrutiny analysis requires that the state demonstrate a compelling state interest and that its action is both closely tailored to effectuate that interest and the least onerous path that can be taken to achieve the State's objective. I am not clear as to how, or whether, private action lends itself to a "compelling state interest" analysis. That is a question that I think would be better left to another day.

¶ 84 Finally, the Court concludes that

> to the extent § 75-5-317(2)(j), MCA (1995), arbitrarily excludes certain "activities" from nondegradation review without regard to the nature or volume of the substances being discharged, it violates those environmental rights guaranteed by Article II, Section 3 and Article IX, Section 1 of the Montana Constitution. Our holding is limited to § 75-5-317(2)(j), MCA

(1995), as applied to the facts of this case. We have not been asked to and do not hold that this section facially implicates constitutional rights.

¶ 85 I do not see how the Court can logically avoid declaring that the statute is unconstitutional on its face. The constitutional infirmity of § 75-5-317(2)(j), MCA (1995), is not limited to the facts in the present case but inheres in the statute's creation of a blanket exception. It creates a blanket exception to the requirements of nondegradation review for discharges from water well or monitoring well tests without regard to the harm caused by those tests or the degrading effect that the discharges have on the surrounding or recipient environment. The fact that there may be water discharges from well tests, say for agricultural purposes, that do not in fact create harm to the environment, does not alter the fact that such discharges are exempted from nondegradation review and that such review is the tool by which the State implements and enforces the constitutional right to a clean and healthy environment. The facial unconstitutionality of § 75-5-317(2)(j), MCA (1995), lies in its exemption of particular water discharges from nondegradation review without consideration of the nature and volume of substances in the water that is discharged. The possibility that some water discharges will not harm the environment does not justify their exemption from careful review by the State to protect Montana's fundamental rights to a clean and healthy environment and to be free from unreasonable degradation of that environment. The whole purpose of the nondegradation review is to determine, in advance, whether a water discharge will be harmful and, if so, is the harm justified and can it be minimized. See § 75-5-303, MCA. In excluding water discharges from well tests from review, the statute makes it impossible for the State to "prevent unreasonable depletion and degradation of natural resources" as required by Article IX, Section 1(3), of the Montana Constitution. Art. IX, Sec. 1(3), Mont. Const.

Chief Justice J.A. TURNAGE [and Justice KARLA M. GRAY] joins in the foregoing specially concurring opinion.

Cape-France Enterprises v. Estate of Peed

305 Mont. 513 (2001)

Justice JAMES C. NELSON delivered the Opinion of the Court.

¶ 1 Cape-France Enterprises brought this action to rescind an agreement between the parties for the sale of a tract of land in Bozeman, Montana. On cross-motions for summary judgment the District Court granted summary judgment in favor of Cape-France. The Estate of Lola Peed and Marthe Moore appeal from the District Court's order granting summary judgment in favor of Cape-France. ***

¶ 4 Cape-France Enterprises (Cape-France), is the owner of a tract of real property in Bozeman, Montana. Lola Peed and her granddaughter Marthe Moore (Peed and Moore) wished to buy a portion of that tract of land in order to build a motel or hotel. The two parties worked through a real-estate agent in the arrangement of this transaction.

¶ 5 Cape-France entered into a buy-sell agreement in 1994 with Peed and Moore for the purchase of a five acre portion of their land that was to be surveyed. The land had not been subdivided at the time of the agreement and needed to be subdivided and re-zoned in order for the sale to be completed. Closing was supposed to take place in September of 1994 but a plat creating the tract at issue was never recorded and the subdivision and closing never took place.

¶ 6 The parties attempted to accomplish subdivision of the property but several obstacles presented themselves. First, difficulties were encountered with the state and local agencies responsible for approving the subdivision. According to the depositions, application files were lost by the state more than once, which caused delays. Second, the parties encountered difficulty in obtaining water, which ultimately needed to be procured in order for subdivision to be approved. Water was not available to the land at the time the agreement was made. According to the agreement, it was the responsibility of Peed and Moore, as buyers, to bring water to the property. City water was not available, so presumably, a well would have to be drilled for that water.

¶ 7 To complicate matters further, a pollution plume was spreading through the groundwater in Bozeman in the area of the tract in question. Sometime during this process, it was discovered that the plume was closer to the land than had been expected. It is not clear where the pollution plume had moved, but state and local officials feared that it may have spread, possibly underneath the tract.

¶ 8 The potential presence of the pollution plume presented an obstacle to the parties' ability to subdivide the property. Ultimately, the Department of Environmental Quality, Water Quality Division (DEQ) warned Cape-France that the subdivision would not be approved unless a well was first drilled and tested. DEQ also warned that the pollution plume may have advanced under Cape-France's property and if the testing of the well water showed pollution in the water, the necessary treatment of this water would be extensive. Further, DEQ warned that if the drilling or pumping of the water caused expansion of the pollution, Cape-France, as the owner of the property, would be held liable for the clean-up costs. This warning took place after the subdivision process was commenced, making it clear to Cape-France that the completion of water drilling and testing was required before subdivision would be approved. According to the record, drilling and testing still have not been completed.

¶ 9 The warning came in December of 1995, when Cape France received a notice from DEQ, which informed it that the property was located within a groundwater contamination site....

¶ 10 Although the parties appear to have been aware of the existence of a pollution plume in Bozeman, presumably originating from a dry cleaner in the area, they believed the property at issue to be unaffected until receiving this notice.

¶ 11 A second letter was sent by DEQ to Cape-France, informing the partners that before subdivision could be approved:

> A well must be drilled and pump tested per WQB 3 3.2.4. Also, the well must be sampled for VOCs in accordance with EPA method 524.2. The well that is drilled and tested should be the proposed well that is closest to the Bozeman Solvent Site. ***

¶ 18 The Montana Code allows for rescission of a contract based on impossibility, under § 28-2-603, MCA, providing:

> Where a contract has but a single object and such object is unlawful, whether in whole or in part, or wholly impossible of performance, or so vaguely expressed as to be wholly unascertainable, the entire contract is void. ***

¶ 26 Moreover... while impossibility or impracticability is a high standard, the application of this doctrine is not limited to cases of literal impossibility. Here, the potential for substantial and unbargained-for damage involved in performing the contract is not only of an economic nature. Just as importantly, environmental degradation with consequences extending well beyond the parties' land sale is also a real possibility.

¶ 27 It is undisputed that the water system required for subdivision may tap into contaminated groundwater and that pumping this water could spread the pollution plume further into other, uncontaminated aquifers. ***

¶ 31 Montana's Constitution, Article II, Section 3, guarantees all persons in this state the right to a clean and healthful environment. This guarantee is a fundamental right that may be infringed only by demonstrating a compelling state interest. *MEIC v. Department of Environmental Quality*, 1999 MT 248 (recognizing that the right to a clean and healthful environment is a fundamental right because it is guaranteed by the Declaration of Rights in Montana's Constitution). We have stated that a compelling state interest is, "at a minimum, some interest 'of the highest order and... not otherwise served'" or "'the gravest abuse[], endangering [a] paramount [government] interest []'." *Armstrong v. State*, 1999 MT 261.

¶ 32 Moreover, interrelated with and interdependent upon Montanans' fundamental Article II, Section 3 right to a clean and healthful environment is the mandate provided in Article IX, Section 1, of our Constitution. This provision provides, in pertinent part, that "the State and each person shall maintain and improve a clean and healthful environment in Montana for present and future generations...." While *MEIC* involved state action, we, nonetheless, recognized that the text of Article IX, Section 1 applies the protections and mandates of this provision to private action—and thus to private parties—as well.

¶ 33 In light of these two provisions of Montana's Constitution, it would be unlawful for Cape-France, a private business entity, to drill a well on its property in the face of substantial evidence that doing so may cause significant degradation of uncontaminated aquifers and pose serious public health risks. As already noted, a contract may be rescinded where the object of the contract is unlawful. Section 28-2-603, MCA.

¶ 34 Moreover, for a court to mandate specific performance of the contract at issue on the record here, would not only be to require a private party to violate the Constitution—a remedy that no court can provide—but, as well, would involve the state itself in violating the public's Article II, Section 3 fundamental rights to a clean and healthful environment, and in failing to maintain and improve a clean and healthful environment as required by Article IX, Section 1.

¶ 35 Furthermore, the law's interest in enforcing a contract for a land sale between two private parties is hardly the sort of compelling state interest under the criteria that we discussed in *Armstrong* that would justify this, or any court, ordering specific performance of the parties' agreement given the fundamental constitutional rights at issue and the substantial risk of violating those rights as demonstrated by the record here.

¶ 36 As already noted, State and local officials required the drilling of a water well on Cape-France property in order for the subdivision to be approved, but warned that if the required well tapped into contaminated water and spread that contamination to the Cape-France property, adjacent property or other aquifers, Cape-France would be liable for the contamination and subsequent cleanup under state and federal laws.

¶ 37 Causing a party to go forward with the performance of a contract where there is a very real possibility of substantial environmental degradation and resultant financial liability for clean up is not in the public interest; is not in the interests of the contracting parties; and is, most importantly, not in accord with the guarantees and mandates of Montana's Constitution, Article II, Section 3 and Article IX, Section 1.

¶ 38 Affirmed. ***

Justice JIM RICE dissenting:

¶ 60 I join in the concerns expressed by Chief Justice Gray and Justice Leaphart [concurrence omitted] regarding the majority's application of constitutional principles herein. This case can be resolved on the contract issues alone, consistent with this Court's long tradition of declining to address constitutional issues where it is unnecessary. Further, while I do not dissent from the principles of environmental protection embodied in the Constitution, I do dissent from the majority's sweeping application of those principles in this case.

¶ 61 First, the majority's discussion of Article II, Section 3, of the Montana Constitution is incomplete. Article II, Section 3, states:

> Inalienable rights. All persons are born free and have certain inalienable rights. They include *the right to a clean and healthful environment* and the rights of pursuing life's basic necessities, enjoying and defending their lives and liberties, *acquiring, possessing and protecting property*, and seeking their

> safety, health and happiness in all lawful ways. In enjoying these rights, all persons recognize corresponding responsibilities. [Emphasis added.]

While the majority discusses the inalienable right to a clean and healthful environment contained in Article II, Section 3, the Court fails to even mention, in a case about acquiring property, the co-existent inalienable right of our people contained in Article II, Section 3, to acquire, possess and protect property. The majority omits any discussion of the interaction or balancing, if any, of these rights, which must occur when they are simultaneously at issue.

¶ 62 Second, the majority today holds that when the anticipated performance of a private, real property contract may potentially impact the environment, the contract's purpose is unlawful, and rescission is the appropriate remedy. Moreover, the majority has unilaterally assessed the potential for environmental contamination, despite the involvement of the regulatory bodies responsible for that determination, and on a record that leaves much in doubt. In the present case, DEQ determined that a test well should be drilled in accordance with established state and federal guidelines to determine whether contamination existed. On the basis of a letter suggesting that liability could be incurred for future contamination, the majority has determined that the DEQ's procedures for testing water pose an unconstitutional threat to the environment.

¶ 63 The decision leaves important questions unanswered. How certain must the potential be before the contract is deemed to have an unlawful purpose? How is a contract's potential adverse impact on the environment to be measured? How significant must that potential impact be? As the record discloses in this case, it has not been established that the plume has actually moved onto the seller's property. A misapprehension of fact—that a test well would exacerbate the existing contamination problem—has barred the test necessary to determine the plume's present location. Is a notice from the State that there may be a pollution issue affecting a parcel of property sufficient enough to prohibit use of the property? While future decisions of the Court may eventually resolve such questions, far too much is today left in doubt.

¶ 64 The environmental provisions of the Constitution may very well apply in this case, and may prohibit development of the proposed subdivision. However, on a record which leaves the question of potential environmental damage unsettled, the applicability of the constitutional protections cannot properly be determined. I would order a remand of this case, and after the material facts are established, the contract and constitutional principles at issue here could be properly adjudicated.

Chief Justice KARLA M. GRAY, dissenting.

*** I strenuously dissent from the Court's insertion—and resolution, on its own and without full briefing—of a nonexistent constitutional issue into this case.

¶ 75 This case was tried and appealed on issues of impracticability/impossibility of performance and specific performance. Whatever our respective views on those matters, the Court resolves the appeal on the basis of impossibility of performance.

Having so resolved the case, however, the Court then improperly inserts a discussion of a critically important constitutional right in Montana, the development of which through case law actually presenting the issue, is in its infancy. To that extent, the discussion is dicta in its entirety and, as a result, not controlling precedent. The problem is that dicta takes on a life of its own. The bigger problem is that the Montana constitutional rights relating to the environment are hugely important and impactful to the citizens of Montana and should not be dallied with by this Court in the absence of issues being raised in the District Court and fully briefed in this Court.

¶ 76 For the reasons stated above, I dissent from the Court's opinion on the issue actually before us and strenuously dissent from its inappropriate insertion of the "clean and healthful" discussion, which will unnecessarily fan the flames of controversy in Montana.

Park County Environmental Council v. Department of Environmental Quality

2020 MT 303

Chief Justice MIKE McGRATH delivered the Opinion of the Court. ***

¶3 Emigrant Gulch lies within of the Greater Yellowstone Ecosystem and is located just outside the Absaroka-Beartooth Wilderness. It is a mere 15 miles north of Yellowstone National Park and its watershed flows into the Yellowstone River, a world-renowned trout fishery. The Absaroka Mountains surrounding Emigrant Gulch are home to bighorn sheep, elk, deer, moose, marmots, coyotes, black bears, and wolves. Emigrant Gulch is within occupied grizzly bear and wolverine habitat as well as Canada lynx designated critical habitat. Emigrant Peak, the most prominent of the mountains flanking Emigrant Gulch, is a popular year-round recreation destination. At the mouth of Emigrant Gulch, residents and visitors have enjoyed the natural mineral pools of Chico Hot Springs for over 100 years. The region's natural beauty is also an important economic driver, supporting tourism that employs large numbers of Park County residents.

¶4 On February 17, 2015, Lucky Minerals, Inc. (Lucky) submitted an exploration license application seeking authorization under the Metal Mine Reclamation Act (MMRA), §§ 82-4-331-32, MCA, to conduct exploration activities within its privately-owned patented St. Julian mine claim block in Emigrant Gulch. Results from the proposed exploration would be used to model subsurface geology and associated mineralization. The St. Julian mine claim block is surrounded by the Custer Gallatin National Forest. Though the original proposal envisioned work on national forest lands, Lucky's revised proposal is for exploration only on its privately-owned patented claims on the St. Julian mine claim block. In its application, Lucky proposed to drill up to 46 holes—expected to average 1,000 feet in depth, with some potentially reaching as deep as 2,000 feet—from 23 drill pads. The work would take place over the course of two field seasons, each anticipated to last from mid-July to mid-October.

Lucky proposed using two drills running two ten-hour shifts per day, the night shift relying on light sources similar to those used by highway construction crews.

¶5 To reach Emigrant Gulch, one must traverse a forest service road that has suffered from rockslides and avalanches and is at times comparable to a Jeep trail not travelable by highway vehicles and best approached by ATV. Lucky's proposed exploration is expected to require the clearing of rocks and debris from the existing Forest Service road in order to access the drilling sight with vehicles and heavy equipment.

¶6 Pursuant to the Montana Environmental Policy Act (MEPA), found under Title 75, chapter one, MCA, the Montana Department of Environmental Quality (DEQ) released a draft Environmental Assessment (Draft EA) in response to Lucky's proposal on October 13, 2016. The Draft EA concluded that Lucky's proposed exploration would not result in significant environmental impacts.

¶7 However, the Draft EA did state that Lucky's proposed exploration would lead to an increase in wildlife disturbance, as road improvements intended to allow Lucky's mining equipment and vehicles to access Emigrant Gulch would also provide easier access for hunters, trappers, and others to enter habitat that has long been inaccessible to many. The Draft EA went on to describe the expected disturbance and displacement of grizzly bears and the potential for den abandonment by female wolverines. Scientific studies in the administrative record confirm that increased human presence in remote areas may have negative effects on wolverine and grizzly bear populations.

¶8 Among the more than 3,000 public comments made on the Draft EA, Montana Fish Wildlife & Parks (FWP) commented that the road improvements could "significantly increase[] [the] level of disturbance and fragmentation" of a presently "very remote and rarely disturbed" habitat. It warned of "a permanent change to the landscape, with long-term implications" for wildlife populations in the area, especially wolverine, lynx, grizzly bear, elk, deer, and moose. FWP recommended altering the project to avoid road improvements or reclaim/close the road after the project's completion.

¶9 On July 26, 2017, DEQ issued its Final Environmental Assessment (Final EA), maintaining that the project posed no significant environmental, and approved Lucky's proposal with slight modifications. In the Final EA, DEQ responded to FWP's comments regarding road improvements by noting that it had "re-evaluated the impact on wildlife resulting from the proposed road improvements and believes that the draft EA overstated the impacts." The Final EA concluded that the road work "may marginally make access to the area easier for hunters and may marginally increase higher mortality" for wildlife in addition to potentially increasing "the harassment or poaching of wildlife." However, DEQ did not expect the proposal to "materially change [the road's] character of an unimproved forest road."

¶10 The Final EA also outlined DEQ's detailed analysis of groundwater quality in the area. DEQ tested groundwater quality at a number of sites in the area, exhibiting a range of water chemistry values. DEQ determined that "[s]ome of the mineralized geologic materials in the Emigrant Mining District are potentially reactive and may produce acid rock drainage or mobilize metals under near-neutral pH conditions. Some water quality samples within the district reflect the reactive nature of the geology. . . ." In particular, DEQ found elevated acidity and concentrations of Total Dissolved Solids (TDS) and sulfites in sights tested to the north of the East Fork of Emigrant Creek (East Fork), which drains the proposed exploration area. Though DEQ identified natural acid rock drainage occurring to the north of the East Fork, the agency concluded that the reactivity of that slope was due to a locally intense pyrite alteration that was not reflective of all subsurface materials in the East Fork drainage. The Final EA noted the presence of disseminated sulfides throughout the Emigrant Mining District deposits.

¶11 The Final EA also analyzed DEQ's groundwater testing on the south side of the East Fork, the same slope upon which the proposed exploration would occur. DEQ collected samples from a spring, two seeps, and three boreholes created during exploration conducted in 1971–73, known as the Duval Corporation Boreholes (Duval Boreholes). DEQ found minimal flow of less than five gallons per minute and no water quality standard exceedances at these sites, with relatively neutral pH values ranging from slightly acidic to slightly basic. DEQ concluded that the samples from the seeps and the Duval Boreholes "represent what is known about the groundwater flowing mid-slope on the south side of the East Fork." Although the "depths of the [Duval] [B]oreholes and the nature of the altered volcanics that were encountered are unknown," the Final EA found it "likely that [Lucky's] proposed boreholes could produce water with chemistry and flow similar to the Duval Corporation boreholes and the seeps below the St. Julian Mine."

¶12 The Final EA concluded that the expected artesian flow from Lucky's proposed drilling would, like the Duval Boreholes, result in "no discernible impact on water quantity or quality in the East Fork of Emigrant Creek drainage, and even less so further downstream in Emigrant Gulch." Not only was the groundwater flowing out of the drill holes expected to be of acceptable quality and limited quantity, but DEQ determined that it could be contained. In addressing potential long term impacts of the proposed boreholes, the Final EA pointed to a regulatory provision (not in existence when the Duval Corporation created its boreholes in the 1970s) requiring Lucky to plug each hole prior to removing the drill rig. *See* Admin. R. M. 17.24.106 (1994). To address the impacts of the expected "artesian conditions" during drilling, the Final EA only noted that Lucky would be required to "develop a mitigation plan to effectively contain flow from artesian boreholes during drilling" and that "procedures for artesian flow containment would be developed prior to commencing drilling operations."

¶13 In the Final EA, DEQ briefly considered completing the exploration project within one year rather than two and eliminating night drilling as alternatives to Lucky's proposal. However, DEQ dismissed these alternatives without significant analysis based on the determination that the impacts would be substantially the same as those envisioned by Lucky's proposal. DEQ determined that, by compressing the exploration project into a single season, Lucky might need to use four drill rigs instead of two, with an attendant increase in traffic, noise, and lighting. Under the other alternative, abandoning night drilling, Lucky's operation could potentially minimize bat disturbances, but would result in the project requiring an additional three or four seasons to reach completion. In addition to a "No Action Alternative," DEQ also considered an "Agency-Modified Alternative" to Lucky's proposal containing minor mitigation measures. The Final EA did not address the potential environmental impacts if Lucky were to use information gained from the proposed exploration to establish vested rights to conduct full scale mining in adjacent federal lands. ***

¶52 *Issue Six: Whether the District Court erred in determining that § 75-1-201(6)(c) and (d), MCA, which bars equitable remedies for a Montana Environmental Policy Act violation, is unconstitutional under Article II, Section 3, and Article IX, Section 1, of the Montana Constitution.*

¶53 Because DEQ concedes that its analysis of road improvement impacts on wildlife and mitigation plans for expected artesian flow during drilling fell short under MEPA, we must now address the issue of appropriate remedies. DEQ asks, and we have agreed, that the matter be remanded to the agency to cure these shortcomings. The issue here centers around the status of Lucky's exploration license while DEQ proceeds to complete its MEPA review. Lucky and the Attorney General contest the District Court order vacating Lucky's exploration license in the interim, pointing to legislative amendments made to MEPA in 2011 (2011 Amendments) prohibiting equitable relief for a MEPA violation. The District Court concluded that the 2011 Amendments violated the Montana Constitution's guarantee of a "clean and healthful environment" and its corollary obligation upon the Legislature to provide "adequate remedies to prevent unreasonable depletion and degradation of natural resources." Mont. Const., art. II, § 3, art. IX, § 1. ***

¶57 The 2011 Amendments to MEPA provide that:

> (c) The remedy in any action brought for failure to comply with or for inadequate compliance with a requirement of parts 1 through 3 of this chapter is limited to remand to the agency to correct deficiencies in the environmental review conducted pursuant to subsection (1).
>
> (d) A permit, license, lease, or other authorization issued by an agency is valid and may not be enjoined, voided, nullified, revoked, modified, or suspended pending the completion of an environmental review that may be remanded by a court.

Section 75-1-201(6), MCA. These provisions allow a project to go forward even when, as here, the agency has conceded that the project was approved without the proper environmental review required by MEPA. A court's only remedy under the 2011

Amendments is to remand to the agency to complete its review, with no ability to halt the project in the interim.

¶58 Article II, Section 3, of the Montana Constitution guarantees Montanans inalienable rights that "include the right to a *clean and healthful environment* and the rights of pursuing life's basic necessities, enjoying and defending their lives and liberties, acquiring, possessing and protecting property, and seeking their safety, health and happiness in all lawful ways." Mont. Const., art. II, § 3 (emphasis added).

¶59 Significantly, Article IX, Section 1, of the Montana Constitution further provides:

> (1) The state and each person shall maintain and improve a clean and healthful environment in Montana for present and future generations.
>
> (2) The legislature shall provide for the administration and enforcement of this duty.
>
> (3) The legislature shall provide adequate remedies for the protection of the environmental life support system from degradation and *provide adequate remedies to prevent unreasonable depletion and degradation* of natural resources.

Mont. Const., art. IX, § 1 (emphasis added).

¶60 Laws implicating either constitutional provision are subject to strict scrutiny. *MEIC* [*v. DEQ* (Mont. 1999)] *I*. Here, neither Lucky nor the Attorney General argue that the 2011 Amendments would survive strict scrutiny review. Instead, they argue that the 2011 Amendments do not implicate the constitutional right or, alternatively, that the Court should apply a lower level of scrutiny by balancing these rights against the right to "possessing and protecting property." Mont. Const. art. II, § 3. ***

¶62 Our conclusions in *MEIC I* are consistent with the constitutional text's unambiguous reliance on preventative measures to ensure that Montanans' inalienable right to a "clean and healthful environment" is as evident in the air, water, and soil of Montana as in its law books. Article IX, Section 1, of the Montana Constitution describes the environmental rights of "future generations," while requiring "protection" of the environmental life support system "from degradation" and "prevent[ion of] unreasonable depletion and degradation" of the state's natural resources. This forward-looking and preventative language clearly indicates that Montanans have a right not only to reactive measures after a constitutionally-proscribed environmental harm has occurred, but to be free of its occurrence in the first place.

¶63 Montanans' right to a clean and healthful environment is complemented by an affirmative duty upon their government to take active steps to realize this right. Article IX, Section 1, Subsections 1 and 2, of the Montana Constitution command that the Legislature "shall provide for the administration and enforcement" of measures to meet the State's obligation to "maintain and improve" the environment. Critically, Subsection 3 explicitly directs the Legislature to "provide adequate remedies to prevent unreasonable depletion and degradation of natural resources." Mont. Const. art. IX, § 3.

¶64 When considering which remedies are "adequate" in this context, we note that equitable relief, unlike monetary damages, can avert harms that would have otherwise arisen. It follows that equitable relief must play a role in the constitutional directive to ensure remedies that are adequate to prevent the potential degradation that could infringe upon the environmental rights of present and future generations. We are not alone in this conclusion. As Delegate Mae Nan Robinson pointed out during the 1972 Constitutional Convention:

> if you're really trying to protect the environment, you'd better have something whereby you can sue or seek injunctive relief before the environmental damage has been done; it does very little good to pay someone monetary damages because the air has been polluted or because the stream has been polluted if you can't change the condition of the environment once it has been destroyed.

¶65 We turn now to MEPA's role in fulfilling this constitutional mandate. MEPA, which requires environmental review prior to government actions that may significantly affect the human environment, § 75-1-201, MCA, was enacted in 1971—just prior to the 1972 Constitutional Convention—with nearly unanimous support from across the political spectrum. MEPA's policy declaration provided that the State will pursue various ends consistent with a thoughtful relationship between the State and Montana's natural environment, including to:

> (a) fulfill the responsibilities of each generation as trustee of the environment for succeeding generations;
>
> (b) assure for all Montanans safe, healthful, productive, and aesthetically and culturally pleasing surroundings;
>
> (c) attain the widest range of beneficial uses of the environment without degradation, risk to health or safety, or other undesirable and unintended consequences....

Section 75-1-103(2), MCA (1971). The provision went on: "The legislature recognizes that each person shall be entitled to a healthful environment and that each person has a responsibility to contribute to the preservation and enhancement of the environment." According to MEPA's 1971 statement of purpose, MEPA would "promote efforts which will prevent or eliminate damage to the environment and biosphere and stimulate the health and welfare of man, to enrich the understanding of the ecological systems and natural resources important to the state."

¶66 These statements of purpose and intent were subsequently amended several times, including in 1995 when the Legislature added language expressing a concern for protecting private property rights from "undue government regulation." A 2003 amendment inserted language stating that the Legislature had enacted MEPA "mindful of its constitutional obligations under Article II, section 3 and Article IX of the Montana constitution," that MEPA "is procedural," and that the purpose of environmental review is to ensure that "environmental attributes are fully considered." The 2003 amendments also recognized that, in addition to the right to a healthful environment, each person has a right to "pursue life's basic necessities" and that the "implementation of these rights requires the balancing of the competing interests" in order "to protect the public health, safety, and welfare." In 2011, MEPA's policy statement was amended to clarify that the purpose of environmental review under MEPA is to better enable the Legislature "to fulfill [its] constitutional obligations" and to "assist the legislature in determining whether laws are adequate to address impacts to Montana's environment and to inform the public and public officials of potential impacts resulting from decisions made by state agencies." The 2011 Amendments also contained the provisions at issue in this dispute, seeking to prevent the grant of equitable remedies for MEPA violations.

¶67 We agree that MEPA serves a role in enabling the Legislature to fulfill its constitutional obligation to prevent environmental harms infringing upon Montanans' right to a clean and healthful environment. The Attorney General points to our language in the 1979 *Kadillak v. Anaconda Co.* [(Mont. 1979)] decision as support for the opposite proposition. There, we held that an EIS was not necessary where the 60 days in which the agency was directed to act by the Hardrock Mining Act were too prohibitively few to allow for a comprehensive EIS to be prepared. While seeking to interpret MEPA in a way reconcilable with the Hardrock Mining Act, we briefly addressed the Montana Constitution's environmental provisions and found:

> no indication that the MEPA was enacted to implement the new constitutional guarantee of a "clean and healthful environment." This Court finds that the statutory requirement of an EIS is not given constitutional status by the subsequent enactment of this constitutional guarantee. If the Legislature had intended to give an EIS constitutional status they could have done so after 1972.

¶68 *Kadillak* is not persuasive here. Subsequent MEPA amendments made clear that the Legislature has shaped MEPA as a vehicle for pursuing its constitutional mandate. *See* § 75-1-102(2), 103(2)(d), MCA (1995 Mont. Laws ch. 352, §§ 1-2) (addressing constitutional property rights); § 75-1-102(1), MCA (2003 Mont. Laws ch. 361, § 5) (providing that Legislature had enacted MEPA "mindful of its constitutional obligations under Article II, section 3 and Article IX of the Montana constitution."); § 75-1-102(1)(a), (3)(a), MCA (2011 Mont. Laws ch. 396, § 1) (declaring the purpose of environmental review under MEPA to better enable the Legislature "to fulfill [its] constitutional obligations" and to "assist the legislature in determining whether laws are adequate to address impacts to Montana's environment"); *see also N. Plains Res. Council, Inc. v. Mont. Bd. of Land Comm'rs*, 2012 MT 234 ("One of the ways that the Legislature has implemented Article IX, Section 1 is by enacting MEPA.").

¶69 The Montana Constitution's framers likely saw MEPA as an essential element of Legislative efforts to meet the government's newly-enshrined constitutional obligations. MEPA's freshly enacted references to an individual right to a healthful environment—vested in present and future generations—and the State's role in preventing degradation and "unintended consequences" to that environment could not have been far from the minds of the delegates who convened in January of the following year to constitutionalize many of these very same environmental principles. The undeniable proximity in time and substance between these two lawmaking efforts informs our conclusion that the constitutional obligations at issue encompass the forward-looking mechanisms found within MEPA.

¶70 We agree that MEPA's role in fulfilling the Legislature's constitutional mandate is essentially procedural. "Procedural," of course, does not mean "unimportant." The Montana Constitution guarantees that certain environmental harms shall be prevented, and prevention depends on forethought. MEPA's procedural mechanisms help bring the Montana Constitution's lofty goals into reality by enabling fully informed and considered decision making, thereby minimizing the risk of irreversible mistakes depriving Montanans of a clean and healthful environment. Therefore, the Legislature cannot fulfill its constitutional obligation to prevent proscribed environmental harms without some legal framework in place that mirrors the uniquely "anticipatory and preventative" mechanisms found in the original MEPA.

¶71 From the 1972 ratification of the Montana Constitution until 2011, MEPA performed an essential part of the Legislature's efforts to meet its constitutional obligations by ensuring that information was gathered and carefully considered *before* committing to an action with potential to cause an environmental harm forbidden by the Constitution. While MEPA's text prior to 2011 did not explicitly provide for equitable remedies, such relief is generally appropriate for violations of the sort and this Court has granted injunctions for MEPA violations prior to the 2011 Amendments. Thus, the 2011 amendments constituted a significant departure from MEPA as it existed since its enactment less than a year prior to Montana's Constitutional Convention.

¶72 Without a mechanism to prevent a project from going forward until a MEPA violation has been addressed, MEPA's role in meeting the State's "anticipatory and preventative" constitutional obligations is negated. Whatever interest might be served by a statute that instructs an agency to forecast and consider the environmental implications of a project that is already underway—perhaps analogous to a mandatory aircraft inspection after takeoff—the constitutional obligation to prevent certain environmental harms from arising is certainly not one of them.

¶73 Here, DEQ has conceded that it failed to conduct the level of review required by MEPA in determining whether to approve Lucky's exploration permit. This information gap occurred within the Greater Yellowstone Ecosystem and the Yellowstone River watershed, in an area that is a mere 15 miles from the national park, home to important habitat for wildlife including grizzly bears and wolverines, and host to one of the most popular year-round recreation destinations in Montana and a tourism-dependent human economy. The need for fully informed and considered decision making could hardly be more pressing.

¶74 DEQ requests a remand to correct this shortfall, gaining the information that it was required under MEPA to collect *prior* to making a permitting decision. However, under the 2011 Amendments, DEQ's early error is essentially irreversible, and the cost of that error will accrue to Montanans' constitutionally-guaranteed environmental rights. Presumably, one of Lucky's first orders of business in proceeding with the proposed exploration will be making improvements to the access road. FWP warned that this undertaking could create a "permanent change to the landscape, with long-term implications" for important wildlife by "significantly increas[ing the] level of disturbance and fragmentation" of a presently "very remote and rarely disturbed" habitat. The 2011 Amendments seek to allow Lucky to commence this work before DEQ completes supplemental review, a review that can be expected to achieve very little beyond informing Montanans—perhaps tragically—of the consequences of actions that have already been taken. Article IX, Section 1, of the Montana Constitution guarantees that the government will provide Montanans with remedies adequate to prevent unreasonable degradation of their natural resources. This guarantee includes the assurance that the government will not take actions jeopardizing such unique and treasured facets of Montana's natural environment without first thoroughly understanding the risks involved.

¶75 The Attorney General does not contest the assertion that the 2011 MEPA amendments render the statute incapable of protecting Council and Coalition's constitutional rights, but, rather, points to the MMRA and a host of other substantive environmental laws as evidence that the Legislature has met its burden of providing Council and Coalition with "adequate remedies," even absent meaningful MEPA remedies. The Attorney General points to various ways in which these provisions protect environmental interests by regulating Lucky's behavior and providing remedies—including injunctive relief—should Lucky violate these provisions.

¶76 These cumulative efforts to meet the Legislature's constitutional obligations, however, fail to show that MEPA is redundant within Montana's ecosystem of environmental protections. MEPA is unique in its ability to avert potential environmental harms through informed decision making. As Delegate Mae Nan Robinson pointed out during the 1972 Constitutional Convention, a remedy implemented only *after* a violation is a hollow vindication of constitutional rights if a potentially irreversible harm has already occurred. Furthermore, MEPA's environmental review process is complementary to—rather than duplicative of—other environmental provisions, functioning to, for example, enable DEQ to make an informed decision in responding to Lucky's operational permit application under the MMRA. Without some other equally proactive and preventative measure in place, injunctive relief available under MEPA *before* action commences remains essential to fulfilling the constitutional mandate.

¶77 The Attorney General's reliance on *N. Plains Res. Council, Inc. v. Mont. Bd. of Land Comm'rs,* where we upheld leases made to Arch Coal prior to environmental review, actually demonstrates this point. There, we upheld the leases at issue because the environmental review would still occur before the permitting stage and the leases themselves allowed for no environmental degradation. *Northern Plains* demonstrates that the relevant question is whether an environmental review occurs at some point *before* decisions are made and actions are taken which have the potential for causing environmental harm. Lucky and the Attorney General's opposite contention, that the environmental review may constitutionally occur *after* the project has begun, is unsupported.

¶78 We are not asked here to engage in a difficult exercise of determining what attributes constitute a "clean" or "healthful" environment, or an "unreasonable" amount of degradation, or what the judiciary's role should be in answering these questions. The question presented to us by this case is straightforward: has the Legislature met its obligation to provide "adequate remedies" with which to prevent potential future environmental harms when it removes what appears to be the *only* available legal relief positioned to do so? We conclude that it has not.

¶79 Having determined that § 75-1-201(6)(c) and (d), MCA (2011 Amendments), fails to meet the State's constitutional obligations and burden constitutional rights, we now turn to selecting the appropriate level of scrutiny with which to analyze these provisions. We have determined that the rights found in Article II, Section 3, and Article IX, Section 1, of the Montana Constitution are fundamental rights and should be subject to strict scrutiny. The Attorney General does not contest the District Court's finding that the 2011 Amendments fail under strict scrutiny but instead asks us to analyze the 2011 Amendments by balancing environmental rights against the private property rights also found in the Montana Constitution. *See* Mont. Const. art. II, § 3 (setting forth inalienable rights including the right of "possessing and protecting property"); Mont. Const. art. II, § 17 (providing the right to due process protection of property); Mont. Const. art. II, § 29 (protecting right to just compensation for taking of private property).

¶80 Balancing may be appropriate when a case presents an irreconcilable conflict between the co-equal rights of the parties. *See, e.g.,* [the right of privacy and the right to know]. Here, however, MEPA's enforcement does not implicate Lucky's private property rights to a constitutionally cognizable degree. When "regulations are designed to have a real and substantial bearing upon the public health, safety, morals and general welfare of a community, such regulations do not unduly interfere with the fundamental nature of private property ownership." *Williams v. Bd. of Cty. Comm'rs of Missoula Cty.,* 2013 MT 243. MEPA poses even less of a burden on private property ownership than regulations designed to protect the general welfare. As the Attorney General points out, MEPA is procedural and contains no regulatory language. While it directs the government to engage in informed decision making, MEPA itself does not restrict Lucky's use of its private property.

¶81 Restrictions on Lucky's ability to conduct mining operations on its private property stem from the MMRA, rather than MEPA. Completely apart from MEPA or its 2011 Amendments, the MMRA forbids Lucky from commencing mining activities until permitted to do so by the State. Government regulation of mining has never been held to pose an undue burden on private property rights. If the MMRA's requirement that Lucky await DEQ approval prior to commencing exploration activities does not cognizably burden a constitutional property right, then MEPA's requirement that DEQ's decision on the matter be well-informed certainly does not either.

¶82 Neither does an equitable remedy for a MEPA violation substantially interfere with constitutionally protected property rights. In essence, it simply requires an applicant to undergo the same wait now that it should have experienced before. There is no argument that simply waiting for DEQ to properly review and act upon an application constitutes an infringement upon property rights. Had DEQ completed the analysis of wildlife impacts and artesian flow containment plans *before* issuing the exploration permit, as required by MEPA, Lucky could not have complained that its private property rights were burdened by being forced to wait for that process to be completed. Waiting while DEQ completes that review *now* does not signify a substantially greater constitutional burden than that which would have been felt while awaiting the completion of that same review process when it should have occurred—*before* the permit was issued. That DEQ's error may give rise to some administrative delay with which to cure the shortfall does not demonstrate an unconstitutional infringement of private property rights.

¶83 DEQ's erroneously premature approval of Lucky's application did not grant Lucky an irrevocable and constitutionally-protected private property right. Even after a permit has been granted, DEQ has broad enforcement powers to address subsequent violations, including through permanent injunctive relief. We do not see why a court-ordered injunction to remedy a MEPA violation poses more of a threat to property rights than an agency-ordered injunction to remedy a substantive violation. Any private property rights implicated by an equitable remedy here are far too minor to be constitutionally cognizable and move us from a strict scrutiny to a balancing analysis.

¶84 As noted previously, the parties do not contest the District Court ruling that the 2011 Amendments fail under strict scrutiny. They do not attempt to demonstrate the 2011 Amendments are narrowly tailored to further a compelling government interest. Because § 75-1-201(6)(c) and (d), MCA, burdens Counsel and Coalition's fundamental constitutional rights and does not withstand strict scrutiny, we hold that these amendments are unconstitutional under Article II, Section 3, and Article IX, Section 1, of the Montana Constitution.

¶85 The parties disagree on whether we should view this as an as-applied or facial constitutional challenge. The distinction is perhaps overstated.

¶86 Courts seek to resolve the controversy at hand, not to speculate about the constitutionality of hypothetical fact patterns. Generally, a statute's facial invalidity does not depend upon the characterization of the challenge brought; rather, it results from our duty to fashion an appropriate remedy in resolving the case before us and to subsequently adhere to the resulting opinion's precedential reasoning. Here, the 2011 Amendments are unconstitutional because they substantially burden a fundamental right and are not narrowly tailored to further a compelling government interest. Thus, our conclusion that § 75-1-201(6)(c) and (d), MCA, is unconstitutional flows from the content of the statute itself, not the particular circumstances of the litigants. This is the hallmark of facial unconstitutionality.

¶87 In *MEIC I,* we held that the challenged statute was subject to strict scrutiny and that it violated environmental rights but limited our decision to the application of the facts of that case. In a special concurrence, Justice Leaphart wrote [that the blanket statutory exception for nondegradation review was facially unconstitutional].

¶88 As in *MEIC I,* the 2011 Amendments at issue here are unconstitutional because they undercut the State's ability to determine in advance whether a given activity will cause environmental harm and thereby take actions to "prevent unreasonable depletion and degradation of natural resources" as required by Article IX, Section 1(3), of the Montana Constitution. Additionally, the 2011 Amendments categorically remove the Plaintiffs' only available remedy adequate to prevent potential constitutionally-proscribed environmental harms, in violation of Article IX, Section 1(3), of the Montana Constitution's guarantee of "adequate remedies." The constitutional infirmities here, as in *MEIC I,* are not limited to the present facts but stem from the statute itself. We find Justice Leaphart's reasoning persuasive and adopt it here.

¶89 MEPA is an essential aspect of the State's efforts to meet its constitutional obligations, as are the equitable remedies without which MEPA is rendered meaningless. Section 75-1-201(6)(c) and (d), MCA, by seeking to deny the people of Montana these remedies, falls short of the constitutional guarantee and is therefore facially unconstitutional. Vacatur of the previously issued exploration permit is an equitable remedy suitable to the present MEPA violations and we affirm the District Court decision to that effect. ***

JAMES JEREMIAH SHEA, BETH BAKER, LAURIE McKINNON, Concur.

Notes on a Clean and Healthful Environment

1. The Court in *MEIC* reads the environmental policy provisions of Article IX, section 1 into the inalienable right provision of Article II, section 3, and therefore finds a fundamental right to a clean and healthful environment, protected by strict scrutiny. How does this work? Consider the following questions.

a. Which parts of Article IX are incorporated into the Article II fundamental right? *MEIC* concerns the non-degradation rule, but does that arise from the underlying statute or the constitutional requirement for the legislation to "provide adequate remedies for the protection of the environmental life support system from degradation and provide adequate remedies to prevent unreasonable depletion and degradation of natural resources"?

b. Relatedly, is the right "self-executing" or does it depend on statutory implementation? In its charges to the Legislature, Article IX, section 1 resembles Article X, section 1 ("educational goals and duties"), which might suggest it, like the educational provisions, is not self-executing. *See Columbia Falls School District*, Chapter 7. But the inalienable rights of Article II, section 3 are self-executing. *See Wadsworth*. In *Sunburst School District No. 2 v. Texaco, Inc.* (Mont. 2007), Chapter 2, the Court avoided the question of "whether Article II, Section 3, is self-executing and consequently could support a private cause of action for monetary damages."

2. What is the scope of strict scrutiny under the right? Must any degradation of natural resources, regardless of ecological or human health impacts, be justified by a compelling state interest? (Or any failure to *improve* the environment?) What might such an interest be, and must all pollution permits pursuant to that interest be narrowly tailored? Recall the degradation in *MEIC* involved naturally occurring arsenic concentrations in pumped water, and these concentrations decreased to natural background levels once they reached the rivers. If local displacement of naturally occurring minerals in groundwater triggers a constitutional prohibition under strict scrutiny, wouldn't anthropogenic pollutants (industrial and agricultural wastes down to household-level garbage and automobile emissions) fail the *MEIC* Court's standard? (Why might plaintiffs not challenge these more pervasive pollutants under strict scrutiny?) Or is the Court's target the narrow "blanket exclusion" from nondegradation review? If so, is strict scrutiny necessary or would such an exclusion also fail intermediate scrutiny, or even the "unreasonable" standard actually expressed by subsection (3)?

3. What other contracts might be unconstitutional, and therefore unenforceable, under *Cape-France*? Would it preclude "brownfields" redevelopment of contaminated lands, leasing of private forest lands for clearcutting, or labor contracts with miners, at least if the court deemed the degradation involved in the execution of such contracts as unreasonable (or lacking a compelling state interest)?

4. In *Cape-France*, Justice Rice suggests a potential conflict among vigorous enforcement of an inalienable right to a clean and healthful environment with the equally inalienable right to acquire, possess and protect property. The court in *Park County*, a four-justice panel that did not include Justice Rice, avoids such a conflict given the procedural posture of the permitting process. In *Wadsworth*, the Court read a right of employment into "pursuing life's basic necessities," which itself might create conflicts with safety and health (consider occupational licensing) or a clean and healthful environment (consider jobs in natural resource development). What additional rights of use and enjoyment might extend from the property right in ways that could conflict with the environmental right? How should the Court resolve such conflicts?

5. In *Park County*, the Court distinguished its holding in *Kadillak* that MEPA was not constitutionally grounded due to an anachronistic 2003 amendment to MEPA: "The legislature, mindful of its constitutional obligations under Article II, section 3, and Article IX of the Montana constitution, has enacted the Montana

Environmental Policy Act." Mont. Code Ann. § 75-1-102(1); *see also* Mont. Code Ann. § 82-4-301(1) (same in the Hard Rock Mining Act). Why might the Legislature have grounded this statute in these constitutional provisions? What difference should this make in how the Court interprets MEPA? If the Legislature repealed these links between MEPA and the "clean and healthful environment" guarantees, what result?

6. Several other states provide environmental protections in their constitutions. Consider *Robinson Township, Washington County, PA v. Commonwealth* (Pa. 2013), which addressed statutes waiving certain state water pollution permitting requirements for, and preempting local government restrictions on, hydraulic fracturing ("fracking") of natural gas deposits in the Marcellus Shale of northeastern Pennsylvania:

> The development of the natural gas industry in the Marcellus Shale Formation prompted enactment of Act 13. *** Section 3215(b)(4) creates a process by which the Department of Environmental Protection grants waivers to oil or gas well permit applicants from statutory protections of certain types of waters of the Commonwealth. Section 3304, meanwhile, implements a uniform and statewide regulatory regime of the oil and gas industry by articulating narrow parameters within which local government may adopt ordinances that impinge upon the development of these resources. *See* 58 Pa.C.S. §§ 3215(b)(4), 3304. ***
>
> The first section of Article I [of the Pennsylvania Constitution] "affirms, among other things, that all citizens 'have certain inherent and indefeasible rights.'" Among the inherent rights of the people of Pennsylvania are those enumerated in Section 27, the Environmental Rights Amendment:
>
> > The people have a right to clean air, pure water, and to the preservation of the natural, scenic, historic and esthetic values of the environment. Pennsylvania's public natural resources are the common property of all the people, including generations yet to come. As trustee of these resources, the Commonwealth shall conserve and maintain them for the benefit of all the people.
>
> Pa. Const. art. I, § 27 (Natural resources and the public estate). ***
>
> Initially, we note that the Environmental Rights Amendment accomplishes two primary goals, via prohibitory and non-prohibitory clauses: (1) the provision identifies protected rights, to prevent the state from acting in certain ways, and (2) the provision establishes a nascent framework for the Commonwealth to participate affirmatively in the development and enforcement of these rights. Section 27 is structured into three mandatory clauses that define rights and obligations to accomplish these twin purposes; and each clause mentions "the people."

A legal challenge pursuant to Section 27 may proceed upon alternate theories that either the government has infringed upon citizens' rights or the government has failed in its trustee obligations, or upon both theories, given that the two paradigms, while serving different purposes in the amendatory scheme, are also related and overlap to a significant degree. Facing a claim premised upon Section 27 rights and obligations, the courts must conduct a principled analysis of whether the Environmental Rights Amendment has been violated. ***

Section 27 is explicit regarding the respective rights of the people and obligations of the Commonwealth, and considerations upon which we typically rely in statutory construction confirm our development of the basic principles enunciated by its drafters. Among the relevant considerations are the occasion and necessity for the constitutional provision, the legislative history and circumstances of enactment and ratification, the mischief to be remedied and the object to be attained. ***

. . . The drafters of the Environmental Rights Amendment recognized and acknowledged the shocks to our environment and quality of life:

> We seared and scarred our once green and pleasant land with mining operations. We polluted our rivers and our streams with acid mine drainage, with industrial waste, with sewage. We poisoned our 'delicate, pleasant and wholesome' air with the smoke of steel mills and coke ovens and with the fumes of millions of automobiles. We smashed our highways through fertile fields and thriving city neighborhoods. We cut down our trees and erected eyesores along our roads. We uglified our land and we called it progress.

1970 Pa. Legislative Journal-House at 2270 (quoting anonymous 1698 description of Penn's Woods air).

With these events in the recent collective memory of the General Assembly, the proposed Environmental Rights Amendment received the unanimous assent of both chambers during both the 1969–1970 and 1971–1972 legislative sessions. Pennsylvania voters ratified the proposed amendment of the citizens' Declaration of Rights on May 18, 1971, with a margin of nearly four to one, receiving 1,021,342 votes in favor and 259,979 opposed.

The decision to affirm the people's environmental rights in a Declaration or Bill of Rights, alongside political rights, is relatively rare in American constitutional law. In addition to Pennsylvania, Montana and Rhode Island are the only other states of the Union to do so. *See* Pa. Const. art. I, § 27 (1971); Mt. Const. art. II, § 3 (1889); R.I. Const. art. I, § 17 (1970). Three other states—Hawaii, Illinois, and Massachusetts—articulate and protect their citizens' environmental rights in separate articles of their charters. *See* Hi. Const. art. XI, §§ 1, 9 (1978); Ill. Const. art. XI, §§ 1, 2 (1971–72); Ma. Const. amend. 49 (1972). Of these three states, Hawaii and Illinois, unlike

Pennsylvania, expressly require further legislative action to vindicate the rights of the people. By comparison, other state charters articulate a "public policy" and attendant directions to the state legislatures to pass laws for the conservation or protection of either all or enumerated natural resources. *See, e.g.*, Ak. Const. art. VIII, §§ 1–18 (1959); Colo. Const. art. XXVII, § 1 (1993); La. Const. art. IX, § 1 (1974); N.M. Const. art. XX, § 21 (1971); N.Y. Const. art. XIV, §§ 1–5 (1941); Tx. Const. art. XVI, § 59 (1917); Va. Const. art. XI, §§ 1–4 (1971). Some charters address the people's rights to fish and hunt, often qualified by the government's right to regulate these activities for the purposes of conservation. *See, e.g.*, Ky. Const. § 255A (2012); Vt. Const. Ch. II, § 67 (1777); Wi. Const. art. I, § 26 (2003). Still other state constitutions simply authorize the expenditure of public money for the purposes of targeted conservation efforts. *See, e.g.*, Or. Const. art. IX-H, §§ 1–6 (1970); W.V. Const. art. VI, §§ 55, 56 (1996). Finally, many of the remaining states do not address natural resources in their organic charters at all. *See, e.g.*, Nv. Const. art. I, § 1 et seq.

That Pennsylvania deliberately chose a course different from virtually all of its sister states speaks to the Commonwealth's experience of having the benefit of vast natural resources whose virtually unrestrained exploitation, while initially a boon to investors, industry, and citizens, led to destructive and lasting consequences not only for the environment but also for the citizens' quality of life. Later generations paid and continue to pay a tribute to early uncontrolled and unsustainable development financially, in health and quality of life consequences, and with the relegation to history books of valuable natural and esthetic aspects of our environmental inheritance. The drafters and the citizens of the Commonwealth who ratified the Environmental Rights Amendment, aware of this history, articulated the people's rights and the government's duties to the people in broad and flexible terms that would permit not only reactive but also anticipatory protection of the environment for the benefit of current and future generations. Moreover, public trustee duties were delegated concomitantly to all branches and levels of government in recognition that the quality of the environment is a task with both local and statewide implications, and to ensure that all government neither infringed upon the people's rights nor failed to act for the benefit of the people in this area crucial to the well-being of all Pennsylvanians. ***

C. Article I, Section 27 Rights in Application

*** Act 13 is not generalized environmental legislation, but is instead a statute that regulates a single, important industry—oil and gas extraction and development. Oil and gas resources are both privately owned and partly public, i.e., insofar as they are on public lands. Act 13 does not remotely purport to regulate simply those oil and gas resources that are part of the public trust corpus, but rather, it addresses the exploitation of all oil and gas resources throughout Pennsylvania. Act 13's primary stated purpose is not to effectuate the constitutional obligation to protect and preserve Pennsylvania's natural environment. Rather, the purpose of the statute is to provide a maximally favorable environment for industry operators to exploit Pennsylvania's oil and natural gas resources, including those in the Marcellus Shale Formation. The authority to regulate the oil and gas industry in this context derives, therefore, from the General Assembly's plenary power to enact laws for the purposes of promoting the general welfare, including public convenience and general prosperity, rather than from its corresponding duties as trustee of Pennsylvania's public natural resources. The public natural resources implicated by the "optimal" accommodation of industry here are resources essential to life, health, and liberty: surface and ground water, ambient air, and aspects of the natural environment in which the public has an interest. As the citizens illustrate, development of the natural gas industry in the Commonwealth unquestionably has and will have a lasting, and undeniably detrimental, impact on the quality of these core aspects of Pennsylvania's environment, which are part of the public trust.

As we have explained, Pennsylvania has a notable history of what appears retrospectively to have been a shortsighted exploitation of its bounteous environment, affecting its minerals, its water, its air, its flora and fauna, and its people. The lessons learned from that history led directly to the Environmental Rights Amendment, a measure which received overwhelming support from legislators and the voters alike. When coal was "King," there was no Environmental Rights Amendment to constrain exploitation of the resource, to protect the people and the environment, or to impose the sort of specific duty as trustee upon the Commonwealth as is found in the Amendment. Pennsylvania's very real and mixed past is visible today to anyone travelling across Pennsylvania's spectacular, rolling, varied terrain. The forests may not be primordial, but they have returned and are beautiful nonetheless; the mountains and valleys remain; the riverways remain, too, not as pure as when William Penn first laid eyes upon his colonial charter, but cleaner and better than they were in a relatively recent past, when the citizenry was less attuned to the environmental effects of the exploitation of subsurface natural resources. But, the landscape bears visible scars, too, as reminders of the past efforts of man to exploit Pennsylvania's natural assets. Pennsylvania's past is the necessary prologue here: the reserved rights, and the concomitant duties and constraints, embraced by the Environmental Rights Amendment, are a product of our unique history.

The type of constitutional challenge presented today is as unprecedented in Pennsylvania as is the legislation that engendered it. But, the challenge is in response to history seeming to repeat itself: an industry, offering the very real prospect of jobs and other important economic benefits, seeks to exploit a Pennsylvania resource, to supply an energy source much in demand. The political branches have responded with a comprehensive scheme that accommodates the recovery of the resource. By any responsible account, the exploitation of the Marcellus Shale Formation will produce a detrimental effect on the environment, on the people, their children, and future generations, and potentially on the public purse, perhaps rivaling the environmental effects of coal extraction. The litigation response was not available in the nineteenth century, since there was no Environmental Rights Amendment. The response is available now. ***

Justice BAER, concurring.

*** I view the substantive due process contentions made by Challengers to be better developed and a narrower avenue to resolve this appeal. ***

Pursuant to Article I, Section 1 of the Pennsylvania Constitution, and the Fifth and Fourteenth Amendments to the United States Constitution, no person may be deprived of his private property without due process of law. In the early years of the Union, this constitutional guarantee translated into the general notion that a landowner had the right to do as he saw fit with his property. As modern American jurisprudence developed, however that constitutional guarantee developed an important limitation: *sic utere tuo ut alienum non laedas*—so use your own property as not to injure your neighbors. As early as 1907, one commentator noted that courts "are not disinclined" to impose damages upon a landowner for use of his property that causes an injustice to his neighbor. ***

. . . Act 13 encroaches upon the substantive due process rights found in Article I, Section 1 of the Pennsylvania Constitution, and the Fifth and Fourteenth Amendments to the United States Constitution. Different landowners, in different parts of the Commonwealth (indeed, different neighborhoods in the same municipality), will be arbitrarily impacted by the imposition of Act 13 upon our political subdivisions. Individual landowners and municipalities alike will be unable to acclimatize to the fledgling world of Marcellus Shale hydrofracturing and drilling and the continuing fluidity of its development, and will be unable to seek recourse for the unquestionable damage to their private enjoyment of property.

Rather, Act 13 promotes and mandates the opposite—it sets static commandments to the municipalities of the Commonwealth in a vacuum, without due consideration for any effect upon those municipalities and the related doctrine of *sic utere tuo ut alienum non laedas*. Indeed, it sets absolute standards rather than minimal guidelines that all municipalities and residents must abide by, without providing for any remedy when the inevitable damage to the enjoyment of private property occurs. Sections 3215(b)(4) and (d), 3303, and 3304 not only allow entry of the pigs into the parlor, but further decree that local governments enact zoning ordinances that expressly permit those intrusions, without exception. Accordingly, because these statutes force municipalities to enact zoning ordinances, which violate the substantive due process rights of their citizenries, they cannot survive constitutional scrutiny.

Justice SAYLOR, dissenting.

*** In summary, I would, as Appellants urge, recognize the authority of the General Assembly to make basic, rational policy choices—through the democratic process—that balance the various and potentially conflicting purposes of Act 13. It is clearly the vision of our Legislature that the Marcellus Shale resource has the potential to be of great benefit to the Commonwealth at large in terms of economic development (to include job creation) and energy self-sufficiency. Furthermore, I would decline to substitute the Court's own wisdom about the merits of Act 13 for that of the General Assembly, in contravention of the limited role of judges upon their review of a duly-promulgated and presumptively valid legislative enactment. To the extent this case is about the hierarchy of municipal power relative to that of the Legislature, I am solidly in the camp supporting sovereign control in furtherance of the interests of the citizenry at large.

Justice EAKIN, dissenting.

*** I find the lead opinion's protracted expression, while thoughtful, to be ultimately inconsistent with the basic relationship between sovereign and subject, and insufficiently considerate of discrete judicial and legislative roles. Its premise conflates individual rights and governmental standing, and the sweeping, general, and necessarily aspirational terms on which the holding is based are too broad and insufficiently defined to provide meaningful guidance in the future. Further, the decision reverses the Commonwealth Court on a theory not presented to us by the parties. While we often affirm decisions using different reasoning than the court below, we should be chary of reversing on theories not raised or argued. ***

And like it or not, the bottom line is this—the gas in question will be extracted. It is going to be removed from the earth, and it is going to be transported to refineries. The question for our legislature is not "if" this will happen, but "how."

The means necessary for making these decisions properly lies in the processes of a different branch of government—our role is to assure those decisions do not violate the Constitution. Our role is not inclusive of balancing all the factors on which a political decision must be made. We have a constitutional duty to afford great deference to the body of government given the power by the Constitution to make decisions about such matters. We should not complain of incursions on judicial independence and of refusals to respect our role when we in turn act legislatively.

> If we limit our role to the evaluation of the constitutionality of this Act, we serve the Commonwealth as we should. And if we do so, this Act withstands our scrutiny. Hence, I must dissent.

How does Pennsylvania's environmental rights provision differ from Montana's? How does the Pennsylvania Supreme Court's "public trust" approach differ from a "fundamental rights" approach? How would *Robinson Township* come out under the Montana Constitution? How would the other cases in this section come out under *Robinson Township*?

7. For a recent overview of Montana's clean and healthful provisions in historical and national context, see Hallee C. Kansman, *Constitutional Teeth: Sharpening Montana's Clean and Healthful Environment Provision*, 81 MONT. L. REV. 247 (2020).

Chapter 10

Dignity & Equality

> **Article II, Section 4. Individual dignity.** The dignity of the human being is inviolable. No person shall be denied the equal protection of the laws. Neither the state nor any person, firm, corporation, or institution shall discriminate against any person in the exercise of his civil or political rights on account of race, color, sex, culture, social origin or condition, or political or religious ideas.
>
> *New provision prohibiting public and private discrimination in civil and political rights.*

The Montana Constitution's equality guarantee contains a familiar equal protection clause bookended by two novel provisions. The opening sentence provides "the dignity of the human being is inviolable" and reflects early humanist values inherited through the Universal Declaration of Human Rights and reflected in the post-war German Constitution. The direct ancestor of Article II, § 4 is the Puerto Rico Constitution, which provides:

> **P.R. Const. Art. II, Sec. 1.** The dignity of the human being is inviolable. All men are equal before the law. No discrimination shall be made on account of race, color, sex, birth, social origin or condition, or political or religious ideas. Both the laws and the system of public education shall embody these principles of essential human equality.

The delegates at the Constitutional Convention understood these values through the lens of Rick Applegate's detailed study of the Bill of Rights, which connected "inalienable rights" to a related conception of dignity:

> If a right is inalienable, it is not the kind which a temporal government can grant or take away. Such inalienable rights were not part of the social contract "bargain": government could at best secure them, but it could provide no substitute for them or impetus to trade them away. To make the point more clear, one might recall the distinction Kant made between "value" and "worth." In Metaphysics of Morals he wrote that
>
> > everything has either a value or worth. What has value has a substance which can replace it as its equivalent; but whatever is, on the other hand, exalted above all values, and thus lacks an equivalent, . . . has no merely relative value, that is, a price, but an inner worth, that is, dignity.

> Kant's typically amazing insight sheds some light on the understanding of the concept of inalienable rights. It is not that the rights could not be transferred without the individual's consent, but that their nature made them fundamentally untransferable in any case. In the sense of the Kantian distinction, they had worth as opposed to value.

Rick Applegate, Montana Constitutional Convention Bill of Rights Study at 82 (1971)

Though its legal meaning is contested, the dignity provision is evidence of the constitutional drafters' deep principles and high aspirations. The closing sentence is more familiar from civil rights laws than from constitutional law, and remarkably applies to private action as well as state action. This anti-discrimination provision protects several standard "suspect classes" but adds "culture" and "social origin or condition," and includes "political or religious ideas" more readily associated with free speech and free exercise of religion.

The following sections unpack each of these sentences, beginning with a canonical overview of the "dignity clause" and its relationship to the equal protection and anti-discrimination provisions. The subsequent section addresses the "equal protection clause," an innovation imported into the 1972 Constitution from federal law, and its relatively more robust form of rational basis scrutiny. The chapter concludes with sections on race, sex, and related classifications under both equal protection doctrine and the anti-discrimination provisions as implemented by the Montana Human Rights Act.

A. Frameworks for Dignity and Equality

Matthew O. Clifford & Thomas P. Huff, *Some Thoughts on the Meaning and Scope of the Montana Constitution's "Dignity Clause" with Possible Applications*

61 Mont. L. Rev. 301, 303–08 (2000)

It is our purpose in this article to clarify the meaning of the dignity clause by appealing to the structure and language of Montana's Constitution, the philosophical background of the Constitutional Convention's ideals, and the historical record of the Convention itself; and then to recommend a strategy for limiting the scope and, therefore, the legal application of this quite remarkable provision. We conclude that the dignity clause expresses a fundamental, if quite ordinary, ideal of post-Reformation, Western ethical and political thought. This ideal provides that human beings have dignity because they have intrinsic worth as individuals, and their dignity is found, in one form or another, in their capacity to live self-directed and responsible lives. To say, as the Montana Constitution does, that "[t]he dignity of the human being is inviolable" is thus to assert that the intrinsic worth, the basic humanity, of persons may not be violated.

I. The Plain Meaning of the Dignity Provision

A. The Structure of Article II, Section 4

The dignity clause of the Montana Constitution is found in Article II, Section 4. This provision reads, in full:

> Section 4. INDIVIDUAL DIGNITY. The dignity of the human being is inviolable. No person shall be denied the equal protection of the laws. Neither the state nor any person, firm, corporation, or institution shall discriminate against any person in the exercise of his civil or political rights on account of race, color, sex, culture, social origin or condition, or political or religious ideas.

At first glance, the structure of this section might seem perplexing. As can be seen, the section consists of three distinct clauses whose exact relationship to each other is not immediately obvious. The first clause is a simple and forceful declaration of the value of human dignity. This is hardly surprising, because, after all, individual dignity is the title of the section. It seems curious, however, that this rather broad reference is the only explicit mention of the word "dignity" in the entire section. The second clause, familiar enough to legally-trained readers, is an equal protection clause essentially identical to the one contained in the Fourteenth Amendment to the United States Constitution. The third clause, which we will call the "anti-discrimination clause," appears to be an extension of the theme of equal protection. It prohibits anyone from discriminating on the basis of certain defined categories. These include familiar categories such as race and sex, but also extend to less familiar ones such as social condition and political ideas.

Any attempt to make some sense of the two references to "dignity" in Article II, Section 4, immediately faces several questions. First and foremost, what is the relationship between the concept of human *dignity* which is expressed in the title and first clause, and the concept of human *equality* which is expressed in the second two clauses? Second, why does the Section 4 provision have *both* an equal protection clause *and* an anti-discrimination clause? After all, the right to equal protection and the right to be free from arbitrary discrimination are normally considered to be the same thing. Third, do the broad references to dignity and equality in the first two clauses *add* anything to the specific prohibitions set forth in the third clause? Or should the third, anti-discrimination clause be considered the only part of the provision with any practical, effective meaning that can be applied in individual cases?

At first blush, it might appear tempting to ignore the first two clauses and concentrate on the third. After all, it will certainly be much easier, in practice, to determine whether persons have suffered discrimination based on the narrowly-drawn categories of race, sex, or political ideas than to determine whether their more nebulous right to "equal protection of the laws" has been violated. And of course, it will be harder still to determine whether "dignity" has been violated. After all, when assessing an equal protection claim, a court can at least look to the rather extensive body of case law interpreting the federal and state equal protection clauses for guidance.

But in assessing a dignity claim, there would seem to be no obvious legal sources to which a court could turn, beyond the bare word "dignity" itself. Surely it would be much easier to treat the title and first two clauses of the dignity provision as mere precatory language—as constitutional "window dressing" so to speak—and treat the third clause as the only portion of the provision with substantive legal force.

Tempting though it might seem, this option is foreclosed to us. One of our oldest and most venerable canons of constitutional interpretation tells us that we must, if at all possible, treat each separate clause of a constitution as both substantively meaningful and not redundant. This principle surely applies with particular force to words which, like "individual dignity," comprise the actual title of the section being interpreted. Daunting though the task may be, we believe Montana courts are compelled, when presented with the appropriate facts, to make some attempt to determine the substantive meaning of the dignity clause.

We would like to propose an alternative and, we think, more defensible reading of Article II, Section 4, a reading that gives meaning to all three clauses. As we see it, the language of the dignity provision moves in a logical progression from the general to the specific. The title of the provision itself is "Individual Dignity;" thus, we must presume that all the language in the provision treats this topic in some respect. The first sentence, the dignity clause, obviously addresses dignity by declaring that human dignity is inviolable. The second sentence, we believe, goes on to declare *one way* in which human dignity can be violated—by denying someone the equal protection of the law based on some sort of arbitrary classification. Our legal tradition has long recognized such classifications as affronts to the dignity of persons. In *Brown v. Board of Education*, for instance, what the United States Supreme Court clearly found wrong with segregated schools, even if they were materially equal, was that segregation itself failed to respect the dignity of African-American children. Indeed, racial segregation degraded them by failing to treat them as *equals*. The Court acknowledged this explicitly, citing social science studies showing that African-American children internalized that degradation. They thought of themselves less worthwhile as human beings, as we might say, lacking the dignity of White children.

The third sentence of Article 4, the anti-discrimination clause, we believe, fleshes out the meaning of the equal protection right by enumerating certain types of classifications which the authors of the dignity provision believed to be arbitrary: race, color, sex, culture, social origin or condition, and political/religious ideas. But this cannot be read as an exhaustive list of all possible arbitrary, and therefore prohibited, classifications. If this list were exhaustive, the equal protection clause in the second sentence would be mere surplusage. By including this separate, more general equal protection clause in Section 4, the framers presumably intended to leave open the possibility that there are other prohibited classifications beyond those which were recognized at that point in history.

By the same logic, and more central to the topic of this paper, the inclusion of a more general prohibition against the violation of human dignity in the first clause of Section 4, we believe, leaves open the possibility that human dignity can be violated in ways that do not involve some sort of arbitrary classification. Indeed, it would seem that in order to give distinct and independent meaning to the dignity clause, avoiding redundancy, this clause should be applied separately when there is a violation of the dignity of persons that does not reflect the forms of unequal treatment or invidious discrimination prohibited by the two subsequent clauses. Presumably anyone could experience such a violation of dignity, not just persons who are members of protected classes.

B. Plain Meaning

What, then, does it mean to violate the dignity of a human being? Thus far, we have simply argued that a reasonable construction of Section 4's structure and language suggests that the dignity clause must refer to treatment violative of individual, human dignity beyond that protected by the equal protection and nondiscrimination clauses. So what does it mean to violate the dignity of a human being?

In our Western ethical tradition, especially after the Religious Reformation of the 16th and 17th centuries, dignity has typically been associated with the normative ideal of individual persons as intrinsically valuable, as having inherent worth as individuals, at least in part because of their capacity for independent, autonomous, rational, and responsible action. Persons, understood as intrinsically valuable because of their capacity for sovereign control over their own lives, claim our respect, and that respect is typically expressed in law through rights to both liberty and fair treatment. Everyone, for example, deserves due process of law. Even persons who have committed heinous crimes deserve due process, because we respect their worth, their dignity *as human beings*. Similarly, no persons deserve different treatment simply because of their race or gender. Such treatment fails to honor their intrinsic worth as human beings, degrading them by reducing them to contingent features of their humanity, such as their race or gender.

Treatment which degrades or demeans persons, that is, treatment which deliberately reduces the value of persons, and which fails to acknowledge their worth as persons, *directly* violates their dignity. But persons' dignity could also be more *indirectly* violated whenever they are denied the opportunity to direct or control their own lives in such a way that their worth is questioned or dishonored. This occurs, for example, any time an important liberty is denied. But it could occur in other circumstances as well, as when the loss of autonomy undermines the fundamental conditions of a self-directed life. Similarly, dignity may be *indirectly*, but more subtly, undermined by treatment which is paternalistic—treating adults like children incapable of making autonomous choices for themselves, or by trivializing what choices they do make about how to live their lives.

In summary, the meaning of the concept of individual human dignity, in traditional Western ethics, imagines human beings as intrinsically worthy of respect, of having dignity, because of their capacity to live self-directed and responsible lives. Dignity may be directly assailed by treatment which degrades, demeans, debases, disgraces, or dishonors persons, or it may be more indirectly undermined by treatment which either interferes with self-directed and responsible lives or which trivializes the choices persons make for their own lives. ***

Notes on Frameworks for Dignity and Equality

1. Clifford & Huff offer a structural analysis of Article II, section 4, in which each provision is increasingly specific but also stands alone as a source of rights. In their study of the convention record:

> We find nothing in the drafting or adoption record, including the very limited debate, which would indicate any sort of novel or radical meaning for the dignity clause. Apparently its ordinary meaning as a principal ideal of our ethical tradition naturally associated with equal protection and non- discrimination was obvious to the delegates. Indeed, in the only formal "Comment" by the Bill of Rights Committee on the entire dignity provision, the committee never mentions the dignity clause, focusing instead on its "intent of providing a Constitutional impetus for the eradication of public and private discriminations based on race, color, sex, culture, social origin or condition, or political or religious ideas." In the course of the only debate over the adoption of Section 4 (a brief discussion which focused on the inclusion of "private action" in the prohibition on discrimination) Delegate Dahood, defending the scope of the proposed provision, did explicitly refer to dignity, stating: "[t]he intent of Section 4 is simply to provide that every individual in the State of Montana, as a citizen of this state, may pursue his inalienable rights without having any shadows cast upon his dignity through unwarranted discrimination."

2. The primary concern of Clifford & Huff is the meaning of the first sentence, the dignity provision. Although they find that the convention debates support an equality-focused reading of dignity aligned with the subsequent provisions, they also suggest a freestanding dignity right could apply to cases of physician-assisted suicide, as well as discrimination on the basis of disability and sexual orientation. These are not expressly protected by the anti-discrimination provision. Might the anti-discrimination classification implicitly protect them? If courts should grapple with the broader dignity principle Clifford & Huff identify, how should they do so?

3. For an overview of dignity in state constitutions, see Michelle Freeman, *The Right to Dignity in the United States*, 68 HASTINGS L.J. 1135 (2017):

> Among the fifty states, twenty-seven make some mention of "dignity" within their respective constitutions. The use of dignity within these twenty-seven states falls into four general categories: (1) seventeen states provide a right to dignity for crime victims; (2) eleven states require that criminal indictments be brought in a just manner as not to offend the dignity of the state; (3) a single state requires the executive to act with dignity; and (4) three states—Illinois, Louisiana, and Montana—provide a right to

> dignity in and of itself, or have guaranteed their citizens' right to dignity through an equal protection clause.

The 1970 Illinois Constitution, Article I, section 20, provides: "To promote individual dignity, communications that portray criminality, depravity or lack of virtue in, or that incite violence, hatred, abuse or hostility toward, a person or group of persons by reason of or by reference to religious, racial, ethnic, national or regional affiliation are condemned." Ms. Freeman finds "legislative intent and subsequent interpretation by the judiciary has rendered this seeming right to be a theoretical principle rather than an actionable right."

4. While equal protection is an innovation in the Montana Constitution, it is a well-developed (if contested) principle in federal constitutional law. *See generally* Neomi Rao, *Three Concepts of Dignity in Constitutional Law*, 86 NOTRE DAME L. REV. 183 (2011). The anti-discrimination provision also draws on anti-discrimination law in federal civil rights laws, though it adds several novel classifications of "culture," and "social origin or condition," and treats "political ideas" the same as more identity-based classifications. In *The Right to Dignity in the United States*, Michelle Freeman examines the delegates' understanding of the dignity clause's relationship to the third sentence's anti-discrimination provision:

> The debate among delegates regarding the adoption of the Individual Dignity Clause into the 1972 Montana Constitution is brief, but provides insight as to the intent of the clause. Overall, the tone of the conversation among the Montana delegates suggests that the Individual Dignity Clause was intended to be an extension of equal protection rights within the State of Montana. As Delegate Mansfield explains in his opening, the clause's intent is to prohibit both private and public discrimination in civil and political rights. To that end, the delegates felt it to be "eminently proper" to include sex in the clause given the testimony heard in favor of its inclusion. Further, the term "culture" was used to "specifically cover groups whose cultural base is distinct from mainstream Montana." "Social origin or condition" were included to reach discrimination on the basis of income and standard of living. Finally, Delegate Mansfield clarified that "political or religious ideas" were not included to afford the right to avoid union membership, but rather to prohibit private and public discrimination on the basis of political or religious beliefs....
>
> During the proceedings only one amendment to the Individual Dignity Clause was proposed. Delegate Habedank moved to delete "by any person, firm or corporation or institution" from the clause for fear that imposing the Individual Dignity Clause on private corporations would force individuals to "have to associate with people that [they] choose not to associate with." In response, Delegate Dahood explained that the Individual Dignity Clause simply intended to provide Montana citizens with the ability to "pursue [their] inalienable rights without having any shadows cast upon [their] dignity through unwarranted discrimination." And to achieve that

end, Delegate Dahood further argued that the clause should apply to both public and private institutions. Upon further objection, Delegate Dahood acquiesced there could be "certain matters" that would allow for specific qualifications (such as gender status to become a member of the Elks or Masons) not in violation of the Individual Dignity Clause. Upon no further objection, Delegate Habedank's amendment to the Individual Dignity Clause was rejected and the clause was adopted as it reads today. ***

Should courts read the anti-discrimination classifications as an exhaustive (or exemplary?) list of "suspect classifications" triggering strict judicial scrutiny according to federal equal protection doctrine? If so, what else would the equal protection provision require of other classifications?

B. Equal Protection of the Laws

Between the principle that "[t]he dignity of the human being is inviolable" and the more detailed policy anti-discrimination on account of status in a protected class lies text borrowed from the Fourteenth Amendment: "No person shall be denied the equal protection of the laws." Despite its federal source, and even as they apply a version of tiered scrutiny modeled on federal doctrine, Montana courts often diverge from federal law in according greater protections for classes not otherwise included in federal "suspect classes" or the specific categories called out in the anti-discrimination provision. Moreover, as several cases in previous chapters demonstrate, the Montana Supreme Court commonly resorts to the language of equal protection and tiered scrutiny in applying distinct state constitutional rights, duties, and limitations on power, sometimes obscuring the plain meaning of the underlying text at issue. Consider how an equal protection doctrine should work in the context of the Montana Constitution, and why state courts and litigants keep coming back to the second sentence of Article II, section 4 with claims that may plausibly sound in more direct provisions elsewhere in the Declaration of Rights and beyond.

State v. Egdorf

2003 MT 264

Justice JIM RICE delivered the Opinion of the Court.

¶ 1 August D. Egdorf (Egdorf), an outfitter, was charged and convicted in the Justice Court of Musselshell County of five misdemeanor offenses involving violations of Montana's fish and wildlife laws and the laws pertaining to outfitters. Specifically, Egdorf was convicted of two counts of failing to report the unlawful taking of wildlife by a client, in violation of §§ 37-47-344 and 37-47-404, MCA (1999); possession of unlawfully taken game, in violation of § 87-3-112, MCA; conspiracy to kill a mule deer without a special permit, in violation of §§ 45-4-102 and 87-2-103, MCA; and solicitation to hunt without a license, in violation of §§ 45-4-101 and 87-2-103, MCA. ***

¶ 13 Does Montana's three-year statute of limitations for misdemeanor violations of fish and game laws, set forth in § 45-1-205(5) and (6), MCA, violate equal protection and due process of law?

¶ 14 Egdorf asserts that § 45-1-205(5) and (6), MCA, unconstitutionally infringes upon his rights to equal protection and due process of law by expanding the period of time allowed for commencing prosecution of misdemeanor violations of fish and game laws. Egdorf notes that while prosecutions for misdemeanors generally must be commenced within one year after commission, § 45-1-205(5) and (6), MCA, extends this period to three years for prosecutions of misdemeanor fish and game violations under Title 87 and Title 37, chapter 47. Egdorf argues that because these statutes allow prosecutions for fish and game violations to be commenced within three years, instead of one year, as for other misdemeanors, the statutes violate both principles of equal protection and substantive due process. [A later chapter considers Egdorf's substantive due process claim.]

A. Equal Protection

¶ 15 The Fourteenth Amendment to the United States Constitution, and Article II, Section 4, of the Montana Constitution guarantee equal protection of the law. The basic rule of equal protection is that persons similarly situated with respect to the legitimate governmental purpose of the law must receive like treatment. That being said, however, the equal protection clause does not preclude different treatment of different groups or classes so long as all persons within a group or class are treated the same. Thus, to prevail on an equal protection challenge, the injured party must demonstrate that the law at issue discriminates by impermissibly classifying individuals and treating them differently on the basis of that classification. If the classes at issue are not similarly situated, then the first criterion for proving an equal protection violation is not met, and we need look no further.

¶ 16 Egdorf correctly notes that the first step in an equal protection analysis is to determine whether similarly situated groups are treated differently. From there he asserts that all misdemeanor offenders form a single similarly situated class for equal protection purposes. However, in [*State v.*] *Renee* [(Mont. 1999)] we noted that "persons convicted of different crimes are not similarly situated and, therefore, may be subjected to different penalties without implicating equal protection concerns." We stated that while persons convicted of the same criminal offense cannot be subjected to grossly disparate sentences without a compelling state justification, "it is quite another [thing] to hold that persons convicted of different criminal offenses. . . must be punished equally."

¶ 17 Although statutes of limitations are procedural in nature and do not define crimes or their punishments, *Renee*'s reasoning is equally applicable to Egdorf's contention that, for equal protection purposes, all misdemeanor offenses must form a similarly situated class. While misdemeanors generally involve offenses of lesser severity than felonies, all misdemeanors do not proscribe the same conduct, and are subject to differing punishments, a factor we relied upon in *Renee*. Indeed, it would be absurd to argue that the penalty for unlawfully taking game must be the same as that for driving under the influence or failing to file a tax return. While all are misdemeanors, they are nonetheless unique and separate offenses. Thus, we conclude that the fish and game offenses at issue herein are, by legislative classification, not similarly situated with all other misdemeanors.

¶ 18 Equal protection does not preclude different treatment of different groups or classes so long as all persons within a similarly situated group or class are treated the same. Here, Egdorf has failed to make the necessary threshold showing that the offenses with which he was charged are part of a similarly situated class of misdemeanor offenses that has subjected him to unequal treatment by the Legislature's determination that a longer period of time should be afforded to commence prosecution of the fish and game violations. Rather, all persons who are alleged to have violated § 45-1-205(5) and (6), MCA—the proper definition of Egdorf's class for purposes of his challenge—are exposed to the same three-year statute of limitations for prosecution. Thus, the challenged statutes do not lay "an unequal hand on those who have committed intrinsically the same quality of offense," and do not violate equal protection. *Renee*, ¶ 34 (citing *Skinner v. Oklahoma* (1942)).

Arneson v. State

262 Mont. 269 (1993)

R.C. McDONOUGH, Retired Justice.

*** In 1989 the legislature passed Chapter 115 Session Laws of 1989 which, for its purpose, provided for a post-retirement adjustment increase in the pensions of the beneficiaries of the Teachers' Retirement System. The law provided that to be eligible for the adjustment, retirees or their beneficiaries must be 55 years of age or older; or, irrespective of age, all those receiving disability or survivorship benefits.

The respondent's benefit was derived from her mother, who was a member of the Teachers' Retirement System, and who had reached retirement age and retired. The mother selected the retirement option that would permit benefits to be paid to her for her lifetime and upon her death continue through the life of her beneficiary (respondent). The mother died shortly after her retirement and the respondent began receiving the benefits. The respondent is 31 years of age.

The respondent has been classified as a beneficiary due to the fact that her mother had retired and was a beneficiary at time of her death, and respondent succeeded to the benefits. Being under 55 years of age she did not receive the adjustment. However, if her mother had continued to work and died while working the respondent would be considered a survivor and would receive the adjustment even though she was 31 years of age. Her request for the post-retirement adjustment was denied and she brought this action.

The respondent contends that the statute violates Article II, Section 4 of the Montana Constitution in that it denies her the equal protection of the laws. ***

This statute, under the equal protection question, does not come under the strict scrutiny test because strict scrutiny of a legislative classification is required only when the classification impermissibly interferes with the exercise of a fundamental right or operates to a peculiar disadvantage of a suspect class. Here the respondent is not a member of a suspect class nor is a fundamental right involved.

In her cross appeal the respondent urges us to adopt the middle-level scrutiny test. The test is applied when the middle level of review is used and is as follows: The means chosen by the legislature (classification) must serve important governmental objectives and must be substantially related to the achievement of those objectives. The middle-level scrutiny test has been recently applied by the U.S. Supreme Court in discussing cases involving such things as gender, alienage and illegitimacy, but the court has specifically refused to invoke it involving age and has applied the rational test thereto. ***

The application of the middle tier scrutiny test in [*Butte Community Union v. Lewis* (Mont. 1986)] was based on a [welfare] benefit directed in our Constitution. Here there is no such constitutional direction. We have previously declined to apply the middle tier scrutiny test to an "age plus" classification, absent a constitutionally based benefit. We also decline to apply it here.

The District Court applied the lowest level of scrutiny, the rational basis test, which determines whether the classification is rationally related to furthering a legitimate state purpose. The trial court found the classification here did not rationally relate to furthering a legitimate state purpose.

The District Court basically found in applying the rational basis test that there was not any reason which was rationally related to the legitimate state purpose to grant a post-retirement adjustment to those who are receiving disability or survivorship allowances and who are under 55 years of age and to deny such adjustment to people in the plaintiff's position under age 55.

We will also apply the rational basis test.

To a certain extent, nearly all legislation classifies or sets forth classifications of applicability, benefits and recipients. If some of these classifications are imperfect they do not necessarily violate the equal protection clauses. ***

The purpose of this law is to grant to the Retirement System beneficiaries, retirees' survivors, and disabled, an amount to alleviate the eroding effect of inflation on their pension. Both the survivor of an employee and the beneficiary of an employee who has retired, are subject to the effect of inflation. But the classification as to who is to receive the post-retirement adjustment does not include the respondent who is the beneficiary of a former employee who had retired. As a result, this legislation is "under inclusive." This differentiation does not create a reasonable classification between such ultimate adult survivor and adult beneficiary. They are both similarly situated with respect to the purpose of this law.

The respondent states that there is no possible purpose which can be conceived to justify such a classification considering the overall purpose of the legislation of post-retirement adjustment to compensate for inflation. The respondent contends no distinction should be made between a beneficiary of a retired employee and the beneficiary of an employee who died while working when the beneficiaries are both under the age of 55. We agree.

We are unable to find any rational relationship to the purpose of the legislation for the establishment of such a classification. It is wholly arbitrary and an example of the legislature picking and choosing who will receive benefits. Such a classification must distinguish one class from another taking into consideration the purpose of the statute.

The granting of a post-retirement adjustment does not come within the approach of considering whether the enactment is experimental or piecemeal, and therefore applying the legislation to one phase of the problem and not affecting others. As we stated above, the legislature cannot arbitrarily pick and choose. The appellant has made such an argument on a money saving basis, but even if the governmental purpose is to save money, it cannot be done on a wholly arbitrary basis. The classification must have some rational relationship to the purpose of the legislation. There is nothing in the record or by conjecture which would justify the differentiation here.

The appellant makes a distinction between the class of service retirees and their beneficiaries and the class of disability and survivorship beneficiaries in that the class of service retirees is based on voluntariness and the class of disability and survivorship beneficiaries is not. That may be true on the basis of the retirees or the disabled, but it is not true as applied to the adult beneficiaries of an employee, a retired employee, or a disabled employee. In addition, there is no record as to what is voluntary and what is not voluntary.

There is no reasonable basis to the classification which permits an adult beneficiary of a disabled or deceased member to receive the adjustment regardless of age, and deny the adult beneficiary of a deceased service retiree who retired under voluntary or involuntary circumstances the adjustment because the beneficiary is under 55 years of age. The constitutional defect of the statute as applied to respondent is revealed when it is reviewed in light of its practical application. We conclude that its application to this respondent whereby the classification excludes her from receiving the post-retirement adjustment, is unconstitutional and in violation of Article II, Section 4 of the Montana Constitution. . . .

TRIEWEILER, Justice.

I rejoice at the majority's re-discovery of the rights provided for in the Equal Protection Clause of Article II, Section 4, of Montana's Constitution. However, I find it peculiar that nowhere in the majority's opinion is any mention made of the majority's decision in *Stratemeyer v. MACO Workers' Compensation Trust* (Mont. 1993). Perhaps that is because the result in this case cannot be reconciled with the majority's decision in *Stratemeyer*. That is because under *Stratemeyer* there is no legislative classification which won't satisfy the toothless rational basis test.

This same majority held in *Stratemeyer* that even where no rational basis for a legislative classification is established by the Legislature or proven in district court, this Court can speculate about why the Legislature acted as it did, and that speculation can serve as the basis for overcoming a constitutional challenge. This Court went on to add that even when the State offers no evidence to justify a legislative classification, a person challenging the legislation has the burden of proving that there is no rational basis. In other words, under the *Stratemeyer* decision, a citizen victimized by legislative discrimination has to, first of all, imagine every conceivable basis for that discrimination about which this Court might speculate and then somehow disprove it. This Court then went on in *Stratemeyer* to conclude that a justification for the classification at issue in that case could have been the Legislature's intention to save money, even though there was no evidence in the record that the classification would save money. This Court held that:

> The exclusion of mental claims rationally relates to the *possible goal* of reducing costs and having a viable program for the State and the enrolled employers and employees in the workers' compensation field. [Emphasis added].

Certainly, by that standard the classification in this case passes any rational basis test. Who can dispute that discriminating against beneficiaries under a certain age "relates to the possible goal of reducing costs" for the teachers' retirement system?

I, of course, have no regard for the *Stratemeyer* decision. I would not follow it and will urge its early demise at every opportunity.

The majority, however, has neither followed it, distinguished it, nor overruled it. Therefore, its decision in this case is both legally and intellectually inconsistent.

Surely this decision must cause a great deal of confusion to those legal scholars and lawyers who follow this Court's decisions for the purpose of discerning reliable legal and constitutional principles upon which to base future advice and conduct. To you, let me simply provide the following explanation. *Stratemeyer* dealt with a classification in the highly political area of workers' compensation law. This case deals with the less politically controversial area of teachers' retirement benefits.

Because of this Court's history of using the rational basis test as a flexible tool for political expediency, I would not base this decision on such a fragile foundation. I believe that the right to be free from discrimination based on age is a significant enough right that classifications based on age warrant middle-tier scrutiny.

The Equal Protection Clause of the Fourteenth Amendment to the U.S. Constitution, and the Equal Protection Clause in Article II, Section 4, of the Montana

Constitution, provide that "[n]o person shall be denied the equal protection of the laws." The equal protection clause guarantees that similar individuals will be dealt with in a similar manner by the government.

Traditionally, the United States Supreme Court has relied on a two-tier system of scrutiny for reviewing whether a state's statutory scheme violates the comparable provision in the Fourteenth Amendment to the United States Constitution. Historically, the two modes of analysis have been strict scrutiny and the rational basis test.

Justice Marshall pointed out the inadequacy of the two-tiered system of scrutiny for analyzing age discrimination cases in his dissent in *Massachusetts Board of Retirement v. Murgia* (1976), as follows:

> If a statute invades a "fundamental" right or discriminates against a "suspect" class, it is subject to strict scrutiny. If a statute is subject to strict scrutiny, the statute always or nearly always, is struck down. Quite obviously, the only critical decision is whether a strict scrutiny should be invoked at all. . . .
>
> But however understandable the Court's hesitancy to invoke strict scrutiny, all remaining legislation should not drop into the bottom tier, and be measured by the mere rationality test. For that test, too, when applied as articulated, leaves little doubt about the outcome; the challenged legislation is always upheld. It cannot be gainsaid that there remain rights, not now classified as "fundamental," that remain vital to the flourishing of a free society, and classes, not now classified as "suspect," that are unfairly burdened by invidious discrimination unrelated to the individual worth of their members. Whatever we call these rights and classes, we simply cannot forego all judicial protection against discriminatory legislation bearing upon them, but for the rare instances when the legislative choice can be termed "wholly irrelevant" to the legislative goal.

Perhaps in response to the legitimate concerns articulated so clearly by Justice Marshall, the U.S. Supreme Court has begun to recognize a third level of scrutiny for rights that are not "fundamental" and classes that are not now considered "suspect," but which deserve more scrutiny than provided for under the rational basis test. ***

It is true that the U.S. Supreme Court has declined to extend this heightened level of scrutiny to classifications based upon age. *Murgia*. However, our Court has developed its own line of authority recognizing a middle-tier of analysis [in *Butte Community Union*] . . . . ***

In this case, the District Court and the majority have declined to apply the middle-tier analysis provided for in *Butte Community Union* based on their conclusion that retirement benefits are not the same as welfare benefits and that there is no requirement in Montana's Constitution that retirement benefits be provided. However, the involvement of an important right or interest is only one of the two circumstances that triggers heightened scrutiny. "A second broad circumstance in which intermediate review has been triggered involves government's use of sensitive, although not necessarily suspect, criteria of classification." L. Tribe, American Constitutional Law, § 16–33 (2d ed. 1988). According to the laws of Montana, age is a "sensitive" if not "suspect" basis for classification. To hold otherwise would be to ignore the import of § 49-1-102, MCA, of the Montana Human Rights Act which provides that "[t]he right to be free from discrimination because of. . . age. . . is recognized as and declared to be a civil right."

Accordingly, I would hold that statutory classifications based upon age involve a sensitive basis for classification and warrant a middle-tier test for determining whether they violate the Equal Protection Clause of Montana's Constitution. I would conclude that the District Court erred when it applied the rational basis test, rather than the middle-tier analysis, to determine whether the age classification in § 19-4-711, MCA (1991), violates equal protection guarantees of the Montana Constitution.

However, I would affirm the result of the District Court's decision. In order to establish that the age classification set forth in § 19-4-711, MCA (1991), does not violate the State's Equal Protection Clause, the State must demonstrate two factors: (1) that its classification on the basis of age is reasonable; and (2) that its interest in classifying entitlement to retirement benefits on the basis of age is more important than plaintiff's interest in obtaining retirement benefits.

The record in this case fails to satisfy either requirement. There is no legislative history which even attempts to set forth the reason for the discriminatory treatment of retiree beneficiaries as opposed to disability or death beneficiaries. Neither was there any evidence offered in the District Court or before the Legislature which would demonstrate on an actuarial basis the State's interest in limiting the post-retirement adjustment to retirees or their beneficiaries who are at least 55 years of age. Without such an evidentiary basis, it is impossible for plaintiff, or for this Court, to compare the interests of the State Retirement System to the interests of retirees and their beneficiaries who are denied benefits because of their age.

On appeal, the attorneys for the Teachers' Retirement System have asserted that voluntary retirees are more likely to be financially prepared to retire than involuntary retirees. It contends that young voluntary service retirees and their beneficiaries who are under 55 years of age may rely on their earning capacity to supplement their retirement benefits. By contrast, the Teachers' Retirement System argues that involuntary retirees (those who are disabled or the beneficiary of deceased employees) have only their retirement allowance to rely on. The problem with the arguments raised by the Teachers' Retirement System on appeal is that they have no factual basis in the legislative history or the record from the District Court.

Without a factual basis for their assertion, these arguments are merely broad generalizations such as those that we condemned in *Butte Community Union*. There, we held that the State employed an arbitrary classification when it asserted, without a factual basis, that "people under the age of 50 are more capable of surviving without assistance than people over the age of 50." Likewise, I would conclude that the age classification in § 19-4-711, MCA (1991), is arbitrary, not grounded in fact, and therefore, invalid. Accordingly, I would hold that to the extent that the age classification in § 19-4-711, MCA (1991), denies a post-retirement benefit to those service retirees and their beneficiaries under the age of 55, the statute violates the Equal Protection Clause of the Montana Constitution.

HUNT, J., joins the foregoing special concurrence.

Oberson v. United States Department of Agriculture, Forest Service

339 Mont. 519 (2007)

Justice BRIAN MORRIS delivered the Opinion of the Court.

¶ 1 Lori Oberson, as legal guardian for Brian Musselman (Musselman), and others, (collectively Oberson), brought an action in the United States District Court for the District of Montana under the Federal Tort Claims Act (FTCA), 28 U.S.C. §§ 2671–2680, alleging that the United States Forest Service (Forest Service) negligently had failed to correct or warn of a dangerous condition on the snowmobile trail where Brian Musselman was injured. Oberson and the Forest Service cross-appealed to the United States Court of Appeals for the Ninth Circuit from the judgment of the District Court following a bench trial.

¶ 2 The Ninth Circuit certified three questions of law to this Court pursuant to Rule 44(c) of the Montana Rules of Appellate Procedure. We accepted the following three questions in our order dated April 5, 2006:

> ¶ 3 Does the gross negligence standard of care in the snowmobile liability statute, Mont.Code Ann. § 23-2-653 (1996), violate the Montana equal protection clause, Mont. Const. art. II, § 4?
>
> ¶ 4 If the snowmobile liability statute's gross negligence standard is unconstitutional, does the recreational use statute's willful or wanton misconduct standard of care, Mont.Code Ann. § 70-16-302(1) (1996), apply in its place?
>
> ¶ 5 If neither the snowmobile liability statute nor the recreational use statute provide an applicable standard of care, does the ordinary care standard, Mont.Code Ann. § 27-1-701, apply?

Factual and Procedural History

¶ 6 In February 1996 Musselman, Patrick Kalahar (Kalahar), Tim Johnson (Johnson), and Jamie Leinberger (Leinberger) were riding their snowmobiles at night on the Big Sky Trail, a trail maintained by the Forest Service on Forest Service land, outside West Yellowstone, Montana. The group came upon a sudden, unmarked, steep decline in the trail. Musselman reached the decline first and safely negotiated the hill, but stopped his snowmobile after Johnson had wrecked. Musselman dismounted from his snowmobile and began to walk across the trail when Kalahar and

Leinberger roared over the hill at approximately 55 mph. One of their two snowmobiles struck Musselman in the head, causing him catastrophic brain injuries.

¶ 7 Oberson brought suit in federal court against the Forest Service under the FTCA. She alleged that the Forest Service negligently had failed to correct or warn of the danger posed by the hill where Musselman was injured, and that its negligence was the proximate cause of Musselman's injuries. The Forest Service filed a third-party complaint against Leinberger, Kalahar, and Johnson, alleging that their negligence had caused Musselman's injuries. Kalahar settled and the court entered a default judgment against Johnson. The case proceeded to trial against the Forest Service with Leinberger as the sole third-party defendant.

¶ 8 The Forest Service argued in pre-trial proceedings that it was immune to liability in light of the fact that its decision not to mark the hazardous hill was "discretionary" within the meaning of 28 U.S.C. § 2680(a). It also argued that §§ 23-2-651, 653–54, MCA (1995) (the snowmobile liability statute), relieved it from a duty to warn of the hazardous hill because "a snowmobile area operator has no duty to eliminate, alter, control, or lessen the risk inherent in the sport of snowmobiling," § 23-2-653(3), MCA. The court rejected both affirmative defenses. The court concluded with respect to the latter that the hill at issue was not one of the risks "inherent in the sport of snowmobiling."

¶ 9 The District Court looked next to Montana negligence law to determine the substantive law governing Oberson's FTCA claim. The court refused the Forest Service's invitation to apply the "gross negligence" standard found in the snowmobile liability statute in light of the fact that this Court in *Brewer v. Ski-Lift, Inc.* (Mont. 1988), had found a similar provision relating to ski area operators to violate the Equal Protection Clause of the Montana Constitution.

¶ 10 The court also barred the Forest Service from arguing that the "willful or wanton" conduct standard found in §§ 70-16-301, 302, MCA (1995) (recreational use statute) applied in place of the "gross negligence" provision in the snowmobile liability statute. The court concluded that the more specific snowmobile liability statute had preempted the willful or wanton standard in the recreational use statute. The court determined, in the absence of any other governing statute, that it would apply the catch-all "ordinary care" standard found at § 27-1-701, MCA. The court applied the ordinary care standard to apportion 40% of the responsibility for Musselman's damages to the Forest Service, 10% to Musselman, and 50% to Kalahar and Leinberger jointly.

¶ 11 The Forest Service appealed the District Court's determination of negligence and its refusal to apply the discretionary function exception of the FTCA. Oberson cross-appealed from the court's liability allocation of 50% to Kalahar and Leinberger. The Ninth Circuit affirmed the District Court "in all respects except that [it left] for future resolution the determinative question of the appropriate standard of care pending the disposition "of this request for certification."

Discussion

¶ 12 Does the gross negligence standard of care in the snowmobile liability statute, Mont. Code Ann. § 23-2-653 (1996), violate the Montana equal protection clause, Mont. Const. art. II, § 4?

¶ 13 Oberson challenges the provisions in the snowmobile liability statute that apply a gross negligence standard of care to snowmobile area operators. The statute provides, in relevant part, that a "snowmobile area operator is liable for death or injury to a snowmobiler or other person or property only for an act or omission that constitutes gross negligence." Section 23-2-653(2), MCA (1995). It also provides that a "snowmobile area operator who attempts to eliminate, alter, control, or lessen the risk inherent in the sport of snowmobiling is liable only for an act or omission that constitutes gross negligence." Section 23-2-653(3), MCA (1995).

¶ 14 We presume that "all statutes are constitutional, and we attempt to construe them in a manner that avoids unconstitutional interpretation." This Court requires a party challenging a statute to prove, beyond a reasonable doubt, that the statute is unconstitutional. [*State v.*] *Trull* [(Mont. 2006)].

¶ 15 Oberson contends that this Court's decision in *Brewer* requires us to hold that the snowmobile liability statute's gross negligence provisions violate equal protection. This Court in *Brewer* held that various provisions in (the skier responsibility statutes), violated the "constitutional guarantee of equal protection." The Court summarized the unconstitutional provisions as "prohibit[ing] the skier from obtaining legal recourse against an operator even if the injury is proximately caused by the negligent or even intentional actions of the operator."

¶ 16 The Court determined that the skier responsibility statutes sought to "protect[] the ski industry from frivolous lawsuits and liability over which the operator has no control." The Court held that "there is no rational relationship between this purpose and requiring that skiers assume all risks for injuries regardless of the cause and regardless of the presence of negligence or intentional conduct on the part of the ski area operator." The Court held that these provisions were "needlessly over broad [, going] . . . far beyond the stated purposes of the statutes. . . ." The Court concluded that the provisions could not "pass even a minimum rationality test."

¶ 17 The snowmobile liability statute's statement of purpose closely mirrors the skier responsibility statute's statement of purpose that this Court analyzed in *Brewer*. The snowmobile liability statute's purpose is stated fairly as "protecting [snowmobile area operators] from frivolous lawsuits and liability over which the operator has no control." Its gross negligence standard of care bears no rational relationship to this purpose for the same reasons we described in *Brewer*. The statute relieves snowmobile area operators of liability for their "negligen[t] or intentional conduct" that is, by definition, within their control.

¶ 18 The Forest Service correctly points out that "the first prerequisite to a meritorious claim under the equal protection clause is a showing that the state has adopted a classification that affects two or more similarly situated groups in an unequal manner." It argues that the "legislature here treated all snowmobilers identically, and thus created no distinction or classification that warrants equal protection review." The Forest Service attempts to distinguish this situation from skiing. It argues that the legislature was justified in treating snowmobilers as a unique class in light of the fact that snowmobilers are "unlike skiers and horseback riders and hikers (for example), . . . because snowmobilers use motorized equipment for high speeds in a natural environment." It also contends that the legislature was particularly concerned with the economic well being of snowmobiling as it has a major effect on the state's economy.

¶ 19 The basic rule of equal protection "is that persons similarly situated with respect to a legitimate governmental purpose of the law must receive like treatment." We do not operate on a blank slate, however, regarding the appropriate classification for our equal protection analysis. We resolved the classifications at issue here in *Brewer* where this Court looked to the statute's purpose in order to determine the threshold question of whether the statute created a discriminatory classification—- i.e. a classification that treats two or more similarly situated groups in an unequal manner. This Court determined in *Brewer* that all inherently dangerous sports, including skiing, were similarly situated with respect to the skier responsibility statute's purpose of immunizing area operators from liability for the inherent risks of the sport for which they provide a venue. The Court concluded that the skier responsibility statute "classif[ied] skiers and treat[ed] them differently than those who engage in other sports activities which are inherently dangerous."

¶ 20 We discern no difference between the snowmobile liability statute's purpose and the skier responsibility statute's purpose. Both statutes seek to prevent frivolous lawsuits by immunizing area operators from the inherent risks of the sport over which the operator has no control. All operators who provide a venue for any inherently dangerous sport are similarly situated with respect to the mischief these statutes propose to remedy. The snowmobile liability statute thus classifies snowmobile area operators and snowmobilers and treats them differently from other similarly situated groups. These other similarly situated groups, including "ski area operator[s]," § 23-2-733, MCA (1995), "persons responsible for equines," § 27-1-725, MCA (1995), and "outfitters, guides and professional guides," § 37-47-402, MCA (1995), operate pursuant to a general negligence standard. We fail to see how either the unique economics of the snowmobile industry or the addition of a motor distinguishes the snowmobilers from other inherently dangerous sports with respect to the snowmobile liability statute's purpose.

¶ 21 The Forest Service lastly attempts to distinguish *Brewer* on the grounds that the *Brewer* Court focused on the fact that the skier responsibility statute had relieved the ski area operators of "all duties otherwise owed by a ski area operator to skiers. . . ." We disagree. The *Brewer* Court focused on the fact that the statute immunized the ski area operator from liability that was within the operator's control—e.g. their own negligence—despite the legislature's expressed intent to protect the area operator only from liability for risks inherent in the sport.

¶ 22 We conclude that Oberson has proven, beyond a reasonable doubt, that the "gross negligence" provision in § 23-2-653, MCA (1995), is "over broad," extends "beyond" its stated purpose and fails to pass rational basis review. The gross negligence standard of care in the snowmobile liability statute, Mont. Code Ann. § 23-2-653 (1996), violates the Montana equal protection clause, Mont. Const. art. II, § 4.

¶ 23 If the snowmobile liability statute's gross negligence standard is unconstitutional, does the recreational use statute's willful or wanton misconduct standard of care, Mont. Code Ann. § 70-16-302(1) (1996), apply in its place?

¶ 24 We next determine what standard of care governs the Forest Service's conduct in the absence of the gross negligence standard. The parties' disagreement on this issue centers around three different statutes, all of which have a different scope of application, and all of which provide a different standard of care. The snowmobile liability statute applies a gross negligence standard to "snowmobile area operators." The "recreational use" statute, § 70-16-302(1), MCA (1995), applies a "willful or wanton" standard to "landowners" who allow individuals to use their land, free of charge, for "recreational uses," such as snowmobiling. Finally, § 27-1-701, MCA, applies an "ordinary care" standard to everyone, "[e]xcept as otherwise provided by law. . . ."

¶ 25 The parties correctly point out that the gross negligence standard in the snowmobile liability statute would govern the actions of the Forest Service if it were constitutional, in light of the fact that the snowmobile liability statute is the most specific of the three statutes with respect to "snowmobile area operators." See § 1-2-102, MCA ("[w]hen a general and particular provision are inconsistent, the latter is paramount to the former. . . ."). The Forest Service argues, however, that the willful or wanton standard described in Montana's recreational use statute, § 70-16-302(1), MCA (1995), should apply in the absence of the snowmobile liability statute's gross negligence standard. It argues that "if the snowmobile statute was unconstitutional, and hence a nullity, at the time of the incident in this case," then the recreational use statute would provide the governing standard of care in light of the fact that it represents the next most specific statute with respect to snowmobilers and snowmobile area operators. The Forest Service's argument hinges, however, upon this Court declaring the entire snowmobile liability statute unconstitutional.

¶ 26 Our decision does not void the entire snowmobile liability statute. A statute "'is not destroyed in toto because of an improper provision unless such provision is necessary to the integrity of the statute or was the inducement to its enactment.'" We cannot say that removing the gross negligence standard destroys the integrity of the snowmobile liability statute in light of the fact that the legislature amended the statute in 1999, following the federal district court's decision in *Riska v. USDA*,

CV-96-63-BU-DWM (D. Mont. Oct 14, 1997). The federal court held that the gross negligence standard violated equal protection pursuant to our decision in *Brewer.* The legislature's amended version contains a general negligence standard. We likewise cannot determine that the gross negligence provision induced the legislature to enact the snowmobile liability statute when the legislature enacted the skier responsibility statute, the equine liability statute, §§ 27-1-725 through 727, MCA (1995), and the outfitter and guide liability statute, §§ 37-47-401 through 404, MCA (1995), with a general negligence standard. As a result, we strike only those provisions that apply a gross negligence standard of care to snowmobile area operators. We leave the remainder of the statute intact, including those provisions in §§ 23-2-653(1) and (3), MCA (1995), describing the duties of snowmobile area operators, and in § 23-2-654, MCA (1995), describing the responsibilities of snowmobilers.

¶ 27 This Court took a similar approach in *Brewer,* when we left the remainder of the skier responsibility statute in force after striking several sections of the statute as unconstitutional. The snowmobile liability statute otherwise continues to control the duties and responsibilities of the Forest Service in this case. The more general recreational use statute's willful or wanton misconduct standard of care, Mont.Code Ann. § 70-16-302(1), MCA (1995), has no application under these circumstances.

¶ 28 If neither the snowmobile liability statute nor the recreational use statute provide an applicable standard of care, does the ordinary care standard, Mont. Code Ann. § 27-1-701, apply?

¶ 29 We address finally the question of what standard to apply to the Forest Service's conduct now that we have declared unconstitutional the only explicit standard of care in the snowmobile liability statute. This Court faced a similar situation in *Mead* [*v. M.S.B., Inc.* (Mont. 1994)] where the plaintiff brought a negligence claim against a ski resort for injuries that he sustained when he struck a rock outcropping while skiing.

¶ 30 The plaintiff claimed that the ski resort negligently had designed, constructed, and maintained the ski trail on which he was injured. The ski resort responded that its duties were limited to those duties enumerated in the 1989 skier responsibility statute. The ski resort noted specifically that the legislature had failed to list the duty of ordinary care among the duties enumerated in the statute. This Court determined that the general statutory duty of ordinary care, as defined in § 27-1-701, MCA, applied to ski area operators even though the skier responsibility statute enumerated no such duty.

¶ 31 Our decision at ¶¶ 13–22 to strike the gross negligence standard in the snowmobile liability statute leaves the statute in a state similar to the skier responsibility statute that we construed in *Mead.* The snowmobile liability statute now enumerates the duties and responsibilities of the snowmobile area operators and snowmobilers without a specified standard of care. Our holding in *Mead* requires, under these circumstances, that the general statutory duty of due care, set forth in § 27-1-701, MCA, provides the standard of care to govern the Forest Service's actions in this case.

¶ 32 For the reasons set forth we answer, "yes," "no," and "yes," respectively, to the three questions certified to this Court by the Ninth Circuit.

Justice W. WILLIAM LEAPHART concurring.

¶ 33 I specially concur only to point out that in ¶ 22, the Court notes that "Oberson has proven, beyond a reasonable doubt, that the 'gross negligence' provision in § 23-2-653, MCA (1995), is 'overbroad,' extends 'beyond' its stated purpose and fails to pass rational basis review." This Court has applied this "beyond a reasonable doubt" standard to constitutional challenges for over 100 years, beginning with *State v. Camp Sing* (Mont. 1896). The standard is applied by many of our sister states, too numerous to cite. It also finds support in a very early decision from the United States Supreme Court:

> "It must be remembered that, for weighty reasons, it has been assumed as a principle, in construing constitutions, by the Supreme Court of the United States, by this court and by every other court of reputation in the United States, that an act of the legislature is not to be declared void unless the violation of the Constitution is so manifest as to leave no room for reasonable doubt;" and, in *Fletcher v. Peck*, Chief Justice Marshall said, "It is not on slight implication and vague conjecture that the legislature is to be pronounced to have transcended its powers and its acts to be considered void. The opposition between the Constitution and the law should be such that the judge feels a clear and strong conviction of their incompatibility with each other." It is incumbent, therefore, upon those who affirm the unconstitutionality of an act of Congress to show clearly that it is in violation of the provisions of the Constitution. It is not sufficient for them that they succeed in raising a doubt.

Legal Tender Cases, Knox v. Lee, Parker v. Davis (1870).

¶ 34 Despite this time-honored and well accepted standard of proving unconstitutionality, I nonetheless find this to be an incongruous standard to apply to the proving of a legal proposition as opposed to an issue of fact. I agree with the New York Federal District Court's observation that the "beyond a reasonable doubt" standard is an "absurd standard of decision" for a question of law. ***

¶ 35 I suggest that the Court adopt a standard whereby we invalidate a legislative enactment only upon a plain showing by the challenger that the legislation in question lacks a rational basis.

¶ 36 However, when reviewing a constitutional challenge under strict scrutiny or middle-tier analysis, the burden to sustain the legislation would be upon the government. For example, to withstand strict scrutiny analysis, the government must demonstrate that the legislation at issue is justified by a compelling state interest and that it is narrowly tailored to effectuate only that interest. Similarly, middle-tier scrutiny requires the State to demonstrate that the law in question is reasonable and its interest in the resulting classification outweighs the value of the right of the individual. Both of these burdens are the State's—not the challenger's.

¶ 37 Therefore, I would apply the "plain showing of unconstitutionality" burden in challenges reviewed for rational basis, but I would continue to hold the State to its different burdens where it is the government's obligation to demonstrate that the challenged statute withstands middle-tier or strict scrutiny analysis.

Justice JAMES C. NELSON and Justice PATRICIA COTTER join in the concurring opinion of Justice LEAPHART.

Justice JIM RICE, dissenting.

¶ 38 The Court fails to properly apply rational basis review, inappropriately relies on *Brewer* to support its holding, and usurps the role of the legislature to create its own broad classification encompassing all "inherently dangerous sports." For these reasons, I dissent.

¶ 39 Despite purporting to apply a rational basis review to the snowmobile liability statute, the Court fails to either enunciate or apply the proper standards for an equal protection challenge.

> "The constitutionality of a legislative enactment is prima facie presumed, and every intendment in its favor will be presumed, unless its unconstitutionality appears beyond a reasonable doubt. The question of constitutionality is not whether it is possible to condemn, but whether it is possible to uphold the legislative action which will not be declared invalid unless it conflicts with the constitution, in the judgment of the court, beyond a reasonable doubt." Every possible presumption must be indulged in favor of the constitutionality of a legislative act. The party challenging a statute bears the burden of proving that it is unconstitutional beyond a reasonable doubt and, if any doubt exists, it must be resolved in favor of the statute. [*Powell v. State Compensation Insurance Fund* (Mont. 2000) (quoting *Stratemeyer v. Lincoln County* (Mont. 1993)).]

We are to declare a statute to be valid "unless the constitutional violation is 'clear and palpable.'"

¶ 40 The Court glosses over the proper rational basis standard of review, never applying it in the subsequent discussion. "As explained by the United States Supreme Court, to survive scrutiny under the rational basis test, classifications must be reasonable, not arbitrary, and they must bear a fair and substantial relation to the object of the legislation, so that all persons similarly circumstanced shall be treated alike." Such a review, by definition, allows for the utmost deference to our legislature's decision: any conceivable purpose will satisfy rational basis review. "The burden is therefore on the one attacking the classification to negative every conceivable basis which might support it, at least where no fundamental right is imperiled."

¶ 41 In my view, the Court has not engaged in the aforementioned analysis, and no such showing has been made by the parties that the snowmobile liability statute represents a "clear and palpable violation" of the Constitution. Rather than apply rational basis review and acknowledge that the legislature is entitled to significant deference under that standard, the Court jumps straight to the conclusion that because "[t]he snowmobile liability statute's statement of purpose closely mirrors the skier responsibility statute's statement of purpose," and because this Court found the skier liability statute in *Brewer* unconstitutional, the same must be true of the snowmobile liability statute at issue here. However, the Court's reliance on *Brewer* is inappropriate, because an essential component to the holding in *Brewer* was the Court's finding that the skier liability statute eliminated all duties a ski area operator owed to its users. Such is not the case here, where the legislature has decided to limit, but not eliminate, the duties a snowmobile area operator owes to its users. To the contrary, an elementary rational basis review leads to the conclusion that the legislature did have a conceivable basis for limiting the liability of snowmobile area operators, including reducing the cost of liability insurance and preventing frivolous lawsuits. As Justice McDonough noted in his dissent to *Brewer*, such purposes have long been recognized by other courts as a valid basis for classification. Furthermore, the statute still provides an avenue for compensating snowmobilers who are injured due to gross negligence. A proper rational basis review clearly distinguishes *Brewer* and clearly satisfies the rational basis test.

¶ 42 It is not supposed to be this Court's role to decide how to classify various groups for the purposes of equal protection. "A legislature must have substantial latitude to establish classifications that roughly approximate the nature of the problem perceived, that accommodate competing concerns both public and private, and that account for limitations on the practical ability of the State to remedy every ill." Such classifications need not be perfect or ideal. Nonetheless, the Court has taken it upon itself to lump all "inherently dangerous sports" into one broad category.

¶ 43 The Court fails to acknowledge that within the spectrum of outdoor recreational activities, some activities are more dangerous than others. As Justice McDonough said in *Brewer*:

> Risk distinctions between sports exist, and rational choices based on the perceived distinctions are made everyday. Sky diving and bull riding are to some people considered dangerous, while football is not. The legislature should be free to recognize the degrees of such risk and impose duties and obligations where needed.

It is the province of the legislature, not this Court, to draw those lines. Traditionally, the legislature has been free to draw those lines in a way that might expand or limit tort liability as it sees fit. As we said in *Meech* [*v. Hillhaven* (1989)], "[l]egislative decisions to expand liability to further various policy objectives are debated and passed almost routinely. In a like manner, for policy reasons, the Legislature debates and passes statutes that take away causes of action and/or constrict liability." This exercise in line drawing obviously includes the task of setting aside particular classes so as to expand or limit tort liability. Provided the classification has a conceivable basis, it does not offend the Constitution "merely because it is not made with mathematical nicety, or because in practice it results in some inequality."

¶ 44 The class at issue in this case should be "snowmobilers," rather than all "inherently dangerous sports," a label for which no definition exists and for which no line has been drawn. [Fn. Is swimming "inherently dangerous" to the same extent that downhill skiing is? What about cross-country skiing? Skydiving? Freestyle motorcycle dirt jumping? Kayaking? And are all such sports as "inherently dangerous" as riding a snowmobile? One who would answer these questions should sit in a legislator's seat.] The reason the legislature should be allowed to distinguish snowmobiling from other dangerous activities is the same reason that snowmobiling is such a popular winter activity: snowmobiles have motors. People want to snowmobile because the machine allows them to go faster, usually over snow, up steeper inclines (possibly resulting in avalanches), and jump farther through the air. Among wintertime activities, snowmobiles are uniquely equipped for these pursuits. Take off the motor, and snowmobiles become considerably less attractive as a recreational device. This one fundamental fact not only draws people to snowmobiling (rather than, say, cross-country skiing), but also warrants and justifies a different classification. Snowmobilers are not "similarly situated" to skiers, horseback riders, or outfitters and guides, as the Court contends. Rather, it is the unique dangers inherent only in snowmobiling that led the legislature to exempt snowmobile area operators from liability, provided they were not guilty of gross negligence. The distinction between snowmobiling and other sports is conceivable and thus capable of satisfying rational basis review—and is precisely the sort of line-drawing the legislature—not this Court—should undertake. To classify all "inherently dangerous activities" as "similarly situated" offends that role which our Constitution has given to the legislature separate and apart from this Court.

¶ 45 The Court, in offering an analysis which relies almost exclusively on *Brewer*, has failed to give any deference to the conceivable purpose behind the snowmobile liability statute, and thus has failed to properly exercise rational basis review. For these reasons, I would answer the Circuit Court's question of whether the gross negligence standard of care in the snowmobile liability statute violates the Montana Constitution's equal protection clause in the negative, and would not reach the remaining two issues.

Chief Justice KARLA M. GRAY and Justice JOHN WARNER join the dissenting opinion of Justice RICE.

Notes on Equal Protection

1. *Egdorf* demonstrates conventional equal protection analysis under Article II, section 4. The threshold element of "similarly situated," however, is tricky and often dispositive. Do you agree with the Court's classification of fish and game misdemeanor offenders as distinct from all other misdemeanor offenders? Could any law violate equal protection if the "similarly situated" class is defined as coinciding with the law's application?

2. What difference does it make if age is a rational basis or middle-tier classification? Does either approach align better with the distinct text and structure of Article II, section 4? Is the classification in *Egdorf* more rational than the classification in *Arneson*?

3. Justice Trieweiler asks whether the Court's application of rational basis in *Arneson* is consistent with an earlier case, *Stratemeyer v. Lincoln Co.* (1993). In that case, the Court denied an equal protection challenge to the Workers' Compensation Court's exclusion of mental stress from covered injuries. Applying the rational basis test, the Court found the mental stress exclusion was rationally related to the legitimate governmental objective of controlling the costs of the workers' compensation program and providing benefits. In later cases, the Court has viewed that objective skeptically, even as a matter of rational basis. *See, e.g., Caldwell v. MACO Workers' Compensation Trust* (Mont. 2011) ("Cost alone does not justify the disparate treatment of similar classes").

4. Is *Oberson* consistent with *Meech v. Hillhaven West* (Mont. 1989) in Chapter 5 (rejecting a claim under Article II, section 16 open courts under the rational basis test) and *Rohlfs v. Klemenhagen* (Mont. 2009) in Chapter 3 (rejecting a claim under Article V, section 12 special legislation and equal protection under the rational basis test)? Are these cases consistent with *Butte Community Union v. Lewis* (Mont. 1986) in Chapter 9, which suggests that all Article II rights are fundamental and require strict scrutiny? Should all denials of "equal protection of the laws" be subject to strict scrutiny?

5. *Oberson* is a federal case certified by the United States Court of Appeals for the Ninth Circuit to the Montana Supreme Court in order to answer the state constitutional question. Montana's equal protection doctrine appears to follow the federal rational basis test for laws that do not discriminate against suspect classes. *Stratemeyer*, cited in the cases above, appears to establish the same deferential approach. If it is still good law, what is the point of certification? Would the federal courts, applying the highly deferential rational basis test under federal equal protection doctrine, reach the same result? If not, does the Montana Supreme Court's tiered scrutiny of equal protection claims not actually march in lock-step with federal law?

C. The Human Rights Act, Race, and Culture

The legal system maintained by the 1972 Constitution is not immune to the racist policies institutionalized in the American legal system for centuries before its adoption, nor to the persistence of subtle and not-so-subtle forms of racism in Montana today. Pauli Murray's definitive compilation *States' Laws on Race and Color* reported in 1951 that Montana was one of thirty states to prohibit marriage between "a white person and a negro or a person of negro blood or in part negro" and one of fifteen states to prohibit marriage between "any white person and a Chinese person" or "Japanese person," provisions imported from California in 1909. An early law required adoptive parents to be "of the same race as the child to be adopted." Article XI, section 7 of the 1889 Constitution required public schools to be "open to all the children and youth between the ages of six and twenty-one years," and in 1921 the Legislature enacted a provision permitting "[t]he Crow Indian children residing in the state of Montana. . . to attend public schools of the state of Montana on the same conditions as the children of white citizens of the said state." State laws prohibited the sale of firearms or liquor to Indians, and prohibited Indians from carrying firearms while away from an Indian reservation. Article III, section 25 of the 1889 Constitution allowed aliens (at statehood, predominantly Chinese immigrants) to hold mining property, an exception to a general rule excluding aliens from real property ownership. The Legislature repealed most of these race laws in 1953. The Montana Supreme Court invalidated the alienage restrictions on real property ownership under the federal Equal Protection Clause, with a nod to similar decisions by the California and Oregon Supreme Courts, in *State v. Oakland* (Mont. 1955). The Legislature repealed the adoption restriction in 1961.

While Montana's 1972 Constitution calls out race classifications as worthy of the highest levels of judicial suspicion, Montana's courts have said little on the subject. Well-worn but still contested issues under the federal Constitution such as disparate impact claims and affirmative action are rarely if ever litigated or reported in Montana. The courts' few encounters with race discrimination under Article II, section 4 are instructive of the difficult questions race presents in law, and the confusing array of doctrinal holdings courts have so far provided in response. Other states have taken different approaches to recurrent issues of race discrimination, and these are explored in the second subsection.

Most discrimination claims, including race discrimination claims, arise under the Montana Human Rights Act as administrative claims, not constitutional cases as such. Most of the basic statutes implementing the Montana Constitution's anti-discrimination guarantees were enacted in 1974 and land in Title 49 of the Montana Code Annotated:

> **Mont. Code Ann. § 49-1-102. Freedom from discrimination.** (1) The right to be free from discrimination because of race, creed, religion, color, sex, physical or mental disability, age, or national origin is recognized as and declared to be a civil right. This right must include but not be limited to:

(a) the right to obtain and hold employment without discrimination; and

(b) the right to the full enjoyment of any of the accommodation facilities or privileges of any place of public resort, accommodation, assemblage, or amusement.

[Montana Human Rights Act] Mont. Code Ann. § 49-2-304. Discrimination in public accommodations. (1) Except when the distinction is based on reasonable grounds, it is an unlawful discriminatory practice for the owner, lessee, manager, agent, or employee of a public accommodation:

(a) to refuse, withhold from, or deny to a person any of its services, goods, facilities, advantages, or privileges because of sex, marital status, race, age, physical or mental disability, creed, religion, color, or national origin; *** [*Cf.* 49-2-303 (employment), -305 (housing), -306 (finance), -307 (education), -308 (public benefits & employment), -309 (insurance).]

[Montana Human Rights Act] Mont. Code Ann. § 49-2-512. Filing in district court—compliance with administrative procedures required. (1) The provisions of this chapter establish the exclusive remedy for acts constituting an alleged violation of chapter 3 or this chapter, including acts that may otherwise also constitute a violation of the discrimination provisions of Article II, section 4, of the Montana constitution or 49-1-102. ***

Complaints arising under the Montana Human Rights Act must be brought before the Human Rights Bureau of the Montana Department of Labor and Industry, where they are investigated and heard administratively, subject to appeal to an appointed Human Rights Commission. The Governmental Code of Fair Practices in Title 49, Chapter 3 establishes a similar process for discrimination claims involving public employment, licensing, services, and funds. Only after this administrative process may a dissatisfied party petition for judicial review. Note that the classifications of the Montana Human Rights Act are not entirely congruent with the anti-discrimination provision of Article II, section 4. For example, the Montana Human Rights Act protects physical or mental disability, marital status, age, and national origin, but not culture, social origin or condition, or political beliefs. Theoretically, these gaps leave paths to enforce those anti-discrimination provisions directly without administrative process, but those paths are unexplored.

1. Montana's Tentative Approach to Race (and Culture)

Indigenous people face a complicated legal status under federal law that in many respects displaces state law. The apparently narrow intersection of Montana Constitutional Law and Federal Indian Law in cases involving classifications of Indigenous people and Indian Tribes is a recurrent source of tension in the law. Meanwhile, the term "culture" promises to elevate indigenous culture to its own privileged constitutional status, and perhaps resolve some of this tension, though it remains undeveloped in the law.

Dupuis v. Board of Trustees

330 Mont. 232 (2006)

Justice BRIAN MORRIS delivered the Opinion of the Court.

*** ¶ 3 The Board of Trustees (Board) for the Ronan School District. No. 30 (District) held a public hearing on May 5, 2003, on the continued use of the "Chief" and "Maiden" mascots and the use of certain Native American symbols on the floor of the Ronan Middle School gymnasium. The District is located entirely within the boundaries of the Flathead Reservation, the current home of the Confederated Salish and Kootenai Tribes. The Board voted five to one in favor of retaining the mascots for the District despite the objections of the Confederated Salish and Kootenai Tribes, the Ronan Indian Education Committee (IEC), and numerous Tribal members.

¶ 4 Dupuis filed an appeal to the Lake County Superintendent of Schools (County Superintendent) alleging that the use of the mascots creates a hostile environment within the District, [and] that the Board's decision violated Article X, Section 1(2) and Article II, Section 4 of the Montana Constitution, § 20-1-501, MCA, and District Policies 2450 and 4150. [After administrative proceedings before the County and State Superintendent of Schools,] Dupuis filed a petition for judicial review in the Twentieth Judicial District, Lake County. The District Court dismissed the petition for lack of jurisdiction without comment on January 14, 2005. This appeal followed. ***

[The Court's discussion of administrative jurisdiction is omitted.]

2. Section 20-1-501, MCA

¶ 14 Section 20-1-501, MCA, provides, in part, that "[i]t is the constitutionally declared policy of this state to recognize the distinct and unique cultural heritage of American Indians and to be committed in its educational goals to the preservation of their cultural heritage." [*Cf.* Mont. Const. Art. X, section 1(2).] Dupuis asserts that § 20-1-501, MCA, creates a privately enforceable right, and that the Board's decision to continue using mascots that are degrading and offensive to the dignity of Native students and the Confederated Salish and Kootenai Tribes violates this right.

¶ 15 Nothing in this statute provides, however, for a right to a hearing before the County Superintendent if an aggrieved party believes that a school district has violated this provision of Montana law. A county superintendent does not have jurisdiction to hear a matter absent a constitutional or statutory right to a hearing. We therefore agree with the State Superintendent and the District Court that nothing in § 20-1-501, MCA, confers jurisdiction on the County Superintendent.

3. Montana Constitution

¶ 16 Dupuis alleges that the Board's decision to continue using "Chiefs" and "Maidens" violates Article X, Section 1(2) and Article II, Section 4 of the Montana Constitution. Article X, Section 1(2) "recognizes the distinct and unique cultural heritage of the American Indians and is committed in its educational goals to the preservation of their cultural integrity." Article II, Section 4, the individual dignity clause, provides, in part, that "[t]he dignity of the human being is inviolable." Dupuis asserts that these constitutional provisions create privately enforceable rights and that the District's use of offensive and degrading mascots violates these rights. She further asserts that these provisions prohibit a school district from choosing a school mascot, team name, or team symbol that the District knows to violate the dignity and cultural traditions of the Tribal people on the reservation. The District argues that the Montana Human Rights Commission provides the proper forum for Dupuis to vindicate her claims. We agree.

¶ 17 The Montana Human Rights Act (MHRA) provides, in part, that it "is an unlawful discriminatory practice for an educational institution: (1) to exclude, expel, limit, or otherwise discriminate against an individual. . . enrolled as a student in the terms, conditions, or privileges of the institution because of race, creed, religion, sex, marital status, color, age, physical disability, or national origin or because of mental disability. . . ." Section 49-2-307, MCA. The MHRA establishes the exclusive remedy for conduct violating this provision. Section 49-2-509(7). An aggrieved party therefore first must file a discrimination claim with the Montana Human Rights Commission before bringing an action in District Court. *Romero v. J & J Tire* (Mont. 1989).

¶ 18 Dupuis's allegations of discrimination and violations of the individual dignity clause first must be brought before the Montana Human Rights Commission. Section 49-2-509(7), MCA. Dupuis's failure to exhaust this administrative remedy precludes our review of her discrimination claims. We therefore affirm the District Court's determination that the County Superintendent lacked jurisdiction to address the merits of Dupuis's discrimination claim. We emphasize that our resolution of this case on procedural grounds should not be interpreted as reflecting our view as to whether the District's use of "Chiefs" and "Maidens" is degrading and offensive to Native Americans.

¶ 19 Affirmed.

State v. Shook

313 Mont. 347 (2002)

Justice JAMES C. NELSON delivered the Opinion of the Court.

*** ¶ 5 On or about November 16, 1997, Shook shot and killed a whitetail buck on private property within the exterior boundaries of the Flathead Indian Reservation. Under Commission hunting regulations, big game hunting privileges on Indian Reservations are limited to tribal members only, thereby closing the hunting season to non-tribal members. Shook is not a tribal member. Further, Shook did not own the private property where she hunted, nor was the property owned by a tribal member. Shook was charged with hunting within a closed area in violation of § 87-1-304, MCA, with the penalty provided in § 87-1-102, MCA. ***

III. Discussion

¶ 10 1. Did the District Court properly conclude that the state's big game hunting closure to non-tribal members on Indian reservations does not violate constitutional guarantees of equal protection?

¶ 11 The 1997 Commission regulation at issue here reads: "Big game hunting privileges on Indian Reservations are limited to tribal members only." While a copy of the regulation at issue was not entered into the trial court record by either party, the parties stipulated to this language in the District Court proceedings. This regulation was promulgated pursuant to § 87-1-304(1)(a)(i), MCA, which reads: "The commission may. . . fix seasons, bag limits, possession limits, and season limits." As mentioned, Shook was prosecuted for hunting during a closed season in violation of § 87-1-304, MCA.

¶ 12 Shook first asserts that the state's big game hunting closure to non-tribal members on reservations is an unconstitutional violation of equal protection because it distinguishes between tribal members and non-tribal members on the basis of race. The State and the Tribes counter that laws that distinguish between persons based on tribal membership have long been held constitutional under equal protection requirements because the distinction is political rather than racial. The District Court agreed with the State and held that tribal membership was a valid political classification.

¶ 13 We agree with the State, with the Tribes, and with the District Court. The United States Supreme Court has already explicitly considered whether laws that distinguish based on tribal membership violate equal protection in *Morton v. Mancari* (1974). In that case, the Court addressed Bureau of Indian Affairs employment preferences for Indians and held that the preferences were not unconstitutional classifications. The Court stated:

> Literally every piece of legislation dealing with Indian tribes and reservations. . . single out for special treatment a constituency of tribal Indians living on or near reservations. If these laws, derived from historical relationships and explicitly designed to help only Indians, were deemed invidious racial discrimination, an entire Title of the United States Code (25 U.S.C.) would be effectively erased and the solemn commitment of the Government toward the Indians would be jeopardized.
>
> . . . .
>
> . . . The preference is not directed towards a "racial" group consisting of "Indians"; instead, it applies only to members of "federally recognized" tribes. This operates to exclude many individuals who are racially to be classified as "Indians." In this sense, the preference is political rather than racial in nature.

The Court went on to hold that laws that afford Indians special treatment are constitutional as long as those laws can be tied rationally to the fulfillment of the unique federal obligation toward Indians. *See also United States v. Antelope* (1977) (federal criminal code applicable in Indian country does not violate equal protection).

¶ 14 The State of Montana is required to follow this federal precedent by the express terms of both our own Constitution and the federal enabling act establishing Montana as a state. Specifically, following the Preamble to the Montana Constitution, Article I, the Compact With the United States, requires that the State abide by "the agreement and declaration that all lands owned or held by any Indian or Indian tribes shall remain under the absolute jurisdiction and control of the congress of the United States." Based on this requirement, we have previously held that Indian treaties are "regarded as a part of the law of the state as much as the state's own laws and Constitution[,] [are] effective and binding on [the] state legislature[] . . . [and are] superior to the reserved powers of the state, including the police power." *State v. McClure* (Mont. 1954).

¶ 15 Consequently, federal Indian law regarding the rights of Indians is binding on the state. Therefore, the state equal protection guarantee under Article II, Section 4, must allow for state classifications based on tribal membership if those classifications can rationally be tied to the fulfillment of the unique federal, and consequent state, obligation toward Indians. Indeed, our own Constitution makes a distinction regarding Indians in Article X, Section 1(2) ("The state recognizes the distinct and unique cultural heritage of the American Indians and is committed in its educational goals to the preservation of their cultural integrity.").

¶ 16 Therefore, we need only address whether the state regulation that prohibits non-tribal members from hunting big game on Indian reservations is rationally tied to the fulfillment of the unique obligation toward Indians. We hold that it is. There are seven Indian reservations in Montana each established by treaty and agreements with the federal government. The majority of the treaties establishing the reservations reserve some type of hunting or fishing rights to the respective tribes. At the same time, we have already held that the state can regulate the hunting activities of non-tribal members on reservations unless precluded by an act of Congress or tribal self-governance matters.

¶ 17 Accordingly, under Article I, the State, and in this case the Commission, has a duty to regulate hunting by non-tribal members in a way that recognizes the Indian hunting privileges protected by federal law. The regulation at issue here deals with the state's obligation by simply prohibiting hunting by non-tribal members on reservations. This is an entirely rational means to preserve wildlife populations for hunting by Indians. Therefore, the regulation is rationally related to the federal, and consequent state, obligation to recognize tribal hunting privileges.

¶ 18 Despite the straightforward approach of the regulation, Shook asserts that the regulation is arbitrary because no studies have been done to show if big game wildlife populations on the reservations are over hunted by tribal members. Shook further asserts that conservation purposes could be accomplished by other legitimate means. While there may be other means to conserve the big game wildlife, we simply disagree this invalidates the regulation. When a law is assessed for a rational basis, exact precision or efficiency is not necessary. *See Baldwin v. Fish & Game Comm'n* (1978) ("That [Montana] might have furthered its underlying purpose more artfully, more directly, or more completely, does not warrant a conclusion that the method it chose is unconstitutional.").

¶ 19 In addition, we agree with the State that the District Court properly denied Shook's request for an evidentiary hearing regarding her argument that the regulation violated equal protection. Such a hearing was not necessary to decide the issues of law presented by Shook to the trial court and this Court. . . .

¶ 20 Finally, we note that while we agree with the amicus Montana-Wyoming Tribal Judges Association that the treaties and agreements involving the seven reservations in Montana are each unique, we do not agree that this prevents the state from designing a big game hunting regulation regarding Indian reservations that applies statewide. Indeed, the regulation at issue serves to assure that big game populations on all the reservations are preserved. See also 2002 Big Game Hunting Regulations, Preparing for Your Hunt, Closed Areas (regulation provides for agreements specific to each tribe). ***

Notes on Race, Culture, and Human Rights

1. In *Dupuis*, the Court appears to frame the claims under the Montana Human Rights Act's educational provision, which prohibits discrimination by schools "because of race, creed, religion, sex, marital status, color, age, physical disability, or national origin or because of mental disability." Is this framing, presumably as race discrimination, a fair reading of a constitutional challenge to "the Board's decision to continue using mascots that are degrading and offensive to the dignity of Native students and the Confederated Salish and Kootenai Tribes"? Could Dupuis bring her claim under the term "culture" in section 4 instead, since it is not covered by the MHRA's exclusive remedy? The Bill of Rights Committee Report explained "[t]he word culture was incorporated specifically to cover grounds whose cultural base is distinct from mainstream Montana, especially the American Indians." Note the use of "culture" in both section 4 and in the Article X commitment "to the preservation of [American Indians'] cultural integrity; could Dupuis bring a claim under Article X? What about under the clause "[t]he dignity of the human being is inviolable"?

2. In 2008, the parties settled the *Dupuis* case before the Montana Human Rights Bureau:

> Pursuant to the Hearing Officer's order of January 8, 2008, the parties to this case having reached an agreement that, in exchange for Dupuis' dismissal of this action and agreement not to file any actions against the

district for use of the names and symbol the district will continue to use, the district will not sanction or use any symbols (other than the "Flying R" with wings consisting of feathers as it currently exists) for any extra or co-curricular programs and will remove such symbols, including arrowheads, etc., on gymnasium floors, at the next regularly scheduled maintenance, while continuing to use the names "Chiefs" and "Maidens" and the "Flying R" symbol, to represent its extra and co-curricular programs....

3. In *Romero v. J & J Tire* (Mont. 1989), the Court upheld the Montana Human Rights Act's exclusive remedy provision against constitutional challenges under Article II, sections 4 (individual dignity), 16 (administration of justice), 17 (due process), and 26 (trial by jury), as well as federal due process and equal protection. The Court held in part:

In *Drinkwalter v. Shipton Supply Co., Inc.* (Mont. 1987), this Court held that a victim of sexual harassment could file her complaint directly in district court, without going through the administrative procedures outlined in the Act. After that decision, the 1987 Legislature enacted § 49-2-509(7), MCA, with an immediate effective date. That section provides that the Act establishes the exclusive remedy for acts constituting a violation thereof and that no claim for relief based upon such acts may be entertained by a district court other than by the procedures the Act specifies. The Act requires that a claimant must file a complaint before the Human Rights Commission, which has 12 months in which to hold a contested case hearing, before a case may be filed in district court. Section 49-2-509(1), MCA. Romero argues that this requirement denies him equal protection of the law and access to the courts as guaranteed under U.S. Const. amend. V and XIV and Art. II, secs. 4, 16, and 17, Mont. Const.

Romero cites *White v. State* (Mont. 1983) and *Pfost v. State* (Mont. 1985) as authority. Both cases were overruled in relevant part in *Meech v. Hillhaven* (Mont. 1989). Moreover, those cases both dealt with limitations on remedies, not procedural requirements.

We look instead to *Linder v. Smith* (Mont. 1981), in which this Court upheld the constitutionality of the Montana Medical Malpractice Act. Under that act, a litigant is required to go through administrative proceedings before the Medical Malpractice Panel before filing a complaint in district court. This Court held that access to the courts may be hindered if another fundamental right is not involved and there exists a rational basis for doing so. We found that the medical malpractice crisis in Montana was a rational basis for hindering access to the courts. We also held that because the requirement that medical malpractice claimants proceed first through the Medical Malpractice Panel operated in the same manner upon all persons in like circumstances, equal protection guarantees

> were not violated. In a similar manner, the requirement that discrimination claimants proceed first through the Montana Human Rights Division operates equally upon all persons in like circumstances. Although Romero argues that freedom from racial discrimination is a fundamental right in Montana, this Court has not previously so held and is not prepared to do so based on the arguments made by Romero. We hold that the State's purpose of combatting illegal discrimination is a rational basis for delaying access to the courts by using a specialized agency to handle discrimination complaints.

How is freedom from racial discrimination *not* a fundamental right in Montana under Article II, section 4? Why would the Court reach such a conclusion?

4. For a look at how racial discrimination claims move through Montana's justice system under the Montana Human Rights Act, see *KB Enters., LLC v. Mont. Human Rights Comm'n*, 2019 MT 131 (contains racial epithets).

5. How does the Court in *Shook* read Article II, section 4 as applying to classifications based on tribal membership? Shook asserts the Commission's rule is race-based, but consistent with federal law, the Court rejects the race-based claim and holds instead that tribal membership is a political classification. What follows, as a matter of state constitutional law? The Court applies rational basis in lock-step with *Morton v. Mancari*, even though cultural and political classifications arguably are suspect classifications under the express terms of the anti-discrimination clause of Article II, section 4. Is the Court required by federal law to apply rational basis scrutiny to *state* classifications based on tribal membership, when such classifications rationally relate to but are not required by federal treaties, notwithstanding the anti-discrimination clause? (Note the Court concedes that only a majority of the treaties of Montana tribes reserve hunting rights, and that each treaty is unique, but disregards the actual terms of those treaties in favor of upholding a blanket statewide rule.) Is the rational basis the Court applies here more like *Arneson* or *Egdorf*? Could the state's policy of providing extra protection for Indian hunting privileges satisfy a stronger form of rational basis, or even strict scrutiny?

6. If you were bringing a discrimination claim under Article II, section 4 on behalf of a member of a tribe, how would you argue that tribal membership is a "cultural" classification instead of a "political" one? What authority would you consider persuasive and where would you look to find it? What about an Indigenous person who is not a member of a recognized tribe?

7. What difference might it make that the rule in *Shook* operated to the benefit of the tribal members it classified? After ratification of the 1972 Constitution, and *Mancari*, the United States Supreme Court held in a 4-1-4 opinion that affirmative action programs based on suspect classifications are subject to strict scrutiny. *University of California Regents v. Bakke* (1978). Does the anti-discrimination clause of Article II, section 4 suggest that affirmative action should be subject to more or less

scrutiny under the Montana Constitution? (Note that a state could not be any more permissive of affirmative action than the Supreme Court's reading of the Fourteenth Amendment would allow as to classes that Court has deemed to be suspect, but these decisions would not be binding as to other classes covered by a state constitution.) With limited exceptions that include certain employment preferences "based on the individual's status as an Indian living on or near a reservation," the Montana Human Rights Act provides "sex, marital status, age, physical or mental disability, race, creed, religion, color, or national origin may not comprise justification for discrimination except for the legally demonstrable purpose of correcting a previous discriminatory practice." Mont. Code Ann. § 49-2-403(1). Is this consistent with Article II, section 4?

2. Other State Approaches to Race

Montana's constitutional law of discrimination is less developed than in other states and at the federal level. Where it is more developed, the law of Article II, section 4 presents questions alongside its answers. Under other state constitutions, some state supreme courts have worked out approaches to racial and other forms of discrimination that provide guidance without lockstepping behind federal doctrine. Consider how the cases below offer distinct perspectives on questions of Indigenous identity and remedying racially disparate impacts of state laws, whether they can inform Montana constitutional law, and what the development of an independent non-discrimination rule of Article II, section 4 might look like.

Malabed v. North Slope Borough

70 P.3d 416 (Alaska 2003)

BRYNER, Justice.

The United States Court of Appeals for the Ninth Circuit certified a question to this court, asking whether a North Slope Borough ordinance enacting a hiring preference in favor of Native Americans violates state or local law. Article I, section 1, of the Alaska Constitution provides that "all persons are equal and entitled to equal rights, opportunities, and protection under the law." *** In addition [to Article I, section 1], Article I, section 3, of the Alaska Constitution categorically prohibits discrimination based on race or national origin: "No person is to be denied the enjoyment of any civil or political right because of race, color, creed, sex, or national origin."

Relying on these provisions, Malabed argues that the borough's hiring preference adopts a racial classification or, alternatively, a classification based on national origin, in violation of the Alaska Constitution. The borough responds by denying that its preference uses a race-conscious classification; instead, the borough insists, the preference adopts a well-accepted and constitutionally permissible political classification based on membership in federally recognized tribes. In advancing this argument, the borough relies chiefly on *Morton v. Mancari*. ***

Assuming for present purposes that the borough's ordinance reflects this kind of political classification [under *Mancari*] and does not discriminate on the basis of race, the ordinance might avoid problems with the Alaska Constitution's bar against racial discrimination. But the political nature of the classification would not necessarily insulate the ordinance from Malabed's equal protection challenge. For the borough, unlike the BIA in *Mancari*, has no obvious governmental interest, as a borough, in furthering Native American self-government; and Native Americans have no explicitly established "unique legal status" under borough law, as *Mancari* found them to have under federal law. Given these disparities between federal and local law, the legitimacy of the borough's hiring preference as a political classification is less apparent than the legitimacy of the BIA's hiring preference in *Mancari*. We must therefore consider whether the ordinance's ostensibly political lines discriminate in a way that offends the Alaska Constitution's guarantee of equal protection.

B. Alaska's Three-Step Equal Protection Standard

We have long recognized that the Alaska Constitution's equal protection clause affords greater protection to individual rights than the United States Constitution's Fourteenth Amendment. To implement Alaska's more stringent equal protection standard, we have adopted a three-step, sliding-scale test that places a progressively greater or lesser burden on the state, depending on the importance of the individual right affected by the disputed classification and the nature of the governmental interests at stake: first, we determine the weight of the individual interest impaired by the classification; second, we examine the importance of the purposes underlying the government's action; and third, we evaluate the means employed to further those goals to determine the closeness of the means-to-end fit.

1. Step 1: individual interests affected by the preference

To determine how the borough's hiring preference fares under this standard, we begin by considering the importance of the individual interests implicated by the preference. Here, the borough's hiring preference impairs Malabed's right to seek and obtain employment in his profession. Under similar circumstances, we have declared the right to employment to be an important right.... [I]ts impairment therefore requires us to give close scrutiny to the borough's hiring preference....

2. Step 2: importance and legitimacy of borough's interests in the preference

a. The borough's interest in the preference is not legitimate ...

In the second part of the equal protection analysis we consider the borough's interests, asking whether it had important and legitimate reasons to adopt the hiring preference. The borough offers several reasons supporting its ordinance: reducing unemployment of the largest group of unemployed borough residents—Inupiat Eskimos; strengthening the borough's economy; and training its workforce....

Though acknowledging these interests as important, we [have] found them to be illegitimate because they favored one class of Alaskans over another. . . .

b. The Alaska Constitution does not give the borough a legitimate interest in adopting the preference.

We reject at the outset the notion that the Alaska Constitution radiates implied guardianship powers allowing the state or its boroughs to treat Alaska Natives as if they were wards. To be sure, the United States Supreme Court has recognized implied powers in the United States Constitution that allow Congress broad latitude to legislate on behalf of Native Americans. The borough reasons that the Alaska Constitution must implicitly grant parallel powers to state and municipal governments. But the federal government's implied powers spring directly from the express powers granted to Congress in the United States Constitution's Indian Commerce and Treaty clauses. . . . In contrast to the federal constitution's provisions dealing with Indian tribes, the Alaska Constitution includes no provisions authorizing state action regarding Alaska Natives and so grants no express powers from which implied powers could arise. Indeed, the only provision of the Alaska Constitution that addresses the state's relations with Alaska Natives is article XII, section 12, which effectively disavows any state authority comparable to the federal government's protective powers. Thus, article XII, section 12, expressly disclaims all "right or title in or to any property, including fishing rights, the right or title to which may be held by or for any Indian, Eskimo, or Aleut, or community thereof," and further specifies "that, unless otherwise provided by Congress, the property, as described in this section, shall remain subject to the absolute disposition of the United States." To the extent that the Alaska Constitution implies anything concerning the state's relations with Alaska Natives, then, it mirrors the constitutional drafters' well-recognized desire to treat Alaska Natives like all other Alaska citizens. The Alaska Constitution thus implies nothing that would give the borough a legitimate interest in enacting the disputed preference.

c. The 703(i) exception does not give the borough a legitimate interest in adopting the preference.

The borough next contends that the Civil Rights Act's 703(i) exception [for employment preferences to individuals who are Indians living on or near a reservation] gives it a legitimate interest in enacting the challenged preference. We agree in theory that Congress can create specific mandates or interests empowering states or units of local government to legislate on behalf of Native Americans without creating suspect classifications. Yet such mandates or interests have been found to arise in two relatively narrow situations: in the first, the state acts under a particularized, state-specific congressional delegation of jurisdiction; in the second, the state acts to accommodate federal supremacy in the field by enforcing congressionally created federal obligations toward Indian tribes that the federal government would otherwise enforce on its own. The borough's reliance on the Civil Rights Act's 703(i) exception presents little in common with these situations. ***

We by no means suggest that boroughs are categorically barred from adopting hiring preferences. Nor do we suggest that all state or local legislation pertaining to Alaska Natives or tribal governments should be assumed to establish suspect classifications presumptively barred by equal protection. Our focus is considerably narrower: we simply hold. . . that the borough has no legitimate basis to claim a general governmental interest in enacting hiring preferences favoring one class of citizens over others; and we find that the borough has failed to identify any source of a legitimate, case-specific governmental interest in the preference it actually adopted—a hiring preference favoring Native Americans. Because the borough is a political subdivision of Alaska, its legitimate sphere of municipal interest lies in governing for all of its people; preferring the economic interests of one class of its citizens at the expense of others is not a legitimate municipal interest, regardless of whether we view its ordinance as drawing distinctions founded on political status or race.

3. Step 3: means-to-end fit

The last step of equal protection analysis under the Alaska Constitution examines the nexus between the state's asserted interests and the means selected to implement those interests. As previously mentioned, even when the state acts for important and legitimate reasons, its action must bear a close connection to those interests to justify impairing an important individual right. Here, of course, because we have found no legitimate borough interest supporting the challenged preference, we need not dwell on the closeness of its means-to-end fit. But a brief comment on the issue is nevertheless important to establish an alternative basis for our equal protection ruling.

For even assuming that the borough had legitimate and important interests in enacting a hiring preference favoring Native Americans, its preference is not closely related to attaining those interests. *** The primary interest asserted by the borough lies in reducing Native American unemployment. But when viewed in light of this purpose, the borough's hiring preference is stunningly broad: it extends borough-wide and to all aspects of borough employment; is potentially limitless in duration; covers not only hiring but also promotions, transfers, and reinstatements; and applies absolutely—even to the extent of requiring Native American applicants without minimum qualifications to be hired over qualified non-Native applicants. Because the borough advances no particular reasons to justify these sweeping provisions, it fails to establish a close fit between its goals and its actions.

IV. Conclusion

We conclude that the borough's hiring preference violates the Alaska Constitution's guarantee of equal protection because the borough lacks a legitimate governmental interest to enact a hiring preference favoring one class of citizens at the expense of others and because the preference it enacted is not closely tailored to meet its goals.

MATTHEWS, Justice, concurring.

I agree with the opinion of the court that the borough hiring preference violates the equal rights clause of the Alaska Constitution and with much of the court's reasoning. But I prefer to address directly the question whether the ordinance discriminates on the basis of race. I believe that it does, for the reasons that follow.

Inupiat Eskimos are a racial rather than a tribal group. The ordinance frankly acknowledges that its goal is to benefit them. In a prefatory clause the ordinance states "that its purpose in establishing an employment preference for Native Americans is to employ and train its Inupiat Eskimo residents in permanent, full-time positions...." Another clause sounds the same theme: "Whereas, to increase the employment of Inupiat Eskimos, the North Slope Borough would like to give an employment preference to Native Americans...." Similarly, the implementation plan for the ordinance expressly states that its purpose is to employ Inupiat Eskimo residents. Further, at oral argument counsel for the borough explained that one reason the term "Native American" was defined in terms of tribal membership was that it served to distinguish eligible Native Americans from others who are not eligible for benefits under the preference ordinance even though they may have some Native American ancestors. Tribal membership was thus used as a convenient mechanism to describe bona fide Native Americans.

Based on the above we can say with confidence that the purpose of the ordinance was to discriminate on the basis of race. Because by the express terms of the civil rights clause of the Alaska Constitution race is a suspect category, the ordinance must be subjected to strict scrutiny in order to determine whether it is permissible under the equal rights and civil rights clauses. But even if there were no clear indicators of an intent to discriminate on the basis of race, I believe that strict scrutiny would still be required because tribal membership is not only a political category but a racial one.

I reach the conclusion that state or municipal laws that grant individual benefits differentially based on tribal membership should be subject to strict scrutiny for a number of reasons. As noted, this is how we treat all race-based classifications. Further, strict scrutiny is well designed to ensure that laws remain race-neutral, as contemplated by the framers of the Alaska Constitution. This case illustrates that tribal membership readily lends itself to use as a proxy for a racial classification and as a pretext for racial discrimination. An effective tool is necessary to prevent these abuses. In addition, strict scrutiny is the approach taken by some federal courts in tribal classification cases when construing the equal protection clause of the Fourteenth Amendment to the federal constitution. Since the federal constitution contains provisions authorizing legislation on behalf of Native Americans, while the Alaska Constitution presumptively prohibits such legislation, it follows that stronger reasons exist for using the strict scrutiny method for state constitutional questions than for those arising under the federal constitution.

Although strict scrutiny review presents a high barrier, it is a barrier that may be overcome in deserving cases. It is impossible to categorize the kinds of cases that might pass strict scrutiny review. But a federal law calling on the state to give preferential treatment to tribal members would almost certainly present a compelling justification for state legislation. On balance, I believe that strict scrutiny properly accommodates the state's strong interest in preventing discrimination on the basis of race and its relatively rare and limited need to act adjunctively with the federal government in programs that favor tribal members over other state citizens.

The present ordinance does not survive strict scrutiny review. As the opinion of the court establishes, the borough had no legitimate interest, much less a compelling one, in adopting the preference. I believe therefore that the ordinance is prohibited by article I, sections 1 and 3 of the Alaska Constitution.

Sheff v. O'Neill

238 Conn. 1 (1996)

PETERS, Chief Justice.

The public elementary and high school students in Hartford suffer daily from the devastating effects that racial and ethnic isolation, as well as poverty, have had on their education. Federal constitutional law provides no remedy for their plight. The principal issue in this appeal is whether, under the unique provisions of our state constitution, the state, which already plays an active role in managing public schools, must take further measures to relieve the severe handicaps that burden these children's education. The issue is as controversial as the stakes are high. We hold today that the needy schoolchildren of Hartford have waited long enough. The constitutional imperatives contained in article eighth, § 1, and article first, §§ 1 and 20, of our state constitution entitle the plaintiffs to relief. At the same time, the constitutional imperative of separation of powers persuades us to afford the legislature, with the assistance of the executive branch, the opportunity, in the first instance, to fashion the remedy that will most appropriately respond to the constitutional violations that we have identified. The judgment of the trial court must, accordingly, be reversed.

[The constitution of Connecticut, article eighth, § 1, provides: "There shall always be free public elementary and secondary schools in the state. The general assembly shall implement this principle by appropriate legislation." The constitution of Connecticut, article first, § 1, provides: "All men when they form a social compact, are equal in rights; and no man or set of men are entitled to exclusive public emoluments or privileges from the community." The constitution of Connecticut, article first, § 20, as amended by articles five and twenty-one of the amendments, provides: "No person shall be denied the equal protection of the law nor be subjected to segregation or discrimination in the exercise or enjoyment of his or her civil or political rights because of religion, race, color, ancestry, national origin, sex or physical or mental disability."]

*** The stipulation of the parties and the trial court's findings establish the following relevant facts. Statewide, in the 1991–92 school year, children from minority groups constituted 25.7 percent of the public school population. In the Hartford public school system in that same period, 92.4 percent of the students were members of minority groups, including, predominantly, students who were either African-American or Latino. Fourteen of Hartford's twenty-five elementary schools had a white student enrollment of less than 2 percent. The Hartford public school system currently enrolls the highest percentage of minority students in the state. In the future, if current conditions continue, the percentage of minority students in the Hartford public school system is likely to increase rather than decrease. Since 1980, the percentage of African-Americans in the Hartford student population has decreased, while the percentage of Latinos has increased. Although enrollment of African-American students in the twenty-one surrounding suburban towns has increased by more than 60 percent from 1980 to 1992, only seven of these school districts had a minority student enrollment in excess of 10 percent in 1992. Because of the negative consequences of racial and ethnic isolation, a more integrated public school system would likely be beneficial to all schoolchildren.

A majority of the children who constitute the public school population in Hartford come from homes that are economically disadvantaged, that are headed by a single parent and in which a language other than English is spoken. The percentage of Hartford schoolchildren at the elementary level who return to the same school that they attended the previous year is the lowest such percentage in the state. Such socioeconomic factors impair a child's orientation toward and skill in learning and adversely affect a child's performance on standardized tests. The gap in the socioeconomic status between Hartford schoolchildren and schoolchildren from the surrounding twenty-one suburban towns has been increasing. The performance of Hartford schoolchildren on standardized tests falls significantly below that of schoolchildren from the twenty-one surrounding suburban towns. ***

The state has not intentionally segregated racial and ethnic minorities in the Hartford public school system. Except for a brief period in 1868, no students in Connecticut have intentionally been assigned to a public school or to a public school district on the basis of race or ethnicity. There has never been any other manifestation of *de jure* segregation either at the state or the local level. In addition to various civil rights initiatives undertaken by the legislature from 1905 to 1961 to combat racial discrimination, the state board of education was reorganized, during the 1980s, to concentrate on the needs of urban schoolchildren and to promote diversity in the public schools. Since 1970, the state has supported and encouraged voluntary plans for increasing interdistrict diversity.

The state has nonetheless played a significant role in the present concentration of racial and ethnic minorities in the Hartford public school system. Although intended to improve the quality of education and not racially or ethnically motivated, the districting statute that the legislature enacted in 1909, is the single most important factor contributing to the present concentration of racial and ethnic minorities in the Hartford public school system. The districting statute and the resultant school district boundaries have remained virtually unchanged since 1909. The districting statute is of critical importance because it establishes town boundaries as the dividing line between all school districts in the state. ***

The defendants maintain that... the plaintiffs are not entitled to judicial relief because the educational disparities of which they complain do not result from the requisite state action. The plaintiffs claim that the state bears responsibility to correct the constitutional violations alleged in their complaint because of the state's failure to "take corrective measures to [e]nsure that its Hartford public schoolchildren receive an equal educational opportunity." That failure is actionable, according to the plaintiffs, because of the state's knowledge of the racial and ethnic isolation in the Hartford schools, combined with the state's extensive involvement in the operations of Connecticut's public schools and the impact of state statutes mandating school attendance within statutorily defined school districts. The defendants maintain, to the contrary, that the state's constitutional duty to provide for the elementary and secondary education of Connecticut schoolchildren is triggered only by state action that is alleged to be intentional state misconduct. The trial court relied on the absence of such intentional state action in denying relief to the plaintiffs. We disagree with the trial court's decision.

The defendants' argument, derived largely from principles of federal constitutional law, founders on the fact that article eighth, § 1, and article first, §§ 1 and 20, impose on the legislature an affirmative constitutional obligation to provide schoolchildren throughout the state with a substantially equal educational opportunity. It follows that, if the legislature fails, for whatever reason, to take action to remedy substantial inequalities in the educational opportunities that such children are being afforded, its actions and its omissions constitute state action. ***

The claims now before us likewise implicate the legislature's affirmative constitutional obligation to provide a substantially equal educational opportunity to all of the state's schoolchildren. The plaintiffs document the existence of an extensive statutory system developed in response to the legislature's plenary authority over state public elementary and secondary schools. As a general matter, the plaintiffs challenge the failure of the legislature to address continuing unconstitutional inequities resulting, de facto, from that scheme. In addition, and more specifically, they point to two statutes that directly impact on their claims of constitutional deprivation. State law sets the borders of school districts to coincide with town boundaries; and requires all children to attend public school within the district in which they reside. ***

[T]he defendants urge us to follow federal precedents that concededly require, as a matter of federal constitutional law, that claimants seeking judicial relief for educational disparities pursuant to the equal protection clause of the fourteenth amendment to the United States constitution must prove intentional governmental discrimination against a suspect class. According to the defendants, because the plaintiffs raise claims of unconstitutional disparities in educational opportunities on the basis of severe racial and ethnic imbalances among school districts, the plaintiffs, too, must prove intentional state action.

For two reasons, we are not persuaded that we should adopt these precedents as a matter of state constitutional law. First and foremost, the federal cases start from the premise that there is no right to education under the United States constitution. *San Antonio Independent School District v. Rodriguez* (1973). Our Connecticut constitution, by contrast, contains a fundamental right to education and a corresponding affirmative state obligation to implement and maintain that right. Second, the federal cases are guided by principles of federalism as "a foremost consideration in interpreting any of the pertinent constitutional provisions under which [a court] examines state action." *San Antonio Independent School District v. Rodriguez.* As the United States Supreme Court noted, "it would be difficult to imagine a case having a greater potential impact on our federal system than the one now before us, in which we are urged to abrogate systems of financing public education presently in existence in virtually every State." *San Antonio Independent School District v. Rodriguez.* Principles of federalism, however, do not restrict our constitutional authority to enforce the constitutional mandates contained in article eighth, § 1, and article first, §§ 1 and 20.

Federal constitutional law, furthermore, has not invariably required intentional state action as a requisite foundation for constitutional remedies. In cases involving the fundamental right to vote, the United States Supreme Court has held state action to be implicated by the legislature's failure to take the proper steps to implement its affirmative constitutional duty. *See Reynolds v. Sims* (1964). We can perceive no principled distinction between judicial intervention to require legislative action to protect the fundamental right to vote and judicial intervention to require legislative action to protect the fundamental right to a substantially equal educational opportunity.

In summary, under our law, which imposes an affirmative constitutional obligation on the legislature to provide a substantially equal educational opportunity for all public schoolchildren, the state action doctrine is not a defense to the plaintiffs' claims of constitutional deprivation. The state had ample notice of ongoing trends toward racial and ethnic isolation in its public schools, and indeed undertook a number of laudable remedial efforts that unfortunately have not achieved their desired end. The fact that the legislature did not affirmatively create or intend to create the conditions that have led to the racial and ethnic isolation in the Hartford public school system does not, in and of itself, relieve the defendants of their affirmative obligation to provide the plaintiffs with a more effective remedy for their constitutional grievances.

We turn now to the merits of the plaintiffs' claims. No statute, no common law precedent, no federal constitutional principle provides this state's schoolchildren with a right to a public education that is not burdened by de facto racial and ethnic segregation. The plaintiffs make no such claim. The issue that they raise is whether they have stated a case for relief under our state constitution, which was amended in 1965 to provide both a right to a free public elementary and secondary education; Conn. Const., art. VIII, § 1; and a right to protection from segregation. Conn. Const., art. I, § 20. This issue raises questions that are difficult; the answers that we give are controversial. We are, however, persuaded that a fair reading of the text and the history of these amendments demonstrates a deep and abiding constitutional commitment to a public school system that, in fact and in law, provides Connecticut schoolchildren with a substantially equal educational opportunity. A significant component of that substantially equal educational opportunity is access to a public school education that is not substantially impaired by racial and ethnic isolation. ***

For Connecticut schoolchildren, the scope of the state's constitutional obligation to provide a substantially equal educational opportunity is informed and amplified by the highly unusual provision in article first, § 20, that prohibits segregation not only indirectly, by forbidding discrimination, but directly, by the use of the term "segregation." The section provides in relevant part: "No person shall be denied the equal protection of the law *nor be subjected to segregation* or discrimination... because of... race [or]... ancestry...." (Emphasis added.)

The express inclusion of the term "segregation" in article first, § 20, has independent constitutional significance. The addition of this term to the text of our equal protection clause distinguishes this case from others in which we have found a substantial equivalence between our equal protection clause and that contained in the United States constitution. Fundamental principles of constitutional interpretation require that "[e]ffect must be given to every part of and each word in our constitution...." In other cases, we have held that, insofar as article first, § 20, differs textually from its federal counterpart, its judicial construction must reflect such a textual distinction.

The issue before us, therefore, is what specific meaning to attach to the protection against segregation contained in article first, § 20, in a case in which that protection is invoked as part of the plaintiff school-children's fundamental affirmative right to a substantially equal educational opportunity under article eighth, § 1. In concrete terms, this issue devolves into the question of whether the state has a constitutional duty to remedy the educational impairment that results from segregation in the Hartford public schools, even though the conditions of segregation that contribute to such impairment neither were caused nor are perpetuated by invidious intentional conduct on the part of the state.

Linguistically, the term "segregation" in article first, § 20, which denotes "separation," is neutral about segregative intent. The section prohibits segregation that occurs "*because of* religion, race, color, ancestry, national origin, sex or physical or mental disability"; without specifying the manner in which such a causal relationship must be established.

Whatever this language may portend in other contexts, we are persuaded that, in the context of public education, in which the state has an affirmative obligation to monitor and to equalize educational opportunity, the state's awareness of existing and increasing severe racial and ethnic isolation imposes upon the state the responsibility to remedy "segregation... because of race [or] . . . ancestry. . . ." We therefore hold that, textually, article eighth, § 1, as informed by article first, § 20, requires the legislature to take affirmative responsibility to remedy segregation in our public schools, regardless of whether that segregation has occurred *de jure* or *de facto.*

The history of the promulgation of article eighth, § 1, and article first, § 20, supports our conclusion that these constitutional provisions include protection from de facto segregation, at least in public schools. That history includes not only the contemporaneous addition, in 1965, of these two provisions to our constitution, but also the strong commitment to ending discrimination and segregation that is evident in the remarks of the delegates to the 1965 constitutional convention.

First, it is undisputed that the duty to provide a public education contained in article eighth, § 1, and the prohibition against segregation contained in article first, § 20, were proposed to and adopted by the voters of this state in response to the constitutional convention of 1965. When the convention delegates debated the desirability of both amendments to our state constitution, they recognized and endorsed the landmark decision in *Brown v. Board of Education* (1954), declaring the unconstitutionality of "separate but equal" public school education. The primary motivation for the addition of article eighth, § 1, to the constitution in 1965 appears to have been the realization that Connecticut was the only state in the nation that did not provide any express right to public elementary and secondary education in its constitution. The delegates' expectation that the proposed amendments to the constitution would secure interrelated constitutional rights was underscored by Bernstein's remark that article first, § 20, was intended to be applied in the context of the "rights of freedom in education."

Second, it is significant that the debate over the amendment of article first, § 20, manifested the intention of the convention delegates to extend broad protection to all persons from all forms of racial and ethnic discrimination and segregation. The debate over the express inclusion of the term "segregation" focused not on whether including such a term might reach too far, but rather on whether it might invite too narrow a construction of the prohibition against discrimination. It was for this reason that the rules committee felt that language regarding segregation was unnecessary. The convention delegates' decision nonetheless to retain the term "segregation" was premised on the acknowledged importance of unequivocal opposition to all that is encompassed by this invidious philosophy and practice. In effect, the convention delegates inserted into article first, § 20, constitutional language that was intended to prohibit not only discrimination, but also segregation on the basis of race or ethnicity.

Finally, the convention delegates' manifest intent that article first, § 20, by prohibiting segregation, should provide "total protection against discrimination"; supports our conclusion that they intended to encompass de facto segregation in the circumstances presented by the present case. If significant racial and ethnic isolation continues to occur within the public schools, for which the legislature has an affirmative constitutional obligation to provide a substantially equal educational opportunity, no special showing of an invidious segregative intent is required.

It would be illogical not to prohibit all such segregation in light of the legislature's otherwise comprehensive assumption of responsibility for the education of Connecticut schoolchildren. The legislature has created the current school districts, has required students to attend school and has determined which students will attend a particular school district. The state cannot now avoid its responsibilities by invoking constitutional restraints articulated for different purposes under different constitutional provisions.

Sound principles of public policy support our conclusion that the legislature's affirmative constitutional responsibility for the education of all public schoolchildren encompasses responsibility for segregation to which the legislature has contributed, even unintentionally. The parties agree, as the trial court expressly found, that racial and ethnic segregation is harmful, and that integration would likely have positive benefits for all children and for society as a whole. Further, as the trial court also expressly found, the racial and ethnic isolation of children in the Hartford schools is likely to worsen in the future.

Racial and ethnic segregation has a pervasive and invidious impact on schools, whether the segregation results from intentional conduct or from unorchestrated demographic factors.... Our state constitution, as amended in 1965, imposes on the state an affirmative obligation to respond to such segregation. ***

Our conclusion finds uncontested factual support in the stipulations of the parties, which provide dramatic documentation of the wide disparities in the racial and ethnic composition of the student populations in the public schools in Hartford and those in the twenty-one surrounding communities. Although we have discussed these statistics previously in this opinion, they bear repeating. The percentage of minorities who attend Hartford public schools is significantly higher than the percentage of minorities who attend schools in the surrounding school districts. In the 1991–92 school year, over 92 percent of the students in the Hartford public school system were members of minority groups. In stark contrast, in that same period, only seven of the twenty-one surrounding suburban towns had a student minority enrollment above 10 percent. We rely also on the findings made by the trial court, which have not been contested by any of the parties, that despite efforts by the state to alleviate the severe racial and ethnic isolation that exists in the Hartford public school system, "[s]tudents in the Hartford schools are racially isolated and are likely to become more isolated in the future" and that "[t]he single most important factor that contribute[s] to the present concentration of racial and ethnic minorities in Hartford [is] the town-school district system which has existed since 1909, when the legislature consolidated most of the school districts in the state so that thereafter town boundaries became the dividing lines between all school districts in the state." This record compels the conclusion that the present state regulation of public elementary and secondary education "emasculate[s] the goal of substantial equality."

We conclude, therefore, that the school districting scheme, as codified at §§ 10-184 and 10-240 and as enforced with regard to these plaintiffs, is unconstitutional. ***

BORDEN, Associate Justice, with whom CALLAHAN and PALMER, JJ., join, dissenting.

The majority has reached a result driven conclusion based on a theory of constitutional liability that was never presented to the trial court or to this court, is ungrounded in the text and history of Connecticut's constitutional provisions regarding the rights to public education and equal protection of the laws and is wholly at odds with the factual record in this case. . . . In its zeal to reach a result that, it envisions, will eliminate racial and ethnic concentration in the public school districts of this state, the majority has "[renounced] this Court's historical commitment to a conception of the judiciary as a source of impersonal and reasoned judgments. . . ." (Internal quotation marks omitted.) *Payne v. Tennessee* (1991) (Marshall and Blackmun, Js., dissenting). In essence, "[p]ower, not reason, is the new currency of this Court's [state constitutional] decisionmaking." *Id.* I therefore dissent. ***

Before analyzing the majority's reasoning and the constitutional claims that the plaintiffs did present in this case, I state the extent of my agreement with the majority. First, I agree that the case is justiciable, and that there is state action. Moreover, and most importantly, I agree with the majority on the desirability—as a matter of public and educational policy—of eliminating from our public schools the type of racial and ethnic concentration demonstrated by this record.

I also agree that racial and ethnic isolation in our public schools is harmful—both to those races and ethnic groups that are so isolated and to the other races and ethnic groups from whom they are isolated. I also agree with the majority's statement, based upon the trial court's finding, that the racial and ethnic isolation of Hartford's schoolchildren is likely to worsen in the future. I agree, furthermore, that racial and ethnic integration of our public schools would be beneficial for all children and society in general. These points of agreement rest on the notions that, as the majority recognizes, schools are important socializing institutions that bear a central responsibility for imparting our shared democratic values to our children, and that the opportunity for children of different races, ethnic backgrounds, economic levels and social groups to get to know each other in school is important if they are to understand and respect each other. Finally, I agree with the majority that the health of the economy of our state requires an educated workforce, which includes "the urban poor as an integral part of our future economic strength." Thus, I agree with the majority on the importance in our state—indeed, in our nation—of finding a way to cross the racial divide.

The majority, however, has transformed a laudable educational philosophy into a constitutional mandate. That philosophy is that racially and ethnically integrated schools are socially and educationally preferable to racially and ethnically concentrated schools, because they confer certain significant social benefits on their students that such concentrated schools cannot, and they avoid certain significant social burdens that such concentrated schools are likely to impose. That belief, however, is utterly without basis as a constitutional claim of deprivation of an equal educational opportunity. Neither the record in this case, the text or history of the Connecticut constitution, nor our case law supports such a claim.

Notes on Other State Approaches to Race Discrimination

1. The Montana Supreme Court in *Shook* holds it must apply rational basis review under *Mancari* because "federal Indian law regarding the rights of Indians is binding on the state," while the Alaska Supreme Court in *Malabed* conducts its own state-specific equal protection analysis. Are the cases inconsistent? If so, who gets the law right?

2. After the Alaska Supreme Court answered the certified state constitutional question, the United States Court of Appeals for the Ninth Circuit rejected a claim that Title VII of the Civil Rights Act of 1964 preempts the state constitution, and invalidated the borough's law under the Alaska Constitution. *See Malabed v. North Slope Borough* (9th Cir. 2003).

3. After ratification of Montana's 1972 Constitution, the United States Supreme Court held that (*de jure*) neutral laws with a (*de facto*) disparate impact on a protected class do not violate the federal Equal Protection Clause. *Washington v. Davis* (1976). In *State v. Spina* (Mont. 1999), the Montana Supreme Court noted, citing *Washington*, that "it is a basic equal protection principle that the invidious quality of a law claimed to be discriminatory must ultimately be traced to an impermissibly discriminatory purpose." Does the same "basic equal protection principle" apply to the distinct text of the anti-discrimination clause of Article II, section 4? (Are you convinced by the Connecticut court's reading of "segregation" in *Sheff*?)

D. Gender, Sex, and Emerging Issues

Although most of the delegates to the Constitutional Convention were men, the nineteen women who drafted the Constitution provided more gender diversity in the convention than was typical in Montana politics at the time. For example, the Legislature appointed only one woman, Margery Hunter Brown Jr., to the Constitutional Convention Commission in 1969. In her 1995 master's thesis "Women in the Montana Legislature: 1941–1993" Laurie Jerin Zimorino reports only two women were elected to seats in 1970 but nine were elected after the Convention in 1972. Four women delegates (Margaret Warden, Better Babcock, Arlyne Reichert, and Dorothy Eck) went on to serve as legislators. At the Convention, many of the women delegates assumed leading roles. Dorothy Eck and Jean Bowman served as officers on the five-member leadership team as Western District Vice President and Secretary of the Convention, respectively. Louise Cross chaired the Natural Resources and Agriculture Committee, and Margaret Warden chaired the Public Information Committee, while Catherine Pemberton vice-chaired the Judiciary Committee, and Virginia Blend vice-chaired the Local Government Committee. Several other women delegates, particularly the youngest delegate Mae Nan (Robinson) Ellingson, shaped debates on critical issues.

Meanwhile, Congress submitted the Equal Rights Amendment to the states for ratification on March 22, 1972, just as Montana's Constitutional Convention was getting underway. The ACLU Women's Rights Project, led by future Justice Ruth Bader Ginsburg, was developing a new equal protection framework for judicial scrutiny of sex discrimination in the United States Supreme Court. These and other advances reflected a broader national movement for women's rights. Parallel calls for equality on the basis of sexual orientation and gender identity emerged in the aftermath of the 1969 Stonewall riots.

Back in Montana, the 1972 Constitution prohibited discrimination "on account of... sex." It would take decades before the law gave life to this text, long after parallel developments in federal constitutional law, in part due to the Montana Human Rights Act's assumption of enforcement. The constitutional meaning of the sex discrimination prohibition remains relatively unexplored notwithstanding the groundbreaking work of the Convention, led by its women delegates.

1. Sex Discrimination (and State Action)

In the Matter of Will of Cram

186 Mont. 37 (1980)

HASWELL, Chief Justice.

Royalston Heywood Cram was a sheep rancher and resident of Cascade County. On March 30, 1948, he executed his Last Will and Testament. He died on January 13, 1954. His Will was admitted to probate on February 17, 1954. The parties do not dispute the validity of Cram's 1948 Will. ***

The trust instrument contains detailed instructions relating to those youths who qualify as eligible recipients of the trust funds, which creates the problem in the instant case. Those instructions are as follows:

> "This trust is to be perpetual and is created for the benefit of members of organizations known as the FUTURE FARMERS OF AMERICA OF MONTANA and the 4-H CLUB OF MONTANA. Persons receiving benefits under the trust shall be members, in good standing, of one of these organizations and bona fide residents of the State of Montana, residents of the County of Cascade to be excluded, however. They shall be boys between the ages of fourteen (14) and eighteen (18) years, both inclusive, of American born parents and such beneficiaries shall be of honest and upright character, worthy of such assistance, and without financial means of his own, and manifest an interest in the sheep raising business."

The instrument provides that on or about September 15 of each year, after $100 has accumulated, the trustee shall determine and notify the state leaders of FFA and 4-H of the number of $100 stipends available to members of those organizations. The FFA and 4-H Club leaders are employees of the State of Montana, and they perform their duties as leaders as a part of their official duties with the University system and the Office of Superintendent of Public Instruction. ***

In the fall of 1977, appellant Donna Bottomly, a member in good standing of FFA, applied for a Cram trust stipend. When the FFA refused to provide any further lists, the trustee petitioned the District Court for instructions. Donna Bottomly, the Montana Human Rights Commission and the Superintendent of Public Instruction all appeared and requested the District Court to reform the trust in order to eliminate the discriminatory provisions. ***

The District Court modified the Cram Will by: (1) removing the provision that the state leaders of the FFA and the 4-H Club be notified of the number of $100 stipends to be made; (2) removing the provision requiring the state leaders to certify a list of names of eligible recipients to the trustee; and (3) removing the provision requiring the trustee to make the state leader a co-payee of the trust checks issued. The District Court instructed the trustee to continue its administration of the Cram trust, as modified. The District Court further instructed the trustee to seek the assistance of other persons from which to obtain the necessary list of names of eligible recipients under the trust, and to make them co-payees on trust checks issued if the state leaders of the FFA and 4-H Club refused to furnish a list of names of eligible recipients. ***

Appellant Bottomly raises three issues on appeal:

(1) Is the Cram Will, as modified by the District Court, discriminatory?

(2) Can the modified Cram trust be enforced in its present form?

(3) Can the Cram Will be reformed so as to be enforceable?

The first issue is whether the Cram Will, as modified by the District Court, is discriminatory. The parties agree that the modified Cram Will is discriminatory; however, the trustee contends that the discrimination is not unlawful, but permissible. We hold that the trust provision of the Cram Will as modified by the District Court is discriminatory. The language contained in the instrument clearly excludes female members of FFA or 4-H from becoming eligible recipients under the Cram trust.

The second issue is whether the modified Cram trust can be enforced in its present form. The District Court modified the original instrument, and the parties agree that the District Court possesses the power to apply deviation and *cy pres* principles in order to modify a Will.... Accordingly, this Court's scope of review is limited to an examination of the Cram trust as modified by the District Court.

The precise issue, as we perceive it, is whether "state action" is involved in the terms and operation of the modified Cram trust rendering it unlawful as a denial of equal protection of the law. Appellant contends that the FFA and 4-H Club are integral parts of the Montana educational system and as such they enjoy a wide variety of federal, state and local financing, assistance and participation. The appellant further contends that by virtue of the organizations' heavy involvement with, and dependence upon federal, state and local assistance, "state action" is present; and it is impossible for the organizations and their members to continue to participate in the benefits derived from the modified Cram trust because it is unlawful discrimination. The trustee contends that the District Court, in modifying the Cram trust, removed the FFA and 4-H organizations from the mechanics of the trust selection process. The trustee further contends that with the removal of the FFA and 4-H state leaders from the mechanics of the Cram trust, "state action" was also removed.

There is an essential dichotomy between discrimination by the State, which is prohibited by the Equal Protection Clause, and private discriminatory conduct, against which that clause erects no shield. *Moose Lodge No. 107 v. Irvis* (1972); *Burton v. Wilmington Parking Authority* (1961); *Shelley v. Kraemer* (1948). It has long been established that private conduct abridging individual rights does not violate the Equal Protection Clause of the Fourteenth Amendment to the United States Constitution. *Civil Rights Cases* (1883). In deciding whether the conduct under attack is governmental or private in nature, the United States Supreme Court has never adopted a precise, rigid test but has relied on a case-by-case approach. Private conduct abridging individual right does no violence to the Equal Protection Clause unless the state in any of its manifestations has been found to have become involved in such conduct to a significant extent. It is only when the State "so far" insinuates itself into a "position of interdependence" that it becomes a "joint participant" in the challenged activity or where private conduct becomes "so entwined" with governmental policies that a constitutional violation occurs. ***

From the principles discussed in the authorities summarized above, and from all the facts and circumstances as developed in this particular case, we cannot conclude that there is "state action" involved in the modified Cram trust.

The intent of Cram to provide stipends to boys between the ages of 14 and 18 is clear and unambiguous. The District Court modified the Cram trust so as to remove the FFA and 4-H Club state leaders from the mechanics of the trust. The District Court modified the Cram trust as nearly in conformity with the intent of the testator as was practicable. With the removal of the FFA and 4-H Club state leaders, "state action" is no longer involved.

Cram established a private trust for the benefit of deserving boys to encourage and assist them so that they could get a start in the sheep and wool raising industry. Cram was a private individual, established the trust with his private funds, appointed a bank as private trustee, and established in his Will a procedure by which the recipients of the trust funds would be selected. Under the modified Cram trust, the FFA and 4-H Club organizations have no involvement in the operation of the trust nor in the beneficiary selection process. The modified Cram trust requires the private trustee to obtain the names of eligible recipients, select the beneficiaries, and to award the stipends. The important distinction is that the modified Cram trust requires the private trustee to award stipends to Individual boys who are members of either the FFA or 4-H Club, and not to the organizations as entities. The fact that the modified Cram trust requires eligible recipients to be FFA or 4-H Club members does not in our opinion rise to the level of "state action." Mere membership and participation in FFA and 4-H Club by eligible boys does not constitute the requisite entwinement between the state and private conduct from which "state action" results.

We hold that the modified Cram trust is enforceable in its present form. A private person has the right to dispose of his money or property as he wishes and in so doing may lawfully discriminate in regard to the beneficiaries of his largess without offending the equal protection clause as long as the State and its instrumentalities are not involved, and unless the trust is unlawful, private trusts are to be encouraged. Our resolution of the second issue renders consideration of the third issue unnecessary. Affirmed.

Notes on Sex & Gender Classifications and State Action

1. Is this a constitutional case? The Court's discussion of state action and discrimination suggests it is, though it only cites the federal Equal Protection Clause (which begins "no state shall"). Presumably because of the involvement of state employees in the administration of the trust, which discriminated on the basis of sex, the district court reformed the trust to exclude the state employees and enforced the remaining provisions. Does Montana's passively voiced equal protection clause ("No person shall be denied. . .") or anti-discrimination clause ("Neither the state nor any person") require a different result? The Delegates debated the applicability of the anti-discrimination clause, with some expressing concern that it would prohibit private associations of men or women. Delegate Wade Dahood, Chair of the Bill of Rights Committee, answered these concerns:

> There is no intent within this particular section to do anything other than to remove the apparent type of discrimination that all of us object to with respect to employment, to rental practices, to actual associationship in matters that are public or matters that tend to be somewhat quasi-public. . . . That type of private organization [the Sons of Norway, for example] is certainly not within the inten[t] of the [Bill of Rights] committee in submitting Section 4.

Does the text of section 4 make that intent clear?

2. The Montana Supreme Court tentatively considered state action issues in *Gazelka v. St. Peter's Hosp.* (Mont. 2018):

> *** ¶ 3 . . . The Montana Preferred Provider Agreements Act (MPPAA), §§ 33-22-1701 to -1707, MCA, permits Preferred Provider Agreements (PPAs) in Montana. A PPA is an agreement between an insurer and a healthcare

provider reducing the amount of money a provider will accept as satisfaction for an insured person's treatment. Thus, two patients may ultimately pay different amounts for treatment depending on whether the patient is insured or uninsured and, if insured, depending on the terms of a particular PPA. *** Gazelka contended that the MPPAA unconstitutionally discriminates against uninsured patients and patients insured by the insurers that did not negotiate the most favorable PPA. ***

¶ 7 . . . By its own terms, Article II, Section 4, protects against two distinct types of unequal treatment. First, it generally provides that "[n]o person shall be denied the equal protection of the laws." Mont. Const. art. II, § 4. The provision then more specifically provides that "[n]either the state nor any person, firm, corporation, or institution shall discriminate against any person in the exercise of his civil or political rights on account of race, color, sex, culture, social origin or condition, or political or religious ideas." Mont. Const. art. II, § 4. The second, more specific guarantee clearly applies to both public and private action; neither the state nor a private party may discriminate against a person in the exercise of his civil or political rights based on an included class. The first, more general guarantee, however, does not name a specific actor. We have never before directly considered whether state action is required for a plaintiff's Article II, Section 4, general equal protection claim.

¶ 8 The 1972 Constitutional Convention's Bill of Rights Committee intended Article II, Section 4, to eradicate "public and private discriminations based on race, color, sex, culture, social origin or condition, or political or religious ideas." The Delegates designed the provision to provide more protection than the federal Equal Protection Clause. The second, more specific equal protection guarantee of Article II, Section 4, effectuates those intentions, and our precedent consistently recognizes that Article II, Section 4, provides even more protection than the federal Equal Protection Clause.

¶ 9 The United States Constitution contains a comparable, general, Equal Protection Clause, which provides, "No State shall. . . deny to any person within its jurisdiction the equal protection of the laws." U.S. Const. amend. XIV, § 1. The provision specifically provides that states cannot deny people equal protection of the laws. . . . Thus, in order to assert a viable federal equal protection claim, a plaintiff must demonstrate that state action, not merely private conduct, denied him equal protection of the laws.

¶ 10 In a similar manner, we consistently state that "the principal purpose of Montana's Equal Protection Clause is to ensure that Montana's citizens are not subject to arbitrary and discriminatory state action." Accordingly, based on the plain language of Article II, Section 4; the Constitutional Convention Transcripts; comparable federal precedent; and our consistent, decades-long interpretation of Article II, Section 4; we conclude that Montana's general

Equal protection Clause, "No person shall be denied the equal protection of the laws," offers protection only against state action.

¶ 11 Thus, as a threshold matter, a plaintiff alleging that she was denied equal protection of the laws under Article II, Section 4's general Equal Protection Clause must demonstrate that the State is responsible for the alleged rights violation. A plaintiff's claim of private discrimination will only prevail if he alleges that he was discriminated against "in the exercise of his civil or political rights on account of race, color, sex, culture, social origin or condition, or political or religious ideas." Mont. Const. art. II, § 4. We have previously stated, while analyzing state action under the federal Equal Protection Clause, that "[p]rivate conduct abridging [an] individual right does no violence to the Equal Protection Clause unless the state in any of its manifestations has been found to have become involved in such conduct to a significant extent." *In re Will of Cram* (Mont. 1980). "It is only when the State 'so far' insinuates itself into a 'position of interdependence' that it becomes a 'joint participant' in the challenged activity or where private conduct becomes 'so entwined' with governmental policies that a constitutional violation occurs." *In re Will of Cram.*

¶ 12 Gazelka bases her equal protection claim on the fact that the MPPAA permits the Hospital to bill insured persons differently than uninsured persons. *** [W]e decline to determine whether the Hospital entering into PPAs with insurers pursuant to the MPPAA constitutes state action. . . . We hold, however, that the general equal protection guarantee of Article II, Section 4, which provides, "No person shall be denied the equal protection of the laws," requires state action. ***

What does the limitation of the anti-discrimination provision to "civil and political rights" mean? As of 1965, the Montana Legislature defined "Basic Personal Rights" to include civil rights protections against discrimination in employment and public accommodations. *See* Mont. Code Ann. § 49-1-102. The original 1895 "Basic Political Rights" provision recognizes the rights of Montana citizens to hold office, but also states "Every person while within the jurisdiction of this state is entitled to its protection." Mont. Code Ann. § 49-1-201. Is there any meaningful difference between the scope of the specific "civil and political rights" in the anti-discrimination clause and the general equal protection clause? Recall the Bill of Rights Committee explained "social origin and condition" specifically covers "discriminations based on status of income and standard of living." Should that change the Court's analysis of an insurance-based classification?

3. In *Geduldig v. Aiello* (1974), the Supreme Court rejected an equal protection challenge to the denial of state disability insurance for pregnancy-related conditions. In *Bankers Life & Casualty v. Peterson* (Mont. 1993), the Montana Supreme Court explained its different approach under the "unisex" insurance statute appended to the Montana Human Rights Act, Mont. Code Ann. § 49-2-309:

In *Mountain States* [*Telephone v. Comm'r of Labor* (Mont. 1980)], this Court determined that distinctions based on pregnancy are sex-linked classifications. Although we were primarily concerned with the question of federal preemption of the Montana Maternity Leave Act, §§ 49-2-310 and -311, MCA, we stated that:

> "[p]regnancy is a condition unique to women, and the ability to become pregnant is a primary characteristic of the female sex. Thus, any classification which relies on pregnancy as the determinative criterion is a distinction based on sex... By definition, [placing pregnancy in a class by itself] discriminates on account of sex; for it is the capacity to become pregnant which primarily differentiates the female from the male."

Citing *Massachusetts Elec.* [*Co. v. Massachusetts Comm'n Against Discrimination* (Mass. 1978)], we stated that the exclusion of pregnancy-related disabilities from a comprehensive disability plan constituted sex discrimination in employment.

In 1984, we reaffirmed the principle that differential treatment of pregnancy is gender-based discrimination because only women can become pregnant. *Miller-Wohl Co., Inc. v. Comm'r of Labor* (Mont. 1984). Again, the primary issue in that case was one of federal preemption. However, in *Miller-Wohl*, we determined that an employer's sick leave policy created a disparate effect on women who became pregnant compared to men who did not. Although the policy was facially neutral, it nonetheless subjected women to job termination on a basis not faced by men. We concluded, therefore, that the policy was gender-based discrimination.

Mountain States and *Miller-Wohl* established that differential treatment of pregnancy constitutes sex discrimination in Montana. Section 49-2-309, MCA, prohibits sex discrimination in the operation, coverage, pricing and benefits of an insurance policy. We conclude, therefore, that § 49-2-309, MCA, prohibits discrimination based on pregnancy in a major medical expense insurance policy. The plain language of § 49-2-309, MCA, and our previous holdings in *Mountain States* and *Miller-Wohl*, amply support our conclusion. ***

Section 49-2-309, MCA, is clear and unambiguous; it prohibits discrimination based on sex in insurance policies. *** As is usually the case, the legislature declined to enumerate all conceivable varieties of sex discrimination, but rather left the interpretation and application of this general anti-discrimination statute to the courts. Our task is merely to interpret § 49-2-309, MCA, to determine whether distinctions based on normal pregnancy and childbirth constitute discrimination on the basis of sex.

We conclude that discrimination on the basis of pregnancy is discrimination on the basis of sex and is, therefore, prohibited by the Montana unisex insurance statute.

Does this suggest the similar constitutional text in the anti-discrimination provision of Article II, section 4 applies to "disparate impact" claims without proof of discriminatory purpose?

4. Consider also *Albinger v. Harris* (Mont. 2002), in which Albinger sued Harris for an engagement ring after they broke the engagement. Although in 1963, the Montana Legislature generally barred causes of action for breach of contract to marry (the "anti-heart balm" statute), Albinger claimed an exception for gifts conditional upon marriage (that is, the engagement ring):

> ¶ 38 Article II, Section 4 of the Montana Constitution recognizes and guarantees the individual dignity of each human being without regard to gender. This Court and the Montana State Bar have recognized the harm caused by gender bias and sexual stereotyping in the jurisprudence and courtroom of this state. . . .
>
> ¶ 39 The Montana Legislature made the social policy decision to relieve courts of the duty of regulating engagements by barring actions for breach of promise. While not explicitly denying access to the courts on the basis of gender, the "anti-heart balm" statutes closed courtrooms across the nation to female plaintiffs seeking damages for antenuptial pregnancy, ruined reputation, lost love and economic insecurity. During the mid-20th Century, some courts continued to entertain suits in equity for antenuptial property transfers. The jurisprudence that rose upon the implied conditional gift theory, based upon an engagement ring's symbolic associations with marriage, preserved a right of action narrowly tailored for ring givers seeking ring return. The bright-line rule of ring return on a no-fault basis, which Albinger urges this Court to adopt, sets forth as a matter of law "proper" post-engagement behavior in regard to this single gifted item. The proposed no-fault adjudication of a disputed engagement ring also ignores the particular circumstances of a couple's decision not to marry.
>
> ¶ 40 Conditional gift theory applied exclusively to engagement ring cases, carves an exception in the state's gift law for the benefit of predominately male plaintiffs. Montana's "anti-heart balm" statute bars all actions sounding in contract law that arise from mutual promise to marry, absent fraud or deceit, and bars all plaintiffs from recovering any share of expenses incurred in planning a canceled wedding. While antenuptial traditions vary by class, ethnicity, age and inclination, women often still assume the bulk of pre-wedding costs, such as non-returnable wedding gowns, moving costs, or non-refundable deposits for caterers, entertainment or reception halls. Consequently, the statutory "anti-heart balm" bar continues to have a disparate impact on women. If this Court were to fashion a special exception for engagement ring actions under gift law theories, we would perpetuate the gender bias attendant upon the Legislature's decision to remove from our courts all actions for breach of antenuptial promises.

> ¶ 35 To preserve the integrity of our gift law and to avoid additional gender bias, we decline to adopt the theory that an engagement ring is a gift subject to an implied condition of marriage. *** We hold that the engagement ring was an unconditional, completed gift upon acceptance and remains in Harris' ownership and control. ***

Is this case about sex discrimination under Article II, section 4? (Or gender discrimination—does it matter that section 4 says "sex"?) If so, is it consistent with the other cases that appear to require a discriminatory purpose to establish unconstitutional discrimination?

2. "Sex," Sexual Orientation, and Suspect Classifications

Snetsinger v. Montana University System

325 Mont. 148 (2004)

Justice JIM REGNIER delivered the Opinion of the Court.

*** ¶ 4 Carol Snetsinger and Nancy Siegel... consider themselves married and hold themselves out to their families and their community as a couple in a committed, marital relationship. They have stated they would marry if legally permitted to do so. They own their home together in joint tenancy with rights of survivorship, have a joint checking account and share all living expenses. Likewise, Grayson and Neff consider themselves married and hold themselves out as such. They own their home together, share living expenses and are raising a child together. ***

¶ 6 As a benefit of employment, the University System provides a group health insurance plan for its employees and their dependents. The University System pays the premium for the employee; if the employee would like coverage for any dependents, the employee must pay an additional premium. The University System's policy defines dependent eligibility. It states:

> An eligible employee... may enroll the following dependents in the Plan.
>
> 1. Spouse—A lawful spouse as defined in Montana law. A Declaration of Common-Law Spouse form may be obtained from the campus payroll/personnel office and must be used if a common-law spouse is to be enrolled in the Plan.
>
> 2. Child(ren)—An unmarried dependent child under age 19.
>
> 3. Student—An unmarried student under age 25, who is a dependent of the employee and/or spouse and dependent on the employee and/or spouse for support and maintenance, and whose time is principally devoted to the attendance of a school or college. The Claims Administrator may periodically require the submission of proof that student status is maintained.

¶ 7 Snetsinger and Grayson are not permitted to enroll their same-sex domestic partners because they are not "dependents" as defined by the University System's policy. They argue the policy impermissibly discriminates against them based on their sex, sexual orientation and marital status and violates their rights to equal protection and dignity provided by Article II, Section 4, the right to privacy provided by Article II, Section 10, and the rights to pursue life's basic necessities and to seek safety, health and happiness provided by Article II, Section 3, of the Montana Constitution because the policy does not extend coverage to same-sex domestic partners. ***

¶ 13 At the outset, it is important to note what this case is not about. Lest there be any doubt, the Appellants clearly stated, both in their brief and in oral argument, that they are not challenging Montana's marriage laws which provide marriage is available only to partners of the opposite sex. Although the constitutionality of such laws has been attacked in various states recently with much national attention, the Appellants emphasized during oral argument that this case does not present such a challenge. Therefore, we have not been asked nor will we address the question of whether Montana's marriage statutes discriminates against same-sex couples by denying them the right to marry. ***

¶ 15 Article II, Section 4, of the Montana Constitution guarantees equal protection of the law to all persons. It provides that "[n]o person shall be denied the equal protection of the laws." "The Fourteenth Amendment to the United States Constitution and Article II, Section 4, of the Montana Constitution embody a fundamental principle of fairness: that the law must treat similarly-situated individuals in a similar manner." [*McDermott v. Montana Dept. of Corrections* (Mont. 2001).] Article II, Section 4, of the Montana Constitution provides even more individual protection than the Equal Protection Clause in the Fourteenth Amendment of the United States Constitution.

¶ 16 When analyzing an equal protection challenge, we "must first identify the classes involved and determine whether they are similarly situated." A law or policy that contains an apparently neutral classification may violate equal protection if "in reality [it] constitut[es] a device designed to impose different burdens on different classes of persons."

¶ 17 Once the relevant classifications have been identified, we next determine the appropriate level of scrutiny. We apply one of three levels of scrutiny when addressing a challenge under the Montana Constitution's Equal Protection Clause: strict scrutiny, middle-tier scrutiny, or the rational basis test. Strict scrutiny applies if a suspect class or fundamental right is affected. Under the strict scrutiny standard, the State has the burden of showing that the law, or in this case the policy, is narrowly tailored to serve a compelling government interest.

¶ 18 We apply middle-tier scrutiny if the law or policy affects a right conferred by the Montana Constitution, but is not found in the Constitution's Declaration of Rights. Under middle-tier scrutiny, the State must demonstrate the law or policy in question is reasonable and the need for the resulting classification outweighs the value of the right to an individual.

¶ 19 The third level of scrutiny is the rational basis test. The rational basis test is appropriate when neither strict scrutiny nor middle-tier scrutiny apply. Under the rational basis test, the law or policy must be rationally related to a legitimate government interest. ***

¶ 21 On appeal, the University System predictably echoes the District Court's conclusion that the policy in question classifies people based on marital status. In arguing the classifications are rational, the University System relies on Montana's statute defining marriage as a relationship between a man and a woman. Section 40-1-103, MCA. The University System also cites to § 40-1-401, MCA, which explicitly states a marriage between persons of the same sex is prohibited. It posits that because state and federal statutes are full of distinctions between married and unmarried individuals (i.e. taxes, inheritance, adoption, rights of witnesses and eligibility for government benefits), the University System's reliance on Montana's marriage statute for its classification is "inherently rational." It argues the marriage distinction provides a rational and administratively simple method to determine eligibility for defining dependent status for health benefits.

¶ 22 In adopting such a policy, the University System rejected the concept of "domestic partners," which would provide same-sex couples the same health benefits as opposite-sex couples. . . . The University System's policy at issue here permits three classes of employees to purchase health benefits for their partners: 1) those, who with their partners, are joined in "solemnized marriage" under § 40-1-301, MCA; 2) those, who with their partners, have elected to enter into marriage using a Declaration of Marriage without solemnization under § 40-1-311, MCA; and 3) those, who with their opposite-sex partners, are not married but who sign an "Affidavit of Common Law Marriage." This third avenue is not provided by statute nor does it satisfy § 40-1-311, MCA.

¶ 23 Although the University System maintains its system is "inherently rational" because it is based on the Montana marriage statutes, we conclude the policy is inherently flawed. The policy allows unmarried opposite-sex couples, who may only have a fleeting relationship, to receive health insurance benefits by signing an Affidavit. The Affidavit is provided by the University System and is typically used to establish benefit eligibility for a partner in a relationship that has not been solemnized or registered as a marriage under Montana law. Presumably, a couple who declines to sign a statutory written declaration of marriage without solemnization, and instead signs the Affidavit provided by the University System, may choose not to marry at all, but rather may choose to sign a document in order to receive employment benefits. ***

¶ 26 A closer look at the University System's policy discloses that marital status, as defined by Montana statutes and case law, plays little if any role in determining who is eligible for benefits. Under the policy, the partner of a non-gay employee would qualify for benefits by signing an Affidavit, when the partner of a gay employee would not qualify for the same benefits when signing the same Affidavit.

¶ 27 Thus, we conclude the District Court erred in its first step of equal protection analysis. In adopting marital status as the litmus test and then reasoning that the classes involved are employees with dependents vs. employees without dependents, the District Court misinterpreted the University System policy. As pointed out above, marital status is not the defining difference. In truth, unmarried opposite-sex couples are able to avail themselves of health benefits under the University System's policy while unmarried same-sex couples are denied the health benefits. These two groups, although similarly situated in all respects other than sexual orientation, are not treated equally and fairly. The principal purpose of the Equal Protection Clause, Article II, Section 4, of the Montana Constitution, is to ensure citizens are not subject to arbitrary and discriminatory state action. Therefore, we conclude there is no justification for treating the two groups differently, nor is the University System's policy rationally related to a legitimate governmental interest. Once the illusory marital status is removed from the analysis, there is no legitimate governmental interest in treating the two groups differently. As former Chief Justice Turnage recognized in his concurrence in *Gryczan v. State* (Mont. 1997), when the State criminalizes sexual acts between persons of the same-sex and decriminalizes the same sexual conduct engaged in by opposite-sex couples, it is "[c]learly. . . a denial of the constitutional guarantee of equal protection of the law in violation of. . . Article II, Section 4 of the Montana Constitution." Similarly, the University System's policy of denying health benefits to unmarried same-sex couples while granting the benefits to unmarried opposite-sex couples results in a denial of equal protection.

¶ 28 Further, we are unconvinced that the University System's policy is justified based on administrative efficiency. Other policies could certainly be adopted without infringing on the important constitutional provisions that protect all Montanans. We are confident the University System can meet this task.

¶ 29 Because we hold that the University System's policy violates equal protection of the laws under the Montana Constitution by impermissibly treating unmarried same-sex couples differently than unmarried opposite-sex couples, we need not address the Appellants' arguments that the policy violates equal protection by classifying them based on sex or that it violates their rights under Article II, Sections 3 and 10, of the Montana Constitution. ***

¶ 35 Our opinion today reiterates and reaffirms existing common law marriage jurisprudence. We haven't changed anything. We do make clear, however, that any organization that adopts an administrative procedure in order to provide employment benefits to opposite-sex partners who may not be in a legal marital relationship, must do the same for same-sex couples. To not do so violates equal protection. ***

Justice JAMES C. NELSON specially concurs.

¶ 69 In my view, this Court's equal protection jurisprudence has been too long bounded by federal equal protection case law where fundamental human rights are at issue. There is no good reason why we should not begin to afford all Montanans the full protections intended by the framers when they adopted Article II, Section 4. As one commentator has suggested, "Montana lawyers should jettison federal discrimination analysis in favor of a Montana analysis free of gender-based standards." . . .

¶ 97 In summary, applying the Clifford and Huff model [*see* Part A, above], I would hold that: (a) laws and policies that make people's rights dependent on gender or sexual orientation violate the inviolable human dignity clause of Article II, Section 4; (b) classifications of persons on the basis of gender or sexual orientation are sex-based and are therefore arbitrary and suspect under conventional equal protection analysis; and, in what I believe to be a better approach, (c) reading Article II, Sections 4 and 34 together, it is appropriate to establish, as a matter of Montana constitutional law, that classifications based on gender or sexual orientation are suspect classifications in their own right and are in addition to those enumerated in the third clause of this State's equal protection provision. ***

¶ 98 Pursuant to this analysis, I would hold that applying strict scrutiny, the Respondents have failed to demonstrate a compelling state interest for treating heterosexual and homosexual couples differently in terms of the benefits relating to employment. ***

Chief Justice KARLA M. GRAY, dissenting.

*** ¶ 168 The fact remains that the Court resolves the present case, and reverses the trial court, on the basis of an issue not presented to the trial court. Our cases holding that we do not consider new issues—or changed theories—on appeal are so legion as to require no citation to authority. [A]s a reviewing Court, it is fundamentally unfair for us to reverse a district court on the basis of arguments not presented to it. In addition, of course, doing so essentially makes this Court the court of first—rather than last—resort in an appeal. . . . Because the Court addresses the new issue, however, I feel compelled to respond. ***

¶ 174 For equal protection purposes, and notwithstanding the Court's statement to the contrary, there is nothing "illusory" about the marital versus non-marital nature of the University System's policy. Indeed, the appellants argued in the District Court, and argue here, a marital versus non-marital classification. The classes created by the policy are based entirely on the kinds of marriages recognized by Montana law, not sexual orientation. For purposes of this case, the difference between the "classes" is that one class involves a spouse in a legally recognized marital relationship and the other class involves a committed partner in a relationship which under current Montana law does not—and cannot—constitute a marriage in any legal sense. Thus, the present case is readily distinguishable from both the Court's and former Chief Justice Turnage's opinions in *Gryczan*, which did not involve a marital classification. Moreover, expressly unlike the present case, *Gryczan* presented a challenge to the constitutionality of a statute criminalizing sexual acts between same-sex people. Here, we all agree the appellants are not directly challenging Montana's laws relating to the definition of marriage. For those reasons, I submit *Gryczan* has no application here.

¶ 175 With regard to the Court's statement that it is unconvinced the policy at issue is justified based on administrative efficiency, surely the Court cannot mean administrative efficiency is not a legitimate governmental interest. Perhaps the Court merely means that it disagrees the policy advances administrative efficiency. If so, I suggest that this Court is not in a position to make such a determination for the University System; nor could we properly conclude that a marital versus non-marital classification is not a rational means of making health benefits available to "dependents" of University System employees. "Rational" does not equate to what this Court might have chosen to do. ***

Justice JIM RICE dissenting.

¶ 112 I respectfully dissent. The Court fails to reference or properly apply the statutes and case law, thereby radically altering common law marriage in Montana, and failing to honor the reliance that many couples place in the law. ***

¶ 152 Appellants contend that the University's policy discriminates on the basis of marital status because it cannot be demonstrated that the policy "was rationally selected to advance an independent, legitimate governmental purpose." However, the legitimate purpose is to provide benefits to the partners of University employees.... [T]he use of marriage to define partner eligibility creates certainty and practicality in administration of a large benefit program because it incorporates existing state law regarding family relationships. As a matter of law, married couples are engaged in a permanent relationship because the relationship cannot be terminated except by operation of law. Thus, there is a legally presumptive stability that attends to the marital relationship that does not exist in other relationships, an important consideration in the administration of health plans. Further, the policy is "rationally related to a legitimate state purpose, the state's interest in promoting marriage." *Hinman v. Dep't of Pers. Admin.* (Cal. Ct. App. 1985) (denying claim for dental benefits for same sex partners of state employees). ***

Justice JOHN WARNER joins in the foregoing dissent of Justice RICE.

Donaldson v. State

367 Mont. 228 (2012)

Chief Justice MIKE McGRATH delivered the Opinion of the Court.

¶ 1 Plaintiffs are individuals from a variety of professional backgrounds who are in committed same-sex relationships. In 2010 they sued the State of Montana, complaining that they are unable to obtain protections and benefits that are available to similarly-situated different-sex couples who marry under State law. Plaintiffs expressly do not challenge Montana law's restriction of marriage to heterosexual couples, do not seek the opportunity to marry, and do not seek the designation of marriage for their relationships. They contend however that there is a "statutory structure" in Montana law that prohibits them from enjoying "significant relationship and family protections and obligations automatically provided to similarly-situated different-sex couples who marry." [Plaintiffs provided the District Court with a list of over 340 Montana statutes that classify based on marital status and that would be impacted by the proposed relief sought.]

¶ 2 Plaintiffs contend that this statutory structure interferes with their rights under Article II of the Montana Constitution, including their rights to equal protection, due process, and the rights to privacy, dignity and the pursuit of life's necessities. They seek a declaration that the State's failure to provide them access to the statutory scheme available to different-sex couples denies them the rights guaranteed by Article II. They seek an injunction prohibiting the State from continuing to deny them access to the statutory scheme. ***

¶ 8 In the past Montana courts have held specific statutes unconstitutional, and in some cases have directed the Legislature to act to comply with specific duties. *Helena Elementary School Dist. No. 1 v. State* (Mont. 1989) (school funding); *Snetsinger v. Mont. Univ. System*, 2004 MT 390. In the present case, however, Plaintiffs do not seek a declaration that any particular statute is unconstitutional or that its implementation should be enjoined. Rather, Plaintiffs seek a general declaration of their rights and seek orders enjoining the State to provide them a "legal status and statutory structure" that protects their rights.

¶ 9 We agree with the District Court that Plaintiffs' requested relief exceeds the bounds of a justiciable controversy, and decline to provide the declaratory relief requested. It is the opinion of this Court that the broad injunction and declaratory judgment sought by Plaintiffs would not terminate the uncertainty or controversy giving rise to this proceeding. Instead, a broad injunction and declaration not specifically directed at any particular statute would lead to confusion and further litigation. As the District Court aptly stated: "For this Court to direct the legislature to enact a law that would impact an unknown number of statutes would launch this Court into a roiling maelstrom of policy issues without a constitutional compass." A district court may refuse to enter a declaratory judgment if it would not terminate the uncertainty or controversy giving rise to the proceedings.... Courts do not function, even under the Declaratory Judgments Act, to determine speculative matters, to enter anticipatory judgments, to declare social status, to give advisory opinions or to give abstract opinions.

¶ 10 In addition, declaring the parameters of constitutional rights is a serious matter. This Court, for example, avoids deciding constitutional issues whenever possible. Statutes are presumed to be constitutional. That presumption can only be overcome after careful consideration of the purpose and effect of the statute, employing the proper level of scrutiny. Broadly determining the constitutionality of a "statutory scheme" that may, according to Plaintiffs, involve hundreds of separate statutes, is contrary to established jurisprudence.

¶ 11 This Court may fashion the relief warranted by any appeal. It is this Court's opinion that Plaintiffs should be given the opportunity, if they choose to take it, to amend the complaint and to refine and specify the general constitutional challenges they have proffered. For example, the record contains several affidavits from the named Plaintiffs and others that assert that they have suffered discrimination from the State's failure to recognize their relationships. While Plaintiffs' brief listed Title 40 of the Montana Code as an area of family law that furthers such discrimination, the dismissal of this action because of Plaintiffs' broad claims has precluded the development of claims that specific statutes promote or cause discrimination. These are important issues and should be decided only after the statutes involved are specifically identified and specifically analyzed in district court proceedings. ***

¶ 13 The Plaintiffs should be afforded the opportunity to amend their complaint and to develop an argument as to the nature of the State's interest in advancing specific laws as well as the level of constitutional scrutiny that should be applied to those laws by the courts. Plaintiffs of course may choose to not amend, and that decision is theirs to make. If they do amend they will need to choose what statute or statutes to put in issue and upon what legal grounds. The dissent may be disappointed in the majority's approach to this case. However, that does not change the fact that the Plaintiffs chose to pursue an overly broad request for a declaratory judgment and injunctive relief, without developing a factual record in the District Court and without identifying a specific statute or statutes that impose the discrimination they allege.

¶ 14 For the reasons set out above, the decision of the District Court is affirmed in part, reversed in part and remanded for further proceedings consistent with this opinion, in a schedule to be determined by the District Court. ***

Justice JIM RICE, concurring.

*** ¶ 32 While Plaintiffs do not claim the right to marry, they are nonetheless claiming constitutional entitlement to all of these same rights and benefits which are provided to married couples on the ground that they are "similarly situated in every material respect." However, this position ignores the historical and long-developed legal foundation and formal structure giving marriage an exclusive legal permanence, which does not exist for other relationships. More importantly, the above discussion, including the precedent addressing marriage and its unique attributes, demonstrates that Plaintiffs' claim to be "similarly situated" to married couples is without merit. This is not meant to disparage Plaintiffs or minimize the contributions they offer, but is simply a statement of the reality that marriage between a woman and man exclusively provides unique and transcendent societal protections vital to human survival which differentiate it and make it dissimilar from other relationships. These protections uniquely provided by marriage form a legitimate and even compelling state interest, and thus a constitutional basis, for the State's exclusive treatment of marriage.

¶ 33 The above discussion of the law of marriage reflects the general state of the law before the Marriage Amendment was adopted by Montanans in 2004. Although some of the cited cases were decided after adoption of the Marriage Amendment, they were premised upon pre-2004 precedent, and marriage was considered to be a fundamental right with constitutionally protected status at the time of the Amendment's adoption. However, several years earlier, legal arguments attacking the exclusive status of marriage began to be offered, and considerable concern was generated over whether the law's exclusive treatment of marriage would remain, or whether courts would begin to overturn long-standing precedent favoring marriage. With all due respect, several courts indicated a willingness to uproot established legal precedent recognizing the uniqueness of marriage between a man and woman, and eliminate the law's exclusive treatment of marriage. *See e.g. Baehr v. Lewin* (Haw. 1993); *Baker v. State* (Vt. 2000); *Goodridge v. Dept. of Pub. Health* (Mass. 2003).

¶ 34 The response of the citizens of the country to these court decisions can only be described as a phenomenon of direct democracy. To counter this threat to established precedent favoring marriage, citizens of some 31 states acted to either reinstate the law's exclusive definition and treatment of marriage in some manner, or to ensure that courts could not eliminate such exclusive treatment, by amending their state constitutions to explicitly protect marriage. Montana was one of those states.

¶ 35 Building on the foundation of historical legal protections for marriage, Montana voters solidified the premise that marriage is between one man and one woman by placing the concept expressly into the Montana Constitution. Mont. Const. art. XIII, § 7. The Voter Information Packet provided voters with the arguments for and against adoption of the Amendment. Proponents stated that the "[t]he time-honored, vital institution of marriage is being threatened.... Special interest groups are constantly seeking to gain special rights that infringe on the rights of the rest of society. Such special rights cost all Montanans.... Voting yes on CI-96 allows the people to give clear direction to judges on this important issue."

¶ 36 Directly related to this case, proponents discussed the issue of benefits which are attendant to marriage. "If CI-96 fails, how will homosexual marriage one day affect your family?... Small business employers in Montana may someday be required to provide expanded health coverage, retirement and fringe benefits to same-sex 'spouses' of employees. The broad subjectivity of such un-funded mandates could hurt Montana's economy and jobs." Opponents likewise also focused on benefits and obligations associated with same-sex couples: "if CI-96 were to pass, the State could nullify the contractual agreements made between same-gender partners. CI-96 would limit innovative and robust companies from treating their employees equitably." As the District Court noted, both sides of the debate acknowledged "that the marriage amendment would have something to do with the benefits and obligations that relate to the status of being married." ***

¶ 40 I appreciate the deeply-held feelings and beliefs of the Plaintiffs and condemn any acts of cruelty they have suffered, some of which are referenced in their affidavits. Yet, given the long-standing legal protections and exclusive treatment of marriage, with its corresponding benefits and obligations, and the incorporation of those principles into the Montana Constitution by the citizens of Montana, Plaintiffs' equal protection claim must fail.

Justice JAMES C. NELSON, dissenting.

¶ 115 Plaintiffs contend that the State's exclusion of same-sex couples from the opportunity to obtain the benefits and protections which the State makes available to different-sex couples violates five fundamental constitutional rights: to pursue safety, health, and happiness (Mont. Const. art. II, § 3), to equal protection of the laws (§ 4), to individual dignity (§ 4), to individual privacy (§ 10), and to due process of law (§ 17). Because I conclude that the Equal Protection Clause (which happens to be Plaintiffs' primary argument) is sufficient to resolve this case, I focus my analysis there and do not address Plaintiffs' arguments under Article II, Sections 3, 10, or 17. At the conclusion of my equal protection discussion, however, I briefly discuss Article II, Section 4's Dignity Clause and the additional support it provides for Plaintiffs' claim.

¶ 120 The United States Constitution and the Montana Constitution both command that no person shall be denied "the equal protection of the laws." U.S. Const. amend. XIV; Mont. Const. art. II, § 4. Although the basic principles underlying these two provisions are the same, this Court has held that Article II, Section 4 provides greater individual protection than the Fourteenth Amendment. *Snetsinger v. Mont. Univ. Sys.*, 2004 MT 390.

¶ 121 "The guaranty of equal protection of the laws is a pledge of the protection of equal laws." *Romer v. Evans* (1996) (internal quotation marks omitted). It is "essentially a direction that all persons similarly situated should be treated alike." *City of Cleburne v. Cleburne Living Ctr.* (1985); *accord Snetsinger*, ¶ 15.

> "[T]here is no more effective practical guaranty against arbitrary and unreasonable government than to require that the principles of law which officials would impose upon a minority must be imposed generally. Conversely, nothing opens the door to arbitrary action so effectively as to allow those officials to pick and choose only a few to whom they will apply

> legislation and thus to escape the political retribution that might be visited upon them if larger numbers were affected. Courts can take no better measure to assure that laws will be just than to require that laws be equal in operation."

Eisenstadt v. Baird (1972) (quoting *Ry. Express Agency, Inc. v. New York* (1949) (Jackson, J., concurring)). The Equal Protection guaranty "requires the democratic majority to accept for themselves and their loved ones what they impose on you and me." *Cruzan v. Dir., Missouri Dept. of Health* (1990) (Scalia, J., concurring).

¶ 122 Of course, the "promise that no person shall be denied the equal protection of the laws must coexist with the practical necessity that most legislation classifies for one purpose or another, with resulting disadvantage to various groups or persons." *Romer.* The general rule, therefore, is that if a law neither burdens a constitutional right nor targets a suspect or quasi-suspect class, then the courts will uphold the legislative classification so long as it bears a rational relationship to some legitimate governmental objective. However, if the classification disadvantages a suspect or quasi-suspect class or impinges upon the exercise of a constitutional right, then the classification is subject to heightened scrutiny. *See Romer*; *Cleburne*; *Snetsinger,* ¶¶ 17–19. ***

¶ 140 . . . Plaintiffs indicate in their affidavits that they share the same interest as different-sex couples in protecting their relationships, their families, and their children. Except for the fact that one partner is the same sex as the other, Plaintiffs' committed intimate relationships are materially indistinguishable from different-sex committed intimate relationships.

¶ 141 Based on these undisputed facts and the foregoing discussion, I conclude and would hold that the pertinent classification here is sexual orientation. I further conclude and would hold that Plaintiffs are similarly situated to, but treated differently than, different-sex couples vis-à-vis the benefits and responsibilities afforded by the State to married persons. I now turn to the question of the appropriate level of scrutiny. ***

¶ 145 Courts have identified four factors or indicia as bearing on whether a class is suspect or quasi-suspect (thus warranting a more exacting constitutional analysis of the legislative classification than that provided by rational basis review). They are (1) whether the class has historically been subjected to discrimination; (2) whether the characteristics that distinguish the class indicate a typical class member's ability to perform or contribute to society; (3) whether the distinguishing characteristic is immutable or beyond the class members' control; and (4) whether the class is a minority or politically powerless. *See In re C.H.* (Mont. 1984) (citing *San Antonio Indep. Sch. Dist. v. Rodriguez* (1973)) . . . .

¶ 146 In the present case, the parties' disagreement centers primarily on the first and fourth factors—history of discrimination and lack of political power. In considering the four factors, therefore, I shall focus primarily on these two.

1. History of Discrimination ***

¶ 149 . . . In 1995, the Montana Senate included homosexual acts in a bill requiring the registration of sexual and violent offenders. Senator Al Bishop, a supporter of the bill, stated on the Senate floor that homosexual sex is "even worse than a violent sexual act." During a 2003 debate over keeping Montana's criminal sodomy law on the books—despite this Court's decision in *Gryczan*—a member of the Coalition for Community Responsibility asserted that "[g]ay men think they are doing children a favor by sodomizing them." During the 2005 legislative session, Senator Dan McGee of Laurel stated, "I'll never be able to support bills which try to overturn centuries of moral ideology. Homosexuality is wrong." In 2010, opponents of the Missoula ordinance prohibiting discrimination based on sexual orientation and gender identity stated that passage of the ordinance would result in "unacceptable loss of safety and privacy for women and children." Numerous bills have been proposed to add sexual orientation to Montana's antidiscrimination laws and to Montana's hate-crimes law, but all have failed. (Christine Kauffman details the repeated defeat of such legislation in Attachment A to her affidavit, at pages 3 to 7.) Earlier this year, the Hamilton School Board voted to remove sexual orientation from a proposed anti-bullying policy and not to include sexual orientation in the district's equal-education and equal-employment policies. See David Erickson, Sexual Orientation Not Included in Hamilton Schools' Anti-Bullying Policy, Ravalli Republic (Mar. 30, 2012). *** The State fails to provide any evidence or sensible argument to refute Plaintiffs' overwhelming showing that homosexuals as a group have historically endured persecution and discrimination.

4. Political Power ***

¶ 158 While the State's central argument on this point is devoted to the proposition that gays and lesbians have achieved some recent political successes, *** the entire underpinning of the Marriage Amendment, discussed in further detail below, was based on attacking and demeaning homosexuals and homosexuality. Accordingly. . . I conclude that gays and lesbians are not in a position to adequately protect themselves from the discriminatory wishes of the majoritarian public.

5. Summary

¶ 162 Based on the foregoing analysis under each of the factors, I conclude and would hold that sexual orientation is a suspect class under Article II, Section 4 of the Montana Constitution. Correspondingly, I would also hold that discrimination based on sexual orientation in the provision of statutory benefits and protections is subject to "strict scrutiny" review. Under the strict-scrutiny standard, the State has the burden of showing that the law or policy is narrowly tailored to serve a compelling governmental interest. I would reverse the District Court's judgment and direct it to enter a declaratory order encompassing these holdings. But for reasons discussed in the Declaratory Judgment section above, I would not order injunctive relief at this time and instead would permit the legislative and executive branches to implement our constitutional interpretation in the first instance.

F. Human Dignity

¶ 163 As just discussed, Plaintiffs are entitled to a declaratory ruling that gay, lesbian, and bisexual persons are a suspect class in Montana and the State's disparate treatment of same-sex couples is subject to "strict scrutiny" review under the Equal Protection Clause of Article II, Section 4. This approach is sufficient to resolve this case in their favor.

¶ 164 That said, however, it is equally important to acknowledge the more fundamental human issue in this case. In addition to guaranteeing "the equal protection of the laws," Article II, Section 4 also provides that "[t]he dignity of the human being is inviolable." I addressed this provision of Montana's Constitution at length in *Baxter v. State*, 2009 MT 449 (Nelson, J., specially concurring). In the interests of brevity, given that this is already a lengthy dissent, I am not going to repeat my entire analysis and discussion of the Dignity Clause here. ***

¶ 167 Without belaboring the point, the State's treatment of the committed couples here based on their sexual orientation is a frontal assault on their dignity as autonomous, rational, independent human beings. The State's public censure effectively conveys to these citizens the message that, as a class, they are inferior, immoral, corrupt, perverted, and sinful—that they are not worthy of sharing in the advantages that the State provides to their "normal," family-oriented, God-fearing, and morally superior heterosexual counterparts. "[T]he failure to provide equal benefits and protections in Montana law to same-sex couples [is] a failure to respect the core humanity of gay and lesbian couples by denying that they can create, for themselves, the same sort of committed, loving relationships which heterosexual couples can create." Matthew O. Clifford and Thomas P. Huff, *Some Thoughts on the Meaning and Scope of the Montana Constitution's "Dignity" Clause with Possible Applications*, 61 Mont. L. Rev. 301, 335 n. 137 (2000). I can think of no better way to attack the right of inviolable human dignity of each of the Plaintiffs in this case. I conclude and would hold that the State's discriminatory refusal to provide the benefits and protections at issue here to the committed intimate same-sex couples violates the Dignity Clause of Article II, Section 4.

V. The Marriage Amendment

*** ¶ 173 The State and several of its amici drape themselves in the mantel of the Marriage Amendment as an underpinning for their arguments. They argue that granting committed intimate same-sex couples any of the statutory benefits and protections which are accorded to different-sex married couples—while still denying same-sex couples the right to marry—may violate the Marriage Amendment. I say "may" because, as noted earlier, the Attorney General's position is difficult to reconcile. On one hand, he seems to contend that the Marriage Amendment precludes Plaintiffs' claims, yet, on the other hand, he concedes that the Legislature could provide same-sex couples with similar protections as are granted to different-sex married couples, by means of a civil-union or domestic-partnership scheme, if it chose to do so. ***

¶ 180 The entire underpinning of the Marriage Amendment is based on attacking and demeaning homosexuals and homosexuality. This is abundantly clear from the 2004 Voter Information Pamphlet provided to voters by the Montana Secretary of State and contained in the record of this case. In their argument for the Marriage Amendment (referred to as Constitutional Initiative 96 or CI-96), Proponents rail against "homosexual activists" who, Proponents claim, are seeking out "activist judges" to force Montanans to become part of "a vast, untested social experiment." Proponents assert that "homosexual activists" are "threatening" not only "the time-honored, vital institution of marriage," but also "the freedom to teach our children as we wish." Proponents warn parents that if CI-96 fails, "[e]very public school in Montana would be required *to teach your children that same-sex marriage and homosexuality are perfectly normal*" (emphasis in original). Proponents use similar scare tactics in an attempt to rally "small business employers," asserting that they "*may someday be required to provide expanded health coverage, retirement and fringe benefits to same-sex 'spouses' of employees*" (emphasis in original), which allegedly "could hurt Montana's economy and jobs." Proponents also warn churchgoers that if CI-96 does not pass, "[y]our church will be legally pressured to perform same-sex weddings" and may lose its "tax exemptions" if it refuses to perform such ceremonies. Finally, Proponents argue that CI-96 is necessary for childrearing:

> Natural marriage is extremely important for future generations. Men and women are distinctly different. Each gender brings vitally important, and unique, elements to a child's development. *Saying that children don't necessarily need fathers or mothers is saying that one gender or the other is unnecessary.* A loving and compassionate society always aids motherless and fatherless families. Compassionate societies never intentionally create families without mothers or fathers, which is exactly what same-sex homes do. [Emphasis in original.] ***

¶ 190 Indeed, the Marriage Amendment is undisputedly grounded in religious doctrine. That much is apparent. . . from the fulminations of numerous religious organizations in the present case, led by the Montana Catholic Conference, against the prospect that gay, lesbian, and bisexual Montanans might enjoy some measure of legal protection for their relationships. If homosexuality and same-sex relationships were not a religious issue, it is highly doubtful that any of these amici would be so actively involved in this case. ***

¶ 196 The Montana Constitution makes it clear that the right and power of government originates with the people, and they may amend the Constitution whenever they deem it necessary. Mont. Const. art. II, §§ 1, 2. Yet, one will search in vain for a provision in the Constitution authorizing the people to amend that document so as to effect some social policy or majoritarian ideology that is, itself, contrary to constitutional principles. Quite simply, "while the people may amend the Constitution, they may not violate it in the process." *Reichert v. State*, 2012 MT 111.

¶ 197 By way of example, the people could not enact additional "General Provisions" in Article XIII that would prohibit marriages between Catholics and Protestants, prohibit women from working outside the home, and create a committee of business and religious leaders to sanitize media stories. Such amendments would clearly run afoul of Article II, Sections 4, 3, and 7, respectively (not to mention their counterparts in the federal Constitution). Such amendments would themselves be inherently unconstitutional.

¶ 198 In the same fashion, the people do not have the power to constitutionalize religious doctrine. Again, by way of example, the people could not adopt an amendment that required all church worship services to be conducted on Sunday, or that denied certain governmental services to persons who were not "born again," or that prohibited women from being ordained as ministers. And for the same reasons, religious teachings that homosexuality is a sin cannot be made part of Montana's secular law—as the proponents of CI-96 have attempted to do through the Marriage Amendment. The Achilles heel of the Marriage Amendment is that it is the wolf of constitutionalized religious doctrine parading in the sheep-suit of social policy.

¶ 199 Unlike the Marriage Amendment, Article II, Section 5 is a "fundamental right." It provides that "[t]he state shall make no law respecting an establishment of religion. . . ." Mont. Const. art. II, § 5. The Montana Constitution itself is "the supreme *law* of this State." *Associated Press v. Bd. of Pub. Educ.* (Mont. 1991) (emphasis added). Thus, when the State, through the initiative process, "makes a law" that serves no purpose other than to codify a religious canon—here, select portions of Genesis and Leviticus—the State clearly violates Article II, Section 5. One can only imagine the uproar if the State began incorporating doctrines from the Koran or some other religion's sacred text into the Constitution. Yet, that is precisely what the Marriage Amendment did. Through the initiative process, the State constitutionalized the biblical abhorrence for homosexuality by prohibiting same-sex couples not only from marrying but, according to the State and its amici, from enjoying any sort of legal protection for their relationships. Such protections are instead to be reserved to the biblically favored class of different-sex couples. ***

¶ 203 In denying Plaintiffs these protections through the conduit of the Marriage Amendment, the State conflates religious canons regarding marriage with the State's own civil laws. This is patently unconstitutional. When the State chooses to enact secular laws for the benefit of different-sex couples, but at the same time denies equal protection of those laws to same-sex couples because of sectarian proscriptions constitutionalized in the Marriage Amendment, the State is engaged in blatant discrimination grounded in religious doctrine. This sort of discrimination is unlawful not only under Article II, Section 5, but also under Article II, Section 4 ("Neither the state nor any person, firm, corporation, or institution shall discriminate against any person in the exercise of his civil or political rights on account of. . . religious ideas.").

Indeed, when, on the basis of religious doctrine, the State denies committed intimate same-sex couples the secular benefits and civil rights incidental to the status of marriage, the State is guilty of at least three abuses of the Constitution: the Equal Protection and Nondiscrimination Clauses of Article II, Section 4; the Dignity Clause of Article II, Section 4; and the Establishment Clause of Article II, Section 5. ***

¶ 206 In conclusion, assuming for the sake of argument that it is even applicable in this case, the Marriage Amendment cannot justify the State's approach. The Marriage Amendment is simply constitutionalized religious doctrine, and it cannot serve as a conduit for providing discretionary statutory benefits to some committed intimate couples while denying them to others. The benefits and obligations which the State creates under its secular law must not first be filtered through the sieve of religious doctrine in order to see who gets what. Article II, Section 5 ensures the separation of church and state. The constitutional quid pro quo is this: While the State is not permitted to be involved in the workings of religious institutions, neither is the State permitted to enforce the doctrines, canons, mandates, or proscriptions of any religion or sectarian organization. The State may not "target" a class of individuals for disparate treatment in order to advance a religious purpose or doctrine, without violating the Establishment Clause. ***

Epilogue

¶ 211 This will be my last opportunity to sit as a member of this Court on a case involving the fight for the dignity and the civil and human rights of lesbian, gay, bisexual, and transgender people. I had hoped—indeed, believed—that the work this Court started 15 years ago in *Gryczan* would be brought to fruition and successfully concluded with our decision in this case. Sadly, that is not to be. As I have, I can strenuously disagree with this Court's decision. Regrettably, however, I have been unsuccessful in doing more than that. I know how frustrating today's decision must be for the committed same-sex couples and for lesbian, gay, bisexual, and transgender Montanans across this State.

¶ 212 Our collective frustration and sadness aside, however, if we have learned anything as an evolving species, it is that no government, no religion, no institution, and no political party can long oppress the inviolable dignity and spirit of human beings in their fight for fairness in the courts, access to justice, and equal protection of the laws. Those are the seminal principles upon which our country was founded, and they are the birthright of every natural person on this planet, without exception. Those rights will not be long denied to those suffering the scourge of discrimination and hatred. The committed couples here—and lesbian, gay, bisexual, and transgender Montanans everywhere—must never lose sight of the fact that although today's battle has been lost, the war has not been. They must remain united in defeat because, in the end, they will overcome; they will prevail. Of that, I am absolutely certain. ***

Notes on "Sex," Sexual Orientation, and Suspect Classifications

1. What's at stake in the level of scrutiny debates? The Court appears to apply rational basis scrutiny in *Snetsinger* more vigorously than the United States Supreme Court did in a series of sexual orientation equal protection cases beginning in *Romer v. Evans* (1996) (holding the breadth of Colorado's Amendment 2 "is so discontinuous with the reasons offered for it that the amendment seems inexplicable by anything but animus toward the class it affects; it lacks a rational relationship to legitimate state interests"). As a result, the *Snetsinger* Court rejects the state's "administrative efficiency" justification without suggesting that the policy was motivated by the illegitimate state interest of animosity toward same-sex couples. In his concurrence, Justice Nelson argues for strict scrutiny, yet finds the policy motivated by the kind of animosity that would fail even the weaker form of federal rational basis review. What are the benefits and costs of each approach?

2. In part at the urging of the plaintiffs, the Court in *Snetsinger* focuses on the technicalities of family law rather than engaging in broader questions of same-sex marriage. In another case, *Kulstad v. Maniaci* (Mont. 2009), the Court upheld the award of a parenting interest in two children to Kulstad, the former same-sex partner of their adoptive parent, Maniaci. It observed, "Far too often this Court faces a situation in which minor children have no adult fit to parent them. This case presents the increasingly unusual situation of two adults fit to parent minor children." In a fact-specific opinion, the Court then deferred to the district court's findings that "it was in the children's best interest to maintain that child-parent relationship" with Kulstad. Justice Nelson concurred, arguing "whether rationalized on the basis of majoritarian morality, partisan ideology, or religious tenets, homophobic discrimination is still bigotry." Justice Rice dissented, citing Maniaci's fundamental rights to parent her adopted children, and arguing "[t]he abandonment of constitutional principle for the expediency of today's decision will have long, far-reaching and negative impacts." Why do the plaintiffs and the Court's majority in these cases not accept these invitations to engage in these big questions of marriage equality?

3. The claim in *Donaldson* is that the state, acting through legislation, denied plaintiffs equal protection of the laws among other rights. (Why not claim discrimination in the exercise of their civil or political rights on account of sex?) A key to equal protection analysis, at least as suggested by the United States Supreme Court in *City of Cleburne v. Cleburne Living Ctr.* (1985) and *Romer v. Evans* (1996), is a finding that the state's interest in enacting or enforcing the legal classification is animosity toward the excluded class. Unlike these cases, or the successful challenges to the federal Defense of Marriage Act in *United States v. Windsor* (2013) or the recently enacted marriage amendments at issue in *Obergefell v. Hodges* (2015), the basic marriage definition at issue in *Donaldson* was codified in 1895. *See* 1895 Mont. Civ. Code § 210 (describing marriage as "[h]usband and wife"). In 1997, the Legislature adopted an unusual prohibition against "a marriage between persons of the

same sex," or any "contractual relationship entered into for the purpose of achieving a civil relationship" between same-sex couples, amending older prohibitions on bigamous and incestuous marriages. Mont. Code Ann. § 40-1-401. How might the Court have decided a challenge focused on this law alone?

4. The 2004 Marriage Amendment in Montana provided "[o]nly a marriage between one man and one woman shall be valid or recognized as a marriage in this state." Mont. Const. Art. XIII, § 7. Unlike Montana, other states adopted express prohibitions on civil unions. *See* Idaho Const. Art. III, § 28 ("A marriage between a man and a woman is the only domestic legal union that shall be valid or recognized in this state."); N. Dak. Const. Art. XI, § 28 ("Marriage consists only of the legal union between a man and a woman. No other domestic union, however denominated, may be recognized as a marriage or given the same or substantially equivalent legal effect."); S. Dak. Const. Art. XXI, § 9 ("Only marriage between a man and a woman shall be valid or recognized in South Dakota. The uniting of two or more persons in a civil union, domestic partnership, or other quasi-marital relationship shall not be valid or recognized in South Dakota."). The state argued Montana's narrower amendment, unlike its neighbors' amendments, permitted legislative recognition of civil unions, but prohibited the Court from expanding marital benefits as such to same-sex couples.

5. According to Justice Nelson's dissent, are all laws supported in part by religious beliefs (even if the laws are justified on facially secular grounds) unconstitutional? Note that the non-discrimination clause also protects the exercise of civil and political rights on account of religious ideas. Do you agree that a constitutional amendment that conflicts with or restricts the scope of a pre-existing provision, but is otherwise duly enacted (for example, it does not contain multiple amendments), can violate the Constitution itself?

6. If discrimination because of sexual orientation is, as Justice Nelson and others have suggested, literally discrimination "on account of sex," would this not implicate the anti-discrimination clause directly, requiring strict scrutiny? Would discrimination on account of gender identity sound in a similar claim? *See Bostock v. Clayton County* (2020) (holding that the similar language of the Civil Rights Act of 1964 prohibited discrimination based on sexual orientation or gender identity). If the plaintiffs framed their challenge this way, would they need to exhaust administrative remedies under the Montana Human Rights Act before bringing their constitutional claims?

7. In 2014, the United States District Court for the District of Montana invalidated Article XIII, section 7 and Mont. Code Ann. § 40-1-401 under the federal Equal Protection Clause:

> Montana's laws that ban same-sex marriage impose a "disfavored legal status" on same-sex couples. The time has come for Montana to follow all the other states within the Ninth Circuit and recognize that laws that ban same-sex marriage violate the constitutional right of same-sex couples to

> equal protection of the laws. Today Montana becomes the thirty-fourth state to permit same-sex marriage.

The federal judge was Brian Morris, a former justice of the Montana Supreme Court who sat in the majority in *Donaldson. See Rolando v. Fox* (D. Mont. 2014).

Chapter 11

Privacy

> **Article II, Section 10. Right of privacy.** The right of individual privacy is essential to the well-being of a free society and shall not be infringed without the showing of a compelling state interest.
>
> *New provision prohibiting any invasion of privacy unless the good of the state makes it necessary.*

The right of privacy is celebrated as one of the Montana Constitution's most notable distinctions. Yet many other state constitutions provide rights of privacy, and privacy doctrine in Montana parallels the structure of what the delegates called "the judicially announced" right of privacy under the federal Constitution. The Bill of Rights Committee Report explained its original purposes in framing a right of individual privacy:

> The committee unanimously adopted this section . . . in order to guarantee the right of privacy. What it accomplishes is the elevation of the judicially-announced right of privacy to explicit Constitutional status. The right has been guaranteed in case law at the federal level [*Griswold v. Connecticut* (1965)] and in Montana [*State v. Brecht* (Mont. 1971)]. The committee believes the Constitution should specify that the only circumstance in which the right of privacy may be infringed is following the showing of a compelling state interest. This is in response to the increasing concern expressed nationwide that the sphere of individual privacy is in danger of eclipse in an advanced technological society. The point of this provision is not to prohibit all invasions of privacy but to require that no invasion of privacy should occur until and unless a compelling state interest has been established.
>
> The committee proposed a broad provision in this area to permit flexibility to the courts in resolving the tensions between public interests and privacy. It is hoped that the legislature will have occasion to provide additional protections for the right of privacy in explicit areas where safeguards are required. An example of a potential legislative subject matter can be seen in Delegate Proposal No. 124 which prohibited requiring submission to a lie detector or similar test as a condition of employment.

As seen by the Montana Supreme Court, the right of privacy displays two facets. The first, informational privacy, addresses concerns about surveillance and invasions of privacy in "an advanced technological society." This was the focus of the delegates' deliberation and the ratification campaign. The second, autonomy privacy, hews to the "liberty interest" analysis of federal substantive due process doctrine, particularly the conception of sexual autonomy and associated reproductive rights developed by the United States Supreme Court in *Griswold v. Connecticut* (1965), *Eisenstadt v. Baird* (1972) during the convention, and, shortly after the Constitution's effective date, *Roe v. Wade* (1973). At the time of the Constitutional Convention, these issues were contested but had not yet become the central controversy of constitutional law nationally, or in Montana.

Even the basic text of the right of privacy raises questions explored below. Is it limited to state action, as discussed in *State v. Long*? In criminal investigations, what is the scope and strength of individual privacy and how is it distinguishable from unreasonable search doctrine, as discussed in *State v. Nelson*? Turning to autonomy privacy, what is its scope and does it have any distinctive form or content beyond the federal *Katz* test as applied in *Gryczan v. State*? If it does, as the Montana Supreme Court suggests in *Armstrong*, how can or should the autonomy concept of privacy shape future decisions such as *Walker v. State* and *Baxter v. State*? What is its relation to dignity and equality?

A. The Origins and Scope of Individual Privacy

In ratifying "the right of individual privacy," the voters fulfilled the framers' intended delegation of privacy's scope to the courts and the Legislature. The text of Article II, section 10 itself raises several questions about the extent of a constitutionally guaranteed privacy interest. Unlike the security against unreasonable searches and seizures established by the federal Fourth Amendment and carried over into Article II, section 11 from the 1889 Montana Constitution, the common law right of privacy can be enjoyed with respect to private as well as state actors. Some early cases arising under section 10 consider whether and how the right of privacy protects against infringement by private parties, including the question of "a compelling state interest" that justifies an infringement of the right. These cases, like most privacy cases, also address the "informational" form of privacy that was the focus of deliberations over the right.

State v. Long

216 Mont. 65 (1985)

MORRISON, Justice.

*** Defendants, Charles and Vicki Long, at the time of the charged offense, were renters of a house in Huntley, Montana. The owner of the house, Millard Hultgren, lived next door. There was no written rental agreement between the parties. The landlord believed he had a right to enter his rental property at will. However, conflicting testimony was presented on whether the tenants ever consented to such an arrangement. The tenant Charles Long testified that there was no such agreement.

A sudden increase in the electricity bill for the rental house, a landlord obligation under the oral tenancy, caused concern. In the evenings, Hultgren noticed a light burning in the attic. On August 4, 1983, he entered, when the defendants were not home, and went to the attic where he discovered a "grow light" shining on what was later determined to be 657 marijuana plants. Hultgren's status at this point was a fact question. The District Court's finding that he was a trespasser is supported in the record.

The Yellowstone County Sheriff's Office was notified and an application made for a search warrant. Subsequently, the warrant was issued and the marijuana plants seized.

The defendants were charged and subsequently filed a motion to suppress. This case presents four-square the issue previously addressed on several occasions, the application of the privacy clause and the exclusionary rule to private action. The narrow issue before the Court in this case is:

> "Are the fruits of a search conducted by a private citizen, without any type of governmental involvement, properly the subject of exclusion?"

This Court has previously held that private searches invade privacy rights protected by the Constitution and are properly the subject of our exclusionary rule. The rule was first articulated in *State v. Brecht* (Mont. 1971). The same principle has been refined, approved or commented upon in [six other] cases. . . .

The last two cases to thoroughly analyze the rationale for the position applying the exclusionary rule to evidence seized by private persons are *State v. Hyem* [Mont. 1981], and *State v. Van Haele* [Mont. 1982]. In *Hyem*, the charges arose when skis, belonging to one Buzz Welch, were found in defendants' residence and seized by officers of the Carbon County Sheriff's Office pursuant to a search warrant issued by the local justice of the peace. The issuance of the warrant was based on affidavits given by two of Welch's friends, who stated they had seen the skis at defendants' rented home in Red Lodge, Montana. The informants had gained entry into defendants' rented residence by telling a local realtor that they were interested in purchasing the home, although in point of fact, they were interested in looking for the skis. Therefore, the informants were technically trespassers.

The majority opinion distinguished the right of privacy in Montana from the right of privacy protected by the Federal Constitution and noted that the right of privacy was specifically guaranteed in Article II, Section 10 of the 1972 Montana Constitution. The majority said:

> "In *Brecht*, it was pointed out that there cannot be a fictional difference between classes of citizens: those who are commanded to obey the constitution and those who are not. Our constitutional prohibition against unreasonable invasion of privacy applies to all persons, whether acting for the state or privately."

This Court, in *Hyem*, indicated a concern with "the ever-increasing presence of private police" and relied upon this concern in shoring up the argument that the privacy provision of the Constitution should be applied to prohibit individual action as well as state action.

Next, the majority opinion in *Hyem* addressed the application of the exclusionary rule to evidence seized illegally by private individuals. Unlike other courts, which have viewed the exclusionary rule as a rule of procedure, this Court indicated that the exclusionary rule was rooted in the Constitution itself. The majority said:

> "The exclusionary rule is not a judicial plaything, casually adopted and casually waived. It is a constitutional answer to unconstitutional activity. It is an affirmation that a free government can no more tolerate the unlawful activities of its agents than crime in the streets. It is paste and cover for the bones of our individual constitutional rights, without which such rights were in danger of becoming an unfleshed skeleton."

The majority noted that a distinction had to be made where the unreasonable search was made by private individuals and not by the police. The Court's opinion, in essence, distinguished federal law denying the application of the exclusionary rule to the fruits of private action by arguing that the Federal Constitution was not violated by private action and that, therefore, the exclusionary rule was not applied. However, this Court noted that, since our State Constitution was violated by a private search, the exclusionary rule should appropriately be applied in order to protect from having the constitutional right invaded. This rationale logically follows if the exclusionary rule itself is implied in the Constitution in order to give meaning to those constitutional rights specifically provided.

The dissent in *State v. Hyem*, was premised upon traditional notions of constitutional principles. Unless specifically provided otherwise, citizens' rights articulated in the Constitution proscribed only state action; therefore, if a private citizen invaded the privacy of another citizen, there was no violation of the Constitution itself. Furthermore, in accordance with the view of all other courts, the dissent viewed the exclusionary rule as a rule of court procedure to deny admission to the fruits of illegally seized evidence in order to deter unlawful police activities and to preserve the integrity of the judiciary itself.

This Court now adopts the rationale of the three dissenters expressed in *State v. Hyem*, and overrules all previous decisions of this Court inconsistent herewith.

Montana is one of a small minority of states to have an express provision for privacy in its Constitution. No other state has followed Montana's lead in interpreting the privacy protections of a state constitution to be applicable to acts of private persons. Other state courts have commented upon the Montana decisions. In fact, a District Court judge in Wyoming was persuaded to follow this jurisdiction. On appeal, the Wyoming Supreme Court said:

> "The sole jurisdiction which we have been able to identify in which a different rule prevails is in our sister state of Montana. The rule in Montana appears to be that the same constitutional protections pertain whether a search and seizure involves private individuals or law enforcement officers.

> The most charitable rationalization of that ruling is that it depends upon a peculiar provision of the Constitution of the State of Montana which is not found in the constitution of this state. Even so, the dissenter to the court's opinion in *State v. Hyem*, points out that other states having the same style of constitutional provision have adhered to the usual rule distinguishing private individuals from law enforcement officers. On the other hand one well could conclude, having perused the somewhat tortured history of that rule in the State of Montana, that the rule is chimerical. Unfortunately in this instance Deon Heiner persuaded the district judge to follow that rule in essence." *State v. Heiner* (Wyo. 1984).

We do not take offense at the Supreme Court of Wyoming terming our rule chimerical, which means fantastic or imaginary. Neither are we afraid to walk alone. Rather, we reverse the previously articulated rule because we believe it unsound.

The privacy section, Mont. Const. Art. II, § 10 (1972), specifically states:

> "The right of individual privacy is essential to the well-being of a free society and shall not be infringed *without the showing of a compelling state interest.*" (emphasis supplied)

The language of the section itself indicates that the framer's contemplated state action by allowing an invasion where there was a compelling state interest.

Historically, constitutions have been means for people to address their government. In rare instances, the constitutional language itself has specifically addressed private action. For instance, Mont. Const. Art. II, § 4 (1972), provides in part:

> "... Neither the state nor any *person, firm, corporation, or institution* shall discriminate against any person...." (emphasis supplied)

Notably, the privacy section does not address private individuals as does the civil rights provision quoted.

Although we do not feel our Constitution is sufficiently ambiguous to require extensive perusal of the constitutional transcripts, we do note that a speech on the floor of the convention by one delegate has been referred to in other decisions of this Court. In *State v. Helfrich* [(Mont. 1979)], this Court [al]luded to the following excerpt from the constitutional debate:

> "'... It isn't only a careless government that has this power to pry; political organizations, private information gathering firms, and even an individual can now snoop more easily and more effectively than ever before ...' Tr. at p. 5182."

This quotation actually resulted from a delegate reading from a newspaper editorial which supported an expanded right of privacy. However, the balance of the delegate's statement is significant. It reads:

> "[I]t produces what I would call a semipermeable wall of separation between individual and state; just as the wall of separation between church and state

is absolute, the wall of separation we are proposing with this section would be semipermeable. That is, as a participating member of society, we all recognize that the state must come into our private lives at some point; but what it says is, don't come into our private lives unless you have a good reason for being there. We feel that this, *as a mandate to our government*, would cause a complete reexamination and guarantee our individual citizens of Montana this very important right. . . ." (emphasis supplied).

There is every indication that the delegates themselves adopted a privacy section which would only proscribe state action. Certainly, there is nothing in the constitutional debate that clearly indicates we should depart from traditional constitutional notions. Therefore, in accordance with well-established constitutional principles, we hold that the privacy section of the Montana Constitution contemplates privacy invasion by state action only.

The second issue which must be addressed is application of the exclusionary rule. Since we have held that the constitutional rights of the defendants have not been violated, the reason for applying the exclusionary rule fades. As a rule of court procedure, the exclusionary rule has been applied to deter illegal police conduct and to preserve judicial integrity. When applied to private action, the deterrence argument is inapplicable. Private individuals are not schooled in the exclusionary rule and most likely would be unaware of its application. Therefore, it would not deter them from engaging in searches that would be illegal if conducted by government officials.

The strongest support for application of the exclusionary rule to the fruits of private action comes from the "silver platter doctrine." In a special concurrence filed to the majority opinion in *State v. Van Haele*, reference was made to that doctrine:

". . . As pointed out in the majority opinion, the United States Supreme Court in *Elkins [v. U.S.]* said in part:

"'If the government becomes a lawbreaker, it breeds contempt for law; it invites every man to become a law unto himself; it invites anarchy. To declare that in the administration of the criminal law the end justifies the means—to declare that the government may commit crimes in order to secure the conviction of a private criminal—would bring terrible retribution. Against that pernicious doctrine this court should resolutely set its face.'

"In *[State v.] Coburn* [(Mont. 1974)], also cited by majority, Justice Daly very logically noted:

"'. . . *[U]nreasonable or illegal intrusions knowingly accepted and used*, from the private sector by the government amount to an extension of the silver platter doctrine condemned by *Elkins*, particularly when viewed in the light of judicial integrity emphasized in *Elkins*.'"

The special concurrence went on to note that:

> "If the 'silver platter doctrine' is to be recognized for the purpose of excluding evidence obtained by private individuals then, in my opinion, it should be confined to instances where the evidence was obtained in violation of criminal statutes thereby rendering the evidence 'illegal.' In this way judicial integrity is preserved by not judicially blessing the fruits of illegal activity. Such an application of the exclusionary rule would not be premised upon an invasion of the accused's constitutional rights. Rather, the exclusionary rule, as a rule of court procedure, would prevent the State from relying upon the illegal conduct of a private citizen." *Van Haele.*

In the case at bar, the evidence was seized by a landlord who was determined by the District Court to be a trespasser. Under such circumstances, judicial integrity does not require exclusion of the evidence. We reserve for another day the determination of whether to apply the exclusionary rule to evidence gathered as the result of felonious conduct.

The order of the District Court suppressing the questioned evidence is reversed. The case is remanded for trial.

WEBER, Justice, concurs as follows:

As pointed out in the majority opinion, starting in 1971 this Court articulated the rule that private searches invade privacy rights protected by Art. II, Sec. 10, Mont. Const. and are therefore properly subject to the exclusionary rule. That rule was set forth in numerous cases, the last of which was decided in 1983. In view of our reversal of that well-established holding I think it appropriate to discuss the rule of stare decisis.

We recognize that a significant change in a basic rule of law unsettles the law and gives rise to criticism. *State ex rel. Sparling v. Hitzman* (Mont. 1935), describes the problems in failing to follow established precedent, as well as the need for evolution of the law:

> "We realize the force and the wisdom of the rule of stare decisis. We are not unmindful of the fact that principles of law should be positively and definitively settled in order that courts, lawyers, and, above all, citizens may have some assurance that important legal principles involving their highest interests shall not be changed from day to day, with the resultant disorders that of necessity must accrue from such changes. We are mindful, however, of the fact, as stated by Mr. Justice Brandeis . . . that 'in the search for truth through the slow progress of inclusion and exclusion, involving trial and error, it behooves us to reject, as guides, the decisions upon such questions which prove to have been mistaken.' *The rule of stare decisis will not prevail where it is demonstrably made to appear that the construction placed upon the constitutional provision in the former decision is manifestly wrong.*" (emphasis supplied)

Principles of law should be definitively settled if that is possible. However, as suggested by Justice Brandeis, the search for truth involves a slow progress of inclusion and exclusion, involving both trial and error. I do not cast any reflection on those justices who participated in the opinions which are being overruled. However, I do believe that the decisions were fundamentally mistaken. I concur with the majority conclusion that Art. II, Sec. 10, Mont.Const. contemplated state action and did not address the question of private action. ***

SHEEHY, Justice, dissenting:

Today's opinion has derailed the one vehicle that gave strength and vitality to the unique right of privacy enshrined in our State Constitution. Our state right of privacy had meaning and force in our lives because this Court excluded evidence obtained in violation of privacy. Until today it was the proud accomplishment of this Court, in the several cases today overruled, that enhanced by judicial decision what the framers proclaimed, that "the right of individual privacy is essential to the well being of a free society, and shall not be infringed without the showing of a compelling state interest." Today the vigor of that ringing proclamation has been drained, leaving it merely a hortative form of words.

The devastation is complete. The immediate effect of today's opinion is to advise tenants that their right to be "secure in their persons, papers, homes, and effects" is subject to the whims of their landlords. But by limiting the application of our constitutional privacy right to state action only, the larger effect of today's decision is to cut the underpinnings from any future claim of invasion of privacy tort under the State Constitution. From today, unless state action is involved a tort claim between individuals for invasion of privacy may not be based on Art. II, § 10 of our State Constitution, but must instead be found in the common law. Tragically, it was not necessary for such a broad sweep of legal decision to set aside the exclusionary rule. In their zeal, the new majority rolled out a cannon to shoot a fly.

The majority opinion today results from a series of misconceptions that distrot the reasoning of our previous cases. One such misconception is that we have held that the exclusionary rule is "rooted" in the Constitution. A second misconception leads the majority to conclude the right of privacy guaranteed by the State Constitution applies only to state action. A third misconception concerns the earlier dissents of the same justices who are now part of the new majority on the exclusionary rule.

It is a given that there is no textual support in our State Constitution for the exclusionary rule. Nowhere, and particularly not in Art. II, § 10, is there found the language "evidence obtained in violation of this section shall be excluded in the courts." But the same is true of the Federal Constitution. We search in vain for the words "right of privacy" in the express provisions of the Federal Constitution. The United States Supreme Court has dug that right out of the "penumbras" of the Bill of Rights. (At oral argument, the Attorney General of this State seemed unwilling to admit such penumbras.) In *Griswold v. Connecticut* (1965), it is said:

"The foregoing cases suggest that specific guarantees in the Bill of Rights have penumbras, formed by emanations from those guarantees that help give them life and substance (citing authority). Various guarantees create zones of privacy. The right of association contained in the penumbra of the First Amendment is one, as we have seen. The Third Amendment, in its prohibition against the quartering of soldiers 'in any house' in time of peace without the consent of the owner is another facet of that privacy. The Fourth Amendment explicitly affirms the 'right of the people to be secure in their persons, houses, papers, and effects, against unreasonable searches and seizures.' The Fifth Amendment in its Self Incrimination Clause enables a citizen to create a zone of privacy which government may not force him to surrender to his detriment. The Ninth Amendment provides: 'The enumeration in Constitution, of certain rights, shall not be construed to deny or disparage others retained by the people.'

"The Fourth and Fifth Amendments were described in *Boyd v. United States*, as protection against all government invasions 'of the sanctity of a man's home and the privacies of life.' We recently referred in *Mapp v. Ohio*, to the Fourth Amendment as creating a 'right to privacy, no less important than any other right carefully and particularly reserved to the people . . .'"

This Court said in *State v. Hyem* (Mont. 1981), that the exclusionary rule "is a constitutional answer to unconstitutional activity." I insist on the integrity of that statement. That the exclusionary rule is constitutionally required, as distinguished from mandated, is supported by Justice Clark who said in *Mapp v. Ohio* (1961), that the exclusionary rule is "that command which this Court has held to be clear, specific, and constitutionally required — even if judicially implied — deterrent safeguard without insistence upon which the Fourth Amendment would have been reduced to a 'form of words' . . ."

Contrary to the misconception of the majority, *Hyem* held not that the exclusionary rule was a constitutional right but a constitutional answer. It is a rule in accord with Art. II, § 16, Montana Constitution, that a speedy remedy be afforded "for every injury to person, property, or character."

The exclusionary rule is the only practicable "speedy remedy." Criminal prosecutions for deprivations of constitutional rights are limited to "willful" violations. *Screws v. United States* (1945). An injunction against violations cannot be obtained unless the party can establish he is likely to be injured by the practices again in the future. *City of Los Angeles v. Lyons* (1983). A civil action against a violator for damages is so obviously impracticable that it needs no discussion.

In view of the fruitlessness of other remedies, any lawyer worth his salt must admit the exclusionary rule is the only effective remedy that will protect against unconstitutional intrusions on privacy by busybodies or snitches.

We were treated by the State in oral argument in this case to a list of frightening possibilities under our exclusionary rule. What, we were asked, would the implications of the exclusionary rule be if the landlord in this case had found a body? The answer of course is simple: A body cannot be suppressed, any more than the body of a prisoner can be suppressed after an illegal arrest. But the exclusionary rule should be applied with might and main when any lesser evidence of criminal conduct is produced through unlawful intrusions into one's privacy, for all of the reasons usually expressed: the growth of technology in electronic eavesdropping; governments should not cooperate with unlawful intruders; no price can be placed on a constitutional right; the exclusionary rule should not depend on the fortuitous circumstance of who and of what quality was the intruder; judicial integrity is involved; and unlawful intrusions should not be encouraged.

Ah, but should the guilty go free? Emphatically yes, where the only evidence of guilt results from an invasion of the home or private precincts of the individual. Only the cases where the intruder discovers criminal activity get into the courts. There must be tens of instances of unlawful intrusions into privacy which do not turn up criminal cases, for most of us obey the laws. The opportunity for courts to stress the heightened privacy right found in our State Constitution will only come in cases, like all other cases on constitutional rights, involving not very nice people. The right of all of us to our privacy weighs greater than the occasional and rare loss of conviction of a criminal. Essentially it preserves judicial integrity for the government not to act in concert with lawbreakers to convict other lawbreakers.

A second misconception of the majority is that the state constitutional right of individual privacy was intended by the framers to be a wall against state action only.

As laws usually reflect the will of the people on social, moral and economic issues, so too do constitutional provisions. The state framers in 1972 were not so far removed from pioneer days in Montana as to have forgotten our traditions of independence and privacy. Even the western usage of hospitality and welcome in remote places for the hungry wayfarer did not displace the duty of the wayfarer to respect the person, home and property of his host. The spirit of neutrality about our neighbor's business was captured by the long-forgotten poet who described the Montana he loved:

> With skies that reach from east to west
>
> And room to go and come
>
> I liked my fellow man the best
>
> When he was scattered some.

That spirit had found its way into the decisions of this Court before the 1972 constitutional convention. In *State v. Brecht* (Mont. 1971), this Court said:

> "... The state admits this, but contends that protection is afforded only against violations by law enforcement officers and not against violations by private citizens.

"We think not. The violation of the constitutional right to privacy and against compulsory self incrimination is as detrimental to the person to whom the protection is guaranteed in one case as in the other. To distinguish between classes of violators is tantamount to destruction of the right itself. This Court in 1952, in a civil case not involving state or federal governmental agents or activity, recognized this principle in the following passage from *Welsh v. Pritchard* [(Mont. 1952)]:

> "'Continuing the article announces:' 'The common law has always recognized a man's house as his castle, impregnable, often even to its own officers engaged in the execution of his commands.'"
>
> "the 'right of privacy' is embraced within the absolute rights of personal security and personal liberty (citing authority.)
>
> "'the basis of the right of privacy is 'the right to be let alone' and is 'a part of the right of liberty and pursuits of happiness.' (Citing authority.)"

Contrary to what is stated in the majority opinion, the constitutional framers certainly contemplated that Art. II, § 10 would be applicable to private as well as state action. In addition to the statement of the delegate quoted in the majority opinion (page 157, supra) that same Delegate Campbell continued:

> ". . . we feel that this, as a mandate to our government, would cause a complete reexamination and guarantee our individual citizens of Montana this very important right—the right to be let alone; and this has been called the most important right of them all. You all had placed on your desk the Montana Standards' editorial of February 3, 1972. I think it states it very well. 'Times change.' That, in a nutshell, is why the Constitutional Convention delegates in Helena are working on a new and more modern governmental charter for Montana. Today, with wire taps, electronic and bugging devices, photo surveillance equipment and computerized data banks, a person's privacy can be invaded without his knowledge and the information so gained can be misused in the most insidious ways. It isn't only a careless government that has this power to pry; political organizations, private organizations, private information gathering firms, and even an individual can now snoop more easily and more effectively than ever before. We certainly hope that such snooping is not as wide spread as some person would have us believe, but with technology easily available and becoming more refined all the time, prudent safeguards against the misuse of such technology are needed. Some may urge and argue that this is a legislative, not a constitutional issue. We think the right of privacy is like a number of other inalienable rights; a carefully worded constitutional article reaffirming this right is desirable. Wade Dahood of Anaconda, chairman of the Bill of Rights Committee, hit the nail on the head when he said: 'As government functions and controls expand, it is necessary to expand the rights of the individual.' The

> right to privacy deserves specific protection. Mr. Chairman, I would recommend adoption of this section."

Beyond cavil, in the light of the holding in *State v. Brecht, supra*, which we must assume the framers knew about, and the direct statement of the delegate proposing Art. II, § 10 for constitutional adoption, a clear intention existed to guarantee individual privacy in Montana from and after 1972 against both state and private action. ***

Perhaps the most telling argument against the State-action-only interpretation of our privacy clause is that the framers gave us a toothless clause if all they intended to cover was state action. Interpreted as a majority today interprets our state privacy clause, it is but the functional equivalent of what is minimally guaranteed to us in the Federal Constitution, but we are entitled to the federal minimums of privacy with or without the Montana Constitution. The Fourteenth Amendment of the U.S. Constitution has, since *Mapp v. Ohio* (1961), guaranteed that states would protect the privacy rights of individuals penumbrally contained in the U.S. Constitution. Those privacy rights existed and still exist before and since the adoption by Montana of Art. II, § 10, and would exist without the State Constitution.

I maintain that the Montana constitutional framers in 1972 wanted to do more for Montanans in the field of privacy. They adopted Art. II, § 10 to give Montanans a heightened right of privacy, beyond the privacy rights found in the U.S. Constitution. That aspiration for a heightened right meant that our State Constitution would afford privacy greater than the minimum guarantees of the Federal Constitution.

There is no force to the majority argument that the Privacy Clause should be applied only to state action because hitherto Montana stands alone in applying it to private action. Montana's constitutional Privacy Clause is unique. No other state has a State Constitution provision exactly like it. The closest is that of Alaska in Art. I, § 22, 1972 Alaska Constitution, which provides:

> "The right of the people to privacy is recognized and shall not be infringed. The legislature shall implement this section."

In *Allred v. Alaska* (Alaska 1976), where one of the questions presented was whether statements made by a defendant to a counselor were protected by Alaska's constitutional provision on privacy, the Alaska Supreme Court seems to assume without discussion that it would take state action to trigger the constitutional privacy guarantee.

In California, in November 1972, the voters amended Art. I, § 1 of their State Constitution to include among the various "inalienable" rights of all people the right of "privacy." Curiously, as far as I am aware, no California case has specifically decided whether the right of privacy in the California Code applies to private action. However, in *White v. Davis* (Cal. 1975), the California Supreme Court identified the principle "mischiefs" at which the privacy right was directed, including "the overbroad collection and retention of unnecessary personal information by government and business interests." To that extent at least, California presumably would recognize that its privacy right precludes business interests from intruding on individual privacy.

Five states, Hawaii, Illinois, South Carolina, Louisiana and Florida as of 1968 included the right of privacy in some form as a part of the traditional constitutional prohibition against unreasonable searches and seizures. Our framers declined that approach.

It is noteworthy that in our 1972 Constitutional Convention, the first draft of the search and seizure provision, Art. II, § 11, included language that "the people shall be secure ... from unreasonable searches and seizures and invasions of privacy ..." The delegates recognized that the modifier "unreasonable" in § 11 weakened the right of privacy they had established in § 10. The convention therefore deleted reference to privacy from § 11.

Two other states have a constitutional provision for privacy, Washington and Arizona. Arizona treats its constitutional provision as the functional equivalent of the Fourth Amendment, *Arizona v. Murphy* (Ariz. 1977). Washington, however, is approaching what had been Montana's position on the effect of its constitutional privacy provision. Art. I, § 7 of Washington's Constitution provides that "no persons shall be disturbed in his private affairs or his home invaded, without authority of law." In *State v. Williams* (Wash. 1984), the Washington Court said:

> "This provision differs from the federal constitution and provides heightened protection to our citizens' privacy rights (citing authority). Where, as here, no probable cause exists to arrest the suspect, we believe that the language of Const. Art. I, § 7 forbids police seizures of this nature."

Although *State v. Williams* addressed police action, and not private action, Washington aligned itself with Montana in determining that the right of privacy afforded by its state constitution is greater than the federal minimums. ***

The importance of the privacy provision to the framers can be assumed from its position in Art. II, relating to the declaration of individual rights. The privacy section preceded the provision against unreasonable search and seizures (§ 11), the right of suffrage (§ 13), the right to justice in the courts (§ 16), the right to due process (§ 17), the privilege of habeas corpus (§ 19), and the right to bail (§ 21). It preceded the right of an accused to meet his witnesses face-to-face (§ 24), the right against self-incrimination and double jeopardy (§ 25) and the right to trial by jury (§ 26). By placing the right of individual privacy before all of those other essential rights, the framers, I submit, meant to evince their intention to give a heightened right to privacy beyond the minimum rights of privacy penumbrally found in the Federal Constitution. It was within the power of the state constitutional framers so to do.

The framers in 1972 had a beautiful conception: They felt the force of our tradition that each person ought to mind his own business; they saw the home as a place of refuge, peace and security. They provided that a wall of law should be erected against all onslaught except when the compelling interest of the State demanded otherwise. Private persons do not act for the State. Intruders into privacy may be nothing more than nosy neighbors, busybodies, or snitches. The framers extended the right of privacy especially against these.

Gone is that beautiful conception. Left only are the minimum protections of the Federal Constitution, which nowhere expressly guarantees individual privacy. Federally, our privacy rights are no more than the shifting courts are inclined to allow. Under our State Constitution, our individual privacy rights are expressly stated to be paramount. The framers unfortunately did not foresee that this Court would dilute their positive declaration in Art. II, § 10, by reading into its clear language some darkling exception. This Court has stamped "approved" on the nettlesome intruders, the nosy ones, the busy ones, the snitches. It has said welcome to the "Big Spy Country."

The third misconception of the majority is embedded in their irresolution about the nature and extent of our state Privacy Clause, as demonstrated by a comparison of the statements of the majority and their earlier dissents.

In the concluding paragraphs of the majority opinion, we are given a moment's glimpse of the monster now penned up in the basement. It may be turned loose again if the State proposes to use evidence obtained in criminal activity.

It defies imagination how a criminal exception can be read into the clear language of Art. II, § 10. The glaring internal inconsistency of the majority is the apparent concession that the Privacy Clause applies to private action if the private actors are criminals.

If the majority does indeed intend that criminal activity shall be the watershed in the future in determining rights under the privacy clause, it is a further sticking inconsistency that the majority glides by the criminal activity of Hultren in this case. The landlord stands before us as a trespasser. He is indeed guilty of criminal trespass under § 45-6-203, MCA. . . . The majority offer no explanation why we must wait for another day for the determination of the effect of criminal activity on the Privacy Clause. This case presents criminal activity to the Court. ***

In light of the present decision, the case at bar, where is the court heading now if the present majority continues to prevail in cases involving private invasions of individual privacy which develop incriminating evidence? In *Hyem*, the justices would not exclude evidence developed by any private action. In *Van Haele*, these justices would exclude evidence if it were developed through a violation of the penal statutes. In this case, *State v. Long*, a violation of the penal statutes occurred, but the question of the application of the exclusionary rule under criminal activity is postponed to another day. Apparently criminal activity does not count unless the perpetrator is actually criminally charged in the courts.

A final evidence of irresolution is that today the majority has overruled *Van Haele*, a decision in which two of the majority justices concurred one and one-half years ago.

I would adhere to our earlier cases and uphold the decision of the District Court to exclude the evidence.

HUNT, Justice, dissenting:

I dissent and concur in the opinion of Mr. Justice Sheehy.

The District Court should be affirmed. Montana has rightfully placed privacy paramount to any illegal public or private intrusion. The constitutional delegates knew Montana when they wrote:

> "The right of individual privacy is essential to the well-being of a free society and shall not be infringed without the showing of a compelling state interest." Mont. Const. art. II, § 10.

This has been the law and should remain the law without exception or qualification.

It is no favor to judicial integrity to use an incident of an illegal intrusion as a substitute for due process. The majority of this Court now allows the trespasser and the snoop to do work properly assigned to lawfully constituted law enforcement. We should leave law enforcement to those legally and rightfully entrusted with that task. It is not an injustice to society to apply the exclusionary rule to private searches. If a private search is a result of illegal or improper conduct, including trespass, all evidence obtained therefrom should be excluded. Law enforcement should be left to law enforcement officers who are not only trained to apprehend the wrongdoer but, just as importantly, to respect the rights of all Montana citizens including what was, before the majority opinion, the constitutional right to privacy.

MORRISON, Justice, concurring:

I am taking the rather unusual step of replying to the dissent of Justice Sheehy in this case. The majority opinion, although authored by this writer, speaks for the majority of the Court. The views herein expressed are my own.

The dissent is an eloquent, if legally unsound, defense of privacy. Its several weaknesses may be readily discernable but I wish to formally join the issue. ***

Our people should not be misl[e]d by this careless characterization of Montana's privacy right. The framers of our constitution intended that privacy be specifically recognized and the right as it exists under Montana law is unquestionably paramount to the privacy right implied in the federal constitution.

In *State v. Solis* (Mont. 1984), this issue was directly confronted. The United States Supreme Court, in *United States v. Caceres* (1979), had said:

> "Neither the constitution nor any act of congress requires that official approval be secured before conversations are overheard or recorded by government agents with the consent of one of the conversants."

We refused to follow the United States Supreme Court in *Solis*. We specifically recognized that the right of privacy in Montana is greater than under the United States Constitution and that we need not, under these circumstances, follow the lead of the United States Supreme Court. The majority of this Court held that electronic eavesdropping, by video taped recording, violated the right of privacy and was subject to exclusion. Thus, this Court firmly recognized the superior right of privacy in Montana.

The dissent again goes awry, in attempting to identify an inconsistency between the dissenter's view as expressed in *State v. Hyem* and *State v. Van Haele*. *** The dissent continues to confuse the privacy clause with the exclusionary rule.

Criminal conduct, unless done with state complicity, does not violate privacy. However, the fruits of felonious action may be excluded as evidence, not because there is a constitutional violation, but because the trial court feels its exclusion necessary to preserve the integrity of the judicial system. "Other crimes evidence" is excluded because the courts have decided that its probative weight is usually less than its potential prejudicial effect. Hearsay evidence is normally excluded because, without the opportunity for cross-examination, its credibility cannot be sufficiently tested. The court excludes evidence for a variety of reasons including preservation of court integrity. On the latter basis a court may feel that a search is so abhorrent that the evidence should be excluded rather than in any way legitimized. This rule has nothing to do with the constitution. The rule can be reworked, shaped, and changed as other rules of evidence.

The dissent's real plea emanates from a public policy concern. The public policy issue of whether the privacy clause should cover private action has not been treated in the majority opinion. Rather, we have sought to determine whether there was a clear intention expressed by the framers to depart from traditional constitutional concepts. We found there was not. Therefore, we have limited the application of the privacy clause to state action.

The battle cry sounded in the dissent may, at first blush, have an alluring ring to liberals and civil libertarians. There is, however, a real danger in extending privacy rights to the interaction of individuals.

Privacy competes with other rights declared by our state constitution to be fundamental. My right to be left alone competes with my neighbor's right for self-expression. The danger of holding that my right to privacy is constitutionally protected from invasion by my neighbor but my neighbor's right of free speech is not protected from my invasion, is apparent.

The rights and responsibilities that we as people have, one to the other, should be competed for in the legislative forum. This better reflects the dynamic nature of our society and gives vibrance to the political process.

State v. Nelson

283 Mont. 231 (1997)

LEAPHART, Justice.

James Nelson (Nelson) appeals from the Seventh Judicial District Court's order denying his motion to quash or to suppress the results of his blood alcohol test obtained by means of an investigative subpoena. We affirm.

The following facts are not in dispute. On December 7, 1994, near Glendive, Montana, Nelson was involved in a motor vehicle accident on Interstate 94 when he drifted off the highway and struck a guardrail. After Nelson received a ride from the accident scene to a friend's residence, Nelson's friend, Mr. Stroh, drove him to the Glendive Medical Center for treatment of facial injuries he sustained in the accident. Emergency room physician Dr. Arthur Fink treated Nelson for a broken jaw and, concerned over Nelson's apparent lack of pain for the injury, ordered a blood test in order to determine his blood alcohol concentration level (BAC).

The following morning, Nelson reported the accident to the Montana Highway Patrol. Highway Patrol Sergeant Jerry Mahlum (Sgt. Mahlum), a Certified Accident Reconstructionist, conducted the investigation of the accident. Sgt. Mahlum viewed the scene of the accident, determined the extent of damage to the guardrail, spoke with the patrolman on duty the night of the accident and independently met with Nelson and Dr. Fink. During Sgt. Mahlum's interview with Nelson, he learned that Nelson had broken his jaw in the accident and that it had to be wired shut as a result. Nelson told Sgt. Mahlum that prior to the accident he had consumed a couple of drinks at a local bar and that he had no recollection of the accident itself. In addition, Sgt. Mahlum determined that Nelson's vehicle had sustained extensive left front-end damage, the type of damage consistent with striking the guardrail. Sgt. Mahlum's findings led him to believe that the driver involved in the accident would have either fallen asleep at the wheel or would have been under the influence of drugs or alcohol.

On December 12, 1994, Sgt. Mahlum met with Dr. Fink. During the interview, and without divulging Nelson's BAC level, Dr. Fink told Sgt. Mahlum that Nelson's BAC level the night of the accident would partly explain Nelson's lack of pain normally associated with his type of injuries.

After Sgt. Mahlum compiled the findings of his investigation, Deputy County Attorney Scott Herrin, reviewed Sgt. Mahlum's report and determined that sufficient facts existed to suggest an "unlawful activity had occurred" and, on December 14, 1994, filed a Motion for Investigative Subpoena Duces Tecum with the District Court. Setting forth the facts recited above, the motion requested that the District Court issue an investigative subpoena to the records keeper at the Glendive Medical Center to require disclosure of all medical records pertaining to Nelson's BAC taken December 7, 1994. On December 16, 1994, the District Court found that sufficient facts were present and granted the motion to issue the Investigative Subpoena Duces

Tecum. On January 3, 1995, the medical reports on Nelson's blood test from December 7, 1994, were provided to the deputy county attorney showing that, shortly after his accident, Nelson's BAC level was .233.

Nelson was charged by Complaint with the offense of driving under the influence of alcohol, a misdemeanor, in violation of § 61-8-401, MCA. Nelson entered a plea of not guilty in Justice Court. Nelson then filed a motion to suppress evidence which was denied by the Justice Court. Nelson then entered a plea of guilty reserving his right to appeal the denial of the motion to suppress to the District Court.

Nelson then appealed to District Court where he filed a Motion to Quash the Investigative Subpoena or, in the alternative, Motion to Suppress Evidence. After entertaining oral argument on the motion, the District Court denied the motion with no findings of fact or conclusions of law. Thereafter, Nelson entered a plea of not guilty and judgment was entered sentencing him to ten days in the Dawson County jail and a fine of $500. The sentence was stayed pending appeal to the Montana Supreme Court. Nelson appealed to this Court and we remanded to the District Court for further proceedings on the question of whether the State had established a compelling state interest justifying the discovery of the BAC test, as required under Article II, Section 10 of the Montana Constitution. Pursuant to this remand order, the District Court conducted a hearing and filed Findings of Fact and Conclusions of Law and Judgment.

The District Court concluded that: (1) a health care provider may disclose health information about a patient without the patient's authorization if the disclosure is made pursuant to § 50-16-530, MCA, which allows for disclosure "to a law enforcement officer about the general physical condition of a patient being treated in a health care facility if the patient was injured on a public roadway or was injured by the possible criminal act of another. . . ." Section 50-16-530(4), MCA. Further, the court recognized that health care information may be disclosed by a health care provider pursuant to § 50-16-535(1)(j), MCA, when "the health care information is requested pursuant to an investigative subpoena issued under 46-4-301."

Section 46-4-301, MCA, provides the authority for the issuance of investigative subpoenas, as follows:

> Whenever a prosecutor has a duty to investigate alleged unlawful activity, any justice of the supreme court or district court judge of this state may cause subpoenas to be issued commanding the persons to whom they are directed to appear before the prosecutor and give testimony and produce books, records, papers, documents, and other objects as may be necessary and proper to the investigation. A subpoena may be issued only when it appears upon the affidavit of the prosecutor that the administration of justice requires it to be issued.

In the instant case, the Dawson County Attorney, relying on Sgt. Mahlum's investigation, filed a motion for an investigative subpoena to the Glendive Medical Center for release of reports of Nelson's blood alcohol level relative to the time of the accident. The District Court found that the "administration of justice" required the subpoena be issued. Pursuant to the subpoena, the County Attorney received Nelson's blood alcohol results from the Glendive Medical Center. ***

Discussion ***

1. Did the taking of a blood sample from Nelson violate his constitutional rights to be free from unreasonable searches?

Nelson contends that, since his blood was drawn at the hospital at a time when law enforcement was not involved, the implied consent law, § 61-8-402(1), MCA, does not apply. He contends, nonetheless, that since the blood was taken by a doctor without first seeking Nelson's consent, that the taking constitutes an illegal search and the results must be suppressed. He cites *State v. Kirkaldie* (Mont. 1978), in support of his contention.

In *Kirkaldie*, the investigating officer and the deputy coroner asked the defendant to submit to a blood alcohol test and the defendant refused. The coroner then requested the assistance of the attending physician who testified that he advised Kirkaldie that he did not have to give blood but that it was in his best interest that he do so. Kirkaldie eventually agreed to the drawing of his blood. He then argued on appeal that his consent was the involuntary product of psychological coercion by the State. We reviewed the voluntariness issue under the "totality of circumstances" test and found substantial evidence to support the trial court's conclusion that the defendant was not coerced into consenting to the test.

The instant case is clearly distinguishable from *Kirkaldie*. Here, in contrast to *Kirkaldie*, there was no State involvement in the taking of the blood sample. The blood was drawn by a doctor at the Glendive Medical Center. The exclusionary rule, which Nelson seeks to invoke, does not apply to evidence resulting from the actions of private individuals unless they are acting as agents of the State. *State v. Christensen* (Mont. 1990); *see also State v. Baker* (Mont. 1995). Here, there is no suggestion or argument that Dr. Fink, in drawing blood from Nelson, was acting at the direction or request of the State. In the absence of any State action or involvement, Nelson's contention that he did not voluntarily consent and that the drawing of his blood constituted an illegal search under the Fourth Amendment to the United States Constitution or Article II, Section 11 of the Montana Constitution, must fail.

2. Did the information provided to Sgt. Mahlum by Dr. Fink exceed the provisions of § 50-16-530(4), MCA ?

Nelson contends that Dr. Fink's comments to Sgt. Mahlum about Nelson's BAC were in excess of the parameters of § 50-16-530(4), MCA, which allows a health care provider to disclose the "general physical condition" of a patient to a law enforcement officer if the patient were injured on a public roadway. Although there is no definition of "general physical condition," general health condition "is defined as the patient's health status described in terms of critical, poor, fair, good, excellent or terms denoting similar conditions. Section 50-16-504(3), MCA. Given this narrow scope of authority, Nelson contends that "the only information that Officer Mahlum should have obtained from Dr. Fink was Nelson's health status." He argues that any information which exceeded the parameters of the general descriptors of critical, poor, fair, good, excellent, etc. must be suppressed.

Nelson's argument ignores the fact that the restrictions imposed by § 50-16-530(4), MCA, are directed not at law enforcement but at health care providers. If, as Nelson posits, Dr. Fink's gratuitous comments to Sgt. Mahlum about Nelson lack of pain exceeded the scope of § 50-16-530(4), MCA, then Nelson's remedy lies with the health care provider, not through a motion to suppress. A motion to suppress must be premised upon illegal conduct by state officials. Section 50-16-530(4), MCA, does not provide a basis for suppressing evidence and, thus, the District Court did not err in denying Nelson's motion in that regard.

3. Did release of the blood alcohol information pursuant to an investigative subpoena violate Nelson's right of privacy under Article II, Section 10 of the Montana Constitution?

Nelson's next prong of attack is aimed at the fact that the State obtained the results of his BAC test through the use of an investigative subpoena. Since an investigative subpoena involves state action, this presents a different issue than Dr. Fink's gratuitous statement to Sgt. Mahlum about Nelson's lack of pain.

In the context of this case, the investigative subpoena finds its roots in a series of statutes starting with § 50-16-530(6), MCA, which provides that the health care provider may disclose information pursuant to compulsory process in accordance with § 50-16-535, MCA. Section 50-16-535, MCA provides, in relevant part, as follows:

> Health care information may not be disclosed by a health care provider pursuant to compulsory legal process or discovery in any judicial, legislative, or administrative proceeding unless:
>
> [***] (c) the patient is a party to the proceeding and has placed his physical or mental condition in issue;
>
> [***] (i) a court has determined that particular health care information is subject to compulsory legal process or discovery because the party seeking the information has demonstrated that there is a compelling state interest that outweighs the patient's privacy interest; or
>
> (j) the health care information is requested pursuant to an investigative subpoena issued under 46-4-301.

In the present case, the County Attorney filed a motion for investigative subpoena thereby invoking subsection (j) of § 50-16-535(1), MCA, which provides for release of health care information pursuant to such a subpoena. The motion recited that the "administration of justice" required the issuance of the subpoena. Further, in issuing the order for the subpoena, the court specifically stated that the "administration of justice" requires that the subpoena be issued. Thus, it is clear that the court employed the "administration of justice" standard of § 46-4-301, MCA, under subsection (j) and that the compelling state interest test of subsection (i) was not at issue.

Nelson contends that the investigative subpoena for release of his health care information violated his right of privacy under Article II, Section 10 of the Montana Constitution. He points out that § 50-16-535(2), MCA, provides that "[n]othing in this part authorizes the disclosure of health care information by compulsory legal process or discovery in any judicial, legislative, or administrative proceeding where disclosure is otherwise prohibited by law." The question presented is whether Nelson's health care information is protected under the constitutional right of privacy and, if so, what effect does this protected status have on the issuance of investigative subpoenas?

We begin our discussion by reviewing our holdings in *State v. Burns* (Mont. 1992) and in *State v. Henning* (Mont. 1993).

In *Burns*, the defendant was charged with deviate sexual conduct. He had provided a list of some fifteen character witnesses. The State, in order to rebut and cross-examine these character witnesses, sought an investigative subpoena to obtain Burns' personnel files from the Catholic Diocese. After conducting an in camera review of the records, the district court barred discovery of the records. On appeal, we reiterated the two-part test from *State ex rel. Great Falls Tribune Co. v. Eighth Judicial District Court* (Mont. 1989), for determining whether privacy interests are protected under Article II, Section 10 of the Montana Constitution. The two prongs of that test are as follows:

1) Whether the person involved had a subjective or actual expectation of privacy; and,
2) Whether society is willing to recognize that expectation as reasonable.

We held in *Burns* that it was apparent that the above test had been satisfied.

> When discovery of documents such as personnel records are at issue, privacy rights are undoubtedly at stake. Montana adheres to one of the most stringent protection of its citizens' right to privacy in the country. Mont. Const. Art. II, Sec. 10. Montana's treatment of privacy rights is more strict than that offered by the Federal Constitution. *Montana Human Rights Division v. City of Billings* (Mont. 1982). It is against this constitutional backdrop that we view the case at bar.

Burns (citations omitted).

We affirmed the district court's holding that, under the circumstances of the case, the State could not show a compelling interest to gain access to Burns' personnel files. *But see Montana Human Rights Div.* (granting Commission access to employment records to investigate possible violations of discrimination) and *Great Falls Tribune v. Sheriff* (Mont. 1989) (holding that the privacy interests of the employee police officers did not exceed the public's right to know).

In *Henning*, the defendant was arrested for DUI and refused a breathalyser test. Instead of submitting to the breathalyser test, he asked the officer to take him to the hospital so that a blood test could be administered at his expense. Accordingly, a blood sample was taken by a registered nurse. The results of the test were obtained by the State pursuant to an investigative subpoena. Henning was convicted in justice court and appealed to district court where he filed a motion in limine asking the court to suppress the results of the blood test as being inadmissible. The district court determined that, pursuant to § 50-16-535(1)(i), MCA, the State had demonstrated a compelling interest which outweighed Henning's privacy interests and therefore the test results were admissible under § 50-16-535(1)(i), MCA. Henning, relying on § 50-16-535, MCA, and not on Article II, Section 10 of the Montana Constitution (Right of Privacy), argued that his medical records were privileged and that the State had not satisfied the statutory "compelling state interest" burden under § 50-16-535(1)(i), MCA. On appeal, we held that § 50-16-535, MCA, pertains to the discovery of health care information but does not control the admissibility of that information as evidence at trial. Since Henning had not challenged the discovery of the test results, we focused on the question of admissibility. We determined that since the blood was drawn with Henning's consent, the result of the blood sample was admissible in evidence. "Once the evidence was discovered, it was no longer privileged information and the State was entitled to move for its admission at trial."

Nelson's appeal differs from Henning's in that Nelson does contend that the medical information was not constitutionally discoverable under Article II, Section 10 of the Montana Constitution which provides: "The right of individual privacy is essential to the well-being of a free society and shall not be infringed without the showing of a compelling state interest."

Nelson's claim of privacy in medical records satisfies the two-part test set forth above in our discussion of Burns. That is, Nelson had a subjective or actual expectation of privacy in his medical records and, society is willing to recognize that expectation as reasonable.

As the California Supreme Court stated in interpreting that state's constitutional guarantee of privacy, Article I, Section 1 of the California Constitution:

> Legally recognized privacy interests are generally of two classes: (1) interests in precluding the dissemination or misuse of sensitive and confidential information ("informational privacy"); and (2) interests in making intimate personal decisions or conducting personal activities without observation, intrusion, or interference ("autonomy privacy").

Hill v. National Collegiate Athletic Ass'n (Cal. 1994).

We agree with the California court that informational privacy is a core value furthered by state constitutional guarantees of privacy and that the zone of privacy created by those provisions extends to the details of a patient's medical and psychiatric history. *Cutter v. Brownbridge* (Cal. 1986). In *Cutter*, the California court explained:

> [T]he right to control circulation of personal information is fundamental. This right reaches beyond the interests protected by the common law right of privacy, and may be protected from infringement by either the state or by any individual. The "zones of privacy" created by article 1, section 1, extend to the details of one's medical history. And, an "individual's right to privacy encompasses not only the state of his mind, but also his viscera, detailed complaints of physical ills, and their emotional overtones."

See also Dr. K v. State Bd. of Physician Quality Assur. (Md. App. 1993) (holding that every citizen has a constitutional right of privacy in his or her medical records).

Although medical records have not been historically protected by the Fourth Amendment's prohibition against unreasonable searches and seizures, *see Whalen v. Roe* (1977), Montana's separate constitutional guarantee of privacy expands the breadth of privacy beyond traditional search and seizure principles derived from the Fourth Amendment and Article II, Section 11 of the Montana Constitution. *See State v. Siegal* (Mont. 1997) and *State v. Bullock* (Mont. 1995) (both decisions holding that Montana's constitutional right of privacy is broader than the right of privacy under the Federal Constitution). We now hold that Article II, Section 10's guarantee of privacy encompasses not only "autonomy privacy" but confidential "informational privacy" as well.

We hold further that, if the right of informational privacy is to have any meaning it must, at a minimum, encompass the sanctity of one's medical records. In contrast to telephone company billing records, for which there is no reasonable expectation of privacy, *Hastetter v. Behan* (Mont. 1982), medical records fall within the zone of privacy protected by Article II, Section 10 of the Montana Constitution. As the Montana Legislature has recognized, "health care information is personal and sensitive information that if improperly used or released may do significant harm to a patient's interests in privacy and health care or other interests." Section 50-16-502(1), MCA. Medical records are quintessentially "private" and deserve the utmost constitutional protection.

Nelson's medical records were discovered via an investigative subpoena under § 46-4-301, MCA. This statute allows an investigative subpoena to be issued if the administration of justice so requires. Although the administration of justice threshold had not been defined, it is safe to conclude that it is considerably less exacting than the "compelling state interest" test demanded by Article II, Section 10's guarantee of privacy. *State v. Baldwin* (Mont. 1990) (the prerequisites for obtaining a search warrant are more stringent than those for acquiring an investigative subpoena). We hold that, as applied to the discovery of constitutionally protected materials such as medical records, the "administration of justice" standard is unconstitutional. Medical records may be discovered through an investigative subpoena only upon a showing of a compelling state interest under Article II, Section 10 of the Montana Constitution. Since this is an issue of first impression in Montana, we must define a test for determining whether a compelling state interest exists.

We note that under similar circumstances, a Pennsylvania court employed a probable cause standard. In *Commonwealth of Pennsylvania v. Moore* (Pa. Super. Ct. 1993), the police sought a subpoena for defendant's medical records. Based upon observations and information given by witnesses to the fatal accident, police were aware that the defendant had been involved in a serious accident in which his vehicle had crossed into the lane for oncoming traffic and that alcohol had been detected on his breath. "This constituted probable cause to believe that a criminal offense had been committed." The court concluded:

> Under these circumstances, we conclude, as did the trial court, that the police use of a subpoena to compel the production of appellant's medical records for the preliminary hearing did not violate any constitutionally protected right of privacy which appellant possessed in his medical records.

As we set forth above, Article II, Section 10 of the Montana Constitution expands the breadth of privacy beyond that recognized under Article II, Section 11 of the Montana Constitution. In requiring a "compelling state interest" it does not, however, establish a new or heightened level of protection for any particular privacy interest. The home, for example, has always been afforded protection under Article II, Section 11 of the Montana Constitution and the Fourth Amendment to the United States Constitution. Although the home likewise comes under the privacy protection of Article II, Section 10, it does not, by virtue of Article II, Section 10 have any "more" protection than it had under Article II, Section 11. Rather, Article II, Section 10 is broader in the sense that it encompasses information and activities in addition to places and persons. Nonetheless, privacy rights, whether under Article II, Section 11 of the Montana Constitution or under Article II, Section 10 of the Montana Constitution are not absolute. They must yield to the State's interest in conducting reasonable searches upon a showing of probable cause.

When an investigative subpoena seeks discovery of protected medical records or information, the subpoena can be likened to a search warrant which must satisfy the strictures of the Fourth Amendment and Article II, Section 11 of the Montana Constitution. A search warrant can only issue upon a showing of "probable cause." In the context of search and seizure law, probable cause exists when facts and circumstances presented to a magistrate would warrant an honest belief in the mind of a reasonable and prudent person that an offense has been, or is being, committed and that property (or information) sought exists at the place designated. Section 46-5-221, MCA. We hold that in order to establish that there is a compelling state interest for the issuance of an investigative subpoena for the discovery of medical records, the State must show probable cause to believe that an offense has been committed and medical information relative to the commission of that offense is in the possession of the person or institution to whom the subpoena is directed.

We turn then to the question of whether, under the facts in this case, there was probable cause to believe that an offense had been committed and that Nelson's medical records contained evidence of the offense. The motion for investigative subpoena was based upon Sgt. Mahlum's report that Nelson was involved in an unreported automobile accident in which Nelson's vehicle was traveling west, drifted left and struck a guardrail and Nelson received injuries; that a Mr. Stroh transported Nelson to the Glendive Medical Center where Nelson received emergency room treatment; and that when interviewed by Sgt. Mahlum, Nelson indicated that he had consumed a couple of drinks prior to the accident. Even if we disregard Dr. Fink's thinly veiled comment to Sgt. Mahlum as to the reason for Nelson's lack of pain, the balance of the information known to law enforcement was sufficient to establish probable cause. That is, that Nelson had consumed a couple of drinks before the accident; that the road was bare and dry; that he ran into a guardrail; that he suffered a broken jaw; and that he had received medical treatment at the Glendive Medical Center.

We reiterate our holding as follows: Medical records and medical information are protected under Article II, Section 10's guarantee of privacy. When an investigative subpoena seeks discovery of medical records, the subpoena can issue only upon a showing of a compelling state interest. In order to establish the existence of a compelling state interest to justify the issuance of an investigative subpoena, the State must demonstrate "probable cause" just as it would if it were seeking issuance of a search warrant under Article II, Section 11 of the Montana Constitution and the Fourth Amendment to the United States Constitution.

The order denying the motion to quash the investigative subpoena, or in the alternative to suppress the evidence is affirmed.

Notes on Origins and Scope of Individual Privacy

1. "The right of individual privacy is essential to the well-being of a free society and shall not be infringed without the showing of a compelling state interest." Unlike the contested unenumerated "right to privacy" in federal constitutional law, Montanans expressed the right in constitutional text. Note the questions raised by the text:

a. How does "individual" limit the right? For example, when if ever would associations of individuals enjoy the right?

b. What work does the "prefatory" clause, "essential to the well-being of a free society," do for the meaning of the right?

c. What should courts make of the incorporation of a "compelling state interest" test into the text? Does the inclusion of an express standard of scrutiny in section 10 suggest it should be applied to other Article II rights as well, or is the omission in other provisions meaningful? And what of the tailoring or fit element of traditional strict scrutiny, from which "compelling state interest" is derived? Must infringements be narrowly tailored to the state interest or merely justified by a rational relationship to the compelling interest?

d. If you agree with the dissents in *Long*, how would you square "compelling *state* interest" with private rights? Would personal interests, no matter how compelling, never trump the privacy right? How would you answer Justice Morrison's concerns?

2. In dissent, Justice Sheehy places section 10 first among privacy protections within the state constitutional tradition, and distinguishes it from the Fourth Amendment and penumbral federal protections. What evidence supports his view that the primary distinction of Montana's right is the applicability to private action? How else might we find grounds to identify a distinctly Montanan right of privacy?

3. The Montana Legislature codified a right of privacy against non-state actors in the Privacy in Communications Act, Mont. Code Ann. § 45-8-213. That law, which raises freedom of expression issues discussed later, creates

> the offense of violating privacy in communications if the person knowingly or purposely:
>
> (a) with the purpose to terrify, intimidate, threaten, harass, or injure, communicates with a person by electronic communication and threatens to inflict injury or physical harm to the person or property of the person or makes repeated use of obscene, lewd, or profane language or repeated lewd or lascivious suggestions;
>
> (b) uses an electronic communication to attempt to extort money or any other thing of value from a person or to disturb by repeated communications the peace, quiet, or right of privacy of a person at the place where the communications are received;
>
> (c) records or causes to be recorded a conversation by use of a hidden electronic or mechanical device that reproduces a human conversation without the knowledge of all parties to the conversation; or
>
> (d) with the purpose to terrify, intimidate, threaten, harass, or injure, publishes or distributes printed or electronic photographs, pictures, images, or films of an identifiable person without the consent of the person depicted that show [nudity or sex acts].

How much of the right of privacy does this protect? What does it leave out?

4. What does the exclusionary rule — a judicial remedy of excluding evidence gathered in violation of the Fourth Amendment — have to do with the right of privacy? If such a remedy is implicit in privacy, why not other rights? For example, should evidence obtained by racial profiling in potential violation of Article II, section 4 be excluded? Note that Montana courts need not apply the exclusionary rule to state searches that do not otherwise violate the relatively narrower scope of federal Fourth Amendment rights, but also may extend the exclusionary rule beyond the federal scope.

5. If probable cause is a compelling state interest (must the subpoena also be narrowly tailored?), does *Nelson* amount to anything more than applying standard Fourth Amendment doctrine to medical records? What role does the Legislature's statutory protections for medical records play in informing whether Nelson had a privacy interest in the records? If such protections had not been enacted, would the result have been the same?

6. *Nelson* holds the "guarantee of privacy encompasses not only 'autonomy privacy' but confidential 'informational privacy' as well." Although the delegates referred in passing to *Griswold*, a federal case recognizing what the Montana Supreme Court would describe as an implied right of "autonomy" privacy to use contraception in marriage, they focused on a more recent state case at the time, *State v. Brecht* (1971), which presented an instance of what the Court would describe as "informational privacy":

> We hold that the admission of Sandra Brumfield's testimony concerning the telephone conversation between defendant and his wife, which she overheard while listening on the extension phone, constitutes prejudicial and reversible error. Admission of this testimony violated the defendant's Fourth Amendment rights under the federal constitution as applied to state court criminal proceedings under the "due process" clause of the Fourteenth Amendment. It equally violated defendant's rights under Article III, Sec. 7 of the Montana Constitution [freedom from unreasonable searches and seizures] .... The violation of the constitutional right to privacy and against compulsory self-incrimination is as detrimental to the person to whom the protection is guaranteed in the one case as in the other.

Are autonomy privacy and informational privacy the same right? Are both equally central to the section 10 guarantee?

7. An earlier case cited in the delegates' debates might more closely resemble the privacy at issue in *Griswold*. *Welsh v. Pritchard* (Mont. 1952) is a colorful case of privacy:

> On June 25, 1949, Pritchard appeared at the Welshs' kitchen door, rapped, walked in and seated himself in the living room....
>
> If Welsh had any idea that his home was his castle, or that he and his family alone would enjoy the privacy and quiet of his domicile, such idea was rudely shattered and took wing when he reached home and found the Pritchards and their belongings cluttering up the living room. Things looked bad and they were to become worse before becoming better. He was in for days and nights that would try any man's soul. ***
>
> The record does not show Griff's fighting weight, but Welsh was a heavyweight at 195 pounds. Without a shake of the hand and before Griff his guard could raise, Welsh, as Griff tells it, "landed on me with all his might," and Griff went down from the dynamite.
>
> Griff pulled himself upright, "hung on to the post for a minute," then staggered to the living room again to face his foe. In that living room he and his wife stayed for 17 days and nights and until July 11, 1949, unwanted guests of unwanted tenants. ***
>
> "The typical privacy cases are those involving the display, sale or publication of one's portrait, the public use of one's name, oppressive publicity

> in connection with the collection of debts, and wire-tapping and other forms of eavesdropping. Superficially, these cases may seem to involve entirely different principles and considerations. Yet, there is a pervading element, common to all the cases, of outraging one's feelings by depriving him of the privacy which most normal persons desire and have a right to demand, whether this deprivation is effected by publishing one's name or picture in an advertisement or by tapping one's telephone line or installing a detectophone so as to listen secretly to one's conversations with family or friends." 138 A.L.R. 25, see annotation.
>
> That Pritchard invaded the privacy and right of privacy of the Welsh's is beyond question. Such invasion, trespass, entry and stay were intentional, wrongful and malicious.

Quite literally, the Welshes asserted a "right to be left alone"! Still, *Welsh* stands for the classical tort-based conception of the right of privacy as protection from "publicity," not the broader constitutional version expressed in *Griswold*. As Warren & Brandeis explained in *The Right to Privacy*, HARV. L. REV. (1890):

> The design of the law must be to protect those persons with whose affairs the community has no legitimate concern, from being dragged into an undesirable and undesired publicity and to protect all persons, whatsoever their position or station, from having matters which they may properly prefer to keep private, made public against their will. It is the unwarranted invasion of individual privacy which is reprehended, and to be, so far as possible, prevented.

Brandeis later dissented as a Supreme Court Justice in *Olmstead v. United States* (1928), arguing for the constitutionalization of this right of privacy under the Fourth Amendment:

> The makers of our Constitution . . . conferred, as against the Government, the right to be let alone — the most comprehensive of rights and the right most valued by civilized men. To protect that right, every unjustifiable intrusion by the Government upon the privacy of the individual, whatever the means employed, must be deemed a violation of the Fourth Amendment.

As we saw earlier in *Bullock* (Chapter 2), the Montana cases consistently assert that Montana's right of privacy is broader than the federal right. But broader in which dimensions?

8. The Montana Supreme Court summarized the relationship of informational privacy to unreasonable seizures in *State v. Staker* (Mont. 2021):

> ¶8 Individuals have a fundamental Montana constitutional right to privacy, subject to government infringement only upon "showing of a compelling state interest." Mont. Const. art. II, §10. In general, privacy is the "ability to control access to information about oneself." Individuals also have a separate but corresponding Montana constitutional right to be free

from "unreasonable searches and seizures." Mont. Const. art. II, § 11. As implementation of its substantive reasonableness requirement, Article II, Section 11 includes a procedural warrant requirement specifying that "[n]o warrant to search any place, or seize any person or thing shall issue without . . . probable cause[] supported by [written] oath or affirmation." Mont. Const. art. II, § 11.

¶9 The fundamental purpose of Article II, Sections 10–11 is "to protect the privacy and security of individuals from unreasonable government intrusion or interference." Together, Article II, Sections 10–11 provide a heightened state right to privacy, broader where applicable than the privacy protection provided under the Fourth and Fourteenth Amendments to the United States Constitution. "When analyzing search and seizure questions that specifically implicate the right of privacy," we thus analyze and apply Article II, Sections 10–11 in tandem.

A. Extent of Montana Right to Privacy and Trigger of Protection Against Unreasonable Search and Seizure in Particular Cases.

¶10 Under Article II, Section 10, a right to privacy exists only to the extent that an individual has or had a reasonable expectation of privacy under the totality of the circumstances at issue. The Article II, Section 11 right to be free from unreasonable searches and seizures similarly applies only to constitutional "searches" or "seizures." A constitutional "search" occurs where government action intrudes or infringes upon an individual's reasonable expectation of privacy.

¶11 For purposes of Article II, Sections 10–11, a reasonable expectation of privacy exists only to the extent that an individual has a subjective expectation of privacy that is objectively reasonable in society. Whether an individual had a subjective expectation of privacy, and whether such expectation was objectively reasonable in society, are mixed questions of fact and law under the totality of the circumstances of each case. Absent a reasonable expectation of privacy, there is no constitutional intrusion, search, or seizure under Article II, Sections 10–11. Even in the presence of a reasonable expectation of privacy, whether a constitutional intrusion or search occurred ultimately depends on whether, based on the nature of the intrusion, the government action substantially infringed or intruded upon the reasonable expectation of privacy.

B. Compelling Government Interest and Constitutional Reasonableness.

¶12 Upon determination of a constitutional search or seizure triggering the protection of Article II, Sections 10-11, the next questions are whether it was both narrowly tailored to further a compelling state interest as required by Article II, Section 10, and constitutionally reasonable as required by Article II, Section 11. While the State generally has a compelling interest in "enforc[ing] its criminal laws for the benefit and protection of other

> fundamental rights of its citizens," warrantless searches and seizures must be narrowly tailored to serve the particular compelling state interest at issue under the circumstances of each case. Thus, based on the heightened individual right to privacy under Article II, Section 10, the government must generally utilize the least intrusive means available to effect a warrantless search under a recognized exception to the warrant requirement of Article II, Section 11.
>
> ¶13 Upon a showing under Article II, Section 10 that the subject search or seizure was narrowly tailored to further a compelling state interest, "the State may [still] not invade an individual's privacy" unless the search or seizure is constitutionally reasonable under Article II, Section 11. In that regard, searches and seizures authorized by judicial warrant, on probable cause of illegal activity and particularly describing the object of the search or seizure, are presumed reasonable under the Fourth and Fourteenth Amendments to the United States Constitution and Article II, Section 11 of the Montana Constitution. In contrast, warrantless searches and seizures are *per se* unreasonable, except as authorized under a recognized and well-defined exception to the respective warrant requirements of the Fourth Amendment and Article II, Section 11. Based on the heightened Montana constitutional right to privacy, "the range of warrantless searches" and seizures permissible under Article II, Sections 10–11 is narrower than the range permissible under the Fourth Amendment. Under the Montana Constitution, we thus assess the reasonableness of a constitutional search or seizure as a function of whether it occurred pursuant to a valid judicial warrant, issued on probable cause and particularly describing the area or person to be searched or seized, or whether it fell within one of the narrower range of recognized exceptions to the warrant requirement of Article II, Section 11. Based on the presumption of unreasonableness, the State bears the burden of demonstrating that a warrantless search or seizure was narrowly tailored to further a particular compelling government interest and accordingly fell within a recognized exception to the warrant requirement of Article II, Section 11.

The Court unanimously held "the warrantless use of a cloaked law enforcement officer under a fake internet advertisement for sexual services, and the responsive text message conversation initiated by Staker to the listed cell phone number in response thereto, did not intrude upon an objectively reasonable expectation of privacy and thus did not effect a constitutional search in violation of his right to privacy under Montana Constitution Article II, §§ 10-11."

In *Staker* the Montana Supreme Court noted the framers' concerns that "the people of Montana should be protected as much as possible against *eavesdropping, electronic surveillance, and such type of activities*" (quoting Delegate Campbell, emphasis in original). The Court then distinguished cases involving "government monitoring or recording of a seemingly private conversation between people by separate surreptitious electronic means," including recordings of telephone and face-to-face conversations, from text messaging. It observed, "the modern analog of the exchange of paper correspondence or notes by traditional mail or courier service by one with another who in fact may or may not be the person who the sender believes them to be." What, then, does Montana's right of individual privacy add to the judicial assessment of a "reasonable expectation of privacy" required by the Fourth Amendment and Article II, section 11?

B. Privacy as Autonomy

The most controversial applications of the right of privacy occur in the area of personal autonomy, or what have developed under federal substantive due process doctrine as "liberty interests." Here, the Montana right of privacy distinguishes itself from federal law, particularly in the area of sexual and reproductive autonomy. Six years before *Lawrence v. Texas* (2003), the Montana Supreme Court in *Gryczan v. State* (Mont. 1997) joined several other state courts in recognizing a right of privacy against government regulation of sexual conduct between partners of the same sex. (The Court in *Lawrence* cited *Gryczan* and other state cases as evidence in support of its holding.) In several cases, most notably *Armstrong v. State*, various Montana courts distinguished federal reproductive rights by invalidating abortion laws previously upheld by federal courts. Notwithstanding the distinct direction Montana courts have taken with respect to privacy's personal autonomy rules, however, they do not necessarily lay new doctrinal foundations in place of the federal approach. Whether it is moored to the dated federal *Katz* rule of "a reasonable expectation of privacy" or drifting toward more abstract and contested jurisprudential conceptions advanced by legal philosophers, the conceptional foundations of Montana's right of privacy, and their implications for privacy as autonomy, remain contested. Consider whether and how the right of privacy in Montana can stand on its own.

Gryczan v. State

283 Mont. 433 (1997)

NELSON, Justice.

The State of Montana appeals a Judgment of the District Court for the First Judicial District, Lewis and Clark County, declaring § 45-5-505, MCA, unconstitutional as a violation of the privacy provision of the Montana Constitution when applied to consensual, private, same-gender sexual conduct between adults. We affirm.

The State raises the following issues:

1. Whether Respondents have standing to maintain an as-applied challenge to the constitutionality of § 45-5-505, MCA.

2. Whether § 45-5-505, MCA, infringes on Respondents' right to privacy under Article II, Section 10 of the Montana Constitution to the extent it prohibits consensual, private, same-gender sexual conduct between adults.

3. Whether § 45-5-505, MCA, violates Article II, Section 4 of the Montana Constitution by infringing on Respondents' dignity as human beings, discriminating against them on the basis of sex, or denying them equal protection of the laws to the extent it prohibits consensual, private, same-gender sexual conduct between adults.

Having affirmed the trial court as to issues 1 and 2, we decline to address issue 3.

Background

On December 6, 1993, Respondents filed a declaratory judgment action, pursuant to Title 27, chapter 8 of the Montana Code, challenging the constitutionality of that portion of Montana's deviate-sexual-conduct statute, § 45-5-505, MCA, that criminalizes consensual sex between adults of the same gender. Respondents contend that § 45-5-505, MCA, is unconstitutional under Article II, Sections 4 and 10 of the Montana Constitution and that it violates the due process clause of the Fourteenth Amendment to the United States Constitution.

Respondents are three men and three women residing in Montana who are homosexuals. They assert that they have in the past and intend in the future to engage in conduct that violates § 45-5-505, MCA. This statute provides:

> Deviate Sexual Conduct. (1) A person who knowingly engages in deviate sexual relations or who causes another to engage in deviate sexual relations commits the offense of deviate sexual conduct.
>
> (2) A person convicted of the offense of deviate sexual conduct shall be imprisoned in the state prison for any term not to exceed 10 years or be fined an amount not to exceed $50,000, or both.
>
> (3) The fact that a person seeks testing or receives treatment for the HIV-related virus or another sexually transmitted disease may not be used as a basis for a prosecution under this section and is not admissible in evidence in a prosecution under this section.

The phrase "deviate sexual relations" is defined at § 45-2-101(20), MCA, as "sexual contact or sexual intercourse between two persons of the same sex or any form of sexual intercourse with an animal." "Sexual contact" and "sexual intercourse" are defined as:

> "Sexual contact" means any touching of the sexual or other intimate parts of the person of another for the purpose of arousing or gratifying the sexual desire of either party.

Section 45-2-101(65), MCA.

> "Sexual intercourse" means penetration of the vulva, anus, or mouth of one person by the penis of another person, penetration of the vulva or anus of

> one person by any body member of another person, or penetration of the vulva or anus of one person by any foreign instrument or object manipulated by another person for the purpose of arousing or gratifying the sexual desire of either party. Any penetration, however slight, is sufficient.

Section 45-2-101(66), MCA.

Section 45-5-505, MCA, was enacted in 1973 as part of the criminal law revision. Prior to 1973, Montana law had prohibited "crimes against nature" with persons or animals. Section 45-5-505, MCA, was amended in 1981 to add a maximum fine of $50,000 as part of the penalty provision. In 1991, a subsection providing a greater penalty when the conduct was nonconsensual was deleted and a subsection prohibiting the use of information regarding the testing of or the treatment for the HIV-related virus as evidence in a prosecution was added. Efforts to repeal the statute were rejected in 1991, 1993, and 1995. ***

Issue 1.

Whether Respondents have standing to maintain an as-applied challenge to the constitutionality of § 45-5-505, MCA.

The State maintains that without a concrete factual context, Respondents' challenge presents a political dispute properly decided in a legislative and not in a judicial forum. The State contends that to establish a justiciable controversy under Article VII, Section 4(1) of the Montana Constitution, Respondents are required to show an "injury in fact" and that no such injury exists here because there is no evidence of a credible threat of prosecution under the statute since no one has been prosecuted for engaging in consensual, adult, private, same-gender sexual conduct since the statute was enacted. The State also contends that Respondents do not have standing to challenge the constitutionality of § 45-5-505, MCA, because they have never been arrested or prosecuted for violating the statute. The State maintains that the mere apprehension of prosecution or the fact that a person may feel denigrated by the law is not sufficient for standing purposes and where an as-applied challenge is at stake, as in this case, resolution of the constitutional issue should await an actual instance of the statute being applied. ***

Respondents argue that, although they have never been arrested or prosecuted under the statute, they have been injured and continue to be injured by the mere existence of the statute. They contend that the damage to their self-esteem and dignity and the fear that they will be prosecuted or will lose their livelihood or custody of their children create an emotional injury that gives them standing to challenge the statute. For example, two Respondents are employed or are seeking employment in positions requiring state licenses. Because they engage in conduct classified as a felony, they fear they could lose their professional licenses. One Respondent is the mother of a five-year old boy. She fears that the statute could be used to limit her relationship with her son. ***

The challenged statute in the case before us is only 24 years old and has been amended as recently as 1991. This, and other prior amendments, make it clear that the Montana Legislature not only contemplates prosecution, but also considers the possibility realistic enough to require the addition of a subsection preventing the use of evidence of testing or treatment for the HIV-related virus or other sexually-transmitted diseases as a basis for prosecution under the statute. Moreover, the legislature has decided three times in the last seven years not to repeal the statute. ***

Because the legislature does not regard the statute as moribund and because enforcement has not been foresworn by the Attorney General, we agree that Respondents suffer a legitimate and realistic fear of criminal prosecution along with other psychological harms. Respondents are precisely the individuals against whom the statute is intended to operate. This is sufficient to give Respondents standing to challenge the constitutionality of the statute. Moreover, to deny Respondents standing would effectively immunize the statute from constitutional review.

Accordingly, we hold that a justiciable controversy exists and that Respondents have standing to challenge the constitutionality of § 45-5-505, MCA.

Issue 2.

Whether § 45-5-505, MCA, infringes on Respondents' right to privacy under Article II, Section 10 of the Montana Constitution to the extent it prohibits consensual, private, same-gender sexual conduct between adults.

In its February 16, 1996 Order on Motions for Summary Judgment, the District Court concluded that § 45-5-505, MCA, violates Respondents' right to privacy guaranteed by the Montana Constitution and that that invasion of privacy is not justified by any compelling state interest. The court recognized that since Respondents did not present a facial attack upon the statute, it could not declare the statute unconstitutional as to any and all sets of circumstances that might arise. However, the court issued a permanent injunction forbidding the State to enforce the statute against Respondents or any other people in the State of Montana who engage in consensual, adult, private, same-gender sexual conduct. In addressing this issue we determine, first, whether Respondents' sexual conduct prohibited by § 45-5-505, MCA, is protected by Montana's constitutional right of privacy and then, if it is protected, whether the State has demonstrated a compelling interest for infringing that right. We begin our discussion with a brief overview of the right of privacy under the federal constitution.

The federal constitution does not explicitly grant citizens the right to privacy. That right has been inferred, however, from other provisions of the constitution and is used particularly in search and seizure contexts. Justice Louis Brandeis, in his dissenting opinion in Olmstead v. United States first argued that the Fourth Amendment protected an individual's right of privacy from invasions by the government.

> The makers of our Constitution . . . conferred, as against the Government, the right to be let alone — the most comprehensive of rights and the right

> most valued by civilized men. To protect that right, every unjustifiable intrusion by the Government upon the privacy of the individual, whatever the means employed, must be deemed a violation of the Fourth Amendment.

Olmstead v. United States (1928), *overruled by Katz v. United States* (1967).

In his concurrence to the majority's opinion in *Katz*, Justice Harlan summarized the rule that has emerged from *Katz* and from prior decisions regarding privacy in the context of a search as requiring, "first that a person have exhibited an actual (subjective) expectation of privacy and, second, that the expectation be one that society is prepared to recognize as 'reasonable.'" This two-prong test was later adopted by the United States Supreme Court in its decision in *Smith v. Maryland* (1979).

In addition to a right of privacy underlying the Fourth Amendment, an aspect of privacy has been tied to an individual's liberty interest. In *Griswold v. Connecticut* (1965), the United States Supreme Court held that laws forbidding the use of contraceptive devices violated the right of marital privacy which the Court determined is within the penumbra of specific guarantees of the Bill of Rights. Six of the justices deciding Griswold recognized the right of privacy to be a fundamental right protected by the federal constitution.

While the right of privacy enunciated in *Griswold* has been recognized by the United States Supreme Court to protect certain personal decisions, other personal choices have been excluded. In *Bowers v. Hardwick* (1986), after being charged with violating a Georgia statute criminalizing sodomy by committing that act with another adult male in the privacy of his home, Hardwick brought suit to challenge the constitutionality of the statute. The United States Supreme Court determined that the federal constitution does not confer a fundamental right upon homosexuals to engage in sodomy, thus the statute was held to be constitutional. However, Justice Blackmun dissenting in *Bowers*, articulated that *Bowers* was not about the right to engage in homosexual sodomy, but rather it was about "the right to be let alone" as enunciated by Justice Brandeis' dissent in *Olmstead*.

Regardless of whether *Bowers* was correctly decided, we have long held that Montana's Constitution affords citizens broader protection of their right to privacy than does the federal constitution. See *State v. Siegal* (Mont. 1997). Unlike the federal constitution, Montana's Constitution explicitly grants to all Montana citizens the right to individual privacy. Article II, Section 10 of the Montana Constitution provides:

> Right of privacy. The right of individual privacy is essential to the well-being of a free society and shall not be infringed without the showing of a compelling state interest.

Since the right to privacy is explicit in the Declaration of Rights in Montana's Constitution, it is a fundamental right and any legislation regulating the exercise of a fundamental right must be reviewed under a strict-scrutiny analysis. To withstand a strict-scrutiny analysis, the legislation must be justified by a compelling state interest and must be narrowly tailored to effectuate only that compelling interest. ***

The State, while acknowledging the existence of an individual's right to privacy under Article II, Section 10, contends that it does not immunize adult same-gender sexual conduct from state regulation. The State maintains that the United States Supreme Court already resolved this issue in *Bowers* and that no right to privacy for this conduct exists. The State also contends that the appropriate test for determining whether a fundamental right to privacy exists is not the two-part test set out in *Katz* regarding informational privacy, but rather, a test regarding personal-autonomy privacy used by the United States Supreme Court in *Bowers* and derived from *Palko v. Connecticut* (1937), overruled on other grounds by *Benton v. Maryland* (1969). This test may be articulated as whether the statute in question "violate[s] those 'fundamental principles of liberty and justice which lie at the base of all our civil and political institutions.'" *Palko.*

We agree with the District Court that under traditional *Katz* analysis, Respondents' same-gender, consensual sexual conduct is protected by Montana's constitutional right of privacy. It cannot seriously be argued that Respondents do not have a subjective or actual expectation of privacy in their sexual activities. With few exceptions not at issue here, all adults regardless of gender, fully and properly expect that their consensual sexual activities will not be subject to the prying eyes of others or to governmental snooping or regulation. Quite simply, consenting adults expect that neither the state nor their neighbors will be co-habitants of their bedrooms. Moreover, while society may not approve of the sexual practices of homosexuals, or, for that matter, sodomy, oral intercourse or other sexual conduct between husband and wife or between other heterosexuals, that is not to say that society is unwilling to recognize that all adults, regardless of gender or marital state, at least have a reasonable expectation that their sexual activities will remain personal and private. Accordingly, we disagree with the State that the *Katz* test is inappropriate. It is, and under that test Respondents' right to privacy in their consensual, non-commercial sexual conduct is protected under Article II, Section 10 of Montana's Constitution.

As to *Palko*, this Court applied a *Palko*-derived test in *Town of Ennis v. Stewart* (Mont. 1991), along with the *Katz* test. In *Ennis*, several property owners refused to hook up to the city water system arguing that they had a privacy right to use the wells in their homes. We stated that under the federal constitution, the right to privacy has been extended only to those rights which are fundamental or implicit in the concept of ordered liberty. We held in *Ennis* that the type of interest being infringed was not the kind sufficient for defendants to invoke the special protections of their privacy right. We stated that because the right being asserted was not of constitutional magnitude the Town need not show a compelling interest to satisfy its ends, rather it need only demonstrate that the ordinance bears a rational relationship to the achievement of a legitimate state interest.

While hooking up to a private well may not be the type of interest sufficient to invoke the special protections of a privacy right, adults engaging in consensual, non-commercial sexual activities in private is sufficient. More importantly, however, regardless of whether same-gender, consensual sexual conduct is accorded federal constitutional, personal-autonomy privacy protection as a fundamental right or as a right implicit in the concept of ordered liberty, Montana's Constitution, as we have already pointed out, explicitly protects individual or personal-autonomy privacy as a fundamental right by its placement in the Declaration of Rights. In fact, it is hard to imagine any activity that adults would consider more fundamental, more private and, thus, more deserving of protection from governmental interference than non-commercial, consensual adult sexual activity.

Accordingly, whether we apply the *Katz* test or the *Palko* test, we conclude that Respondents' right of privacy under Article II, Section 10 of Montana's Constitution includes the right to engage in consensual, non-commercial, private, same-gender sexual conduct with other adults free of governmental interference or regulation.

Finally, the State points out that the delegates to the 1972 Montana Constitutional Convention defeated a proposal to include a provision in the Declaration of Rights stating that "[p]rivate sexual acts between consenting adults do not constitute a crime." The State contends that this reflects an unwillingness to protect this type of conduct, even under the privacy clause. We do not agree. The verbatim transcript of the 1972 Constitutional Convention is bereft of any discussion as to why the proposal was defeated. While the State can speculate that this reflects an unwillingness to protect this type of conduct, one can also speculate that the delegates believed it was already protected under the privacy clause.

In summary, and regardless of the sort of legal test used, we agree with the statement of the Tennessee Court of Appeals when faced with a similar question of the extent of an individual's right to privacy under the Tennessee Constitution:

> We think it is consistent with this State's Constitution and constitutional jurisprudence to hold that an adult's right to engage in consensual and non-commercial sexual activities in the privacy of that adult's home is a matter of intimate personal concern which is at the heart of Tennessee's protection of the right to privacy, and that this right should not be diminished or afforded less constitutional protection when the adults engaging in that private activity are of the same gender.

Campbell v. Sundquist (Tenn.Ct.App.1996). We hold that Respondents' sexual conduct which is prohibited by § 45-5-505, MCA, is protected by Article II, Section 10 of Montana's Constitution.

It follows then that since we have concluded that § 45-5-505, MCA, constitutes a governmental intrusion into Respondents' right to privacy, we must next determine whether the State has a compelling interest warranting this intrusion. The State contends that this compelling interest includes protecting public health by preventing the spread of the HIV-related virus and by protecting public morals.

The State's assertion that the statute protects public health by containing the spread of AIDS relies on faulty logic and invalid assumptions about the disease. To begin with, § 45-5-505, MCA, was enacted in 1973, almost ten years before the first AIDS case was detected in Montana. Despite the two-plus decades that the statute has been in effect, HIV infection is currently a significant cause of illness and death in this State, and AIDS is now the sixth leading cause of death among middle-aged Montanans.

Moreover, the State's rationale assumes that all same-gender sexual conduct contributes to the spread of the disease. This is grossly inaccurate. ***

Section 45-5-505, MCA, targets a wide range of behavior unrelated to the spread of HIV. For example, the term "sexual contact" in the statute encompasses touching, caressing and kissing, activities that do not spread HIV. Moreover, if two people are not infected with HIV, they cannot spread it, yet sexual conduct between the two is prohibited under the statute. In addition, the statute does not account for "safe" versions of the activities, i.e., use of a condom during any "sexual contact" which greatly reduces or eliminates the risk of HIV transmission. Thus, the inclusion of behavior not associated with the spread of AIDS and HIV and the exclusion of high-risk behavior among those other than homosexuals indicate the absence of any clear relationship between the statute and any public health goals. *** Accordingly, we conclude that public health goals attributed to § 45-5-505, MCA, do not support a compelling interest for the infringement of Respondents' privacy rights.

The State also argues that it has a compelling interest in protecting public morals and that § 45-5-505, MCA, advances that interest. The State contends that "societal notions" of appropriate sexual conduct provide rational grounds for § 45-5-505, MCA, and that this is simply one of many areas of the law where legislative majorities have made moral choices contrary to the desire of minorities. In a similar vein, *amicus* Montana Citizens for Decency Through Law argues that this statute is deeply rooted in the values of the citizens of this State and that the legislature's prohibition against homosexual sex is a proper exercise of the decision-making power of that branch—as opposed to the judicial branch—on what is an important political, moral and public policy issue. We disagree.

We do not deny the legislature's public policy-making power, nor do we dispute that public policy and the laws implementing it may often reflect majority will and prevailing notions of morality. Nevertheless, it is axiomatic that under our system of laws, the parameters of the legislature's policy-making power are defined by the Constitution and that its ability to regulate morals and to enact laws reflecting moral choices is not without limits. As the Tennessee Court of Appeals pointed out in *Campbell*:

> With respect to regulation of morals, the police power should properly be exercised to protect each individual's right to be free from interference in defining and pursuing his own morality but not to enforce a majority morality on persons whose conduct does not harm others. ... Indeed, what is considered to be "moral" changes with the times and is dependent upon societal background. Spiritual leadership, not the government, has the responsibility for striving to improve the morality of individuals.

We agree with the State and with amicus that it is not the function of this or of any court to interpret the law on the basis of what may be morally acceptable or unacceptable to society at any given time. It is not the judiciary's prerogative to condone or condemn a particular lifestyle and the behaviors associated therewith upon the basis of moral belief. That said, it does not follow, however, that simply because the legislature has enacted as law what may be a moral choice of the majority, the courts are, thereafter, bound to simply acquiesce. Our Constitution does not protect morality; it does, however, guarantee to all persons, whether in the majority or in a minority, those certain basic freedoms and rights which are set forth in the Declaration of Rights, not the least of which is the right of individual privacy. Regardless that majoritarian morality may be expressed in the public-policy pronouncements of the legislature, it remains the obligation of the courts—and of this Court in particular—to scrupulously support, protect and defend those rights and liberties guaranteed to all persons under our Constitution. The oath of office taken by every justice and every judge in this state (not to mention every legislator as well) demands precisely that Art. III, Sec. 3, Mont. Const.

As we have already stated, in this State, under Montana's Constitution, the right of individual privacy—that is, the right of personal autonomy or the right to be let alone—is fundamental. It is, perhaps, one of the most important rights guaranteed to the citizens of this State, and its separate textual protection in our Constitution reflects Montanans' historical abhorrence and distrust of excessive governmental interference in their personal lives. That such interference is because the majority wills it is no less pernicious.

James Madison decried the potential for a tyranny of the majority, pointing out that it was as important in our system of government to guard the minority in our society against injustice by the majority, as it was to guard society from the oppression of its rulers. The Federalist, No. 51 (James Madison). Moreover,

> [o]f all tyrannies a tyranny sincerely exercised for the good of its victims may be the most oppressive. It may be better to live under robber barons than under omnipotent moral busybodies. The robber baron's cruelty may sometimes sleep, his cupidity may at some point be satiated; but those who torment us for our own good will torment us without end for they do so with the approval of their own conscience.

C.S. Lewis, *The Humanitarian Theory of Punishment* (1970).

The right of consenting adults, regardless of gender, to engage in private, non-commercial sexual conduct strikes at the very core of Montana's constitutional right of individual privacy; and, absent an interest more compelling than a legislative distaste of what is perceived to be offensive and immoral sexual practices on the part of homosexuals, state regulation, much less criminalization, of this most intimate social relationship will not withstand constitutional scrutiny. Quite simply, while legislative enactments may reflect the will of the majority, and, arguably, may even respond to perceived societal notions of what is acceptable conduct in a moral sense, there are certain rights so fundamental that they will not be denied to a minority no matter how despised by society. In Montana, the right of privacy is such a right. While nothing in this opinion should be construed to countenance nonconsensual sexual activity, sexual contact with a minor, or any form of sexual conduct for commercial purposes, Montana's constitutional right of privacy—this right of personal autonomy and right to be let alone—includes the right of consenting adults, regardless of gender, to engage in non-commercial, private, sexual relations free of governmental interference, intrusion and condemnation.

Having concluded that § 45-5-505, MCA, constitutes a governmental intrusion into Respondents' right to privacy, guaranteed by Article II, Section 10 of Montana's Constitution, and finding no compelling state interest for such an intrusion, we hold that § 45-5-505, MCA, is unconstitutional as applied to Respondents and other consenting adults engaging in private, same-gender, non-commercial, sexual conduct, and we affirm the decision of the District Court. ***

TURNAGE, Chief Justice, concurring and dissenting.

I agree with the result of this case declaring § 45-5-505, MCA, unconstitutional. However, I dissent to the majority's ruling basing unconstitutionality on Article II, Section 10 of the Montana Constitution.

The majority has unnecessarily and unwisely used privacy as the basis for its decision. ***

The statutory scheme of the legislature clearly criminalizes sexual acts between persons of the same sex and decriminalizes the same sexual conduct engaged in by persons of opposite sexes. Clearly, this is a denial of the constitutional guarantee of equal protection of the law in violation of the Fourteenth Amendment to the United States Constitution and Article II, Section 4 of the Montana Constitution.

To be treated equally under the law is a far broader constitutional right, together with the right of due process, than any other constitutional guarantee in either the federal or state constitution.

I agree with the majority that § 45-5-505, MCA, is unconstitutional as applied to noncommercial homosexual activity engaged in by adults consensually and in private. However, unlike the majority, I would base that determination on violation of constitutional guarantees of equal protection under the Fourteenth Amendment to the United States Constitution and Article II, Section 4 of the Montana Constitution.

The Equal Protection Clause prohibits any classification scheme which fails a rational basis analysis. Under rational basis analysis, the Court's inquiry must be whether there exists a legitimate government objective which bears some identifiable rational relationship to the classification made.

As is discussed at some length in the majority opinion, § 45-5-505, MCA, bears no rational relationship to either of its suggested government purposes, as an expression of societal mores or to protect public health. As an expression of societal mores, the statute is both overbroad and under inclusive, forbidding consensual intimate touching between homosexuals without any evidence that such conduct was historically forbidden, yet permitting heterosexuals to engage in conduct long deemed inappropriate by some segments of society, such as anal sex, sex outside of marriage, and non-procreative sex. Furthermore, the State has not demonstrated, nor can it demonstrate, that the purpose of § 45-5-505, MCA, was or is to protect public health. Not one of the three public health experts who testified in this case suggested that § 45-5-505, MCA, offered any benefit to the public health.

In *Com. v. Wasson* (Ky. 1992), the Supreme Court of Kentucky struck down a statute similar to § 45-5-505, MCA, which defined as a misdemeanor criminal offense "deviate sexual intercourse with another person of the same sex." In doing so, the court reasoned:

> In the final analysis we can attribute no legislative purpose to this statute except to single out homosexuals for different treatment for indulging their sexual preference by engaging in the same activity heterosexuals are now at liberty to perform. By 1974 [when the Kentucky statute was enacted] there had already been a sea change in societal values insofar as attaching criminal penalties to extramarital sex. The question is whether a society that no longer criminalizes adultery, fornication, or deviate sexual intercourse between heterosexuals, has a rational basis to single out homosexual acts for different treatment. Is there a rational basis for declaring this one type of sexual immorality so destructive of family values as to merit criminal punishment whereas other acts of sexual immorality which were likewise forbidden by the same religious and traditional heritage of Western civilization are now decriminalized? If there is a rational basis for different treatment it has yet to be demonstrated in this case. We need not sympathize, agree with, or even understand the sexual preference of homosexuals in order to recognize their right to equal treatment before the bar of criminal justice.

No rational basis has been demonstrated for the classification created under § 45-5-505, MCA. I conclude that the statute is violative of the Equal Protection Clauses of the Montana and the United States Constitutions as applied to persons of the same sex engaging in noncommercial, consensual, private sexual conduct, and is therefore unconstitutional. I therefore dissent and specially concur that § 45-5-505, MCA, is unconstitutional as a denial of equal protection.

So much for the unnecessary reliance by the majority on Article II, Section 10 of the Montana Constitution and now as to the basis for the majority opinion being unwise.

The opinion of the majority, I submit, is an open-door invitation to challenges of legislative enactments by the people of Montana, through their constitutionally-empowered legislature, prohibiting conduct that they believe to be destructive to Montana's society as a whole. There are many such statutes on the books that not only have a rational basis but are very important to the people of Montana.

I submit that this Court should not be surprised if one of the first challenges under the theory espoused by the majority in this case will be to § 45-5-105, MCA, which provides severe criminal sanctions for a person who purposely aids or solicits another to commit suicide. The majority opinion cites with approval the District Court's statement that "a person's decision as to sexual matters is probably one of the most private areas of a person's life." This statement is correct. However, there is something in the lives of people equally private and more important — the right to life or death.

I respectfully concur as to the result and dissent as to the reasoning used by the majority.

Armstrong v. State

296 Mont. 361 (1999)

Justice JAMES C. NELSON delivered the Opinion of the Court

¶ 14 . . . [A]rticle II, Section 10 of the Montana Constitution broadly guarantees each individual the right to make medical judgments affecting her or his bodily integrity and health in partnership with a chosen health care provider free from government interference. More narrowly, we conclude that Article II, Section 10, protects a woman's right of procreative autonomy — i.e., here, the right to seek and to obtain a specific lawful medical procedure, a pre-viability abortion, from a health care provider of her choice.

¶ 15 Importantly, this case requires that we decide who should set the standards for reasonable medical practice and procedure in this State. As in the case at bar, should legislators determine these standards based upon prevailing political ideology, personal values and beliefs, and under pressure from a vocal and powerful constituency? Or, should these standards be set by the medical community in the exercise of its collective professional expertise and judgment, acting through the state's medical examining and licensing authorities, and after taking into consideration the education, training, experience and skills of the health care provider and the patient's health interests?

¶ 16 Finally, we must decide whether, in the case before us, the government has demonstrated a compelling state interest for infringing women's right of procreative autonomy guaranteed under Article II, Section 10 of the Montana Constitution. In this regard, we conclude that it has not.

Factual and Procedural Background

¶ 17 To place the challenged legislation in proper perspective, we review the history and evolution of the related statutory provisions. In response to the United States Supreme Court's decision in *Roe v. Wade* [(1973)], the Montana Legislature enacted the Montana Abortion Control Act (the Act), Title 50, Chapter 20 of the Montana Code Annotated. Included in that legislation were the following provisions:

> Control of practice of abortion. (1) No abortion may be performed within the state of Montana:
>
> (a) except by a licensed physician;
>
> (b) after the first 3 months of pregnancy, except in a hospital licensed by the department;
>
> . . .
>
> (4) No physician, facility, or other person or agency shall engage in solicitation, advertising, or other form of communication having the purpose of inviting, inducing, or attracting any person to come to such physician, facility, or other person or agency to have an abortion or to purchase abortifacients.

Section 50-20-109, MCA (1991).

¶ 18 In December 1992, Arlette Randash (Randash), Executive Director of the Montana Right to Life Association, and Charles Lorentzen (Lorentzen), President of Flathead Pro-Life, began writing letters to various individuals in state and local government arguing that criminal charges should be brought against Dr. Armstrong and P.A. Cahill. In a December 7, 1992 letter to then Attorney General Marc Racicot, Randash asked Racicot to investigate the performance of abortions by a physician assistant working at Dr. Armstrong's office and for Racicot to inform Randash of his findings. Randash alleged that the abortions were being performed in violation of § 50-20-109, MCA.

¶ 19 In March 1993, Lorentzen sent similar letters regarding Dr. Armstrong to Racicot, who by then was Governor of Montana, to Flathead County Attorney Tom Esch, and to Eleanor Parker, Montana Department of Health and Environmental Sciences counsel. Lorentzen alleged that Dr. Armstrong had violated the Act, specifically §§ 50-20-109(1)(a), (b) and (4), MCA. Parker referred the letter to Attorney General Joe Mazurek who referred the matter to Esch. On April 9, 1993, Esch asked Detective Ron Fredenberg of the Kalispell Police Department to investigate the performance of abortions at Dr. Armstrong's office by a person other than a licensed physician and the performance of second-trimester abortions outside of a hospital.

¶ 20 Dr. Armstrong and P.A. Cahill, the only physician assistant in the State performing abortions, challenged various provisions of the Act in federal court. Subsequently, the State stipulated to a permanent injunction prohibiting enforcement of Montana's requirement that abortions be performed only by licensed physicians as well as a permanent injunction against the second-trimester hospitalization requirement and the ban on advertising.

¶ 21 In 1995, Representative Susan Smith (Smith) of Kalispell, sponsored House Bill 442 to amend § 37-20-103, MCA (a portion of the Montana Code regulating physician assistants-certified), and § 50-20-109, MCA, to specifically exclude physician assistants-certified from performing abortions. Ch. 321, L.1995. Thus, as noted by

District Judge Sherlock, these amendments trace their genesis to the complaints and demands addressed to county and state officials by certain anti-abortion groups operating in the Flathead Valley of northwestern Montana.

¶ 22 Smith contended in hearings before the House Committee on Human Services and Aging, and the Senate Committee on Public Health, Welfare & Safety, that HB 442 was intended to protect women who are seeking abortions from possible complications and that the legislation was a women's health and safety issue. However, at the hearings, Smith and other proponents of the legislation failed to relate any complications or problems encountered by patients of P.A. Cahill during the more than twenty years that P.A. Cahill has been performing abortions.

¶ 23 Furthermore, those testifying in support of HB 442 during the February 10, 1995 hearing before the House Committee on Human Services and Aging, and the March 10, 1995 hearing before the Senate Committee on Public Health, Welfare and Safety, failed to give any medical justification for excluding physician assistants-certified from performing abortions. Moreover, none of the proponents of HB 442 testifying before the House Committee and only one of the proponents of HB 442 testifying before the Senate Committee was a licensed physician. Instead, those testifying in favor of HB 442 included representatives of the Montana Right to Life Association, the Montana Catholic Conference, and Eagle Forum, as well as the Executive Director of the Montana Christian Coalition.

¶ 24 Opponents of HB 442 testified that, since there were no medical reasons why physician assistants-certified could not perform abortions, HB 442 was just another obstacle to affordable health care for women. Those testifying against HB 442 included both current and former members of the Montana Board of Medical Examiners, the Executive Director of the American Civil Liberties Union of Montana, and the President of the Montana Academy of Physician Assistants, as well as representatives of the Montana Women's Lobby, the Montana Business and Professional Women's Association, the Center for Reproductive Law and Policy, and the National Abortion and Reproductive Rights Action League.

¶ 25 HB 442 was passed by the Montana Legislature and signed into law by Governor Racicot on April 3, 1995. Through the passage of this bill, § 37-20-103, MCA, was amended to include the following sentence: "A physician assistant-certified may not perform an abortion." And, § 50-20-109, MCA, was amended to include a new subsection (5) that provides: "The utilization plan of a physician assistant-certified may not provide for performing abortions." In addition, such conduct was criminalized as a felony. Section 50-20-109(6), MCA. Passage of HB 442 also effectively re-enacted the provisions requiring second trimester abortions to be performed in a hospital and banning advertising.

¶ 26 Dr. Armstrong and P.A. Cahill, along with various other abortion providers, responded to the amendment of § 37-20-103, MCA, and § 50-20-109, MCA, by filing suit in federal court to prevent enforcement of the amended statutes regarding physician assistants. They also sought to prevent the enforcement of the second trimester hospitalization requirement and the ban on advertising which were re-enacted by the amendment of the statute. The trial court enjoined enforcement of the re-enacted abortion restrictions, but declined to grant a preliminary injunction against enforcement of the ban on Dr. Armstrong's utilization of P.A. Cahill to perform abortions. *Armstrong v. Mazurek* (D.Mont.1995).

¶ 27 On appeal, the Ninth Circuit vacated the District Court's denial of a preliminary injunction against enforcement of the statutes restricting the performance of abortions to licensed physicians and remanded the case to the District Court. *Armstrong v. Mazurek* (9th Cir.1996). On November 5, 1996, the State consented to an injunction against enforcement of the Act while the State sought review by the United States Supreme Court. The Supreme Court, by a 6-3 vote, determined that Plaintiffs failed to establish the likelihood of prevailing on the merits of their claim that the statutory provisions violated due process by imposing an undue burden on a woman's right to choose to terminate a pregnancy prior to the viability of the fetus, and thus, Plaintiffs were not entitled to preliminary injunctive relief. *Mazurek v. Armstrong* (1997).

¶ 28 On October 1, 1997, following the Supreme Court's ruling, Respondents filed the instant case in the District Court for the First Judicial District, Lewis and Clark County, contending that HB 442 violated Montana's constitutional provisions regarding privacy, due process, and equal protection of the laws. On November 25, 1997, the District Court granted Plaintiffs' motion for a preliminary injunction, but limited the scope of the injunction to Dr. Armstrong and P.A. Cahill. The District Court found that the Act affects a woman's constitutional right to obtain a first trimester abortion and that the State had advanced no compelling interest to justify prohibiting P.A. Cahill from performing abortions as she has safely done for the past twenty years. The State appeals the court's order granting Plaintiffs' motion for a preliminary injunction.

Discussion

I.

¶ 29 Article II, Section 10 of the Montana Constitution provides:

> Right of privacy. The right of individual privacy is essential to the well-being of a free society and shall not be infringed without the showing of a compelling state interest.

¶ 30 Modern legal notions of the right of privacy trace their roots to the political theory of English philosopher John Locke. Locke's concept of "liberty" was prevalent in colonial America and significantly influenced the framers of this country's foundation documents, including the United States Constitution. Among other things, this philosophy holds that the laws of nature require that each individual has an inherent property interest in his own person and has the capacity for and the right of rational self-determination which must be promoted and protected by civil society and political institutions. *See* Larry M. Elison and Dennis NettikSimmons,

Right of Privacy, 48 Mont. L.Rev. 1, 17–19 (1987) (hereafter, Elison); Jeffrey S. Koehlinger, *Substantive Due Process Analysis and the Lockean Liberal Tradition: Rethinking the Modern Privacy Cases*, 65 Ind. L.J. 723 (1990).

¶ 31 John Stuart Mill recognized this fundamental right of self-determination and personal autonomy as both a limitation on the power of the government and as principle of preeminent deference to the individual. He stated:

> [T]he only purpose for which power can be rightfully exercised over any member of a civilised [sic] community, against his will, is to prevent harm to others. His own good, either physical or moral, is not a sufficient warrant. He cannot rightfully be compelled to do or forbear because, it will be better for him to do so, because it will make him happier, because, in the opinion of others, to do so would be wise, or even right.

Mill, *On Liberty*, 43 Great Books of the Western World 271 (R. Hutchins ed.1952) (quoted in *Brophy v. New England Sinai Hospital* (1986).

¶ 32 Despite prior judicial recognition of this general "liberty interest" or right of privacy by both the United States Supreme Court and this Court, the delegates to Montana's 1972 Constitutional Convention viewed the textual inclusion of this right in Montana's new constitution as being necessary for the protection of the individual in "an increasingly complex society . . . [in which] our area of privacy has decreased, decreased, decreased." This "right to be let alone . . . the most important right of them all," as Delegate Campbell put it, "produces . . . a semipermeable wall of separation between individual and state" in much the same fashion that a constitutional wall separates church and state. Montana Constitutional Convention, Verbatim Transcript, March 7, 1972, p. 1681.

¶ 33 Furthermore, it is clear from their debates that the delegates intended this right of privacy to be expansive — that it should encompass more than traditional search and seizure. The right of privacy should also address information gathering and protect citizens from illegal private action and from legislation and governmental practices that interfere with the autonomy of each individual to make decisions in matters generally considered private. Elison, at 11–13.

¶ 34 With this background, and as correctly noted by Judge Sherlock, Montana adheres to one of the most stringent protections of its citizens' right to privacy in the United States — exceeding even that provided by the federal constitution. Indeed, since the right of privacy is explicit in the Declaration of Rights of Montana's Constitution, it is a fundamental right. *Gryczan v. State* (Mont. 1997). It is,

> perhaps, one of the most important rights guaranteed to the citizens of this State, and its separate textual protection in our Constitution reflects Montanans' historical abhorrence and distrust of excessive governmental interference in their personal lives.

For this reason, legislation infringing the exercise of the right of privacy must be reviewed under a strict-scrutiny analysis — i.e., the legislation must be justified by a compelling state interest and must be narrowly tailored to effectuate only that compelling interest.

II.

¶ 35 As noted, Article II, Section 10 of the Montana Constitution was intended by the delegates to protect citizens from illegal private action and from legislation and governmental practices that interfere with the autonomy of each individual to make decisions in matters generally considered private. However, it was not until our decision in *Gryczan* that this Court directly addressed and judicially recognized this "personal autonomy" component of Montanans' fundamental constitutional right of individual privacy. *See also* Elison, at 13 n. 83; Scott A. Fisk, *The Last Best Place to Die: Physician-Assisted Suicide and Montana's Constitutional Right to Personal Autonomy Privacy*, 59 Mont.L.Rev. 301, 323–25 (1998) (hereafter, Fisk). In *Gryczan*, we held that the personal autonomy component of the right of individual privacy includes the right of consenting adults to engage in private, same-gender, non-commercial sexual conduct free from governmental interference, intrusion and condemnation. Beyond that, however, we made no attempt to define personal autonomy as a component of the right of individual privacy or to articulate its scope.

¶ 36 While some suggest that this was an oversight — see Fisk, at 326 — neither did the delegates to Montana's Constitutional Convention attempt to circumscribe the right to privacy. Rather the Bill of Rights Committee proposed "a broad provision . . . to permit flexibility to the courts in resolving the tensions between public interest and privacy." As Delegate Campbell noted:

> We had much discussion before [the Bill of Rights Committee], and why not try to define the right, to put in specific examples. But it was our feeling that once you do that, you are running a risk that you may eliminate other areas in the future which may be developed by the court.

In truth, that the Convention delegates deliberately drafted a broad and undefined right of "individual" [fn. 5 "A term added on the floor of the Convention."] privacy was more a testament to and culmination of Montanans' continuous and zealous protection of a core sphere of personal autonomy and dignity than it was an attempt to create a greater right than that which already existed by historical precedent. *See* William C. Rava, *Toward a Historical Understanding of Montana's Privacy Provisions*, 61 Alb. L.Rev. 1681, 1716–17 (1998).

¶ 37 Yet, defining personal autonomy has and continues to challenge courts, philosophers and authors. For example, the United States Supreme Court has stated that the right involves "intimate and personal choices" that concern "the right to define one's own concept of existence, of meaning, of the universe, and of the mystery of human life," *Planned Parenthood v. Casey* (1992). It may also be that, as Fisk suggests, personal autonomy encompasses

> [t]he complex human capacities that . . . include language, self-consciousness, memory, logical relations, empirical reasoning about beliefs and their

> validity (human intelligence), and the capacity to use normative principles . . . [and] . . . rational choice, to decide which among several ends may be most effectively and coherently realized.

Fisk, at 327 (*quoting* David A.J. Richards, *Sex, Drugs, Death and the Law* 8 (1982)). Or, more simply, as John Stuart Mill stated: "Over himself, over his own body and mind, the individual is sovereign." Mill, *On Liberty* (*quoted in Thor v. Superior Court* (Cal. 1993)).

¶ 38 Attempts to define this right notwithstanding, we conclude that, while it may not be absolute, no final boundaries can be drawn around the personal autonomy component of the right of individual privacy. It is, at one and the same time, as narrow as is necessary to protect against a specific unlawful infringement of individual dignity and personal autonomy by the government—as in *Gryczan*—and as broad as are the State's ever innovative attempts to dictate in matters of conscience, to define individual values, and to condemn those found to be socially repugnant or politically unpopular.

III.

¶ 39 And that brings us to the matter at bar: broadly, the right of each individual to make medical judgments affecting her or his bodily integrity and health in partnership with a chosen health care provider free from the interference of the government; and, more narrowly, a woman's right to seek and obtain pre-viability abortion services. The former is protected under the personal autonomy component of the fundamental right of individual privacy set out in Article II, Section 10 of the Montana Constitution. The latter—procreative autonomy—is a protected form of personal autonomy. Since the primary focus of this case is the latter, we begin with that.

¶ 40 There is no doubt that a woman's right to choose to have an abortion before fetal viability and to obtain it without "undue interference" or "undue burden" from the state is protected under the federal constitution. *Planned Parenthood.* This federal constitutional right is grounded in privacy and is protected under the Due Process Clause of the Fourteenth Amendment. *Roe*; *Planned Parenthood.*

¶ 41 Notwithstanding, and independently of the federal constitution, where the right of individual privacy is implicated, Montana's Constitution affords significantly broader protection than does the federal constitution. Article II, Section 10, requires more than that the State simply not impose an undue burden on a person's exercise of his or her right of individual privacy. Rather, under Montana's Constitution, the government must demonstrate a "compelling state interest" for infringing this right. [Fn. 6 We have not, heretofore, specifically defined what makes a state interest "compelling," rather, leaving that determination to be made case by case. . . . Some inkling of the Constitutional Convention's view of how serious a situation must exist before the government has a "compelling" interest for infringing the right of individual privacy can be gleaned from delegate comment of electronic surveillance. There, Delegate Dahood noted that, if it should ever be allowed at all, "electronic surveillance shall be justified only in matters involving national security, perhaps in matters involving certain heinous federal crimes where the situation is such that in those instances we must risk the right of individual privacy because there is a greater purpose to be served."]

¶ 42 Judge Sherlock determined that "if the right to privacy includes anything, it includes the decision of a woman whether or not to beget or bear a child . . . [and it] encompasses a woman's choice of whether or not to end her pregnancy." The court was correct in this statement of the law as derived from federal authorities. *See Eisenstadt v. Baird* (1972); *Roe*. Facially, then, procreative autonomy being grounded in the right of privacy, there is no reason why this right would not also be encompassed within the broader personal autonomy protections afforded by the fundamental right of individual privacy guaranteed by Article II, Section 10 of the Montana Constitution.

¶ 43 The State in this case disagrees, however. Rather, it contends that Montana's Constitution does not protect women's right to obtain a pre-viability abortion and that this right is subject to legislative determination and regulation within the parameters of the weaker protections afforded by the federal constitution and federal law. The State argues that Article II, Section 10, excepts a woman's choice to obtain a pre-viability abortion because of the Constitutional Convention's rejection of Delegate Kelleher's attempt to confer constitutionally protected status on a fetus at the time of conception. The government is wrong.

¶ 44 Significantly, the Convention determined not to deal with abortion in the Bill [Declaration] of Rights "at this time" and rather chose to leave the matter to the legislature because of the historical debate as to "when a person becomes a person." *Roe*, handed down a year after the Convention, resolved this debate from the legal standpoint, concluding that a fetus does not enjoy a constitutionally protected status—i.e., that a fetus is not a constitutional person—until "viability" (at about 26 weeks or the third trimester). *See* . . . Ronald Dworkin, *Freedom's Law: The Moral Reading of the American Constitution* 87–90 (1996) (hereafter, Dworkin, Freedom).

¶ 45 Importantly, there is nothing in the Constitutional Convention debates which would logically lead to the conclusion that Article II, Section 10, does not protect, generally, the autonomy of the individual to make personal medical decisions and to seek medical care in partnership with a chosen health care provider free of government interference. Nor is there any reason to conclude, in light of *Roe* and post-*Roe* cases, that a woman's right to obtain a pre-viability abortion—part and parcel of her right of personal/procreative autonomy—likewise would not be encompassed within the protection of Montana's constitutional right of individual privacy. In fact, given the delegates' overriding concern that government not be allowed to interfere in matters generally considered private, and given the delegates' specific determination to adopt a broad and undefined right of individual privacy grounded in Montana's historical tradition of protecting personal autonomy and dignity, the opposite conclusion must be reached.

¶ 46 This determination is further supported by the Bill of Rights Committee's favorable reference to *Griswold v. Connecticut*, underlying its determination that the judicially-recognized right of privacy be elevated to explicit constitutional status. *Griswold* acknowledged the privacy interest inherent in contraception and procreation. Moreover, *Griswold* has been recognized to protect both "the individual interest in avoiding [accumulation and] disclosure of personal matters, and . . . the interest in independence in making certain kinds of important [personal] decisions," *Whalen v. Roe* (1977), including those "relating to marriage, procreation, contraception, family relationships, and child rearing and education," *Paul v. Davis* (1976).

¶ 47 Similarly, in the floor debates, Delegate Campbell, emphasizing Montana's historical commitment to the right of privacy and arguing for the core "right to be let alone," cited *Griswold*. [Fn. 7 Delegate Campbell also referred to the 1890 law review article on privacy authored by Samuel Warren and Louis Brandeis (*The Right to Privacy*, 4 Harv. L. Rev. 193, 195, 205 (1890)), which asserted that the right of privacy encompasses "[t]houghts, emotions, and sensations" and the principle "of an inviolate personality"—concepts which deeply influenced the later development of American privacy jurisprudence. These references to *Griswold* in the proceedings of the Constitutional Convention are important because

> *Griswold* and [] other [federal] privacy decisions can be justified only on the presumption that decisions affecting marriage and childbirth are so intimate and personal that people must in principle be allowed to make these decisions for themselves, consulting their own preferences and convictions, rather than having society impose its collective decision on them.

Ronald Dworkin, *Life's Dominion: An Argument About Abortion, Euthanasia, And Individual Freedom* 106 (First Vintage Books ed. 1994) (hereafter, Dworkin, Life's Dominion). Moreover,

> [t]he Supreme Court, in denying the state the specific power to make contraception criminal, presupposed the more general principle of procreative autonomy. . . . The law's integrity demands that the principles necessary to support an authoritative set of judicial decisions must be accepted in other contexts as well. It might seem an appealing political compromise to apply the principle of procreative autonomy to contraception, which almost no one now thinks states can forbid, but not to abortion, which powerful constituencies violently oppose. But the point of integrity—the point of the law itself—is exactly to rule out political compromises of that kind.

Dworkin, *Life's Dominion*, at 158.

¶ 48 Accordingly, given Montana's broad, yet undefined, concept of individual privacy—historically predating even the 1972 Constitution; given the Constitutional Convention's unmistakable intent to textualize this tradition by explicitly protecting citizens from legislation and governmental practices that interfere with the autonomy of each individual to make decisions in matters generally considered private; given the Convention's reliance on *Griswold*; and given jurisprudential recognition, following the close of the Constitutional Convention, of a woman's right to seek and obtain a pre-viability abortion, it is clear that the procreative autonomy component of personal autonomy is protected by Montana's constitutional right of individual privacy found at Article II, Section 10.

¶ 49 Implicit in this right of procreative autonomy is a woman's moral right and moral responsibility to decide, up to the point of fetal viability, what her pregnancy demands of her in the context of her individual values, her beliefs as to the sanctity of life, and her personal situation. Moreover, the State has no more compelling interest or constitutional justification for interfering with the exercise of this right if the woman chooses to terminate her pre-viability pregnancy than it would if she chose to carry the fetus to term. Recognition of this point is important—especially for those who reject abortion. For if the State has the power to infringe the right of procreative autonomy in favor of birth, then, necessarily, it also has the power to require abortion under some circumstances. If one accepts the former, then imposition of the latter is no more remote than a change in prevailing political ideology.

¶ 50 And, if the reader finds this farfetched or shocking, consider that in 1927 the United States Supreme Court ruled that eugenics by involuntary sterilization of the mentally retarded was constitutionally permissible. According to that Court, "[i] t is better for all the world, if instead of waiting to execute degenerate offspring for crime, or to let them starve for their imbecility, society can prevent those who are manifestly unfit from continuing their kind." *Buck v. Bell* (1927). Or, consider the United States Congressional Office of Technology Assessment's 1988 discussion of "Social and Ethical Considerations" raised by the Human Genome Project:

> Human mating that proceeds without the use of genetic data about the risks of transmitting diseases will produce greater mortality and medical costs than if carriers of potentially deleterious genes are alerted to their status and encouraged to mate with noncarriers or to use artificial insemination or other reproductive strategies.

See George J. Annas, *Standard of Care: The Law of American Bioethics* 156 (1993) (quoting U.S. Congress, Office of Technology Assessment, *Mapping Our Genes: Genome Projects, How Big, How Fast?* 84 (U.S. Govt. Print Office 1988)).

¶ 51 Unless fundamental constitutional rights—procreative autonomy being the present example—are grounded in something more substantial than the prevailing political winds, Huxley's Brave New World or Orwell's 1984 will always be as close as the next election. Fortunately, as demonstrated above, the roots of Montana's constitutional right of procreative autonomy go much deeper and are firmly embedded in the right of individual privacy guaranteed under Article II, Section 10 of the Montana Constitution.

IV.

¶ 52 Similarly, in the broader context of one's right to choose or refuse medical treatment, we must likewise conclude that these sorts of decisions are protected under the personal autonomy component of the individual privacy guarantees of Montana's Constitution. And properly so.

¶ 53 Few matters more directly implicate personal autonomy and individual privacy than medical judgments affecting one's bodily integrity and health. Joel Feinberg, a philosophy professor at the University of Arizona, describes the interrelationship between privacy and personal or "bodily" autonomy as follows:

> After all, we speak of "bodily autonomy," and acknowledge its violation in cases of assault, battery, rape, and so on. But surely our total autonomy includes more than simply our bodily "territory," and even in respect to it, more is involved than simple immunity to uninvited contacts and invasions. Not only is my bodily autonomy violated by a surgical operation ("invasion") imposed on me against my will; it is also violated in some circumstances by the withholding of the physical treatment I request (when due allowance has been made for the personal autonomy of the parties of whom the request is made). For to say that I am sovereign over my bodily territory is to say that I, and I alone, decide (so long as I am capable of deciding) what goes on there. My authority is a discretionary competence, an authority to choose and make decisions.

3 Joel Feinberg, *Harm to Self* 53 (1986). *See also* Fisk, at 326–27.

¶ 54 Indeed, medical treatment decisions

> are, to an extraordinary degree, intrinsically personal. It is the individual making the decision, and no one else, who lives with the pain and disease. It is the individual making the decision, and no one else, who must undergo or forego the treatment. And it is the individual making the decision, and no one else, who, if he or she survives, must live with the results of that decision. One's health is a uniquely personal possession. The decision of how to treat that possession is of a no less personal nature.
>
> ... The decision can either produce or eliminate physical, psychological, and emotional ruin. It can destroy one's economic stability. It is, for some, the difference between a life of pain and a life of pleasure. It is, for others, the difference between life and death.

Andrews v. Ballard (D.C.S.D. Tex. 1980) (holding that the decision to obtain or reject medical treatment is encompassed by the right of privacy and that, absent evidence showing that they were narrowly drawn to achieve a compelling state interest, Texas regulations requiring acupuncturists to be licensed physicians imposed a burden on and significantly interfered with the patient's decision to obtain acupuncture treatment and were, therefore, unconstitutional).

¶ 55 Recognition of these inherent rights to make medical judgments affecting one's bodily integrity and health and the right to choose and to refuse medical treatment are certainly not creatures of recent invention, however. Rather, like America's historical legal tradition acknowledging the fundamental common law right of self-determination, acceptance of the right to make personal medical decisions as inherent in personal autonomy is a long-standing and an integral part of this country's jurisprudence.

¶ 56 Over a century ago, the Supreme Court observed:

> No right is held more sacred, or is more carefully guarded by the common law, than the right of every individual to the possession and control of his own person, free from all restraint or interference of others, unless by clear and unquestionable authority of law.

Union Pacific Railway Co. v. Botsford (1891). Eighty-five years ago, Justice Cardozo noted that, "[e]very human being of adult years and sound mind has a right to determine what shall be done with his own body." *Schloendorff v. Society of New York Hosp.* (N.Y. 1914), overruled in part by *Bing v. Thunig* (N.Y. 1957). And, more recently, the Supreme Court has reaffirmed that the right to control fundamental medical decisions is an aspect of the right of self-determination and personal autonomy that is "deeply rooted in this Nation's history and tradition." *Moore v. City of East Cleveland* (1977).

¶ 57 In the context of "informed consent" cases, Montana, too, has recognized that each individual is the sovereign of his or her own body. *Collins v. Itoh* (Mont. 1972) ("Each man is considered master of his own body and may request or prohibit even lifesaving surgery. The law will not allow a physician to substitute his own judgment, no matter how well founded, for that of his patient.") (citing *Natanson v. Kline* (Mont. 1960)). *See also* Dworkin, *Freedom*, at 134 ("The law of most American states seems settled that the autonomy of a competent patient will be decisive . . . and that doctors may not treat him against his will either for his sake or for the sake of some social interest in keeping him alive").

V.

¶ 58 Acknowledging these precepts of patient autonomy, however, is not to deny the obvious—that medical decisions affecting one's bodily integrity and health must often and necessarily be made in partnership with a health care provider. In those instances, the individual typically seeks out and may consent to the most risky and intimate invasions of body and psyche, largely upon her or his personal trust in the education, training, experience, advice, and professional integrity of the health care provider he or she has chosen. This truism points up the seriousness of the infringement of personal autonomy and privacy that accompanies the government usurping, through laws or regulations which dictate how and by whom a specific medical procedure is to be performed, the patient's own informed health care decisions made in partnership with his or her chosen health care provider.

¶ 59 Certainly, this right of choice in making personal health care decisions and in exercising personal autonomy is not without limits. In narrowly defined instances the state, by clear and convincing evidence, may demonstrate a compelling interest in and obligation to legislate or regulate to preserve the safety, health and welfare of a particular class of patients or the general public from a medically-acknowledged, bona fide health risk. Subject to this narrow qualification, however, the legislature has neither a legitimate presence nor voice in the patient/health care provider relationship superior to the patient's right of personal autonomy which protects that relationship from infringement by the state.

¶ 60 Worse, when, as in the case at bar, the legislature thrusts itself into this protected zone of individual privacy under the guise of protecting the patient's health, but, in reality, does so because of prevailing political ideology and the unrelenting pressure from individuals and organizations promoting their own beliefs and values, then the state's infringement of personal autonomy is not only constitutionally impermissible, it is, as well, intellectually and morally indefensible.

¶ 61 Long ago, this Court declared that "the State Constitution is a limitation upon the power of the legislature and not a grant of power to that body." *State v. Aronson* (Mont. 1957) (citing *State ex rel. DuFresne v. Leslie* (Mont. 1935)). Just as the government has no business in the bedrooms of consenting adults, *Gryczan*, neither does it have any business in the treatment rooms of their health care providers, except under the very narrowly defined circumstances referred to above.

¶ 62 Simply put, except in the face of a medically-acknowledged, bona fide health risk, clearly and convincingly demonstrated, the legislature has no interest, much less a compelling one, to justify its interference with an individual's fundamental privacy right to obtain a particular lawful medical procedure from a health care provider that has been determined by the medical community to be competent to provide that service and who has been licensed to do so. To this end, it also logically and necessarily follows that legal standards for medical practice and procedure cannot be based on political ideology, but, rather, must be grounded in the methods and procedures of science and in the collective professional judgment, knowledge and experience of the medical community acting through the state's medical examining and licensing authorities.

VI.

¶ 63 The case at bar, unfortunately, exemplifies the gross violation of these principles. Based upon P.A. Cahill's education, training and experience, the Board of Medical Examiners, in its professional judgment, determined that, under the supervision of a licensed physician, she was competent to perform certain types of abortions and other even more risky medical procedures. In the District Court, the government failed utterly to demonstrate why this determination was wrong or that the State had a compelling interest for effectively infringing the right of procreative autonomy of women to obtain a pre-viability abortion and their right of personal autonomy to choose P.A. Cahill, under the supervision of Dr. Armstrong, to perform this lawful medical procedure.

¶ 64 Rather, the record shows that the legislature chose to prohibit P.A. Cahill from performing abortions, yet made no attempt to prohibit her from performing other more risky medical procedures such as uncomplicated deliveries of babies, inserting IUDs, and prescribing and administering most drugs. The record also shows that the legislature chose to prohibit P.A. Cahill from executing various procedures at the direction of the doctor performing a medical abortion, yet did not prohibit registered nurses or others with less training than P.A. Cahill from executing those same procedures. The record shows that P.A. Cahill has been performing abortions with the approval of the Montana Board of Medical Examiners since 1983; that she has performed approximately 3,000 abortions; that she has never been sued for malpractice or disciplined; and that Dr. Armstrong's rate of complications for patients obtaining abortions from him is the same as the rate for patients obtaining abortions from P.A. Cahill. The record shows, and Judge Sherlock found, that "[t]here is simply no evidence to support the contention that this practice by Cahill and Armstrong in any way endangers women's health." In short, the record shows that "protecting women's health" served as little more than a rhetorical guise for enacting the 1995 amendments to § 37-20-103, MCA, and § 50-20-109, MCA, and that this legislation was not justified by any constitutionally legitimate interest of the State, compelling or otherwise.

¶ 65 Indeed, the history of the 1995 amendments to § 37-20-103, MCA, and § 50-20-109, MCA, and the record of this case demonstrate how unrelenting pressure from individuals and organizations promoting their own particular values influence politicians to legislate, often via the back door, in matters of personal conscience, belief and choice and, concomitantly, infringe the zone of personal autonomy and procreative autonomy protected by the right of individual privacy. The reality of this case is that, while the legislature could not make pre-viability abortions facially unlawful, it could, and did — under the facade of "protecting women's health" and the lesser "undue burden" test of Planned Parenthood — attempt to make it as difficult, as inconvenient and as costly as possible for women to exercise their right to obtain, from the health care provider of their choice, a specific medical procedure protected by the Due Process Clause of the federal constitution and, independently of the Fourteenth Amendment, protected by their greater right of individual privacy under Article II, Section 10 of the Montana Constitution. Furthermore, that the 1995 amendments to § 37-20-103, MCA, and § 50-20-109, MCA, may have been narrowly drawn is irrelevant, where, as here, there was no predicate compelling state interest justifying the amendments in the first place.

¶ 66 There is simply no evidence in the record of this case that laws requiring pre-viability abortions be performed only by a physician to the exclusion of a trained, experienced and medically competent physician assistant-certified, working under the supervision of a licensed physician, are necessary to protect the life, health or safety of women in this State. Indeed, there is overwhelming evidence to the contrary and that the 1995 amendments to § 37-20-103, MCA, and § 50-20-109, MCA, were the product of and grounded in nothing other than the divisive and vocal politics of abortion.

VII.

A.

¶ 67 That said, we close with two final observations. First, from our foregoing discussion, it should be apparent that this opinion is about the government's infringement of certain fundamental rights of individual privacy—personal and procreative autonomy—guaranteed under Article II, Section 10 of the Montana Constitution. From this same discussion, it should be equally obvious, what this opinion is not about. For the reasons hereafter set forth, the latter needs to be underscored, nonetheless. This opinion is not a comment, pro or con, on the merits of sectarian doctrine or on the deep and sincerely held personal beliefs, values and convictions of those who either favor abortion or who oppose it on moral or religious grounds.

¶ 68 Unfortunately, however, it is these doctrines, values, beliefs and convictions which invariably fuel the hurricane of legal debate on this issue. And that, of course, is precisely the problem. The government can demonstrate no compelling interest for legislating on the basis of any sectarian doctrine nor may the state infringe individual liberty and personal autonomy because of majoritarian demands to safeguard some intrinsic value unrelated to the protection of the rights and interests of persons with constitutional status. The fundamental right to personal and procreative autonomy and, in the broader sense, to individual privacy, prohibits the government from dictating, approving or condemning values, beliefs and matters ultimately involving individual conscience, where opinions about the nature of such values and beliefs are seriously divided; where, at their core, such values and beliefs reflect essentially religious convictions that are fundamental to moral personality; and where the government's decision has a greatly disparate impact on the persons whose individual beliefs and personal commitments are displaced by the State's legislated values. *See* Dworkin, *Life's Dominion*, at 157; Dworkin, *Freedom*, at 101–102.

¶ 69 That is not to say that matters involving religious values and individual conscience are not appropriately addressed by churches, other organizations and individuals in both sectarian and secular forums. Indeed, such expression aimed at changing individual values and convictions and at fostering respect for the intrinsic value of all life is protected by the First Amendment and, independently of the federal constitution, by Article II, Sections 5 and 7 of the Montana Constitution. However the doctrine of separation of church and state which is also embodied in the First Amendment and, independently, in Article II, Section 5, makes theology an impermissible basis on which to make law or interpret the Constitution. Religious arguments do not count as legal arguments. *See* Dworkin, *Life's Dominion*, at 110.

¶ 70 For this reason, and without abandoning their own personal beliefs and convictions, those in government who make, execute and interpret the law and who are sworn to support, protect and defend the Constitution may not, except in violation of their oaths of office, succumb to the pressure of those who would engraft the sectarian tenets and personal values of some onto the laws which govern all.

B.

¶ 71 Our second observation concerns the manner in which the matters discussed in this opinion arise under Montana's Constitution. In keeping with the way in which the issues were argued to and decided by the trial court, we have directed our focus in this opinion to the right of individual privacy found at Article II, Section 10. It bears noting, however, that Montana's Constitution, and especially the Declaration of Rights, is not simply a cook book of disconnected and discrete rules written with the vitality of an automobile insurance policy. Rather, our Constitution, and in particular its Declaration of Rights, encompasses a cohesive set of principles, carefully drafted and committed to an abstract ideal of just government. It is a compact of overlapping and redundant rights and guarantees. *See* Dworkin, *Freedom*; Dworkin, *Life's Dominion*. Thus, the rights of personal and procreative autonomy at issue here also find protection in more than just Article II, Section 10. Without attempting to exhaustively plumb the depths of the Constitution in this regard, several provisions of the Declaration of Rights deserve mention.

¶ 72 Respect for the dignity of each individual—a fundamental right, protected by Article II, Section 4 of the Montana Constitution—demands that people have for themselves the moral right and moral responsibility to confront the most fundamental questions about the meaning and value of their own lives and the intrinsic value of life in general, answering to their own consciences and convictions. Equal protection, also protected by Article II, Section 4, requires that people have an equal right to form and to follow their own values in profoundly spiritual matters. *See* Dworkin, *Life's Dominion*, at 165–67. Article II, Section 3, guarantees each person the inalienable right to seek safety, health and happiness in all lawful ways—i.e., in the context of this case, the right to seek and obtain medical care from a chosen health care provider and to make personal judgments affecting one's own health and bodily integrity without government interference. As already noted, Article II, Sections 5 and 7, protect, respectively, the freedom to accept or reject any religious doctrine, including those about abortion, and the right to express one's opinion in all lawful ways and forums. The right to due process of law, Article II, Section 17, protects those rights—including rights of personal and procreative autonomy—inherent in the historical concept of "ordered liberty." Finally, the right of individual privacy guaranteed by Article II, Section 10, requires the government to leave us alone in all these most personal and private matters.

¶ 73 Having made this observation, though, we must also note that each person's enjoyment of these various constitutional rights is not without a corresponding cost. In fact, Article II, Section 3, requires that those enjoying the inalienable rights set forth in that section "recognize corresponding responsibilities." Whatever may be this cost or corresponding responsibility, however, it does not include the demonization of women who choose to terminate their pregnancies at a time the law allows nor does it mandate the criminalization of providers of abortion services to these women. Likewise, this cost does not require the denigration and condemnation of those who, as a matter of their own good consciences, either favor or reject abortion.

Most importantly, this cost does not permit the government's infringement of personal and procreative autonomy in the name of political ideology.

¶ 74 Rather, the price—the corresponding responsibility—for our commitment to the values and ideals of just government and for our enjoyment of our individual rights protected by Montana's Constitution is simply tolerance. And indeed, that is a token sum for, among other freedoms, the right to be let alone.

Summary

¶ 75 We hold that the core constitutional right infringed by the legislation at issue in the case at bar is the fundamental right of individual privacy guaranteed to every person under Article II, Section 10 of the Montana Constitution. We hold that the personal autonomy component of this right broadly guarantees each individual the right to make medical judgments affecting her or his bodily integrity and health in partnership with a chosen health care provider free from the interference of the government, except in very limited circumstances not at issue here. More narrowly, we hold that Article II, Section 10, protects a woman's right of procreative autonomy—here, the right to seek and to obtain a specific lawful medical procedure, a pre-viability abortion, from a health care provider of her choice. We also hold that the government has failed to demonstrate a compelling state interest for infringing upon these rights of privacy and that, therefore, the amendments to § 37-20-103, MCA, and § 50-20-109, MCA, enacted pursuant to Ch. 321, L.1995, prohibiting a physician assistant-certified from performing a pre-viability abortion under the supervision of a licensed physician are unconstitutional under Article II, Section 10, of the Montana Constitution. ***

Justice KARLA M. GRAY, specially concurring.

¶ 77 I concur in the Court's opinion to the extent it addresses the issue before us in this case. That is, I agree that the challenged statutory amendments are unconstitutional because they violate a woman's right of procreative autonomy protected by Article II, Section 10 of the Montana Constitution and the State has not demonstrated a compelling state interest for infringing on that right. I cannot join in other parts of the Court's opinion which, although scholarly written, are overly broad and far outside the scope of the issue actually before us. In concluding that Article II, Section 10 broadly guarantees each individual the right to make medical judgments affecting his or her bodily integrity and health in partnership with a chosen health care provider free from government interference, the Court's opinion sweeps so broadly as to encompass and decide such issues as the right to physician-assisted suicide and other important health and medical-related issues which simply were not litigated in this case. I cannot agree that it is appropriate to address such matters in this case and, indeed, it is my view that much of the Court's opinion is dicta.

¶ 78 I am particularly troubled by that portion of the Court's opinion which states—without any analysis whatsoever—that the rights of personal and procreative autonomy at issue in this case also find protection in the individual dignity and equal protection rights set forth in Article II, Section 4; the inalienable right to seek safety, health and happiness in all lawful ways contained in Article II, Section 3; the religious and speech freedoms set forth in Article II, Sections 5 and 7; and the due process right contained in Article II, Section 17. That discussion is far beyond the scope of this case as presented and, in any event, is totally unsupported by the Court. While such thoughts appropriately might be included in a concurring opinion if supported by legal analysis, it is my view that they have no place in an opinion addressing and resolving the issue before us under the right to privacy contained in Article II, Section 10 of the Montana Constitution.

¶ 79 Finally, it is necessary to comment on those portions of the Court's opinion which discuss the propriety of leaving the determination of standards for medical practice in the hands of the medical community—acting through the medical examining and licensing authorities. I generally agree with the Court's discussion in those regards but I do not agree with any implicit notion therein that the Legislature has no place at all in the equation. It is important to keep in mind that the practice of medicine is a privilege, not a right, in Montana and that it is generally subject to legislative oversight in order to protect the health, safety, and welfare of the people of Montana. *See* § 37-3-101, MCA. Indeed, the Montana Board of Medical Examiners (Board) is an entity created by the Legislature via § 2-15-1841, MCA, and given the powers and duties set forth in § 37-3-203, MCA, for the purpose of ensuring that medical licensees conform to appropriate standards of conduct and exercise the privileges granted to them "in the greatest public interest." Section 37-3-302, MCA.

¶ 80 In discharging its oversight responsibility in the area of medical care for Montanans, however, the Legislature has expressly provided for the licensing of certified physician assistants who practice under the supervision of physicians pursuant to the terms of "utilization plans" approved by the Board. See §§ 37-20-101, 37-20-203, and 37-20-301, MCA. As provided by the Legislature, a certified physician assistant is "a member of a health care team, approved by the board, who provides medical services that may include examination, diagnosis, prescription of medications, and treatment, as approved by the board, under the supervision of a physician licensed by the board." Section 37-20-401, MCA. The utilization plan requiring Board approval must set forth the scope of the physician assistant's practice, and can be approved only if the physician assistant's practice is within the scope of the training, knowledge, experience and practice of the supervisory physician and also within the scope of the training, knowledge, education and experience of the certified physician assistant. Sections 37-20-301(2)(c), (3)(b), and (3)(c), MCA.

¶ 81 In the context of the present case, I agree with the Court that, once the statutory requirements for licensure of a certified physician assistant and for approval of the utilization plan covering that certified physician assistant have been satisfied, the Legislature cannot indirectly intrude into a utilization plan setting forth the scope of practice for that physician assistant which has been approved by the medical authorities empowered by the Legislature to do just that. Here, the Board had approved Cahill's utilization plan which permitted her to perform abortions, and it was inappropriate for the Legislature to substitute its judgment for that of the Board it created to oversee such matters involving the practice, training, knowledge, education and experience of medical personnel.

¶ 82 In summary, I join in those portions of the Court's opinion which address and resolve the issue actually before us. I do not join in those portions of the opinion which cast too wide a net and which implicitly suggest that the Legislature has no role at all in matters relating to the health care to be provided to the people of Montana.

Chief Justice J.A. TURNAGE joins in Justice GRAY's foregoing special concurrence.

Notes on Privacy as Autonomy

1. Which privacy test does the Court apply in *Gryczan*, the *Katz* "reasonable expectation of privacy" (derived from the Fourth Amendment's Search and Seizure Clause) or the *Palko* "implicit in the concept of ordered liberty" (derived from the Fourteenth Amendment's Due Process Clause)? Why would either be the correct test, if neither is a construction of a right of *privacy*? These tests not only march in lock-step with the Supreme Court's interpretation of the federal Constitution, they also construe clauses that already have their own versions in the Montana Constitution. Should the Montana Supreme Court look instead to the *Griswold* statement of "penumbras, formed by emanations from those guarantees that . . . create zones of privacy" because it was mentioned in the drafting process? (Does delegate intent matter in this case? Would it matter in others?) Note that while *Griswold* defined an unenumerated marital right to use contraceptives in the Federal Constitution, the point of section 10 was to enumerate a broad standalone right. What, then, is the scope of the privacy right incorporated into section 10?

2. How should readers of *Gryczan* interpret the fact that the delegates rejected a proposal that would have protected "private sexual acts" expressly? Would it matter if the delegates rejected the proposal because they thought private sexual acts were not protected as a fundamental right?

3. Does Chief Justice Turnage's concurrence in *Gryczan* offer a better alternative to the privacy rationale? (Why doesn't the Court join him?) He applies rational basis scrutiny, rejecting the law as singling out only one kind of sexual activity without any public health benefit. Note the plaintiffs raised a sex-discrimination claim too — doesn't the law also discriminate based on the sex of the participants, and shouldn't this subject it to strict scrutiny under section 4?

4. *Roe v. Wade* was first argued in December 1971, on the eve of the Montana Constitutional Convention. As *Armstrong* notes, the Convention did not address abortion specifically in the context of the right to privacy. Yet *Armstrong* also says *Roe v. Wade* "resolved the debate from the legal standpoint," six months after the Convention. Which debate, state or federal? Is it surprising, on the eve of *Roe*, that

abortion was not a major issue in debates over the right of privacy in Montana? Consider the same question asked of *Gryczan*: would it matter if the delegates (or ratifiers) understood the right of privacy to exclude (or include) a right to an abortion? Why or why not?

5. After identifying both *Katz* and *Palko* as potential tests for the scope of privacy in *Gryczan*, *Armstrong* discusses neither. (*Katz* appears only in a footnoted string cite.) So which test does the Court apply in *Armstrong*? The Court reframes *Gryczan* as recognizing a "personal autonomy" component of privacy, and draws a comparison to several theories of liberty. These include the *per curiam* opinion in *Planned Parenthood v. Casey* ("intimate and personal choices" that concern "the right to define one's own concept of existence, of meaning, of the universe, and of the mystery of human life"), John Stuart Mill's libertarianism, Ronald Dworkin's liberal conception of "law as integrity," Joel Feinberg's harm principles, and common law rules of informed consent. The concluding sections cite no other authority but Dworkin, who is one of the most influential legal philosophers of the late Twentieth Century. Are any of these sources either authoritative with respect to the Montana Constitution, or helpful in understanding when the right of privacy is or is not infringed?

6. What is the scope of the right recognized in *Armstrong*? First, "the right to make medical judgments affecting her or his bodily integrity and health in partnership with a chosen health care provider free from the interference of the government, except in very limited circumstances not at issue here." Recall from Chapter 9 discussing inalienable rights *Wiser v. State* (2006) and *Montana Cannabis Industry Association v. State* (2012), which also asserted this right unsuccessfully; are they distinguishable? Are the "very limited circumstances" of "a medically-acknowledged, *bona fide* health risk," that the Court addresses in its opinion, "clearly and convincingly demonstrated"? Second, privacy "protects a woman's right of procreative autonomy—here, the right to seek and to obtain a specific lawful medical procedure, a pre-viability abortion, from a health care provider of her choice." How much of this protection depends on abortion being "lawful" under state statute or federal constitutional law? How much depends on the procedure or the provider's certification by the medical community, in this case the Board of Medical Examiners? (By statute, the Board is appointed by the Governor, and fewer than half are medical doctors.)

7. More broadly, the Court in *Armstrong* concludes that, while the right of privacy may not be absolute, "no final boundaries can be drawn around the personal autonomy component of the right of individual privacy. It is, at one and the same time, as narrow as is necessary to protect against a specific unlawful infringement of individual dignity and personal autonomy by the government—as in *Gryczan*—and as broad as are the State's ever innovative attempts to dictate in matters of conscience, to define individual values, and to condemn those found to be socially repugnant or politically unpopular." What legal principle or principles are at play here?

8. The Court in *Armstrong* describes the Declaration of Rights as encompassing "a cohesive set of principles, carefully drafted and committed to an abstract ideal of just government," and "a compact of overlapping and redundant rights and guarantees." Or more colorfully, that it "is not simply a cook book of disconnected and discrete rules written with the vitality of an automobile insurance policy." The authority for this is Dworkin's theory of "law as integrity," not the Constitution itself, which expressly provides in section 2 of the Declaration of Rights that the people "may alter or abolish the constitution and form of government whenever they deem it necessary." Does *Armstrong* suggest the right it recognizes cannot be overruled by constitutional amendment, at least without violating the separate amendment rule? (Consider Justice Nelson's dissent in *Donaldson v. State* in Chapter 10, as well as the Court's opinion in *Montana Ass'n of Counties* in Chapter 1.)

9. *Armstrong* also suggests that religious reasons are inadmissible in the making and enforcement of law, citing the religiously affiliated proponents of the law at issue in contrast to the medical organizations that opposed it. "[T]hose in government who make, execute and interpret the law and who are sworn to support, protect and defend the Constitution may not, except in violation of their oaths of office, succumb to the pressure of those who would engraft the sectarian tenets and personal values of some onto the laws which govern all." Justice Nelson also made this point in his *Donaldson v. State* dissent (Chapter 10). This rationale appears to extend beyond the Court's concerns about the law's lack of medical justification. Would the same rationale apply to the abolition of the death penalty if the only proponents were religiously affiliated, or the only reasons given by proponents sounded in sanctity, a religious term sometimes invoked by the Court itself?

10. After *Armstrong*, the Montana Supreme Court has not revisited abortion rights in detail. *Cf. Planned Parenthood of Montana v. State* (Mont. 2015) (holding issue preclusion not met in challenges to the 2011 Parental Notification Act and the 2013 Parental Consent Act). Instead, lower courts invalidated several abortion regulations, and those rulings were not appealed by the Attorney General to the Supreme Court. *See Jeannette R. v. Ellery* (Mont. 1st Dist. 1995) (with respect to Medicaid funding for abortions, "although the state is under no obligation to fund an individual's choice to a right of privacy, once it has entered an area that is covered by the zone of privacy, the state must be neutral. . . ."), *contra Harris v. McRae* (1980); *Wicklund v. Lambert* (Mont. 1st Dist. 1999) ("Defendants have not shown a compelling state interest in requiring parental notification of a minor's intent to terminate her pregnancy. Furthermore, the Act does not enhance the protection of minors."), *contra Lambert v. Wicklund* (1997).

11. Most recently, in *Weems v. State* (Mont. 2019), a challenge brought by a Certified Nurse Practitioner and Certified Nurse Midwife, the Montana Supreme Court affirmed a preliminary injunction against enforcement of a 2005 law limiting the performance of pre-viability abortions to licensed physicians and physician assistants, citing *Armstrong*. Justice Rice, joined by Justices McKinnon and Shea, dissented: "the interest the State seeks to protect is much narrower [than the rights of

women patients to obtain the lawful medical procedure recognized in *Armstrong*], that is, ensuring that the proper regulatory authority affirmatively determines that individuals offering the medical procedures in question are both licensed and competent to provide that type of care in order to 'safeguard life and health'."

12. The separate opinions in both *Gryczan* and *Armstrong* worry that the cases' broad holdings extend to physician aid in dying. Do they?

C. Privacy's Frontiers and Dignity, Revisited

The frontiers of the right of privacy lie beyond issues of sexual and reproductive rights in more general questions of personal autonomy. Here, issues of privacy connect to distinct but related concerns of bodily integrity and individual dignity. These concerns pervade the law's treatment of persons across the range of personal conduct. They gain particular salience for both individuals and lawmakers at the extremes of life and liberty. In the following cases, consider the relevant legal scope of privacy and dignity, as well as which government interests might satisfy a court's scrutiny of cases invading these rights.

Walker v. State

316 Mont. 103 (2003)

Justice JAMES C. NELSON delivered the Opinion of the Court.

¶ 1 Mark Edward Walker appeals an order of the District Court for the Eighth Judicial District, Cascade County, denying Walker's Petition for Postconviction Relief. Walker had alleged in his petition that he was the victim of cruel and unusual punishment at the hands of Montana State Prison (MSP) officials. We reverse and remand for further proceedings consistent with this Opinion.

¶ 2 We address *** [w]hether "Behavior Management Plans" constitute cruel and unusual punishment when such plans exacerbate an inmate's mental health condition.

Factual and Procedural Background

¶ 6 On December 13, 1994, Walker was charged in Cascade County with felony forgery, arson, and two counts of criminal mischief. Walker admitted forging his brother's signature on several checks. The other two charges stemmed from a fire started on a tarp covering a motorcycle in his parents' garage. Walker claimed that the fire was an accident.

¶ 7 At the time, Walker had been diagnosed with Attention Deficit Hyperactive Disorder (ADHD) for which he was taking Ritalin. Walker pleaded guilty to negligent arson and felony forgery on July 25, 1995, in exchange for dismissal of the criminal mischief charges. On December 18, 1995, the District Court sentenced Walker to five years with the Department of Corrections with all five years suspended. Walker subsequently violated the terms of his probation and the State filed a petition to revoke his suspended sentence.

¶ 8 While awaiting revocation proceedings, Walker absconded. He was arrested in Colorado on December 29, 1997, on a charge of giving false information to a pawn broker. Walker remained incarcerated in Colorado until November 6, 1998, when he was extradited to Montana.

¶ 9 While incarcerated in Colorado, Walker underwent a mental health evaluation and was diagnosed with Hebephrenic Schizophrenic Disorder. That diagnosis was later changed to Bipolar Disorder. Between April 19, 1998, and November 6, 1998, the psychiatric staff of the Colorado Department of Corrections prescribed various medications to treat Walker's mental disorder. They eventually settled on a regimen which included Lithium. Walker was taking 300 milligrams of Lithium three times a day for a total of 900 milligrams each day. For the seven months Walker was taking Lithium while incarcerated in Colorado, the staff reported that his mood was more predictable and he did not receive any major disciplinary write-ups.

¶ 10 On November 6, 1998, Walker was transported from Colorado to the Cascade County Detention Center. On December 8, 1998, after a hearing, the District Court revoked Walker's suspended sentence and resentenced him to five years with the Department of Corrections. Walker was transferred to MSP on February 5, 1999.

¶ 11 Walker is six feet two inches tall. Because he is hypoglycemic, Walker has difficulty keeping on weight. At the time of the hearing on his petition for postconviction relief, Walker weighed 140 pounds. While incarcerated, his weight fluctuated from a high of 155 pounds while in Colorado, to a low of 129 pounds while locked down in maximum security (Max) at MSP. In addition, Walker is legally blind. The vision in his left eye measures 1/100, while the vision in his right eye measures 20/80. Walker does not have peripheral vision. Besides his regular corrective lenses, Walker uses a "funnel scopic lens" on top of his glasses which acts like binoculars.

¶ 12 Walker also suffers from a nystagmus problem which makes both of his eyes twitch constantly and forces him to turn his head to the side when speaking to other people. Also, Walker's mode of speech is "pressured," meaning that his speech and thought processes are so rapid that it is difficult to keep up with him. A prison psychologist described Walker's thoughts as coming out like "a fire hose rather than a garden hose" and that it was difficult to slow or stop the stream of thought, "like trying to cap a fire hydrant while it's flowing."

¶ 13 While at the Cascade County Detention Facility, Walker was taking his Lithium only sporadically. On February 5, 1999, Walker's first day at MSP, the intake officer described him as quiet, timid and cooperative. In his intake form, Walker notified MSP that he had been diagnosed as Bipolar and that he was receiving Lithium for his condition. On February 10, 1999, Walker notified MSP staff psychiatrist, Dr. David Schaefer, that he was experiencing stomach pains due to the Lithium. He requested that a snack be provided to accompany his medication and alleviate the nausea associated with taking his Lithium. Walker also requested that Dr. Schaefer review his medical records. Shortly after these requests, Walker stopped taking his Lithium. Thereafter, Walker's behavior showed a progressive decline.

¶ 14 For the first six months after his arrival at MSP, Walker averaged only two severe disciplinary infractions a month. Then, in August 1999, Walker was moved to Max after he broke a sprinkler head and claimed that he had swallowed it. For the next six months, Walker averaged eleven severe disciplinary infractions a month. According to various correctional officers, Walker had transformed from a timid and quiet inmate into an excited, belligerent, hostile, disruptive and suicidal inmate.

¶ 15 The officer who initially processed Walker on his arrival at MSP, later observed that Walker was refusing to eat and was losing a lot of weight. Although that officer said he tried to convince Walker to eat, Walker refused claiming that the slot that his food was passed through was filthy. Another officer testified that Walker would holler for hours, sometimes for the entire length of the officer's eight-hour shift. Still another officer reported that Walker was one of the most disruptive inmates that he had seen in five years of working in Max. That officer notified the mental health staff three or four times about Walker, but he did not see any follow up. Other inmates reported that Walker would scream all night long and one inmate reported that Walker would pound continuously on his sink. An inmate housed near Walker described Walker's moods as ranging from depressed and moody to "happy as shit."

¶ 16 Other instances of Walker's disruptive behavior consisted of spitting on officers; covering his cell walls with ketchup, mustard and mayonnaise; throwing his food tray out his food slot and onto the floor; covering his cell window to prevent officers from seeing in; and purposely flooding his cell. Walker also refused to comply with direct orders from the officers. On two occasions, officers had to use pepper spray on Walker and forcibly remove him from his cell.

¶ 17 Walker's behavior culminated in three suicide attempts. On October 7, 1999, Walker was evaluated by medical staff for swallowing a staple. The psychiatrist noted in his report following that incident that Walker was a chronic risk for self-harm. On October 8, 1999, Walker tried to hang himself with a sheet. And, on October 12, 1999, he tried to hang himself with his prison overalls.

¶ 18 Both the guards and the inmates quickly tired of Walker's behavior. Hence, Walker was put on a series of Behavior Management Plans (BMPs). In its response brief on appeal, the State agreed with the characterization in Walker's brief concerning the BMPs on which the prison placed Walker. These BMPs were characterized by Walker as follows:

> ¶ 19 BMPs are prison management tools using "a carrot-and-stick approach" of withdrawing and returning privileges based on conduct. BMPs are supposed to be "a tool of last resort" when all other options for discipline have been exhausted. To prevent abuse, BMPs cannot be initiated by a single guard, and are supposed to have other fail-safe measures in place, such as review by mental health staff.

¶ 20 BMPs are only implemented and completed in the A-block area of Max. A-block is a detention unit designed for disciplinary punishment. The inmates in A-block are only provided with the bare necessities. Each cell has a cement bed, a cement table or desk, a stainless steel sink, a stainless steel toilet and a stainless steel plate that serves as a mirror. None of these fixtures are removable. The cell has an intake vent and an exhaust vent to circulate air. The cell does not have a window to the outside, so no natural light enters the cell. There is a single light fixture in the ceiling and the guards control the lighting. The light remains on 12 to 16 hours a day. No recreation yard time is allowed for inmates in A-block.

¶ 21 BMPs further curtail the already restricted detention created in A-block and are designed to last 24 to 48 hours. BMPs are not meant to be therapeutic, they are used as a tool to manage dangerous behavior. If a BMP continues beyond a week, prison mental health services are supposed to conduct a formal review of the plan.

¶ 22 Walker was transferred to A-block on August 25, 1999. While on A-block, MSP officials implemented five separate BMPS for Walker even though they conceded that Walker did not respond well to progressive discipline. Walker's first BMP was initiated on September 6, 1999, after he flooded his cell. This BMP lasted until September 11, 1999.

¶ 23 Walker was placed on another BMP on October 8, 1999, after he attempted to hang himself with a sheet. The previous day, Walker swallowed a metal staple and attempted to block his window. On October 10, 1999, Walker cut himself by breaking off a piece of his food tray and concealing the sharp piece in his cell. On October 12, 1999, Walker tried to hang himself with his coveralls, hence he was sent to the infirmary for several days. On October 18, 1999, Walker was returned to his cell in A-block. He was stripped of all of his clothing and put in his cell naked. He was not permitted to have bedding or a pillow and the water to his sink and toilet were turned off. The guards controlled the water and turned it on at regular intervals. Walker was given a "space" or "suicide" blanket consisting of two wool blankets sewn inside a canvas cover. Walker remained in his cell, naked, with only his suicide blanket for four days.

¶ 24 As part of the BMP, Walker was not allowed to have hot meals. Instead, he was provided with "finger food"—individually wrapped slices of meat and cheese served with bread. The guards would order Walker to the back of his cell and tell him to face the wall. They would then place the food on a slot in the door. Sometimes the food was wrapped in plastic and other times the officers would unwrap the food before placing it on the slot. This was the same slot where toilet cleaning tools and other cleaning supplies were passed through prompting Walker's refusal to eat unwrapped food placed on the slot claiming that the slot was filthy.

¶ 25 BMPs were only designed to last for 24 to 48 hours. On this BMP, Walker had to have 24 hours of clear conduct before clothing and other necessities would be returned to him. However, on October 20, 1999, Walker received additional write-ups for trying to block his cell window, thus no items were returned to him. On

October 22, 1999, Walker's mattress was returned to him and, on October 23, 1999, his pillow was returned to him. Walker was still naked and he received another disciplinary write up for again trying to cover his window. On October 27, 1999, prison officials returned control of the sink and toilet water to Walker. On October 28, 1999, Walker began receiving regular hot meals served on a tray. On October 29, 1999, after eleven days of being naked in his cell, Walker received underwear, coveralls and thermal underwear. MSP officials then returned Walker to regular detention status.

¶ 26 On December 9, 1999, MSP officials forced Walker into a third BMP after Walker covered his cell window, threatened to harm himself, and flooded his cell block. Prison officials once again removed Walker's clothing and placed him in his cell with only his underwear, a suicide blanket and a mattress. In this BMP, prison officials determined that Walker needed 72 hours of clear conduct, rather than the previously established 24 hours, before returning any basic items. This BMP ended on December 15, 1999, when Walker was transported to Great Falls for a court date.

¶ 27 On January 1, 2000, prison officials commenced a fourth BMP against Walker because he wrote a threatening letter to MSP staff. Once again Walker was stripped naked and only given a suicide blanket to keep warm. Again, his access to water was restricted and he was given only finger foods. On January 12, 2000, MSP officials returned Walker's mattress, and the following day, they returned his pillow. On January 15, 2000, his clothing was returned. For two weeks, Walker had remained in his cell naked. MSP records indicate that while on this BMP, mental health staff did not review Walker's mental health status every seven days as required by prison policy. Walker completed this BMP on January 18, 2000.

¶ 28 On February 26, 2000, MSP officials started Walker's fifth BMP because Walker claimed to have taken some pills in another suicide attempt. All of Walker's clothing and bedding were taken away. Walker was again forced to sleep naked on a concrete bunk with nothing but a suicide blanket for warmth for over a week. On March 4, 2000, Walker's mattress was returned to him. On March 5, 2000, he received his pillow. On March 6, 2000, after nine days of being naked in his cell, MSP officials returned his coveralls. Walker completed this BMP on March 11, 2000.

¶ 29 Several correctional officers later testified that they noticed no difference in Walker's behavior whether he was on or off a BMP. They also reported that the BMPs often failed to prevent further disruptive or dangerous behavior by Walker.

¶ 30 In January 2000, Walker, while on a BMP, filed a pro se petition with this Court. Because he was without any writing utensils or paper, Walker dictated his petition to a neighboring inmate. In his petition, Walker alleged that he was the victim of cruel and unusual punishment at the hands of MSP officials. He reported that while placed on "lock-up status," his clothes were taken away, he was housed in a cell with human blood and waste, he was forced to sleep naked on a concrete slab without a mattress, his food was served in an unsanitary manner, and he was deprived of drinking water. [The Court appointed counsel who brought a postconviction relief petition in district court.] ***

¶ 35 Walker now appeals the District Court's conclusions of law that the prison's BMPs and the conditions in A-block do not constitute cruel and unusual punishment. Walker was discharged from MSP on August 10, 2001, after he filed his notice of appeal. He has completely discharged his sentence and is not on probation or parole. Consequently, the State moved to dismiss Walker's appeal as moot. In an Order dated September 18, 2001, we denied the State's motion as premature because Walker had not yet filed his brief on appeal. However, we denied that motion "without prejudice to the State's right to renew its motion after the issues on appeal are more clearly defined." The State has again raised that issue in its Response brief on appeal. ***

¶ 52 The District Court determined that Walker had not met his burden of proof to succeed on any of the issues in his petition for postconviction relief and that Walker was not subject to cruel and unusual punishment under either the Eighth Amendment to the United States Constitution or Article II, Section 22 of the Montana Constitution. Hence, the court denied all relief requested by Walker.

¶ 53 The State argues on appeal that the District Court was correct in concluding that MSP's treatment of Walker did not amount to cruel and unusual punishment. The State maintains that MSP did not deliberately disregard an excessive risk to Walker's health or safety, but only made an informed decision to employ BMPs to try to control Walker's aberrant, disruptive, and dangerous behavior.

¶ 54 Walker argues, on the other hand, that the District Court erred in failing to find that imposing BMPs on mentally ill inmates amounts to cruel and unusual punishment in violation of the cruel and unusual punishment provisions of both the Eighth Amendment and Article II, Section 22 of the Montana Constitution. The Eighth Amendment provides: "Excessive bail shall not be required, nor excessive fines imposed, nor cruel and unusual punishments inflicted." Article II, Section 22 is nearly identical.

¶ 55 Walker also argues that the District Court erred by failing to apply the "deliberate indifference test" appropriately to BMPs. He maintains that pursuant to the United States Supreme Court's decision in *Farmer v. Brennan* (1994), the deliberate indifference test provides that "an Eighth Amendment claimant need not show that a prison official acted or failed to act believing that harm actually would befall an inmate; it is enough that the official acted or failed to act despite his knowledge of a substantial risk of serious harm."

¶ 56 *Madrid v. Gomez* (N.D. Cal. 1995), sets forth the standard for determining deliberate indifference as it applies to improper psychological or psychiatric care in violation of the Eighth Amendment. First, the inmate must demonstrate that "the levels of medical and mental health care are constitutionally inadequate from an objective standpoint — based on either a 'pattern of negligent conduct' or 'systematic deficiencies.'" Second, the inmate must show that the correctional institution "knew the risk to inmate health" due to this inadequacy, and "acted with disregard for this risk." In short, a plaintiff must show that the defendants "'consciously disregard[ed]' a substantial risk of serious harm to plaintiffs' health or safety."

¶ 57 While at MSP, Walker was evaluated by four psychological experts. Dr. David Schaefer, MSP staff psychiatrist, was informed as early as February 20, 1999, that Walker complained of stomach pains associated with taking Lithium. Nevertheless, Dr. Schaefer did not evaluate Walker until March 11, 1999. That evaluation lasted less than 30 minutes. By that time, Walker had discontinued taking his Lithium because of the stomach problems he experienced. Consequently, Dr. Schaefer discontinued prescribing Lithium for Walker without reviewing Walker's medical records and without completing any psychological testing. He concluded that Walker did not have a serious mental illness, but rather an antisocial personality with narcissistic traits, typical with the things Dr. Schaefer sees at the prison on a daily basis. *** He concluded that Walker was not Bipolar.

¶ 59 Dr. Andrew Schoening, a psychologist who worked at MSP along with Dr. Schaefer, also diagnosed Walker with antisocial personality disorder. He concluded that Walker fit into the category of a "self-mutilator." At the hearing on Walker's petition for postconviction relief, Dr. Schaefer explained that self-mutilators in a prison context usually injure themselves to obtain transfer to a less restrictive setting. He concluded that Walker was harming himself in an attempt to control the situation even though Walker's self harm always placed him in a more restrictive setting. Dr. Schoening also concluded that Walker's behavior, such as yelling all night long and then being assaulted by the inmate he was yelling at, was not psychotic, but just poor judgment.

¶ 60 Dr. William Stratford . . . was asked by Walker's attorney to evaluate Walker's current diagnosis of mental health; the possibility that Walker may have suffered from fetal alcohol syndrome; and Walker's mental state at the time he committed the crimes that sent him to MSP. *** Based on his evaluation, Dr. Stratford concluded that Walker suffers from Bipolar Disorder. *** Dr. Stratford opined that Walker had been properly treated for mental illness while in the Colorado correctional system, but that he was neglected while at MSP. In Colorado, treating physicians reported that the Lithium effectively controlled Walker's moods and behaviors. In Montana, Walker was not taking Lithium and he received more than 100 disciplinary write-ups. *** According to Dr. Stratford, MSP officials didn't adequately treat Walker, but they continued to discipline him, consequently "the guy got worse and worse and worse."

¶ 63 Dr. Terry Kupers, is a board-certified psychiatrist specializing in correctional psychology. *** Dr. Kupers concluded that it was "absolutely clear" that Walker suffers from a serious mental illness, most likely Bipolar Disorder. . . . Dr. Kupers also testified that it was "inexcusable" that Walker was not on medications considering they were effective in the past. He concluded that the diagnosis from MSP's mental health staff that Walker did not have a mental illness was "preposterous" and fell below the ethical standards for practicing medicine in this field. *** Dr. Kupers also discussed the psychological harm caused by placing inmates in a severely restrictive setting for nearly 24 hours a day. . . . Dr. Kupers testified that the restrictive BMPs imposed on Walker were the most counter-therapeutic, punitive and cruel plans that he had witnessed in all the states that he had reviewed. He stated: "If it's a security program, I think it's just cruel and inhumane. If it's a treatment, it is ethically wrong and far below the standard in terms of all of the fields of mental health."

¶ 68 MSP did nothing to treat Walker. Rather, prison officials responded to Walker's behavior by giving Walker well in excess of 100 disciplinary write-ups and placing him in disciplinary detention or "lock down" for six months. While in lock down, Walker was placed on a number of BMPs and with each successive BMP, Walker's behavior got increasingly worse.

¶ 69 Walker was placed on one BMP after he made three suicide attempts on October 7, 8 and 12, 1999. Rather than rendering psychiatric or psychological treatment to Walker, prison officials placed him on a BMP and took away his mattress, pillow and all of his personal items including his clothing. This pattern continued when Walker again threatened self-harm and he was placed on another BMP on December 9, 1999. He received another BMP after threatening suicide in February 2000. Prison officials stated that BMPs are intended to manage dangerous behavior, they are not intended to be therapeutic. Walker's suicide attempts did not result in psychiatric or psychological help. Instead, they resulted in BMPs which admittedly are not therapeutic and are not a substitute for mental health assistance.

¶ 70 Other Max inmates reported that Walker would scream and pound on objects in his cell for hours at a time, often for entire shifts. One inmate recalled an episode where, after being deprived of his clothing and underwear, Walker yelled for two days. Walker's behavior was so aberrant that some Max inmates reported that Walker should have been placed in a psychiatric ward. However, prison officials chose to label Walker as a bad person rather than treat the mental health problems that were apparent to inmates and staff. ***

¶ 72 When the people of Montana ratified a new State Constitution in 1972, they recognized that all human beings have an innate dignity:

> Individual dignity. *The dignity of the human being is inviolable.* No person shall be denied the equal protection of the laws. Neither the state nor any person, firm, corporation, or institution shall discriminate against any person in the exercise of his civil or political rights on account of race, color, sex, culture, social origin or condition, or political or religious ideas.

Art. II, Sec. 4, Mont. Const. (emphasis added).

¶ 73 In *State v. Siegal* (Mont. 1997), we held that because Article II, Section 10 of the Montana Constitution explicitly grants to all Montana citizens the right to individual privacy, the Montana Constitution affords citizens broader protection at the hands of the government in search and seizure cases than does the federal constitution. Just as we read the privacy provision of the Montana Constitution in conjunction with the provisions regarding search and seizure to provide Montanans with greater protections from government intrusion, so too do we read the dignity provision of the Montana Constitution together with Article II, Section 22 to provide Montana citizens greater protections from cruel and unusual punishment than does the federal constitution. The federal constitution does not expressly provide for the right to human dignity.

¶ 74 We have repeatedly recognized the rights found in Montana's Declaration of Rights as being "fundamental," meaning that these rights are significant components of liberty, any infringement of which will trigger the highest level of scrutiny, and, thus, the highest level of protection by the courts.

¶ 75 Thus, while we will analyze most cruel and unusual punishment questions implicating Article II, Section 22 of Montana's Constitution by reference to that section alone, in certain instances where Montana's constitutional right to individual dignity (Article II, Section 4) is also specially implicated, we must, of necessity, consider and address the effect of that constitutional mandate on the question before us.

¶ 76 Walker agrees that the prohibitions against cruel and unusual punishment do not guarantee that he will not suffer from some psychological effects from incarceration or segregation, however, "if the particular conditions of segregation being challenged are such that they inflict a serious mental illness, greatly exacerbate mental illness, or deprive inmates of their sanity, then [prison officials] have deprived inmates of a basic necessity of human existence—indeed, they have crossed into the realm of psychological torture." *Madrid.*

¶ 77 In addition to the problems associated with BMPs, Walker asserted that the living conditions in A-block were intolerable. Numerous inmates who resided in A-block testified about the filthy, uninhabitable cells. These inmates testified that the cells commonly had blood, feces, vomit and other types of debris in the cells they were forced to inhabit. One inmate recounted an instance where he was placed in a cell with human waste rubbed all over the walls and vomit in the corner. He claims the corrections staff ignored his complaints and told him to "live with it."

¶ 78 Another inmate testified that he had bloodied a cell by smashing his head against the wall. His blood remained in the cell until Walker eventually inhabited the cell. After Walker was removed from that cell sometime later, the inmate who originally bloodied the cell was moved back in. He testified that the blood streaks and the words he previously had written in blood on the wall of the cell remained unchanged.

¶ 79 Walker also complained that the correctional staff mishandled his food. Correctional officers passed the food through the same hatch in which toilet brushes and other cleaning supplies were passed through. While on a BMP, an inmate's food consisted of bread, lunch meat and cheese. Often this food was placed on the dirty food hatch, unwrapped. Walker also contended that on several occasions, correctional officers threw his food into the cell onto the floor where it occasionally landed under the toilet and in one instance landing in the toilet. While correctional officers testified that these incidents never occurred, other A-block inmates testified that they had either seen it happen or had heard Walker complain when it happened. One inmate described life in A-block as follows:

> My feeling of worth, you know, was just—I didn't feel worth anything, you know, I didn't want to—I didn't want to carry on. When I finally went to the mental health block [in Max], I didn't care whether I lived or died.
>
> It's—eating like a dog, eating your food off the ground, and really, you know, you don't even feel human after a while....

¶ 80 When any state, in the exercise of its police powers, receives an individual into its residential correctional systems as an inmate, it assumes responsibility for that person's general well being and for his basic human needs—e.g., food, clothing, shelter, medical care, and reasonable safety.

¶ 81 Moreover, "[t]reatment which degrades or demeans persons, that is, treatment which deliberately reduces the value of persons, and which fails to acknowledge their worth as persons, directly violates their dignity." Matthew O. Clifford & Thomas P. Huff, *Some Thoughts on the Meaning and Scope of the Montana Constitution's "Dignity" Clause with Possible Applications* (Summer 2000), 61 Mont.L.Rev. 301, 307 (hereafter, Clifford). These authors went on to examine Montana's dignity clause in the context of mentally ill individuals and prisoners:

> [I]n the case of the mentally ill, basic human needs must be met, along with adequate opportunity to develop capacities, and adequate mental health care must also be provided to treat the illness. It is natural to speak of the inherent dignity of such developmentally disabled or mentally ill persons, and to speak of the requirement that such vulnerable persons be treated with dignity.
>
> For those imprisoned for crimes, complementary application of the dignity clause would be more appropriate. The reformation and prevention functions of punishment both express the community's disrespect for the actions of the criminal, but the processes of punishment must never disrespect the core humanity of the prisoner. Section 22 of Article II prohibits the infliction of cruel and unusual punishment on persons. Section 28 mandates "reformation" as one of the foundations of punishment for crimes. Part of what these rights proscribe and mandate should be informed by the complementary application of the dignity clause. However we punish, whatever means we use to reform, we must not punish or reform in a way that degrades the humanity, the dignity, of the prisoner. Protecting dignity should include, for example, security from physical harm, including security from sexual violation, by other prisoners or guards. It should also include attention to such basic human needs as adequate medical care, humane rules for visitation, adequate exercise, and adequate opportunity for education or other capacity-developing activity. Prisoners may not claim that their punishment, itself, violates the dignity clause, unless the

> conditions of that punishment violate the cruel and unusual punishment prohibition, and that violation might most easily be elaborated by asking whether the core humanity of the prisoner is being treated with dignity.

Clifford, pp. 331–32.

¶ 82 Our Constitution forbids correctional practices which permit prisons in the name of behavior modification to disregard the innate dignity of human beings, especially in the context where those persons suffer from serious mental illness. We cannot sanction correctional practices that ignore and exacerbate the plight of mentally ill inmates like Walker, especially when that inmate is forced to rely on the prison for his care and protection. The plain meaning of the dignity clause commands that the intrinsic worth and the basic humanity of persons may not be violated. Moreover, if the particular conditions of confinement cause serious mental illness to be greatly exacerbated or if it deprives inmates of their sanity, then prison officials have deprived inmates of the basic necessity for human existence and have crossed into the realm of psychological torture.

¶ 83 Walker is

> part of a growing population of faceless, powerless, voiceless, warehoused people whose rights are paid lip service but rarely taken seriously by the institutions responsible for their custody. The only check on that indifference is the judiciary. Sometimes the system works. Sometimes it does not.... When the rights of even the most disrespected among us are ignored, all of society is diminished.

Campbell v. Mahoney, 2001 MT 146 (Trieweiler, J., dissenting).

¶ 84 Accordingly, we hold that, reading Article II, Sections 4 and 22 together, BMPs and the living conditions on A-block constitute an affront to the inviolable right of human dignity possessed by the inmate and that such punishment constitutes cruel and unusual punishment when it exacerbates the inmate's mental health condition.

¶ 85 We reverse and remand to the District Court for entry of an order requiring MSP to conform the operations of its administrative segregation units to the requirements of this Opinion and to report, in writing to that court within 180 days as to the actions taken. The District Court may, thereafter, order inspections or further remediation as in that court's discretion is necessary under the circumstances.

Chief Justice KARLA M. GRAY, dissenting.

¶ 86 ... It is my view that this case is now moot and that many of the procedural approaches by the Court ... have been totally lacking in legal authority. The result is that this Court has improperly intruded into issues involving conditions at the Montana State Prison (MSP) and reversed the District Court without determining that any of its extensive findings of fact are clearly erroneous or that its conclusions of law are incorrect. The Court also has placed that same District Court Judge in the position of undertaking further inspections and remediation regarding conditions of confinement at the MSP. I cannot agree. ***

¶ 88 [T]he Court concluded that if Walker's allegations were true, his constitutional rights to be free from cruel and unusual punishment might be implicated, but conceded that it was not authorized to collect the information and resolve the factual issues which might arise from the investigation. The Court then stated that persons imprisoned in Montana are not without "a remedy when or if their civil rights are violated." I agree wholeheartedly with both of those statements in the Court's order of March 9, 2000. Indeed, both this Court and Montana inmates are aware that the remedy for alleged violations of civil rights is 42 U.S.C. § 1983. With full knowledge of § 1983 actions to protect civil rights, however, the Court did not state that to be the available remedy. . . .

¶ 89 . . . Such challenges, under either the law or common sense, simply are not seeking "review of a criminal sentence" in any form or fashion. Notwithstanding, the Court concluded, without any applicable legal authority whatsoever, that Walker's challenge to the conditions of his confinement "is a critical stage related to the penalty phase of the criminal proceedings against him" (emphasis added) and, consequently, Walker was entitled to appointment of counsel. The potential consequences of that conclusion — essentially, that appointed counsel is required whenever an inmate challenges conditions of confinement — cannot be calculated. Suffice it to say that costs for appointed counsel, now a state funded cost, will skyrocket and, almost without doubt, both district court case loads and this Court's case load will do the same. ***

¶ 95 . . . In my view, Walker having sought relief from certain conditions he experienced while in the MSP, no effective relief can be granted by this Court now that he has been released, notwithstanding the Court's holding . . . that it is Walker's appeal the Court is addressing. [In an omitted section, the Court held Walker's appeal was not moot "merely because he had been released from custody."] I submit that, in essence, the Court is issuing an advisory opinion, which courts have no jurisdiction to do. Absent a showing in this case that either the BMPs or the conditions on A-block have exacerbated any inmate's mental health condition, this case simply does not meet the "capable of repetition, yet evading review" test necessary to avoid mootness.

¶ 96 Mootness aside, the Court totally disregards the District Court's 56 findings of fact, covering 18 pages, and its conclusions of law. While stating the proper standard of review regarding the clearly erroneous test for findings of fact and the "correct" standard for conclusions of law, the Court never addresses a single one of the District Court's 56 findings, much less determines that any of them are clearly erroneous. Indeed, many of the so-called facts presented throughout the Court's opinion are at odds with those found by the District Court. Nor does the Court address any errors it has discovered in the District Court's conclusions of law which, of course, are premised on that court's findings of facts. Finally, with regard to the Court's reliance on the Montana constitutional right to individual dignity, Walker did not raise "dignity" or "humanity" in the District Court until filing his Proposed Findings of Fact and Conclusions of Law and even there, he did not cite to Article II, Section 4 of the Montana Constitution. For that reason, I disagree with the Court's reliance on that particular constitutional right in its opinion.

¶ 97 More importantly, the Court's vague and conclusory statements about this constitutional right do little to provide guidance in defining that right. Nor does the Court present the ordinary analysis of whether any violations of the right to dignity which might occur in prison settings can withstand our usual constitutional scrutiny. And while "some thoughts on the meaning and scope of the Montana Constitution's dignity clause" by noted academics are of interest, they do not provide the needed analytical structure for addressing that right as it relates to the surely undisputed need of correctional officials to run prisons confining many violent and manipulative inmates.

¶ 98 The Court concludes broadly that "[o]ur Constitution forbids correctional practices which permit prisons in the name of behavior modification to disregard the innate dignity of human beings." Such a conclusion fails to take into account or balance other constitutional rights which may be at issue in an appropriate case, such as those inalienable rights guaranteed by Article II, Section 3, held by other inmates, correctional staff and the Montana public. Virtually every aspect of being incarcerated may, to some extent, degrade and demean persons. Certainly any member of this Court would find it so. But no legal authority is presented, and I daresay none can be found, which even begins to support the breadth of the Court's conclusion. It is not enough to say that no other state has a comparable constitutional right and then just "take the ball and run with it."

¶ 99 In this latter regard, the Court does not look to the source of the dignity right found in Article II, Section 4 of the Montana Constitution — namely, the verbatim transcript of the Montana Constitutional Convention. That transcript for March 7, 1972, where the Convention delegates unanimously adopted Section 4, captures the clear intent of the Convention with regard to the dignity right contained in Section 4 — an intent totally at odds with the Court's discussion of the right in this case:

> DELEGATE MANSFIELD: The committee unanimously adopted this section with the intent of providing a constitutional impetus for the eradication of public and private discrimination based on race, color, sex, culture, social origin or condition, or political or religious ideas. The provision, quite similar to that of the Puerto Rico declaration of rights, is aimed at prohibiting private as well as public discrimination in civil and political rights. Considerable testimony was heard concerning the need to include sex in any equal protection or freedom from discrimination provisions. The

> committee felt that such inclusion was eminently proper and saw no reason for the state to wait for the adoption of the federal equal rights amendment or any amendment which would not explicitly provide as much protection as this provision. The word "culture" was incorporated specifically to cover groups whose cultural base is distinct from mainstream Montana, especially the American Indians. Social origin or condition was included to cover discriminations based on status of income and standard of living. Some fears were expressed that the wording "political or religious ideas" would permit persons who supported the right to work in principle to avoid union membership. Such is not the intent of the committee. The wording was incorporated to prohibit public and private concerns discriminating against persons because of their political or religious beliefs. The wording of this section was derived almost verbatim from the Delegate Proposal Number 61. The committee felt that this proposal incorporated all features of all the delegate proposals, numbers 10, 32, 50 and 51, on the subjects of equal protection of the laws and the freedom from discrimination. The committee is well aware that any broad proposal on these subjects will require considerable statutory embellishment. It is hoped that the Legislature will enact statutes to promote effective eradication of the discriminations prohibited in this section. The considerable support for and the lack of opposition to this provision indicates its import and advisability....
>
> DELEGATE DAHOOD:... There is no intent within this particular section to do anything other than to remove the apparent type of discrimination that all of us object to with respect to employment, to rental practices, to actual associationship in matters that are public or matters that tend to be somewhat quasi-public..... The intent of Section 4 is simply to provide that every individual in the State of Montana, as a citizen of this state, may pursue his inalienable rights without having any shadows cast upon his dignity through unwarranted discrimination....

It is my view that Delegates Mansfield and Dahood presented Section 4 as a package intended in its entirety to prohibit intrusion on a person's dignity through discrimination, and the Convention accepted it as presented. Nothing in the transcripts supports a free-standing, separate dignity right.

¶ 100 As its last "act" in the present case, the Court puts the District Court in charge of such "inspections or further remediation as in that court's discretion is necessary under the circumstances." I suspect that, like myself, the District Court will have no idea what to do, when to do it, or how to respond to what may well be hundreds of petitions addressed to it requesting inspections into, investigations of, or challenges to conditions of confinement at any of Montana's correctional facilities. Nor, I expect, will that court have a clue how it is to fund such matters. ***

Baxter v. State

354 Mont. 234 (2009)

Justice W. WILLIAM LEAPHART delivered the Opinion of the Court.

*** ¶ 5 This appeal originated with Robert Baxter, a retired truck driver from Billings who was terminally ill with lymphocytic leukemia with diffuse lymphadenopathy. At the time of the District Court's decision, Mr. Baxter was being treated with multiple rounds of chemotherapy, which typically become less effective over time. As a result of the disease and treatment, Mr. Baxter suffered from a variety of debilitating symptoms, including infections, chronic fatigue and weakness, anemia, night sweats, nausea, massively swollen glands, significant ongoing digestive problems and generalized pain and discomfort. The symptoms were expected to increase in frequency and intensity as the chemotherapy lost its effectiveness. There was no cure for Mr. Baxter's disease and no prospect of recovery. Mr. Baxter wanted the option of ingesting a lethal dose of medication prescribed by his physician and self-administered at the time of Mr. Baxter's own choosing.

¶ 6 Mr. Baxter, four physicians, and Compassion & Choices, brought an action in District Court challenging the constitutionality of the application of Montana homicide statutes to physicians who provide aid in dying to mentally competent, terminally ill patients. The complaint alleged that patients have a right to die with dignity under the Montana Constitution Article II, Sections 4 and 10, which address individual dignity and privacy.

¶ 7 In December 2008, the District Court issued its Order and Decision, holding that the Montana constitutional rights of individual privacy and human dignity, together, encompass the right of a competent, terminally ill patient to die with dignity. The District Court held that a patient may use the assistance of his physician to obtain a prescription for a lethal dose of medication. The patient would then decide whether to self-administer the dose and cause his own death. The District Court further held that the patient's right to die with dignity includes protection of the patient's physician from prosecution under the State's homicide statutes.... The State appeals. ***

Discussion

¶ 9 The parties in this appeal focus their arguments on the question of whether a right to die with dignity—including physician aid in dying—exists under the privacy and dignity provisions of the Montana Constitution. The District Court held that a competent, terminally ill patient has a right to die with dignity under Article II, Sections 4 and 10 of the Montana Constitution. Sections 4 and 10 address individual dignity and the right to privacy, respectively. The District Court further held that the right to die with dignity includes protecting the patient's physician from prosecution under Montana homicide statutes. The District Court concluded that Montana homicide laws are unconstitutional as applied to a physician who aids a competent, terminally ill patient in dying.

¶ 10 While we recognize the extensive briefing by the parties and amici on the constitutional issues, this Court is guided by the judicial principle that we should decline to rule on the constitutionality of a legislative act if we are able to decide the case without reaching constitutional questions. Since both parties have recognized the possibility of a consent defense to a homicide charge under § 45-2-211(1), MCA, we focus our analysis on whether the issues presented can be resolved at the statutory, rather than the constitutional, level.

¶ 11 We start with the proposition that suicide is not a crime under Montana law. In the aid in dying situation, the only person who might conceivably be prosecuted for criminal behavior is the physician who prescribes a lethal dose of medication. In that the claims of the plaintiff physicians are premised in significant part upon concerns that they could be prosecuted for extending aid in dying, we deem it appropriate to analyze their possible culpability for homicide by examining whether the consent of the patient to his physician's aid in dying could constitute a statutory defense to a homicide charge against the physician.

¶ 12 The consent statute would shield physicians from homicide liability if, with the patients' consent, the physicians provide aid in dying to terminally ill, mentally competent adult patients. We first determine whether a statutory consent defense applies to physicians who provide aid in dying and, second, whether patient consent is rendered ineffective by § 45-2-211(2)(d), MCA, because permitting the conduct or resulting harm "is against public policy."

¶ 13 Section 45-5-102(1), MCA, states that a person commits the offense of deliberate homicide if "the person purposely or knowingly causes the death of another human being. . . ." Section 45-2-211(1), MCA, establishes consent as a defense, stating that the "consent of the victim to conduct charged to constitute an offense or to the result thereof is a defense." Thus, if the State prosecutes a physician for providing aid in dying to a mentally competent, terminally ill adult patient who consented to such aid, the physician may be shielded from liability pursuant to the consent statute. This consent defense, however, is only effective if none of the statutory exceptions to consent applies. Section 45-2-211(2), MCA, codifies the four exceptions:

> Consent is ineffective if: (a) it is given by a person who is legally incompetent to authorize the conduct charged to constitute the offense; (b) it is given by a person who by reason of youth, mental disease or defect, or intoxication is unable to make a reasonable judgment as to the nature or harmfulness of the conduct charged to constitute the offense; (c) it is induced by force, duress, or deception; or (d) it is against public policy to permit the conduct or the resulting harm, even though consented to.

The first three statutory circumstances rendering consent ineffective require case-by-case factual determinations. We therefore confine our analysis to the last exception and determine whether, under Montana law, consent to physician aid in dying is against public policy. For the reasons stated below, we find no indication in

Montana law that physician aid in dying provided to terminally ill, mentally competent adult patients is against public policy.

¶ 14 Section 45-2-211(2)(d), MCA, renders consent ineffective if "it is against public policy to permit the conduct or the resulting harm, even though consented to." We addressed the applicability of this provision in *State v. Mackrill*, 2008 MT 297. This Court held that the consent of a victim is not a defense to the charge of aggravated assault under § 45-5-202(1), MCA. The *Mackrill* decision, while not limiting the exception's reach, applied the "against public policy" exception to situations in which violent, public altercations breach public peace and endanger others in the vicinity. Physician aid in dying, as analyzed below, does not fall within the scope of what this Court has thus far identified as "against public policy."

¶ 15 The *Mackrill* case arose from a particularly violent altercation between Jason Mackrill and Robert Gluesing outside a Livingston bar. Mackrill, who had been drinking heavily, spent the better part of the evening disrupting other bar-goers, including Gluesing. When a bartender refused to serve Mackrill, Gluesing offered Mackrill a few dollars and encouraged him to go elsewhere. Mackrill became obstinate and refused to leave. When the bartender picked up the phone to call the police, Gluesing escorted Mackrill out of the bar. Once outside, Mackrill began punching Gluesing, including a "very solid shot" that caused Gluesing's feet to come off the ground and the back of his head to hit the pavement. A witness called 9-1-1 and paramedics arrived on the scene. They found Gluesing unconscious and bleeding in the street. He was transported to the hospital and treated for head injuries, including a skull fracture.

¶ 16 The State charged Mackrill with one count of aggravated assault, a felony under § 45-5-202, MCA. He pleaded not guilty and filed a Notice of Affirmative Defenses, in which he stated he would argue consent as a defense at trial. The jury found Mackrill guilty. He then filed a post-trial motion claiming the State failed to introduce evidence upon which the jury could conclude Gluesing did not consent to the fight. After a hearing on the matter, the district court denied the motion. Mackrill appealed. This Court concluded that consent is not an effective defense against an assault charge under § 45-5-202(1), MCA.

¶ 17 The *Mackrill* decision is the only Montana case addressing the public policy exception to consent. It demonstrates one set of circumstances in which consent as a defense is rendered ineffective because permitting the conduct or resulting harm is "against public policy." This "against public policy" exception to consent applies to conduct that disrupts public peace and physically endangers others. Clearly, under *Mackrill*, unruly, physical and public aggression between individuals falls within the parameters of the "against public policy" exception. The men were intoxicated, brawling in a public space, and endangering others in the process. ***

¶ 23 In contrast, a physician who aids a terminally ill patient in dying is not directly involved in the final decision or the final act. He or she only provides a means by which a terminally ill patient himself can give effect to his life-ending decision, or not, as the case may be. Each stage of the physician-patient interaction is private, civil, and compassionate. The physician and terminally ill patient work together to create a means by which the patient can be in control of his own mortality. The patient's subsequent private decision whether to take the medicine does not breach public peace or endanger others.

¶ 24 Although the "against public policy" exception of § 45-2-211(2)(d), MCA, is not limited to violent breaches of the peace as discussed in the above cases, we see nothing in the case law facts or analysis suggesting that a patient's private interaction with his physician, and subsequent decision regarding whether to take medication provided by a physician, violate public policy. We thus turn to a review of Montana statutory law.

¶ 25 We similarly find no indication in Montana statutes that physician aid in dying is against public policy. The Montana Rights of the Terminally Ill Act (Terminally Ill Act) and the homicide statute's narrow applicability to "another" human being, do not indicate that physician aid in dying is against public policy.

¶ 26 Under § 45-5-102, MCA, a "person commits the offense of deliberate homicide if: (a) the person purposely or knowingly causes the death of another human being...." In physician aid in dying, the physician makes medication available for a terminally ill patient who requests it, and the patient would then choose whether to cause his own death by self-administering the medicine. The terminally ill patient's act of ingesting the medicine is not criminal. There is no language in the homicide statute indicating that killing "oneself," as opposed to "another," is a punishable offense, and there is no separate statute in Montana criminalizing suicide. There is thus no indication in the homicide statutes that physician aid in dying — in which a terminally ill patient elects and consents to taking possession of a quantity of medicine from a physician that, if he chooses to take it, will cause his own death — is against public policy. ***

¶ 38 There is no indication in the Rights of the Terminally Ill Act that physician aid in dying is against public policy. Indeed, the Act reflects legislative respect for the wishes of a patient facing incurable illness. The Act also indicates legislative regard and protection for a physician who honors his legal obligation to the patient. The Act immunizes a physician for following the patient's declaration even if it requires the physician to directly unplug the patient's ventilator or withhold medicine or medical treatment that is keeping the patient alive. Physician aid in dying, on the other hand, does not require such direct involvement by a physician. Rather, in physician aid in dying, the final death-causing act lies in the patient's hands. In light of the long-standing, evolving and unequivocal recognition of the terminally ill patient's right to self-determination at the end of life in Title 50, chapter 9, MCA, it would be incongruous to conclude that a physician's indirect aid in dying is contrary to public policy.

¶ 39 There are three central problems with the Dissent's response. First, the Dissent applies § 45-5-105, MCA — a statute that factually does not apply to Mr. Baxter's appeal. This statute only applies if the suicide does not occur. Second, the Dissent massages the statute's legislative history into makeshift legislation, which it then proffers as public policy. Such analysis directly violates this Court's precedent regarding statutory interpretation.

¶ 40 The Dissent first cites § 45-5-105, MCA, stating that a person may be prosecuted for aiding or soliciting suicide only if the individual does not die. The statute's plain meaning is clear. It is also inapplicable. The narrow scenario we have been asked to consider on appeal involves the situation in which a terminally ill patient affirmatively seeks a lethal dose of medicine and subsequently self-administers it, causing his own death. Section 45-5-105, MCA, unambiguously applies only when the suicide does not occur. ***

¶ 44 Even if this Court were to extend consideration to § 45-5-105, MCA, as a generalized reflection of the legislature's views on third party involvement in suicides, there remains no indication that the statute was ever intended to apply to the very narrow set of circumstances in which a terminally ill patient himself seeks out a physician and asks the physician to provide him the means to end his own life. As the Dissent states, the original enactment addressed situations of a third party "encouraging" a suicide. The present version reflects the same focus in the "soliciting" language. The statute's plain language addresses the situation in which a third party unilaterally solicits or aids another person. In physician aid in dying, the solicitation comes from the patient himself, not a third party physician.

¶ 45 There is no indication that the 1973 Montana legislators contemplated the statute would apply to this specific situation in which a terminally ill patient seeks a means by which he can end his own incurable suffering. In fact, it was not until twelve years later in 1985, that the legislature enacted the Rights of the Terminally Ill Act, which squarely addresses the modern complexities of physician- and technology-dependent end-of-life care provided to terminally ill Montanans. Since then, the legislature—as illustrated in the Terminally Ill Act analysis above—has carefully cultivated a statutory scheme that gives terminally ill Montanans the right to autonomously choose what happens to them at the end of painful terminal illness. ***

¶ 49 In conclusion, we find nothing in Montana Supreme Court precedent or Montana statutes indicating that physician aid in dying is against public policy. The "against public policy" exception to consent has been interpreted by this Court as applicable to violent breaches of the public peace. Physician aid in dying does not satisfy that definition. We also find nothing in the plain language of Montana statutes indicating that physician aid in dying is against public policy. In physician aid in dying, the patient—not the physician—commits the final death-causing act by self-administering a lethal dose of medicine.

¶ 50 Furthermore, the Montana Rights of the Terminally Ill Act indicates legislative respect for a patient's autonomous right to decide if and how he will receive medical treatment at the end of his life. The Terminally Ill Act explicitly shields physicians from liability for acting in accordance with a patient's end-of-life wishes, even if the physician must actively pull the plug on a patient's ventilator or withhold treatment that will keep him alive. There is no statutory indication that lesser end-of-life physician involvement, in which the patient himself commits the final act, is against public policy. We therefore hold that under § 45-2-211, MCA, a terminally ill patient's consent to physician aid in dying constitutes a statutory defense to a charge of homicide against the aiding physician when no other consent exceptions apply. ***

Justice JOHN WARNER concurs. ***

¶ 53 The Court's opinion today answers the statutory question: is it, as a matter of law, against the public policy of Montana for a physician to assist a mentally competent, terminally ill person to end their life? The answer provided is: "No, it is not, as a matter of law."

¶ 54 This Court correctly avoided the constitutional issue Baxter desires to present. No question brought before this Court is of greater delicacy than one that involves the power of the legislature to act. If it becomes indispensably necessary to the case to answer such a question, this Court must meet and decide it; but it is not the habit of the courts to decide questions of a constitutional nature unless absolutely necessary to a decision of the case.

¶ 55 This Court has done its job and held that pursuant to § 45-2-211, MCA, a physician who assists a suicide, and who happens to be charged with a crime for doing so, may assert the defense of consent. I join the opinion, and not the thoughtful and thought provoking dissent, because the Legislature has not plainly stated that assisting a suicide is against public policy. This Court must not add such a provision by judicial fiat. Section 1-2-101, MCA.

¶ 56 The logic of the Court's opinion is not necessarily limited to physicians. In my view, the citizens of Montana have the right to have their legislature step up to the plate and squarely face the question presented by this case, do their job, and decide just what is the policy of Montana on this issue.

¶ 57 As for the constitutional analysis requested by Baxter, I have found many times in my judicial career that Viscount Falkland is correct: when it is not necessary to make a decision, it is necessary to not make a decision. A question of constitutional law should not be anticipated in advance of the necessity of deciding it.

Justice JAMES C. NELSON, specially concurring. ***

¶ 59 With the exception of the Court's decision to vacate the District Court's ruling on the constitutional issues . . . I otherwise join the Court's Opinion. For the reasons which follow, I agree with the Court's analysis under the consent statute (§ 45-2-211, MCA), and I further conclude that physician aid in dying is protected by the Montana Constitution as a matter of privacy (Article II, Section 10) and as a matter of individual dignity (Article II, Section 4). ***

II. CONSTITUTIONAL ANALYSIS

¶ 64 Although the Court has chosen to decide this case on the narrow statutory ground suggested by the State of Montana (as an alternative approach) in its briefs on appeal, and although physician aid in dying is protected statutorily (as the Court holds under this alternative approach), physician aid in dying is also firmly protected by Montana's Constitution. In this regard, I compliment District Court Judge Dorothy McCarter for her well-written, compassionate, and courageous—indeed, visionary—interpretation of our Constitution. The parties have extensively briefed the constitutional issues, and the Dissent touches on them as well. For these reasons, and because I so passionately believe that individual dignity is, in all likelihood, the most important—and yet, in our times, the most fragile—of all human rights protected by Montana's Constitution, I proceed to explain what I believe the right of dignity means within the context of this case—one of the most important cases the courts of this state have ever considered.

¶ 65 The District Court's decision is grounded in both the right of individual dignity guaranteed by Article II, Section 4 and the right of individual privacy guaranteed by Article II, Section 10. Likewise, the Plaintiff-Appellee patients (Patients) and their amici present arguments under both provisions. With regard to Article II, Section 10, they persuasively demonstrate that under *Gryczan v. State* (Mont. 1997), and *Armstrong v. State*, 1999 MT 261, physician aid in dying is protected by the right of individual privacy. Indeed, this Court held in *Armstrong* that "the personal autonomy component of this right broadly guarantees each individual the right to make medical judgments affecting her or his bodily integrity and health in partnership with a chosen health care provider free from the interference of the government...." As noted, however, I believe that this case—aid in dying so as to die with dignity—is most fundamentally and quintessentially a matter of human dignity. Accordingly, it is to that right that I direct my comments below. ***

B. Construction of Article II, Section 4

¶ 74 Article II, Section 4 of Montana's 1972 Constitution provides:

> Individual dignity. The dignity of the human being is inviolable. No person shall be denied the equal protection of the laws. Neither the state nor any person, firm, corporation, or institution shall discriminate against any person in the exercise of his civil or political rights on account of race, color, sex, culture, social origin or condition, or political or religious ideas.

While there are differing interpretations of this language, which I note below, it is my view that the first clause of Article II, Section 4 (the Dignity Clause) is a stand-alone, fundamental constitutional right. *See Walker v. State*, 2003 MT 134 (explaining that the rights found in Article II are "fundamental" and that the plain meaning of the Dignity Clause "commands that the intrinsic worth and the basic humanity of persons may not be violated").

¶ 75 First, I categorically reject the notion that the Dignity Clause is merely some "aspirational introduction" to the equal protection and nondiscrimination rights which follow it—a proposition for which there is no authority. Our Constitution is "a limitation upon the powers of government," and in construing a constitutional provision, we are required "to give meaning to every word, phrase, clause and sentence therein, if it is possible so to do." Accordingly, the command that "[t]he dignity of the human being is inviolable" must be acknowledged as the freestanding limitation it is on the power of the government—much in the same way we recognize that trial by jury, which is similarly "inviolate" (Mont. Const. art. II, § 26), is not merely "aspirational" but is in fact a concrete right guaranteed by the Constitution.

¶ 76 Second, I likewise reject the notion that the right of dignity is fully implemented by the Equal Protection and Nondiscrimination Clauses or that these clauses are the sole "operative vehicles" for achieving dignity. In other words, I cannot agree that the inviolable dignity of a human being is infringed only when the person is denied equal protection of the laws or suffers discrimination for exercising his or her civil or political rights. Indeed, such an interpretation of Article II, Section 4 attributes an implausibly narrow meaning to the term "dignity." As the Dissent notes, the Dignity Clause can be traced to West Germany's 1949 Constitution, which was developed in response to the Nazi regime's treatment of the Jewish people (as well as homosexuals, Gypsies, persons with disabilities, and political opponents). These "inferior" people (so-called "useless eaters") were not merely denied equal protection of the laws. The government placed them in concentration camps and used them for slave labor. Medical experiments were performed on them. They were persecuted and killed. They were viewed and treated as subhuman, without any dignity. The West German Constitution and its command that "[t]he dignity of man shall be inviolable" must be understood in this context. Doing so, it simply cannot be maintained that Article II, Section 4 prohibits only discrimination and the denial of equal protection. The Dignity Clause broadly prohibits any law or act that infringes upon our inviolable dignity as human beings. This is not some "vague, lurking" right as the Dissent suggests. Rather, it is an imperative; an affirmative and unambiguous constitutional mandate. ***

¶ 79 This interpretation is consistent with the debate on Article II, Section 4 at the 1971–1972 Constitutional Convention. During the debate, Delegate Jerome T. Loendorf inquired whether the express prohibition against discrimination was necessary, given that the right of equal protection already prohibits discrimination. Delegate Wade J. Dahood (chair of the Bill of Rights Committee) acknowledged that the Nondiscrimination Clause was "subsumed in" the Equal Protection Clause, but he explained that "when we're dealing with this type of right, Delegate Loendorf, and we are dealing with something that is this basic, to an orderly and progressive society perhaps sometimes the sermon that can be given by constitution, as well as the right, becomes necessary." Thus, the delegates decided that it was preferable to include the additional language making certain facets of the equal protection right explicit. This same principle supports the notion that denying someone the equal protection of the laws is but one way in which human dignity can be violated, as discussed above.

¶ 80 In arguing against this interpretation of Article II, Section 4, the Dissent points to Delegate Dahood's statement that "[t]here is no intent within this particular section to do anything other than to remove the apparent type of discrimination that all of us object to with respect to employment, to rental practices, to actual associationship in matters that are public or matters that tend to be somewhat quasi-public." This statement, however, must be understood in context. Dahood was not purporting to limit the scope of Article II, Section 4. In fact, he was trying to keep the provision broad. Delegate Otto T. Habedank had voiced a concern that the language "any person, firm, corporation, or institution" in the Nondiscrimination Clause would prohibit private organizations from limiting their membership and would force individuals to associate with people they otherwise would choose not to associate with. Habedank therefore had moved to delete the "any person, firm, corporation, or institution" language from the Nondiscrimination Clause, thereby rendering the clause applicable to only the state. Dahood, in turn, argued against this amendment (which ultimately was defeated 76 to 13) and in favor of applying the nondiscrimination prohibition to entities other than the state, such as employers, landlords, and public or quasi-public associations. Dahood made no remarks about the Dignity Clause itself.

¶ 81 In contrast, Delegate Proposal No. 33 specifically recognized an independent right of individual dignity. It stated: "The rights of individual dignity, privacy, and free expression being essential to the well-being of a free society, the state shall not infringe upon these rights without the showing of a compelling state interest." This proposal was referred to the Bill of Rights Committee, which adopted the proposal in its entirety. The right of individual dignity, the right of privacy, and the right of free expression were then incorporated, respectively, into Sections 4, 10, and 7 of Article II.

¶ 82 In sum, given the plain language of Article II, Section 4 and the structure of this provision, I conclude that the Dignity Clause—stating that the dignity of the human being is inviolable—is a stand-alone, fundamental constitutional right. This conclusion is supported by the record from the Constitutional Convention. I now turn to the substance of this right.

C. The Right of Human Dignity

¶ 83 Human dignity is, perhaps, the most fundamental right in the Declaration of Rights. This right is "inviolable," meaning that it is "[s]afe from violation; *incapable* of being violated." Black's Law Dictionary 904 (Bryan A. Garner ed., 9th ed., West 2009) (emphasis added). Significantly, the right of human dignity is the only right in Montana's Constitution that is "inviolable." [Fn. As noted, the right of trial by jury is "inviolate." Mont. Const. art. II, § 26. "Inviolate," however, means "[f]ree from violation; not broken, infringed, or impaired," Black's Law Dictionary 904, which is not the same as "incapable of being violated."] It is the only right in Article II carrying the absolute prohibition of "inviolability." No individual may be stripped of her human dignity under the plain language of the Dignity Clause. No private or governmental entity has the right or the power to do so. Human dignity simply cannot be violated — no exceptions. *Snetsinger v. Montana University System*, 2004 MT 390 (Nelson, J., specially concurring). ***

¶ 86 Given its intrinsic nature, it is entirely proper, in my view, that the right of dignity under Article II, Section 4 is absolute. Indeed, human dignity transcends the Constitution and the law. Dignity is a fundamental component of humanness. It is inherent in human self-consciousness. Dignity belongs, intrinsically, to our species — to each of us — as a natural right from birth to death. It permeates each person regardless of who that person is or what he does. It cannot be abrogated because of one's status or condition. While the government may impinge on privacy rights, liberty interests, and other Article II rights in proper circumstances (e.g., when one becomes a prisoner), the individual always retains his right of human dignity. So too with persons suffering from mental illness or disability and involuntary commitment: Each retains the right to demand of the State that his dignity as a human being be respected despite the government's sometimes necessary interference in his life.

¶ 87 I am convinced that each of us recognizes this intrinsic, elemental nature of human dignity. Indeed, that recognition explains why we collectively recoil from the pyramid of naked enemy soldiers prodded by troops with guns and dogs at Abu Ghraib; why disgust fills most of us at the descriptions and depictions of water boarding and torture; and why we revolt from ethnic cleansing and genocide. It is why we should collectively rebel, as well, when we see our fellow human beings in need from lack of food, clothing, shelter, medical care, and education.

¶ 88 Experience teaches, and we understand innately, that once we strip an individual of dignity, the human being no longer exists. A subhuman is easy to abuse, torture, and kill, because the object of the abuse is simply that — an object without worth or value and devoid of the essential element of humanness: dignity. Six million Jewish people, along with homosexuals, Gypsies, and persons with disabilities stand as mute testament to what happens when human beings are stripped of their dignity.

¶ 89 I believe this is why we also collectively recoil from accounts of our fellow human beings forced to endure the humiliation and degradation of an agonizing death from an incurable illness. Pain may, in theory, be alleviated to the point of rendering the person unconscious. But in those circumstances, we still cannot deny that the individual's human dignity has been dealt a grievous blow long before death claims her body. ***

¶ 90 Few of us would wish upon ourselves or upon others the prolonged dying that comes from an incurable illness. And it is for this reason that some of our fellow human beings demand—rightfully, in my view—that we respect their individual right to preserve their own human dignity at a time when they are mentally competent, incurably ill, and faced with death from their illness within a relatively short period of time.

¶ 91 The State asserts that it has compelling interests in preserving life and protecting vulnerable groups from potential abuses. This broad assertion, however, is entirely inadequate to sustain the State's position in opposition to physician aid in dying. We are dealing here with persons who are mentally competent, who are incurably ill, and who expect death within a relatively short period of time. The State has failed to explain what interest the government has in forcing a competent, incurably ill person who is going through prolonged suffering and slow, excruciating physical deterioration to hang on to the last possible moment. Moreover, the State has not come close to showing that it has any interest, much less a "compelling" one, in usurping a competent, incurably ill individual's autonomous decision to obtain a licensed physician's assistance in dying so that she might die with the same human dignity with which she was born. In point of fact, the State's position in this appeal is diametrically in opposition to the public policy reflected in the Montana Rights of the Terminally Ill Act: that a mentally competent, incurably ill individual should have autonomy with regard to end-of-life decisions and should be afforded respect and assurance that her life-ending wishes will be honored.

¶ 92 Furthermore, it must be remembered that an individual's right of human dignity is inviolable; it is incapable of being violated. Thus, there is absolutely no merit to the State's suggestion that it may strip a human being of his dignity in order to satisfy an interest that the government believes is "compelling." The right of dignity is absolute, and it remains absolute even at the time of death. It may not be stripped from the individual by a well-meaning yet paternalistic government. Nor may it be stripped by third parties or institutions driven by political ideology or religious beliefs. *Cf.* Clifford and Huff, 61 Mont. L.Rev. at 330 ("To be forced into degrading or dehumanizing pain or suffering because of someone else's conception of a good or proper death exacerbates the loss of dignity. . . ."). Dignity defines what it means to be human. It defines the depth of individual autonomy throughout life and, most certainly, at death. Usurping a mentally competent, incurably ill individual's ability to make end-of-life decisions and forcing that person against his will to suffer a prolonged and excruciating deterioration is, at its core, a blatant and untenable violation of the person's fundamental right of human dignity.

III. Conclusion

¶ 93 In conclusion, while I join the Court's decision, I also would affirm the District Court's ruling on the constitutional issues. I agree with the Court's statutory analysis, but I also agree with Judge McCarter that physician aid is dying is firmly protected by Article II, Sections 4 and 10 of the Montana Constitution. Under these sections, individuals who are mentally competent and incurably ill and face death within a relatively short period of time have the right to self-administer, at a time and place of their choosing, a life-ending substance prescribed by their physician. The physician simply makes the medication available to the patient who requests it and the patient ultimately chooses whether to cause her own death by self-administering the medicine.

¶ 94 This right to physician aid in dying quintessentially involves the inviolable right to human dignity—our most fragile fundamental right. Montana's Dignity Clause does not permit a person or entity to force an agonizing, dehumanizing, demeaning, and often protracted death upon a mentally competent, incurably ill individual for the sake of political ideology, religious belief, or a paternalistic sense of ethics. Society does not have the right to strip a mentally competent, incurably ill individual of her inviolable human dignity when she seeks aid in dying from her physician. Dignity is a fundamental component of humanness; it is intrinsic to our species; it must be respected throughout life; and it must be honored when one's inevitable destiny is death from an incurable illness.

Justice JIM RICE, dissenting.

¶ 96 The prohibition against homicide—intentionally causing the death of another—protects and preserves human life, is the ultimate recognition of human dignity, and is a foundation for modern society, as it has been for millennia past. Based upon this foundation, Anglo-American law, encompassing the law of Montana, has prohibited the enabling of suicide for over 700 years. *Wash. v. Glucksberg* (1997). However, in contradiction to these fundamental principles, the Court concludes that physician-assisted suicide does not violate Montana's public policy. In doing so, the Court has badly misinterpreted our public policy: assisting suicide has been explicitly and expressly prohibited by Montana law for the past 114 years. More than merely setting aside the District Court's order herein, I would reverse the judgment entirely.

¶ 97 A flaw that underlies the Court's analysis is its failure to distinguish between the physician's basic intention in the assisted-suicide case from the physician's intention while rendering treatment in other cases. As developed further herein, the intentions in these two cases are diametrically opposed, and create the very difference between a criminal and noncriminal act. Physician-assisted suicide occurs when a physician provides a lethal drug with the intent to cause, when the drug is taken by the patient, the patient's death. With palliative care, the physician does not intend his or her actions to cause the patient's death, but rather intends to relieve the patient's pain and suffering. For this reason a physician providing palliative care, even in cases where the treatment arguably contributes to the patient's death, lacks the requisite mental state to be charged under homicide statutes. A similar distinction arises in the withholding or withdrawal of medical treatment that merely prolongs the dying process, pursuant to the Montana Rights of the Terminally Ill Act.

Under the Act, a patient may refuse treatment and allow death to occur naturally, and physicians incur no liability, having not administered any death-causing treatment. Sections 50-9-103, -204, MCA.

¶ 98 Criminal acts may be defended on the basis of a victim's consent to the act in certain circumstances. Section 45-2-211(1), MCA. However, this statute makes consent "ineffective" if "it is against public policy to permit the conduct or the resulting harm." Section 45-2-211(2), MCA. The Court concludes from its review of Montana law that "it would be incongruous to conclude that a physician's indirect aid in dying is contrary to public policy." Because, generally, "the public policy of the State of Montana is set by the Montana Legislature through its enactment of statutes," I turn to the very statutes which address the assisting of suicide.

The Statutory Prohibition on the Aiding or Soliciting of Suicide

> "If the conduct of the offender made him the agent of the death, the offense is criminal homicide notwithstanding the consent or even the solicitations of the victim." Commission Comments, § 45-5-105, MCA.

¶ 99 Montana originally enacted a prohibition on the aiding or soliciting of suicide statute in 1895, providing that "[e]very person who deliberately aids, or advises or encourages another to commit suicide is guilty of a felony." Section 698, Mont. Penal Code (1895). The prohibition on aiding suicide has been the formally enacted public policy of our state for the succeeding 114 years. Under the 1895 enactment, the death or survival of the victim was irrelevant, as the crime only required that a defendant deliberately aid, advise, or encourage another to commit suicide. The Legislature left the statute untouched for over seventy years.

¶ 100 In 1973, the Legislature revised the statute to read:

> (1) A person who purposely aids or solicits another to commit suicide, but such suicide does not occur commits the offense of aiding or soliciting suicide.
>
> (2) A person convicted of the offense of aiding or soliciting a suicide shall be imprisoned in the state prison for any term not to exceed ten (10) years.

Section 94-5-106, RCM (1973). The Legislature codified this provision within the homicide statutes. The current version of the statute is the same as the 1973 version, except that the Legislature has increased the potential punishment for the crime by authorizing a $50,000 penalty. Section 45-5-105(2), MCA (2007).

¶ 101 Under the wording of the current version of the statute, a person may be prosecuted for aiding or soliciting another to commit suicide only if the victim survives. The purpose of this change of the statutory language from the pre-1973 version was explained by the Criminal Code Commission that proposed it. When the victim dies, the act is to be prosecuted as a homicide. "If the conduct of the offender made him the agent of the death, the offense is criminal homicide...." Commission Comments, § 45-5-105, MCA (emphasis added). The Commission Comments then direct attention to the other crimes codified within the same homicide section—deliberate homicide, mitigated deliberate homicide, and negligent homicide. Commission Comments, § 45-5-105, MCA (citing §§ 45-5-102, -103, -104, MCA). Like the other homicide statutes, the statute prohibiting the aiding or soliciting of suicide makes the offense a felony. Sections 45-5-102(2), -103(4), -104(3), -105(2), MCA. The justification for the felony designation of the offense, despite the fact the victim has survived, was provided by the Commission: "The rationale behind the felony sentence for the substantive offense of aiding or soliciting suicide is that the act typifies a very low regard for human life." Commission Comments, § 45-5-105, MCA (emphasis added). This clear statement of the State's policy to protect human life is steadfastly avoided by the Court in its analysis.

¶ 102 Thus, under Montana law, physicians who assist in a suicide are subject to criminal prosecution irrespective of whether the patient survives or dies. If the patient survives, the physician may be prosecuted under aiding or soliciting suicide. Section 45-5-105, MCA. If the patient dies, the physician may be prosecuted under the homicide statutes. Commission Comments, § 45-5-105, MCA (citing §§ 45-5-102, -103, -104, MCA).

¶ 103 Importantly, it is also very clear that a patient's consent to the physician's efforts is of no consequence whatsoever under these statutes. The Commission Comments explain that a physician acting as the agency of death may not raise "consent or even the solicitations of the victim" as a defense to criminal culpability. Commission Comments, § 45-5-105, MCA (emphasis added). This principle has likewise been stated and restated by courts around the country: *Mich. v. Kevorkian* (Mich. App. 2001) ("consent and euthanasia are not recognized defenses to murder"); *Gentry v. Ind.* (Ind.App. 1st Dist.1993) ("consent is not a defense to conduct causing another human being's death") (citation omitted); *Pa. v. Root* (Pa. Super. 1959) ("The Commonwealth is interested in protecting its citizens against acts which endanger their lives. *The policy of the law is to protect human life, even the life of a person who wishes to destroy his own.* To prove that the victim wanted to die would be no defense to murder." (Emphasis added.)), *overruled on other grounds*, *Pa. v. Root* (Pa. 1961). ***

The Montana Rights of the Terminally Ill Act

¶ 106 In 1991, the Legislature enacted the Montana Rights of the Terminally Ill Act (Montana Act) by substantially adopting the Uniform Rights of the Terminally Ill Act (Uniform Act). Secs. 1–16, Ch. 391, L. 1991 (codified at §§ 50-9-101 to -206, MCA). The Prefatory Note in the Uniform Act explains that "[t]he scope of the Act is *narrow*. Its impact is limited to treatment that is *merely life-prolonging*. . . ." Uniform Rights of Terminally Ill Act (1989), 9C U.L.A. 311, 312 (2001) (emphasis added) . . . . And, as the Court acknowledges, the Montana Act is careful to explain that it "does not condone, authorize, or approve mercy killing or euthanasia." Section 50-9-205(7), MCA.

¶ 107 The operative words in the Montana Act are those permitting a patient to "withhold" and "withdraw" life-sustaining treatment. *See* §§ 50-9-103(2), -106, -204,

-205, MCA. Largely self-evident, to "withhold" means "to desist or refrain from granting, giving, or allowing." Webster's Third New International Dictionary of the English Language 2627 (Philip Babcock Gove ed., G. & C. Merriam Co. 1971). Similarly, "withdraw" is defined as "to take back or away (something bestowed or possessed)." Webster's Third New International Dictionary of the English Language at 2626. Neither word incorporates the concept of affirmatively issuing a life-ending drug to a patient. Rather, the plain language permits only the taking away of, or refraining from giving, certain medical treatment—that which merely prolongs the dying process. Sections 50-9-102(9), -103(2), -106, -204, -205, MCA.

¶ 108 Although the Court reasons that because the Montana Act permits the withholding or withdrawal of treatment prolonging the dying process, "it would be incongruous to conclude that a physician's indirect aid in dying is contrary to public policy," the opposite is true: it is incongruous to conclude there is no legal distinction between the withdrawal of life-prolonging medical treatment and the provision of life-ending treatment. This distinction is clearly recognized by the wording of our statutes, discussed above, and by the courts. *See e.g., Vacco v. Quill* (1997) (distinguishing between physician-assisted suicide and refusal of medical treatment does not violate equal protection); *and compare Glucksberg* (holding there is no constitutional right to physician-assisted suicide) *with Cruzan v. Mo. Dept. of Health* (1990) (assuming a constitutional right for competent person to refuse unwanted medical treatment). ***

¶ 110 Thus, the law accommodating a patient's desire to die of natural causes by withholding treatment does not, as the Court posits, support a public policy in favor of the deliberate action by a physician to cause a patient's pre-natural, or premature, death.

The 1972 Montana Constitution

¶ 111 Montana's longstanding public policy against the assistance of suicide was continued by adoption of the 1972 Constitution. It supports neither the Court's public policy determination, nor the District Court's constitutionally based decision.

¶ 112 No statement concerning a "right to die" is included within the Constitution's Declaration of Rights. This absence is neither accidental nor the product of ignorance. In this regard, it is important to note that "[n]o proposal was adopted or rejected without considered deliberation."

¶ 113 One of the proposals receiving such careful deliberation was Proposal No. 103. Submitted to the Bill of Rights Committee by Delegate Robert L. Kelleher, Proposal No. 103 would have included a right to die within the Constitution's Declaration of Rights.

¶ 114 Delegate Kelleher's proposal provided, in pertinent part, "The incurably ill have the right not to be kept alive by extraordinary means." Delegate Kelleher testified before the Bill of Rights Committee, "that the person with an incurable disease should have the right to choose his own death." Alternatives offered to Kelleher's proposal covered the broad spectrum of "right to die" scenarios. Joe Roberts testified on the same day as Delegate Kelleher, advocating for broader language: "There shall be a right to die. The legislature shall make appropriate provisions therefore." Mr. Roberts referenced the "very poignant testimony" of witness Joyce Franks and her "personal encounter with the agonizing death of her father." Ms. Franks' testimony had described the death of her 86-year-old father and his wish that a doctor "give him something to put him to sleep right then." Ms. Franks stated to the Bill of Rights Committee, "What I am working for is that every person shall have the right to determine, barring accident, the manner of his dying. And then, I am advocating the twin right to make it legal, if he desires this type of death, for a person to receive a quick and easy medicated death somehow." Ms. Franks therefore urged adoption of an amendment stating: "Every citizen shall be allowed to choose the manner in which he dies."

¶ 115 However, the Bill of Rights Committee rejected Kelleher's proposal in its entirety and also rejected all of the alternatives which had been offered in conjunction with Kelleher's proposal to incorporate a "right to die" of any kind within the new Constitution.

¶ 116 Nor were other provisions of the Constitution, such as the Individual Dignity and the Right of Privacy provisions, drafted to include a right to die. The Constitutional Convention adopted the Individual Dignity Section for the express purpose of providing equal protection and prohibiting discrimination. The Bill of Rights Committee proposed the Individual Dignity Section "with the *intent* of providing a Constitutional impetus for the eradication of public and private discriminations based on race, color, sex, culture, social origin or condition, or political or religious ideas." During the floor debate on the provision, Delegate Otto Habedank expressed concern that he would be required "to associate with people that I choose not to associate with." Delegate Wade J. Dahood, Chairman of the Bill of Rights Committee, responded to Delegate Habedank's concern by stating, "There is no intent within this particular section to do anything other than to remove the apparent type of discrimination that all of us object to with respect to employment, to rental practices, to actual association in matters that are public or matters that tend to be somewhat quasi-public." Delegate Dahood's statement was consistent with the expressed intent of the Bill of Rights Committee Proposal, which was, in consideration of the entirety of Article II, Section 4, to provide "a Constitutional impetus for the eradication of public and private discriminations. . . ." Nothing within these discussions or explanations suggests even a thought that the dignity clause contained vague, lurking rights that might someday manifest themselves beyond what the delegates or the citizens of Montana who approved the Constitution believed, and overturn long-established law, here, the policy against assisted suicide. The reference to dignity therefore provides an aspirational introduction to the already well-established substantive legal principles providing the operative vehicles to achieve dignity: equal protection and the prohibition upon discrimination.

[Fn. The historical origins of the dignity clause are enlightening. At the Constitutional Convention, delegates reviewed two foreign constitutions, the 1949 West Germany Constitution and the 1951 Puerto Rico Constitution. The West German Constitution, the eldest of the two, provided, "The dignity of man shall be inviolable." The Montana Constitution contains the identical provision, adopted word-for-word except for the use of the gender-neutral "human being" instead of "man." The West German Constitution was developed in response to the Nazi regime's unequal treatment, persecution, and ultimate killing of the Jewish people.]

Likewise, the right to privacy did not alter the State's policy against assisted suicide. There is nothing within either the language of the provision or the convention proceedings which would reflect any such intention. For such reasons, not one court of last resort has interpreted a constitutional right of privacy to include physician-assisted suicide. *Krischer v. McIver* (Fla. 1997); *Sampson v. Alaska* (Alaska 2001); *Glucksberg*. No evidence exists that the delegates intended the right of privacy to change the state's longstanding public policy. Since adoption of the 1972 Constitution, the Legislature has continued to enact legislation prohibiting assisted suicide. Indeed, the Legislature directed the Department of Public Health and Human Services to "implement a suicide prevention program by January 1, 2008," including a plan that must delineate "specific activities to reduce suicide." Sections 53-21-1101(1), -1102(2)(b), MCA. This is further indication of a state public policy against assisted suicide.

¶ 117 Because we live in a democracy, this policy may someday change. Controlling their own destiny, Montanans may decide to change the State's public policy after what would be, no doubt, a spirited public debate. In fact, efforts in that regard have already started. See e.g. Bill Draft LC1818, 61st Leg., Reg. Sess. (Jan. 9, 2008) (The proposed "Montana Death with Dignity Act" had the stated purpose of "allowing a terminally ill patient to request medication to end the patient's life."). This Court should allow the public debate to continue, and allow the citizens of this State to control their own destiny on the issue.

¶ 118 Until the public policy is changed by the democratic process, it should be recognized and enforced by the courts. It is a public policy which regards the aiding of suicide as typifying "a very low regard for human life," Commission Comments, § 45-5-105, MCA, and which expressly prohibits it. Instead, the Court rejects the State's longstanding policy. It ignores expressed intent, parses statutes, and churns reasons to avoid the clear policy of the State and reach an untenable conclusion: that it is against public policy for a physician to assist in a suicide if the patient happens to live after taking the medication; but that the very same act, with the very same intent, is not against public policy if the patient dies. In my view, the Court's conclusion is without support, without clear reason, and without moral force. ***

Hon. JOE L. HEGEL, District Court Judge, sitting in place of Chief Justice MIKE McGRATH, joins in the dissenting Opinion of Justice JIM RICE.

Notes on Privacy's Frontiers and Dignity, Revisited

1. In *Walker*, what does the dignity provision add to the cruel and unusual punishment analysis under the Montana Constitution or the federal Constitution's Eighth Amendment? (Section 1983 is the federal civil rights law providing a claim for damages arising from violations of constitutional rights by state officials.) Conversely, why would a federal civil rights action, and its highly technical standards for stating a claim arising out of imprisonment, displace Walker's claims under the Montana Constitution? If "the dignity provision of the Montana Constitution together with Article II, Section 22 [provides] Montana citizens greater protections from cruel and unusual punishment than does the federal constitution," because "[t]he federal constitution does not expressly provide for the right to human dignity," along which dimensions are those protections greater in the context of punishment? How does it help distinguish between the ordinary indignities of imprisonment and the extraordinary treatment the Court finds in *Walker*, beyond the terms "cruel and unusual"?

2. Is the *Walker* Court's extension of the dignity provision beyond the equality and anti-discrimination provisions of section 4 faithful to its text, structure, and history? How might Walker's claims fare if framed under the equal protection or anti-discrimination provisions? What about a claim that Walker's treatment was inconsistent with the "rights of the convicted" in section 28? (*See* Chapter 14.)

3. Walker himself raised a cruel and unusual punishment claim; it was Walker's appointed counsel who framed it as a petition for post-conviction relief. Procedurally, does *Walker* make sense as a post-conviction relief proceeding? Should it matter in a case such as this? Why not bring a damages claim against the state, similar to the federal civil rights action suggested by Chief Justice Gray?

4. The Court's decision in *Baxter* that physician aid in dying is not "against public policy" under the general criminal consent defense statute avoided the question of whether it is also a privacy or dignity right under the Montana Constitution. As Justice Warner observed, this constitutional avoidance allowed the Legislature to "step up to the plate and squarely face the question presented by this case, do their job, and decide just what is the policy of Montana on this issue." Twelve years and six legislative sessions later, multiple bills attempting to regulate, clarify, or prohibit the right to physician aid in dying have failed. Does this suggest the *Baxter* Court got the law right, shortcut the democratic process, or should have reached the constitutional question anyway?

5. Justice Rice provides extensive evidence of the Constitutional Convention proceedings, including rejected proposals and citizen testimony at the committee level. (The latter is recorded only in state archives; the published transcripts only identify the names of those who testified at each committee.) After *Gryczan*, *Armstrong*, and *Baxter*, is there a settled approach for how the Court regards (or disregards) deliberations of specific issues during the Constitutional Convention? How is such

evidence probative of constitutional meaning? Where should it fall within the hierarchy of constitutional sources?

6. As justices predicted in *Gryczan* and *Armstrong*, the "right to die" issue was framed not just as a novel instance of personal dignity, but also an application of individual privacy recognized in *Armstrong*, ¶ 59:

> Certainly, this right of choice in making personal health care decisions and in exercising personal autonomy is not without limits. In narrowly defined instances the state, by clear and convincing evidence, may demonstrate a compelling interest in and obligation to legislate or regulate to preserve the safety, health and welfare of a particular class of patients or the general public from a medically-acknowledged, bona fide health risk. Subject to this narrow qualification, however, the legislature has neither a legitimate presence nor voice in the patient/health care provider relationship superior to the patient's right of personal autonomy which protects that relationship from infringement by the state.

Would *Baxter* have come out differently under the right of privacy standing alone? What is the privacy analysis supporting Justice Nelson's concurrence?

Chapter 12

Freedoms of Religion and Expression

1889 MONT. CONST. Article III, Section 4. The free exercise and enjoyment of religious profession and worship, without discrimination, shall forever hereafter be guaranteed, and no person shall be denied any civil or political right or privilege on account of his opinions concerning religion, but the liberty of conscience hereby secured shall not be construed to dispense with oaths or affirmations, excuse acts of licentiousness, by bigamous or polygamous marriage, or otherwise, or justify practices inconsistent with the good order, peace, or safety of the state, or opposed to the civil authority thereof, or of the United States. No person shall be required to attend any place of worship or support any ministry, religious sect, or denomination, against his consent; nor shall any preference be given by law to any religious denomination or mode of worship.

Article II, Section 5. Freedom of religion. The state shall make no law respecting an establishment of religion or prohibiting the free exercise thereof.

Revises 1889 constitution by using wording of the U.S. constitution to guarantee free exercise of religion and prohibit the state from establishing a religion.

Article II, Section 6. Freedom of assembly. The people shall have the right peaceably to assemble, petition for redress or peaceably protest governmental action.

No change except in grammar. Retains basic rights to assemble and to petition or protest for redress of grievances.

Article II, Section 7. Freedom of speech, expression, and press. No law shall be passed impairing the freedom of speech or expression. Every person shall be free to speak or publish whatever he will on any subject, being responsible for all abuse of that liberty. In all suits and prosecutions for libel or slander the truth thereof may be given in evidence; and the jury, under the direction of the court, shall determine the law and the facts.

Revises 1889 constitution by enlarging a citizen's freedom to express himself and allowing the truth to be given in evidence in slander as well as libel cases.

The Montana Constitution takes what most Americans consider the (federal) "First Amendment" freedoms of religion and speech and splits them three ways. In a rare example of reverse textual "lockstepping," section 5 expressly adopts the language of the federal Religion Clauses, though at a time when the courts read them differently than they read them now. Like most state constitutions, the Montana Constitution also includes more detailed prohibitions on religious aid and discrimination, particularly in education, beyond free exercise and establishment. Conversely, the Montana Constitution maintained its distinctive approach to freedom of assembly and the right to "peaceably protest governmental action," and added "expression" to its freedom of speech and press guarantees. Yet neither of these innovations have prompted departures from federal free speech doctrine. Twice in the past decade, however, the United States Supreme Court has held the Montana Supreme Court's interpretations of religious and expressive freedom to conflict with the First Amendment. In *Espinoza v. Department of Revenue* (2020), the Court held that Montana's prohibition on financial aid to religious education violated the Free Exercise Clause as applied to a scholarship program for private schools. In *American Tradition Partnership v. Bullock* (2012), the Court held that Montana's interests in preventing corporate corruption of elections did not satisfy strict scrutiny under the First Amendment for campaign expenditure restrictions. Consider whether it is desirable, or even possible, for Montana to forge its own conceptions of these highly contested freedoms.

A. Freedom of Religion

Section 5 of the Declaration of Rights converts the detailed but limited historical protections for "liberty of conscience" in the 1889 Constitution to an apparently simple restatement of the federal Religion Clauses in the First Amendment. Those clauses have been debated for decades by the United States Supreme Court, which has driven sharp shifts in the federal rules governing religious freedom. At the time of the Montana Constitution's ratification, the federal approach favored separation between church and state. More recently, the United States Supreme Court has moved to require neutrality in government's approach to religion. In some areas, the Court appears to suggest a requirement of government accommodation of religion. What course does the Montana Constitution chart for religious freedom in Montana? Should that course shift with the shifts in the meaning of the First Amendment? Between what the Free Exercise Clause requires and the Establishment Clause prohibits, what room has federal constitutional law left for state constitutions — the origins of the American tradition of religious freedom — to strike different balances involving the complications of what conscience demands?

1. Free Exercise and Establishment of Religion

Big Sky Colony, Inc. v. Montana Department of Labor and Industry

368 Mont. 66 (2012)

Justice BRIAN MORRIS delivered the Opinion of the Court.

¶ 1 Appellant Montana Department of Labor and Industry (the Department) appeals from the order of the Ninth Judicial District Court, Glacier County, that granted summary judgment to Appellees Big Sky Colony, Inc., and Daniel E. Wipf (collectively Colony). The District Court [then-Judge Laurie McKinnon] determined that the requirement to provide workers' compensation coverage for the Colony's members engaged in certain commercial activities contained in House Bill 119 (2009 Mont. Laws, ch. 112 § 30) (HB 119) violated the Colony's rights under the Free Exercise Clause and the Establishment Clause of the First Amendment to the U.S Constitution, and also violated the Colony's right to equal protection of the laws under the U.S. Constitution and the Montana Constitution. We reverse. ***

Factual and Procedural Background

¶ 6 The Hutterite Brethren Church originally formed in the 16th century as part of the Anabaptist movement during the Protestant Reformation in Europe. Anabaptists rejected infant baptism as "unbiblical" and instead renewed the practice of adult baptism. Anabaptists live a life of pacifism. Jacob Hutter and his followers eventually broke away from other Anabaptists over a dispute regarding communal living.

¶ 7 Jacob Hutter suffered a violent end as he was burned at the stake in a public square in Innsbruck, Austria, in 1536. Austro-Hungarian authorities held Hutter in freezing water and then placed him in a hot room. Authorities further tortured Hutter by pouring brandy on his wounds before burning him to death.

¶ 8 Hutterite believers moved across Europe for the next several centuries in search of a safe place in which to practice their faith and live their communal life. This wandering eventually brought the Hutterites to North America in the 19th century in search of religious freedom. Hutterites continue to practice their faith and live a communal lifestyle in colonies in Minnesota, North Dakota, South Dakota, Montana, Washington, and parts of Canada.

¶ 9 The Colony, a signatory to the Hutterian Brethren Church Constitution, organizes itself as a religious corporation under Montana law. The Colony's Articles of Incorporation provide that it was formed for the purpose of operating "a Hutterische Church Brotherhood Community." All members of the Colony must belong to the Hutterische Church Society and all members agree to "live a communal life and follow the teaching and tenets of the Hutterische Church Society." Daniel Wipf serves as the Colony's first minister and corporate president.

¶ 10 The Department initially determined that the Workers' Compensation Act did not apply to the Colony or its members due to the fact that the Colony did not pay "wages" to its members. The Department based this determination on the fact that the Colony did not fall within the definition of "employer" set forth at § 39-71-117, MCA, and that the Colony's members did not fall within the definition of "employee" set forth at § 39-71-118, MCA. The 2009 Montana legislature enacted HB 119.

¶ 11 HB 119 worked a laundry list of changes to the Workers' Compensation Act, including revised claims handling practices (§ 39-71-107, MCA), and revised accident reporting requirements for employers (§ 39-71-307, MCA). Pertinent to our analysis, Section 6 amended the definition of "employer" to include:

> a religious corporation, religious organization, or religious trust receiving remuneration from nonmembers for agricultural production, manufacturing, or a construction project conducted by its members on or off the property of the religious corporation, religious organization, or religious trust.

Section 39-71-117(1)(d), MCA. Section 7 of HB 119 amended the definition of "employee" to include:

> a member of a religious corporation, religious organization, or religious trust while performing services for the religious corporation, religious organization, or religious trust, as described in 39-71-117(1)(d).

Section 39-71-118(1)(i), MCA. ***

Discussion

¶ 17 Issue 1. Whether the provisions in HB 119 that incorporate the Colony into the definition of "employer" and the Colony's members into the definition of "employee" under the Workers' Compensation Act violate the Free Exercise Clause.

¶ 18 The District Court determined that the practice of the Hutterite faith demands that its members engage in commercial activities with nonmembers for remuneration. This determination prompted the District Court to analyze the statute based on the strict scrutiny standard applied in the U.S. Supreme Court's decision in *Church of the Lukumi Babalu Aye, Inc. v. City of Hialeah* (1993). The Court in *Lukumi Babalu* struck down a group of municipal ordinances that banned animal sacrifice[, one of the principal forms of devotion of the Santeria church]. ***

¶ 21 The requirement that a religious corporation provide workers' compensation coverage for its members differs markedly from the outright ban of an activity central to the Santeria faith. Unlike the prohibitions in *Lukumi Babalu* and *McDaniel* [*v. Paty* (1978)], the workers' compensation requirement does not prohibit the Colony members from engaging in the commercial activity. HB 119 regulates the Colony's engagement in commercial activities in the same manner that the workers' compensation system regulates the commercial activities of other employers in Montana. The Colony, like all other employers in Montana, simply will make less money on these commercial endeavors once it pays the workers' compensation premiums.... These distinctions lead us to reject the strict scrutiny analysis from *Lukumi Babalu* as the appropriate lens through which to analyze the Colony's claim.

¶ 22 We instead apply the standard used by the Court in *Dept. of Human Resources of Oregon v. Smith* (1990). The workers' compensation requirement must be facially neutral and serve a secular purpose in order to survive a Free Exercise challenge. The requirement also must impose only an incidental burden on religious conduct as opposed to a prohibition on religious conduct.

Facially Neutral and Secular Purpose.

¶ 23 The District Court concluded that HB 119 "unquestionably targets only the Hutterite religious practice of communal living." This conclusion ignores the fact that the workers' compensation requirement in Montana applies generally to multiple types of entities. See § 39-71-117, MCA. The legislature did not conceive of the workers' compensation system as a means to shackle the religious practices of Colony members. HB 119 simply adds to the scope of the workers' compensation system religious corporations that engage in commercial activities with nonmembers for remuneration through its expansion of the definition of "employer" contained in § 39-71-117, MCA.

¶ 24 No doubt exists that the workers' compensation requirement would apply if the Colony employed its members to work for wages on these commercial activities. Indeed, in *St. John's Lutheran Church v. State Comp. Ins. Fund* (Mont. 1992), this Court rejected a Free Exercise challenge to the requirement that the church provide workers' compensation coverage to its pastor on the basis that the provision of workers' compensation represents "an overriding governmental interest." No doubt exists that the workers' compensation requirement would apply if the Colony opted to establish separate commercial entities to perform the type of work at issue here. *See Ridley Park United Methodist Church v. Zoning Hearing Board* (Pa. Cmwlth. 2007) (denying zoning variance to operate a daycare on church site did not impinge on religious activities of church as operation of the daycare "is not a fundamental religious activity of a church").

¶ 25 The Dissent suggests that HB 119 would not capture the activities of the other religious employers, in part, because they do not engage in the types of economic activities enumerated by HB 119. HB 119 did not need to capture these other religious employers, however, to incorporate them into the workers' compensation system. Section 39-71-117(1)(a), MCA, already captures other religious employers who engage in commercial activities. Subsection (a) includes within the definition of "employer" "all public corporations and quasi-public corporations," religious or otherwise. Subsection (a) further includes within the definition of "employer" "each firm, voluntary association, limited liability company, limited liability partnership, and private corporation," religious or otherwise. Finally, subsection (c) defines employer to include "any non-profit association, limited liability company, limited liability partnership, or corporation or other entity," religious or otherwise, that receives federal, state, or local government funds to be used for community service programs.

¶ 26 The Department of Labor and Industry previously did not consider the Colony subject to the workers' compensation system due to the fact that the Colony did not pay "wages" to its members as part of its communal living system. The Colony nevertheless engaged in commercial activities. The Colony instead provides food, shelter, clothing, and medical care to its members who engage in these commercial activities. HB 119 clarified that religious corporations, organizations, or trusts that engage in specified commercial activities, who do not pay "wages" to their members for labor on these commercial activities, but who receive remuneration from non-members, qualify as "employers" for purposes of the workers' compensation system. Section 39-71-117(1) (d), MCA. HB 119 does not lose its facial neutrality or shed its secular purpose due to the fact that it sought to include the colony's commercial activities, as opposed to its religious practices, within the scope of the workers' compensation system.

Incidental Burden or Prohibition on Religious Conduct.

¶ 27 The District Court pronounced that the communal lifestyle represents the Hutterites' "most distinguishing feature." This communal lifestyle merges religious exercise and labor as a member voluntarily contributes all of his property and labor to the Colony "as an expression of faith and worship." This attribute led the District Court to determine that application of HB 119 to the Colony's commercial activities transformed a potentially valid regulation into an outright prohibition on religious conduct. Courts uniformly have rejected the notion that a party's religious motivation for undertaking an act can transform a generally applicable regulation into a prohibition on religious conduct. Other courts have recognized that this logic, taken to its extreme, would subsume every facet of a religious organization into a religious activity. *** The Court in *Smith* dismissed the notion that the "religious motivation" for using peyote placed the two employees beyond the reach of a criminal law not directed specifically at their religious practice. ***

¶ 41 The legislature's regulation of the activities of Colony members would violate the right of members to exercise freely their religion only when the regulation impermissibly singles out "some or all religious beliefs or regulates or prohibits conduct because it is undertaken for religious reasons." *Lukumi Babalu*. The workers' compensation system in Montana generally applies to all employers engaged in commercial activities. Section 39-71-401, MCA. The inclusion of religious organizations that engage voluntarily in commercial activities within the workers' compensation system does not single out religious beliefs. And neither does HB 119's inclusion of religious organizations within the workers' compensation system regulate or prohibit any conduct "because it is undertaken for religious reasons." *Lukumi Babalu*.

¶ 42 Courts routinely have rejected Free Exercise challenges to compelled participation by religious organizations in a wide variety of social welfare programs.... Each of these religious organizations presented sincere and heartfelt beliefs that its participation in the governmental program violated its religious beliefs. The courts rejected each claim. We, too, reject the Colony's Free Exercise challenge to its participation in Montana's workers' compensation system for Colony members engaged in commercial activities with nonmembers for remuneration. The decision of the legislature to include in the definition of "employer" religious corporations that voluntarily engage in commercial activities with nonmembers for remuneration fails to establish evidence of discrimination against religious organizations.

¶ 43 Issue 2. Whether the provisions in HB 119 that incorporate the Colony into the definition of "employer" and the Colony's members into the definition of "employee" under the Workers' Compensation Act violate the Establishment Clause.

¶ 44 *Lemon* [*v. Kurtzman* (1971)] provides the test to analyze government conduct under the Establishment Clause of the First Amendment. The government conduct at issue must (1) have a secular purpose, (2) not have as its principal or primary effect inhibiting religion, and (3) not foster excessive entanglement with religion. Courts most commonly apply *Lemon* to situations in which the government allegedly has given preference to a religion. The *Lemon* test likewise accommodates evaluation of a claim brought under the theory of hostility to religion. ***

¶ 63 The information necessary for the Colony to comply with participation in the workers' compensation system would not delve into the religious beliefs of the Colony or its members. It further appears that the requirement to provide workers' compensation coverage for its members engaged in commercial activities poses no more burdensome recordkeeping requirement than those outlined in *Stahl* [*v. United States* (9th Cir. 2010)]. The Colony presently maintains financial records based on its status as a religious corporation so that its members, similar to the religious corporation in *Stahl*, may file tax returns. Finally, as the Department asserts, the Colony retains the option to self-insure as a means to limit excessive entanglement. Section 39-71-2101, MCA. We cannot agree with the District Court's conclusion that "a comprehensive, discriminating, and continuing state surveillance will inevitably be required to ensure that only particular areas of Hutterite activity are scrutinized." The recordkeeping required to establish compliance with Montana's workers' compensation system constitutes a valid regulation of the Colony's commercial activities.

¶ 64 Issue 3. Whether the provisions in HB 119 that incorporate the Colony into the definition of "employer" and the Colony's members into the definition of "employee" under the Workers' Compensation Act violate the Colony's right to equal protection of the laws. ***

¶ 71 Section 39-71-117, MCA, sets forth in mind-numbing detail the full definition of "employer" for purposes of the workers' compensation system. This extensive definition, including subsections (a), (b), and (c), all of which predated HB 119, applies generally to religious and non-religious entities alike. The definition of "employer" includes the state, counties, cities, public corporations, quasi-public corporations, private corporations, individual people, associations, limited liability companies, and nonprofit associations, as well as numerous other entities. Section 39-71-117(a), (b), and (c), MCA. HB 119 simply adds religious organizations to the types of entities that qualify as an "employer" for purposes of the workers' compensation system. HB 119 treats religious organizations no differently than any other employer under the workers' compensation system. A review of the complete list of entities that qualify as an "employer" for purposes of the workers' compensation system reveals that the Workers' Compensation Act creates no separate classification under HB 119 that singles out religious groups for different treatment.

¶ 72 The Colony's failure to establish that HB 119 creates "two separate similarly situated groups" that receive unequal treatment under the Workers' Compensation Act ends our inquiry. This failure to establish two separate groups relieves the Court of the need to evaluate whether the alleged disparate treatment rationally relates to any legitimate governmental interest. ***

Justice JIM RICE, dissenting.

*** ¶ 81 A law affecting the constitutional guarantee of free exercise of religion is to be both facially neutral and generally applicable. A law failing to satisfy the requirements of neutrality and general applicability "must be justified by a compelling governmental interest and must be narrowly tailored to advance that interest." A law is not neutral if the text of the law has a targeting effect or a discriminatory object as discerned from direct and circumstantial evidence. The Court in *Lukumi Babalu* stated:

> Official action that targets religious conduct for distinctive treatment cannot be shielded by mere compliance with the requirement of facial neutrality. The Free Exercise Clause protects against governmental hostility which is masked as well as overt. 'The Court must survey meticulously the circumstances of governmental categories to eliminate, as it were, religious gerrymanders.'

Lukumi Babalu. In determining that the contested ordinances in *Lukumi Babalu* were not neutral, the Court reviewed the legislative record and history surrounding the enactment of the ordinances, stating, "the effect of a law in its real operation is strong evidence of its object." The Court found that the four contested ordinances created an impermissible religious gerrymander because they "were drafted in tandem" to "target petitioners and their religious practices." ***

¶ 83 . . . [T]he record establishes that a hallmark of the Hutterite religion is the communal lifestyle where religious exercise and labor are not divisible because "[a]ll labor and support provided by members to the Colony is done for their own personal religious purpose without promise or expectation of compensation. The performance of labor and support for the Colony is an act of religious exercise." Hutterites eat meals, worship, work, and are educated entirely communally and they do not associate with "non-members." The Membership Declaration, to which every member of the Colony must subscribe, affirms each member's responsibility to relinquish current and future property rights to the Colony, and members are not permitted a wage or salary. In fact, the Hutterite faith prohibits the payment of wages for labor performed by its members. At oral argument, the State conceded that the wage replacement component of workers' compensation coverage would not be applicable to Colony members because, pursuant to their tenets of faith, they cannot receive wages. Farming and agricultural production has been a part of the Hutterite lifestyle for hundreds of years and is specifically named in the Colony's Articles of Incorporation and the Hutterian Brethren Church Constitution as a central component of the Colony's livelihood. The Colony also participates in manufacturing and construction projects. ***

¶ 85 In addition to the communal lifestyle that requires renouncement of wages and the ownership of property, and critical to an understanding of the conflict presented by their inclusion into the Workers' Compensation Act, is the tenet that making a legal claim is a violation of fundamental Hutterian doctrine. Daniel Wipf's affidavit states that "Christians shall not sue one another at law nor sit in judgment of one another. Hutterites cannot make claims against others for wrongs done to them." The Membership Declaration, which every member of the Colony must sign, states:

> I declare that my acceptance of membership and the terms and conditions of membership is a matter of my religious beliefs . . . Among those beliefs is the commandment to live at peace with fellow believers, to resolve disputes within the Church, and *not to seek redress before secular authorities whether related to secular or sectarian issues.*

(Emphasis added.) Wipf's affidavit explains that a member who does not convey his or her "ownership" of a legal claim to the Colony, like other property, would be subject to excommunication, or essentially termination from membership in the Colony. He states, "I do not know of any Hutterite member who has made any workers' compensation claim against a Hutterite colony in Montana or against the Uninsured Employers['] Fund."

¶ 86 HB 119's legislative history must be considered in order to understand the impact of the bill. The United States Supreme Court has looked both to the text and to the legislative history of a law to determine whether legislators intended to target religious practices, although the Court fails to do so here. The Department proposed HB 119 to address complaints received "about Hutterite colonies competing with other Montana businesses, such as contractors, without having to provide workers' compensation insurance." The only religious group named in the legislative debates surrounding HB 119 was the Hutterites, and both the House and the Senate specifically discussed the impact HB 119 would have on Hutterite colonies. Representative Hunter said, "[i]n particular, we are speaking of, in [Sections 6 and 7], about Hutterite colonies" when he introduced HB 119 in the House Committee and reiterated this concept to the Senate Committee. Senator Stewart Peregoy characterized HB 119 and the corresponding Legislative debate as "targeting" the Hutterites, stating, "if we're going to target a group, we should have just put Hutterite religious organizations and let's be done with it. . . . [W]e are targeting a group and I just wanted that for the record." Additionally, Senator Balyeat acknowledged HB 119 was really "aimed" at the Hutterite religious colonies near Great Falls. The legislative record clearly shows that the objective intent of the legislators was none other than to target the Hutterites.

¶ 87 In response to this expressed legislative intention, the text of HB 119 was amended throughout the legislative process to focus more and more narrowly on the Hutterites. Language was inserted within Section 6's definition of employer to read "a religious corporation, religious organization, or religious trust receiving remuneration *from nonmembers for agricultural production, manufacturing, or a construction project* conducted by its members on or off the property of the religious corporation, religious organization, or religious trust." Section 39-71-117(1) (d), MCA (emphasis added). The language "agricultural production, manufacturing, or a construction project"—instead of all commercial activities—was inserted into HB 119 to incorporate only those specific business enterprises in which the Hutterites engaged. Here, the Court's tactic of ignoring the facts and over-generalizing HB 119 and the Act as a whole in order to give the appearance that the Act applies equally to all employers is well illustrated. The Court repeatedly states that HB 119 applies to all "commercial activities" and bases its analysis thereon. However, the text of HB 119 does not apply to "commercial activities" generally, nor does HB 119 use the term "commercial activities" at all. Rather, it employs the phrase "agricultural production, manufacturing, or a construction project"—only those economic activities that the Legislature knew the Hutterites to be engaged in.

¶ 88 Similarly, the Court makes repeated statements to the effect that all religious employers are treated the same as other employers. However, these statements are not supported by the text of HB 119. Religious employers such as a Presbyterian Day Care, a Mormon Cleaning Service, or a Catholic Social Agency would not satisfy HB 119's definition of religious "employer" for multiple reasons, the first being that they are not engaged in the economic activities targeted by the bill—"agricultural production, manufacturing, or a construction project." ***

¶ 91 Some of these provisions could be potentially innocuous methods of defining a religious entity for incorporation within the workers' compensation system as part of a broad inclusion of all religious organizations within the system. However, the Legislature did not broadly incorporate all religions. Rather, it enacted these provisions to define and target only the Hutterite religion for inclusion within the system. While the text of HB 119 is not facially discriminatory, its history and text reveal that it nonetheless fails to be neutral and generally applicable. "Official action that targets religious conduct for distinctive treatment cannot be shielded by mere compliance with the requirement of facial neutrality." *Lukumi Babalu*. The effect of HB 119 is to create a religious gerrymander that improperly singles out one religion. The significance of a religious gerrymander under the proper legal analysis is that it must sustain strict scrutiny review. ***

¶ 93 That being so, the State argues that [HB 119 protects] the Uninsured Employers' Fund (UEF) from potential liability for a catastrophic injury claim filed by a Hutterite member and ensuring fair competition among businesses by eliminating the Hutterites' perceived advantage. Regarding the first, the UEF only applies to uninsured "employers" who are subject to the Act but have not provided coverage for their employees. Consequently, prior to HB 119, a claim could not have been filed by a Hutterite member against the UEF because the Colony was not an "employer" subject to the Act—and none have been filed.... Additionally, ... a fundamental tenet of the Hutterites' faith is that they cannot make legal claims against others. The Hutterite faith includes "the commandment to ... not to seek redress before secular authorities whether related to secular or sectarian issues." A governmental interest in protecting the UEF from claims that are prohibited as a matter of law, made by people whose faith forbids them to make such claims, can hardly be considered "legitimate."

¶ 94 The State's second argument that HB 119 was enacted for a legitimate government purpose pertained to complaints from businesses about unequal competition with the colonies. We recognize that the State has legitimate interests in the financial viability of the workers' compensation system, in controlling costs, and in providing benefits. However, the State has provided no authority for the proposition that ensuring "competitive fairness" among the state's businesses is an objective of the workers' compensation system.... [W]hether or not "fairness" among competing businesses is a viable goal of the workers' compensation system, it pales in comparison to "one of the most cherished and protected liberties in our society," *St. John's Lutheran Church*, and cannot be accomplished by legislation that targets a particular religious group and intrudes upon their internal religious practices. The State's interest in insuring a viable workers' compensation system or creating a "level playing field" is not legitimized by HB 119 in a way that satisfies the rigorous standards protecting the free exercise of religion.

¶ 95 ... HB 119 [also] fails to prohibit nonreligious conduct that endangers the State's purported government interests of preventing a catastrophic claim against the UEF and address the perceived business advantage enjoyed by the Hutterites by not participating in the workers' compensation system. The Workers' Compensation Act currently exempts other areas of employment in agriculture, manufacturing, and construction that could affect the UEF or the viability of the workers' compensation system. For example, § 39-71-401(2), MCA, exempts certain employments from the Act, unless the employer elects coverage and the insurer allows coverage, including: household or domestic employment (§ 39-71-401(2)(a)), casual employment (§ 39-71-401(2) (b)), employment of a person performing services in return for aid or sustenance only (§ 39-71-401(2)(h)), a person who is employed by an enrolled tribal member or an association, business, corporation, or other entity that is at least 51% owned by an enrolled tribal member or members, whose business is conducted solely within the exterior boundaries of an Indian reservation (§ 39-71-401(2)(m)), and a person who is an officer or manager of a ditch company (§ 39-71-401(2)(s)). Similarly, independent contractors may waive rights and benefits of the Act if they obtain an independent contractor exemption (§ 39-71-401(3)). These exemptions are contrary to the governmental interests asserted by the State, and lend further credence that the Legislature's intent, as demonstrated above, was to pursue "governmental interests only against conduct motivated by religious belief."

¶ 96 HB 119 is likewise not narrowly tailored and it places an impermissible burden on the Hutterite religion. A law is narrowly tailored when the law achieves its stated ends without unduly burdening religion. Following the United States Supreme Court, this Court has previously applied the *Thomas* [*v. Review Bd. of Ind. Employment Sec. Div.* (1981)] test to determine whether there is a burden on the free exercise of religion:

> Where the state conditions receipt of an important benefit upon conduct proscribed by a religious faith, or where it denies such a benefit because of conduct mandated by religious belief, thereby putting substantial pressure on an adherent to modify his behavior and to violate his beliefs, a burden upon religion exists.

Griffith v. Butte Sch. Dist. No. 1, 2010 MT 246. There is a burden on the free exercise of religion when the state causes an "internal impact or infringement" on the relationship between a religious entity and its members or "on their sincerely held religious beliefs." ***

¶ 99 I would thus reject the State's argument that the burden imposed here is incidental. HB 119 creates a substantial burden on the Colony's religious practice because, in order for the Colony and its members to actually participate under the Act, they must violate their sincerely held religious beliefs. HB 119 creates substantial internal intrusion into the religious practices of the Colony and its members, burdening the Hutterites' religious practices. Strict scrutiny review is not satisfied because the law is neither justified by a compelling state interest nor narrowly tailored to advance that interest.

¶ 100 In my view, the Court fails in its duty to properly undertake the necessary constitutional inquiry. The Court's over-general statements do not acknowledge the facts of the record. The Court's reliance on *Lyng v. Northwest Indian Cemetery Protective Association* (1988), where the United States Supreme Court rejected a challenge to the government's use of its own property for road construction and the property was deemed sacred by non-owners, provides little authority for this case and less consolation. Our Court has held that "only those interests of the highest order and those not otherwise served can overbalance legitimate claims to the free exercise of religion." *St. John's Lutheran Church*. However, in my view, such protection has not been provided herein. Had this been the status of religious freedom in 1620, the Pilgrims may well have sailed right by. ***

Justice PATRICIA O. COTTER and Justice JIM NELSON join in the dissenting Opinion of Justice RICE.

Notes on Free Exercise and Establishment of Religion

1. The Montana Constitution was ratified the year the United States Supreme Court decided *Wisconsin v. Yoder* (1972), which tested a generally applicable compulsory schooling law for a compelling state interest and found none, citing *Sherbert v. Verner* (1963). *Sherbert* held that, for a law to withstand scrutiny under the Free

Exercise Clause, "it must be either because [Sherbert's] disqualification as a beneficiary represents no infringement by the State of her constitutional rights of free exercise, or because any incidental burden on the free exercise of [her] religion may be justified by a 'compelling state interest in the regulation of a subject within the State's constitutional power to regulate. . . .'" *Employment Division v. Smith* (1990) sounded the end of *Sherbert*'s broad applicability under the Free Exercise Clause, holding "the right of free exercise does not relieve an individual of the obligation to comply with a valid and neutral law of general applicability on the ground that the law proscribes (or prescribes) conduct that his religion prescribes (or proscribes)." *Smith* came down two years before *St. John's Lutheran*, yet there, the Montana Supreme Court applied the *Sherbert* line of cases without mentioning *Smith*. In fact, the Court did not apply the *Smith* test until two decades later in *Big Sky Colony* (2012). The United States Supreme Court's religious liberty doctrine is contested among the justices and therefore somewhat hard to pin down; if Montana's Court is going to march in lock-step with federal religious liberty, should Article II, section 5 be read in the context of the doctrine as of 1972 or today?

2. The Colony brought a freedom of religion claim under the Montana Constitution as well as the federal Free Exercise and Establishment Clauses. Yet the majority and the dissent in *Big Sky Colony* barely mention the Montana Constitution. Should the Montana Constitution make a difference to these claims? How?

3. Is the debate in *Big Sky Colony* about targeting the Hutterite Colonies (a violation of current federal doctrine under *Lukumi Babalu*) or about failing to accommodate the Hutterite Colonies under a generally applicable law (a violation of prior federal doctrine under *Sherbert* before *Smith*)? The law at issue was drafted in a way that calls out a "religious organization . . . receiving remuneration from nonmembers for agricultural production, manufacturing, or a construction project conducted by its members" as an exception to the exception for religious organizations under the Workers Compensation Act. If HB 119 instead removed the broader exception for all religious organizations, so the Act was generally applicable regardless of an organization's religious purposes, would that resolve the dissent's concerns?

4. In 2021 the Montana Legislature enacted a "religious freedom restoration act" patterned after the federal law enacted after *Smith*. It provides in part:

> **Section 5. Free exercise of religion protected.** (1) State action may not substantially burden a person's right to the exercise of religion, even if the burden results from a rule of general applicability, unless it is demonstrated that applying the burden to that person's exercise of religion:
>
> (a) is essential to further a compelling governmental interest; and
>
> (b) is the least restrictive means of furthering that compelling governmental interest.
>
> (2) A person whose exercise of religion has been substantially burdened or is likely to be substantially burdened . . . may assert the violation or impending violation as a claim or defense in a judicial or administrative

> proceeding, regardless of whether the state of Montana or one of its political subdivisions is a party to the proceeding. The person asserting such a claim or defense may obtain appropriate relief, including relief against the state of Montana or its political subdivisions. Appropriate relief includes but is not limited to injunctive relief, declaratory relief, compensatory damages, and costs and attorney fees.

What does the restoration of religious freedom in Montana mean given the cases interpreting Article II, section 5? In other words, how does this law change preexisting free exercise doctrine in Montana? What exceptions to generally applicable rules would this law require? The debate on the bill centered on implications for civil rights laws in general, and protections for gay, lesbian, and transgender persons in particular. In light of this new law, and given Montana's distinct constitutional protections against private discrimination in Article II, section 4, where does free exercise of religion end and prohibited class discrimination begin?

5. State courts that did not follow *Smith* have developed an extensive jurisprudence of state interests that, when sufficiently tailored, justify substantial burdens on free exercise. Consider *Attorney General v. Desilets* (Mass. 1994):

> The defendants have a policy of not leasing an apartment to any person who intends to engage in conduct that violates their religious principles. The defendants' sole reason for declining even to consider Lattanzi and Tarail as tenants was that religion-based policy. The defendants, who are Roman Catholics, believe that they should not facilitate sinful conduct, including fornication. Since developing the policy at least a decade earlier, the defendants have applied it ten or more times to deny tenancies to unmarried couples. ***
>
> In interpreting [our Free Exercise Clause], we prefer to adhere to the standards of earlier First Amendment jurisprudence.... In each opinion, we used the balancing test that the Supreme Court had established under the free exercise of religion clause in *Wisconsin v. Yoder* (1972), *Sherbert v. Verner* (1963), and subsequent opinions. By applying the balancing test as we do, we extend protections to the defendants that are at least as great as those of the First Amendment. No further discussion of rights under the First Amendment is, therefore, necessary.
>
> Our tasks are to determine whether the defendants have shown that the prohibition against housing discrimination based on marital status substantially burdens their free exercise of religion, and, if it does, whether the Commonwealth has shown that it has an interest sufficiently compelling to justify that burden. *** In short, on the summary judgment record, we conclude that the uncontested material facts disclose no basis for ruling that the Commonwealth can or cannot meet its burden of establishing that it has a compelling interest that can be fulfilled only by denying the defendants an exemption from [the housing discrimination law]. ***

See also Swanner v. Anchorage Equal Rights Commission (Alaska 1994) (holding housing discrimination laws do not burden the religious exercise of plaintiff who refuses to rent to cohabiting couples in his property-rental business). *Compare Catholic Charities v. Serio* (N.Y. 2006):

> In interpreting our Free Exercise Clause we have not applied, and we do not now adopt, the inflexible rule of *Smith* that no person may complain of a burden on religious exercise that is imposed by a generally applicable, neutral statute. Rather, we have held that when the State imposes "an incidental burden on the right to free exercise of religion" we must consider the interest advanced by the legislation that imposes the burden, and that "[t]he respective interests must be balanced to determine whether the incidental burdening is justified."
>
> The burden the [Women's Health and Wellness Act] places on plaintiffs's [faith-based social service organizations] religious practices is a serious one, but the WHWA does not literally *compel* them to purchase contraceptive coverage for their employees, in violation of their religious beliefs; it only requires that policies that provide prescription drug coverage include coverage for contraceptives. *** It is also important, in our view, that many of plaintiffs' employees do not share their religious beliefs.... [W]hen a religious organization chooses to hire nonbelievers it must, at least to some degree, be prepared to accept neutral regulations imposed to protect those employees' legitimate interests in doing what their own beliefs permit....
>
> Finally, we must weigh against plaintiffs' interest in adhering to the tenets of their faith the State's substantial interest in fostering equality between the sexes, and in providing women with better health care. The Legislature had extensive evidence before it that the absence of contraceptive coverage for many women was seriously interfering with both of these important goals. The Legislature decided that to grant the broad religious exemption that plaintiffs seek would leave too many women outside the statute, a decision entitled to deference from the courts. Of course, the Legislature might well have made another choice, but we cannot say the choice the Legislature made has been shown to be an unreasonable interference with plaintiffs' exercise of their religion. The Legislature's choice is therefore not unconstitutional.

The United States Supreme Court came to the opposite conclusion in applying strict scrutiny to substantial burdens on religious exercise under the federal Religious Freedom Restoration Act. *See Burwell v. Hobby Lobby* (2014) (assuming the federal contraceptive mandate served a compelling interest, but holding that it was not the least restrictive means of doing so).

6. The *Big Sky Colony* Court analyzed the Establishment Clause claim exclusively under the federal test in *Lemon v. Kurtzman* (1971), a case the Supreme Court "has either expressly declined to apply ... or has simply ignored" for decades, according

to the Court itself. *American Legion v. American Humanist Ass'n* (2019). Why should the Montana Supreme Court rely on outdated federal law when, like the Free Exercise Clause, a distinction could be made between the federal Establishment Clause and analogous state provisions? Due to evolving concerns about state support of religion, many state challenges to religious aid are brought under more specific clauses.

2. Other Religion Clauses and "the Play in the Joints"

Most state constitutions contain additional detailed provisions concerning religion beyond the federal clauses. Some of these provisions date back to admission to statehood, at a time when Congress was more active in religious freedom debates and the Supreme Court was all but silent. The 1889 Enabling Act requires, in addition to a state constitution that is not "repugnant to the Constitution of the United States," that "[t]hat perfect toleration of religious sentiment shall be secured" and that public schools be "open to all the children of said States, and free from sectarian control." Others are innovations, such as the unexplored prohibition in Article II, section 4 against all discrimination "on account of ... religious ideas." Many of these more specific religion clauses originated in the 1889 Constitution but were revisited in the 1972 Constitutional Convention, sometimes after substantial debate. These include the Article V, section 11 prohibition on appropriations to private persons "for religious, charitable, industrial, educational, or benevolent purposes," the Article VIII, section 5 permissive property tax exemption for "places for actual religious worship," and the Article X, section 7 prohibition on "religious or partisan test or qualification" and advocacy of "sectarian tenets" in public education. The most debated religion clause at the 1972 Constitutional Convention was the "no-aid" prohibition of Article X, section 6, discussed in the following case.

Espinoza v. Montana Department of Revenue

393 Mont. 446 (2018)

Justice LAURIE McKINNON delivered the Opinion of the Court.

¶ 1 The Montana Department of Revenue (the Department) appeals from an order of the Eleventh Judicial District Court, Flathead County, granting Kendra Espinoza, Jeri Ellen Anderson, and Jaime Schaefer (collectively, Plaintiffs) summary judgment. The Department is responsible for administering § 15-30-3111, MCA (the Tax Credit Program), which provides a taxpayer a dollar-for-dollar tax credit based on the taxpayer's donation to a Student Scholarship Organization (SSO). SSOs fund tuition scholarships for students who attend private schools meeting the definition of Qualified Education Provider (QEP). The Legislature instructed the Department to implement the Tax Credit Program in compliance with Article V, Section 11(5), and Article X, Section 6, of the Montana Constitution. Pursuant to that grant of authority, the Department implemented Admin. R. M. 42.4.802 (Rule 1), which it believed was necessary to constitutionally administer the Tax Credit Program. Rule

1 adds to the Legislature's definition of QEP and excludes religiously-affiliated private schools from qualifying as QEPs.

¶ 2 Plaintiffs are parents whose children attend a religiously-affiliated private school. Because Rule 1 precludes religiously-affiliated private schools from the definition of QEP, SSOs cannot fund tuition scholarships at the school Plaintiffs' children attend. Plaintiffs filed this proceeding challenging Rule 1. The Department responded, arguing Rule 1 was necessary because the Tax Credit Program as enacted by the Legislature violates Montana's Constitution. The District Court determined the Tax Credit Program was constitutional without Rule 1 and accordingly granted Plaintiffs summary judgment. ***

Discussion

¶ 15 The First Amendment's Religion Clauses — the Establishment Clause and the Free Exercise Clause — are "frequently in tension." *Locke v. Davey* (2004). Yet, "there is room for play in the joints" between them. *Walz v. Tax Comm'n of N.Y.* (1970). A state's constitutional prohibition against aid to sectarian schools may be broader and stronger than the First Amendment's prohibition against the establishment of religion. Where a state's constitution "draws a more stringent line than that drawn by the United States Constitution," the "room for play" between the Establishment and Free Exercise Clauses narrows. *See Locke*. The Montana Constitution broadly and strongly prohibits state aid to sectarian schools, leaving a very limited amount of "room for play." See Mont. Const. art. X, § 6 (hereinafter, Article X, Section 6).

¶ 16 Our analysis, therefore, considers Article X, Section 6, within a narrower "room for play" between the federal Religion Clauses and, consequently, we do not address federal precedent. We conclude that Montana's Constitution more broadly prohibits "any" state aid to sectarian schools and draws a "more stringent line than that drawn" by its federal counterpart. Therefore, the sole issue in this case is whether the Tax Credit Program runs afoul of Montana's specific sectarian education no-aid provision, Article X, Section 6. For the following reasons, we conclude the Tax Credit Program aids sectarian schools in violation of Article X, Section 6.

I. Article X, Section 6, broadly and strictly prohibits aid to sectarian schools.

¶ 17 Article X, Section 6, of the Montana Constitution, entitled "Aid prohibited to sectarian schools," provides:

> (1) The legislature, counties, cities, towns, school districts, and public corporations shall not make any direct or indirect appropriation or payment from any public fund or monies, or any grant of lands or other property for any sectarian purpose or to aid any church, school, academy, seminary, college, university, or other literary or scientific institution, controlled in whole or in part by any church, sect, or denomination.
>
> (2) This section shall not apply to funds from federal sources provided to the state for the express purpose of distribution to non-public education.

¶ 18 The Constitutional Convention Delegates' (Delegates) intent controls our interpretation of a constitutional provision. We primarily discern the Delegates' intent "from the plain meaning of the language used." However, we define the Delegates' intent "not only from the plain meaning of the language used, but also in light of the historical and surrounding circumstances under which the [Delegates] drafted the Constitution, the nature of the subject matter they faced, and the objective they sought to achieve." Accordingly, we "determine the meaning and intent of constitutional provisions from the plain meaning of the language used without resort to extrinsic aids except when the language is vague or ambiguous or extrinsic aids clearly manifest an intent not apparent from the express language."

¶ 19 In determining what the Delegates intended Article X, Section 6, to mean, we first observe that the plain language of the provision's title is expansive and forceful: "Aid prohibited to sectarian schools." The title clearly manifests the Delegates' intent to broadly prohibit aid to sectarian schools. The provision's text is equally expansive, prohibiting numerous types of state actors, including the "legislature, counties, cities, towns, school districts, and public corporations" from making "any direct or indirect appropriation or payment from any public fund or monies, or any grant of lands or other property for any sectarian purpose or to aid any ... school ... controlled in whole or in part by any church, sect, or denomination." Mont. Const. art. X, § 6(1).

¶ 20 The provision's plain language begs three main inquiries, each of which cast a broad net clearly intended to prohibit "any" type of state aid being used to benefit sectarian education. First, the provision's plain language identifies the entity that is prohibited from providing the aid: Article X, Section 6, prohibits the "legislature, counties, cities, towns, school districts, and public corporations" from aiding sectarian schools. Second, the provision's plain language identifies the type of aid it prohibits: Article X, Section 6, broadly prohibits any type of direct or indirect aid to sectarian schools — "any direct or indirect appropriation or payment from any public fund or monies, or any grant of lands or other property." Third, the provision's plain language specifies that the aid is prohibited "for any sectarian purpose or to aid any church, school, academy, seminary, college, university, or other literary or scientific institution, controlled in whole or in part by any church, sect, or denomination."

¶ 21 The Delegates adapted Article X, Section 6, of the Montana Constitution from the 1889 Constitution's broad and general no-aid provision, recognizing that it was already "among the most stringent [no-aid clauses] in the nation."

¶ 22 The Delegates' strong commitment to maintaining public education and ensuring that public education remained free from religious entanglement is evident from the Constitutional Convention Transcripts; the Delegates wanted the public school system to receive "unequivocal support." Delegate Burkhardt noted, "Under federal and state mandates to concentrate public funds in public schools, our educational system has grown strong in an atmosphere free from divisiveness and fragmentation." He further emphasized, "*Any diversion of funds or effort from the public school system* would tend to weaken that system in favor of schools established for private or religious purposes."

¶ 23 A minority of Delegates sought to delete the language prohibiting indirect aid from Article X, Section 6. Those Delegates wanted to ensure private school students could receive federal aid under the United States Supreme Court's child-benefit theory, which allows federal aid as long as it directly supports the child and not the religious school. Delegate Blaylock, however, expressed concern that deleting the indirect language would make it "fairly easy to appropriate a number of funds ... to some other group and then say this will be done indirectly." The Delegates ultimately maintained the indirect language and instead added a separate subsection specifically addressing federal aid: "[Article X, Section 6] shall not apply to funds from federal sources provided to the state for the express purpose of distribution to non-public education." Mont. Const. art. X, § 6(2). Notably, the Delegates understood that Montana could prohibit forms of state aid that were otherwise permissible as federal aid. Our conclusion that Article X, Section 6, more broadly prohibits aid to sectarian schools than the federal Establishment Clause is consistent with the Delegates' intent of the provision.

¶ 24 It is also worth observing that Montana's no-aid provision is unique from other states' no-aid provisions. Article X, Section 6's prohibition of "any direct or indirect appropriation or payment from any public fund or monies, or any grant of lands or other property for any sectarian purpose or to aid any ... school ... controlled in whole or in part by any church" make it a broader and stronger prohibition against aid to sectarian schools than other states. Even other states whose no-aid provisions also contain "indirect" language only prohibit aid in the form of the direct or indirect taking of money from the public treasury. See Ga. Const. art. I, § II, ¶ VII ("No money shall ever be taken from the public treasury, directly or indirectly, in aid of any church. ..."); Fla. Const. art. I, § 3 ("No revenue of the state or any political subdivision or agency thereof shall ever be taken from the public treasury directly or indirectly in aid of any church. ..."). Such language is distinct from and less stringent than Montana's prohibition on any type of aid, whether it be a "direct or indirect appropriation or payment from any public fund or monies, or any grant of lands or other property." Mont. Const. art. X, § 6(1).

¶ 25 As a Court, we have not yet interpreted Article X, Section 6. However, the 1972 Constitutional Convention Delegates intended Article X, Section 6, to retain the meaning of Article XI, Section 8, of the Montana Constitution of 1889. See Convention Transcript, p. 2014. Accordingly, this Court's pre-1972 precedent analyzing Article XI, Section 8, of the Montana Constitution of 1889 remains helpful to our analysis of Article X, Section 6. In *State ex rel. Chambers v. School Dist. No. 10* (Mont. 1970), the Court considered whether a tax levy intended to fund general teaching positions at a religiously-affiliated private school violated Article XI, Section 8, of the Montana Constitution of 1889. The Court observed that the tax levy permitted a religiously-affiliated school to unconstitutionally obtain teachers at public expense. Even though the teachers would have taught general, secular subjects, the Court noted that the funding nonetheless aided sectarian schools, as there was no way to determine "where the secular purpose ended and the sectarian began." Accordingly, the Court determined Article XI, Section 8, of the Montana Constitution of 1889 prohibited "a public school board from making a levy for, or expending funds for the employment of teachers to teach in a parochial school."

¶ 26 The plain language of Article X, Section 6, and the Constitutional Convention Transcripts demonstrating the Delegates' clear objective to firmly prohibit aid to sectarian schools lead us to the conclusion that the Delegates intended Article X, Section 6, to broadly and strictly prohibit aid to sectarian schools.

II. The Tax Credit Program aids sectarian schools in violation of Article X, Section 6, of the Montana Constitution.

*** ¶ 28 To analyze the Tax Credit Program under Article X, Section 6, first, we identify the entity providing the aid; second, we identify the type of aid; and third, we consider whether the entity provided the aid "for any sectarian purpose or to aid any . . . school . . . controlled in whole or in part by any church. . . ." We ultimately conclude the Tax Credit Program aids sectarian schools in violation of Article X, Section 6, and that it is unconstitutional in all of its applications.

a. The Legislature aided sectarian schools when it enacted the Tax Credit Program.

¶ 29 Article X, Section 6, directly prohibits various entities, including the Legislature, from aiding sectarian schools. Preliminarily, we recognize that an individual taxpayer may give money to any cause she wishes. A taxpayer is free to donate to an SSO, a QEP, or any other charitable cause of her choice. There is no prohibition on a taxpayer giving her money away, nor would such prohibition be constitutional.

¶ 30 In this case, the action under scrutiny is the Legislature's provision of a tax credit to taxpayer donors. The Legislature, by enacting the Tax Credit Program, involved itself in donations to religiously-affiliated private schools. The Tax Credit Program provides a dollar-for-dollar incentive of up to $150 for taxpayer donations to SSOs. The tax credit encourages the transfer of money from a taxpayer donor to a sectarian school because the taxpayer donor knows she will be reimbursed, dollar-for-dollar, for her donation to an SSO. SSOs, in turn, directly fund tuition scholarships at religiously-affiliated QEPs. The Legislature, by enacting a statute that provides a dollar-for-dollar credit against taxes owed to the state, is the entity providing aid to sectarian schools via tax credits in violation of Article X, Section 6.

b. The Tax Credit Program permits the Legislature to indirectly pay tuition at private, religiously-affiliated schools.

¶ 31 Article X, Section 6, broadly prohibits any type of direct or indirect aid: the Legislature may not make "any direct or indirect appropriation or payment from any public fund or monies, or any grant of lands or other property."

¶ 32 The Tax Credit Program permits the Legislature to indirectly pay tuition at private, religiously-affiliated schools. Parents owe a certain amount of tuition to the QEP their child attends. If a child receives a tuition scholarship from an SSO, the scholarship decreases the amount of tuition that child's parents owe to the QEP. Many of the taxpayer donors who would donate to SSOs would be parents of children who attend QEPs. When parents donate to an SSO, they receive a dollar-for-dollar tax credit of up to $150. If the parents' child also receives a tuition scholarship from an SSO in the amount of, for example, $150, the parents' tuition obligation to the QEP decreases by $150—the exact amount the parents received as a tax credit for their donation to an SSO. The parents donated $150 to an SSO, received a dollar-for-dollar reimbursement for that donation in the form of a tax credit, and subsequently owed $150 less in tuition to their child's QEP. The Legislature indirectly payed $150 of that student's tuition by permitting his or her parents to claim a tax credit instead of paying that amount of tuition to the QEP.

¶ 33 The Legislature attempted to sever the indirect payment by requiring taxpayer donors to donate to an SSO generally and prohibiting them from directing or designating contributions to specific parents, legal guardians, or QEPs. See § 15-30-3111(1), MCA. Therefore, parents cannot donate to an SSO, claim a tax credit for their donation, and then directly designate the funds they donated to their own child's scholarship. However, an indirect payment still exists, as described above, when a student whose parents claimed the tax credit receives a scholarship from an SSO. The simple fact that parents who donate to SSOs cannot directly designate the scholarship funds to their own child or to their child's school does not defeat the fact that the Legislature indirectly pays tuition to the QEP....

¶ 34 The Tax Credit Program permits the Legislature to subsidize tuition payments at religiously-affiliated private schools. A subsidy is a "grant, usu[ally] made by the government, to any enterprise whose promotion is considered to be in the public interest." Subsidy, Black's Law Dictionary (10th ed. 2014). "Although governments sometimes make direct payments (such as cash grants), subsidies are usu[ally] indirect. They may take the form of... tax breaks...." Subsidy, Black's Law Dictionary (10th ed. 2014). When the Legislature indirectly pays general tuition payments at sectarian schools, the Legislature effectively subsidizes the sectarian school's educational program. That type of government subsidy in aid of sectarian schools is precisely what the Delegates intended Article X, Section 6, to prohibit.

¶ 35 While $150 may seem like a small sum of money when compared to the State's overall operating budget, the amount of aid is wholly insignificant to an Article X, Section 6, analysis. The Legislature violates Article X, Section 6's prohibition on aid to sectarian schools when it provides any aid, no matter how small. Further, the $150 indirect payments certainly add up over time, especially as the aggregate limits on the tax credits increase from $3 million each year the limit is met. See § 15-30-3111(5)(a)(i)-(iii), MCA. The Tax Credit Program creates an indirect payment: the program reduces "the net price of attending private school . . . for students who receive scholarships and whose families claim the credit." Fiscal Note, at 2. Article X, Section 6, expressly prohibits that type of indirect payment to sectarian schools.

¶ 36 Importantly, for purposes of examining the facial constitutionality of the Tax Credit Program, the schools meeting the Legislature's definition of QEP may be—and, in fact, the overwhelming majority are—religiously affiliated. There is simply no mechanism within the Tax Credit Program itself that operates to ensure that an indirect payment of $150 is not used to fund religious education in contravention of Article X, Section 6. The Department, in administering the Tax Credit Program pursuant to the Legislature's definition of QEP, § 15-30-3102(7), MCA, has no ability to ensure that indirect payments are not made to religious schools. Or, as this Court has previously cautioned, there is no mechanism within the Tax Credit Program to identify "where the secular purpose end[s] and the sectarian beg[ins]." The Department cannot discern when the tax credit is indirectly paying tuition at a secular school and when the tax credit is indirectly paying tuition at a sectarian school. Because the Tax Credit Program does not distinguish between an indirect payment to fund a secular education and an indirect payment to fund a sectarian education, it cannot, under any circumstance, be construed as consistent with Article X, Section 6.

c. The Legislature provided the tax credits to aid schools controlled in whole or in part by churches.

¶ 37 Article X, Section 6, prohibits aid used "for any sectarian purpose or to aid any . . . school . . . controlled in whole or in part by any church, sect, or denomination." In *Chambers*, we explained that public funds could not be used to pay teachers' salaries at a religiously-affiliated private school, even if those teachers provided standard, non-religious instruction. In support of that conclusion, we reasoned that the school was sectarian as a whole, and therefore there was no way to determine "where the secular purpose ended and the sectarian began."

¶ 38 Under the Legislature's definition of QEP, the majority of QEPs are private schools controlled by churches. SSOs pay scholarship funds directly to QEPs and the funds offset scholarship recipients' general tuition obligations. General tuition payments fund the sectarian school as a whole and therefore may be used by the school to strengthen any aspect of religious education, including those areas heavily entrenched in religious doctrine. Religious education is a "rock on which the whole [church] rests, and to render tax aid to [a religious school] is indistinguishable . . . from rendering the same aid to the [c]hurch itself." *Chambers* (*quoting Everson v. Bd. of Educ.* (1947) (Jackson, J., dissenting)). The Tax Credit Program aids schools controlled by churches, in violation of Article X, Section 6.

¶ 39 "The most effective way to establish any institution is to finance it." *Chambers* (*quoting Sch. Dist. of Abington Twp. v. Schempp* (1963) (Douglas, J., concurring)). The Legislature's enactment of the Tax Credit Program is facially unconstitutional and violates Montana's constitutional guarantee to all Montanans that their government will not use state funds to aid religious schools. This basic notion of separation of church and state is a foundation of our Nation's federal Constitution, but is more fiercely protected by Montanans through the broader prohibitions contained in Article X, Section 6. Although the Tax Credit Program provides a mechanism of attenuating the tax credit from the SSO's tuition payment to a religiously-affiliated QEP, it does not comport with the constitutional prohibition on indirectly aiding sectarian schools. We conclude, following consideration of both the plain language of the provision and the Delegates' intent as discerned from their discussion when drafting Montana's 1972 Constitution, that such attenuation remains inconsistent with Article X, Section 6's strict and broad prohibition on aid to sectarian schools. The Tax Credit Program constitutes the precise type of indirect payment the Delegates sought to prohibit in their formulation of Article X, Section 6. Based on the Legislature's definition of QEP, the Department cannot constitutionally implement or administer the Tax Credit Program. Because Senate Bill 410 contained a severability clause, we conclude the Tax Credit Program, § 15-30-3111, MCA, must be severed from the remainder of Part 31, §§ 15-30-3101 to -3114, MCA.

¶ 40 Having concluded the Tax Credit Program violates Article X, Section 6, it is not necessary to consider federal precedent interpreting the First Amendment's less-restrictive Establishment Clause. Conversely, however, an overly-broad analysis of Article X, Section 6, could implicate free exercise concerns. Although there may be a case where an indirect payment constitutes "aid" under Article X, Section 6, but where prohibiting the aid would violate the Free Exercise Clause, this is not one of those cases. We recognize we can only close the "room for play" between the joints of the Establishment and Free Exercise Clauses to a certain extent before our interpretation of one violates the other.

III. Rule 1 is unnecessary because the underlying Tax Credit Program is unconstitutional and, further, the Department exceeded its rulemaking authority when it enacted Rule 1.

¶ 41 The Department enacted Rule 1 in its efforts to constitutionally implement the Tax Credit Program, which we have now determined is unconstitutional. We severed the Tax Credit Program from the remainder of Part 31. See *supra*, ¶ 39. As a result, Rule 1 is superfluous. However, we further note that, in enacting Rule 1, the Department exceeded the Legislature's grant of rulemaking authority. See § 15-30-3114, MCA (granting the Department rulemaking authority to adopt rules that are necessary to implement and administer Part 31). ***

Conclusion

¶ 45 We conclude the Tax Credit Program violates Article X, Section 6's stringent prohibition on aid to sectarian schools. Because the Tax Credit Program is unconstitutional, Rule 1 is superfluous and, further, the Department exceeded the scope of its rulemaking authority when it enacted Rule 1. We accordingly reverse the District Court's order granting Plaintiffs summary judgment and determine the Tax

Credit Program, § 15-30-3111, MCA, must be severed from the remainder of Part 31, §§ 15-30-3101 to -3114, MCA.

Justice INGRID GUSTAFSON, concurring.

¶ 46 I concur in the Majority's Opinion and agree the Tax Credit Program violates our Constitution's prohibition against providing aid to religious schools, and this constitutional deficiency cannot be cured via administrative rule. I write separately to discuss additional grounds upon which the Tax Credit Program creates an indirect payment under Article X, Section 6(1), of the Montana Constitution. ***

¶ 51 The [Tax Credit Program] was explicitly designed as a tax expenditure. Section 5-4-104(2), MCA, defines "tax expenditures" as "those revenue losses attributable to provisions of Montana tax laws that allow a special exclusion, exception, or deduction from gross income or that provide a special credit . . . including: . . . (d) credits allowed against Montana personal income tax or Montana corporate income tax." . . . Moreover, many of the items enumerated under § 5-4-104(2), MCA, while not appropriations, are nonetheless expenditures. *** Thus, Article X, Section 6(1), prohibits not only appropriations, but also payments.

¶ 53 By creating a diversionary scheme whereby money otherwise bound for the public treasury is diverted, the Legislature has created an indirect payment. Moreover, as noted above, the [Tax Credit Program] does require "funding," with the State setting aside $3 million to cover the anticipated revenue shortfall this statutory scheme is expected to cause in its first year — in addition to the substantial administrative costs described in the Majority Opinion. ***

Chief Justice MIKE McGRATH and Justice Dirk Sandefur join in the concurring Opinion of Justice GUSTAFSON.

Justice DIRK SANDEFUR, concurring.

*** ¶ 77 Plaintiffs assert, inter alia, that the program does not violate Article X, Section 6, of the Montana Constitution because the purpose and effect of the program is not to further a sectarian purpose or aid religiously-affiliated schools but, rather, merely to facilitate parental educational choice without regard for the choice made. They assert that any secondary benefit to religiously-affiliated schools is only incidental or de minimis. Despite the superficial appeal of this argument, closer examination quickly unveils the false distinction on which it is premised. Religiously-affiliated schools exist for the purpose of providing a quality general education, but with a specific emphasis on religious beliefs and values not taught in public schools. It is certainly conceivable that some parents, even though they do not subscribe to the affiliated religion, may nonetheless choose a religiously-affiliated school in pursuit of a quality general education perceived to be unavailable in public schools. However, the obvious and indisputable fact is that most, if not all, parents choose to send their children to a religiously-affiliated school for the specific purpose of educating their children with an emphasis on particular religious beliefs and values not taught in public schools. Providing children with particular religious instruction or emphasis incident to general education unquestionably aids and benefits the exercise and proliferation of those religious beliefs and values—the very raison d'être for religiously-affiliated schools. Tuition aids also help maintain enrollment in religiously-affiliated schools, thereby helping facilitate their continued existence and administration. However neutrally characterized, a law diverting money otherwise earmarked and accrued to the public purse to allow parents to choose religiously-affiliated schools is clearly tantamount to an indirect payment of government monies for a sectarian purpose and aids schools controlled in whole or in part by a particular church, religious sect, or religious denomination. ***

Justice BETH BAKER, dissenting.

*** ¶ 86 The Court begins with a fundamental mistake that permeates the remainder of the Opinion and flaws its conclusions. Relying in part on the title of Section 6, the Court makes a sweeping statement that the provision broadly prohibits "aid" to sectarian schools. Recognizing the first principle of statutory construction—to examine the plain meaning of the words used—it nonetheless skips over the words used in Section 6 to divine the Delegates' intent. Throughout the Opinion, the Court then applies its broad construct of "aid" to draw conclusions on each element within its outlined framework.

¶ 87 Let's back up a step. Article X, Section 6, says that the government "shall not make any direct or indirect appropriation or payment from *any public fund or monies*, or any grant of lands or other property *for any sectarian purpose or to aid* any church, ... or other ... institution, controlled in whole or in part by any church, sect, or denomination." (Emphasis added). In purporting to identify the "three main inquiries" required in its analysis, the Court applies the sweeping term "aid" instead of the textual "appropriation or payment from any public fund or monies." Opinion, ¶ 20. As an established principle of statutory construction, we do not rely on a provision's title over the language contained within its text. *Bates v. Neva*, 2014 MT 336, ¶ 21 (recognizing that titles "are subordinate to statutory text and cannot be used to create ambiguity"). The operative language in the text is "direct or indirect appropriation or payment from any public fund or monies." Without examining what that language plainly means, the Court employs a broad meaning of "aid" for its analysis. I begin with the plain language.

¶ 88 Article X, Section 6(1) prohibits four actions:

(1) direct appropriations;

(2) indirect appropriations;

(3) direct payments; or

(4) indirect payments

from public funds or monies. The first step is to examine what is an "appropriation" and what is a "payment." "A long line of Montana cases has established that 'appropriation' refers only to the authority given to the legislature to expend money from the state treasury." ***

¶ 89 A "payment" is the "[p]erformance of an obligation by the delivery of money or some other valuable thing. . . ." Payment, Black's Law Dictionary (10th ed. 2014). The Constitution likewise extends this prohibition to "any grant of lands or other property"—other items of value that the government must own, or be entitled to, before it can effectuate a delivery to another. Article X, Section 6, using the disjunctive "or," distinguishes an "appropriation" from a "payment." As discussed above, an appropriation comes "from the law-making body" or the "legislature" to "expend" or "apply" money "from the state treasury." A "payment," in contrast, is attenuated from the law-making body. The Legislature cannot "appropriate" funds "to any private individual, private association, or private corporation not under control of the state." Mont. Const. art. V, § 11(5). "Payments" are made by the Executive Branch carrying out its appropriated spending authority, for example, by spending on contracts or by awarding grants.

¶ 90 For illustrative purposes, using the SSO Program as an example, the plain language of Article X, Section 6, would apply to the following:

1. Direct Appropriation: the Legislature appropriates $3 million to QEPs as defined in the statute, including religious schools;

2. Indirect Appropriation: the Legislature appropriates $3 million to SSOs, which then award the funds to QEPs, including religious schools;

3. Direct Payment: (a) the Office of Public Instruction (OPI) implements a grant program to award grants from its general fund budget to QEPs, including religious schools, or contracts with religious schools to hire teachers, or (b) the State Land Board donates a section of state trust land to a QEP on which to build a religious school;

4. Indirect Payment: (a) OPI grants funds to SSOs to provide teachers to religious schools, or (b) the State Land Board donates a section of state trust land to an SSO, which then auctions the land to support QEPs, including religious schools, or conveys the land for a sectarian school building site.

¶ 91 There is little dispute that the Tax Credit Program's tax credit does not constitute a direct appropriation or payment. The Department argues instead that the District Court erred by failing to consider the indirect impact that targeted tax breaks have on the public fisc. It emphasizes that the tax breaks indirectly aid sectarian schools. This argument becomes the lynchpin for the Court's holding. The argument may be correct, as far as it goes. But a theory based upon "indirect impacts" or "indirect effects" of the Tax Credit Program diverges from the constitutional text. Unambiguous constitutional language must be given its plain, natural, and ordinary meaning. ***

¶ 96 The concern about "indirect payments" that undergirded the Delegates' decision to re-adopt the subject provisions in the 1972 Constitution was the possibility that government would appropriate funding for religious schools through intermediaries, necessitating retention of the language prohibiting "indirect" payments. "[I]t would be fairly easy to appropriate a number of funds and then—to [sic] some other group and then say this will be done indirectly." The Constitutional Convention was held one year after this Court had decided *Montana State Welfare Board v. Lutheran Social Services* (Mont. 1971)—in which we rejected the State Welfare Board's argument that payment of medical benefits to a woman using a religiously affiliated adoption agency would violate the Constitution—and two years after this Court's decision in *Chambers*, in which we distinguished property tax exemptions from impermissible property tax levies in support of religious schools. Delegate Loendorf, sponsor of the proposal to retain the "indirect" language that the Convention ultimately adopted, stated that, under his proposal, the provision "will continue to mean and do whatever it does now," expressing an apparent desire to preserve the status quo so recently stated by this Court. Beyond indirect payments, the delegates did not discuss tax credits or deductions for private donations to religious schools. ***

¶ 105 The Court today holds that a tax credit—granted to a private individual for a donation that may or may not be directed to a religious entity—violates the State Constitution, even though it is clear under the law that a direct tax exemption by the State to a church does not. Mont. Const. art. VIII, § 5(1)(b) .... Although the Court does not mention them, its ruling calls into question numerous other state laws granting tax credits that may benefit religious entities, among them Montana's College Contribution Credit, § 15-30-2326, MCA, and Qualified Endowment Credit, § 15-30-2328, MCA.

¶ 106 At the end of the day, this case—like others involving the religion clauses—may be made more difficult by the circuitous path a legislative body designs in attempting to advance policy within its constitutional limits. It is in those instances that the Court's examination must be particularly precise. Tax policy is within the Legislature's wheelhouse.... The Montana Constitution does not bar the Legislature from setting tax policy to encourage any manner of private action, including incentivizing individuals to support certain philanthropic undertakings, religious or otherwise....

Justice JIM RICE joins in the dissenting Opinion of Justice BAKER.

Justice JIM RICE, dissenting.

*** ¶ 111 The Court summarily declares that the subject Scholarship Program "aids sectarian schools" in violation of Article X, Section 6, of the Montana Constitution, a conclusion that is factually and legally incorrect. *** [T]he beneficiary of the Program is not the school, but the student/family receiving the scholarship, because they are relieved of a portion of their financial obligation for the student's attendance at a private school. This is separate from the private school itself, which must be paid the same tuition regardless of any assistance from the Program. Other courts have widely recognized this principle. *See Simmons-Harris v. Goff* (Ohio 1999) ("The primary beneficiaries of the School Voucher Program are children, not sectarian schools."); *Meredith v. Pence* (Ind. 2013) (scholarship program not violative of no-aid provision because "[t]he direct beneficiaries under the voucher program are the families of eligible students and not the schools selected by the parents for their children to attend"); *Kotterman v. Killian* (Ariz. 1999) ("The primary beneficiaries of this credit are taxpayers who contribute to the [SSOs], parents who might otherwise be deprived of an opportunity to make meaningful decisions about their children's educations, and the students themselves.... Private and sectarian schools are at best only incidental beneficiaries of [the] tax credit...."); *see also Zelman v. Simmons-Harris* (2002) (distinguishing between "government programs that provide aid directly to religious schools" and scholarship programs based upon "genuine and independent choices of private individuals"). ***

¶ 114 Because the scholarships are directed by students and families, and there is no government action endorsing or directing funds for sectarian or religious purposes, there is no significance to the fact that more Program options are currently available for students choosing to attend private religious schools than private non-religious schools. The same was true for the private religious adoption agencies at issue in *Lutheran Soc. Servs.* Other courts have widely recognized this principle. *See Oliver v. Hofmeister* (Okla. 2016) (finding no "constitutional significance" in the fact that there are "more students attending sectarian private schools than non-sectarian" private schools); *Simmons-Harris* (finding the fact that "[m]ost of the beneficiaries" of a neutral school scholarship program "attend sectarian schools" not relevant or persuasive). The Program simply creates a neutral opportunity for genuine independent choices of donors and scholarship recipients, and provides that the beneficiaries of the program are the scholarship recipients. *See Oliver* (upholding a student scholarship program because it was "completely neutral with regard to religion and that any funds deposited to a sectarian school occur as the sole result of the parent's independent decision completely free from state influence.... The parent, *not the State*, determines where the scholarship funds will be applied.") (emphasis in original).

¶ 115 ... The Department's view, that "'[t]ax expenditures' are monetary subsidies the government bestows on particular individuals or organizations by granting them preferential tax treatment ... the various deductions, credits and loopholes [] are just spending by another name," might be correct for purposes of internal state government budgeting, § 5-4-104, MCA, but it is an utter misstatement of the fundamental right of private property ownership. A citizen's income—all income of each year, every year—belongs to the citizen until such time the proper portion thereof becomes owed to the government; the government does not own all income until the citizen demonstrates otherwise.... "[U]nder such reasoning all taxpayer income could be viewed as belonging to the state because it is subject to taxation by the legislature." *Kotterman*; *accord Ariz. Christian Sch. Tuition Org. v. Winn* (2011) ("Private bank accounts cannot be equated with the [] state treasury.").

¶ 116 A study of history reminds us that governments have oppressed or discriminated against citizens based upon their religious faith over millennia. Today, courts are to ensure that the citizen's free exercise of religion is not violated by the government. As the U.S. Supreme Court has stated in a recent religious rights case, "all officials must pause to remember their own high duty to the Constitution and to the rights it secures." *Masterpiece Cakeshop, Ltd. v. Colo. Civil Rights Comm'n* (2018). I thus disagree with the Court's determination that it need not entertain the Plaintiffs' pled free exercise claims because "this is not one of those cases."

Notes on Separationism and the Play in the Joints

1. Montana's 1972 Constitution, like its federal counterpart, contains an Establishment Clause. Unlike the United States Constitution, many state constitutions also contain "no-aid" clauses that presumably have a distinct meaning from framing-era debates about established churches. Consider Michael P. Dougherty, *Montana's Constitutional Prohibition on Aid to Sectarian Schools: "Badge of Bigotry" or National Model for the Separation of Church and State?*, 77 Mont. L. Rev. 41 (2016):

> The delegates debated the majority of the Convention's final drafting of Article X, Section 6, over a single day on March 11, 1972. The primary focus of the debate centered on the adoption of the 1889 section, as well as an amendment to allow non-public schools to accept federal funds. Ultimately, delegates discussed multiple proposed versions of the section. Delegate Burkhardt, speaking on behalf of the majority proposal produced by the Education and Public Lands Committee, started the debate by moving for the adoption of the 1889 language and a title. Delegate Burkhardt explained the majority proposal recommended retention of the section for a few key reasons.
>
> First, the 1889 provision provided unequivocal support for free public education by reinforcing the important American tradition of the separation of church and state. Delegate Burkhardt warned that "[a]ny diversion of funds or effort from the public school system would tend to weaken that system in favor of schools established for private or religious purposes." Second, the majority committee recognized that it is the State's function to provide public education. The third issue the majority noted involved the fear that if any changes were made to the section, it could "endanger passage of the entire Constitution." Delegate Burkhardt noted the issue of church and state is an emotional area for the public, and that this emotionalism could cloud people's feelings about the proposed Constitution. Changes to a similar provision, Delegate Burkhardt argued, were thought to have led to the defeat of the 1967 New York Constitution. The majority proposal's final reason for adopting the 1889 provision involved the threat government poses when it gets involved with religious groups and their

educational systems. The recommendation to keep the section as-is was not met with universal acceptance.

In response to the majority proposal, Delegate Harbaugh introduced the minority proposal and moved for the adoption of a proposed amendment to the 1889 language. This amendment would have removed the term "indirectly" from the section and added language that would have provided: "[t]his section shall not apply to funds from federal sources provided to the state for the expressed purpose of distribution to nonpublic [sic] education." The primary reasons for this amendment, Delegate Harbaugh argued, were twofold: (1) to legitimize receipt of indirect federal aid by non- public schools, something that had already been occurring under "questionable methods"; and (2) to ensure sectarian schools would receive any federal funds made available in the future. Interestingly, Delegate Harbaugh also stated the intention behind removing the indirectly language from the provision was to allow indirect aid to be permissible under the "child-benefit theory." This, he clarified, "would make it possible for the state to authorize other forms of indirect aid permissible under the First Amendment."

The delegates continued to debate the amendment until Delegate Loendorf moved to introduce a substitute amendment that appeared to compromise between the majority and minority proposals. This amendment retained the majority proposal's use of the term indirectly but, like the minority proposal, added language exempting distribution of federal funds for non-public education. The Convention ultimately adopted Delegate Loendorf's version in a roll call vote of 53–40.

A review of the transcripts of the debate and the corresponding votes clearly show a coalition of delegates came together to adopt Delegate Loendorf's compromise proposal. Two main camps can be seen in this coalition. The first group consisted of individuals who supported the language as it existed in 1889—and thus the majority proposal—but ultimately voted for the compromise proposal. Although these individuals may have initially supported the majority proposal, they undoubtedly changed their votes after Delegate Loendorf's compromise version was introduced. Delegate Blaylock, who expressed opposition to deleting "indirectly" from the current provision, voted for the compromise proposal. He, like many other delegates, would fit squarely into the first camp. The second group forming the final majority coalition consisted of individuals who initially backed the minority proposal but changed their support after the clause allowing federal funds was added. Delegates Toole and Brown, who initially urged the adoption of the minority proposal, both voted to adopt the compromise proposal and would be included with this second group. However, delegates voiced additional reasons for and against the provision.

Many of the delegates who initially supported the minority proposal expressed hesitation about the provision's infamous history as a "Blaine Amendment." Delegate Harbaugh, who introduced the minority proposal, criticized the 1889 provision and as being a product of 19th century hysteria in opposition to Catholics. The delegate lamented how "80 years later, the State of Montana still retains in its constitution remnants of a long-past era of prejudice." Delegate Driscoll, a Catholic mother of ten, criticized the majority proposal for "retain[ing] an archaic provision in our Constitution." Some of the most compelling testimony came from Delegate Schiltz's description of the anti-Catholic harassment he witnessed as a boy:

"I've lived with the Blaine Amendment and the philosophy of the Blaine Amendment all the days of my life. I can remember during the Al Smith campaign when they burned crosses on the rim-rocks [sic] in Billings. I can remember being let out of school in the fourth grade to erase three 'Ks' on the front doors of the Catholic Church in Billings.... To me, the Blaine Amendment is a badge of bigotry, and it should be repealed."

Interestingly, all three of these delegates ultimately voted to adopt Delegate Loedorf's compromise amendment. It appears these delegates put their apprehensions about bigotry aside in order to secure federal funds for non-public education. The delegates who voiced support for the minority proposal did not universally echo the anti-Catholic animus. An express concern was the detrimental effects that occur when church and state "get mixed up." Delegate Harper, who was a minister, stated many of the delegates who supported the minority proposal were dedicated to the separation of church and state. In fact, as Delegate Harper pointed out, supporters of the minority proposal did not ask to remove the entire 1889 provision. Their goal was to merely ensure that federal funds would be consistently available to non-public institutions, such as Rocky Mountain College. These delegates did not want to remove the wall separating church and state from the constitution; they just wanted to amend the 1889 language to declare federal aid available to private schools.

One theme throughout the debate was the strictness of the 1889 language. Delegate Toole called it "an especially stringent section that perhaps is among the most stringent in the nation." This description was echoed by Delegate Harbaugh who noted the provision's "extreme inflexibility." Delegate Harbaugh, who begrudgingly accepted the deletion of "or indirectly" in the minority proposal, felt the addition of the language was overly repetitious because two other clauses in the Montana Constitution already addressed state support for religion. "[I]f you put it in there three times, you've really got the message across," he quipped.

> However, some delegates felt that the amended majority proposal did not go far enough. At least a few delegates, like Delegate McNeil, voted against the compromise proposal because of the addition of the federal funds provision. He felt it was "fundamentally wrong to take any tax money . . . and apply it to any church purpose." Representatives from three church denominations echoed this view in testimony before the convention. These individuals expressed opposition to all government funds, federal or state, being allocated to churches and religious schools. These groups did not want the government getting involved with their "church work." Speaking for one of the churches, Delegate Conover reiterated: "If we cannot support our private schools, then it's our fault. We are the ones that's [sic] running it, and we don't want nobody [sic] to interfere with us. We teach our religion and we want it this way." Delegate Conover, like Delegate McNeil, voted against the compromise proposal, which would be ratified later that year. ***

This debate exemplifies the complexity of Constitutional Convention deliberations, even just to revise a provision from the 1889 Constitution. Does it help answer the question posed in *Espinoza*?

2. The United States Supreme Court granted plaintiffs' petition for *certiorari* on claims that the Montana Supreme Court's decision—and potentially the Montana Constitution itself—violated the Free Exercise Clause of the United States Constitution. *See Espinoza v. Montana Dep't of Revenue* (2020). In a remarkable brief *amici curiae*, ten of the surviving delegates to the 1972 Constitutional Convention argued:

> In adopting a no-aid clause to serve the lofty goals they set for education in Montana, the delegates were not blind to the concerns voiced by some delegates that some of the support for late nineteenth century no-aid provisions in the United States was based on anti-Catholic animus. But they repudiated any such history—consistent with their rejection of provisions from the 1889 Constitution that were biased against religious groups viewed as outside the mainstream in the nineteenth century, such as Mormons.
>
> Rather than being motivated by anti-religious animus, many delegates urged adoption of the no-aid clause to protect religious institutions from government interference. Some of those delegates, echoing testimony from religious groups within Montana, would have favored prohibiting even the pass-through of federal funds. For the majority of delegates, however, the no-aid clause that emerged from extensive debate struck the right balance by protecting state funds for public education while ensuring religious schools could avail themselves of federal resources.
>
> This sovereign choice regarding how to fund and structure education, endorsed by the people of Montana in a ratification vote, is precisely the sort of choice that the federal constitution leaves to the authority of the States. Nothing in the federal constitution requires commitment to use state public funds for state public programs. On the contrary, our federalist structure

dictates deference to the choices made by Montana citizens through a deliberative and democratic process.

3. The United States Supreme Court reversed. Several of the opinions of the justices raise questions about state constitutionalism in a federal system.

a. Chief Justice Roberts, writing for the Court, held:

> The Free Exercise Clause, which applies to the States under the Fourteenth Amendment, "protects religious observers against unequal treatment" and against "laws that impose special disabilities on the basis of religious status." *** Montana's no-aid provision bars religious schools from public benefits solely because of the religious character of the schools. The provision also bars parents who wish to send their children to a religious school from those same benefits, again solely because of the religious character of the school. This is apparent from the plain text. The provision bars aid to any school "controlled in whole or in part by any church, sect, or denomination." Mont. Const., Art. X, § 6(1). The provision's title—"Aid prohibited to sectarian schools"—confirms that the provision singles out schools based on their religious character. *Ibid.* And the Montana Supreme Court explained that the provision forbids aid to any school that is "sectarian," "religiously affiliated," or "controlled in whole or in part by churches." The provision plainly excludes schools from government aid solely because of religious status. ***
>
> The Department argues that a tradition against state support for religious schools arose in the second half of the 19th century, as more than 30 States—including Montana—adopted no-aid provisions. Such a development, of course, cannot by itself establish an early American tradition.... [M]any of the no-aid provisions belong to a more checkered tradition shared with the Blaine Amendment of the 1870s. That proposal—which Congress nearly passed—would have added to the Federal Constitution a provision similar to the state no-aid provisions, prohibiting States from aiding "sectarian" schools. "[I]t was an open secret that 'sectarian' was code for 'Catholic.'" The Blaine Amendment was "born of bigotry" and "arose at a time of pervasive hostility to the Catholic Church and to Catholics in general"; many of its state counterparts have a similarly "shameful pedigree." The no-aid provisions of the 19th century hardly evince a tradition that should inform our understanding of the Free Exercise Clause.
>
> The Department argues that several States have rejected referendums to overturn or limit their no-aid provisions, and that Montana even re-adopted its own in the 1970s, for reasons unrelated to anti-Catholic bigotry. But, on the other side of the ledger, many States today—including those with no-aid provisions—provide support to religious schools through vouchers, scholarships, tax credits, and other measures. According to petitioners, 20 of 37 States with no-aid provisions allow religious options in publicly

funded scholarship programs, and almost all allow religious options in tax credit programs.

All to say, we agree with the Department that the historical record is "complex." And it is true that governments over time have taken a variety of approaches to religious schools. But it is clear that there is no "historic and substantial" tradition against aiding such schools comparable to the tradition against state-supported clergy invoked by *Locke* [*v. Davey* (2004)]. ***

... When the Court was called upon to apply a state law no-aid provision to exclude religious schools from the program, it was obligated by the Federal Constitution to reject the invitation. Had the Court recognized that this was, indeed, "one of those cases" in which application of the no-aid provision "would violate the Free Exercise Clause," the Court would not have proceeded to find a violation of that provision. And, in the absence of such a state law violation, the Court would have had no basis for terminating the program. Because the elimination of the program flowed directly from the Montana Supreme Court's failure to follow the dictates of federal law, it cannot be defended as a neutral policy decision, or as resting on adequate and independent state law grounds. ***

What is the impact of *Espinoza* on state constitutions? The majority holds that Montana's "no-aid" clause is unconstitutional as applied by the Montana Supreme Court. Does any constitutional application of Article X, section 6 remain? Consider Justice Baker's options in her dissent: direct appropriations, indirect appropriations, direct payments, and indirect payments. Under *Espinoza*, could the "no-aid" clause restrict any of these forms of aid to religious schools in a generally available educational program, even if the aid were used for religious purposes? What does it take to establish a "historic and substantial" tradition in state constitutions with respect to the prohibitions of federal constitutional law?

b. Justice Alito concurred:

*** Respondents and one dissent argue that Montana's no-aid provision was cleansed of its bigoted past because it was readopted for non-bigoted reasons in Montana's 1972 constitutional convention. They emphasize that the convention included Catholics, just as the constitutional convention that readopted Louisiana's purportedly racist non-unanimous jury provision included black delegates. As noted, a virtually identical argument was rejected in *Ramos*, even though "'no mention was made of race'" during the Louisiana convention debates. Under *Ramos v. Louisiana* (2020) [in which Justice Alito dissented], it emphatically does not matter whether Montana readopted the no-aid provision for benign reasons. The provision's "uncomfortable past" must still be "[e]xamined." And here, it is not so clear that the animus was scrubbed.

Delegates at Montana's constitutional convention in 1972 acknowledged that the no-aid provision was "a badge of bigotry," with one Catholic delegate recalling "being let out of school in the fourth grade to erase three 'Ks' on the front doors of the Catholic church in Billings." Nevertheless the convention proposed, and the State adopted, a provision with the *same* material language, prohibiting public aid "for any *sectarian* purpose or to aid any... school... controlled in whole or in part by any church, sect, or denomination." Mont. Const., Art. X, § 6(1) (1972) (emphasis added). A leading definition of "sect" at the time, as during the Blaine era, was "a dissenting religious body; *esp: one that is heretical in the eyes of other members within the same communion.*" Webster's Third New International Dictionary 2052 (1971) (emphasis added).

Given the history above, the terms "sect" and "sectarian" are disquieting remnants. And once again, there appears to have been little doubt which schools this provision would predominantly affect. In 1970, according to the National Center for Educational Statistics, Montana had 61 religiously affiliated schools. Forty-five were Roman Catholic. Not only did the convention delegates acknowledge the no-aid provision's original anti-Catholic intent, but the Montana Supreme Court had only ever applied the provision once—to a Catholic school, and one that had "carrie[d] a sizeable portion of the total educational load" in Anaconda, Montana. *State ex rel. Chambers v. School Dist. No. 10 of Deer Lodge Cty.*, (Mont. 1970) (per curiam). The Montana Catholic Conference also voiced concerns about access to school funds, and a convention delegate proposed removing the no-aid provision's restriction on "indirect" aid. That amendment was rejected.

Thus, the no-aid provision's terms keep it "[t]ethered" to its original "bias," and it is not clear at all that the State "actually confront[ed]" the provision's "tawdry past in reenacting it." After all, whereas the no-aid provision had originally been foisted on Montana, the State readopted it voluntarily—"sectarian" references included. Whether or not the State did so for any reason that could be called legitimate, the convention delegates recognized that the provision would "continue to mean and do whatever it does now," Convention Tr. 2014 (statement of Delegate Loendorf), and the discrimination in this case shows that the provision continues to have its originally intended effect. And even if Montana had done more to address its no-aid provision's past, that would of course do nothing to resolve the bias inherent in the Blaine Amendments among the 17 States, by respondents' count, that have not readopted or amended them since around the turn of the 20th century. ***

Justice Alito's concurrence pays closer attention to the framing of the provision at issue. He calls for a law's "uncomfortable past" to be examined, adopting an approach he criticized the same year in *Ramos v. Louisiana* (2020) ("Too much public discourse today is sullied by ad hominem rhetoric, that is, attempts to discredit an argument not by proving that it is unsound but by attacking the character or motives of the argument's proponents."). What more should the 1972 Montana

Constitutional Convention have done to confront that past? Should Congress, or the President, or the Supreme Court satisfy the same standard when amending or interpreting laws arguably rooted in discrimination? Why or why not?

c. Justice Ginsburg dissented:

> *** Petitioners argue that the Montana Supreme Court's decision fails when measured against *Trinity Lutheran*. I do not see how. Past decisions in this area have entailed differential treatment occasioning a burden on a plaintiff's religious exercise. This case is missing that essential component. Recall that the Montana court remedied the state constitutional violation by striking the scholarship program in its entirety. Under that decree, secular and sectarian schools alike are ineligible for benefits, so the decision cannot be said to entail differential treatment based on petitioners' religion. Put somewhat differently, petitioners argue that the Free Exercise Clause requires a State to treat institutions and people neutrally when doling out a benefit—and neutrally is how Montana treats them in the wake of the state court's decision.
>
> Accordingly, the Montana Supreme Court's decision does not place a burden on petitioners' religious exercise. Petitioners may still send their children to a religious school. And the Montana Supreme Court's decision does not pressure them to do otherwise. Unlike the law in *Trinity Lutheran*, the decision below puts petitioners to no "choice": Neither giving up their faith, nor declining to send their children to sectarian schools, would affect their entitlement to scholarship funding. There simply are no scholarship funds to be had. ***
>
> Nearing the end of its opinion, the Court writes: "A State need not subsidize private education. But once a State decides to do so, it cannot disqualify some private schools solely because they are religious." Because Montana's Supreme Court did not make such a decision—its judgment put all private school parents in the same boat—this Court had no occasion to address the matter. On that sole ground, and reaching no other issue, I dissent from the Court's judgment.

Justice Ginsburg's dissent points to the possibility of harmonizing state and federal constitutional law. Would or should the United States Supreme Court have treated the Montana Supreme Court as more of a partner in achieving any possible harmonization if the state court had paid more attention to the demands of federal free exercise doctrine?

d. Justice Sotomayor also dissented:

> *** The Court typically declines to read state-court decisions as impliedly resolving federal questions, especially ones not raised by the parties. Indeed, to honor principles of comity, this Court generally dismisses writs of certiorari from a State's highest court where, as is true here of the Court's

> bespoke inquiry, "the sole federal question" the Court seeks to decide was not "raised, preserved, or passed upon in the state courts below." ***
>
> These principles exist to prevent this Court from issuing advisory opinions, sowing confusion, and muddying the law. This is case in point. Having held that petitioners may not be "exclu[ded] from the scholarship program" that no longer exists, the Court remands to the Montana Supreme Court for "further proceedings not inconsistent with this opinion." But it is hard to tell what this Court wishes the state court to do. There is no program from which petitioners are currently "exclu[ded]," so must the Montana Supreme Court order the State to recreate one? Has this Court just announced its authority to require a state court to order a state legislature to fund religious exercise, overruling centuries of contrary precedent and historical practice? Indeed, it appears that the Court has declared that once Montana created a tax subsidy, it forfeited the right to eliminate it if doing so would harm religion. This is a remarkable result, all the more so because the Court strains to reach it. ***
>
> In sum, the decision below neither upheld a program that "disqualif[ies] some private schools solely because they are religious," nor otherwise decided the case on federal grounds. The Court's opinion thus turns on a counterfactual hypothetical it is powerless (and unwise) to decide. ***

The majority opinion frames the issue as the state court contradicting the state legislature. But the law at issue contained not only a severability clause but an unusual constitutional proviso: "[t]he tax credit for taxpayer donations under this part must be administered in compliance with Article V, section 11(5) [prohibiting appropriations to private religious organizations], and Article X, section 6 [the "no-aid" clause], of the Montana constitution." If the Montana Supreme Court held the tax credit could not be administered in compliance with the Montana Constitution, did it have any choice but to invalidate the entire program consistent with this expression of legislative intent? Or would the proviso itself be an unconstitutional application of the "no-aid" clause? If so, what remedy should the United States Supreme Court provide? Is Justice Sotomayor correct that the repeal of the tax credit program, citing the "no-aid" clause would raise the same constitutional issues? Ultimately, how do state and federal constitutions interact to bind state actors to their respective guarantees?

B. Freedom of Speech, Press, and Expression

The Montana Constitution's freedom of assembly and expression provisions echo and extend related federal rights. While the ratifiers were told these rights would "enlarg[e] a citizen's freedom to express himself," the courts have struggled to find points of departure from the complexities of federal doctrine expounding the freedoms of speech, press, and assembly. At times, such as in *City of Billings v. Laedeke*, the Montana Supreme Court has declined to recognize any greater protections for self-expression in the state Constitution. Other times, such as in *City of Helena v. Krautter*, the Court tries to march with federal precedent precisely in lock-step. As the cases recounted in *State v. Dugan* suggest, the Court has at times fallen a few steps short of basic First Amendment protections. The relative rarity of free speech cases in Montana may be explained, in part, by the procedural and remedial complexities discussed in *Griffith v. Butte School District*. Federal free speech doctrine strongly protects free expression in general, though it is controversial and contingent in many details. Consider whether there is an opportunity for Montana constitutional law to blaze a different trail. (Note some of these cases contain offensive language, including a sexist epithet in *Dugan*.)

1. A Distinct Freedom of Expression?

Montana's free speech guarantee of Article II, section 7 is textually distinct from the First Amendment. The final two sentences reflect traditional protections of speech and press against defamation actions. The first sentence, however, contains two deliberate innovations: "impair" (instead of "abridge") and "expression" (in addition to speech). In *Trailing in the Wake: The Freedom of Speech in Montana*, 77 MONT. L. REV. 61 (2016), John Wolff explores these potential distinctions:

> It has been noted that, at least in theory, impair provides a broader protection than abridge because prohibiting impairment is more comprehensive than prohibiting abridgment. Despite this textual difference, the Montana Supreme Court has held the two words mean the same thing.
>
> To abridge means to shorten. In the First Amendment, this word has been understood to mean no speech within the freedom may lose its First Amendment protections by being placed outside the freedom. This idea is consistent with the Supreme Court's unwillingness to create new categories outside the freedom. Speech within the freedom is still subject to regulation, but the freedom provides the speech within its cloak varying levels of protection that regulations must satisfy.
>
> To impair means to make worse, diminish in quantity or value, or to deteriorate. Textually, impair is a more comprehensive protection than abridge for at least three reasons. First, similar to the First Amendment, Article I, Section 10 [the Freedom of Speech guarantee of the proposed 1884 Montana Constitution] protects speech within the freedom. Second, similar to the prohibition on abridgment preventing the government from shrinking the freedom, the prohibition on impairment likewise prevents shrinking the freedom because "impair" means "deteriorate." Third, and most importantly, the prohibition on impairment protects the quality and value of the speech within the freedom, which indicates a more precise and exacting level of protection that speech regulations must satisfy. Thus, the prohibition on impairment takes its protections one step further by providing not

only shall no speech within the freedom be placed outside the freedom, but also no speech within the freedom may be diminished in quality or value.

These definitions, however, are not always consistent with the 1884 Constitution's other uses of impair and abridge. The 1884 Constitution used the term impair three other times, and abridge twice (unfortunately, impair and abridge were never used within the same section). *** The contemporaneous definition of impair; its use in Article I, Section 28; and Article XV, Section 9's use of abridge lead to the conclusion impair was intended to provide more protection than abridge in Article I, Section 10 of the 1884 Montana Constitution. The two terms' coexistence in the same document underscores this point. While a prohibition on abridging a right protected any acts within that right from being placed outside of the right, a prohibition on impairing a right went one step further by providing the right may not be deteriorated or diminished in quality either. Thus, the 1884 Constitution provided a heightened layer of protection against regulations that might chill, *i.e.* deteriorate or diminish in quality, speech. [The 1889 Constitutional Convention rejected a proposal that would have replaced the word "impair" with "abridge."] ***

[The 1972 Constitutional Convention record] indicates that progressively protecting the freedom of speech, whether spoken or through expression, is within the original meaning of the section. This meaning, combined with the heightened protection already provided by impair, is a directive to the Montana Supreme Court to proactively protect speech, rather than merely following federal precedent. The ratification record indicates the voters also understood and believed that the freedom of expression contained in their constitution was a more protective right, separate and independent of the First Amendment. ***

The document that most likely helped voters understand the new freedom of speech provision was a voter pamphlet containing the official proposed text with accompanying explanations, published by the 1972 Convention for the voters of Montana. Although newspapers at the time generally stated the freedom of speech had been "broadened," the voter pamphlet provided voters with context for the new constitution they were considering by explaining the differences between the 1889 and 1972 constitutions. The voter pamphlet explicitly differentiated between rights retained from the 1889 Constitution and new rights added to the proposed 1972 Constitution. . . . In contrast [to rights retained as identical to the 1889 Constitution like suffrage or keeping and bearing arms], the Explanation section of the freedom of speech explains that the right has not remained the same, and instead is more protective. The Explanation section states "[r]evises 1889 constitution by enlarging a citizen's freedom to express himself[.]" Voters would understand the explanation to mean the 1972 Constitution offered a more protective freedom of speech than the 1889 Constitution.

> The text of the 1972 Constitution, the 1972 Constitutional Convention's debates, and the ratification record are all seemingly in agreement that the 1972 Constitution's freedom of speech provision stands on its own with heightened protections, separate and distinct from the First Amendment....

Consider these potential distinctions in the following two cases.

City of Billings v. Laedeke

247 Mont. 151 (1991)

TURNAGE, Chief Justice.

*** In 1987, Jimmy Lee Laedeke worked as a male revue dancer at the Club Carlin, d/b/a Big Daddy's, an establishment licensed by the state to sell alcoholic beverages, in Billings, Montana. As a male revue dancer, Laedeke entertained the Club Carlin patrons by performing burlesque-type dance routines to music. Laedeke designed his own dance costumes, which consisted of various layers of clothing that he would progressively remove as his dance routines unfolded.

Laedeke began one of his dance routines dressed in a raincoat. Underneath his raincoat, Laedeke wore a bikini brief, equivalent to a speedo swimsuit, which was embellished with portrayals of Groucho Marx's nose, mustache and glasses on the front portion of the bikini. Underneath his "Groucho" bikini, Laedeke wore two overlapping G-strings. A G-string, designed for a male, is a garment consisting of a pouch that covers the genital area with a narrow string attached to the pouch which runs up the buttocks and attaches to a narrow belt worn around the waist. Laedeke's top G-string was of slightly larger proportions than the bottom G-string. The arresting police officer testified that the smaller G-string's pouch barely covered Laedeke's genital area and its string was approximately one-eighth inch wide. Laedeke would complete his routine by wearing only the smaller G-string.

On the evening of November 6, 1987, the arresting police officer observed Laedeke while he was performing this particular dance routine. After viewing Laedeke's performance, the police officer left the Club Carlin to review relevant ordinances in connection to this performance. The police officer returned approximately one-half hour later and cited Laedeke with a violation of § 3-304, BMCC [Billings, Montana City Code], which prohibits certain forms of nude and semi-nude dancing while Laedeke was again performing the same routine. Additionally, the arresting officer cited four other female performers that night, as well as the manager of the Club Carlin, for violating § 3-304, BMCC, and in one instance, § 3-301, BMCC, which requires live entertainment to remain on a platform or within an exclusive area while performing. ***

Following a trial on January 11, 1990, the District Court found that the City of Billings had the authority to enact § 3-304, BMCC, and that this ordinance was constitutional; the court also found Laedeke guilty of violating the ordinance, fined him $130.00, and assessed him a $20.00 court surcharge. From this decision, Laedeke further appeals. ***

2. Did the District Court err in concluding that the municipal ordinance did not violate federal and state constitutional provisions relating to freedom of speech, freedom of expression, equal protection, due process, and vagueness and over-breadth?

Laedeke argues that restricting burlesque-type dancing is a violation of the First Amendment of the United States Constitution, as well as Article 2, § 7 of the Montana Constitution, which states that "[n]o law shall be passed impairing the freedom of speech or expression." Laedeke asserts that nude dancing, as a visual representation, is a form of protected expression if it is not found to be obscene citing 41 Op. Att'y Gen. 75 (1986), and here, uncontroverted evidence establishes that burlesque-type dancing featured at the Club Carlin was viewed by the performers as a form of artistic self-expression. Furthermore, Laedeke argues that no evidence exists in the record to establish that Laedeke's performance was obscene. ***

Laedeke's constitutional argument based on a First Amendment violation lacks merit in light of a series of three United States Supreme Court cases. Those cases clearly establish that an ordinance regulating nude and semi-nude dancing is constitutional under the broad language of the Twenty-first Amendment of the United States Constitution, which grants the states the power to regulate the sale of liquor. ***

Therefore, a municipality may enact an ordinance regulating nude and semi-nude dancing if the state has delegated its regulatory authority under the Twenty-first Amendment to the municipality. Here, the City of Billings is a municipality with self-government powers. In Montana, a municipality with self-government powers "may exercise any power not prohibited by this constitution, law, or charter." Mont. Const. Art. XI, § 6. A Montana municipality with self-government powers is not expressly prohibited from regulating nude and semi-nude dancing in establishments state-licensed to sell liquor. Therefore, the City of Billings, a municipality with self-government powers, may enact an ordinance that regulates nude and semi-nude dancing under the broad regulatory powers of the Twenty-first Amendment.

Laedeke further argues that Article II, § 7 of the Montana Constitution, the "freedom of speech or expression" clause, provides greater protection for individual expressive activity than the First Amendment's "freedom of speech" clause of the United States Constitution. In the past, this Court has discussed the First Amendment and its state counterpart without distinguishing between the two provisions. Several state courts, however, have developed state constitutional protections which limit state authority over nude entertainment apart from the Twenty-first Amendment. Some of these courts have held that the state's police power, though possibly not limited under the United States Constitution, is limited by the state constitution's free expression protections. *See Mickens v. City of Kodiak* (Alaska 1982); *Bellanca v. New York State Liquor Authority* (N.Y. 1981); *Harris v. Entertainment Sys. Inc.* (Ga. 1989).

We, however, concur with the Florida Supreme Court's analysis in *City of Daytona Beach v. Del Percio* (Fla.1985), where, in upholding a municipal ordinance banning certain forms of nude and semi-nude dancing, the court stated:

> Assuming that Florida's constitutional protection of nude barroom dancing is coextensive with the federal protections (and we are not inclined to find a greater state protection in this instance), a municipality's inherent police power, exercised for the public health and welfare, may outweigh the minimal speech protection at stake here. "The regulation of activity which has demonstrated a capacity to induce breaches of the peace is a traditional and legitimate subject for the exercise of a municipality's police power." [citations omitted.] . . . While some may question the wisdom of regulating crime such as this, which said detractors might term victimless, the decision lies with the legislative body, not the courts.

Here, we are also inclined not to find a greater state protection of nude and semi-nude dancing in establishments state-licensed to sell alcoholic beverages than what is afforded by the United States Constitution. Accordingly, we hold that the municipal ordinance in question is constitutionally sound under the Montana Constitution. ***

HUNT, Justice, dissenting:

. . . There are many ways to express an opinion. Some people wrap themselves in the flag. Others burn it. But the majority of us silently regard it as an emblem of the freedom to express ourselves as we see fit. In dancing, there are many ways to express oneself, ways that the rest of us do not always regard as "our way." Some put on a pair of tights and perform classical ballet. Others attire themselves in fancy dress and promenade on a ballroom floor. Jimmy Lee Laedeke dons a Groucho Marx bikini and two G-strings and prances before the patrons of The Club Carlin.

The Majority has danced the wild fandango in its zeal to ensure that Laedeke's routine shall never again see the footlights of Billings. *** The ordinance could not pass scrutiny under this test because, as the City acknowledged in its brief, it has failed to make a showing of any governmental interest furthered by the law.

What I find most disturbing about the Majority's thinly veiled attempt to uphold this ordinance at any price is its failure to take this opportunity to put some teeth into our state constitutional guarantee of freedom of expression. 1972 Mont. Const. Art. II, § 7. In voting unanimously to include a specific provision for the freedom of expression in the Montana Constitution, the Bill of Rights Committee stated:

> Hopefully, this extension [of freedom of expression] will provide impetus to the courts in Montana to rule on various forms of expression similar to the spoken word and the ways in which one expresses his unique personality *in an effort to re-balance the general backseat status of states in the safeguarding of civil liberties. The committee wishes to stress the primacy of these*

> *guarantees in the hope that their enforcement will not continue merely in the wake of the federal case law.* (Emphasis added.)

Bill of Rights Committee Proposal, II Mont. Const. Convention 630 (Feb. 23, 1972).

Although the committee expressed the hope that the Montana Constitution's freedom of expression would give broader guarantees than the U.S. Supreme Court had accorded the right, this Court has refused to listen to this desire. Instead, the Majority today bestows lesser protection to the freedom of expression than that accorded by the federal court. The Majority has not required the City to demonstrate any governmental interest forwarded by this ordinance. Instead, it has placed the burden of proving unconstitutionality on Laedeke. And the standard the majority has demanded that he use, that of a reasonable doubt, is the most stringent standard of all. What a sad day it is when we allow a law that on its face constricts so fundamental a right to pass muster under the lowest possible scrutiny available.

The fact that Laedeke dances to a different choreographer should not be a reason to deny him, and inferentially all of us, the basic constitutional right to express our feelings whether they are about the flag, dancing or Groucho Marx. ***

City of Helena v. Krautter

258 Mont. 361 (1993)

HARRISON, Justice.

*** Krautter was arrested at the Intermountain Planned Parenthood Clinic in Helena, Montana, on December 6, 1991, for violating § 45-6-203, MCA. This statute makes it a crime to enter or remain unlawfully on the premises of another. The primary issue on appeal is whether Krautter had a constitutional right of access to private property for the purpose of exercising her right of free speech.

At the time of her arrest, Krautter was sitting on a concrete step at the west door of the clinic. She was part of an anti-abortion demonstration that included approximately forty people. With Krautter at the west door was a group of three people who had locked themselves together with bicycle locks. Krautter had not locked herself to this group.

"No trespassing" signs were posted around the perimeter of the clinic property. Like most of the other people at the demonstration, Krautter had stationed herself within the area defined by those signs. Shortly after the demonstration began, and before any patients had arrived at the clinic, the clinic manager and a police officer asked everyone to leave. About twenty-five people moved from the clinic property to the sidewalk or street. The remaining demonstrators, including Krautter, were arrested and charged with trespass and disorderly conduct.

The Helena Municipal Court found that Krautter was not guilty of disorderly conduct but guilty of criminal trespass, for which she was fined $240. Krautter appealed to the District Court, which heard the case on August 3, 1992. Shortly after the hearing, Krautter moved to dismiss the charge against her on the grounds that she was on the clinic property to exercise her constitutional right of free speech by discussing "physical, emotional, and psychological injuries that have occurred to other women at women's health clinics" with any interested women entering the clinic that day, and that she had no other reasonable opportunity to convey her message to her intended audience.

On August 21, 1992, the District Court issued its decision, denying Krautter's motion and finding her guilty of trespass. Krautter appealed. ***

Krautter admits that she trespassed but contends that the fine was improper because she entered and remained on the clinic property to exercise the right of freedom of speech guaranteed by the First Amendment and by the Montana Constitution, Art. II, § 7. She argues that § 45-6-203, MCA, is unconstitutional because it does not allow for protected speech on private property. ***

Although no Montana case addresses the relation between property rights and freedom of speech, we concluded in *City of Billings v. Laedeke* (Mont. 1991) that Art. II, § 7 provides no greater protection for free expression than does the United States Constitution. Thus, if the trespass statute is constitutional under the First Amendment, it is also constitutional under Art. II, § 7, Mont.Const., which provides in pertinent part that:

> No law shall be passed impairing the freedom of speech or expression. Every person shall be free to speak or publish whatever he will on any subject, being responsible for all abuse of that liberty.

The constitutionality of a statute is presumed; the party challenging it must prove beyond a reasonable doubt that it is unconstitutional. *Laedeke*. The United States Supreme Court has held that "[i]t would be an unwarranted infringement of property rights to require them to yield to the exercise of First Amendment rights . . . where adequate alternative avenues of communication exist." *Lloyd Corp., Ltd. v. Tanner* (1972). Here, the District Court found that Krautter did have alternative avenues of communication. We conclude that Krautter has not proved that she had no alternative avenue of communication and that the Montana trespass statute does not violate the First Amendment.

The question remains as to whether Krautter has a constitutional right of access to private property for the purpose of exercising her right of free speech.

Krautter relies on United States Supreme Court cases, particularly *Amalgamated Food Employees Union Local 590 v. Logan Valley Plaza, Inc.* (1968); and *Lloyd*. In both cases the Supreme Court recognized that a privately-owned shopping center has many of the attributes of a public forum. In *Logan Valley*, it held that "the State may not delegate the power, through the use of its trespass laws, wholly to exclude those members of the public wishing to exercise their First Amendment rights on the premises in a manner and for a purpose generally consonant with the use to which the property is actually put." But in *Lloyd* the Court effectively overruled *Logan Valley*. *** Unless a shopping center has assumed "all of the attributes of a state-created municipality, . . . performing the full spectrum of municipal powers," the Court held, members of the public do not have the same right of free speech in the streets and sidewalks of a shopping center as they would have in similar public facilities in the streets of a city or town. *Lloyd* (distinguishing *Marsh v. Alabama* (1945), which held that a state could not enforce a prohibition of expressive activity in a shopping center or "company town" with attributes of a municipality).

Here, Krautter has not shown or even argued that the Intermountain Planned Parenthood Center is a public facility. It is not even the type of quasi-public facility that figured in *Logan Valley* and *Lloyd*. Even if it were, Krautter still would have to show that no reasonable alternative to convey her message existed. She asserts that "the only way for her to communicate her information to the target audience who could most benefit from her information was to be on the property of the Planned Parenthood clinic." As the District Court pointed out, however, "nothing . . . has been shown to this court that persons driving up to the clinic could not see her picketing in the street and would not have been able to stop and talk with her if they so desired."

. . . The United States Supreme Court held, in *Pruneyard Shopping Center v. Robins* (1980), that a state could adopt in its own constitution "individual liberties more expansive than those conferred by the Federal Constitution," and affirmed a California Supreme Court decision holding that a privately owned shopping center could not prevent speech and petitioning, reasonably exercised, within the shopping center. The Court clearly distinguished *Lloyd*, where the state constitution did not create "rights to the use of private property by strangers, comparable to those found to exist by the California Supreme Court."

We do not find in Art. II, §7 of the Montana Constitution any right to "the use of private property by strangers" that would entitle Krautter to access to clinic property for purposes of conveying a message to the clinic's invitees. *** We hold that neither the First Amendment nor Art. II, §7 of the Montana Constitution entitles Krautter to have access to Planned Parenthood's property in order to exercise her right of free speech.

Notes on a Distinct Freedom of Expression

1. In *Laedeke*, the Montana Supreme Court declines to distinguish Article II, section 7 from federal expressive conduct doctrine, although it acknowledges both that other states have done so and that Montana distinctly protects "expression." What is its reasoning? Assuming impairments of the freedom of expression are, like other provisions in the Declaration of Rights, subject to strict scrutiny, would the city's "police power" to protect public health, safety, and welfare satisfy it? After *Laedeke*, what does "the freedom of expression" add to Montana constitutional law that is not already protected (or unprotected) by federal law?

2. In *Krautter*, the Montana Supreme Court declines to distinguish Article II, section 7 from federal public forum doctrine. Although (again) it acknowledges that it has the authority to depart from that doctrine, it reads *Laedeke* to hold that "Art. II, §7 provides no greater protection for free expression than does the United

States Constitution." Is that a fair reading of *Laedeke*? Would Krautter have had more success with an Article II, section 6 claim to the "right peaceably to assemble [or] peaceably protest governmental action"? Recall Article II, section 4 from Chapter 10: "Neither the state nor any person, firm, corporation, or institution shall discriminate against any person in the exercise of his civil or political rights on account of . . . political . . . ideas." Through the Governmental Code of Fair Practices, the Legislature has provided a remedy for public but not private political discrimination. Could Krautter have brought a private political discrimination claim on these facts?

3. In addition to textual distinctions, some states have recognized historical and cultural distinctions in the expression protected. For example, Article I, section 8, of the Oregon Constitution provides: "No law shall be passed restraining the free expression of opinion, or restricting the right to speak, write, or print freely on any subject whatever; but every person shall be responsible for the abuse of this right." In *State v. Henry* (Or. 1987), the court invalidated an obscenity prosecution of an adult bookstore owner:

> [T]he state claims that "obscenity" would have been a conventional crime when Oregon's Bill of Rights was adopted in 1857. *** The only relevant Oregon territorial legislation enacted before Article I, section 8, included prohibitions against the sale, distribution and possession of obscene writings or pictures which manifestly tended to corrupt the morals of youth. *** The territorial statute, which contained no definition of "obscene" and which was directed primarily to the protection of youth, certainly does not constitute any well-established historical exception to freedom of expression and that statute is in no way the equivalent of statutes punishing libel, perjury, forgery and the like. ***
>
> In *Roth* [*v. United States* (1957)], Justice Douglas [dissenting] observed that the First Amendment was a product of a robust, not a prudish age. Likewise, although Oregon's pioneers brought with them a diversity of highly moral as well as irreverent views, we perceive that most members of the Constitutional Convention of 1857 were rugged and robust individuals dedicated to founding a free society unfettered by the governmental imposition of some people's views of morality on the free expression of others. We conclude as we did in reviewing English and American history that restrictions on sexually explicit and obscene expression between adults were not well established at the time of the adoption of Article I, section 8, of the Oregon Constitution. The history of restriction on undefined obscenity contrasts sharply with the Oregon and common law crimes involving expression such as perjury, theft, forgery and fraud that were well established by 1859. The very fact that "obscenity" originally was pursued and repressed for its "anti-establishment" irreverence rather than for its bawdiness elsewhere and only to protect the morals of youth in this state leads us

to conclude that no broad or all-encompassing historical exception from the guarantees of free expression was ever intended. ***

We hold that characterizing expression as "obscenity" under any definition ... does not deprive it of protection under the Oregon Constitution. Obscene speech, writing or equivalent forms of communication are "speech" nonetheless. We emphasize that the prime reason that "obscene" expression cannot be restricted is that it is speech that does not fall within any historical exception to the plain wording of the Oregon Constitution that "no law shall be passed restraining the expression of [speech] freely on any subject whatsoever." ***

How might such an analysis inform the meaning of Montana's 1972 free expression provision, or other rights? Montana's current obscenity statute was enacted in 1973; is that of any significance?

2. The Current Scope of the Freedom of Expression

This chapter surveys only a few approaches to Article II, section 7 rights of expression. As with the equal protection and anti-discrimination rights of Article II, section 4, there are many ways in which practitioners might successfully distinguish federal freedom of speech doctrine. If anything, federal doctrine in this area is even more dynamic than federal equal protection doctrine. Consider, for example, what a distinct vision of the Montana Constitution might have to say about defamation and emotional distress, obscenity, false speech, expressive conduct, commercial speech, prior restraints, forum analysis, government speech, compelled speech, expressive association, or political speech. Current case law in Montana, however, locksteps with the basic federal "categorical" freedom of speech rule: heightened protection for regulations targeting the content or viewpoint of speech with exceptions, as the United States Supreme Court put it in *Chaplinsky v. New Hampshire* (1942), for "certain well-defined and narrowly limited classes of speech, the prevention and punishment of which have never been thought to raise any Constitutional problem." The door appears to have closed for new categories of less-protected speech in federal law, and courts construe the preexisting categories narrowly. Is Montana constitutional law lockstepping with these developments, trailing in the wake (in John Wolff's words), or charting some other course?

State v. Dugan

369 Mont. 39 (2013)

Justice PATRICIA O. COTTER delivered the Opinion of the Court.

*** ¶ 7 On October 21, 2009, Dugan visited the office of the Gallatin County Victim Assistance Program (Victim Services) and requested assistance with filling out and filing paperwork for obtaining an order of protection against the mother of his children, who was about to be released from prison. Victim Services is a joint effort of Gallatin County, the City of Bozeman, and the private nonprofit Network Against Sexual and Domestic Violence. It is located in the Law and Justice Center in Bozeman, Montana. The office door is locked and controlled by a video-monitored entry system. Dugan was not allowed to enter the office because he had been loud and disruptive in the past. An employee of Victim Services, Jan Brownell, informed Dugan that the person with whom he needed to speak, Krystal Redmond-Sherrill, was not in the office at that time. Brownell told Dugan to call Redmond-Sherrill and make an appointment to discuss the order of protection.

¶ 8 On October 28, 2009, Dugan contacted Gallatin County Dispatch to attempt to obtain an order of protection. Dispatch contacted Deputy Mayland of the Gallatin County Sheriff's Office and asked him to get in touch with Dugan. Deputy Mayland spoke with Dugan and Dugan told him that he was afraid the mother of his children would try to take his children when she was released from prison. Dugan reported that he spoke with Redmond-Sherrill at Victim Services, but she refused to provide him with the necessary paperwork or assistance to obtain an order of protection. Deputy Mayland contacted Victim Services to investigate Dugan's claims. Redmond-Sherrill informed Deputy Mayland that Dugan had stopped by the office a week ago and was told to make an appointment. Deputy Mayland also talked to Brownell, who told him about Dugan's past behavior. Brownell reported that the Victim Services' office staff felt threatened by Dugan.

¶ 9 Later that same day, Redmond-Sherrill contacted Deputy Mayland and reported that Dugan had just called her. Once again, Dugan requested assistance obtaining an order of protection. When Redmond-Sherrill informed Dugan that she could not help him and suggested that he obtain the necessary paperwork directly from the clerk of court, Dugan became aggressive and agitated. Dugan continued to argue with Redmond-Sherrill, and called her a "fucking cunt" as he hung up the phone. When Redmond-Sherrill described the conversation to Deputy Mayland, her voice was shaky and soft and he believed she was about to cry. Brownell observed that Redmond-Sherrill was visibly upset following the conversation. However, Redmond-Sherrill reported that Dugan did not threaten her or anyone else in the office. Redmond-Sherrill told Deputy Mayland that Dugan was "just really upset that — that [she wasn't] going to hand him an order of protection . . . and basically wasn't getting what he was wanting out of that conversation."

¶ 10 Deputy Mayland issued a citation to Dugan for violating the Privacy in Communications statute. On the citation, Deputy Mayland wrote that Dugan "called victim on telephone and used obscene, lewd and profane language, offending the victim." *** Dugan was sentenced to 180 days in jail with all but five suspended, and ordered to pay fines and fees totaling $585. ***

Discussion

¶ 15 Did the State violate Dugan's right to free speech under the First Amendment to the United States Constitution and Article II, Section 7 of the Montana

Constitution when it charged him with violating the Privacy in Communications statute, § 45-8-213, MCA?

¶ 16 The statute under which Dugan was charged is § 45-8-213, MCA. It reads in pertinent part as follows:

> 45-8-213. Privacy in communications. (1) Except as provided in 69-6-104, a person commits the offense of violating privacy in communications if the person knowingly or purposely:
>
> (a) with the purpose to terrify, intimidate, threaten, harass, annoy, or offend, communicates with a person by electronic communication and uses obscene, lewd, or profane language, suggests a lewd or lascivious act, or threatens to inflict injury or physical harm to the person or property of the person. The use of obscene, lewd, or profane language or the making of a threat or lewd or lascivious suggestions is prima facie evidence of an intent to terrify, intimidate, threaten, harass, annoy, or offend.
>
> ...
>
> (4) "Electronic communication" means any transfer between persons of signs, signals, writing, images, sounds, data, or intelligence of any nature transmitted in whole or in part by a wire, radio, electromagnetic, photo-electronic, or photo-optical system.

As backdrop to our discussion of whether this statute infringed Dugan's free speech rights, we will analyze the protections historically accorded free speech under the United States and Montana Constitutions.

¶ 17 The First Amendment to the United States Constitution and Article II, Section 7 of the Montana Constitution both protect the right to free speech. The First Amendment to the United States Constitution provides that "Congress shall make no law . . . abridging the freedom of speech." Montana is bound to the guarantees of the First Amendment by the Due Process Clause of the Fourteenth Amendment. Article II, Section 7 of the Montana Constitution states that "[n]o law shall be passed impairing the freedom of speech or expression." Additionally, under Article II, Section 7, "[e]very person shall be free to speak . . . whatever he will on any subject, being responsible for all abuse of that liberty."

¶ 18 The right to free speech is a fundamental personal right and "essential to the common quest for truth and the vitality of society as a whole." The "vast majority" of speech enjoys constitutional protection. However, neither the First Amendment nor Article II, Section 7, provide unlimited protection for all forms of speech. The United States Supreme Court has explained that the right of free speech is not absolute at all times and under all circumstances:

> There are certain well-defined and narrowly limited classes of speech, the prevention and punishment of which have never been thought to raise any Constitutional problem. These include the lewd and obscene, the profane,

> the libelous, and the insulting or "fighting" words—those which by their very utterance inflict injury or tend to incite an immediate breach of the peace. It has been well observed that such utterances are no essential part of any exposition of ideas, and are of such slight social value as a step to truth that any benefit that may be derived from them is clearly outweighed by the social interest in order and morality. Resort to epithets or personal abuse is not in any proper sense communication of information or opinion safeguarded by the Constitution, and its punishment as a criminal act would raise no question under that instrument.

Chaplinsky v. N.H. (1942) (internal quotations omitted). The District Court relied on the "fighting words" categorical exception to conclude that Dugan's speech was not protected by the First Amendment.

A. The "Fighting Words" Doctrine and the United States Supreme Court

¶ 19 The United States Supreme Court first declared that "fighting words" is a category of speech not protected by the First Amendment in *Chaplinsky.* Chaplinsky was a Jehovah's Witness preacher who caused a disturbance after distributing religious literature on public streets and denouncing all religion as a "racket." A police officer escorted Chaplinsky to the police station, and Chaplinsky told the officer "[y]ou are a God damned racketeer" and "a damned Fascist and the whole government of Rochester are Fascists or agents of Fascists." . . . The United States Supreme Court upheld Chaplinsky's conviction, holding that his speech constituted "fighting words," which can be prevented and punished without raising any First Amendment problems. ***

¶ 21 Since the *Chaplinsky* decision in 1942, the United States Supreme Court has never again upheld a conviction based on the "fighting words" categorical exception. *** A review of post-*Chaplinsky* Supreme Court decisions reveals the limited scope of the "fighting words" categorical exception. *** The Supreme Court's more recent decisions discussing fighting words demonstrate that even when narrowly drawn, "fighting words" statutes will not be upheld unless they are content neutral. *** Despite the narrowness of the categorical exception for "fighting words," the Supreme Court has made clear that First Amendment concerns do not prevent a state from outlawing speech that constitutes a "true threat." *See Virginia v. Black* (2003) ["'True threats' encompass those statements where the speaker means to communicate a serious expression of an intent to commit an act of unlawful violence to a particular individual or group of individuals."] *** When evaluating the scope of protection afforded to Dugan's speech, we must consider the First Amendment concerns in light of the Supreme Court's historically narrow application of the "fighting words" categorical exception.

B. The "Fighting Words" Doctrine in Montana

¶ 28 Montana has demonstrated a greater willingness to uphold convictions based on "fighting words." Montana cases discussing free speech rights and "fighting words" have arisen out of charges for disturbing the peace, disorderly conduct, and intimidation. These cases have often involved speech directed at police officers.

¶ 29 In *City of Whitefish v. O'Shaughnessy* (Mont. 1985), a police officer heard "loud hollering" at around 2:00 a.m. and went to investigate. The officer approached O'Shaughnessy and his group of friends on a city street and asked them to "hold it down." O'Shaughnessy told the officer that he could not "hold it down" because it was such a "beautiful day." After asking O'Shaughnessy to "keep it down" several more times and warning him of a possible arrest, O'Shaughnessy entered the back of the patrol car and was asked to get out. O'Shaughnessy exited the vehicle, then re-entered the car. When the officer refused to shake hands with O'Shaughnessy, O'Shaughnessy stated: "Well, [m.f.], I will holler and yell when and wherever I want if I want to." O'Shaughnessy was arrested and charged with disturbing the peace under a Whitefish municipal ordinance, and was convicted following a jury trial. *** This Court held that O' Shaughnessy's speech constituted unprotected "fighting words" pursuant to *Chaplinsky*. ***

¶ 31 Later that same year, the Court decided another "fighting words" case, *City of Billings v. Batten* (Mont. 1985). In *Batten*, an argument broke out between neighbors and Batten called his neighbor "a communist government worker, no good son-of-a-bitch, chickenshit, and m-—r" and stated: "Fight me. Hit me. You have a golf club. Come on. I want to fight you." While the face-to-face confrontation ensued, Batten yelled "come back and fight you m-—r." Batten was found guilty of disorderly conduct following a jury trial. On appeal, this Court held that Batten's speech constituted "fighting words" because he directly challenged a person to and nearly provoked a fight, causing such concern that one of the neighbors ran away from the confrontation. ***

¶ 32 In *State v. Lance* (Mont. 1986), a defendant challenged his conviction for intimidation under § 45-5-203(1)(b), MCA, on First Amendment grounds. Lance was found guilty of intimidation for sending multiple letters in which he described his plans to take hostages to gain media attention for what he perceived were wrongs committed against him by judges and attorneys. First, this Court held that the statute was not facially overbroad because it only prohibited speech in the form of threats to subject any person to physical confinement or restraint, without lawful authority, with the purpose of causing another to perform or omit the performance of any act. The Court determined that the State had a legitimate and considerable interest in preventing persons from threatening to take hostages for the purpose of attaining some end, and Lance failed to identify any substantial application of the statute to constitutionally protected speech. Next, we held that the type of "true threat" prohibited by the statute was not speech protected by the First Amendment.

¶ 33 This Court's most recent "fighting words" case involved a disturbing the peace charge arising from a confrontation with a police officer. *State v. Robinson*, 2003 MT 364. Robinson was crossing an intersection in front of a police car when he glared at the waiting police officer and called him a "fucking pig." The officer parked his car and approached Robinson. The officer asked Robinson if there was anything he wanted to talk about, to which Robinson replied "[f]uck off, asshole." The officer arrested Robinson for disorderly conduct, in violation of § 45-8-101, MCA.... We affirmed the district court's determination that his speech constituted "fighting words" because it was "sufficiently and inherently inflammatory." The Court explained:

> If the statements in question had been uttered in the context of a political rally or protest, free speech concerns might well prevail. However, we fail to see how randomly goading a police officer by calling him a "f*** *** pig" adds to our constitutionally-protected social discourse.

[Fn. The author of this Opinion dissented in *Robinson*, disagreeing with the majority on the basis that "a trained officer should be expected to exercise a higher degree of restraint than the average citizen." *Robinson*, ¶ 31 (Cotter, J., dissenting).]

¶ 34 Though this Court has addressed "fighting words" in other contexts, it has never discussed this categorical exception in connection with Montana's Privacy in Communications statute, § 45-8-213, MCA.

C. The District Court Erred in Deeming Dugan's Speech "Fighting Words" ***

¶ 43 Words spoken over the telephone are not proscribable under the "fighting words" doctrine because the person listening on the other end of the line is unable to react with imminent violence against the caller. Redmond-Sherrill was in her office at the time of the phone call. Her office is located behind locked doors controlled by a video-monitored entry system. Nothing in the record suggests that she knew Dugan's location when he called her, and no facts indicate that Dugan was located near the Law and Justice Center when he placed the phone call. Under these circumstances, the face-to-face requirement of the "fighting words" doctrine cannot be satisfied. ***

¶ 44 While Dugan's utterance was certainly not of high social value, essential in any sense, or beneficial to the pursuit of truth, it is not automatically rendered proscribable on the basis of these shortcomings. *** Though Dugan's choice of words was among the most distasteful in our vocabulary, if we are to preserve the free speech rights enshrined in the Montana and United States Constitutions, we must recognize that "the State has no right to cleanse public debate to the point where it is grammatically palatable to the most squeamish among us." The context suggests that Dugan's speech was uttered in exasperation and frustration.... Expletives and insults, no matter how distasteful, can be constitutionally proscribed only if they fall within one of the narrow and limited categories of unprotected speech.

¶ 46 We are likewise not persuaded by the State's argument that Dugan's speech was punishable under the captive audience doctrine. The Supreme Court has applied the captive audience doctrine "sparingly to protect unwilling listeners from protected speech." The ability of the government to constitutionally shut off discourse solely to protect others from hearing it depends on "a showing that substantial privacy interests are being invaded in an essentially intolerable manner." While the government may act in limited situations to prohibit intrusion into the privacy of the home, the Supreme Court has "consistently stressed that we are often captives outside the sanctuary of the home and subject to objectionable speech."

¶ 47 Given the Supreme Court's sparing application of the captive audience doctrine, we conclude that it does not apply under these circumstances. Redmond-Sherrill was not in her home when she received the telephone call from Dugan. Redmond-Sherrill was using a business phone at Victim Services, an entity that holds itself out to the public to provide assistance. Dugan's phone call was made to elicit those services. The charges against Dugan stem from a single phone call. Dugan immediately hung up the phone after making his objectionable utterance, but even if he had not done so, Redmond-Sherrill had the power at any moment to end the communication by simply hanging up the phone. The privacy interests of a public employee at Victim Services are certainly less substantial than the privacy interests that a private citizen enjoys while in her residence. Under these facts, the State has failed to show that Redmond-Sherrill's substantial privacy interests were invaded in an essentially intolerable manner.

¶ 48 Dugan's speech did not constitute an unprotected "true threat." Calling Redmond-Sherrill a "fucking cunt" is not a statement meant to communicate an intent to commit an act of unlawful violence against her. Redmond-Sherrill admitted that Dugan did not threaten her or anyone else at Victim Services during the phone call. Furthermore, Dugan's words were not unprotected obscenity. Obscene material must be erotic in some significant way and appeal to the prurient interest in sex. See § 45-8-201(2), MCA. The words used by Dugan could constitute obscenity under different circumstances, but the context suggests that he uttered the words in frustration and his use is not subject to a literal interpretation.

¶ 49 We hold that the District Court erred in deeming Dugan's speech unprotected "fighting words." This Court and the United States Supreme Court have applied the "fighting words" doctrine only to face-to-face interactions and in circumstances likely to cause an immediate breach of the peace. We see no reason to extend the doctrine beyond its historically narrow and limited reach. Thus, Dugan's words do not fall under one of the categorical exceptions to free speech protections guaranteed by the Montana and United States Constitutions.

¶ 50 It is important to note that in reaching the foregoing conclusion, we do not foreclose Dugan's prosecution under the statute. Prosecution for his actions in this case does not violate Dugan's free speech rights because the statute only proscribes communication made "with the purpose to terrify, intimidate, threaten, harass, annoy or offend." Section 45-8-213(1)(a), MCA. As further explained below, the requirement that the State prove Dugan's statement was made with a specific intent removes the danger of criminalizing protected speech.

¶ 51 Is the Privacy in Communications statute, § 45-8-213, MCA, facially overbroad in violation of the First Amendment to the United States Constitution and Article II, Section 7 of the Montana Constitution? ***

¶ 61 . . . Montana's Privacy in Communications statute, § 45-8-213, MCA, makes the "use of obscene, lewd, or profane language . . . prima facie evidence of an intent to terrify, intimidate, threaten, harass, annoy, or offend" with no regard to the circumstances and facts of the particular case. As such, it presents a substantial and real danger of infringing on the free speech rights of others. For example, a person who was talking on the phone and accidentally stubbed his toe might inadvertently say a profane word. The prima facie provision would ignore the facts of the case and automatically presume that he uttered the profane word with "an intent to terrify, intimidate, threaten, harass, annoy, or offend." [I]t is not rational to assume based on mere use of certain types of language over the telephone that the person is doing so with the intent proscribed by the statute. ***

¶ 63 We hold that the prima facie provision of the Privacy in Communications statute, § 45-8-213, MCA, is facially overbroad. It is well-established that "the same statute may be in part constitutional and in part unconstitutional, and that if the parts are wholly independent of each other, that which is constitutional may stand while that which is unconstitutional will be rejected." We strike the following language from § 45-8-213, MCA, as unconstitutionally overbroad: "The use of obscene, lewd, or profane language or the making of a threat or lewd or lascivious suggestions is prima facie evidence of an intent to terrify, intimidate, threaten, harass, annoy, or offend."

¶ 64 Though the statute was only designed to burden or punish activities which are not constitutionally protected, the statute includes within its scope activities which are protected by the First Amendment. Therefore, the statute sweeps within its prohibitions speech which may not be punished constitutionally. With the prima facie provision invalidated, Montana's Privacy in Communications statute legitimately encompasses only those electronic communications made with the purpose to terrify, intimidate, threaten, harass, annoy, or offend. Such communications can be proscribed without violating the Montana and United States Constitutions. ***

Conclusion

¶ 73 For the foregoing reasons, we reverse the District Court's conclusion that Dugan's speech constituted "fighting words." Next, we strike the prima facie provision of Montana's Privacy in Communications statute, § 45-8-213, MCA, as unconstitutionally overbroad. Lastly, we remand to the District Court to allow Dugan to withdraw his nolo contendere plea pursuant to § 46-12-204(3), MCA, and proceed to trial. At trial, the State must prove that Dugan violated the Privacy in Communications statute by "knowingly or purposely" using "obscene, lewd, or profane language" on the telephone with Redmond-Sherrill "with the purpose to . . . offend" her.

Justice JIM RICE concurring in part, dissenting in part.

¶ 74 The Court concludes that Dugan's statement did not constitute fighting words, is not punishable under the captive audience doctrine, is not a true threat, is not obscenity, and is "certainly not of high social value." Although the Court may have established what Dugan's statement is not, I would like to discuss what it is and call it for what it is. My conclusion is based upon and limited to the specific facts of this case, of one person speaking directly and individually to only one other person who was duty-bound to receive communication, with no other intended audience.

¶ 75 As alleged, Dugan's statement was a direct, individual, and personal attack upon Redmond-Sherrill. It was demeaning, degrading, and debasing. It included only words "which by their very utterance inflict injury." It bore "no essential part of any exposition of ideas." It was utterly without any social value whatsoever. It truly constitutes, as used here and in this context, "no part of the expression of ideas." It had only one purpose: to injure and abuse Redmond-Sherrill, to reduce her human dignity to nothing more than a sexual act or a sexual body part. "Resort to epithets or personal abuse is not in any proper sense communication of information or opinion safeguarded by the Constitution, and its punishment as a criminal act would raise no question under that instrument." *Chaplinsky.* ***

¶ 77 . . . There is no necessity of weighing Dugan's statement against "the social interest in order and morality," *Chaplinsky*, because under the facts of this case it holds no weight at all. On its face, the statement offered absolutely no social value, and no justification whatsoever can be offered for it. It communicated no thought or expression to any audience or any person beyond Redmond-Sherrill, who was on the phone with Dugan pursuant to her public duty. The statement was, as alleged, intended to be personally injurious only to her. The right of free speech should not extend to Dugan's individually directed, personally debasing, and injurious statement to duty-bound Redmond-Sherrill that had no part of any exposition of ideas.

¶ 78 Dugan could have sought to verbally injure Redmond-Sherrill without using "obscene, lewd, or profane language," and he would not have violated the criminal statute. Section 45-8-213(1)(a), MCA. Or, he could have used these particular words without intending to injure Redmond-Sherrill, and he likewise would not be guilty of violating the statute. However, as alleged, if he used these words and intended to injure Redmond-Sherrill, then he used his speech "as an integral part of conduct in violation of a valid criminal statute," for which the Supreme Court has approved criminal sanction. Thus, Dugan's motion to dismiss was properly denied.

¶ 79 "The right to free speech is not absolute." We have often quoted *Chaplinsky* as the basis that the First Amendment does not protect all speech. All 50 states, the District of Columbia, and the federal government have some form of criminal statute prohibiting harassing or obscene communication through the telephone. In Montana, we have previously held that harassment and intimidation fall outside the protection of the First Amendment, independent from analyses examining whether the words were unprotected "fighting words," obscenity, or threats, or were made to a captive audience. Further, the Montana Constitution provides that "[e]very person shall be free to speak or publish whatever he will on any subject, *being responsible for all abuse of that liberty.*" Mont. Const. art. II, § 7 (emphasis added).

¶ 80 Dugan chose to speak in a manner that was as debasing, injurious, and abusive as can be spoken in our society, in a direct, personal, and individual attack on a public employee who was duty-bound to receive communications from Dugan. I would hold that Dugan's speech was integral in harassing Redmond-Sherrill, as "an activity illegal throughout the Nation," and is "a previously recognized, long-established category of unprotected speech" by this Court. Dugan's words should be deemed unprotected speech and he should now be held "responsible for all abuse of that liberty." Mont. Const. art. II, § 7.

¶ 81 As to Issue 2, whether the statute is overbroad, the Court today strikes the prima facie language in § 45-8-213, MCA. However, a narrow application would be more appropriate where the prima facie evidence at issue is similar to other mental state requirements. To remedy the problem that a statute may not set forth a prima facie intent provision to conclusively prove the defendant's mental state, I would construe the prima facie evidence sentence in § 45-8-213, MCA, as permissive rather than mandatory. This Court presumes that statutes enacted by the Legislature are constitutional and we "must adopt a construction of the statute which renders the statute constitutional in preference to one which renders it invalid." *** The state would need to prove that the defendant formulated the specific intent "to terrify, intimidate, threaten, harass, annoy, or offend" in order to be proven guilty. This approach would follow our mandate to uphold legislative enactments while adopting an interpretation of the statute that is constitutional. ***

Notes on the Current Scope of Freedom of Expression

1. The Court in *Dugan* observes "Montana has demonstrated a greater willingness to uphold convictions based on 'fighting words,'" particularly for "speech directed at police officers." Is this just a polite way of saying Montana has fallen behind *federal* freedom of speech rights? The Court is free to do so with respect to the Montana Constitution, even if it comes at a cost to faithful interpretation of Montana's distinct text and history, but it also must respect the federal floor of free speech rights recognized by the United States Supreme Court. Why wouldn't the defendants in these cases vindicate their federal rights in federal court?

2. After the invalidation of the prima facie intent provision, can the state still punish the use of "obscene, lewd, or profane language" if it can prove (rather than presume) a purpose to "annoy" or "offend" in an "electronic communication" [defined by the statute as "any transfer between persons of signs, signals, writing, images, sounds, data, or intelligence of any nature transmitted in whole or in part by a wire, radio, electromagnetic, photoelectronic, or photo-optical system"]? If you were a prosecutor, under which circumstances would you bring such charges? *See also State v. Lilburn* (1994) (rejecting freedom of speech challenge to conviction under hunter harassment law for "disturb[ing] an individual engaged in the lawful

taking of a wild animal with intent to dissuade the individual or otherwise prevent the taking of the animal.").

3. In *State v. Nye* (1997), the Montana Supreme Court affirmed a conviction under Montana's "hate crimes" statute when "Nye and four other individuals affixed bumper stickers that read 'NO I do not belong to CUT' on state and county road signs near Gardiner, Montana [and] affixed them to property belonging to the Church Universal and Triumphant (CUT)." It held:

> "free speech does not include the right to cause substantial emotional distress by harassment or intimidation." Activities which are intended to embarrass, annoy or harass, as was the case here, are not protected by the First Amendment.

Given the separate constitutional protection of Article II, section 4 for private discrimination on account of various classes including religion (*Nye*) and sex (*Dugan*), should "hate speech" be treated differently under the Montana Constitution? How?

4. One area in which the Montana Supreme Court has diverged from federal doctrine, in both more and less speech-protective directions, is campaign finance regulation. In *Montana Auto. Ass'n v. Greely* (Mont. 1981), the Court invalidated under Article II, section 6 (freedom of assembly) and section 7 (freedom of speech) significant portions of a political reform initiative focused on lobbyist disclosure. In several instances, the Court went beyond what the United States Supreme Court has prohibited under the First Amendment, including a recognition that out-of-state lobbyists should enjoy the same rights as Montanans to influence the Legislature, but did not explain any grounds for distinguishing the federal and state speech rights at issue. In contrast, in *Western Tradition Partnership v. Attorney General* (Mont. 2011), the Court rejected a challenge to a corporate electioneering prohibition similar to the federal law invalidated by the United States Supreme Court in *Citizens United v. FEC* (2010). Conceding that the law must meet strict scrutiny under *Citizens United*, the Montana Court upheld it on First Amendment grounds:

> ¶ 36 Based upon the background of §13-35-227(1), MCA, the State of Montana, or more accurately its voters, clearly had a compelling interest to enact the challenged statute in 1912. At that time the State of Montana and its government were operating under a mere shell of legal authority, and the real social and political power was wielded by powerful corporate managers to further their own business interests. The voters had more than enough of the corrupt practices and heavy-handed influence asserted by the special interests controlling Montana's political institutions. Bribery of public officials and unlimited campaign spending by the mining interests were commonplace and well known to the public. Referring to W.A. Clark, but describing the general state of affairs in Montana, Mark Twain wrote in 1907 that Clark "is said to have bought legislatures and judges as other men buy food and raiment. By his example he has so excused and so

> sweetened corruption that in Montana it no longer has an offensive smell." Mark Twain, Mark Twain in Eruption, 72 (Harper & Bros. 1940).
>
> ¶ 37 The question then, is when in the last 99 years did Montana lose the power or interest sufficient to support the statute, if it ever did. If the statute has worked to preserve a degree of political and social autonomy is the State required to throw away its protections because the shadowy backers of WTP seek to promote their interests? Does a state have to repeal or invalidate its murder prohibition if the homicide rate declines? We think not. Issues of corporate influence, sparse population, dependence upon agriculture and extractive resource development, location as a transportation corridor, and low campaign costs make Montana especially vulnerable to continued efforts of corporate control to the detriment of democracy and the republican form of government. Clearly Montana has unique and compelling interests to protect through preservation of this statute. ***
>
> ¶ 48 *Citizens United* does not compel a conclusion that Montana's law prohibiting independent political expenditures by a corporation related to a candidate is unconstitutional. Rather, applying the principles enunciated in *Citizens United*, it is clear that Montana has a compelling interest to impose the challenged rationally-tailored statutory restrictions. ***

The United States Supreme Court reversed the judgment in a one-paragraph opinion, without argument. *American Tradition Partnership v. Bullock* (2012). The plaintiffs in *Western Tradition Partnership* did not bring a state claim under Article II, section 7. If they did, should the Montana Court have held the law did not violate the Montana Constitution?

3. Religion, Speech, and Civil Rights, Revisited

The federal First Amendment reflects how freedoms of conscience, expression, and assembly intertwine in practice. Cases such as *Big Sky Colony* raise questions of discrimination that also sound in equal protection doctrine. As noted above, Article II, section 4 of the Montana Constitution protects against public and private discrimination on grounds of religious, as well as political, expression. This provision also introduces the exclusive remedy of the Montana Human Rights Act and related state civil rights statutes for some but not all claims. In the background of these overlapping state guarantees stands far more developed federal freedom of speech and religion doctrine, as well as the promise of attorneys fees for prevailing parties through the complex of federal civil rights statutes. The following case demonstrates the opportunities and challenges of litigating free speech claims under Montana law.

Griffith v. Butte School District No. 1

2010 MT 246

Justice PATRICIA O. COTTER delivered the Opinion of the Court.

*** ¶ 5 The parties do not dispute the material facts. During the 2007–2008 academic year, Griffith was a senior at Butte High School (BHS), which is a school in the School District. Metz was the principal of BHS and Uggetti was the superintendent of the School District. Griffith, along with several classmates, achieved the distinction of being named valedictorians of the class of 2008, and was invited to speak at the May 29, 2008 graduation ceremony. Griffith was one of the valedictorians who expressed a desire to deliver a speech.

¶ 6 Neither the School District nor BHS had written guidelines for student speakers addressing the content of valedictory speeches. The students were told their remarks had to be "appropriate, in good taste and grammar, and should be relevant to the closing of [their] high school years." The style and topic of the speech was left to each speaker. Since there were several valedictorians, Griffith was asked to give her remarks jointly with another student, Ethan Keeler. Together, Griffith and Keeler decided to give a speech in an alternating fashion on the topic of what they learned in high school.

¶ 7 Among the remarks Griffith wrote and intended to deliver at the graduation ceremony, she included the following passage:

> I learned to persevere these past four years, even through failure or discouragement, when I had to stand for my convictions. I can say that my regrets are few and far between. I didn't let fear keep me from sharing Christ and His joy with those around me. I learned to impart hope, to encourage people to treat each day as a gift. I learned not to be known for my grades or for what I did during school, but for being committed to my faith and morals and being someone who lived with a purpose from God with a passionate love for Him.

Griffith felt she could not accurately convey her high school experience without mentioning these motivations for her accomplishments, actions, and life purpose.

¶ 8 In the days prior to the graduation ceremony, the student speakers met with Stephen Riordan, a speech coach asked by the school to assist the students with their speeches. During their second meeting, Riordan relayed a message from Superintendent Uggetti to Griffith—she must omit the references to "God" and "Christ" in her speech because religious references were not permitted in graduation speeches.

¶ 9 Two days before the graduation ceremony, Griffith and her father met with Uggetti, who gave them a copy of the School District's policies. Uggetti reiterated that religious references would not be allowed in students' graduation speeches. *** Consequently, one day before the graduation ceremony, Uggetti summoned Griffith to his office and proposed the following changes to her remarks:

> I learned to persevere these past four years, even through failure or discouragement, when I had to stand for my convictions. I can say that my regrets are few and far between. I didn't let fear keep me from sharing *my faith* with those around me. I learned to impart hope, to encourage people to treat each day as a gift. I learned not to be known for my grades or for what I did during school, but for being committed to my faith and morals and being someone who lived with a purpose *derived from my faith and based on a love of mankind.* (Emphasis added.)

¶ 13 Griffith informed Uggetti she would not change her original remarks because she believed she could not speak of what she had learned in high school without acknowledging Christ and God. Uggetti told Griffith that, while he was ultimately in charge of the School District, he would defer to the judgment of Principal Metz concerning whether or not Griffith would be allowed to speak. He repeated, however, that it was unlikely she would be allowed to speak unless she removed the religious references.

¶ 14 At the graduation practice, Metz called Griffith and Keeler aside and told Griffith she had to either remove the religious references from her remarks or not speak at all. Griffith responded that she would not change her speech. *** During the graduation ceremony, Keeler gave his valedictory speech with another partner. Griffith was not permitted to speak because she would not remove the religious references from her speech.

The Human Rights Bureau Administrative Proceedings

¶ 16 On July 23, 2008, Griffith filed a timely complaint with the Montana Human Rights Bureau (HRB). She alleged Uggetti, Metz, and the School District had discriminated against her in her education on the basis of creed or religion in violation of the Montana Human Rights Act (MHRA), specifically § 49-2-307, MCA. Pursuant to § 49-2-504(1), MCA, an HRB investigator conducted an informal investigation of Griffith's allegations of discrimination in education based on her religion. The investigator took statements from all of the parties, reviewed pertinent documents, and interviewed witnesses.

¶ 17 The investigator filed a Final Investigative Report with the HRB recommending a finding of "no cause to believe unlawful discrimination occurred as set forth in Griffith's complaint." On January 20, 2009, Griffith received a two-page letter from the HRB entitled "Notice of Dismissal and Notice of Right to File Civil Action in District Court."

The District Court Proceedings

¶ 18 Upon receipt of the notice of dismissal from the HRB and pursuant to § 49-2-511, MCA, Griffith filed a timely complaint in the Thirteenth Judicial District, Yellowstone County. Griffith claimed the School District, Uggetti, and Metz violated her state and federal constitutional rights to free speech and freedom of religion. Her complaint alleged, in six counts, that the defendants violated: (I) the MHRA, Title

49, chapter 2, MCA; (II) the Governmental Code of Fair Practices, Title 49, chapter 3, MCA;[1] (III) Article II, Section 5 of the Montana Constitution; (IV) Article II, Section 7 of the Montana Constitution; (V) the First Amendment to the United States Constitution; and (VI) the Fourteenth Amendment to the United States Constitution. Griffith's complaint prayed for nominal and compensatory damages, as well as attorney fees.

¶ 19 On cross-motions for summary judgment, the District Court found in favor of the School District. The court determined the exclusivity provision of the MHRA barred Counts III through VI because, while Griffith pled these claims as constitutional tort actions, the gravamen of the claims was discrimination. As to Count I, violation of the MHRA, the District Court found the School District did not violate the First Amendment to the United States Constitution or § 49-2-307(1), MCA, when it prohibited Griffith from delivering her unedited remarks. ***

Discussion ***

¶ 25 Issue One. Did the District Court err in ruling the exclusivity provision of the Montana Human Rights Act barred Griffith's claims for violation of her state and federal constitutional rights to free speech and freedom of religion? ***

¶ 36 The statutory language of §§ 49-2-504, -511 and -512, MCA, is unambiguous. The statutes permit a party to take a case to district court for a trial on the merits once the action is dismissed from the HRB. There is no provision that allows a district court to essentially remand a case back to the HRB if it disagrees with the HRB and finds the complaint sounds in discrimination. In this situation, §§ 49-2-511(3)(a) and -512(3), MCA, specifically state the district court may provide the same relief to the prevailing party as would have been received in the administrative process.

¶ 37 Accordingly, Griffith was entitled to a trial in district court addressing the merits of all of her claims, including her discrimination allegations. Griffith complied with § 49-2-501, MCA, and filed a timely complaint with the HRB. Upon concluding its investigation, the HRB issued a notice of dismissal and right to sue in district court, in compliance with the plain language of § 49-2-504(7)(b), MCA. *** Therefore, we reverse the District Court and hold that Griffith's claims were not barred by the exclusivity provision of the MHRA.

¶ 40 Issue Two. Did the District Court err in concluding that the School District's refusal to permit Griffith to state her personal religious views during her valedictory speech did not violate Griffith's state and federal constitutional rights to free speech and freedom of religion?

¶ 41 Before turning to the substantive merits of Griffith's appeal, we address two preliminary issues. First, for the reasons set forth below, Griffith's claims were properly pled as constitutional tort actions. We agree with the HRB that her claims did not allege discrimination within the meaning of the MHRA.

¶ 42 Second, the parties present several undeveloped arguments that we decline to consider. *** Griffith presents a two-paragraph, undeveloped argument that the

School District violated her right to free speech under Article II, Section 7 of the Montana Constitution. The School District does not address Article II, Section 7 of the Montana Constitution at all, except to assert it did not violate Griffith's right to free speech under the provision. We will not formulate arguments for the parties; we therefore decline to consider this issue further. ***

¶ 45 With those preliminary matters addressed, for the reasons discussed herein, we hold: (1) the School District violated Griffith's right to freedom of speech under the First Amendment of the United States Constitution, entitling her to relief under 42 U.S.C. § 1983 (2006); and (2) the School District did not violate Griffith's right to freedom of religion under either Article II, Section 5 of the Montana Constitution or the First Amendment of the United States Constitution.

A. The School District violated Griffith's constitutional right to freedom of speech when it imposed a non-neutral, viewpoint-based limitation on the content of her valedictory speech

¶ 46 "It is axiomatic that the government may not regulate speech based on its substantive content or the message it conveys." Viewpoint discrimination is "an egregious form of content discrimination," and "the government must abstain from regulating speech when the specific motivating ideology or the opinion or perspective of the speaker is the rationale for the restriction." These basic principles of constitutional law forbid the government from practicing viewpoint discrimination in any forum — public, limited public, or non-public.

¶ 47 Students' free speech rights in a school setting have not historically turned on the type of forum created by a graduation ceremony, or the degree of regulatory control school officials have in each of those various forums. As discussed more fully below, the extent of a student's right to free speech is determined on a case-by-case basis, in light of the special circumstances of a school environment. Because questions regarding forum (public, limited public, or non-public) have not formed part of the analysis in free speech cases arising in the school environment, the parties' arguments asserting general First Amendment forum concerns are inapposite.

¶ 48 The United States Supreme Court's present approach to a student's right to free speech was first articulated in *Tinker v. Des Moines Indep. Community Sch. Dist.* (1969). *** Students "do not shed their constitutional rights to freedom of speech or expression at the schoolhouse gate," but their rights are not commensurate with the rights of adults and "must be applied in light of the special circumstances of the school environment." *Hazelwood Sch. Dist. v. Kuhlmeier* (1988). School officials may not impose viewpoint-based limitations on student speech in the school setting unless (1) school officials reasonably conclude the speech will "materially and substantially disrupt the work and discipline of the school," *Tinker*; (2) the student's expression in a school-sponsored activity may reasonably be "perceive[d] to bear the imprimatur of the school," *Hazelwood*; or (3) the expression can be "reasonably viewed as promoting illegal drug use." *Morse v. Frederick* (2007).

¶ 50 Applying this analytical framework to Griffith's case, we conclude the School District violated Griffith's constitutional right to free speech because this matter does not fall within any of the three recognized situations in which it is permissible for school officials to impose a viewpoint-based limitation on student speech. First, the *Morse* exception is clearly inapplicable because Griffith's religious references in her valedictory speech are wholly unrelated to illegal drug use. Second, it would be unreasonable to conclude that Griffith's brief mention of her personal religious views would materially and substantially disrupt the graduation ceremony, and indeed the School District never argues as such. Finally, we address the only exception argued by the parties — whether Griffith's passing references to God and Christ could "be perceived to bear the imprimatur of the school."

¶ 51 We find it unreasonable for the School District to conclude that Griffith's cursory references to her personal religious beliefs could be viewed by those in attendance at the BHS graduation ceremony as a religious endorsement by the School District. *** In a two-page speech, given jointly with another student and premised on a theme of what they learned in high school, Griffith references God or Christ three times. Moreover, each of those references is prefaced by "I learned," or "my faith," and each is unmistakably directed to her personal life and beliefs. Not once did Griffith use the term "we" or "you"; her passing references to her personal beliefs cannot be construed as proselytizing; and her remarks were not part of a group exercise and did not elicit audience participation.

¶ 55 Furthermore ... no objectively reasonable observer could perceive that Griffith's religious references bore the imprimatur of the School District. In fact, the School District explicitly dissociated itself from Griffith's speech by printing the unambiguous Disclaimer in each graduation program pursuant to Policy No. 2333 stating "any presentation by participants ... is the private expression of the individual participants and does not necessarily reflect any official position of the District, its Board, administration, or employees, or indicate the views of any other graduates." More to the point, the second paragraph of the printed Disclaimer avows that any religious expression by students is not endorsed by the School District and then goes on to clarify that individuals "have the freedom to express their individual political, social or religious views, for this is the essence of education." Under these circumstances, there is no real likelihood Griffith's passing religious references in her valedictory speech would have been construed by any in attendance as an endorsement of religious views by the School District.

¶ 56 Finally, the School District violated its own written policies of non-censorship when it prohibited Griffith from giving her chosen remarks. Policy No. 2333, which explicitly addresses content for graduation speeches, states "the school administration shall not censor any presentation or require any content" and that students who are selected to speak may choose to deliver "an address, poem, reading, song, musical presentation, prayer or any other pronouncement of their choosing." The School

District ignored this policy by requiring Griffith to remove the words "God" and "Christ" from her speech.

¶ 57 For the aforementioned reasons, we reach a narrow holding based on the particular facts of this case. We hold that the School District violated Griffith's right to freedom of speech under the First Amendment of the United States Constitution when it impermissibly censored the content of her valedictory speech based on the viewpoint she expressed.

B. Griffith is entitled to relief under 42 U.S.C. § 1983 because the School District, a governmental entity, violated her constitutional right to free speech

¶ 58 Since we find that School District deprived Griffith of a federal constitutional right, she is entitled to seek relief under 42 U.S.C. § 1983 (§ 1983). "Section 1983 'is not itself a source of substantive rights, but merely provides a method for vindicating federal rights elsewhere conferred.'" *Jones v. Mont. Univ. Sys.*, 2007 MT 82. To evaluate a § 1983 claim, the first step is to identify the specific federal constitutional violation, and the second step is to determine whether the officials who violated a plaintiff's constitutional rights were acting under the color of state law.

¶ 59 Griffith satisfies the first part of the § 1983 analysis because her federal constitutional right to free speech, as guaranteed by the First Amendment, was violated when she was prohibited from delivering her valedictory speech. We conclude that the second part of the analysis is satisfied as well. The School District is a government entity. Sections 2-9-101(3) and (5), MCA. During the 2007–2008 academic year, Uggetti and Metz, as employees of the School District, were acting in their official capacities as School District superintendent and BHS principal, respectively. Section 2-9-101(2)(a), MCA. The constitutional violation occurred when Uggetti and Metz precluded Griffith from delivering her chosen remarks at the graduation ceremony. It is undisputed that this was done during the course and scope of their employment as school officials. Because the School District, through the actions of Uggetti and Metz, violated her First Amendment right to free speech, Griffith is entitled to relief under her § 1983 claim.

¶ 60 The District Court did not reach the question of whether Uggetti and Metz as individually-named defendants, are individually liable for their actions against Griffith. We conclude they are not and they should be dismissed from the action. Section 2-9-305(5), MCA, serves as a complete bar to holding Uggetti and Metz individually liable because it provides immunity from suit to individually-named defendants for actions performed within the course and scope of the official's employment. All of Griffith's allegations turn on actions performed by Uggetti and Metz, as school officials, in the course and scope of their employment. On remand, we instruct the District Court to dismiss Uggetti and Metz as individual defendants pursuant to § 2-9-305(5), MCA.

C. The School District did not violate Griffith's state and federal constitutional right to freedom of religion because it neither compelled Griffith to violate the tenets of her religion nor denied her an important governmental benefit

¶ 61 Griffith argues that the School District infringed on her right to free exercise of religion in violation of Article II, Section 5 of the Montana Constitution and the First Amendment of the United States Constitution. She claims the School District unduly burdened her religious practice when it prohibited her from saying "God" and "Christ" in her valedictory speech. The School District argues that Griffith has not demonstrated that her religious beliefs mandate she include personal religious expression in her valedictory speech, nor has she shown that her religious beliefs proscribe delivery of a valedictory speech free of personal religious expression. On this issue, we agree with the School District.

¶ 62 "A facially neutral regulation impermissibly infringes on the constitutional requirement of government neutrality if it unduly burdens the free exercise of religion." *Valley Christian Sch. v. Montana High Sch. Assoc.*, 2004 MT 41 (*citing Wisconsin v. Yoder* (1972)). To determine whether there is a burden on the free exercise of religion, this Court adopted the *Thomas* test established by the United States Supreme Court:

> Where the state conditions receipt of an important benefit upon conduct proscribed by a religious faith, or where it denies such a benefit because of conduct mandated by religious belief, thereby putting substantial pressure on an adherent to modify his behavior and to violate his beliefs, a burden upon religion exists.

Id. (*quoting Thomas v. Review Bd. of Indiana Empl. Sec. Div.* (1981)).

¶ 63 The first part of the analysis under the *Thomas* test is to determine whether being permitted to deliver a valedictory speech at a high school graduation ceremony is an important benefit. A benefit is an "advantage or privilege." Black's Law Dictionary 166 (Bryan A. Garner ed., 8th ed., West 2004). We have previously recognized student participation in extracurricular activities as an important benefit. *Valley Christian School*, ¶ 8 (*citing State ex. rel. Bartmess v. Bd. of Trustees* (1986)). A student's invitation to deliver a valedictory speech is an honor conferred on the student based on the student's academic success throughout high school. An academic award is a privilege and is certainly analogous to the privilege of participating in extracurricular activities. It follows that delivering a valedictory speech is an important benefit.

¶ 64 The second part of the *Thomas* analysis focuses on whether Griffith's conduct—expressing her personal religious views in her valedictory speech—was "proscribed by a religious faith" or "mandated by a religious belief." Nothing before this Court indicates either that Griffith's religious faith mandates she include personal religious expressions in a speech or that her faith proscribes delivering a speech devoid of personal religious expression. Griffith's personal belief that she could not speak without mention of God and Christ during her speech is not equivalent to a mandate by her religious faith that she do so.

¶ 65 Therefore, Griffith cannot meet the second prong on the *Thomas* test because she cannot demonstrate that the School District's request that she omit "God" and "Christ" from her speech is incompatible with the tenets of her religious faith. Griffith has not shown that the School District unduly burdened her free exercise of religion when it conditioned the delivery of her valedictory speech on omitting "God" and "Christ" from the text. We hold the School District did not violate Griffith's constitutional right to freedom of religion.

D. Griffith may be entitled to an award of attorney fees because she is the prevailing party under her 42 U.S.C. § 1983 claim

¶ 66 A prevailing party in a § 1983 claim may be awarded reasonable attorney fees as part of the costs pursuant to 42 U.S.C. § 1988(b). While the power of a court to award attorney fees under 42 U.S.C. § 1988(b) is discretionary, "a prevailing plaintiff in a § 1983 claim should ordinarily recover an attorney's fee 'unless special circumstances would render such an award unjust.'" A party is considered to "prevail when actual relief on the merits of [the plaintiff's] claim materially alters the legal relationship between the parties by modifying the defendant's behavior in a way that directly benefits the plaintiff." "A plaintiff who wins nominal damages is a prevailing party under § 1988" because an award of damages, in any amount, changes the legal relationship in favor of the plaintiff "by forcing the defendant to pay an amount of money [the defendant] otherwise would not pay."

¶ 67 Pursuant to the foregoing statutory law and caselaw, Griffith may be entitled to an award of attorney fees since we conclude she is the prevailing party. We instruct the District Court to determine whether to award attorney fees under the law, and if so, to conduct a hearing on the amount.

Conclusion

¶ 68 In sum, we hold Griffith's constitutional claims were not barred by the exclusivity provisions of the MHRA and that the School District violated Griffith's First Amendment right to free speech. Furthermore, we reverse and remand for entry of summary judgment in Griffith's favor, consistent with this Opinion. We remand for a determination (1) of the amount of damages to which Griffith is entitled under 42 U.S.C. § 1983; and (2) of whether Griffith is entitled to attorney fees, and, if so, for a hearing and determination of the amount. ***

Justice W. WILLIAM LEAPHART, dissenting.

*** ¶ 79 The Court here reasons that the school, through a disclaimer in the graduation program, made it clear that it was not sponsoring the speech. The disclaimer, although it may have alleviated concerns of school "sponsorship" or "entanglement," does not address the coercive effect on dissenters. In *Lee* [*v. Weisman* (1992)], the Court held that a school district violated the Establishment Clause when it invited a rabbi to deliver a nonsectarian, nonproselytizing prayer at its graduation ceremony. The Court noted the singular importance of a high school graduation as a once-in-a-lifetime event and the susceptibility of adolescents to peer and social pressure. This left a dissenting student with the unduly coercive dilemma of participating in the prayer against her conscience or missing her own high school graduation. Because this dilemma gave the dissenting students no legitimate alternative to attending their graduation, the Court concluded the school district had in effect compelled participation in an explicit religious exercise. The dissenting students in Griffith's class were in the same untenable dilemma. They were part of a captive audience and had to choose between attending the ceremony and turning the other way when the speaker sought to "share Christ and His Joy" or not attending their high school graduation.

¶ 80 Although Griffith's speech was not as blatant in its proselytizing as the speech the Court uses for contrast from Cole, it graphically illustrates the impracticality of having school administrators walk this Constitutional tightrope. What if three of four valedictorians made personal references to Christ or one speaker made five references to Christ? What if a speaker used ten references to "sharing the joy of Allah," would that be free speech or proselytizing? The question is answered in the asking. The line drawing will necessarily be subjective depending upon the administrator. The point being that school districts have a constitutional obligation to avoid violating the Establishment Clause. In honoring that obligation, school districts are entitled to a degree of latitude. The proper test is not whether the speech in question would be constitutionally permissible; rather, it is whether the District "acted reasonably to avoid violating the Establishment Clause." There is "no doubt that compliance with the Establishment Clause is a state interest sufficiently compelling to justify content-based restrictions on speech." *Capitol Square Review & Advisory Bd. v. Pinette* (1995). Here the District was not engaging in viewpoint discrimination. In demanding that there be no sectarian religious references, it was properly imposing content-based restrictions. It had no other means of preventing the coerced participation in this "sharing" of a sectarian religious experience. The Butte School District did not act unreasonably.

Notes on Religion, Speech, and Civil Rights, Revisited

1. *Griffith* demonstrates some of the procedural complexities of bringing a free speech claim (or any mixed federal-state civil rights claim) in state courts.

a. Given that the Court previously held it does not distinguish between a state free expression claim and a federal free speech claim, what more would Griffith need to do beyond "a two-paragraph, undeveloped argument" to properly present the state claim?

b. What is the extent of Montana Human Rights Act preemption of state freedom of expression claims, where the Act serves as the exclusive remedy for religious discrimination (but not free exercise or establishment of religion) and the Governmental Code of Fair Practices serves as the exclusive remedy for political discrimination, both of which may also sound in freedom of expression? (Note the MHRA exclusivity provision only includes "acts that may otherwise also constitute a violation of the discrimination provisions of Article II, section 4, of the Montana constitution," Mont. Code Ann. § 49-2-512.)

c. The immunity and fees issues discussed in Chapter 2 both arise in *Griffith*. Put yourself in Griffith's counsel's shoes: how would you have litigated her claims, all things considered?

2. Recall that the federal *Tinker* doctrine considers minors' rights as "not commensurate with the rights of adults." If Griffith had brought a claim under Article II, section 7, should the Court apply the *Tinker* doctrine as to school speech, or would Article II, section 15 ("The rights of persons under 18 years of age shall include, but not be limited to, all the fundamental rights of this Article unless specifically precluded by laws which enhance the protection of such persons") require a different analysis?

3. The Court entertains Griffith's Article II, section 5 freedom of religion claim alongside her free exercise claim. Is the test it applies consistent with *Big Sky Colony*? (Note Justice Cotter, writing here for the majority, joined the dissent in that case.) Would the analysis change under Montana's Religious Freedom Restoration Act?

4. Justice Leaphart's dissent would reach a different conclusion as to a potential violation of the Establishment Clause that would have justified restricting Griffith's speech. Note Article X, section 7 provides:

> **Nondiscrimination in education.** No religious or partisan test or qualification shall be required of any teacher or student as a condition of admission into any public educational institution. Attendance shall not be required at any religious service. No sectarian tenets shall be advocated in any public educational institution of the state. No person shall be refused admission to any public educational institution on account of sex, race, creed, religion, political beliefs, or national origin.

If the parties had raised this issue, which way would it cut? (Would a claim under this provision be preempted by the Montana Human Rights Act?)

Chapter 13

Rights to Participate & Know

> **Article II, Section 8. Right of participation.** The public has the right to expect governmental agencies to afford such reasonable opportunity for citizen participation in the operation of the agencies prior to the final decision as may be provided by law.
>
> *New provision creating a right of the people to participate in the decision making process of state and local government.*
>
> **Article II, Section 9. Right to know.** No person shall be deprived of the right to examine documents or to observe the deliberations of all public bodies or agencies of state government and its subdivisions, except in cases in which the demand of individual privacy clearly exceeds the merits of public disclosure.
>
> *New provision that government operations be open to public scrutiny except when the right to know is outweighed by the right to individual privacy.*

The complementary right of participation and right to know are two of the Montana Constitution's truly distinctive rights. These precede the right of privacy in the Declaration of Rights and may be understood in sequence. The right of participation ensures that citizens are at the table for any state or local government decision. The right to know ensures that persons (broader than citizens) can inform citizens about what is at issue in those decisions. The right of privacy is the only limit on the right to know, and then only when it "clearly exceeds the merits of public disclosure."

The rights to know and participate are linked in a shared purpose to open government processes to public scrutiny. There are some important distinctions between the two rights that reflect their different functions. The right to know is broad, applying to "documents" and "deliberations" of "all public bodies" as well as "agencies of state government and its subdivisions," and is limited where "the demand of individual privacy clearly exceeds the merits of public disclosure." The right of participation is narrower, guaranteeing a "reasonable opportunity for citizen participation" and applying only to "governmental agencies . . . prior to the final decision as may be provided by law."

As with the Montana Human Rights Act, the state Legislature has provided a detailed statutory scheme to implement both the right of participation and the right to know. Although these laws resemble the public meeting and public record laws of other states, they are constitutionally grounded and therefore must provide at least as much access as the right of participation and right to know require. Unlike the

Human Rights Act or many other areas of civil rights enforcement, the Legislature also provided for award of attorneys fees. (Consider the separation of powers and local government dynamics that may lead the Legislature to encourage enforcement of these rights more than other rights.) This provides an incentive for citizens and other eligible persons (including the media) to litigate these rights, and an incentive for state and local agencies to heed them. The courts therefore see many more cases presenting the right of participation and right to know relative to other constitutional rights.

A. The Rights to Participate and Know

Both the right of participation and the right to know are implemented by statutes and rules promulgated under them. These laws define the governmental agencies and public records subject to the rights, outline basic procedures for open meetings and public information requests, and provide enforcement mechanisms, all subject to interpretation and the supremacy of the underlying constitutional rights. Peter Michael Meloy, a leading practitioner of the right to know, summarizes the origin of the open government provisions in the Montana Constitution, including the surprising opposition of the news media, as well as its initial implementation in the Montana Code Annotated. *Bryan v. Yellowstone County Elementary School District No. 2* demonstrates these provisions in action at the local level. As you read the cases in this chapter, consider how the original meaning, legislative implementation, and judicial interpretation of the rights to know and participate value open government relative to other values, including but not limited to individual privacy.

Peter Michael Meloy, *Double and Nothing: Open Government in Montana Under Article II, Section 9 and Section 10*

79 Mont. L. Rev. 49, 52–54, 56–64 (2018)

After the Second World War, a non-partisan group of professional women and homemakers joined together as the Montana League of Woman Voters, taking the motto "Democracy is not a spectator sport." The League appeared before the Montana Legislature throughout the late 1950s and 1960s on matters related to open government and public participation. Most of the testimony was given by members who appeared before the Legislature without pay, promoting the public interest. But in 1967, the League sent part-time lobbyists to Helena, one of whom, Dorothy Eck, became a full-time lobbyist in 1969.

During those years, the Montana Legislature was a "good old boy" club. It had few women and was dominated by hard-drinking cowboys in smoke-filled rooms where important legislative policy was made in secret. Until the late 1960s, the lobbyists for the Northern Pacific railroad, the Anaconda Company, and the Montana Power Company made or influenced virtually all legislative decision-making. But the decline of the railroads and the collapse of the copper industry in the late 1960s loosened the grip of corporate interests on the reins of public policy and created a vacuum in Montana politics. ***

. . . Gallatin County elected Dorothy Eck as its delegate [to the 1972 Constitutional Convention]. When the Convention met, she was elected to the Convention leadership as Western District Vice President and appointed to the Bill of Rights Committee. Prior to her service as a delegate, Dorothy Eck lobbied for the League, and experienced, firsthand, a governmental apparatus that was closed to public influence. The Convention delegates wrote:

> Public trust does not come from just a matter of confidence in the integrity of public officers, but rather it comes from knowing that public affairs are placed in the public eye. This can only occur when the activities of government are visible and when there are ways of checking on what our public officials are doing.

Delegate Eck introduced Proposal No. 57, "A Proposal for a New Constitutional Section Providing for Citizen Rights of Access to Government Documents and Procedures." Seven other delegates, including Bob Campbell from Missoula, co-sponsored the proposal. Campbell became the primary sponsor of a subsequent proposal, which eventually became Article II, Section 10, the right to privacy, which added significance to his co-sponsorship for the right to know. The text of Proposal 57 read:

> Section _____. No person shall be deprived of the right to examine documents or to observe the actions and deliberations of all public officials or agencies of state government and its subdivisions, except in cases in which the demand of individual privacy exceeds the merits of public disclosure.

In approving this proposal, the Bill of Rights Committee recommended passage of the proposal with minor changes:

> Section 9. RIGHT TO KNOW. No person shall be deprived of the right to examine documents or to observe the deliberations of all public bodies or agencies of state government and its subdivisions, except in cases in which the demands of individual privacy exceeds the merits of public disclosure.

The Committee Comments reflect the intent and purpose of the provision:

> In the main, the provision is from Delegate Proposal 57. It is a companion to the preceding right of participation. Both arise out of the increasing concern of citizens and commentators alike that government's sheer bigness threatens the effective exercise of citizenship. . . . The committee intends by this provision that the deliberation and resolution of all public matters must be subject to public scrutiny. It is urged that this is especially the case in a democratic society wherein the resolution of increasingly complex questions lead to the establishment of a complex and bureaucratic system of administrative agencies. The test of a democratic society is to establish full citizen access in the face of this challenge.

During the Style and Drafting process, the word "clearly" was added to the balancing provision: "except in cases in which the demand of individual privacy clearly exceeds the merits of public disclosure." According to the sponsor, "clearly" was inserted to assure that the balance would favor disclosure: "[W]e added the word 'clearly', with the intention of tipping the balance in favor of the right to know." ***

Delegate Eck rephrased the Committee comments when moving to adopt Article II, Section 9. She expressed the concern of citizens and commentators alike, that the government's enormity threatens the effective exercise of citizenship:

> The committee notes this concern and believes that one step which can be taken to change this situation is to *constitutionally presume the openness of government documents and operations.* [Section 9 of Article II] stipulates that persons have the right to examine governmental documents and the deliberation of all public bodies or agencies, except to the extent that the demands of individual privacy clearly outweigh the needs of the public right of disclosure. The provision applies to state government and its subdivisions. The committee intends by this provision that the deliberations and resolution of all public matters must be subject to public scrutiny.

Addressing the tension between the right to know and the right of privacy contained in Article II, Section 9, Delegate Eck explained:

> We do recognize, however, that there are some cases where the right to know what is in a document that might be classified may exceed the right of privacy. There are times when the right to know what is going on in a deliberation regarding personnel, which ordinarily would be classified and would not be public — we considered it private — but there are times when the public right to know clearly exceeds the individual person's right to privacy in this case. You might have an agency head, for instance, whose dismissal is being considered. If there is — if he is being dismissed for cause, I would think that the public has a right to know that reason of dismissal.

Since the provision was clearly "self-executing," the Committee appointed the courts as the governmental body responsible for enforcing the public's right to know:

> We had assumed that the court also would pretty well define the exceptions; in other words, they would determine what the cases are in which the demands of privacy exceed the demands of public disclosure; and I think it was pretty well the agreement of our committee that we would prefer this method of determination.

Shortly before taking a vote on the proposed Article II, Section 9, Delegate George Heliker inquired of Delegate Dahood as to whether the privacy exception included corporations:

> CHAIRMAN GRAYBILL: Mr. Heliker, for what purpose do you arise?
>
> DELEGATE HELIKER: I would like to ask Mr. Dahood a question.
>
> CHAIRMAN GRAYBILL: Okay. (Laughter) Mr. Dahood.

DELEGATE DAHOOD: I yield, Mr. Chairman.

DELEGATE HELIKER: Mr. Dahood, being an ignorant nonlawyer, what is an individual?

DELEGATE DAHOOD: What is an individual?

DELEGATE HELIKER: Is it by any chance also a corporation?

DELEGATE DAHOOD: A person can, of course, Dr. Heliker, as you well know, be defined to include a corporation under the law.

DELEGATE HELIKER: I know a person can, but can an individual?

DELEGATE DAHOOD: An individual, in my judgment, would not be a corporation, no.

There were some Delegates who thought it was more advantageous to authorize the legislature to define the exception. In pursuit of this preference, Delegate Jerry Cate moved to add language to the provision "except as may be provided by law." He explained his amendment: "[i]t has the effect of putting the Legislature in as the arbiter of the cases excepted."

Before Delegate Cate's amendment was considered, however, Delegate Fred Martin made a substitute motion to delete the right-to-know section in its entirety. Delegate Martin was a career newsman who, at the time of his service in the Convention, was the editor of the *Livingston Enterprise* and *Park County News*. While the Montana Press Association appeared in support of the provision earlier when it was heard in the Bill of Rights Committee, it now called the provision the "right-to-conceal" and was lobbying hard to kill it. The concern was that the exception for individual privacy was a loophole that "could be interpreted to allow almost any public board, agency or administrator to cover up vital private matters." The newspapers thought the public would be served better without any constitutional provision at all. In 1963, the press had successfully engineered the passage of § 82-3401 of the Revised Codes of Montana, which required open meetings subject to a list of exceptions, preferring to take chances with the Legislature rather than the courts. However, Delegate Martin's substitute motion was rejected on a vote of 76-14.

Thereafter, the Convention debated and voted on Delegate Cate's motion to let the Legislature define what would be open or closed to the public. His motion drew more votes than Delegate Martin's had, but the motion still failed 56-30. Delegate Eck's motion to adopt the right-to-know provision as reported by the Bill of Rights Committee passed on a voice vote.

As the Convention continued its business constructing the rest of the new charter, the Montana news media relentlessly pressured the delegates to abandon the right-to-know section. Indeed, almost all of the daily newspapers editorialized against the provision. The harshest criticism was expressed in an editorial published on the front page of the *Billings Gazette*, in which the editor threatened that opposition to this right-to-know provision would jeopardize ratification of the entire Constitution.

Concerned that this threat might be realized, the Chair of the Bill of Rights Committee, Delegate Dahood, moved to reconsider the section during the Style and Drafting sessions of the Convention. He did so to insert language which would give the Legislature the power to define the bounds of privacy which would justify closing a meeting or denying access to a document. Delegate Dahood proposed to insert, in lieu of the privacy exception, the phrase: "except in cases in which the Legislature, subject to court interpretation, shall have determined that the demands of individual privacy exceed the merits of public disclosure." The original sponsor of the proposal, Delegate Eck, supported Delegate Dahood's amendment.

Before the Convention could vote on that amendment, Delegate Carl Davis, the long-time Beaverhead County Attorney, moved to delete the entire section. He reasoned the Legislature would implement the right to know, whether or not it was specifically authorized to do so. He thought deletion of the entire section would let the press "go and lobby the Legislature on how they want this done." His motion failed 56-33, but the proposed deletion received 19 more votes than Delegate Martin's earlier motion.

Considerable discussion on the Dahood motion ensued. Delegate Donald R. Foster argued in support of the amendment because of concerted pressure from the newspapers. He did not think the amendment made any substantive change, but was willing to accept it to ameliorate the press. Some opposed the motion because of the heavy media lobbying. Some opposed based on a mistrust of the Legislature. Delegate Noel D. Furlong contended, tongue in cheek, that the best option was to eliminate freedom of the press altogether. He felt the original provision "has to do with the right of the people, the little guy, to find out what's going on, and I resist the motion to be stampeded into changing this thing.... The press will take care of itself, lets [sic] us take care of the people."

President Leo Graybill yielded the chair to Delegate Magnus Aasheim so he could speak on the motion. Of all the speakers that afternoon, President Graybill articulated the clearest rationale for the section as it was originally proposed and adopted:

> What's going to happen is the Legislature's going to pass a statute of some kind, that's going to list all of the incidences that it thinks should be secret. Now if you know the Legislature as I do, they're not going to do that in one line; there's going to be a lot of different things that are secret. They're going to have the same trouble we're going to have, or we're having. They're going to put a lot of words in that statute. And when somebody comes to the agency and wants to know—let's say it's the reporter or let's say it's a person—when they come to the agency and want to know, or when they try to get into the agency meeting, who's the first person that's going to interpret the Legislature's language? It ain't going to be the courts, it's going to be the agency. So the more language you give that agency to work with, the less to know there's going to be left, because they'll be able to interpret it right out of the window. So if the press really wants to lock this state up, just let them have the Legislature pass a nice, long-as-your-arm statute

> about what's secret; and everything will be secret by the time the agency, or the agency head, or the agency lawyer get his hands on it and advises whether the people can come to the meeting or whether the papers can be shown to the press. I don't think the press has yet thought this thing through. The press has to go and demand what it wants, and if an agency makes an unreasonable determination, the press has to take them to court and whip them; that's the only way this thing's going to work. But the way the committee originally drew it, at least the little guy's got something to say to that agency man when he goes to the door; he's got the Constitution. But he hasn't got anything when we get through amending it. So I think, Mr. Foster, you could do the press a big favor, and I'm sure we could all help Mr. Furlong protect the people, if they'll just let us write the Constitution and they'll write the articles.

Even with the majority of the Bill of Rights Committee voting aye on the motion to put the Legislature in charge of implementing the privacy exception, it failed, 70-18. As a result, the judiciary would decide when and under what circumstances the right-to-know guarantee would be trumped by a right of privacy. The original language of Article II, Section 9, was adopted and voters ratified the new Constitution in November of 1972.

The Convention transcript of the debates on the new right-to-know guarantees shows how the delegates envisioned it would be applied. The section, like its neighbors in the Bill of Rights, is clearly self-executing. The resounding defeat of Delegate Cate's initial amendment, and Delegate Dahood's later proposal to put the Legislature in charge of what would be private, emphasizes that reading. The Convention delegates intended to start with a balance tipped in favor of openness ("clearly exceeds") and the courts would enforce the guarantee:

> DELEGATE WILSON [to Delegate Berg]: Would you foresee a lot of litigation, separate litigations on these particular issues?
>
> DELEGATE BERG: No, I foresee that there will be litigation. I foresee that there will be interpretations, and that final decisions will be achieved through the courts.

When the Legislature met in 1973, subcommittees were formed to work during the interim between the 1973 and 1974 annual sessions to prepare any necessary legislation precipitated by the new Constitution. The Subcommittee on Constitution, Elections, and Federal Relations was commissioned to "conduct a detailed study leading to draft legislation implementing article II, sections 8 and 9 of the 1972 Montana constitution."

The study was completed in December of 1973. It concluded that while Article II, Section 9, was self-executing: "[t]here is no inherent prohibition in the section itself against any statute or regulation which deprived a person of the right to observe public deliberations or documents as long as (1) the statute or rule was consistent with the proviso protecting individual privacy and (2) authorized a case by case determination as to whether the demands of individual privacy exceeded the merits of disclosure." However, the purpose of the study was to determine whether existing statutes were valid in view of the new constitutional provision.

The study identified three categories of existing statutory law governing the right to know: "(1) those that authorized closed meetings, (2) those that protect documents in the custody of a public body which relate to individual people, and (3) those that protect documents in the custody of a public body which relate to corporations." In the first category was Rev. Codes of Mont. § 75-6127 (permitting school boards to close collective bargaining strategy sessions) and § 82-3402 (requiring open meetings subject to certain exceptions).

According to the study, because § 75-6127 did not involve a question of individual privacy, it "clearly violates the 'right to know' and should be repealed." Section 82-3402 authorized a closed meeting when the discussion pertained to:

1. National or state security;
2. Disciplining of a public officer or employee;
3. Employment, appointment, promotion, dismissal, demotion or resignation of any public officer or employee;
4. Purchasing of public property, investing of public funds which might adversely affect the public security of financial interest of state or political subdivisions of the state;
5. Revocation of any license of any person licensed under the state;
6. Law enforcement, crime prevention probation or parole.

According to the study, "[i]tems one and four do not in any way relate to individual privacy.... The items, then, are clearly unconstitutional." Items two, three, five and six do relate to individual privacy and would have to be determined on a case-by-case basis "to determine whether: 1. The case involved a question of individual privacy, and 2. whether the demands of individual privacy clearly exceeded the merits of public disclosure." Since the statute created absolute exceptions, not subject to the discretionary language of the new constitutional provision, amendments to existing statutes were necessary to comply with the new constitutional guarantee. Those amendments would, at a minimum, contain: (1) "A definition of what constitutes a 'deliberation,'" (2) "A method of enforcing the provision," and (3) "A general statement authorizing the body holding the meeting" or agency possessing a record to make the balancing test on a case-by-case basis. At the time, the Legislature did not consider (nor has it ever considered) establishing a set of factors by which privacy and disclosure would be balanced. The Legislature seemed to presume the courts would undertake this task on a case-by-case basis.

The study also identified statutes protecting documents concerning natural persons, e.g. Rev. Codes of Mont. § 7-147 (records of borrowers of building and loan associations), § 10-703 (adoption records), § 48-139 (marriage applications), and § 71-1520 (welfare records). Indeed, the study listed 28 separate statutes prohibiting release of certain public records. There were also at least 15 separate statutes under which records of corporations could not be publicly disclosed: § 3-709 (bean dealer records), § 3-1721 (commercial fertilizer records), § 50-1221 (hard-rock mining permit applications), § 84-3406 (records of produce dealers), etc.

According to the study, it was necessary to distinguish between laws governing natural persons and corporations because the Convention debates made it clear that a corporation was not an "individual" with protected privacy interests under Article II, Section 9. The Heliker/Dahood exchange The Heliker/Dahood exchange, *supra*, was quoted verbatim in the study. Unfortunately, before legislative action was taken on the study, Attorney General Robert Woodahl issued an official AG opinion construing the word "individual" in Article II, Section 9, to apply to corporations as well as natural persons.

Two "implementation" bills accompanied the report. One recast the existing open meeting statute by imposing the Article II, Section 9, constitutional mandate, providing a definition of "deliberation" (two or more members of a body discussing public business) and "public body" (any policy-making body of the State or its subdivisions, including bodies "supported in whole or in part by public funds") and imposing a criminal penalty for violation of the right to know. Sections 82-3402 and 75-6127 of the Revised Codes of Montana were both repealed under the bill.

The second bill implemented the right-to-examine-documents portion of Article II, Section 9. Its operative provision established a process by which the custodian of a document would disclose a document containing information related to individual privacy. The constitutional balancing test was included in the statute. The balancing test additionally required the custodian of the document to notify the individual about whom the information pertained that the custodian would release the document unless the in- dividual (within five days of the notice) established that the demands of privacy clearly exceeded the merits of disclosure. All records of any public body, without exception, were covered by the bill. Forty-one existing confidentiality statutes would be repealed, including those related to marriage and adoption records.

The bills (H.B. 720 and 721) were assigned to Rep. Michael Greely to carry in the 1974 second annual session. Both bills passed the house, but were killed in the Senate. Constituent groups of those protected by the respective confidentiality statutes vigorously opposed the open records bill. Opposition to the open records bill, particularly by the adoptive parents' organization, was so vociferous that Greely, a popular Cascade County native in an overwhelmingly Democratic county, came within fifteen votes of losing his bid for election to the Montana Senate in the fall of 1974 (Greely received 1,756 votes. His opponent, Dr. M.F. Keller, received 1,742.).

In the 1975 session of the Montana Legislature, HB 412 was introduced. HB 412 was virtually identical to HB 720 from the previous session. HB 412 passed the Legislature. The bill also added a provision to the criminal code making it "official misconduct" to close a meeting in violation of the law. In 1977, HB 302 again amended

Rev. Codes of Mont. § 82-3402 by deleting the specific exceptions and adding a general balancing test similar to Article II, Section 9. This general section also contained a provision authorizing an individual to waive the right of privacy, causing the meeting to be open. However, it also permitted closing a meeting when a public body discussed collective bargaining or litigation strategy. It included a new section defining a meeting as the convening of a quorum of the body either in person or by electronic means. Cell phones and email were still in the future in 1977. An enforcement feature was also added permitting a district court to set aside a decision made in violation of the law. Interestingly, the Senate amended the bill to exclude the Legislature's caucuses and conference committees. A conference committee rejected this effort. (Ironically, the conference committee meeting was held without any public notice as allowed by legislative rules at the time.) The bill adopted in 1977 remains the law today, with a few minor changes made in the subsequent 40 years. [The current statutes are codified at Title 2, Chapters 3 (Public Participation in Governmental Operations) and 6 (Public Records).]

Bryan v. Yellowstone County Elementary School District No. 2

312 Mont. 257 (2002)

Justice JIM REGNIER delivered the Opinion of the Court.

*** ¶ 6 In the summer of 2000, in anticipation of a budget shortfall for the 2001–02 school year, the District directed a group of principals, referred to as the Principals' Committee, to investigate alternative methods of "delivering education," aside from the traditional K–6 model. The Principals' Committee sought to reduce operating expenses and maintain student-teacher ratios without necessitating school closures. On February 12, 2001, the Principals' Committee, now referred to as the Reconfiguration Committee, presented a report to the Billings Public School Board. This report introduced three models to reduce expenditures and maintain optimal student-teacher ratios: cluster schools, kindergarten centers, and sister schools. ***

¶ 8 On March 5, 2001, the School Board established another committee, the Facilities Committee, to review the reconfiguration proposals and consider the option of school closures. The Facilities Committee consisted of the principals from the Principals' Committee, Nilo Cabrera, two teachers, and four members of the public from various geographical areas of town. The Facilities Committee was to gather information and provide a recommendation to the School Board on April 2, 2001.

¶ 9 The Facilities Committee first convened on March 19, 2001. From that date to April 9, 2001, the Facilities Committee met approximately eight times to synthesize a multitude of information in support of its ultimate recommendation. Sometime between the 19th and 21st of March 2001, Cabrera, a computer professional by trade, utilized a spreadsheet program to summarize information regarding various schools in the district. The spreadsheet contained, in part, information about each school's: capacity; per capita expenditures for gas, water, and electricity; square footage; maintenance costs; projected cost of repairs; percentage of students bused to school; special education requirements; growth potential; and average class size.

¶ 10 Based on this and other information, Cabrera developed a rating system which assigned points to each respective school. Purportedly, the schools which received the highest point totals were those which were the least cost-effective for the District to operate. Between March 19 and April 9, 2001, Cabrera distributed several copies of this spreadsheet to the Facilities Committee, the public, and the School Board. However, the copies varied in format and content. For instance, some versions contained the names of the schools, others substituted an objective identification number for the school names. Further, some versions did not incorporate the rating system or explanation of the point allocation.

¶ 11 On March 29, 2001, the School Board hosted a public forum to address the budget issues confronting the District for the 2001–02 school year. The School Board disseminated budget information to Bryan and the rest of the general public in attendance, which included one version of Cabrera's spreadsheet. This version of the spreadsheet did not reference the rating system or otherwise indicate any prioritizing scheme regarding the schools in the district. Following this meeting, the Facilities Committee completed its deliberations and submitted its recommendation to the School Board at another public meeting on April 2, 2001. The Facilities Committee proposed two closure options both proposals contemplated the closure of Rimrock School and Beartooth School, and recommended alternative options for the closure of at least one other school.

¶ 12 On April 3, 2001, the School Board sent a letter to parents which outlined the Facilities Committee's recommendation. The letter indicated that the School Board would hold another meeting on April 9, 2001, for the public to attend and provide comment before the School Board reached its final decision. Upon receiving the letter, Bryan joined with a coalition of Rimrock parents to rebut the recommendation to close Rimrock School. On April 4, 2001, one of the Rimrock parents, Lisa Schroeder, spoke with the District's superintendent and requested a "head-to-head comparison" of the schools based on the criteria examined by the Facilities Committee. The superintendent claimed that she did not have such a comparison and was not certain whether one even existed.

¶ 13 On April 5, 2001, Schroeder observed Cabrera in a television interview standing next to a stack of documents. According to Schroeder, Cabrera stated that each of the local schools had been itemized on a spreadsheet and compared to one another. Therefore, on April 6, 2001, Schroeder called the superintendent's office with another request for the purported comparison. Again, the office denied having any knowledge about such a comparison. Schroeder also sent an email request for the comparison to a member of the School Board but received no response.

¶ 14 On April 9, 2001, the School Board held its final meeting on the school closure issue. Members of the public, including Bryan, addressed the School Board about the recommendation and urged the Board not to close Rimrock School. After the public comment period concluded, the School Board began its discussion on the school closure recommendation. At that point, Cabrera distributed spreadsheets to the School Board which contained the rating system. Cabrera then described the point allocation to the School Board but did not distribute this version of the spreadsheet to the public. The Rimrock parents did not obtain the spreadsheet containing the rating system until the morning of April 10, 2001. However, by that point, the School Board had already voted to accept the Facilities Committee's recommendation and close Rimrock, Beartooth, and Garfield Schools. ***

Issue One

¶ 17 Is an advisory committee, established by a school board, subject to the constitutional mandates prescribed in Article II, Section 9 of the Montana Constitution? ***

¶ 22 Bryan states that the delegates to the 1972 Montana Constitutional Convention enacted Article II, Sections 8 and 9 of the Montana Constitution to increase public involvement in the decision making processes of unelected, bureaucratic entities. Bryan argues that "[t]o allow a public body to evade the right to know and the right to participate by delegating the bulk of its work to committees . . . would be to sanction the abdication of sovereignty and responsibility" that the delegates and Legislature rejected. Bryan insists that the Facilities Committee was subject to the mandates of Article II, Section 9 of the Montana Constitution. Bryan does not address whether the Facilities Committee was subject to the Article II, Section 8, right of participation.

¶ 23 The Montana Constitution is to be given a broad and liberal interpretation. While the Legislature is free to pass laws implementing constitutional provisions, its interpretations and restrictions will not be elevated over the protections found within the Constitution. In resolving disputes of constitutional construction, this Court applies the rules of statutory construction. Under those rules, the intent of the framers of the Constitution is controlling and that intent must first be determined from the plain language of the words used.

¶ 24 Article II, Section 8 of the Montana Constitution provides:

> Right of participation. The public has the right to expect governmental agencies to afford such reasonable opportunity for citizen participation in the operation of the agencies prior to the final decision as may be provided by law.

The Legislature has codified guidelines to protect the Article II, Section 8, guarantees at § 2-3-101, et seq., MCA. Article II, Section 9 of the Montana Constitution provides:

> Right to know. No person shall be deprived of the right to examine documents or to observe the deliberations of all public bodies or agencies of state government and its subdivisions, except in cases in which the demand of individual privacy clearly exceeds the merits of public disclosure.

The Legislature has promulgated guidelines to protect the Article II, Section 9, guarantees in Montana's open meeting statutes, codified at § 2-3-201, et seq., MCA. One of these open meeting statutes, § 2-3-203(1), MCA, provides:

> All meetings of public or governmental bodies, boards, bureaus, commissions, agencies of the state, or any political subdivision of the state or organizations or agencies supported in whole or in part by public funds or expending public funds must be open to the public.

Further, § 2-3-203(5), MCA, provides that "[a]ny committee or subcommittee appointed by a public body ... for the purpose of conducting business which is within the jurisdiction of that agency is subject to the requirements of this section."

¶ 25 As indicated in the language in the constitutional provisions, Article II, Section 9, is broader in application than Article II, Section 8. Article II, Section 9, applies to public bodies as well as governmental agencies. In *Common Cause v. Statutory Committee* (Mont. 1994), we defined "public or governmental body" as a group of individuals organized for a governmental or public purpose.

¶ 26 The Legislature has instilled in the trustees of a school district the authority to close schools in the district. See §§ 20-3-324(7) and 20-6-509, MCA. Here, the District assembled a group of individuals to research and prepare a recommendation on the very closure issue which the Legislature assigned to the District itself. Therefore, for purposes of the above described duties, the Facilities Committee assumed the identity of the District, albeit through a different composition of constituents. In researching the school closure proposition and submitting a recommendation to the School Board, the Facilities Committee performed a legislatively designated governmental function. This function served a clear public and governmental purpose to assist the District in its school closure determination. Accordingly, we hold that the Facilities Committee constituted a "public or governmental body" subject to the strictures of Article II, Section 9 of the Montana Constitution.

Issue Two

¶ 27 Did the District violate Bryan's constitutional right to know and participate?

***

¶ 29 ... Bryan contends that Article II, Sections 8 and 9, are inextricably linked by way of Article II, Section 8's, "reasonable opportunity" proviso. The District, on the other hand, insists that the Article II, Section 8 and 9, rights "are separate and distinct." It argues that neither Article II, Section 8, nor its implementing statutes, condition participation on a prior review of documents.

¶ 30 The delegates' discussions regarding the adoption of Article II, Sections 8 and 9, do not appear to support the District's "separate and distinct" proposition. Admittedly, the delegates did not often refer specifically to the two provisions' interrelationship during their open discussions. However, there are several references in the Constitutional Convention transcripts which reveal the fundamental link between the right to know and participate. In expressing reservations about the privacy exception contemplated in the right to know, Delegate Martin claimed that an exception "could close much of government to all citizens, frustrating their ability to *participate* in the decision making process. . . ." Later, Delegate Ask reiterated that "we have in the Bill of Rights . . . that they want . . . to participate in government the right to know, the right to participate."

¶ 31 Perhaps we find little discussion regarding the provisions' interrelationship because of the resounding clarity in the comments to Article II, Section 9. In the comments accompanying Article II, Section 9, the Bill of Rights Committee stated:

> The committee, with two dissenting votes, and after considerable reflection, adopted this provision explicitly establishing a public right to know. . . . *It is a companion to the preceding right of participation.* Both arise out of the increasing concern of citizens and commentators alike that government's sheer bigness threatens the effective exercise of citizenship. The committee notes this concern and believes that one step which can be taken to change this situation is to Constitutionally presume the openness of government documents and operations. [Emphasis added.]

While the two provisions do contain somewhat different language and prescribe somewhat different rights, the above comment clearly indicates that the Bill of Rights Committee, and subsequently the delegates as a whole, acknowledged the inextricable association between the "companion" provisions. For, as some commentators have noted, "[t]o participate effectively and knowledgeably in the political process of a democracy one must be permitted the fullest imaginable freedom of speech and one must be fully apprised of what government is doing, has done, and is proposing to do." Larry M. and Deborah E. Elison, *Comments on Government Censorship and Secrecy*, 55 Mont. L.Rev. 175, 177 (1994). Therefore, we will not analyze the two provisions in a vacuum, "separate and distinct" from one another, as urged by the District. We now turn our attention to the particulars of the purported violations.

A. Right to Know

¶ 32 As indicated above, Article II, Section 9, contains two components: the right to examine documents and the right to observe the deliberations of public bodies or agencies. Bryan argues that the spreadsheet which contained the rating system was a public document subject to public examination. Therefore, Bryan alleges that the District violated her right to examine documents when it failed to distribute the rating system version of the spreadsheet following the Rimrock parents' request.

¶ 33 As we stated in *Becky v. Butte-Silver Bow Sch. Dist. 1* (Mont. 1995):

> Any review of Article II, Section 9, of the Montana Constitution necessarily involves a three-step process. First, we consider whether the provision applies to the particular political subdivision against whom enforcement is sought. Second, we determine whether the documents in question are "documents of public bodies" subject to public inspection. Finally, if the first two requirements are satisfied, we decide whether a privacy interest is

> present, and if so, whether the demand of individual privacy clearly exceeds the merits of public disclosure.

We have already determined that Article II, Section 9, applied to the actions of the Facilities Committee. Further, this case does not implicate the "privacy interest" prong of the three-part test, nor does the District assert otherwise. Therefore, for purposes of Bryan's Article II, Section 9, allegation, we need only examine whether the requested spreadsheet was a "document of a public body" subject to public inspection.

¶ 34 The District and Amicus Curiae indicate that the Legislature has promulgated statutes to implement an individual's right to examine documents at § 2-6-101, et seq., MCA. According to the District and Amicus Curiae, the public is entitled to examine only those documents which constitute "public writings," pursuant to § 2-6-101(2), MCA. The District insists that "the spreadsheet did not constitute a public writing until it was considered and relied upon by Board members to make their decision at the April 9, 2001 meeting" and, therefore, not subject to the right of examination until that time.

¶ 35 In *Becky*, this Court acknowledged that "the Montana Constitution does not define 'documents . . . of . . . public bodies.'" We noted that the definition of "public writings," contained in § 2-6-101(2), MCA, proved useful in interpreting the constitutional language. However, we then departed somewhat from the narrowly crafted definition of "public writings" and stated:

> Although "documents of public bodies" is not defined in the Montana Constitution, it must reasonably be held to mean documents generated or maintained by a public body which are somehow related to the function and duties of that body.

Therefore, while we did discuss the "public writings" factors delineated in § 2-6-101(2), MCA, we ultimately interpreted the constitutional "documents of public bodies" much more broadly than the legislative construct.

¶ 36 As indicated above, the Facilities Committee was a public body. Further, Cabrera generated the spreadsheet and rating system to assist in the function of that body's charge, while acting in his capacity as a member of the Facilities Committee. Therefore, we conclude that the spreadsheet was a document of a public body subject to public inspection prior to the April 9, 2001, board meeting.

¶ 37 In apparent anticipation of this conclusion, the District claims that it did not violate Bryan's right to know because the Rimrock parents did not make an "intelligent request" for the document. The District indicates that the Rimrock parents contacted the superintendent's office and requested a "head-to-head comparison" of the schools which contemplated some thirty-five various criteria. The District insists that no such document existed. Therefore, as the parents did not submit an intelligent request for the desired spreadsheet, the District maintains that it did not violate Bryan's right to examine public documents.

¶ 38 As indicated above, the Rimrock parents contacted the District's chief administrator on April 4, 2001, and requested a head-to-head comparison of the affected schools. The District denied knowledge of any information regarding such a comparison. On April 6, 2001, the Rimrock parents again phoned the superintendent's office with a request for the purported comparison. However, this time, the parents propounded a more specific request they requested a copy of the spreadsheet to which Cabrera referred in his April 5, 2001, television interview. Again, the District claimed ignorance but now implies that had the parents framed their request in a different manner, they may have achieved a better result.

¶ 39 When the delegates adopted Article II, Section 9, they essentially declared a constitutional presumption that every document within the possession of public officials is subject to inspection. Yet, the District would purport to temper the constitutional right of inspection based on the gatekeeper's interpretation of the request. To impose such a hypertechnical constraint on the lay public would frustrate the maxim of liberal interpretation and subvert the constitutional mandate on open government. Here, it certainly does not shock the bounds of reason to consider that one might contact a school district's chief administrator in an effort to acquire information on school closures. Further, the Rimrock parents' request for "Cabrera's head-to-head comparison" is not so unintelligible that it justifies nondisclosure. Therefore, we hold that the District violated Bryan's right to examine public documents when it failed to divulge the rating system version of the spreadsheet for public inspection upon request. Consequently, the District Court erred when it concluded otherwise.

B. Right to Participate

¶ 40 Before we delve into the merits of the parties' arguments on Article II, Section 8, we find it useful to reference the provision's genesis and the delegates' motivation for memorializing such a protection. In its accompanying comments to the proposed text of Article II, Section 8, the Bill of Rights Committee stated:

> The committee unanimously adopted this section in response to the increased public concern and literature about citizen participation in the decision-making processes of government. The provision is in part a Constitutional sermon designed to serve notice to agencies of government that the citizens of the state will expect to participate in agency decisions prior to the time the agency makes up its mind. In part, it is also a commitment at the level of fundamental law to seek structures, rules and procedures that maximize the access of citizens to the decision-making institutions of state government. The committee believes that this is eminently proper and that it will have a salutary effect not only on the quality of the final decisions, but more important, on the deliberative and political capabilities of the citizenry. It is hoped that this provision will play a role in reversing the dissatisfactions increasingly expressed regarding bureaucratic authority insulated from public scrutiny and participation.

Further, in deliberations prior to the adoption of Article II, Section 8, delegates offered the following insight into the scope of the right of participation:

> Delegate Dahood: What is intended by Section 8 is that any rules and regulations that shall be made and formulated and announced by any governmental agency, which of course are going to affect the citizens of this state and the common welfare, shall not be made until some notice is given so that the citizen will have a reasonable opportunity to participate with respect to his opinion, either for or against that particular administrative action.
>
> . . . .
>
> Delegate Foster: . . . I think that we should be very well aware of what this committee is attempting to do. The continuing growth of bureaus has brought a new dimension to our representative form of government. We have drawn clearer lines of election for legislative officials. We have devised a more responsive system of selection and election for judicial officials. We have retained an extensive elective process for our executive officials. But what of the bureaus, the long arm of government with which the average citizen most often comes in contact; the long arm of government which is not responsive to elective officials; the long arms of government with which many, if not most, of our Montana citizens have met frustrating resistance and/or indifference? Elections do not materially affect the bureaus. Political pressures are not sufficient to juvenate [sic] response to public need. Public awareness and access seem to be the only tools to remind the great mass of public servants that their job is to serve the needs of the public and no other; they are paid by tax dollars to benefit the public above all else.

¶ 41 Using the aforementioned directives as a backdrop, we now turn to the parties' Article II, Section 8, contentions. Since the District failed to disclose the requested information, Bryan insists that the District did not afford her a reasonable opportunity to participate on April 9, 2001. In other words, Bryan claims that she could not effectively exercise her Article II, Section 8, right to participate on April 9, 2001, because the District violated her Article II, Section 9, right to examine public documents. The District concedes that a school board is an agency subject to the provisions of Article II, Section 8. However, the District suggests that an individual's reasonable opportunity to participate is satisfied when the "person succeeds in submitting her views to the agency." The District claims that it fulfilled its obligations to Bryan as it distributed the information considered by the School Board and provided her with an opportunity to speak at its April 9, 2001, meeting.

¶ 42 Essentially, the parties' dispute hinges on the interpretation of the "reasonable opportunity" language found in Article II, Section 8, and § 2-3-111, MCA. In discussions prior to the provision's adoption, Delegate Garlington expressed similar concerns regarding the opportunity prescribed in Article II, Section 8:

> Mr. Chairman, I have said before, I think it is the responsibility of this body to be to deliberate carefully and not to do things that are going to create a

> lot of difficulty and confusion in the future. I am concerned about what is meant by the phrase "opportunity for citizen participation in the operation of government." ... And I bring this up so that we can look at these words and make sure that whatever we draft here really states what our intention is and if there are limits to what we're authorizing.

While the delegates did not specifically debate the definition of "reasonable," Delegate Dahood did offer this in[sight] into the term:

> Mr. Chairman, I do not experience any particular problem in having the word "reasonable" substituted. I'm sure that my committee would not have any particular difficulty. I think, in our judgment, feasible was synonymous with reasonable but somewhat more expansive; but I think, as a lawyer, having been confronted with the use of the word "reasonable" so many times, having seen it defined so many times, that I think the definition that the law would give it would certainly serve the purpose that we intend to serve by Section 8.

¶ 43 Black's Law Dictionary defines "reasonable" as "1. Fair, proper, or moderate under the circumstances...." Black's Law Dictionary 1272 (7th ed.1999). Within the context of Rule 12(c), M.R.Civ.P., this Court has stated that a party has a "reasonable opportunity" to act if he or she is "fairly apprised." Other jurisdictions have expanded upon these equitable notions to include a "meaningful" component to the "reasonable" standard.

¶ 44 While we decline this opportunity to adopt some mechanical formula interpreting "reasonable opportunity," we conclude that, at a minimum, the "reasonable opportunity" standard articulated in Article II, Section 8, and § 2-3-111, MCA, demands compliance with the right to know contained in Article II, Section 9. It is evident from the comment to Article II, Section 8, that the delegates sought to expose the activities of those bureaucratic authorities which were once isolated from public scrutiny. However, if we adopt the District's position, agencies could once again invoke the autonomy of the long arm government structure through delegation. Such a superficial interpretation of the right to participate to simply require an uninformed opportunity to speak would essentially relegate the right of participation to paper tiger status in the face of stifled disclosure and incognizance. Given the tenor of the delegates' insistence upon open government and citizen participation, we find it improbable that they envisioned and subsequently memorialized such a hollow right.

¶ 45 Certainly, as the District suggests, Bryan was given the opportunity to voice her concern regarding the school closure recommendation. However, she participated under a distorted perspective in light of the District's partial disclosure of information. At the evidentiary hearing, Bryan testified that upon receiving the rating system, following the April 9, 2001, meeting, she identified many serious flaws and errors in its analysis. She claims that "she could have undermined the basis for the committee's recommendation if she had had the opportunity . . . [and] might have swayed the one vote that was needed to keep her children's school from being closed."

¶ 46 As the United States Supreme Court stated:

> The right to a hearing embraces not only the right to present evidence, but also a reasonable opportunity to know the claims of the opposing party and to meet them. The right to submit argument implies that opportunity; otherwise the right may be but a barren one. Those who are brought into contest with the Government in a quasijudicial proceeding aimed at the control of their activities are entitled to be fairly advised of what the Government proposes and to be heard upon its proposals before it issues its final command.

Morgan v. United States (1938). In essence, when the District violated Bryan's right to know, it reduced what should have been a genuine interchange into a mere formality. Therefore, we hold that the District did not provide Bryan with a "reasonable opportunity" to participate at the April 9, 2001, meeting. Consequently, the District Court erred when it concluded that the District did not violate Bryan's Article II, Section 8, right of participation.

Issue Three

¶ 47 If the District violated Bryan's constitutional right to know and participate, to what remedy is Bryan entitled?

¶ 48 In light of the constitutional violations referenced above, Bryan requests that we void the School Board's decision pursuant to § 2-3-114, MCA. In the alternative, Bryan requests that a "declaratory judgment be entered that she was denied the right of participation." The District, relying upon *Common Cause*, claims that if we determine the Facilities Committee violated Bryan's constitutional rights discussed herein, we should void the Facilities Committee's report and recommendation and not the School Board's final decision.

¶ 49 The District's reliance on *Common Cause* is misplaced. In *Common Cause*, a committee was established, pursuant to § 13-37-102, MCA, to submit a list of candidates for the office of Commissioner of Political Practices to the governor for consideration. Ultimately, the governor interviewed all five of the recommended candidates and announced the appointment of one of the nominees. The plaintiffs filed suit against the committee and governor and sought to void the committee's submission of the list and the governor's appointment. The plaintiffs asserted that, in compiling the list of candidates, the committee violated Montana's open meeting statutes and Article II, Section 9 of the Montana Constitution.

¶ 50 This Court held that the committee did in fact violate the open meeting statutes. However, as to the remedy for the violation, we concluded:

> [B]ecause the Committee's submission of the names is statutorily independent of the governor's choice and not in any way binding on that choice, we also conclude that the Committee's statutory violation does not require that the entire appointment process be voided....
>
> Notwithstanding the unique circumstances of this case, open meetings violations remain of utmost concern to this Court. Nothing in this opinion should be interpreted to suggest that violations of open meeting laws by any entity subject to those laws will not result in voiding decisions so reached. We will not hesitate to affirm a district court's determination to void such decisions or reverse a court's refusal to do so.

Therefore, we clearly limited the effect of our holding in *Common Cause* to the "unique circumstances" of that case, i.e., the statutory independence of the committee and its recommendation. This case simply has not presented similar circumstances. Further, unlike Bryan, the plaintiffs in *Common Cause* did not allege a violation of their right of participation. For the foregoing reasons, *Common Cause* proves inapposite to our consideration of an appropriate remedy in the case at bar.

¶ 51 Section 2-3-114, MCA, provides:

> Enforcement. The district courts of the state have jurisdiction to set aside an agency decision under this part upon petition made within 30 days of the date of the decision of any person whose rights have been prejudiced.

There is no dispute in this case that Bryan filed the petition within thirty days of the School Board's decision. Further, Bryan's rights have clearly been prejudiced as indicated in our analysis of the constitutional violations. Therefore, the question presented becomes one of redress, i.e., should we void the School Board's decision and force the parties to start anew or should we simply issue a declaratory judgment and permit the decision to stand?

¶ 52 We conclude that the facts in this case and its implications on future conduct compel the former remedial measure. While the District did notify the public about the April 9, 2001, meeting and allow for public comment prior to reaching its decision, the public was not provided all of the information presented to the School Board for its consideration. Therefore, the constitutional violation "taint[ed] the entire process from start to finish." *See Common Cause* (Hunt, J., dissenting). To simply declare a constitutional violation and yet allow the decision to stand would set a regrettable precedent. In the future, we presume that the prospect of negligible consequences would invoke concomitantly negligible deterrence. Here, we simply are not prepared to sacrifice Bryan's constitutionally prescribed right to know and participate for the sake of convenience. Therefore, we declare the School Board's closure decision null and void and hold that the District Court erred when it failed to do so.

¶ 53 We in no way mean to insinuate that a devious intent mobilized the District to appoint the Facilities Committee for the designated task. Likewise, we do not intend to suggest that the District deliberately concealed information or disingenuously evaded the Rimrock parents' requests. To the contrary, the record indicates that the District undertook extraordinary measures to reach a thoughtful, albeit difficult, determination. However, regardless of the inadvertent nature of the omission, the procedure to which Bryan was subjected did not comport with the constitutional safeguards prescribed by Article II, Sections 8 and 9 of the Montana Constitution. This actuality leaves us with no viable option other than voiding the District's decision. While the circumstances of this case compel an unfortunate result, the vigilant protection of one's constitutional rights warrants such a disposition.

¶ 54 So as to obviate the likely alarm generated by our holding, we believe it is important to articulate what this Opinion does and does not require of the parties on remand. This Court in no way intends to express an opinion about the school closure determination, or impose our will regarding the same upon the District. Therefore, this Opinion does not command the District to reopen those schools it has already closed. In fact, Bryan has not requested such relief on appeal.

¶ 55 At oral argument, this Court inquired of Bryan, "What happens if we agree with your argument here, and agree with your remedy which is to void that order? In a practical sense, what happens?" Bryan responded as follows:

> In a practical sense, we go back to the Board . . . and make the argument that she made in court . . . on the merits . . . with this [new] information. The Board can then decide whatever they want to do. . . . If they want to reaffirm the decision, that is their prerogative. But at least then she will have had the opportunity to say her piece with the information that she needed.

Therefore, per Bryan's request, this Opinion effectively voids the School Board's April 9, 2001, closure decision. On remand, the School Board shall allow Bryan another opportunity to rebut the closure recommendation. It is then within the School Board's discretion to reexamine the closure determination, in light of Bryan's fully informed presentation, and affirm or modify its prior decision. ***

Notes on the Rights to Participate and Know

1. Both the right to know and the right of participation require basic procedures for open meetings such as notice. In *Jones v. County of Missoula* (Mont. 2006), the Court provided some guidance for when final agency action triggers a right to participate and associated duties to notify.

> Plaintiffs learned from a fellow church member that Missoula County was considering amending its Missoula County Employee Benefits Plan to extend dependent coverage to domestic partners. On Wednesday, March 12, 2003, Plaintiffs attended the Missoula County Commission's regularly scheduled meeting and they openly voiced their objections to including domestic partners in the Missoula County Employee Benefits Plan. *** At the meeting on April 3, 2003, Missoula County extended dependent coverage to domestic partners of county employees. ***

Plaintiffs filed a complaint in District Court alleging that Missoula County failed to give them proper notice of the vote regarding domestic partner benefits, thereby depriving them of their constitutional right to participate in the operation of government. They sought to void the action of the county commission making such benefits available. ***

The Montana Public Meeting Act . . . requires each public agency to adopt policies that permit and encourage public participation in agency decisions and also to assure adequate notice is given before a final agency action of significant public interest is taken. *** With all the public attention and scrutiny attendant to government decisions surrounding health insurance benefits for domestic partners, we conclude that the issue of extending health insurance benefits to the domestic partners of Missoula County employees is an issue of significant public interest. Notice and an opportunity for public participation were required before the action of Missoula County. This does not, however, automatically translate to a holding that the decision of Missoula County was in violation of the law. ***

In the case before us, the County posted a schedule of the meetings for the week of March 31 to April 4, 2003, on the previous Friday. The schedule merely stated that an administrative meeting would be held on Thursday, April 3, 2003, in room 204 from 10:00 a.m. to 11:00 a.m. The actual agenda for the meeting was posted on April 2, 2003, 24 hours prior to the meeting, and was e-mailed to The Missoulian. The agenda clearly stated that three amendments would be discussed with regards to the Missoula County Employee Benefits Plan. One of the amendments involved "Domestic Partner Benefits." ***

. . . [W]hen the facts in the case before us are taken together, they establish sufficient notice to satisfy the requirements of § 2-3-103(1), MCA. Missoula County afforded Plaintiffs an opportunity to voice their opposition to the domestic partner inclusion on March 12, 2003, even though the issue was not on the agenda for that meeting. Also, Plaintiffs, who were aware of the fact that the issue was being considered by the county commission, could have requested that they be advised when the matter again came up for discussion. There was certainly no need for them to be "glued to the Commissioners' bulletin board" as suggested by the dissent.

Then, on March 14, 2003, The Missoulian published an article which stated that the County would be making a decision on the issue sometime in April. On April 2, 2003, the County Commissioners posted notice that the issue would be discussed at the administrative meeting on April 3, and e-mailed the agenda to The Missoulian. The County Commissioners used the same procedures they follow for posting notice of all regularly scheduled business. The commissioners voted on the issue at a meeting that was open to the public on April 3. While the dissent takes issue with Missoula

County's procedures for notice, and complains about the size of the typeface, its placement on the agenda, and the wording used, it ignores the undisputed fact that these procedures were successful in giving notice to these interested Plaintiffs that the issue was on the table. It appears, however, that Plaintiffs' interest was not significant enough in their minds to move them to request that they be given notice of any further discussions and action. In no way did the commissioners "hide the ball" as suggested by the dissent. Accordingly, the Court concludes that in this instance the notice afforded the public on the issue in question was sufficient to satisfy the requirements of § 2-3-103(1), MCA.

Justice Nelson, joined by Chief Justice Gray and Justice Rice, dissented:

*** I cannot, in good conscience, agree that the public meeting notice requirements utilized by the Missoula County Commissioners are in any way adequate to protect the public's right to participate; are in any way adequate to give the public adequate notice of the Commissioners' decision to take final action on matters of significant interest to the public; are in any way adequate to allow public comment before that decision is made; are in any way adequate to protect the public's right to observe the deliberations of their public officials; are in any way adequate to encourage public participation in the Commissioners' decisions on matters of significant interest to the public; or, are in any way adequate to promote the effective exercise of citizenship.

Missoula County can, and in my view, must, do a better job of notifying its citizens when matters of significant public interest are to be deliberated and decided by the County Commissioners. Pinning a notice to a bulletin board may have been adequate when Missoula's streets were covered in dirt and there were hitching posts outside the courthouse. This is not an adequate means of notice in the information age where people are accustomed to getting their news primarily from television, radio, newspapers and on-line.

The letter of §§ 2-3-103 and 2-3-104, MCA, and the spirit of Article II, Sections 8 and 9, require that the Commissioners develop procedures for permitting and encouraging the public to participate in decisions that are of significant interest to the public. These procedures must ensure adequate notice and assist public participation before a final decision is made on such a matter. These procedures must assure specific notice and public comment before the final decision is made on a matter of significant interest to the public. These procedures, in the words of the Bill of Rights Committee, must encourage the "effective exercise of citizenship." ***

"Significant interest to the public," the concept debated in *Jones*, is a statutory gloss on the constitutional right "to observe the deliberations of all public bodies."

Other than for reasons of privacy discussed in the next subsection, is it constitutional to exempt *any* public meeting from the requirements of the right to know?

2. Open meeting requirements in Montana are a product of both the right of participation (applicable to "governmental agencies") and the right to know (applicable to "all public bodies"). Although the specific requirements of these provisions remain open to interpretation, the courts and the Attorney General have broadly interpreted the applicability of these provisions and their implementing legislation, as Prof. Fritz Snyder explains:

> A committee is a "public or governmental body" if it has a clear public and governmental purpose and was created for a specific governmental purpose; e.g., a committee to recommend a list of persons from whom the Governor may select the Commissioner of Political Practices. A Board of Education advisory committee, the Facilities Committee, is "a public or governmental body." Quasi-judicial boards are public bodies and subject to Montana's open-meeting and public-notice laws. The Attorney General found that the Montana Life and Health Insurance Guaranty Association is a public body statutorily organized to protect insured members of the public from insurance company insolvency, and, as such, the Association's board of directors is subject to the Open Meeting Law. By accepting public funds and deciding how those funds are to be spent, a convention and visitors bureau became subject to the Open Meeting Law. Meetings of private corporations under state contract are to be open to the public. Deliberations of the Human Rights Commission are subject to the Open Meeting Law unless demands of individual privacy clearly exceed the merits of public disclosure. Without public notice, though, a meeting is open to the public in theory only, not in practice.

The Right to Participate and the Right to Know in Montana, 66 MONT. L. REV. 297 (2005).

3. Advances in information technology shape what is or is not a public document or deliberation, and how citizens access those documents or participate in those deliberations. During the COVID-19 pandemic, public bodies from the Montana Legislature to school boards moved meetings to online platforms. Public officials and citizens learned to adapt, more or less, to video presentations, shared screens, and chat functions. The constitutional mandates of "reasonable opportunity for citizen participation," "examine documents," and "observe deliberations," appear to permit adaptations, and in many ways, government is more open now than ever. But these advances raise new questions about citizens' access to the internet and about the increasing documentation of public officials' interactions when text messages and video sessions displace phone calls and office visits. Some of these questions will test the demands of individual privacy, addressed below. Under the open text of Article II, sections 8 and 9, and the broad terms of the implementing statutes, however, these questions also stand at the threshold of what the public and public officials should expect in the basic operations of government. How, if at all, should

the meaning of "documents" and "deliberations" reflect the evolution of workplace technology and culture since 1972?

B. Limits on the Right to Know

The most commonly litigated issue in right to know cases is not whether information is within the broad scope of public documents or deliberations, but instead whether some other interest overrides the public's interest in that information. This includes the right of individual privacy, which Article II, section 9 expressly recognizes as an exception to the right to know, at least when it "clearly exceeds the merits of public disclosure." Consider how the right to know and the right of privacy weigh in the balance with the section 9 "clearly exceeds" thumb on the scale replacing the compelling state interest of the section 10 privacy framework. Notwithstanding this single textual exception, the Montana Supreme Court has implied several additional exceptions to the right to know beyond individual privacy. Along with the expressly overriding right of privacy, these implied limits on the right to know keep important information held by the government out of public view. For the public to access this information, a court must hold that the information is within the scope of the right to know to begin with, then must also hold that there is no right of privacy implicated which clearly exceeds the merits of public disclosure. These cases take these two steps in sequence.

1. Implicit Limits on the Right to Know

Nelson v. City of Billings

2018 MT 36

Justice BETH BAKER delivered the Opinion of the Court.

¶ 1 Kevin Nelson filed a Petition for Release of Documents with the Thirteenth Judicial District Court requesting "everything related to" a civil judgment the Montana Municipal Interlocal Authority (MMIA) paid on behalf of the City of Billings (City). The City and MMIA released to Nelson all non-privileged documents and provided privilege logs describing those documents withheld on the ground of attorney-client or attorney-work-product privilege.... Nelson argu[es] that Montana's constitutional right to know forecloses the City's and MMIA's privilege claims. ***

¶ 12 Montana Constitution Article II, Section 9, provides: "No person shall be deprived of the right to examine documents ... of all public bodies or agencies of state government and its subdivisions, except in cases in which the demand of individual privacy clearly exceeds the merits of public disclosure." We have held that the language of Article II, Section 9, is unique, clear, unambiguous, and speaks for itself without requirement for "extrinsic aids or rules of construction." Pursuant to the plain meaning of the language of Article II, Section 9, we have construed the term "documents . . . of . . . public bodies or agencies" to mean documents "generated or maintained" by the bodies or agencies in relation to their "function and duties."

¶ 13 As a right expressly enumerated in the Montana Constitution, the right to know is a fundamental right subject to the highest degree of protection. Like other constitutional rights, however, the right to know is not absolute.

¶ 14 In construing constitutional provisions, we apply the same rules used in construing statutes. The intent of the Framers controls the Court's interpretation of a constitutional provision. Borrowing from the rules of statutory construction, we often declare that we must discern the Framers' intent from the plain meaning of the language used and may resort to extrinsic aids only if the express language is vague or ambiguous. Even in the context of clear and unambiguous language, however, we have long held that we must determine constitutional intent not only from the plain meaning of the language used, but also in light of the historical and surrounding circumstances under which the Framers drafted the Constitution, the nature of the subject matter they faced, and the objective they sought to achieve.

¶ 15 "In determining the meaning of the constitution, the Court must keep in mind that it is not the beginning of law for the state, but a constitution assumes the existence of a well understood system of law which is still to remain in force and to be administered, but under constitutional limitation." The constitution refers to many terms and concepts that it does not define. The Court examines these concepts in the context of "'the previous history' of this community [and] 'the well-understood system' then in use." We have not considered previously whether any privileges protected by statute or common law at the time of adoption survived enactment of the 1972 Constitution. Nelson's appeal presents that question.

¶ 16 As with statutory interpretation, constitutional construction should not "lead to absurd results, if reasonable construction will avoid it." The principle of reasonable construction "allows courts to fulfill their adjudicatory mandate and preserve the [Framers'] objective." Thus, a fundamental rule of constitutional construction is that we must determine the meaning and intent of constitutional provisions from the plain meaning of the language used without resort to extrinsic aids except when the language is vague or ambiguous or extrinsic aids clearly manifest an intent not apparent from the express language.

¶ 17 The Framers drafted Article II, Section 9, in broad and general terms. In its report to the whole convention, the Bill of Rights Committee explained that the purpose of the provision was to "presume the openness of government documents and operations" to combat "government's sheer bigness[, which] threatens the effective exercise of citizenship." The Bill of Rights Committee of the 1972 Constitutional Convention clearly modeled the language of Article II, Section 9, on Montana's 1963 open meeting law, which applied to "[a]ll meetings of *public or governmental bodies,* boards, bureaus, commissions [and] *agencies of the state or any political subdivision.*" See § 82-3402, RCM (1947) (emphasis added). The Committee intended that Article II, Section 9, would expand the availability of government documents beyond the more narrow 1895 statutory definitions of public and private writings then codified at Title 93, chapter 1001, §§ 2-3, RCM (1947). We thus have construed Article II, Section 9, as creating "a constitutional presumption that every document within the possession of public officials is subject to inspection."

¶ 18 The Bill of Rights Committee cautioned, however, that the right to know is not absolute. Recognizing that they were defining a constitutional right and not drafting a statute, the Chair of the Bill of Rights Committee, Wade Joseph Dahood, explained to the other delegates that Article II, Section 9, is

> stated in a broad principle form. It's the type of constitutional right that must necessarily be expressed in general terms; the specific guidelines that perhaps some of the critics would like cannot be stated within that particular section if it's to fall within the framework of a true constitutional principle. It's a principle that must endure for the decades and the ages.... [T]he court shall interpret within this particular doctrine.

¶ 19 Though largely focused on balancing with the individual right to privacy protected by Article II, Section 10 ... the Framers understood that the right to know would be subject to interpretation and considered together with other constitutional rights and existing laws. The Framers recognized that, like other fundamental rights protected in the federal and state constitutions, the parameters of the right to know would be interpreted over time in the context of particular factual situations.

¶ 20 Importantly, during debate on Article II, Section 9, the delegates acknowledged instances, unrelated to individual privacy concerns, in which the right to know would not apply: when "necessary for the integrity of government." For example, the delegates acknowledged the then-existing open meeting laws and existing exceptions to open meetings. Multiple delegates expressed the intention that Article II, Section 9, did not abrogate those laws; no delegate spoke to the opposite conclusion. Further, the delegates discussed multiple other instances in which they did not intend for Article II, Section 9, to change current law and practice. Of singular import here, convention deliberations clearly indicate that the Framers did not intend for Article II, Section 9, to abolish, supersede, or alter preexisting legal privileges applicable to government proceedings and documents.

¶ 21 For example, opposing a motion to revise the language of Article II, Section 9, to allow the Legislature to define privacy exceptions to the public's right to know as advocated by press interests, the Chairman of the Bill of Rights Committee stated:

> How about the *confidential relationships* that are *set by statute* that are zealously guarded? Should they not be protected? Should not communication with respect to a private matter that deals with some governmental concern between attorney and client not be protected? Perhaps there's some

disclosure between priest and penitent, doctor and patient, the sacred relationships that are so important in a free society; should they not be paramount? Should they not be supreme?

In response to concerns that the broad language of Article II, Section 9, would upset preexisting privileges protecting the integrity of government operations, the Chairman of the Bill of Rights Committee advised the Committee that it would not:

DELEGATE SKARI: Mr. Dahood, in Section 82-3402, Revised Codes of Montana, in Section 4, they say that one of the exceptions is "the purchasing of public property, the investing of public funds, or other matters involving competition or bargaining which, if made public, may adversely affect the public security or financial interest of the state or any political subdivision or agency of the state." Does your Bill of Rights Section 9 cover that sort of thing? In other words, *can the state's interest be protected here?*

DELEGATE DAHOOD: *Yes, I think the state's interest is protected* in those instances where there's a need for that protection. Where you've got a bidding situation, of course, that particular matter must be kept confidential until the bidding is over. * * *

DELEGATE SKARI: Well, as I read it, Section 9 states "except in the case where the demand of individual privacy exceeds the merits of public disclosure." I have a little trouble with that.

DELEGATE DAHOOD: Well, Delegate Skari, what we are talking about here, of course, is protecting basically the right of the individual with respect to those matters that may affect him. I think *what you're talking about is the statute that has to do with certain functions of government* in securing property for the operation of government to serve the citizen.... I think, as you read it, that indicated *that there must be some confidentiality up to a particular point*; is that not true?

DELEGATE SKARI: Yes.

DELEGATE DAHOOD: And I think *that's necessary for the integrity of government within that particular area.* I do not think that anyone would expect to have information before a particular point of decision is reached in that situation, because the reason for it, of course, is to secure property for the government at the best obtainable price.

DELEGATE SKARI: Thank you. * * *

DELEGATE DAVIS: Mr. Dahood, ... *is it your intention on this to repeal* the *existing statutes* on open hearings, or do you feel that they would still remain in full force and effect?

DELEGATE DAHOOD: I feel they would still remain in full force and effect.

Addressing similar concerns that the undefined and unqualified reference to "public bodies" in Article II, Section 9, would require deliberations of juries, grand juries, and this Court to be open to the public contrary to established law, the Chairman of the Bill of Rights Committee advised the Committee that it would not:

> DELEGATE BERG: I have been concerned as a lawyer about the use of the word "public bodies" . . . When I think of a public body deliberating, I think first of a jury . . . I think also of grand juries. . . . Those deliberations ought not to be open. . . . For that reason I think we should strike the words "bodies or," because . . . that terminology . . . is clearly broad enough to include the deliberations of a . . . jury. Similarly, . . . take the deliberations of the Supreme Court. That's a public body. Is it to be understood that Mr. Davis, or Mr. Dahood, or myself, if we're on opposite sides of the case, having finished the argument, may then go into chambers with the court and observe their deliberations in the judgment of the case we just argued? . . . Now I want to see all agencies, in particular, opened up to the public. I want their documents examined; I want their deliberations open. I am particularly interested in the operations of the city councils and boards of county commissioners, as well as all other agencies and commissions and forms of government. . . . But I do not think that the term "public bodies" adds anything, and it may create problems which we do not otherwise envisage. . . . * * *
>
> DELEGATE DAHOOD: I think [Delegate Berg's] concern is one that should concern us all. And I think the interpretation that he has given could possibly be laid against this section, but . . . *I'm not satisfied in my mind and judgment that a court could conceivably give that interpretation to "bodies."* We are referring there to public bodies; perhaps city councils, perhaps some bureaucratic groups or some bureau that may have been established perhaps for some particular special public purpose that may not fall within the term of "agencies." . . . I think our comments clearly indicate that *we are not trying to upset any traditional rule of procedure with respect to anything within the judiciary. . . . I just do not think that that problem would arise.* And with those comments in the record and in the journal, I would stand with the present language.

¶ 22 Consistent with the Framers' manifest intent that Article II, Section 9, would not affect preexisting legal privileges against public disclosure, the 1972 Constitution included a Transition Schedule that, in pertinent part, provided:

> All laws . . . and rules of court not contrary to, or inconsistent with, the provisions of this Constitution shall remain in force, until they shall expire by their own limitation or shall be altered or repealed pursuant to this Constitution.

The Transition Schedule "presuppose[d] that the laws . . . in force upon the effective date of the new Constitution [were] those which [were] not contrary to or inconsistent with" the Constitution. ***

¶ 25 Evidentiary privileges—like the attorney-client and attorney-work-product privileges—protect governmental agencies and employees like any other party to civil litigation to ensure "broader public interests in the observance of law and administration of justice." Attorney-client and attorney-work-product privileges are integral to the operation of our legal system and encourage an attorney's candid advice to prevent or resolve disputes.

¶ 26 The inviolate nature of these privileges is a cornerstone of our judicial system, reflecting "the policy of the law to encourage confidence and to preserve it inviolate."

¶ 27 What's more, both privileges were ingrained in Montana's legal landscape at the time the 1972 Montana Constitution was drafted and ratified. The attorney-client privilege was first adopted in Montana in 1867—twenty-two years before statehood. Montana adopted the Federal Rules of Civil Procedure in 1961, which the United States Supreme Court had interpreted fourteen years earlier to include an attorney-work-product privilege.

¶ 28 The Constitution vests this Court with authority over procedural rules for the judicial system under Article VII, Section 2(3). Evidentiary privileges long have been protected in the Montana Rules of Civil Procedure, preventing opposing parties from discovering privileged documents during litigation. Such protections were in the Montana Rules of Civil Procedure both before and after the 1972 Constitution was adopted. It is not reasonable to conclude that the Framers intended to eliminate these privileges for public bodies in Montana without a single acknowledgment of such an intention during the convention debates.

¶ 29 Further, the Framers validated this Court's historical authority to set procedural rules to perpetuate and maintain the legal system of this state. In fact, the Framers chose to strengthen this Court's role in the rulemaking process by eliminating the statutory requirement for legislative approval of court rules. But they left in place a constitutional check on judicial rulemaking: our rules are subject to *disapproval* by the Legislature within two legislative sessions of their passage. Mont. Const. art. VII, § 2(3). Importantly, the Legislature did not disapprove of court rules that retain these privileges.

¶ 30 Given this history, the 1972 Convention proceedings, and the Constitution's own Transition Schedule, we conclude that the Framers' intent is manifest that the preexisting attorney-client and work-product privileges would carry forward inviolate as essential components of the preexisting legal system regardless of the broad, clear, and unambiguous language of Article II, Section 9. Therefore, we hold that documents protected by the attorney-client or attorney-work-product privileges are not subject to disclosure under Article II, Section 9.

¶ 31 Pointedly, just as the fundamental right to know is not absolute, neither are these privileges. And just as the right to know is not a tool for private litigation interests, neither are these privileges a means for public bodies and government agencies to impede transparency. We construe the attorney-client privilege narrowly because it obstructs the truth-finding process. As such, "the [attorney-client] privilege protects only those disclosures—necessary to obtain informed legal advice—which might not have been made absent the privilege." Too, the attorney-work-product privilege does not grant absolute protection.

¶ 32 Courts assess privilege claims carefully in the context of litigation discovery disputes, and they should follow the same course when privilege is asserted in response to a right-to-know request. Because of its "presumption" of disclosure, Article II, Section 9, embodies the principle that "the agency would be the one which would have to prove the burden" that a privilege applies.

¶ 33 It is plain, then, that in a court's review of a claimed privilege when a citizen seeks government information, it should not treat the privileges as sacrosanct. Particularly in light of the presumption of openness the Constitution endows, a reviewing court must examine whether the claimed privilege in a given document is sufficient to keep that document from public disclosure. The attorney-client privilege raises special concerns when the client is a government entity. Though the attorney-client and work-product privileges apply equally to government entities as well as private entities, we must recognize the peculiar nature of government entities vis-à-vis the privileges and the public's right to know. As a threshold matter, the attorney-client and work-product privileges belong to, and benefit, their public sector clients, not the lawyers. Unlike their private adversaries, state and local government entities exist for the sole purpose of serving the public. As corporate entities, state and local governments can act only through their authorized officers and agents. Because public officers and agents hold their positions as "a public trust, created by the confidence that the electorate reposes in [their] integrity," those officers and agents act in their official capacities solely "for the benefit of the people." Section 2-2-103(1), MCA.

¶ 34 Consequently, because they obstruct "the truth-finding process" and—as applied to government agencies and public bodies—collide with the public's fundamental right to know under Article II, Section 9, the attorney-client and work-product privileges must be narrowly construed to effect their limited purposes. The attorney-client "privilege protects only those disclosures" made by the client "to obtain informed legal advice" and the legal advice given. For example, the California Supreme Court has held that the attorney-client privilege "is not applicable when the attorney acts merely as a negotiator for the client or is providing [non-legal] advice." That Court also has held that, except to the extent that they directly or indirectly disclose the substance of legal advice given or facts communicated by the client to the attorney for the purpose of obtaining legal advice, the attorney-client privilege does not protect attorney-client billing records.

¶ 35 As with other evidentiary privileges, the attorney-client and work-product privileges must cease to exist when they no longer serve their underlying purposes.

¶ 36 Upon a demand for public documents under Article II, Section 9, the government entity asserting the attorney-client or work-product privilege has the burden of proving the application and the scope of the asserted privilege to the court upon *in camera* inspection. Upon finding privileged material, the reviewing court must—as possible based on the nature and substance of the documents—give effect to both the subject privilege and the public's right to know by ordering appropriate redaction of the privileged information and disclosure of the unprivileged balance of the document, if any.

¶ 37 The City and MMIA produced detailed privilege logs from which the validity of their privilege claims could be evaluated. In response, Nelson simply presented a blanket challenge, insisting that no documents could be withheld on privilege grounds consistent with Article II, Section 9. The case thus does not require us to determine under what circumstances the City's and MMIA's claimed privileges could yield to the right to know, and we decline to speculate. The District Court appropriately recognized that Nelson's position that the government cannot withhold privileged documents would be "antithetical to" the public interests the privileges serve and would "render[] the attorney client privilege [and attorney-work-product privilege] meaningless." Nelson was free to object to MMIA's and the City's claims of privilege on the legal grounds that the privileges should not apply to protect particular documents. But he did not do so. Based on the record before it, the District Court correctly determined that documents protected by the attorney-client and attorney-work-product privileges were not subject to release under Article II, Section 9, of the Montana Constitution.

Justice LAURIE MCKINNON, specially concurring.

*** ¶ 41 It is my opinion that the Court errs, first, by concluding that documents created out of the government's relationship with counsel are *not* documents of public bodies subject to disclosure under Article II, Section 9. Second, the Court errs when it unconditionally subjugates an express constitutional right to a statutory privilege, thus excepting from judicial scrutiny any consideration of the public's right to know and monitor a particular activity of governance. Finally, the Court's analysis categorically adopts general principles of a statutory privilege to circumscribe a constitutional right—without regard to the public nature of the client. The Court's "back door" approach of defining a constitutional right by a statutory privilege is unsound and compromises fundamental principles underlying the right to know. Such an approach will prove difficult when citizens have a need, for example, to learn of government practices that can only be ascertained by examining documents created in the context of the government's relationship with counsel. Under the Court's approach, the statutory privilege takes priority over the constitutional right, thus directing the inquiry and precluding any judicial review of the public's constitutional right to know the contents of the documents.

¶ 42 The starting point for any right-to-know analysis is the constitutional provision itself. The Montana Constitution, Article II, Section 9, provides:

> No person shall be deprived of the right to examine documents or to observe the deliberations of all public bodies or agencies of state government and its

> subdivisions, except in cases in which the demand of individual privacy clearly exceeds the merits of public disclosure.

There is no dispute that MMIA and the City are government entities subject to the disclosure requirements of Article II, Section 9. Further, this Court has recognized that the Delegates' adoption of Article II, Section 9, created a "constitutional presumption that every document within the possession of public officials is subject to inspection." If the issue could be resolved completely within the confines of Article II, Section 9, then Nelson would be entitled to the documents in MMIA and the City's possession because the privacy protection included in the latter section of Article II, Section 9, does not pertain to non-human entities, such as MMIA and the City. However, Nelson's claim made pursuant to his presumptive right to inspect the documents is only the starting point for the inquiry. The analysis must thereafter consider the government's potentially countervailing confidentiality privileges, which are substantial and exist outside the parameters of Article II, Section 9.

¶ 43 However, the Court completely excludes the documents from disclosure under Article II, Section 9, by finding that documents protected by the attorney-client and attorney-work-product privileges are not documents of public bodies. To support its finding that the privileged documents are not subject to Article II, Section 9, scrutiny, the Court considers the historical roots of the privileges, the 1972 Convention proceedings, and the Constitution's Transition Schedule. While recognizing that Article II, Section 9, contains "broad, clear, and unambiguous language" requiring disclosure of all public documents, the Court maintains that the privileges were "essential components" of the legal system prior to 1972 and thus privileged documents are not subject to disclosure under Article II, Section 9. I disagree with the Court's reasoning that privileged documents are not documents of public bodies due, almost exclusively, to the fact that the privileges predated the 1972 Constitution. ***

¶ 45 I find the Court's analysis of the Transcripts inconsistent with the context of the Delegates' discussions. For example, the Court extensively quotes and cites from the Delegates' discussion on March 7, 1972, in support of its conclusion that the Delegates did not intend for the right to know to affect the existing privileges. However, that debate was solely focused on whether the right to know should contain an explicit exception for cases in which the demands of individual privacy exceeded the merits of public disclosure. Some Delegates were concerned that the individual privacy exception was too subjective and that public bodies would be able to cover up "vital public matters" by hiding information within the exception. Proponents of the exception went on to explain that the exception was necessary because certain documents, such as an individual's welfare application containing personal and sensitive information, should not be available for public inspection.

¶ 46 It was within that conversation, focused on the right to know's exception for individual privacy, that the Chairman of the Bill of Rights Committee stated that confidential relationships set by statute should be "zealously guarded." The Chairman opined that the attorney-client relationship should protect communication between attorney and client "with respect to a private matter that deals with some governmental concern." The Chairman was not contemplating a situation where the government is the client and commenting on whether the right to know applies to that attorney-client relationship; instead, he was commenting on instances in which the demand of an individual's privacy, which is undisputedly not at issue here, may exceed the merits of public disclosure.

¶ 47 Similarly, the Court's quoted material regarding protecting the integrity of government operations, was also pulled from the Delegates' debate over the individual privacy exception. Further, that conversation was focused on open meetings and the Delegates were specifically discussing whether the right to know would alter or limit existing statutes as they relate to open meetings. The Court's conclusion that the Delegates intended all statutes to remain in full effect, despite the new right to know provision, is inconsistent with the Delegates' actual conversation, which was simply a discussion regarding different Delegates' opinions on how the right to know, as drafted with an exception for individual privacy, would limit or otherwise affect existing open meeting laws.

¶ 48 Further, the Court cites the Transcript . . . for the proposition that "the delegates discussed multiple other instances in which they did not intend for Article II, Section 9, to change current law and practice." However, during those debates, the Delegates were considering whether the right to know's exception for individual privacy should be amended to add language that "*the Legislature, subject to court interpretation, shall have determined that* the demands of individual privacy exceed the merits of public disclosure" (emphasis added). Thus, that conversation was, again, focused on the individual privacy exception to the right to know. One Delegate also proposed amending Section 9 to rephrase "public bodies or agencies" to "public agencies," based on concerns for individual privacy. The amendment ultimately failed, but it was sought to clarify that certain deliberations, including those of juries, grand juries, and the Supreme Court, were not subject to public viewing under the right to know. The Court inappropriately takes bits-and-pieces of specific Delegates' opinions, as stated during Convention debate, and asserts those opinions as the intent of all of the Delegates. In doing so, the Court takes the Delegates' statements out of the contexts in which they were made.

¶ 49 The Court states that it "is not reasonable to conclude that the Framers intended to eliminate these privileges for public bodies in Montana," and I agree that the privileges, as applied to public bodies, surely survived enactment of the 1972 Constitution. In my opinion, however, the Court's decision today neglects the fact that the 1972 Constitution contains a right-to-know provision requiring disclosure of documents of public bodies. The Bill of Rights Committee presented the right to know to the rest of the Convention as creating a general constitutional presumption that government documents and operations would be open to the public. The Committee intended the provision to be "a long step forward" in assuring government openness to increase the public's confidence in government operations. The Court's decision goes against the Committee's stated interests by completely excluding privileged documents of public bodies from Article II, Section 9, scrutiny. As the Court recognizes, "a constitution assumes the existence of a well understood system of law which is still to remain in force and to be administered, *but under constitutional limitation.*" The Court further relies on the Constitution's Transition Schedule, which states, in part, that laws and rules in existence prior to the Constitution's enactment "remain in force, *until they . . . shall be altered or repealed pursuant to this Constitution.*" Accordingly, while I agree that enactment of the right-to-know provision in 1972 did not eliminate public bodies' privileges, I believe that we must determine whether documents protected by the privileges are subject to Article II, Section 9, scrutiny, and, if subject to the right to know, how the privileges are now limited or altered by the constitutional right. ***

¶ 56 In my opinion, the right to know is a fundamental constitutional right that may sometimes demand public disclosure of attorney-client privileged documents. Instead of recognizing that the attorney-client privilege may now be limited by the right to know, the Court completely excludes the privileged, public documents from Article II, Section 9, scrutiny. The Court's blanket exclusion of all privileged documents from Article II, Section 9, analysis is unwarranted, as there are some instances where the merits of public disclosure may indeed exceed the asserted privilege. To use a current national event as an example, it was recently revealed that Stormy Daniels (Stephanie Clifford) was paid $130,000 in the fall of 2016 to keep quiet about an alleged on-again, off-again affair between herself and Donald Trump. Daniels received the payment from a shell company in Delaware; a company set up by Trump's lawyer, Michael Cohen, for the sole purpose of passing the payment to Daniels. Cohen, in a recent statement, indicated that he used personal funds to *facilitate* the payment, but it is still unclear who actually paid Daniels the $130,000. It is also unclear whether and to what extent Trump himself was personally involved in any negotiation discussion or payment. Because Cohen is Trump's attorney, the attorney-client privilege likely protects most of the information regarding Trump's potential involvement. Under the Court's decision, if a similar matter was at issue in Montana, the public would be excluded from requesting any information regarding the monetary exchange pursuant to Article II, Section 9, if the information is protected by the attorney-client privilege. However, it is my view that the public should be able to utilize its right to know and ask for privileged information if the public's interest in the information is sufficiently weighty or compelling. Accordingly, in situations where attorney-client privileged documents are requested pursuant to Article II, Section 9, I believe the appropriate approach is to balance the public's right to know with the weighty and compelling attorney-client privilege to determine whether, in that case, the merits of public disclosure exceed the privilege's protections.

¶ 57 Such an analysis is consistent with our Article II, Section 9, precedent. Significant to our discussion here, the right to know "can be properly circumscribed when the right or interest against which it competes is weighty or compelling." For example, we recognized that the public's right to know was not absolute and that a defendant's constitutional rights to a fair and speedy trial must be balanced against the public's right to know.... [W]e [have also] observed that a power company may assert a claim of confidentiality if the documents in question constituted a [trade secret] property right which was protected under constitutional due process requirements. *** Similarly, we balanced the defendant's right to a fair and impartial trial against the public's constitutional right to know... and decided that the public may be excluded from an otherwise public hearing "only if dissemination of information acquired at the hearing would create a clear and present danger to the fairness of defendant's trial and no reasonable alternative means can be utilized to avoid the prejudicial effect of such information." *** In determining whether a right or interest is weighty or compelling enough to overcome the public's right to know, we must balance various factors while looking at the totality of the circumstances.... For example, the Court [has] considered factors such as "the type of taxpayer involved..., the source of the information provided by the taxpayer, and the public's interest in the information" to determine "whether a taxpayer's right of privacy outweighs the public's right to know." ***

¶ 61 In these proceedings, I would clarify that documents appropriately protected by the attorney-work-product privilege are not documents of public bodies and thus not subject to Article II, Section 9, analysis. I would then reaffirm that the right to know, like all constitutional rights, is not absolute, as there could be instances where the public has the right to know information which is also protected by the statutory attorney-client privilege. Under such circumstances, the statutory privilege should not automatically preclude a court's consideration of a litigant's constitutional right to know. Rather, as our well-established jurisprudence recognizes, we should balance the statutory attorney-client privilege asserted by MMIA and the City to determine whether the privilege constitutes an interest weighty or compelling enough to overcome the constitutional presumption of the public's right to inspect the documents. Here, Nelson presented a blanket challenge to MMIA and the City's claims of privilege. Based on the record, I would affirm the District Court's determination that the documents are protected by the attorney-work-product and attorney-client privileges. I would further hold that any documents covered only by the attorney-client privilege were properly withheld by MMIA and the City because, in this case, the parties' interest in protecting the documents under the attorney-client privilege is weighty and compelling enough to exceed the merits of public disclosure. ***

Notes on Implicit Limits on the Right to Know

1. What are the stakes of the disagreement between the Court and Justice McKinnon's concurrence? Consider the ways in which a traditional attorney-client or work-product privilege analysis would differ from a constitutional balancing test under the right to know, particularly if the court's privilege analysis would take account of the public status of any claimant. Does it make a difference if the privilege analysis displaces the right-to-know analysis?

2. The majority and concurrence pore through the Constitutional Convention transcripts and reach divergent conclusions about the priority of the privilege or the right to know. How should a court approach apparent conflicts between some delegates' expressed intent and the plain text ratified by the people? Is it really "absurd" to read the 1972 Constitution as invalidating law in place at the time? The transition provision cited by both opinions says "All laws, ordinances, regulations, and rules of court not contrary to, or inconsistent with, the provisions of this Constitution shall remain in force, until they shall expire by their own limitation or shall be altered or repealed pursuant to this Constitution." Does that help answer the question presented by the case? (To take a sharp example from federal constitutional law, do laws on the books segregating schools by race or prohibiting interracial marriage in 1868 mean the Equal Protection Clause permits such laws?)

3. The "demand of *individual* privacy" in section 9 anticipates "the right of *individual* privacy" in section 10. After some debate, the Court settled on a holding that "the state constitutional right of privacy is afforded only to natural human beings and not to non-human entities such as corporations." *Great Falls Tribune v. Montana Public Serv. Comm'n* (Mont. 2003). However, the Court went on to hold:

> While non-human entities do not enjoy privacy rights under the right of privacy provision of the Montana Constitution, nothing in Article II, Section 9 requires disclosure of trade secrets and other confidential proprietary information where the data is protected from disclosure elsewhere in the federal or state constitutions or by statute. For example, a non-human corporate entity may enjoy confidentiality of its property interests under Montana statutory law, such as the Uniform Trade Secrets Act, Title 30, Chapter 14, Part 4, or protection against the "taking" of private property for public use without just compensation under the federal and state constitutions. Such cases implicate the due process and equal protection clauses of the state and federal constitutions and form the legal grounds through which non-human entities can seek protection of confidential information.

After *Great Falls Tribune*, corporate entities invoke private property rights to limit the public's right to know with respect to documents they provide to public bodies for official government business such as rate regulation or taxation. If corporations cannot have a reasonable expectation of privacy in their information, when if ever should they have a constitutionally protected property interest in information they provide to public bodies in order to do business with the state? *Cf. Elliot v. Montana Dep't of Revenue* (Mont. 2006) (raising but not deciding the question of whether a state legislator had the right to know and disclose to his constituents tax information of major corporations doing business in Montana). There are other exceptions to the right to know (and the right to participate) for "confidential" information defined by statute; what might be the constitutional basis for these?

4. A recurrent issue under the right to know is the treatment of "criminal justice information," including confidential criminal justice information (CCJI)

such as investigative files. Many records containing confidential criminal justice information would be protected as a matter of the individual privacy of victims, suspects, and, to a lesser extent, persons convicted of crimes. Yet the agencies possessing such information have reasons other than privacy, such as public safety and ongoing investigations, to keep it confidential. Prosecutors also may have additional reasons other than the right to know to disseminate such information regardless of a suspect's privacy interests, such as dissemination of mugshots directly or through broadcast or online media. The Montana Criminal Justice Information Act of 1979, codified at Title 44, chapter 5 of the Montana Code Annotated, details the regulation of criminal justice information. Does the right to know contain any "compelling interest" exception for public safety or ongoing investigations when individual privacy is not implicated? Consider *Crites v. Lewis & Clark County* (Mont. 2019):

> ¶ 4 On June 28, 2011, Crites was reported missing. On October 8, 2011, Crites's dismembered remains were found in black plastic trash bags near MacDonald Pass. Crites's skull was later found on the west side of MacDonald Pass. To date, nobody has been charged with Crites's murder.
>
> ¶ 5 On March 27, 2012, the County issued a death certificate for Crites. On April 19, 2012, Crites's sister, Connie Crites, was appointed personal representative of his Estate. On January 9, 2018, the Estate requested that the County release Crites's investigative file for the purposes of defending itself in the ongoing lawsuit and to pursue a civil wrongful death action. On January 19, 2018, the County responded to the Estate's request with a letter from County Attorney Leo Gallagher that it could not release Crites's investigative file because release "would jeopardize the State's ability to prosecute someone for the homicide and the investigation is ongoing." ***
>
> ¶ 19 We have held that Article II, Section 9 creates "'a constitutional presumption that every document within the possession of public officials is subject to inspection.'" But in crafting the "right to know," the Framers recognized that Article II, Section 9 may yield to countervailing societal interests — beyond the right to individual privacy — that were recognized at the time the Montana Constitution was adopted.
>
> ¶ 20 One specific interest the Framers considered as "necessary for the integrity of government" was that "'all rights have to be balanced against a police power.'" Pertinent to the issue before us, the Framers explicitly considered how the "right to know" would apply to the protection of CCJI. The Framers' deliberations on CCJI and "the right to know" indicate that they did not intend for the drafting of Article II, Section 9 "to abolish, supersede, or alter preexisting legal privileges applicable to government proceedings and documents."

¶ 21 In that vein, we have previously observed in our application of §44-5-303, MCA, that "[p]ublic exposure of law enforcement files relating to ongoing criminal investigations would . . . have a disastrous effect upon law enforcement agencies in the performance of their duty. . . ." ***

¶ 25 . . . [I]t was entirely correct, and indeed necessary, for the District Court to consider the prosecutor's assertion to that effect, which was supported by an affidavit from the detective assigned to the case. Such consideration is consistent with both the Framers' intent that "all rights have to be balanced against a police power," and our concern that "public exposure of law enforcement files relating to ongoing criminal investigations would have a disastrous effect upon law enforcement agencies in the performance of their duty."

¶ 26 The circumstances of the present case do not demonstrate that the District Court erred in declining the Estate's request for an in camera review before denying its application for the CCJI. The record before us supports the County's determination in its letter to the Estate, and in Detective O'Malley's affidavit, that dissemination of the CCJI contained in Crites's investigative file would jeopardize its murder investigation. The County's affidavit specifically illustrates the vast nature of Crites's investigative file, the substantial amount of time needed to conduct a review of the file, and that the County is actively investigating Crites's murder. Crites's murder occurred in 2011. Though eight years is a noteworthy length of time, there is no statute of limitations on homicide, and the Estate does not dispute that the investigation is ongoing.

¶ 27 "Because the judiciary has authority over the interpretation of the Constitution, it is the courts' duty to balance the competing rights at issue in order to determine what, if any information, should be given to a party requesting information from the government." Irrespective of whether or not a prosecutor asserts that dissemination of CCJI would jeopardize a criminal investigation, a district court always retains the authority to conduct an in camera review, and to determine what, if any, information should be released to the requesting party. . . . The Estate's interest in the CCJI contained in Crites's investigative file must yield to the State's police power to conduct investigations in this instance, which includes the County protecting CCJI of its active investigation into Crites's murder. . . .

Compare State ex rel. The Missoulian v. Montana Twenty-First Jud. Dist. Ct. (Mont. 1997) (requiring that a "gag order" against dissemination of information about a criminal trial by participants must meet "heightened scrutiny" balancing the public's right to know and a defendant's right to a fair trial). Conventionally, enumerated rights are understood to restrain the state's general police power, not the other way around. What are the limits to an investigative or "police power" exception to the right to know? What other limits to the right to know might follow from the "police power"?

2. Privacy and the Merits of Public Disclosure

Billings Gazette v. City of Billings

372 Mont. 409 (2013)

Justice JIM RICE delivered the Opinion of the Court.

¶ 5 Between March and June of 2012, the City discovered five city employees (Employees) had possibly been using their respective public City computers to access adult and/or pornographic material on the Internet during work hours. The City conducted separate internal investigations into the Internet activity of each Employee. Upon conclusion of each investigation, the City issued a written corrective action determination to each Employee, setting forth a summary of the evidence gathered during the investigation and the disciplinary action being taken by the City as a result. Each of the Employees was suspended for five days without pay.

¶ 6 On August 24, 2012, the Gazette requested copies of "all written reprimands or records of other disciplinary actions affecting employees of the City Attorney's office between February 1, 2012 and August 24, 2012." On August 28, 2012, the Gazette requested the City provide a list of all city employees who had been disciplined within the prior six months. On August 31, 2012, the Gazette requested "documentation of the searches/filtering that indicated a pattern of attempts to access blocked sites in the cases involving the five city workers suspended for accessing (or attempting to access) inappropriate websites[;] any reports by [the City's Chief Information Office] regarding such searches; any communications between city employees ... [and] any due process letters resulting from these incidents." The City denied the first two requests, citing the employees' privacy rights but, in response to the third request, provided copies of its investigative documents relating to the Internet activity of the Employees and email correspondence sent in connection with the City's internal investigation of the Employees. These documents were redacted to omit the names and other identifying information of the Employees and uninvolved third persons. The City did not provide copies of the disciplinary corrective action forms for any of the Employees. ***

Discussion

¶ 11 1. Did the District Court err by ordering that identifying information for five City employees disciplined for accessing pornography on their government computers be released to the Gazette?

¶ 12 Montana's right to privacy is established in Article II, Section 10 of the Montana Constitution:

> Right of privacy. The right of individual privacy is essential to the wellbeing of a free society and shall not be infringed without the showing of a compelling state interest.

¶ 13 Often at issue with this provision is the public right to know, also established in the Montana Constitution. Article II, Section 9 of the Montana Constitution provides:

> Right to know. No person shall be deprived of the right to examine documents or to observe the deliberations of all public bodies or agencies of state government and its subdivisions, *except in cases in which the demand of individual privacy clearly exceeds the merits.* [Emphasis added.]

¶ 14 We have held that these competing interests must be balanced "in the context of the facts of each case, to determine whether the demands of individual privacy clearly exceed the merits of public disclosure. Under this standard, the right to know may outweigh the right of individual privacy, depending on the facts."

¶ 15 An examination of a request under the public right to know provision of the Montana Constitution requires a three-step process:

> First, we consider whether the provision applies to the particular political subdivision against whom enforcement is sought. Second, we determine whether the documents in question are "documents of public bodies" subject to public inspection. Finally, if the first two requirements are satisfied, we decide whether a privacy interest is present, and if so, whether the demand of individual privacy clearly exceeds the merits of public disclosure.

Becky v. Butte-Silver Bow Sch. Dist. No. 1 (Mont. 1995). No single rule or policy can be used to determine what information may be released upon public request because each request requires a fact specific, case-by-case analysis of the interests at issue and a balancing of the demands of individual privacy and the merits of public disclosure. ***

¶ 17 We decline to address the issue of whether the documents requested by the Gazette are public documents because all of the requested documents have already been disclosed. The investigative records were voluntarily released to the Gazette with only Employee and third-party names and identifying information redacted. Additionally, the corrective actions forms with redactions only for Employee identifying information (name, job title, and department) have been turned over to the Gazette. Though the corrective action forms were disclosed by the District Court in its order granting a stay, rather than by the City, the forms have nevertheless been disseminated and any further discussion as to whether these forms are considered public documents has been rendered moot. Thus the only remaining issue is whether the Employees had a reasonable expectation of privacy in their identifying information in relation to the internal disciplinary proceedings that outweighs the public's right to know.

A. Constitutionally Protected Privacy Interest

¶ 18 To determine whether a person has a constitutionally protected privacy interest, we consider (1) whether the person has a subjective or actual expectation of privacy, and (2) whether society is willing to recognize that expectation as reasonable. *Mont. Human Rights Div. v. City of Billings* (Mont. 1982). Actual expectation of privacy is necessarily a question of fact that requires a determination of whether the individual whose privacy is at issue had notice of possible disclosure.

¶ 19 The District Court found "the Employees did expect the fact they were disciplined for having misused public computers and the specifics regarding that misuse would be and remain private." The Gazette counters that no actual expectation of privacy could exist here because the City's Internet use policy for employees provides that "[u]sers using City-provided Internet accounts should not assume they are provided any degree of anonymity." Additionally, the policy states that "[u]se of the Internet may be monitored by the City."

¶ 20 The precise question is whether the Employees had an actual expectation of privacy in their identities in relation to internal disciplinary proceedings, not as to their employer's knowledge of their Internet usage. Only the latter is addressed by the City's policy. If the question was whether they held an actual expectation that the City would not monitor their usage, clearly the answer would be no. However, the City's Internet usage policy alone is insufficient to render clearly erroneous the District Court's finding that the Employees had an actual expectation that "the fact they were disciplined for having misused public computers . . . would be and remain private."

¶ 21 Having concluded the Employees had an actual or subjective expectation of privacy, we next must determine whether society would be willing to recognize that expectation as reasonable. Whether society is willing to accept an expectation of privacy as reasonable is a determination of law that requires

> reasoned consideration of the specific facts underlying the dispute. To provide but a few examples, the following inquiries may prove relevant in evaluating the reasonableness of an individual's expectation of privacy: (1) attributes of the individual . . . and whether the individual holds a position of public trust; (2) the particular characteristics of the discrete piece of information; and (3) the relationship of that information to the public duties of the individual.

Havre Daily News [*v. Havre* (Mont. 2006)], ¶ 23. The reasonableness of an expectation of privacy "may vary, even regarding the same information and the same recipient of that information."

¶ 22 In order to examine this fact specific question of law, it is important to undertake a review of our prior decisions relating to the reasonableness of public employees' expectations of privacy when balanced against the public's right to know.

¶ 23 In *Montana Human Rights Division*, the Human Rights Commission (HRC) requested personnel records of complainants and certain other employees in order to investigate allegations of discrimination based on sex, race, marital status, and/or union membership. The City refused to release non-complainant files, citing those individuals' right to privacy. We noted that employment records reasonably contain references to family, health, or substance abuse problems, employer criticisms, test scores, prison or military records, and many other things an employee would reasonably expect to be confidential.

¶ 24 We ultimately held that, though the information being requested was subject to the right to privacy, the right was nevertheless outweighed by other considerations, including the right to equal protection and the HRC's authority to investigate claims of discrimination. We rejected the City's argument that redaction of the names could reduce the intrusion on the non-complainants' privacy because the names alone could be indicators of sex, race, or even marital status, information which may not be available in the rest of the file. Though we found that the right to privacy was outweighed by the HRC's right to know, we required a protection order to restrict release of identifying information to the public.

¶ 25 Two years later, in *Missoulian* [*v. Bd. Of Regents* (Mont. 1984)], we held that the individual privacy interests of six university presidents in confidential job performance evaluations clearly exceeded the merits of public disclosure. The Missoulian had sought access to a meeting of the Board of Regents (Board) and the Commissioner of Higher Education (Commissioner) where the presidents' job performance was discussed, as well as evaluation documents considered by the Board. The request was denied by the Board due to privacy concerns.

¶ 26 We held that "time, place and status are factors in the reasonableness determination.... [T]he determination should include consideration of all relevant circumstances, including the nature of the information sought." "[M]ere status does not control the determination. University presidents do not waive their constitutional protections by taking office." Confidentiality in personnel records and evaluations is especially important because such records include subjective opinions of the employee's performance that will vary with the person evaluating the employee, public disclosure could impede candid communication between employer and employee, and a supervisor could use the public nature of evaluations or ratings as a vindictive mechanism against employees she disliked. We found it reasonable to expect that information that has a "'lack of objective criteria, the potential for vindictiveness, the lack of an opportunity for the employee to rebut statements ... and a substantial potential for abuse'" will be kept confidential. We concluded the presidents' right to privacy clearly outweighed general assertions that public disclosure would "foster[] public confidence in public institutions, maintain[] the accountability of public officials, assur[e] public access to information to allow evaluation of public expenditures, and prevent[] the secret conduct of government and usurping of the people's sovereignty," without a showing of how any of these interests would be furthered or hindered by public disclosure.

¶ 27 In *Great Falls Tribune v. Cascade County Sheriff* (Mont. 1989), we held that the privacy interests in the identity of law enforcement officers disciplined for unlawful acts while on duty did not clearly exceed the merits of public disclosure. City police officers and county sheriff's deputies were involved in a chase to apprehend a suspect. A deputy sheriff ran his car up onto a city sidewalk and struck the suspect, then on foot, but did not take him for medical treatment. An investigation into the suspect's injuries resulted in one deputy being suspended, one police officer being fired, and two other police officers resigning when given the option to resign or be discharged. The Great Falls Tribune sought the names of the disciplined officers.

¶ 28 We affirmed the District Court's conclusion that society would not recognize a very strong expectation of privacy in the identity of law enforcement officers disciplined for serious misconduct while in the line of duty. Law enforcement officers occupy positions of public trust because the "public health, safety, and welfare are closely tied to an honest police force. The conduct of our law enforcement officers is a sensitive matter so that if they engage in conduct resulting in discipline for misconduct in the line of duty, the public should know."

¶ 29 In *Flesh v. Board of Trustees of Joint School Dist. No. 2* (Mont. 1990), we concluded that an assistant school administrator had a reasonable expectation of privacy in a meeting to discuss allegations of wrongdoing that outweighed the public's right to know. Robert Flesh (Flesh) filed a complaint to void any decision made during the closed portion of a meeting where the school board heard a grievance filed by Flesh alleging that the assistant school administrator had maliciously made false statements against him. Over Flesh's objections, the school board closed the presentation and deliberation portions of the meeting to the public.

¶ 30 We noted that the grievance specifically asked the school board to take disciplinary action against the administrator, a request that would necessitate a review of his personnel record. We held that "society is willing to recognize a privacy interest in a public employer's consideration of allegations involving an employee's character, integrity, honesty, and personality." Since there was no showing of any public interest to be served by opening the meeting to the public, the privacy interest of the employee clearly outweighed the public's right to know.

¶ 31 In *Citizens to Recall Mayor Whitlock v. Whitlock* (Mont. 1992), we held that a mayor, as an elected official, has no reasonable expectation of privacy in regard to an investigation of allegations of "sexually harassing public employees or of other misconduct related to the performance of his official duties." Then-Mayor James Whitlock of Hamilton had been accused by City Judge Martha Bethel of sexual harassment and discrimination. A citizens group filed suit seeking release of the investigatory report.

¶ 32 In affirming the District Court's order to release the report, we noted two important reasons that the mayor could not allege a reasonable expectation of privacy. First, an elected official must be subjected to public scrutiny because it is the public that has the responsibility for "hiring, disciplinary action, and supervision." Second, we noted that the nature of the information being sought was the result of an investigation into misconduct related to the performance of his official duties, rather than general performance evaluations or discussion of Whitlock's character, integrity, honesty, or personality. We held that sexual harassment allegations went directly to Whitlock's ability to properly carry out his public duties, and the report was therefore properly disclosed.

¶ 33 In *Bozeman Daily Chronicle v. Bozeman Police Department* (Mont. 1993), a cadet at the Law Enforcement Academy in Bozeman made an allegation of sexual intercourse without consent against an off-duty Bozeman city police officer. Following investigation, no criminal charges were filed, but the special prosecutor opined that "[the police officer] should not be allowed to continue working as a law enforcement officer because of inappropriate use of his position in relation to his contacts with women." The officer resigned the next day. The Bozeman Daily Chronicle (Chronicle) sought the name of the officer and the investigative documents.

¶ 34 We upheld the District Court's order to release the name, and reversed its order shielding the investigative documents. Though the officer had been off duty at the time of the alleged misconduct, and had resigned by the time of the Chronicle's request, we noted that "the nature of the alleged misconduct ran directly counter to the police officer's sworn duty to uphold the law, to prevent crime, and to protect the public.... [S]uch alleged misconduct went directly to the police officer's breach of his position of public trust [and] therefore, this conduct is a proper matter for public scrutiny."

¶ 35 In *Jefferson County* [*v. Montana Standard* (Mont. 2003)], the Montana Standard sought information regarding the arrest for DUI of Beaverhead County Commissioner Donna Sevalstad (Sevalstad). Sevalstad pled guilty to driving under the influence of alcohol and driving with an expired license. We cited our decision in Whitlock in affirming the District Court's order to release the requested information. Because Sevalstad was an elected official, the public had the responsibility in hiring, supervising and disciplining her actions, which requires that the public be informed of her actions and conduct. Even though her driving habits didn't pertain directly to her duties as County Commissioner, "her decision to violate the law directly relate[d] to her ability to effectively perform her job duties. That is, Sevalstad's decision to violate the law questions her judgment."

¶ 36 We have also held that teachers hold positions of public trust because they are entrusted with the care and instruction of children. *Svaldi v. Anaconda-Deer Lodge Co.*, 2005 MT 17. Antoinette Svaldi (Svaldi), a teacher in the Anaconda public school system for approximately 25 years, was alleged by several parents to have assaulted or verbally abused their children. Svaldi filed an action against the County alleging that her right to privacy was violated when the County Attorney informed a reporter from a local paper that his office was discussing a deferred prosecution agreement with Svaldi's attorney in exchange for Svaldi's promise to resign from teaching. We affirmed the District Court's grant of summary judgment in favor of the County, even though no criminal charges were ultimately filed and no deferred prosecution agreement was ever entered, because she was in a position of public trust and the allegations of assault against her students "went directly to her ability to properly carry out her duties."

¶ 37 In *Yellowstone County v. Billings Gazette*, 2006 MT 218, we held that an interim chief public defender did not have a reasonable expectation of privacy in his deposition testimony for an employment discrimination lawsuit that outweighed the public right to know. Following the resignation of the Yellowstone County Chief Public Defender, Curtis Bevolden (Bevolden) was hired as the interim chief. Bevolden fired the Deputy Chief Defender, Roberta Drew (Drew), who had also applied for the interim chief position, but an internal grievance proceeding resulted in Drew's reinstatement. Drew filed a federal discrimination suit against the County, Bevolden, and other officials. The Gazette requested Bevolden's unredacted deposition transcript from the suit.

¶ 38 In holding that the public right to know was not clearly outweighed by any privacy interest Bevolden may have in the redacted information, we noted that public defenders have the duty to safeguard the constitutional rights to counsel and a fair and speedy trial, and are essential to preserving public trust in our judicial system. We also held that the redacted information of the transcript "bears directly on Bevolden's professional judgment, the management decisions he made as Interim Chief Public Defender, and his official conduct." Because the information being sought related directly to the official duties of a person in a position of public trust, Bevolden could not assert a right to privacy that outweighed the public's right to know.

¶ 39 In 2011, we decided *Billings Gazette v. Billings*, 2011 MT 293. Deanna Anthony (Anthony), a Police Department Senior Administrative Coordinator authorized to use a police department credit card, was investigated for allegations that she had made thousands of dollars of personal purchases using the card. Following the investigation, Anthony was issued a 16-page "due process letter" notifying her of a due process hearing to respond to the allegations against her, and detailing the evidence gathered during the investigation. The City denied the Gazette's request for the letter.

¶ 40 We held that even though she was an administrative employee, Anthony held a position of public trust because she was in a job that "allowed her to spend large amounts of public monies." Because the information being sought related directly to an investigation for allegations of misappropriating public funds, "the very aspect of her job that render[ed] it a 'position of public trust,'" the due process letter was properly subject to public disclosure. However, we also pointed out that not "every public employee with purchasing power can have no expectation of privacy in her personnel matters." Based on the facts of the case ("the alleged embezzlement of large sums of [public] money over a protracted period of time"), we held that information relating to a public employee's violation of the public trust implicit in her duties should be released to the public.

¶ 41 Having reviewed our prior cases, we turn to the case at bar. The information at issue in this case is limited to the identity of the Employees, including identifying information such as job title and department, as all other aspects of the misconduct, including the nature of the misconduct, the websites visited, the investigation process, and the discipline issued, has been disclosed to the Gazette. Initially, we note that the specific allegations of misconduct, accessing adult or pornographic websites, are not a focus of this analysis. We have held that a public employee is not entitled to heightened privacy protections simply because the information at issue was sexual in nature. *Harris v. Smartt*, 2002 MT 239 (Justice of the Peace not entitled to heightened privacy rights in pornography downloaded to his county-owned computer). However, neither is a public employee given less of a privacy right due to the sexual nature of the information. The fact that the images viewed on the Employees' computers "had sexual content does not influence the privacy analysis."

¶ 42 The City averred that the Employees were not elected officials, department heads, or high management. After in-camera review of the unredacted Corrective Action Forms, the District Court did not make any finding that any of the Employees hold any particular position of trust with regard to public spending or public safety. Our review of the unredacted forms does not convince us otherwise. Additionally, the Internet usage of the Employees was not related to their public duties. The Gazette has not argued to this Court that disclosure of the Employees' positions or titles, separate and distinct from the Employees' names, was necessary in order to analyze their respective expectations of privacy.

¶ 43 Rather, the Gazette argues that there can be no reasonable expectation of privacy in the identity of any public employee if the employee was disciplined for misconduct. The Gazette argues that this holding follows from our decision in *Great Falls Tribune* where we stated: "it is not good public policy to recognize an expectation of privacy in protecting the identity of a law enforcement officer whose conduct is sufficiently reprehensible to merit discipline." We reiterated this in *Bozeman Daily Chronicle*, However, there are key distinctions between those cases and this one.

¶ 44 First, in both prior cases the discipline was severe. *See Great Falls Tribune* (one officer was fired and two others were given the option to resign or be terminated); *Bozeman Daily Chronicle* (officer resigned after it was recommended that he not be allowed to continue in law enforcement). Here the employees were given a five-day suspension without pay, a far cry from being discharged or forced to resign. If we were to give the statement from *Great Falls Tribune* the meaning urged by the Gazette, any disciplinary action, no matter how trivial, would trump an employee's right to privacy.

¶ 45 Other important distinctions in the case here are the positions held by the disciplined Employees and the relation of their positions to the alleged misconduct. In *Great Falls Tribune*, the employees whose identities were being sought were law enforcement officers who had engaged in misconduct in the line of their official duties. We held that law enforcement officers hold a particular position of public trust due to their sworn duty to protect the public health, safety, and welfare. Allegations of misconduct in apprehending a suspect and failing to seek medical attention for his injuries clearly violate this duty. Similarly, in *Bozeman Daily Chronicle*, we noted that allegations of criminal conduct, even while off duty, ran directly counter to the officer's duty to uphold the law and prevent crime. Also, the officer's position was implicated by the victim's status as a police cadet. No similar connection can be made with regard to the Employees in this case.

¶ 46 The Dissent argues that the Employees' actions could be considered illegal conduct under the Computer Fraud and Abuse Act, as well as Montana's Unlawful Computer Use, Theft, and Official Misconduct statutes. However, no criminal charges have been filed or are contemplated in this case. Notably, the Ninth U.S. Circuit Court of Appeals has held that an employee's misuse of an employer's computer is not a crime under the Computer Fraud and Abuse Act. In any event, the misconduct in this case does not rise to the level of illegal conduct that was present in *Great Falls Tribune*, *Bozeman Daily Chronicle*, or *Billings Gazette*.

¶ 47 Additionally, we have previously held that matters relating to employee misconduct can be protected from the public right to know. In *Montana Human Rights Division*, we held that public employees possess a privacy right in their personnel files. The Court noted that personnel files can include sensitive information such as drug and alcohol problems, prison records, poor work performance, and tardiness—all forms of wrongful conduct. "A discussion regarding an employee's alleged wrongful conduct constituted precisely the type of communication that frequently occurred between the employer and employee." *Billings Gazette* (Morris, Rice, Baker, JJ., dissenting). The Court in *Montana Human Rights Division* recognized the fact that there is frequently pressure upon an employee to "communicate these matters to his employer in the privacy of his boss's office. . . ." Even without any assurance of confidentiality, the Court nevertheless concluded that "employees would reasonably expect such communication normally would be kept confidential." Thus, an allegation of misconduct by a public employee does not summarily end the privacy analysis.

¶ 48 The Gazette also argues, and the District Court agreed, that the City's Acceptable Use Policy demonstrates that the public placed its trust in the Employees with respect to Internet usage. It further argues that misuse of the Internet, a City resource, while at work is a violation of that public trust that relates directly to their fitness to perform a public duty. However, evident from the above discussion of our cases, not all public employees hold the same level of privacy in all disciplinary matters simply on the basis of having a public employer. We are not prepared to say that providing public employees with access to a computer on which to do their work itself "evinces a public trust" that can be breached by a violation of an Internet use policy. Nor are we prepared to hold that any violation of office policy by any government employee results in a violation of public trust simply because tax dollars pay that employee's salary. To do so would be tantamount to a holding that all citizens lose their constitutionally guaranteed right to privacy on the day they enter public employment. If university presidents do not automatically lose their constitutional protections by taking office, *Missoulian*, the same would certainly be true for the thousands of other public employees.

¶ 49 Our past cases have held, and we reaffirm today, that the "'right of privacy turns on the reasonableness of the expectation, which may vary, even regarding the same information and the same recipient of that information' . . . [T]ime, place and status are factors in the reasonableness determination." Where the status of the employee necessitates a high level of public trust, such as an elected official or high level employee, the expectation of privacy in misconduct may be found to be significantly lower than for an administrative employee. Similarly, an employee may have a lower expectation of privacy in misconduct related to a duty of public trust, such as responsibility for spending public money or educating children.

¶ 50 Here, the Employees are not elected officials, high-level management, or department heads, nor is there evidence that any specific duty alleged to have been violated related to the performance of a public trust function. The information being sought is merely their identities in relation to internal disciplinary action for a violation of office policy. We hold that society would be willing to accept as reasonable a public employee's expectation of privacy in his or her identity with respect to internal disciplinary matters when that employee is not in a position of public trust, and the misconduct resulting in the discipline was not a violation of a duty requiring a high level of public trust.

¶ 51 The Dissent employs a Fourth Amendment analysis and concludes that the Employees had no reasonable expectation of privacy in their computer misuse. The Fourth Amendment protects persons from unreasonable searches and seizures in the criminal context. The misconduct in this case involved no criminal conduct. Further, the civil cases cited by the Dissent . . . involve employee privacy claims raised against employers who sought information. Rejection of such claims by the courts in these cases was appropriately premised upon the employees' lack of an expectation of privacy as to their employers. Unlike these cases, there is here no privacy claim by the Employees against the City. The City obtained the information from the Employees' computers pursuant to the computer use policy, and proceeded to discipline the Employees. The question is whether the Gazette—a third party—is entitled to the identifying information about the Employees.

¶ 52 Montanans are provided a "heightened expectation of privacy" under the Montana Constitution in comparison to the U.S. Constitution, and Article II, Sections 9 and 10 of the Montana Constitution explicitly require that a balancing of the right to know and the right to privacy be conducted in this case. This Court's precedent provides the appropriate analysis of the particular state constitutional provisions that govern here, without regard to Fourth Amendment jurisprudence or federal approaches to the issue.

¶ 53 Having found that the Employees had an actual or subjective expectation of privacy that society is willing to find reasonable, we must balance the Employees' right to privacy against the merits of public disclosure.

B. Balancing Privacy with the Public Right to Know

¶ 54 The City argues that the risks mentioned in *Missoulian* with respect to performance evaluations are present in this case and necessitate a need for confidentiality in internal disciplinary matters. Specifically, it asserts that it has an interest in the confidentiality of disciplinary measures in order to effectively address and react to misconduct without fear that employer criticisms and disciplinary actions will be publicly disseminated. It argues that honest and critical communications between employers and employees will suffer, and there could be a risk of vindictive use of the discipline process, which lacks an opportunity for the employee to rebut the alleged misconduct, if disciplinary actions are subjected to public scrutiny.

¶ 55 The only argument offered by the Gazette in favor of public disclosure is that "[o]penness promotes fairness and thwarts cronyism." It argues that without knowing the name and status of each disciplined Employee, the public cannot determine why each Employee was given the same punishment, or why an employee of a different public agency was given a harsher punishment for similar conduct. The District Court agreed, holding that public disclosure of the corrective action forms and identifying information would "foster[] a public confidence in public institutions and maintain[] the accountability of public officers."

¶ 56 However, as we held in *Missoulian*, general assertions that public disclosure will foster public confidence in public institutions and maintain accountability for public officers are not sufficient to establish a strong public interest. The Gazette has already received information regarding the misconduct of the Employees, the investigation by the City, and the discipline meted out to each Employee. If the public is dissatisfied with the discipline chosen by the City, it has all the information it needs to voice its opinions and objections to the City Council, the Mayor, or the newspaper. Public knowledge of the names of the individuals disciplined will not provide the public with any greater opportunity to participate in the internal employment decisions of the City.

¶ 57 Unlike public officials, over whom the public has responsibilities regarding "hiring, disciplinary action, and supervision," it is the responsibility of the City to hire, fire, and discipline its employees. Such decisions necessarily involve a subjective determination on the part of the supervisor. The nature of the work to be done, the alleged misconduct, and the person making the disciplinary decision will all affect the type of discipline meted out, even for the exact same violation. As we noted in *Flesh*, these disciplinary decisions necessitate a review of the employee's entire personnel file.

¶ 58 Finally, to hold that the general interests of "fairness and prevention of cronyism," absent any allegations that such has occurred, is sufficient to outweigh an employee's privacy interest would open all public employment decisions to public scrutiny. Decisions of whom to hire, promote, discipline, or terminate are all decisions that require a subjective evaluation by supervisors based upon past performance, personality, character, test scores, etc. Our past cases preclude such an expansive holding.

¶ 59 We conclude that the Employees' reasonable expectation of privacy in their identities with regards to internal disciplinary proceedings clearly outweighs the limited merits of public disclosure. "This information may make interesting or sensational news copy, but we conclude that public disclosure is not in the public interest." ***

Justice LAURIE McKINNON, dissenting.

¶ 62 In my view, a City employee has no reasonable expectation of privacy in viewing pornographic materials over the Internet using a City computer during work hours—particularly when there is a policy in place which specifically advises employees that use of the Internet is not anonymous and may be monitored. Moreover, placement of a final disciplinary report (the Corrective Action Form) into an employee's personnel file does not transform the employee's open and pervasive access to pornographic material over the Internet into a private activity. The Court, by misstating the question as "whether the Employees had an actual expectation of privacy in their identities in relation to *internal disciplinary proceedings*, not as to their employer's knowledge of the Internet usage," redefines the inquiry in order to recognize a privacy interest that other courts have uniformly held to be unreasonable. After finding that the Employees were "not in a position of public trust" and that "the misconduct resulting in the discipline was not a violation of a duty requiring a high level of public trust," the Court concludes that the name, position, and department of a City employee accessing pornography may not be disclosed to the public. In my view, it is not necessary to decide whether the Employees are in positions of "public trust," because the Employees do not have an expectation of privacy, which Montanans are willing to accept as reasonable, in the fact that they accessed, posted, and enjoyed pornographic material while working for a public employer with an Internet use policy.

¶ 63 All City employees are subject to the City's "Acceptable Use" policy, which applies to "all equipment, systems and tools used for electronic communication, local area networks, computer networks, the Internet and e-mail." Among other things, the policy prohibits use of City computers to access or store "offensive graphical images." It also prohibits "[u]sing any means to defeat security systems on any computer network" and the "propagation of computer worms and viruses." Employees are advised that "[u]se of the Internet may be monitored by the City." Moreover, the policy states:

> The City's Internet hosts are traceable to the City. *Users using City-provided Internet accounts should not assume they are provided any degree of anonymity. Outside users who want to identify machines associated with the City can do so easily.* [Emphasis added.]

¶ 64 In the spring of 2012, the City conducted internal investigations into the Internet activity of five City employees on City-provided computers and ultimately issued written Corrective Action Forms suspending each employee for five days without pay. The nature of the violations were set forth in the Corrective Action Forms as follows:

1. Daily logs of each of the five employees showed a pattern of "[s]eeking out pictures of women on the internet that were sexual in nature." These images included "nude adults," "pictures that were pornographic in nature," and "scantily clad adults that were inappropriate for the workplace."

2. Daily logs also showed a pattern of "[e]xcessive amounts of time being spent on non-work related searches while . . . being compensated to perform . . . assigned duties."

3. One of the employees had conducted "[s]earches on blog, foreign country and image hosting sites. Specifically, links were found to a Polish site with adult content that contained file sharing functionality, subsequently increasing the potential of a virus threat to the City's computer network."

4. Another employee had saved four images of "scantily clothed and nude adults and pictures that were pornographic in nature."

5. Yet another employee had sought out "pictures of women associated with escort services."

As noted, the City disciplined the Employees by imposing five days of suspension on each. Although the suspensions were without pay, the City did not dock any pay of the employees for the "excessive" amount of work time they had spent viewing pornography.

¶ 65 As the Court observes, the documents requested by the Gazette have already been disclosed. However, certain information has been redacted from those documents — information that the Gazette contends the public has a constitutional right to know. Specifically, the information redacted in the Corrective Action Forms includes the employee's name, the employee's position, the employee's department, and the name of the employee's supervisor.

¶ 66 Despite this Court's knowledge — acquired through our in-camera review of the unredacted Corrective Action Forms — that some of the disciplined employees held upper-level positions and/or were involved in law enforcement, we refuse to apply that knowledge and analysis in resolving this case. We avoid the analysis by stating: "The City averred that the Employees were not elected officials, department heads, or high management." But the Court knows what positions the Employees held because we, like the District Court, reviewed the documents, which are part of the record on appeal. We nevertheless ignore the Employees' positions in spite of our precedent and the Gazette's argument that the public has a constitutional right to assess whether the City meted out discipline fairly. We avoid an analysis that incorporates consideration of the Employees' specific positions by determining that the Gazette did not advance this argument (How could it, given that the Gazette was not privy to that information?) and that "the District Court did not make any finding that any of the Employees hold any particular position of trust with regard to public spending or public safety." In failing to recognize the significance of the redacted information to the Gazette's investigation, we have subjectively limited the Gazette's inquiry and decided the direction the Gazette's investigation and reporting should take. Montana's constitutional provision embracing the citizenry's right to know is premised on the right to have information disseminated and available so that the public — not this Court — may draw its own inferences and conclusions from the information and thereby make informed decisions regarding their governmental bodies. The unfiltered dissemination of information is fundamental to the exercise of Montana's constitutional right to know and is limited only where an individual has a reasonable privacy interest that "clearly exceeds" the merits of public disclosure. Mont. Const. art. II, § 9.

¶ 67 Although the Court states that "[t]he only argument offered by the Gazette in favor of public disclosure is that '[o]penness promotes fairness and thwarts cronyism,'" the Gazette has actually advanced several arguments in support of its request for disclosure—arguments which the Court fails to acknowledge. First, the Gazette has argued that in violating the City's Acceptable Use policy, the Employees acted to defeat the security system on the City's computer network and potentially compromised the City's workplace by breaching security devices and introducing viruses from international pornography websites. While the Court states that "the specific allegations of misconduct, accessing adult or pornographic websites, are not a focus of this analysis," the Gazette argues that the pornographic nature of the material and the potential for security breaches are relevant in determining what society recognizes as a reasonable expectation of privacy. We are required to examine the privacy interest "'in the context of the facts of each case.'" Accordingly, we cannot avoid examining the content of the material at issue and the security threats posed by the individuals' actions when assessing whether society would recognize the privacy interest as reasonable. I thus do not agree that "[t]he fact that the images viewed on the Employees' computers 'had sexual content does not influence the primary analysis.'" I seriously question whether society is willing to protect the privacy of a public employee who breaches security devices, thus exposing the City's computer network to damage from viruses and other malware, in order to view pornography on a public computer during work hours. The pornographic nature of the material is important, in the context of all other factors.

¶ 68 Second, the Gazette maintains that the public has an interest in knowing whether public employees are violating the law. The Gazette argues that although no charges have been filed, the Employee's conduct can be characterized as illegal under the Computer Fraud and Abuse Act, 18 U.S.C. § 1030. The Gazette points to several court decisions which have held that violating the terms of an "acceptable use" policy may constitute a federal offense. Significantly, Montana has its own criminal offenses relating to the unlawful use of a computer. Section 45-6-311(1)(a), MCA, prohibits a person from knowingly or purposely "obtain[ing] the use of any computer, computer system, or computer network without consent of the owner." The City's Acceptable Use policy clearly establishes that employees are not authorized to use City computers to access pornographic materials over the Internet. Arguably, Montana's theft statute is likewise implicated by the Employees' conduct. Pursuant to § 45-6-301(2)(a), MCA, a person commits the offense of theft when the person purposely or knowingly obtains, by deception, control over another's property (money paid in the form of wages) with the purpose of depriving the owner (the City) of that property. Montana additionally has an "official misconduct" statute that makes it unlawful for a "public servant" to "knowingly perform[] an act in an official capacity that the public servant knows is forbidden by law." Section 45-7-401(1)(b), MCA. "Public servant" means "an officer or *employee of government*." Section 45-2-101(64)(a), MCA (emphasis added). This Court's precedent establishes that the public has the right to know about unlawful activity of public employees. Furthermore, our constitutional right to know protects the right to receive information about decisions of government officials to prosecute or commence a criminal investigation. The fact that "no criminal charges have been filed or are contemplated," puts the cart before the horse—this is precisely the information the public has the right to know in order to evaluate the conduct of public officials.

¶ 69 Third, the Gazette also maintains that the public has the right to scrutinize whether the discipline the City imposed on the Employees was fair. While the Court seemingly finds it significant that the punishment meted out in other cases was "severe" while the punishment meted out in the present case was less so, I believe such an assessment of government discipline is best left for citizens to determine after being presented with adequate information. The Gazette specifically argued before the District Court that during the same timeframe when the Employees here were given five-day suspensions, five employees with the City landfill also received five-day suspensions for taking trash outside the City during off-work hours. The Gazette maintained that the public has a right to scrutinize the discipline imposed and to question whether there is "some distinction between high-level employees" who got the same punishment "as the people in the landfill." Likewise, on appeal, the Gazette again questions whether "the status of the employees" accounts for the punishments that the City imposed—information which the Gazette maintains the public has a constitutional right to know.

¶ 70 Lastly, the Gazette argues that a substantial amount of taxpayer money was wasted on time the Employees spent accessing pornographic materials and that the investigation likewise has cost taxpayers money and public resources. The Gazette maintains that the public has an interest in how their government spends public funds, just as the public had a right to know the identity of the police department employee who misappropriated public funds in *Billings Gazette v. City of Billings*, 2011 MT 293.

¶ 71 In light of the foregoing, the Gazette's arguments for public disclosure cannot be dismissed as merely seeking to promote fairness and thwart cronyism. Rather, in my opinion, the Gazette has set forth these particular arguments as components of a more general argument that disclosure fosters public confidence in public institutions and maintains accountability of public officers.

¶ 72 Determining whether public documents must be disclosed requires a balancing of the public's right to know with any competing privacy interests. Mont. Const. art. II, §§ 9, 10. Again, the balancing must be done in the context of the facts of each case. A person has a constitutionally protected privacy interest when (1) the person has an actual or subjective expectation of privacy and (2) society is willing to recognize that privacy expectation as reasonable.

¶ 73 In this case, the District Court observed that neither party had disputed the first prong of the test—actual or subjective expectation of privacy—and the District Court thus found that "the Employees did expect the fact they were disciplined for having misused public computers and the specifics regarding that misuse would be and remain private." The District Court further determined, however, that the Employees' subjective expectations of privacy were unreasonable in light of their knowledge that the City had the right to monitor their Internet usage and that they had no anonymity with respect to the sites they visited. In my judgment, the District Court's conclusion was not only correct, but also consistent with that of numerous courts which have considered a public employee's expectation of privacy and decided that an Internet use policy negates any such expectation. ***

¶ 76 Although [these cases are] largely in the context of Fourth Amendment jurisprudence, the reasonableness of an expectation of privacy—that is, what society will recognize as legitimate—does not vary depending upon whether the argument is made under the Fourth Amendment or under Montana's constitutional provision regarding an individual's right of privacy. Our precedent recognizes the validity of federal caselaw in the context of a right-to-know analysis, regarding whether a privacy interest is one that society is willing to recognize as reasonable. In *Mont. Human Rights Div. v. City of Billings* (Mont. 1982), we applied the standard set forth by the Supreme Court in *Katz v. U.S.* (1967), to evaluate what constituted a reasonable expectation of privacy in relation to the right to know. *Katz* was the landmark case that defined a constitutionally protected expectation of privacy, under the Fourth Amendment, as consisting of a subjective component and a reasonableness component. This Court has applied that test in search-and-seizure cases....

¶ 77 I cannot accept that Montana citizens would recognize as reasonable, under *Katz, Mont. Human Rights Div.*, or any other precedent, this Court's willingness to shield the identities, positions, departments, and supervisors of public employees who access pornographic material on their work computers during work hours after having been warned that their computer usage would be monitored and that they cannot expect anonymity. I also am not willing to carve out an exception to the well-established test for determining a constitutionally protected expectation of privacy because we want to protect particular employees from embarrassment. The reasonableness of an expectation of privacy depends on what society deems is legitimate, and such a test cannot logically depend on whether a claim is asserted pursuant to search-and-seizure jurisprudence or precedent interpreting the right to know.

¶ 78 Contrary to the Court's reasoning, the City's placement of the final disciplinary report in each Employee's personnel file does not give the document protections that it otherwise would not have. The Employee's privacy expectation has been extinguished by the Acceptable Use policy and is not resurrected by placing the Corrective Action Form into a personnel file. Actions of the Employees in choosing to access websites at work on a City computer with an Internet use policy in effect, for which there was no reasonable expectation of privacy, cannot subsequently be made private through actions of the City in placing the disciplinary report into the protective confines of the Employees' personnel files. To allow a public employer to potentially subvert the right to know by concealing the contents of the objectionable material in a personnel file would undermine the public's ability to evaluate the functioning of government and whether it is meting out discipline fairly and evenhandedly.

¶ 79 The rationale for protecting from disclosure the contents of a personnel file does not exist in this case. Arguably, the Corrective Action Form is more akin to the "due process letter" in *Billings Gazette*, which we noted was different from the job performance evaluations of university presidents in *Missoulian*, and the employment applications in *Mont. Human Rights Div.* As we stated in *Mont. Human Rights Div.*:

> Employment records would reasonably contain, among less sensitive information, references to family problems, health problems, past and present employers' criticism and observations, military records, scores from IQ tests and performance tests, prison records, drug or alcohol problems, and other matters, many of which most individuals would not willingly disclose publicly. Some testing and disclosure (e.g., past employment records, prison records, drug or alcohol use) is a necessary part of many applications for employment; other information may be compiled by present employers or may be submitted by an employee in explanation of absence from work or poor performance on the job. It is clear that there is frequently pressure upon an employee to communicate these matters to his employer in the privacy of his boss's office or on an application for employment or promotion. And while, as far as we know, respondents gave their employees no specific assurances of confidentiality, we believe that employees would reasonably expect such communication normally would be kept confidential.

¶ 80 Significant to our decision in *Missoulian* was a written policy that provided for confidentiality of self-evaluations. We noted that

> the Board's written evaluation policy stated that the self-evaluations would be confidential and the evaluation meetings would be conducted in "executive session." The anonymous interviewees who commented on the presidents' performance were promised confidentiality. It is undisputed that the six university presidents actually expected that the job performance evaluations would be private. [They] submitted their self-evaluations expecting confidentiality.

We held that these expectations of privacy were reasonable.

¶ 81 In contrast, the Acceptable Use policy here specifically advises that there is no confidentiality in the materials and the activities conducted on an employee's computer. Furthermore, nothing in the Corrective Action Form contains sensitive information akin to an employment record, such as family references, health problems, prison records, or drug and alcohol issues. The Corrective Action Form is the final report of the discipline a public employer has imposed on its employee. The Gazette is not requesting the Employees' entire personnel files, employment records, or performance evaluations; it is requesting the final report—the end product—of the City's investigation into misconduct of its employees.

¶ 82 "Government offices are provided to employees for the sole purpose of facilitating the work of an agency. The employee may avoid exposing personal belongings at work by simply leaving them at home." *O'Connor v. Ortega* (1987) (plurality). Likewise, a public employee who is paid by taxpayers does not have a reasonable expectation of privacy in viewing pornography during work hours on a City computer, particularly when he/she has been advised by the City that computer use is not anonymous.

¶ 83 The District Court concluded that because "the Employees' privacy expectations were unreasonable under these circumstances, their privacy rights do not clearly exceed the merits of public disclosure." Mont. Const. art. II, § 9. I agree with this conclusion. Although public humiliation may be an unfortunate consequence of disclosure, it is not a defense to disclosure. . . .

Justice PATRICIA O. COTTER joins the Dissent of Justice LAURIE McKINNON.

Notes on Privacy and the Merits of Public Disclosure

1. The Court in *Billings Gazette* (a common plaintiff in Montana right-to-know cases) reviews the balances it has struck in the past between the right to know and the right to privacy. Consider the elements of a right to know claim as applied to this case.

a. Are employee disciplinary records "documents" of "public bodies" subject to the right? The city itself conducted the investigation, so its reports appear to qualify for disclosure, particularly to the extent they reflect the internal disciplinary processes of a local government. Do records generated by individual employees by web browsing, emailing, or phoning at work also qualify as "documents" of "public bodies," if they do not otherwise "relate to the transaction of official business"? *See* Mont. Code Ann. § 2-6-1002(11) ("public information"). At least under the right to know statutes, personal information of public employees is not necessarily public information, unless it becomes the subject of "official business" through disciplinary proceedings. (Is this definition constitutional?) Even then, does the right to know extend to all personal information subject to the city's investigation (e.g., the full investigative file), only the personal information relied upon by the city's investigation (e.g., a non-redacted report), or none of the personal information once the city discloses its official disciplinary actions (e.g., a redacted report or disciplinary letter)? Note how these alternatives raise questions about the purpose underlying the right to know: is it the public's interest in the employees' conduct or is it the public's interest in the city's investigation that triggers the right to know? (Why does the Court not answer this question? Or does it?) These are threshold questions of personal and public information that arise before any privacy inquiry.

b. If the right to know extends to a document, there is a three-step test to protect individual privacy: (1) there is a "demand of individual privacy," measured by reasonable expectations under current doctrine; (2) that privacy interest "clearly exceeds," (3) "the merits of public disclosure." What are these merits? The Court rarely discusses the privacy exception in these terms, but there are a few possible approaches to the text. "The merits of public disclosure" may simply refer back to the right to know, so that all public documents or deliberations are presumptively disclosed unless a sufficient privacy interest overrides that right. To borrow the dissent's terminology, the merits would be the same for an "upper-level" full-time employee or a "lower-level" temporary worker with the same privacy demands. Or "the merits" may refer to a qualitative assessment of how important the right to know is in a particular instance, so that once there is a demand of individual privacy, a court should consider how important the public documents or deliberations are in light of the political accountability or other principles underlying the right to know. In this case, the merits would be greater for an "upper-level" employee than a "lower-level" employee with the same privacy demands. Finally, "the merits" may refer to some other consideration entirely. What might that be?

2. The Court frames its "public trust" inquiry as a matter of privacy, but it is not always clear why a university president or a police officer, for example, should expect less privacy of at least some personal information than an office clerk or a government contractor. "The merits of public disclosure" might be a better fit for this inquiry. If this is so, is "public trust" an elaboration of the right to know (under the second approach above) or some other value (under the third approach above)?

3. Note the similarities between *Billings Gazette* and *State v. Nelson* (Chapter 11) in how they look to substantive law or policy (employee handbooks and criminal law in *Billings Gazette*, health records confidentiality laws in *Nelson*) to determine whether society would be willing to recognize an expectation of privacy as reasonable. Consider again the benefits and costs of such a statutorily grounded approach relative to judicially determined "reasonableness" standing alone.

4. In *Krakauer v. State* (2016), the Montana Supreme Court considered a Colorado-based journalist's request for records of the state Office of the Commissioner of Higher Education pertaining to an appeal of the University of Montana's expulsion of an unnamed student-athlete for sexual assault. A district court ordered disclosure of the requested records subject only to the redaction of student identification information. The Court first rejected the Commissioner's argument that out-of-state residents lacked standing to assert a right to know. After a review of federal and state student privacy laws, the Court reversed the district court and required it to reconsider the privacy interests including "information pertaining to student members of the University Court, the victim, and other University students who acted as witnesses in the multiple-step process . . . and in the event it determines to release any document after conducting the balancing test, every precaution should be taken to protect the personal information about other persons contained in the documents." On remand:

> The [district] court conducted an in-camera review of Doe's educational records. First, the District Court did not make a finding about whether an adverse ruling against Doe existed that would have permitted the release of limited information from Doe's records. Second, although recognizing students' enhanced privacy interests in their educational records, the court found Doe's personal information in the records was already substantially available to the public through unsealed court records and significant media coverage of Doe's contemporaneous public criminal trial. Therefore, it held Doe did not have a subjective or actual expectation of privacy in the records at issue, which rendered the issue of redaction moot. Third, the District Court concluded that even if Doe had a privacy interest in his records, his privacy interest did not clearly exceed the merits of public disclosure due to Doe's status as a high-profile student-athlete at the time of the disciplinary proceedings, the scholarships he received from the University, the attendant publicity of the alleged sexual assault, and the public's compelling interest in understanding the disciplinary procedures employed by a state university.

Krakauer v. State II (2019). The Montana Supreme Court reversed. It held the district court "fundamentally erred by holding the public's knowledge of the personal information in Doe's records negated his expectation of privacy in them." The Court then held that Doe's expectation of privacy was reasonable and clearly exceeded the merits of public disclosure:

> [E]ven a student who is a "public representative" of a university plainly does not occupy a position of public trust. Doe was not, for example, a law enforcement officer, teacher, or government official, nor was he charged with performing public duties. Doe was a student. Even if, as Krakauer suggests, his popularity benefited both the University and himself (and even though Doe was an especially prominent sports figure), Doe simply was not a public official; as a student, he was entitled to an enhanced privacy interest in his educational records. ***
>
> We therefore recognize the strong merits of publicly disclosing information pertaining to the University's handling of sexual assault allegations, but we must also "honor the unique privacy protection legislatively cloaked around the subject records . . . ," *Krakauer I*, ¶ 37, Doe's continued defense of his privacy interest, and the necessity to maintain confidentiality for student disciplinary proceedings. Accordingly, under the particular facts of this case, we conclude Doe's demand of individual privacy clearly exceeds the merits of public disclosure.

Justice Rice, joined by Chief Justice McGrath and Justice Baker, dissented:

> . . . Review of the record convinces me that the public's right to know the basis for the Commissioner's decision outweighs even the enhanced right to privacy in this case. The Commissioner's decision makes clear that it is premised on matters of process in the University's handling of the matter,

> and includes very little discussion of the underlying facts. Redactions may be viable within that document to ensure protection of any private information, such as information provided by or about, or the identity of, other parties, or of the nature of specific evidence. I would remand for the District Court to further consider any appropriate redactions.

Krakauer sharpens the question raised in *Billings Gazette* around privacy and the merits of public disclosure in the context of the right to know: to what extent does the public interest in public policy decisions (including disciplinary proceedings) override the privacy interests of those implicated in those decisions?

5. In implementing the Code of Ethics for public officials pursuant to Article XIII, section 4 of the Montana Constitution, the Legislature required "[t]he complainant and the person who is the subject of the complaint shall maintain the confidentiality of the complaint and any related documents released to the parties by the commissioner [of political practices] until the commissioner issues a decision." A state legislator filed an ethics complaint against the Governor and a cabinet member, publicly disclosed it the week before a general election in which the Governor sought re-election, and challenged the confidentiality requirement as a violation of his First Amendment freedom of speech. The federal courts accepted the state's defense that its restriction on speech was justified by a compelling interest in protecting the privacy of unelected employees, but invalidated the law as not narrowly tailored because "[t]here is no attempt in the provision to distinguish between constitutionally protected personal information and information that may be revealed without violating [privacy rights]." *Tschida v. Motl* (9th Cir. 2019). Would the result be the same under the right to know? *Cf. Goldstein v. Commission on Practice* (Mont. 2000) (rejecting a right to know challenge to the confidentiality of preliminary lawyer disciplinary proceedings); *see also* Mont. Const. Art. VII, § 11(4) ("The proceedings of the [judicial standards] commission are confidential except as provided by statute.").

Chapter 14

Due Process of Law and Other Guarantees

Article II, Section 17. Due process of law. No person shall be deprived of life, liberty, or property without due process of law.

Identical to 1889 constitution.

Article II, Section 34. Unenumerated Rights. The enumeration in this constitution of certain rights shall not be construed to deny, impair, or disparage others retained by the people.

Identical to 1889 constitution.

So far, this part of the book has focused on the first ten amendments, more or less, of the Declaration of Rights in Article II of the Montana Constitution. This is only the beginning of the Montana Constitution's wide range of guarantees. There are twenty-five additional rights provisions in the Declaration of Rights, and several more rights-like guarantees elsewhere in the document. To conclude the book, this chapter gathers these provisions to hint at the vast constitutional territory left to explore in Montana. It begins with the foundational concept of "due process of law," a right that also sometimes serves as a catch-all for other unenumerated rights. Then it turns to the other rights in Article II, which address criminal justice, carry over relatively undeveloped and sometimes curious rights from the 1889 Constitution, and assert a few novel but limited rights. The chapter, and book, concludes with a brief discussion of some novel rights that most distinguish the state constitutional law tradition from its federal counterpart.

A. Due Process of Law

As noted in Chapter 9, due process of law is rooted in a lineage as old as the concept of inalienable rights and "the law of the land." Today, this is understood as requiring government to apply law according to basic procedural safeguards of fair notice and a hearing before an impartial tribunal. As "the law of the land" suggests, and the federal *Mathews v. Eldridge* (1976) balancing test requires, "what process is due" depends on the context. Whether something qualifies as a liberty or property interest, and the weight it should be accorded relative to government interests and available procedures, varies according to the situation and the community in which the situation occurs. When it comes to due process, the law of the land arguably depends on the land.

Due process and inalienable rights are connected in another way. Federal courts enforce unenumerated rights embedded in the substantive due process doctrine. In *Washington v. Glucksberg* (1997), the case in which the United States Supreme Court rejected a "right to die" similar to that raised in *Baxter v. State* from Chapter 11, Justice David Souter examined the state origins of substantive due process:

> Before the ratification of the Fourteenth Amendment, substantive constitutional review resting on a theory of unenumerated rights occurred largely in the state courts applying state constitutions that commonly contained either due process clauses like that of the Fifth Amendment (and later the Fourteenth) or the textual antecedents of such clauses, repeating Magna Carta's guarantee of "the law of the land." On the basis of such clauses, or of general principles untethered to specific constitutional language, state courts evaluated the constitutionality of a wide range of statutes.
>
> Thus, a Connecticut court approved a statute legitimating a class of previous illegitimate marriages, as falling within the terms of the "social compact," while making clear its power to review constitutionality in those terms. *Goshen v. Stonington* (Conn. 1822). In the same period, a specialized court of equity, created under a Tennessee statute solely to hear cases brought by the state bank against its debtors, found its own authorization unconstitutional as "partial" legislation violating the State Constitution's "law of the land" clause. *Bank of the State v. Cooper* (Tenn. 1831). And the middle of the 19th century brought the famous *Wynehamer* case, invalidating a statute purporting to render possession of liquor immediately illegal except when kept for narrow, specified purposes, the state court finding the statute inconsistent with the State's due process clause. *Wynehamer v. People* (N.Y. 1856). The statute was deemed an excessive threat to the "fundamental rights of the citizen" to property.

Justice Souter quoted the New York Court of Appeals (its highest court) in explaining, "the form of this declaration of right, 'no person shall be deprived of life, liberty or property, without due process of law,' necessarily imports that the legislature cannot make the mere existence of the rights secured the occasion of depriving a person of any of them, even by the forms which belong to 'due process of law.' For if it does not necessarily import this, then the legislative power is absolute." In the words of the second Justice Harlan, dissenting in *Poe v. Ullman* (1961), "[w]ere due process merely a procedural safeguard it would fail to reach those situations where the deprivation of life, liberty or property was accomplished by legislation which by operating in the future could, given even the fairest possible procedure in application to individuals, nevertheless destroy the enjoyment of all three."

Contemporary state constitutional law, particularly in Montana, is rich in enumerated rights. Consider whether that should change a state court's acceptance of substantive due process modeled on what has become the most contested doctrine in federal law. According to the United States Supreme Court's opinion in *Glucksberg*, that federal model "specially protects those fundamental rights and liberties which are, objectively, 'deeply rooted in this Nation's history and tradition,' and 'implicit in the concept of ordered liberty,' such that 'neither liberty nor justice would exist if they were sacrificed'." A state court engaged in a substantive due process inquiry, and looking to federal law for guidance, might decide to identify ordered liberty and tradition at the state level or accept the current roster of federal liberty interests. This is a choice the United States Supreme Court wrestled with in considering whether to "incorporate" certain federal rights against the states under the Fourteenth Amendment's Due Process Clause, and it may still hold lessons for states.

1. "Procedural" Due Process

State v. Stanko

292 Mont. 192 (1998)

Justice TERRY N. TRIEWEILER delivered the opinion of the Court.

¶ 1 The defendant, Rudy Stanko, was charged by a complaint filed in the Justice Court for Garfield County with failing to drive in a reasonable and prudent manner in violation of § 61-8-303(1), MCA. Following trial by jury, he was found guilty of that offense and was sentenced. He appealed his conviction to the District Court for the Sixteenth Judicial District in Garfield County where he was recharged by information with the same offense. In District Court, he again pled not guilty, moved to dismiss the charge against him on the basis that the statute pursuant to which he was charged was unconstitutionally vague, and following denial of that motion, received a second jury trial. He was again convicted and sentenced and now appeals that conviction to this Court. We reverse the judgment of the District Court.

¶ 2 The dispositive issue on appeal is whether § 61-8-303(1), MCA, is so vague that it violates the Due Process Clause found at Article II, Section 17, of the Montana Constitution.

Factual Background

*** ¶ 4 Kenneth Breidenbach is a member of the Montana Highway Patrol who, at the time of trial and the time of the incident which formed the basis for Stanko's arrest, was stationed in Jordan, Montana. On March 10, 1996, he was on duty patrolling Montana State Highway 24 and proceeding south from Fort Peck toward Flowing Wells in "extremely light" traffic at about 8 a.m. on a Sunday morning, when he observed another vehicle approaching him from behind. [The vehicle passed him, and he clocked it "at a steady 85 miles per hour during the time that he followed it."] ***

¶ 6 When Stanko's vehicle reached a point where the road was wide enough to pull over safely, Officer Breidenbach signaled him to pull over and issued him a ticket for violating § 61-8-303(1), MCA. The basis for the ticket was the fact that Stanko had been operating his vehicle at a speed of 85 miles per hour at a location where Officer Breidenbach concluded it was unsafe to do so.

¶ 7 The officer testified that the road at that location was narrow, had no shoulders, and was broken up by an occasional frost heave. He also testified that the portion of the road over which he clocked Stanko included curves and hills which obscured vision of the roadway ahead. However, he acknowledged that at a distance of from 249 to 374 feet behind Stanko, he had never lost sight of Stanko's vehicle. The roadway itself was bare and dry, there were no adverse weather conditions, and the incident occurred during daylight hours. Officer Breidenbach apparently did not inspect the brakes on Stanko's vehicle or make any observation regarding its weight. The only inspection he conducted was of the tires, which appeared to be brand new. He also observed that it was a 1996 Camaro, which was a sports car, and that it had a suspension system designed so that the vehicle could be operated at high speeds. He also testified that while he and Stanko were on Highway 24 there were no other vehicles that he observed, that during the time that he clocked Stanko on Highway 200 they approached no other vehicles going in their direction, and that he observed a couple of vehicles approach them in the opposite direction during that eight-mile stretch of highway.

¶ 8 Although Officer Breidenbach expressed the opinion that 85 miles per hour was unreasonable at that location, he gave no opinion what would have been a reasonable speed, nor did he identify anything about Stanko's operation of his vehicle, other than the speed at which he was traveling, which he considered to be unsafe.

¶ 9 Stanko testified that on the date he was arrested he was driving a 1996 Chevrolet Camaro that he had just purchased one to two months earlier and which had been operated fewer than 10,000 miles. He stated that the brakes, tires, and steering were all in perfect operating condition, the highway conditions were perfect, and he felt that he was operating his vehicle in a safe manner. He conceded that after passing Officer Breidenbach's vehicle, he drove at a speed of 85 miles per hour, but testified that because he was aware of the officer's presence he was extra careful about the manner in which he operated his vehicle. He felt that he would have had no problem avoiding any collision at the speed that he was traveling. Stanko testified that he was fifty years old at the time of trial, drives an average of 50,000 miles a year, and has never had an accident.

Discussion

¶ 10 Is § 61-8-303(1), MCA, so vague that it violates the Due Process Clause found at Article II, Section 17, of the Montana Constitution?

¶ 11 Stanko contends that § 61-8-303(1), MCA, is unconstitutionally vague because it fails to give a motorist of ordinary intelligence fair notice of the speed at which he or she violates the law, and because it delegates an important public policy matter, such as the appropriate speed on Montana's highways, to policemen, judges, and juries for resolution on a case-by-case basis.

¶ 12 The State denies that Montana's "basic rule" is unconstitutionally vague, but contends that even if it is impermissibly vague as applied in some situations, Stanko does not have standing to challenge the statute facially because his conduct in this case was clearly prohibited by the statute and "[o]ne to whose conduct a statute clearly applies may not successfully challenge it for vagueness." *Parker v. Levy* (1974).

¶ 13 We conclude that operating a relatively new motor vehicle, which is concededly in excellent condition, at a speed of 85 miles per hour, on a clear day during daylight hours, on a dry road in rural Montana with no significant traffic in the area, is not so clearly prohibited by the speed restriction found in § 61-8-303(1), MCA, that Stanko lacks standing to challenge that statute for facial vagueness. ***

¶ 17 A vagueness challenge to a statute or ordinance may be raised on two different bases: (1) because the statute or ordinance is so vague that it is rendered void on its face; or (2) because it is vague as applied in a particular situation.

¶ 18 Stanko contends that § 61-8-303(1), MCA, to the extent that it regulates speed at which vehicles can be operated on Montana's highways without providing a numerical limit, is facially vague and, therefore, violates Article II, Section 17, of Montana's Constitution, which guarantees to Montana's citizens due process of law.

¶ 19 Section 61-8-303(1), MCA, provides as follows:

> A person operating or driving a vehicle of any character on a public highway of this state shall drive the vehicle in a careful and prudent manner and *at a rate of speed no greater than is reasonable and proper under the conditions existing at the point of operation*, taking into account the amount and character of traffic, condition of brakes, weight of vehicle, grade and width of highway, condition of surface, and freedom of obstruction to the view ahead. The person operating or driving the vehicle shall drive the vehicle so as not to unduly or unreasonably endanger the life, limb, property, or other rights of a person entitled to the use of the street or highway.

(Emphasis added.)

¶ 20 Since there is no evidence in this case that Stanko lost control of his vehicle, or that he endangered any other person or any other person's property, it is clear that he was arrested, charged, and prosecuted for operating his vehicle at a speed that Officer Breidenbach considered unreasonable. The question is whether a statute which regulates speed in the terms set forth above gave Stanko reasonable notice of the speed at which his conduct would violate the law.

¶ 21 The United States Supreme Court has established the following test for whether penal statutes are void for vagueness in violation of the Due Process Clause of the Fourteenth Amendment to the United States Constitution:

> As generally stated, the void-for-vagueness doctrine requires that a penal statute define the criminal offense with sufficient definiteness that ordinary people can understand what conduct is prohibited and in a manner that does not encourage arbitrary and discriminatory enforcement. Although

> the doctrine focuses both on actual notice to citizens and arbitrary enforcement, we have recognized recently that the more important aspect of the vagueness doctrine "is not actual notice, but the other principle element of the doctrine—the requirement that a legislature establish minimal guidelines to govern law enforcement." Where the legislature fails to provide such minimal guidelines, a criminal statute may permit "a standardless sweep [that] allows policemen, prosecutors, and juries to pursue their personal predilections."

Kolender v. Lawson (1983).

¶ 22 In Montana, we have established the following test for whether a statute is void on its face for vagueness:

> "A statute is void on its face if it fails to give a person of ordinary intelligence fair notice that his contemplated conduct is forbidden." No person should be required to speculate as to whether his contemplated course of action may be subject to criminal penalties.

State v. Crisp (Mont. 1991). ***

¶ 25 We conclude that, as a speed limit, § 61-8-303(1), MCA, does not meet these requirements of the Due Process Clause of Article II, Section 17, of the Montana Constitution, nor does it further the values that the void-for-vagueness doctrine is intended to protect.

¶ 26 For example, while it was the opinion of Officer Breidenbach that 85 miles per hour was an unreasonable speed at the time and place where Stanko was arrested, he offered no opinion regarding what a reasonable speed at that time and place would have been. Neither was the Attorney General, the chief law enforcement officer for the State, able to specify a speed that would have been reasonable for Stanko at the time and place where he was arrested. ***

¶ 28 It is evident . . . that the average motorist in Montana would have no idea of the speed at which he or she could operate his or her motor vehicle on this State's highways without violating Montana's "basic rule" based simply on the speed at which he or she is traveling. Furthermore, the basic rule not only permits, but requires the kind of arbitrary and discriminatory enforcement that the due process clause in general, and the void-for-vagueness doctrine in particular, are designed to prevent. It impermissibly delegates the basic public policy of how fast is too fast on Montana's highways to "policemen, judges, and juries for resolution on an ad hoc and subjective basis."

¶ 29 For example, the statute requires that a motor vehicle operator and Montana's law enforcement personnel take into consideration the amount of traffic at the location in question, the condition of the vehicle's brakes, the vehicle's weight, the grade and width of the highway, the condition of its surface, and its freedom from obstruction to the view ahead. However, there is no specification of how these various factors are to be weighted, or whether priority should be given to some factors as opposed to others. This case is a good example of the problems inherent in trying to consistently apply all of these variables in a way that gives motorists notice of the speed at which the operation of their vehicle becomes a violation of the law. For all practical purposes, there was no other traffic on the highway at the time that Stanko was arrested, the condition of his vehicle was excellent, the surface of the road was dry, and the view ahead was unobstructed for a distance of at least 249 to 374 feet. On the other hand, the road was narrow, there were hills and curves which presented some degree of obstruction to the view ahead, and there was an occasional frost heave on the surface of the road. A reasonable speed under these circumstances would require a calculation of sight distances and stopping distances for the particular vehicle. These functions are normally provided by engineers employed by highway departments who then post signs indicating when it is necessary to reduce speed on a curve or hill crest in order to safely operate a motor vehicle. It is not the kind of decision that the average motor vehicle operator is qualified to make, and not the kind of decision that policemen or highway patrolmen should be called upon to make. Most importantly, for constitutional purposes, even if law enforcement officials were qualified to make those kinds of judgments, the statute would not satisfy the requirement that a motor vehicle operator of average intelligence know what conduct is prohibited and when his or her conduct is going to be subject to criminal penalties.

¶ 30 For these reasons, we conclude that that part of § 61-8-303(1), MCA, which makes it a criminal offense to operate a motor vehicle "at a rate of speed . . . greater than is reasonable and proper under the conditions existing at the point of operation" is void for vagueness on its face and in violation of the Due Process Clause of Article II, Section 17, of the Montana Constitution.

¶ 31 We do not, however, mean to imply that motorists who lose control of their vehicle or endanger the life, limb, or property of others by the operation of their vehicle on a street or highway cannot be punished for that conduct pursuant to other statutes, such as § 61-8-301, MCA (reckless driving), or § 61-8-302, MCA (careless driving). We simply hold that Montanans cannot be charged, prosecuted, and punished for speed alone without notifying them of the speed at which their conduct violates the law. ***

Chief Justice J.A. TURNAGE dissenting. ***

¶ 34 This important statutory provision of our motor vehicle traffic regulations has been the law of Montana since it was enacted by the legislature in 1955 as Section 41, Chapter 263, 1955 Session Laws of Montana. This important traffic regulation has remained unchanged as the law of Montana (with the exception of a minor gender change by the legislature in 1995) since that time.

¶ 35 Appellant Rudy Stanko challenged this statute as being unconstitutional in 1998 because of vagueness. Apparently for the past forty-three years, other citizens driving upon our highways had no problem in understanding this statutory provision.

¶ 36 Section 61-8-303(1), MCA, is not vague and most particularly is not unconstitutional as a denial of due process. Therefore, I dissent.

Justice JIM REGNIER dissenting. ***

¶ 40 In my view, Stanko's speed on the roadway where he was arrested clearly falls within the behavior proscribed by the statute. Operating a vehicle at 85 miles per hour on a two-lane highway with frost heaves, steep hills, and curves, where farm vehicles may unexpectedly appear, is not reasonable and proper under the conditions. Therefore, I conclude that Stanko has no standing to attack the facial validity of this statute.

Justice KARLA M. GRAY joins in the foregoing dissenting opinion.

In the Matter of the Mental Health of K.G.F.

306 Mont. 1 (2001)

Justice JAMES C. NELSON delivered the Opinion of the Court.

*** ¶ 3 K.G.F. raises the following issue:

Did her counsel render ineffective assistance of counsel in violation of her rights guaranteed under the Sixth Amendment to the United States Constitution and Article II, Section 24, of the Montana Constitution?

Factual and Procedural Background

¶ 4 It is undisputed that the condition of K.G.F.'s mental health [severe bipolar disorder] in October of 1999, reached a critical point that led her to voluntarily seek treatment at St. Peter's Community Hospital in Helena, Montana. She was admitted into the hospital on October 21, 1999. ***

¶ 8 On October 26, 1999, a deputy county attorney filed a petition with the District Court "alleging mental disorder that requires commitment." The petition relied on the findings and request made by a case coordinator, Nancy McVean, at St. Peter's who was also a certified "professional person" under § 53-21-106, MCA. The primary focus and concern was that K.G.F. planned to commit suicide, and that once released from the hospital she would implement her plan. The petition also reported that K.G.F. was indigent and therefore unable to afford an attorney, and that she was "presently detained" at the hospital. The petition requested that K.G.F. be held at the hospital for further evaluation and treatment until a commitment hearing took place.

¶ 9 That same day, the District Court issued an order finding probable cause that K.G.F. had a mental disorder requiring commitment. Counsel was appointed pursuant to this order. An initial appearance took place later that same day some time in the afternoon, according to a court reporter minute entry. At that time, with counsel present, K.G.F.'s constitutional rights were explained to her as well as the substantive effects of the petition. A hearing was set for the next morning, on October 27, 1999, at 11:30 a.m.

¶ 10 Two medical professionals were called to testify at the hearing the next day, one by the State and one by counsel for K.G.F. Both experts had interviewed K.G.F. and reviewed her records. K.G.F. was also called to testify. Although present at the hearing, K.G.F.'s husband was not called to testify.

¶ 11 McVean, the case coordinator who had requested the petition and who in turn served as a "professional person" as required by law, recommended that based on her interview with K.G.F., K.G.F. should be committed to a community facility, as opposed to the State Hospital at Warm Springs.

¶ 12 Nancy Adams, who had spent approximately one hour with K.G.F. the day before, recommended that K.G.F. remain in the hospital for a few days, so that a community-based treatment plan in Bozeman—nearer to where K.G.F. lived—could be arranged. She testified that "being pulled away from her closest support, her husband, and staying in a strange place might do more harm than good."

¶ 13 K.G.F. was called to testify on her own behalf. She agreed that the Bozeman option would be best for her, and explained that she had private financial and insurance resources to cover the expenses. She further testified that "my husband is there and he is with me every night and every morning." She indicated that she would voluntarily remain at the St. Peter's facility until such arrangements could be worked out. ***

¶ 15 The court . . . ordered that she be committed to Golden Triangle Mental Health, in Helena, for a period of 90 days for "care, treatment and evaluation of the respondent's mental health needs. . . ."

Discussion

*** Did K.G.F.'s counsel render ineffective assistance of counsel in violation of her rights guaranteed under the Sixth Amendment to the United States Constitution and Article II, Section 24, of the Montana Constitution? ***

¶ 25 This Court has not previously addressed whether a person subjected to an involuntary commitment proceeding has a constitutional right to effective assistance of counsel, and, if so, how such effectiveness should be measured.

A. The right to effective assistance of counsel

¶ 26 Involuntary civil commitments in Montana are governed by Title 53, Chapter 21, MCA (codified in 1975). Our initial review of this matter is guided by § 53-21-101(4), MCA, which expressly provides that one purpose of our laws governing the treatment of "seriously mentally ill" persons is to "ensure that due process of law is accorded any person coming under the provisions of this part." Further, under § 53-21-115, MCA, a person who is involuntarily detained or against whom a commitment petition is filed is expressly afforded numerous due process rights including the right to be represented by counsel.

¶ 27 In turn, the foregoing statutory rights explicitly and implicitly garner protection under both the federal and the Montana constitutions. We disagree with

K.G.F., however, that the protection of those rights flows from the express constitutional provisions addressing persons subject to criminal prosecution. ***

¶ 31 Therefore, we hold that the right to counsel, as provided under our Title 53, Chapter 21 statutes, provides an individual subject to an involuntary commitment proceeding the right to effective assistance of counsel. In turn, this right affords the individual with the right to raise the allegation of ineffective assistance of counsel in challenging a commitment order.

¶ 32 The fundamental question that must be resolved, as addressed by the parties and Amicus, is how effective counsel must be when representing an individual who is facing an involuntary commitment.

B. The *Strickland* standard is an inappropriate threshold

¶ 33 Although in numerous respects the procedural due process rights of an involuntary commitment patient-respondent are identical to those afforded an accused criminal defendant, we disagree with K.G.F. that the application of the *Strickland* [*v. Washington* (1984)] standard is appropriate in involuntary civil commitment proceedings. We conclude that the standard under *Strickland* [which requires showings of both deficient performance by counsel and resulting prejudice to the defendant] simply does not go far enough to protect the liberty interests of individuals such as K.G.F., who may or may not have broken any law, but who, upon the expiration of a 90-day commitment, must indefinitely bear the badge of inferiority of a once "involuntarily committed" person with a proven mental disorder. ***

¶ 40 Thus, we turn as suggested by the State and Amicus, to the due process clause of the Montana Constitution.

C. Due process and fundamental rights

¶ 41 Under Article II, Section 17, the Montana Constitution provides that "No person shall be deprived of life, liberty, or property without due process of law."

¶ 42 As a starting point, it is safe to say that in purportedly protecting the due process rights of an individual subject to an involuntary commitment proceeding—whereby counsel typically has less than 24 hours to prepare for a hearing on a State petition that seeks to sever or infringe upon the individual's relations with family, friends, physicians, and employment for three months or longer—our legal system of judges, lawyers, and clinicians has seemingly lost its way in vigilantly protecting the fundamental rights of such individuals.

¶ 43 In the case sub judice, for example, the public defender appointed to represent K.G.F. had, from the close of the initial appearance to the commencement of the commitment hearing, at best four or five working hours—amidst his usual case load of criminal matters—to prepare for what can only be described as a perfunctory process that lasted minutes.

¶ 44 Our Legislature has, however, expressly provided that an individual who may be suffering from a mental disorder and who, as a result, may be involuntarily committed must be afforded care and treatment that fully respects that person's "dignity and personal integrity." See § 53-21-101(1), MCA. Once admitted to a mental health facility, whether voluntarily or involuntarily, a patient has the right to "privacy and dignity," under § 53-21-142(1), MCA. These legislative mandates, in turn, invoke fundamental rights under our state constitution.

¶ 45 Respect for a person's dignity invokes Article II, Section 4, under this state's constitution, which provides that "dignity of the human being is inviolable." See *Armstrong v. State*, 1999 MT 261 (stating that "[r]espect for the dignity of each individual—a fundamental right, protected by Article II, Section 4 of the Montana Constitution—demands that people have for themselves the moral right and moral responsibility to confront the most fundamental questions about the meaning and value of their own lives and the intrinsic value of life in general, answering to their own consciences and convictions"). ***

¶ 47 In *Armstrong*, this Court identified an individual's medical decisions affecting "bodily integrity" as a fundamental right under the personal autonomy component of the constitutional right to privacy set out in Article II, Section 10, of the Montana Constitution. See *Armstrong*, ¶ 39. Respect for a patient-respondent's medical-decision personal autonomy has likewise been expressed by our Legislature under § 53-21-115(11) and (12), MCA, which provide that a person has the right to either refuse or voluntarily take medications prior to any hearing, and the right to be examined by a professional person of the respondent's choice, under §§ 53-21-115(9) and 53-21-124(3), MCA.

¶ 48 That these fundamental constitutional rights are at issue during all phases of the involuntary commitment process, including prior to a hearing when counsel is either appointed or obtained, is self evident. Thus, we agree that the "[q]uality counsel provides the most likely way—perhaps the only likely way" to ensure the due process protection of dignity and privacy interests in cases such as the one at bar. ***

D. Individual liberty and the *parens patriae* doctrine

¶ 51 In articulating a standard for effective counsel, it is necessary to recognize and dispel certain stereotypes that serve only to frustrate the legal process that purports to secure the skillful and humane care and treatment of individuals suffering from mental disorders. ***

¶ 63 We must recognize, after all, that an involuntary commitment is supposed to help, not punish, the person who "may be suffering from a mental disorder." See § 53-21-101, MCA. As discussed by numerous scholars, the legislated involuntary commitment process must, as a matter of public policy, strive to maintain the "therapeutic influence" of the legal system on the individual. However, as argued by Amicus, rather than helping the individual afflicted with a mental disorder, the legal system's paternalistic influence too often turns such individuals away from seeking treatment due to the imminent fear of involuntary commitment.

¶ 64 Thus, with the foregoing in mind, it is imperative that we construct a constitutionally sound framework detailing the deliberate steps counsel should take to effectively protect his or her client's best interests — in particular the liberty interests addressed herein — and ensure that the client receives a formal and fair adversarial hearing at which the State bears the burden of proof. See § 53-21-126(2), MCA.

¶ 65 Further, it is incumbent upon courts to meaningfully respect and facilitate the exercise of the following requisite standards, in fully discharging the responsibility of safeguarding the due process rights of individuals "at every stage of the proceedings." Thus, it is imperative in applying the following standards to the matter at bar, and all subsequent cases, that the constitutional and legislated rights discussed herein are formally and fairly balanced with the State's ultimate power to protect both the individual and the public from actual or perceived harm.

E. The role of effective counsel in involuntary civil commitment proceedings

¶ 66 As acknowledged by all parties concerned here, our statutory guidelines under Title 53, Chapter 21, offer little assistance in determining the requisite scope of duties of effective counsel in involuntary commitment proceedings. Nevertheless, the Legislature has provided clear procedural opportunities for counsel to pursue an adversarial role in such proceedings that adequately serve as a framework for our due process analysis.

¶ 67 Once counsel is appointed, pursuant to § 53-21-122, MCA, counsel "shall meet with the respondent, explain the substance of the petition, and explain the probable course of the proceedings." Ordinarily, the commitment hearing must take place within five days of a respondent's initial appearance. Under this statute, however, counsel may request additional time.

¶ 68 Under § 53-21-124(1), MCA, the court may not order detention of a respondent pending the hearing on the petition unless requested by the county attorney and upon the existence of probable cause for detention. At that time, counsel for the patient-respondent may request a detention hearing, which "must be held forthwith." Further, under § 53-21-124(3), MCA, counsel for the patient-respondent may also object to the continued evaluation and treatment by a professional person selected by the patient-respondent pending the hearing.

¶ 69 Under § 53-21-125, MCA, a patient's counsel may in lieu of a hearing request a jury trial, "whereupon the time set for hearing shall be vacated and the matter set on the court's jury calendar at the earliest date possible, the matter taking precedence over all other matters." Upon a finding that a patient-respondent requires commitment, a court must hold a post-trial "disposition" hearing, pursuant to § 53-21-127(2), MCA. Apparently, in the case at bar, this second mandatory hearing was simply combined with the hearing on the petition, pursuant to § 53-21-126, MCA.

¶ 70 In order to further enhance the due process protections under the foregoing statutory mandates, as Amicus suggests, we adopt certain portions of the National Center for State Courts' Guidelines for Involuntary Civil Commitment. Thus, the following critical areas shall serve to better define the scope of effective representation in involuntary commitment proceedings, under Article II, Section 17, of the Montana Constitution.

[The court then adopts several of the Guidelines verbatim as requirements of due process, including: the training of appointed counsel; an attempt to interview all persons who have knowledge of the circumstances surrounding the commitment petition; a prehearing client interview; the assistance of counsel along with the (statutory) right to remain silent at any court-ordered examination; and vigorous argument for the patient-client under a presumption against involuntary commitment, such that "evidence that counsel independently advocated or otherwise acquiesced to an involuntary commitment — in the absence of any evidence of a voluntary and knowing consent by the patient-respondent — will establish the presumption that counsel was ineffective."]

F. Conclusion

¶ 90 In summary, we hold that the right to counsel, as provided under Title 53, Chapter 21, provides an individual subject to an involuntary commitment proceeding the right to effective assistance of counsel. This right affords the individual with the right to raise the allegation of ineffective assistance of counsel in challenging a commitment order.

¶ 91 We further hold that the foregoing five critical areas of representation define, generally but not exclusively, the scope of effective counsel pursuant to Article II, Section 17, of the Montana Constitution. In turn, the due process afforded individuals under the foregoing standards must serve to protect the fundamental individual liberty interests of dignity and integrity as identified under Title 53, Chapter 21, and Article II, Sections 4 and 10, of the Montana Constitution. We hold that upon a substantial showing of evidence, presented to the issuing district court, or this Court, pursuant to § 53-21-131, MCA, that counsel did not effectively represent the patient-respondent's interests pursuant to the foregoing standards, an order of involuntary commitment should be vacated.

¶ 92 In so holding here today, we again emphasize that it is not only counsel for the patient-respondent, but also courts, that are charged with the duty of safeguarding the due process rights of individuals involved at every stage of the proceedings, and must therefore rigorously adhere to the standards expressed herein, as well as those mandated under Title 53, Chapter 21.

¶ 93 Finally, the record before this Court, particularly any evidence of the critical pre-hearing investigation, is insufficient. Accordingly, this matter is reversed and remanded for a fact finding hearing and further proceedings consistent with this opinion.

Justice TERRY N. TRIEWEILER dissents.

¶ 99 *** My problem with the majority opinion is that I can find no evidence in the record that K.G.F.'s counsel was ineffective. There is no indication in the pleadings, transcript, nor briefs filed on appeal that any of the procedural rights statutorily afforded to K.G.F. were denied based on ineffective assistance of counsel. Furthermore, it is clear from the transcript of the hearing that the State was held to its burden of proving that K.G.F. suffered from a mental disorder which threatened her own well being. ***

¶ 107 Counsel had an obligation to serve his client effectively, however, effective representation cannot change reality. In a civil commitment proceeding, if there is no question about a person's mental disorder and no question about the fact that that person presents a danger to herself, then counsel is left to argue for the least restrictive form of commitment. That is exactly what K.G.F.'s counsel did. ***

¶ 110 My concern is this. Having adopted the five-part criteria for evaluating effective assistance of counsel, does this now mean that following every civil commitment proceeding, a separate hearing will be required to determine the extent of counsel's experience in civil commitment proceedings, the nature and extent of his initial investigation, and the detail provided during his client interview? None of these facts will be apparent from the record and in this record there is nothing to indicate that any of these responsibilities were performed inadequately. How then is this case to be distinguished from any civil commitment appealed in the future?

¶ 111 While I agree with the general principles established in the majority opinion and applaud the majority's efforts to guarantee consistently capable representation for those people subject to civil and voluntary commitment proceedings, I am concerned about some of the practical effects of the majority opinion and particularly disagree that there is any basis for reversing and remanding the District Court's order in this case. After thoroughly reviewing the record, I can find no evidence that the attorney who represented K.G.F. acted ineffectively or that K.G.F. was denied any of the procedural rights to which she is entitled pursuant to Article II, § 17 of the Montana Constitution and Title 53, Chapter 21, Part 1, of the Montana Code. Therefore, I dissent from the majority's decision to reverse the order of the District Court and remand to the District Court for further proceedings.

Notes on Procedural Due Process

1. In *Stanko*, the challenge to the "basic rule" is a "facial" challenge to the law in all of its applications (to his and everyone else's potential conduct subject to the law). A successful "facial" challenge invalidates the law completely. Stanko also brought an "as-applied" challenge to the reckless driving statute in a separate case decided the day after the case above (on December 24). *See State v. Stanko*, 292 Mont. 214 (1998):

> ¶ 45 . . . Stanko imagines himself to be a "champion race-car driver" because he won a few stock-car races in Oregon almost twenty years ago. He testified that he was consciously driving 117 mph and 121 mph at the times he was cited, but that this conduct was not reckless because he is

accustomed to driving at high speeds. While Stanko's driving abilities may be legend in his own mind, we are not impressed. Unfortunately, Stanko fails to realize that racing conditions are far different from highway conditions and that Montana highways are not controlled racetracks. While Stanko may be willing to risk his own life and property traveling the highways at grossly excessive speeds as though he is still on a racetrack, other motorists do not assume the risk of driving in racetrack conditions when they travel Montana's highways. In point of fact, Montana's highways are used by senior citizens, parents hauling small children, farmers and ranchers moving machinery, school buses, commercial vehicles, and bicyclists, all of whom typically drive at less than "racetrack" speeds. Other motorists, as well, in driving and in overtaking and passing vehicles rightfully expect that following and oncoming traffic will be moving at a reasonably prudent and safe speed. Few would gauge their driving in anticipation that coming over the crest of the next hill will be a car traveling at well over 100 mph being driven by one who believes that he is on the Autobahn. Moreover, even if Stanko were to only injure or kill himself in a high-speed crash, his conduct still would be responsible for putting on the highway and at risk the emergency personnel and vehicles that would most surely have to respond. Furthermore, any person who drives in this State is aware that wild and domestic animals frequently cross Montana's roads and highways. It is common experience that trying to avoid wildlife or livestock on a road, without crashing, is difficult enough while driving at a reasonable and prudent highway speed; it is nearly impossible while driving at speeds well over 100 mph.

¶ 46 In short, it is clear that, under the conditions at issue here, Stanko unquestionably operated his vehicle "in willful or wanton disregard for the safety of persons or property." Section 61-8-301, MCA. Accordingly, we hold that the District Court was correct in denying Stanko's Motion to Dismiss for Failure to Establish the Necessary Elements of the reckless driving offenses with which he was charged. *** Accordingly, we hold that § 61-8-301, MCA, is not unconstitutionally vague as applied to the facts in this case.

Is the Court's "void for vagueness" doctrine clear? Would the Court have upheld Stanko's conviction under the basic rule if he were driving 117 mph instead of 85? If so, would that undermine the facial challenge to the basic rule? The prevailing speed on many Montana (and other American) highways is often five to ten miles-per-hour above the posted speed limit, which is only sometimes enforced within that range. Although the speed limit is clear on its face, should this raise similar vagueness problems?

2. Does the Court's interpretation of due process in *Stanko* march in lock-step with federal due process law? Should it? Chief Justice Turnage's dissent may seem

to rely only on common sense, but is there a reason laws that might comport with due process in some jurisdictions might not comport with due process in others? In other words, in a given context (like driving), is what is "reasonable" or "arbitrary" to a Montanan the same to a Californian or New Yorker?

3. In *K.G.F.*, neither the Montana Constitution nor the Montana Legislature had adopted the National Center for State Courts' Guidelines for Involuntary Civil Commitment. Why should the Court find these detailed guidelines in the general guarantee of due process of law? What role do the rights of privacy and dignity play in the Court's analysis?

4. The Court in *K.G.F.* notes that the Legislature provides detailed procedural protections for civil commitment by statute. It then proceeds to use these statutes' invocation of constitutional standards to elaborate its own requirements as a matter of due process. Could the Legislature repeal these statutory requirements and would it change the result in a future constitutional claim? Is a future Legislature more or less likely to detail procedural protections after a decision like *K.G.F.*?

5. The Court unanimously overruled the Guidelines approach in *K.G.F.* in *Matter of JS*, 2017 MT 214:

> We affirm *K.G.F.* to the extent it recognized a statutory right to effective assistance of counsel and a right to counsel premised upon the federal Due Process Clause and Montana's right of due process contained in Article II, Section 17. We also affirm the conclusion reached in *K.G.F.* that a respondent in a civil commitment proceeding does not have a Sixth Amendment right to counsel. We clarify *K.G.F.* by holding that, while our civil commitment statutes and jurisprudence are rooted in the right to dignity (Article II, Section 4) and right of privacy (Article II, Section 10), the effectiveness of counsel in protecting the guarantee of a fair trial is based on principles of due process. We overrule *K.G.F.* to the extent that it requires a formalistic approach to measure counsel's effectiveness; that "critical areas" of representation must be assessed in measuring counsel's performance; and that it repudiates application of *Strickland* in civil commitment proceedings. The standards and principles enunciated in *Strickland* for measuring the effectiveness of counsel are henceforth to be applied in civil commitment proceedings. Finally, we conclude the statutory rights embedded in Title 53, chapter 21, MCA, inform the inquiry of whether a respondent has received the effective assistance of counsel, although the enumerated statutory safeguards are not exclusive and circumstances of a particular case may dictate other considerations.

Why, do you think? Is the demanding federal *Strickland* test for ineffective assistance of counsel in criminal proceedings faithful to due process under the Montana Constitution in civil commitment proceedings?

2. "Substantive" Due Process

State v. Egdorf

2003 MT 264

[In the portion of *Egdorf* reproduced in Chapter 10, the Montana Supreme Court held the 3-year statute of limitations for misdemeanor violations of fish and game laws did not violate the Article II, section 4 equal protection clause.]

Justice JIM RICE delivered the Opinion of the Court. ***

B. Substantive Due Process

¶ 19 Both the Fourteenth Amendment to the United States Constitution and Article II, section 17 of the Montana Constitution provide that no person shall be deprived of life, liberty, or property without due process of law. The guarantee of due process has both a procedural and a substantive component. The process requirement necessary to satisfy procedural due process comes into play only after a showing that a property or liberty interest exists. Substantive due process bars arbitrary governmental actions regardless of the procedures used to implement them and serves as a check on oppressive governmental action.

> The theory underlying substantive due process reaffirms the fundamental concept that the due process clause contains a substantive component which bars arbitrary governmental actions regardless of the procedures used to implement them, and serves as a check on oppressive governmental action.... Substantive due process primarily examines underlying substantive rights and remedies to determine whether restrictions are unreasonable or arbitrary when balanced against the purpose of the legislature in enacting the statute.

Newville v. State, Dept. of Family Services (Mont. 1994).

¶ 20 In this case, Egdorf argues that § 45-1-205(5) and (6), MCA, violates substantive due process by needlessly extending the statute of limitations for prosecutions of misdemeanor fish and game offenses to three years. He asserts that the legislative purpose behind § 45-1-205(5) and (6), MCA — to facilitate the prosecution of misdemeanor violations by out-of-state offenders or those which are not readily apparent within the first year of the violation or require extensive investigation — can be accomplished within the general one-year time frame. Egdorf notes, for instance, that the law tolls the time period for commencing prosecutions against offenders when the offender is beyond the State's jurisdiction. Section 45-1-206(1), MCA. In cases of more serious offenses, requiring a longer period of investigation, Egdorf contends that the offenses may be treated as felonies, thus invoking a longer statute of limitations. Egdorf concludes that the expanded period for commencing prosecutions of misdemeanor fish and game violations is arbitrary and unsupported by a rational legislative objective and therefore violates substantive due process.

¶ 21 In *Raisler v. Burlington N. Ry. Co.* (Mont. 1985), this Court set forth the following analysis for evaluating a substantive due process claim:

> A substantive due process analysis requires a test of reasonableness of a statute in relation to the State's power to enact such legislation. "The essence of substantive due process is that the State cannot use its police power to take unreasonable, arbitrary or capricious action against an individual." . . . In order to satisfy substantive due process guarantees, a statute enacted under a state's police power must be reasonably related to a permissible legislative objective.

Accordingly, we turn to the legislative history of § 45-1-205(5) and (6), MCA, to determine whether the extended statute of limitations for commencing prosecution of misdemeanor fish and game offenses is reasonably related to a permissive legislative goal.

¶ 22 Historically, misdemeanor fish and game offenses were prosecuted under a one-year statute of limitations. In 1991, the Legislature amended § 45-1-205, MCA, providing a three-year statute of limitations for misdemeanor fish and game violations under Title 87. Testimony presented to the Senate Fish and Game Committee identified the special circumstances surrounding prosecution of fish and game offenses. According to Bob Lane of the Department of Fish, Wildlife & Parks:

> These violations, by the nature of hunting and fishing, are not always readily discoverable, undercover operations frequently must span more than one hunting or fishing season, and many suspected violators are from out-of-state. All of these factors make it difficult, and sometimes impossible, to complete investigations and bring charges within a one year period of time.

¶ 23 Additionally, K.L. Cool, Director of the Department of Fish, Wildlife & Parks, testified before the Senate committee that 'many times investigations into serious wildlife violations take longer than a year to discover or complete and prosecution is not possible within the current one-year limitations. This is compounded by the fact that many sportsmen and sportswomen are from out-of-state."

¶ 24 In 1993, with the urging of the Montana Outfitters and Guides Association, the Legislature again amended § 45-1-205, MCA, similarly providing a three-year statute of limitations for commencing prosecution of misdemeanor fish and game offenses under Title 37, chapter 47, which specifically applies to the activities of outfitters. According to the testimony presented by the Montana Outfitters and Guides Association to the House Fish and Game Committee, the one-year statute of limitations was often inadequate because of the nature of the activities giving rise to the offense. The outfitters explained:

> Often it is necessary to extend an investigation well over a year because of additional violations which may also be more severe in nature, such as felony game violations tied to the Lacey Act. The nature of these violations may cause the investigation to be extended to account for all the illegal activities. It was this same logic that enabled the Dept. of Fish, Wildlife and

Parks to extend their statute of limitations to three years. Game violations are often tied to illegal outfitting activities.

¶ 25 In this case, Egdorf's act of assisting a client in the unlawful taking and possessing of a mule deer, in violation of Title 87 and Title 37, chapter 47, is precisely the type of offense contemplated by the outfitters and the Department of Fish, Wildlife & Parks, in extending the statute of limitations for misdemeanor fish and game offenses. As revealed by the legislative history, these offenses are not always readily discoverable and often times require more than one year to complete investigation. Compounding this problem is the fact that frequently the perpetrators reside out-of-state. Further, undercover operations necessary to identify violations may span over the course of several hunting seasons.

¶ 26 The United States Supreme Court has recognized that "[t]he protection and preservation of the state's wildlife is peculiarly within its police power and the state has great latitude in determining by what means are appropriate for protecting wildlife." *Baldwin v. Fish and Game Commission of Montana* (1978). Numerous Montana cases have additionally recognized the State's power to protect public wildlife resources through regulations designed for that purpose.

¶ 27 We conclude, therefore, that the State has a legitimate governmental interest in preserving its wildlife. Extending the period prescribed for prosecuting misdemeanor violations of fish and game laws to three years is a reasonable exercise of the State's legitimate police power. The statute of limitations set forth in § 45-1-205(5) and (6), MCA, is reasonably related to a permissive legislative purpose and, accordingly, does not violate principles of substantive due process. Consequently, the District Court did not err in denying Egdorf's motion to dismiss.

Notes on Substantive Due Process

1. Would Egdorf have a better chance under Article II, section 3 "inalienable rights" or Article V, section 12 "special legislation"? In light of these specific provisions (as well as the Article II, section 10 guarantee of individual privacy), is there any additional work for substantive due process to do in Montana constitutional law?

2. Is there any difference between the rational basis test for equal protection and the similar test the *Egdorf* Court applies for substantive due process? Consider United States Supreme Court Justice Robert H. Jackson's concurrence in *Railway Express Agency v. New York* (1949):

> Invalidation of a statute or an ordinance on due process grounds leaves ungoverned and ungovernable conduct which many people find objectionable. Invocation of the equal protection clause, on the other hand, does not disable any governmental body from dealing with the subject at hand. It merely means that the prohibition or regulation must have a broader impact.... [T]here is no more effective practical guaranty against arbitrary and unreasonable government than to require that the principles of law which officials would impose upon a minority must be imposed generally.

3. The incorporation of most of the Bill of Rights against the states under the Fourteenth Amendment's Due Process Clause requires state courts to protect federal constitutional rights against state action in the same way federal courts would protect the same rights against federal action. The second Justice Harlan opposed this "jot-for-jot incorporation" in favor of a "fundamental rights" approach more akin to general substantive due process doctrine. As he concurred in *Pointer v. Texas* (1965):

> I agree that in the circumstances the admission of the statement in question deprived the petitioner of a right of "confrontation" assured by the Fourteenth Amendment. I cannot subscribe, however, to the constitutional reasoning of the Court.
>
> The Court holds that the right of confrontation guaranteed by the Sixth Amendment in federal criminal trials is carried into state criminal cases by the Fourteenth Amendment. This is another step in the onward march of the long-since discredited "incorporation" doctrine, which for some reason that I have not yet been able to fathom has come into the sunlight in recent years. *See, e.g., Mapp v. Ohio* (1961).
>
> For me this state judgment must be reversed because a right of confrontation is "implicit in the concept of ordered liberty," *Palko v. Connecticut* (1937), reflected in the Due Process Clause of the Fourteenth Amendment independently of the Sixth.
>
> While either of these constitutional approaches brings one to the same end result in this particular case, there is a basic difference between the two in the kind of future constitutional development they portend. The concept of Fourteenth Amendment due process embodied in *Palko* and a host of other thoughtful past decisions now rapidly falling into discard, recognizes that our Constitution tolerates, indeed encourages, differences between the methods used to effectuate legitimate federal and state concerns, subject to the requirements of fundamental fairness "implicit in the concept of ordered liberty." The philosophy of "incorporation," on the other hand, subordinates all such state differences to the particular requirements of the Federal Bill of Rights and increasingly subjects state legal processes to enveloping federal judicial authority. "Selective" incorporation or "absorption" amounts to little more than a diluted form of the full incorporation theory. Whereas it rejects full incorporation because of recognition that not all of the guarantees of the Bill of Rights should be deemed "fundamental," it at the same time ignores the possibility that not all phases of any given guaranty described in the Bill of Rights are necessarily fundamental.
>
> It is too often forgotten in these times that the American federal system is itself constitutionally ordained, that it embodies values profoundly making for lasting liberties in this country, and that its legitimate requirements demand continuing solid recognition in all phases of the work of this

> Court. The "incorporation" doctrines, whether full blown or selective, are both historically and constitutionally unsound and incompatible with the maintenance of our federal system on even course.

Should Harlan's reasoning at least support a distinctive reading of a *state* Due Process Clause?

4. Abortion rights are the most controversial application of substantive due process doctrine, though under *Armstrong v. State* (Chapter 11), abortion rights in Montana are protected under the individual right of privacy. In many states, opponents of abortion rights have sought "personhood amendments" to their state due process clauses. The 2021 Montana Legislature considered the following "personhood amendment":

> **Section 17. Due process of law.** (1) No person shall be deprived of life, liberty, or property without due process of law.
>
> (2) As used in this section, the word "person" applies to all members of mankind at any stage of development, beginning at the stage of fertilization or conception, regardless of age, health, level of functioning, or condition of dependency.
>
> (3) No cause of action may arise as a consequence of harm caused to an unborn baby by an unintentional act of its mother.
>
> (4) The legislature shall implement this section by appropriate legislation.

The proposal fell five votes short of the two-thirds legislative majority needed to ballot a constitutional amendment. If it were ratified, what result?

5. In *Dorwart v. Caraway* (Chapter 2), Justice Nelson specially concurred on the issue of unenumerated rights under Article II, section 34. While noting the provision had not been applied, he referenced the Bill of Rights Committee's report, which deemed the provision "a crucial part of any effort to revitalize the state government's approach to civil liberties questions," and "may be the source of innovative judicial activity in the civil liberties field." Yet the section itself was not an innovation. As the voter information pamphlet explained, it is "[i]dentical to the 1889 Constitution." In light of the undeveloped doctrine of substantive due process, and the extensively enumerated Declaration of Rights, what might "enumerated rights" mean in the Montana Constitution, and how might courts apply them, if at all?

B. Other Rights in the Montana Constitution

Recall the map of rights charted by the Montana Supreme Court and summarized in the equal protection analysis of *Snetsinger v. Montana University System* (Chapter 10):

> We apply one of three levels of scrutiny when addressing a challenge under the Montana Constitution's Equal Protection Clause: strict scrutiny, middle-tier scrutiny, or the rational basis test. Strict scrutiny applies if a suspect class or fundamental right is affected. *** We apply middle-tier scrutiny if the law or policy affects a right conferred by the Montana Constitution, but is not found in the Constitution's Declaration of Rights. The rational basis test is appropriate when neither strict scrutiny nor middle-tier scrutiny apply. Under the rational basis test, the law or policy must be rationally related to a legitimate government interest.

Although these tiers are framed by the Equal Protection Clause, they recognize the Montana Constitution confers rights in at least two places: the Declaration of Rights (perhaps with the addition of other "fundamental" unenumerated rights) and elsewhere in the document. They also suggest a priority of rights by the overlay of strict scrutiny on Article II rights and of middle-tier (something like intermediate) scrutiny on other rights "conferred by the Montana Constitution." The section 10 right of individual privacy, after all, is the only constitutional right that expressly calls for some form of conventional scrutiny analysis in its instruction that it "shall not be infringed without the showing of a compelling state interest." Consider how this tiered structure shapes the interpretation of enumerated rights throughout the Montana Constitution, and whether such a scrutiny-based equal protection analysis is appropriate for all of the rights we might find there, including the provisions briefly noted below. More generally, consider how a lawyer equipped with the interpretive tools applied in the book to this point might breathe distinctly Montanan meanings into these sometimes neglected constitutional rights.

1. The Declaration of Rights

The first two sections of the Declaration of Rights, popular sovereignty and self-government (Chapter 2), and arguably the third section inalienable rights (Chapter 9), set the stage for the other rights by expressing the purpose of government as "instituted solely for the good of the whole," subject to the people's "exclusive right of governing themselves," in order to secure the enjoyment of "certain inalienable rights." The next eight rights of individual dignity (equality and anti-discrimination); freedom of religion; freedom of assembly; freedom of speech, expression, and press; right of participation; right to know; and right of privacy round out the major rights in the Declaration. The associated privacy protection against unreasonable searches and seizures follows in section 11. Suffrage, open courts, due process, sovereign immunity, and unenumerated provisions are addressed above and elsewhere in this book. The majority of remaining rights are the criminal justice provisions, most with analogues in the United States Constitution, which run from section 19 through section 28. Two other provisions with federal analogues concern private property (section 29) and contract (section 31) rights. Several "military" provisions address the right to bear arms (section 12), "importation of armed persons" (section 33), civilian control of the military (section 32), and veteran preferences (section 35). Two more novel rights round out the Declaration: adult rights (section 14) and rights of persons not adults (section 15), which is also the latest to be amended. Consider the approaches taken by the majority and dissenting opinions in the following case, and how they might inform the development of less familiar constitutional rights.

Buhmann v. State

2008 MT 465

Justice PATRICIA O. COTTER delivered the Opinion of the Court.

¶ 1 Bruce and Shirley Buhmann (Buhmanns), owners and operators of the Circle Eagle Game Farm, and Len and Pamela Wallace (Wallaces), owners and operators of the Big Velvet Ranch, appeal an order of the First Judicial District Court which denied their takings claims under the Fifth Amendment to the U.S. Constitution and Article II, Section 29 of the Montana Constitution. These claims alleged that the enactment and enforcement of initiative measure no. 143 (I-143), which was approved by the citizens of Montana on November 7, 2000, constituted a taking of their private property and that they were entitled to just compensation for this taking. For the reasons set forth below, we affirm the District Court. [In a companion case, *Kafka v. Mont. Dept. of Fish Wildlife & Parks* (Mont. 2008), the Court rejected a federal Fifth Amendment regulatory taking challenge to I-143.]

Factual and Procedural Background ***

¶ 3 The appellants in this case were owners and operators of alternative livestock game farms (Game Farms) within the state of Montana. The Game Farm industry is premised on the notion that individuals are willing to pay significant amounts of money to shoot captive animals, primarily elk, within the confines of a Game Farm. Since 1917, it has been lawful for individuals to own alternative livestock, such as elk, and keep them in captivity. Game Farms are heavily regulated by the Montana Department of Fish, Wildlife, and Parks (FWP) because of the threat posed by chronic wasting disease (CWD), a fatal disease of the central nervous system of captive and free-ranging animals such as mule deer, white-tailed deer, and Rocky Mountain elk. To operate a Game Farm, the owner/operator must possess an alternative Game Farm license and comply with the rigorous and extensive licensing requirements set forth in Title 87, chapter 4, part 4, MCA.

¶ 4 On November 7, 2000, the voters of Montana passed I-143, which made two significant changes to the regulation of Game Farms in Montana. First, it prohibited fee-shooting on Game Farms in Montana. Second, I-143 prohibited licensees from transferring their alternative livestock licenses to others. These changes had a significant impact on the Game Farm industry in Montana because the vitality of the Game Farm industry was premised upon the profits derived from fee-shooting. The ban on the transfer of licenses was significant because it essentially prohibited Game Farm owners from selling those Game Farms to others, since a Game Farm could not operate without a valid license. I-143 did not, however, eliminate all uses of alternative livestock as it still permitted Game Farm operators to own herds, harvest the animals for their meat or antlers, or sell them in out-of-state markets where fee-shooting was legal. ***

¶ 61 . . . Appellants . . . assert that Article II, Section 29 of the Montana Constitution provides greater protection than the Fifth Amendment, thus requiring a different analysis. This provision reads as follows:

> **Eminent domain.** Private property shall not be taken or damaged for public use without just compensation to the full extent of the loss having been first made to or paid into court for the owner. In the event of litigation, just compensation shall include necessary expenses of litigation to be awarded by the court when the private property owner prevails.

Mont. Const., Art. II, § 29.

¶ 63 [W]e have generally looked to federal case law for guidance when considering takings claims brought under Article II, Section 29—a practice that is consistent with that of other states with similar or identical language in their state constitutions. Appellants and the Dissent have seized upon the "damaging" language in Article II, Section 29 to argue for a sweeping new interpretation of this provision.

¶ 64 It is important to bear in mind that Article II, Section 29 protects against a "taking" and "damaging" of private property. We take this occasion to reaffirm . . . that the protection against a "taking" of private property under Article II, Section 29 is coextensive with the protection given under the Fifth Amendment. In other words, a takings analysis based on federal law under *Penn Central* [*Trans. Co. v. New York City* (1978)] or *Lucas* [*v. South Carolina Coastal Council* (1992)] is to be applied to takings claims whether brought under the U.S. or Montana Constitutions. This practice is in accord with the overwhelming majority of states that have similar or identical language in their state constitutions. ***

¶ 67 It thus appears that the "or damaged" language of the provision has been interpreted to apply to eminent domain proceedings, including inverse condemnation proceedings, where private property is taken or damaged for public use. In fact, during the debate over the 1972 Montana Constitution, the committee discussed this provision strictly in the context of eminent domain proceedings, using property taken for highway construction as the primary example in explaining what occurs when the offer by the government is, for example, too low or too high. ***

¶ 69 The point of the foregoing discussion is that the "or damaged" language of Article II, Section 29 is intended to apply to damage to real and private property occasioned by a taking of real property for public use. Neither the 1889 or 1972 Montana Constitutions evince any intent that it apply to regulatory takings or damages resulting therefrom. Moreover, the provision mandates that private property not be taken or damaged for public use without just compensation "having been first made to or paid into court for the owner." This language obviously contemplates a condemnation of property by the State, and the recognition that the appropriation will cause determinable consequential damages to property owners affected thereby—damages which can be ascertained at the time of the taking. Simply put, the plain language of Article II, Section 29 does not suggest that the provision was intended to apply to the types of damages a regulatory taking might arguably cause over time, after a regulation has taken its toll on a property owner. And, notably, neither the appellants nor the Dissent have cited a single case for the proposition that the "or damaging" language—which, incidentally, is present in roughly half of the state constitutions in this country—is intended to provide any greater protections in the regulatory taking context than does the Fifth Amendment to the U.S. Constitution, or that it applies to anything other than the consequential damages to the property of persons affected by a physical condemnation, or similar actions, initiated by the State. ***

Justice JAMES C. NELSON, dissenting.

¶ 135 . . . [T]he fundamental right to just compensation to the full extent of the loss for a taking or damaging of private property must be interpreted mindful of other pertinent rights in the Montana Constitution. One such right is the "inalienable" right of "acquiring, possessing and protecting property." Mont. Const. art. II, § 3 . . . . [W]e have never excluded other types of property—e.g., personal, intangible, and intellectual—from the principle that "any statute which allows a condemnor to take a person's property must be strictly construed, giving the statute its plain interpretation, but favoring the person's fundamental rights." Indeed, there is no basis in the constitutional text for limiting this principle to "real property," given that Article II, Section 3 recognizes the inalienable right to acquire, possess, and protect "property," not just "real property."

¶ 140 The Montana Code defines "property" broadly. It is not simply land, a fence, a car, or some office furniture. It is anything that a person has the right to possess and use to the exclusion of others. By way of example, property interests exist in "all inanimate things which are capable of appropriation or of manual delivery," "all domestic animals," "all obligations," "such products of labor or skill as the composition of an author, the goodwill of a business, trademarks, and signs," and "rights created or granted by statute." Nothing in Montana property law, however, suggests that the meaning of "property" depends on arbitrarily drawn lines or rigidly constrictive tests devised by the federal courts. . . .

¶ 141 In the present case, the Ranchers seek just compensation for the taking or damaging of several property interests: "their alternative livestock business, inventory, and equipment," which includes "fixtures," "facilities," and the alternative livestock. The State, the Sportsmen, and the Court do not dispute that these are compensable property interests; however, before proceeding to the question of whether a part or a whole of these interests has been taken or damaged for public use, I note the following considerations regarding the Ranchers' businesses. In the same way that the opportunity to pursue employment is a necessary incident to the fundamental right (under Article II, Section 3) to pursue life's basic necessities,

Wadsworth, the opportunity to operate one's business as a going concern is a necessary incident to the fundamental right (also under Article II, Section 3) to acquire, possess, and protect property. Indeed, operating one's business as a going concern is, like employment, the vehicle by which many Montanans pursue life's basic necessities; and the property interests associated with a going business are, therefore, entitled to the highest level of protection by this Court. ***

¶ 152 The Court's contrary interpretation, limiting the reach of Article II, Section 29 to direct appropriations, amounts to the improper insertion of language into the provision. Article II, Section 29 does not in any way describe, define, or circumscribe the ways in which private property may be "taken or damaged." It simply states, "Private property shall not be taken or damaged for public use. . . ." Clearly, property is "taken" for public use in an eminent domain proceeding. Property may also be "damaged" as a result of a public works project. But I reject the Court's assertion that property cannot be "taken or damaged" for public use by government regulation. Nothing in the text of Article II, Section 29 requires such a construction. In fact, given that the Fifth Amendment's Takings Clause reaches regulatory takings, and given that Article II, Section 29 is facially broader than the Fifth Amendment, the logical conclusion is that Article II, Section 29 also reaches regulatory takings (and damagings). ***

¶ 160 . . . [T]he Court today eviscerates the protections of Article II, Section 29 by declaring this section to provide no more protection than does the Fifth Amendment. To make matters worse, the Court chooses to march lockstep with the confused muddle of Fifth Amendment jurisprudence. I simply cannot abide the Court's decision. It ignores the plain language of Article II, Section 29. It ignores the interconnectedness of the Article II rights — in particular here, the right to acquire, possess, and protect property (Article II, Section 3) and the right to just compensation for a taking or damaging of that property (Article II, Section 29). It ignores the broad property rights statutorily defined in §§ 70-1-101 and -104, MCA. And it ignores the overriding theme and fabric of the Declaration of Rights: to protect the fundamental rights of Montanans irrespective of how those rights may be interpreted under like provisions of the federal constitution and to "revitalize" the government's approach to civil liberties.

¶ 161 Long ago, when Montana first joined the Union, the citizens of this state were unwilling to leave their property rights to the whims of the property-related provisions of the federal constitution and the Supreme Court's interpretations of those provisions. Rather, they included in our Constitution an explicit assurance that private property would not be taken or damaged for public use without just compensation. This provision was carried forward into the 1972 Montana Constitution, with the additional requirement that compensation be provided "to the full extent of the loss" — language which clarifies unequivocally that whether property was taken or damaged depends not on what the government got, but on what the property owner lost.

¶ 162 It is this Court's responsibility—indeed, its obligation—to acknowledge Article II, Section 29 as the free-standing provision it is and not relegate it to the status of a mere constitutional redundancy. We previously recognized this obligation in *Gas Products Co. v. Rankin* (Mont. 1922), when we refused to ignore our own Constitution and simply adopt the Supreme Court's holding in a closely related case:

> Were we content to accept the views expressed by the Supreme Court of the United States as the rule of property rights in this state, our task in determining the questions presented would be comparatively easy. However, the danger of establishing such a principle in this state is apparent, and although we entertain the very highest regard and respect for the decisions of the Supreme Court of the United States, we do not feel constrained to follow blindly its determinations affecting the rights of our citizens, especially in view of our own constitutional guaranties....
>
> Since the constitutionality of the act is attacked, both under the federal and state Constitution, we believe it to be our duty, irrespective of the holdings of other courts, to consider and apply the provisions of our own Constitution and general statutes thereto, and declare the rule of property for Montana.

¶ 163 Thus, some 86 years ago, this Court announced that it would not blindly follow the determinations of the Supreme Court affecting the property rights of our citizens, and we acknowledged our duty, irrespective of the holdings of other courts, to declare the rule of property for Montana based on the provisions of our own Constitution and general statutes thereto. We have utterly failed in recent years to abide by this approach, choosing instead, as the Court does today, to "look[] to federal case law for guidance when considering takings claims brought under Article II, Section 29." As a result, the confusion and uncertainty encumbering federal regulatory takings jurisprudence have infected our own takings jurisprudence. This situation is untenable. It is long past time that we articulate appropriate standards for analysis under Article II, Section 29 and quit allowing federal court decisions to dictate the meaning and substance of Montana's Constitution.

¶ 164 Construing Article II, Section 29 in light of the coordinate guarantees in Article II, I conclude that this provision applies to situations in which property is taken or damaged by virtue of government regulation. I further conclude that this provision affords broader protections than the Fifth Amendment's Takings Clause. Based on these conclusions and the foregoing discussion, I now address whether a part or a whole of the Ranchers' property interests has been taken or damaged, entitling them to just compensation to the full extent of the loss pursuant to Article II, Section 29. Given the impact of I-143 on the alternative livestock industry—outright obliteration—I consider this to be a relatively easy question to answer.

¶ 165 I-143 forced the Ranchers out of business, as it was intended to do. Consequently, the goodwill and going-concern value of the Ranchers' businesses have been totally destroyed. In this respect, I-143's effect is dramatic. For all intents and purposes, the Ranchers have been "ousted" from their domain vis-à-vis the goodwill and going-concern value of their businesses. I would hold that this constitutes not merely a damaging of their businesses, but an outright taking of them. ***

Judge WM. NELS SWANDAL, sitting for Justice BRIAN MORRIS, joins the Dissent of Justice JAMES C. NELSON.

Notes on the Declaration of Rights

1. The opinions in *Buhmann* serve as a reminder that state constitutional interpretation is more than a matter of following federal law or providing greater protection under state constitutional rights. Marching in lock-step in constitutional law almost always requires some improvisation. Federal doctrine under the Takings Clause, if not a "confused muddle," may be read more and less broadly on its own terms, and always can be overturned by a changing United States Supreme Court. Distinguishing a state constitutional right, even when a court is working with different text (here, "damaging" and "the full extent of the loss"), requires more than a holding that a state constitutional claim wins where a federal constitutional claim loses. Text and history may be equivocal, and precedent may be relatively rare compared with analogous federal case law. Either way a court goes, particularly with less developed state constitutional rights, faithful interpretation is a demanding task.

2. A detailed account of constitutional criminal procedure is beyond the focus of this book, but the rights of persons prosecuted and convicted by the state for crimes are fertile ground for state constitutional development due to variations in the texts of the relevant provisions in the Montana Declaration of Rights and the United States Bill of Rights, the frequency with which such issues are litigated, and the dynamism of both federal and state doctrine in the area. A few clear textual distinctions stand out in habeas corpus (section 19 prohibits suspension of the writ in all circumstances), initiation of criminal proceedings (section 20 allows charging by information), double jeopardy (section 25 prohibits double jeopardy regardless of jurisdiction), and certain trial rights (e.g., sections 24 and 26 provide a right to trial by jury for misdemeanor defendants in justice and district court). Some rights may be starting to break away from lock-step, or may be falling back in line. *See, e.g., State v. Bailey* (Mont. 2021) (holding two-way video testimony of a state expert witness violated the section 24 right "to meet the witnesses against him face to face," but applying a federal Confrontation Clause standard); *State v. Yang* (Mont. 2019) (holding a sentencing judge, when imposing a mandatory fine, must be allowed to consider the financial resources of the offender and the burden the fine will impose, citing both the Eighth Amendment and section 22); *State v. Betterman* (Mont. 2015) (holding the speedy trial right of the Sixth Amendment and section 22 does not apply to postconviction, presentencing delay), *affirmed by Betterman v. Montana* (2016). As discussed in Chapters 2 and 11, the intersection of the right of privacy and

security from unreasonable searches and seizures offers regular opportunities for distinction, hybridization, or convergence of federal and state law.

3. Article II, section 28 of the 1972 Constitution originally provided:

> **Rights of the Convicted.** Laws for the punishment of crime shall be founded on the principles of prevention and reformation. Full rights are restored by termination of state supervision for any offense against the state.
>
> *Revises 1889 constitution by deleting reference to capital punishment and providing that rights a person loses when convicted of a crime are automatically restored when he has served his sentence.*

In 1998 voters approved a legislatively proposed amendment:

> <u>Criminal justice policy—</u>**rights of the convicted.** <u>(1)</u> Laws for the punishment of crime shall be founded on the principles of prevention, reformation<u>, public safety, and restitution for victims</u>.
>
> <u>(2)</u> Full rights are restored by termination of state supervision for any offense against the state.

In the voter information pamphlet, proponents of the amendment observed "more than 20 states have adopted victims' rights amendments to help restore balance to their [criminal justice] systems," and:

> The approval of this Constitutional amendment would be one step in reforming a criminal justice system which far too often focuses only on the rights of the criminal. Focusing our lawmakers['] attention upon the safety of the public, upon the losses of crime victims, and upon restitution of those losses by those who cause them, is an important step that this State should take to improve our criminal justice system and make it more responsive to the needs of all Montanans.

Opponents, including Delegate Mae Nan (Robinson) Ellingson, argued "Montana statutes have many penalties including fines, jail sentences, community service, treatment programs, as well as restitution." At the time of the proposed amendment, the Montana Supreme Court had not applied the principles expressed in "the rights of the convicted" to invalidate any law, conviction, or sentence, and has not done so since. What kind of state actions might violate the original and amended "rights of the convicted"? What did the proponents of the amendment accomplish? Recall the Montana Supreme Court invalidated under the separate amendment rule a more elaborate statement of crime victims' rights in *Montana Ass'n of Counties v. State* (Chapter 1).

What is now the second subsection of section 28 provides for full restoration of rights to persons convicted of crime after the conclusion of "state supervision." The Montana Supreme Court reads this provision to refer "to those rights commonly considered political and civil rights incident to citizenship such as the right to vote, the right to hold public office, the right to serve as a juror in our courts and the panoply of rights possessed by all citizens under the laws of the land." *State v. Gafford* (Mont. 1977); *see also State v. Mount* (Mont. 2003) (rejecting restoration of rights challenge to sexual offender registration law enacted after the predicate conviction).

4. A contemporary observer may be surprised by the number of civil- and self-defense provisions in the Declaration of Rights, especially given its reframing in 1972. None of these provisions have been substantially developed in case law. All but section 35 are identical to the 1889 Constitution.

a. **Section 12. Right to Bear Arms.** Unlike the federal Second Amendment right, section 12 expressly protects a right to bear arms "in defense of his own home, person, and property" as well as "in aid of the civil power when thereto legally summoned." Section 12 uses the unusual phrasing of "[t]he right . . . shall not be called into question." Notably it does not protect "the carrying of concealed weapons," reflecting some statehood-era perceptions of concealed-carry as dishonorable. In the only extended discussion of the provision in the 1889 Convention, Delegate Burleigh expressed "[t]he object of the law to prevent the carrying of concealed weapons is to obviate and prevent these quarrels in the streets, by which many lives are lost, and great danger to . . . persons is inflicted."

b. **Section 33. Importation of Armed Persons.** Professor Robert G. Natelson concludes this provision, similar to provisions in the constitutions of Wyoming, Idaho, and Kentucky, prohibits both public and private importation of armed persons. *"No Armed Bodies of Men"—Montanans' Forgotten Constitutional Right*, 63 MONT. L. REV. 1 (2002). Although it is one of the Montana Constitution's more arcane provisions, consider how it might apply to contemporary circumstances of a Governor importing police or the National Guard from other states to protect the border or suppress protests. Would it apply to prohibit the deployment of private paramilitary groups to protect protesters or property? Its complementary provision is section 32, civilian control of the military.

c. **Section 35. Servicemen, Servicewomen, and Veterans.** This is a new provision authorizing preferences for servicemen, servicewomen, and veterans. Does section 35 have implications for other class-based public preferences under the anti-discrimination provisions of section 4?

5. The year before the 1972 Constitutional Convention, Montana's United States Senator Mike Mansfield had led the effort to propose and ratify the Twenty-Sixth Amendment, lowering the voting age in state and federal elections to eighteen. Courts were beginning to recognize the rights of minors in various proceedings. Several young delegates in the Constitutional Convention were ready to capitalize on the cultural moment.

> a. **Section 14. Adult Rights.** A person 18 years of age or older is an adult for all purposes, except that the legislature or the people by initiative may

establish the legal age for purchasing, consuming, or possessing alcoholic beverages *and marijuana*.

New provision. Self explanatory. [With 1978, 1986, and 2020 (*in italics*) amendments.]

The 1972 aspiration to provide full adult rights to 18-year-olds yielded twice for alcoholic beverages. Montanans raised the drinking age to 19 in 1978 and, with encouragement from Congress's threat to withhold highway funding, left it to the Legislature entirely in 1986. In 2020 the approval of "adult-use marijuana" by statutory initiative was accompanied by a constitutional initiative conforming section 14 to the proposal's 21-year-old age limit.

b. **Section 15. Rights of Persons Not Adults.** The rights of persons under 18 years of age shall include, but not be limited to, all the fundamental rights of this Article unless specifically precluded by laws which enhance the protection of such persons.

New provision giving children all of the rights that adults have unless a law meant to protect children prohibits their enjoyment of the right.

This provision guarantees persons under 18 the same constitutional rights as adults in Montana, and additional rights as may be appropriate to juveniles, unless the Legislature expressly restricts such rights by law, and such laws actually protect those persons. *See generally* Rebecca Stursberg, *Still-in-Flux: Reinterpreting Montana's Rights-of-Minors Provision*, 79 MONT. L. REV. 259 (2018). For example, the state cannot add an adult sentence to a juvenile disposition, where unlike rehabilitative institutionalization, such retributive sentencing decreases rather than increases the protection of those juveniles. *See In the Matter of S.L.M.* (Mont. 1997); *see also Wicklund v. State* (Mont. 1st. Dist. 1999) (holding the Parental Notice of Abortion Act violated the right of privacy incorporated into section 15 for juveniles and did not enhance their protection).

2. Rights Elsewhere in the Montana Constitution

Beyond the Article II Declaration of Rights lie several distinctive rights, as well as duties imposing correlative rights. These rights and duties include Article IX, section 1 "clean and healthful environment," and the Article X, section 1 "[e]quality of educational opportunity," previously covered in Chapters 9 and 7, respectively. The right to public use of water, which was so important at statehood as to merit a place in section 15 of the 1889 Constitution's Declaration of Rights, is now placed in Article IX, section 3. Although these rights lack federal counterparts in the United States, many of them appear in many state constitutions, as well as in other national constitutions. Many are "positive" rights, imposing affirmative duties on state government to fulfill citizens' constitutional entitlements, or protect citizens from private action, rather than "negative" rights of noninterference with citizens by state action. Often they are non-self-executing instructions to the legislature, primarily implemented by and litigated under detailed statutes. Courts rarely adjudicate these rights directly. Major cases like *MEIC* (Chapter 9) and *Columbia Falls Elementary School District No. 6* (Chapter 7) are the exceptions that prove the rule. Consider how these rights function in a state's law and politics, how they relate to the other rights and powers considered in the book, and whether the entrenchment of detailed positive rights represents a deviation from or complement to the American constitutional tradition.

Emily Zackin, *Looking for Rights in All the Wrong Places: Why State Constitutions Contain America's Positive Rights*

207–09, 217 (2013)

. . . [W]hen we include state constitutions in our view of American constitutionalism, many successful movements for positive constitutional rights become immediately apparent. These positive rights were by no means as widely embraced or strongly enforced in America as they might have been. However, the lengthy and enduring American practice of writing and amending state constitutions to include mandates for protective, welfarist governance demonstrates that the American rights tradition is more complicated and less libertarian than many have argued. Like the fundamental laws of countries all over the world, American constitutions contain rights to protection *by*, and not merely *from*, government.

The particular controversies that have shaped state constitutions (whether to mandate the construction of escapement shafts in mines or provide detailed instructions about the management of school funds, for instance) might seem trivial and mundane at first blush. However, the proponents of these policies were quite clear that big principles were at stake in their struggles. American campaigns for positive rights have varied across states and over time, but each has worked for a more expansive government, one that would protect people from threats other than a tyrannical state, and often from the dangers associated with unfettered capitalism. Whether activists wanted the state to offer protection from the environmental degradation caused by unregulated industrial practices, the lack of educational opportunity available to children of the poor, or the dehumanizing conditions established by labor markets, all wanted government to intervene on behalf of those in danger. Through constitutional conventions and/or referenda, reformers added mandates to their state constitutions, demanding that government intervene in social and economic life. These efforts to secure governments' protection created positive constitutional rights.

In the context of American politics, constitutional change has often appeared to offer tactical advantages that other kinds of politics alone could not. Thus, this study of state constitutional development not only revises the prevailing interpretation of American political culture, but also enhances our understanding of the strategic calculations that can give rise to constitutional change. Scholars of constitutionalism, and of rights in particular, have sometimes claimed that constitutional drafting and change should occur through some form of higher lawmaking, distinct from the ordinary, interest-based bargaining through which legislatures make statutes. However, the champions of positive rights understood their efforts both as a form of higher lawmaking and as a means to further their legislative agendas. Thus, this analysis of positive-rights movements suggests that constitutions are different from statutes not because they transcend the struggles of ordinary politics, but because they play a different role in resolving those struggles.

While there are certainly important differences between statutory and constitutional politics (even at the state level), the differences are not those of ordinary versus higher politics. Instead, the differences between state constitutions and statutes lie in their different institutional capacities. One well-understood advantage of constitutional politics (over statutory politics alone) is that when a policy has been added directly to a constitution, courts can nullify any legislative attempts to tinker with that policy. Thus, by ushering courts into particular policy battles, constitutions can render policies more stable over time by entrenching them against the wishes of changing legislative majorities. State-level activists certainly understood and attempted to exploit this property of constitutional politics. However, they also articulated other (less documented) advantages that a constitutional strategy held over statutory change alone. For instance, even the environmental movement, which used constitutions to facilitate litigation, was not hoping to entrench the status quo, but to achieve policy reform through public interest lawsuits. In addition, just as constitutions can be used to switch courts on, ushering them into particular policy battles, constitutional provisions (unlike statutes) can also be used to switch courts off, excluding courts from specific fights.

The strategic appeal of constitutional provisions was not limited to constitutions' effect on the judiciary. In fact, many of the movements that shaped state constitutions were motivated largely by calculations that had little to do with courts. For example, constitutional provisions struck political organizers as valuable and highly visible banners for their cause. Not only did movement leaders believe that citizens would rally around the constitutional provisions they drafted, they also hoped that successful constitutional change would demonstrate their movement's electoral strength to the states' legislatures. Thus, when it was difficult to get legislation through state legislatures, reform-oriented organizations used constitutions to speak directly to those legislatures, writing explicit mandates for action into constitutions, while simultaneously demonstrating the political power of their supporters. ***

Rather than considering the state and federal constitutional traditions in isolation from one another, or describing American constitutional development as a steady triumph of the federal Constitution over state practices, it may be more fruitful to explore the many, mutually influential connections between constitutional development at the state and federal levels. After all, each time the boundary between state and federal authority has been a source of controversy, the resolution of that controversy has simultaneously shaped both state and federal constitutions. The state and federal constitutions have therefore developed together as a single system (albeit an overlapping and often disorderly one) of laws and institutions.

Notes on Rights Elsewhere in the Montana Constitution

1. One example of positive rights is *Butte Community Union* (Chapter 9), where the Montana Supreme Court, applying "middle-tier" scrutiny, invalidated welfare reforms under "[t]he legislature shall provide" public assistance provisions of Article XII, section 3. In *Harper v. Greely* (Chapter 1), the Court let stand an amendment that "[t]he legislature may provide such economic assistance. . . ." Several other provisions provide instructions to the Legislature with less substantive policy content.

a. Article XII, section 1 (Agriculture) provides in part: "[t]he legislature shall provide for a Department of Agriculture and enact laws and provide appropriations to protect, enhance, and develop all agriculture." What types of laws and appropriations does the "shall" require? Could any law or budget violate this provision?

b. Article XII, section 2 (Labor) requires the Legislature to provide a Department of Labor and Industry, and further provides "A maximum period of 8 hours is a regular day's work in all industries and employment except agriculture and stock raising. The legislature may change this maximum period to promote the general welfare." In *Kuhr v. City of Billings* (Mont. 2007), the Montana Supreme Court rejected a firefighter group's challenge to an extended work day because the Legislature had changed the 8-hour maximum in certain jobs subject to a collective bargaining agreement, including firefighters. Does "promote the general welfare" provide any justiciable limits on the Legislature's ability to extend the workday?

c. Article XIII, section 1 (Non-Municipal Corporations) requires the Legislature to "provide protection and education for the people against harmful and unfair practices by either foreign or domestic corporations, individuals, or associations." The Voter Information Pamphlet explained this "[n]ew provision requir[es] the legislature to pass consumer protection laws." When if ever could a person challenge Montana consumer protection laws as inadequate? *See also* Mont. Const. Art. IX, § 4 ("The legislature shall provide for the identification, acquisition, restoration, enhancement, preservation, and administration of scenic, historic, archeologic, scientific, cultural, and recreational areas, sites, records and objects, and for their use and enjoyment by the people.").

2. The Montana Constitution provides other entitlements in the form of trust funds of "inviolate" principal from dedicated revenue sources, the income from which is dedicated to specific policy programs. Two of the first four amendments after ratification in 1972 established trust funds. The resource indemnity trust, ratified in 1974, amended the natural resource reclamation requirement of Article IX, section 2 to provide funding to support reclamation of disturbed lands. The coal severance tax trust fund (discussed in *White v. State*, Chapter 3) of Article IX, section 5, ratified in 1976, arises from a specific source but supports general programs

from its interest and income. The Montana tobacco settlement trust fund of Article XII, section 4, ratified in 2000, supports programs "related to the health care needs of the people of Montana." The most targeted constitutional trust fund is the noxious weed management trust fund of Article IX, section 6, ratified in 2004, with a purpose "to fund the noxious weed management program." Fiscal amendments protecting particular interests work both ways, as demonstrated by the 2010 amendment prohibiting "real property transfer taxes" in Article VIII, section 17, a tax of little interest to the Legislature (which had not enacted such a tax) but of great interest to real estate agents (who funded the campaign).

3. In 2004, the Legislature proposed, and Montana voters ratified, a constitutional amendment to Article IX, a new section 7:

> **Preservation of harvest heritage.** The opportunity to harvest wild fish and wild game animals is a heritage that shall forever be preserved to the individual citizens of the state and does not create a right to trespass on private property or diminution of other private rights.

In the Voter Information Pamphlet proponents argued:

> ***In other states hunting/fishing opportunities have been steadily eroded by anti-hunting, anti-fishing, "animal rights" extremists,*** with endless legal challenges to hunting/fishing culture. C-41 gives Montana the legal foundation to resist these challenges in court as they arise—and they WILL inevitably happen here eventually. Rather than be on the defensive, we must be proactive. We must give future generations legal ammunition now to defend our heritage against outside attacks. ***
>
> The purpose of enumerating rights in state constitutions is to protect minority groups against the political whims of the majority. ***While today hunting/fishing are enjoyed by large numbers of Montanans, there may come a day when harvesting wild fish and game is practiced by only a small minority,*** because the hunting population is shrinking. We must pass C-41 today, while we still have the political will to do so....

Opponents argued "[e]ither this proposed amendment allows current and future laws and regulations to manage and regulate hunting and fishing, or it does not. It cannot be both." What aspects of state fish and wildlife regulation does a harvest heritage amendment preserve from revision? Would the answer change if it amended Article II? Why do you think the proponents did not do so?

After efforts by opponents of trapping to ban the practice on public lands, the 2015 Legislature enacted "An Act Clarifying the Types of Fish and Game Harvest Protected Under the Montana Constitution." The law adds "harvest" to the definitions of fishing, hunting, and trapping in the chapter regulating fishing, hunting, and trapping languages. Supporters of the bill included the original proponents of the harvest heritage amendment, who testified that their original intent was to include trapping under the amendment, notwithstanding the lack of any mention of trapping in the voter materials. Would a statute enacting strict new limits on trapping be constitutional?

Index

1884 Montana Constitution, 21, 24–25, 55, 202, 666–667
1889 Montana Constitution, 21–23, 25–26, 32–33, 39–41, 55, 67, 79–81, 97, 121, 131–132, 134, 141–143, 146, 149, 154, 163, 167–168, 172, 174, 181, 190, 199–200, 202, 204, 212, 214, 234, 245, 250, 255, 259, 277–279, 286–287, 312, 315, 325–326, 328, 343, 351, 353, 387, 396, 483, 534, 629–630, 644, 646–648, 660, 667, 757, 777, 785–787

Accused, rights of the (Article II, section 24), 59–60, 78, 80, 764–766, 784
Acquire, possess, and protect property, right to, 275, 325, 387, 390–391, 400, 404–405, 414–415, 434–435, 440, 445, 448, 781–782; *see* Inalienable rights (Article II, section 3)
Administration of justice (Article II, section 16), 106, 108–110, 113, 120–121, 128, 199, 245–262, 266–267, 269–274, 276–279, 482, 490, 541, 788
Adult rights (Article II, section 14), 779, 786–787
Agriculture (Article XII, section 1), 53, 144, 790
Aid prohibited to sectarian schools (Article X, section 6), 325–327, 644–665
Alaska, 9, 11, 492–497, 505, 544, 625, 643, 669
Albinger v. Harris (Mont. 2002), 513–514
Alden v. Maine (1999), 100
Alderson, State v., (Mont. 1914), 49–51, 55
Allgeyer v. Louisiana (1897), 417–418
Almendarez-Torres v. United States (1998), 78, 80
Amendment by initiative (Article XIV, section 9), 39, 52, 54, 56–57, 62, 236
Amendment by legislative referendum (Article XIV, section 8), 38–39, 44, 52, 236–237
Amendments (U.S. Const. art. V), 39
American Cancer Society v. State (Mont. 2004), 287–294, 296
American Tradition Partnership v. Bullock (2012), 630, 686
Anderson v. Board of Commissioners of Cloud County (Kan. 1908), 160
Anderson v. Celebrezze (1983), 354–355
Andrews v. Ballard (S.D. Tex. 1980), 407, 584
Apprendi v. New Jersey (2000), 78
Arizona, 11, 25, 56, 545, 584, 656
Armatta v. Kitzhaber (Or. 1998), 50–51, 56, 63
Arms, right to bear (Article II, section 12), 778, 786
Armstrong v. State (Mont. 1999), 64, 111, 406–407, 412, 433–434, 563, 574–595, 615, 626–627, 767–777
Arneson v. State (Mont. 1993), 466–472, 482, 491
Ashcraft v. Montana Power Company (Mont. 1971), 257–258, 266, 272
Assembly, freedom of (Article II, section 6), 629–630, 665, 674, 685, 778

Associated Press v. Board of Public Education (Mont. 1991), 111, 114, 528
Attorney conduct, *see* Supreme court jurisdiction (Article VII, section 2)

Bacus v. Lake County (Mont. 1960), 191–193
Bail, right to (Article II, section 21), 58, 60, 545
Baker v. Carr (1962), 338
Baker, Beth, 122, 189, 221, 237, 239, 354, 653, 721
Balanced budget (Article VIII, section 9), 173, 175
Baldwin v. Fish & Game Commission of Montana (1978), 489, 775
Baldwin, State v., (Mont. 1990), 555
Ballot (Article IV, section 1), 351, 353
Bankers Life & Casualty v. Peterson (Mont. 1993), 511–512
Barenblatt v. United States (1959), 222
Barker v. Manchin (W. Va. 1981), 195–196
Barnett, Randy E., 390, 416–417
Bartmess v. Board of Trustees (Mont. 1986), 316–325, 327–328, 693
Basic system of free quality public elementary and secondary schools, *see* Educational goals and duties (Article X, section 1)
Batten, City of Billings v., (Mont. 1985), 679
Baxter v. State (Mont. 2009), 128, 232, 526, 534, 609–627, 758
Becky v. Butte-Silver Bow School District No. 1 (Mont. 1995), 710–711, 737
Benderson Development Co. v. Sciortino (Va. 1998), 161–162
Big Sky Colony, Inc. v. Montana Department of Labor and Industry (Mont. 2012), 310, 631–641, 643, 686, 696
Billings Firefighters Local 521 v. City of Billings (Mont. 1999), 288, 292
Billings Gazette v. City of Billings (Mont. 2011), 742, 744, 750, 752
Billings Gazette v. City of Billings (Mont. 2013), 736–754, 756
Bills (Article V, section 11), 20, 44, 48–51, 55–57, 60, 64, 131–139, 144–146, 185, 220, 362, 644, 654, 665
Bivens v. Six Unknown Named Agents of Federal Bureau of Narcotics (1971), 104–106, 109–110
Blue in Color, 1993 Chevrolet Pickup, State v., (Mont. 2005), 82, 86–94
Board of Commissioners, State v., (Mont. 1906), 49–51, 55
Board of land commissioners (Article X, section 4), 64, 165, 168
Board of Regents of Higher Education v. Judge (Mont. 1975), 170–179, 183, 185, 232, 349
Boards of education (Article X, section 9), 170–172, 175–176, 179–183, 317–318, 324, 335, 348
Boreen v. Christensen (Mont. 1994), 399, 404
Bostick, Florida v., (1991), 70
Bowers v. Hardwick (1986), 567–568
Bowsher v. Synar (1986), 188–189
Bozeman Daily Chronicle v. Bozeman Police Department (Mont. 1993), 741, 743–744
Brecht, State v., (Mont. 1971), 533, 535, 542, 544, 559
Brewer v. Ski-Lift, Inc. (Mont. 1988), 473–477, 479–481
Brown v. Board of Education (1954), 460, 502
Brown v. Gianforte (Mont. 2021), 233–234
Bryan v. Yellowstone County Elementary School District No. 2 (Mont. 2002), 698, 706–717
Budget and messages (Article VI, section 9), 173, 185–186

Buhmann v. State (Mont. 2008), 78, 779–784
Bullock, Governor v. Fox, Attorney General (Mont. 2019), 167–170, 178–179
Bullock, State v., (Mont. 1995), 79, 82–86, 91–94, 111, 555, 560
Burdick v. Takushi (1992), 354–355, 357
Burgan & Walker v. State Highway Commission (Mont. 1943), 48
Burger v. Judge (D. Mont. 1973), 35–38
Burns, State v., (Mont. 1992), 553–554
Butte Community Union v. Lewis (Mont. 1986), 42, 111, 261, 318, 320, 325, 391–396, 398, 415, 423–424, 467, 470–471, 482, 790
Butte Community Union v. Lewis (Mont. 1987), 42–43, 47

C.H., In the Matter of, (Mont. 1984), 392, 423–424, 524
Caceres, United States v., (1979), 547
California, 10–11, 13, 39–40, 65, 87, 91, 93, 124, 182, 210, 213, 329, 337, 483, 519, 544–545, 554, 580, 600, 673, 727
Campbell v. Mahoney (Mont. 2001), 605
Campbell v. Sundquist (Tenn. Ct. App. 1996), 569, 570
Cape-France Enterprises v. Estate of Peed (Mont. 2001), 431–436, 448
Caperton v. A.T. Massey Coal Co. (2009), 217–218
Cashmore v. Anderson (Mont. 1972), 36
Castles, Wesley, 170, 184
Catholic Charities v. Serio (N.Y. 2006), 643
Cecil v. Allied Stores (Mont. 1973), 404
Chambers v. School District No. 10 (Mont. 1970), 326, 647, 650, 655, 663
Chaplinsky v. New Hampshire (1942), 675, 678–679, 683
Charvat, State v., (Mont. 1978), 85–86
Chatton, State v., (Ohio 1984), 69
Chovanak v. Matthews (Mont. 1948), 235
Christensen, State v., (Mont. 1990), 551
Church of the Lukumi Babalu Aye, Inc. v. City of Hialeah (1993), 632, 634, 636, 638, 641
Citizens to Recall Mayor Whitlock v. Whitlock (Mont. 1992), 740, 741
Citizens United v. FEC (2010), 122, 127, 208, 685–686
City of Daytona Beach v. Del Percio (Fla. 1985), 670
City of Whitefish v. O'Shaughnessy (Mont. 1985), 679
Civilian control of military (Article II, section 32), 779, 786
Clean and healthful environment, maintain and improve, *see* Protection and improvement (Article IX, section 1)
Clean and healthful environment, right to a, 110, 119–120, 290, 387–388, 390, 419–423, 425, 428–431, 433–436, 439–443, 445–449; *see* Inalienable rights (Article II, section 3)
Cleburne Living Center, City of Cleburne v., (1985), 523–524, 530
Clifford, Matthew O., 458, 462, 518, 526, 604–605, 619
Coate v. Omholt (Mont. 1983), 208–215, 231–232, 240
Coburn, State v., (Mont. 1974), 538–539
Code of ethics (Article XIII, section 4), 180, 402, 414, 756
Collier v. Civil Service Commission (Tex. Ct. App. 1989), 403
Colorado, 11, 24, 231, 313, 451, 530, 596, 601, 754
Columbia Falls Elementary School District No. 6 v. State (Mont. 2005), 240, 329, 337–349, 395, 448, 788
Common Cause v. Statutory Committee to Nominate Candidates for

Commissioner of Political Practices (Mont. 1994), 111, 709, 715–716
Commonwealth of Pennsylvania v. Moore (Pa. Super. Ct. 1993), 556
Compact with the United States (Article I), 26–27, 488
Conflict of interest, *see* Code of ethics (Article XIII, section 4)
Connecticut, 246, 497–505, 758
Constitutional convention (Article XIV, section 1), 52
Consumer counsel (Article XIII, section 2), 52–53
Convicted, rights of the, *see* Criminal justice policy (Article II, section 28)
Cooney, State v., (Mont. 1924), 49–51, 55
Corrigan v. Janney (Mont. 1981), 249, 260, 269–270, 277
Cotter, Patricia O., 86, 153, 291, 675, 687, 779
Covington, State v., (Mont. 2012), 77–80
Crawford v. Marion County Election Board (2008), 363
Criminal justice policy (Article II, section 28), 110, 604, 626, 785
Crisp, State v., (Mont. 1991), 762
Crites v. Lewis & Clark County (Mont. 2019), 734–735
Cruel and unusual punishment, *see* Excessive sanctions (Article II, section 22)
Cruzan v. Director, Missouri Department of Health (1990), 524, 623
Cultural heritage of the American Indians, 315–317, 332, 336, 342, 349–350, 485, 488; *see* Educational goals and duties (Article X, section 1)
Cultural resources (Article IX, section 4), 790
Cutter v. Brownbridge (Cal. 1986), 554–555
D & F Sanitation Service v. City of Billings (Mont. 1986), 143, 282–286, 288, 291, 296
Davidson v. Rogers (Or. 1978), 251
Dennis v. United States (1951), 220
Desilets, Attorney General v., (Mass. 1994), 642
Detention (Article II, section 23), 110
Dignity, individual (Article II, section 4), 48, 110, 141–145, 149, 152–153, 156, 161–162, 255, 261–264, 270–271, 274–275, 277, 283–284, 318, 321–322, 328, 334, 362–363, 387, 391–395, 424, 457–532, 537, 564, 572–573, 579–581, 587, 589–590, 592–593, 595, 602–605, 607–627, 631, 642, 644, 674–675, 685–686, 696, 739, 767, 769, 772–773, 775, 778, 786
Dignity, right to, 110, 142, 387, 457–464, 485–486, 489–490, 515, 518, 523, 526, 529, 564, 579–581, 589–590, 593, 595, 602–605, 607–627, 767, 769, 772, 778; *see* Dignity, individual (Article II, section 4)
Disqualification (Article V, section 9), 185
District court jurisdiction (Article VII, section 4), 169, 565
Districting and apportionment (Article V, section 14), 351–352, 365–369
Dixson, State v., (Or. 1988), 85
Donaldson v. State (Mont. 2012), 520–530, 532, 594
Dorwart v. Caraway (Mont. 2002), 102–117, 119–121, 128, 777
Double jeopardy, 80, 545, 784; *see* Self-incrimination and double jeopardy (Article II, section 25)
Douglas v. Judge (Mont. 1977), 136
Drinkwalter v. Shipton Supply Co. (Mont. 1987), 490
Driscoll v. Stapleton (Mont. 2020), 354–357, 362–363

Due Process Clause, 217–218, 265, 390, 417–418, 453, 559, 564, 587, 592, 677, 758-761, 773, 776; *see* Fifth Amendment; Fourteenth Amendment
Due process of law (Article II, section 17), 47–48, 58, 64, 103, 106, 110, 116, 362, 445, 523, 589, 591, 757, 759–763, 766, 769–770, 772–773, 777
Dugan, State v., (Mont. 2013), 666, 675–685
Duke Power Co. v. Carolina Environmental Study Group (1978), 262, 265
Dunn, United States v., (1987), 84, 85
Dupuis v. Board of Trustees (Mont. 2006), 485–486, 489–490

Economic assistance, *see* Institutions and assistance (Article XII, section 3)
Educational goals and duties (Article X, section 1), 132, 315–350, 485, 488, 787
Egdorf, State v., (Mont. 2003), 464–466, 482, 491, 773–775
Eighth Amendment (U.S. Const. amend. VIII), 105, 600, 626, 784
Eisenstadt v. Baird (1972), 523–524, 534, 581
Elections (Article III, section 6), 312
Elections Clause (U.S. Const. art. I, § 4, cl. 1), 369–370, 381–383
Elections, suffrage (Article IV, section 3), 193, 351–356, 363
Electors Clause (U.S. Const. art. II, § 1, cl. 2), 193, 382, 383
Eleventh Amendment (U.S. Const. amend. XI), 96, 97
Elison, Larry M., 23, 98, 121, 390, 577–579, 710
Elkins v. United States (1960), 538
Eminent domain (Article II, section 29), 78, 110, 445, 779–783
Employment Division, Department of Human Resources of Oregon v. Smith (1990), 633–634, 641–643
Employment, opportunity to pursue, *see* Pursuing life's basic necessities, right of
Enabling Act, 22, 26, 29, 35, 81, 316, 388, 488, 644
Environmental degradation, *see* Protection and improvement (Article IX, section 1)
Equal Protection Clause, 149, 161–162, 329, 362–363, 380, 392–393, 395, 458–460, 464–465, 469–470, 482–483, 487–488, 490, 493, 496, 499, 505–506, 508–511, 515, 523–524, 530–531, 572–573, 623, 631, 675, 733, 775; *see* Fourteenth Amendment (U.S. Const. amend. XIV)
Equal protection, 141–145, 149, 152–153, 156, 161–162, 255, 261–264, 270–271, 274–275, 277, 283–284, 318, 321–322, 328, 334, 362–363, 391–395, 424, 457–482, 488, 490, 505, 509–511, 515, 517–518, 520, 523, 526, 529–530, 572–573, 589–590, 608, 615–616, 624, 631, 675, 733, 775, 778; *see* Dignity, individual (Article II, section 4)
Equality of educational opportunity, *see* Educational goals and duties (Article X, section 1)
Erdmann, Charles E., 404
Espinoza v. Montana Department of Revenue (2020), 630, 660–665
Espinoza v. Montana Department of Revenue (Mont. 2018), 644–657, 660
Establishment Clause, 327, 529, 630–631, 635, 641, 643–645, 647, 651, 694–696; *see* Religion Clauses
Ex post facto, obligation of contracts, and irrevocable privileges (Article II, section 31), 208, 211–213, 276, 283, 291

Excessive sanctions (Article II, section 22), 111, 595, 599–600, 603–606, 626, 784
Executive Duties (Article VI, section 4), 163, 168–169, 187, 189
Expression, freedom of, 558, 665–667, 669–675, 684, 695–696; *see* Freedom of speech, expression, and press (Article II, section 7)

Federal judicial power (U.S. Const. art. III, § 2), 96, 169, 200, 234, 242
Fifteenth Amendment (U.S. Const. amend. XV), 359
Fifth Amendment (U.S. Const. amend. V), 73, 105, 390, 490, 541, 758, 779–784
Finke v. State ex rel. McGrath (Mont. 2003), 125, 362
First Amendment (U.S. Const. amend. I), 124, 225, 319, 327, 338, 541, 588, 600, 630–631, 635, 642, 645, 651, 658, 666–669, 672–674, 677–679, 682–683, 685–686, 689–690, 692–694, 756
Flesh v. Board of Trustees of Joint School District No. 2 (Mont. 1990), 740, 746
Florida, 11, 70, 72, 246, 399, 545, 625, 649, 670
Forms of government (Article XI, section 3), 287, 301
Fourteenth Amendment (U.S. Const. amend. XIV), 13, 35, 37, 68, 74, 80, 96, 110, 142, 145, 149, 161–162, 329, 338, 362–363, 380, 392–393, 418, 453, 459, 464–465, 469–470, 483, 490, 492–493, 496, 499, 505, 508–511, 515, 523, 526, 531, 544, 559, 562, 564, 572, 580, 587, 592, 661, 677, 689, 758–759, 761, 773, 775–776
Fourth Amendment (U.S. Const. amend. IV), 70–72, 74, 83–87, 90, 93, 104–105, 110, 534, 541, 545, 551, 555–560, 562–563, 566–567, 592, 745, 751
Fox, City of Missoula v., (Mont. 2019), 298–299
Free Exercise Clause, 629–633, 636, 640–643, 645, 651, 657, 660–662, 664, 693–695; *see* Religion Clauses
Freedom of speech, expression, and press (Article II, section 7), 388, 416–417, 558, 629–630, 665–692, 695–696, 702–703, 710, 756, 778
Full educational potential, *see* Educational goals and duties (Article X, section 1)
Full legal redress, right to, *see* Administration of justice (Article II, section 16)
Fuller, State v., (Mont. 1996), 73

Gambling (Article III, section 9), 28, 35–36, 287–290, 292, 294, 297
Gas Products Co. v. Rankin (Mont. 1922), 783
Gazelka v. St. Peter's Hospital (Mont. 2018), 509–511
General Agriculture Corp. v. Moore (Mont. 1975), 342–344, 428–429
General powers (Article XI, section 4), 281–282, 287, 294–297, 304–308
Glucksberg, Washington v., (1997), 81, 417, 620, 623, 625, 758–759
Granger v. Cascade County School District (Mont. 1972), 328–329
Gray, Karla M., 120, 291, 326, 435, 518, 590, 605
Great Falls Tribune v. Cascade County Sheriff (Mont. 1989), 533, 739–740, 743–744
Great Falls Tribune v. Eighth Judicial District Court (Mont. 1989), 553
Great Falls Tribune v. Montana Public Service Commission (Mont. 2003), 733

Greens at Fort Missoula, LLC v. City of Missoula (Mont. 1995), 306
Greenwood, California v., (1988), 87–88, 91, 93–94
Gregory v. Ashcroft (1991), 288
Griffith v. Butte School District No. 1 (Mont. 2010), 640, 666, 687–696
Griswold v. Connecticut (1965), 533–534, 540, 559–560, 567, 582, 592
Gryczan v. State (Mont. 1997), 111, 517, 519, 525, 529, 534, 563–574, 578–580, 586, 592–593, 595, 615, 626–627
Gulbrandson, L.C., 395
Gunwall, State v., (Wash. 1986), 81
Gustafson, Ingrid G., 652

Habeas corpus (Article II, section 19), 545, 784
Hamilton, State v., (Mont. 2003), 92
Harlow v. Fitzgerald (1982), 108, 109
Harper v. Greely (Mont. 1988), 41–48, 396, 790
Harper v. Virginia State Board of Elections (1966), 359, 362–363
Harrison, John C., 41, 277, 671
Haswell, Frank I., 506
Havre Daily News v. Havre (Mont. 2006), 738
Hawaii, 9, 11, 13, 450, 522, 545
Hay, see Alderson, State v., (Mont. 1914)
Hazelwood School District v. Kuhlmeier (1988), 690
Health, right to seek, 325, 387, 390–391, 410–412, 414–515, 523, 589, 591; *see* Inalienable rights (Article II, section 3)
Heiner, State v., (Wyo. 1984), 536–537
Helena Elementary School District No. 1 v. State (Mont. 1989), 329–337, 340, 342, 344, 347–349, 520
Helfrich, State v., (Mont. 1979), 537
Henning, State v., (Mont. 1993), 553, 554
Henry, State v., (Or. 1987), 674–675
Hester v. United States (1924), 84–85, 93
Hill v. National Collegiate Athletic Association (Cal. 1994), 554
Hill v. Rae (Mont. 1916), 134, 283
Hollow v. State (Mont. 1986), 135–136
Hotel Dorset Co. v. Trust for Cultural Resources of City of New York (N.Y. 1978), 160
Houston v. Williams (Cal. 1859), 210
Huber v. Groff (Mont. 1976), 134–138
Huff, Thomas P., 458, 462, 518, 526, 604–605, 619
Human Rights Act, 275, 458, 471, 483–484, 486, 489–492, 506, 511, 531, 686, 688–689, 694–698
Hunt, William E., 190, 547, 670
Hyem, State v., (Mont. 1981), 535–537, 541, 546, 548

Idaho, 11, 25, 92, 182, 196, 531, 786
Illinois, 7, 11, 24–25, 143, 246–247, 426–427, 450, 462–463, 545
Immunity (Article V, section 8), 223
Impairment of contracts, *see* Ex post facto, obligation of contracts, and irrevocable privileges (Article II, section 31)
Impeachment (Article V, section 13), 233
Importation of armed persons (Article II, section 33), 778, 786
Imprisonment for debt (Article II, section 27), 110
Inalienable rights (Article II, section 3), 47, 110, 113, 119–120, 275, 290, 387–392, 395–396, 398–402, 404–405, 407–408, 410–425, 428–430, 433–435, 439–442, 445–448, 457, 515, 523, 543, 589–591, 607, 775, 781
Indiana, 10–11, 89, 202, 240, 279, 363–364, 399, 622, 656
Individual privacy, *see* Privacy, right of (Article II, section 10)

Information for governor (Article VI, section 15), 182
Initiation of proceedings (Article II, section 20), 59, 60
Initiative (Article III, section 4), 236
Initiative and referendum (Article XI, section 8), 281, 301, 304, 311–313
Institutions and assistance (Article XII, section 3), 41–43, 45, 47, 391–396, 398, 790
Investment of public funds and public retirement system and state compensation insurance fund assets (Article VIII, section 13), 135, 138

Jackson v. Porter (Mont. 1920), 212
Jackson, State v., (Mont. 1983), 75–77
Jefferson County v. Montana Standard (Mont. 2003), 741
Jimeno, Florida v., (1991), 71
Johnson, State v., (Mont. 1986), 77
Johnson, State v., (Wash. 1994), 85–86
Johnstone, Anthony, 40, 95, 179, 201
Jones v. County of Missoula (Mont. 2006), 717–719
JS, Matter of, (Mont. 2017), 772
Judge v. Legislative Finance Committee (Mont. 1975), 173, 183–188
Judicial appointment, *see* Selection (Article VII, section 8)
Judicial power (Article VII, section 1), 199–200, 210, 224, 234
Judicial salaries, *see* Terms and pay (Article VII, section 7)
Judicial standards commission, *see* Removal and discipline (Article VII, section 11)
Jury trial, right to a, *see* Trial by jury (Article II, section 26)

K.G.F., In the Matter of the Mental Health of, (Mont. 2001), 764–770, 772
Kadillak v. Anaconda Co. (Mont. 1979), 442, 448
Kafka v. Montana Department of Fish, Wildlife & Parks (Mont. 2008), 779
Kansas, 24, 305, 309, 311–312
Kaptein v. Conrad School District (Mont. 1997), 322–328, 339, 341
Katz v. United States (1967), 84–85, 91–93, 534, 563, 567–569, 592–593, 751
Kentucky v. Graham (1985), 100
Kirkaldie, State v., (Mont. 1978), 551
Kirtley v. State (Ind. 1949), 399
Know, right to (Article II, section 9), 30, 47, 59–60, 62, 110–111, 183, 186, 320, 445, 553, 697–706, 708–717, 719–756, 778
Kolender v. Lawson (1983), 761–762
Kottel v. State (Mont. 2002), 140–145, 149
Kotterman v. Killian (Ariz. 1999), 656, 657
Krakauer v. State (Mont. 2016), 754–755
Krakauer v. State (Mont. 2019), 755–756
Krautter, City of Helena v., (Mont. 1993), 666, 671–674
Kuhr v. City of Billings (Mont. 2007), 790
Kulstad v. Maniaci (Mont. 2009), 530
Kvaalen v. Graybill (Mont. 1972), 29, 38

Labor (Article XII, section 2), 790
Laedeke, City of Billings v., (Mont. 1991), 665–666, 668–674
Lame Deer, In the Petition to Transfer Territory from High School District No. 6 (Mont. 2000), 190–193
Lance, State v., (Mont. 1986), 679
Larson v. State (Mont. 2019), 356–357
Lawrence v. Texas (2003), 563
League of Women Voters of Indiana v. Rokita (Ind. 2010), 363–364

League of Women Voters v. Commonwealth (Pa. 2018), 369–382
Leaphart, W. William, 48, 90, 114, 153, 287, 290, 322, 337, 430, 478, 549, 609, 694
Lee v. Delmar (Fla. 1953), 399
Lee v. Weisman (1992), 694–695
Legislation, general or special, *see* Local and special legislation (Article V, section 12)
Lemon v. Kurtzman (1971), 635, 643
Libertarian Party of Wisconsin v. State (Wis. 1996), 147
Linder v. Smith (Mont. 1981), 143, 490–491
Litchfield v. State (Ind. 2005), 89
Lloyd Corp. v. Tanner (1972), 672, 673
Local and special legislation (Article V, section 12), 132–133, 143–144, 149–150, 153–157, 159–162, 284, 482, 775
Lochner v. New York (1905), 196, 396, 417–418
Locke v. Davey (2004), 645, 662
Long, State v., (Mont. 1985), 534–548, 557
Louisiana, 8, 10–11, 39, 65, 247, 338, 451, 462, 545, 662
Lowery v. Garfield County (Mont. 1949), 155–156
Lyng v. Northwest Indian Cemetery Protective Association (1988), 640
Lyons, City of Los Angeles v., (1983), 541

Mackrill, State v., (Mont. 2008), 611
Madison, James, 6, 132–133, 162, 228, 571
Madrid v. Gomez (N.D. Cal. 1995), 600, 603
Malabed v. North Slope Borough (Alaska 2003), 492–497, 505
Mapp v. Ohio (1961), 541, 544, 776
Marriage (Article XIII, section 7), 522–532
Marshall v. Cooney (Mont. 1999), 48–57, 60, 62–64
Massachusetts, 3, 7, 10–11, 399, 450, 512, 522, 642
Mathews v. Eldridge (1976), 757
McCabe, Matter of, (Mont. 1975), 214, 240
McDonough, Russell C., 133, 248, 466
McGrath, Mike, 167, 186, 309, 436, 520
McKinney, State v., (Mont. 1904), 44–45
McKinnon, Laurie, 54, 227, 644, 728, 747
McLaughlin v. Montana State Legislature (Mont. 2021), 221–229, 233–234, 239–240, 242
McNair v. School District No. 1 (Mont. 1930), 317–318, 321, 328
Mead v. M.S.B., Inc. (Mont. 1994), 477
MEA-MFT v. McCulloch (Mont. 2012), 169, 186–190
Means v. Montana Power Co. (Mont. 1981), 337
Meech v. Hillhaven West (Mont. 1989), 246, 248–279, 480, 482, 490
Meyer v. Nebraska (1923), 319
Michigan v. Long (1983), 71–73, 76–77
Michigan, 11, 174–175, 177, 182, 194, 622
Midwest Institute of Health v. Governor (Mich. 2020), 194
Miller v. Fallon County (Mont. 1986), 253–254
Miller-Wohl Co. v. Commissioner of Labor (Mont. 1984), 512
Minielly v. State (Or. 1966), 399
Minnesota, 7, 11, 56, 165, 176, 631
Minors, rights of, *see* Persons not adults, rights of (Article II, section 15)
Miranda v. Arizona (1966), 72
Missoulian v. Board of Regents (Mont. 1984), 739, 744–746, 752
Missouri River Power Co. v. Steele (Mont. 1905), 252
Missouri, 11, 56, 358–361, 364

Montana Administrative Procedure Act, 195
Montana Association of Counties v. State (Mont. 2017), 54–64, 234, 594, 785
Montana Automobile Association v. Greely (Mont. 1981), 138–139, 685
Montana Cannabis Industry Association v. State (Mont. 2012), 409–415, 419, 593
Montana Environmental Information Center v. Department of Environmental Quality (Mont. 1999), 119, 420–431, 433, 440, 447–448, 788
Montana Human Rights Division v. City of Billings (Mont. 1982), 553, 737–738, 744, 751–752
Montana State Welfare Board v. Lutheran Social Services (Mont. 1971), 655, 656
Montana Stockgrowers Association v. Department of Revenue (Mont. 1989), 144–145
Montana tobacco settlement trust fund (Article XII, section 4), 791
Montanans for the Responsible Use of the School Trust v. State ex rel. Board of Land Commissioners (Mont. 1999) [*Montrust*], 124–127, 342
Moore v. City of East Cleveland (1977), 585
Moran v. School District # 7, Yellowstone County (D. Mont. 1972), 317, 328
Morgan v. United States (1938), 715
Morris, Brian M., 77, 117, 153, 472, 485, 631
Morris, Petition of, (Mont. 1978), 405
Morris, State v., (Vt. 1996), 91, 92
Morrison, Frank B., 319, 391, 534, 547
Morse v. Frederick (2007), 690, 691
Morton v. Mancari (1974), 487, 491, 493, 505
Mountain States Telephone v. Commissioner of Labor (Mont. 1979), 512
Murgia, Massachusetts Board of Retirement v., (1976), 470

Natural resources, degradation of, *see* Protection and improvement (Article IX, section 1)
Nehring v. LaCounte (Mont. 1986), 151
Nelson v. City of Billings (Mont. 2018), 721–732
Nelson, James C., 52, 89, 110, 120, 126, 140, 154, 192, 215, 235, 291, 325, 342, 397, 413, 431, 486, 518, 523, 563, 574, 595, 614, 719, 764, 781
Nelson, State v., (Mont. 1997), 534, 549–559, 563, 754
New Hampshire, 38, 93–94, 231
New York, 11–12, 38, 85, 92, 94, 104, 160, 451, 478, 585, 643, 657, 669, 758, 772
Newville v. State, Department of Family Services (Mont. 1994), 773
Ninth Amendment (U.S. Const. amend. IX), 121, 416, 541
Nixon, State v., (Mont. 2013), 80
No-aid provision, *see* Aid prohibited to sectarian schools (Article X, section 6)
Nondegradation, *see* Protection and improvement (Article IX, section 1)
Nondiscrimination Clause, 48, 142, 395, 457–464, 483–484, 490–492, 505–506, 509–514, 528–531, 592, 602, 607–608, 615–617, 624, 626, 642, 644, 674–675, 685–686, 696, 778, 786; *see* Dignity, individual (Article II, section 4)
Nondiscrimination in education (Article X, section 7), 315, 644, 696
Nonmunicipal corporations (Article XIII, section 1), 144, 790
North Dakota, 11, 22–23, 25, 531, 631
Northern Plains Resource Council, Inc. v. Montana Board of Land

Commissioners (Mont. 2012), 442, 445
Noxious weed management trust fund (Article IX, section 6), 791
Nye, State v., (Mont. 1997), 685

Oath of office (Article III, section 3), 67, 571
Oberson v. U.S. Department of Agriculture, Forest Service (Mont. 2007), 156, 472–482
Obligation of contracts, 208, 211–213, 283; *see* Ex post facto, obligation of contracts, and irrevocable privileges (Article II, section 31)
Ohio, 11, 56, 68–74, 656
Oliver v. United States (1984), 84
Olmstead v. United States (1928), 84, 560, 566–567
Olson v. Cory (Cal. 1980), 213
One subject, 20, 44, 49–51, 55–57, 60, 64, 131–132, 138, 144–145, 220, 241, 362; *see* Bills (Article V, section 11)
Open courts, *see* Administration of justice (Article II, section 16)
Oregon, 11, 14, 50, 56–57, 63, 85, 92, 94, 250–251, 276, 279, 312–313, 399, 451, 483, 674–675, 770
Organization and procedure (Article V, section 10), 175, 185, 233

Palko v. Connecticut (1937), 568–569, 592–593, 776
Park County Environmental Council v. Department of Environmental Quality (Mont. 2020), 436–448
Participation, right of (Article II, section 8), 47, 110–111, 320, 697–710, 712–720, 733, 778
Patel v. Texas Department of Licensing (Tex. 2015), 418–419
Patrick v. State (Mont. 2011), 229–231
Pennsylvania, 11, 24–25, 143, 232, 289, 369–383, 449–453, 455, 556, 622, 633
People v. Scott (N.Y. 1992), 85, 86
Periodic submission (Article XIV, section 3), 28, 294
Persons not adults, rights of (Article II, section 15), 110, 594, 779, 786–787
Pfost v. State (Mont. 1985), 249, 255, 257–261, 269, 271, 274, 393, 490
Phillips v. City of Whitefish (Mont. 2014), 301–312
Planned Parenthood v. Casey (1992), 579–580, 587, 593
Plyler v. Doe (1981), 319
Pointer v. Texas (1965), 776–777
Popular sovereignty (Article II, section 1), 45, 67, 112–113, 387–388, 778
Powder River County v. State (Mont. 2002), 287
Powell v. State Compensation Insurance Fund (Mont. 2000), 479
Power and structure (Article V, section 1), 131, 136, 138, 172, 187, 189, 221, 259, 304
Preamble, 3, 428–429, 488
Preservation of harvest heritage (Article IX, section 7), 791–792
Press, freedom of, 416–417, 630, 665–666, 702–703, 778; *see* Freedom of speech, expression, and press (Article II, section 7)
Privacy, right of (Article II, section 10), 59–60, 64, 79, 86–87, 91–93, 110–111, 406, 412, 515, 523, 533–627, 697, 699, 721, 723, 733, 736, 744–745, 750–751, 753, 767, 772, 775, 777–778, 784
Prohibition on real property transfer taxes (Article VIII, section 17), 791
Property tax administration (Article VIII, section 3), 141–143
Property tax exemptions (Article VIII, section 5), 644, 655
Protection and improvement (Article IX, section 1), 420–423, 425–431, 433–436, 439–448, 787
Prout v. Sears (Mont. 1989), 265, 266

Public employees, code of ethics for, *see* Code of ethics (Article XIII, section 4)
Public land trust, disposition (Article X, section 11), 144
Public purpose, taxes levied for, *see* Tax purposes (Article VIII, section 1)
Puerto Rico, 457, 607, 625
Pursuing life's basic necessities, right of, 42, 47, 110, 275, 325, 387–388, 390–392, 396, 398–402, 404, 407–408, 410–411, 413–415, 424–425, 442, 448, 515, 781–782; *see* Inalienable rights (Article II, section 3)

Qualifications (Article VII, section 9), 216, 219–220, 236–237
Qualifications Clause (U.S. Const. art. I, § 2), 352, 359
Qualified elector (Article IV, section 2), 351

Railway Express Agency v. New York (1949), 524, 775
Raisler v. Burlington Northern Railroad Co. (Mont. 1985), 774
Ramos v. Louisiana (2020), 662, 663
Reclamation (Article IX, section 2), 52–53, 790
Redman v. Meyers (Mont. 1922), 155–156, 284
Reeves v. Ille Electric Co. (Mont. 1976), 252, 255, 262
Referendum (Article III, section 5), 236, 238, 304, 308–309, 311–313
Regents of University of Michigan v. State (Mich. Ct. App. 1973), 174, \177
Regents, board of, *see* Boards of education (Article X, section 9)
Regnier, Jim, 365, 514, 706, 764
Reichert v. State (Mont. 2012), 215–221, 232–242, 527
Religion Clauses (U.S. Const. amend. I), 327, 529, 629–657, 660–665, 693–696; *see also* First Amendment (U.S. Const. amend. I)
Religion, freedom of (Article II, section 5), 528–529, 588, 629–630, 641–642, 644, 657, 688–690, 693–696, 778
Remedy, right to a, *see* Administration of justice (Article II, section 16)
Removal and discipline (Article VII, section 11), 209, 211, 223–227, 233, 756
Renee, State v., (Mont. 1999), 465, 466
Republican Party of Minnesota v. White (2002), 220, 225
Resource indemnity trust, *see* Reclamation (Article IX, section 2)
Reynolds v. Sims (1964), 359, 363, 500
Rice, James A., 61, 116, 301, 344, 405, 434, 464, 479, 519, 521, 620, 636, 655, 682, 736, 773
Robinette, Ohio v., (1996), 68, 71–74
Robinette, State v., (Ohio 1995), 68–71, 74
Robinette, State v., (Ohio 1997), 68, 74–75
Robinson Township v. Commonwealth (Pa. 2013), 449, 455
Robinson, State v., (Mont. 2003), 679–680
Roe v. Wade (1973), 534, 574, 580–581, 592
Rohlfs v. Klemenhagen (Mont. 2009), 149–158, 482
Romer v. Evans (1996), 523–524, 530
Romero v. J & J Tire (Mont. 1989), 486, 490
Roth v. United States (1957), 674
Rules of procedure, *see* Supreme court jurisdiction (Article VII, section 2)

Salary, diminution of, *see* Terms and pay (Article VII, section 7)

San Antonio School District v. Rodriguez (1973), 317, 319, 329, 348, 500, 524
Sandefur, Dirk M., 229, 356, 652
Sawyer Stores v. Mitchell (Mont. 1936), 50, 51
School district trustees (Article X, section 8), 315, 320, 322, 333–334
School funding, adequacy and equity of, 316, 329–348; *see* Educational goals and duties (Article X, section 1)
Searches and seizures (Article II, section 11), 79, 83–93, 102–103, 106, 110–111, 120, 534, 536–537, 545, 551, 555–557, 559–563, 602–603, 778, 784–785
Second Amendment (U.S. Const. amend. II), 786
Secret ballot, *see* Ballot (Article IV, section 1)
Selection (Article VII, section 8), 199, 205, 233–234
Self-government (Article II, section 2), 38, 46, 63, 387–388, 778
Self-government charters (Article XI, section 5), 282, 285, 294–295
Self-government powers (Article XI, section 6), 281–282, 285–292, 298, 669
Self-incrimination and double jeopardy (Article II, section 25), 73, 80, 545, 559, 784
Self-incrimination, *see* Self-incrimination and double jeopardy (Article II, section 25), 73, 80, 559
Separate amendment, *see* Submission (Article XIV, section 11)
Separation of powers (Article III, section 1), 124, 163, 172, 176, 185–197, 200, 208–211, 214–215, 221, 227–228, 233, 259–260, 304
Serrano v. Priest (Cal. 1977), 124, 329, 337
Servicemen, servicewomen, and veterans (Article II, section 35), 786
Severance tax on coal — trust fund (Article IX, section 5), 134–135, 138–139, 145–146, 790
Shaw v. Reno (1993), 366
Shea v. North Butte Mining Co. (Mont. 1919), 251–252, 254–256, 258, 260, 265
Shea, Daniel J., 208
Sheehy v. Commissioner of Political Practices (Mont. 2020), 179–183
Sheehy, John C., 46, 139, 266, 282, 320, 394, 540
Sheff v. O'Neill (Conn. 1996), 497–505
Sherbert v. Verner (1963), 640–642
Shook, State v., (Mont. 2002), 486–489, 491, 505
Siegal, State v., (Mont. 1997), 87, 111, 555, 567, 602
Simmons-Harris v. Goff (Ohio 1999), 656
Single subject, *see* One subject
Sixth Amendment (U.S. Const. amend. VI), 77–81, 764–766, 772, 776, 784, 786
Snetsinger v. Montana University System (Mont. 2004), 514–520, 523–524, 530, 618, 777–778
Snyder, Fritz, 23, 98, 121, 390, 720
Sofie v. Fireboard Corp. (Wash. 1989), 276
Solis, State v., (Mont. 1984), 547, 548
South Dakota, 22–23, 25, 531, 631
Sovereign immunity, *see* State subject to suit (Article II, section 18)
Sparling v. Hitzman (Mont. 1935), 539
Special legislation, *see* Local and special legislation (Article V, section 12)
Speech, freedom of, 388, 629–630, 665–669, 671–673, 675–692, 695, 710, 756, 778; *see* Freedom of speech, expression, and press (Article II, section 7)

Spina, State v., (Mont. 1999), 505
St. John's Lutheran Church v. State Compensation Insurance Fund (Mont. 1992), 633, 639–641
Stafford v. Fox-Great Falls Theatre Corp. (Mont. 1942), 338, 343
Stahl v. United States (9th Cir. 2010), 635
Staker, State v., (Mont. 2021), 560, 562–563
Stanko, State v., (Mont. 1998), 759–764, 770–771
State Public Employee's Association v. Office of Governor (Mont. 1995), 169
State subject to suit (Article II, section 18), 51–52, 94–101, 108, 110, 114, 128, 247, 778
Sterling v. Regents of University of Michigan (Mich. 1896), 174, 182
Stewart v. Standard Publishing (Mont. 1936), 252, 255–256, 568
Stratemeyer v. Lincoln County (Mont. 1993), 469, 479, 482
Strickland v. Washington (1984), 722, 766
Strict accountability (Article VIII, section 12), 172–173, 175, 211
Submission (Article XIV, section 11), 39–41, 48–64, 145, 241, 594, 785
Suffrage, right of (Article II, section 13), 47, 320, 351–357, 362–363, 365, 382
Sunburst School District No. 2 v. Texaco, Inc. (Mont. 2007), 117–121, 448
Supremacy Clause (U.S. Const. art. VI, cl. 2), 19, 67–68, 382, 414
Supreme court jurisdiction (Article VII, section 2), 58, 60, 199, 213–215, 224, 231, 234, 243–245, 343, 726
Supreme court organization (Article VII, section 3), 218
Svaldi v. Anaconda-Deer Lodge County (Mont. 2005), 741
Tackitt, State v., (Mont. 2003), 91
Takings Clause, 782–784; *see* Fifth Amendment (U.S. Const. amend. V)
Tate, Commonwealth ex rel. Carroll v., (Pa. 1971), 232
Tax purposes (Article VIII, section 1), 132–133, 135, 141–149
Teague, see Board of Commissioners, State v., (Mont. 1906)
Tennessee, 7, 11, 242, 569–570, 758
Terms and pay (Article VII, section 7), 208, 211–213, 232
Terry v. Ohio (1968), 69, 89
Texas, 8, 11, 329, 403, 407, 418–419, 584, 776
Third Amendment (U.S. Const. amend. III), 541
Thomas v. Review Board of Indiana Employment Security Division (1981), 640, 693–694
Tinker v. Des Moines Independent Community School District (1969), 690, 696
Town of Beloit v. County of Rock (Wis. 2003), 147–149
Town of Ennis v. Stewart (Mont. 1991), 568
Town of Milton v. Civil Service Commission (Mass. 1974), 399
Trial by jury (Article II, section 26), 49, 77–80, 276, 490, 545, 616–618, 784
Trieweiler, Terry N., 82, 102, 115, 402, 420, 468, 759, 769
Trump for President v. Bullock (D. Mont. 2020), 193, 194
Trump v. Mazars (2020), 221–222, 226–227, 233
Turnage, J. A., 572, 668, 763
Twenty-Sixth Amendment (U.S. Const. amend. XXVI), 351, 786

Unenumerated rights (Article II, section 34), 42, 112–114, 121, 390, 395, 415, 757–758, 777–778
Union Pacific Railway Co. v. Botsford (1891), 585
University of Minnesota v. Chase (Minn. 1928), 176
Utah, 11, 25, 56

Valley Christian School v. Montana High School Association (Mont. 2004), 693
Van Haele, State v., (Mont. 1982), 535, 538–539, 546–548
Vermont, 91–94, 247, 451, 522
Veto power (Article VI, section 10), 51–52
Virginia v. Black (2003), 678
Virginia, 10, 11, 38, 161–162, 262, 389, 451
Vote, right to, *see* Suffrage, right of (Article II, section 13)
Voter review of local government (Article XI, section 9), 294, 301

Wadsworth v. State (Mont. 1996), 397–405, 407–408, 410–411, 414–415, 417–419, 424–425, 429–430, 448, 781–782
Walker v. State (Mont. 2003), 48, 534, 595–608, 615, 626
Waltermire, Montana Citizens for the Preservation of Citizens' Rights v., (Mont. 1986), 46, 238
Waltermire, Montana Citizens for the Preservation of Citizens' Rights v., (Mont. 1987), 44, 52, 260
Walz v. Tax Commission of New York (1970), 645
Warner, John, 149, 292, 614
Washington, 11, 22–23, 25, 56, 81, 85–86, 92–94, 276, 370, 449, 545, 631
Wasson, Commonwealth v., (Ky. 1992), 573
Water rights (Article IX, section 3), 787
Weatherwax, City of Billings v., (Mont. 1981), 286
Weber, Fred J., 316, 330, 539
Weems v. State (Mont. 2019), 594–595
Weinschenk v. State (Mo. 2006), 358–364
Welfare, right to, *see* Institutions and assistance (Article XII, section 3)
Welsh v. Pritchard (Mont. 1952), 93, 543, 559–560
Western Tradition Partnership v. Attorney General (Mont. 2011), 122, 208, 685–686
Western Tradition Partnership v. Attorney General (Mont. 2012), 122–128
Whalen v. Roe (1977), 555, 582
Wheat, Michael E., 409
White v. Davis (Cal. 1975), 544
White v. State (Mont. 1983), 249, 255–261, 263, 269–271, 274, 490
White v. State (Mont. 1988), 133–139, 145–146, 164, 234, 790
Whitehall v. Preece (Mont. 1998), 304–309, 311–312
Whiteside v. District Court of First Judicial District (Mont. 1900), 243–245, 343
Wichita v. Kansas Taxpayers Network (Kan. 1994), 305, 309
Will of Cram (Mont. 1980), 506–509, 511
Williams v. Board of County Commissioners of Missoula County (Mont. 2013), 445
Williams, State v., (Wash. 1984), 545
Wisconsin v. Yoder (1972), 640, 642, 693
Wisconsin, 10, 56, 147, 240
Wiser v. State (Mont. 2006), 405–409, 411–415, 419, 593

Woirhaye v. Montana Fourth Judicial District Court (Mont. 1998), 78, 79
Workers' Compensation Act, 309, 482, 631–632, 635–639, 641
Wynehamer v. People (N.Y. 1856), 758
Wyoming, 11, 25, 92, 489, 536–537, 786

Yellowstone County v. Billings Gazette (Mont. 2006), 741–742

Zobrest v. Catalina Foothills School District (1993), 327